MOTHER WIT
FROM
THE LAUGHING
BARREL

Readings in the Interpretation
of Afro-American Folklore

ALAN DUNDES
University of California at Berkeley

PRENTICE-HALL, INC., ENGLEWOOD CLIFFS, NEW JERSEY

© 1973 by Prentice-Hall, Inc., Englewood Cliffs, N.J.

Library of Congress Catalog Card Number: 77–164923

Printed in the United States of America

ISBN: C 0–13–603019–x
        P 0–13–603001–7

10 9 8 7 6 5 4 3 2 1

PRENTICE-HALL INTERNATIONAL, INC., London
PRENTICE-HALL OF AUSTRALIA, PTY. LTD., Sydney
PRENTICE-HALL OF CANADA, LTD., Toronto
PRENTICE-HALL OF INDIA PRIVATE LIMITED, New Delhi
PRENTICE-HALL OF JAPAN, INC., Tokyo

Folklore is not as easy to collect as it sounds. The best source is where there are the least outside influences and these people, being usually under-privileged, are the shyest. They are most reluctant at times to reveal that which the soul lives by. And the Negro, in spite of his open-faced laughter, his seeming acquiescence, is particularly evasive. You see we are a polite people and we do not say to our questioner, "Get out of here!" We smile and tell him or her something that satisfies the white person because, knowing so little about us, he doesn't know what he is missing. The Indian resists curiosity by a stony silence. The Negro offers a feather-bed resistance. That is, we let the probe enter, but it never comes out. It gets smothered under a lot of laughter and pleasantries.

The theory behind our tactics: "The white man is always trying to know into somebody else's business. All right, I'll set something outside the door of my mind for him to play with and handle. He can read my writing but he sho' can't read my mind. I'll put this play toy in his hand, and he will seize it and go away. Then I'll say my say and sing my song."

Zora Neale Hurston, *Mules and Men* (Philadelphia, 1935), pp. 18–19.

Contents

FOLK BELIEF, 357

FOLK MUSIC, 429

Preface

       With the increasing interest in Afro-American culture, there has been an outpouring of books devoted to black history and the black experience. This is a healthy sign both for those whites who sincerely wish to remedy their enormous lack of knowledge of black culture and for those Negroes who are tired of reading "whites only" accounts of American history. But if history is crucial, so also is folklore.

       American Negro folklore is every bit as important as black history in the overall order of things in black culture. One must remember that many American Negroes have relatively little knowledge of black history—thanks to the unfortunate editorial bias inherent in most of the textbooks which have been employed in American education for the past hundred years. But all American Negroes have some personal knowledge of the folk music, folktales, and folk speech which have not only contributed to the vitality of American folklore but which have had an impact upon musical traditions all over the world. Jazz, blues, and spirituals, at this point, belong to all mankind.

       Yet despite the undeniable importance of American Negro folklore, much of it remains largely unknown to whites and even to some Negroes. One reason for the latter's lack of knowledge is the association of folklore with the white stereotype of the Negro. Part of the racist white stereotype speaks of the Negro's "natural" sense of rhythm as reflected in song and dance. Another facet of the stereotype describes the alleged superstitious nature of the Negro. Thus folklore, which includes folksong, folk dance, and superstitions, was and is viewed as something for educated Negroes to demean. And it is true that folklore in many parts of the world is associated with "error"—as in the phrase "That's (just) folklore". If folklore is regarded as a synonym for ignorance, then one can easily understand why American Negroes have been slow to study their own folklore and, moreover, why they have bitterly resented the attempts of white folklorists to collect and analyze it. To the extent that folklore has been used as the tool of racists (in attempting to validate the stereotypes), these misgivings are perfectly justified. But to the extent that a people have been led to turn their backs upon their own heritage, such a situation is sad.

The present volume seeks to raise some of the critical theoretical issues involved in the study of American Negro folklore. The anthology is *not* one of mere folklore texts. There are already sampler collections of raw folklore data available, e.g., Langston Hughes and Arna Bontemps, eds., *The Book of Negro Folklore* (New York, 1958) or J. Mason Brewer, *American Negro Folklore* (Chicago, 1968). Rather, the concern here is for the meaning and significance of the folklore. Obviously, as soon as one enters the area of interpretation, one runs the risk of error. No doubt some of the interpetations expressed by authors represented in this anthology will strike some readers as being far-fetched or absurd. Inasmuch as there has been a conscious effort to include a wide variety of interpretations, this type of reader response is probably inevitable. One can only hope that readers who become sufficiently annoyed will be stimulated enough to try to "correct" what they believe to be a misinterpretation.

As there is no such thing as "the American Negro," there is similarly no such thing as "American Negro folklore" in the sense of one large body of folklore known to *all* American Negroes. Black ghetto folklore is quite different from rural folklore, for example. And both are in turn quite different from middle-class Negro folklore. To be sure, there are elements common to all these traditions, but there can be no question that there are considerable differences. Middle-class Negroes, for example, might resent the implication that rural Negro folklore is "their" folklore just as much as they might resent the thought that urban Negro ghetto street talk is "their" folklore. Unfortunately, since there has been relatively little study of middle-class Negro folklore, most of the scholarly discussion has been focused upon rural and ghetto traditions. It should also be noted that the folklore of Negroes living in the United States is quite different from the folklore of Latin American Negroes and from the rich folklore of the Caribbean. However, many of the theoretical issues raised with respect to American Negro folklore are also relevant to the study of folklore in Brazil and the West Indies, to mention just two areas.

The variety of American Negro folk groups is exceeded only by the variety of genres of Negro folklore. Whole books could be, and in fact have been, devoted to just one genre, e.g., Richard M. Dorson, *American Negro Folktales* (New York, 1967) or to several, e.g., Harold Courlander, *Negro Folk Music U.S.A.* (New York, 1963). In the present volume, the scholarship dealing with a particular genre may be represented by a single essay. Clearly, one essay cannot hope to cover subjects not adequately treated in entire books. Nevertheless, it is hoped that some inkling of the range of American

Negro folklore genres will be communicated to the reader. Bibliographical suggestions for further discussion will be available for the reader who is specially interested in a particular genre or topic.

One indication of the range of materials included in the anthology is the large number of sources. Important contributions to the study of American Negro folklore have appeared in popular literary magazines, American Negro periodicals, and sociology and psychology journals, as well as in conventional folklore journals. If one of the responsibilities of academic scholarship is to make the results of research known, then perhaps one accomplishment of the present anthology is simply the collection of writings widely scattered in extremely diverse publications. Surely this will aid relatively small educational institutions with limited libraries, not to mention those members of the general public who desire to learn something about American Negro folklore.

The organization of the book is roughly as follows: The selections are divided into eight sections. The first, "Folk and Lore," concerns the attitudes, positive and negative, toward American Negro folklore. The crucial question raised is that of the relationship between folklore and a sense of group identity. The second section samples the longstanding and ongoing debate about the origins of American Negro folklore. The third section deals with folk speech with special reference to traditional names and slang. In the fourth section, there is a consideration in some detail of many of the most important forms of traditional word play, e.g., of "signifying" and "playing the dozens." The fifth section treats custom and belief and the sixth section attempts to examine the incredibly rich area of American Negro folksong. The seventh section investigates narrative forms which include folktales, legends, and memorates. The eighth and final section is devoted to analyses of traditional humor.

It will soon become obvious to the reader that the organizational divisions are far from perfect. There is much obvious overlapping of topics. There are essays on the blues, for example, in the sections on origins and on verbal art in addition to the essay in the folk music section. The reader should bear in mind that it is the selections, not their organization, which are of primary importance. If, through his reading, he gains a better understanding of the nature of American Negro folklore and a better idea of what the critical questions are with respect to the interpretation of that folklore, then the ultimate goal of the anthology will have been reached.

Having explained the organizational plan of the book, I should like to add a final word about the title. In slavery times and afterward, Negroes were not always free to laugh (or sing) openly. If a Negro wished to laugh out loud at his master, he might do so only at considerable risk. So he suppressed the desire to laugh and went instead to the "laughing barrel," where he could laugh to his heart's content without fear of being heard. This traditional outlet is strikingly similar to the custom of placing an inverted wash kettle in the center of the floor during a prayer meeting so that the sounds of the singing might go into the pot and thereby not disturb the white folks at the plantation house. It is that laughter which once echoed in the imaginary laughing barrel and those songs once directed into the kettle which form a large part of American Negro folklore. Mother wit is a popular term in black speech referring to common sense. Mother wit is the kind of good sense not necessarily learned from books or in school. Mother wit with its connotation of collective wisdom acquired by the experience of living and from generations past is often expressed in folklore. This is why the image of tapping the laughing barrel to search for mother wit is hopefully an appropriate metaphor for the study of American Negro folklore.

ACKNOWLEDGMENTS

I thank all the authors, editors, and publishers who were kind enough to give their permission to reprint copyrighted materials. I also wish to thank many of my colleagues and students for their thoughtful suggestions and criticisms. Among those to whom I am especially indebted are Roger Abrahams, Dorothy Atkins, Sarah Baker, William Bascom, Elizabeth Colson, Jerry Davis, Richard Dorson, Victoria Durant, Bill Ferris, Gladys Fry, Kenny Goldstein, Bess Hawes, Ernest Jackson, Willie Mae Kelley, Tom Kiefer, Barbara Kirshenblatt-Gimblett, Larry Levine, Dennis McDonald, Christine Milner, Doris North, John Ogbu, Eleanor Mason Ramsey, Neil Rosenberg, Anya Peterson Royce, Dolores Ruff, William Shack, John Szwed, Peter Tamony, and Bob Toll. Very much appreciated was Madeleine Hall's invaluable assistance in reading the galley proofs.

I should like to express my gratitude to Ed Stanford of Prentice-Hall for his initial encouragement of the project and Bill Oliver, English editor, of Prentice-Hall for all his assistance. I am grateful to Robb Reavill and the other Prentice-Hall staff members who contributed their talents to the design and production of the book.

To my wife Carolyn and to our children three: Alison, Lauren, and David, I owe special thanks. Moments taken from the precious time of being a husband and father were spent hunting on dusty library shelves for relevant materials. I can only hope the final result justifies my selfish sacrifice of time and energy. To the extent that the book stimulates a better understanding and appreciation of American Negro folklore on the part of both Negroes and whites, I shall feel my hours in the library and at the typewriter were not in vain.

ALAN DUNDES

Berkeley, California

FOLK & LORE

In most countries of the world there is an ambivalence toward folklore and there has been ever since the science of folkloristics began to develop in the nineteenth century. At that time, folklore was wrongly defined exclusively in terms of survivals from the ancient past. As a people moved from a "primitive" or "savage" state toward "civilization," they were assumed to be losing their folklore, that is, their myths, folktales, legends, songs, customs, games, proverbs, riddles, etc. According to nineteenth century folklore theory, folklore still survived in less civilized areas, e.g., among isolated rural peasant groups in Europe. The feelings of ambivalence occurred because on the one hand the materials of folklore were despised as the antithesis of knowledge and learning (e.g., compare folk medicine to "scientific" medicine) and thus something to be stamped out if possible. On the other hand, these "remnants" or "fossils" from times past were held to be part of the national or racial heritage from the past which in one sense belonged to all generations no matter how civilized they might pretend to be. This identification of folklore with romanticism and nationalism was clearly a positive one. Herder's earlier assertion that folksongs reflected the soul of a people, inspired the Grimm brothers to collect folklore in a nationalistic attempt to salvage and reconstruct the essence of German or Teutonic character.

We know today that this definition of folklore was much too narrow. We do not limit folklore to the notion of survivals. Neither do we limit the definition of "folk" to "rural peasant." Any group of people who share at least one linking factor—be it occupation, religion, or ethnicity—qualify as a "folk" and it is easy to find lumberjack or Jewish folklore. All of us are members of at least one folk group and most of us belong to several. Thus I might know examples of military folklore, campus folklore, and California folklore. Yet in spite of the more flexible definition of folk groups and the extension of rural folklore to urban folklore (e.g., the folklore of labor unions or of the civil rights movement),

1

the feeling of ambivalence toward folklore continues. There is frequently both shame and pride felt about one's folklore. One may be ashamed of practicing or even knowing about a superstitious ritual—at least in front of someone who is not a member of the "in-group" —but at the same time there may be pride in singing a particular folk song with one's family or with members of one's folk group.

There is no better example of the ambivalent attitudes toward folklore than those found among American Negroes. The critical question of the relationship between folklore and race pride (which corresponds to the relationship between folklore and nationalism in the nineteenth century) is a thorny one. One argument is that folklore is an indispensable means of promoting group solidarity. Accordingly, pride in folklore leads to pride in race. A contrary argument is that folklore is essentially a negative factor, especially as it perpetuates such racist notions that "white" is pure and good and that "black" is evil. With this reasoning, race pride can only develop as folklore is eradicated. These two views exist side by side and this is why some American Negroes have been anxious to investigate folklore while others have had as little to do with folklore as possible.

Perhaps the moderate position would be that folklore provides a mirror for the rest of culture. Folklore *per se* is neither good nor evil. It can be used to promote either group pride or group shame. The fact that folklore reflects racism should come as no surprise. To the extent that there is racism in American society, one would expect that American folklore, both black and white, would reflect this racism. While it is probably true that some folklore may aid the cause of racism, it is also true that the mere elimination of racist folklore would not necessarily eliminate the racist conditions which led to the creation of the folklore in the first place. It is obviously those conditions which need to be altered. One they are altered, the *raison d'être* for racist folklore would in theory exist no longer. In any case, it is impossible to stamp out folklore, racist or otherwise, even if one wanted to. Folklore is transmitted from person to person, often orally, and there is no way to effectively stop its transmission. In this respect, folklore differs from printed material, which can be subjected to various types and degrees of censorship. Folklore always tells it like it is or at least tells it as some people think it is or as they would like it to be. So since there is no question of eliminating folklore, and since folklore is a kind of popular pulse, ever indicating what is on a people's mind and in a people's heart, we might just as well look into the mirror of a people that folklore provides.

Race Pride & Folklore

NEWBELL NILES PUCKETT

Here is a representative statement of the positive attitude toward folklore. The late Newbell Niles Puckett, Professor of Sociology at Western Reserve University, spent many years studying American Negro folklore, especially superstitions. He is perhaps best remembered for his Yale University doctoral dissertation Folk Beliefs of the Southern Negro (*Chapel Hill, 1926*), *which has been reissued in paperback (New York: Dover, 1969). Puckett does appear to associate folklore with the past and to identify the folk as the rural illiterate. (In modern folklore scholarship, there is a recognition of urban folklore, e.g., superstitions believed by the astronauts, street games and sidewalk rhymes of urban school children. It is also recognized that folklore reflects the present as well as the past.) Although there is an occasional hint of patronizing condescension in some of his verbiage, it is also quite clear that Professor Puckett genuinely loved folklore and sincerely believed in its intrinsic beauty and worth.*

For other essays by Puckett, see his "Religious Folk Beliefs of Whites and Negroes," Journal of Negro History, *16 (1931), pp. 9–35. "Negro Character as Revealed in Folklore,"* Publications of the American Sociological Society, *28 (1934), pp. 12–23, and his study of slave names reprinted in this volume.*

Reprinted from *Opportunity: A Journal of Negro Life*, vol. 4, no. 39 (1926), pp. 82–84, by permission of the National Urban League.

IT IS truly remarkable how quickly the stately old grandfather-chair haughtily chooses the ostracism of the attic rather than association with some new-fledged nondescript of plush and ugliness. Years later the fickle hand of fortune, attracted by the glamor of the antique, arouses the complaining old chair from its couch of dust and props its century-racked limbs into their former place of honor. But the years are careless and the elements gluttonous—countless thou-

3

sands of individual masterpieces have returned forever to the dust from which they sprang.

This slaughter of the first born vents its wrath upon Children of the Mind as well as upon Children of the Hands. The collector of folklore will often burst upon Coöperation in some lowly corner, while Antagonism and Race-Pride stalk hand in hand along the main highways of Negro thought. I intentionally say, "the main highways of Negro thought"—the illiterate Negro, as a rule, will generously share with you his treasure of unwritten lore, while, too often, colleges and cultured individuals regard Race-Pride and Folk-Lore as irreconcilable enemies. It is, to say the least, disquieting to the student of race, who is earnestly seeking opinions from fact rather than prejudice, to have some unthinking custodian of hundreds of living volumes of rapidly disappearing lore lock the library door in his face with a superficial, "We desire to forget the past in pressing forward to the future." As if the past could by simple willing be forever erased! Even in the material world certain features of the discarded grandfather's chair peep out in modern chair structure, though one could scarcely expect the clumsy, gear-fingered hand of industry to reproduce the individuality of the old master. There is no single institution, no single bit of knowledge in today's civilization but what has been erected with incredible slowness and with an almost incalculable cost of human time and energy from the material of yesteryears. Remove the past from our civilization and the whole structure crumbles into dust—it is as foolish as trying to extract a house from its outside shell of paint.

Those who ignore the past never really understand the present; for the past gives shape to the present just as the house gives shape to the covering of paint. Such ultra-modern worshippers of race-pride would do well to visit again the great Kindergarten of Folk-Thought as evidenced, for instance, in the unwritten social philosophy of the Georgia Negro: "Never despise a bridge that carries you safely over." How much better would it be if those who are ashamed of their folk-heritage could but realize the truth that folk-beliefs and superstitions are *normal* stages of development through which *all* peoples have passed and are passing in their societal evolution. Given accurate folk-data instead of pride-warped sophisms and the sociologists of the future may in time be well enough informed regarding the laws and principles governing human development to remove intelligently certain hindrances which prevent these natural forces from working at their maximum efficiency. The United States is a great laboratory with a gigantic experiment in race-contact, working itself out before the very eyes of the student of race. In order to understand and interpret this experiment our knowledge of the conditioning facts must be as accurate and as complete as possible. Differences in cultural background are all-important causes of friction and prejudice between groups and folk-lore is an essential part of these backgrounds. At the present time these rough timbers of early thought are being rapidly veneered with the culture of today— there is need of haste if we are to study them at first hand instead of vaguely guessing at the influences beneath certain traits of later culture. What is the African contribution to this folk-background, and what particular needs have preserved these special folk-beliefs after other African beliefs have been more or less completely dropped? What elements of European lore have been assimilated by the Negro, and why these particular items instead of others? In what portion of the societal organization does this seepage of lore from group to group occur, and in what section of Negro society are the agents most responsible for the transmission of these beliefs? The answers to these and similar questions depend upon a careful survey of the field of folk-beliefs, but once such answers are forthcoming the task of removing the people from the spell of certain undesirable beliefs may proceed with a certitude and efficiency far superior to that of aimless repression.

From the viewpoint of the development of race-pride alone, a study of ethnocentrism as evidenced in folk-lore would be both interesting and instructive. At first there is apparently that African pride of race, traces of which still remain in the folk-lore of the Southern Negro, which assumes that all men were created black to begin with but that the white man originated when Cain turned pale from fright after murdering his brother Abel. In time

lighter colored race-egotism teaches the Negro that angels are white and devils black, and depreciates dreams of black as ill luck, while welcoming dreams of white. Generations of caricatures in black sometimes force lighter pigments into folk-masterpieces, as where the Negro poet sings:

"You needn't think jes' caze I's black,
I'se gwinter ax you ter take me back;
Fool gal, you ain' got no sense."

Or again:

"You needn't think jes' caze you's
        yelluh,
You gwinter git you anuther felluh;
Fool gal, you ain't got no sense."

Although the Negro in his rhymes sometimes declares definitely, "I wouldn' marry a black gal," he also sings, "I wouldn' marry dat yelluh Nigger gal," or, "I wouldn' marry dat white Nigger gal," and decides with emphasis, "I'd druther be a Nigger dan a po' white man," showing clearly that race-pride had not been completely blanched.* Chromatic folk-lore is an interesting field and could teach us much regarding these important group-attitudes which make for fighting or friendship.

---

* In the South, the classic retort to being called "nigger" by some white person was the couplet:

    I had a little dog, his name was Dash;
    I'd ruther be a nigger than poor white trash.

See Arthur P. Davis, "When I Was in Knee Pants," *Common Ground*, vol. 4 (Winter, 1944), p. 50. See also Thomas W. Talley, *Negro Folk Rhymes Wise and Otherwise* (New York, 1922), pp. 42–43. Newman I. White in his *American Negro Folk-Songs* (Hatboro, Pennsylvania, 1965), p. 170, reports "My name is Sam, I don't give a damn, I'd rather be a nigger'n a po' white man." Nearly the same rhyme was recorded by Lafcadio Hearn in his article "Genius Loci" which appeared in the *Cincinnati Commerical* on August 12, 1877: "I'm Rag-a-back Sam, And I don't care a damn, Fur I sooner be a nigger dan a poor white man." See Lafcadio Hearn, *Children of the Levee* (Lexington, Kentucky, 1957), p. 104. This suggests that the Negroes' feelings of superiority to "crackers," "peckerwoods" or "poor white trash" may go back to ante-bellum times. —ED.

Again it would seem that race-pride could be more rationally and effectively fostered, not by blotting out the footprints of the past, but by graving them indelibly upon the minds of the people and emphasizing the distance travelled as well as the heights attained. Truly this is a matter for pride—the Negro has advanced more in the last half-century or so than did the Germans during the eight centuries between the time of Julius Caesar and the ascension of Charlemagne, and this development promises to continue. The social scientists in their study of group development would be able to speak more definitely concerning the direction and degree of societal evolution were these footprints clearly mapped out. The only way of estimating the degree of change is to compare accurately the present with the past. If the change indicates what we would call progress then there are grounds for a real race-pride.

Presumably a flourishing race-pride aims at group improvement, and in this undertaking a study of folk-lore offers valuable assistance in that it brings definite knowledge to bear upon certain conditions relating to the less advanced classes and indicates the lines along which a more rational education is required. It is a short-sighted policy to conceal a festering sore beneath a silken cover of hypocrisy and pharisaism— far better to recognize the truth as such and deal with it straight from the shoulder without equivocation. No mere buncombe or cant can cope with the murderous lore of mid-wifery, for instance, and the sooner this is recognized the sooner will such superstitions be replaced by modern scientific knowledge.

Perhaps some day a broader spirit of tolerance will elbow out the feeling of shame apparently associated with superstition. Every single folk-belief is thoroughly justifiable in the light of its times and meets a definite need on the part of the individual or group, whether it be illiterate Negro farmers or students at our most advanced universities. One should always be swift to collect and slow to criticize—even such falsisms as burying a murdered man face downward in order to catch the murderer or throwing the stem of a stolen melon into the creek to cause the thief to die, are light-footed policemen of the first order where the regulative organization of society is not developed more highly. Perhaps the uninformed may be inclined to scoff at the red-flannel hoodoo-bag, containing such waifs and estrays as lodestone, steel filings, graveyard dirt, red pepper, gunpowder, anvil-dust, bluestone, nail trimmings and the thousand and one roots individualized as "Red Shanks," "Devil's Shoe String," "Angel's Turnip," "Purpose of the World," "Cruel Man of the Woods," and such like, but no careful observer in the field can deny the fact that these various conjures in many cases *actually work*. In this sense they represent means of faith-healing or faith-harming, admirably adapted to the temperament of an uneducated folk. Nor are these conjures entirely without their sound advice. One New Orleans hoodoo-man sold an anxious suitor some "French Love Powder" (sugar of milk in this case) which was to be sprinkled upon everything he gave to his elusive sweetheart. "But," the conjurer added, "gib de 'oman ebbything she laks and lots uv hit—nebber cross her er make her mad no mattah how much she pesters you er flirts wid other men. Show her all de time dat she's de onliest 'oman you wants." Of course such sensible instructions in wife-winning were entirely successful, and the client was well satisfied with his "Love Powder."

The home missionary worker would find it worth his while to study carefully the folk-creed of the rural Negro before he attempts further lessons in Christianity. He would find that Negro Christianity is not identical with white Christianity, because the folk-background of the Negro is not identical with that of the white man. Negro Christianity is often Christianity in convulsions, and this religious frenzy of the rural Negro offers much interesting material to the student of religious development or of psychology applied to groups. The devil often assumes an importance entirely unbecoming to one who has been summarily "kicked outer heaven." Saints and biblical characters are shamelessly called upon through conjuration to assist in the myriad petty and even unholy affairs of life, while legends are woven around them to explain such phenomena as the peculiar bark of the scaley-bark tree, the trembling of the cottonwood, and the origins of the cat and the boarding house. Dream signs are often carefully observed when "gittin' 'ligion," and when the lightning strikes near a house where a man is dying, the devil is said to have come for his soul. The Christian deities, including angels and devils, shade off imperceptibly into the great ghost-world, querulous with vaguely draped figures, headless men, calf-size dogs with flaming red eyes, Jack-o'-my-lanterns and

other unnumbered specters which in one way or another are meddling constantly with the affairs of man. A discerning race-pride would glory in the fact that the overswarmed African ghost-heritage has been decimated to such scanty proportions. After all, these remaining Negro ghosts are to a certain degree promoters of folk-virtues. One heartless woman of Alabama was beating an innocent orphan child. Suddenly the wrathful fist of the ghost-mother smote the wicked woman violently in the jaw, knocking her face entirely lopsided and sounding a warning to all unscrupulous mortals who are tempted to violate the trust placed in them.

The conscientious objector to folklore should also realize that not all of folk-knowledge is pure chaff. For instance, the Negro farmer says that when the smoke falls towards the ground, or when moisture gathers on an iron vessel, or when the sky is grey in the evening, it is a sign of rain. Careful scientific investigation has brought to light natural laws behind these observations which establish them as scientific facts. Other items of lore are of value from the point of view of our civilization because of the sentiments they express. Thus it is considered "bad luck ter sit in de house wid yo' hat on or ter sass de ole folks," while a person who eats too fast "will sho marry too young." Rhymes such as:

"Whiskey nor brandy ain' no fren'
　　ter my kind,
Dey kilt my po' daddy an' dey trubbl'
　　my mind,"

are not without their value in folk-discipline. Indeed the friendly eye cannot but see many general aspects of folk-thought which might greatly bolster up the racial self-esteem. The countless unique methods employed in conjuration, for instance, speak with convincing eloquence of a wealth of originality. I have collected from the Negroes some twenty-three or more separate and distinct methods of avoiding death when an owl hoots near one's house. These beliefs do not mutter to me of a sterility of folk-thought—could the same mental torrent in some way be turned from avoiding death to avoiding debt the visible increase in material prosperity would leave no question as to its power.

But, after all, life is something more than meat and money, as important as these factors are in conditioning other societal activities. Man shows his need for self-gratification by the energy he expends for the means of pleasure, and my final appeal is for the preservation of the beauty-things of folk-life—those priceless pearls of folk-thought which daily are being crushed beneath the feet of the unthinking. Apart from the beauty and simplicity of many of the concepts hidden in this treasure-chest of the past, there are those unmatched gems of spontaneous expression which enrich the stilted formalism of today like dew upon a dusty spider web. "Dear Sir, the precise meaning of your state-ment is not entirely clear to me." Such is the leaden phraseology of today. In contrast the sprightly, "Sir, you is a huckleberry beyon' my persimmon," capers out and "surprises de mind," as the Negro would say, leaving the world happier for its having been said. Negro folk-songs are receiving more attention than ever before, but great is the power of the hymn-book and phonograph. The quavering whispers of the old "songster" can no longer be heard above the uncouth blare of modern music—daily, almost hourly, these superb rhythmic masterpieces die down to golden echoes and pass un-written to the Land of Forgotten Things. The true lover of Negro achievements will preserve not only the song but also the habit of singing—he will face the trials and disappointments of life with his buckler of song, and glory in the exploits of a Singing Race.

There is a need for men—men who will build honestly and completely—men with foresight who scorn a race-pride founded upon half-truths—proud men who will record without shame the flaws and the flowers of folk-life, that generations yet to come may look back with enduring pride upon quagmires safely crossed as well as upon mountains ascended.

As Crinkly as Yours

ELDRIDGE CLEAVER

Here is an eloquent statement of some of the negative aspects of folklore. Not all folklore is indicted. Only those portions which reflect racism, e.g., the traditional symbolic associations of the colors black and white, are strongly condemned. It certainly cannot be denied that the folkloristic dichotomy of "white as good" and "black as evil" is a contributing factor to the formation of racial prejudice. Cleaver attempts to pinpoint this factor with the hope of weakening its baneful influence. In fact, the creation in the 1960's of the slogan "Black is beautiful" is a conscious attempt to undo some of the damage caused by the traditional symbolism of black and white. In this context, one can see that it would be naive to claim that all folklore was supportive of race pride. Some folklore is; some is not.

The critical problem with Cleaver's bold suggestion that Negroes "root-out" from their thinking and folklore those pernicious elements which have robbed them of their race pride is that it is extremely difficult either to self-consciously create new folklore or to self-consciously destroy old folklore. Individuals can write songs modeled after folksongs or compose proverbs similar to traditional ones, but such artificial "literary" folksongs or proverbs rarely ever enter the folk's repertoire. Similarly, while one can rightfully resent such racist rhymes as "If you're white, you're right. . . but if you're black, get back," it is quite another matter to rescind oral tradition. It is virtually impossible to effectively censor oral tradition. Moreover, one could even argue that the very act of citing such rhymes in the vain attempt to mitigate their destructive influence does little more than give them added prominence and ensure their further continuity in tradition.

The particular thrust of Cleaver's essay concerns the Negro's reluctance or

Reprinted from *The Negro History Bulletin*, vol. 25 (1962), pp. 127–32. Copyright © by Association for the Study of Negro Life and History.

unwillingness to accept his own hair style. Malcolm X in his powerful and poign-
ant Autobiography *also condemned the "conk," describing in detail the*
painful process of hair straightening. It has been precisely this type of behavior
which has lent support to the controversial "self-hate" hypothesis proposed by
Kardiner and Ovesey. (The self-hate hypothesis argues that Negroes have
internalized white values to such an extent that they, like some whites, have
come to hate Negroes, i.e., themselves, and nearly all elements of Negro
culture.) Inasmuch as hair which has been altered in conformity with
"straight" white culture is obviously visible for all to see, it has become a spe-
cially important topic among those in favor of a "Black is beautiful" philosophy.

    For further discussion of the self-hate hypothesis, see Abram Kardiner and
Lionel Ovesey, The Mark of Oppression: Explorations in the Personality of
the American Negro (*Cleveland: Meridian, 1962). For the description of*
conking by Malcolm X, see The Autobiography of Malcolm X (*New York:*
Grove Press, 1966), pp. 52–55. For additional consideration of the importance
of hair styles, see Hylan Lewis, Blackways of Kent (*Chapel Hill, 1955), pp.*
56–61. For more essays by Eldridge Cleaver, see his best-seller Soul on Ice
(*New York: McGraw-Hill, 1968).*

IN EVERY society, in every historical period, it is demonstrable that human beings have always made some type of judgment as to what is beautiful and what is not beautiful. The things, or aspects of things, esteemed as beautiful have changed; but always men have looked upon some things as beautiful and others as unbeautiful or, condemnatorily, as ugly. Indeed, an entire branch of philosophy—Esthetics—has this phenomenon as its subject-matter.

As time goes by, these judgments seep into, and become deeply entrenched in, the culture of a people, and are looked upon as standards by which value judgments are made. To each cultural group, the acceptance of these traditional standards is as natural and unquestioned as is the acceptance by the group of any other aspect of its culture.

It seems that, from time immemorial, mankind has passed judgment on the human body, pronouncing these characteristics and traits beautiful and these unbeautiful—or ugly. As the judgments are reiterated over the years, they become objectified into standards by which the merits and demerits of individual human beings are determined. This practice can be observed amongst all people, be they so-called civilized or so-called primitive. They all ornament themselves in various ways—in conformity to an accepted standard of beauty: and failure to do so marks one as an oddity, an eccentric, or one type of freak or another.

This phenomenon would not be the subject of remark which embraces it, were it not for the fact that the traditional judgments which Western Man has made, and still tenaciously clings to, are now (and, indeed, have been) the cause of very serious maladjustments in our society and, much more seriously, in the world at large. In this essay, the attempt will be made to show that the continued application of these judgments is the cause of an untold amount of mental illness and frustration.

In our culture, the recognized standard of beauty—one could just as well say, "the official standard of beauty"—

is that of the Caucasian peoples; and since the Caucasian has possessed hegemony over the world for the duration of the epoch which is now drawing to a close, along with other values of Western culture, he has also exported *his* standard of beauty. In a profound sense, the Caucasian standard of beauty has been—and is now—one of the corner-stones of the doctrine of "White Supremacy." We have only to observe in order to see the destructive psychological impact of this standard of beauty on the people around the world who have unknowingly fallen under its subtle influence. In this essay, the discussion will be confined chiefly to the situation as it relates to the American Negro; but by extension, most of what is said here can be applied in a general way.

It is generally held that the first incidence of Africans being seized and abducted from their native soil and brought to America and enslaved, occurred in the year 1619; if that is so, then that is the date on which the traditional standard of beauty of the transplanted African was first undermined and the corroding process of subversion began. Certainly, up until that time, the Africans had their own standards of beauty, and they accepted them just as naturally, proudly, and unquestioningly as all other people accepted their own.

But after being crushed down into a position of slavery, degradation, poverty and general wretchedness—but most important, after the arbitrary and more or less total disruption of his cultural continuity, due largely to the indiscriminate and unceremonious mixing of different tribes and cultural groups by the Slavers, who cared not a tack for the cultures of their prey—the

black slave began to identify everything that fell to his lot with the conditions under which he suffered. The lodging that was forced upon him; the food that was parceled out to him; the crude work-a-day clothing that he was obliged to wear—all of these items became in his eyes, badges of bondage; and therefore he passionately hated them.

Under the harsh physical brutality, the taunts, castigations and deprecatory harassments of his slavemasters, who looked upon the black man as a sub-human beast of burden, after generation on top of generation of slaves, born into slavery and knowing nothing but the miseries of their state and the constant brain-washing of their every-day life, totally stripped of their own culture —under that pressure the slaves began to identify everything that is good and desirable with the Caucasians for whom they toiled. It was the Caucasians whom they saw dressed in the finest garments and attire that the fabulous profits of slavery could command; it was the Caucasians whom they saw inhabiting the palatial mansions of the plantations in the "great white world beyond . . ." —consequently the slaves came to regard the surroundings of the "whites" as a veritable heaven on earth; something to dream of, yet never attain. The pomp and show of the ostentatious Southern Aristocracy served to hammer the Black man down, dwarfing his pride and extirpating his self-esteem by shackling to his neck the huge, iron collar of the inferiority complex. This went on for some 240 years, and after this blanket annihilation of his traditional way of life, the black man was set free in a "white" oriented society. With the advent of freedom, the adverse effects of the Caucasian standard of beauty on the black men upon whom it had been imposed became more apparent.

Following the Civil War, the great mass of "Freedmen," now designated as "Negro," were able, in a quasi-free way, to determine their own destiny. For the first time in the history of the race, black men found themselves 'free' en masse in the midst of Western culture and civilization. And if Negroes, while in slavery, identified the fabled 'Good Life' with the standards of the Caucasians, after freedom was achieved the desires and dreams of attaining this "Good Life" mushroomed and took on new tantalizing proportions in their minds by virtue of the fact that the actual conditions to which they aspired were ever-present and all around them, as it were "so near and yet so far."

Negroes migrated to the big cities, to the fashion capitals of the nation, there to be fascinated and dazzled by, what must have seemed to them, splendor and finery fit for kings— treasures unparalleled in their most inspired dreams. And who possessed the objects of these dreams? The Caucasians. (It is important to remember that the ideals and values which were born in slavery were carried over and persisted into the new era.)

There were deeply imbedded in the thinking and folklore of the race such adages and beliefs as: "If you're white you're all right; if you're brown stick around; but if you're black—GET BACK!" And some of these same old sayings are still current in the Negro community.*

Think on it: this was the era of the camera. Negroes saw photographs, paintings and portraits in which the beauty of the Caucasian was extolled

---

* This is invariably quoted as a prime example of "self-hate" folklore. Like all folklore, there is some textual variation. The version in William H. Grier and Price M. Cobbs, *Black Rage* (New York, 1968), p. 66, is: "If you're white, you're right. If you're brown, hang around. If you're black, get back." The version cited in the first pages of Philip Sterling, ed., *Laughing on the Outside: The Intelligent White Reader's Guide to Negro Tales and Humor* (New York, 1965), is:

> If you're white, you're right.
> If you're yellow, you're mellow.
> If you're brown, stick aroun'.
> If you're black, brother, get back!

For other versions, see J. Mason Brewer, *Humorous Folk Tales of the South Carolina Negro*, Publications of the South Carolina Negro Folklore Guild, no. 1 (Orangeburg, South Carolina, 1945), p. 45; Ralph Ellison, *Shadow and Act* (New York, 1964), p. 173; Harold R. Isaacs, *The New World of Negro Americans* (New York, 1964), p. 84; Kenneth Clarke, "Folklore of Negro Children in Greater Louisville Reflecting Attitudes Toward Race," *Kentucky Folklore Record*, 10 (1964), p. 6; Nathan Hare, "The Plasma of Thinking Black," *Negro Digest*, vol. 18, no. 3 (January, 1967), p. 14; H. Rap Brown, *Die Nigger Die* (New York, 1969), p. 2. For the version used by blues singer Bill Broonzy, see the article "Protest and Irony in Negro Folksong" by Russell Ames, reprinted in this volume. Versions of the rhyme are also included in Zora Neale Hurston's "Story in Harlem Slang" and Langston Hughes, "Jokes Negroes Tell on Themselves," both of which are reprinted in this volume. Note that the rhyme does suggest that there are gradations between black and white. One itemization of these gradations was given as follows: "black, chocolate-brown, sepia, bronze-skin, seal-skin, high brown, yaller, high yaller," although the inadequacy of the listing was noted by the compiler. See "Some Negro Slang," in Nancy Cunard, ed., *Negro* (London, 1934), p. 77. —ED.

saturatingly throughout the land. Negroes witnessed beauty contests in which Caucasian men and women were held up and proclaimed the most beautiful creatures that God had fashioned and placed upon the face of the earth (it never dawning on the Negroes that it was the Caucasians themselves who were pinning roses on their own lapels). Great numbers of Negroes were learning to read and write: and in the books which they read, the process took on a sweeping new dimension. When a Negro retired in solitude to relax and enjoy a *great* book, it was the Caucasian standard of beauty which was flaunted before him and held up for him to praise —and praise it he did, unable to resist or dispute, having no criterion by which to refute. In the novels, he met heroines with *creamy white skin, sparkling blue eyes, and long flowing blonde tresses;* and heroes with *rugged Roman noses, wavy black hair* and perhaps a *gentle* sun-tan. And then the motion-picture industry sprang into being, and with it, a constant deluge reiterating and indisputably establishing the Caucasian standard of beauty.

At this point let it be recalled that *physical appearance*, i.e., skin color and texture of hair, is what primarily distinguishes the great majority of Negroes from other Americans. It is this salient factor—physical appearance —which points out the Negro and makes him readily available as a target of abuse and a more vulnerable mark for exploitation. Significantly, the historical fact is that the other despised minority groups which America has known were able, after a comparatively brief time, to disappear into the main-stream of our national life and take active parts in the social, political and economic affairs of the country. Unlike the Negro, the other minority groups could not be identified as such merely on the basis of physical appearance. For those minorities, assimilation was an accomplished fact simply by learning to speak English and smoothing out the family name from Schmidt to Smith.

To an excruciatingly painful degree, Negroes were very much aware of their "burden of color and bad hair."

How can the effects of the Caucasian standard of beauty be identified in the thinking and actions of Negroes? Why, observe the great vogue of hair-straighteners, wigs, and skin-bleaches that sprang into being! Great geniuses were at work! One such savant, after much pondering and tedious toil, emerged and created a revolution amongst Negro women when he introduced that Magic Wand—the Straightening Comb:

"After one preparation, Madam, you too can have *silky-straight* flowing tresses, just as *beautiful* and *lovely* as your pale sister. Or perhaps you *require* a hank of this *flattering* Store Bought Hair? Just come as you are and when we are finished with you—well just come in to see us—then you be the judge!"

Another great benefactor was at work, but due to the fact that the Negro male would run the risk of burning out his brains if he took to the Hot Comb, this Einstein had a more difficult, arduous and exacting quest. But not to be daunted, he experimented, researched and concocted: and then one fateful day he returned victorious and announced to the world that, at long last, the Negro male, too, could have *silky-straight* locks, wavy and curly which, if you master the technique, you can even toss around a bit; it will even fall down in front of your eyes, just like the movie stars—that is, if you are prudent and do not overdo it.

"All you have to do, Sammy, my boy, is go see your barber, or go to the Beauty Parlor (oh, it's all right); just tell them to "tighten" your mop for you, man, and when they get through applying their Lye Solutions, their Caustic Soda Preparations, their Miracle Acids and Combinations of Acids—after that, you will be just like Boss Charlie! You will have such Beautiful Straight Hair!"

Ah! Love that scientific spirit.

"After Madam and Monsieur have finished their coiffure, why go right around the corner to the Drug Store and buy a big fat bottle of Skin Bleach! Get the six-month economy size! Oh, don't worry about which brand, all of them are medically tested, proven, and guaranteed to bleach your dull skin Pretty-Pink and White!"

According to Ebony's Hall of Fame, Madame C. J. Walker, the "founder of the world's oldest and biggest Negro cosmetics company," became "the first Negro woman millionaire," after starting business with $2 and an original formula for "refining the scalp and straightening hair," (as if the Negro's head was an unfinished product!). Madame Walker is acclaimed as a "pioneer in the field of Negro beauty culture," and was elected to the Hall of Fame for her "contributions to the progress of the Negro and the American way of life." Incidentally, Madame Walker mixed her first batch of hair straightener in a washtub; and her last prayer went thus:

"Not for me, O Lord, but for my race."

Apparently she felt that her "formula" had delivered the Negro from all evil.

Now it is not surprising that the Negro reacted so. That is the logical outcome of his historical experience.

But it is time that he checked himself. That he should continue to react in this way is not only surprising—it is beginning to be something of a scandal. Do not think that the reasons for such behavior have disappeared: on the contrary, they have gathered force and broadened. All of the mass media are constantly busy publicizing the Caucasian standard of beauty: the motion pictures, magazines, newspapers, television, literature, illustrated wall posters and bill boards—an unthinking (or money-hungry) Negro press—and most obvious and telling of all, the beauty contests.

What reaction do you think a young Negro girl has when a blonde haired, blue eyed "white" girl is held up and proclaimed as Miss America, or Miss Universe? When this is done, implicitly they are saying:

"This type of female is the ideal, the most beautiful female on earth, and the more closely you approximate her characteristics the more beautiful you will be, otherwise, my dear little black girl, you are just plain ugly!"

What unspoken and unspeakable wretchedness must scorch and flame in the heart of the young black girl when she witnesses this type of thing! Especially when the values of her friends, the Negro press—and in many cases—her own values, seem to acquiesce in applauding the Caucasian standard of beauty.

What Negro is there who has not felt an inarticulate questioning—deep down inside—upon being confronted with the Caucasian standard of beauty, especially if he has to make a decision, in his own mind, as to whether or not this is really beauty upon which he is looking? What rationalizations he is forced to make! And oh! What frustration and feelings of inferiority result! How much pathological, insane, peculiar behavior, do you think, is a direct result of this frustration caused by the standard of beauty which Negroes have accepted? Undoubtedly the proportion would prove alarming. With all the mass media disseminating this doctrine, it would be difficult, if not impossible, to find a Negro who has not been influenced by it.

Implicit in the very acceptance of the Caucasian standard of beauty is the negation of typical Negroid traits. If it is believed that blue eyes, long straight blonde hair, and non-colored skin are the component parts of beauty —then it logically follows that since Negroes generally do not share this particular variety of attributes, Negroes generally are not beautiful. To be sure, Negroes have eyes, and hair, and skins; but if you will just think about the words which Negroes employ to describe themselves, you will see that the words reflect degrees and gradations *away* from the Caucasian ideal of beauty.

Eye color does not present much of a problem, but notice that a Negro who possesses blue eyes, grey eyes, hazel eyes, light-brown eyes—a Negro with eyes of either of these colors is generally looked upon as being fortunate, whereas the majority of Negroes have eyes of a dark hue. It is axiomatic of the eye that when we look at it in search of beauty, we look for such things as the clearness—the sparkle, as it were—of the eyeball; the length and density of the eye-lashes and eye-brows, and the general contour of the eye. And it does not matter too much what the type of face is in which a beautiful eye is set. But still, when we consider the eye, we take our cue from the Caucasian standard of beauty.

But what happens when we consider skin color and hair texture? The very words that we use indicate that we have set a premium on the Caucasian ideal of beauty. When discussing interracial relations, we speak of "white people" and "non-white people." We will refer to people all over the world as "white" and "non-white." Notice that that particular choice of words gives precedence to "white people" by making them a center—a standard— to which "non-white" bears a negative relation. Notice the different connotations when we turn it around and say "colored" and "non-colored," or "black" and "non-black." Our thinking is so foggy on this issue that we describe our complexions as if they are qualities strewn along a yard-stick, the opposite ends of which are painted black and white respectively—black being the negative end. In this type of thinking, to be black is extremely unfortunate, and the higher up towards the white end of the yard-stick your complexion is located, the better off you are. We have a host of terms to fit the ascending graduations of the yard-stick: passing for white, high-yellow, real-light, high-brown, dark-brown, dark, black, blue-black, jet-black. In a sense these descriptive terms are accurate, because the complexions of those designated as 'Negro' run the gamut of the spectrum from 'jet-black' to 'passing for white.' However, it is our thinking—the relative value which we set on these various hues: and the fact that we do set *values* on them—that is what we are concerned with herein.

Now, when we consider the hair, we reach a topic on which we are extremely sensitive. This is because of the obvious variation between the texture of the typical Negro's hair and that of the typical Caucasian. But if Negroes are going to adhere to the Caucasian standard of beauty, must they not also pass judgment on the hair? Of course we must, and we have: we look upon our texture of hair as an affliction, a fiendish mockery of us by Mother Nature. Consequently we have another yardstick for *evaluating* the relative *quality* of our hair. This one progresses from "bad hair" to "good hair." The straighter the hair—that is to say, the more one's hair resembles that of the Caucasian—the "better" it is. Good hair, bad hair, nappy hair, kinky hair and so on. And *short-haired women*? Good Gravy! (God bless the soul to whom we must forever be humble for inventing the "Boyish Bob") Short hair is looked upon as an especial abomination. We do not have even any flattering words with which to describe our hair: but this is not surprising since we do not look upon our hair as being particularly flattering.

In her brilliant play, *A Raisin in the Sun*, Lorraine Hansberry focuses the spotlight squarely on this problem. But as it turned out, the lady Hansberry filed charges against the American Negro woman, and then refused to prosecute. In Act One, Scene Two, she has Asagai, the young Nigerian student who symbolizes the rebirth of Africa, tell Beneatha, an American Negro girl who is looking for her *identity*, that she has "mutilated" her hair; and this is what follows:

BENEATHA (Turning suddenly): My hair— what's wrong with my hair?

ASAGAI (Shrugging): Were you born with it like that?

BENEATHA (Reaching up to touch it): No ... of course not.
(She looks back to the mirror, disturbed.)

ASAGAI (Smiling): How then?

BENEATHA: You know perfectly well how ... as crinkly as yours ... that's how.

ASAGAI: And it is ugly to you that way?

BENEATHA (Quickly): Oh, no—not ugly ... (More slowly, apologetically) But it's so hard to manage when it's well—raw.

ASAGAI: And so to accommodate that— you mutilate it every week?

BENEATHA: It's not mutilation!

ASAGAI (Laughing aloud at her seriousness): Oh ... please! I am only teasing you because you are so very serious about these things. (He stands back from her and folds his arms across his chest as he watches her pulling at her hair and frowning in the mirror.)

How much worry, frustration—and wasted money—is a direct result of our attempts to run away from ourselves! We can pick up any issue of probably any Negro newspaper, and we will see a report of some opportunistic itinerant witch doctor, or perhaps an entire troup of witch doctors, touring the country, hitting the big "progressive" cities, teaching the eager populace the latest methods of becoming carbon copies of the Caucasian via the "last word" in beauty culture.

That the Negro press is a primary sower of these seeds of inferiority complexes, feelings of rejection and self-rejection, can be seen at a glance. Open almost any one of the Negro publications which carry advertisements of skin bleaches and skin lighteners, hair straighteners, false hair and wigs, etc., all with an emotion-charged indictment such as "Why should you *suffer* with hard to manage kinky ugly hair? Use Dr. Flop's Hair Straightener and become a big hit!" "Do you suffer from dull ugly skin? Get Hosana Bleaching Cream and have a fair, beautiful complexion!"

This type of advertising is usually accompanied by one of those convincing "Before and After" illustrations of some wretched, despondent young Negro girl or boy who, immediately after applying the product advertised, is suddenly transformed into a sparkling young center of attraction.

Ebony Magazine, which is probably the most widely read Negro magazine, periodically runs a feature which it presumptuously entitles "The World's Most Beautiful Negro Women" or something to that effect.

And what are the contents of this feature? Why the Caucasian standard of beauty, of course! Invariably, they will crown Lena Horne, Dorothy Dandridge, or someone else whose appearance would nominate them to compete rather for the title of Miss Scandinavia, Miss Greater Europe, or Miss Anything—other than that which is indicated by the title of the feature. And what emotions do you think the typical Negro girl experiences when she reads this feature? Why obviously, exactly the ones that are evoked when she sees the results of the Miss America or Miss Universe contests!

Thus, it is obvious that while on one hand, through no fault of his own, the Negro is a victim of a set of cultural values—on the other hand it is equally true that the Negro's response to this vicious situation has been to adjust to the environment through the dubious process of "mutilating" his natural ethnic characteristics in order to conform as best he could, to the Caucasian standard of beauty.

Of course, it would be facetious of us to campaign for a law to ban the Caucasian standard of beauty; but it is of paramount importance that we realize that there is absolutely no such thing as a universal standard of beauty for all people—black, brown, red, yellow, white—measuring up to which they stand or fall. The standards of beauty which exist in the world today are nothing but manifestations of ethnocentrism. Our concepts of beauty enter our minds through social indoctrination. We think a person with a certain complexion, a certain type of hair, a certain shape of nose, a certain color of eyes— we think that person possessed of beauty, not because he is beautiful per se, but rather because we have been culturally conditioned to look upon the particular traits of which he is possessed as being the most desirable, the most becoming: the beautiful. Let it be remembered that, historically, each ethnic group has looked upon its own characteristic traits as being beautiful.

If Negroes continue to respond blindly and unthinkingly to this indoctrination, then they as surely will continue to be plagued by the divisive self-hatreds, feelings of inferiority, etc., which are vestiges of the bygone days of the unchallenged sway of the odious doctrine of "White Supremacy." When we judge ourselves by the Caucasian standard of beauty and find that it does not fit us, if we have accepted that standard as absolute, then our reaction is not merely that we think our own individual selves ugly, it extends much farther than that: it touches every facet of our existence, it influences the very value which we set on ourselves as individuals, it colors our thinking and our opinion of the race as a whole— in short—it has a disastrous effect. This confusion pursues many of us all through life, "like the Furies in a Greek play," driving us deeper into a private hell.

To be sure, it is a hyper-ethnocentric

act—but one consonant with the doctrine of "White Supremacy"—for the
Caucasian to hold up one of his members
and crown him or her Mister or Miss
Universe; but it is *something else* when
the Negro accepts this standard, and
then proceeds with a host of contrivances
to warp his natural characteristics in
a vain effort to measure up to that alien
standard. Until the social values of
human beings evolve to the point where
we no longer feel the need to aggrandize
ourselves above our fellow men on the
quicksand ground of ethnic superiority,
until that time, we will have with us the
spectacle of the Eskimos in Alaska
saying that they are the most beautiful
people in creation; the Chinese in China
saying that they alone are beautiful;
the Japanese, the Arabs, the Australian
Aborigines, all in their own lands saying
the same thing, while the Caucasian
proclaims it to the entire world. But
let us hope that the Negro will not still
be running along behind in the "white
shadows" with his Hot Combs and
Bleaching Creams in an orgy of self-
destroying mimicry.

It is superficially absurd for a given
ethnic group to judge itself by the standard of some other group. If we were
to take a Caucasian man and woman
and judge their beauty by a people's
standard other than their own, that
Caucasian man and woman would be
judged as ugly. The same will be the
result when we judge others by the
Caucasian standard of beauty, or when
we judge a member of one ethnic group
by the prevailing standard of another
ethnic group.

Would it not be superfluous for the
Pygmies to take for their standard of
beauty that of the Watusi? The average
height of the Watusi is about 7 feet,
while that of the Pygmy is about 4 1/2
feet! In addition, the Watusi are rather
large of body while the Pygmies are rather
small. Would it not be a fallacy for the
Pygmy to set about inventing contrivances with which to eradicate their
natural physical endowments in order
to measure up to the Watusi ideal of
beauty? They could invent stretching
machines to elongate their diminutive
bodies: and they could inflate their
torsos with helium and become Watusi-
like! And wouldn't the Watusi seem
ridiculous to try to approximate the
ideal of the Pygmy? They would have
quite a shrinking job on their hands!
But should either of them consider
himself inferior because of their differences? This is analogous to the Negro's
present position.

Let it be remembered that the purpose of this essay is to call attention to
certain unhealthy concepts and ideals
which currently are held by all too many
Negroes. Essentially, the problem is
a psychological one. It concerns unexa-
mined ideals and practices which are an
integral part of our social heritage,
and which are fostered and inculcated
by the white-oriented culture of which
we are members. By becoming aware
of the nature and origin of our beliefs
and ideals, we are better able to understand and manipulate them if it becomes
apparent that they need readjustment.
When a group of ideals and beliefs
become the authors of as much evil
as the ones under discussion, then it is
obvious that they require examination
and readjustment. If there is a general
stigma attached to the Negro because
of his previous condition of servitude,
and if the Negro does have something
of an inferiority complex, it is composed

of elements such as the ones isolated in this essay. We try to escape this stigma and complex by becoming "passively Negro," i.e., we accept our status as Negroes only because we can not escape it. The danger lies in the fact that there are only three main positions from which one must choose on the issue of belonging to a particular ethnic group: there is a positive, a neutral, and a negative position. The ethnocentric bigot will take the positive; he who realizes that all men are brothers and that they are all of the same moral value must, in order to be consistent, take the neutral position; the negative is owned by those who despise what they are, consciously or subconsciously, their vociferations to the contrary notwithstanding.

Psychologically, a Negro of the negative position, i.e., a Negative Negro, attempts to purge himself of any and all traits which identify him as Negro. This brings us to a very important point, one which goes hand in hand with the Caucasian standard of beauty, and yet runs deeper and cuts deeper than any other facet of the entire affair.

THE POLARIZED WESTERN MIND

What we term as *The Polarized Western Mind* derives from the symbolism attached to the two colors, black and white, in the mind of Western man. These two colors are highly charged and the symbolization is deeply ingrained in the thinking and culture of the West. Everything that is good, desirable, beautiful, morally elevated, pure—in short, the highest abstractions of the Western mind are denoted by the celestial hue of white. And at the opposite end of the pole lies the degrading shade of black. Everything that is debased, corrupt, feared, evil, and ugly, is identified with the color black.

Even in those activities which touch us deepest, such as religion, we find manifestations of this polarization. For an instance, when persons are united in the *sacred* rites of matrimony the traditional garments worn by the bride to symbolize her virtue and chastity are of the color white. While at the other end of the pole, at the time of death, or rather the funeral following death, the traditional attire of those in mourning is of the *dreary* hue of black. Instances of this polarization could be cited from now until doomsday: there is an old Negro Spiritual which calls upon Jesus to "wash my sins away and make me white as snow." We speak of black cats causing bad luck, and black magic, and individuals with malignant black hearts.*

This polarization affects the mind in very subtle ways. We are not conscious of it, as such, when it is in motion, but it colors our thinking just the same.

---

* Several writers have pointed out the bias implicit in English by examining the words and phrases containing "black." They invariably have an unfavorable connotation: blackmail, black-hearted, blackguard, black list, etc. White, on the other hand, often has a positive connotation, e.g., even lies which are "white" are thought to be acceptable. There are occasional exceptions to these general trends, e.g., to be in the black—as opposed to being in the red (in debt), or to white-wash (cover over) a scandal or to buy a white elephant (something useless), but generally the white/good and black/bad dichotomy is consistent. For further discussion, see Ossie Davis, "The English Language is My Enemy," *The Negro History Bulletin*, vol. 30, no. 4 (1967), p. 18; Simon Podair, "Language and Prejudice Toward Negroes," *Phylon*, vol. 17 (1956), pp. 390–94; and Eric Berne, "The Mythology of Dark and Fair: Psychiatric Use of Folklore," *Journal of American Folklore*, 72 (1959), pp. 1–13. —ED.

An obvious and striking example of polarized thinking came to our attention recently. It concerned an illustrated cartoon satirizing the fallacious stupidity of the non-policy of segregation. The artist presents Jesus Christ hanging sufferingly from his cross; there ran a barbed wire fence through the center of Jesus and the cross, bisecting them; on one side of the fence kneeled a black man, and on the other side kneeled a white man; everything on the black man's side was painted black to symbolize the separation, and everything on the other side was painted white to further emphasize the separation; the cross, too, was painted black and white on the respective sides—but Jesus himself was pure white! If the artist had been logically consistent, he would have painted Jesus one-half black and one-half white. But the artist's polarized mind would not allow him to represent the Savior in the infamous hue of despised black.

And just as the Negro lives in the shadows cast by the connotations of the terms Negro and black, the Caucasian is living in the reflected glory of the term white. By describing himself as white, the Caucasian associates himself with the highest ideals and values in our culture.

Have you ever seen such a thing as a *white* man? Wow, what a sight that would be! Actually, if the Caucasian were forced to describe his hue realistically, he would be hard pressed to discover a hue in the spectrum that would plausibly coincide with his own. But, having labled himself *white*, whenever he hears that name called, a flattering process of association goes on in his mind. And whenever a non-Caucasian with a polarized mind utilizes the term

white in referring to the Caucasian, the same associations are made.

When the term *black* is applied to the Negro (Negro being the Latin for black), the process is reversed. Along with all of the unsavory connotations of the word *black*, in the polarized mind, the Negro is subconsciously condemned and degraded. Not that the term *black* is, in itself, derogatory, but rather that it is incumbent upon the polarized mind to make the associations that the connotations of the term carry, and through those associations, the imperative condemnation follows.

A Negro with a polarized mind is daily committing a type of mental suicide on the installment plan. The component parts of his polarization are constantly gnawing away at his sanity. He has to make myriad rationalizations; but there are times when the mind is unable to come up with the appropriate rationalization; these are the times when the conscious mental aberrations occur, the crushing of the personality under the leaden weight of the inferiority complex, the slow burn of suppressed rage; and these are the times when the black hand will reach for the bottle of whiskey, narcotics, or what have you, to blot out the insupportable reality which hovers above one in a stultifying cloud of condemnation, and one is further crushed when this occurs because one will describe the burdensome reality as: "Ah, the *black* clouds!"

It is manifest, then, that for the sake of the people who are the victims of this polarization, they must shatter these antiquated cliches of thought and, as it were, de-polarize their minds. It is not to be supposed that values so deeply rooted in our culture can be re-fashioned over night; but, by realizing that the problem exists the job is half-done.

What we must do is stop associating the Caucasian with these exalted connotations of the word *white* when we think or speak of him. At the same time, we must cease associating ourselves with the unsavory connotations of the word *black*. "A house divided against itself cannot stand," how much truer this must be for the mind! We can talk, preach, and write about race pride and self-respect interminably, but in the last analysis, if we are indeed to have any pride, we must root-out from our thinking and folklore those elements which have robbed us of our pride.

When a black President Kwame Nkrumah of Ghana, arrayed majestically in colorful tribal robes, can stride in towering dignity and pride onto the highest rostrum of the United Nations General Assembly, and deliver a rousing, epoch-making speech—without first pausing to either "straighten" his hair or "bleach" his skin, the unspoken message to his brethren is unmistakable: Black is Coming Back! The rebirth of Africa, black dignity and black power, is destined to raise the black end of the yard-stick from the depths to which it was crushed by the oppressive weight of the doctrine of "White Supremacy" —raise it back into proper equilibrium. And then when Africa asks the American Negro with what type of hair was he born, he will answer loud and clear, with dignity and pride: "As crinkly as yours."

My People! My People!

ZORA NEALE HURSTON

Perhaps one of the best discussions of the relationships between folklore and race pride is that of Zora Neale Hurston, who has been one of the most eloquent and insightful American Negro folklorists to date. Trained in part by anthropologist Franz Boas at Columbia University, Miss Hurston was one of the few American Negro writers who did not turn their back on the rich traditions of Afro-American folklore. Although much of her energy was devoted to creative writing, Miss Hurston never lost her interest in collecting folklore. Many of her collections still stand as major documents in American Negro folklore, e.g., Mules and Men *(Philadelphia and London, 1935; paperback edition New York, 1970), which contains her intensive investigation of hoodoo first published in the* Journal of American Folklore *in 1931.*

The present essay appeared originally as a chapter in her autobiography and it is a marvelous statement by a sensitive spirit who was proud of being a Negro and of being a folklorist. For more about Zora Neale Hurston, see Hugh M. Gloster, "Zora Neale Hurston, Novelist and Folklorist," Phylon, *4 (1943), pp. 153–59; James W. Byrd, "Zora Neale Hurston: A Novel Folklorist,"* Tennessee Folklore Society Bulletin, *21 (1955), pp. 37–41; Alan Lomax, "Zora Neale Hurston—A Life of Negro Folkore,"* Sing Out, *10 (October–November, 1960), pp. 12–13; Emma L. Blake, "Zora Neale Hurston: Author and Folklorist,"* Negro History Bulletin, *29 (1966), pp. 149–50, 165. See also Clarence Merton Babcock,* A Word-List from Zora Neale Hurston, *Publication of the American Dialect Society, no. 40 (University: University of Alabama Press, 1963), and Darwin T. Turner, "Introduction to the Perennial Edition," in the paperback edition of* Mules and Men *(New York: Harper and Row, 1970), pp. 6–15.*

"MY PEOPLE! My people!" From the earliest rocking of my cradle days I have heard this cry go up from Negro lips.* It is forced outward by pity, scorn and hopeless resignation. It is called forth by the observations of one class of Negro on the doings of another branch of the brother in black. For instance, well-mannered Negroes groan out like that when they board a train or a bus and find other Negroes on there with their shoes off, stuffing themselves with fried fish, bananas and peanuts, and throwing the garbage on the floor. Maybe they are not only eating and drinking. The offenders may be "loud-talking" the place, and holding back nothing of their private lives, in a voice that embraces the entire coach.† The well-dressed Negro shrinks back in his seat at that, shakes his head and sighs, "My people! My people!"

Now, the well-mannered Negro is embarrassed by the crude behaviour of the others. They are not friends, and have never seen each other before. So why should he or she be embarrassed? It is like this: the well-bred Negro has looked around and seen America with his eyes. He or she has set himself to measure up to what he thinks of as the white standard of living. He is conscious of the fact that the Negro in America needs more respect if he expects to get any acceptance at all. Therefore, after straining every nerve to get an education, maintain an attractive home, dress decently, and otherwise conform, he is dismayed at the sight of other Negroes tearing down what he is trying to build up. It is said every day, "And that good-for-nothing, trashy Negro is the one the white people judge us all by. They think we're all just alike. My people! My people!"

What that educated Negro knows further is that he can do very little towards imposing his own viewpoint on the lowlier members of his race. Class and culture stand between. The humble Negro has a built-up antagonism to the "Big Nigger." It is a curious thing that he does not resent a white man looking down on him. But he resents any lines between himself and the wealthy and educated of his own race. "He's a nigger

* There is some evidence that this phrase goes back at least to the turn of the century. It is used, for example, in a 1907 complaint about Negro leaders who feign friendliness to other Negroes but who give their business exclusively to white doctors, lawyers, merchants, etc. Part of the critical comment is: "You can hear a great deal of talk about 'my people,' and high-sounding gush about race pride from many colored folks, but what the race needs is not so much loud talk, but some doing . . ."—"doing" referring to supporting *Negro* doctors, lawyers, merchants, etc. See "The 'Lemon' Handshake," *The Colored American Magazine*, 13 (1907), pp. 168–69. —ED.

† This technique of Negro speech has begun to receive the attention of linguists. See "louding" in the unpublished Columbia University study by William Labov, Paul Cohen, Clarence Robins, and John Lewis, "A Study of the Non-Standard English of Negro and Puerto Rican Speakers in New York City," vol. II, *The Use of Language in the Speech Community* (1968), pp. 77, 114, 129, or the fuller discussion of "loud-talking" in Claudia Mitchell-Kernan's unpublished 1969 doctoral dissertation at the University of California, Berkeley: "Language Behavior in a Black Urban Community," pp. 129–37. (The thesis has been issued as Working Paper No. 23 of the Language-Behavior Research Laboratory at the University of California, Berkeley.) In a novel describing the lifestyle of Negro pimps, there is an interesting reference to a "loud-talk session": " 'Talk loud and draw a crowd' was the motto of the super-cool characters. The louder one talked the more the onlookers thought one was saying." See Nathan C. Heard, *Howard Street* (New York: Signet Books, 1970), p. 227. —ED.

just like us," is the sullen rejoinder. The only answer to this is, "My people! My people!"

So the quiet-spoken Negro man or woman who finds himself in the midst of one of these "broadcasts", as on the train, cannot go over and say, "Don't act like that, brother. You're giving us all a black eye." He or she would know better than to try that. The performance would not only go on, it would get better, with the "dicky" Negro as the butt of all the quips.* The educated Negro may know all about differential calculus and the theory of evolution, but he is fighting entirely out of his class when he tries to quip with the underprivileged. The bookless may have difficulty in reading a paragraph in a newspaper, but when they get down to "playing the dozens" they have no equal in America, and, I'd risk a sizeable bet,

in the whole world.† Starting off in the first by calling you a seven-sided son-of-a-bitch, and pausing to name the sides, they proceed to "specify" until the tip-top branch of your family tree has been "given a reading".‡ No profit in that to the upper-class Negro, so he minds his own business and groans, "My people! My people!"

It being a traditional cry, I was bound to hear it often and under many circumstances. But it is not the only folk label that I heard. "Race Pride", "Race Prejudice", "Race Man", "Race Solidarity", "Race Consciousness", "Race".

"Race Prejudice", I was instructed, was something bad that white people used on us. It seemed that white people felt superior to black ones and would not give Negroes justice for that reason. "Race Pride" was something that, if we had it, we would feel ourselves

---

* "Dicty" means haughty or snobbish. For illustrations of "dicty," see Horace R. Cayton, *Long Old Road* (New York, 1965), p. 51; Harold Wentworth and Stuart Berg Flexner, *Dictionary of American Slang* (New York, 1960), p. 146; and Clarence Major, *Dictionary of Afro-American Slang* (New York, 1970) p. 46. Miss Hurston also uses the term in her "Story in Harlem Slang" reprinted in this volume.

Other common adjectives for someone who puts on airs include "uppity", "hinkty" or "hincty", and "siditty." For examples of the use of "siditty," see Maya Angelou, *I know Why the Caged Bird Sings* (New York, 1969), pp. 62, 232: Nathan C. Heard, *Howard Street* (New York, 1970), p. 31. "Siditty," though often pronounced with the primary stress on the second syllable may derive from "side" as in "High-siding" which Eldridge Cleaver defines as cutting up, having fun at the expense of another. See *Soul on Ice* (New York, 1968), p. 27. "High-siding" in turn may be a transformation of "High Society." "High-Societying" would thus refer to someone trying to put on airs and/or act condescending toward another person with the latter person feeling that the condescension was not appropriate.

In connection with the above discussion, it may be worth noting that there appears to be a common theme in Negro folklore which warns against acting "high and mighty." I am indebted to Willie Mae Kelley for the following two proverbs which illustrate this theme. In Sulphur Springs, Texas, circa 1920, Mrs. Kelley remembers her mother saying "There never was a bird that flew so high that it didn't have to come down to earth to drink water." Around the same period, she recalls the president of Jarvis Christian College in Hawkins, Texas, saying "Don't ever let your clock strike twelve." The metaphor warns against placing oneself up on a pedestal, as it were, because, although one may feel safe, superior, and removed on the hands at high noon, one is bound to descend when the hands go down. —ED.

† For further discussion of "playing the dozens," see the essays by Dollard and Abrahams in this volume. —ED.

‡ It is possible that "specify" means much the same thing as "signify." For an analysis of "signifiyin'" see the essay by Claudia Mitchell-Kernan in this volume. —ED.

superior to the whites. A black skin was the greatest honour that could be blessed on any man. A "Race Man" was somebody who always kept the glory and honor of his race before him. Must stand ever ready to defend the Negro race from all hurt, harm and danger. Especially if a white person said, "Nigger", "You people", "Negress" or "Darkies". It was a mark of shame if somebody accused: "Why, you are not a Race Man (or woman)." People made whole careers of being "Race" men and women. They were champions of the race.

"Race Consciousness" is a plea to Negroes to bear their color in mind at all times. It was just a phrase to me when I was a child. I knew it was supposed to mean something deep. By the time I got grown I saw that it was only an imposing line of syllables, for no Negro in America is apt to forget his race. "Race Solidarity" looked like something solid in my childhood, but like all other mirages, it faded as I came close enough to look. As soon as I could think, I saw that there is no such thing as Race Solidarity in America with any group. It is freely admitted that it does not exist among Negroes. Our so-called Race Leaders cry over it. Others accept it as a natural thing that Negroes should not remain an unmelting black knot in the body politic. Our interests are too varied. Personal benefits run counter to race lines too often for it to hold. If it did, we could never fit into the national pattern. Since the race line has never held any other group in America, why expect it to be effective with us? The upper-class Negroes admit it in their own phrases. The lower-class Negroes say it with a tale.

It seems that a Negro was asked to lead the congregation in prayer. He got down on his knees and began, "O Lawd, I got something to ask You, but I know you can't do it."

"Go on, Brother Isham, and ask Him."

"Lawd," Brother Isham began again, "I really want to ask You something but I just know You can't do it."

"Aw, Brother Isham, go on and tell the Lawd what you want. He's the Lawd! Ain't nothing He can't do! He can even lead a butt-headed cow by the horns. You're killing up time. Go 'head on, Brother Isham, and let the church roll on."

"Well then, Lawd, I ask You to get these Negroes together, but I know You can't do it." Then there is laughter and, "My people! My people!"

Hearing things like this from my childhood, sooner or later I was bound to have some curiosity about my race of people.

What fell into my ears from time to time tended more to confuse than to clarify. One thing made a liar out of the one that went before and the thing that came after. At different times I heard opposite viewpoints expressed by the same person or persons.

For instance, come school-closing time and like formal occasions, I heard speeches which brought thunderous applause. I did not know the word for it at the time, but it did not take me long to know the material was traditional. Just as folk as the songs in church. I knew that because so many people got up and used the same identical phrases: (a) The Negro had made the greatest progress in fifty years of any race on the face of the globe. (b) Negroes composed the most *beautiful* race on earth, being just like a flower garden with every color and kind. (*c*) Negroes were the bravest men on earth, facing every danger like lions, and fighting with demons. We must remember with pride that the first blood spilled for American Independence was that of the brave and daring Crispus Attucks, a Negro who had bared his black breast to the bullets of the British tyrants at Boston, and thus struck the first blow for American liberty. They had marched with Colonel Shaw during the Civil War and hurled back the forces of the iniquitous South, who sought to hold black men in bondage. It was a Negro named Simon who had been the only one with enough pity and compassion in his heart to help the Saviour bear His cross upon Calvary. It was the Negro troops under Teddy Roosevelt who won the battle of San Juan Hill.

It was the genius of the Negro which had invented the steam-engine, the cotton gin, the air-brake, and numerous other things—but conniving white men had seen the Negro's inventions and run off and put them into practice before the Negro had a chance to do anything about it. Thus the white man got credit for what the genius of the Negro brain had produced. Were it not for the envy and greed of the white man, the Negro would hold his rightful place—the noblest and the greatest man on earth.

The people listening would cheer themselves hoarse and go home feeling good. Over the fences next day it would be agreed that it was a wonderful speech, and nothing but the God's truth. What a great people we would be if we only had our rights!

But my own pinnacle would be made to reel and rock anyway by other things I heard from the very people who always applauded "the great speech", when it was shouted to them from the schoolhouse rostrum. For instance, let some member of the community do or say something which was considered either dumb or underhand: the verdict would be "Dat's just like a nigger!" or "Nigger from nigger leave nigger" —("Nothing from nothing leave nothing.") It was not said in either admiration or pity. Utter scorn was in the saying. "Old Cuffy just got to cut de fool, you know. Monkey see, monkey do. Nigger see de white man do something, he jump in and try to do like de white man, and make a great big old mess." "My people! My people!"

"Yeah, you's mighty right. Another monkey on de line. De white man, you understand, he was a railroad engineer, so he had a pet monkey used to take along wid him all de time. De monkey, he set up there in de cab wid de engineer and see what he do to run de train. Way after while, figger he can run de train just as good as de engineer his own self. He was just itching to git at dat throttle and bust dat main line wide open. Well, one day de engineer jumped down at de station to git his orders and old monkey seen his chance. He just jumped up in de engineer's seat, grabbed a holt of dat throttle, and dat engine was splitting de wind down de track. So de engineer sent a message on ahead, say, 'Clear de track. Monkey on de line!' Well, Brer Monk he was holding de throttle wide open and jumping up and down and laughing fit to kill. 'Course, he didn't know nothing about no side tracks and no switches and no schedules, so he was making a mile a minute when he hit a open switch and a string of box cars was standing on de siding. Ker-blam-er-lam-er-lam! And dat was de last of Brer Engine-driving Monk. Lovely monkey he was, but a damned poor engineer."

"My people! My people!"

Everybody would laugh at that, and the laughter puzzled me some. Weren't Negroes the smartest people on earth, or something like that? Somebody ought to remind the people of what we had heard at the schoolhouse. Instead of that, there would be more monkey stories.

There was the one about the white doctor who had a pet monkey who wanted to be a doctor. Kept worrying his master to show him how, and the doctor had other troubles, too. Another man had a bulldog who used to pass the doctor's gate every day and pick a fight with the monkey. Finally, the doctor saw a way to stop the monkey from worrying him about showing him how to be a doctor. "Whip that bulldog until he evacuates, then bring me some of it, monkey. I'll take it and show you how to be a doctor, and then I'll treat it in a way so as to ruin that bulldog for life. He won't be no more trouble to you."

"Oh, I'll git it, boss. Don't you worry. I sho' wants to be a doctor, and then again, dat old bulldog sho' is worrisome."

No sooner did the bulldog reach the gate that day than the monkey, which could not wait for the bulldog to start the fight as usual, jumped on the dog. The monkey was all over him like gravy over rice. He put all he had into it and it went on until the doctor came out and drove the dog off and gave the monkey a chance to bolt into the office with what he had been fighting for.

"Here 'tis, boss. It was a tight fight, but I got it."

"Fine! Fine!" the doctor told him. "Now, gimme that bottle over there. I'll fix that bulldog so he'll never be able to sit down again. When I get through with this, he'll be ruined for life."

"Hold on there, boss! Hold on there a minute! I wish you wouldn't do dat, boss."

"How come? You want to get rid of that old bulldog, don't you?"

"Dat's right, I sho' do."

"Well, why don't you want me to fix him, then?"

"Well, boss, you see, it's like dis. Dat was a tight fight, a mighty tight fight. I could have been mistaken about dat bulldog, boss, we was all tangled up together so bad. You better leave dat fixing business alone, boss. De wrong man might git hurt."

There were many other tales, equally ludicrous, in which the Negro, sometimes symbolized by the monkey, and sometimes named outright, ran off with the wrong understanding of what he had seen and heard. Several white and Negro proposals of marriage were compared, and the like. The white suitor had said his love had dove's eyes. His valet had hurried to compliment his girl by saying she had dog's eyes, and so on.

There was a general acceptance of the monkey as kinfolks. Perhaps it was some distant memory of tribal monkey reverence from Africa which had been forgotten in the main, but remembered in some vague way. Perhaps it was an acknowledgement of our talent for mimicry with the monkey as a symbol.

The classic monkey parable, which is very much alive wherever the Negroes congregate in America, is the one about "My people!"

It seems that a monkey squatted down in the middle of a highway to play. A Cadillac full of white people came along, saw the monkey at play and carefully drove around him. Then came a Buick full of more white people and did the same. The monkey kept right on playing. Way after a while a T-model Ford came along full of Negroes. But instead of driving around the monkey, the car headed straight for him. He only saved his life by a quick leap to the shoulder of the road. He sat there and watched the car rattle off in the distance, and sighed, "My people! My people!"

A new addition to the tale is that the monkey has quit saying, "My people!" He is now saying, "Those people! Those people!"*

I found the Negro, and always the blackest Negro, being made the butt of all jokes—particularly black women.

They brought bad luck for a week if they came to your house of a Monday morning. They were evil. They slept with their fists balled up ready to fight and squabble even while they were asleep. They even had evil dreams. White, yellow and brown girls dreamed about roses and perfume and kisses. Black gals dreamed about guns, razors, ice-picks, hatchets and hot lye. I heard men swear they had seen women dreaming and knew these things to be true.

"Oh, gwan!" somebody would chide, laughing. "You know dat ain't so."

"Oh, now, he ain't lying," somebody else would take up the theme. "I know for my own self. I done slept wid yaller women and I done slept wid black ones. They *is* evil. You marry a yaller or a brown woman and wake her up in de night and she will sort of stretch herself and say, 'I know what I was dreaming when you woke me up. I was dreaming I had done baked you a chicken and cooked you a great big old cake, and we was at de table eating our dinner out of de same plate, and I was sitting on your lap and we was just enjoying our-selves to death!' Then she will kiss you more times than you ask her to, and go on back to sleep. But you take and wake up a black gal, now! First thing she been sleeping wid her fists balled up, and you shake her, she'll lam you five or six times before you can get her awake. Then when she do git wake she'll have off and ast you, 'Nigger, what you wake me up for? Know what I was dreaming when you woke me up? I dreamt dat you shook your old rusty black fist under my nose and I split your head open wid a axe.' Then she'll kick your feets away from hers, snatch de covers all over on her side, ball up her fists agin, and gwan back to sleep. You can't tell me nothing. I know." "My people!"

This always was, and is still, good for a raucous burst of laughter. I listened to this talk and became more and more confused. If it was so honorable and glorious to be black, why was it the yellow-skinned people among us had

* In another version of this classic, a monkey observes a beggar successfully stop a passing wagon to receive a dime. The monkey does the same thing and also receives a dime. At that point, a wagon with a Negro driver comes along and drives right over the monkey. Suddenly, the wagon stops and returns. The monkey assumes the driver intends to apologize or to offer asistance, but instead the driver simply takes the dime. The story ends with the monkey shaking his head sadly, saying, "Our race won't do." See K. Leroy Irvis, "Negro Tales from Eastern New York," *New York Folklore Quarterly*, vol. 11 (1955), pp. 170–71. —Ed.

so much prestige? Even a child in the first grade could see that this was so from what happened in the classroom and on school programs. The light-skinned children were always the angels, fairies and queens of school plays. The lighter the girl, the more money and prestige she was apt, and expected, to marry. So on into high-school years, I was asking myself questions. Were Negroes the great heroes I heard about from the platform, or were they the ridiculous monkeys of everyday talk? Was it really honorable to be black? There was even talk that it was no use for Negro boys and girls to rub all the hair off of their heads against college walls. There was no place for them to go with it after they got all this education. Some of the older heads held that it was too much for Negroes to handle. Better leave such things for the white folks, who knew what to do with it. But there were others who were all for pushing ahead. I saw the conflict in my own home between my parents. My mother was the one to dare all. My father was satisfied.

This Negro business came home to me in incidents and ways. There was the time when Old Man Bronner was taken out and beaten. Mr. Bronner was a white man of the poor class who had settled in aristocratic Maitland. One night, just after dark, we heard terrible cries back in the woods behind Park Lane. Sam Moseley, his brother Elijah, and Ike Clarke hurried up to our gate and they were armed. The howls of pain kept up. Old fears and memories must have stirred inside of the grown folks. Many people closed and barred their doors. Papa and the men around our gate were sullen and

restless as the cries churned over the woods and lake.

"Who do you reckon it is?" Sam Moseley asked.

"I don't know for sure, but some thinks it's Jim Watson. Anyhow, he ain't home yet," Clarke said, and all of them looked at each other in an asking way.

Finally Papa said, "Well, hold on a minute till I go get my rifle."

"'Tain't no ifs and buts about it," Elijah Moseley said gravely. "We can't leave Jim Watson be beat to death like that."

Papa had sensed that these armed men had not come to merely stand around and talk. They had come to see if he would go with the rest. When he came out shoving the sixteen bullets into his rifle, and dropping more into his pocket, Mama made no move to stop him. "Well, we all got families," he said with an attempt at lightness. "Shoot off your gun, somebody, so de rest will know we ready."

Papa himself pointed his Winchester rifle at the sky and fired a shot. Another shot answered him from around the store and a huddle of figures came hurrying up the road in the dark.

"It's Jim Watson. Us got to go git him!" and the dozen or more men armed with double-barrelled shotguns, breech-loaders, pistols and Papa's repeating Winchester hurried off on their grim mission. Perhaps not a single one of them expected to return alive. No doubt they hoped. But they went.

Mama gasped a short sentence of some sort and herded us all into the house and barred the door. Lights went out all over the village and doors were barred. Axes had been dragged in from woodpiles, grass-hooks, pitchforks and scythes were ranked up in corners behind those barred doors. If the men did not come back, or if they only came back in part, the women and children were ready to do the best they could. Mama spoke only to say she wished Hezekiah and John, the two biggest boys, had not gone to Maitland late in the afternoon. They were not back and she feared they might start home and—— But she did not cry. Our seven hounds, with big, ferocious Ned in the lead, barked around the house. We huddled around Mama in her room and kept quiet. There was not a human sound in all the village. Nothing had ever happened before in our vicinity to create such tension. But people had memories and told tales of what happened back there in Georgia and Alabama and West Florida that made the skin of the young crawl with transmitted memory, and reminded the old heads that they were still flinchy.

The dark silence of the village kept up for an hour or more. The once loud cries fell and fell until our straining ears could no longer find them. Strangest of all, not a shot was fired. We huddled in the dark and waited, and died a little, and waited. The silence was ten times more punishing than the cries.

At long last, a bubble of laughing voices approached our barn from the rear. It got louder and took on other dimensions between the barn and the house. Mama hissed at us to shut up when, in fact, nobody was saying a thing.

"Hey there, Little-Bits," Papa bellowed. "Open up!"

"Strike a light, Daught," Mama told my sister, feeling around in the dark to find Sarah's hand to give her the matches which I had seen clutched in her fingers before she had put out the light. Mama had said very little, and I could not see her face in the dark; somehow she could not scratch a match now that Papa was home again.

All of the men came in behind Papa, laughing and joking, perhaps more from relief than anything else.

"Don't stand there grinning like a chessy cat, Mr. Hurston," Mama scolded. "You ain't told me a thing."

"Oh, it wasn't Jim Watson at all, Lulu. You remember 'bout a week ago Old Man Bronner wrote something in de Orlando paper about H.'s daughter and W.B.G.'s son being seen sitting around the lakes an awful lot?"

"Yeah, I heard something about it."

"Well, you know those rich white folks wasn't going to 'low nothing like dat. So some of 'em waylaid him this evening. They pulled him down off of a load of hay he was hauling and drug him off back there in de woods and tanned his hide for him."

"Did y'all see any of it?"

"Nope, we could hear him hollering for a while, though. We never got no further than the lake. A white man, one of the G——boys, was standing in the bushes at de road. When we got ready to turn off round de lake he stepped out and spoke to us and told us it didn't concern us. They had Bronner down there tied down on his all-fours, and de men was taking turns wid dat bull whip. They must have been standing on tip-toes to do it. You could hear them licks clear out to de road."

The men all laughed. Somebody mocked Bronner's cries and moans a time or two and the crowd laughed immoderately. They had gone out to rescue a neighbour or die in the attempt, and they were back with their families. So they let loose their insides and laughed. They resurrected a joke or two and worried it like a bone and laughed some more. Then they just laughed. The men who spoke of members of their race as monkeys had gone out to die for one. The men who were always saying, "My skin-folks, but not kinfolks; my race but not my taste," had rushed forth to die for one of these same contemptibles. They shoved each other around and laughed. So I could see that what looked like ridicule was really the Negro poking a little fun at himself. At the same time, just like other people, hoping and wishing he was what the orators said he was.

My mother eased back in her chair and took a dip of snuff. Maybe she did not feel so well, for she didn't get tickled at all. After a while, she ordered us off to bed in a rough voice. Time was, and the men scattered. Mama sat right where she was until Hezekiah and John came home around ten o'clock. She gave them an awful going over with her tongue for staying out late, and then she eased to bed.

I was dredged up inside that night, so I did not think about the incident's general connection with race. Besides, I had to go to sleep. But days later it was called to my recollection again. There was a program at the Methodist Church, and Mrs. Mattie Moseley, it was announced, was to have a paper. She was also going to have a fine new dress to read it in. We all wanted to see the dress.

The time came and she had the dress on. The subject of her paper was, "What will the Negroes do with the Whites?" I do not know what she decided was

to be done. It seemed equally unimportant to the rest of the town. I remember that everybody said it was a fine subject. But the next week the women talked about nothing else but the new wristwatch she had on. It was the first one ever seen in our town.

But in me, the affair stirred up more confusion. Why bring the subject up? Something was moving around me which I had no hooks to grasp. What was this about white and black people that was being talked about?

Certainly nothing changed in the village. The townspeople who were in domestic service over in Maitland or Winter Park went to work as usual. The white people interested in Eatonville came and went as before. Mr. Irving Bacheller, the author, who had a show place in Winter Park, petted up Willie Sewell, who was his head gardener, in the same old way. Bishop Whipple petted Elijah Moseley, and Mrs. Mars, who was his sister, did lots of things for Lulu Moseley, Elijah's wife. What was all the talk about? It certainly was puzzling to me.

As time went on, the confusion grew. By the time that I got to high school I was conscious of a group that was neither the top nor the bottom of Negrodom. I met the type which designates itself as "the better-thinking Negro". I was thrown off my stride by finding that while they considered themselves Race Champions, they wanted nothing to do with anything frankly Negroid. They drew color lines within the race. The Spirituals, the Blues, *any* definitely Negroid thing was just not done. They went to the trouble at times to protest the use of them by Negro artists. Booker T. Washington was absolutely vile for advocating industrial education. There was no analysis, no seeking for merits. If it was old cuffy, down with it! "My People! My people!"

This irritated me until I got to the place where I could analyze. The thing they were trying to do went wrong because it lacked reason. It lacked reason because they were attempting to stand equal with the best in America without having the tools to work with. They were attempting a flight away from Negrodom because they felt that there was so much scorn for black skin in the nation that their only security was in flight. They lacked the happy carelessness of a class beneath them and the understanding of the top-flight Negro above them. Once, when they used to set their mouths in what they thought was the Boston Crimp, and ask me about the great differences between the ordinary Negro and "the betterthinking Negro", I used to show my irritation by saying I did not know who the better-thinking Negro was. I knew who the think-they-are-better Negroes were, but who were the better-thinkers was another matter. But when I came to understand what made them make their useless motions, and saw them pacing a cage that wasn't there, I felt more sympathy than irritation. If they want to establish a sort of fur-coat peerage, let 'em! Since they can find no comfort where they happened to be born, no especial talents to lift them, and other doors are closed to them, they have to find some pleasure somewhere in life. They have to use whatever their mentality provides. "My People! My People!"

But one thing and another kept the conflict going on inside me off and on for years. Sometimes I was sure that the Negro race was all that the platform speakers said. Then I would hear so much self-deprecation that I would be deflated. Over and over I heard people shake their heads and explain us by the supposed prayer of a humble Negro, who got down on his knees and said: 'Lawd, you know I ain't nothing. My wife, she ain't nothing. My chillun ain't nothing, and if you fool 'round us, Lawd, you won't be nothing neither."

So I sensed early that the Negro race was not one band of heavenly love. There was stress and strain inside as well as out. Being black was not enough. It took more than a community of skin color to make your love come down on you. That was the beginning of my peace.

Light came to me when I realized that I did not have to consider any racial group as a whole. God made them duck by duck and that was the only way I could see them. I learned that skins were no measure of what was inside people. So none of the Race clichés meant anything any more. I began to laugh at both white and black who claimed special blessings on the basis of race. Therefore I saw no curse in being black, nor no extra flavor by being white. I saw no benefit in excusing my looks by claiming to be half Indian. In fact, I boast that I am the only Negro in the United States whose grandfather on the mother's side was *not* an Indian chief. Neither did I descend from George Washington, Thomas Jefferson, or any Governor of a Southern state. I see no need to manufacture me a legend to beat the facts. I do not coyly admit to a touch of the tarbrush to my Indian and white ancestry. You can consider me Old Tar Brush in person if you want to. I am a mixed-blood, it is true, but I differ from the party line in that I neither consider it an honor

nor a shame. I neither claim Jefferson as my grandpa, nor exclaim, "Just look how that white man took advantage of my grandma!" It does not matter in the first place, and then in the next place, I do not know how it came about. Since nobody ever told me, I give my ancestress the benefit of the doubt. She probably ran away from him just as fast as she could. But if that white man could run faster than my grandma, that was no fault of hers. Anyway, you must remember, he didn't have a thing to do but to keep on running forward. She, being the pursued, had to look back over her shoulder every now and then to see how she was doing. And you know your ownself how looking backwards slows people up.

In this same connection, I have been told that God meant for all the so-called races of the world to stay just as they are, and people who say that may be right. But it is a well-known fact that no matter where two sets of people come together, there are bound to be some in-betweens. It looks like the command was given to people's heads, because the other parts don't seem to have heard tell. When the next batch is made up, maybe Old Maker will straighten all that out. Maybe the men will be more tangle-footed and the women a whole lot more faster around the feet. That will bring about a great deal more of racial and other kinds of purity, but a somewhat less exciting world. It might work, but I doubt it. There will have to be something harder to get across than an ocean to keep East and West from meeting. But maybe Old Maker will have a remedy. Maybe even He has given up. Perhaps in a moment of discouragement He turned the job over to Adolf Hitler and went on about His business of making more beetles.

I do not share the gloomy thought that Negroes in America are doomed to be stomped out bodaciously, nor even shackled to the bottom of things. Of course, some of them will be tromped out, and some will always be at the bottom, keeping company with other bottom-folks. It would be against all nature for all the Negroes to be either at the bottom, top, or in between. It has never happened with anybody else, so why with us? No, we will go where the internal drive carries us like everybody else. It is up to the individual. If you haven't got it, you can't show it. If you have got it, you can't hide it. That is one of the strongest laws God ever made.

I maintain that I have been a Negro three times—a Negro baby, a Negro girl, and a Negro woman. Still, if you have received no clear-cut impression of what the Negro in America is like, then you are in the same place with me. There is no *The Negro* here. Our lives are so diversified, internal attitudes so varied, appearances and capabilities so different, that there is no possible classification so catholic that it will cover us all, except My people! My people!

The Negro Folk Cult

HAROLD PREECE

In trying to understand the relationship between a folk and that folk's lore, one may need to raise the question of what good, if any, the collection and analysis of folklore do the folk from whom the folklore comes? Harold Preece writing in the 1930's suggests that the folklorists' scholarly interest in American Negro folkore has not helped American Negroes one whit. Basically, the issue is whether the folklorist is really interested in the "folk" or in the "lore" if we may divide the word "folklore" to make the point. It would appear that the majority of folklorists are more concerned with the lore, with collecting, preserving, classifying, and occasionally analyzing it, than with the folk. The "folk" or the actual people who possess the lore are forgotten as soon as the precious folksongs or folktales are once safely recorded in notebook or on tape. In such cases, the folklorist can be said to be practicing the longstanding exploitative tradition of academic colonialism in which investigators receive and justify their financial support in the form of fieldwork grants by amassing a sufficiently impressive quantity of raw data. But while the investigator gets something from the experience, usually prestige or status rather than financial reward, the poor informant remains exactly as he was before the folklorist entered the scene. In this plea for political and social activism, Preece takes conventional folklorists, including Zora Neale Hurston, to task for "merely" collecting folklore.

Although it is abundantly clear that Preece had definite leftist leanings—he speaks of the impossibility of the development of Negro culture under capitalism and even claimed that folk cultures in the Soviet Union were flowering—it is the validity of his particular criticisms which is important, not his political beliefs. While many of the references are to events of the 1930's, the general thrust of his argument remains very timely.

For a reference to Preece as an emancipated white Texas communist, see

Reprinted from *The Crisis*, vol. 43 (1936), pp. 364, 374, by permission of the author and *The Crisis*.

J. G. St. Clair Drake, Jr., "Communism and Peace Movements," The Crisis, 43 (1936), pp, 44–45. See also Preece's letter to the editor in The Crisis, 43 (1936), pp. 123. Preece was a frequent contributor to The Crisis, though rarely on the subject of folklore. Other articles by Preece include "Confession of an Ex-Nordic," Opportunity, 13 (1935), pp. 232–33; "Fascism and the Negro," The Crisis, 41 (1934), pp. 355–66; "The Klan's 'Revolution of the Right,' " The Crisis, 53 (1946), pp. 202–3, 219–20; "Klan, 'Murder, Inc.' in Dixie," The Crisis, 53 (1946), pp. 299–301.

THE AMERICAN Negro has been able to make himself felt as a cultural entity, even if his artistic contributions have been rewarded with hemp and pellagra. No critic, not even an instructor of literature in the University of Georgia, can deny that the folk culture of the black race early possessed an originality totally lacking among the dominant white group. One need only contrast the didactic doggerel of Michael Wigglesworth or the imitative *opera* of James Fenimore Cooper with the Negro spirituals and folksay to appreciate this invidious distinction. Nor is it surprising that Dvořák should have incorporated the melodies of the American Negro, rather than the borrowed elegiac music of the Southern planter, into his composition dealing with the life of that particular region.

These are musty commonplaces needful only for purposes of background. Unfortunately, most of us have accepted uncritically all the stock premises concerning the Negro folk culture. Indeed, too many Negroes have hoped subconsciously for social acceptance on the basis of a traditional culture which was being cleverly exploited and distorted by white authors. Thus, Carl Van Vechten presented Harlem to the neurotic white middle class during the cultural upheaval that accompanied the spurious prosperity of Mr. Coolidge. Caucasian dowagers, some of them no doubt on Mr. Stark Young's calling list, flocked to Negro cabarets, drank gin supplied by Negroes with more business acumen than the race is generally credited with having, and patronizingly gave individual Negroes bids to their homes. Nothing was too good for the black man—as long as he expended his energies in song and dance.

One need not deprecate Mr. Van Vechten's genuine interest in Negro culture to draw analogies. In the seventeenth century, the sophisticated gentry of Great Britain was highly amused when it discovered that unwashed peasants had a strong tradition of balladry and story-telling. The folklore school has never outgrown this snobbish origin. Today, it is still mainly a cult of sophisticates whose patronizing interest in folklore obscures the basic creative instincts of the masses. "*Green Pastures* is *so* amusing—and aren't the Negroes *such* childlike, lovable people?" I have heard this expression over teacups a hundred times. More sickening, I have attended meetings of professional folklorists where all the ancient jokes about the Negro's supposed incompetence and unthinking amiability were told with the usual gusto of the educated illiterate.

SUPERIORITY COMPLEX

I can see very little difference between such an attitude and that of the yokel who applauds the annual minstrel-show. Each expression of this interest in the Negro is the manifestation of a definite superiority complex. The professional collector of Negro folklore simply capitalizes upon the artificial peculiarities of a group kept in systematic impoverishment and ignorance. Minstrelsy was originally a definite expression of the southern land-owners, who defended slavery by adorning it with the mellifluous phrases of Stephen Collins Foster and Daniel Emmett. Today it is most popular in the villages of the Hookworm Belt and shares honors with lynching as an expression of the South's deep concern for the colored man.

If the Negro ever hoped for salvation through his culture, he should be thoroughly disillusioned by the status of the race during this particular phase of American capitalism. When hungry Negroes defended their rights in Harlem two years ago, the hangers-on of the cabarets were not in sight. When black share-croppers were massacred in Alabama and Arkansas for demanding living wages, neither Mr. Roark Bradford nor Miss Julia Peterkin uttered a murmur of protest. Scottsboro became a symbol equal in importance to Harper's Ferry, but this passional of a race evoked no response from those who have written pages of sirupy fable about the Negro. Angelo Herndon was condemned to break rocks in Georgia; but a member of his own race, Miss Zora Neale Hurston, was devoting her literary abilities to recording the legendary amours of terrapins.

Nor can these events be explained as so much short-sightedness upon the part of the resplendent folklorists. We have lost sight of the rather elementary fact that those who profit from Negro primitivism have an obvious interest in preserving that primitivism. Thus, Miss Peterkin sits on the front porch of her South Carolina manor and concocts "Roll, Jordan, Roll."* It must be a pleasant situation for any author to be supported economically by the same group from which she draws material. And all metaphors about "the universality of art" aside, one can well understand that any change in the fundamental status of the Negro might affect the pocketbooks of the folklorists.

Indeed, one is strongly tempted to believe that the folklorists have been more concerned with their pocketbooks than with the authentic life of the race. Mr. Langston Hughes describes rather wittingly in one of his stories the attitude of two white artists who are rather confounded when their Negro servants refuse to be perpetual "models" of what "a simple race" should be. Certainly, Mr. Bradford, doing his nickel-a-word articles for *Collier's* would not care to offend the good southern ladies who read the magazine with religious devotion. Our indictments of the professional Negrophiles need not even be so personal; we could pardon them their incomes if they only told the truth.

* For a survey of some of the useful folkloristic data recorded by Miss Peterkin, see Irene Yates, "Conjures and Cures in the Novels of Julia Peterkin," *Southern Folklore Quarterly*, 10 (1946), pp. 137–49. For an analysis which reveals some condescension verging on racism in Miss Peterkin's work, see the review of *Roll, Jordan Roll*, "The Big House Interprets the Cabin," *The Crisis*, 41 (1934), pp. 37–38. For a similar commentary on another white female collector who couldn't understand how for eighteen years her "faithful" servant kept from her the secret that she knew the slave songs her mistress had been seeking all the time, see the review of Lydia Parrish's *Slave Songs of the Georgia Sea Islands* by Bernard Katz, "Songs That Will Not Die," *Negro Quarterly*, 1 (1942), pp. 283–88. —ED.

NEGRO CULTURE EVASIVE

For there are traditions of the Negro people which have been neglected with good reason by white writers. "Uncle Remus" is a familiar symbol to every American schoolboy, but Nat Turner remains a vague figure on the edge of history. Innumerable volumes have been written about the religious life of the Negro, but no author has dared mention the revolutionary significance of certain sects existing before the Civil War.

When one surveys the development of the Negro culture, he realizes that it has been one of evasion whatever its intrinsic beauty. The educational and economic limitations of a dominantly white society have forced the Negro to express himself in ambiguous terms. Thus the folk-hero, *John*, always outwits his master through cunning; thus, Negro songs often satirize the white man without the latter's being aware of any mockery. And while this quality is highly admirable for protective purposes, it obviously impedes further cultural development.

Under the circumstances, one can sympathize with the northern Negroes who attempt so strenuously to escape the traditional culture, and who justly avoid the conventional folklorist. The resentment of some Negro circles toward the work of Miss Hurston is easily explained on the same grounds. For when a Negro author describes her race with such a servile term as "Mules and Men," critical members of the race must necessarily evaluate the author as a literary climber.*

But there is another viewpoint which recognizes the value of the past as well as the promise of the future. However archaic some cultural forms may appear, they are indissolubly a part of the racial heritage. We should oppose the vulgarity of those who would discard altogether the spirituals and the old dances as much as we oppose those clever sentimentalists who strive to make over the Negro according to their own likings. Recognizing fully that the same element which burned Harriet Beecher Stowe in effigy also buys tickets to hear Paul Robeson, we should rather use that troubled past as an implement for the future.

---

* In fairness to Zora Neale Hurston, it might be pointed out that Preece may well have simply failed to fully comprehend the nature of the Negro's attitude toward mules. There is considerable evidence that southern Negroes sometimes tended to identify with the mule. On the one hand, mules were bought and sold by plantation owners just as slaves were. Mules were forced to work long hours with little reward just as slaves were. On the other hand, the mule demonstrated some characteristics which Negroes could appreciate. As Mississippian David L. Cohn observed, the mule "has more mother wit than the horse." The mule was always an individualist blessed with proverbial stubbornness and strength. His behavior was not always predictable and though he might toil willingly for a while, there was invariably that moment when he would refuse to do more or when he would lash his hooves at a too demanding overseer. See David L. Cohn, *Where I Was Born and Raised* (Notre Dame, 1967), p. 300.

There is even more direct evidence of the symbolic significance of the mule. For example, there is a blues line in which the singer complains that another man is with his woman and the image employed is "There was another mule in my stall." Perhaps one of the best overt statements of the sense of identification is the short poem by Langston Hughes which ends "I'm like that old mule ... Black/ And don't give a damn!/ So you got to take me/ Like I am." See Newman I. White, *American Negro Folk-Songs* (Hatboro, Pennsylvania: Folklore Associates, 1965), p. 334; Langston Hughes, "Me and the Mule," *The Negro Quarterly* 1 (1942), p. 37. —ED.

As a white man, I use the term "we" with all deference. But as a folklorist of a different school from Miss Peterkin, Miss Hurston, and Mr. Bradford, I am convinced that any culture divorced from its human origins must end in inglorious imitation. It is not the cultural traditions of the Negro which are inadequate; it is his lack of economic and political power which makes him the water-bearer of our moneyed Olympians.

STRUGGLE GIVES NEW IMPETUS

Indeed, in this period of struggle for the liberation of twelve million people, it is all important that the cultural tradition progress with the advancement of the race. In the states where the Share Croppers' Union extends like an unbreakable network, the spirituals are being rewarded to fit the demands of a new situation. Nor should we, living on the eve of great class battles into which the Negro will be drawn inextricably, despise the worksongs. True, the traditional "Cap'n," will become the capitalist while Angelo Herndon* and Ralph Gray will probably replace Nat Turner and Denmark Vesey in the folk-myths. These are questions which will be decided by time and the perspective of events.

Negro folk culture can very well dispense with the professional collectors of songs and proverbs. But if the folklorists themselves wish to preserve any professional integrity, then they must cast their lot with the folk. The time has passed for haphazard collecting of queer idioms and simple tales. The time has come for the abolition of social factors which threaten the existence of all culture whether its source be white or black.

Any extensive development of Negro culture under capitalism is, of course, impossible. For precisely as the economic system becomes more chaotic, the Negro, as the constant scapegoat, will suffer physically and intellectually. We face the further danger of having the white folk-tradition used as a club in the hands of our potential Hitlers unless socially-minded writers and artists appropriate that tradition first. Certainly, the Negro culture will be damaged and further degraded unless the working-classes to which most Negroes belong, become the masters of the future.

Limitations of space prevent me from discussing the creative opportunities for the Negro in a collective America. I may use as a brief analogy the flowering of the folk-cultures in the Soviet Union. The growth of the American Negro culture has been too long stunted.

---

* For more about Angelo Herndon who later became editor of the short-lived *Negro Quarterly* (1942), see Angelo Herndon, *Let Me Live* (New York, 1937). —ED.

Background of Folklore in Negro Literature

STERLING A. BROWN

With regard to the question of whether American Negroes should take pride in their folklore or whether they should deny it, one of the most critical issues has to do with the authenticity of what is said to be Negro folklore. Since many of the hitherto published collections of Negro "folklore" have been made by whites—either white folklorists or white writers of fiction—there is some doubt as to whether or not such materials are in fact bona fide folklore. An extreme position would be that no white is capable of collecting, or at any rate of fully understanding, American Negro folklore in all its subtlety. But even with a more moderate view that to some extent any member of any group can collect folklore from members of another group, the fact remains that there is always the possibility of bias creeping in. Bias, after all, does not have to be conscious to qualify as bias.

In the following excerpt from an address given at Jackson College, Mississippi, Professor Sterling A. Brown, a distinguished member of the faculty of Howard University, demonstrates the striking contrast between what some white writers have "reported" as Negro folklore and Negro folklore as it really exists. White writers, even those with the best will in the world, frequently cannot escape the bias of the white stereotype of the Negro. It is both startling and frightening to see how white racist stereotypes were insidiously put into the mouths of Negro characters in books written by white authors. True American Negro folklore, however, as it is told by and to American Negroes certainly gives quite a different picture. The point is then that the relationship of folklore to race pride cannot be intelligently discussed until the matter of the accuracy and authenticity of the folklore is firmly established.

Reprinted from the *Jackson College Bulletin*, vol. 2, no. 1 (September, 1953), pp. 26–30, by permission of the author.

I DO not want to give you a catalog of authors and books; it is also hard to do justice to novels and drama; even summaries take much time. I think, then, there will be an over-stress on poetry because poetry does say briefly and vividly many of the things I want to point out as characteristic of these seventy-five years. . . . First of all I am going to look at the beginning of these seventy-five years and see what was the literary picture then.* I want to notice some of the authors who were handling the Negro characters, and Negro life. I am dealing here chiefly, as you know, with Negro writers. But Negro writers have been much influenced both positively and negatively by the white authors who have set up certain stereotypes of Negro life. Publishers and readers have been so influenced.

What we had right after Emancipation was a prevailing illiteracy. We had few men who could write books; we had a very small audience of Negroes to read them. The audience then was chiefly white and that would govern much of what the authors were attempting to say. The division after that, however, is what the Negro was contributing himself; if not through writing, through what we call oral literature—folk literature—and we'll get a picture of the folk Negro as he reveals himself.

The next division is devoted to Dunbar and Chesnutt who, in a way, could be called pioneers or forerunners of the many authors of the present. We go then to what is called the New Negro Movement, then to Regionalism,

Social Protest, the Present Experimentation, and the Present Scene which makes us believe that perhaps we are getting near the integration of the Negro author in the American literary scene.

I want to look at what was the literary picture seventy-five years ago. There was a young white man over at Port Gibson, Mississippi, who was very interested in conveying to America what he knew, or what he felt he knew, about Negro folk life. This man's name was Irwin Russell and he is important in American literary history because he is the first to make a literary use of Negro dialect. He wanted to do what Burns had done for Scotland. He had a fairly good ear; he had a good eye, and he had had some experience.

We find that to be quite the story in American literary history. From the very start, almost all of the major novelists have at one time or another tried to interpret the Negro. They don't have to know much about him, but they believe that they can tell the truth about him. And that happened from James Fenimore Cooper right down to a neighbor of yours who has won the Nobel Award—William Faulkner—who paid much attention to Negro life in those sagas of the country there around Oxford, Mississippi.

Now, Irwin Russell is one of the men from the outside trying hard to get inside and reveal a new sort of local color. A new sort of character. He was praised by Joel Chandler Harris of Georgia for having a perfect knowledge of Negro character. I doubt if any

---

* The reader should keep in mind that this selection is only one portion of Professor Brown's address "Seventy-five Years of the Negro in Literature" which was presented at Jackson College. Furthermore, the selection was printed as transcribed from a tape recording of the address and for this reason it bears the style of oral rather than written discourse. —ED.

single author could have such knowledge, and certainly Irwin Russell did not have it. Maybe Joel Chandler Harris had a little more. What we get is a fairly young man writing a book called *Christmas Night in the Quarters*. To show you how incomplete it was, almost all of it is on the joyous side, on the happy side. The only trouble I've been able to find in the book is that one man comes too near a mule's rear end and is kicked across the street. He wakes up on the other side. That's the only tragedy in the book. Now, everybody knows that there was much more tragedy around Port Gibson. But he, of course, could not sense it. By and large, what he gave was a jocular picture of people whom he liked, whom he was amused by; and whose speech, outside appearance and behavior he could catch.*

Much more important would be a man named Thomas Nelson Page. Now at this time there was tremendous drama. Here you have a newly-freed people. Here was a subject crying for literary treatment. Instead, it got argument. The writers were white. They were the sons of the generation that had gone down with Lee at Appomattox. Here you have the young men looking back at slavery from the viewpoint of the master. Looking back from the viewpoint of the lost cause, at the old South, and at the present. In the present, they could find nothing good. In the old South they could find nothing bad. Listen to one of Thomas Nelson Page's characters speak. Uncle Sam is talking

of slavery, and he says:

Dem wuz good ole times, marster. De bes' Sam evah seed. . . . Ah wuz settin' in de do' wid mah pipe, an' ah heah dem settin' dar on de frunt steps—day voices soundin' lo, lak bees, an' de moon sorta mellow ovuh de ya'd—an' ah sorta got to studyin'. An' hit 'peared lak de plantation live once mo'; an' dere ain't no mo scufflin'; an' de ole good times done cum back agin.

He dreamed of the "good old times" of slavery coming back again. What we get, then, is a man proving a point. Arguing about these people, instead of showing the rich drama that was in their lives.

The last of these that I want to take up is Joel Chandler Harris. Now Joel Chandler Harris, as a boy, was very lonely. And on the plantation, he went down to the cabins to visit. Particularly did he visit the cabin of an old man whom he called "Uncle George Terrell" (but whom I prefer calling Mr. Terrell) who told these fine stories about Brer Rabbit, Brer Wolf, Brer Bear, and the rest of them. He told him these stories, and this boy had a quick mind and a good ear. He remembered these. And later he became famous in American literary history because of the faithfulness in reproduction, the good memory he had, and the catching of the cadence in the speech and the idiom.

And so we get him saving these Uncle Remus stories for us; but by and large, altering them—not making them what the folk really tell when nobody is around. What we get here is the folk story being altered for the little white

---

* For more about Russell's contribution to folklore data, see James Wilson Webb, "Irwin Russell and Folk Literature," *Southern Folklore Quarterly*, 12 (1948), pp. 137–49. For further detail about Russell, see Laura D. S. Harrell, "A Bibliography of Irwin Russell, with a Biographical Sketch," *Journal of Mississippi History*, 8 (1946), pp. 2–23. —ED.

boy. The teeth are pulled out of many of the stories.* At any rate, Joel Chandler Harris' heart was right, and he saved much of value for American Literature.

When Uncle Remus is not telling about Brer Rabbit, however, Uncle Remus gets very much like a Thomas Nelson Page dummy. Very much like the ventriloquist act. Here is Uncle Remus talking to a cop in Five Points, Atlanta. He is discussing one of our problems, the problem of the education of Negroes:

Hit de ruination ob dis country. Put a spellin' book in a Negro's han', and right den an dere you lost a plow han'. Whut's a Negro (he didn't say "Negro," however) gonna larn outtn books? Ah kin tak a barrel stav' an fling mo sense in a Negro in a minute, dan all deir schoolhouses 'twixt heah an de state o' Michig'n. Wid one barrel stav', ah kin fa'ly lif de veil o' ig'nance.

Here we get an old fool saying what Joel Chandler Harris wants him to say, of course: that when you educate a Negro you lose a plowhand.

It was only recently that throughout America, the States have come around to the fact that we must have for all the citizenry a first class education. What we get, then, is these men taking over and having Negroes plead their cause.... It sounded something like folk speech, and therefore people accepted it.

Now in opposition to that, there was a man writing in Louisiana who was named George Washington Cable. He did a better job. And we had Mark Twain who wasn't fooled by that nonsense. But by and large, these are the stereotypes: the Negro was contented in slavery; he was unhappy if free.

Let us look at the Negro folk themselves and see how they stepped out of this picture.... The spirituals had nothing of that contentment with slavery which belongs with the great tragic lines in American Literature—not folk literature—but American literature. In the spirituals you have an oppressed people . . . :

I don't know what my mother wants to
    stay here for, this old world
    ain't been no friend to her.

. . . rolling through an unfriendly world

. . . Didn't my Lord deliver Daniel,
    why not every man?

Go down, Moses, way down in Egypt
    land. Tell ole Pharoah, let
    my people go.

Before we go on, bear with me on just two folk tales depicting characters with a new note. Here is one appearing after slavery. You can tell as soon as it is set up. You have Brother Bear who is powerful, strong—but a little dumb. Then there is Brother Rabbit. He is weak but smart. Slaves had to use smartness to outwit physical strength—brute strength.†

---

* For further discussion of this point, see Bernard Wolfe, "Uncle Remus and the Malevolent Rabbit," *Commentary*, 8 (July, 1949), pp. 34–41, which is reprinted in this volume. —ED.

† This folktale is a version of tale type 1030, The Crop Division, a tale which appears to be a European rather than an African story. Of course, the question of origin is not as important as the function of the tale as social protest against the evils of sharecropping contracts with wealthy landowners. For a rough indication of the tale's distribution, see Antti Aarne and Stith Thompson, *The Types of the Folktale*, 2nd revision (Helsinki, 1961), pp. 350–51. —ED.

Brother Bear has a sharecropping contract with Brother Rabbit and in it, a clause that Brother Bear will get the top of the crop. Brother Rabbit, who has a very large family and is very poor, will get the bottom. The bear owns so much land (he is one of those huge landowners) that he doesn't get around to the crop until harvest time comes and he finds that Brother Rabbit has planted *potatoes*. So all he gets is green tops—so Brother Rabbit wins (which is not completely stupid).

Brother Bear then says, "All right, this year I get the bottom and you get the top." But he's got many acres and he doesn't get down to that lower forty until the end of the year at harvest time. Then, lo and behold, Brother Rabbit has planted oats. So he gets the roots and Brother Rabbit gets the grain.

But then, Brother Bear—he's got everything on his side. Brother Rabbit's got a huge family. It's even larger now, and so he's got to sign up for whatever "the man" says. Brother Bear says, "All right, this year I get both top and bottom." And so Brother Rabbit said: "What am I going to get?" And he said, "You gets the middle!" And so at the end of the year when Brother Bear gets around there, he looks and he says, "Well! That low down scoundrel! He done planted all those acres in *corn*!"

So Brother Bear gets the tassels and the roots. And from the middle, Brother Rabbit gets all those fine ears. . . . That is not the kind of thing Joel Chandler Harris got. What he pictures is largely an animal beating (winning out over) another animal. But right here you've got *people* called Brother Bear and Brother Rabbit, but you know who it is he's talking about.

The last one is about Sister Goose, one of those fine individualistic people.* She had courage. She had intelligence. She wouldn't let anybody kick her around (something like the New Negro). One day she was floating on a lake and it was fine.

She was just paddling on the lake. It was a beautiful day, like today, and she was just swimming on the lake. It was really nice. All of a sudden she gets too near some reeds, and Brer Fox reaches out and grabs her.

He says, "Uh-huh, I got you! You swimming on my lake." She says, "Un-unh! This ain't none of your lake. . . . I got civil rights. . . . I got just as much right to swim on this lake as you got!"

Brer Fox says, "No you ain't! It's my lake. I'm goin' to kill you. I'm going to execute you. I'm goin' to pick your bones!" Sister Goose says, "Oh no, you can't kill me. You can't execute me. You can't pick my bones. I'm going to take you to court!" So she took Brer Fox to court. And in the court the Sheriff was a fox, the jurymen were foxes, everybody who came to see the trial—all were foxes. The prosecuting lawyer was a fox, and the defending lawyer was a fox.

So they tried her. They gave her a fair trial. They executed her. And they all sat around and picked her bones.

Then the teller of this yarn (first version that I heard comes from the grass-roots

---

* There is little question but that Professor Brown has retold both folktales and updated them for his audience. This may be seen by comparing his versions with those found in Langston Hughes and Arna Bontemps, eds., *The Book of Negro Folklore* (New York, 1958), pp. 13–16, or the original source, A. W. Eddins, "Brazos Bottom Philosophy," *Publications of the Texas Folklore Society*, no. 2 (Austin, 1923), pp. 50–51, no. 9 (1931), pp. 153–56. On the other hand, there is no doubt that Sterling Brown is a superb storyteller. See Hoyt W. Fuller, "The Raconteur," *Negro Digest*, 16 (April, 1967), p. 50. —ED.

section of Texas, but it is probably told all over) says, "Sisters and brothers, when all the courthouse is foxes—and you ain't nothing but a poor goose—ain't much chance for you and me."*

Now those people, you see, are not fooled and there is a quality there, a quality of the folks, that appears also in the legends of John Henry—that heroic man of courage and stamina.

* There is some evidence that the goose was a traditional victim figure. For another tale in which Miss Goose was duped, see Daniel Murray, "Three New Folk-Lore Stories (Current in Maryland in Colonial Times)," *Colored American Magazine*, 14 (1908), pp. 104–9 (see esp. pp. 107–8). On the other hand, there is the indestructible figure of "The Grey Goose" who though shot, picked, pickled, and boiled, etc. couldn't be stopped. At the end of the folksong, the Grey Goose flies away from all its tormentors and escapes to freedom. See John Greenway, "The Flight of the Gray Goose: Literary Symbolism in the Traditional Ballad," *Southern Folklore Quarterly*, 18 (1954), pp. 165–74. —Ed.

The Negro Writer in America: An Exchange

I. THE FOLK TRADITION
Stanley Edgar Hyman

II. CHANGE THE JOKE AND SLIP THE YOKE
Ralph Ellison

The attitudes of some American Negroes toward their folklore appear to have been tempered by their perception of the literary derivatives of that folkore. To the extent that folklore has proved to be an inspiration for literary creativity, folklore possesses a positive value over and above its intrinsic worth. In other words, folktales and blues are not only beautiful, exciting materials; they are also the direct sources of beauty and excitement in literature. However, to the extent that racist stereotypes present in folklore are perpetuated in literature, folklore continues to carry negative connotations.

The nature of the relationship between American Negro literature and American Negro folklore is explored by literary critic Stanley Edgar Hyman and by novelist Ralph Ellison in a brilliant debate which originally appeared in the Partisan Review. *One of the bones of contention is the universality or at least widespread distribution of certain folkloristic elements, e.g., the trickster and the "smart man playing dumb" theme. The question in essence is: if a given folktale is found in fifty different cultures, how can its manifestation in any one of these cultures be said to reflect the values or mores of that one culture? Doesn't the tale's existence in several cultures rule out the possibility of analyzing the tale as a reflection of just one culture? It is true that "nationalists" around the world are unhappy when comparative folklorists point out "parallels" to local folklore because without knowledge of such parallels, nationalists are free to assume that local folklore is utterly unique and, hence, a mark of national identity. The fact is that Turks and Greeks share many of the same Hodja folktales; Arabs and Jews share much folklore (e.g., the greetings "Salaam" and "Shalom"), etc.*

On the other hand, even if different cultures share the same folkloristic

Reprinted from *Partisan Review*, vol. 25 (1958), pp. 197–222, by permission of Phoebe P. Hyman, and Random House, Inc.

elements, the local manifestations almost certainly differ with respect to numerous details. And it is precisely these differences which are often critical with respect to the study of national or ethnic character. However, it is obviously only after the cross-cultural comparisons have been made and the cognates or parallels noted that it becomes possible to identify exactly those details which are reflective of local problems and values.

In this fascinating literary debate, Hyman attempts to find parallels for American Negro folklore in the folk literatures of other cultures. Ellison, in contrast, focuses upon the unique cultural-historical features underlying American Negro folklore and stresses in particular how the whole matter of group identity is central to a proper understanding of folklore. Ellison's eloquent critique of Hyman's essay demonstrates once more the unfortunate influence of the white stereotype of the Negro as a factor, a negative factor, which not only impedes white comprehension of Negro folklore but also tends to discourage the Negro's appreciation of his own folklore.

I

"AMERICAN NEGRO Literature"—by which I do not mean any special body of writing but only that varied American literature produced by Negroes—has, or at least some of it has, a relation to a living folk tradition that is rare in American writing, and very much worth our study.* By folk tradition, I do not mean a folksy tradition. I have in mind the dependence of writers like Yeats and Synge on Irish folk culture, not of James Whitcomb Riley or Edgar Guest on Hoosier corn. There is a whole spectrum of possible relations to a folk tradition, ranging from such unpromising connections as simple imitation and fakery, archaism or sentimentalizing, to a number of complicated, ironic, and richly rewarding connections. I propose as much as possible to confine myself to some of the latter.

Without attempting any sort of historical survey of Negro writing, I would suggest that several obviously different strains are visible. One is a body of writing largely indistinguish-able from white writing, with no specifically Negro character at all, which exists in an unbroken line from the poems of Phillis Wheatley, an eighteenth-century slave and apologist for slavery, to the historical novels of Frank Yerby. A second strain has a specifically Negro character, or at least subject matter. It is the naturalism of the social protest or documentary, the account of lynching, passing, discrimination, or varieties of resistance, and its examples are legion. A third is the naturalism of the regional or folksy, which was once about watermelon eating on the old plantation, and now seems to be mostly about hair straightening and razor fighting in Harlem. I want to bypass these modes, and to discuss the half-dozen or so Negro writers who seem to me largely to have gone beyond any sort of mimicry or naturalism, and who in their use of literary form as an act of the moral imagination have joined the mainstream of symbolism and irony in modern literature. These Negro writers, although not all of them are from the South, clearly relate to the

* This is a shortened version of a paper read at Brandeis University.

renaissance of white Southern writing we have seen in our day, particularly in fiction, from Faulkner to Flannery O'Connor. I shall discuss this small group of Negro writers in relation to two forms of Negro folk literature: the folk tale and the blues. Other forms, among them spirituals and ballads, sermons and speeches, rhymes and games, have comparable literary extensions, but these two must suffice to suggest some of the possibilities.

. . .To talk about the folk tale, oddly enough, we have to begin with the familiar figure of the "darky" entertainer: Stepin Fetchit, Rochester, the Kingfish of the Amos and Andy program. His role is to parody the familiar stereotype of the Negro: stupid, ignorant, lazy, fraudulent, cowardly, submoral, and boundlessly good-natured. The comic point of the act is that the performer is not really this subhuman grotesque, but a person of intelligence and skill; in other words, a performer. Assuming this role, a smart man playing dumb, is a characteristic behavior pattern of Negroes in the South (and often in the North) in a variety of conflict situations. In *No Day of Triumph*, the reporting by a brilliant and sensitive Negro of a trip through the South in 1940, J. Saunders Redding gives us a typical example. He was driving into Kentucky with a Negro hitchhiker he had picked up when they were stopped in a strike-bound mining town by a guard with an automatic rifle. Before Redding could say anything, the hitchhiker shifted automatically into just such a "coon" act:

"Cap'n, we'se goin' to Kintucky. See all dat stuff back dere, Cap'n? Well, dat stuff 'longs ter Mista Rob French, an'

he sho' will raise hell ef we don' git it to him," Bill lied convincingly.

"That gittar too?" the guard questioned, already softened to a joke.

Bill grinned. "No, suh, Cap'n. Dis yere box is mine. Dis yere's ma sweetheart! If we-all hed time an' you hed time, I'd beat one out fer you," Bill said.

"G'on. But don' stop nowheres. Don' even breathe hard," the guard said, grinning.

"No, suh, Cap'n. I ain't much of a breever noway. Jus' 'nough ter live on. No, suh. I don' want no mo' o' white folks' air den I just got ter have."

One of the memorable characters in Richard Wright's autobiography, *Black Boy*, is a Memphis elevator operator called Shorty, who specializes in playing what Wright calls "the role of a clown of the most debased and degraded type." Shorty gets quarters from white passengers by an obsequious clown act that culminates in his inviting the white man to kick his rump. When Wright, full of "disgust and loathing," asks him, "How in God's name can you do that?" Shorty answers simply, "Listen, nigger, my ass is tough and quarters is scarce." Wright's fictional use of the stereotype constitutes something like Shorty's revenge. In Wright's recent novel, *The Outsider*, the hero, Cross Damon, is a Negro intellectual and existentialist criminal of terrifying literacy and paranoia. At one point in his criminal career he needs a false birth certificate and gets it by the same darky act. Cross thinks: "He would have to present to the officials a Negro so scared and ignorant that no white American would ever dream that he was up to anything deceptive." He does so, batting his eyes stupidly, asking for "the paper that say I was born," explaining in answer to every question only that his white boss said he had better have it right away. Of course he gets it immediately. The novel explains:

And as he stood there manipulating their responses, Cross knew exactly what kind of man he would pretend to be to kill suspicion if he ever got into trouble. In his role of an ignorant, frightened Negro, each white man—except those few who were free from the race bias of their group—would leap to supply him with a background and an identity; each white man would project out on him his own conception of the Negro and he could safely hide behind it. . . . He knew that deep in their hearts those two white clerks knew that no human being on earth was as dense as he had made himself out to be, but they wanted, needed to believe it of Negroes and it helped them to feel racially superior. They were pretending, just as he had been pretending.

A comically related use of the darky act appears in Rudolph Fisher's *The Conjure-Man Dies*, which so far as I know is the only Negro detective story.* Here there are no whites at all: victim, murderer, detective, police, and all the other characters are Negro. The darky act is thus directed not at a character in the book, but at the white reader. Shortly after the murder, an uncouth kinky-haired buffoon appears, exclaiming:

"Great day in the mornin'! What all you polices doin' in this place? Policeman outside d' front door, policeman in d' hall, policeman on d' stairs, and hyer's another one. 'Deed I mus' be in d' wrong house! Is this Frimbo the conjure-man's house, or is it the jail?"

He turns out, of course (and I hope you will forgive me for giving away the plot

of a twenty-five-year-old mystery), to be the murderer, an intelligent and literate man, disguised in a wig and a "coon" act. The point here seems to be that for a Negro reader, no Negro ever talked like that to his fellows, and the character is immediately suspicious. To a white reader, Fisher apparently assumes (and probably with justice), the disguise is impenetrable because it fits white stereotypes. Writing a mystery that would mystify whites but convey the essential clue to Negro readers seems an odd burlesque equivalent to Cross Damon's obsequious aggressions.

The fullest development I know of the darky act in fiction is Ralph Ellison's *Invisible Man*, where on investigation every important character turns out to be engaged in some facet of the smart-man-playing-dumb routine. The narrator's grandfather, who was "the meekest of men," confesses on his deathbed:

"Son, after I'm gone I want you to keep up the good fight. I never told you, but our life is a war and I have been a traitor all my born days, a spy in the enemy's country ever since I give up my gun back in the Reconstruction. Live with your head in the lion's mouth. I want you to overcome 'em with yesses, undermine 'em with grins, agree 'em to death and destruction, let 'em swoller you till they vomit or bust wide open."

Dr. Bledsoe, the president of the college, a tough and unscrupulous autocrat, pretends to be a simple pious Negro for the schools's white trustees, explaining to the narrator: "I had to be strong and purposeful to get where I am. I had to wait and plan and lick around. . . .

---

* A number of the many novels written by Chester B. Himes might be considered Negro detective stories. See, among others, *Cotton Comes to Harlem* (New York, 1965). —ED.

Yes, I had to act the nigger!" Tod Clifton, a young intellectual in the Brotherhood, perversely turns to peddling black Sambo dolls on the street, singing and making them dance, and is thus himself a kind of Sambo doll when he is shot down. Rinehart, like his prototype, Melville's Confidence Man, has so many disguises—from the Reverend B. P. Rinehart, Spiritual Technologist, to Rine the sweet man and numbers runner—that we see only comic masks, and have to conjecture the master illusionist behind them. And so on, from character to character, with the narrator himself the ultimate darky act, an invisible blackness that conceals a sentient human being.

The origins of this figure in clown makeup are many. He comes immediately from vaudeville, burlesque, and the minstrel show, but behind those sources he is an authentic figure of folk tale, in fact the major figure of Negro folk tale. In one form, he is Brer Rabbit (more accurately, "Ber" or "Buh" Rabbit), who appears an innocent but can outwit fox and wolf; in another form he is John, who appears an ignorant slave but can always outwit Ole Massa. When Richard M. Dorson was collecting folk tales in Michigan, an informant told him "Rabbit always the schemey one," and an informant in Florida similarly told Zora Neale Hurston "John was too smart for Ole Massa. He never got no beatin'!"* Behind both figures in American Negro tales there is the prototype of the West African trickster hero of so many cycles:

Spider on the Gold Coast, Legba the creator god's son in Dahomey, Rabbit or Tortoise elsewhere. Like other trickster heroes in other folklores, he is not quite animal, man, or god, but partakes of all three natures.

If Wright, Fisher, and Ellison get the darky act from the realities (and travesties) of Negro life in America, from folk tales of Buh Rabbit and John, and ultimately from West African mythology, those are still not the only sources. The same mocking figure dances through Western literature from the *Eiron* in Greek old comedy and the Fool in *Lear* down to Holden Caulfield in J. D. Salinger's *Catcher in the Rye* and Kingsley Amis's Lucky Jim. We see a related figure called into being by the hard doctrine of I Corinthians 3:19, "For the wisdom of this world is foolishness with God."

In other words, when the Negro writer retreats furthest from white models and deepest into Negro folk tradition, back in fact to African myth, he is paradoxically not furthest from Western literature, but finds himself sharing a timeless archetype with Aristophanes, Shakespeare, and St. Paul, who in turn derived it from *their* folk sources in myth and ritual. High Western culture and the Negro folk tradition thus do not appear to pull the writer in opposite directions, but to say the same thing in their different vocabularies, to come together and reinforce insight with insight. Prince Myshkin in *The Idiot* derives identically from the *Eiron* and Fool of drama, the Fool in

---

* For more on the trickster John, see Zora Neale Hurston, "High John de Conquer," *The American Mercury*, vol. 57 (1943), pp. 450–58, and Harry Oster, "Negro Humor: John and Old Marster," *Journal of the Folklore Institute*, vol. 5 (1968), pp. 42–57. Both of these essays are reprinted in this volume. —ED.

Christ, and a folk figure of wisdom-in-stupidity out of Russian peasant life and lore instead of Negro.

...The relationship of Negro writing to the blues is, if anything, even more immediately visible than its relationship to the folk tale, although it is much harder to describe, since the blues is an extraordinarily complicated and subtle form, much of it depending on the music, which I shall have to ignore here. Most blues songs seem to divide readily into two types, a slow lament and a faster and gayer form.* The slow lament says, with Ma Rainey:

Easy rider, see what you done done,
Easy rider, see what you done done;
You made me love you, now my man
      done come.

or with Bessie Smith:

I was with you, baby, when you didn't
      have a dime,
I was with you, baby, when you didn't
      have a dime;
Now since you got plenty money you
      have throwed your good gal
      down.

The fast blues says, with Joe Turner:

You so beautiful, but you gotta die
      someday,
Oh, you so beautiful, but you gotta
      die someday;
All I want's a little lovin', baby, just
      before you pass away.

or with Jabo Williams:

Please, fat mama, take those big legs
      off of me,

Please, fat mama, take those big legs
      off of me. . . .
Those great big legs gonna drive me
      away,
Those big legs drive me away.

or with Rosetta Crawford:

I'm gonna get me a razor and a gun,
Cut him if he stand still, shoot him if
      he run;
'Cause that man jumped salty on me.

Superficially, the choice seems to be the impossible pair of alternatives Freud gave us in *Beyond the Pleasure Principle*, destroy others or turn the destruction inward. Yet beyond it in the memorable blues performance there seems always to be a resolution, a transcendence, even a catharsis and cure.

The themes of the blues appear everywhere in Negro literature. One of the most predominant is the theme of leaving, travel, journey: "I'm gonna move to Kansas City"; "Some day, I'll shake your hand goodbye"; "Well, babe, goin' away and leave you by yourself"; "Pick up that suitcase, man, and travel on." Walter Lehrman, in an unpublished study of the blues (to which I am considerably indebted), finds some sort of movement away from here in eighty-three out of one hundred lyrics. This sort of aimless horizontal mobility is a constant in American Negro life, substituting for frustrated possibilities of vertical mobility: if a Negro cannot rise in a job, he can change jobs; if he cannot live well here, he can try elsewhere. The major theme of Wright's *Native Son* is Bigger's aimless running;

---

* There is an enormous literature devoted to studies of the blues. For samples, see Janheinz Jahn, "Residual African Elements in the Blues," and Alan Lomax, "I Got the Blues" in this volume. For a discussion of types of blues, see Harry Oster, "The Blues as a Genre," *Genre*, vol. 2 (1969), pp. 259–74. —ED.

in *The Outsider* it is the journey from Chicago to New York to start a new life that proves the impossibility of any such rebirth. In Ellison's *Invisible Man*, the movement is first the great Exodus out of the South north to the Promised Land. Then, when that fails its promises, it is a random skittering up and down Manhattan, between Harlem and "downtown," until the narrator achieves his only possible vertical mobility, significantly *downward*, into a sewer (an ironic verticality already anticipated in Wright's story "The Man Who Lived Underground").

The dramatic self-pity* of the blues, as we hear it in Billie Holiday's:

My man don't love me, treats me oh
    so mean,
My man he don't love me, treats me
    awful mean;
He's the lowest man that I've ever seen.

or Pine Top Smith's:

Now my woman's got a heart like a
    rock cast down in the sea,
Now my woman's got a heart like a
    rock cast down in the sea;
Seems like she can love everybody
    and mistreat poor me.

is the constant note in the work of such a writer as James Baldwin. In *Go Tell It on the Mountain*, the adolescent hero, John, is ugly, friendless, and always the smallest boy in each class. When he encounters *Of Human Bondage* he identifies (almost inconceivably) with Mildred. In Baldwin's "Autobiographical Notes" in *Notes of a Native Son*, the author identifies himself with Caliban, and says to white Prospero, "You taught

me language, and my profit on't is I know how to curse." In *Giovanni's Room* the book's most contemptible-pathetic character, Jacques, retires "into that strong self-pity which was, perhaps, the only thing he had which really belonged to him."

Accompanying the self-pity is a compensatory grandiose fantasy. In the blues, Bessie Smith sings:

Say, I wisht I had me a heaven of my
    own,
Say, I wisht I had me a heaven of my
    own;
I'd give all the poor girls a long lost
    happy home.

In Negro writing, the grandiose fantasy is often upward, but rarely so otherworldly as a private heaven. The nameless Negro protagonist of "The Man Who Lived Underground," after a casual and pointless robbery, papers the walls of his sewer cavern with hundred-dollar bills, hangs gold watches and rings from nails all around him, and makes the dirt floor a mosaic of diamonds. The narrator of *Invisible Man* wires *his* hole in the ground with 1,369 light bulbs covering every inch of the ceiling, and plans on five phonographs simultaneously playing Louis Armstrong's record of "Black and Blue" while he eats pink and white, vanilla ice cream covered with sloe gin. In *Go Tell It on the Mountain*, John lives in a fantasy world where he is "beautiful, tall, and popular." In his daydreams he feels "like a giant who might crumble this city with his anger; he felt like a tyrant who might crush this city beneath his heel; he felt like a long-

---

* One of the first to investigate the theme of "self-pity" in Negro folksong was John A. Lomax. See his "Self-Pity in Negro Folk-Songs," *The Nation*, vol. 105 (August 9, 1917), pp. 141–45. —ED.

awaited conqueror at whose feet flowers would be strewn and before whom multitudes cried, Hosanna!" Sometimes John fancies, in the direct imagery of the blues, that he has "a closet full of whisky and wine," at other times, in his family's imagery, that he is the John of Revelation, or St. Paul. His identification with Maugham's Mildred is not only self-pity but power fantasy. Baldwin writes: "He wanted to be like her, only more powerful, more thorough, and more cruel; to make those around him, all who hurt him, suffer as she made the student suffer, and laugh in their faces when they asked pity for their pain."

The long monologue by "Flap" Conroy in Redding's *No Day of Triumph,* in its combination of bitter misery with high-spirited defiance, is almost an extended blues. Flap opposes the reality principle to blues fantasy, *"White folks* got the world in a jug an' the stopper in their hand," and then immediately denies it, "That's what *they think*." Bigger and his friend Gus in *Native Son* daydream of flying planes and dropping bombs on the white world. In *The Outsider*, this has become a vision, by a Negro in a bar, of flying saucers landing from Mars and disembarking *colored* men, come to put the white overlords of earth in their place. In Langston Hughes's *Simple Speaks His Mind*, Simple, who alternates between feeling "like I got the world in a jug and the stopper in my hand" and varieties of depression, also alternates between fury that Negroes are not allowed to run trains and fiy planes,

and fantasies of space flight:

Why, man, I would rock so far away from this color line in the U.S.A., till it wouldn't be funny. I might even build me a garage on Mars and a mansion on Venus. On summer nights I would scoot down the Milky Way just to cool off. I would not have no old-time jet-propelled plane either. My plane would run on atom power. This earth I would not bother with no more. No, buddy-o! The sky would be my roadway and the stars my stopping place. Man, if I had a rocket plane, I would rock off into space and be solid gone. Gone. Real gone! I mean *gone*!"

Balancing this complex of misery and compensation in the slow blues, we have the abuse and bawdry of the fast blues. Georgia White sings:

When we married, we promised to stick
    through thick and thin;
When we married, we promised to stick
    through thick and thin.
But the way you thinned out is a
    lowdown dirty sin.

"Speckled Red" sings:

Now you're a dirty mistreater, a robber
    and a cheater,
I slip you in the dozen, your pappy
    is your cousin,
Your mama do the Lordy-Lord.

(The reference is to "the dozens," a formalized Negro game, particularly common among children, creating what John Dollard calls "a pattern of interactive insult" by exchanging slurs on the cleanliness, odor, legitimacy, fidelity, and heterosexuality of the opponent's immediate family.)* Simple and

* For further discussion of the dozens, see John Dollard, "The Dozens: Dialectic of Insult" and Roger Abrahams, "Playing the Dozens," in this volume. —ED.

Hughes's narrator slip each other repeatedly in the dozens, as do the college boys in Redding's novel *Stranger and Alone*, along with the characters in many other Negro works. There is a particularly interesting example in *Invisible Man*. The nameless protagonist, brought up on charges before a committee of the Brotherhood, is asked indignantly where he got the "personal responsibility" he claims, and automatically answers "From your ma," before he corrects himself.

Related to the theme of obscenity and abuse in the blues is a pervasive cynicism, the cynicism of "If you don't like my peaches, don't shake my tree; I ain't after your woman, she's after me"; or "Papa, papa, you in a good man's way; I can get one better than you any time of day." The Negro poet who has made this note uniquely his own is Fenton Johnson. I quote part of his poem "Tired," which catches the fast blues' mingled tones of despair and mean comedy:

I am tired of work; I am tired of
    building up somebody else's
    civilization.
Let us take a rest, M'Lissy Jane.
I will go down to the Last Chance
    Saloon, drink a gallon or two of
    gin, shoot a game or two of dice
    and sleep the rest of the night
    on one of Mike's barrels.
You will let the old shanty go to rot,
    the white people's clothes turn
    to dust, and the Calvary Baptist
    Church sink to the bottomless
    pit.
You will spend your days forgetting
    you married me and your nights
    hunting the warm gin Mike
    serves the ladies in the rear of
    the Last Chance Saloon.

Throw the children into the river;
    civilization has given us too
    many.

Along with the themes and attitudes of the blues, their techniques and diction are equally pervasive in Negro writing. In the folk blues, the formal unit is not the song but the individual stanza (what in ballad study is called the "commonplace"), and the composer or singer strings traditional stanzas together to produce his own composition. The formal organization of the blues is thus not narrative, dramatic, or logical; but lyric, thematic, and associative, like a good deal of modern poetry. A typical folk blues is "Little Brother's Blues," recorded by the Lomaxes for the Library of Congress at Texas State Penitentiary in 1934 (I omit the repeated first lines of each stanza):

Lord, you light weight skinners, you
    better learn to skin,
Old Mister Bud Russell, I tell you, he
    wants to starve the men.

O my mama, she called me, I'm gonna
    answer "Mam?"
Lord, ain't you tired of rollin' for that
    big-hat man?

She's got nine gold teeth, long black
    curly hair,
Lord, if you get on the Sante Fe, find
    your baby there.

I been prayin' Our Father, Lord, Thy
    kingdom come,
Lord, I been prayin' Our Father, let
    Your will be done.

One, two, three, four, five, six, seven,
    eight, nine,
I'm gonna count these blues she's got
    on her mind.

Here motifs of work, compulsion and

hunger, mother and rebellion, nine gold teeth and long black curly hair, train journey and baby, God's will and counting the digits, all associate thematically with doing time in a prison camp and the contrasted pole of freedom and gratifications, as T. S. Eliot associates garlic and sapphires in the mud.

The Negro poet most obviously identified with this sort of thematic and associative organization is Melvin B. Tolson, in his remarkable long poem *Libretto for the Republic of Liberia.* Allen Tate in a preface places the poem "in the direct succession" from Hart Crane's *The Bridge,* and other critics have identified its techniques with those of Eliot's *Waste Land* or Pound's *Cantos.* Reinforcing rather than denying these analogies, I would insist on its kinship to the associative organization of the blues. In any case, it is an intricate and sophisticated work, and the advance in complexity it represents can best be shown by comparing a stanza with one from its obvious predecessor, Paul Laurence Dunbar's "Ode to Ethiopia." Dunbar writes:

> On every hand in this fair land,
> Proud Ethiope's swarthy children stand
>   Beside their fairer neighbor;
> The forests flee before their stroke,
> Their hammers ring, their forges
>   smoke,—They stir in honest
>   labor.

Tolson writes:

> And now the hyenas whine among the
>   barren bones
> Of the seventeen sun sultans of Songhai,
> And hooded cobras, hoodless mambas,
>   hiss
> In the gold caverns of Falémé and
>   Bambuk,

And puff adders, hook scorpions,
    whisper
In the weedy corridors of Sankoré.
    Lia! Lia!

Negro writers have ceaselessly attempted to define the emotional ambivalence of the blues: "grief-gayety," "melancholy-comic," "wistfulness-laughter," "making light of what actually is grave," or the blues line itself, "I'm laughing just to keep from crying." In his *Libretto,* that treasure-ship of plunder from the world's cultures and languages, Tolson uses a Yiddish phrase for this ambivalence, *"lachen mit yastchekes,"* which he translates in the notes as " 'laughing with needles being stuck in you'; ghetto laughter." "As for the laughter," a character in Redding's *Stranger and Alone* thinks, "unless one had experienced it, he cannot imagine how it rips and tears you with pain." In an interview in the *Times,* Baldwin stated what are clearly his intentions as a writer: "I have always wondered why there has never, or almost never, appeared in fiction any of the joy of Louis Armstrong or the really bottomless, ironic, and mocking sadness of Billie Holiday."

Ellison made the first critical attempt I know to relate the blues to specific Negro literature in an article on *Black Boy* entitled "Richard Wright's Blues" in *The Antioch Review,* Summer, 1945. He began by defining the form as a symbolic action:

> The Blues is an impulse to keep the painful details and episodes of a brutal experience alive in one's aching consciousness, to finger its jagged grain, and to transcend it, not by the consolation of philosophy, but by squeezing from it a near-tragic, near-comic lyricism.

and concluded:

Let us close with one final word about the Blues: Their attraction lies in this, that they at once express both the agony of life and the possibility of conquering it through sheer toughness of spirit. They fall short of tragedy only in that they provide no solution, offer no scapegoat but the self.

This conception did not really fit Wright's *Black Boy* very well, but it turned out to be a remarkably accurate manifesto for Ellison's novel, *Invisible Man*, published seven years later. If we want "a near-tragic, near-comic lyricism" in a fictional image we need go no further than its final tableau of the Harlem riot of 1943. Here Ras the Exhorter, a bitter Negro nationalist, arrays himself as an Abyssinian chieftain, armed with spear and shield, and rides out against the police guns. We see the scene through the eyes of an anonymous Harlem citizen:

"Hell, yes, man, he had him a big black hoss and a fur cap and some kind of old lion skin or something over his shoulders and he was raising hell. Goddam if it wasn't a *sight*, riding up and down on this ole hoss, you know, one of the kind that pulls vegetable wagons, and he got him a cowboy saddle and some big spurs."

"Aw naw, man!"

"Hell, yes! Riding up and down the block yelling, 'Destroy 'em! Drive 'em out! Burn 'em out! I, Ras, commands you.' You get that, man," he said, "I *Ras*, commands you—to destroy them to the last piece of rotten fish!" And 'bout that time some joker with a big ole Georgia voice sticks his head out the window and yells, 'Ride 'em cowboy. Give 'em hell and bananas.'"

Finally, "riding like Earl Sande in the fifth at Jamaica," Ras charges to his death.

... Negro writing, because of the special vulnerabilities and resources of Negro writers, is in a position to deal with certain ironies and ambivalences of American condition as most white writers (at least outside the South) are not. Negro writers are, as it were, a special kind of radar to extend our vision. Wright in "The Ethics of Living Jim Crow" and *Black Boy*, Tolson in the *Libretto*, Ellison in the Prologue and Epilogue to *Invisible Man*, Baldwin in *Notes of a Native Son*, have all tirelessly articulated this peculiar role, with its consequent responsibilities. The social and racial relations of America are changing radically. One has only to read Toomer's 1923 portrait of Negro life in the South in *Cane*, and its 1942 equivalent, Redding's *No Day of Triumph*, to see the changes wrought by two decades, and a comparable 1958 book would show changes about again as great. Nor does this process go on only in the United States. Any daily paper will show the varieties of ferment of the world's Negro peoples, and we can see its articulate consciousness in such fiction as *In the Castle of My Skin* by George Lamming of the Barbados, or *The Palm-Wine Drinkard* and *My Life in the Bush of Ghosts* by the Nigerian writer Amos Tutuola.

"The artist must lose such lesser identities [as Negro] in the great well of life," Waldo Frank says in his foreword to *Cane*. That has not been the view of many Negro artists of our time. In Paris, Baldwin reports, the American Negro "finds himself involved, in another language, in the same old battle: the battle for his own identity," and this turns out to be part of a larger American quest: "The American in

Europe is everywhere confronted with the question of his identity." There is a Negro character in Claude McKay's *Home to Harlem* for whom identity is largely a matter of cuisine: "He would not eat watermelon, because white people called it 'the niggers' ice-cream.' Pork chops he fancied not. Nor corn pone. And the idea of eating chicken gave him a spasm." Ellison has written exhaustively on the identity problem in "Richard Wright's Blues" and elsewhere, but his most graphic account of it is a similarly culinary identification in *Invisible Man*. The narrator had always scorned Negro food, along with other backward "darky" trappings, in his effort to rise in the white world, until a moment in the middle of the book when on impulse he buys a yam from a peddler and eats it on the street. At that moment, in the magical equation of "yam" with "I am," he comes to terms with his Negro identity and folk tradition, while maintaining his quest for a fully developed human consciousness. In other words, he wants yams, but he wants to be a twentieth-century Western man eating them. It is in just this fashion that the blues, say, develop in significance; starting with the specific lament for lost love, calamity, or hard times, and ending with these events metaphoric for the most universal human condition.

The folk tradition, for the Negro writer, is like Ellison's yams, not the regression or reversion it appears to be, but another path to the most ironic and sophisticated consciousness. Tate's preface to *Libretto for the Republic of Liberia* finds that full utilization of the resources of modern poetry and language has made Tolson "not less but more intensely *Negro*." There is an almost unavoidable unconscious pun in dealing with Negro culture. A silly white Negrophile in Fisher's *The Walls of Jericho* says she prefers Negroes to whites because "You see, they have so much color." Margaret Just Butcher, the Negro author of *The Negro in American Culture*, makes the pun continually in what I take to be entire innocence: "The Negro observably colored the general temper and folkways of the American South"; Negro comedy "richly colored Southern local and regional culture, and eventually that of the whole nation"; a work typifies "the well-meaning, somewhat colorless accounts by white authors"; *Uncle Tom's Cabin* is written in "sharp blacks and whites, no shadings." The reality behind the pun is that Negro life in America, Negro folk literature, and some Negro writing does have color in every sense; not only skin pigment, but all the rich pigmentation of the fullest possible awareness. The best Negro literature and folk literature extends our perception to a far wider spectrum. "Who knows," the narrator of *Invisible Man* asks in the book's last line, "but that, on the lower frequencies, I speak for you?" Perhaps, we can add, on some of the higher, the almost inaudible frequencies as well?

II

Stanley Edgar Hyman's essay on the relationship between Negro American literature and Negro American folklore concerns matters in which my own interest is such that the very news of his piece aroused my enthusiasm. Yet after reading it I find that our conceptions of the way in which folk tradition gets into literature—and especially into the novel; our conceptions of just what is *Negro* and what is *American* in Negro American folklore; and our conceptions of a Negro American writer's environment—are at such odds that I must disagree with him all along the way. And since much of his essay is given over so generously to aspects of my own meager writings, I am put in the ungrateful—and embarrassing—position of not only evaluating some of his statements from that highly dubious (but privileged) sanctuary provided by one's intimate knowledge of one's personal history, but of questioning some of his readings of my own novel by consulting the text.

Archetypes, like taxes, seem doomed to be with us always, and so with literature, one hopes; but between the two there must needs be the living human being in a specific texture of time, place, and circumstance; who must respond, make choices, achieve eloquence, and create specific works of art. Thus I feel that Hyman's fascination with folk tradition and the pleasure of archetype-hunting leads to a critical game that ignores the specificity of literary works. And it also causes him to blur the distinction between various archetypes and different currents of American folklore, and, generally, to over-simplify the American tradition.

Hyman's favorite archetypical figure is the trickster, but I see a danger here. From a proper distance *all* archetypes would appear to be tricksters and confidence men; part-God, part-man, no one seems to know he–she–its true name, because he–she–it is protean with changes of pace, location, and identity. Further, the trickster is everywhere and anywhere at one and the same time, and, like the parts of some dis-

membered god, is likely to be found on stony as well as on fertile ground. Folklore is somewhat more stable, in its identity if not in its genealogy; but even here, if we are to discuss *Negro* American folklore let us not be led astray by interlopers.

Certainly we should not approach Negro folklore through the figure Hyman calls the " 'darky' entertainer." For even though such performers as he mentions appear to be convenient guides, they lead us elsewhere, into a Chthonic labyrinth. The role with which they are identified is not, despite its "blackness," *Negro* American (indeed, Negroes are repelled by it); it does not find its popularity among Negroes but among whites; and although it resembles the role of the clown familiar to Negro variety-house audiences, it derives not from the Negro but from the Anglo-Saxon branch of American folklore. In other words, this " 'darky' entertainer" is white. Nevertheless, it might be worthwhile to follow the trail for a while, even though we seem more interested in interracial warfare than the question of literature.

These entertainers are, as Hyman explains, professionals, who in order to enact a symbolic role basic to the underlying drama of American society assume a ritual mask—the identical mask and role taken on by white minstrel men when *they* depicted comic Negroes. Social changes occurring since the 1930's have made for certain modifications (Rochester operates in a different climate of rhetoric, say, than did Stepin Fetchit) but the mask, stylized and iconic, was once required of anyone who would act the role— even those Negroes whose natural coloration should, for any less ritualistic purposes at least, have made it unnecessary.

Nor does the role, which makes use of Negro idiom, songs, dance motifs, and word-play, grow out of the Negro American sense of the comic (although we too have our comedy of blackness), but out of the white American's Manichean fascination with the symbolism of blackness and whiteness expressed in such contradictions as the conflict between the white American's Judeo-Christian morality, his democratic political ideals and his daily conduct—indeed in his general anti-tragic approach to experience.

Being "highly pigmented," as the sociologists say, it was our Negro "misfortune" to be caught up associatively in the negative side of this basic dualism of the white folk mind, and to be shackled to almost everything it would repress from conscience and consciousness. The physical hardships and indignities of slavery were benign compared with this continuing debasement of our image. Because these things are bound up with their notion of chaos it is almost impossible for many whites to consider questions of sex, women, economic opportunity, the national identity, historic change, social justice— even the "criminality" implicit in the broadening of freedom itself—without summoning malignant images of black men into consciousness.

In the Anglo-Saxon branch of American folklore and in the entertainment industry (which thrives on the exploitation and debasement of all folk materials), the Negro is reduced to a negative sign that usually appears in a comedy of the grotesque and the unacceptable. As Constance Rourke has made us aware, the action of the early minstrel show—with its Negro-derived choreography, its ringing of banjos and rattling of bones, its voices cackling jokes in pseudo-Negro dialect, with its nonsense songs, its bright costumes and sweating performers—constituted a ritual of exorcism.* Other white cultures had their gollywogs and blackamoors but the fact of Negro slavery went to the moral heart of the American social drama and here the Negro was too real for easy fantasy, too serious to be dealt with in anything less than a national art. The mask was an inseparable part of the national iconography. Thus even when a Negro acted in an abstract role the national implications were unchanged. His costume made use of the "sacred" symbolism of the American flag—with red and white striped pants and coat and with stars set in a field of blue for a collar—but he could appear only with his hands gloved in white and his face blackened with burnt cork or greasepaint.

This mask, this willful stylization and modification of the natural face and hands, was imperative for the evocation of that atmosphere in which the fascination of blackness could be enjoyed, the comic catharsis achieved. The racial identity of the performer was unimportant, the mask was the thing (the "thing" in more ways than one) and its function was to veil the humanity of Negroes thus reduced to a sign, and to repress the white audience's awareness of its moral identification with its own acts and with the

---

* The reference is presumably to Chapter Three, "That Long-Tail'd Blue," in Constance Rourke, *American Humor: A Study of the National Character* (New York, 1931). —ED.

human ambiguities pushed behind the mask.

Hyman sees the comic point of the contemporary Negro's performance of the role as arising from the circumstance that a skilled man of intelligence is parodying a subhuman grotesque; this is all very kind, but when we move in from the wide-ranging spaces of the archetype for a closer inspection we see that the specific rhetorical situation involves the self-humiliation of the "sacrificial" figure, and that a psychological dissociation from this symbolic self-maiming is one of the powerful motives at work in the audience. Motives of race, status, economics, and guilt are always clustered here. The comic point is inseparable from the racial identity of the performer—as is clear in Hyman's example from Wright's *Black Boy*—who by assuming the group-debasing role for gain not only substantiates the audience's belief in the "blackness" of things black, but relieves it, with dream-like efficiency, of its guilt by accepting the very profit motive that was involved in the designation of the Negro as national scape-goat in the first place. There are all kinds of comedy: here one is reminded of the tribesman in *Green Hills of Africa* who hid his laughing face in shame at the sight of a gun-shot hyena jerking out its own intestines and eating them, in Hemingway's words, "with relish."

Down at the deep dark bottom of the melting pot, where the private is public and the public private, where black is white and white black, where the immoral becomes moral and the moral is anything that makes one feel good (or

that one has the power to sustain), the white man's relish is apt to be the black man's gall.

It is not at all odd that this black-faced figure of white fun is for Negroes a symbol of everything they rejected in the white man's thinking about race, in themselves and in their own group. When he appears, for example, in the guise of Nigger Jim, the Negro is made uncomfortable. Writing at a time when the blackfaced minstrel was still popular, and shortly after a war which left even the abolitionists weary of those problems associated with the Negro, Twain fitted Jim into the outlines of the minstrel tradition, and it is from behind this stereotype mask that we see Jim's dignity and human capacity—and Twain's complexity—emerge. Yet it is his source in this same tradition which creates that ambivalence between his identification as an adult and parent and his "boyish" naiveté, and which by contrast makes Huck, with his street-sparrow sophistication, seem more adult. Certainly it upsets a Negro reader, and it offers a less psychoanalytical explanation of the discomfort which lay behind Leslie Fiedler's thesis concerning the relation of Jim and Huck in his essay "Come Back to the Raft Ag'in, Huck Honey!"*

A glance at a more recent fictional encounter between a Negro adult and a white boy, that of Lucas Beauchamp and Chick Mallison in Faulkner's *Intruder in the Dust*, will reinforce my point. For all the racial and caste differences between them, Lucas holds the ascendency in his mature dignity over the youthful Mallison and refuses to

---

This essay appeared in the *Partisan Review*, vol. 16 (1948), pp. 664-671, and was reprinted in Leslie Fiedler, *An End to Innocence* (Boston, 1955), pp. 142-151. —ED.

lower himself in the comic duel of status forced on him by the white boy whose life he has saved. Faulkner was free to reject the confusion between manhood and the Negro's caste status which is sanctioned by white southern tradition, but Twain, standing closer to the Reconstruction and to the oral tradition, was not so free of the white dictum that Negro males must be treated either as boys or "uncles"—never as men. Jim's friendship for Huck comes across as that of a boy for another boy rather than as the friendship of an adult for a junior; thus there is implicit in it not only a violation of the manners sanctioned by society for relations between Negroes and whites, there is a violation of our conception of adult maleness.

In Jim the extremes of the private and the public come to focus, and before our eyes an "archetypal" figure gives way before the realism implicit in the form of the novel. Here we have, I believe, an explanation in the novel's own terms of that ambiguity which bothered Fiedler. Fiedler was accused of mere sensationalism when he named the friendship homosexual, yet I believe him so profoundly disturbed by the manner in which the deep dichotomies symbolized by blackness and whiteness are resolved that, forgetting to look at the specific form of the novel, he leaped squarely into the middle of that tangle of symbolism whichh e is dedicated to unsnarling, and yelled out his most terrifying name for chaos. Other things being equal he might have called it "rape," "incest," "parricide," or— "miscegenation." It is ironic that what to a Negro appears to be a lost fall in Twain's otherwise successful wrestle with the ambiguous figure in blackface is viewed by a critic as a symbolic loss

of sexual identity. Surely for literature there is some rare richness here.

Although the figure in blackface looks suspiciously homegrown, Western, and Calvinist to me, Hyman identifies it as being related to an archetypical trickster figure, originating in Africa. Without arguing the point I shall say only that it *is* a trickster; its adjustment to the contours of "white" symbolic needs is far more intriguing than its alleged origins, for it tells us something of the operation of American values as modulated by folklore and literature. We are back once more to questions of order and chaos; illusion and reality; nonentity and identity.

The trickster, according to Karl Kerenyi (in a commentary included in Paul Radin's study, *The Trickster*), represents a personification of the body

which is . . . never wholly subdued, ruled by lust and hunger, forever running into pain and injury, cunning and stupid in action. Disorder belonging to the totality of life . . . the spirit of this disorder is the trickster. His function in an archaic society, or rather the function of his mythology, of the tales told about him, is to add disorder to order and to make a whole, to render possible, with in the fixed bounds of what is permitted, an experience of what is not permitted. . . .

But ours is no archaic society (although its archaic elements exert far more influence in our lives than we care to admit), and it is an ironic reversal that, in what is regarded as the most "open" society in the world, the license of the black trickster figure is limited by rigidities of racial attitudes, by political expediencies, and by the guilt bound up with the white compulsion to identify with the ever present man of flesh and blood whose irremediable features have been expropriated for "immoral" purposes. Hyman, incidentally, would have found in Louis Armstrong a much better example of the trickster, his medium being music rather than words and pantomime. Armstrong's clownish license and intoxicating powers are almost Elizabethan; he takes liberties with kings, queens, and presidents; emphasizes the physicality of his music with sweat, spittle, and facial contortions; he performs the magical feat of making romantic melody issue from a throat of gravel; and some few years ago was recommending to all and sundry his personal physic, "Pluto Water," as a purging way to health, happiness, and international peace.

When the white man steps behind the mask of the trickster his freedom is circumscribed by the fear that he is not simply miming a personification of his disorder and chaos but that he will become in fact that which he intends only to symbolize; that he will be trapped somewhere in the mystery of hell (for there is a mystery in the whiteness of blackness, the innocence of evil, and the evil of innocence, though, being initiates, Negroes express the joke of it in the blues) and thus lose that freedom which, in the fluid, "traditionless," "classless," and rapidly changing society, he would recognize as the white man's alone.

Here another ironic facet of the old American problem of identity crops up. For out of the counterfeiting of the black American's identity there arises a profound doubt in the white man's mind as to the authenticity of his own image of himself. He, after all, went into the business when he refused the king's shilling and revolted. He had put on a mask of his own, as it were; and

when we regard our concern with identity in the light of what Robert Penn Warren has termed the "intentional" character of our national beginnings, a quotation from W. B. Yeats proves highly meaningful:

There is a relation between discipline and the theatrical sense. If we cannot imagine ourselves as different from what we are and assume the second self, we cannot impose a discipline upon ourselves, though we may accept one from others. Active virtue, as distinct from the passive acceptance of a current code, is the wearing of a mask. It is the condition of an arduous full life.

For the ex-colonials, the declaration of an American identity meant the assumption of a mask, and it imposed not only the discipline of national self-consciousness, it gave Americans an ironic awareness of the joke that always lies between appearance and reality, between the discontinuity of social tradition and that sense of the past which clings to the mind. And perhaps even an awareness of the joke that society is man's creation, not God's. Americans began their revolt from the English fatherland when they dumped the tea into the Boston Harbor, masked as Indians, and the mobility of the society created in this limitless space has encouraged the use of the mask for good and evil ever since. As the advertising industry, which is dedicated to the creation of masks, makes clear, that which cannot gain authority from tradition may borrow it with a mask. Masking is a play upon possibility and ours is a society in which possibilities are many. When American life is most American it is apt to be most theatrical.

And it is this which makes me question Hyman's designation of the "smart man playing dumb" role as primarily

Negro, if he means by "conflict situations" those in which racial pressure is uppermost. Actually it is a role which Negroes share with other Americans, and it might be more "Yankee" than anything else. It is a strategy common to the culture, and it is reinforced by our anti-intellectualism, by our tendency toward conformity and by the related desire of the individual to be left alone; often simply by the desire to put more money in the bank. But basically the strategy grows out of our awareness of the joke at the center of the American identity. Said a very dark southern friend of mine in laughing reply to a white business man who complained of his recalcitrance in a bargaining situation, "I know, you thought I was colored, didn't you." It is across this joke that Negro and white Americans regard one another. The white American has charged the Negro American with being without past or tradition (something which strikes the white man with a nameless horror), just as he himself has been so charged by Europeans and American critics with a nostalgia for the stability once typical of European cultures; and the Negro knows that both were "mammy-made" right here at home. What's more, each secretly believes that he alone knows what is valid in the American experience, and that the other knows he knows but will not admit it, and each suspects the other of being at bottom a phony.

The white man's half-conscious awareness that his image of the Negro is false makes him suspect the Negro of always seeking to take him in, and assume his motives are anger and fear—which very often they are. On his side of the joke the Negro looks at the white man and finds it difficult to believe that the "grays"—a Negro term for white people—can be so absurdly self-deluded over the true interrelatedness of blackness and whiteness. To him the white man seems a hypocrite who boasts of a pure identity while standing with his humanity exposed to the world.

Very often, however, the Negro's masking is motivated not so much by fear as by a profound rejection of the image created to usurp his identity. Sometimes it is for the sheer joy of the joke; sometimes to challenge those who presume, across the psychological distance created by race manners, to know his identity. Nonetheless, it is in the American grain. Benjamin Franklin, the practical scientist, skilled statesman, and sophisticated lover allowed the French to mistake him for Rousseau's Natural Man. Hemingway poses as a non-literary sportsman, Faulkner as a farmer; Abe Lincoln allowed himself to be taken for a simple country lawyer—until the chips were down. Here the "darky" act makes brothers of us all. America is a land of masking jokers. We wear the mask for purposes of aggression as well as for defense; when we are projecting the future and preserving the past. In short, the motives hidden behind the mask are as numerous as the ambiguities the mask conceals.

My basic quarrel with Hyman is not over his belief in the importance of the folk tradition; nor over his interest in archetypes, but that when he turns to specific works of literature he tends to distort their content to fit his theory. Since he refers so generously to my own novel, let us take it as a case in point. So intense is Hyman's search for archetypical forms that he doesn't see that the narrator's grandfather in *Invisible Man* is no more involved in a "darky" act than was Ulysses in Polyphemus' cave. Nor is he so much a "smart-man-playing-dumb" as a weak man who knows the nature of his oppressor's weakness. There is a good deal of spite in the old man, as there comes to be in his grandson, and the strategy he advises is a kind of jiu jitsu of the spirit, a denial and rejection through agreement. Samson, eyeless in Gaza, pulls the building down when his strengh returns; politically weak, the grandfather has learned that conformity leads to a similar end, and so advises his children. Thus his mask of meekness conceals the wisdom of one who has learned the secret of saying the "yes" which accomplishes the expressive "no." Here too is a rejection of a current code and a denial become metaphysical. More important to the novel is the fact that he represents the ambiguity of the past for the hero, for whom his sphinx-like deathbed advice poses a riddle which points the plot in the dual direction which the hero will follow throughout the novel.

Certainly B. P. Rhinehart (the P. is for "Proteus," the B. for "Bliss") would seem the perfect example of Hyman's trickster figure. He is a cunning man who wins the admiration of those who admire skulduggery and know-how; an American virtuoso of identity who thrives on chaos and swift change; he is greedy, in that his masquerade is motivated by money as well as by the sheer bliss of impersonation; he is god-like, in that he brings new techniques—electric guitars, etc.—to the service of God, and in that there are many men in his image while he is himself unseen; he is phallic in his role of "lover"; as a numbers runner he is a bringer of manna and a worker of miracles, in that

he transforms (for winners, of course) pennies into dollars, and thus he feeds, (and feeds on), the poor. Indeed, one could extend this list in the manner of much myth-mongering criticism until the fiction dissolved into anthropology, but Rhine's role in the formal structure of the narrative is to suggest to the hero a mode of escape from Ras, and a means of applying, in yet another form, his grandfather's cryptic advice to his own situation. One could throw Rhinehart among his literary betters and link him with Mann's Felix Krull, the Barron Clappique of Malraux's *Man's Fate* and many others, but that would be to make a game of criticism and really say nothing.

The identity of fictional characters is determined by the implicit realism of the form, not by their relation to tradition; they are what they do or do not do. Archetypes are timeless, novels are time-haunted. If the symbols appearing in a novel link up with those of universal myth they do so by virtue of their emergence from the specific texture of a specific form of social reality. The final act of *Invisible Man* is not that of a concealment in darkness in the Anglo-Saxon connotation of the word, but that of a voice issuing its little wisdom out of the substance of its own inwardness—after having undergone a transformation from ranter to writer. If, by the way, the hero is pulling a "darky act" in this, he certainly is not a smart man playing dumb. For the novel, his memoir, is one long, loud rant, howl, and laugh. Confession, not concealment, is his mode. His mobility is dual; geographical, as Hyman points out, but, more importantly, it is intellectual. And in keeping with the reverse English of the plot, and with the Negro

American conception of blackness, his movement vertically downward (not into a "sewer," Freud notwithstanding, but into a coal cellar, a source of heat, light, power and, through association with the character's motivation, self-perception) is a process of *rising* to an understanding of his human condition. He gets his restless mobility not so much from the blues or from sociology but from the circumstance that he appears in a literary form which has time and social change as its special province. Besides, restlessness of the spirit is an American condition that transcends geography, sociology, and past condition of servitude.

Discussions of folk tradition and literature which slight the specific literary forms involved seem to me questionable. Most of the writers whom Hyman mentions are novelists, workers in a form which has absorbed folk tradition into its thematic structures, its plots, symbolism and rhetoric; and which has its special way with folklore as it has with manners, history, sociology and psychology. Besides, novelists in our time are more likely to be inspired by reading novels than by their acquaintance with any folk tradition.

I use folklore in my work not because I am Negro, but because writers like Eliot and Joyce made me conscious of the literary value of my folk inheritance. My cultural background, like that of most Americans, is dual (my middle name, sadly enough, is Waldo).

I knew the trickster Ulysses just as early as I knew the wily rabbit of Negro American lore, and I could easily imagine myself a pint-sized Ulysses but hardly a rabbit, no matter how human and resourceful or Negro. And a little later I could imagine myself as Huck Finn (I so nicknamed my brother) but not, though I racially identified with him, as Nigger Jim, who struck me as a white man's inadequate portrait of a slave.

My point is that the Negro American writer is also an heir of the human experience which is literature, and this might well be more important to him than his living folk tradition. For me, at least, in the discontinuous, swiftly changing and diverse American culture, the stability of the Negro American folk tradition became precious as a result of an act of literary discovery. Taken as a whole, its spirituals along with its blues, jazz, and folk tales, it has, as Hyman suggests, much to tell us of the faith, humor, and adaptability to reality necessary to live in a world which has taken on much of the insecurity and blues-like absurdity known to those who brought it into being. For those who are able to translate its meanings into wider, more precise vocabularies it has much to offer indeed. Hyman performs a service when he makes us aware that Negro American folk tradition constitutes a valuable source for literature, but for the novelist, of any cultural or racial identity, his form is his greatest freedom and his insights are where he finds them.

ON ORIGINS

The newcomer to folklore almost inevitably begins by asking questions about origins. When and where did a particular folksong originate? How old is a given folktale? Unfortunately, discussions of origins are nearly always doomed to failure or at least inconclusiveness. The printed record only goes back so far, and many of the most popular folktales or games clearly date from times well before the invention of writing. Thus while it may be possible in a given instance to suggest that folklore item "x" was probably borrowed by people B from people A, This does not solve the ultimate-origin question of how people A (or the original people in the chain of borrowers) happened to tell the tale or sing the song in the first place.

Actually, contemporary folklore scholarship has tended to turn away from questions of origins in favor of analyses of form and function. The interest has shifted to focus upon the nature of folkloristic phenomena and their function—what the folklore does for and to the people who have it. The nagging question of where a folksong

originated has been replaced by more answerable questions such as how that folksong reflects the ideology of the folksinger who sings it or how the folksong serves as a vehicle of interpersonal communication or as a dynamic expression of social protest.

One reason why the question of origins has remained a vital issue in the study of American Negro folklore is racism. If one assumes that there are, generally speaking, three possible origins for an individual item of American Negro folklore: (1) it comes from African folklore; (2) it comes from European folklore; and (3) it comes from neither Africa or Europe but developed indigenously in the New World; one can easily see how racism and race pride could have entered into the origins scholarship. White scholars, consciously or unconsciously racist, argued that Negro spirituals were essentially derived from a European heritage and that Gullah, the dialect spoken by the inhabitants of the Sea Islands, was nothing but a degenerate dialect of English. The debates have not ended but it has become obvious to anyone who takes the time to examine the available evidence that the African contributions to the musical performance style of the spirituals are considerable and certainly that many of the African-derived lexical and grammatical features of Gullah were overlooked or ignored by many early white scholars. Honest mistakes are sometimes forgivable, but attempts to use specious arguments about origins to demonstrate racial superiority or racial inferiority are contemptible. It is the worst form of academic colonialism for a "scholar" to try to rob a people of their folklore, e.g., by claiming that it is only a poor imitation of the "scholar's" own folklore! For this reason, even though discussions of origins have become somewhat passé in the mainstream of folklore scholarship, it is essential for anyone truly interested in the historical development of the study of American Negro folklore to become thoroughly familiar with the various heated debates having to do with origins.

The Negro-White Spiritual

D. K. WILGUS

    Nowhere has the question of origins been debated more hotly than over the spirituals. D. K. Wilgus, Professor of English and Folk Music at UCLA, has ably summarized the debate as an appendix to his full length discussion of the history of Anglo-American folksong scholarship. From this survey, the reader should be able to see that origins questions are rarely all-or-nothing propositions. Negro spirituals owe something to the European tradition—they do, after all, reflect Christianity and are in English, but they also owe a great deal to African rhythms and singing performance style. On the other hand, as John Lovell, Jr. points out in his excellent essay "The Social Implications of the Negro Spiritual" (reprinted in this volume), it is perhaps the interpretation of the Negro spirituals in the light of American history and in the context of American Negro life in the United States which must take precedence over questions of European versus African origins. In that sense, American Negro folklore should never be considered European folklore or African folklore. Rather it is, simply stated, American Negro folklore!

THE DISPUTE over the origin of the Negro spiritual has many points in common with Ballad War. At the heart of the Anglo-African contention has been the confusion of origin and essence. The antithesis of spontaneity and borrowing pervades the air. Early evidence is scanty and confused; the authority of print has been opposed to internal evidence; and both sources have been variously interpreted. In fact, the same evidence has nourished both sides. Etymologies have been constructed to support opposing views.

Students have misunderstood or mis-stated opponents' arguments. Folk authority has been advanced. But this major dispute has unfortunately involved sectional and racial friction, pride and prejudice. Furthermore, the issue is not resolved. Like the problem of "original form" of the English and Scottish popular ballads, the origin of the Negro spiritual may be past determination; but opposing forces are not completely convinced.

A full history of the slave-song controversy may someday be written. But because of the part the Afro-American argument played in the broad field of twentieth-century folksong scholarship, it must be considered here, if only in this brief essay. The final history may present the dispute in the light of the sympathies and prejudices of those involved. The present discussion will make every effort not to do so. Too many opinions have been judged on these grounds already. Certain motives existed, stimulated the disputants, and possibly colored their judgments. Beyond that this brief outline cannot go.

To define the nature of the argument, one may pose the problem: what elements in the Negro spiritual have been borrowed from the music of the North American whites and what are due to an African heritage and/or the Negroes' own creation in America? Whatever the confusion in some minds, no serious student has imagined that Negroes disembarked in Virginia singing "Deep River" or "Roll, Jordan." And whatever the confusion in some minds, no reputable scholar who has studied the problem has ever said that Negroes merely imitated or echoed white song. The

issue lies between the extremes; and it is unfortunate that a few early commentators and the hysterical fringes of both sides have obscured the problem.

The problem and its history are difficult because of the nature of the songs and their record, and because of the nature of their critics. There is no trustworthy evidence before the Civil War. There are few examples of American Negro tradition that we can accept as pure. Too little is known of African song, and analyzable elements seem to prove little. Critics of Negro song have not been competent in all the required fields and have usually based their arguments on only a part of the evidence. Even all the evidence is not enough, for there are elements in the songs to which we are not yet able to apply objective analysis. As long as a subjective chink remains, the argument will continue.

Although there are earlier references to Negro song, the record begins in the "crossed and disguised" songs of the blackface minstrels of the second decade of the nineteenth century (unless we hold with certain students that turn-of-the-century hymn books also give white versions of Negro songs)[1]. How many and what elements the minstrel stage borrowed from the Negro will probably remain in dispute. But it is clear that the Ethiopian song craze resulted in a stream of burlesques entering folk tradition—Negro and white. And this exchange of material must have only added to a mutual influence which had been occurring for over a century.

Negro song next came into wide public notice through contacts of

---

[1] Miles Mark Fisher, *Negro Slave Songs in the United States* (Ithaca, 1953), pp. 37ff.

Northern soldiers and civilians with the Southern Negro during the Civil War. "O Let My People Go," from the singing of "contrabands" at Fortress Monroe, was published in 1861, and the following year Lucy McKim printed in *Dwight's Journal of Music* a small collection made at Port Royal. Out of experiences with Negroes during and after hostilities grew *Slave Songs of the United States* (1867), bearing the names of William Francis Allen, Charles Pickard Ware, and Luck McKim Garrison, but containing songs gathered by many other collectors.

Considering the sympathies and understandable ignorance of these collectors, their conclusions are surprisingly moderate. They were not folklorists, anthropologists, or musicologists. They knew little of the South, their acquaintance with the "Western and Southern Camp-meetings" must have been superficial, and they knew nothing of folksongs among the white population. But they recorded a body of song, religious and secular, that differed from any they knew. They discovered the shout and the work song. They described the nonpart harmony of the singers. They heard irregularities, *slides*, and *turns*, and noted what they could. They recognized adaptations of camp-meeting hymns, such as "The Ship of Zion," and rejected some songs paralleled in Methodist hymnals. For the rest, they turned to the only authorities they knew, the Negroes themselves.

We recognize as reasonable Allen's conclusion that

the chief part of Negro music is *civilized*—partly composed under the influence of the whites, partly actually imitated from their music. In the main it appears to be original in the best sense of the word. . . . In a very few songs . . . strains of a familiar tune can be traced; and it may easily be that others contain strains of less familiar music, which the slaves heard their masters sing or play (p. vi).

He found the words to be from Scripture and from the hymns heard at church, but he discovered few tune analogues. The sad songs of slavery then seemed to be the creation of a race "imbued with the mode and spirit of European music—often, nevertheless, retaining a distinct tinge of their native Africa" (p. viii).

The period which followed was one of popularization of the spirituals and general praise, slight study, but growing emphasis on their African nature. In 1871 the Fisk Jubilee Singers made their first tour to raise funds for their school, and *Jubilee Songs* was published the following year. *Cabin and Plantation Songs as Sung by the Hampton Students* appeared in 1874, and similar collections followed. Though the emphasis was on religious song, some attention was given to secular music, particularly in David C. Barrow's description of "A Georgia Cornhusking"[2] and in George W. Cable's articles on New Orleans secular music.[3] Commentators generally agreed on Negro origin and African survival of duple rhythm and pentatonic scales.

[2] David C. Barrow, "A Georgia Corn-Shucking," *Century Magazine* 24 (1882), 873–78. [This essay is reprinted in Bruce Jackson, ed., *The Negro and His Folklore in Nineteenth-Century Periodicals* (Austin, 1967), pp. 168–76. —ED.]

[3] George W. Cable, "The Dance in Place Congo," *Century Magazine*, 31 (1886), pp. 517–32; and "Creole Slave Songs," *Century Magazine*, 31 (1886), pp. 807–28. [Both these essays are also reprinted in Jackson, pp. 189–210, 211–42. —ED.]

The Negroes told how the songs grew spontaneously or were brought from Africa; whites repeated the stories. By 1914 the African-Negro origin of the spirituals was widely held, and the presence of Negroid elements in "popular songs of the day" was being noticed.[4] It seemed that there was "no true American music but the wild sweet melodies of the Negro slave."[5]

There were two important dissenting opinions, however, both from foreign observers. Julien Tiersot in his *La Musique chez les peuples indigènes de l'Amérique du Nord* (1911) failed to find African survivals in American Negro songs; and earlier Richard Wallashek in his *Primitive Music* (1893) had stated crushingly that, "speaking generally, these negro-songs are very much overrated and . . . as a rule they are mere imitations of European composition which the negroes have picked up and served again with slight variations" (p. 60). But Wallashek did not pretend to have examined the problem. The only other dissent came from scattered American writers who took another tack and denied that slave songs were American. Therefore Henry Edward Krehbiel had few challenges to meet, but had to meet them on a wide range. In *Afro-American Folk Songs* (1914) he set out to show that the songs of American Negroes are folksongs, that they are American folksongs, and that they contain certain "idioms that were transported hither from Africa" (p. 22).

Krehbiel experiences little difficulty in establishing his first two contentions, but he does so in a way that points out the fundamental basis of the argument. To prove that Negro songs are American folksongs (i.e., spontaneous utterances voicing the joys, sorrows, and aspirations of a people[6]), he maintains that they are the *only* American folksongs.

Nowhere save on the plantations of the South could the emotional life which is essential to the development of the true folksong be developed; nowhere else was there the necessary meeting of the spiritual cause and the simple agent and vehicle. The white inhabitants of the continent have never been in the state of cultural ingenuousness which prompts spontaneous emotional utterance in music. . . .
It did not lie in the nature of the mill life of New England or the segregated agricultural life of the Western pioneers to inspire folksongs; those occupations lacked the romantic and emotional elements which existed in the slave life of the plantations in the South and which invited celebration in song—grave and gay. Nor were the people of the North possessed of the ingenuous, native musical capacity of the Southern blacks (pp. 22–23).

And to justify his attribution of an African background to the idioms of the slave songs he writes:

There is but one body of specifically national song with which the slave of the United States could by any possibility have become

---

[4] Natalie Curtis [Burlin], "Folk Music of America; Four Types of Folk-Song in the United States Alone," *The Craftsman*, 21 (1912), pp. 414–20; "The Negro's Contribution to the Music of America," *The Craftsman*, 23 (1913), pp. 660–69.
[5] William E. Burghardt Du Bois, *The Souls of Black Folk* (Chicago, 1903), p. 11.
[6] Krehbiel does not deny individual authorship; he insists only that the folk poet must speak for his people in their idiom and about their lives, and that the song must be submitted to anonymous oral tradition. See *Afro-American Folksongs* (New York, 1914), p. 4.

familiar—the Scottish, with its characteristic pentatonic scale and rhythmical snap; but the singing of Scottish ballads was not so general in the South that their peculiarities could become the common property of the field-hands on the plantations (p. 83).

In fairness to Krehbiel we must recognize that the existence and character of American folksong had not then been widely recognized. Still, by 1913 sufficient criticism, texts, and even tunes were in print to challenge Krehbiel's statements. His approach became typical of those who supported the autochthonous character of the slave songs. The proponents of Negro genesis were to remain largely outside the official tradition of folklore study in the United States. They tended to consider the Negro song in relative isolation from other American song and looked to Africa alone for parallels. They saw no link between white and Negro song—and looked for none.

Therefore, Krehbiel's recognition of the wide occurrence of many elements common to the slave songs—gapped scales, unorthodox intervals, the snap or syncopation, the solo and chorus organization, for example—did not deter him from seeking Africa as the sole source of influence. Though he found numerous technical correspondences between the meager record of African song and the slave song, he failed even to look for parallels in Anglo-American tradition. His emphasis was, at least in part, due to ignorance. Among his successors, the ignorance hardened into a refusal to consider the possibility of other influences.

Krehbiel's emphasis on religious song also influenced the course of the argument. Though he provides references to secular songs and summarizes the available material on New Orleans and West Indian dances, he is interested in them only as a background for the important creations, the spirituals; and the spirituals turned out to be the weak link in the African chain. For more than a decade Krehbiel's study remained the point of departure for discussions of Negro song, and the commentators did not depart very far.

Behind the rhapsodies of John Wesley Work's *Folk Song of the American Negro* (1915), whatever their validity, lies too little evidence. The important matters of rhythmic emphasis, "turns, twists, and intonations," and the characteristic use of the voice are dealt with only in generalities. And there is no recognition of parallels in Anglo-American tradition for the verse and chorus plan, introduction of extra syllables, the "African" pentatonic scale with added flat seventh, and the chant with interjections. John Work presents folk authority for the origin of many songs, but does not take a full view of the tradition in which the songs were composed. The narrowness of his approach extends even to Negro tradition. Though he refers to African secular and work songs, he slights the secular tradition of American Negro song. He writes of the "uncommon character" of the Negro's religious songs and "the paucity and utter worthlessness of his secular songs. So few and so inferior are these latter that we may justly state that the Negro Folk Music is wholly religious" (p. 27).

James Weldon Johnson's introduction to *The Book of American Negro Spirituals* (1925) is an excellent recapitulation of the evidence and does emphasize the distinction between the spiritual and the ring shout, but it offers little that is new. The only truly independent work was done by Natalie Curtis Burlin[7] and Nicholas George Julius Ballanta[8]. Mrs. Burlin, who had done fieldwork in Indian music, recorded and transcribed both African and American Negro songs. Her findings, in terms of "intuitive harmonies," rhythm, and tonality, tend to confirm those of Krehbiel, though she concedes a good deal of white influence and calls for more evidence. This was provided by Ballanta's theory of African music, which he found demonstrated in his American collection as well. Briefly, he holds that the African pentatonic results not from any concept of the scale, but from a rudimentary harmonic sense of a fifth above and a fourth below any given tone. The rhythm he finds based on vibration rather than division of the pulse, thus explaining the effect of two or four against three. These concepts he finds reflected in the American Negro song. But his contrasts with European music fail to take into account the evidence of Cecil Sharp and other collectors of Anglo-American folk music.

Despite the emphasis on religious song, students were beginning to notice other manifestations in folk and popular song. Collectors such as Odum and Johnson and Dorothy Scarborough were bringing to light all sorts of secular song. Jazz had succeeded ragtime, and the Krehbiel-Ballanta evidence was applied to the "new" manifestations

very effectively by Abbe Niles in his introduction to W. C. Handy's *Blues: An Anthology* (1926).

A reaction from the Krehbiel school was inevitable. Whatever the validity of their evidence, proponents of Negro-African genesis seldom looked outside their chosen field. They tended to sneer at any suggestion of white influence, but sometimes displayed almost total ignorance of white folksong. Thomas W. Talley, for example, illustrates a "Negro rhyming pattern" with a version of "Froggie Went A-Courting" and finds that a rhyme entitled "Bought Me a Wife" preserves African social patterns.[9] But "Bought Me a Wife" is a version of the Anglo-American "Barnyard." Some of the musical examples in other collections were to turn out no better. Furthermore, folklorists and cultural historians were beginning to discover evidence which considerably enlarged the picture drawn by the Krehbiel school.

The enlargement came from the discovery of parallel songs and parallel song-making conditions in white tradition. Works such as Louis F. Benson's *The English Hymn* (1915) called attention to the crude songs springing from the early nineteenth-century revivals, compositions called *spiritual songs*. In 1918 Louise Pound noted that one of the Negro spirituals printed by Krehbiel, "Weeping Mary," had been learned by her mother at a New York Methodist revival between 1826 and 1830.[10] But if we except the usual

---

[7] *Negro Folk-Songs, Hampton Series*, 4 vols. (New York, 1918–1919); *Songs and Tales from the Dark Continent* (New York, 1920).

[8] *Saint Helena Island Spirituals* (New York, 1925).

[9] Thomas W. Talley, *Negro Folk Rhymes* (New York, 1922), pp. 228ff.

[10] Louise Pound, "The Ancestry of a Negro Spiritual," *Modern Language Notes*, 33 (1918), pp. 442–44.

forcefulness of Miss Pound's style and the unfortunate language of Edmund S. Lorenz,[11] the attitude of those opposing the Krehbiel thesis was conciliatory. They sought not to displace but to modify.

The storm of protest broke in 1928. In January, E. M. von Hornbostel printed an article on African music in which, after outlining what was known of the subject, he wrote that

the negro slaves in America and their descendants, abandoning their own musical style, have adapted themselves to that of their white masters and produced a new kind of folk-music in that style.[12]

These words from a student of African music were perfectly timed to introduce the rebellion. Edward Sapir, in a review of James Weldon Johnson's *Book of American Negro Spirituals*, paid tribute to the musical gifts of the Negro, but found both the "poetic titles" and the music itself within the European tradition. That another group under the same conditions could have developed the spirituals and blues, he wrote,

is all but inconceivable. [But] it does not follow . . . that American negro music is merely a carry-over of a specifically African tradition, that it owes little or nothing to the white man's musical stock in trade. The truth seems to be far from simple and not at all easy to state either historically or psychologically. No doubt the African tradition as such was entirely lost or nearly so. . . . It is simply not true . . . that the rhythms of American Negro music are African rhythms.[13]

James Weldon Johnson had issued a challenge:

The Negro Spirituals are as distinct from the folksongs of other peoples as those songs are from each other; and, perhaps, more so. One needs to be only ordinarily familiar with the folk music of the world to see that this is so.[14]

Scholars began to compare, and found likenesses instead of differences.

First in the field was Newman Ivey White, whose *American Negro Folk-Songs* (1928) embraced a collection begun in 1915 and a study pursued in the American academic tradition, textual and historical. White does not hold with the theory that Negro song is mere imitation or borrowing. He finds that assumption "fully as unjust and inaccurate, in the final analysis, as the Negro's assumption that his folk-song is entirely original" (p. 19). Disqualifying himself as a judge of the musical evidence, he adds only an emphasis on the strong Scottish element in American songsters and in white songs in the slave-holding areas. He finds it "reasonable to conclude that the Negro brought African music with him to America, and that it is a considerable element in the songs he sings today," and his over-all conclusion is that the "songs of the Negro today are beyond question the Negro's songs, not the white man's" (pp. 24-25). But to the Krehbiel school White's words seemed but an uncharitable concession. He had discovered a "white man in the woodpile."

White's textual and historical studies

---

[11] Edmund S. Lorenz, *Church Music* (New York, 1923), p. 377.

[12] "African Negro Music," *International Institute of African Languages and Cultures, Memorandum IV*, p. 33. (Reprinted from *Africa*, 1 (1928), pp. 30–62.) See also "American Negro Music," *The International Review of Missions*, 15 (1926), pp. 748–53.

[13] *Journal of American Folklore*, 41 (1928), p. 173.

[14] *The Book of American Negro Spirituals* (New York, 1925), p. 14.

reveal that from the very first, the Negro's songs have been influenced by the songs of the white people. Through variational imitation of the revival songs of the early nineteenth century, the early minstrel songs (only 10 per cent of which seem to have been actually Negro), and the later "coon" songs, the Negro created his own distinctive music. The core of the argument emerges in White's re-creation of the milieu out of which the Negro spiritual grew: the primitive religious practices of the whites during the camp-meeting period, which produced crude spiritual songs. These songs, with their references to spiritual bondage, were taken over by the Negroes and perhaps reinterpreted in terms of physical bondage. This conclusion White documents with contemporary description of the emotional fervor of the camp meetings, a few hymn books containing examples of "less illiterate" spiritual songs, and a few survivals among the "backwoods" whites. "The American Negro song was not at first original with the Negro. It originated in an imitation frustrated by imperfect comprehension and memory, and by a fundamentally different idea of music" (p. 25).

Similar opinions were being advanced by other students. Robert W. Gordon, for example, wrote in a similar vein in his *New York Times* articles of 1927–1928, although he found some indication of an older stratum of Negro religious songs.[15] But the next step was to include the music in "the white man's burden." Milton Metfessel made an attempt to transcend the limits of conventional notation in determining the African and European qualities of American Negro song. But, as he reports in *Phonophotography in Folk Music* (1928), comparison was made only between Negro folksinging and European-style art singing. Important contributions however, used the forms of analysis developed by students of folksong.

The musical approach was pioneered by Anne G. Gilchrist, who discovered folk tunes in the hymn books of the Primitive Methodists and analogues in American Negro songs.[16] Two years later, in 1930, Guy B. Johnson attacked the problem in a study of *Folk Culture on Saint Helena Island.* For comparative purposes, Johnson used two camp-meeting song books and Cecil Sharp's collection and conclusions drawn from the Southern Appalachians. He found the subject matter and words similar, sometimes identical. The tunes themselves are markedly similar. The distribution of major and minor tunes shows no significant difference. Every deviation from conventional scale in Negro song is also found in the white song. The Negro spirituals employ a higher percentage of pentatonic tunes than do the white religious songs which Johnson examined, but almost the same proportion as do the secular songs found by Sharp. Absence of the fourth and seventh tones is not distinctive of Negro song; and the flat seventh is rarer in Negro than in white song. The results of Johnson's study of tempo and rhythm

[15] Robert W. Gordon, *Folk-Songs of America*, National Service Bureau Publication no. 73-S (New York, 1938), pp. 20–26. See also Gordon's chapter on "The Negro Spiritual" in Augustine T. Smythe, *et al., The Carolina Low Country* (New York, 1931), pp. 191–222.

[16] Anne G. Gilchrist, "The Folk Element in Early Revival Hymns and Tunes," *Journal of the Folk-Song Society*, 8 (1928), pp. 61–95.

are less conclusive. He is willing to connect the preponderance of duple rhythm in the Negro songs with the Negro habit of bodily motion, but notes that fewer than 10 per cent of the most "folksy" of the published white songs have triple time. Although syncopation is present in white song, Johnson concedes it to be "one of the few elements in the spirituals which is (*sic*) unmistakably traceable to African patterns" (p. 115).

The remaining element is that of possible melodic relationship. On the basis of his limited material, Johnson discovers four tunes "undoubtedly borrowed" by the Negroes, and eight more traceable "in whole or part" to white song. An effort, writes Johnson, "to check up on the relations between 500 spiritual tunes and about as many white religious tunes, to say nothing of the vast possibilities of white secular music, is a task which might well require ten years of study" (p. 115). And Johnson was right, for George Pullen Jackson's summation of his own studies of *White and Negro Spirituals* was published in 1943.

Though Jackson was not the only scholar establishing white sources for Negro spirituals,[17] his work is the most complete. It has firmly established the contention that the melodic core of Negro religious songs developed from white spirituals. His textual and musical analysis is set in the frame of American religious folksong, whose history he has written. His examination of the tunes is both analytic and genetic.

In *White and Negro Spirituals*, Jackson gives the results of a comparison (of 892 Negro tunes with 555 white spirituals) which reveals 116 genetic relationships. These relations are the heart of the argument, for sixty of the tunes have been collected from oral tradition in the British Isles, fifteen more are widespread in the secular tradition of the whites of North America, and seventeen are by known composers of the nineteenth century; fifteen are what Jackson terms *general melodizing*, and the source of the remaining nine is unknown. But who made the rest of the Negro songs? The Negro, writes Jackson, just as the whites made their songs "by endless singing of heard tunes and by endless, inevitable, and concomitant singing differentiation" (p. 267).

Jackson's analysis of the tunes generally confirms Guy B. Johnson's earlier study. Jackson finds that the Negro tends to borrow more pentatonic tunes and in singing to slenderize their tonal content still further. The Negroes have preferred more major sequences than have the whites, but the Negroes have seldom altered modes, tending to sing the songs as they heard them. Jackson identifies Krehbiel's "wild tones" (weak or variable thirds and sevenths, and raised sixths) in both singing traditions, as well as in all folksong "since time immemorial," but he gives the Negro credit for bringing about the reintroduction of these deviations into modern art music.

Jackson goes further than some other writers in accounting for other features of Negro spirituals. The call and response, the repetition, the syncopation more prevalent in Negro song he holds not to be connected with Africa. These he finds grew from white singing

---

[17] See especially Phillips Barry, "Negro Folk-Songs from Maine," *Bulletin of the Folk-Song Society of the Northeast*, no. 8 (1934), pp. 13ff; no. 9, pp. 10ff; no. 10, pp. 21ff.

in the camp-meeting period heightened by the Negro's racial emphasis. This emphasis may correspond with a similar one in Africa, but it did not necessarily come from Africa. The most exotic and "African-sounding" of Negro songs are the *surge songs*, which Jackson identifies as a survival of the old-style country manner of singing eighteenth-century psalm tunes, now reserved by the Negro for "Dr. Watts."

Jackson's writing is not always urbane, but his tone is easily accounted for. This transplanted New Englander became a champion of the Southern yeoman class, the poor white. His early writing, if directed against anyone, chastised "the professional Southerners of big-plantation presumptions" and "the Southern urban church folk," although his reference to those with a "vested interest in the perpetuation of the *un*truth" cuts a wider swath. But his "Farewell to Africa" chapter of *White and Negro Spirituals* was called forth by the attacks, many of them personal, which had arisen as he published his various studies. Followers of the Krehbiel school never contradicted his evidence. They first merely repeated and expanded Krehbiel's one-sided argument, adding a few sneers at "library scholars" and "paper scholarship." They next intimated that the white hymns were borrowed from the Negro. One might ignore such hysterical works as Maud Cuney Hare's *Negro Musicians and Their Music* (1936), but the investigations of Melville J. Herskovits are another matter.

Herskovits is hunting bigger game,

of course. His studies of the influence of Africanisms on New World civilization are distinguished. His most important observation on the Negro-white controversy concerns the over-emphasis on religious songs and on the Negro songs of the United States. But Herskovits is not willing to write off the spirituals and devote himself to other manifestations of Negro song. Faced with the patent connection of Negro religious song with the American revivals, he seeks to show that the revivals themselves are a "reflex of those Africanisms in Negro behavior which, in a particular social setting, take the form of hysteria."[18] He maintains that European religious possession was a private, not a social phenomenon and that there is an intrinsic difference between the manifestations of the Great Awakening and those of the later camp meeting. Herskovits' suggestion is not exactly new, for William Edward Burghardt Du Bois wrote in 1903 that "the religion of the poor whites is a plain copy of Negro thought and methods,"[19] but it has a firmer and more far-reaching basis. Herskovits provides much evidence from Africa and the New World which establishes at least an independent Negro basis of many elements—musical and behavioral —found in the spirituals. But his own evidence reveals that the shouting spiritual is found only after exposure to Protestant revivalism. Herskovits is careful to recognize parallels in African and European tradition that "have coalesced and reinforced each other in New World Negro music,"[20] but he

[18] *The Myth of the Negro Past* (New York, 1941), p. 225.
[19] *The Souls of Black Folk*, p. 192.
[20] *The Myth of the Negro Past*, p. 267.

seems to impute to Negro influence on white revivalism an importance out of proportion to the probabilities. On the other hand, unacknowledged borrowings by white tradition had received too little attention. Music knows no color line, but to attribute to Negro influence elements possibly developed in white tradition is as erroneous as to postulate the Negro's borrowing of elements which can be African survivals.

Important discussion has been contributed by investigators of the genesis of jazz. Though all such writers are not agreed on origins, they have generally viewed jazz as largely a development from Negro—and hence African—art. They have had the advantage of recent recordings of African and American Negro folk music and have been basically interested in performance, rather than written music. Further, they have seen the spiritual as a small part of the larger picture, and therefore more objectively.

One of the most important students has been Rudi Blesh, whose *Shining Trumpets* (1946) is the most thorough treatment of the problem. Blesh depends to a great extent on the African and New World materials of Herskovits and the unpublished studies of M. Kolinski. He seeks not to discredit the conclusions of Jackson and George Herzog,[21] but to supplement and interpret them. He thus accepts without question the melodic origin of many spirituals in the white hymn, but he emphasizes the adoption of "white melodies and harmony that are amenable to the peculiar scalar, tonal, antiphonal or polyrhythmic treatment of African music" (p. 343)—

a selective borrowing and transformation. Consequently the investigator finds African or European elements, depending on which he is seeking. *Matter* tends to be European, and *manner* African. Blesh—to oversimplify his discussion—finds predominantly African elements in the early rural work songs and in the spirituals and their offspring, the blues, a process of adaptation and transformation that creates a new musical form in the African tradition of songs intimately related to daily living.

With all due respect to Blesh's evidence and careful investigation, his work reveals the fault common to most proponents of African genesis, a failure to take into account the characteristics of Anglo-American folk music, a consideration of which might even strengthen his theory of selective borrowing and transformation but would reveal the greater complexity of the problem. Blesh's listing of African survivals is most soundly based in the areas of "the hot concept" (variation and improvisation of melody and rhythm), rhythmic patterns, and timbre or tone quality. In other areas he fails to note correspondences with Anglo-American folksong. His comparisons are almost invariably with European cultivated music, not folk music. Pentatonic and hexatonic scale structures and microtonal flatting, especially of thirds and sevenths, may be African survivals; they are also a part of Anglo-American folk music. Glissandi, pitch wavering, and wide vibrato are distinctive of Negro singing, but their occurrence in lesser degree in white folksong must also be observed. And antiphony (call and response) is an African technique that

---

[21] See *Journal of American Folklore*, 48 (1935), pp. 394ff.

has some slight parallel in the rendition of the American white folk hymn. Blesh's list of types of Negro folk music prior to jazz is enough to indicate many possible interrelationships with white folksong. A small indication of the problem is his dismissal as "pseudo-blues" of "a rural type of song the white singers call blues and which certain writers designate as white blues. This . . . is not blues, nor is it even an established form. It preserves faint echoes of the real Negro blues, but in mountain districts it is hill-billy song and in the Southwest it is a cowboy tune" (p. 146). But is it parallel to or derivative from Negro singing? Though the latter seems likely, the concept of "white blues" cannot be summarily dismissed, nor can those elements of contemporary American white folksinging not found in Great Britain. The problem of their origin is tied up in one way or another with the problem of African survivals. When Blesh treats "Casey Jones" as a Negro adaptation of a white ballad, he unwittingly points out the difficulty. Blesh's "white ballad" is an adaptation of a Negro ballad, itself widespread in a railroad tradition shared by Negroes and whites. The age and character of the blend assumes great importance.

Marshall W. Stearns' recent *The Story of Jazz* (1956), though less technical than Blesh's study, is an improvement in that it takes more direct account of the white folk tradition and certain similarities of European folk and West African music that enter into the blend of Afro-American music. Stearns notes the presence in both traditions of the diatonic scale and "a certain amount of harmony. . . . The main difference is that European folksong is a bit more complicated harmonically and African

tribal music is a little more complicated rhythmically. . . . When the African arrived in the New World the folk music that greeted him must have sounded familiar enough, except for a lack of rhythm. The blending has proceeded on many levels and in a variety of ways" (p. 14). He points out how the white religious tradition in its lining out "confirmed the West African in his use of the call-and-response pattern" (p. 10) and in its part singing and freedom from other than accidental harmony "gave a melodic and rhythmic liberty which proved attractive to the West African ear" (p. 82). But when, describing the growth of revival song in camp-meetings, he writes that "the blend of British hymn and folk song became partly Africanized" (p. 83), is he speaking of a parallel development or of the influence of Negro participants? On the one hand he seems to be merely saying that the Negro adopted and adapted the type of worship and song with which he was most familiar and at which he excelled. Yet he writes later, "searching for the origin of the harmony of the spiritual (and sometimes its melody) *as written down* can lead to the conviction that all spirituals were taken from the Protestant hymn. But the truth is that only the harmony of the spiritual could have come directly from the Protestant hymn, and even that was transformed at once by the cry into an over-all blue tonality that is unknown in the Old World" (p. 138).

One of the problems (in addition to Stearns' failure to comment on intervals common to white and Negro song) is the term *spiritual*. Stearns differentiates roughly among ring shout, song-sermon, jubilee, and spiritual. In discussing the evolution of the last, he does not always differentiate clearly between the folk process and the interference of the recorder who wrote down one of a number of tunes for the words. In fact, he leaves the impression that the pioneers created the spirituals by noting fragments of ring shouts or jubilees. Granting that little can be proved by citing the origin of a term, one could wish that Stearns in his many references to the Protestant hymn would note that the term *spiritual* was applied by the whites to their camp-meeting songs. And, "searching for the origin of 'fixed' melodies," Stearns adopts the "spontaneous combustion" theory, improvisation "along traditional lines within a fixed form" (p. 134), making no reference to Jackson's researches. But his over-all position that many types of American music and the widespread shanty as well are a blend of European and West African elements seems sound, even if it still leaves much of the analysis of the blend incomplete.

The implication of Herskovits's suggestion that American revivals derive at least in part from Africanisms has been developed in another direction by Miles Mark Fisher. The thesis of his *Negro Slave Songs of the United States* (1953) is that, although there has been some influence of European song, the slave songs are historical documents created by the Negroes to record contemporary happenings and to pass on a record to future generations. The songs preserve the Negroes' reaction to everyday events of slavery, slave uprisings, the efforts of the African Colonization Society, the secret meetings continuing the African cult. This is the most ingenious interpretation of the spirituals yet seen. The proof is even more interesting.

Fisher has first the evidence of African song and cult, which supports a "worldly" interpretation of Negro song. He has a bit of external evidence in that Negroes sometimes served as choir singers in early Southern churches. But his proof comes largely from the internal evidence of the spirituals themselves. He connects specific songs with events many years prior to the appearance of the cognate white songs— a sort of "higher chronology." But he must date the songs by interpreting their symbolism, which is not static.

Moses was understood in the eighteenth century to be Bishop Francis Asbury. Later he stood for a Negro and frequently attended camp meetings. All at once he was transported to Africa.... Such evolution gave color to the spirituals (p. 178).

Fisher also gives color by his restoration of texts to what he considers their original form.

I am huntin' for a city, to stay awhile,
I am huntin' for a city, to stay awhile,
I am huntin' for a city, to stay awhile,
O believer got a home at las',

becomes

I see home,
I see home,
I see home,
O Believer (Po' Sinner) got a home
    at las' (p. 45).

The voice of the euhemerist and the hand of the solar mythologist!

According to Fisher, the slaves first created songs in which *heaven* meant the North or Africa; then the whites, to whom *heaven* meant heaven, borrowed the songs. It is difficult to believe, even with Fisher's help, that the slaves created and communicated this symbolism. Fisher has amassed a good deal of evidence to show that the religious songs may have had a private meaning, and no one doubts that many of the songs were symbolically understood or that certain of the slave songs were in code, but the theory seeks to prove too much.

Fisher's approach is fortunately not typical of recent criticism. Though hysterical outbursts appear from time to time,[22] the strongest position is that of the "compromise theorists" who, as Bruno Nettl writes in *Music in Primitive Culture* (1956), "do not hold that the melodies of the American Negroes originated in Africa, but assume that the Negroes have taken over tunes of the whites and combined with them African stylistic traits—hot rhythm, much variation, preference for part-singing, antiphony, and response" (p. 129). Nettl accounts for the survival of African traits by Richard A. Waterman's theory of syncretism—that traits in African music similar to features in European music tend to survive—and by the postulation of strong traits that defy acculturation. Taking another point of view, we might add that strong traits in African music have tended to reinforce and heighten corresponding traits in American white folk music. Thus study is revealing that a simple concept of *origin* is not only misleading, but nonsensical.

To America from Africa the Negro brought a song tradition differing from and yet in some respects resembling the European folk tradition (with which, in fact, it had some historic connections). From the songs of the whites, the Negro borrowed what was congenial to him, and the whites were debtors as well as creditors. The resulting hybrid is a folk music which sounds African in the Negro tradition and European in the white tradition. There are certainly African survivals, even in tunes, as Lydia Parrish has recently demonstrated.[23] The ring shout undoubtedly has African ancestors (the attempt to connect it with shouting in the Old Testament seems beside the point[24]); yet we need not derive *shout* from *saut*[25] or connect the circular dances of the Shakers with African songs. Though a West African river cult may help to explain the popularity of the Baptist sect among the Negroes, it has no necessary connection with the number of Southern white Baptists; rather, the efforts of the Southern Baptists may have reinforced an African survival. The Negro has preserved, borrowed, and re-created, as has the white. The two races share a tradition which they tend to treat distinctively. In the absence of trustworthy reports from the eighteenth and nineteenth centuries, we can only hope that an increasing knowledge of African music and study of recent field reports from American areas will enable us not merely to sort our elements, but to understand the hybridization of not only the spiritual but all American folk and popular music.

---

[22] For example, in *The Armed Vision* (New York, 1948), p. 138, Stanley Edgar Hyman writes, "Jackson is a Southern white chauvinist who has tricked out with trappings of pseudo-musicology his conviction that the Negro, as an inferior human, could hardly produce a first-rate art like the spirituals."

[23] Lydia Parrish, *Slave Songs of the Georgia Sea Islands* (New York, 1942), pp. 45ff.

[24] Barry, *Bulletin of the Folk-Song Society of the Northeast*, no. 9 (1935), p. 10.

[25] Parrish, *Slave Songs of the Georgia Sea Islands*, p. 54.

African Influence
on the Music
of the Americas

RICHARD ALAN WATERMAN

Having been introduced to the European-African origin question with respect to spirituals by an expert in Anglo-American folksong, the reader should, in fairness, read an essay by a convincing advocate of the Africanist position. Richard Waterman, Professor of Anthropology at the University of South Florida, was greatly influenced by Melville Herskovits whose Myth of the Negro Past *and other writings represent the most detailed documentation of the African origins of American Negro culture. Waterman's discussion of some of the distinctive differences between African and European rhythms is particularly illuminating and should be helpful even to those readers who lack sophistication in ethnomusicology.*

It might not be amiss to point out that studies of African origins have not always been hailed with enthusiasm by all members of the Negro community. One reason for this is that many American Negroes essentially "bought" the white stereotype of Africa as a very primitive, "savage" place. Negroes holding this false, stereotyped attitude toward Africa were not anxious to be in any way associated with such a place and, in fact, tended to regard the attempts of white scholars to locate African origins as one more instance of the white's denigrating Negro culture, that is, to the extent that American Negro culture was African it was "primitive," "savage," etc.

In view of this, one can more easily understand why Negroes had little reason to be interested in disputes about European versus African origins. European origins were insulting in that there was invariably an implication that "inferior" Negroes could only borrow or imitate "superior" European culture; African origins were considered to be demeaning in that such origins were construed to be prima facie evidence of primitivism. In other words, neither European nor African origins did much for race pride. Unfortunately, it has taken literally decades to undo the damage caused by this stereotypic thinking— among both whites and blacks—and it is only relatively recently that the genius and creativity involved in the Negro transformation of European musical forms (such as the "spiritual") and the marvelous cultural achievements of the different African cultures (e.g., in art and in music) have begun to be recognized. Finally, the earlier unfavorable image of Africa has begun to fade and is being replaced by a new, exciting and more positive image.

For a discussion of the white stereotype of Africa, see Katherine George, "The Civilized West Looks at Primitive Africa: 1400–1800, A Study in Ethnocentrism," Isis, *49 (1958), pp. 62–72, reprinted in Alan Dundes, ed.,* Every Man His Way *(Englewood Cliffs, N. J., 1968), pp. 22–35. For considerations of American Negro attitudes toward Africa, see Earl E. Thorpe, "Africa in the Thought of Negro Americans,"* The Negro History Bulletin, *23 (October, 1959), pp. 5–10, 22; Melville J. Herskovits, "The Image of Africa in the United States,"* Journal of Human Relations, *10 (1962), pp. 236–45; Harold R. Isaacs, "Negroes and Africa," in his* The New World of Negro Americans *(New York, 1963), pp. 105–322; St. Clair Drake, "Negro Americans and 'The Africa Interest,' " in John P. Davis, ed.,* The American Negro Reference Book *(Englewood Cliffs, N. J. 1966), pp. 662–705; Sterling Stuckey, "Du Bois, Woodson and the Spell of Africa,"* Negro Digest, *16 (February, 1967), pp. 60–74; Henry E. Cobb, "The African Background of the American Negro: Myth and Reality,"* Black Experience, A Southern University Journal, Bulletin Southern University and A. & M. College, *vol. 55, no. 7 (June, 1969), pp. 9–20; Felix N. Okoye,* The American Image of Africa: Myth and Reality *(Buffalo: Black Academy Press, Inc., 1971).*

For a more technical treatment of some of the characteristics of Afro-American music, see Richard A. Waterman, " 'Hot' Rhythm in Negro Music," Journal of the American Musicological Society, *1 (1948), pp. 24–37. For other representative samples of the considerable literature devoted to identifying African origins of American Negro folk music, see Barbara Greene,* African Music Survivals in the Songs of the Negro in Haiti, Jamaica, and the United States *(Chicago, 1956); Paul Oliver,* Savannah Syncopators: African Retentions in the Blues *(New York, 1970); and Alan Lomax, "The Homogeneity of African–Afro-American Musical Style," in Norman E. Whitten, Jr. and John F. Szwed, eds.,* Afro-American Anthropology: Contemporary Perspectives *(New York, 1970), pp. 181–201. Although Afro-American art has not been as well studied as Afro-American music, it is clear that this is a productive area of research. See Robert Farris Thompson, "African Influence on the Art of the United States," in* Black Studies in the University, *eds. Armstead L. Robinson, Craig C. Foster, and Donald H. Ogilvie (New Haven, 1969), pp. 122–70, and especially Thompson's book,* Esthetic of the Cool: Towards a History of African and Afro-American Art *(In press).*

THERE ARE two reasons why African musical elements have influenced the musical styles of the Americas.[1] In the first place, American Negro groups have remained relatively homogeneous with regard to culture patterns and remarkably so with respect to in-group solidarity. This has almost guaranteed the retention of any values not in conflict with the prevailing Euro-American culture pattern. Second, there is enough similarity between African and European music to permit musical syncretism. This has put some aspects of African musical style in the category of traditions not destined to be forced out of existence because of their deviation from accepted norms. The first factor has been dealt with adequately by Herskovits (8, 5, 9, 10, 11). The second, less well known because of the lack, until recently, of reliable data concerning the music of Africa, will be given consideration here.

In some respects, the western one-third of the Old World land mass is musically homogeneous, for it is set off from the other major musical areas by the extent of its reliance on the diatonic scale and by its use of harmony. Although the former appears sporadically elsewhere, as, for example, in China, it has not, except in the West, been used as the basis for musical development, and is to be distinguished sharply from the microtonal scalar system of the Indo-Arabic area. Harmony, on the other hand, appears in aboriginal music nowhere but in the western one-third of the Old World, where it is common in European folk music and African tribal music. Three points must be made here in amplification and clarification of this statement. In the first place, no reference is intended to the European school of literate music and musical theory; this has developed many aspects of music, and harmony in particular, to a point of complexity where it can scarcely be compared to either European folk music or African tribal music. Second, there exists a broad intrusive belt of Arabic and Arabic-influenced music which stretches across the middle of the western area, along both shores of the Mediterranean. Since the times of ancient history this alien musical outcropping has masked the fact of the previous existence of a continuous harmony-using bloc of cultures established earlier in the area.

The third point concerns the oft repeated assertion that Africans, except those who have been in contact with European music, use harmony only as the accidental result of polyphonic overlapping of leader and chorus phrases. This last fact merits closer examination, since it contradicts—by fiat, as it were—the evidence now available in many recordings of African music. It seems to have stemmed from certain preconceptions concerning the evolution of music which have proved inapplicable to the present case. The

[1] The writer gratefully acknowledges the aid of the Carnegie Corporation of New York in providing a field grant for ethnomusicological study among African-derived religious cults in Cuba during the summers of 1946 and 1948, from which stemmed many of the insights documented in this paper. He is even more deeply indebted to the Social Science Research Council of Northwestern University and to the Graduate School of that institution for their financial support over a period of years of a program of research which has resulted in the establishment of the Laboratory of Comparative Musicology and in most of the work in the field of Afro-American music which is summarized here.

argument, in terms of these preconceptions, is simply that Africans had not developed enough culturally to be expected to have harmony. Given this bias, it is easy to see, in view of some factors immediately to be adduced, how an ethnomusicologist of a decade or two ago could have listened to African music, and even have transcribed African music, without ever hearing harmony used, even though harmony may actually have been present.

Let us first consider the nature of the machines used in gathering early recordings of African music. These necessarily were acoustical rather than electrical. A singer whose voice was being recorded had usually to be carefully placed in front of the horn. He had to sing loudly, and, even so, a deviation of any magnitude from the correct position might serve to put his voice out of collecting range. Since the usual field-musicological task is looked upon simply as the collection of melodies, it is not difficult to comprehend how choral backgrounds, possibly harmonized, could elude the ear of the laboratory musicologist who heard only the recorded result, although he might be making use of the best equipment available at the time. Coupled to this consideration is the circumstance that most studies of African music were done by trained music analysts using phonographic materials provided by other, perhaps even "nonmusical" researchers. Purely as a practical matter this division of labor between the collector in the field and the analyst in the laboratory, so unfortunate for the development of ethnomusicology as a branch of cultural anthropology, has been, until recently, a standard arrangement for the conducting of

research in this discipline and is, of course, very effective in those rare cases in which true collaboration has been achieved between collector and analyst.

The fact that many African tribal styles actually do not use harmony to any great extent bolstered the accepted position. "Negro Africa" encompasses a number of peoples, and while, as will be seen presently, certain generalizations may be made concerning the musical style of the whole area, the great variety of styles actually present must never be lost sight of. The peoples of a large section of Dahomey, for example, manage to do almost entirely without harmony, while the Ashanti, in the neighboring West African territory of the Gold Coast, seem to employ at least two-part, and frequently three- and four-part, harmony for almost all of their music. It may be, therefore, that the notion of the absence of harmony in African music was connected initially with the fact that early samples came from non-harmonizing areas. Also, although this can by no means be used as a valid explanation of African harmony, it is true that the ubiquitous "overlapping call-and-response" pattern provides many instances of a sort of sporadic, although accidental, harmony when the beginning notes of the chorus refrain happen to harmonize with the simultaneously sounded terminal tones of the soloist's phrase.

That a hypothesis concerning the absence of harmony in African music could have been framed on the basis of early data presented, then, is completely understandable; how the hypothesis came to be accepted as fact and how it managed to persist to this day are less readily understood. Yet we must realize that not only in ethnomusicology does it occur that an authoritatively stated, although invalid, generalization comes to have considerable inertia of its own. Nevertheless, facts, in the form of phonographic recordings, indicate that singing in harmony is common among African tribesmen. The presumption that the development of African music must of necessity be following the same evolutionary path blazed by European academic music is, furthermore, seriously undermined by recorded examples of the facile use by non-Europeanized African tribesmen of intervals considered extremely "modern" when encountered in European harmony.[2] African harmony, while it has remained simple, as has that of most European folk-songs, nevertheless seems in some areas to have had certain striking autonomous developments.

The presence of the same basic concept of scale and the use of harmony in both Europe and Africa have made easy and inevitable the many varieties of Euro-African musical syncretism to be observed in the New World. It is, for example, easy to understand how, to a member of an early American Negro group steeped in the value and behavior patterns of West African musical tradition, the European music which came to his attention must have appeared mainly as a source of new musical ideas to be worked out in terms of African concepts and techniques. Almost nothing in European folk music, to phrase the matter cautiously, is incompatible with African musical style, and much of the European material fits readily into the generalized African musical mold. An indicator of the fact

that this is not true of any two styles of music taken at random is afforded by the rarity of examples of genuine syncretization between American Indian music and the music of either Europe or Africa.

Thus, in the United States as in other New World areas controlled by English-speaking Europeans, folk tunes and hymns stemming from the British Isles were often seized upon by African slaves and their descendants and, after suitable remodeling, adopted as American Negro tunes. The remodeling process was one of Africanization, and the tunes which emerged are best to be interpreted as European-inspired African music. In the Iberian-controlled areas of the New World, an additional factor facilitated the process of syncretization. The fact that the music of Spain and Portugal had already, over a period of several generations before the beginning of the slave trade with the Americas, been influenced by African musical traits imported along with West African slaves, was something that gave Euro-African musical syncretization in Latin America a head start, so to speak.

Both of the criteria offered above for the persistence of a tradition in an acculturative situation are thus seen to have been fulfilled in the case of the African musical style in the Americas. There has been sufficient density of Negro population, sufficient Negro group-consciousness, and sufficient homogeneity with respect to African musical values in most of the Negro areas of the New World to permit the transmission of these values to the young in consistent fashion. The socio-

---

[2] Observe, for example, the use of parallel seconds in the choral music of the Babira of the Belgian Congo (1, side No. 2).

logical isolation of some of these Negro groups without relation to the actual proportions of African ancestry in the genealogies of members of the groups, as is the case in the United States, must not be overlooked as an important factor in maintaining relatively inviolate the African musical values in spite of a considerable infusion of non-African genetic strains. The ease with which many European musical traits could be incorporated into the African patterns simply permitted, through the processes of reinterpretation and syncretization, a retention of African musical formulae in bodies of New World Negro music which have become, if we start with African music, more and more European with each generation as the blending progressed.

This statement has been intended to show how African musical tradition, or at least, certain aspects of it, could persist in the New World. There would be no reason for the explanation, since such persistences of tradition are commonplace in acculturative situations, were it not for the fact that a sort of *academic* tradition has been in force which, placing emphasis on the many changes in the lives of the American Negroes brought about first by slavery, and later by the exigencies of life as a member of a minority underprivileged group, has systematically denied both the fact and the possibility of such persistence of African tradition.

This is not to say, of course, that American Negro music must be derived entirely from Europe or entirely from Africa. Since the music actually is, for the most part, a blend of both African and European idioms, the answer to the question of derivation may well depend largely on the initial direction of approach to the problem. Thus, Negro

spirituals have been pronounced by some scholars to be derived solely from Europe because they contain a great many Euro-American elements; the problem of the provenience of jazz, on the other hand, has been muddled by the proclamations of certain writers who, discerning Africanisms in that form of music, insist that jazz is purely African.

Attention thus far has been concentrated upon the aspects of African music which coincide with European; however, African music, obviously, is not European music. The European folk song is typically more complex harmonically and simpler rhythmically than African tribal song. Modulation from key to key, for example, is virtually unknown in African tribal music, while the consistent use of multiple meter— two or three time-signatures at once, as it were—is equally unknown in European songs. Melodic structure, however, seems to be at about the same level of complexity in both areas, although different forms are utilized.

The outstanding feature of African music which sets it most apart from that of Europe is the rhythm, a focal value which is implemented in a great number of ways. As Herskovits (7, p. 3) has written, "for the African, the important thing about rhythm is to have it, regardless of how it is produced." African rhythms have been spoken of (13, p. 61) as "incredible and incomprehensible to us." While this may be rejected as the counsel of defeat, it is undoubtedly true that the appreciation of African rhythms requires the development of a musical sense that, in the individual conditioned only to the norms of European music, usually lies somewhat dormant.

This may be spoken of as the *metronome sense*. Until it is developed, much of the aspect of African music most important to the African may well remain incomprehensible to the most careful investigator. From the point of view of the listener, it entails habits of conceiving any music as structured along a theoretical framework of beats regularly spaced in time and of co-operating in terms of overt or inhibited motor behavior with the pulses of this metric pattern whether or not the beats are expressed in actual melodic or percussion tones. Essentially, this simply means that African music, with few exceptions, is to be regarded as music for the dance, although the "dance" involved may be entirely a mental one. Since this metronome sense is of such basic importance, it is obvious that the music is conceived and executed in terms of it; it is assumed without question or consideration to be part of the perceptual equipment of both musicians and listeners and is, in the most complete way, taken for granted. When the beat is actually sounded, it serves as a confirmation of this subjective beat. And because it amounts to an unverbalized point of view concerning all music, this traditional value which differentiates African from "pure" European systems of musical appreciation is a typical example of the variety of subliminal culture pattern most immune to the pressures of an acculturative situation.

The metronome sense is not limited to the African; one variety of it is necessary in playing or listening to Hindu music, for example. But complete reliance on it, as a part of the standard musical equipment of every individual in making music, is an exclusively African musical trait. The metronome sense, in an extremely limited way, is also necessary in appreciating European music, particularly European social dance music and marching tunes. The rhythmic music of Europe, however, is so structured as to emphasize the very metric elements which African music is most likely to take for granted—the up-beat and the down-beat. The assumption by an African musician that his audience is supplying these fundamental beats permits him to elaborate his rhythms with these as a base, whereas the European tradition requires such close attention to their concrete expressions that rhythmic elaboration is limited for the most part to mere ornament. From the point of view of European music, African music introduces a new rhythmic dimension.

Additional features of African music which set it off markedly from that of Europe may be summarized as follows:

DOMINANCE OF PERCUSSION

Most African music includes, and depends upon, percussion instruments. Indeed, most African musical instruments are of this type, including a bewildering array of drums, rattles, and gongs. These are the necessary implements for the peculiarly African elaboration of rhythmic and metric constellations. Melodic instruments, also, are utilized for their percussive value, as in the case of "thumb pianos," xylophones, and, for the last three centuries or so, the European guitar. Conversely, the gongs and drums frequently have melodic and harmonic importance. The percussive effect of hand-clapping, often in intricate rhythmic patterns, is also utilized constantly in African music.

POLYMETER

European rhythms are typically based on single metrical schemes, more or less elaborated according to the types of music the rhythms are used to reinforce. In European folk and popular music, particularly that used as accompaniment to the dance, the tempo is steady; in academic forms, the tempo may be varied greatly. African music, on the other hand—based, as we have seen, on the invariant or accelerated tempo consistent with the metronome sense—uses the interplay of two or more metrical frameworks as the primary material out of which the music is built. While the individual components may be quite simple, the combination is likely to sound to European-trained ears completely puzzling, particularly when, as often happens, rhythmic emphasis shifts back and forth from meter to meter. Anyone who cares to attempt to perform a $\frac{6}{8}$ beat with one hand, a $\frac{4}{4}$ beat with the other, and a $\frac{3}{4}$ tap with the toe of one foot will be convinced of the complexity, and will learn something about the character, of African multiple meter. This particular relationship of time signatures is a common pattern in African musical rhythm. The various rhythms are usually expressed by drums or other percussion instruments, but they need not be. Signs that these complex patterns pervade all of the African feeling for music are to be read in the accent patterns of melodies both instrumental and vocal and are likewise evident in the motor behavior of participants in African dance.

OFF-BEAT PHRASING OF MELODIC ACCENTS

From the African tradition of taking for granted the presence of a basic musical beat in the mind of the performer and auditor alike has stemmed not only the elaboration of meters just discussed, but also a quite different artistic technique completely dependent for its effect on the metronome sense. Syncopation, as utilized in European music, is in a way the simplest form of this technique, but in the absence of the metronome sense further development could hardly occur. In popular writings on the subject of jazz, the term "syncopation" has been used to characterize the technique as it appears in that form of music. However, in terms of total musical effect this label is felt to be misleading, and the more cumbersome but more general designation, "off-beat phrasing of melodic accents," is preferred by the author.

In transcriptions of African music this pattern appears in the form of notes tied together across bar lines or across other main beats. Melodic tones, and particularly accented ones, occur between the sounded or implied beats of the measure with great frequency. The beat is, so to speak, temporarily suspended, i.e., delayed or advanced in melodic execution, sometimes for single notes (syncopation), sometimes for long series of notes. The displacement is by no means a random one, however, for the melodic notes not coinciding with the beat are invariably sounded, with great nicety precisely on one of the points of either a duple or a triple division of the beat. Viewed a different way, this may be seen as a placement of tones *on* the beat of an implied meter at a tempo twice or thrice that of the controlling rhythm.

Certain psychological aspects of African off-beat phrasing must be considered if the pattern is to be fully understood. The maintenance of a subjective meter, in terms of the metronome sense, requires effort and, more particularly, a series of efforts regularly spaced in time. The regular recurrence of these "rhythmic awarenesses" involves the expectancy, at the moment of any beat, that the next beat will occur precisely at some succeeding moment determined by the tempo. Subjectively, the beat does occur. If it is reinforced by an objective stimulus in the form of a percussive or melodic tone, the metronome sense is reassured, and the effort involved in the subjective beat is masked by the effort of perceiving the objective pulse. If the objective beat is omitted, however, the co-operating auditor becomes very much aware of the subjective beat, which thus attains for him greatly increased significance. If the objective beat occurs ahead of time, the auditor, unprepared for it, perceives it and assigns to it the additional importance always accorded the unexpected, further reinforcing it with his subjective pulse which occurs at the "proper" time in terms of his experience. If the objective beat is delayed, the period of suspense between subjective and objective beats likewise increases the auditor's awareness of the rhythm. When the objective, audible beat occurs halfway between two subjective pulsations, as is frequently the case, both mechanisms operate to give the off-beat tone heightened significance.

On the other hand, it is apparent that if a whole tune were to be sung in such a way that each note occurred a half-beat ahead of a corresponding beat established by the subjective metronome on the basis of cues from, say, the initial beats of a percussion instrument, the subjective beats would sooner or later, depending on the degree of intransigence of the metronome sense of the auditor, come to be interpreted as off-beats, and hence would be realigned so as to coincide with the new beat pattern.

In other words, complete "off-beating" has the same effect as complete lack of off-beat patterns; it is, in these terms, meaningless.

The off-beat phrasing of accents, then, must threaten, but never quite destroy, the orientation of the listener's subjective metronome. In practice, this means that a sufficient number of notes of varying degrees of importance in the structure of the melody must coincide with the auditor's rhythmic set to validate the gestalt through reinforcement of key points. A very few notes so placed will suffice for a listener whose metronome sense is highly developed, particularly since at least one percussion instrument is likely to reinforce the main beat. Occasions where melodic notes are on the beat, and percussion notes are off, are more trying to the metronome sense than the usual situation just sketched, and of course, melodic notes may be in an off-beat relationship to one meter in such a way as to suggest even more complex relationships with other simultaneous meters. Theoretically, elaborations of the combination of polymeter with off-beat phrasing are almost endless. In practice, however, limits are set to this development by the fact that, regardless of conditioning, no musician's and no listener's metronome sense operates beyond a certain point of complexity. This point, however, is likely to be far beyond anything the European tradition would consider rhythmically intelligible.

OVERLAPPING CALL-AND-RESPONSE PATTERNS

While antiphonal song-patterning, whereby a leader sings phrases which alternate with phrases sung by a chorus, is known all over the world, nowhere else is this form so important as in Africa, where almost all songs are constructed in this manner. A peculiarity of the African call-and-response pattern, found but infrequently elsewhere, is that the chorus phrase regularly commences while the soloist is still singing; the leader, on his part, begins his phrase before the chorus has finished. This phenomenon is quite simply explained in terms of the African musical tradition of the primacy of rhythm. The entrance of the solo or the chorus part on the proper beat of the measure is the important thing, not the effects attained through antiphony or polyphony. Examples of call-and-response music in which the solo part, for one reason or another, drops out for a time, indicate clearly that the chorus part, rhythmical and repetitive, is the mainstay of the songs and the one really inexorable component of their rhythmic structure. The leader, receiving solid rhythmic support from the metrically accurate, rolling repetition of phrases by the chorus, is free to embroider as he will.

The metronome sense, then, together with these four basic characteristics related to or derived from it, accounts for the major differences between tribal African and European folk and popular music. In attempting to trace the influence of African musical ideas on the music of the Americas, we must, therefore, pay particular attention to these features. The extension of purely rhythmic aspects of African musical style to Western Hemisphere music has already been discussed at some length (19). Certain additional musical and allied practices of that area may, however, be mentioned here, and the fact of

their appearance in the Americas simply indicated. While, as has been mentioned, the African scale is diatonic like that of Europe, the tendency toward variable intonation of the third and seventh of the scale has occasionally been noted in West African music.[3] This is the "blues" scale. West African song often utilizes the device of contrapuntal duet, with or without an additional recurrent chorus phrase (21, Album II, record 6). This pattern is important in the religious singing of southern United States Negroes. The use of song as a device for social control and for the venting of aggression and the traditional contests of virtuosity in singing and playing are functioning elements of West African culture today, as they are of such musical styles as the Trinidad "calypso" in the New World. The counterclockwise circle dance, in which the dancers make up a part of the singing chorus, is common both in West Africa and in the New World, as is the custom of singing in falsetto. Finally, there is, in West Africa, little difference, in purely musical terms, between sacred and secular usage; this is mirrored in all the areas of Negro settlement in the Americas.

There are two aspects of the problem of African influence on the music of the Americas. One concerns the music of predominantly Negro populations, the other the spread of stylistic elements from American Negro music to the music of New World populations in general. Also, two distinct geographical areas— roughly, North American and Latin American—must be considered separately since they have had different acculturation histories.

In the Negro population of Brazil

---

[3] For a typical example of this, hear 21, Album I, song 5C.

all traits[4] of African music have been retained, and many songs are sung in West African languages.[5] Negro songs of Dutch Guiana exhibit all the listed traits of West African music; they are, however, sung in a creolized language compounded, for the most part, of English vocabulary and West African phonetics and grammar (10; 14). In Haiti, songs of the *Vodun* cult show all traits of African music, as do many secular songs (3; 2). In Jamaica, both sacred and secular music of the Negroes of the Port Morant district frequently show the five "basic" African traits.[6] Found here also is the use of a large African vocabulary, both in songs and in actual conversation. Negro music of the Island of Trinidad ranges from the religious songs of the Shango Cult of Port-of-Spain, conceived in purely African style, through the various urban secular styles, including the "calypso," in which all the basic African traits are to be observed, to the "reels," "quadrilles," "bongos," and "beles" of the rural districts, in which European and African traits are commingled, although all the basic African traits are likely to appear (17). Most of the folk music of Puerto Rico is derived from Spain, although the style called "la bomba" is of purely African conception, while the popular urban Negro style, the *plena* (Puerto Rican equivalent of the calypso) sometimes shows all

the African traits (18). Percussion instruments of African origin are used in connection with all the above styles.

In United States Negro musical styles, one of the main African components, polymeter, is usually absent except by implication, and there is a dearth of African-type musical instruments.[7] Metronomism, however, is present in all Negro sacred and secular styles, as is the importance of percussion (wherever percussion instruments or effects are not proscribed by circumstances) and the overlapping call-and-response pattern.

In modern American Negro spirituals and, to a greater degree, in the urban gospel hymns, percussion effects are stressed even in the absence of actual instruments, and the instruments (sometimes, but rarely, the pipe-organ, usually the piano, and frequently the guitar and tambourine) used are, in general, exploited to the full extent of their percussive possibilities (20). The overlapping call-and-response and the off-beat phrasing of melodic accents are important features of the religious music of the United States Negro, and a well-developed metronome sense is required for its appreciation.

It is evident, then, that in the regions mentioned, which span the habitat of the Negro in the Americas, music associated with Negroes is, in terms of the five dominant values listed, predominantly African. There are, even in the

---

[4] "All traits" of African music, in the present list, must be taken to mean those basic traits discussed above as distinguishing tribal African from European folk music: the metronome sense, dominance of percussion, polymeter, off-beat phrasing, and overlapping call-and-response patterns.

[5] See 12. Research now being conducted by A. P. Merriam, using a larger sample of Afro-Bahian cult music, confirms these findings (personal communication).

[6] Recorded 1950, by Joseph G. Moore. To be deposited with the Laboratory of Comparative Musicology, Department of Anthropology, Northwestern University.

[7] See, however, Courlander's convincing derivation of the United States Negro "tub" from the West African "earth bow" (4, p. 5).

United States, cases of Negro songs with melodies almost identical to recorded African songs.[8] These identities must be laid to the fact that the songs have sprung from similar roots.

The music of these same areas which is *not* specifically identified with Negro populations likewise shows, in many instances, the same African traits. The diagnostic rhythm schemes of the Brazilian *samba* and the Cuban *rumba* and *conga*, to mention only three examples, are common in West African music. In general, most styles of popular dance music in these Latin American countries where the Negro population is at all dense have been strongly influenced by the basic African musical patterns listed, and many African musical instruments, such as drums, calabashes, etc., are used.

The areas referred to are those in which research has been done specifically from the point of view of African acculturation. There are undoubtedly many other instances of African musical influence in Latin America. For example, the Guatemalan "national instrument" is the *marimba*—an instrument certainly derived from Africa. In Mexico, especially in the region of the former slave port of Vera Cruz, African elements appear strongly in the rhythms of the folk music. The Argentine *maxixe*, to mention another example, probably can be considered as of partly African origin.

A major artistic product of the United States is the music called "jazz." Jazz is an intricate blend of musical idioms and has also had its own evolution as an art form. It is, of course, no one thing; yet any attempt to frame an all-inclusive definition points up the fact that those elements that mark off any kind of jazz from the rest of the popular music of the United States are precisely those we have cited as diagnostic of West Africa music.

For example, jazz depends, for its effect, largely on the metronome sense of its listeners and its players. Jazz terminology makes constant reference to this metronome sense. Musical terms like "rock" and "swing" express ideas of rhythm foreign to European folk tradition, and stem from African concepts, as does the extremely basic idea of the application of the word "hot" to musical rhythms. The development of a "feeling for the beat," so important in jazz musicianship, is neither more nor less than the development of the metronome sense.

The tremendous importance accorded to complex percussion patterns is another basic trait of African music to appear in jazz. An appreciable proportion of African dance music is entirely drum music; the tradition of long drum solos appears in all jazz styles, and, in the United States, only in the jazz styles.

The overlapping call-and-response pattern has, in jazz, been reworked in accordance with jazz instrumentation and orchestration. Typically, a soloist plays the call phrases as an improvised variation on the melody, while an appropriate section of instruments plays the chorus pattern, repeated with only those minimal changes forced by the changing harmonies, as a "riff." Most jazz band records contain examples of this use of the riff; since it is a pattern which gives a good deal of "rock" to the music, it is frequently reserved for the last, hottest chorus.

The off-beat phrasing of melodic

---

[8] Hear, for example, "Run Old Jeremiah" (16) and compare with "Bahutu Dance" (1). Also compare the "Mossi Chant" (21, Album 1) with "Long John" (15).

accents is a stylistic trait which functions in jazz in unusually clear-cut fashion perhaps because of the absence of poly-metric formations, which tend to make the off-beats equivocal. Syncopation has often been spoken of as an earmark of jazz melodies; of importance here is the fact that, in addition, jazz makes con-stant use of the more extended off-beat phrasing patterns. It is these, rather than syncopation per se, which give to the melodic line of jazz its characteristic impelling rhythmic quality.

In this short paper it has been possible to illustrate in only the most general way the character of African influences on the music of the Americas. To summarize: in areas (e.g., in Brazil, Haiti, and Cuba) where the official European religion permitted the syncre-tism of deities with the saints of the Church, African religious music has persisted almost unchanged, and African influence upon secular music has been strong. In Protestant areas where such syncretism has not been possible, the influence of African musical patterns on both religious and secular music has hinged upon a more extensive process of reinterpretation but is nonetheless considerable, in that fundamental char-acteristics of West African music have been retained.

In the case of the music of the Negro in the New World, we have an ideal situation for the study of musical change. We know, in general, the African side of the equation, although much field work must be done before specific tribal styles—the real raw data for our study—can be described. We also know the European side, and we are in a position to study the American results of musical acculturation. We also know enough about the general cultural con-texts of the various American Negro musical styles to be able to assess both historical and contemporary factors bear-ing on change. Furthermore, among the less tangible aspects of culture, music is unique in that it can readily be quanti-fied and submitted to rigid statistical analysis, although nothing of this sort has been attempted in this paper. The objective demonstration of the retention and reworking of West African tribal musical styles in the Americas, which seems likely to follow the collection of sufficient field data from specific African groups, may be expected to have rele-vance for the study of other cultural intangibles which, while not so easily subjected to quantitative treatment, are, like musical patterns, carried largely below the level of consciousness.

BIBLIOGRAPHY

1. "The Belgian Congo Records," *Denis Roosevelt Expedition Album*. New York: General Records, Inc.
2. COURLANDER, H. *Folk Music of Haiti*, Album No. 1407. New York: Ethnic Folk-ways Library.
3. ———. *Haiti Singing*. Chapel Hill: University of North Carolina Press, 1939.
4. ———. Pamphlet accompanying *Folk Music of Haiti*, Albums Nos. 1417 and 1418. New York: Ethnic Folkways Library.
5. HERSKOVITS, MELVILLE J. *Life in a Haitian Valley*. New York: A. A. Knopf, 1937.
6. ———. *Man and His Works*. New York: A. A. Knopf, 1948.

7. ———. "Music in West Africa." Pamphlet accompanying *Tribal, Folk, and Cafe Music of West Africa*. New York: Field Recordings, Inc.

8. ———. *The Myth of the Negro Past*. New York: Harper & Row., 1941.

9. HERSKOVITS, MELVILLE J. and FRANCES S. *Rebel Destiny*. New York: McGraw-Hill Book Company 1934.

10. ———, eds. *Suriname Folklore*. New York: Columbia University Press, 1936.

11. ———. *Trinidad Village*. New York: A. A. Knopf, 1947.

12. HERSKOVITS, MELVILLE J., and WATERMAN, R. A. "Musica de culto Afro-Bahiana," *Revista de estudios musicalos* (Mendoza, Argentina), I (1949), pp. 65–127.

13. JONES, A. M. *African Music*. Livingstone, Northern Rhodesia: Rhodes–Livingstone Museum, 1949.

14. KOLINSKI, M. "Suriname Music." In HERSKOVITS, M. J., and F. S., eds., *Suriname Folklore*, pp. 489–740. New York: Columbia University Press, 1936.

15. LOMAX, JOHN A., and ALAN. "Long John." In *Afro-American Spirituals, Work Songs, and Ballads*. "Library of Congress, Archive of American Folk Song," Album 3.

16. ———. "Run Old Jeremiah," *ibid.*

17. WATERMAN, R. A. "African Patterns in Trinidad Negro Music." Unpublished doctoral dissertation, Northwestern University, 1943.

18. ———. *Folk Music of Puerto Rico*. "Library of Congress, Archive of American Folk Song," Album 17. Washington, D. C.: Government Printing Office, 1947.

19. ———. "Hot Rhythm in Negro Music," *Journal of the American Musicological Society* (New York), I (1948), pp. 3–16.

20. ———. "The Role of Spirituals and Gospel Hymns in a Chicago Negro Church," *Journal of the International Folk Music Council* (London), III (1951).

21. *West African Folk, Tribal, and Cafe Music*. 2 albums. New York: Field Recordings, Inc., 1950.

Residual African Elements in the Blues

JANHEINZ JAHN

In this provocative and surely controversial discussion of possible African elements in the blues written by a leading contemporary student of African literatures and cultures, we find our attention drawn to some of the more rhetorical and philosophical aspects of American Negro folksong. And it is certainly plausible that the total significance of folksong cannot be measured solely in terms of mere words and music. In the performance of any item of folklore, there is always the matter of strategy and motivation, though these factors may not always be explicit or conscious. Janheinz Jahn, from his analysis of African philosophical principles or categories, is able to look at the blues in a new way.

In order to understand Jahn's approach as found in his book Muntu, we must briefly consider several terms. From the treatise by Alexis Kagame, La philosophie băntu-rwandaise de l'Être (Brussels, 1951), in which the philosophy of the Bantu of Ruanda is analyzed by a member of that culture, Jahn borrows four concepts: Muntu (human being), Kintu (thing), Hantu (place and time), and Kuntu (modality). These concepts represent not substance but force. The stem "-ntu" common to all these categories refers to the universal force present in all its various manifestations (Muntu, p. 101). There is also the driving power that gives life and efficacy to all things. This is termed "Nommo" (pp. 124–25). Jahn explains that "Muntu" cannot really be defined as "human being" but rather as a "force endowed with intelligence" or as an entity which is a force that has control over Nommo. Often Nommo is controlled or invoked through the power of words (p. 135). Perhaps the most difficult category for the Western reader to comprehend is "Kuntu," the modal force. Jahn gives examples of "laughing" and "beauty" as forces, as modal forces.

From *Muntu: An Outline of the New African Culture*. Reprinted by permission of Grove Press, Inc. Translated by Marjorie Grene. Copyright © 1961 by Faber and Faber .

In this system of thought, art, for example, is the transformation of a thing, "kintu," through the designating power of Nommo. The resultant image receives its meaning from its designation but it is "kuntu," or the modality, which determines the form of the image. One illustration of "kuntu" is rhythm. Thus the Nommo word (one which controls or invokes Nommo) cannot be uttered without rhythm and this is true whether the rhythm is polymetric—in which several different meters are heard simultaneously—or polyrhythmic—in which a single basic meter is accented and syncopated in different ways (p. 165). The reader interested in fuller explanations of these different concepts should consult Janheinz Jahn, Muntu *(New York, 1961).*

The potential implications of Jahn's analysis for American Negro folklore are immense. One of the most striking points concerns personal interrelationships. In white European culture, God commands man, and leaders command subordinates. Thus in religion, God calls individuals—they are summoned to service as was Jonah in the Old Testament. In musical performance, a God-like conductor creates music or silence with the movement of his badge of authority, a baton. There is one leader who commands his musical followers in a single rhythm. This monolithic, monotheistic, monorhythmic tendency is not characteristic of African music. Instead of God summoning men, men summon God. God or rather gods are summoned by the followers through the power of the word (Nommo is controlled by Muntu). Thus as Jahn points out, God, or a religious presence, is produced by a congregation during the act of worship. In singing, one does not have one individual singing at or over his fellows. Rather there is antiphonal singing with everyone participating. (This is also true of Negro sermons in which the congregation answers or punctuates the preacher's words and of children's singing ring games in which little girls chant responses and follow the actions of a temporary leader.) The lack of rigid unitary form (so common in European music) is reflected in polymeter and polyrhythm and in the general widespread penchant for improvisation.

The sense of personal participation in American Negro folk music is also signalled by what has been termed by folklorists "the intrusive I." In blues as in other forms of Negro music, the singer or singers make the song an individual, personal account. It is "my" story or "my" blues. This subjectivity is in marked contrast to the objective, third-person technique found in Anglo-American folksong. Anglo-American ballad singers are removed from their subject matter both by the third person reportorial technique ("he" or "she" not "I") and by their actual singing stance which normally includes an impassive, unmoving face. (Just watch a traditional Anglo-American folksinger sing a ballad of murder or incest or the like. The singer's face shows little or no emotion. Then observe a Negro blues singer and watch his personal identification with the content of his song.)

The stylistic feature of personal identification through the use of the "intrusive I" pronoun is found in a variety of Negro folklore genres. Roger Abrahams, who noted the phenomenon in narratives, remarked upon the similarity of his finding to what Odum and Johnson had termed "The Dominant Self" in Negro folksong. The identical stylistic feature is found in sacred as well as secular folksong and Miles Mark Fisher, for example, specifically commented upon its presence in spirituals. See Roger D. Abrahams, Deep Down in the Jungle (Chicago, 1970), pp. 58–59; Howard W. Odum and Guy B. Johnson,

The Negro and His Songs (*Chapel Hill, 1925*), *pp. 279–83; Miles Mark Fisher,* Negro Slave Songs in the United States (*New York, 1969*), *p. 180.*

There is even some interesting evidence from riddles that the "intrusive I" is African in origin. In African riddles, there is frequently an introductory formula referring to "my father" or "my mother." And in a great number of riddles the subject of the action of the metaphor is in the first person singular. (See, for example, P. D. Beuchat, "Riddles in Bantu" in Alan Dundes, ed., The Study of Folklore (*Englewood Cliffs, 1965*), *p. 197. In New World Negro riddles, especially from the West Indies, the same formulas are found. (See Archer Taylor,* English Riddles from Oral Tradition [*Berkeley and Los Angeles, 1951*], *pp. 185, 187, 191, 362–63, 370, 375–76, etc.)*

In any event, even if one wishes to dispute some of Jahn's definitions of African philosophic concepts or to argue about whether or not they are pan-African, his insights into the nature of the blues remain exciting ones. Readers especially intrigued with Jahn's discussion may wish to look at his later consideration of "blues form and blues logic" as well as his similar treatment of the Negro spiritual in his Neo-African Literature: A History of Black Writing (*New York: Grove Press, 1968*), *pp. 155–75.*

To keep from cryin' I opens my mouth an' laughs.

LANGSTON HUGHES

THE PECULIAR development of African culture in North America began with the loss of the drums. The Protestant, and often Puritan, slave owners interfered much more radically with the personal life of their slaves than did their Catholic colleagues in the West Indies or in South America. The slaves were allowed no human dignity and their cultural past was ignored; or else it was considered a humane task to educate them into being "better" human beings, and this process was initiated by teaching them to be ashamed of their African heritage. And to forbid the drums was to show a keen scent for the essential: for without the drums it was impossible to call the orishas, the ancestors were silent, and the proselytizers seemed to have a free hand. The Baptists and Methodists, whose practical maxims and revivals were sympathetic to African religiosity quickly found masses of adherents.

Their nearness to God, their intimately personal relation to Him, and their ecstatic possession by the Holy Ghost won the highest praise for the converts in many Christian circles. People talked of the renewal of Christianity, of a "fervour of faith akin to early Christianity,"[1] and the like. And certainly, the intensity of this religious feeling cannot be doubted, but the question whether it is really Christian might well provoke some theological dispute. According to Christian doctrine man designates by the word "God" that unworldly–supraworldly (transcendent) reality by which he knows that the experienced world including his own being is governed and sustained.[2] But of what sort is the transcendence of the Christian God in the Negro churches of the United States, when the Pulitzer Prize winner Gwendolyn Brooks in one

[1] Joachim Ernst Berendt, *Blues* (München, 1957), p. 80.
[2] Cf. Oskar Simmel and Rudolf Stahlin, *Christliche Religion* (Frankfurt am Main, 1957), p. 111.

of her poems makes the preacher murmur at the end of his sermon:[3]

> Picture Jehovah striding through the hall
> Of His importance, creatures running
>   out
> From servant-corners to acclaim, to
>   shout
> Appreciation of His merit's glare.
> But who walks with Him?—dares
>   to take His arm,
> To slap Him on the shoulder, tweak
>   His ear,
> Buy Him a Coca-Cola or a beer,
> Pooh-pooh his politics, call Him a
>   fool?

Gwendolyn Brooks' preacher positively feels sorry for the Good Lord, because—to use our Haitian expression—he has to remain "Bon Dieu" and is not allowed to become a loa like his son Jesus or the Holy Ghost. The revivalist ceremonies in the Negro churches, which no one describes better than the Afro-American poet James Baldwin in his novel *Go Tell it on the Mountain*, contain so many residual African elements, that the comparison with the Arada rite of Voodoo is inevitable. However, we are concerned here with the differences. In the first place the drums are missing. The percussion instruments are replaced by hand-clapping and foot-stamping. But no polymetry can be produced in this way and there are no specific formulas permitting the invocation of a number of loas. The singing is therefore directed to the *one* Christian divinity, to whom the sermon was also addressed, and the faithful, usually many of them at a time, are "ridden" by a single divinity. The procedure which in the African orisha cult evokes ecstatic immobility, and in Haitian Voodoo different types of ecstatic movement, produces, in the Negro churches, "mass ecstasy."[4]

A faith, like African art, is an attitude. It is the relation between men on the one hand and one or more divine or deified beings on the other. In Christianity this relation is unequivocally determined by God alone: God created man, commanded him, forbade him; God enlightens, punishes and redeems him. The bond of man with God (*religio*) is expressed in man's obedience. In African religion this relation is reversed: *religio*, active worship, "creates" God, as the expression "She Orisha"[5] puts it: that is, the living person (muzima) in his active worship installs the divine being as such. Analogously to the designation of an image[6] we may speak of the *designation of divinity*. Necessarily, therefore, this divinity must be other than transcendent, for it is concretely present during the act of worship—or better, it is produced by the congregation during the act of worship. This occurs in the African cults, in Haitian Voodoo, in the Cuban santería, in the Jamaican pocomania, in the Brazilian macumba,[7] in the Winti cults of Guiana and in the Negro churches of the United States. But while the cults of the West Indies and South America have remained polytheistic, through the equation of the loas and

---

[3] Gwendolyn Brooks, *A Street in Bronzeville* (New York and London, 1945), p. 13.
[4] Cf. Chapter 2, "Voodoo: The Embodiment of the Gods" in Janheinz Jahn, *Muntu* (New York, 1961), especially pp. 39ff.
[5] Cf. *Muntu*, pp. 63 and 115.
[6] Cf. *Muntu*, p. 157.
[7] Cf. Pierre Verger, *Dieux d'Afrique* (Paris, 1954).

orishas with saints (the equation is a pure act of designation), the Negro churches perform the designation of a single divinity.

With the designation of a Christian God, Christian standards penetrate the cult, above all the sharp separation of good and evil; but the nature of worship, the *service* of God, remains to a great extent African. For God is not only served but invoked, called up and embodied by the faithful. As in art, so also in religion, the Kuntu is unchanging and remains the hallmark of African culture. Even the Christian images are treated in prayer in the African manner. Thus an old woman in Baldwin's novel *Go Tell it on the Mountain* prays: "Lord, sprinkle the door-post of this house with the blood of the Lamb to keep all the wicked men away."[8]

Musically, the change is expressed by the fact that with the loss of the drums, the polymetry which carries polytheism is lost, and all that remains is polyrhythm, which is constructed on the basis of a single meter. The hymns of Christian European origin used by the missions are Africanized, producing *jubilees*, "original songs of praise, in which, as they are sung stanza after stanza, a more and more marked Africanization takes place, sometimes leading in the end to sporadic outbreaks of possession."[9] Kuntu, the manner of singing, remains African, and where European melody and harmonics begin to penetrate, in the ballads, spirituals and blues, this becomes apparent through the fact that the African *way*

of singing alters the melody in many ways unknown in Europe. First of all there is that melodic technique which Dauer calls "heterophony of variants," impromptu variations by means of "singing separately," for which in classical jazz "the misleading title improvization has become widespread."[10] Then there are changes of tone, of intonation, of pitch and timbre, variations, paraphrases and slurring of the text and many other African devices which Dauer expounds in detail.

Nor did the Afro-Americans have to wait to learn melody and harmony from European Americans. The very first slaves brought to America and passed on to their descendants their own tonality, harmony and a rich treasure of musical means of expression. "If in this connection anything had surprised them in 'white' music," Dauer believes, "it would have been at the most the fact of an amazingly large tonal and harmonic kinship."[11] Yet the familiarization of the Afro-Americans with European church music (which was by no means always voluntary) produced "a perceptible approach to the European melodic form and a new type of Afro-American harmony"[12] in the true spirituals, which differ considerably from the concert hall spirituals as they are presented by concertizing Negro choirs and soloists. For between 1860 and 1870 University choirs like the Fisk Jubilee Singers or the Hampton Student Singers began to collect spirituals in great numbers, to "purify" them of "ugly and unlovely" Africanisms and then to copy and record

[8] James Baldwin, *Go Tell It on the Mountain* (New York, 1952), p. 59.
[9] Alfons M. Dauer, *Der Jazz, seine Ursprunge und seine Entwicklung* (Kassel, 1958), p. 61.
[10] Dauer, p. 59.
[11] Dauer, p. 183.
[12] Dauer, p. 63.

them in choral fashion. Through this "purification" all the basic elements were destroyed.[13] The definiteness prevents designation; Nommo cannot take shape or be given shape; in the concert hall Kuntu freezes into a dead form. The true folk spirituals, on the other hand, are residual African folk art, and the part played in their origin by Christian influences is still considerably exaggerated.

The secular parallel to the jubilee and the spiritual is that music which is usually so completely misunderstood: the blues, "A white song—black: that is, reduced to a simplified formula, blues."[14] This is a widespread view. People also think that the *blue notes* and the modulation of tone exhaust the African part of the blues.[15] What is correct in all this is the fact that the blues did originate from the contact of African and European music. How the different contributions are divided, in what way these two very different styles affected one another, Dauer has described and determined. It is not the formula of the blues that is the true hallmark of blues but the sequence of voices, which is founded on the African antiphony. "This consists in appeal and answer and explains the division of phrases in blues singing, as well as the function of the individual phrases. In the simplest case the phrase sequence runs A B and corresponds to the functions of an appeal and an answer. In the 12-beat blues, which have become classic, the sequence runs A A B, which

corresponds to two appeals and one answer."[16] Only in the blues the separate events of appeal by the first singer and answer by the chorus are "consolidated into a single event, since they are all executed by a single voice."[17] One song *in* the community becomes one song *before* the community, for the community is now only a listener. Instead of a chorus answering the singer, there are instruments accompanying the singing. In Africa the drums lead the singer's performance; one might say that the song accompanies the drums. In the blues this relation is reversed. First there is unaccompanied singing, then in the course of the development the instruments are added, but they are only accompaniment and the singing remains the most important part of the performance.

The texts of the blues follow the African narrative style almost entirely. They stem from the Afro-American ballads, which in turn continued the tradition of the African fable. "In the fable," writes Senghor, "the animal is seldom a totem; it is this or that one whom every one in the village knows well: the stupid or tyrannical or wise and good chief, the young man who makes reparation for injustice. Tales and fables are woven out of everyday occurrences. Yet it is not a question of anecdotes or of 'material from life.' The facts are images and have paradigmatic value."[18] The boll weevil ballad, which comes from Texas, may serve as an example.[19] The weevil is the arch enemy

---

[13] Cf. Dauer, p. 64.

[14] Berendt, *Blues*, p. 11.

[15] Cf. Berendt, p. 12.

[16] Alfons M. Dauer, *Knaurs Jazz-Lexikon* (München, 1957), p. 53.

[17] Dauer, *Der Jazz*, p. 74.

[18] Léopold Sédar Senghor, "L'esprit de la civilisation ou les lois de la culture négro-africaine," *Présence Africaine*, VIII-X (1956), p. 60.

[19] Original in Dauer, *Der Jazz*, pp. 145ff.

of the cotton planter.

> Fahmah say to de weevil
> "whut makes yore head so red,"
> weevil say to de fahmah
> "it's wonder ah ain't dead,
> lookin' foh a home, lookin' for a
>   home!"
>
> Nigger say to de weevil,
> "ah'll throw yo in de hot san'!"
> Weevil say to de nigger
> "ah'll stand it like a man,
> ah'll have a home, ah'll have a home!"
>
> Say de Capt'n to de Mistis
> "what do yo think ob dat?
> Dis Boll Weevil done make a nes'
> inside my Sunday hat;
> he will have a home, he'll have a
>   home!"

The weevil, which bores into the bolls of cotton with its proboscis, is the plantation worker in his eternal search for a home. In the farmer's Sunday hat, his best piece of property, the weevil will have a home. Here again is the imperative future, which, in the form "has made a nest," is set back into the perfect tense but means that the weevil *is to* make a nest there.[20] It is the same technique that Césaire uses. The ballad is a song that invokes liberation; in the most harmless fable it conceals the call to rebel.

The old ballad was later turned into a blues song, for the two types fade imperceptibly into one another. In the Boll Weevil Blues the weevil then becomes the living symbol of liberation.[21] The blues cannot therefore be reduced to the formula: "a white song —black"; for both textual and musical structure stem from African traditions.

Nor are the blues "sad," although the legend of "melancholy" blues has been influential for a century and for a couple of decades there have in fact been melancholy blues. In accordance with the common view we do indeed find in the *Negro Caravan* of 1941 the statement: "In contrast to the spirituals, which were originally intended for group singing, the blues are sung by a single person. They express his feelings and ideas about his experience, but they do this so fundamentally, in an idiom so recognizable to his audience, that this emotion is shared as theirs."[22] But this is the exact contrary of the real situation.

For the blues singer does not in fact express *his* personal experiences and transfer them to his audience; on the contrary, it is the experiences of the community that he is expressing, making himself its spokesman.[23] Even when there is talk of loneliness, of the beloved who has run away, of the neglected wife, of nostalgia for the South, it is not the personal experience that is emphasized, but the typical experience of all those rejected by society in the Negro districts of the North. And even though indirectly, the note of rebellion is always heard too:

> I'd rather drink muddy water, sleep in a
>   hollow log,
> dan to stay in dis town, treated like a
>   dirty dog.[24]

---

[20] Cf. *Muntu*, pp. 136ff.

[21] Dauer, *Der Jazz*, p. 60.

[22] Sterling A. Brown, Arthur P. Davis, and Ulysses Lee, *The Negro Caravan* (New York, 1941), p. 426.

[23] Cf. *Muntu*, p. 149.

[24] Sterling A. Brown, et *al.*, *The Negro Caravan*, p. 429.

The melancholy is a camouflage, the "plaint" hides a *com*plaint.

If we read the text of the blues songs without prejudice and notice the double meaning, which all authors emphasize, we find them mocking, sarcastic, tragi-comic, tragic, dramatic and accusing, often crudely humorous—there is only one thing that they are only exceptional-ly, and then usually when they have been turned into a cabaret number, and that is—melancholy. Yet we read in the *Negro Caravan*: "The mood is generally a sorrowful one; the word 'blues' is part of the American vocabulary now as a synonym for melancholy, for un-happy moodiness."[25] This widespread misinterpretation has various causes. The *blue notes* characteristic of the blues, which go back to the middle pitch of the West African tonal languages,[26] and have a modality between sharp and flat, sound sad to European ears. Besides, we are accustomed in Europe to interpret poetry and music psychologi-cally as expressions of an individual soul. For African art, on the other hand, this means a confusion of means and meaning. Of the Afro-American *Work Songs*, which go back to the traditional form of communal work, and which are called *dokpwe* in Da-homey, *egbe* in Yoruba, *coumbite* in Haiti, *troca dia* in Brazil, and *gayap* in Trinidad, even Dauer writes:

The basic law of the work song is to increase energy through music. Its effect consists in turning work into a kind of game or dance which in turn invokes an excitement that cannot be produced by pack mule work. This excitement increases energy and when reduced to a form that excludes all unneces-sary movements itself becomes a driving force. The constant sequence of game and dance distracts the mind from the burdens of labour, the evenly rhythmic singing and playing becomes a (pretended) reality, work goes on automatically, and becomes subconscious.[27]

This interpretation of Dauer's correctly perceives the effects but not the causes. Song and dance do not have the purpose of lightening the work, but in song and dance Nommo is doing the real work, and conjuring up the latent forces of nature, while the work itself is only an addition.[28] The meaning of the work lies in the song and dance; they are not a purposive means for the end of lightening the work, even though their influence has that effect. The song is not an aid to the work, but the work an aid to the song.

The same is true of the blues. The blues are sung, not because one finds oneself in a particular mood, but because one wants to put oneself into a certain mood. The song is the Nommo which does not reflect but creates the mood. And this mood is melancholy only from the romantic point of view current since the time of the abolitionists. The picture of the poor slave full of yearning, singing his sad song, corresponded to the mood awakened by Harriet Beecher Stowe with *Uncle Tom's Cabin*. Much as we may admire the sentiments of the abolitionists, we must not overlook the fact that they saw the slaves as alienated, helpless beings who were longing for freedom but ought not to rebel: enslaved by white men, they

[25] Brown, *et al.*, p. 426.
[26] Dauer, *Der Jazz*, p. 31.
[27] Dauer, p. 53.
[28] Cf. *Muntu*, pp. 124ff.

should also be set free by them. So they were drawn as patiently suffering lambs, helpless, pitiable and sad. Help and support was to be given the slaves, but from agitators one kept one's distance and tried to pacify them. This attitude was apparent as late as the beginning of this century in the generous help that was given to the pacifist Booker T. Washington, while every possible obstacle was put in the way of W. E. B. DuBois, who made rigorous demands.

The abolitionists opposed their picture of the sad slave with his melancholy songs to the picture of the willing, confident, happy slave which the slave owners habitually drew. For the latter, the song of the disenfranchised sounded by no means melancholy; they considered it the expression of a carefree and happy mood. But both pictures are distorted. Frederick Douglass, the runaway slave, writes in his autobiography the telling sentences:

The remark is not infrequently made, that slaves are the most contented and happy labourers in the world. They dance and sing, and make all manner of joyful noises—so they do; but it is a great mistake to suppose them happy because they sing. The songs of the slave represent the sorrows, rather than the joys, of his heart. Slaves sing to *make* themselves happy rather than to express their happiness through singing.[29]

The blues do not arise from a mood, but produce one. Like every art form in African culture song too is an attitude which effects something. The spiritual produces God, the secularized blues produce a mood. Even there residual-African Nommo is still effective.

[29] Douglass quoted from Sterling A. Brown, *et al.*, p. 726.

Jazz Choreology

GERTRUDE P. KURATH
AND NADIA CHILKOVSKY

A consideration of the origins of American Negro music leads quite logically to the subject of American Negro dance. Unfortunately, the study of dance is somewhat handicapped by the intrinsic difficulties involved even in the mere recording of dance data. Yet these difficulties are not insuperable, though the transcription problem remains a serious one.

One reason why there has been relatively little first-rate scholarship devoted to folk dance in general and to American Negro dance in particular is that the majority of dance specialists tend to be performance-oriented. Their objective in the analysis of a dance is to be able to perform it or to teach others to perform it. There is nothing wrong with this—without the performance of dance and other forms of folklore, there would be nothing for the academic folklorist to study! Nevertheless, there is a difference between dancing folk dances or singing folksongs and the scholarly study of traditional dance and song.

Gertrude Kurath, a leading scholar in the field of dance and perhaps the authority on American Indian dance, attempts in the following brief discussion to pinpoint some of the critical characteristics of some of the best known American Negro dances. Of particular interest in the present context are her remarks about possible African origins of some of these characteristics. While the details of Labanotation, one of the most widely used conventional systems of movement notation, will in all likelihood be beyond the competence of most readers, the concluding note on "dance notation" by Nadia Chilkovsky may help to demonstrate the empirical basis for analyses of American Negro dance forms.

For a general survey of research in folk and primitive dance, see Gertrude P. Kurath, "Panorama of Dance Ethnology," Current Anthropology, *1* (*1960*),

Reprinted from *Men and Cultures*, ed. Anthony F. C. Wallace (Philadelphia, 1956), pp. 152–60, by permission of the authors and the University of Pennsylvania Press.

pp. 233–54. For further consideration of the mixtures of European, African, and American Indian elements in New World dances, see her articles, "Stylistic Blends in Afro-American Dance Cults of Catholic Origin," Papers of the Michigan Academy of Science, Arts, and Letters, 48 (1963), pp. 577–81, and "African Influences on American Dance," Focus on Dance, 3 (1965), pp. 35–40. For additional discussion of American Negro dance, see Chadwick Hansen, "Jenny's Toe: Negro Shaking Dances in America," American Quarterly, 19 (1967), pp. 554–63. See also Nadia Chilkovsky, "Analysis and Notation of Basic Afro-American Movements," in Marshall and Jean Stearns, Jazz Dance: The Story of American Vernacular Dance (New York, 1968), pp. 421–49.

COMPARATIVE ANALYSIS

BY GERTRUDE P. KURATH

THE HOT rhythms of jazz have set fire to most corners of the globe within fifty years. They have emerged from slave quarters and honky-tonks to respectable society and to learned circles. Only the music, however, has engrossed historians and musicologists and has engendered a voluminous literature. The indispensable concomitant, the dance, has remained neglected as a field of serious study. It deserves investigation by sociologists as well as by specialists in African, Afro-American, and jazz dance over a wide area. Someone has to get started on its choreology, its scientific analysis, albeit a specialist in the field of Amerindian dance, a jazz practitioner for the fun of it.

First of all, we need some kind of definition. Is jazz dance simply dancing to jazz music? Is it ballroom, folk dancing, or a form of degenerate professionalism? Without much ado one can answer that jazz dancing is always done to jazz, but not necessarily vice-versa. Much of the pushing around to jazz bands on ballroom floors is not dancing at all. Some of it is based on Latin American styles, which are related but peripheral. Peripheral are also the dilutions taught in dancing schools, the vulgarizations in night clubs, and the creative elaborations of stage professionals. Jazz dancing is a twentieth-century American product, with distinctive qualities and heritage to be identified presently, and with vast diffusion. It is primarily a dance of the people, hence a folk form, though it is often adapted to commercial purposes.

Stylistic Nucleus. To define the stylistic qualities I have notated the most important step patterns, have analyzed them and extracted essential characteristics. Most typical is the category known as jitterbugging,[1] which has many variants, antecedents, and developments, which differs by location, social and age group, and predominant color of a gathering, Negro or white. The fundamental, recurrent qualities can be identified as follows:

1. Rhythmic, often syncopated knee flexion.
2. Basic two-step pattern, in various tempi and directions.
3. Weight on heel or full foot.
4. Frequent foot twists.
5. Hip swaying and torsion, motivated by foot action.
6. Frequent sway back (Negro), forward torso tilt, or hunching (white).

[1] Murray, 1946, p. 33.

7. Opposition between leg and shoulder-arm movements.
8. Syncopated hand-clapping, finger-snapping, or thigh-swatting.
9. Aliveness of the entire body, with awareness of each part.
10. Relaxation to the rhythmic impulse.
11. Alternation of subtle and violent acrobatic movements.
12. Absence of set spatial or temporal form, with improvisation.
13. Frequent counterpoint with musical rhythms.

Jitterbugging is a couple dance, though not in the embrace position. The boy may hold one of the girl's hands to pull, push, and twirl her about. After releasing hold, they can continue with the basic pattern of two-step and balancing or they can string together any of the jazz steps in their repertoire.

With this brief stylistic definition as starting point, it will be easier to trace developments, to identify ethnic components, and to suggest ways of comparative analysis.

Development.[2] I have mentioned the two-step (or change-step) as the foundation of jitterbugging. The ballroom two-step of 1890–1910 was a dull step-close-step with rigid body. The one-step or turkey trot of the Irene and Vernon Castle team was little more than a smooth walk.[3] In the era of ragtime music the younger set began "ragging the two-step" with knee flexions and syncopations, and devised the foxtrot with its broken rhythm (see Fig. 1).[4] Ball-

room dances were performed in an embrace which was intensified into the dead clinch of the Californian Grizzly Bear.

The embrace and other restraints were shaken off after the first World War, in an epidemic of angular, foot-twisting gyrations—the Charleston, Snake Hips, Susie-Q, and Truckin'. The Charleston, after seething in the Southland as a Negro round dance, was discovered in 1923 among Negro dock workers of Charleston, S.C., and by 1926 had infected higher society.[5] The Susie-Q and Truckin' are said to have developed in New York's Negro quarter, Harlem,[6] when jazz musicians had spread from the Mississippi River and Chicago to the East. The "boll weevil" in Truckin' is a particularly entertaining and absurd step, a glide from heel to flat foot with a twist, a rear-protruding posture, and wicked shaking index finger. From these seeds sprang the Lindy Hop, named after Colonel Lindbergh's long hop across the Atlantic Ocean in 1927.[7]

In the middle thirties one of the Lindy steps, the kick, became the basis of the Big Apple. It has been rumored that the Big Apple originated with the Gullah Negroes of Georgia.[8] It seems a fact that Arthur Murray discovered it in a barn in Columbia, S.C. and popularized it, particularly in collegiate circles, by means of his national dance school. He considered it important, as the nearest approach in years to an original and native American dance.[9] It certainly is the only jazz dance which

[2] See development traced in Kurath, 1949.
[3] Shawn, 1956, pp. 8, 34.
[4] Davis, 1923, p. 44; Murray, 1946, p. 32; Shomer, 1943, p. 26.
[5] Avakian, 1956; Johnson, 1935, pp. 16–17.
[6] Shomer, 1943, pp. 15–18, 21–23.
[7] Avakian, 1956; Murray, 1946, p. 33.
[8] Green, 1951, p. 444.
[9] Murray, 1938, p. 183.

unites an entire assembly in one circle dance, with figures borrowed at times from square dancing, and which also incorporates solo or couple improvisations similar to the instrumental solos in jazz orchestras. The group figures had names like Peelin' the Apple, Kickin' the Mule, Organ Grinder, Praise Allah, Swing High Swing Low; and used all of the popular jazz steps. The soloists in center could give free rein to their imaginations. It roused wild enthusiasm among participants, including myself; yet it has become extinct. Perhaps it became too eclectic.

Jitterbugging has, however, survived three decades, with constant modifications. After the Lindy period it was standardized into the Swing Break; during the Boogie-Woogie musical period it was known as Boogie, and it accumulated substeps, the Mooch, the dragging Sand, the Camel Walk, and the strutting Duck Walk, which recalls the Rumba in its hip action.[10] After the forties it took the name of Bop, no matter what music was used.[11] The Jersey Bounce, Detroit Jump, Huckabuck, and others came and went. Now it's the Chicken, miming rooster and hen, and Drivin' Home, with its suggestions of starting and steering a car.[12] Today the sequences are freer and more improvisatory than in the forties, while the style is more sedate.

All of these variations exhibit the same fundamental qualities. These we will now try to identify racially and historically.

Antecedents and Ethnic Components. As in the study of jazz music, we can ask, "To what extent is jazz dancing a Negro legacy from the importation of Negro slaves to the American South in the eighteenth century?" An answer requires examination of African and Afro-American as well as white and jazz dance styles, to support the traditions of Negro provenience for many of the steps.

Africa displays innumerable dance styles.[13] But certain qualities seem to predominate in the western slave coasts, among the Yoruba for instance. These are whole-bodied movements, flat feet, flexible knees, sway back or forward tilt, dynamics from pussyfooting to violent acrobatics, rhythmic complexity, improvisation, an unconcern for set structure or ground plan save a counterclockwise circle.[14] These resemble the characteristics of jazz dance. Two striking, culturally determined differences are Africa's virtual neglect of couple dancing, and its emphasis on religious function as opposed to the secular purpose of jazz.

Analogous characteristics, plus a religious motivation, survive in Haitian dancing[15] and other Negro-derived dances of the Americas. Oderigo's equation of the Carolina "shout" and the Brazilian "candomblé" also suggests jazz analogies.[16] As shown by Dr. Lorenzo Turner, the female devotees in the candomblé for the water deity Oshun shuffle with small two-stepping foot twists in a counterclockwise circle,

---

10 Dorothy Arnette and Shirley Wright, Negro informants 1948.
11 Ruby Hunter and Horace Soward, Negro informants, 1956.
12 Ruby Hunter. Photos in *Detroit News*, *Pictorial Magazine*, June 3, 1956.
13 Murray, 1952, pp. 44–45.
14 Gorer, 1944, pp. 20–21.
15 Courlander, 1944, p. 37.
16 Oderigo, 1956, p. 317.

while their leader gyrates herself into a frenzy. The Holy Dance or Shout of the Gullah and other southern Negroes proceeds in a heel-shuffle, with hand clapping called "patting the juba."[17] Today this can also be observed in northern cities, Chicago, Detroit. In Ann Arbor I have witnessed at services of the Holiness church such syncopated knee flexions and hand-clappings, two-steps with foot twists and low kicks, and spasmodic jerking.[18]

Recreational dances of plantation Negroes commenced with a prayer and worked up to considerable enthusiasm, even ecstasy. The slaves ragged and syncopated their clog dances, frenzied stamps with hand-clapping, and less frenzied, prancing cake walks.[19] Around 1876 dances on the Cincinnati levees opened with a quadrille, borrowed from Europe, perhaps Spain. They culminated in a roar of song, stamping, patting juba, and acrobatics.[20] In New Orleans the Calinda was a contradanza in two rows (originally a stick dance). The women writhed with dragging steps, and the men leaped like savages.[21] This, the Bamboula, and other dances derived from the Spanish-influenced West Indies, especially after the Louisiana Purchase in 1803.[22] There was always a stylistic difference between men and women—observations confirmed by paintings of the period.[23]

These historical descriptions can readily be visualized by any observer of the Lindy in Harlem's Savoy Ballroom, when band and dancers warm up after midnight.

The white masters were fascinated by the slaves' antics.[24] In Cincinnati some whites took part, appearing clumsy next to the lithe Negroes. Whites started the vogue of minstrel shows. In recreation they clung to European-derived dances, French quadrilles, English country dances with set figures and erect, proper posture, precise Scotch reels and flings, Austrian couple waltzes, and later on, the two-steps. Quadroon balls in New Orleans imprinted a Negro flavor on the international assortment of quadrilles, polkas, waltzes, and Latin-American songs.[25] At times high society accepted one of the exotic dances and promptly dehydrated it. But one may suppose that the dockhands and their girls on Mississippi River boats performed turkey trot and tango with zest.[26] After decades of disdain, educated whites of the late twenties yielded to the captivation of jazz rhythms.

When they did so, they contributed their own mannerisms, exaggerating the Charleston and putting it on high heels, hunching shoulders in the Truckin'. White professionals have often created a pleasing style of their own within the

---

[17] Chase, 1955, p. 256.
[18] Kurath, 1951, p. 179.
[19] Chase, 1955, pp. 83, 439–40.
[20] Chase, 1955, pp. 436–37, quoting Lafcadio Hearn.
[21] Chase, 1955, pp. 77, 312; Harris, 1952, p. 49.
[22] Harris, 1952, p. 48.
[23] Photographic reproductions: for instance, in *Caribbean Quarterly* 3: 1, Frontispiece (E. Bridgens' "Negro Dances"); and in Abby Aldrich Rockefeller Folk Art Collection, Williamsburg, Va., Cat. 301.29 (The Old Plantation) from plantation between Orangeburg and Charleston, S.C.
[24] Chase, 1955, pp. 77–78.
[25] Chase, 1955, p. 304; Terral, 1954, p. 9.
[26] Harris, 1952, pp. 88–89.

medium of jazz, notably Fred Astaire and Ginger Rogers, more freely also "modern creative" dancers.[27] But the most exciting jazz dancing must still be sought in the streets and ballrooms and homes of the Negro population.

Though the obvious white contributions are limited to couple patterns, to figures of the Big Apple, and to secularization, yet jazz dance can be considered a racial hybrid, with the two-step rhythm as common denominator. The forms stem from the clash and fusion of races and cultures. Though jazz dance proper does not celebrate the economic and religious pursuits of life, it has its roots in such functional activities. Its analysis may hence prove useful in the study of seething racial problems.

Analysis through Symbols. The present modest paper cannot touch the wider ethnological or psychological implications.[28] Limited to the formal aspects, it will proceed to provide a firm foundation and to show a few tricks of the trade in dealing with forms. As in musicology these tricks consist in notation on paper by symbols, in juxtaposition of similar forms in a sort of tabulation, and in interpretation. A number of dance notation systems are available, including a convenient one of my own. In this article it is best to use Labanotation, which is widely known in many countries. Its symbols, here somewhat simplified, can reveal essential characteristics shared by African, Afro-American, and jazz dances.

The illustration aligns a few typical steps from personal observation. Always read from bottom to top and from left to right of the page, they represent the following steps:

a. Two-step (ragged)
b. Foxtrot
c. Duck Walk
d. Double Lindy
e. Lindy kick
f. Chicken
g. Truckin'
h. Step in a Holiness Negro service
i. Step in the Brazilian candomblé

They represent the girl's part, usually only the right foot sequence, to be reversed on the other foot. Bilateral sequences are shown in (d), (f), (g), and (i).

The selected symbols show the salient characteristics noted as common denominator, as follows:

1. Rhythmic, often syncopated knee flexions (flexion shown by black symbols), in all examples.
2. Prevalent two-step, in various arrangements of short-short long and various tempi (relative length of symbols, fortified by musical notes written at the right of the column), in all except (g).
3. Shift from heel to flat foot (hooks on symbols), in (g) and (i).
4. Foot twists (oblique rectangle), in (g), (h), and (i).
5. Sympathetic hip movement (dotted line), shown for (g), also evident in (c) and others, though not shown.
6. Sway back (key signature at bottom of page), in (c).
7. Opposition of raised leg and shoulder (reversed symbols, shoulder and arm written outside three lines of staff), in (f).
8. Alternate extension and flexion (bent horizontal line and X), in (d).
9. Syncopated finger snap (here written by musical notes on right), in (c).

---

[27] A Labanotation record, *Better Dancing with Fred Astaire*, is in preparation, M. Witmark, New York.
[28] Kurath, 1956, states various applications of choreology.

The Afro-American steps are so placed as to show the similarity between Lindy kick (e) and Holiness step (h), Truckin' (g) and candomblé (i). Other similarities and features will be apparent to a reader of Labanotation, or a student who consults one of the publications on the system, listed below. It is hoped that the general features will be apparent to all readers.

The musical accompaniment is not included with the tabulation; but some

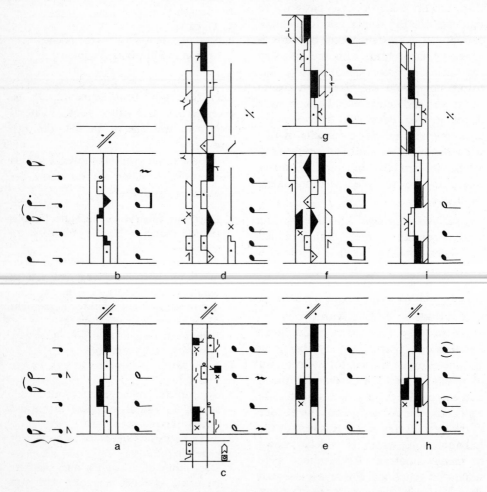

Fig. 1. Shared Features in Typical Dances

typical tunes and accompaniments are written to the extreme left. Suitable musical sources are appended to the bibliography.

Thus the illustration reinforces the remarks put forth in the written words of this article. The argument would be even more forceful when extended to a large number of dances and to the study of motion pictures, photographs, and descriptions, insofar as these are clear enough.

DANCE NOTATION

By Nadia Chilkovsky

The ethnologist will easily recognize the value of recording not only the music and a word description of folk and ethnic dances but the movements themselves, if he wishes to study the influence of the movement behavior of the transplanted African Negro upon the music and dance of America, and, indeed, upon that of the entire contemporary world.

Almost 500 years of trial and error

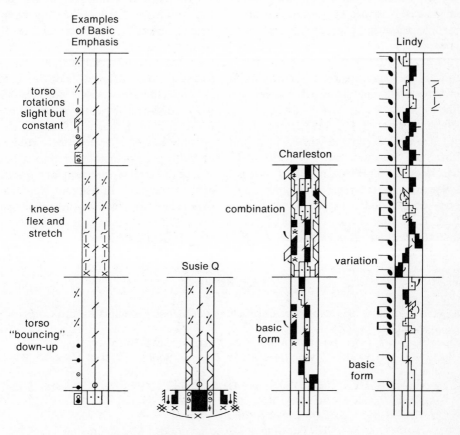

Fig. 2. Distinctive Features in Typical Dances

preceded the system of movement notation known in this country as Labanotation and abroad as Kinetographie Laban. Rudolf Laban devised an alphabet of movement notation in which there is a separate symbol for each motion within the framework of a tightly knit, logical, simple set of visual signs.[29] He discarded all previous efforts which either used letters as symbols for ideas of movement or which used symbols or words to represent combinations of

[29] Hutchinson, 1954.

movements, and set about the task of devising a movement alphabet which could record accurately the flow of time, effort and spatial path of all movement regardless of style. It can adapt itself to new ideas and needs for expression. The terminology can identify specific styles of dance as practiced by people of a variety of nationalities and languages, or codes of gesture language used by adjacent people with different languages.

Labanotation is read from the bottom of the page up, on a vertical staff of three main lines of which the center line represents the body's division of left and right.[30] On the center staff are marked off units of time which, in turn, are marked off by horizontal bar lines to represent meter. There is a separate location for each joint and body area, aided by a set of pre-signs. Eight basic direction symbols, all of them direct variations of a simple rectangle, are placed upon this staff. Each symbol indicates the duration of movement (by its length), the direction of movement (by its shape), the level of movement (by its shading), and the part of the body (by its location on the staff). These symbols are capable of infinite combinations.

The choice of illustrations has here been limited to a few of the steps known to one observer. The study can readily be extended not only to her full repertoire, but also to variants and to unique forms in many locations. For thousands of dance-literate students are now able to set down their observations and to make use of published tests. With a proved movement notation, students of culture comparisons can thus have source materials from many areas, as far apart as Nigeria, Brazil, and New York City. They can combine these with their own data towards the solution of ethnological problems.

REFERENCES

AVAKIAN, GEORGE, 1956. Notes for *Cakewalk to Lindy Hop*. Columbia Record Corporation, CL782.

CHASE, GILBERT, 1955. *America's Music*. New York, McGraw-Hill Book Co.

CHILKOVSKY, NADIA, 1955–1956. *Three R's for Dancing*, Books I-IV. New York, M. Witmark.

COURLANDER, HAROLD, 1944. "Dance and Dance Drama in Haiti," *The Function of the Dance in Human Society*. New York, Boas Studio, pp. 35–45.

DAVIS, HELENE, 1923. *Guide to Dancing*. Chicago, Regan.

GORER, GEOFFREY, 1944. "The Function of Dance in Primitive African Communities," *The Function of the Dance in Human Society*. New York, Boas Studio, pp. 19–34.

GREEN, ABEL, and JOE LAURIE, 1951. *Show Biz*. New York, Henry Holt & Co.

HARRIS, REX, 1952. *Jazz*. Harmondsworth, Penguin Books.

HUTCHINSON, ANN, 1954. *Labanotation*. New York, New Directions.

JOHNSON SMITH Co., 1935. (no author) *The Art of Dancing*. Detroit.

KURATH, GERTRUDE, 1949. "Jazz," *Dictionary of Folklore*. New York, Funk and Wagnalls, Vol. I, 545–46. 1951. "Syncopated Therapy," *Midwest Folklore*, 1: (3) 179–86. 1956. "Choreology and Anthropology," *American Anthropologist*, 58: (1) 177–79.

[30] Chilkovsky, 1955, 1956.

MURRAY, ARTHUR, 1938. *How to Become a Good Dancer.* New York, Simon and Schuster. 1946. *Dance Instructor.* New York, Robbins.

MURRAY, K. C., 1952. "Music and Dancing in Nigeria," *African Music Society News Letter* 1: (5) 21–30.

ORTIZ ODERIGO, NESTOR R., 1956. "Notas de Etnografia Afro-Brasileña: El Candomblé," *Ciencias Sociales*, Pan-American Union, 6: (36) 310–19.

SHAWN, TED, 1956. *16 Dances in 16 Rhythms.* New York, M. Witmark.

SHOMER, LOUIS, 1943. *Swing Step.* New York, Padell.

TERRAL, RUFUS, 1954. "Lo Llaman Jazz," *Américas*, Pan-American Union, 6: (9) 9–12, 30–31.

RECORDS AND MUSIC

Field recordings, inter'alia
KURATH, GERTRUDE, 1951. Services of the Holiness Church in Ann Arbor. Kurath.

TURNER, LORENZO, n.d. Brazilian and African Dances from field trips.

Commercial recordings
ETHNIC FOLKWAYS, 1899. New York, *Jazz 6* (FP 65), I, 7, *Maple Leaf Rag.* (Publ. *Ragtime Folio, Blues Stomps and Ragtime*, Melrose, n.d., 1–3; cop. Scott Joplin 1899, Melrose.) Suited to Two-step.

Other good selections in this jazz series:
COLUMBIA RECORD CORP., New York, n.d. *Cakewalk to Lindy Hop* (CL782), (Wally Rose), *Charleston* I, 6, *Truckin'*, II, 5, *That Lindy Hop* II, 6. 1946. *The Great Benny Goodman* (CL820), I, 2, *Stompin' at the Savoy.* (Publ. in Murray 1946, 36–38, cop. 1936 Robbins.) Suited to Jitterbug.

JAZZTONE SOCIETY, New York, n.d. *Jelly Roll Morton* (J-1211), *King Porter Stomp*, II, 5 and others. Suited to Two-step and Foxtrot. n.d. *Rex Stewart* (J-1202), *Basin Street Blues*, I, 2. (Publ. *The Dixieland*, I, Melrose, 2–3, cop. 1929.) Suited to Foxtrot or Duck Walk. n.d. *Sam Price* (J-1207), *Jumpin' on 57th*, I, 1. Suited to Lindy or Big Apple.

African Tales Among the North American Indians

ALAN DUNDES

While it is true that the bulk of the discussion about the origins of American Negro folklore has been concerned with music, there has been some treatment of verbal forms of folklore. As it happens, the existence of several key technical folkloristic tools of the trade makes it possible in the case of folktales to make some fairly objective determinations of the possible origins of individual stories. These tools include various tale type indices and motif indices. Those unfamiliar with the discipline of folklore are not likely to know about these tools and how to use them, but even the beginning student of folklore soon discovers the enormous utility of these standard aids.

The positions regarding the origin of American Negro folktales fall along the all too familiar traditional lines. Africanists generally claim that the tales are African survivals while specialists in European folklore argue that the majority of American Negro folktales are borrowed from the European repertoire. Melville J. Herskovits in The Myth of the Negro Past, *probably the best single work delineating the African retention argument, more or less assumes that American Negro tales are African in origin. However, although Herskovits recognizes that there are objective means available to facilitate rigorous comparative studies, he does not really take advantage of them. The section of his book which deals with folktales is much less convincing than his discussion of religion and other aspects of culture. In contrast, Richard M. Dorson in his anthology* American Negro Folktales *makes a strong case for the European origin of the majority of American Negro tales. By using tale type and motif indices, Dorson is able to demonstrate the European provenience of the greater portion of the tales in his collection and he thereby presents considerable documentation in support of his assertion that the basic corpus of American Negro*

Reprinted from *Southern Folklore Quarterly*, vol. 29 (1965), pp. 207–19, by permission of *Southern Folklore Quarterly*.

tales "*does not come from Africa.*" On the other hand, he is careful to state that each individual tale must be studied separately if one is interested in discerning its history.

The present essay is not concerned solely with the African origin of American Negro folktales but rather with those particular folktales which are shared by American Negroes and several Indian tribes residing in the southeastern United States. The inquiry started with the given fact that a number of folktales were told both by American Negroes and by southeastern Indians. The question raised was whether the Negroes borrowed the tales from the Indians or whether the Indians borrowed the tales from the Negroes. The essay tries to show that previous scholarship devoted to the question was often subjective and frankly racist in denying the African origin of some of these tales. The objective techniques available to the modern professional folklorist make it possible to eliminate much of the subjectivity and guesswork from such considerations of origins.

For Herskovits' statements on folktales, see The Myth of the Negro Past (*Boston, 1958*), *pp. 18, 272–75. See also Daniel J. Crowley, "Negro Folklore; An Africanist's View,*" Texas Quarterly, *5 (1962), pp. 65–71. For Dorson's view, see the section entitled "Origins of American Negro Tales" in his* American Negro Folktales (*New York, 1967*), *pp. 12–18. For an introduction to tale type and motif indices, see Stith Thompson,* The Folktale (*New York, 1951*), *pp. 413–27, or Jan Harold Brunvand,* The Study of American Folklore (*New York, 1968*), *pp. 103–23.*

EVER SINCE the partial publication of Stith Thompson's 1914 doctoral dissertation in 1919, *European Tales Among the North American Indians*, there has been no doubt that American Indians borrowed a good many European tale types. What is not so well known is that American Indians, particularly those located in the southeastern portion of the United States, have borrowed a considerable number of African tale types as well. That the identification of European rather than African tale types should have been made first is in keeping with the European-centered orientation of American folklorists coupled with their tendency to neglect African folklore.

Perhaps the first indication that American Indians had borrowed African tales from Negro slaves and ex-slaves was the noting of a large number of parallels in Joel Chandler Harris's "Uncle Remus" tales and the tales collected from the Cherokee and the Creek. Of course, most of the early interest was centered on the possible if not probable African origin of the Negro tales themselves rather than the relation of these tales to American Indian narratives.[1] In an important review article in 1881 by one of the first great American folklorists, T. F. Crane, a number of parallels between South American Indian tales and American Negro tales were carefully considered.

[1] Typical are T. F. Crane, "Plantation Folk-Lore," *Popular Science Monthly*, 18 (1880–81), 824–33; Robert Lee J. Vance, "Plantation Folk-Lore," *The Open Court*, 2 (1888), 1029–32, 1074–76, 1092–95; A. B. Ellis, "Evolution in Folklore: Some West African Prototypes of the Uncle Remus Stories," *Popular Science Monthly*, 48 (1895–96), 93–104, and A. Gerber, "Uncle Remus Traced to the Old World," *Journal of American Folklore*, VI (1893), 245–57.

Crane pointed out that it was absurd to think that the American Negroes had obtained these stories from South American Indians and that it was perfectly clear that South American Indians heard these stories from African slaves in Brazil, who like their counterparts in North America had brought their tales over with them from Africa.[2] Shortly thereafter in 1883, Joel Chandler Harris published *Nights with Uncle Remus* in which he wrote a scholarly introduction. In this short folkloristic treatise, Harris considered the question of Negro and Creek parallels. After pointing out a number of African parallels for his Negro tales, Harris stated that many of the Creek stories were "undoubtedly" borrowed from the Negroes.[3] Harris, however, was well aware of the alternative theory and he cited J. W. Powell of the Smithsonian Institution as one authority who suspected that the Negroes had obtained their tales from the Indians.[4] In 1888, in the first volume of the *Journal of American Folklore*, James Mooney observed that certain myths of the Cherokee resembled the Uncle Remus stories and he said that he hoped to prove that these stories were of American Indian origin.[5] In 1891, Alexander F. Chamberlain, who was the following year to be awarded the first American Ph.D. in Anthropology, presented a paper on the contact between Negro and Indian in which he reviewed both Crane's and Mooney's positions. Chamberlain called for an investigation of the influence of the Indian upon Negro folklore and the influence of the Negro upon Indian folklore.[6] Adolf Gerber at the Fourth Annual Meeting of the American Folklore Society in 1892 gave a paper tracing the Uncle Remus stories back to both African and European sources. Working in the same comparative tradition as Crane and Harris, Gerber argued along similar lines. Negro tales with African or European analogs could hardly have originated with American Indians. The direction of migration was clearly from the Old to the New World and not the other way around.[7] Gerber, however, did not discuss any of the Negro-American Indian parallels in particular as his purpose was to investigate the origin of Negro tales, not American Indian tales.

The documentation offered by Crane, Harris, and Gerber did not end the controversy. Consider, for example, a statement made by Mooney in his important collection of Cherokee tales published in 1900. "The negro, with his genius for imitation and his love for stories, especially of the comic variety, must undoubtedly have absorbed much from the Indian . . . , while on the other hand the Indian, with his

---

[2] Crane, "Plantation Folk-Lore," p. 832.

[3] Joel Chandler Harris, *Nights with Uncle Remus* (Boston and New York, 1883), p. xxix.

[4] Harris, p. xxviii.

[5] James Mooney, "Myths of the Cherokees," *Journal of American Folklore*, I (1888), 106.

[6] A. F. Chamberlain, "African and American: The Contact of Negro and Indian," *Science*, 17 (1891), 90.

[7] Gerber, "Uncle Remus Traced to the Old World," pp. 244–45. Unfortunately, Gerber never completed his promised memoir on the subject of the origins of the Uncle Remus stories. The accuracy of Gerber's scholarship is truly amazing considering the limited African materials available to him at that time.

pride of conservatism and his contempt for a subject race, would have taken but little from the negro. . . . ,"[8] In 1905, Frank G. Speck, writing a Master's thesis on southeastern American Indian mythology at Columbia University finessed the question of the African origin of American Indian materials by saying that the time was not yet ripe for definite opinions on the matter. More collections from West Africa were needed to settle the question.[9] The anti-African, pro-American Indian position was forcefully reiterated by Hartley B. Alexander in the volume on North American Indian mythology which appeared in *The Mythology of All Races* in 1916: "The *Brer Rabbit* stories, made famous as Negro tales by Joel Chandler Harris, appear as a veritable saga cycle among the Cherokee, from whom they are *doubtless* borrowed."[10] In 1919, Stith Thompson touched upon the problem in passing. In his discussion of animal tales in the monograph

European Tales Among the North American Indians, Thompson declared that "The larger number of the animal stories are probably of Spanish origin, though many of them come to the Indian directly from the Negro." The final sentence in the monograph summarizes Thompson's position. "The animal tales here treated are usually of Negro and Spanish origin—all of them ultimately belonging to European tradition."[11] Thompson's views appear to have influenced Franz Boas who in his article entitled "Romance Folk-Lore among the American Indians," devoted some attention to the vexing question of the possible Negro contributions to American Indian narrative repertoires. After agreeing with Gerber that American Indian tales in the southeast were affected by Negro contact, Boas made the following statement, "Espinosa and myself have held to the theory that most of these tales are of Spanish provenience and came to America in part

---

[8] James Mooney, *Myths of the Cherokee*, Nineteenth Annual Report of the Bureau of American Ethnology, Part I (Washington, 1900), p. 233.

[9] Frank G. Speck, "A Comparative Study of the Native Mythology of the South-Eastern United States," unpublished M.A. thesis (Columbia, 1905), pp. 14, 20. Speck reiterated these sentiments several years later. See "The Negroes and the Creek Nation," *Southern Workman*, 37 (1908), 109. See also Speck's "Notes on Creek Mythology," *Southern Workman*, 38 (1909), 9–11.

[10] Hartley B. Alexander, *North American Mythology*, The Mythology of All Races, X (Boston, 1916), p. 67. The emphasis on "doubtless" is added. Alexander was "doubtless" paraphrasing Mooney's views. One sees in the controversy that collectors tend to identify with their informants. Anthropologists are wont to speak of "their" people or "their" village referring to a people or a village with which they became familiar during extensive fieldwork. It is often hard to refrain from protecting or defending one's people when an occasion to do so arises. Surely, it is no accident that J. W. Powell, Mooney, and Alexander, all of whom worked with American Indians, believed that the Negro-Indian tales were Indian rather than Negro tales. In contrast, Harris, who worked with Negro informants, favored a Negro origin. Some of the arguments adduced, for example, those uttered by Mooney, verge on racism. When Mooney speaks of a "subject race" with a "genius for imitation," he implies that the Negroes were perhaps incapable of originating such tales. They could not invent; they could but borrow and imitate.

[11] Stith Thompson, *European Tales Among the North American Indians* (Colorado Springs, 1919), pp. 449, 457. This is, of course, a different position. Animal tales in both Negro and Indian tradition are considered to be borrowings from European folklore. The Negro versus the Indian origin is thus not an issue.

directly and part indirectly from Spain, the latter group brought here by Negroes who learned the tales in Africa from Spaniards and Portuguese."[12] Thus, like Thompson, Boas maintained that the Negroes were but carriers of the European tradition and thus the apparent African origin was really a European origin in disguise.

During the next few years, there were a number of important studies which confirmed beyond all reasonable doubt that there had in fact been extensive contact and intermarriage between Negroes and Indians in the southeast and elsewhere. Representative studies include Johnston's essay, "Documentary Evidence of the Relations of Negroes and Indians," which appeared in the *Journal of Negro History* in 1929; Laurence Foster's University of Pennsylvania doctoral dissertation, *Negro-Indian Relationships in the Southeast* in 1935; and George Herzog's interesting paper on "African Influences in North American Indian Music," presented at the 1939 International Congress of Musicology in New York City.[13] However, no specific studies of Negro-Indian folktale parallels were undertaken with respect to the "who-borrowed-from-whom" question. Not until 1959 was there any further serious attempt made to unravel the origin of those tales found among both American Negro and American Indian groups.

In 1959, Celia Blackmon Taylor wrote a Master's thesis at Alabama Polytechnic Institute entitled "Cherokee and Creek Folklore Elements in the Uncle Remus Stories: A Comparison of the Tales by Joel Chandler Harris and Legends of the Southeast." As the title of the thesis indicates, Taylor was attempting to show the American Indian origin rather than the African origin of the Negro-Indian parallels. Of the forty-six parallel tales, Taylor claims that only fourteen have African origins. The rest, she contends, in the light of their apparent absence in African tradition strengthen the argument "that Harris, in collecting 'Negro' stories, inadvertently included an appreciable number of stories that had trickled into Negro lore through contact with the Southeast Indians."[14] Taylor's study is the first of the Indian-origin school to employ the comparative method in detail. Unfortunately, Taylor did not utilize either the tale type index or the motif-index and this was a serious mistake inasmuch as even these tools could have demonstrated the absolute falsity of many of her conclusions. (It is a sad commentary on the state of the discipline of folklore when folklore theses can be written and then approved

[12] Franz Boas, *Race, Language and Culture* (New York, 1940), pp. 519–20. However, Boas at least considers an alternative theory in which an African origin is hypothesized. He suggests that perhaps African tales were imported into Europe by African slaves employed in Portugal as early as the fifteenth century. See pp. 520–21.

[13] J. H. Johnston, "Documentary Evidence of the Relations of Negroes and Indians," *Journal of Negro History*, 14 (1929), 21–43; Laurence Foster, *Negro-Indian Relationships in the Southeast* (Philadelphia, 1935); and George Herzog, "African Influences in North American Indian Music," in *Papers Read at the International Congress of Musicology Held at New York, September 11th to 16th, 1939* (New York, 1944), pp. 130–43.

[14] Celia Blackmon Taylor, "Cherokee and Creek Folklore Elements in the Uncle Remus Stories. A Comparison of the Tales by Joel Chandler Harris and Legends of the Southeast," unpublished M. A. thesis (Alabama Polytechnic Institute, 1959), pp. vi, 78.

by five faculty members without apparent knowledge of such standard aids. There may have been an excuse for Stith Thompson not to have known about Aarne's 1910 tale type index in 1919 when he published his *European Tales Among the North American Indians*, but there is none whatsoever for a study like Taylor's written in 1959.) Thus, for example, some of the tales which Taylor ascribes to American Indian sources are in fact European tale types originating from neither Indian nor African oral tradition. Taylor asserts, for instance, that the Uncle Remus tale "In Some Lady's Garden" in which Brer Rabbit, captured by Mr. Man, dupes Brer Fox into taking his place in a box by pretending that Mr. Man will force him to eat lots of mutton, comes from a Creek tale in which Rabbit, trapped in a box and about to be thrown into a stream, dupes a child into exchanging places in order to listen to the sweetest music in the world.[15] Yet, this is clearly motif K 842, Dupe persuaded to take prisoner's place in a sack: killed, which is very popular in European tradition.

In order to have proven her thesis, Taylor should have done the following: (1) establish that the Negro-Indian parallels were not European tale types; (2) demonstrate that the supposed native American Indian tales were found among American Indian peoples other than the Cherokee and Creek Indians; and (3) check to see whether or not the tales were African tale types. In other words, in order to settle the question of the origin of the Negro-Indian parallels, one must have a competent knowledge of European, African, and American Indian narrative traditions.

Having sketched some of the history of the problem, we may now examine some specific American Indian tales or tale elements with respect to a possible African origin. There is a tale type in which the hero in order to obtain either wisdom or a wife is required to capture a series of animals such as a large snake (e.g., a python or boa constrictor), a ferocious animal (e.g., a leopard), and a sack of biting insects (e.g., ants or hornets). A characteristic trait of the tale type is the trick used to trap the snake. The trickster plays upon the serpent's vanity and pretends to wish to measure and verify its great length. The serpent foolishly agrees and stretches out along a stick. The protagonist, using the pointed end of the stick, pierces it or ties the snake to the stick. There are Creek, Natchez, Hitchiti, Seminole, and Potawatomi versions of this tale.[16] If one looks up Motif H1154.6, Task: capturing squirrel and rattlesnake, one finds only one reference and that is to Harris's "Brother Rabbit Submits to a Test," in *Nights with Uncle Remus*. In his 1883 "Introduction," Harris refers to

---

[15] Harris, *Nights with Uncle Remus*, pp. 177–85; John R. Swanton, *Myths and Tales of the Southeastern Indians*, Bureau of American Ethnology Bulletin 88 (Washington, 1929), pp. 70–71. (For references to Alabama, Koasati, and Yuchi versions, see Swanton, p. 274, no. 66.); Taylor, pp. 27, n. 10, 75.

[16] For the Hitchiti, Natchez, and three Creek versions, see Swanton, p. 273, no. 54; for a Seminole version, see Robert F. Greenlee, "Folktales of the Florida Seminole," *Journal of American Folklore*, LVIII (1945), 144; a Potawatomi version is contained in Margaret Pearson-Speelman's unpublished 1922 University of Kansas M.A. thesis, "A Collection of Folk Stories of the American Indian," pp. 31–32.

this tale specifically as one which the Creeks must have borrowed from the Negroes and Gerber in 1893 suggested an African origin for the tale, citing a single African parallel.[17] On the other hand, Celia Blackmon Taylor cites this tale as a prime example of Harris's borrowing from a Creek original. The question is then whether the tale is an American Indian tale type or an African tale type? (It is clearly not a European tale type.) Although in the absence of an African tale type index or motif indexes for parts of Africa other than West Africa, one cannot easily find all available versions of a tale in print, one can with little difficulty locate a half dozen African texts.[18] It becomes clear that this is a popular West African tale type which diffused to southeastern American Indian groups via American Negro tradition in which the tale is also common. The tale is *not* found among the majority of American Indian tribes and as Gerber pointed out in 1893, it is hard to

imagine that an American Indian tale diffused to many parts of Africa by those few American Negroes who returned to Africa. In short, the American Indian origin theory for this particular tale is untenable.

Another tale type found among the American Indians is one in which a trickster dupes two animals into a tug-of-war in which each animal believes he is pulling against the trickster. Swanton reports eight versions, most of them Creek.[19] However, the tale is not reported from other American Indian groups. It is not a European tale type. From the list of references in the *Motif-Index* under K 22, Deceptive tug-of-war, one can easily ascertain the African origin of this tale. Kenneth Clarke in his 1958 doctoral dissertation, "A Motif-Index of the Folktales of Culture Area V, West Africa," lists eleven references and there are many others from other parts of Africa not listed by Clarke.[20] In the great majority of African texts,

---

[17] Harris, p. xxix; Gerber, p. 249.

[18] Taylor is unaware of this tale's existence in Africa and thus she can contend that Harris copied the tale from a Creek source (pp. 31, 75). Typical African versions include; Richard C. Bundy, "Folk-Tales from Liberia," *Journal of American Folklore*, 32 (1919), 416; W. H. Barker and Cecilia Sinclair, *West African Folk-Tales* (London, 1917), pp. 29–31; R. S. Rattray, *Akan-Ashanti Folk-Tales* (Oxford, 1930), pp. 54–59; Harold Courlander and Albert Kofi Prempeh, *The Hot-Shaking Dance and Other Tales from the Gold Coast* (New York, 1957), pp. 3–5; Melville J. Herskovits and Frances S. Herskovits, "Tales in Pidgin English from Ashanti," *Journal of American Folklore*, L (1937), 53–57. For additional versions, mostly American Negro, see Elsie Clews Parsons' note in "Folk-Tales from Students in the Georgia State College," *Journal of American Folklore*, XXXII (1919), 404, n. 2. For a garbled South American Indian Version, see Johannes Wilbert, *Warao Oral Literature* (Caracas, 1964), pp. 177–80.

[19] Swanton, p. 274, no. 70.

[20] Kenneth W. Clarke, "A Motif-Index of the Folktales of Culture Area V, West Africa," unpublished Ph.D. dissertation (Indiana University, 1958) cites sources of eleven texts. Other African texts include; Bufe's "Die Poesie der Duala-Neger in Kamerun," *Archiv für Anthropologie*, N.S. 13 (1914), 33–34; Wilhelm Lederbogen, "Duala-Märchen," *Mitteilungen des Seminars für Orientalische Sprachen*, 4, part 3 (1901), 170–73; Hugh Stannus, "The Wayao of Nyasaland," *Harvard African Studies*, 3 (1922), 334–35; Karl Gengenbach, "Märchen in der Nyang-Sprache," *Zeilschrift für Eingeborenen-Sprachen*, 29 (1938–39), 1–2, 219–22; E. Schuler, "Aus der Volkslitteratur der Yabakalaki-Bakoko in Kamerun," *Zeitschrift für afrikanische und ozeanische Sprachen*, 3

it is the tortoise which fools a hippopotamus and an elephant. Interestingly enough, the tale has been included in the 1961 revision of the tale type index as tale type 291. However, the references listed there are misleading. Reference is made to only three African versions and one could conclude that the tale was an Indo-European tale rather than an African tale type. This has important implications for origin studies of American Negro tales. The unwary folklorist might assume that if he finds a tale type number in the Aarne-Thompson index for an American Negro text that this means that the Negroes must have borrowed it from European rather than African tradition. There is, of course, nothing wrong with having African tale types included in the tale type index so long as it is clear that they are African, not European tale types.

A third African narrative element occurs in the widespread southeastern tale of Orphan and the Origin of Corn. In Creek, Alabama, Koasati, and Natchez versions, the trickster, usually Rabbit, tricks the orphan boy into diving into a stream to catch turtles.

While the boy is under the water, Rabbit runs off with the boy's clothes. A similar tale, "Old Brother Terrapin Gets Some Fish," appears in *Nights with Uncle Remus* and once again Joel Chandler Harris himself pointed out a clear Kaffir parallel in his 1883 "Introduction," a parallel which was also noted by Gerber.[21] References listed for motif K 16.2, Diving match: trickster eats food while dupe is under water, include only African and American Negro texts with no mention of the American Indian versions.[22] There can be no question as to the African origin of this element in American Indian folklore.

The Seminole have a tale in which there is a fasting contest between a rattlesnake and an owl in which the snake wins. The tale is paralleled in part by "The Wise Bird and the Foolish Bird," in *Nights with Uncle Remus*. This tale was one of the ones for which Gerber could find no Old World source, either European or African. However, the tale appears to be a version of motif K 53, Deceptive contest in fasting, which looks like an African tale. In one

---

(1897), 275–76; Louis Tardy, "Contributions à l'étude du folklore Bantou: Les fables, devinettes et proverbes fãng," *Anthropos*, 28 (1933), 292.

For additional references, see Elsie Clews Parsons, *Folk-Lore from the Cape Verde Islands*, *Memoirs of the American Folklore Society*, 15, Part I (Cambridge, 1923), p. 83, n. 1. It might be noted that Gerber called attention to the African origin of this tale before the turn of the century. See Gerber, p. 250. In terms of plot structure, this African tale type may well be one of the sources of the American Negro toast of "The Signifying Monkey." In both a small weak trickster succeeds in duping two strong rivals into fighting one another. The fact that one of the dupes is frequently the elephant in both the African tale type and the American Negro toast supports the hypothesis. For texts of the toast, see Roger D. Abrahams, *Deep Down in the Jungle* (Hatboro, 1964), pp. 136–57.

[21] Harris, p. xix; Gerber, pp. 248–49. For the American Indian texts, see Swanton, pp. 11, 14 (Creek); 135, 136 (Alabama); 179 (Koasati); and 232, 235 (Natchez).

[22] For an additional African text in which the trickster takes the victim-elephant's clothes, the same object of theft as in the American Indian tales, see Ludwig Kohl-Larsen, *Das Zauberhorn. Märchen und Tiergeschichten der Tindiga* (Eisenach and Kassel, 1956), pp. 105–6.

African version, a kingfisher deceives an owl who dies. The similarity of the owl victim in both this and the Seminole tale strengthens the probability of its African origin.[23]

Another possible African element occurs in the southeastern American Indian tale in which Rabbit gets Man-eater beyond the ocean. In Natchez and Creek versions of the tale, there is an episode in which the trickster asks his victim what sort of noise he makes when he sleeps. Some sort of onomato-poeic snoring sound is given in response. The trickster also tells the dupe what sound he makes. Later he makes the sound and the dupe, thinking the trick-ster is asleep, feels it is safe to fall asleep too. This episode occurs as a separate tale among the Alabama. In an African tale, an identical dialogue occurs between a dog and a leopard concerning the sounds made when sleeping. Since this episode does not appear to be in general North Ameri-can Indian tradition nor in European folklore, one can reasonably assume that this element came to the New World from Africa.[24]

Still another African element is found in a Cherokee tale in which Possum and Terrapin are out after persimmons. When a greedy wolf comes along to intercept the persimmons being thrown down by Possum who is up in the tree, Possum manages to drop a large one into the wolf's mouth which kills the interloper. Taylor in her thesis argues that this Cherokee tale is the origin of the Uncle Remus tale, "The Pimmerly Plum," in which Brer Tarrypin fools Brer Fox into waiting below a tree with an open mouth for a plum which never falls. However, the Cherokee tale ap-pears to be motif K 1035, Stone (hard fruit) thrown into greedy dupe's mouth, which is a tale not reported among other North American Indian groups but a tale extremely popular in East Africa. Taylor could more correctly have noted Creek and Natchez tales in which a rabbit waits in vain for syca-more balls to fall as parallels for "The Pimmerly Plum." And as a matter of fact, this too may be an African tale, motif J 2066.3, Men (animals) wait in vain for nuts to fall from a tree.[25]

One of the most widely diffused African elements in American Indian oral tradition is probably the account of the origin of the different races in which white men, Indians, and Negroes bathe successively in a river. Quite obviously, the highly developed sensi-tivity to racial differences in the southeast made the borrowing of this

[23] The Seminole tale is summarized in Louis Capron, *The Medicine Bundles of the Florida Seminole and the Green Corn Dance*, Anthropological Papers, 35, Bureau of American Ethnology Bulletin 151 (Washington, 1953), p. 164. The African text in question is in John H. Weeks, *Jungle Life and Jungle Stories* (London, 1923), p. 415.

[24] For the Creek and Natchez versions, see Swanton, pp. 43, 45, and 260. For the Alabama tale, see p. 161. The African tale cited is in Karl Gengenbach, "Märchen in der Nyang-Sprache," *Zeit-schrift für Eingeborenen-Sprachen*, 29 (1939), 224.

[25] For the Cherokee tale, see Mooney, p. 278; for the tale of "The Pimmerly Plum," see Harris, pp. 223–30; for Taylor's faulty argument, see her thesis, pp. 8, 75. Additional parallels for motif K 1035 may be found in Gerhard Lindblom, *Kamba Folklore, I. Tales of Animals*, Archives D'Etudes Orientales, 20 (Upsala, 1928), p. 101. For the Creek and Natchez versions of motif J 2066.3, see Swanton, pp. 61, 255.

motif, A 1614.2, Races dark-skinned from bathing after white men, almost automatic.[26]

The task of assigning an African origin to the narrative elements discussed thus far has been greatly facilitated by the general absence of these elements in European tradition. It is much more difficult a task to determine the origin of a tale found among the North American Indians which is reported in both Europe and Africa. For example, there is a Creek and Cherokee tale in which a bat participates in a game played with birds and quadrupeds on opposing sides. In a Creek version, bat wins the game for the animals; in Cherokee versions, bat wins the game for the birds. This is motif B 261.1 or tale type 222A, Bat in War of Birds and Quadrupeds, reported in Europe and Africa. One might presume an African origin in view of the tale's popularity in West Africa, but one must also note its absence in American Negro tradition.[27] The point is really that for a number of tales, it is extremely hard to say whether it is a European or an African tale type. The well known tale of tarbaby,

tale type 175, and the race won by using identical-looking relatives, tale type 1074, are both just as popular in Africa as in Europe, if not more so. One could argue that in view of the incontrovertible evidence that some African elements did diffuse into southeastern American Indian tradition, that these tale types could just as well have been introduced from Africans as from Europeans. It is also possible that tale type 72, Rabbit Rides Fox A-Courting, which Thompson lists as a European tale among the North American Indians, may be in fact an African tale among the American Indians. Similarly, Aarne-Thompson tale type 73, Blinding the Guard, a tale found among the Hitchiti and the Natchez, a tale which Thompson considered as a European tale among the North American Indians, is almost certainly an African tale type and it was almost certainly borrowed from African tradition, not European.[28] Thus one can conclude that not only are there African tales among the North American Indians but that some of Thompson's European tales among the North American Indians may in fact be African tale types.[29]

[26] For additional texts, see William C. Sturtevant, "Seminole Myths of the Origin of Races," *Ethnohistory*, 10 (1963), 80–86. Swanton, pp. 74–75, gives two versions.

[27] For the Creek version, see Swanton, p. 23; for Cherokee versions, see Mooney, pp. 286–87; John B. Davis, "Some Cherokee Stories" *Annals of Archaeology and Anthropology*, 3 (1910), 40–41; and David W. Owl, "How the Bat Got His Wings," *The Indian Leader*, 26, no. 27 (March 30, 1923), p. 7.

[28] For southeastern American Indian texts of tarbaby and the race won by using relative helpers, see Swanton, pp. 273, 274, no.'s 57, and 63. For American Indian versions of Rabbit Rides Fox A-Courting, see Swanton, p. 274, no. 61; for Blinding the Guard, see Swanton, pp. 107 (Hitchiti), and 257 (Natchez).

[29] Thompson has been consistent in his consideration of what is a European tale and what is not. Not only did he list tale types 72, 73, 175, and 1074, among others, as European tales among the North American Indians in 1919, but in a summary table in his textbook on the folktale published in 1946, he lists the same tales as "Borrowings of European-Asiatic tales" by Africans and Indians. See Stith Thompson, *The Folktale* (New York, 1951), pp. 288–93. While there is an Indo-European tale tradition, it should be realized that there is an African tradition and even an Indo-African tradition (cf. motif K 944, Deceptive agreement to kill wives (children) which is independent of

This consideration of the African influence upon American Indian folk narrative cannot end without a brief mention of the rabbit-trickster dispute. Mooney's exaggerated statement continues to be accepted. Mooney opposed the notion that Cherokee rabbit trickster was a borrowing from Negroes. He spoke of a Great White Rabbit who he claimed was the hero-god, trickster, and wonder-worker of all the tribes east of the Mississippi from Hudson bay to the Gulf.[30] Hartley B. Alexander, obviously influenced by Mooney stated that "There can be little question that "Brer Rabbit"—vain, tricky, malicious —is a Southern and humorous debasement of the Great Hare, the Algonquian demiurge and trickster."[31] Even John Swanton, greatest of all the students of southeastern American Indian folklore, was convinced that the rabbit was an aboriginal trickster although he was a much too sophisticated folklorist not to realize that many of the tales in which the rabbit figured were not aboriginal.[32]

Taylor in her thesis goes so far as to declare that "Brer Rabbit's prominence as trickster is not paralleled in African lore."[33] In view of such strong statements, can a case in fact be made for the African origin of the southeastern American Indian rabbit trickster? Well, for one thing, the rabbit does *not* figure as a trickster in most North American Indian folklore repertoires. Mary R. Haas in her survey of southeastern Indian folklore specifically remarked that among some of the Gulf Coast tribes, e.g., the Tunica, there were very few Rabbit stories and that there appeared to be no animal trickster cycle.[34] The second point is that many folklorists have assumed, wrongly in my opinion, that all African origins must be in West Africa. In West Africa, the most common trickster figure is the tortoise. But it is a known fact that Negro slaves came from East Africa as well and in East Africa it is the hare which is the principal trickster figure.[35] Therefore since the rabbit is not a trickster figure outside

European tradition. Moreover, for tales in Asia, Europe and Africa, there is no reason to assume in every case that the versions in Africa represent a borrowing from "European-Asiatic" tales. A tale which diffuses from India to Europe and to Africa might better be termed an Indo-European-African tale type than an African borrowing of an Indo-European tale type.

[30] Mooney, p. 232.

[31] Alexander, *North American Mythology*, p. 67. For a more recent uncritical regurgitation of Mooney's views, see Marshall Fishwick, "Uncle Remus vs. John Henry; Folk Tension," *Western Folklore*, 20 (1961), 78.

[32] Swanton in his article, "Animal Stories from the Indians of the Muskhogean Stock," *Journal of American Folklore*, 26 (1913), 193, said that "Whatever the origin of the separate Rabbit tales, there seems to be every reason to believe that Rabbit was the trickster or one of the tricksters of the Southern Indians in pre-Columbian times."

[33] Taylor, p. 52.

[34] Mary R. Haas, "Southeastern Indian Folklore," *Journal of American Folklore*, 60 (1947), 405–6.

[35] For some consideration of the importance of the hare as trickster in East Africa, see Alice Werner, "Some Notes on East African Folklore," *Folk-Lore*, 26 (1915), 60–75. In a recent short study, Hugh Tracey suggests a possible East African source for a Georgian Negro lullaby and he remarks that there were nearly a hundred shiploads of slaves from the Zambezi basin which went around the Cape to join the slave ship convoys from West Africa. Tracey is probably right when he says that this small East African contribution to the total slave trade has frequently been overlooked. See Hugh Tracey, "Tina's Lullaby," *African Music: Journal of the African Music Society*, 2 (1961), 99–101.

the southeast in American Indian folklore and since there can be no question that African narrative elements were introduced into American Indian tales, one can plausibly argue that the rabbit trickster figure so popular in American Negro tradition is African, not American Indian. In any case, the burden of proof should be on those espousing an American Indian origin theory. Let them show aboriginal White Rabbit trickster tales similar to those tales collected from southeastern Indians. No doubt when some enterprising student undertakes a tale type index for Africa or even just East Africa, the amount of evidence for the African influence on American Indian folklore will be overwhelming.

Problems Confronting the Investigator of Gullah

LORENZO D. TURNER

    The identification of Africanisms in American Negro folk music and folk-tales should not surprise anyone. No amount of inhumanity could destroy the delight in a good story or obviate the need to sing. Quite the contrary. The deplorable conditions of slavery made tales and songs even more essential as a means of venting emotions and anger. But the search for African survivals in language might strike the uninitiated as a wild goose chase. We know that peoples and families were cruelly separated, often making it difficult for an individual to continue to speak his native tongue. Moreover, the slaves were expected to learn English (to speak English, that is,—reading and writing were discouraged, to say the least!). To what extent then is it reasonable to look for Africanisms in American Negro speech?
    Again we find European-oriented scholars arguing that American Negro speech is a clear-cut derivative from "standard" English. Perhaps the classic case is that of Gullah, a dialect spoken by the inhabitants of the Sea Islands off the coast of Georgia. Typical was the statement made by Professor George Krapp of Columbia University in 1924:

The Gullah dialect is a very much simplified form of English, with cases, numbers, genders, tenses reduced almost to the vanishing point .... Generalizations are always dangerous but it is reasonably safe to say that not a single detail of Negro pronunciation or Negro syntax can be proved to have other than an English origin.

As Professor Lorenzo Dow Turner has pointed out, Krapp made these pronouncements without benefit of a personal knowledge of Gullah and without benefit of the languages spoken in West Africa! Just as white historians have, until recently, ignored black history, so white students of language have categorically denied the African contributions to black speech.
    Fortunately, Professor Lorenzo Turner spent a number of years investigating

Reprinted from *Publications of the American Dialect Society* no. 9 (1947), pp. 74–84, by permission of the author and the American Dialect Society.

the Gullah question. Not only did he undertake extensive fieldwork among Gullah speakers, he also studied many African languages. The culmination of his research was Africanisms in the Gullah Dialect *(Chicago, 1949) which is not likely to be superseded. Professor Turner's thorough and detailed comparative studies revealed a large number of parallels between Gullah and West African languages. Some of these Africanism-parallels have even been borrowed by white Americans, e.g., "tote" (meaning to carry), "goober" (peanut), "juke"— as in juke box, etc. The Negro use of "tote" was noted in November, 1863, by Thomas Wentworth Higginson. See his* Army Life in a Black Regiment *(New York, 1962), p. 178. Earlier it was cited by Solomon Northup in his slave narrative published in 1853. See* Puttin' On Ole Massa, *ed. Gilbert Osofsky (New York, 1969), p. 315. But "tote" is much older than that. It appeared in the* Boston Gazette *for August 7, 1769, which refers to someone being "toated" on board a ship. The* Oxford English Dictionary *(Oxford, 1933) even cites a similar instance of "toat" from 1676–1677, but claims that the "alleged Negro origin" is without foundation. However, Professor Turner's evidence in* Africanisms in the Gullah Dialect, *p. 203, is extremely convincing.*

The following essay represents a most summary account of Professor Turner's research. Although it is in parts somewhat technical for readers unacquainted with linguistics and phonetic transcription, it does provide an excellent example of the necessity for both fieldwork and library research if one is seriously interested in studying questions of origins. For additional discussion of possible African retentions with respect to individual lexical items, see "Africanisms in the Plantation Vocabulary," in M. M. Mathews, Some Sources of Southernisms *(University, Ala.: University of Alabama Press, 1948), pp. 86–129, as well as Professor Turner's magnum opus* Africanisms in the Gullah Dialect. *For the full text of the outrageous statement by Professor Krapp, see "The English of the Negro,"* American Mercury, *2 (1924), pp. 190–95. For further research on Africanisms in Gullah, see P. E. H. Hair, "Sierra Leone Items in the Gullah Dialect of American English,"* Sierra Leone Language Review, *4 (1965), pp. 79–84; Heinz Rogge, "Das Erbe Afrikas in Sprache und Kultur der nordamerikanischen Gullahs,"* Zeitschrift für Volkskunde, *61 (1965), pp. 30–37.*

THE PROSPECTIVE investigator of Gullah[1] should not be misled by the popular view that the African languages have exerted little or no influence on this dialect, but that it is derived entirely (or practically so) from English, especially that of the seventeenth and eighteenth centuries. There is no basis in fact for this view. Persons responsible for spreading it obviously lacked certain important requisites for an objective approach to the study of Gullah.[2]

One of these requisites is adequate knowledge of the conditions surrounding the importation of slaves to the United States. It is not true that most of

---

[1] Gullah is the name given the dialect spoken by the ex-slaves and their descendants who live on the Sea Islands off the coast of South Carolina and Georgia and on the mainland nearby.

[2] Cf., for example, George P. Krapp, "The English of the Negro," *American Mercury* (June, 1924); Ambrose E. Gonzales, *The Black Border* (Columbia, S. C., 1922), 17, 18; Reed Smith, *Gullah* (Columbia, S. C., 1926), 22, 32; Guy B. Johnson, *Folk Culture on St. Helena Island, South Carolina* (Chapel Hill, N. C., 1930) and "St. Helena Songs and Stories," in T. J. Woofter, Jr., *Black Yeomanry* (New York, 1930), 49, 51, 53; and Mason Crum, *Gullah: Negro Life in the Carolina Sea Islands* (Durham, N. C., 1940), 111, 121, 123.

the slaves who came to South Carolina and Georgia had previously lived in the British West Indies, where they learned English and were seasoned or otherwise fitted for plantation life, or that after reaching the Gullah region they were so distributed that any Africanisms which might previously have been observed in their speech soon disappeared. On the contrary, reliable documents reveal that a large majority of the slaves came direct from Africa to Charleston and other southern ports.[3] In many instances, slave-traders did not care to purchase slaves from the West Indies because taxes on them were prohibitive; and, in addition, they were thought to be instigators of slave revolts. In 1768 Georgia placed a duty on incoming Negroes who had been more than six months in any of the West India or Continental colonies,[4] and in 1803 the legislature of South Carolina passed an act prohibiting the importation of all Negroes from the West Indies.[5] Moreover, a careful study of the speech of the Gullahs reveals many African linguistic survivals.

Another of these requisites for the proper approach to the study of Gullah is some acquaintance with the speech of Negroes in areas of the New World where they could have had no contact with the English language of the seventeenth and eighteenth centuries—such areas, for example, as Haiti, Brazil, and other non-English regions of the New World. A study of the speech of the Negroes in these areas reveals the same characteristics that one finds in the non-English portions of Gullah.[6]

A third requisite for an adequate study of Gullah, and a highly important one, is some familiarity with African culture, especially with the African languages spoken in those areas from which the slaves were brought to the United States.[7] In this requirement the advocates of the theory that Gullah is merely the English of the seventeenth and eighteenth centuries were conspicuously lacking.

If one has met these requirements, he has gone a long way toward solving the first problem confronting the investigator of this dialect—that is, the problem of acquiring an adequate background for the study. With such preparation the investigator is not inclined at the outset to the assumption that every strange Gullah word he encounters is an English word which the Gullah speaker is unable to pronounce intelligibly. For example, one of the Gullah

---

[3] See Elizabeth Donnan, *Documents Illustrative of the History of the Slave Trade to America* (Washington, D. C., 1935), 4. 278–587.

[4] *Ibid.*, 624.

[5] W. E. B. Du Bois, *The Suppression of the African Slave Trade to the United States* (New York, 1896), 240.

[6] See Suzanne Sylvain, *Le Créole Haïtien* (Port-au-Prince, 1936); Renato Mendonça, *A Influência Africana no Português do Brasil* (São Paulo, 1935); Manuel Querino, *Costumes Africanos no Brasil* (Rio de Janeiro, 1935); Jacques Raimundo, *O Elemento Afro-Negro na Lingua Portuguesa* (Rio de Janeiro, 1933); Arthur Ramos, *O Negro Brasileiro* (São Paulo, 1940); João Ribeiro, *O Elemento Negro* (Rio de Janeiro, 1939); and Nelson de Senna, *Africanos no Brasil* (Bello Horizonte, 1938). See also M. J. and F. S. Herskovits, *Suriname Folk-Lore* (New York, 1936), 117–35.

[7] Among these languages are the following: Wolof (Senegal and Gambia), Bambara (French West Africa), Mende (Sierra Leone), Mandinka (Gambia), Fula (West Africa), Vai (Liberia and Sierra Leone), Twi, Fante, and Gã (Gold Coast), Ewe (Togo and Dahomey), Fɔ̃ (Dahomey), Hausa (Northern Nigeria), Yoruba, Ibo, Efik, and Ibibio (Southern Nigeria), Kongo (Belgian Congo and Angola), Tshiluba (Belgian Congo), Kimbundu and Umbundu (Angola).

words for "tooth" is [bɔɲ]. Investigators have assumed that this is merely the Gullah speaker's pronunciation of the English word "bone," not realizing that in the Wolof language of Senegal and Gambia, from which areas several thousand slaves were brought to Charleston, the word for "tooth" is [bɔɲ]. The Gullah expression for "a hard rain," frequently of several days' duration, is [dɛt] or [dɛt ren]. This has been taken by investigators to be the English word "death," the assumption being that to the Gullahs a hard rain foreshadows the death of someone. As a matter of fact, the Wolof word for "a hard rain" is [dɛt]. Again, the Gullah expression for "pregnancy" is [enu ꞌΦole]. Investigators of the dialect have identified this with the English phrase *in foal*, used in reference to pregnant animals of the horse family. If these investigators of Gullah had been acquainted with the vocabulary of the Ewe language, spoken in Togo and Dahomey, they would have known that the word for "pregnancy" in that language is [Φo₁le₁e₃nu₁],[8] lit., "She is with child." One of the Gullah words for "any alcoholic beverage" is

[maꞌlaβu] (written in several lists of Gullah words prepared by investigators of the dialect as if pronounced [malafi]). Dr. Guy Johnson says that the word "could be an English dialectal pronunciation of *malvesie* and might have entered this country with the English.... At any rate," he continues, "this word affords an excellent illustration of the need for caution in the study of strange words found in American Negro speech."[9] Here again the African languages furnish the solution to the difficulty. The word [malavu], meaning "wine," "beer," or "any alcoholic drink," is found in the Kongo language, spoken in Angola and the Belgian Congo,[10] the very areas from which thousands of slaves were being brought direct to South Carolina throughout the eighteenth century and the first half of the nineteenth. Since Kongo has supplied Gullah with several hundred other words, it is not at all unreasonable to suppose that [maꞌlaβu] got into Gullah in a similar manner. Such Gullah words and expressions as the following the investigators either did not know existed, or, being unable to explain them on

---

[8] Tones are given for words from the following West African languages: Vai, Gã, Ewe, and Yoruba. The low, mid, and high level tones will be indicated, respectively, by the inferior numerals 1, 2, and 3 placed after the syllables whose tones they represent. Glides from one tone level to another will be indicated as follows:

> 3–1 = a tone falling from high to low
> 3–2 = a tone falling from high to mid
> 2–1 = a tone falling from mid to low
> 1–3 = a tone rising from low to high
> 1–2 = a tone rising from low to mid
> 2–3 = a tone rising from mid to high

The accentuation of Gullah words of more than one syllable is indicated by the mark (ꞌ) placed before the syllable for the main stress and (ˌ) placed before the syllable for the secondary stress, when it is thought necessary to indicate the secondary stress. The accentuation and intonation of Gullah words vary somewhat with individual speakers. A word is given the pronunciation used by the particular speaker from whom it was obtained. In the case of many Gullah words the syllables differed not so much in stress as in tone. These differences are indicated by inferior numerals placed after the syllables.

[9] *Folk Culture on St. Helena Island, South Carolina*, 56.

[10] In Tshiluba, also spoken in the Belgian Congo, the word for "palm wine" is [maluvu].

the basis of English, they probably took them to be nonsense words and accordingly omitted them from their lists:

['agogo] "cow-bell"*	Yoruba, [a₂go₂go₂] "a bell"; "a metal musical instrument made in the shape of a cow-bell"
['anduɲu] "I am not with you"	Wolof, [anduɲu] "We not unite"
['bara ('bala)] "xylophone"	Bambara and Mandingo, [bara (bala)] "xylophone"
['binda] "a kite"	Vai, [bin₂da₃] "a kite, a sail"
['bɒbɒbɒ] "a woodpecker"	Kongo, [mbɔbɔbɔ] "a woodpecker"
['bumbu] "to lift"	Mende, [mbumbu] "to lift"
[do] "child"	Mende [ndo] "child"
['duŋgu] "pepper"	Kongo, [nduŋgu] "pepper"
['gulu] "pig"	Kongo, [ŋgulu] "pig, hog"; Umbundu, [oŋgulu] "pig"
['ʃamba] "elephant"	Umbundu, [ondʒamba] "elephant"
[ʃoso] "witchcraft"	Mende, [ndʒoso] "magic"
[ka'luŋga] "sea"	Kongo and Kimbundu, [kaluŋga] "sea"
[kiɲ'kβaβi] "partridge"	Kongo, [kiŋkwavi] "partridge"
['muŋgaβa] "salt" (taken from the ocean and used for cooking)	Kongo and Kimbundu, [muŋgwa] "salt"
['sɒ ɛ a 'duɸe] "Put wood on the fire"	Vai, [sɔ:₃₋₁ɛ₁a₁du₁fe₁] "The fuel has been consumed"
['βaŋga] "witchcraft"	Kimbundu, [waŋga (ɔwaŋga)] "witchcraft"
['yambi] "sweet potato"	Mende, [yambi] "the wild yam"

* It is tempting to speculate as to the possible relationship of "agogo" to such phrases as "Whiskey a-go-go" and "Go-go girls."—ED.

That this background information which I have been emphasizing is all-important for the prospective investigator of Gullah is illustrated further by the ways in which certain syntactical features of the African languages have influenced Gullah—as, for example, in the Gullah speaker's employment of compound words,[11] in his comparison of adjectives,[12] in his use of verbal adjectives,[13] in his word order,[14] and in the frequent repetition of words and phrases throughout his sentences.*

As regards the forms of words,

[11] Cf. [i Φa go go ʃvm] "He goes to see her," lit., "He takes go go see her" (showing the influence of such West African languages as Ewe, Twi, and Fante).
[12] For example, [i tɒl pas unə] "He is taller than you," lit., "He is tall, surpasses you." Cf. Ewe [sɔ₃ lo₃lo₁ wu₃ te₃dzi₃] "The horse is larger than the donkey," lit., "The horse is large, surpasses the donkey."
[13] Cf. Gullah [i tɒl] "He is tall," lit., "He tall," with Ewe [a₁ti₃ la₃ kɔ₃] "The tree is high," lit., "Tree the high"; Kimbundu [ene makamba] "They are friends," lit., "They friends"; Kongo [kiadi] "It is sad," lit., "It sad," etc.
[14] Cf. Gullah [rol raʊŋ] "roll round," i.e., "round roll, biscuit" and [de klinbrɒd] "day clean broad," i.e., "broad daylight" with Gã [gbe₃kɛ̃₂kpa₂kpa₂] "child good," i.e., "good child"; Yoruba [o₂hũ₂ bu₂bu₂ru₃] "thing bad," i.e., "bad thing"; Tshiluba [mitʃi mile] "sticks long," i.e., "long sticks," etc.
* For further discussion of the frequent repetition of words and phrases, see Lorenzo Dow

Gullah reveals the influence of the African languages in distinguishing between the singular and plural of nouns solely by the use of a qualifying demonstrative pronoun or a numeral adjective rather than by a change in the form of the noun; in the phenomenon of the verb form remaining unchanged throughout the singular and plural, distinction being made only by the personal pronoun preceding the verb; in the employment of aspect rather than tense as we know it in English[15]; in the fact that the nominative or subjective forms of the personal pronouns are practically the same as the objective forms and the forms of the possessive; in the fact that nouns have the same form in all cases; and in the method of indicating the gender of a noun—that is, by prefixing to the noun the word "man" or "woman" or some other word meaning "male" or "female."[16]

In order to appreciate many of the sounds of Gullah, an investigator of the dialect needs to have some acquaintance with the sounds of those African languages that were spoken by the Gullahs who were brought here as slaves. I refer especially to their substitution of the ejective *p, t,* and *k* for the English *p, t,* and *k* at the beginning of a stressed syllable; their occasional employment of the combination of initial nasal plus another consonant, such as [mb], [mp], [mw], [nd], [ns], [nt], [ŋd], [ŋk], [ŋg], etc.; their substitution of the voiceless bilabial fricative [Φ] for the English *f* and the voiced bilabial fricative [β] for the English *v* and *w*; their use of the voiceless and voiced palatal plosives [c, ɟ] instead of the English palato-

---

Turner, *Africanisms in the Gullah Dialect* (Chicago, 1949), pp. 220–22. It is quite possible that this characteristic of repetition is found outside of the Gullah-speaking area. For example, in several speeches recorded in the early 1860's by Thomas Wentworth Higginson from Negro soldiers under his command and published in his *Army Life in a Black Regiment* in 1869, we find comparable repetitions; "Fus' ting I shoot, and den I shoot, and den I shoot again. Den I creep-creep up near de boat. . . ." In another report, we learn that "Mas'r stand in de wood, peep, peep, faid for truss [afraid to trust] . . . ." See Higginson, *Army Life in a Black Regiment* (New York, 1962), pp. 149, 168.—ED.

15 In Gullah, as in many West African languages, little importance is attached to the actual time when an event takes place. It may be the manner of the action (mood), or the character of it (aspect), or possibly both as they impress the speaker at the moment that are important. Accordingly, the form of the verb used to refer to present time is frequently the same as that used in reference to the past, and often there is no change in form when the future is intended. If necessary for clearness a statement may be added by the speaker that will specify the time intended. In the Ewe language, the aorist form of the verb does not indicate any particular time, but can represent the present, past, or even future, according to the context. For example, [me₁yi₁] can be translated "I go," "I went," or "I am going." (See Diedrich Westermann, *A Study of the Ewe Language*, London, 1930, 73ff.) In the Mandinka language, there are three aspects of the verb; the first represents an action without reference to its completeness or incompleteness; the second describes an action which is being continued; and the third describes one which has been completed. In each of these aspects are found varying degrees of time—present, past, and future. The simple past form of transitive verbs is employed to refer to present, past, and future time; whereas the past form of intransitive verbs refers only to the past. (See W. T. Hamlyn, *A Short Study of the Western Mandinka Language*, London, 1935, 11ff.)

16 Cf. Gullah *man chicken* "rooster" and [ʊmə] (*woman*) *chicken* "hen" with Gã [wu₁ɔ₂nũ₁] "rooster," lit., "man chicken," and [wu₁ɔ₂yo₁] "hen," lit., "woman chicken"; Mandinka [diŋmuso] "girl," lit., "child woman," and [diŋke] "boy," lit., "child man," etc. [This construction might account for the neologism "manchild" as in Claude Brown, *Manchild in the Promised Land* (New York, 1965).—ED.]

alveolar affricates [tʃ] and [dʒ] and the voiced palato-alveolar fricative [ʒ]; the very common use among them of the palatal nasal [ɲ], especially in many words in which y or n would be heard in cultivated English[17]; their failure to aspirate a voiceless plosive at the beginning of a stressed syllable; the tendency on the part of Gullah speakers when pronouncing English words or syllables that end in a consonant, either to add a vowel or to drop the consonant, as well as the tendency to avoid certain consonant clusters common in English, either by inserting a vowel between the consonants or, more frequently, by dropping one of them; and finally their substitution of d and t for the voiced and voiceless varieties of the English th sound.[18]

Mr. Cleanth Brooks, in his monograph entitled *The Relation of the Alabama-Georgia Dialect to the Provincial Dialects of Great Britain* (Baton Rouge, 1935), reveals some confusion in his discussion of the Negro's substitution of initial d for th in such words as *this, that, them, then, there,* etc. Assuming that all the peculiarities of the Negro's pronunciation stem from the British dialects of the seventeenth and eighteenth centuries, he devotes several pages (75 to 81, to be exact) to an attempt to show that the use of initial d for th in such words occurred in certain British dialects probably early enough for the white settlers in Alabama and Georgia to pass it on to the Negroes. He obviously did not realize that in *none* of the West African languages spoken by the Negroes who were coming to Georgia direct from Africa until

practically the beginning of the Civil War does the *th* sound occur. The Gullahs regularly substitute d and t, respectively, for the voiced and voiceless varieties of th in *all* positions. Moreover, when the native West African today first encounters the English *th* sounds, whether in the United States, the Caribbean, West Africa, or elsewhere, he substitutes for them d and t, with which he is thoroughly familiar and which he considers closer to the English *th* than any of the other sounds of his language. This is true whether he is literate or illiterate. All of my African informants who have recently learned to speak English use these substitutes, and it is reasonable to suppose that their ancestors who came to Georgia from Africa as slaves reacted similarly to the English *th* sounds when encountering them for the first time. It is likely that they would have done this even if they had heard these substitutions in the speech of some of the white people; but no evidence is available that they heard them.

The indebtedness of the Gullahs to the African languages is also unmistakable when one considers the methods they use to form words. Among these are (1) the employment of groups of words for nouns, verbs, adverbs, adjectives, or other parts of speech (such as *a-beat-on-iron* for "a mechanic"; *day-clean* for "dawn," being a translation of the Wolof expression [bɔr bu sɛt] "dawn," lit., "the day clean"; [Φula 'ΦaΦa] "woodpecker," being the Mende term [fulafafa] "to bore into a tree"; *to sweet mouth* "to flatter," resembling the Twi expression [no ano yɛdɛ] "He

---

[17] Cf. [ɲuz] "use"; [ɲɒŋ] "young"; [reɲɟ] "reins," etc.
[18] For an analysis of the vowel and consonant phonemes of Gullah, see my "Notes on the Sounds and Vocabulary of Gullah," *Publication of the American Dialect Society*, No. 3, May, 1945.

is a flatterer," lit., "His mouth is sweet"; *a bad mouth* "a curse," being the Vai expression [da₃ ɲa₃ ma₃] "a curse," lit., "a bad mouth," etc.)* (2) the Gullah's use of reduplicated forms (such as the following personal names: ['baŋgu'baŋgu]—cf. Kongo, [mbaŋgubaŋgu) "the bark of the [mbaŋgu] tree," given to patients suffering from [nsaku], an ailment characterized by pains in the back; ['didi'didi]—cf. Twi, [didididi] "to feed"; [i'yami-i'yami]—cf. Yoruba, [i₁ya₃mi₂-i₁ya₃mi₂] "my mother-my mother"; ['tɒtɒtɒ]—cf. Ewe, [tɔ₃tɔ₃tɔ₃] "in great numbers"; ['yoyoyo]—cf. Ewe, [yo₁yo₁yo₁] "dripping," heard frequently in the sentence [e₃le₁nu₃ Φom₃ yo₁ yo₁ yo₁] "He is talkative"); (3) onomatopoetic expressions (such as 'blʌdinɒŋ] "frog," ['bɒbɒbɒ] "woodpecker," ['ΦugΦug] "the lungs of an animal," ['pakpakpak] "to knock," and [βulisãkpãkpã] "woodpecker," being the Mende term [wulisãkpãkpã] "woodpecker," lit., "to pound the tree quickly").

As a final illustration of the fact that the prospective investigator of Gullah should have some acquaintance with the Gullah's African background, I should mention briefly the intonation of the dialect. Probably no characteristic of the Gullah Negro's speech appears so strange to one who hears it for the first time as its intonation. To understand fully the intonation of Gullah one will have to turn to those West African tone languages spoken by the slaves who were brought to South Carolina and Georgia. Among these are Mende, Vai, Twi, Fante, Gã, Ewe, Ibo, Bini, Efik, Ibibio, and a few others. So far as my own observation is concerned, features of tone in Gullah are not used as primary phonemes, i.e., the tones of Gullah words do not distinguish meanings as do tones in the African tone languages. There are in Gullah, however, several intonation patterns, used in sentences, phrases, and words, that are quite common in the African languages but are not used in English under similar conditions. Among these are (1) the use of a high or mid level tone at the end of a declarative sentence in which no implication or special meaning is intended; (2) the use of a rising tone at the end of a declarative sentence when no special meaning is intended; (3) the use of level tones—mid, high, or low—throughout a statement; (4) the alternation of low and mid or low and high tones throughout a statement; (5) the use of tones that fall from high to mid; (6) the use of tones that rise from low or mid to high, or from low to mid, when no special meaning is implied, or when the tone does not occur at the end of an unfinished tonal group, such as at the end of a subordinate clause that does not end the sentence; (7) the use of non-English tones in Gullah words and short phrases (such as in the word [bʌ₁krʌ₁] "white man"); (8) the use of a level tone at the end of

---

* It seems likely that to "bad mouth" someone, meaning to speak ill of, or more commonly, to jinx or put the whammy on someone, is nearly a direct translation of the African idiom. The sense in American Negro folk speech is typically that suggesting an evil contingency will cause it to happen. For examples of usage, see Harold Wentworth, *American Dialect Dictionary* (New York, 1944), p. 39; Claude Brown, *Manchild in the Promised Land* (New York, 1965), pp. 26, 41, 46, 277; and Harry Middleton Hyatt, *Hoodoo-Conjuration-Witchcraft-Rootwork*, Memoirs of the Alma Egan Hyatt Foundation, vol. I (Washington, D.C.: American University Bookstore, 1970), pp. 255–56. Similarly, to "sweet-talk" someone appears to be an English reworking of an Africanism. —Ed.

a question whether or not "yes" or "no" is required for an answer and when no special meaning is implied. Examples of all these varieties of tones are numerous in the African tone languages.

So far my discussion has been concerned with one important problem involved in the study of Gullah. I have emphasized the fact that any study of this dialect is sure to be inadequate and superficial without the investigator's having certain important information regarding the Gullah's African background. This information will contribute greatly toward making intelligible the non-English portions of the dialect.

There is another problem which I shall dispose of very briefly. It has to do primarily with the collection of Africanisms in Gullah. The investigator of Gullah should know his Gullah informants so well that they will feel no necessity for using a form of speech which they commonly reserve for strangers. This form may be almost wholly English; whereas when speaking to friends and relatives they will employ language which contains many Africanisms. Mr. Leonard Bloomfield has called to the attention of investigators of languages and local dialects the danger of having merely a superficial acquaintance with their informants who speak a strange dialect:

Indeed, diffidence as to one's speech is an almost universal trait. The observer who sets out to study a strange language or a local dialect often gets data from his informants only to find them using entirely different forms when they speak among themselves. They count these latter forms inferior and are ashamed to give them to the observer. An observer may thus record

a language entirely unrelated to the one he is looking for.[19]

This observation, it would appear, is applicable to the experience of many of the investigators of Gullah. The Gullah Negroes are extremely cautious when talking to strangers. They say they have fared so badly at the hands of strangers that they are suspicious of anyone whom they do not know very well. Again, the curiosity always displayed by a stranger on hearing Gullah and frequently his lack of understanding of the temperament of the Gullah Negroes are a source of great annoyance to them and increase their reticence and sensitiveness.

Moreover, as already indicated, when talking to strangers the Gullah Negro is likely to use speech that is essentially English in vocabulary. When he talks to his friends, however, or to the members of his family, his language is different. One striking example of the superficial contact which the investigators of Gullah had with this dialect, even though many of them believed that they knew the Gullah Negro intimately, is the fact that not one of them observed any African personal names among the Gullahs. These names are so numerous, both on the Sea Islands and on the mainland nearby, that it is difficult for one to conceive of an investigator's not observing them. It is true that in almost all of their dealings with white people the Gullahs use their English names if they have any. Many, however, have never been given an English name. At school their children are not allowed to use their African names because the teacher, who is usually not a native

[19] *Language* (New York, 1933), p. 497.

islander, supposes that they are nonsense words and refuses to record them. If the child has no English name, the teacher will give him one. If, therefore, a field-worker does not come in contact with these people in their homes, but merely consults the class-rolls of the teachers or other records, he will assume that they have only English names. Mr. John Bennett, Ambrose Gonzales, George Philip Krapp, Reed Smith, Mr. Guy Johnson, Mr. Mason Crum, and others who contend that Gullah is derived wholly (or practically so) from English reveal in their writings no knowledge whatsoever of the several thousand African personal names still used by the Gullahs. Most of the Gullahs use two kinds of given-names. One is English, and they call it their real or true name and use it at school, in their correspondence, and in their dealings with strangers. The other is the nickname known also as the pet name or basket name.* In their homes and among their friends and acquaintances they use the nickname almost exclusively. In fact, so general is its use that many of the Gullahs have difficulty in recalling their English given-name. The nickname is nearly always a word of African origin. When not African it is likely to be an English word revealing methods used by the Africans in naming their children —that is, it may indicate something regarding the nature of the weather at the time of the child's birth; or the appearance, temperament, or health of the child; or the time of its birth;

or some particular incident or object with which the child or his parents were associated at the time of the child's birth or later (such as some superstition, or a place, person, animal, or plant). In many instances both the given-name and surname are African words. Some of my ex-slave informants explain this by saying that during slavery they used for their surname the surname of their owner. After slavery, many of them refused to use any longer the name of their former enslavers. Likewise, many former slave-holders refused to allow the freedmen to use their names. Thereupon, the former slaves chose their nickname for their surname and gave themselves another nickname. This also is frequently an African word. Many have only one name, which they may use both as the given-name and surname.

In conclusion, I should like to call attention to the fact that even though this discussion has been confined to Negroes in the Gullah region, it is not wholly inapplicable to Negroes in other parts of the South. The Gullahs are and have been continually moving westward and northward. Since in doing so they carry their speech habits with them, persons investigating Negro speech in Alabama, Mississippi, or elsewhere may find it to their advantage to be acquainted with the Negro's African background and to know the Negro informant so well that there will be no occasion for him to use the language which he commonly reserves for strangers.

* According to one account, basket names were given to babies so that the Evil Spirit might not know the infant's right name. This suggests that the basket name provided a form of protection for the newborn child. See Rossa B. Cooley, "Aunt Jane and Her People; The Real Negroes of the Sea Islands," *The Outlook*, 90 (1908), pp. 425–32. For additional discussion of Sea Islands names with particular reference to West African naming practices, see Melville J. Herskovits, *The Myth of the Negro Past* (Boston, 1958), pp. 190–94.—ED.

Americanisms
That May Once
Have Been Africanisms

DAVID DALBY

    Lest anyone think the question of origins is a dead one, the following brief, but suggestive, essay by David Dalby, Reader in West African Languages at the British School of Oriental and African Studies in London ought to set the record straight. It is quite likely that Dalby's speculations concerning possible influences of Wolof, one of the principal languages of Senegambia, will infuriate both proponents of "European" origins of American Negro speech and advocates of an African origin, though for somewhat different reasons. Professional students of the history of English and American slang will surely take issue with Dalby on the discussions of many if not most of the particular words he treats. On the other hand, it should be pointed out that merely finding a nineteenth-century citation or even an eighteenth-century citation of a particular slang item in an English language source would not necessarily rule out the possibility of an African origin for that term.

    Since Dalby is arguing in favor of African origins, it may not be altogether clear why scholars generally sympathetic to espousals of African origin hypotheses might object to his conjectures. No doubt some scholars will be dismayed by Dalby's failure to provide full comparative data from languages other than Wolof. It does seem incredible in view of the diversity of the African peoples from whom slaves were taken that a single language, Wolof, should have been the sole source for so many important slang terms. One recalls that Professor Turner in his studies of Africanisms in Gullah often found possible sources in as many as seven or eight different African languages. In comparison, Dalby's cursory treatment of numerous lexical items seems almost cavalier; and, for this reason, scholars may fear that his essay, despite the fact that it appeared in a newspaper rather than an academic journal, may tend to weaken the plausibility of other, more rigorous African origin studies. However, should there be cognate

Reproduced from *The Times* of London (July 19, 1969, p. 9) by permission.

terms in other African languages for some of the derivations proposed by Dalby, this would make his fascinating suggestions ever so much more convincing.

The reader should probably be urged to keep in mind that even if a number of Dalby's projected etymologies/parallels should ultimately prove to be completely wrong, there is still the possibility that he may be right about some of them. In any case, the reader should try to keep an open mind until such time as definitive studies of more West African languages become available and the life-histories of American slang items like "dig," "honkie," and "jam session" can be reconstructed in more detail.

For more information about the Wolof, see David P. Gamble, The Wolof of Senegambia *(London, 1957) and the various sources listed in Ruth Jones, comp.,* Africa Bibliography Series: West Africa *(London, 1958), pp. 50–52.*

THERE HAS been much speculation about the origin of such well-known Americanisms as OK, guy, jive, hippy, cat (meaning "person"), and dig (meaning "to understand"). Fanciful explanations have sometimes been proposed, like the traditional derivation of OK from a misspelling of "all correct," but generally there has been agreement in regarding these words as indigenous to America. It would seem, however, that these and certain other Americanisms may originally have been Africanisms, taken to the new world by West African slaves.

Although many items of American vocabulary were first used by American Negroes—or black Americans as they are now known—the historical role of black speech in the development of American English appears to have been underestimated. Just as black Americans have often been unjustly regarded as passive agents in the course of American history, so they have been regarded as largely passive agents in the shaping of the American language.

The traditional belief was that slaves lost all trace of their original African languages when they arrived in the new world, and that they were forced to imitate the language of their white captors as best they could. This belief was first challenged by Lorenzo D. Turner, a black American scholar, who drew attention to many African survivals in the "Gullah" language of isolated black communities on the South Carolina coast: Gullah is a form of creolized English taken to the United States by slaves from West Africa, however, rather than a regular dialect of black American English. Only in the past few years have linguists begun to demonstrate that black American English has a complex grammatical structure of its own rather than being a mangled form of white speech, and it is scarcely a coincidence that this structure should frequently be reminiscent of West African languages. This leads one to investigate the degree to which African vocabulary also may have survived in black American English, and hence may have contributed to the American language at large.

MAIN LANGUAGES

Slaves were taken to the Americas from all over West Africa and beyond, and spoke many different languages. Some already had a knowledge of the creolized English which had come into use along the Guinea coast as a trade language. Senegambia, the nearest part of the African coast to North America, was a major source of slaves for the former English colonies, and many of these slaves were therefore conversant with the two main languages of Senegambia: Wolof and Mandingo. When a runaway slave who could speak no English was arrested in Pennsylvania in 1731, for example, his white interrogators had no difficulty in finding another Wolof-speaking slave to act as an interpreter.

The importance of the Wolof in linguistic contact between black people and white stems also from the fact that they are the nearest Negro African people to Europe (as well as to North America), and that they were frequently employed as interpreters and mariners during early European voyages along the African coast. As a result, the Wolof names of several African foodstuffs, including banana and yam, were taken into European languages. It therefore seems reasonable to look for a possible Wolof influence on the development of American English vocabulary, and the initial results of this investigation have been most encouraging. A number of resemblances have already been found between the two languages, and most relate to forms whose origin in American English has not yet been adequately explained.

The verb "dig," as used in American —especially black American—English to mean "to understand" and hence "to appreciate" occurs in such phrases as "d'ya dig black talk?" (do you understand black English?): there is thus a similarity in sound and meaning, to the Wolof verb *dega*, pronounced close to English "digger" and meaning "to under-

stand"—as in *dega nga olof*? (do you understand Wolof?). In the same way the American term "guy," especially as used in informal address is paralleled by Wolof *gay* (pronounced between English gay and guy), used also as a term of address meaning "fellows, guys," although restricted to the plural.

JAZZ ERA TERMS

Several terms popularized during the jazz era also resemble words in Wolof. "Jive" had the original meaning in black American English of "misleading talk," which it retains, and can be compared to the Wolof *jev*, meaning "to talk disparagingly." The American forms hep, hip, and hippy have a basic sense of "aware" or "alive to what is going on" (including heightened awareness from drugs), while in Wolof the verb *hipi* means "to open one's eyes." The American use of cat to mean "person," as in hep-cat or cool-cat, can be likened to the Wolof *kat*, used as an agentive suffix after verbs: *hipi-kat* in Wolof means "a person who has opened his eyes."

The verb "sock," in the sense of "to strike," especially with something, has recently been popularized in the black American phrase "sock it to me" (with an obscene connotation), and is reminiscent of a similar-sounding verb in Wolof meaning "to beat with a pestle." In American slang, the suffix bug (as in jitter-bug) denotes a person with an enthusiastic desire or liking for something; in Wolof a similar sounding form means "to desire, like."

"Honkie" is used by black Americans as a term of abuse for "white man," and—since white men are often described as "red" in African languages—one may compare the term to the Wolof *hong*, meaning "red, pink" (the English word "pink" has also been used by black Americans as a term for a white man). A term of abuse in the reverse direction, namely Sambo, is similar in form to a common Wolof family name, Samb or Samba (existing also in the neighbouring Mandingo languages as *sambu*).

The term "fuzzy" is used in the United States to describe either a range horse or a sure bet at a horse race. In both cases one is reminded of the Wolof *fas* (pronounced between fass and fuss), meaning "horse," and it even becomes possible that the American term fuzz, used to describe a policeman, may have originated in the days when runaway slaves were hunted down on horseback. On a more domestic note, the word "cush" is used in the American South to describe "corn-meal soaked in water," whereas a similar word is used by the Wolof for millet meal soaked in water.

The most interesting American item with a parallel in Wolof is "OK," the origin of which has been much debated but never convincingly explained. In Wolof a common word for "yes" is *waw* (pronounced wow), and this is combined with an emphatic particle *kay* to convey the sense of "all right, certainly." The resulting form *waw kay* thus corresponds closely, in both sound and meaning, to OK, and would have required only a slight change of pronunciation (by analogy with the letters O and K) to have produced the modern American word.*

African usage can also explain the frequent use by Americans of the interjections uh-huh, for "yes," and uh-uh for "no." Similar forms, especially for "yes," occur in scattered parts of the world, but nowhere as frequently and as regularly as in Africa, where not only Wolof but most other African languages make extensive use of "yes" and "no" words of the general *uh-huh/uh-uh* type. The fact that these same items are used far more frequently in American than in British English, and in Afrikaans (South African Dutch) than in Netherlands Dutch, points to an African influence in both cases.

The study of Wolof may also throw light on the term "jam" as used in "jam music" and "jam session," and in the American slang term "jamboree" (now made famous by the Scout movement). "Jam session" and "jam music" refer to the uninhibited playing of jazz musicians for their own entertainment, and "jamboree" had the original meaning of "noisy carousal" or "revel." Recalling that the few opportunities which slaves had for self-entertainment were normally riotous and uninhibited, one is inclined to speculate whether these terms might not go back to the old slave-plantations, and to the Wolof word *jaam*, meaning "slave."

"CODE" FOR SLAVES

In considering the old plantations, one should not forget that attempts were made to prevent newly arrived slaves from speaking African languages, in the fear that they might be used for secret communication. At the same time, the slaves had a legitimate interest in deceiving their white captors, and the examples we have considered indicate that a partial code may have been

---

* For a sample of the scholarly debate about "OK," see Allen Walker Read, "The Folklore of O.K.," *American Speech*, 39 (1964), pp. 5–25.—ED.

established among them by concealing African words, with their original African meanings, behind similar sounding words already existing in English: dig, cat, sock, bug, fuzz(y) and jam may be vestiges of such linguistic subterfuge.

It would of course be rash to suggest that all the American items discussed here can be derived with certainty from Wolof. On the other hand the frequency of these resemblances is unlikely to be the result of chance and points to the contribution of at least one African language to American (and hence also British) vocabulary. There is now need for more detailed research, on both sides of the Atlantic, into the influence of African languages on the development of the English language at large.

There has been contact between English and West African languages for more than 400 years, and it is a sad reflection of old attitudes towards Africans and black Americans that the possible effects of this contact on the English language should have received so little attention. It should not be forgotten that black Americans represented the largest non-British ethnic group in the North American colonies during the formative years of American English, and that the last African-speaking ex-slaves in the United States were still alive at the beginning of this century.

FOLK SPEECH

Of all the areas of American Negro folklore, none has piqued more interest and produced more arguments than folk speech. Despite all the popular interest in spirituals, blues, and animal tales, it is the common everyday folk speech which must take precedence. After all, days and days can go by without reference to a spiritual or Brer Rabbit, but it is impossible to transact the ordinary daily routine business of living without using words.

In casual conversation, one cannot avoid using names, epithets, and slang. And it is precisely these names, epithets, and in-group lingo that perhaps more than any other single element of folklore help to create (or destroy) a sense of group identity. The language of a folk must be understood by anyone who wishes to communicate with members of that folk group. Thus a Negro child is required to learn the folk speech of his peer group or of his elders if he wishes to speak with them. On the other hand, if he wishes to communicate in a schoolroom dominated by middle-class white speech habits, he finds he must use another set of lexical items with another set of linguistic rules. If he does not make the effort to use the white idiom, he runs the risk of being branded by his white teacher as being verbally unskilled or inarticulate. This is unfortunate inasmuch as the mastery of black folk speech requires every bit as much verbal skill, if not more, than the mastery of white folk speech. Nevertheless, the white teacher who knows little or nothing about black folk speech is often quick to criticize his black students for their failure to master their "second" language, that is, idiomatic white speech which is graced with the white label of "*Standard* English."

In this section, it is hoped that the reader may obtain a glimpse of the range and richness of American Negro folk speech. In the following section devoted to "Verbal Art," a sample of some of the special techniques and forms of extended word play should convince even the most adamant sceptic that no black child who can signify or play the dozens can rightly be called lacking in verbal skills.

141

Designations
for Colored Folk

H. L. MENCKEN

    It is likely that in all societies there is a word which means "us" as opposed to "them." Often it is this word which is critical in the process of an individual's gaining a sense of group identity. The history of culture contact around the world reveals that the conquering of one people by another has frequently been accompanied by a renaming process in which the conqueror forces the conquered to call himself by a "foreign" word from the conqueror's vocabulary. All over the earth, peoples are stuck with names for themselves imposed by unthinking colonialist rulers. An obvious example is the American Indian who bears a generic name stemming from a fundamental error made by Columbus who, upon his arrival in the New World, thought he had arrived in India. Even the names of many specific tribes, e.g., the Nez Percé—a French designation intended to describe people with the custom of piercing the nasal septum in order to hold nose ornaments—reflect this colonialist tendency.

    The American Negro is another victim of colonial "namism." Forcibly cut off from his original African tribal identity and from his language which surely included a term for that identity, the individual American Negro had to find a new term for group identity, and he had to find it in a European tongue. One solution was simply to accept the term or terms used by whites, but inasmuch as such terms often carried pejorative connotations, this solution has been far from satisfactory.

    In view of all this, it should come as no surprise to learn that over the years there has been a continuous debate about what American Negroes should call themselves. Inasmuch as there has not been agreement among American Negro leaders, it is no wonder that many whites have been confused. At one point, a member of the U.S. House of Representatives concerned about what term to use in drafting federal legislation wrote directly to Booker T. Washington and asked him what term to use. The reply indicated a personal preference for

Reprinted from *American Speech*, vol. 19 (1944), pp. 161–74, by permission of Columbia University Press.

Afro-American, which would have the advantage of being political rather than racial. Nevertheless, Booker T. Washington reluctantly suggested the term Negro be employed. In his words: "Rightly or wrongly, all classes have called us Negroes. We cannot escape from that name if we would." Less conciliatory leaders and certainly modern militants could not accept the status quo as willingly as Booker T. Washington did. W. E. B. Du Bois in an eloquent response to a letter written by a high school student claimed that the name wasn't what was important but that having pride in one's race was. This point of view was echoed by James W. Ivy, editor of The Crisis *in his review of Richard B. Moore's* The Name "Negro": Its Origin and Evil Use, *when he remarked that the name question was really a futile one. In his words, "To avoid the name 'Negro' is not to void our semi-pariah status . . . . What American Negroes must continue fighting for is not substitution of 'Afroamerican' for 'Negro,' but complete equality in American life. Achieve that and any group name will have dignity."*

The issue is far from dead as both Negroes and whites continue to wrestle with it. Some of the lexical choices are partly determined by age. For example, many members of the older generation of both Negroes and whites are comfortable with the term "colored." Middle-aged people tend generally to use "Negro" while the younger generation is leaning strongly toward "black." Not only is there the age factor, but there is the more crucial matter of geographical area and particular social situation. The term used depends upon who is speaking to whom in the presence of what third parties. It is probably safe to assume that no one term is likely to please everyone.

The following discussion by H. L. Mencken, one of the leading pioneers in the study of American speech provides a useful historical survey. Mencken was famous for his frankness and his vitriol. No doubt some readers will find some of the discussion distasteful. However, the issue continues to be a viable one, and it cannot be swept under the rug.

For a sample of the endless debate, see W. A. Domingo, "What Are We, Negroes or Colored People?" The Messenger, *2 (May–June, 1919), pp. 23–25; J. A. Rogers, "What Are We, Negroes or Americans?"* The Messenger, *8 (1926), pp. 237–38, 255; and Richard B. Moore,* The Name "Negro," Its Origin and Evil Use *(New York, 1960). For the review by Ivy, see* The Crisis, *67 (1960), pp. 680–81. For a rebuttal by Moore pointing out that it is unlikely that any amount of equality could ever make "such vile names" as "nigger," "coon," "shine," etc. appear dignified, see his letter to the Editor,* The Crisis, *68 (1961), pp. 185–86. For Booker T. Washington's letter to Representative T. W. Simms, see "Negro or Colored,"* The Colored American Magazine, *11 (1906), pp. 7–8. For Du Bois's view, see "The Name 'Negro,'"* The Crisis, *35 (1928), pp. 96–97. For more of Mencken, see his* The American Language, *4th ed. (New York, 1936) with the 1945 Supplement I and the 1948 Supplement II. For biographical details, see Mencken's own statements, e.g.,* Happy Days, 1880–1892 *(New York, 1940); Heathen Days, 1890–1936 (New York, 1943); or Newspaper Days, 1899–1906 (New York, 1945), or any of the many books written about him, e.g., Edgar Kemler,* The Irreverent Mr. Mencken *(Boston, 1950); William R. Manchester,* Disturber of the Peace; The Life of H. L. Mencken *(New York, 1951); Charles Angoff,* H. L. Mencken: A Portrait from Memory *(New York, 1956); Marvin Kenneth Singleton,* H. L. Mencken and the American Mercury Adventure *(Durham, 1962); William G. Nolte,* H. L. Mencken,

Literary Critic (*Middletown, 1966*); *and Sara Mayfield*, The Constant Circle:
H. L. Mencken and His Friends (*New York, 1968*). *For bibliography see
Betty Adler, comp.*, H. L. M. The Mencken Bibliography (*Baltimore, 1971*).
Also useful is Betty Adler, comp., A Descriptive List of H. L. Mencken Col-
lections in the U. S. (*Baltimore, 1967*).

WHEN THE *New York Times* announced
in an editorial on March 7, 1930, that it
would capitalize the word *Negro* thereafter, there were loud hosannahs from
the Aframerican intelligentsia, for (with
an exception to be noted) they seemed
to be convinced that lifting the word
out of lower case would also give a leg
up to its bearers. The decision of the
Times was inspired, according to its
own account, by Major Robert Russa
Moton, then principal of Tuskegee
Institute, but he was by no means the
originator of the movement, nor was the
Times the first American newspaper to
yield. The true pioneer seems to have
been Lester Aglar Watson, a colored
journalist hailing from St. Louis, who,
after a varied career on both Negro
and white newspapers, was made minister to Liberia in 1935. "In 1913," he says
of himself in *Who's Who in America*,
"with coöperation of Associated Press,
started movement for capitalization of
N in *Negro*." He does not give the name
of the first newspaper to be fetched, but
by the time the *Times* succumbed there
were already some important ones in
his corral—among them, the New York
World, Herald Tribune and *Telegram*, the
Chicago *Herald-Examiner* (Hearst), the
Christian Science Monitor of Boston,
the Springfield (Mass.) *Republican*, and
the Brooklyn *Eagle*. Moreover, he had
made some converts in the South, even
in the Deep South—for example, the
Montgomery (Ala.) *Advertiser* (then
edited by the late Grover Hall), the
Durham (N.C.) *Sun*, and the Columbus
(Ga.) *Ledger*. Yet more, he had persuaded a number of national magazines,

including the *Atlantic Monthly*, the *Nation*, the *New Republic*, the *American
Mercury*, and *Time*. Finally, he had
rounded up several government agencies
—for example, the Census Bureau, the
Bureau of Education and the whole
Department of Commerce. But the
surrender of the *Times* was hailed as a
crucial victory in the long war, and when
it was followed three years later by that
of the Style Manual of the Government
Printing Office, which sets the style for
the *Congressional Record* and is generally followed by other government
publications, there was a renewal of
the rejoicing.

The one dissentient was George
S. Schuyler, columnist since 1924 for the
Pittsburgh *Courier*, contributor to many
white magazines, author of "Black-No-
More," father of the *Wunderkind*, Phi-
lippa Schuyler, and the best Negro
journalist, and by long odds, ever heard
of. On March 15, 1930, only a week
after the *Times* had come into camp, he
broke out in the *Courier* with the following:

It really doesn't matter a tinker's damn
whether *Negro* is spelled with a small or
large *N*, so far as the Negro's economic,
political and cultural status is concerned.
The gabble, mostly senseless, to the contrary has vastly amused me; for, if anything, it is worse to spell *Negro* with a large
N than with a small one, and if I had my
way I would discontinue it. . . .

The truth is that the American Negro is
an amalgam of Caucasian, Amerindian
and African, there being but 20 per cent
"pure," and those are the only ones entitled to the term *Negro* when used as a descriptive adjective. Geographically, we are

neither Ethiopians or Africans, but Americans. Culturally, we are Anglo-Saxons.

Used as a noun, the term is therefore a designation of a definite social caste, an under-dog, semi-serf class which believes it is dignifying its status by a capitalization of the term by which it is called and recognized. This is the same thing as arguing that an imbecile is somewhat ennobled by spelling the word with a capital *I* or that a convict has his status improved by spelling the word with a capital *C*. Lifting *Negro* from the lower case to the upper typographically does not in the least elevate him socially. As a matter of fact, it fits right in with the program of racial segregation. As *negroes* we are about 3,000,000 strong, as *Negroes* we are 12,000,000 strong; as *negroes* we are a definite physical type, as *Negroes* we are a definite social class. It is significant that Southern newspapers and magazines were more ready and willing to make the change in *Negro* than the Northern publications. The former are ever eager to make the Negro satisfied with his place; the latter based their objections on etymological and grammatical grounds. . . .

The possession of physical characteristics or ancestry different from other people by any citizen should not be constantly emphasized and brought to the attention of newspaper readers, especially in this country. The interests of interracial peace demand the abolition of such references and we ought to fight for that and lose no time trying to get white folks to "dignify" a socio-chromatic caste system established and maintained by them for their own convenience and economic advantage. There is something ridiculous about a so-called *Negro* bellowing against color discrimination and segregation while wearing out his larynx whining for a glorification of his Jim Crow status in society through capitalization of the *N* in *Negro*.

Mr. Schuyler returned to the subject many times afterward. Thus on July 17,

1937:

> Negro clearly belongs with *blonde, brunette, ruddy, mulatto, octoroon* and such descriptive terms, and has no stronger claim on capitalization. . . . Capitalized, it tends to bolster the *status quo*, and thus is at best conservative and at worst reactionary, for it discourages differentiation and strengthens the superstition that "all coons are alike."

And again on March 20, 1943:

> *Negro* is either an adjective meaning black or it is a caste name like *Sudra*. When we eagerly accept it as a group designation, regardless of our skin tint, we are accepting all the "racial" nonsense of Hitler, Bilbo, and the myriads who believe as they do—at least in the day time.

But Mr. Schuyler's iconoclastic position got no support from the general run of American colored folk, nor from their accepted fuglemen and haruspices. Even so generally non-conforming a spokesman of the race as the late Dr. Kelly Miller was moved, in 1937, to argue for *Negro* in *Opportunity*, the organ of the National Urban League:[1]

> A printed list consisting of Englishmen, Germans, Italians, Jews and *negroes* would evidently be a case of unexplained typographical discrimination. If it be said that *Negro* is not derived from a country or geographical division, as other racial designations are, an adequate rejoinder would be that neither is *Jew*.[2]

In the first days of slavery, Dr. Miller said, the slaves were called simply *blacks*, and even after interbreeding lightened their color the term continued in use "in a generic sense." Then came *African*, which "was accepted by the race in the early years, after it first came to self-consciousness, "and still survives

---

[1] "*Negroes* or Colored People?" May, 1937, pp. 142–46.
[2] Here Dr. Miller slipped. The *New English Dictionary* says that *Jew* was "originally a Hebrew of the kingdom of Judah."

in the titles of some of its religious organizations, *e.g.*, the *African* Methodist Episcopal Zion Church. (This, according to the *Dictionary of American English*, was during the first half of the Eighteenth Century.) A bit later *darky* or *darkey* began to be used, and "at first it carried no invidious implication." (The *DAE's* first example is dated 1775.) Then came *Africo-American* (1835 or thereabouts), but it was too clumsy to be adopted.[3] After the Civil War *freedman* was in wide use, but it began to die out before the end of the 70's.[4] In 1880 *Afro-American* was invented by T. Thomas Fortune, editor of the New York *Age*, and it still survives, but only in rather formal usage.[5] "Mr. Fortune," said Dr. Miller, "repudiated the word *Negro* because of the historical degradation and humiliation attached to it." At some undetermined time after 1900 Sir Harry Johnston, the English African explorer and colonial administrator, shortened *Afro-American* to *Aframerican*, but the latter has had but little vogue.[6] After rehearsing, in his article, the history of all these appellations, Dr. Miller turned to *Negro* and *colored*, and proceeded to discuss their respective claims to general adoption. The latter, he concluded, could not qualify, for it was properly applicable to any person not white, including Chinese, Japanese, Indians and Mexicans, and had been so applied in various State laws, and even, at least by inference, in Federal population statistics.[7] Thus his reasoning:

[3] It survives, however, in the name of the *Africo-American Presbyterian*, a weekly published since 1879 by the Negro Presbyterian Church at Charlotte, N. C.

[4] Many other terms, now obsolete, were used in that era, *e.g.*, the abbreviation *f.m.c.* (free man of color). Carl Sandburg says in his *Abraham Lincoln: the War Years* (New York, 1939), vol. II, p. 137; "Demurrings arose to Lincoln's progressions in styling the Negroes, in 1859, *negroes;* in 1860, *colored men;* in 1861, *intelligent contrabands;* in 1862, *free Americans of African descent.*" *Contraband* came into use in 1861, when General Benjamin F. Butler issued a proclamation declaring slaves owned by Confederates contraband of war, but it was forgotten by 1870.

[5] It is the name of a Negro newspaper of wide circulation and influence, published in Baltimore with local editions in other places. The readers of the paper in Baltimore call it the *Afro*, and it so refers to itself. "It is interesting to note," said Dr. Miller, "that the *Africo-American Presbyterian* and the *Afro-American*, which stress their names in heavy type at the head of their papers, rarely use these terms in their news service or editorial columns."

[6] It was preceded, and probably suggested, by *Amerindian*, a name for the American Indian coined by Major J. W. Powell, of the Bureau of American Ethnology, in 1899. *Amerindian* was quickly displaced by *Amerind*, which is still in use. In South Africa a similar quest for a sonorous designation for themselves has been carried on by the natives. "Their latest choice," said J. A. Rogers in *Sex and Race* (New York, 1941). p. 131, "is *Eur-African.*" But this is objected to by the whites, who say that they are the only real *Eur-African*. The term *Afrikander*, which might well designate the blacks, is already monopolized by the whites. In Liberia the descendants of returned American slaves who constitute the ruling caste of the country used to call themselves *Americo-Liberians* to distinguish their group from the general mass of blacks. But I am informed by Mr. Ben Hamilton, Jr., formerly of the Liberian consulate in Los Angeles, that this compound is now out of favor. He says: "Because of the great amount of intermarriage between the descendants of colonists to Liberia from America with aborigines of the Negro republic, and because of a wave of nationalism that is sweeping the country, Liberians consider the term *Americo-Liberian* opprobrious as reflecting upon their [ancestors'] condition of servitude in the States. Hence they prefer to be called *civilized* or *Monrovian Liberians* to distinguish them from the natives of the hinterland, who are generally called by their tribal names." Monrovia is the capital of Liberia, and the home of virtually all its *noblesse*.

[7] Mexicans were not formally classified as white until the 1940 Census. Before that they were lumped with "other races." Very few of them, of course, are actually white, even in part. The change was made in furtherance of the Good Neighbor policy.

Try, if you will, to express the idea involved in *Negro* art, *Negro* music, *Negro* poetry, *Negro* genius, the *Journal of Negro History*, the *Journal of Negro Education* and the *Negro Handbook* in terms of the word *colored* and see what a lamentable weakness would result from this substitution. . . . The term *Negro* is far superior to the term *colored* in grammatical inflection, for it may be used either as a noun or as an adjective, whereas *colored* has no nominal equivalent. Unlike the words *black* and *white*, it does not pluralize into a noun. . . . The word *people*, *race* or *persons* must be added to give collective or plural effect. . . . This handicap is seen in the possessive case. . . . Again, the word *Negro* may be easily inflected into *Negroid* by adding the Greek ending *-oid*, which implies likeness or resemblance to. This term may be used either as a noun or an adjective, and forms an apt designation of the derivatives of African blood now scattered through the world.

Dr. Miller admitted that "such terms as *colored lady*, *colored gentleman* and *colored society*" sounded "more polite than the corresponding Negro equivalents," but argued that the preference for them probably grew out of "that to which the ear is accustomed." He went on:

Many of the off-colored group object to the term *Negro* because it serves as a reminder of the humiliation and degradation through which the race has passed. The fact that *Negro* is now used to describe the group does not indicate any lesser degree of appreciation or esteem. . . . Any race or group, in the long run, will derive its reputation from its character and worth, and not from the appellation by which it is known. . . . Sensitiveness about a name is always a sign of the inferiority complex.

Dr. Miller, going further than most other advocates of *Negro*, was also willing to accept *Negress*, which is intolerably offensive to most high-toned colored folk. Here the iconoclastic Schuyler agreed with him, saying,

If we accept the term *Negro* there is no sound reason for spurning *Negress*, and yet its use is discouraged and condemned without, of course, any sensible argument being advanced for this position. I understand Jews are similarly unreasonable about the term *Jewess*.[8]

But despite this agreement of two high Negro authorities, the *Atlantic Monthly* got into hot water when, in October, 1935, it used *Negress* in an editorial reference to a colored contributor, Miss Juanita Harrison, author of a serial entitled "My Great, Wide, Beautiful World." Moreover, it added to its offense by speaking of the lady by her given name alone, without the *Miss*.[9] Protests came in promptly, and one of them, from Isadore Cecilia Williams, of Washington, was printed in the issue for December, along with an editorial explanation. I take the following from Miss (or Mrs. ?) Williams's letter:

Negress . . . is obnoxious to Negroes chiefly because of the sordid, loose, and often degrading connotations it has been forced to carry. From the standpoint of etymology I believe I am right in saying that the use of *ess* as a suffix to designate the women of any race is practically obsolete. Out of courtesy to a race and a sex I suggest that you hereafter discard the offensive term *Negress*.

It was petty, to say the least, to refer to Miss Harrison as *Juanita* in the editorial

---

[8] "Views and Reviews," Pittsburgh *Courier*, July 17, 1937.
[9] Some of the Negro papers carry their liking for this honorific so far that they apply it to lady criminals. I take the following, for example, from the New York *Amsterdam News*, Jan. 15, 1944, p. 8-B: "On the eve of her trial for fatally bludgeoning another woman to death [*sic*] last April, Beatrice Watson, 23, avoided a possible life term in prison last week by pleading guilty to second degree manslaughter. As a result Miss Watson will be faced with a penalty of not more than 15 years."

preface to her letters. Perhaps it is mere class distinction, but class distinction should be beneath the dignity of your pages. A witness in a recent kidnapping case, though only a nursemaid, was referred to as *Miss* Betty Gow. Certainly Miss Harrison, whose honesty you commend and whose native intelligence merited a place in your pages, deserves at least common courtesy at your hands.

To this the editor of the *Atlantic* replied somewhat lamely that he "really did not know that the word *Negress* carried a derogatory connotation." "I suppose," he went on, "that the feeling must come from the analogy of the suffix *-ess* being used throughout the animal kingdom." In further confession and avoidance he cited the parallel terms, *Jewess* and *Quakeress*, conveniently overlooking the fact (maybe also unknown to him) that the former is vastly disliked by Jews. As to the use of her simple given-name in referring to Miss Harrison he said:

In the correspondence regarding her which came from a former employer she was continually referred to as *Juanita*, and it was natural to transfer this designation to the *Atlantic*. We certainly meant no disrespect, for as you surmise, we thought her an honest, interesting and able character.

Other Negro publicists have proposed various substitutes for any designation pointing directly to color, among them *race* and *group*. According to Dr. Miller, *racemen* was suggested in 1936 or thereabout by Robert L. Abbot, editor of the Chicago *Defender*. Dr. Miller himself rejected it as equally applicable to a white man or an Indian

and predicted that it would "fall under the weight of its own ineptness." It has, however, survived more or less, and *group* is really flourishing. Many of the Negro newspapers use *our group*, *group man*, *group leader*, etc. Some of them also use such terms as *brown-skinned* and *sepia* to get away from the forthright but usually inaccurate *black*, and in 1944 there was a *Sepia* Miss America contest operated by a committee in Boston.[10]

At present the surviving objection to *Negro*, now capitalized by nearly all American publications, takes two forms. First, there is a campaign against using it whenever a person of color comes into the news, on the ground that calling attention to his race is gratuitous, and usually damaging to the other members of it. Second, there is resentment of the unhappy fact that the word is frequently mispronounced, and tends to slide into the hated *nigger*. In the South it is commonly heard as *nigrah*,[11] and not only from white lips. Indeed, *nigrah* is also used by Northern Negroes, including some of the most eminent, as witness the following protest from a reader of the Pittsburgh *Courier*.

A great many professional Negro orators, prominent speakers, leaders and so on are speaking on the radio all over the country—on forums, "March of Time" programs, etc. Nearly all make the one big noticeable error of pronouncing *Negro* as if it were spelled *nigro* or *nigraph*. ... It is all the more noticeable when white people are on the same program. They pronounce *Negro* correctly, with the emphasis on *ne* and not *nig*.[12]

[10] "Miss America Contest Plans Given to Public," by Paul Davis, New York *Amsterdam News*, March 18, 1944, p. 6-A.

[11] In *The Field, the Dungeon and the Escape*, by Albert D. Richardson (Hartford, Conn., 1865), p. 37, a Southern planter was made to use *nig-roe*. I have heard *niggero*, but only in sportive use.

[12] This protest appeared May 15, 1943, in "Yes! We All Talk," a philological column conducted by Marcus H. Boulware. Mr. Boulware, in a note appended to the letter, said that "*ne* in *Negro* should rime with *see*, and *gro* with *grow*."

Worse, even the abhorred *nigger* is in wide use among the colored people themselves, especially on the lower levels. Said Lucius Harper, managing editor of the Chicago *Defender*, in 1939:

It is a common expression among the ordinary Negroes and is used frequently in conversation between them. It carries no odium or sting when used by themselves, but they object keenly to whites using it because it conveys the spirit of hate, discrimination and prejudice.[13]

Nigger is so bitterly resented by the more elegant members of the race that they object to it even in quotations, and not a few of their papers spell it *n——r* when necessity forces them to use it.[14] On March 4, 1936, Garnet C. Wilkinson, first assistant superintendent of schools of Washington, in charge of the Negro public schools of the District of Columbia, actually recommended to Superintendent F. W. Ballou that *Opportunity*, for years a recognized leader among Negro magazines, be barred from the schools of the District on the ground that it used "the opprobrious term *N——* in its publications on Negro life." When news of this recommendation reached Elmer A. Carter, the editor, he naturally protested, and under date of March 11 received the following from Dr. Wilkinson:

It is contrary to a long established administrative policy, initiated and fostered by the school teachers and officers of Divisions 10–13 of the public schools of the District,[15] to recommend to the Board of Education the adoption of any textbook, basic or supplementary, magazine, or periodical known to make use of the term *N——* in its publication.

Textbooks published by white authors and making use of such material have been refused for adoption in our public schools. Textbooks have been withdrawn from the approved list for the same reason. Obviously, a textbook, magazine, or periodical published by a Negro should be subject to the same administrative policy. There can be no double standard of evaluating such school materials—one standard for white authors, another standard for Negro authors.

You are now advised that this office would be willing to recommend the placing of *Opportunity* on the approved list of magazines and periodicals for the public schools of the District if you, as editor, will give us the assurance that *Opportunity* will discontinue the policy of using any opprobrious term or terms in referring to the Negro.

Mr. Carter replied to this curious communication under date of March 17, as follows:

Even a casual examination of the magazine will reveal that your recommendation has been based on a total misconception of the use of the term *nigger* when it appears in *Opportunity*. That use is limited to quotations from other writers or is the reproduction in poem or story of the speech and conversation of characters who commonly use this term, and in both cases the word or the line in which it occurs is always set off by quotation marks, italics, or other literary and printing insignia.

It should not be necessary for me to direct your attention to the fact that there is a vast and obvious difference in the use of a word or phrase in quotation and its use

---

[13] Quoted in "Journalistic Headache," by R. E. Wolseley, *Ken*, March 9, 1939.
[14] For example, I find the following on p. 1 of the Pittsburgh *Courier*, Nov. 1, 1941, in a dispatch from Due West, S.C., reporting the beating of a colored pastor, the Rev. B. J. Glover, Jr., "because law officers of this prejudice-ridden town thought he was too uppity for a *N——r*." Here, it will be noted the offending word was given a capital *N*. In the same dispatch occurred the following: "Another officer said, Let's teach that *D . . . N . . . . .* a lesson, and struck Rev. Glover."
[15] These divisions are made up of Negro elementary and high schools.

as a definitive term in the editorial contents of a publication, nor to affirm that *Opportunity* never employs any epithet of opprobrium in its columns except under the limitations mentioned above.

If impartially applied, the ruling of the Board of Education will achieve astonishing if not fantastic results. For by the same standards the *Nation*, the *New Republic*, *Harper's*, *Time*, the *Literary Digest*, the *Forum*, in fact, almost every magazine which on occasion publishes stories or articles involving the Negro, must likewise be removed from the list of magazines approved for the children in the Negro schools of Washington. By the same token the most authoritative books on the Negroes' status in America must of necessity fail of approval as suitable reading matter for Negro children in the District of Columbia. For this incredible decision would refuse approval to "The Souls of Black Folk" and "Black Reconstruction," by DuBois; "The Black Worker," by Harris; "Shadow of the Plantation," by Johnston; the autobiography of Frederick Douglass; "The Life and Works of Booker T. Washington," the novels of Walter White, Chesnutt and Dunbar, and the poetry of Countee Cullen, Sterling Brown, Langston Hughes, to mention only a few.[16]

Nothing came of this effort to purge *Opportunity* of *nigger*. I am told by Lester B. Granger, executive secretary of the National Urban League, that it is still used whenever required by "a faithful description of real life situations," though "where it adds nothing to the context it is sometimes eliminated." The same failure marked an effort to work up a boycott against Noxzema, a lotion popular among Negroes as among whites, because the credit manager of the manufacturing company had used the phrase *nigger in the woodpile* in a dunning circular to slow-paying druggists. This boycott was launched by an organization calling itself the National Commission on Negro Work, affiliated with the International Workers Order, and for a while a committee collected signatures to a paper demanding that the company "apologize publicly," discharge the offending credit manager, and "open job opportunities for Negroes in your plant." Every signer was invited to make a contribution to "a collection to defray costs of promotion only" and so deliver "a sock at Hitlerism," but the company refused to be intimidated, and nothing came of the boycott. Nor did any greater success attend an attack by the same National Commission on the A. & P. stores for selling a *Niggerhead* stovepolish. But a year before this the New York *Amsterdam News* apparently had better luck with a crusade against the American Tobacco Company for offering a *Niggerhead* smoking-tobacco, for on March 20, 1943 the *Nation* announced that the brand would be withdrawn. *Nigger in the woodpile* is traced by the *DAE* to 1861, and is defined by it as "a concealed or inconspicuous but highly important fact, factor or catch in an account, proposal, etc." Of the six examples that it gives, two are from the *Congressional Record*. *Niggerhead*, in the more refined form of *negrohead*, is traced to 1833, and defined as "a low grade of strong, dark-colored tobacco." It was used by Huckleberry Finn in contradistinction to store-tobacco. *Niggerhead*, in the sense of a piece of extraordinarily hard rock, goes back to 1847, and has been used in a report of the Smithsonian; it also appears in "Chicago Poems" by Carl Sandburg, 1916.

[16] This correspondence was published in full in *Opportunity*, April, 1936, pp. 126–27.

Negro is not, of course, an Americanism. It is simply the Spanish and Portuguese word for "black," and was borrowed by the English during the sixteenth century. By 1587 a Northern English form, *neger*, had appeared, and it was from this that both the Irish *naygur* and the English-American *nigger* were derived. The *New English Dictionary's* first example of *nigger* comes from a poem by Robert Burns, published in 1786. In the United States, in the spelling of *niger*, the *Dictionary of American English* traces it to Samuel Sewell's diary, 1700. But after that the *DAE* offers no example until the nineteenth century. *Nigger-boy* is traced to 1825, *nigger-wench* to 1837, *nigger-regiment* to 1863, *nigger-talk* to 1866 (*nigger* alone, meaning the manner of speech of Negroes, goes back to 1825), *niggerish* to 1825, *nigger-killer* to 1856, *nigger-luck* (meaning good luck) to 1851, and *nigger-heaven* (the top gallery in a theatre) to 1878. *Nigger-stealer*, once a term of opprobrium comparable to the *isolationist* of today, is not listed, and neither are *nigger-lover*, *nigger-job*, *nigger-mammy* and *nigger-gal*. There are many other derivatives. I have mentioned *niggerhead* in the sense of a lump of hard rock, and in that of coarse chewing and smoking tobacco. It is also used to designate the common black-eyed Susan, a variety of greenbrier, and one of cactus. After the Civil War it was used for a person in favor of full political equality for Negroes. There are a *nigger-duck*, a *nigger-goose*, a *nigger-weed*, and

several kinds of *nigger-fish*. *To nigger off* means to divide a log into convenient lengths by burning through it, to *nigger out* means to exhaust the soil by working it without fertilizer, and *to nigger it* means to live meagrely. A *nigger* is a device used in sawmills to turn a heavy log, and also a defect in an electrical conductor, causing a short circuit. *Niggertoe* is a dialect name, in rural New York, Ohio and Pennsylvania, for a Brazil nut, and was once used to designate a variety of potato. *To work like a nigger* is traced by the *DAE* to 1836, and *to let off a little nigger* to 1828. The use of *niggerhead* to signify a hard stone was no doubt suggested by the old American belief that the skull of the Negro is extraordinarily thick, and hence able to stand hard blows without cracking. That superstition is accompanied by one to the effect that the shins of the colored folk are extremely tender. The notion that they have an inordinate fondness for watermelon belongs to the same category. This last is so far resented by high-toned Negroes that they commonly avoid *Cirtullus vulgaris* in their diet as diligently as the more elegant sort of German-Americans used to avoid Limburger cheese.[17]

Before 1890, according to Dr. Miller, the Census Bureau "sought to sub-divide the Negro group into *blacks*, *mulattoes*, *quadroons* and *octoroons*," but found it "impossible to make such sharp discriminations, since these divisions ran imperceptibly into one another." It was upon the advice of Booker T. Washing-

[17] From "Journalistic Headache," by R. E. Wolseley, already cited, I take the following: "The sports editor of a small Midwestern daily learned this unforgettably one Fall when he jokingly suggested that a good way to stop Ozzie Simmons, the great Negro football star from Iowa, was to roll a number of big juicy watermelons out on the field. . . . Telephone calls, letters and personal visits from the Negroes of the city made him realize he had hurt some feelings. A formal protest—a petition—from the local Inter-Racial Council brought the matter to the attention of the newspaper's managing editor."

ton that it began calling all colored persons of African blood *Negroes*. *Mulatto, quadroon* and *octoroon* have now almost disappeared from American speech. Of them, only *octoroon* seems be an Americanism. *Mulatto*, which comes from the Spanish and Portuguese *mulato*, signifying a young mule, and hence a half breed, is traced by the *NED* in English use to 1595. Originally, the word meant the immediate offspring of a Negro and a white person, but by the beginning of the eighteenth century it was being applied to anyone of mixed white and Negro blood. In the early chronicles and travel-books it was spelled in a dozen different ways, some of them quite fantastic, *e.g.*, *malatta, melatto, muletto* and *mulattoe*. *Quadroon* is a loan from the *quateron* of the Louisiana French, who borrowed it in turn from the Spanish *cuarterón*. The *NED*'s first example of *quarteron* is dated 1707; Thomas Jefferson used it in that form in 1793. In the form of *quatroon* it goes back to 1748 in English usage and to 1808 in American, and in the form of *quadroon* to 1796 and 1832 respectively. *Octoroon* is apparently more recent. There is no recorded trace of it before 1861, when Dion Boucicault used it in the title of a play. *Griffe*, another loan from the French of Louisiana, is now obsolete. It signified, according to Miss Grace E. King, quoted by the *DAE*,[18] a mixed breed one degree lighter than an *octoroon*, the series being *mulatto, quadroon, octoroon, griffe*.

The irreverent Schuyler, who does not hesitate to refer to the members of his race, in his column in the Pittsburgh *Courier*, as *Senegambians, tarbrushed folk* and so on, frequently discusses the opprobrious names that have been applied to them, *e.g.*, *darkey, coon, shine, smoke, woolly-head, dinge* and *boogie*, In 1936, when the Baltimore *Afro-American* started a holy war against "My Old Kentucky Home" because *darkey* occurs in it, and the National Association for the Advancement of Colored People denounced the Rev. Charles E. Coughlin for using it in a radio speech, he said:

Will some one who has the gift of logic and intelligence tell me what is the difference between *darkey* and *Negro?*... There can be no more real objection to *darkey* than there can be to *blondie*. It is a far more acceptable term than *wop* or *kike*. As my friend J. A. Rogers[19] once profoundly remarked, the difference between *Negro* and *nigger* is the difference between *sir* and *sah*. Granted that the overwhelming majority of Negroes are opposed to the use of these terms, I can see no point in constantly making a wailing protest against their use.

Coon, though it is now one of the the most familiar designations for a Negro, apparently did not come into general use in that sense until the 80's; Thornton's first example is dated 1891 and the *DAE*'s 1887.[20] For many years before that time the term had been used in the sense of a loutish white man, and in Henry Clay's day it had designated a member of the Whig party. It came originally, of course, from the

18 *New Orleans: The Place and the People* (New York, 1895), p. 333.
19 A Negro historian, already mentioned. He has published a number of valuable books on the history of his people, and accumulated an enormous store of illustrative material.
20 Walter D. Edmonds says in *American Notes and Queries*, May, 1941, p. 23, that "Zip Coon, the blackface song, was being sung in 1834," but it apparently did not lead to the application of *coon* to Negroes.

name of the animal, *Procyon lotor*, which seems to have been borrowed from the Algonquian early in the seventeenth century, and was shortened from *raccoon* to *coon* before 1750. "How the Negro Got the Name of Coon" is the title of one of the stories in a collection of Maryland folk-lore published by Mrs. Walter R. Bullock, Jr., in 1898,[21] but all it shows is that the Negro who is the chief figure called himself a *coon*, and that the name was afterward applied to others. Why he did so is not explained, nor when. The popularity of the term seems to have got a lift from the vast success of Ernest Hogan's song, "All Coons Look Alike to Me," in 1896. Hogan, himself a colored man, used it without opprobrious intent, and was amazed and crushed by the resentment it aroused among his people. Says Edward B. Marks in *They All Sang*:[22]

The refrain became a fighting phrase all over New York. Whistled by a white man, it was construed as a personal insult. Rosamond Johnson[23] relates that he once saw two men thrown off a ferry-boat in a row over the tune. Hogan became an object of censure among all the Civil Service intelligentsia, and died haunted by the awful crime he had unwittingly committed against his race.

"All Coons Look Alike to Me" was followed in 1899 by "Every Race Has a Flag But the Coon," by Heelan and Helf, two white men, and in 1900 by "Coon, Coon, Coon," by two others, Jefferson and Friedman, and from that time forward *coon* was firmly established in the American vocabulary.[24] The history of the other more or less opprobrious synonyms for *Negro* is mainly obscure. The *DAE* does not list *boogie* and its congeners, but reports that *booger* is an Americanism, traced to 1866, for a bogy. In 1891 a writer in *Harper's Magazine*,[25] quoted by the *DAE*, defined *boogahhole* as "the hiding place of cats and of children fleeing from justice" and of *boogars* or *boogahs*, "whatever these mysterious beings may be." It is possible that the suggestion of darkness developed *boogie* from *booger* or *boogah*. The latter form, however, hints at a Southern variant of *bogy* or *bogey*, which has been traced in England by the *NED*, in the sense of the devil, to 1836, in the sense of a goblin to 1857, and in that of a bugbear to 1865. In Baltimore, in my childhood, *boogieman* was one of the names of the devil.

Buffalo as a designation for a Negro is not listed by the *DAE*, but it gives the word as used to designate a North

---

[21] *Journal of American Folk-Lore*, Jan–March, 1898, 13, 14.

[22] New York, 1935, p. 91.

[23] The colored composer of "Under the Bamboo Tree," "Oh, Didn't He Ramble," "Lazy Moon," and other songs of the 90's, and also of the Negro anthem, "Lift Every Voice and Sing." The words of some of his songs were written by his brother, James Weldon Johnson (1871–1933), the best poet the race has yet produced.

[24] In South Africa the term is sometimes used by the newspapers to designate a black native, apparently without derogatory intent. The following is from "Stilt-Walker of Serowe," by Norman Howell, *Cape Times* (Cape Town), Aug. 22, 1936: "Why is stilt-walking a common thing among the *coons* of the Cape?" In the Virgin Islands, formerly under the Danish flag, the blacks are called *goons* or *goonies*. In "Lazy Islands Come to Life," Baltimore *Sunday Sun*, March 22, 1942, Lawrence H. Baker suggested that the *g* may be "a gutteralizing of the *c* in *coon*, arising out of the Danes' attempts to pronounce the latter word."

[25] Oct., 1891, p. 825.

Carolina Unionist during the Civil War; it has also been applied to the people of seaboard North Carolina in general. From the early eighteenth century down to 1880 or thereabout *Cuffy* was a generic name for a Negro, comparable to *Pat* for an Irishman. George Philip Krapp says in *The English Language in America*[26] that "it is said to be derived from Dutch *Koffi*, in Guiana a common name for Negroes and by custom applied to anyone born on Friday." The *DAE* calls it "of African origin" and traces it to 1713. It had a rival in *Sambo*, which apparently arose, not in the United States, but in England. The *DAE* traces it to 1748 there and to 1806 here. In my boyhood *Cuffy* had disappeared and *Sambo* was being supplanted by *Rastus*.[27] During the same era *Liza* or *Lize* was the common name for a colored girl. The *DAE* omits *dinge* and lists *dinkey* only in the adjectival sense of small, trifling. *Dinkey*, in the Baltimore of my nonage, meant a colored child. Webster's *New International*, 1934, lists *dinge*, but omits *dinkey* in the sense here considered. *Kink* shows an obvious allusion to the Negro's hair; the *DAE* says that *kinky*, as applied to it, is an Americanism, and traces it to 1844. When, in 1936, Cab Calloway, the Negro musician, used *kinky-head* in a broadcast, he was violently belabored by the radio critic of one of the Negro weeklies.[28] *Woolly-head* is first found by the *DAE* in Cooper's *The Prairie* in 1827; it was also used by Harriet Beecher Stowe in *Dred: a Tale of the Great Dismal Swamp* in

1856. During the Civil War era the term was applied, like *buffalo*, to Unionists.

Moke is traced by the *DAE* to 1856, but the word was used in England before this in the sense of a donkey. An amateur lexicographer calling himself Socrates Hyacinth, writing in 1869,[29] sought to derive it "from Icelandic *möckvi*, darkness," and called it "a word chiefly in use among the Regulars stationed in Texas and in the Territories." He added that it also had "Cymric affinities, and was probably brought into currency by Welsh recruits who have occasionally drifted into the Army from New York City." This suggestion of a possible Welsh origin was supported by an anonymous writer in the London *Daily Mirror* on November 28, 1938, who said that the etymology "Which receives the greatest expert support derives *moke* from the Welsh gipsy *moxio* or *moxia*, a donkey." "*Moxio*," he continued, "existed some fifty years before the first recorded instance, in 1848, of *moke*. Moreover, about 1839 somebody of the name of Brandon records *moak* as a cant word of gipsy origin, and, at that time, mainly gipsy use." The *NED* calls *moke* "of unknown origin," and Webster's *New International* marks it "origin uncertain." Ernest Weekley, in his *Etymological Dictionary of Modern English*,[30] suggests that it is "perhaps from some proper name (?*Moggy*) applied to the ass," and says that *Mocke*, *Mok*, *Mog* and *Mug* "all occur as personal names in the thirteenth century and survive in the surnames *Mokes*

[26] New York, 1925, vol. I, p. 256.
[27] The once very popular song, "Rastus on Parade," by Kerry Mills, was published in 1896.
[28] The episode is recorded by Schuyler in the Pittsburgh *Courier*, Nov. 7, 1936.
[29] "South-Western Slang," *Overland Monthly*, Aug. His article is reprinted in full in *The Beginnings of American English*, by M. M. Mathews (Chicago, 1931), pp. 151–63.
[30] New York, 1921, p. 942.

and *Moxon.*" *Moke* was thrown into competition with *coon* in 1899 by the success of "Smoky Mokes," a popular song by Holzmann and Lind, but is now heard only seldom. *Pickaninny*, in the sense of a Negro child, is not an Americanism. It was in use in England so long ago as 1657, whereas the *DAE*'s first American example is dated 1800. The English prefer the spelling *piccaninny;* the word, in the past, was variously spelled *piccanini, pickoninnie, pick'ny, piccanin* and *picannin*. It appears to be derived from the Cuban Spanish *piquinini*, meaning a small child, and it was taken into English in the British West Indies. It is used in South Africa precisely as we use it, but is commonly spelled *piccanin*. In Australia it designates a child of the aborigines, and has there produced a derivative, *piccaninny-daylight*, signifying dawn.[31] In the Baltimore of my youth *pickaninny* was not used invidiously, but rather affectionately. So, indeed, was *tar-pot*, also signifying a Negro child.

The *DAE* does not list such vulgar synonyms for *Negro* as *ape, eight-ball, jazzbo, jigabo* (with the variants, *jibagoo, jig, zigabo, zigaboo, zig*), *jit, seal, shine, skunk, smoke, snowball, spade, squasho* and *Zulu. Crow* is traced to 1823, when it was used by Cooper in *The Pioneers*, the first of the Leatherstocking tales. Whether it suggested *Jim Crow* or was itself suggested by *Jim Crow* I do not know. The *DAE*'s first example of *Jim Crow* is dated 1838, but that example includes the statement that "'Zip Coon' and 'Jim Crow' are

hymns of great antiquity." The *DAE* says, however, that Thomas D. Rice's song and dance, "Jim Crow," was written in 1832.[32] The verb phrase, *to jump Jim Crow*, appeared a year later. By 1838 *Jim Crow* had become an adjective and it was so used by Harriet Beecher Stowe in *Uncle Tom's Cabin*, 1852; of late it has also become a verb. The *DAE*'s first example of *Jim Crow car* is dated 1861; of *Jim Crow school*, 1903; of *Jim Crow bill*, 1904; of *Jim Crow law*, 1904, and of *Jim Crow regulations*, 1910. On April 10, 1943, the *Nation* used *Jap Crow* in the title of an article on the internment of the Japanese of the Pacific Coast, but this Winchellism did not catch on. *Eight-ball*, without doubt, is derived from the game of pool, which is played with fifteen numbered and vari-colored balls, No. 8 being black. The *DAE* lists *blueskin* as an early synonym for Negro. It occurs, in Cooper's *The Spy*, 1821, but had become obsolete before the Civil War. In Baltimore, in the 80's of the last century, the German-speaking householders, when they had occasion to speak of Negro servants in their presence, called them *die blaue*. In the 70's *die schwarze* had been used, but it was believed that the Negroes had fathomed it. In the Bronx, so I am informed by a correspondent, the Jewish housekeepers use *die gelbe*, with *ein gelber* in the singular. Without doubt *gelbe* has failed of its purpose as miserably as *blaue*, for the colored folk always penetrate the stratagems of the Caucasian, and chuckle over them in a sad but amiable manner.

[31] *A Popular Dictionary of Australian Slang*, by Sidney J. Baker (second ed., Melbourne, 1943), p. 58. See also *Australian English*, by Edward E. Morris (London, 1898), p. 350.

[32] Rice (1808–1860) was a comedian, playwright and song-writer, and "Jim Crow" was only one of his songs that became popular. He is not to be confused with Dan Rice (1822–1900), an acrobat, circus clown and temperance orator.

Names of American
Negro Slaves

NEWBELL NILES PUCKETT

The generic name of a people is very important, but to an individual, his personal name may be even more important. It is probably universally the case that the bestowing of a name upon an individual has ritual or symbolic implications. Whether a person is named for an ancestor or for an event or for the day on which he was born, the name selection process is almost certainly in accordance with a conscious or unconscious cultural pattern.

The following detailed essay by Professor Puckett attempts to survey the naming patterns evident from the names of slaves. Although the emphasis is upon nineteenth-century data, there are no doubt some elements of the pattern which are applicable to current American Negro naming practices.

For other studies of American Negro names, see Naomi C. Chappell, "Negro Names," American Speech, *4 (1929), pp. 272–75; Urban T. Holmes,* "A Study in Negro Onomastics," American Speech, *5 (1930), pp. 463–67; Arthur Palmer Hudson, "Some Curious Negro Names,"* Southern Folklore Quarterly, *2 (1938), pp. 179–93; Howard F. Barker, "The Family Names of American Negroes,"* American Speech, *14 (1939), pp. 163–75; Ruby Terrill Lomax, "Negro Nicknames,"* Publications of the Texas Folklore Society, *18 (1943), pp. 163–71; and Hennig Cohen, "Slave Names in Colonial South Carolina,"* American Speech, *28 (1952), pp. 102–7. For discussions of African origin of American Negro names, see Melville J. Herskovits,* The Myth of the Negro Past *(Boston, 1958), pp. 190–94, and especially Lorenzo Dow Turner,* Africanisms in the Gullah Dialect *(Chicago, 1949).*

From *Studies in the Science of Society*, ed. George Peter Murdock, pp. 471–94. Copyright © 1937 by Yale University Press. Reprinted by permission of the Yale University Press.

HUMAN SOCIETY not only creates the necessity for personal names, but it establishes group patterns of nomenclature through which this necessity is met. Nominal folkways, like all others, are subject to societal variation, and the individual is thereby afforded at least some opportunity for personal distinction. In the last analysis, however, names are group products. Taking on a folk flavor in a fashion similar to language, they usually label the person as a member of a specific society and a participant in a particular culture.[1] Individual and group interests are not always in harmony,[2] but in cases of conflict group control is ordinarily dominant. The individual seeking social recognition through the use of an "outlandish" name is apt to encounter only ridicule, and the immigrant to this country rapidly warps his traditional name into an Americanized form less indicative of membership in an alien culture group.[3] Such names as André or Madeleine suggest membership in one social group; Giovanni or Vicenzina, in another; Lars or Sigrid, in still another. But what of such names as Bituminous, Snowrilla, Vanilla, Precious Pullins, Jeremiah Chronicles, or Magnolia Zenobia Pope? Some might be tempted to say immediately: "These are typical of the American Negro."

But one should not be too hasty in expressing such an opinion. Group patterns do not mushroom into being overnight. Are such names found among other American groups? How common are they in colored nomenclature? When did they first come to be used by the Negro? What role do they play in the adjustment of the colored group to American culture? In view of the fact that the Negro, unlike the average foreigner, is labeled socially by color more prominently than by name or by speech, and that his system of nomenclature has had to adjust to such varying social situations as the movement from Africa to America, from slavery to freedom, and from illiteracy to relative literacy, the Negro would seem to afford excellent material for the study of a larger topic, the social role of names in general. The present article, dealing with names of American slaves, is a first step towards this broader subject.

Since no adequate list of slave names was available, our first problem was one of collection. The names of approximately 7,000 slaves were tabulated from Mississippi probate records, will books, and deed registers in Monroe, Lowndes, and Hinds counties, and from plantation records, old church minute books, the files of the Mississippi State Department of Archives and History, and the files of the Vicksburg *Republican* and *Eagle*. Of this list, covering the period from 1803 to 1865, approximately 5,600 names came from Lowndes County. A survey

[1] Concerning the significance of the name in primitive society, see Miller, N., *The Child in Primitive Society* (New York, 1928), pp. 70–88; idem, "Some Aspects of the Name in Culture-History," *American Journal of Sociology*, XXXII (1927), pp. 585–600; Sumner, W. G., and Keller, A. G., *The Science of Society* (4 vols., New Haven, 1927), II, pp. 810–14; IV, index, *s.v.* "names"; Ploss, H., *Das Kind in Brauch und Sitte der Völker* (2 vols., Leipzig, 1911), chaps. XXIII-XXIV.

[2] See Keller, A. G., *Social Evolution* (2d ed., New York, 1931), pp. 73–76, 265 ff.

[3] For examples of the Americanization of foreign names, see Mencken, H. L., *The American Language* (4th ed., New York, 1936), pp. 505 ff.; Reuter, E. B., and Hart, C. W., *An Introduction to Sociology* (New York, 1933), pp. 359–64.

of available published sources[4] brought
the total number of slave names to
approximately 12,000, distributed geographically as follows: Alabama 350,
Georgia 644, Kentucky 489, Louisiana
571, Massachusetts 120, Mississippi
7,258, North Carolina 806, South Carolina 507, Tennessee 272, Virginia 640,
state unknown 61, and all others 229.
The list, though admittedly inadequate
and probably more typical of Mississippi
than of the country at large, is still a
considerable improvement over no list
at all.

This collection includes only 65
names of slaves prior to 1700—36 from
Virginia, 27 from New York, and 2
from Maryland. In the hands of the
earlier slave traders slaves seem to have
been simply merchandise *en masse*,
not distinguished by individual names
until they had entered into the occupational life of their subsequent owners.
Thus a slave ship's journal (1675) might
mention that "a neaggerman dep'ted
this life whoe died suddenly,"[5] or a New
England slave notice might announce
"a very likely negro man" for sale. A
name gives individuality and character
even to animals.[6] The slave, until his
purchase, had neither. A dog in a pet
shop is just a dog, but when we have
purchased him and taken him into our
own home and named him, he is set

apart so far as we are concerned from
the rest of the canine world.

In the group of Negro slaves
originally brought into Virginia in 1619
there seem to have been three Anthony's,
two John's, and an Angelo, Isabella,
William, Frances, Edward, and Margaret. Angelo is a very uncommon name
in England, and the rest may represent
Anglicizations of original Spanish
names.[7] Slave women Couchaxello and
Palassa are mentioned in a Virginia
inventory of 1644, possibly indicating
antecedent Spanish baptism, while two
children born in Virginia received the
English names Mary and Elizabeth.
Bastiaen, Fernando, Figa, Francisco,
Gasinte, Madelina, and Paulo also
indicate non-English influence, but only
Mookinga and Sambo (Maryland, 1692)
seem to offer possibilities of an African
origin. John 10[8] is the commonest
name, with Maria 4 and Antonio 4
next in order. A few surnames appear
among slaves even prior to 1700. Andrew
Moore and Philip Gowen, who probably
took their masters' surnames, show
rather complete Anglicization. John
Pedro (Virginia, 1623) may have received
an earlier Spanish baptism; his name is
only partially Anglicized. Edward
Mozingo (Virginia, 1672) may well have
had the English Edward added to an
original African name.

---

[4] Caterall, H. T., *Judicial Cases Concerning American Slavery and the Negro* (3 vols., Washington,
1926–32), the most important source; Donnan, E., *Documents Illustrative of the History of the Slave
Trade to America* (4 vols., Washington, 1930–35); various articles on the subject in *Journal of
Negro History;* Mencken, *op. cit.*, p. 524; Phillips, U. B., *A Documentary History of American
Industrial Society* (Cleveland, 1909), vols. I–II; Weld, T.S., *American Slavery as It Is* (New York,
1839).
[5] Donnan, *op. cit.*, I, p. 199.
[6] Schmidt, W., *Die Bedeutung des Namens in Kult und Aberglauben* (Darmstadt, 1912), p. 5.
[7] Caterall, *op. cit.*, I, pp. 55–56.
[8] Throughout this article numerals following a name indicate the number of persons bearing that
name in the list under discussion at the time. Thus, in the present instance, John appears ten times
in the list of slave names prior to 1700.

For the eighteenth century the names of 703 slaves were available, including 100 from Louisiana of definitely non-English origin. The remaining 603 names indicate that the period was one of continued transition, since they conform in most cases to the patterns of the dominant group. The names of possible African derivation are perhaps the most interesting because of their divergence from Negro naming usage today. The stereotype, Sambo, occurs four times, although it does not appear at all either in our list of slaves after 1800 or in an intensive study of modern Negro names. Its use in a ridiculous way by white men in minstrels and in connection with Negro jokes may well have operated as a deterrent.[9] Cuffy[10] (Cuffey, Cuffee) occurs five times in our small eighteenth-century sample, but only four times in the much larger nineteenth-century tabulation. The African practice of naming a child according to the day of the week on which he was born persisted in Jamaica, and a number of these traditional Jamaican names[11] are found in the United States, e.g., Quashe, Cudjo, Quaco, and Cuffee among male slaves and Juba, Beneba, Cooba (spelled Cubah or Cubbah), and Abba (spelled Abah) among female slaves. Coffee,

Quashey, and Quashoo are mentioned among the slaves of the Royal African Company in Africa about 1680.[12] Phillips[13] attributes the continuation of some few African names to the persistence of the maritime slave trade, bringing new slaves of the same name from Africa. But Cobb,[14] in mentioning four native Africans, named Capity, Saminy, Quominy, and Quor, who were slaves in Georgia, states that they had facial tattooing and "were treated with marked respect by all the other Negroes for miles and miles around." This suggests that the cultural value of American names may not have been the same with the slave as with the modern immigrant. African captions may even have conferred a certain amount of distinction among the slaves, and thus have continued where the master allowed it. In fact, freedom from the control of white owners, in addition to a slowly forming family tradition, may have been one reason why the free Negroes of 1830[15] seem to have possessed a larger assortment of African names than did the slaves of that period.

Other slave names of the eighteenth century which suggest a possible African origin include: Abanna, Abnabea, Abra, Ankque, Annika, Bamba, Bayna, Bilah,

[9] Rastus occurs in none of our Negro lists, although one case was found among white school children in Mississippi. It would seem that such stereotypes frequently do not follow actual Negro naming usage.

[10] Possibly derived from the Dutch *koffie* (coffee). See Mencken, *op. cit.*, p. 524.

[11] Beckwith, M. W., *Black Roadways* (Chapel Hill, 1929), p. 59; Pitman, F. W., "Slavery on British West India Plantations in the Eighteenth Century," *Journal of Negro History*, XI (1926), p. 641. See also Clodd, E., *Magic in Names and Other Things* (London, 1920), p. 66. For similar usages among the Saramacca Negroes of Suriname, see Herskovits, M. J., and F. S., *Rebel Destiny* (New York, 1934), pp. 222–23.

[12] Woodson, C. G., "Extracts from the Records of the African Companies," *Journal of Negro History*, XIII (1928), pp. 290 ff.

[13] Phillips, U. B., *Life and Labor in the Old South* (Boston, 1935), p. 195.

[14] Cobb, J. B., *Mississippi Scenes* (Philadelphia, 1851), p. 173.

[15] For a comprehensive list of free Negroes of this period, see Woodson, C. G., *Free Negro Heads of Families in the United States in 1830* (Washington, 1925).

Binah, Boohum, Braboo, Bumbo, Bungoh, Comba, Cudah, Cumba, Curiarah, Demeca, Ducko, Fantee, Gumba, Lango, Monimea, Mowoorie, Ocra, Ocrague, Ocrasan, Ocreka, Oessah, Pattoe, Quack, Quaco, Quamana, Quamno, Quash, Quoney, Samba, Sena, Simbo, Simboh, Tanoe, Temba, Warrah, Yamboo, Yaumah, Yearie, Yonaha, and Yono Cish. To these Mencken,[16] from a list compiled by Miss B. B. Armfield, adds Cavannah, Cotica, Cush, Dunke, Guela, Liceta, Limus, Maneta, Mood, Moosa, Mozingo, Paya, Sauny, Sebany, and Tremba, but he mentions the possibility that at least some of them may be of Indian origin.

Louisiana offers an interesting illustration of the alteration of slave names in response to changes in cultural surroundings. Of 115 slaves listed there prior to 1800,[17] 100, or 87 per cent, had names of French or Spanish provenance, whereas, of 339 Louisiana slaves listed after 1800, only 47, or 14 per cent, had such names.[18] The free Negro seems again to have been more conservative than the slave in the matter of name changes.[19] In other localities, non-English influence appears to have declined during the eighteenth century, although Acavan, Agonna, Anthony 5, Antonio 2, Arneda, Bannia, Bongeos, Elecata, Emanuel, Habella, Kauchee, Lysett, Maison, Mamillus, Manuel, Marie, and Pamo occur in our list.

Most of the other names of slaves prior to 1800 persist after that date, and will be discussed in connection with the later group. Cherry (North Carolina, 1789) occurs eight times after 1800 and fourteen times in a list of modern Negro names.[20] Dinah 4, a Biblical name which became a great favorite in England dur-

[16] Op. cit., p. 524.

[17] Tabulated from Caterall, op. cit., Vol. III. Doubtful names such as Louis, Maria, and Marie, which might possibly be of English derivation as well as French or Spanish, are omitted altogether in this analysis.

[18] For the sake of record, these non-English names may be listed here; Aimée 2, Alexandro, Alphonse, Anaïse, Andres, Angelica, Angélique, Antonio 2, Arsène, Augustine, Bambara, Bernardine, Bernardo, Biron, Boucaud, Brunet, Calais, Carlos, Carmelite, Catalina, Catarina, Catin, Celesie, Celeste, Célestine, Cesard, Changereau, Charlot 2, Choucoura, Colas, Crusquet, Cupidon, Delphine 2, Dominic, Eugenie, Felicité, Florestine Cécile, Française Gabrielle Lorio, Franchon, Franchonet, Francisco 6, François 5, Frosina, Gil La Rose, Gonzalo, Guaissecamant, Guela, Hélène, Hibou, Honorato, Isabella 2, Jacques, Janot, Jasmin, Jean 5, Jeanneton, Jeannot, Juan Luis, Juana 2, Junon 2, Langulo, Leon 2, Lizeta, Louison, Lubin, Luis, Magdalena 2, Maillon, Manon 4, Maranthe, Marguerita, Mariana 2, Màrie Aram (Jeanne and Louise 2), Mariquina, Maturina, Maturine, Melite, Meme, Miguel La Rose, Modeste, Morieux, Mulet, Myrthée, Naneta 3, Narcisse, Paya, Pedro 3, Petit, Pierre 3, Pierrot, Pistolet, Raphael, Reynaldo, Robinette, Rosine, Rosette 2, Sans Quartier, Sebany, Songot, Thérèse. For slave names in French Canada during the same period, see Riddell, W. R., "Notes on the Slave in Nouvelle-France," Journal of Negro History, VIII (1923), pp. 316–30; for those in Jamaica, see Pitman, op. cit., pp. 584–668; for those in the Virgin Islands, see Westergaard, W., "Account of the Negro Rebellion on St. Croix, Danish West Indies," Journal of Negro History, XI (1926), pp. 50–61.

[19] Of some 2,360 Louisiana free Negroes listed by Woodson (Free Negro Heads of Families) in 1830, 1,647, or 70 per cent, possessed names of French or Spanish origin, suggesting that name changes were frequently forced upon slaves by their masters.

[20] Unless qualified, all references herein to names of contemporary Negroes are based upon a collection of several hundred thousand Negro names assembled by the author through field work; from Polk's city directories of Columbus, Miss. (1926), and of Montgomery, Ala. (1920); from the Lowndes County, Miss., school enumeration of 1936; from the student lists of 31 Negro colleges,

ing the Elizabethan age,[21] occurs 31 times after 1800 and 9 times among modern Negroes. Pero, though absent in the slave list after 1800, was very common among the free Negroes of 1830, and is found occasionally today. Lemon runs through all groups; in the modern list there are thirteen cases, including such absurdities as Lemon Brown (Mississippi), Lemon Freeze (Alabama), and Lemon Custer (Alabama).[22] Punch, Guy (Gye), Ulysses, and Orange do not occur in the list of slaves after 1800, although found both prior to that date and today. The classical influence appears before 1800 in such names as Caesar 2, Cato 5, and Jupiter 3, and the Biblical influence in Balthazar, Meriah, Hager 3, Jeremiah, and many others. Names exhibit interesting differences in vitality. Sambo lives a brief moment and expires. Prince occurs 5 times before 1800, 19 times between 1800 and 1865, and 20 times in the contemporary list. The Johns, Marys, Marthas, and Williams are always with us.

The names of slaves appearing prior to 1800 but not thereafter include such diminutives as Addy, Deddie, Lando, and Tance, and many names probably derived from masters' surnames, e.g., Bass, Bromley, Claus, Combwood, Fuller, Marlborough, Tower, and Young. Certain unusual names likewise disappear in the list of slaves after 1800.

Some are place names, e.g., Limehouse and Portsmouth. Bacches may be a clerk's attempt at Bacchus, and there is perhaps also a flavor of the classics in Pater, Primax, and Quod. Boatswain is probably occupational, whereas Jade, Sham, Tomboy, Yalluh, and possibly Young are descriptive. Battah, Boomy, Mink, Paddle, Shante, Such, and Ventured may refer to some personal trait or episode in the life of the slave. Anbe, Durah, Farih, Fassiah, Ishener, Jackes, Sherry, Silph, Sive, Sook, Taynay, Temperence, Theribah, and Tobias are the remaining names not found in the list of later slaves, although some persist today. The only definite case of a male slave given a feminine name is Carolina (South Carolina, 1799); this may have referred to the state whence he came, and was possibly followed by Tom or some other name not included in the listing. Taken as a whole, the group of slave names prior to 1800, although too small to be regarded as entirely typical of the period, indicates a gradual transition from a foreign to English setting, with the African element still fairly strong.

Our list of 10,954 slaves[23] after 1800, containing 5,920 male and 5,034 female names, represents a more adequate sample. For purposes of comparison, the 100 names of male slaves occurring most frequently in this list are presented

---

containing some 25,000 names; from more than 50 lists of unusual Negro names from Family Welfare agencies all over the country and from settlements and clinics in Cleveland, Ohio; from lists of Cleveland, Ohio, school children; from Boris, J. J., *Who's Who in Colored America, 1928–1929* (New York, 1929); and from published sources, the most detailed of which is Holmes, U. T., "A Study in Negro Onomastics," *American Speech*, V (1930), pp. 463–67. This collection will serve as a basis for a continuation of the present study.

[21] Bardsley, C. W., *Curiosities of Puritan Nomenclature* (London, 1880), p. 72.

[22] There was a Lemon Peel among the English Puritans of the seventeenth century. See Train A., *Puritan's Progress* (New York, 1931), pp. 131 ff.

[23] Hereinafter, "slaves" or "slave Negroes," when used without further qualification, will refer to this list of slaves, covering the period between 1800 and the close of the Civil War.

in Table I along with the 100 commonest masculine names in a selected list of educated Negroes of today,[24] and a similar comparison of feminine names is made in Table II, In both tables, names are italicized unless they appear among the 100 most common names in both the slave and the modern lists. In other words, italicized names in the slave column, e.g., *Sam* and *Maria*, are those that seem to have been decreasing in use with the Negro since Emancipation, while those italicized in the modern column, e.g., *Walter* and *Annie*, are those that appear to be growing more common.[25]

A disproportionate number of the male slave names are shortened forms, such as Bob, Bill, Sam, and Tom, which seem designed primarily for efficient identification by the master. While they bestow a degree of personal individualization, they do not convey a sense of dignity or of equality; they are names that might well be used by an adult in addressing a child. Some of the names that are common in one group do not occur at all in the other. The slave name Ellick, for instance, does not appear in our total list[26] of contemporary Negroes, while Cato, Mingo, Nat, Ned, and Primus are exceedingly rare. The modern names Alonzo, Carl, Cecil, Chester, Claude, Clifford, Clifton, Donald, Edgar, Elmer, Harold, Herbert, Hubert, Kenneth, Leon, Leonard, Leroy, Leslie, Lloyd, Luther, Melvin, Otis, Reginald, Roscoe, Roy, Vernon, and

Wilbur do not occur at all in our list of 5,920 male slaves, while Clarence, Curtis, Ernest, Nathaniel, and Raymond appear only once each. The main trend among Negro males seems to have been a shift from Biblical and classical names to the more current English ones. Of the former, only Isaac[27] and Solomon retain a place among the more common names, and both show a decline in relative position. The modern Ulysses and Theodore do not appear in the total slave list, suggesting that Ulysses refers to President Grant rather than to the Homeric hero and that Theodore rode into popularity with the late President Roosevelt.

The slave women, like the men, show a tendency toward the use of familiar forms of address, such as Betsy, Judy, and Milly, instead of a more formal nomenclature. The slave names Becky, Ginny, Mima, and Sukey do not appear in our complete modern list, while Dinah, Dorcas, Patience, and Venus[28] are rare. Addie, Alberta, Alma, Beatrice, Bernice, Bertha, Blanche Carolyn, Carrie, Cleo, Doris, Dorothy, Edna, Eloise, Ernestine, Essie, Ethel, Eunice, Eva, Geneva, Gladys, Gwendolyn, Hattie, Hazel, Irma, Juanita, Maggie, Mamie, Marion, Maude, Myrtle, Naomi, Pearl, Ruby, Thelma, Viola, Vivian, Willie, and Willie Mae, although common Negro names today, do not appear at all in our slave list, while Daisy, Effie, Florence, Irene, Lena, Marguerite, Mildred, Rosa,

---

[24] Compiled from student directories of fourteen Negro colleges, located in Ala., Ark., D. C., Fla., Ga., La., Miss., N. C., Okla., S. C., Tenn., Tex., and Va. This list includes 6,014 male and 6,248 female names.

[25] For a comparison with the most popular names among white males, see Simon Newton's table in the *World's Almanac and Enyclopedia for 1921* (New York, 1921), p. 150.

[26] I.e., the the complete list mentioned in footnote 20, not the selected list here under discussion.

[27] A very common name in England about 1300. See Bardsley, *op. cit.*, p. 3.

[28] Although Venus occurred among English Puritans in 1756, and Dorcas was a great favorite (Bardsley, *op. cit.*, pp. 48, 70).

Table I: The 100 Most Common Given Names of Male Slaves
and of Negro Male College Students

Slaves	Modern	Slaves	Modern
1. John 221	James 411	51. *Green 23*	Philip 18
2. Henry 191	William 357	52. *Reuben 23*	*Ralph 18*
3. George 164	John 277	53. *Dennis 22*	*Luther 17*
4. *Sam 121*	Robert 163	54. *Abraham 21*	*Clyde 16*
5. *Jim 119*	Charles 162	55. *Ephraim 21*	Daniel 16
6. Jack 118	George 150	56. *Jeff 21*	Lewis 16
7. *Tom 118*	Edward 115	57. *Jordan 20*	*Claude 15*
8. Charles 115	Joseph 106	58. *Nathan 20*	*Eddie 15*
9. *Peter 109*	Thomas 97	59. Solomon 20	*Lee 15*
10. Joe 93	Henry 90	60. *Jackson 19*	*Melvin 15*
11. *Bob 88*	Samuel 76	61. *Prince 19*	Solomon 15
12. William 88	*Walter 67*	62. Edward 17	*Ulysses 15*
13. Isaac 81	*Willie 66*	63. Thomas 17	*Vernon 15*
14. *Bill 80*	Arthur 63	64. *Amos 16*	*Alonzo 14*
15. *Moses 78*	*Clarence 60*	65. Charlie 15	*Chester 14*
16. *Dick 74*	Frank 58	66. *Edy 15*	*Clifton 14*
17. James 67	Albert 53	67. Joseph 15	*Curtis 14*
18. Lewis 65	Richard 43	68. *Sampson 15*	Jack 14
19. *Ben 64*	David 44	69. Wesley 15	*Milton 14*
20. Frank 60	*Ernest 41*	70. *Andy 14*	*Wilbur 14*
21. Harry 58	*Benjamin 40*	71. *Cato 14*	*Alvin 13*
22. *Jacob 58*	*Nathaniel 37*	72. *Elias 14*	Charlie 13
23. *Ned 51*	*Eugene 35*	73. *Elijah 14*	Joe 13
24. *Simon 48*	Jesse 35	74. *Isham 14*	*Kenneth 13*
25. *Abram 47*	*Leroy 35*	75. *Madison 14*	Oscar 13
26. Daniel 47	*Harold 34*	76. *Nat 14*	Wesley 13
27. *Jerry 47*	*Lawrence 33*	77. *Pleasant 14*	*Wallace 12*
28. *Washington 43*	*Theodore 32*	78. *Primus 14*	*Augustus 11*
29. *Billy 42*	*Howard 31*	79. Alexander 13	*Carl 11*
30. *Stephen 40*	*Raymond 31*	80. *Eli 13*	*Reginald 11*
31. *Anthony 39*	*Paul 30*	81. *Henderson 13*	*Roscoe 11*
32. David 39	*Earl 29*	82. Philip 13	Allen 10
33. Andrew 38	Harry 29	83. *Pompey 13*	*Clifford 10*
34. Alfred 36	*Louis 29*	84. *Wash 13*	*Donald 10*
35. Jesse 36	*Fred 27*	85. *Calvin 12*	*Edwin 10*
36. *Nelson 35*	*Frederick 27*	86. *Harrison 12*	*Elmer 10*
37. Willis 33	*Herbert 25*	87. *Jake 12*	*Floyd 10*
38. *Adam 30*	Andrew 23	88. *Jefferson 12*	*Harvey 10*
39. *Will 30*	*Johnnie 23*	89. *Miles 12*	*Jasper 10*
40. *Edmond 28*	*Booker 22*	90. *Mingo 12*	*Otis 10*
41. Allen 27	*Herman 22*	91. *Robin 12*	*Cecil 9*
42. *Ellick 27*	Isaac 22	92. *York 12*	*Hubert 9*
43. Robert 27	Alexander 21	93. Arthur 11	*Jerome 9*
44. *Dave 26*	*Leon 21*	94. *Berry 11*	*Leslie 9*
45. *Davy 24*	*Leonard 19*	95. *Caleb 11*	*Lloyd 8*
46. *Phil 24*	*Matthew 19*	96. *Gilbert 11*	Martin 8
47. *Aaron 23*	Alfred 18	97. Martin 11	*Irvin 8*
48. Albert 23	*Edgar 18*	98. Richard 11	*Roy 8*
49. *Anderson 23*	*Julius 18*	99. Samuel 11	*Wendell 8*
50. *Caesar 23*	Oliver 18	100. *Sidney 11*	Willis 8

Table II: The 100 Most Common Given Names of Negro Female
Slaves and of Negro Female College Students

Slaves	Modern	Slaves	Modern
1. Mary 241	Mary 247	51. Hester 19	Ida 31
2. Maria(h) 146	Annie 119	52. Venus 19	Juanita 31
3. Nancy 125	Ruth 109	53. Becky 18	Maggie 31
4. Lucy 117	Helen 87	54. Emma 18	Sadie 31
5. Sarah 116	Dorothy 80	55. Rebecca 18	Clara 30
6. Harriet 103	Thelma 75	56. Lydia 17	Eleanor 30
7. Hannah 99	Louise 67	57. Violet 16	Esther 30
8. Eliza 98	Alice 66	58. C(K)aty 15	Hattie 30
9. Martha 86	K(C)atherine 66	59. Isabella 15	Josephine 30
10. Jane 82	Elizabeth 65	60. Molly 15	Pauline 30
11. Amy 80	Lillian 64	61. Patience 15	Cora 29
12. Ann 80	Ethel 63	62. Dorcas 14	Laura 29
13. Rach(a)el 80	Gladys 62	63. Elvira 14	Lula 28
14. Caroline 76	Mildred 61	64. Emiline 14	Vivian 28
15. Betsy 71	Carrie 60	65. Laura 14	Addie 26
16. Milly 71	Ruby 57	66. Minerva 14	Essie 25
17. Sally 66	Emma 56	67. Anna 13	Viola 25
18. C(S)harlott(e) 65	Grace 55	68. Dolly 13	Alma 24
19. Fanny 65	Evelyn 54	69. Phebe 13	Eva 24
20. Louisa 60	Margaret 54	70. Priscilla 13	Sallie 24
21. Matilda 58	Mabel 53	71. Sukey 13	Katie 23
22. Rose 57	Marie 52	72. Aggy 12	Naomi 23
23. Margaret 55	Sarah 49	73. Jinn(e)y 12	Irene 22
24. Betty 52	Julia 48	74. Leah 12	Doris 21
25. Emily 46	Edna 46	75. Letty 12	Florence 21
26. Lucinda 46	Pearl 46	76. Nanny 12	Marguerite 21
27. Susan 46	Bernice 44	77. Sary 12	Myrtle 21
28. Judy 45	Frances 44	78. Chloe 11	Alberta 20
29. Peggy 43	Mattie 44	79. Delia 11	Geneva 20
30. Polly 39	Bessie 43	80. Clara 11	Susie 20
31. Frances 38	Martha 42	81. Lavinia 11	Willie Mae 20
32. Charity 37	Hazel 41	82. Alice 10	Blanche 19
33. Ellen 37	Beatrice 39	83. Aurelia 10	Lois 19
34. Nelly 34	Bertha 39	84. Bella(h) 10	May(e) 19
35. Phillis 34	Marion 38	85. Eveline 10	Charlotte 18
36. Adaline 32	Rosa 38	86. Henrietta 10	Eloise 18
37. Amanda 31	Jessie 37	87. Mima 10	Georgia 18
38. Dinah 31	Minnie 37	88. Agnes 9	Maude 18
39. Elizabeth 31	Willie 37*	89. Biddy 9	Nellie 18
40. Clarissa 29	Anna 34	90. Clary 9	Ernestine 17
41. Esther 28	Fannie 34	91. Doll 9	Eunice 17
42. Kitty 28	Lucille 34	92. Eve 9	Effie 16
43. Malinda 26	Edith 33	93. Hetty 9	Gwendolyn 16
44. Catharine 24	Lillie 33	94. Phoebe 9	Elsie 15
45. Grace 23	Mamie 33	95. Ginny 8	Irma 15
46. Flora 21	Virginia 33	96. Josephine 8	Lena 15
47. Winn(e)y 21	Gertrude 32	97. May 8	Carolyn 13
48. Patsy 20	Lucy 32	98. Patty 8	Henrietta 13
49. Silvey 20	Daisy 31	99. Rhoda 8	Cleo 13
50. Celia 19	Ella 31	100. Sophia 8	Leola 13

* Willie in this case does not include Willie Mae.

Sadie, and Susie occur only once each. Annie, second most common among modern Negro names for girls, occurs only three times in the slave list, and Ruth, the third in frequency today, appears only seven times. A marked falling off is apparent, not only in Biblical names, but also in Puritan names such as Charity and Patience. Only 23 of the 100 names most common among female slaves are still among the most common with Negro college girls, while 33 male names out of 100 survive from the earlier to the later list. This suggests that the masculine names are the more conservative, and the feminine more susceptible to change.

Of our 5,034 female slaves, 1,352, or 27 per cent, had names which would be considered unusual according to present-day white standards in the South; 1,018 of these, however, had names, like Abigail, Deborah, and Saphronia, which would today be regarded merely as old-fashioned. This leaves only 334 female slaves, or 6.7 per cent, with names unusual *per se* according to present standards. Of 18,870 contemporary Negro females,[29] 2,653, or 14.2 per cent, have unusual names; these are merely old-fashioned in 430 cases, leaving 2,223 persons, or 11.9 per cent, with names unusual in themselves. Thus, while it is difficult to project oneself backward into an earlier period and to determine just what would or would not have been considered normal then, there is some reason to believe that unusual names are more common among Negro women today than under slavery. The difference in the case of Negro men is less marked.[30] Of 5,920 male slaves, 1,174, or 19.8 per cent, had unusual names according to present southern white standards, 809 having old-fashioned names and 365, or 6.2 per cent, having names unusual in themselves. Of 15,879 male Negroes of today, 1,390, or 8.7 per cent, have unusual names—old-fashioned in 370 cases, unusual *per se* in 1,020, or 6.4 per cent. The rate of unusualness is higher among females than among males in all cases, though less markedly so in the slave than in the modern group.

The 5,034 female slaves had 901 distinct names, while the 5,920 male slaves had 1,112. Of these, 219 feminine and 259 masculine names—24.3 and 23.2 per cent, respectively—do not appear at all in our complete list of modern Negro names.[31] From this point on, to avoid needless cross-classification, all slave names that do not appear in our list of contemporary Negroes will be italicized.

Seventy-four individuals in our slave list, less than one per cent of the total, reveal names derived from either African or Indian sources. Among these names are *Affa, Agga, Anaka* 4, *Anecky, Anika, Ara, Cavannah, Chena, Claniho, Conder, Congo, Cotta* 3, Cudjo, Cuff, Cuffee 3, Cuffy, *Ganza, Kumba, Lappo, Maina, Manga* 2, Mingo 12, *Monda, Nong,* Quash 8, *Quay, Quico* (or *Quaccoo*),

---

[29] Compiled, like the list of Negro males mentioned below, from the student lists of 30 Negro colleges, the 1926 city directory of Columbus, Miss., and the 1936 school enumeration of Lowndes County, Miss.

[30] A preliminary study of name changes indicated in the alumni lists of Negro colleges seems to indicate a tendency for unusual names to increase more rapidly among women than among men.

[31] This does not necessarily mean, of course, that these names are absolutely unknown among modern Negroes. Since, however, our list is the large one mentioned above in footnote 20, the presumption is that they are at least very uncommon.

Quinny, *Quomana*, *Rattra*, *Saby*, *Sango*, *Toosh*, and *Websha*. Of the 116 last African slaves brought to this country on the voyage of the *Clotilde* in 1859, the sole survivor in 1927, living in Plateau, Alabama, bore the name Cudjo. Six others were named *Abache*, *Kanko*, *Monachee*, *Polute*, *Shamber*, and *Zoomm*, although in the course of time *Abache* became Clara Turner, and *Monachee*, Kitty Cooper.[32] Herskovits[33] derives "Jim Crow" from *nyonkro*, the name of a play given by women on the Gold Coast of West Africa in which "there are dancing and sexual extravaganza in word play, mimicry, and general ridicule." If this derivation is correct, the names Jimie Crow (Mississippi, 1836) and Jim Crack (Louisiana, 1852, and Mississippi, 1856) should perhaps be added to the above list of African names, although the minstrel influence was probably decisive in these particular instances. *Juba 3* and its relatives, *Jub*, *Jube 2*, *Juby*, and perhaps *Jubis*, continue with the slaves and appear in folk-rhymes formerly used in connection with the Juba dance in Mississippi:

> Juba dis an' Juba dat,
> Juba kilt a yalluh cat.[34]

As the proportion of African names declines after 1800, so also does the proportion of names derived from other non-English sources, indicating a more complete titular adjustment on the part of the slave to his new environment. The following names,[35] however, give indication of possible outside origin: Amand, *Amces*, *Albinus*, *Amoritt*, Antoney 3, Antonio, *Bartee*, Battiste, Danrille, *Francesco*, *Frelingheizsen*, *Freno*, Ganze, *Goservar*, Jeffoy, Jenz, *Macia*, Manuel 6, *Mensoza 2*, *Nicolis*, Roblein, Sancho, *Sanco*, *Trussvan; Andrienette*, Angelia, Angelina, Angeline 2, Angila, Antoinette 4, *Antona*, *Antonia*, *Bellesames*, Bridget 3, Cebille, Celesta, Celestia, Delphine, Dolphin, *Euphemie*, *Fernaster*, Frenoli, Georgiana 2, Gracieuse, Jeanett, Jeanette, Jeannet, Jenette, Jennett 2, Jennetta 2, Justine, *Kanzada*, *Luida* 2, Mahalz, *Marena*, Margarita, Marz, *Muttpuin*, Syvill.

In these slave lists it has seemed best to record the name as listed on the individual document, even though owners and overseers obviously twisted identical names into many curious forms. The orthographic situation with the slaves resembles that in early England, when spelling was roughly phonetic. Even up to the Elementary Education Act of 1870 a considerable proportion of the English people did not spell their own names but trusted to the parson and the clerk, who wrought strange and wonderful creations from unfamiliar names.[36] Similarly, among our slave names we find Liz 2, ·Liza 6, Lizar, Lize 2, Lizee, Lizy, Lizza, Lizzie 5, and Lizzy 9, making it sometimes difficult to say just where Eliza ends and Lizzie be-

[32] Hurston, Z. N., "Cudjo's Own Story of the Last African Slaves," *Journal of Negro History*, XII (1927), 648–63.
[33] *Op. cit.*, pp. 354–55.
[34] Informant Mr. John Sale, Columbus, Miss.
[35] In this and following tabulations, male slave names will be listed first, followed by female. Occasional errors in sex classification seem unavoidable, owing in part to the character of the sources.
[36] Weekley, E., *The Romance of Names* (London, 1922), pp. 27–28.

gins, Rachel 60 blossoms forth into Rachael 20, Racchel, Rachell, and Rachiel, while *Cina* 2, *Cind*, *Cinda* 3, *Cindy* 3, Sina 2, Sinah, Sinda, and *Sindy* 5 leave one wondering whether to blame Cindarella or Lucinda for such cryptographic confusion. Lucy 117 appears also as Lussee and Luce; Sarah 116, as Sara, Saraugh, and Sary; Charlotte 47, as Chalath, Charlette, Charlott 12, Scharlotte, Sharlot, Sharlott, and Sharlotte 5; *Sukey* 13, as *Soockey*, *Sookey* 4, Suck 2, Sucky 8, and *Sucy*; and Violet 16, as Vilet 3, Vilett 4, and Violette. Lucretia 6 is not only the mother of Lucresha but also the stepmother of Creacy, Creasey, Creasy 2, Creecy 2, Cresa, Crese, Cresy 2, Cricy, *Crissy*, and perhaps even Cretia 2 and Critty. The names of male slaves seem to run into fewer vagaries of spelling, although we do find Peter 109 appearing as Peater, and Caesar 23 as Caezar, Cesar 4, and Seasar 2.

The slave himself may well have enjoyed playing around with the spoken word. Slave boy Malachi, for instance, "was baptized seven times, under different names, and with different sponsors, the good rector, to whom all young negroes looked alike, not recognizing him,"[37] although in this case the enticement may have been the ceremony rather than a delusion of nomenclatural grandeur expressing itself in terms of quantity rather than quality. Quite possibly many slave names were developed by the Negroes themselves and used to express social distinctions current in slave society. Just as younger slaves were required to show respect to older ones by addressing them as "Uncle,"[38] so other factors, such as differences in occupation, led to social distinctions. House servants, drivers (foremen), carpenters, carriage drivers, fiddlers, cart-wrights, and shoemakers were high in the slave aristocracy, color entering in indirectly through the fact that mulattoes were more often chosen to be domestics and artisans. Moreover, slaves of "quality folk" held themselves above those owned by "trash,"[39] Something of this element of social distinctions among slaves is expressed in a Mississippi Negro folk-rhyme formerly used in connection with cake walks. The latter, being "pay parties," required a doorkeeper possessing a sense of both financial and social discrimination. The rhyme runs as follows:

"Is dat you, Sambo?" "No, dis am Cin."
"You'se pooty good lookin', but you can't come in."[40]

In order to use the name as a mark of social distinction among his fellows, the slave had to have freedom of choice. When this was allowed, as happened in at least some cases, it resulted, sometimes, in the selection of a master's given name, perhaps in the hope of receiving a special gift;[41] sometimes, in such descriptive names as Monday

---

[37] Clayton, F., "A Sketch in Black and White," *Atlantic Monthly*, XCVII (1906), 605.

[38] Frazier, E. F., "The Negro Slave Family," *Journal of Negro History*, XV (1930), p. 213.

[39] *Ibid.*, p. 209; *Harper's Monthly Magazine*, XVII (1858), p. 422; Mallard, R. Q., *Plantation Life before Emancipation* (Richmond, 1892), p. 46.

[40] Informant Colonel W. A. Love, Columbus, Miss.

[41] "Gift-names" are still found among Virginia Negroes. One colored woman named her daughter Annie Virginia Cordelia Idella Pigram, received a gift from each white person included in this list, and then called the child Tumps "for short" (Informant Miss S. F. Barrow, Cleveland, Ohio).

("He oughter been name' Sunday, de day o' rest! He been sittin' down all his life."); and sometimes in such combinations as Willis Silblumus Quintellius Cerlarius Thomas William, called "literally 'fo' short,' Willis."[42] Such slave names as April, August 3, *Friday* 7, *January* 3, July 5, June, March 7, Monday, *Morning*, *Winter* 2, and, for women, Easter 7, Easther, July, and *Morning*, may refer to events associated with birth, as was true in England at the eve of the Reformation, where Easter was the name longest to survive.[43]

Certain slave names on our list refer to localities: Aberdeen 3, Alabama, *Baltimore*, Boston 2, Dallas, *Dublin* 2, Erie, French 2, *Galilee*, *Glascow*, Holland 5, *Jersey*, *London* 5, *Newport*, Paris, Richmond 8, *Scotland* 4; Carolina 4, Dallas, Georgia 2, Holland, India 2, Indiana 2, Louisiana, Louisianna, Misourie, Missouria, Savannah 2, Tennessee, *Venice* 2, Virginia 9, Virginie. Some may have been chosen by slave parents in reference to place of birth; some, by masters to indicate place of purchase. Others refer to localities known by name rather than through contact. In the rice plantation section there was much coming and going of ships from England, and slave mothers sometimes named their children York, London, or the like, according to the port of sail or destination of various vessels.[44] Holland was a fairly common name among whites in England[45] and in colonial Massachusetts, where London, Boston, America, and many similar names were also found.[46]

Nicknames might come either from a slave source or from the masters. They are, of course, common all over the world, being used frequently by uncivilized folk for the purpose of concealing their true names from the machinations of sorcerers. Ordinarily they were too informal to be entered in official records, although in the Esher Parish Register we do find "Bacchus *alias* Hogtub *alias* Fat Jack *alias* John from Ld. Clive at Claremont, buried 1772."[47] Relatively few traces survive of the nicknames used among plantation Negroes in addressing other slaves. Carmer,[48] however, cites the following from Thorn Hill Plantation in Alabama: Pie ya, Puddin'-tame, Frog, Tennie C., Monkey, Mush,

---

[42] Armstrong, O. K., *Old Massa's People* (Indianapolis, 1931), p. 59.

[43] Bardsley, *op cit.*, pp. 36, 96. [However, the practice of having "day names" is almost certainly African in origin. For example, Turner reports that "kofi" is a name given to a boy born on Friday among the Temne, Ewe, Fante, and Ga. This is unquestionably the source of the name Cuffee or Cuffy, which has even become a general term in Negro speech for a Negro. Similarly, "kojo," a Ga and Ewe name for a male born on Monday became "Cudjo." In 1774, Edward Long writing about Jamaica noticed that Jamaican Negroes named their children on the basis of the African day of the week on which they were born and he even compiled a chart of male and female names corresponding to the seven days of the week. See Edward Long, *History of Jamaica* (London, 1774), p. 427; Hennig Cohen, "Slave Names in Colonial South Carolina," *American Speech*, 28 (1952), p. 104 where the chart is reproduced; or the more recent survey, David DeCamp, "African Day-Names in Jamaica," *Language*, 43 (1967), pp. 139–49. For Turner's data, see *Africanisms in the Gullah Dialect* (Chicago, 1949), pp. 114–15. —ED.]

[44] Armstrong, *op. cit.*, p. 62.

[45] Weekley, *op. cit.*, p. 98.

[46] Bowditch, N. I., *Suffolk Surnames* (Boston, 1858), pp. 16–18.

[47] Ewen, C. L., *A History of Surnames of the British Isles* (London, 1931), pp. 203, 330, 328.

[48] Carmer, C., *Stars Fell on Alabama* (New York, 1934), p. 96.

Cooter, John de Baptist, Fat-man, Preacher, Jack Rabbit, Sixty, Pop Corn, Old Gold, Dootes, Tangle-eye, Bad-Luck, Fly-up-de-Creek, Cracker, Jabbo, Cat-fish, Bear, Tip, Odessa, Pig-lasses, Rattler, Pearly, Luck, Buffalo, Old Blue, Red Fox, Coon, Jewsharp. Several of these suggest personal traits or episodes in the life of the individual, and hence approach closely the character of certain types of primitive names. Some nicknames occurring in our own list are: *Bap*, *Bebb*, *Bingo*, *Binkey* 2, *Bipy*, Bus, *Fell*, *Fodder*, *Fute*, *Gallon*, *Jacko*, Luck, *Money*, *Moon*, *Nig*, *Pillow*, *Pool*, Quince 2, *Ratler*, *Rep*, *Roller*, Sandy 10, *Tabs*, *Tell*, *Tink*, *Tip*, *Top*, *Town*, Toy; *Bis*, Icy, *Mopsy*, *Munny*, Pussy (2), *Spice*, Spicy.

Such titular nicknames among men as Dock 6, Doctor 5, Esquire, General, Govenor, Judge 5, King 6, Major 8, Parson, and Squire 8 seem to indicate a recognition of slave social distinctions, although both Squire and Major were common among ordinary folk in England before the death of Queen Elizabeth.[49] Possible slave derivation is also indicated in those names that seem to be based on personal peculiarities,[50] of which the following occur in our list: Baldy 2, *Bellow*, *Bold*, *Boney*, Brag, *Brave Boy*, Crip, *Grizzy*, Hardtimes, Junior, *Live*, *Lively*, *Mangy*, *Muss*, *Polite*, *Racket*, *Senior*, Short, Smart 6, Tartar; Babe, Bitsey 2, Bonny, *Grief*, *Happy* 2, *Mourning*, Peachy, Queen, and Sis.

There remain a considerable number of other names which seem unusual to us today. Some are old-fashioned forms probably perfectly normal for the period; others are apparently diminutives or nicknames; still others may be due to distortions in spelling. These names perhaps reflect about equally the influence of slave and master. The list follows: *Ager*, *Ails* 2, *Ailsey*, Aller, *Alphaid*, *Altamont*, *Baltissum*, *Bann*, *Batsey*, *Bazie*, *Benbow*, Blunt, *Bonum*, *Bosum*, Braters, *Brigut*, Buck 8, *Buny*, Butter, *Caro*, *Chain*, Chance, *Chang*, *Chanty*, *Clander*, *Coateen*, *Comas*, Coon, *Creed*, *Dago*, *Dedon*, *Die*, *Dilas*, *Dine*, *Eben*, *Edom*, *Eincline*, *Elizus*, *Ember* (a slave blacksmith), *Enox*, *Exom*, Feber, *Flander*, Fountain 3, *Fravas*, Freling, Gosh, Gosport, *Grundy*, *Gruss*, *Hamet*, *Hasty* 2, *Healen*, Horatio, *Hover*, Huger, *Ian*, *Isare*, Ishum, Isom, Isum 2, *Jacksoney*, *Jeffro*, *Jimboy*, Jubiter, *Juble*, Junius 2, Justine, *Keas*, *Kertus*, *Kinder*, *Kindy*, *Knap*, Leathy, *Lenias*, *Limerick*, *Lurse*, *Luturn*, *Mahaly*, *Mance*, *Marmaduke*, *Martesia*, Micajah, *Milus* 2, *Myal*, *Naise*, *Nicker* 2, *Nonen*, *Onash*, Oney, Orange 6, Organ, *Osmgon*, *Pagy*, Pall, Philander, Phylander, *Polydore*, Ransom 2, *Rastin*, *Rolla*, *Rosey*, Rucker 2, *Rue*, *Rusus* *Saman*, *Sanney*, Sanny, *Sawney* 4, *Scearse*, *Seac*, *Seantry*, Seller, *Sharper*, *Shorum*, Sipio, *Surry*, *Teams*, *Teener* 2, Thamer, *Thamil*, *Tumer*, Valentine, *Vind*, *Visa*, *Wasset;* Abbergall 2, *Abiail*, Acie, Aggaby, *Airy*, Aleathea, Almyra 3, *Alzeria*, *Anada*, *Anonicat*, *Aphnah*, Arabella 6, Arena, Armmitta, *Arteta*, *Artimesia* 2, *Arzilla*, *Avarilla* 2, *Azilla*, *Barsilla*, *Barzella*, Bina 3, Binah 3, Biner 4, Calidonia 4, Candes 2, Canna, Cardine, Catrane, Cherry 8, Cherrylane, *Chima*, *Chitta*, Clemensa, *Cleonder*, *Coteler* 2, *Dausey*, *Delitha*, *Delpha*, Delphia, *Docia* 2, *Dyche*, Elena, *Ellender* 2,

[49] Bardsley, *op. cit.*, pp. 196–97.
[50] W. F. Allen (*Slave Songs of the United States* (New York, 1867), p. xxxiii) mentions a slave named After-dark, "so called because he was so black than 'you can't sh'um 'fo' day-clean.' "

Elvia, Elvina 2, *Elvine*, Eulalie 2, *Fender*, Fillis 3, Fiscal 2, *Flerah*, *Florinda*, *Hemutal*, *Inda* 2, *Jeine*, *Jelia*, Jemima, *Jincey*, Jinsey, Joaney 3, *Juda* 3, *Jude*, *Judea* 3, *Kanice*, *Kasina*, *Kinah*, Kissee, *Klima*, *Larnia*, *Latria*, *Lavinera*, *Lesa Ann*, Liggina, *Loticia*, *Luci*, Lytha, Mahala 4, Mahaly 2, *Mahola*, *Maisa*, *Malsa*, Manda 4, *Mandana*, *Manzy*, *Marteria* 2, *Martille*, *Matta*, Melvina 2, *Mema*, *Menia*, *Merilla*, *Meroh*, *Messeniah*, *Mima* 3, *Mimey*, Minda 3, Minty 2, Mira 2, Mirah 2, Mirnia, *Missoney*, *Monah*, *Mooning*, *Morina*, Nicey, Nicy 4, *Nilla*, *Nine*, Notice, *Oney* 2, Palsey, *Pamela*, Pamelia 3, Paralee, Parthenia 2, *Pauladore*, Pheby 6, *Pheraby*, *Pherady*, Phereby, *Phillissia*, *Plina*, *Preepey*, *Reanna*, *Reuta*, Rhina, *Rhinor*, Rihna, Rina 2, Riney, Rosalinda, *Saby*, *Safrona*, Salena 3, Samantha, Saphroney, Saphronia, Sarena, *Satira*, *Satirah* 3, *Savinia*, *Savory*, *Scamby*, Selina, Seloy, Serena 3, *Sinethas*, *Sobuty*, Sofa 2, *Spinar*, *Syphax*, Syrena, *Szela*, *Tandy*, Taner, Tena, Tenah 3, Tener, Tenor 2, Thena, Tina, Tumps, Tyrah 2, *Unis*, *Usly*, *Vennah*, Virgin, *Viza*, *Winnia*, Woody, *Writ*, Zera, Zilphy, *Zinny*, Ziphy, Zody. Although some of the unusual modern Negro names appear in our slave list, the slaves had fewer unusual names in proportion and did not exhibit the bizarre and fantastic extremes of modern Negro nomenclature.

Biblical names among the slaves are probably attributable more to the masters than to the slaves themselves. In addition to those mentioned above,

the following occur in our list: Abel 7, Absolom 6, Aron 3, *Baal*, *Cain* 5, *Celim* 2, Cimon, Cornelius 3, Elisha 7, Enoch 5, Esau, Faro, Ezekiel 3, Gabriel 9, *Ham* 2, Hezekiah, Hosea, Isaiah 5, Ishmael 5, Ishmel 2, Isiah 2, Israel 2, Jeremiah, *Jerusha*, Jethro, Job 6, Jonas 8, Joshua 9, Josiah 6, *Judah* 4, Levi 6, *Lot*, Luke 3, Mark 9, Mathew 2, Mathias, Michael, Nazareth, Nehemiah 2, Nimrod 3, Noah 4, Obadiah, Paul 9, Pharo, Samson, Saul 2, Shadrach 3, Silas 5, Simeon 2, Solimon, Thaddeus, Theophilus, Timothy 4, Titus 3, Uriah, Zachariah; Abigail, Deborah 2, Delila 4, Dorcus 4, *Dosh*, Doshia, Dosia, Drucilla 2, Ester 5, Hagar 6, Hagur, Hanah 2, Hanna 4, *Judah*, Kesiah, Kessiah, Keziah 2, Kissiah, Kiziah, Kizziah, Lidia, *Moriah*, Selah, Tabitha, Tamar 2, Tamer 2. To this group should perhaps be added names reflecting Puritan influence, e.g., Amis, Fortune 6, *Providence*, Candis 6, Comfort 2, *Piety*, Pleasant 2 (females), Prosper, Prudence 7, and its derivative Prudy 4. Biblical and Puritan names were at one time exceedingly common among the English,[51] and they appear frequently in colonial New England,[52] in the roll of the United States Congress, in *Who's Who in America*,[53] and among contemporary southern mountaineers.[54] Although they are less prominent in the South than in early New England,[55] most of those mentioned above for slaves were also found among the early whites of Columbus, Mississippi, as revealed by probate records.

The direct or indirect influence of the

[51] Bowman, W. D., *The Story of Surnames* (London, 1931), pp. 89–90, 250 ff.; Bardsley, *op. cit.*, pp. 38–116; Train, *op. cit.*, pp. 131 ff.; Weekley, *op. cit.*, pp. 85–89.

[52] Bowditch, *op. cit.*, pp. 12–20.

[53] See Mencken, *op. cit.*, p. 515.

[54] Campbell, J. C., *The Southern Highlander and His Homeland* (New York, 1921), p. 2.

[55] Bowman, *op. cit.*, p. 92.

master in the naming of the slave child is reflected in three large classes of slave names: those, like Eugene, Nathaniel, and Ella, which were clearly identical with white nomenclature at the time; given names, such as Addison, Campbell, and Robinson, which were apparently derived from white surnames; and diminutives, such as Dan, Pete, Nell, and Tabby, which followed patterns current in the white population. Limitations of space prevent the listing of these names. They nevertheless constitute, together with the 100 commonest names already cited, the great bulk of slave nomenclature and indicate the growing affiliation of the Negro with American usage in this respect. Slave children, in fact, were often, if not usually, actually named by the master or mistress. In this way they received, not only names current in the master's family,[56] but also such appellatives as Fed[57] or Last Night, the master in the latter case having been roused from his morning sleep by the news that Clementine "had a little boy last night."[58] Classical names, although less numerous than certain writers on plantation life would have us think, also probably reveal the hand of the master class. Our slave list includes the following: *Achilles*, Augustus 5, Bachus, Brutus 2, *Calypso*, Cassius, Cicero 2, Cupid 2, *Esop*, Felix 8, Hannibal 5, *Harculos*, Hector 10, Horace 7, Jupiter 4, Mars, Nero 8, *Ovid*, Plato, Pliny, Pompy, Scipio 8, *Seneca*, *Telmachus*; Augusta, Ceries, Cornelia 3, Daphna 2, Daphne 3, Daphney 2, Diana 4, Dianna 3, *Dido* 2, *Juno* 6, Lethe 3, Manerva, Mernervey, Minervi, Narcissa

3, Octavia 2, Penelope, Penny 8, Scylla, Silla 6, Siller 5, Sylla 2. More recent names of prominence include: Byron, Columbus 2, *Dumas*, Erasmus, Gen'l Washington, Hamlet, Lafayette 2, *Lear*, Napoleon 3, and Van Buren.

Fundamentally, however, the attitude of master toward slave was less that of a parent toward his child than that of an owner toward his property. Probate records reveal a tendency to personalize and identify accurately by name all livestock, human or otherwise; mules and cows are often listed by name, and are distinguished from slaves mainly in terms of appraised value. To furnish an interesting comparison, 235 names of mules were abstracted from the Lowndes County, Mississippi, Probate Record for 1858. Of this number, 197, or 84 per cent, occur also as slave names, including not only such common names as Bet, Eliza, Jinny, and Tobe, but also such classical names as Cato, Dianna, Hector, and Pompey. The ten most common mule names were, in order of frequency, Jack, Kitt, Beck, John, Mike, Ned, Tom, Bill, Jim, and Dolly—and most of these also occur among the most common slave names. Certain names, on the other hand, seem to have been distinctive to mules, e.g., Blaze, Dragon, Five Cents, Fly 3, Lightfoot, Pick, Rock, Shot, Telegraph, Value, and Yanky. In general, however, mule names resemble many of the slave diminutives in being short and terse, designed rather for property distinction than for personal distinction.

As long as a farmer had but five or six mules, Betty, Fanny, Matilda, or

---

[56] Armstrong, *op. cit.*, p. 59.
[57] Frazier, *op. cit.*, p. 229.
[58] "Negro Minstrelsy, Ancient and Modern," *Maga Social Papers* (New York, 1867), p. 286.

Henry would serve fairly well as titles, but on plantations with more abundant mule-power, we find appearing on the records such secondary descriptions as Young Beck, Old Dick, Little John, Big Kitt, Yellow Jim, Leader Kit, and even such regular surnames in muledom as Jane Henkel, Sam Nelson, and Pol Jones, which may or may not have been patterned after the surname of the owner. Precisely the same tendency, of course, appeared in the case of slave names.

A glance at the development of secondary distinctions in English history will shed light on this tendency. In the eleventh century the majority of people in England had but a single name, but with the rise of large towns and a growing country population it became increasingly difficult to identify an individual with only one name.[59] Hence, by the end of the twelfth century it had become exceptional for a person to lack an official description or surname.[60] These were at first of secondary importance, being placed after the frontname. They were derived mainly from the individual's personal appearance, from his place of residence, from his parentage, and from his occupation, and it was not uncommon for a person to have several such additions. Secondary appellatives, first noticed as hereditary in 1267, gradually became recognized as family names, and eventually became more important than the forename.[61]

A very similar situation existed among American Negro slaves. The development of names among slaves followed essentially the same pattern as that of surnames in early England if we include another category, the assumption by the freed slave of the surname of his former owner. In Johnson v. Field (Louisiana, 1827) it was ruled: "Slaves being men, are to be identified by their proper names . . . and when there are two or more of the same name, by some other, which distinguishes them in relation to physical, or, perhaps, moral qualities."[62] But again in 1831, in Louisiana, we find that "the slaves had so many *sobriquets*, and were known by so many names that . . . embarrassment remains, from the designation in the . . . deeds, not corresponding."[63] Into the property records crept a great many aliases in an effort to identify slaves more exactly. Some were simply diminutives, as Alexander or Aleck, Alice or Else, Appling or App, Charlotte or Lotty, Doritha or Doll, Francis or Franky, Simon or Si, Sucky or Susan. Others possibly represent differences due to transfer of ownership and change of name, as Clara or Hager, Henrietta or Mary, John or Jupiter, Juba or Jupiter. Still others represent nicknames, as as Anthony or Nig, and Old Nat "commonly called Capt. Nat."

Secondary names became almost a necessity on the larger plantations. In the will of Nathaniel H. Hooe (Louisiana, 1844) three slaves named Bill were distinguished as Blacksmith Bill, Billy Monroe, and Bill Beverly.[64] Age was often made a basis for such distinctions, and in the slave lists we find

[59] Bowman, *op. cit.*, p. 5.
[60] Ewen, *op. cit.*, p. 218.
[61] *Ibid.*, pp. 47, 90–92, 218–19.
[62] Caterall, *op. cit.*, III, 482.
[63] *Ibid.*, III, 493–94.
[64] Caterall, *op. cit., III*, 315.

such descriptions as Old Isaac, Young Ned, Old Man Peter, Granny Sarah, James the Babe, Andrew (7 yrs.), Paul (born March, 1839), and Benty (purchased Feb'y, 1837). The terms "big" and "little," which were used very frequently, usually refer to age rather than to physical size, and sometimes lead to such curiosities as Big Patience and Little Patience (Mississippi, 1838). In England, even as late as 1545, the will of John de Gyton refers to his two sons as "Olde John" and "Young John," and "John the Bigg" is used in other instances.[65] In France, such names as Grandjacques and Petitjean were fairly common.[66] Personal traits other than age also served to distinguish between slaves, as in the cases of Jack (short), Jenny (blind), Miley (prime), Long Poll, and possibly Blush Billy. Reference is made to Mulatto Will or Will Brown, and to Yellow Jane, and color may even have given rise to an actual surname in the case of John Mulatto or Joe Creole. Location figures in such names as Guinea Jack, Kentucky Tom, Pararie Jim (possibly from the prairie section of Mississippi), Columbia Bitsey (from Columbia, Mississippi?), and, perhaps, John Kentuck. On the plantation of John Palfred in Louisiana, in 1807, American Hercules "was so styled to distinguish him from an African of the same name."[67] America, a name in use in England four centuries ago,[68] was a fairly common name among female slaves and also occurs with modern Negroes.

Occupation and working ability served as a basis for many secondary distinctions among slaves, as in the cases of Tinker Jack, Isaac the Potter, Preaching Dick, Captain (Chimney Sweep), George (carpenter), Fortune (Head Bird-Minder with Gun), Stephney (best ploughman), John (Driver), Clary (Plantation Cook), Dolly (in house), and Miller Joshua (at mill). Ben Shipman and Isaac Butcher may conceivably have derived their surnames from occupations as truly as did the early English Cooks, Fishers, or Smiths. Genealogical relationships were sometimes noted, e.g., Rose's Giney, Ann (Mingoe's mother), Pompey (Phillis's son), Katrina's York, Jenny's Dolly, and in some instances these maternal[69] descriptives may have laid the basis for a true surname, such as Julianna Eliza or Lindsey Walton (son of Lindsey). With an increase in numbers came a need for still further differentiation, and we find a few cases of double distinctions, e.g., Black Fat, Eliza's Rattra (child), Old Penny Boon and Old Penny at Mill, Old Cook Woman Jinny. The case of "Old Woman named Little Mary" shows that the childhood distinction "Little" was sometimes difficult to shake off in later life. These double distinctions, all from Mississippi after 1840, give some indication of the need for actual surnames.

"Even during slave days the surname of the master was used for identification purposes among servants. . . . 'Who dat?' you say. 'Dat William Dunbar.'

---

65 Bardsley, *op. cit.*, p. 4.
66 Weekley, *op. cit.*, p. 59.
67 Phillips, *Life and Labor in the Old South*, p. 293.
68 Bardsley, *op. cit.*, p. 212.
69 The slave child in many cases had little or no contact with his father, who might be unknown to him or be living on some other plantation. For illustrations, see Frazier, *op. cit.*, p. 228.

'An' you know he b'long to de Dun-
bars.' "[70] Thus Matilda Davis was the
slave of Thomas Davis (Kentucky,
1855), William Isaac Rawlings (Tennessee, 1837) was the son of his master
Isaac Rawlings by a slave mother, and
Isaac of Cowling (Virginia, 1800)
belonged to Thomas Cowling. In the
cases of Jane Harper, owned by a Mr.
Wallis, and of Mary Harry, owned by
the McCants, the surname was probably
that of a former owner. In some instances
a double name may have been amalga-
mated into a single one by an owner or
overseer. Thus Jimboon (Mississippi,
1840) might originally have been Jim
Boone.

With freedom, these simple distinctions of slavery days were naturally
expanded. Romeo Jones now signed his
name Romey O. Jones, and Pericles
Smith became Perry Class Smith. A boy
who had always been known as Polly's
Jim, having learned to read the New
Testament, became Mr. Apollos James.[71]

Slave Sam of Mississippi became Sam
Buck when his master acquired another
Sam, but under the exhilaration of freedom he expanded into Sam Buck Jeemes
Ribber Highoo, and indulged in other
vagaries, such as feeding his dog gunpowder to make him brave.[72] Corinthia
Marigold Wilkinson Ball Wemyss
Alexander Jones Mitchell owed her
collection of names to the fact that she
had been owned successively by half
a dozen families and after Emancipation
took the names of them all.[73] But this
brings us down to a type of nomenclature developed under a situation
where social contacts and group responsibilities were much wider in scope than
those engendered in the simple plantation society of slavery days. It has
been our purpose here to show the
characteristics and trends of Negro
nomenclature under slavery. The reactions of the freed slave and of the
modern Negro must come later.

---

[70] Armstrong, *op. cit.*, p. 60.
[71] Harrison, J. B., "Studies in the South," *Atlantic Monthly*, L (1882), p. 477.
[72] Informant Colonel W. A. Love, Columbus, Miss.
[73] Macrae, D., *The Americans at Home* (2 vols., Edinburgh, 1870), II, p. 332.

On the Grammar of Afro-American Naming Practices

J. L. DILLARD

If there are patterns in personal names, there are also patterns in other kinds of names, for example, the names of objects such as boats or cars or of institutions such as churches. In this essay, Professor Dillard of Yeshiva University examines some names of store-front churches and attempts to delineate possible patterns.

The role of religion in American Negro culture continues to be significant. Although there has always been a strong sense of resentment of Christianity as the white man's religion, there has also been an equally strong theme of commitment to Christianity or a modified form thereof. Thus, despite the fact that preachers in slavery times were often little more than the paid hirelings of plantation masters charged with urging their parishioners to "obey the master," the rise of American Negro churches with their own ministers has had an enormous impact upon American Negro life. Many of the acknowledged leaders of American Negro movements, including civil rights, have been ministers (e.g., Martin Luther King).

So although there continues to be a religious/non-religious split—as exemplified in the musical preferences for religious spirituals or for secular blues—the church remains a vital force for many American Negroes. If identity includes membership in a church, then obviously the name of the church may well reflect that sense of identity. As Professor Dillard demonstrates, the individual words in store-front church names may be SE (Standard English), but the combinations of these words appear to be Afro-American.

For an initial entrée into the vast liteature on American Negro religion, some of the following studies may be of interest: Christopher Rush, A Short Manual of the Rise and Progress of the African M. E. Church in America (*New York,*

Reprinted from *Names*, vol. 16 (1968), pp. 230–37, by permission of the author and the American Name Society.

1843); Carter G. Woodson, The History of the Negro Church (*Washington, 1921); Benjamin E. Mays and Joseph W. Nicholson*, The Negro's Church (*New York, 1933); Benjamin Mays*, The Negro's God as Reflected in His Literature (*Boston, 1938); Arthur Huff Fauset*, Black Gods of the Metropolis: Negro Religious Cults of the Urban North (*Philadelphia, 1944); E. Franklin Frazier*, The Negro Church in America (*New York, 1963); and Joseph R. Washington, Jr.*, Black Religion (*Boston, 1966*).

Readers especially interested in the folk sermon, a too often neglected but nevertheless crucial genre of religious folklore, might wish to consult any of the following: James Weldon Johnson, God's Trombones (*New York, 1932); William H. Pipes*, Say Amen, Brother (*New York, 1951); Henry H. Mitchell*, Black Preaching (*Philadelphia, 1970); and Bruce A. Rosenberg*, The Art of the American Folk Preacher (*New York, 1970). See also such articles as Floyd C. Watkins, "De Dry Bones in De Valley," Southern Folklore Quarterly, 20 (1956), pp. 136–49, and Nancy B. McGhee, "The Folk Sermon: A Facet of the Black Literary Heritage," CLA Journal, 13 (1969), pp. 51–61.*

IT IS well known that names are somehow related to grammar, and it is often suspected that linguistics may somehow be able to furnish the solution to any grammatical problem. Francis Lee Utley has dealt in general terms with the relationship between linguistics and names,[1] with some suggestion of syntactic analysis—limited therein, however, primarily to such formulations as that regarding co-occurrence of articles with naming nouns. The present essay deals with a more specific naming problem, limited to what is regarded for these purposes as one specific community, and with a somewhat broader approach to syntactic analysis.

The community selected may be called a part of the Afro-American (in the Herskovitsian sense) community, although the discussion here is limited almost entirely to the Negro community within the United States. Although I believe that a wider discussion of naming practices within an Afro-American cultural group would be valuable, the paper will center on the names of store-front churches in the Negro community in the U.S. It is the belief here that these naming practices are a peripheral manifestation of the linguistic differences which have motivated Stewart[2] to write of the language of the "culturally disadvantaged Negroes of a lower socioeconomic stratum" as a "quasi-foreign language." The differences between these church naming practices and those of standard English speaking communities is obvious to anyone looking over a list of names.[3] Naturally, ghetto naming practices are not characteristic of middle-class Negroes closer to the mainstream of American culture—and incidentally, speakers of standard American English. Obviously peripheral linguistic phenomena of Non-standard

---

[1] "The Linguistic Component of Onomastics," *Names*, XI (1963), 145–76.
[2] William A. Stewart, *Non-Standard Speech and the Teaching of English*, Center for Applied Linguistics (Washington, D. C., 1964).
[3] Excellent lists have been published by James B. Strong, "Chicago Store Front Churches: 1964," *Names*, XII (1964), 127–28; and R. S. Noreen, "Ghetto Worship; A Study of Chicago Store Front Churches," *Names*, XIII (1965), 19–38.

Negro English (NNE) are the result of orderly historical processes,[4] not of "distortion" of either language or naming practices by any presumptive ecological factors in the urban ghetto. Regrettably, but undeniably, the culturally and linguistically naive members of the mainstream culture tend to view such a list with amusement. Writers such as Octavus Roy Cohen[5] and the creators of the even less accurate Amos n' Andy comedy show[6] have given unfortunate emphases to such tendencies. Although distressing from the point of view of racial relations, there is a core of fact upon which they could build.

It is my belief that there is a causative analogy between the humorous reactions felt toward NNE naming practices and the "Spanglish" naming practices in Puerto Rico.[7] The primary difference is that the isolation and description of the interfering language is a much subtler and more difficult problem where NNE is concerned.

Using the native mainstream speaker's reaction as a kind of linguistic discovery device, we may begin analyzing names on the order of:

SACRED HEART SPIRITUAL CHURCH OF JESUS CHRIST, INC.

(This is a genuine name—some noted in Appendix A are even longer and more complex.) Length might be the first objective factor to be isolated as "different" in some way. In the more ordinary syntactic terms, there is nothing particularly unusual structurally. A singular noun preceded by modifiers and followed by a prepositional modifier is customary. *Inc.* may mark a somewhat unusual lexical item in this particular context, but it certainly occurs where *Inc.* would occur in any normal firm name, so that only in its occurrence in the church-naming field of discourse is it in any way unusual in English.

However, some of the same reactions are produced by the following names, without *Inc.*:

TRAVELING SOULS SPIRITUAL CHURCH (Washington, D.C.) THE TRUE TABERNACLE CHURCH OF THE FIRST BORN (Washington, D.C.)

[4] For a perceptive preliminary statement of the historical pattern indicated (creolization of a slave pidgin by field servants of slavery days, the ancestors in most cases of ghetto inhabitants, with subsequent decreolization in most areas except for Gullah territory), see W. A. Stewart, "Sociolinguistic Factors in the History of American Negro Dialects," *Florida FL Reporter*, V: 2 (Spring, 1967).

[5] See Inez Lopez Cohen, (Mrs. Octavus Roy Cohen), *Our Darktown Press* (New York, 1932).

[6] See, however, Marshall and Jean Stearns, "Frontiers of Humor: American Vernacular Dance," *Southern Folklore Quarterly*, XXX (1966), 227–35, an article in which there is more than a suggestion that white "blackface" comedy is based upon a genuine Negro comic tradition. The Kingfish and his wife Sapphire of the Amos n'Andy show seem, on this evidence, to be modeled upon Stringbean and Sweetie May or Butterbeans and Susie. The store-front church names under discussion here are superficially similar to the *Mystic Knights of the Sea*, although a really good grammar of NNE naming practice would probably not generate that name. The Amos and Andy taxi cab company, *The Fresh Air Taxicab Company of America "Incorpulated"* is an approximately equal mixture of real and phony traditions. (Charles J. Correll and Freeman F. Gosden, *Here They Are . . . Amos' n' Andy* (New York, 1931), p. 163.)

[7] See my articles in *Names*, XII (1964), 98–102; and XIV (1966), 178–80.

THE OLD SAMARITAN
BAPTIST CHURCH
(Washington, D.C.)
THE TRUE LEE BAPTIST
CHURCH (Dallas, Texas)

In order to cope with this problem in some kind of objective manner, a corpus of ghetto store-front church names (Appendix A) from the Washington, D.C. area was selected and compared with 20 names (Appendix B) taken from traditional churches from the Washington metropolitan and surrounding areas, where the congregations are middle-class, or mainly so, and mostly white.* An attempt was made to study these names through a phrase structure analysis, primarily through the device of *branching*, right or left, with the word *church* (or *temple*, etc.) considered as head. This process involves simply selecting a noun as "head"—or nuclear component—by arbitrary if intuitively reasonable procedures and counting as "branching" structures any components which occur to the left or to the right. Conventionally, a prepositional phrase would be considered as one component, even though composed of three or four words; a one-word adjectival modifier of the head noun would also be considered as one component. It is, of course, possible to write more complicated "generative" formulas; but it hardly seems necessary in the course of this discussion.

For the store-front churches, the left-branching expansion was far more numerous. It was made of noun forms and other premodifiers of mainly the adjectival type, with the occurrence of other form classes not generally part of nominal structure in standard English. Concerning the number of pre-modifiers of the head, it can be seen that, where standard English tends to use not more than one to three pre-modifiers, store-front churches generally use from three to five of them e.g.,

CHESTER GRAHAM RESCUE
MISSION
EAST FRIENDSHIP BAPTIST
CHURCH
MOUNT SION CHRISTIAN
SPIRITUAL CHURCH
MOUNT ZION UNITED HOLY
CHURCH
NEW MOUNT NEBO BAPTIST
CHURCH
THE OLD SAMARITAN
BAPTIST CHURCH
FIRST RISING MOUNT ZION
BAPTIST CHURCH

Where right-branching is concerned, differences in usage from what is usual in standard English are often to be found. These discrepancies are mainly of the type where the head of the nominal group is followed by two prepositional phrases, sometimes containing as many as nine words in post-modifiers like these two prepositional phrases. This is clearly observable in the following:

CANNANITE (sic) TEMPLE OF
THE CHURCH OF GOD
CHURCH OF GOD OF TRUE
HOLINESS
THE CHURCH OF GOD
UNIVERSAL HOLINESS NO. 1

* For an earlier comparative study of white and Negro church names in one city, see G. Thomas Fairclough, " 'New Light' on 'Old Zion,': A Study of the Names of White and Negro Baptist Churches in New Orleans," *Names*, 8 (1960), pp. 75–86. —ED.

THE REFUGE CHURCH OF
OUR LORD JESUS CHRIST
OF THE APOSTOLIC FAITH

It will be noted of course, that these examples are not without left-branching as well. The most usual case, indeed, is multiple branching, which may be the chief source of the intuition that these practices are different from those of standard English. There are frequent nominal strings which not only offer from three to four pre-modifiers—with the inclusion even of verb forms—but also a post-modifier consisting of two prepositional phrases. Examples are:

THE HOLY EVANGELISTIC
CHURCH NO. 2 OF NORTH
AMERICA
THE SACRED HEART
SPIRITUAL CHURCH OF
JESUS CHRIST, INC.
MOUNT CALVARY HOLINESS
CHURCH OF DELIVERANCE
OF THE APOSTOLIC FAITH
BETHLEHEM FIRE BAPTIZE
HOLINESS CHURCH OF GOD
OF THE AMERICANS

The "traditional" churches chosen for this comparison do have much more simplified names (see Appendix B), than those of the Negro store-front churches. It will be noted, particularly, that right-branching is an uncommon device; where utilized, it consists entirely of institutionalized sequences like *of the Latter-Day Saints* and *of Jehovah's Witnesses*. Although the traditional, predominantly white middle-class churches display both right- and left-branching, the former is quite limited. Multiple branching, is almost nonexistent, except where there are institutionalized forms on the right.

Noticeable differences are to be found in the number of pre-modifiers of the head of the nominal group. In opposition to the four and even five pre-modifiers of Negro store-front churches, the traditional ones do not appear to favor long strings of pre-modifiers. Three appears to be the maximum in this limited comparative list, with a frequency of usage of only one or two premodifiers being the most common. Most modifiers tend to be limited to the institutionalized forms.

A facile assumption would be that the store-front church naming practice reflects a kind of exuberance of language —and, elsewhere popular writers apply such terms as *exuberant*[8] to the Afro-American dialects. After checking hundreds of city telephone books (including those from certain cities in the South where Baptist churches for example, are still listed under *Negro* and *White*), I am inclined to believe that, insofar as *exuberant* has implications of "spontaneous improvisation," the truth may be a more pedestrianly grammatical one. Components like *Bethel* (*Church of XYZ*) recur very frequently, modified into *New Bethel XYZ* and *Greater New Bethel XYZ No. 2*, etc. As is the case with NNE in general, the components do not differ from those of SE; it is the putting together, the syntax, which differs. (A striking non-onomastic case is NNE *You been*

---

[8] Noreen, p. 19, writes of the "vitality and imagination expressed in the names of these churches," compared to which "traditional church names of established, sophisticated denominations are somber and colorless."

know that.) A few cases of deviational morphology (*Fire Baptize* in store-front names; *he brother* in the NNE of relatively early age grades,[9]) call attention to themselves rather strikingly, yet their complete implications are not apparent until they have been placed in the total context. Admittedly this paper is only a halting first step in that placing in context for store-front church naming practices. By implication, however, it would extend to other naming practices.

An additional dimension in grammatical complexity is suggested by a few names in Noreen's list

THE LORD IS ABLE HOUSE
   OF PRAYER
LOOK AND LIVE COMMUNITY
   CHURCH
RISE AND SUN SPIRITUAL
   CHURCH

where the first, particularly, is grammatically unlike the names of middle-class churches. All three examples are apparently unembedded sentences, the last two being imperatives (not so unusual, admittedly, in standard English naming practices as is the first) and the last being perhaps an original *Rising Sun* which was made to conform to the pattern. The use of the untransformed sentence as a modifier is the feature which I wish to call attention to, and hesitantly to compare to naming practices of the same type in West Africa and in the Caribbean. These are vehicles, and the head noun which would presumably be modified by the sentence is usually not overtly expressed. It would be easy to supply *Bus*, *Mammy Wagon*, *Voiture* or some other such name. Bus ("Mammy Wagon") names from West Africa include

People Will Talk of You[10]
Love is Nice
Life is War
All Shall Pass[11]
If It Must It Will[12]
Rien n'est total dans la vie[13]

even omitting the very frequent use of imperative sentences in such function. Equivalent unembedded sentences used in naming structures, again apparently without head noun, occur in Martiniquan canoe names:

Dieu Seul Sait
Le Jour est Arrive
Ç.A.Q.F.CA Ç. D. LAR D
   (Initial name, interpreted by owner as "Ça qui fait ça a cent dollars")[14]

Whether these naming patterns are to be explained as cultural survivals or in some other way, they provide interesting departures from "traditional" (European) naming practices.

APPENDIX A

The Bible Way Church of Our Lord Jesus Christ World Wide, Inc.

---

[9] Noreen, p. 26, cites *State Street Move of God Church*, where *Move* is apparently *mother*—reflecting a well-known and very widespread NNE dialect pronunciation.
[10] Jan Harold Brunvand, "A Note on Names for Cars," *Names*, X (1962), 279–84.
[11] N. T. Keeney, "The Winds of Freedom Stir a Continent," *National Geographic*, vol. 118, no. 3 (Sept. 1960), 303–59.
[12] Langston Hughes, *An African Treasury* (New York, 1960).
[13] J. L. Dillard, *Afro-American and Other Vehicle Names*, Institute of Caribbean Studies, Special Study no. 1 (March 1965). Several other names of this type, primarily from Haiti, are included.
[14] Richard and Sally Price, "A Note on Canoe Names in Martinique," *Names*, XIV (1966), p. 160.

Bethel Commandment Church of the Living God

Bethlehem Fire Baptize Holiness Church of God of the Americans

Brookland Union Baptist Church

Brown Memorial AME Church

Cannanite (sic) Temple of the Church of God

Chester Graham Rescue Mission

Church of God of True Holiness

Deliverance Church of God in Son

Emmanuel Church of God in Christ

East Friendship Baptist Church

First Rising Mount Zion Baptist Church

Full Speed Gospel Church

Georgetown Psychic Healing Church

Gospel Union Church of Christ

Gospelite Full Gospel Church

Holy Mount Olives Church of Christ of the Apostolic Faith

International Constitutional Church Organitional

Marantha Gospel Hall

Montell Avenue Baptist Church

Mount Calvary Holiness Church of Deliverance of the Apostolic Faith

Mount Pleasant Baptist Church Inc.

Mount Tabor Baptist Church

Mount Zion United Holy Church

New Bethel Baptist Church

New Mount Nebo Baptist Church

Old Way Baptist Church

Peoples Church

Royal Fellowship Center

Second Eureka Baptist Church

The Church of God Universal Holiness No. 1

The Full Gospel Baptist Church

The Holy Evangelistic Church No. 2 of North America

The Old Samaritan Baptist Church

The Refuge Church of Our Lord Jesus Christ of the Apostolic Faith

The Sacred Heart Spiritual Church of Jesus Christ, Inc.

True Baptist Church

United House of Prayer

APPENDIX B*

Foundry Methodist Church

Cathedral of Sts. Peter and Paul

St. Dunstan's Episcopal Church

St. Alban's Episcopal Church

Kingdom Hall of Jehovah's Witnesses

Washington Cathedral

Church of the Epiphany

Walker Methodist Church

St. Dominic's Church

The National Methodist Church

Metropolitan Memorial Methodist Church

Grace Lutheran Church

Epiphany Episcopal Church

St. John's Church

Trinity Episcopal Church

St. Agnes Catholic Church

St. Mary's Church

Immanuel Presbyterian Church

Langley Hill Meeting of the Religious Society of Friends

* Appendix B is shorter than Appendix A because of special conditions in the District of Columbia, which make it difficult to find "traditional" churches about which one can be certain that there is no mixture of store-front tradition. A few articles have appeared on names of "traditional" churches; e.g., Charles A. Ferguson, "Saints' Names in American Lutheran Church Dedications," *Names*, vol. 14, no. 2 (June, 1966), 76–82.

Black Ulysses in Camp

HOWARD W. ODUM

    Folk speech consists of far more than names. Rather, it includes the vast number of idioms and slang terms which enliven everyday spoken discourse. In the following essay, a white sociologist who spent many years studying American Negro folksong and folk speech describes the life of a black soldier around the time of World War I. While some may object to the feigned auto-biographical stream-of-consciousness technique employed by Professor Odum, it is hoped that they will appreciate both the richness of the folk speech and of the specific details of army and post-war life.

    Those who particularly like the style of this type of "poetic sociology" may wish to refer to the several books which Professor Odum wrote in this vein. Both the articles and the books were apparently based upon a mixture of fact and fiction. The fact consisted of real-life stories of a one-armed wandering Negro laborer who was called "Left-Wing Gordon"; the fiction was Professor Odum's rendering of these stories. For other samples, see "Black Ulysses Goes to War," American Mercury, *17 (August, 1929), pp. 385–400;* Rainbow Round My Shoulder: The Blue Trail of Black Ulysses *(Indianapolis, 1928);* Wings on My Feet: Black Ulysses at the Wars *(Indianapolis, 1929);* Cold Blue Moon: Black Ulysses Afar Off *(Indianapolis, 1931). For more conventional academic works by Odum, see* Social and Mental Traits of the Negro *(New York, 1910); "Religious Folk-Songs of the Southern Negroes,"* American Journal of Religious Psychology and Education, *3 (1909), pp. 265–365; "Folk Song and Folk Poetry as Found in the Secular Songs of the Southern Negroes,"* Journal of American Folklore, *24 (1911), pp. 255–94, 351–96; and* Race and Rumors of Race *(Chapel Hill, 1943). There were also his joint works with Guy B. Johnson,* The Negro and His Songs *(Chapel Hill, 1925), and* Negro Workaday Songs *(Chapel Hill, 1926). For further details about Professor Odum and a bibliography of his writings, see* Folk, Region, and Society: Selected Papers of

Reprinted from *The American Mercury*, vol. 18 (September, 1929), pp. 47–59, by permission of *The American Mercury*.

Howard W. Odum, *arranged and edited by Katharine Jocher, Guy B. Johnson, George L. Simpson, and Rupert B. Vance (Chapel Hill, 1964).*

For earlier accounts of black soldier life, there is Thomas Wentworth Higginson, Army Life in a Black Regiment *(Boston, 1869, paperback edition, New York: Collier Books, 1962), with its important discussion of spirituals. For more recent reports of Negro military life, see Seymour J. Schoenfeld, "Present Status of the Negro in the Armed Forces,"* The Negro History Bulletin, *8 (November, 1944), pp. 29–30, 43–47; L. D. Reddick, "The Negro in the United States Navy During World War II,"* Journal of Negro History, *32 (1947), pp. 201–19; John P. Davis, "The Negro in the Armed Forces of America," in John P. Davis, ed.,* The American Negro Reference Book *(Englewood Cliffs, N. J., 1966), pp. 590–661; Richard Stillman II, "Negroes in the Armed Forces,"* Phylon, *30 (1969), pp. 139–59. For additional references, see the section "The Negro as a Soldier," in Monroe N. Work,* A Bibliography of the Negro in Africa and America *(London, 1965), pp. 397–404. For a somewhat anecdotal, but nonetheless valuable, reporting of songs sung by black soldiers during World War I, see John J. Niles,* Singing Soldiers *(New York, 1927).*

BEEN MIGHTY change since I been born. Change where I been, never changed me. I been to war an' I been back. Already told about it. War change times, never changed me. Like I say, me an' war same things. Had it all my day, gonna have it till I die. War never got me, never will. Got my buddies, never got me. Had some turrible times in France, diggin' an' workin' an' fightin'. Maybe I done forgot about it, maybe I recollects some things. Howsomever, hard times in American camps whut I'm talkin' about. Hard times after war whut's blowin' me down.

> I been down so long,
> Down don't worry me.
> Lawd, don't you grieve after me!

Wus drafted in service at 3:30 P.M. for Camp Meade. Thought army life mus' be good. Nothin' to it for travellin' man like me. Gonna take it easy, didn't give a dam. Gonna see does the Kaiser know right from wrong.

> Joinin' Army to git free clothes;
> What war's about nobody knows.
> Lawd, don't you grieve after me!

First thing when we come into camp boys begin hollerin' at us. Hollerin' dam if they didn't send for train load of po'k an' beans an' here we come pokin' ourselves in camp instead! Some boys gittin' mad an' fightin'. Me, I ain't bother yet, I ain't bother yet.

So officer says, "What in the hell you doing standing here? Forward march!" So I marched up to 37 company D. P. o. p. B. B. II. There I had to fix up my bed. Went 'bout mile away to horse barns to get a tick of wheat straw and come back and went 'bout two miles to get a blanket. Then line up for supper at 11 o'clock that night. This was quite a nuisance to me, so I had in mind to leave and go back home the next day with my little white straw hat on and Norfolk coat.

> Ruther be in cornfield workin' hard,
> Than be buck private in National
>   Guard,
> Lawd, I'm on my way an' can't turn
>   back.

Company commander come in and he says, "Any of you boys leave this camp without orders means A. W. O. L.

If so you gonna ketch hell." And I thought to myself if I should ketch hell on this side and misfortune and die and go to hell on other side it would be two hells in one. So it paid me to stay in camp.

On the first morning they gave me ten minutes to dress for reverlee and five minutes thereafter. Next morning at 5 o'clock the bugle blowed for reverlee, I arose and dressed in ten minutes, and went out, not knowing where to go, not even where I was. I dropped in line with some soldiers.

One boy says, "You can't stand here."

I says, "I stand where I please, ain't I in the Army?"

'Bout that time sargent come to me and say, "What in the hell you doing standing here? Get over yonder with them ruckeys."

I says, "I guess I am a ruckey then."

"Yes," says he, "a dam ruckey."

So after reverlee we goes in for mess and after that we goes to the supply-house, and gets clothing, returning to barret an' goes to Marnel Station for examination. Passed 20:20 in every thing, returned back to barret, goes to insurance offices and rested the rest of the day excepting standing retreat.

Next morning, risin' up early, goes back to Marnel Station and taking a 'noculation, restin' remainder of the day. And for six weeks couldn't wash my face.

Camp sholy was roughish place. Some boys would form circle to say prayers at night. Whilst they was down to pray before taps, other boys was busy shootin' craps. Some old hero from Florida rose up and says, "Boys, why don't you get up? Look here who's serving the Lawd. Dam if you got any

time to serve the Lawd," he says, "Serve Uncle Sam, he is our best friend."

This big sargent wus jes' too mean to live. Too turrible to talk about. Would say to us boys. "Well, damit, I'm here to-day. World's in trouble. I don't keer if sun never shine. I don't give a dam 'bout my mother, neither God. To hell with God an' Devil both! I looks toward risin' sun an' tells both God an' Devil to go to hell." Lawdy, any man would cuss his mama an' God won't have no luck!

After this I taken the flu, but they never would let me be excused. I served in all the drills and the medicine they give me wusn't nothing but pills. I served on detail three weeks building a road from the camp eight miles from town. In five days I couldn't eat neither drink. Made me stay on duty. And when I would report on the sick list sayin' I was sick they would say, "Die and prove it!" Lawdy, Lawd, jes' like times I worked on chain-gang! Foreman would say, "Damit, die, an' prove it." War camp ain't nothin' new to me. Buildin' roads is my middle name.

> It takes the rock an' gravel,
> To make this solid road;
> It takes a good-lookin' woman
> To satisfy my soul.

Jes' bound to git in devilment. Don't mean no harm, jes' feel my hell a risin'. Way it wus, officers started after me an' jes' 'bout time they gonna ketch me, I stoops down low an two officers go pilin' over me on groun'. Reason I wus runnin' wus officers took us out on parade an' tells us to right face. Some boys face about, some lef' face, an' I makes out like I don't know nothin' an' so starts runnin' like hell. Never could tell whether officers tickled at my funny ways or whether wus mad. Leastwise made me do without supper, double time two hours next day, an' give me ten days' kitchen duty.

So they seen couldn't do nothin' else with me an' transferred me back to my company. One night me and Jesse wus on guard an' we both got mean an' wished we wus in France on the firing line. As we walked our post late that night the day officer and his wife and little black dog come tramping along. Of course we hollered, "Halt! who comes there?" and the officer said, "Friend of the camp." So we said, "Advance and be recognized." So he comes little closer, an' we says, "Halt! who comes here?" He said, "Officer of day, wife, and dog." So I hollered out, "If you the officer of the day, what in hell you doin' out here this time o' night?"

The next morning early after reverlee we goes in for mess and wus ordered to fall in line an' march to the supply-house for oversea equipments. Then after returnin', goes out on drill-field. Drill from nine in the mornin' till five-thirty without eatin' or drinkin'. Look like I jes' can't make it. Next mornin' 'bout 4 o'clock sargent blowed his whistle, and every devil fall out with his pack rifle .45. Then we had a thirty-mile straight hike, return back on that night about 10 o'clock. Every devil fall out in line with bag and equipments. Here we had a three-mile hike to another barret. Jes' natchelly went to sleep with my pack on.

Next mornin' commander called us out, fall out in column twos, an' general lectured to us. Told us we had to be booked in a few days for overseas. Said we boys been seein' easy time on this side, and when we found it bad over there make the best out of it we can.

Said he wanted every soldier to get a man before he died. So I said I'm goin' over there and get as many as I can put in a tank an' dam if I ain't comin' back home.

Next morning after reverlee boarded train for Camp Afervail. Landed at Camp Afervail one night, booked next day. But never did sail that time. Turned back in few days to Camp Afervail and transferred back to old camp. Boys mad as hell. When came to town near camp, boys decided gonna have some liquor an' so tore out to barroom worser than bloodhounds after raw beef. We act sociable long as money last, then we went snatching and jerking. In few minutes every barroom wus closed. But believe me, we soldiers had our shear!

> Well, me name is Uncle Sam,
> And I don't give a dam,
> If I takes a toddy now and then.
> Ain't been sober since last October,
> An' I don't know the reason why.

So next day company commander had all soldiers form circle an' lectured to 'em. Called 'em all sorts an' kinds o' names. Told us if any of us go A. W. O. L. we gonna ketch hell. An' all time we thought we wus already ketchin' hell now! So we returns to barret singin':

> All we do is sign pay-roll,
> All we do is sign pay-roll,
> Lawd, all we do is sign pay-roll,
> An' never draw a doggone cent!

Thought officers mad as hell, didn't know what to do. Boys gittin' mighty rough. Oughta heard them dices ring, oughta heard them singin' blues, drinkin', cussin', gamblin'. Lawd, Lawd, makes me think 'bout old times in construction camps and women comin' out from town.

Wouldn't give my high brown Belle,
For all madomesells this side o' hell.
Got them awful deep sea blues!

We had hard time gettin' back to
camp some nights. One night old James
got hold of wrong girl an' some ole
servitor beat him up so bad till he didn't
know where he wus at, neither who
he wus. Took me to call him home to
Promised Land with my good right
fist. Brought him home, laid other
fellow low. One time I got so drunk
couldn't tell where I wus, neither who I
wus, an' next day caught hell.

Done give myself to Uncle Sam,
Now I ain't worth a good goddam,
I don't want no mo' camp,
Lawd, I want to go home!

One night I wus out on guard duty
an' been goin' on so till I wus tired an'
sleepy. So I went to sleep settin' up'
gainst pile o' wheat straw. So some big
officer comes by an' hollers to me,
askin' who I is an' what I'm doin'.

So I rises up, steadyin' myself an'
says, "I am some sort of soldier. Who
the hell are you?"

Officer replies, "I am some sort of
major-general." So I says, "I guess I
better bring you some sort o' salute,
then." So I had company punishment
ten days. I jes' *would* be gittin' into
devilment all time.

Howsomever, I seen one white boy on
sentry duty standing an' leanin' 'gainst
haystack up 'bout Norfolk, froze stiff
an' dead befo' he wus found. Mus a
jes' got sleepy like I did an' in cold
Winter of 1917. Jes' went to sleep an'
never did wake up, leastwise 'scusin'
it be in Heaven or Hell. War got that
buddy, never got me.

One time crowd of us boys wus in
town waitin' for way to git back to
camp. So we gets 'round in circle an'
starts rollin' them bones. Policeman
comes 'long, sorter oldish captain, an'
says to us, boys, he knows he can't
arrest us but we got to stop shootin'
dices. So we asks him what the hell he's
gonna do. So he walks over and says
he can take our dices. An' so he does.
I gits up in front of him an' tells him
he's gonna give us our dices or me or
him one gonna eat breakfast or dinner
in Hell, don't make no difference to
me which one. So other boys git up an'
tells him that's right, we gonna have our
dices back. So old man jes' grins an'
hands 'em back to us, an' goes off mutterin' 'bout niggers runnin' this country,
dam if they ain't.

'Nother time one Sat'day night I
wus goin' cross bridge of creek hollerin'
and singin', namin' name of soldier,
'bout fohty wid breaks on. So Law
come up to me an' says I better watch
my step. So I don't do nothin' but pick
officer up an' throw him over bridge in
creek.

Oh, I'm mighty warrer in the Army,
I'm mighty warrer for my Lawd,
I'm fightin' soldier in the Army,
I'm soldier in Army of the Lawd.

Got in trouble one time. Wus goin'
on an' raisin' hell. Knowed officers
couldn't 'rest me. Told 'em I wus in
Army now, couldn't touch me. 'Bout
that time seen M.P.'s comin'. Actual fact,
chased me five miles up creek. Them wus
hard boys! So I got to stop, either be
blowed down, either got to go with
them.

'Bout that time moved me to 'nother
camp. Thought they move me more'n
other boys, leastwise took me to seven
camps, maybe eight, 'scusin' all I been

in after I goes over seas. Can't name 'em all, take me till tomorrow night to tell 'bout it. Thought I jes' bound to be travellin' soldier, ruckey or no ruckey, feel my hell a risin'. Me and war same thing.

II

One time in camp up 'bout Portsmouth I wus walkin' along an' white lieutenant hollers at me. "Where the hell you goin'?" So I says, "Where the hell you think I'm goin'?" Neither does I salute him.

So he asks me if I knows I'm talkin' to officer, an' I says, yes, hell, does he know he's talkin' to enlisted man. So he stands there starin' at one 'nuther' He takes matter up with officers but nothin' to do 'bout it, 'cause he started ruckus not treatin' me like soldier.

One evenin' late, boys all wet an' cold an' tired from workin' in rain all day, loadin' box cars. So wus gettin' late an' boys didn't work very fast. Boys jes' natchelly tired an' don't want to work no-how. So lieutenant comes up an' hollered at boys callin' 'em goddam niggers an' all sorts an' kind o' names. Wus white officer done it.

So we didn't do nothin' but beat that lieutenant up an' throw him in box car. Well, they had whole batallion 'rested, which I was one. Had hard time gittin' matter fixed up.

One day big white officer comes over to camp to see what could he do 'bout fixin' things up. So he comes on over to where big colored superior officer wus standin' an' comes up from behind an' hollers at him natural like, jes' same as if he wus in Birmingham or some place. Big colored officer don't do nothing but walk off with one o' them big short cigars in mouth whut he always smokin'. So white officer comes on over further an' hollers again. Colored officer don't look 'round but asks him if he knows he's speakin' to superior officer.

So white officer has to go 'round in front of colored officer an' salute. Colored officer takes his time, puffin' big cigar, then takes cigar out of his mouth an' salutes. Then he tells white officer to stand at 'tention till he gits back. So he walks off an' stays 'bout half hour, which he then tells major he can go. So after that thought we didn't have no mo' trouble, only moved us to 'nother camp. Lawdy, Lawd, always movin' on, but just suit me, just suit me!

Howsomever, had some mighty fine officers, both colored and white. Like I say if officers treat me right seem to take a likin' to me with my winnin' ways. Would let me git 'way with most anything. Howsomever, done sumpin' to fine captain one time didn't aim to do.

Wus this way. I wus pretty good fighter an' boys always havin' fights. Jes' scrappin' an' also fights with gloves on. If boys jes' have to fight would git gloves, give 'em to boys, an' tell 'em to go to it, damit, to fight. Would have time watchin' 'em bust one 'nuther open. Like I wus sayin' I wus pretty good fighter an' would step out an' holler. "Anybody better fighter than I is ain't no wall between us." So nobody would step out.

One day, whilst I wus steppin' 'round talkin' 'bout it, little black boy runs up an' hits me upper cut an' knocks me flat. Boy slips out an' runs like rabbit. But I seen which way he goes an' so I jumps up an' starts after him. I wus mad as wet hen an' sholy gonna lay his body down. Boys hollerin' an' laughin' 'cause little fellow first one to git me. So I runs 'round corner where I seen him go and rushes up behin' him an' hits him on side o' head with left an' right, *bam, bam*, like pile-driver or sumpin'. Falls down like tree.

Howsomever, wus white captain I hit, neither wus it little black boy. Way it wus, this little fellow dodge behin' captain when he seen me comin' an' I wus so mad didn't see nothing but man standin' there. Lawd, thought I wus skeered o' myself! Didn't mean to hit captain. Oh my God, what shall I do?

Never did know how mad captain wus, never done much to me. Captain always bettin' on me an' would talk 'bout what good fighter I wus. How-somever, had to do something with me, everybody laughin' at him. Thought it must abeen funny sight big black buck private knockin' white captain down, with *bam, bam* on side of head. So told me if I had to be knockin' sumpin' I could kill three hundred flies 'fo' I got any supper. Didn't, I would ketch hell.

Thought I wus gonna git off easy, but told me when I got through killin' all flies in world gotta peal four thousand potatoes. Reason kep' on givin' me mo' punishment wus other white officers would rag him 'bout gittin' knocked out by Tiger Gordon, champeen black boy fighter of world. Heard one officer come up to him an' say, "Well, Captain, that black boy knocked hell out o' you, didn't he?"

Captain didn't say nothin'. So other officer repeats, "Well, Captain, I say, that nigger got a clean knockout, eh?" So captain says, "Yes, by God, and I'm gonna get one, too," but he misses other officer. Howsomever, captain don't hold no grudge 'gainst me and wus always whoopin' 'em up when I would git in good fight.

Had some big fights in Camp. One black boy wus mighty hard for me to kill, but knowed I would git him some day. Name wus Job Jenkins, but called him Battlin' Cowboy 'cause he come from Texas. So fixed up ringside seats an' had big Sat'day night fight. Called me Tiger Gordon. One crowd hollerin' fer me an' 'nother crowd hollerin' fer Cowboy. Lawdy, Lawd, could fight better hearin' crowd yellin'. If yelled fer me, made me fell like bear-cat huggin' lion. If yelled for Cowboy made me so mad could see dry land through muddy water. Gonna knock hell out of Cowboy sho'!

Boys would say to me, "Oh, you Tiger, that Battlin' Cowboy sho' is hard. He's a son-of-a-gun. He boxed all over New York. Cowboy jes' gonna be too smart for you. You jes' natchelly too slow for Cowboy."

So I would say, "Yes, by God, I'm a Sunrose, I'm Hell, I'm yeller-hammer goin' North, I'm sober-headed big boy gonna shoot into him. Gonna bust him so dam hard till he's like scrambled eggs. Gonna hit 'im on side of head till he can't guide hisself. Gonna tear his rump."

So crowd would start hollerin' "Hurry up, Cowboy, hit 'im in that one spot! . . . Kill 'im, Cowboy! . . . I'd kill that ole crutch boy any time! . . . That got 'im! . . . See that Cowboy comin'!"

Boys would holler to me, "Whoopee, Tiger, I want you to cut his throat this time! . . . I ain't satisfied! . . . Break his neck! . . . Reason I went to church Sunday, was prayin' for you! . . . Step out, Tiger, he ain't no woman! . . . Hit 'im! . . . Give him jes' one mo' like that an' I'll be satisfield! . . . Hee, hee, ketch, 'im Tiger, tear 'im in the rump!"

'Bout that time I seen Cowboy stop an' shake his head, look like he don't know where he is at. So I shoots him on other side of head, *bam, bam.* Sound like hame-string poppin'. Cowboy shakes his head like dog comin' up out of water. So I lands big uppercut an' Cowboy goes down. Won't be so iron-jawed with me no mo'.

I'm fightin' man, from Devil's Land,
I'm greasy streak o' lightenin', don't
    you see?
Lawd, don't you grieve after me!

We had heap other fights, big boys an' little boys. One of funniest sights I ever seen since I been born wus little black boy 'bout five feet high knockin' big black boy over six feet tall cold as monkey wrench. Little fellow wus too quick fer him, Lawd, Lawd. 'Nother funny sight wus when two boys been fightin', one boy knocked other down. Referee held up this fellow's arm signi-fyin' he wus winner. Bout' that time other boy got up an' wus so mad knocked winner cold an' started fightin' referee an' eveybody else in ring. Took 'bout four men to cool him off.

Boys mighty rough in war camp, same as wus in road-gangs an' construc-tion camps. One night in camp boys got to playin' game called dozen. Jes' *would* play dozen 'scusin' captains an' lieutenants not bein' 'round, cause been told not to do it. Mighty roughish game, boys talkin' 'bout other boys' folks. So one big boy tells 'nother big boy no use him worryin' 'bout his lovin' wife back home, 'cause somebody else shovelin' coal in his furnace. Told him she jes' like street-car, anyhow plenty folks payin' fare an' she ain't gonna starve. So this boy gits so mad he jumps up an' takes shoe-heel and busts other boy's head wide open an' kills him dead. After that captain tells boys he's jes' natchelly gonna shoot next man goes to playin' dozen. Oh, my Lawd, wonder does my baby know right from wrong!

Rocks on mountain,
Fishes in sea,
Slacker got my woman,
Army got me.

'Nother thing would do in camp wus singin'. Whenever major or general would come 'round captain would have boys sing. Maybe would be out on field drillin'. So would be 'bout thousand men, some singin' bass, some tenor, some other kinds, an' sholy would harmonize. Wished I could be settin' off on hill somewhere jes' listenin' to 'em sing. Had all sorts an' kinds o' songs, take me till tomorrow night to count 'em. Couldn't name 'em all. Some Army songs an' some religious songs. Look like boys just made to sing, forgits troubles an' Army an' everthing. Singin' an' war same things.

Officers like to hear soldiers sing with deep-rollin', boomin' voices. Would sing special war songs, like "Goodbye, Broadway; Hello, France," "Long Trail A-Windin'," an' others same as white soldiers sung. But what officers like to hear wus songs like "I Am Climbin' Jacob's Ladder," "Do You Think I'll Make a Soldier," "I Been Fightin' in Army of Lawd All My Life," "Do Lawd Remember Me," "Jesus Is Listenin' All Night Long" or maybe

I want to be ready, I want to be ready,
Walkin' to Jerusalem just like John;
Oh Lawd, won't you come by here,
Lawd, won't you hear my prayer?—
Oh yes, Lawd, I want to be ready,
Yes, walkin' to Jerusalem just like
    John.

Some boys would sing an' some would shout, "Lawd, Lawd!" "Yes, oh my Lawd!" an' would go trampin' on, little further on, marchin' an' singin' till visitin' officers jes' could hear 'em.

We'll roll the old chariot along,
We'll roll the old chariot along,
We'll roll the old chariot along,
And we won't drag on behind.

III

'Bout that time moved us to 'nother camp. Told us we wus gettin' ready to go overseas. Howsomever, we stayed in that camp long time befo' moved us to last one. Had sorrowful thing happen. One of my chiefest buddies, Charley Alexander Hoofer, got killed, neither could police find out who killed him. Boys called him Hoof, an' sho' wus some hoofer. Me an' Hoof made powerful pair buddies. Found him all shot up one mornin' 'bout risin' of sun. Law can't find out who done it. I'm gonna git that dam rascal if last thing I do. Ruther stick man killed my buddy wid bayonet than shoot Kaiser Bill fohty-fo'.

Wus this way. Hoof wus big high-brown boy. Women belong to him wid his winnin' ways. Wus hawk like pizen to men foolin' wid him. Maybe Hoof would come to new town. 'Nother black boy would come up to him an' say he wus rooster on the roost, an' was 'bout time Hoof be gittin' along, 'scusin' he don't want no spurs stuck in his belly. So Hoof would say, hell, he wus hawk whut *eats* roosters, and any black roosters 'round better watch out. Look like they jes' skeered of him; leastwise nobody could run him off.

If Hoof wanted girl would jes' say, "Well, I believe I'll git that baby."

So she would fall in love with him an' leave husband or sweetheart. Hoof would have mo' sweet mamas than he could be sweet papa to. Would give him money an' likker an' be sweet mama to him. Howsomever, in this town near new camp Hoof found him pretty high-brown. Thought he would leave all other women alone. Hoof wus crazy 'bout this teasin' brown an' she wus crazy 'bout Hoof. Everybody else crazy 'bout her likewise an' Hoof scattered niggers like hawk swoopin' down on chickens. Still, this girl so foolish in her head 'bout Hoof wouldn't let other boys touch her. Would call 'em cheap skates, signifyin' she had handsome high-brown soldier hero. Would jes' go blind an' rave over Hoof. If he jes' look at her she jes' open up an' fall in his arms. Jes' wouldn't let him go, would do anything for him an' never tire. Hoof swear he's gonna stay with her till Hell freeze over.

Some black devil slacker bound to git po' Hoof, gonna lay his body down. Played bad on him. Must a sneaked up from behind an' shot him down. Onliest way could git him. So found him with hole in his head 'bout risin' of sun. Said I wus gonna git dam scoundrel shot. I'm bad man, bad as hell I know. Gonna find him out. Gonna lay his body down some day.

So I feels my hell a risin'. I gits soldier blues, homesick blues, railroad blues, ain't got no fare. Got every kind o' blues anybody ever had, cryin' blues, swearin' blues, don't-care blues, 'fo-day blues, down-hearted blues.

Oh my baby, Lawd,
You don't know my mind,
When you think I'm laughin',
Laughin' to keep from cryin'.

Wus bound to git in trouble some way. Me an' war buddies, fightin's my middle name. So I seen big black preacher settin' up to this brown baby, talkin' sweet honey 'bout restin' in bosom of Jesus. I'm watchin' this black scoundrel. Don't like 'im, thinkin' 'bout po' Hoof. Got them crazy blues, hey baby, hey honey, don't know whether I'm gittin' sleepy, else gittin' hard as blue steel!

So I straggles 'long followin' black preacher an' high-brown lady takin' walk. I hears po' girl weepin' an' moanin' sayin' she ain't got nothin' to live fer. Wants po' Hoof. Say she don't believe Jesus is listenin' all day long, an' she don't give a dam if He is. Preacher says Hoof wus sinner-man gone to Judgment Day.

'Bout that time I feels my hell a risin', got crazy blues. Got ramblin' blues, got bad-man blues, gonna have them chain-gang blues. So I goes trompin' 'round, gonna git in front of dam nigger. Gonna call him ever name 'scusin' Son of God.

So I comes staggerin' up bellowin' like a bull. 'Bout that time me feets nearbout freeze to ground. I don't know whether I'm in Heaven or Hell. Don't know whether I'm skeered or fightin' mad. Me an' war same thing. Got fightin' blues, can't be satisfied. Oh my God, seen po' Hoof come floatin' in between big preacher an' high-brown girl, floatin' in coffin, lid poppin' off, oh my God! Seen hole in his head, seen blood gushin' out. 'Seen po' Hoof signifyin' to me big black devil whut done it.

Got them crazy blues, done gone mad, yellin' an' hollerin'. "Oh my God. po' Hoof, is you hurt? Is you shot? Where is you at? I'm comin', Buddy, gonna kill that black nigger sho' as Hell!" So high-brown lady gits to scream-

in'. I'm comin' on tryin' to git my hands on nigger. Got him by throat, gonna choke him till eyeballs pop out, gonna break his neck jes' like chicken. Thought preacher begin to pray, Oh Lawd, to have mercy on him. Thought Hoof wus breathin' fire on him, eyes look like little red balls o' lightnin' flashin'. Oh my God, never seen such a sight since I been born. Preacher hollerin', lady screamin', I'm cussin' an' fightin' an' yellin' like Devil hisself.

Shot my pistol in heart of town,
Big chief holler, "Don't you blow me
    down."
Oh, which a-way did po' girl go?
She left here runnin' is all I know.

'Bout that time M.P.'s come up. Big black nigger went crashing through fence palin' an' woods like bear on hillside. Never did ketch him. Made his getaway like greasy streak o' lightnin'. But I'm gonna git him dam skin yet. M.P.'s got me an' took me back to camp. Good thing locked me up. Had them crazy blues, gonna raise hell. Been in Army longer than I stays in camp. Never stays more'n three weeks, leastwise never mo'n four in no one place. But I'm in Army now, nothin' to do 'bout it. Made me tote big rocks weighin' 'bout 150 pounds; made me carry wood mile an' half, made me cut cord wood, made me do all sorts an' kind o' things.

Lawd, wish I wus in Georgia,
Singin' jail-house blues.
Lawd, don't you grieve after me!

Howsomever, got letter from my mother. Gits me to thinkin' 'bout sompin' else. Like I told you, las' time she was mighty fine lady, always helpin' somebody an' always talkin' 'bout how good Lawd been to her. So she wrote me to do best I could. Told me 'bout me sister's husband dyin' with flu an' said she had letter from her. My sister wus in Washington an' Mama says hopes charity folks won't let her suffer. Wus writin' her to come on home and would take keer of her an' children. Wus always doin' things like that.

Howsomever, in a few days got 'nother letter from my sister tellin' 'bout Mama dyin' with flu. Captain won't give me no leave, can't go home. Always tellin' me he's gonna see what could he do. Never done it. Signified gonna take us to last camp befo' we goes over. Can't go home.

That old letter read 'bout dyin',
Boy, did you ever think about dyin'?
Then I can't read it now for cryin',
Tears run down, Lawd, tears run
        down!

Make me think how mean I been, mean as hell I know. Jes' old Kid Bad workin' in me. Never meant no harm, jes' feel my hell a risin', always some other place better'n this, some other work easier, road callin' me on. This old worl' been a hell to me ever since I left my mama's house. Now she's done dead an' gone, sleepin' in her grave, I want to go home, Lawd, I want to go home! Funny how colored soldiers always wonderin' will they ever git back home to see sweet old mommer. Always singin' 'bout best friend in this world, somebody to tell trouble to. Then treat po' mother like fatherless child. I'm same way. Can't tell you reason why, can't name it. Must be me an' war same thing. Other boys same way, sorrowful, an' blue, singin',

I'm gonna meet me mother,
Some day in Promised Land.

She stole away an' went to Heaven,
Hope I join her in the band.

Soldiers got homesick blues, got faraway blues, got cemetery blues. Jes' set an' droop around, head hung down studyin'. Somebody would come 'round, tryin' to cheer 'em up. Wouldn't say nothin'. Can't see how other boys laughin' an' goin' on. Howsomever, don't do no good mopin' 'round, can't go home, jes' make matters worse.

If blues wus whiskey
I'd be drunk all the time.

Heap of boys skeered. Never seen much of world like I has, never been travellin' man. Skeered of everything. Skeered poison gas in water, think German spies gonna blow 'em up at night. Wus skeered to put lights out at night, skeered to cross that big water, can't study nothin' but wantin' to go home. Lawd, wantin' to go home. Boys would git mad cause wus skeered an' would start joreein' an' braggin' 'bout whut they gonna do on the other side.

Did you hear whut become of long tall boy called Spider Brown started off with us? He wus powerful funny boy. Would dance an' sing and carry his box everywhere he went. Nobody couldn't git his banjo 'way from him. Love to play. Could step on it, wus some musicianer, and songster. Wus big talker, too, but always singin' an' lookin' 'way off like wus seein' sumpin' couldn't tell 'bout.

Went with us to Jacksonville. Wus mighty sad case. Couldn't do nuthin' with him. Got so homesick wouldn't eat, wouldn't drink, neither would he sleep. Said home folks died. Wouldn't let him go home to funeral. Officer couldn't talk to him. Red Cross man couldn't do nothin' with him jes' 'bout loses his mind, eyes stare an' look different. Worrination jes' got him. Officers would try everything. Couldn't do nothin' with him. Would cry an' holler. Give him box an' told him to sing. Didn't do nothin' but play an' sing homesick blues:

Wish to God some old train would
　　run,
Carry me back where I come from.

Mighty sorry to hear 'bout po' Spider. Thought a heap of that old boy. I seen other boys tryin' to get away, makin' excuses an' tryin' all sorts an' kinds o' tricks to get back home. Remember old boy called Gus Bigun, big boy from Mississippi. Well, Gus told 'em he couldn't hear nothin'. Couldn't prove he wus lyin'. Would ask him all sorts an' kinds of questions. Wouldn't open his mouth, neither signify that he wus hearin' whut they ask. So one officer says to leave it to him an' he'll fix up this boy. So he does. They puts Gus in room where he can hear 'em talkin'. So they begins talkin' loud an' sayin' well they is sorry but have to send Gus back home. Says he can't hear and don't want no deef soldiers in Army. So this officer goes in room where Gus is an' says right sudden like, "Well, Gus, what you gonna do when you git home?" An' Gus he says, "I don't know yet, Captain." So they puts him in labor batallion an' first makes him work at hard labor for week.

Heard 'bout other boys tryin' all sorts an' kinds of ways to git out of Army. Would play sick. Would tie rubber bands 'round legs to make 'em swell up. Would put soap under arms. Would smoke asthma tablets rolled up in cigarette to see could they git fever. No need to play sick, gonna make you sorry sho'.

Did you hear about old boy called Enoch Hoop? Well, would jes' leave camp an' couldn't keep him from it. Maybe would slip out one way today an' nother way tomorrow. Would put on citizens' clothes an' get away. Punished him same as other boys but couldn't stop him. So they filled up tank of water and put Enoch in tank. Then let water run in till gits nearly to his mouth. Then gives him thimble to scoop it up with. Howsomever, water runnin' in faster than he can scoop it out. Boy gits skeered an' strangled an' begins hollerin', oh Lawdy, will he ever get out. But never cured him. Look for him to go A.W.O.L. when he gits on ship. Don't know how he's gonna do it but sho'ly look for him to git away with sumpin'.

Yeh, we had big boy in one camp jes' like that. Jes' would slip out, like magic. Couldn't tell where he got out an' how he would get back. Tried all sorts punishment. So one time officer got man an' made him dig big grave. Stood over him with guns and made him dig his own grave. When got grave dug, made him stand up at end so would fall in it when firin' squad shot.

So gets six men with rifles lined up an' tells boy to git ready to tell his Jesus good-mornin', 'cause he ain't got long to stay here. Boy swears he won't *never* leave no mo' without orders if they jes' spare his life. So lets him off. Never did aim to kill him. All boys with guns wus on to trick.

'Bout that time boys dyin' with flu like hogs with cholera back on Tello's farm in Mississippi. Captain told me to drive truck-load colored soldiers piled up dead; said thought that might keep me out o' meanness while. Lawd, never seen like since I been born!

> I looks into the East,
> I looks into the West;
> Lawd, I sees dead a risin',
> From every graveyard.

Look like Judgment Day. Folks dyin' back home an' writin' pitiful letters. Soldiers dyin' in camp. Boys sick in tents an' camp hospital. Hospital for sick, graveyard for dead. Couldn't count 'em, loaded 'em off in boxes. Never seen like since I been born.

Onliest one thing help po' boys in time of trouble. Red Cross officers in camp an' Red Cross ladies back home wus whut done it. Officers would help out in camp an' would git white folks to help back home. When my mama died an' captain won't let me go home, Red Cross man sends telegram. In 'bout two days he gits telegram back sayin' mama had good funeral, both white an' colored folks helpin', an' my sister is well an' takin' keer of all folks. So I feels better an' havin' telegram work for me helps my feelin's a heap. Thought I would try to do better.

Would say to myself, damit if I ain't patriot. Heard band play, got to marchin', buddies dyin' made me think maybe neither would I ever git back again. So I says to myself, any man that is of this country got to go an' sacrifice his life. I got to do the same. I wus principled up like this, if I had to go I could do it. Wan't no hero, wan't no coward. I can do what I have to do. Got to luck it. If I'm gonna git killed I'm gonna git killed. Howsomever, war never got me, never will.

IV

Like I'm sayin' I been to war an' I been back. Been mighty change since I been born. Change where I been, never changed me. I disremembers most things I done in France. Done told about some of them. Told about comin' back on big ship. Well, big ship docks. Whistles blowin', bands playin', everbody talkin' an' goin' on. Red Cross an' Salvation Army meets us an' passes out things to soldiers, both colored an' white. Big crowds cheerin'. Feel like soldier in Army of the Lawd. Feel like patriot, proud to have name of soldier. Gonna have good time, ain't gonna work no mo'. Howsomever, glad we gonna git our discharge, won't be long. Lawd, won't be long!

> I'm gonna lay my burden down,
> Ain't gonna study war no mo'.
> Down by the river side.

So we takes ferry an' train an' goes over to same camp which we wus in befo' we sailed for overseas. Been mighty change since we been gone. Many long weary days have passed. Some buddies never did come back. Po' Shorty Geech an' Funny Sam an' other boys sleepin' in their graves in France. Feel powerful sorrowful, 'scusin' glad to git back. War never got me, never will. Got my buddies, never got me.

We stayed there from Wednesday 'bout three o'clock till Friday mornin' 'bout ten, when we left on train for Camp Gordon. Wus long train Pullman cars windin' 'round them curves. Boys mighty glad to git on board. Ridin' them cushions, settin' rared back. Ridin' them Pullman cars to the Promised Land. Mighty different now from whut wus when we started to camp, crowded all up in day-coaches like I told 'bout. Sho God different from ridin' in French box-cars.

So we goes on out to Camp Gordon on good old Southern road. Got in them good old cantonment barracks. Goodbye France, Hello Georgia, goodbye rain an' goodbye mud! Won't be long now, Lawd, I'm on my way an' can't turn back! Lord, sun don't set in the morning. Got rainbow round my shoulder, wings on my feet.

> Some o' these mornin's bright an' fair
> Gonna hitch my wings an' try the air.
> Lawd, don't you grieve after me!

We stayed there jes' precisely one week. Didn't know what day neither hour would we git discharged. So boys stayed in camp. No trouble at all keepin' 'em in line. So they gives us uniform, maybe two shirts an' underwear, hat an' overcoat. Salvation Army done give us socks an' handkerchiefs. So treated us fine, better than we been treated befo'. Thought we gonna be livin' easy, gonna be livin' high.

> Well, ain't no use me workin' so,
> 'Cause, Lawd, I ain't gonna work no
> mo'.
> Tain't nobody's business but my own.

Thought I would go see my sister, also mother of white captain got killed, lived in same town my mama did. Been mighty change since I been gone, felt sorry for myself, my mama bein' dead an' buried whilst I been in Army. Nobody to carry my troubles to. Found my sister an' her children doin' very well. Leastwise, had used all money I sent home to keep till I come back.

Went to see white lady, mother of white captain got killed in France and lady my mama worked for. Told him when he died I would do so. Felt mighty sorry for po' lady. Ask me how did her son die? Did I see him? Wus he sufferin'? Did he talk about his mother befo' he died? an' heap mo' questions which I wus tellin' her yes'm best way I could.

So I didn't stay there long. White lady an' husband told me would give me good job at house or workin' on college grounds. Howsomever, I wus not ready to settle down. Wus too restless, neither had I been to see my old friends, neither had I found black scoundrel that shot my buddy.

So I starts on road again. Thought I would ride cushions till my money give out. So first place I stops at wus town I worked in befo'. My friends showed me good time treatin' me better, maybe better than I been treated befo'. Had my uniform on, told 'em 'bout France, made 'em think I wus talkin' French. Lawd, I wus boy back home, jes' natchelly been mo' places than anybody else.

Howsomever, white folks told me would give me half hour, whether would I take my uniform off or leave town. I tells 'em I'm soldier of Uncle Sam. I been fightin' in France, can't do nothin' with me. They tells me they don't give a dam, I ain't no soldier neither, nothin' but dam nigger an' can't have me wearin' uniform. So they sends crowd of boys askin' me will I leave or will I not. Nothin' to do 'bout it, 'scusin' maybe I'm mutterin'.

> 'Scuse me mister, don't git mad,
> Gonna raise a ruckus to-night,
> 'Cause you look like sumpin, buzzard
> had,
> Gonna raise ruckus tonight.

So I leaves there, walkin' an' talkin' to myself, feels my hell a risin'. Nothin' to do 'bout it. I can do what I have to do an' maybe time come when I have to do it. Heard 'bout other boys in Tennessee an' Mississippi an' other States. Tore uniform off one boy. Nothin' to do 'bout it. White folks principled up like this, they don't keer if we been good soldiers or bad, we jes' come befo' them as man with black skin.

So we had some hard times jes' after war in South. White folks lookin' for nigger soldiers to raise ruckus. Heard 'bout sheriff's gittin' machine-gun, gittin' ready to blow us down, did we make attack. Heard 'bout whole town gittin' het up, thought colored people wus drillin' at night. Way it wus lodge wus havin' big initiatin' ceremony, marchin' round an' singin' an' goin' on.

So I starts out. Thought I would go back up North. Thought I would ride cushions till my money give out. Goin' to see my friends an' buddies, ain't gonna work no mo'. So I gits off at Philadelphia, place I been befo.' Too many soldiers back all come under same gourd vine. Jes' lak never been to war. Nothin' to do 'bout it. So I'm movin' on, always some place better, road callin' me on.

Thought I would go to California. Been there one time. Thought I would like that better. Would walk away from bein' mistreated soldier. So I rides cushion some an' works my way some. Howsomever, don't like it out there, neither can I git much to do. Feels like po' boy long way from home, ain't got a friend in this world.

I'm out in this wide world alone,
Got nobody to carry troubles to,

Good man jes' ain't treated right,
Oh, look down that lonesome road
    an' cry!

So I feels my hell a risin'. Gonna roll them bones. Gonna git some money an' play bad. So I'm gamblin' man, startin' with little money an' raisin' 'em higher. Black cat-bones an' Adam an' Eve charm workin' this time.

Come on, bones, an' treat me nice,
Roll' em, soldier, roll them dice!
Tain't nobody's business but my own.
Lawd, don't you grieve after me!

'Scusin' I ain't soldier no mo'. Been mighty change since I been born. Change where I been, ain't changed me. I'm travellin' man, I'm high brown, lean an' mean, ain't no soft-bellied green ruckey. Me an' war same thing. I been in all States an' foreign land. Been had trouble all my day. Nothin' to do about it. I'm on my way, Lawd, I'm on my way. Gonna ride them cushions to the Promised Land. Goin' where water taste like wine. Gonna see does my honey know right from wrong. Gonna hoo-doo black devil shot my buddy.

Thought I heard that K. C. whistle
    blow
Blow like she never blow befo';
Oh, she blow like she never blow
    befo'.

So my money lasts till I gits 'bout to Wyoming. An' I works little an' gambles some mo' an' goes on to North Dakota through Minnesota an' Omaha workin' on Great Northern an' on wheat fields an' whatever I could git to do. So I works an' gambles my way back through

Minnesota, an' Ohio. Won't be long, Lawd, won't be long!

> I'm goin' back to sunny South
> Where sun shines on my honey's
>   house;
> Tain't nobody's business but my own.

So I comes back to Virginia an' North Carolina, then goes on to Georgia an' Alabama an' back up Mississippi to Memphis, Tennessee. Thought Memphis good place if know how to git on, 'scusin' also I stayed in Memphis little while in trainin' an' guardin' big bridge. So thought I would go on up to Tennessee see could I be satisfied. Had them Memphis blues, Lawd, an' can't be satisfied.

> Well, it's come an' go to sweet
>   Tennessee
> Where the money grows on trees,
> Where the women do as they
>   please,
> Lawd, come an' go to sweet Tennessee.

Howsomever, got railroad blues, can't be satisfied. So I goes on back to North Carolina an' Virginia, then on up to Philadelphia an' New Jersey. Thought I would road hustle to see if times be like used to be. Seen many buddies back from war. Can't be satisfied. Some boys say ruther be shot than go to war again. Some boys say they learned heap 'bout world in war, ain't so bad, Lawd, ain't so bad. Some buddies mighty bitter. Say country don't treat 'em right over fightin' in Army. Say don't see why should fight fer Uncle Sam if Uncle Sam always 'busin' them.

Me, I ain't bother yet. I ain't bother yet. War don't make things no better, maybe neither worse. Well, I don't know, Lawd, I don't know. Heard some boys cussin' 'bout it. I don't give a dam. If I gits to thinkin' 'bout it, gits me mad as hell. So I ain't bother yet, I ain't bother yet.

Thought 'bout old times, workin' an' gamblin'. So I starts in road gang. Lawd, Lawd, look jes' like war. A man jes' natchelly don't count. Men an' mules an' wheelers an' captain an' walkin' boss hollerin' an' cussin'. Let wheelers roll, let wheelers roll! So I wus thinkin' 'bout all them times we had in France, an' 'bout all places I been to an' all things I done. Must a got keerless 'cause 'bout that time stonecrusher come down on my arm. Thought it smashed it clean off. Captain hollerin' at me what hell I'm doin'. Oh my Lawd, how in hell I know whut I'm doin'? So I lost my left arm. Nothin' to do about it, goddam.

> Trouble, trouble been had it all my
>   days,
> Trouble meet me at the do',
> I'm goin' where trouble ain't no mo',
> Lawd, don't you grieve after me.

So I starts again as hustlin' sport. Maybe women's treat me little better with one arm, like po' boy needin' a friend. Can shoot with my good right hand an' maybe don't git in so many fights. Leastwise, I ain't bother yet, I ain't bother yet. Seen mo' buddies travellin' 'round. Heard 'em talkin' 'bout war. All come under same gourd vine. Heard Pullman porters an' cooks an' hustlin' sports an' rum-runners. Thought they have hard time.

White man gives me job as night watchman at 'lectric plant. Thought he treated me fine. He wus pleasant to me an' I wus pleasant to him. Thought maybe I would be satisfied. So one night somebody come prowlin' 'round. I been guardin' in Army an' so I says, "Halt, who goes there?" He don't say nothin' an' starts runnin'. So I tells him to halt, which he don't. So I shoots. Wus white man! Oh my Lawd, trouble, trouble! Been had it all my day, gonna have it till I die!

So Law 'rested me an' put me in jail. Big crowd white folks gatherin'. Crowd kept comin' thought better call out company of soldiers. Could look out of jail bars an' see soldiers settin' 'round an' standin' up. Thought about me bein' soldier, proud of name of soldier workin' an' fightin' in France. Now soldiers guardin' me to keep folks from stringing me up, all jes' cause I done whut I wus told to do in Army. Wus some other colored boys in prison. Oh my Lawd, hear 'em singing:

> I am climbing Jacob's ladder,
> I am climbing Jacob's ladder,
> I am climbing Jacob's ladder,
> Soldier of the cross!
>
> Do you think I'll make a soldier,
> Do you think I'll make a soldier,
> Do you think I'll make a soldier,
> Soldier of the cross?

Never hurt white man much. Jes' shoot 'im through chest. So good white folks got me off. Thought about it, Lawd, thought about it. Been mighty change since I been born. Change where I been, never changed me. Thought about trainin' in camp. Thought about war in France. Thought about my mama's papa's tellin' me 'bout fightin' tribes of Africa. Me an' war same thing. Been had it all my day. Gonna have it till I die. Howsomever, war never got me. Got my buddies, never got me.

Lawd, been mighty change since I been born. Lawd, I wonder is good old U. S. A. gonna blow me down. Thought about marchin' in New York, peoples cheerin' colored soldiers. Thought about singin' on boat goin' over when torpedo missed us. Thought 'bout singin' on ship back an' train goin' home.

Thought about boys singin' in France 'bout pack up yo' troubles in yo' old kit bag, an' me yodlin', "Oh, where shall I go for to ease my trouble in mind?" Well I don't know, Lawd, I don't know. Been mighty change since I been born. Change where I been, never changed me. Maybe some other crowd git me some other day. Maybe neither will they blow me down. Well, I don't know, Lawd, I don't know. I'm leavin' here, won't be long now, won't be long. Gonna rock trouble to sleep, rainbow 'round my shoulder, wings on my feet. Well, don't you grieve after me.

> I'm gonna lay my burden down,
> Ain't gonna study no mo'.
> Yes, by God, I'll be in Heaven
> When I lay my burden down,
> Ain't gonna study war no mo'
> Down by the riverside.

Dialogues of the Old and the New Porter

A. PHILIP RANDOLPH

One of the great struggles in the twentieth century has been the Negro's attempt to join the ranks of organized labor. Although there remain numerous labor unions which continue to discriminate against Negroes, by and large there has been some improvement. Part of the credit for this improvement belongs to the small but active band of Negro labor leaders, and, of these, surely one of the most eminent is A. Philip Randolph.

The organization of the Pullman sleeping car porters into a labor union was accomplished to a great extent by the dedicated and zealous work of A. Philip Randolph. Just one of the many persuasive techniques he employed was the following fictional dialogue sequences which he published in The Messenger *in 1927. In the dialogues, we find a "New Porter" representing, in a way, the "New Negro" who has realized the necessity of having strong unions in order to better the Negro worker's lot. The pro-union porter tries— successfully—to induce the old "Uncle Tom" porter to join the union. Aside from the obvious historical interest of the content of the dialogue, there is for the present context a useful illustration of the importance of folk speech. The dialogues are chock-full of proverbs and colorful idioms. It is not entirely clear whether the abundance of slang was intentional or not, but judging from the definite distinction between the heavy rural dialect of the Uncle Tom porter and the smart citified speech of the New Negro porter, one might hazard a guess that the extended use of folk speech was part of Randolph's verbal strategy. In any case, much of the vitality of the dialogues comes from the presence of the folk speech of the period.*

For more information about Randolph and the union, see Brailsford R. Brazeal, The Brotherhood of Sleeping Car Porters (*New York, 1946*). For an appreciation of Randolph, see John Henrik Clarke, "Portrait of an Afro-American Radical," Negro Digest, 16 (March, 1967), pp. 16–23.

Reprinted from *The Messenger*, vol. 9 (1927), pp. 94, 131–32, by permission of the author.

I

UNCLE TOM PORTER: How is you, son?
NEW PORTER: Can't say it, Pop.

U. T. P.: Can't say what? What's th' matter wid you? 'Specks you got dat Randolph fever, too, eh?

N. P.: What d'you mean?

U. T. P.: Don't try to fool de ole fox, son. Bin heah too long. You know what I mean. What about dat Brotherhood?

N. P.: Well, what about it? Anything wrong with it?

U. T. P.: I ain't saying no or yes. Is you joined yet?

N. P.: Why do you want to know? Did Mitchell or Burr tell you to ask me?

U. T. P.: Now, look heah, son, you muss think I is a stool pigeon.

N. P.: Well, I wouldn't know, Uncle. I ain't taking no chances.

U. T. P.: Now, sho nuf, son; 'twixt you, me and the gate post, what do you think about dis Union business?

N. P.: Well, since you have asked me, I'll tell you. I think it's the best thing that could ever happen.

U. T. P.: But suppose dat Randolph fellow should run away wid de money? I done heah dat he went to Russia or was gwine to.

N. P.: Don't be a dummy, Pop. That's Pullman propaganda. Don't you know if Randolph *only wanted money*, he wouldn't have to run away with the porters' little money they pay to join and in dues. He could get plenty money from *those* who want to *stop* the Union.

U. T. P.: You know, son, I never thought of dat.

N. P.: Well, Pop, you want to get your thinking cap on or you'll be in Dutch.

U. T. P.: But son, do you think you kin win agin des white folks?

N. P.: White folks are no different from any other kind of folks, pop. It all depends on how much *power* you got, and you can't get power unless you are *organized*. You know the old joke about the farmer not bothering *one hornet* because of fear of the *rest* of the *hornets standing behind him.** Well, that's all we porters got to do. That's all the Negro race has got to do—*stick together;* be *all for each and each for all.*

U. T. P.: But, son, you know des "*niggers*" ain't like *hornets*, dey ain't gwine to *stick*.

N. P.: That's nothing but the slave psychology in you, Pop. You don't think a black man can do anything a white man can do. That's all bunk, pop. Get that stuff out of your noodle. This is the 20th Century. Understand that "a man's a man." A Negro can do anything he is big enough to do. When you're right, pop, and got "guts," you can stand up and look any man in the face and spit right square in his eyes if he tries to give you any *hot stuff* about your rights.

U. T. P.: Yes, boy, but suppose des white folks hot-foot you off des cars?

N. P.: That's all pure moonshine, put out by such spineless Negroes as Perry Howard, I. Garland Penn, Bishop A. J. Carey, Melvin Chisum and their ilk. That crowd is no good. Nobody pays them any mind, any more. Everybody knows they sold out to the Pullman Company. Don't be an old fool. The Pullman Company *couldn't* put anybody else in the Negroes' place if they *would*, and *wouldn't* if they *could*.

U. T. P.: But son, dey done already put some of dem Filipinos, whatever you call 'em, on club cars.

N. P.: And now you're scared stiff. That's

---

* For a full text of this exemplum in which a Negro coachman hits a horsefly and bumblebee but refuses to strike a hornet, see the tale entitled "Dey's Auganized," in J. Mason Brewer, "Juneteenth," *Publications of the Texas Folklore Society*, 10 (1932), pp. 23–24. (Also reprinted in *Publications of the Texas Folklore Society*, 26 [1954], pp. 57.) —ED.

just like those ghost stories about old slaves scared to death at a bed-sheet over the head of their masters.* There's nothing to it. Just a trick to frighten you away from the Union. It's just like this: The Pullman Company will use Negroes against white workers when white workers try to organize and they'll use Filipinos against Negroes when Negroes try to organize. But that didn't keep white workers from organizing and it won't keep Pullman porters from organizing. Besides, I am not going to lose any sleep over losing a job because I join a Union, as white men do, to get a living wage. Suppose they put Filipinos on the cars, what of it? They'll organize, too. Don't you forget it, Pop.

U. T. P.: Specks you's right, son. But I'm old and feeble; won't be heah long, and I can't fool around wid no Union dis late date, 'cause I mightn't get no pension.

N. P.: Get that rabbit out of you, old man, and be a real man. It's all bosh about the Company not paying you your pension if you join the Union. Look at Dad Moore of Oakland and "Cy" Taylor of the Pennsylvania District. They are two of the biggest Brotherhood men in the country, and they receive their pension, too. Listen, Pop, because you are about to be pensioned is just the reason why you ought to have brains enough to ditch that Employee Representation Plan sham and get into a regular Union. Don't you know that if porters get more wages, you'll get more pension? You ought to see that. It's as plain as the nose on your face.

U. T. P.: Look heah, son, do you know I never thought of that before. You sho is telling the truth.

N. P.: Sure, nothing but these Uncle Toms and stool pigeons are putting out that nonsense.

U. T. P.: Look out, son, hold dat Uncle Tom, stool pigeons stuff, hold it. I ain't none of dem things. I is a man.

N. P.: Well, Uncle, don't go hand me no lip service on this man business. Our slogan is, if you ain't for us, you are against us. I've got a blank right here with me. *Put up or shut up.*

U. T. P.: Wait a minute, son. I's wid you.

N. P.: Can that bunk. You ain't with us unless you lay the cold cash on the wood. No use beating around the bush. The Brotherhood can't print booklets, leaflets, circulars, pay organizers, railroad and Pullman fares, stenographic services, expenses of expert economists and Donald R. Richberg, on *air pudding and wind sauce*. It requires money and the porters must supply it for they benefit from the work. The time is here when Negroes must fight for their liberty and pay for it, too. We've been begging long enough. Get that.

U. T. P: I don't miss it. But, son, suppose des white folks find out I'se jined dis Brotherhood?

N. P.: They won't find out unless you tell 'em. The Company hasn't got enough money to buy a name of a Brotherhood man from the Brotherhood. This is a New Negro steering this ship, now, Pop.

U. T. P.: Suppose des white folks ask me whether I'se a member?

N. P.: Well, you don't have to tell 'em you're a member. They lied to you for over 50 years.

U. T. P.: Son, you's jist too radical anyhow. Whar in the devil did you come from? Well, the truth is the truth. Des white folks sho is bin lying to us "niggers" and robbing us, too.

N. P.: Well, it doesn't matter to me what you call me. I know this. The New Negro

---

* For further discussion of the bed-sheet hoax, see H. Grady McWhiney and Francis B. Simkins, "The Ghostly Legend of the Ku-Klux Klan," *The Negro History Bulletin,* 14 (February, 1951), pp. 109–12, reprinted in this volume. —Ed.

does not propose to permit white folks to flim flam him any longer, job or no job, Filipino or no Filipino. Organization certainly can't make things any worse. And you've got to take a chance just as white workers have done. Nothing ventured, nothing gained. Of course today you're not taking any chance. Success is a sure thing with organization. You can't fail.

U. T. P.: Well, son, you think I's an Uncle Tom, don't you? Now I want you to show me everything, all the cards. Now put up or shut up. You're suppose to know everything and so radical and everything.

N. P.: What d'you say? You don't mean to tell me you're there. Good night, Pop! Well, there is everything!

U. T. P.: All right, son. Now shove me your mit and slip me the pass word, and I don't mean maybe.

N. P.: I ain't giving you nothing different. I'm coming 'cross with the whole works.

U. T. P.: Everything is pretty, old top. I'm bluffing these white folks to death. They think I'm the worst enemy of the Union in the service. Good night, lower 8 is ringing me again. We got to hit the ball, you know, and give 'em service jam-up, 'cause we are loyal Brotherhood men. If we do our work right, pay our dues, pay our assessment and get the slackers to join, we can't lose.

II

NEW PORTER: All made down, Pop?

OLD TIME PORTER: Go on back in yo' car. Whatcha up to now, Mr. Smart Aleck?

N. P.: Oh, is that the way you feel about it. I was going to give you a lift—but—.

O. T. P.: Why, what d' you say, Sonnie. Don't be so quick to fly off de handle. I was jes runnin' on wid you. You done made down a'ready? Aint feeling so good, son. Shake some of dem sheets for yo' uncle.

N. P.: Sure. I'm a good Brotherhood man, Pop.

O. T. P.: What dat yo' say about dat Brotherhood? You's jined? Don' come foolin' roun' me if you done jined dat crazy bunch.

N. P.: Oh don't get excited, Pop. You're all made down, now. Is that the way you gointa talk to your friend? What about this talk of reviving the old Employee Representation Plan? You ain't votin' for it, are you, Pop?

O. T. P.: I ain't excited, but I jest don' want no talk in my car 'bout no Brotherhood, dat settles dat cause de white folks ain't gointa let you organize no union, no how. Is I gointa vote fer de Plan? Course I'se goin' vote fer de Plan and you is too. No you ain't goin' miss.

N. P.: No Employee Plan for me, Pop. It's nothing but pure slavery. If it was any good, why did the Pullman conductors can it? They saw it was nothing but a joker.

O. T. P.: Now, Son, don' lose yo' head. De Plan was fixed up by de Company fer you.

N. P.: That's just the trouble. It was fixed up for us by the Company, and for cryin' out loud, we're fixed, too. Pop, you're a whole lot older than I am, but I want to tell you one thing. Beware of anybody who always wants to *give you something*—nothing to it. You'll pay a bigger price than when you're told you got to pay. You know that.

O. T. P.: Yes, 'specks you'se right deah, Son. Nobody's gwine to give you something for nothin'. But de Pullman Company is our friend 'case it gives us jobs and says so.

N. P.: Cut that stuff out, Pop. It makes me sick. Don't you know the Pullman Company isn't in business for love and it wouldn't keep you one minute if you didn't make profits for it? The Pullman Company has made a higher rate of profit out of our sweat and toil than any other corporation in America has made out of its employees. We made the Pullman Company what it is today. You ought to have brains enough to see that.

O. T. P.: Look out deah, now, hold dat

brains stuff. I ain't nobody's dummy Sonnie. Ain't gointa stand fer nobody sayin' I is, neither. You ain't no Solomon yourself.

N. P.: What's that?

O. T. P.: You ain't deef.

N. P.: Well, Pop, I didn't intend to insult you. You don't deny that the Pullman Company wouldn't hire you if it couldn't make money out of your labor do you? You don't deny that a good friend is one who is interested in your getting a good living do you? You don't deny that the conductors who turned down the Plan, get a better living out of $150 a month and 240 hours work than you do out of $72 a month and 11 thousand miles or 366 hours work, do you? Then there is nothing to show that the Company is any better friend of the porters than it is of the conductors, is there? If you gotta decide by wages whom the Company loves more, you'll have to agree that it is the better friend of the conductors, isn't that so? It's foolish to contend that any one is your friend who tries to hold your wages down and keep your hours of work up. This is common sense. Now, Mr. Hard-boiled Company man, let me see you do your stuff and get out and from under that.

O. T. P.: Yea, it sho is common sense, all right. But you got me wrong, Son, I ain't no Company man. Well, Son, I was in a meetin' where Mr. Simmons called dat Randolph fellow everything but a chile of God. But, you know, Son, I thought it was funny too, dat a white man should take up so much of his good time knocking a young Negro. Dat Randolph man sho is got des white folks scared to death.

N. P.: Yes, and that ain't all. They got to come across for once and lay it on the wood for black men according to Hoyle. They got to put the cards on the table and let us cut 'em. And, of course, it's a bitter pill for white folks to be jacked up by black folks, you know that. But Pop, times have changed.

O. T. P.: Well, Son, I is gointa leab it to you young folks. So far as dis Plan goes, I don knowed it was no good, but Son, I jest bin scared to say so. De "nigger" members of de committees is agin you whetter you right or wrong, case dey is scared ob de white folks, too. You can't 'speck des "nigger" bosses to speak up for our rights when it mought cos dey jobs.

N. P.: That's no reason why you should support the Plan, but a mighty good reason why you should join the Brotherhood. Self-organization is the only thing which will ever free you from the tyranny of petty Pullman officials. They will be compelled to respect you when they realize that you have the guts to stick together, take it from your Uncle Dudley who knows his onions, Pop.

O. T. P.: What is I gotta pay to jine dat Union anyhow, Son?

N. P.: Oh, don't let that worry you. It's only five bones. You know, Pop, the New Negro realizes that he has not only got to fight for his freedom, but that he must pay for his freedom too, if he expects to get it. You heard the saying, "He who pays the fiddler will call the tune," haven't you? Well, nuf sed. Your move.

O. T. P.: Yea, Son, but you don't have to pay anything to jine dat Plan.

N. P.: Oh, yes you do. Don't put that noise out. You pay a price you can't afford to pay, for you give up your liberty, your manhood, your independence, when you accept the Plan. Don't be deceived that because you don't pay out any money you are not paying a price to join the Plan. There is no such thing as getting something for nothing. You've got to suffer and sacrifice, fight and put your hands in your jeans and give up the hard cash for your rights or you get none, that's all, Pop. It may sound hard but it's fair. Other people had to do it, why not we. That's why you can't trust the Plan. It is bought and paid for, organized, controlled and operated by the Company and for the Company. Whichever way these committees vote on your case, you lose, the Company always wins. How I'm doin', yours truly?

O. T. P.: Look out Son, hear comes one of dem stool pigeons. Hold your horses. I know 'em if I lamp 'em a mile off. Dey jest ain't got 'em in de looks, you know. Done lied so much they can't look you straight in de eyes.

N. P.: There you are, Pop. Think of a condition where a Negro will have to sneak around to get news on a member of his own race to trot back with it to the Pullman Company, and for what; just because Pullman porters want to do what Pullman conductors and other railroad workers have done, namely, organize. It proves that organization is the only thing for you. If it wasn't the Company wouldn't fight it so hard.

O. T. P.: Yea, Son. You's tellin' the truth and nothin' but de truth. A stool pigeon represents the lowest dregs of human beings. Any man who will try to cause another man to lose his job cause that man tries to better his condition ain't fit to associate with a dog.

N. P.: Now you're signifying, Pop.* You almost got the Brotherhood religion.

O. T. P.: Well, Son, I'm for right and nothin' but right.

N. P.: But Pop, isn't it right that Pullman porters should get a living wage?

O. T. P.: Yea.

N. P.: Isn't it right that porters, as other railroad workers, should have the right to organize if they want to?

O. T. P.: Yea.

N. P.: Isn't it wrong that you should be compelled to rely on a tip here and a tip there according as a man's stomach is good or bad, for means with which to support your wife and children?

O. T. P.: Yea.

N. P.: Well, that's all the Brotherhood is contending.

O. T. P.: Watch your step. Close up your trap. Heah comes the train conductor.

N. P.: Oh, you needn't lose your nerves on account of him. The train conductors are all with you because they are organized themselves. They want to see every train 100 per cent union. Furthermore, no white man has said a word against this union; only spineless Negroes sell their souls to the Pullman Company to oppose the Brotherhood.

O. T. P.: I ain't heard no white man say nothin' 'gin the union.

N. P.: But you heard plenty of your folks and my people knocking it, haven't you, Pop?

O. T. P.: Lawd a mussy, ha, ha! Yo' sho is right. I ain't missed hearin' 'em.

N. P.: Look out, old top. Here comes a snitch. Well, how've you been, Pop? (Spoken in loud voice to throw the snitch off.)

O. T. P.: Fairly middlin', fairly middlin', Son. (In loud voice as though he didn't see the snitch. Snitch passes.)

N. P.: I hope he'll fall down and break a leg.

O. T. P.: I don't wish nobody no harm, Son, but I hope to God he slips up on a banana peelin' and breaks his bloomin' neck.

N. P.: Pop, you better sign up—you got everything.

O. T. P.: Quit your kiddin', what kind of evarthin'? Wait a minute, Son, I'm comin' in, cause I'm wid you.

N. P.: That's what they all say. You ain't with me unless you're in the Union, Pop. We can't buy no literature with "I'm wid you."

O. T. P.: But, I ain't hauling nobody, Son,

* For a further consideration of "signifying," see the essay by Claudia Mitchell-Kernan in this volume. —ED.

now, and my pockets is jest as clean as a hound's tooth.

N. P.: Well, Pop, I'm game. To show you I'm a good Brotherhood man, I'll lend you a dollar on your application.

O. T. P.: All right, Son. You got de ole man cornered. Gimme de blank. I'll pay you back next pay day. Tips pretty slow now. You're right, we got to hang together or we'll be hung separately.

N. P.: All right, Pop. Give me five; time to receive passengers, now, and keep my lamps on the stools 'cause they're trying to frame me.

O. T. P.: I'm all de way wid you, Son, and if we fight on and faint not, we will reap our reward in due season. (Turning to passenger approaching the car.) What's your berth, sir?

PASSENGER: Lower seven.

The Technique of Jive

DAN BURLEY

 Here is an entertaining and instructive attempt to communicate the nature of American Negro speech spoken in Harlem in the 1940's. Dan Burley who was managing editor of the New York Amsterdam News, one of the leading Negro newspapers, was fascinated by "Jive," and he frequently featured it in his column "Back Door Stuff." In his valuable Handbook of Harlem Jive, he gives many examples of dialogues in slang—with translations as well as a full glossary, "The Jiver's Bible."

 In the selection presented here, Burley tries to articulate some of the governing principles of jive. For readers who may have mistakenly imagined that "hip," "groovy," etc. were created in the 1960's, Burley's essay should prove a useful corrective. Not only do many slang terms enjoy a long life, but a goodly number of the "rules" delineated by Burley appear to be applicable to contemporary urban American Negro speech.

 On the other hand, some of Burley's ideas, e.g., that jive came into being because of the inadequacy of the vocabularies of its users, are open to question. There is also the matter of just how widespread some of the lexical items cited by Burley were. One reviewer suggested that the dialect reported by Burley was perhaps no more familiar to the proverbially average Harlemite than to average white New Yorkers. The same reviewer also wondered how much of the lingo was Harlemese and how much Burleyese. Nevertheless, there is little doubt that many of the terms and constructions discussed by Burley were and are part of modern American Negro folk speech.

 For the above mentioned review of Burley's Handbook, written by James W. Ivy, see The Crisis, 52 (1945), pp. 180–81. For appreciations of Dan Burley, *see Earl Conrad's "Foreword" to Burley's* Handbook, *pp. 3–7 or his "The Philology of Negro Dialect,"* Journal of Negro Education, *13 (1944), pp. 150–54, or Chuck Stone's "A Tribute to Dan Burley," in his* Tell It Like It Is *(New York: Trident Press, 1968), pp. 186–89. For some biographical details, see Stanley Frank, "Now I Stash Me Down to Nod,"* Esquire, *21 (June, 1944), pp. 53, 168–70.*

LESSON NO. 1

"IF YOU'RE a hipped stud, you'll latch on; but if you're a homey, you ain't nowhere, ole man, understand? Like the bear, nowhere. And, ole man, why can't you dig this hard mess I'm laying down when the whole town's copping the mellow jive? Are you going to be a square all you days? Ain't you gonna click your gimmers, latch onto this fine pulp I'm dropping on you and really knock yourself out as you scoff, ace-deuce around the chiming Ben? You dig, ole man, that, from early bright to late black, the cats and the chippies are laying down some fine, heavy jive; most of it like the tree, all root; like the letter all wrote; like the country road, all rut; like the apple, all rot; like the cheese, all rat! Understand, ole man?"

That, dear reader, is pure jive. However, we'll play around with it and translate that paragraph later. Don't worry, we'll come back to it.

1. INTRODUCTION TO BASIC JIVE

Before entering on the details of the System of Basic Jive, it seems appropriate to answer here those general questions and inquiries which everyone hearing of Jive for the first time is inclined to ask. These questions may be summed up roughly as follows:

How and why the System developed? How the principles on which it is evolved have been established? What are the needs and purposes which it professes to serve, the methods by which it may be learned, its value to the individual, its place in education, the agencies through which it may be spread, and its advantages as an auxiliary medium of expression.

What is jive? Jive is a distortion of that staid, old, respectable English word "jibe" (jibber—Speak fast and inarticulately, chatter; such speech or sound. Jibberish—unintelligible speech, meaningless sounds, jargon, blundering or ungrammatical talk).

In the sense in which it came into use among Negroes in Chicago about the year 1921, it meant to taunt, to scoff, to sneer—an expression of sarcastic comment. Like the tribal groups of Mohammedans and people of the Orient, Negroes of that period had developed a highly effective manner of talking about each other's ancestors and hereditary traits, a colorful and picturesque linguistic procedure which came to be known as "putting you in the dozens." Later, this was simply called "Jiving" someone.

Subsequently, ragtime musicians picked up the term and it soon came to mean "all things to all men," it began to express many things, to describe many new things, and since 1930 Jive has been accepted as the trade-name for "swing" music, for the "jitterbug" population, and as the key to a complete new world in itself. Today, instead of bearing a connotation concerning one's parents, one's appearance, or one's knowledge, Jive, instead of being used disparagingly, as a term of opprobrium, has acquired honor, dignity—class.

2. WHAT IS THE PURPOSE OF JIVE?

Basic Jive has two main purposes:

1. To serve as an auxiliary slanguage, one that is easily and quickly learned, in which the rules of grammar and sentence construction are so simple they are practically non-existent. This "second" language can be picked up with very little effort for use in general communication and social intercourse.
2. As a means of providing a rational—or irrational if you prefer—introduction to basic American slang for those who, because of lack of time or money, find it impossible to concentrate on learning the routine principles of grammar, verb conjugation, sentence construction, etc. Jive requires very little concentration but serves to develop clarity of thought and expression for English speaking people at any stage of proficiency in the mother tongue.

The proponents of Harlem jive talk do not entertain any grandiose illusions about the importance or durability of jive. They do not hope that courses in the lingo will ever be offered at Harvard or Columbia University. Neither do they expect to learn that Mrs. Faunteen-Chauncey of the Mayfair Set addresses her English butler as "stud hoss," and was called in reply, "a sturdy ole hen." However, they do cherish some fond dreams. They hope that some day, the cats who lay that larceny in the book of many pages (dictionary) will give the jivers a break and substitute the phrase, "twister to the slammer," for the word, "key"; use the word "jive" in their definition of "slang"; and, otherwise, give notice to those hipped studs who have

collared such a heavy slave to add color to the American language.

3. THE ORIGIN AND DEVELOPMENT OF JIVE

Jive is the product of slang parlance from all over the country from cities, hamlets and villages where Negroes meet and gather. It undergoes a certain purifying process in which extraneous expressions, such as, "kicking the gong around," "Minnie the Moocher," "Flatfoot Floogie with the floy-floy" are tried and discarded, or used and retained. Some of the expressions cannot be used in polite conversation; others have slipped into the English language and are now more or less accepted universally, and by the most severe critics as a fundamental part of the language.

Jive has been in the process of evolution from the early years following World War I. The Prohibition Era, the Gangster Period, the Age of Hardboiled, Quick-shooting Heroes, and their seductive molls contributed to it. So did the decade known as the Great Depression. All this led inevitably to the Age of the Jitterbug, a spasmodic era with a background of World War II and swing music contributing to its use and popularity.

The teacher who marked zero after little Johnny's name when he used slang terms in the class-room is no longer perturbed by the vividness of his vocabulary. In all probability she used a little Jive herself without being aware of it. For Jive, like cussing, is a language of emotion; a means of describing how one is affected by certain experiences or situations. Among those who contributed largely to the vocabulary of Jive and helped build it up to its present-day fluency, were many with little or no knowledge of formalized and classical English. The twisting of the language to suit the user has been one of the things that brought Jive to its highest development.

4. BASIC BACKGROUNDS OF JIVE

Perhaps the greatest attribute of the Negro is his universal mimicry; the ability to make himself understood among his own people no matter from what clime or country he may hail. This calls for pantomime and acting ability. As pointed out by Zora Neale Hurston, the eminent Negro novelist,*

The Negro's universal mimicry is not so much a thing in itself as an evidence of something that permeates his entire being and that thing is drama, and emotional intensity. His (the Negro's) very words are action words. His interpretation of the English language is in terms of pictures (remember the vivid portrayal of biblical scenes in "Green Pastures?") One act described in terms of another. Hence, the rich metaphor and simile.

The metaphor is, of course, very primitive. It is easier to illustrate than to explain, because action came before speech. Every phase of Negro life is highly dramatized. No matter how joyful or sad the case may be, there is sufficient scope for drama. Everything is acted out. Unconsciously for the most part, of course. There is an impromptu ceremony always ready for every hour of life. No little moment passes unadorned.

Now the people with highly developed languages have words for abstract, detached ideas. But the primitive man relies on descriptive words. His terms are all tightly integrated, close-fitting. Frequently the Negro, even with abstract words in his vocabulary, not inherent to him, but transposed to his vocabulary through contact, must add action to make these words have meaning to him. The white man thinks in written language. The Negro thinks in hieroglyphics.

There might be a further explanation to the fact that the white man thinks objectively, the Negro subjectively— that is the dark-skinned man throws words deep into his subconscious mind and when they come out of his mouth later the results are something startling.

The Negro, it seems, knows so well the power, the magic, the witchery of words —not the words themselves, but the feelings evoked by the sound of certain words. The witch-doctor with his savage and barbaric costume relied on the power of words in his mysterious chants and incantations to the gods. He was a highly respected member in an African tribal community. And since civilization is only a very thin veneer over most of our subconscious instincts, Jive might be a reversal back to that old love of chant, or mumbo-jumbo, etc.

All this has to do with venture here into the higher and more exalted realms of Jive, where the fancy floats about as though reposing on pink edged clouds, and the senses are beguiled and hypnotized by the soothing cadence of matchless phrases and delightful rhythm. To an outsider this might sound like the most utter, complete and childish nonsense.

As pointed out by Miss Hurston, the Negro's reaction to language is an emotional, not an intellectual one. It is the sound of words, their flexibility, and the way in which they may be combined with other similar words that impresses him—not their meaning. This might be due to the fact that the subconscious

* The remarks quoted by Burley come from Zora Neale Hurston, "Characteristics of Negro Expression," in Nancy Cunard, *Negro* (London, 1934), pp. 39–46. —ED.

mind of the Negro is much nearer the surface of his actual life and actions, than in the white man. Which would explain why the average Negro is such a complex and complicated person, with many sides and phases to his character.

5. THE SYSTEM—THE A B C OF BASIC JIVE

On learning the basic words and terms. It is not necessary that you have a college degree in English in order to learn and appreciate Basic Jive, nor is it required that you renounce your present conventional and introspective habits and go jitterbugging at the nearest dance hall, in order to become an adept in its use. All that is needed is a good memory plus a sense of rhythm. At the same time, it will be of great help to the student if he puts every word he learns into actual use by memorizing some simple phrase or statement at this early stage in order that he may get an idea of its ordinary use in talking and writing. Within a relatively few weeks one may develop an amazing proficiency in Jive talk.

The learning of the System of Basic Jive may be accomplished in this manner:

1. By familiarizing oneself with the vocabulary.
2. Expansion of the words in form and sense.
3. Special uses of the words and their application for special purposes.

6. FIRST STEPS IN JIVE

Names of things. Since Jive talk came into being because of the paucity of words and inadequacy of the vocabularies of its users, it is of primary interest that we get a good working knowledge of the Jive names for things. It is also essential to understand here that really good Jive talk is also accompanied by appropriate gestures, inflections of the voice, and other aids toward making one's meaning clear.

The simplest words in Jive are those relating to things—inanimate objects, the furniture in a room, objects which can be moved, sold, bought, exchanged, all concrete and tangible objects. Once mastered, one feels that he is fairly launched on a career as a Jive linguist.

Basic vocabulary. Are you one of those people whose mind quickly associates related objects one with the other? For example, do you associate the following automatically, coupling them up subconsciously, without any effort? boy-and-girl, door-and-knob, horse-and-wagon, subway-and-nickel, man-and-woman, pen-and-ink, pencil-and-paper, knife-and-fork. If you are, then you should make a list of the words below that naturally go together. Definitions are in italics.

Avenue—*Main Trill, Stroll*
Alarm Clock—*Chimer*
Automobile—*Gas buggy*
Bed—*Softy*
Boy—*Cat, skull*
Body—*Frame*
Coffee and doughnuts—*slops and slugs*
Corner—*Three-pointer*
Cigarette—*Long white roll*
Chinese—*Riceman*
Door—*Slammer*
Dress—*Drape*
Double-decker Bus—*Avenue tank*
Ears—*Flaps*
Elderly man—*Poppa Stoppa*
Eyes—*Gims*
Face—*Pan, mug*
Fingers—*Wigglers*
Feet—*Groundpads*
Fur Coat—*Fine Fur*
Frankfurter—*Pimp-steak*

Girl—*Chick, chippie, scribe, banter*
Gun—*Bow-wow*
Hair—*Moss*
Hat—*Sky*
Hands—*Grabbers*
Head—*Conk, thinkpad, knowledge-box*
House—*Pad, crib, pile-of-stone, layout*
Indian—*Jin*
Juke-box—*Piccolo*
Jail—*House of Many Slammers*
Key—*Twister*
Knees—*Dukes, knobs, benders*
Knife—*Chib or chiv, switch*
Legs—*Gams, stems, props*
Liquor—*Lush, juice*
Magazine—*Rag*
Marijuana-Weed—*Reefer, roach, Hemp, Rope, Tea*
Moon—*Pumpkin*
Movie—*Flicker*
Match—*Snapper*
Notebook—*Snitchpad*
Nose—*Sniffer*
Negro—*Mose, Spade, Cluck, Clink*
Newspaper—*Rag or Snitchpad*
Overcoat—*Benny*
Pants—*Pegs*
Rain—*Heavy Wet, Light Drip-drizzle*
Road—*Stroll*
Socks—*leg sacks*
Street—*Stroll*
Suit—*Drape*
Sun—*Beaming-Bean*
Sky—*Blue*
Toes—*Wigglers*
Trill—*Stroll, street*
Trousers—*Pegs*

With the above words at your disposal, try your hand at constructing sentences employing them in place of the words you would use ordinarily. For example: Instead of saying: "I'm going home," you say: "I'm going to my pile of stone." When you reach your "pile of stone," if you didn't have a "twister to the slammer," you would naturally have to knock on the "slammer," would you not? Your "thinkpad" would in-struct you do to that. And in going to your "pile of stone", your groundpads would bear your "frame" to that place. Suppose you decided to ride instead of walking, then you would take "an avenue tank". You may note from the above list of Jive names that there is a complete absence of verbs or words denoting action. But in the next phase of Jive we discuss verbs and their forms.

7. Verbal Nouns

These are the words that move and "jump," the Jive Verbs that give the language its appeal and spontaneity, that make Jive flexible.

Here we are dealing with the words which describe bodily motion, the movement of arms, legs, hands and feet. They also denote intangible action having to do with thought, comprehension, a very important phase of Jive.

We start off by naming simple acts. In the preceding portion of this chapter we discussed the name of things, we had you going home; and, instead of saying, "I am going home," you said, "I'm going to my pile of stone." "Am going" is a perfectly legitimate expression in English denoting an intention and describing an act already taking place. In Jive you would substitute the words "cop" and "trill" in place of "am going," and your statement would be: "I'm copping my trill for my pile of stone." Simple, isn't it? Even your great-aunt Hannah could understand that, couldn't she?

There are relatively few Jive verbs, since Jive is primarily a language consisting of descriptive adjectives, rather than being replete with verbs denoting action. However, the few Jive verbs to balance the enormous number of nouns, or names of things, are thrillingly competent, graphic and commanding. Two in particular are worthy of our attention. The verbs "knock" and "lay" are the basis of Jive. "Knock" in particular is found all through the process of a Jive conversation. It is one of the key words.

"Knock a nod," says the Jiver. He means going to sleep. "Knock a scoff," he says. He means, eat a meal. "Knock a broom" is found to mean a quick walk or brisk trot away from something. "Knock me down to her" means to introduce me to a young lady; "knock off a riff," in musical parlance means for a musician to play a musical break in a certain manner. "Knock a jug" means to buy a drink.

The verb, "Lay," is another vitally important verb in the Jiver's vocabulary. It also denotes action. For example: "Lay some of that cash on me," says a Jiver. His statement means literally what it says. But if he says, "he was really laying it," he means someone was doing something out of the ordinary, as in a stage performance or musical program, or a well-dressed person entering a room and suddenly becoming the object of all eyes.

Here are some other important verbs:

Blow—*To leave, move, run away*
Broom—*To walk, leave, run, stroll*
Cop—*To take, receive, understand, do*
Dig—*To understand, take, see, conceive, perceive, think, hand over*
Drag—*To disappoint, humiliate, upset, disillusion*
Fell—*To be put in prison, or durance vile*
Kill—*To thrill, fascinate, enthrall*
Jump—*To move, dance*
Latch—*To understand, take, perceive, think, meet*
Rock—*To move, dance*
Rug—*To dance, gambol, to frolic*
Stumble—*To get into trouble, misfortune, dire predicament*

Stash—*To lay away, hide, put down, stand, a place*
Take a powder—*leave, disappear*
Trilly-walk—*To leave, move on foot, run, flee*

8. JIVE ADJECTIVES, OR WORDS SIGNIFYING QUALITY

Before the names of things, or objects, as in standard English we need to know a special state or condition regarding them in order to get a clear mental picture in our minds. For example, a *blue* sky, a *soft* chair, the *hot* sun, etc. The language of Jive has plenty of such adjectives, more of which are constantly being added every day. The following list may prove helpful:

Anxious—*Wonderful, excellent*
Fine—*All right, okay, excellent*
Frantic—*Great, wonderful*
Groovy—*To one's liking, sensational, outstanding, splendid*
Mad—*Fine, capable, able, talented*
Mellow—*State of delight, beautiful, great, wonderful*
Oxford—*Black, Negro*
Righteous—*Pleasing to the senses, glorious, pretty, beautiful, mighty*
Solid—*Very fine, okay, great, terrific*

9. JIVE PHRASES, SIMILE AND HYPERBOLE

As in standard English, Jive is flexible and infinitely capable of expressing phrases of rare harmonic beauty and rhythmical force. The language of the hepsters is constantly acquiring new descriptive phrases, narrative and explanatory in content, which constitute an integral and necessary part of one's equipment for gaining proficiency in talking and writing Jive. Here are a few, some of which are self-explanatory, and others of which are translated into

English in italics:

Fine as wine

Mellow as a cello

Like the bear, nowhere

Playing the dozens with my uncle's cousins
—*doing things wrong*

Hard as Norwegian lard—*In reality, soft. The phrase is used mainly to express perfection, i.e., "I was laying down a line of jive, hard as Norwegian lard," in which case soft, deft skill is indicated.*

"I'm like the chicken, I ain't stickin"—*broke*

"Dig what I'm laying down?"—*understand what I'm saying?*

"I'm chipper as the China Clipper and in the mood to play"—*flying high and personally feeling fine*

"Swimps and wice"—*shrimps and rice*

"Snap a snapper"—*light a match*

"Like the farmer and the 'tater, plant you now and dig you later"—*means, "I must go, but I'll remember you."*

10. Jive Rhyming and Meter

The language of Jive presents an unusual opportunity for experimentation in rhymes, in fact, a lot of it is built on rhymes which at first hearing might be considered trite and beneath the notice. However, Jive rhymes and couplets are fascinating and comparatively easy to fashion. As to meter, it is desirable that the syllables form a correct measure, but this is not essential. All that is necessary is that the end words rhyme; they do not necessarily need to make sense. Here are some examples:

"Collars a broom with a solid zoom"—*left in a hurry*

"No lie, frog eye"

"What's your duty, Tutti-Frutti?"

"Joe the Jiver, the Stranded Pearl-Diver"

"I'm getting a brand new frail, cause the one I've got can't go my bail"—*means getting a new girl because the one he has is broke and can't help him out in a pinch*

"Had some whiskey, feel kind o' frisky"

"Swing and sweat with Charley Bar-net"—*means dance to Barnet's music*

"Are you going to the function at Tuxedo Junction?"—*Tuxedo Junctions are places, dancehalls, candy-stores, etc., where hepsters gather*

"My name is Billie, have you seen Willie?"—*used as a greeting or salutation among accomplished hepcats*

"Ain't it a pity, you're from Atlantic City?"—*salutation*

"I can't frolic, I got the colic"—*I drank too much*

"Let's dip and dive on this mess of jive"—*Let's have some fun*

"Jack, the bean is beaming, and I'm really steaming—*sun shining hot and I'm sweating.*"

"I'm a solid dreamer, you're a low-down schemer"—*I'm innocent, you're not*

"I've got a mellow banter, a real enchanter"—*I have a pretty girl friend*

"As I was saying on the jive I was laying. I at last found the pad but the pickings were sad and the chippies ain't playing it straight; so I stretched out at eight, still looking for a mate, and playing the game like a lad"—*Translated this means, "I visited the place but the girls all said, 'No', so I left at 8 P.M. still looking for a girl friend just like any young boy"*

"I digs all jive, that's why I'm alive"

"Where did you get that drape? Your pants look like a cape"

"Let's get racy with Count Basie"

"Cut out the rootin' and tootin', and there's won't be any shootin' and bootin'"—*means stop so much loud noise and you won't get hurt*

To attain any degree of proficiency in Jive talking, one has to keep at it. An hour a day will "boot" it your way. That's why, dear reader, you must constantly review what has gone before, and why you must insist on perfection before attempting ambitious steps in this hitherto uncharted division of Americana.

Soon you will be able to write letters to your friends in Jive that no one but you and those who have a knowledge of it can understand. Soon you will be talking in such a manner that your friends will think you have gone completely looney and belong in a strait-jacket. But don't let that worry you. They tried to put Shakespeare in the dog-house, and even attempted it with Edgar Allan Poe. Now while you may not be in the league where Shakespeare and Poe make up the battery, your day is coming and then you'll be a candidate for a sanitarium, but wait; don't get impatient.

We now go into the construction of simple statements in jive.

11. Simple Construction of Statements in Jive

Suppose your baby (if you are a mother) should be a hepcat. As you came by to feed the little darling lying in his crib, you would croon:

"Pick up on the scoff, cherub, pick up on the double click."

Wouldn't you be mortified (as well as frightened out of your wits) if your offspring retorted with this snappy comeback:

"Lay it on me, ole hen. It's strictly in there, ready and righteous, and I'm gonna knock it out, but solidly."

The "scoff" or "scarf" in the above simple statement is dinner food, meals. "Pick up" means just that in this instance; and, of course, "cherub" is baby-angel (or is your offspring something else?). The "double click" is right away: quickly, hurriedly. The baby's reply doesn't mean to spread a blanket on him. Instead, he calls you an old woman when he calls you "ole hen." That it's "strictly in there" means it is acceptable, all right, fine, excellent. "Ready and righteous" is the degree of acceptance at which he gauges your action. "Knock it out" means to eat.

Herewith are several simple statements written in ordinary English first, then translated into Jive. Study them carefully and then construct some of your own and read them aloud for cadence, harmony, and lilt.

I walked slowly to the corner where I awaited the coming of a bus.

"I trilled to the three-pointer and stashed my frame on the flag spot waiting for the avenue tank."

I was standing on the corner one night very late, two or three weeks ago, when I heard a rather fanciful conversation about a girl and her boyfriend. The boy, it seems, attempted to dominate her.

"I'm stiffing the stroll on the three-pointer on the late dark a deuce or tray of haircuts ago, when I latched on to this hard, mad spiel about the chippie and the cat that cracks the whip."

Suppose you went into a restaurant and asked the waiter for a glass of water. All you would say would be: "Lay a light splash of spray on me, ole man."

If you wanted to touch your best friend for a loan of two dollars you would say:

Jack, knock me out with a brace of chollies."

If he was broke and couldn't loan you anything, he would answer:

"Jeeze, Jake, I'm a snake; my bags are slick as rat holes, and I'm really suffering with the shorts."

If you caught a trolley and didn't have change for a dollar, you would ask the motorman: "Say, Poppa Stoppa, can you crack this cholly for me? Knock it out in a few double ruffs, a few sous and brownies."

In introducing yourself to another person, presumably as adept in Jive talk as yourself, you would announce: "I'm a hip kitty from the big city, quite witty, dig my ditty?" What you said in this instance was: "I'm competent to understand completely anything you may say, or attempt to say in Jive, so it shouldn't be hard for you to see that I'm your equal."

To do away with the conjugating of verbs, which would be complicated in the extreme, most of Jive is in the present tense which strikes the ear pleasantly, and adds infinitely to its rhyming possibilities. The Jive addict experiences a sense of accomplishment and delight in being able to translate it correctly. Let's translate lesson No. 1 in jive as presented in the opening paragraph of this introduction:

If you're a hipped stud—*a well-informed person*

You'll latch on—*you'll understand everything quickly*

But if you're a homey—*uninitiated*

Like the bear, you just ain't nowhere—*just don't fit in, since, obviously the bear would be out of place in any social gathering*

And ole man—*my friend*

Why can't you dig this hard mess?—*perceive this heavy discourse*

When the whole town's copping—*enjoying and understanding*

The mellow jive—*the finest things in life*

Are you going to be a square all your days? —*a person completely unaware of what's going on*

Ain't you gonna click your gimmers?—*open your eyes*

Latch on to this fine pulp I'm dropping on you—*try to understand this book I've written for you*

As you scoff, ace-deuce around the chiming Ben—*eat three square meals daily*

You dig, ole man—*you understand, my friend*

That from early bright to late black—*early morning until late night*

The cats and chippies—*the boys and the girls*

Are laying down (using) some fine, heavy jive—*the best of the new fad*

Most of it like the tree, all root—*universally okay, since tree roots spread underground in many directions*

Like the country road, all rut—*it's in a regular groove*

Like the apple, all rot—*superlative of rut*

Like the cheese, all rat—*definition obscure, but used in the comparative sense to add color to the series*

The tendency toward rhyming which has been noted before, is to be found more especially among members of the Negro theatrical and musical fraternities. These people travel more extensively than the average Harlemites and, since they are engaged, more or less, in work that has to do with the lyrical and poetic, such expressions as "like the bear, I ain't nowhere"; "like the bear's brother, Freddie, Jack I ain't ready"; "like the chicken, I ain't stickin,'" (broke); "Home from Rome" (Georgia); "Lane from Spokane," (Lane is the same as home); and innumerable others are widely used.

The inventive genius of the jiver is shown in his current attack on the standard classics. All regard for the sanctity of the ancient and best loved masterpieces of English prose and poetry, is discarded completely as Harlem lexicographers busily burn the midnight oil and turn out parodies on all subjects, religious and secular. Remember your nursery prayer: "Now I lay me down to sleep. I pray the Lord my soul to keep" etc.

In Harlemese it would read: "Now I stash me down to nod; my mellow frame upon this sod. If I should cop a drill before the early toot, I'll spiel to the Head Knock to make all things root." In this the definitions are:

Stash—*lay down*
Mellow frame—*the body*
Cop a drill—*leave quickly, disappear, or walk away, saunter, stroll, meander, pass away, succumb, die.*
Early toot—*morning, the next day, bright and early*
Spiel—*speech, prayer, supplication, discourse, soliloquy, plea*
Head Knock—*The Lawd!*

As already noted, Hamlet, in his Soliloquy, according to the Harlemese version says: "To dig, or not to dig, that is the question; whether 'tis the proper play to eat onions and wipe the eyes (endure the trials and tribulations of the times), or to snap open one's switchblade, turn out the joint, making cats take low by much head cutting."

Whittier's "Barefoot Boy" is changed to read: "Blessings on thee, little square, barefoot cat with the unconked hair" (unstraightened hair).

The variations, parodies and innovations in Jive are endless. When someone says: "She laid the twister to her slammer on me, ole man, understand, and I dug the jive straight up and down, three ways sides and flats," he means: His girl friend let him have the key to her apartment and he played her for all she was worth.

Other jivers have concocted such expressions as "Diggeth thou this jive?" "Canst thou latch on to yon fine, young hen?" (Greet, make contact with a pretty woman, 23 to 27 years old). "Woe to ye rugcutters who choppeth the carpet, maketh much dust and purchaseth not any lush!" (dancers who fail to buy wine and beer at a party).

Since its introduction to Harlem (the expression was imported from Chicago at the time of the Joe Louis–Tony Galento fight in 1939), "Gimme some skin"—which simply means shake hands with me—is almost universally understood among jive-conscious Negroes. The act of "Gimme some skin" involves some theatricals, an intricate sense of timing, plenty of gestures. For example: You are standing on the corner. You see a friend approaching. You bend your knees halfway and rock back and forth on your heels and toes with a swingy sway like the pulsing of a heartbeat. You hold your arms closely to your sides with index fingers pointing rigidly toward the sidewalk. You say to your friend as he comes up: "Whatcha know, ole man, whatcha know?" He answers: "Can't say, Jackson, (pal, buddy, etc.) whatcha know?"

You say: "Tell me something, studhoss, whatcha know?"

He says again: "I don't know, ole man, whatcha know?" Then he says: "Gimme some skin, ole man; gimme some of that fine skin!"

You bend your knees in a gentle sag. Your upper right arm is held close to your side, but the forearm, with the palm of the hand open, is thrust out like a motorist flagging on a left turn. You both swing around and your palms collide in a resounding whack. You both then shake your hand violently in the air as though the sting upset you. You dance in a bandy-legged stance in a semi-circle. Then in a satisfied manner of a man who has finally talked his creditor out of a ten-spot, loaned a year ago, you thrust your hand in your trouser pocket—"so it won't get wet" (in order to save and preserve this token of good fellowship).

"Gimme some skin" now calls for such artistry that it is a delight to watch kids or oldsters going through the motions. In some instances, the palm is held up in the manner of a Congressman voting to adjourn, and suddenly brought forcefully to the other fellow's in a quick, staccato blow. Other variations have been added, noticeably: "Gimme some skin, (hands are smacked); now gimme some nail, (fingernails are rubbed lightly across each other); and gimme some fist, (fists are touched); now gimme some elbow, (elbows are touched or bumped); and a little shoulder, (shoulders are nudged); now a little head, (heads are touched ever so slightly); and now, ole man, kick me lightly with some of that fine heel (heels are kicked)." Each is then ready to buy the other a drink.

12. JIVE EXCURSIONS

Back in 1924, in the prohibition era, when Jive was in the incipient stages, its early advocates described something that pleased them, whether a free dinner, a pretty girl, a new suit or a pocket full of "easy" money as being "forte" or "forty." This term of approval was also known as "twice twenty," or "thirty-eight and two," for both of these terms added up to mean satisfaction or a situation that was distinctly "o.k." In reality, "forte" meant strong, loud, forceful. But jivers had their own way about it. Today "forty" has come through such stages as "okey doke," "well, all right then," "the last word," "killer-diller," "solid" and others, including my own, "all reet, all root, and all rote," to the "really booted," "frantic," and "foxy" terms of approbation, the dream of the perfectionist, which may be summed up in the succinct phrase of being "really in there."

"All reet" means o.k., today as last year. This phrase, like any verb phrase, has its tenses so that "all reet" is the present, "all root" the past, and "all rote" the superlative.

"Hepcat" or "Hipcat" indicates one who has been around, and who, as a result knows most of the questions, and most of the answers. The fellow "with his boots on," however, is the ultimate in worldly wisdom. He knows *all* the answers and a few questions that have never been thought of. To the uninitiate a "hepcat" is sometimes confused with a "Swing-music" fan, but the real "hepcat" is something more than just a foot-nervous listener to hot music; he is a superior sort of individual, with real standing in his particular clan. His opinion and approval are eagerly sought by lesser members, or less knowing members of his fraternity.

At one time the term "thinkpad" in conjunction with various verbs was considered sufficient to describe various processes of mental cerebration. The term, however, has been proven inadequate. The jiver's insatiable thirst for newness and for more vivid means of expression brought forth the word "wig" to describe an individual's head, hair or brain, or contents of his skull— a word that is the twin of "cap," or its co-descriptives, "top" and "sky." To "lift the wig" does not actually imply the process of scalping, or snatching off one's hair. Instead it is an indication that one is suddenly "surprised," "overjoyed," or "thrilled" at something potent, unbelievably fresh, or "surprising" as to automatically "lift the wig." Similarly, to "snap the cap" means to be startled with something new or unexpected: whereas to "blow the sky" means to lose the mind, to get drunk, to be rendered unconscious.

Jive has some picturesque terms for

describing the physical characteristics of the female sex. Since the most important thing about a female, in the genuine Jiver's estimate, is her age and degree of availability, the age of these dear ones figures prominently in the terms used to describe them. Most of these terms have to do with "chickens" for the Jiver persists in the notion that womenfolk come in the same category as the barnyard's feathered inhabitants. So he describes the youngest of them, the least experienced, and hence the most dangerous, if he's in California, as "San Quentin Quail," or "Wings Over Sing Sing," if you are in New York. The pretty, youthful female, aware of her charms is known as a "fine young bantam." She is in the 15 to 20 year old class. Those from 18 to 20 are designated as "fine young chicks." Between 20 and 25 they are simply "chicks." The 25 to 30 bracket takes in the "fine young hens." Between 30 and 33 they are just "fine hens," and over 35 they are plain "hens."

In rare instances, an extraordinarily handsome or desirable member of the 33 to 45 group is considered worth "broiling" or "frying." The Jiver expresses his condemnation of the female of 45 and up, who has a yen for the company of young males half her age, by designating her as a "stewer," or in some cases, just plain "harpy," which is another type of fowl that has not yet encountered a hot pan of grease, or been put to the acid test of a pot full of hot water very heavily salted.

There are also other assorted names definitely not of the barnyard variety, which befit the female in the Jiver's sight. For example, "chippie" is commonly used to designate a racy, rather slender type of girl, who is good company, who can dance expertly, who has the money to pay her own way, who has a job, or is looking for one, and whose very attitude of independence makes her desirable.

"Scribe" is another way of describing the same sort of young woman. But carries with it a connotation of affection. A "scribe" is a young woman definitely dear to the Jiver's heart. "Saw" is more of a derogatory term. It refers to the wife, or some other nagging female, whose tongue has that sawing quality, which would arouse goose pimples along the hearer's spine when her shrill voice is heard raised in protest against something or other.

Masculine nouns are entirely different, of course. They begin with "cat," which was a descriptive term originally used to designate a "hot" musician, improvising a number on his favorite instrument. But later this term was used to designate mankind, inclusive, all those whose imagination worked above a certain more or less ordinary mental level.

"A Square" is the poor chap who works for a living, who does not know any of the "angles," and who comes home to *find* his dinner eaten, or his wife seduced, by a more Knowing Cat.

"A Lane" is too smart for himself, in most instances, but is usually capable of being handled successfully by a smarter "Skull," the latter being on his way toward becoming the proud possessor of well-laced boots.

"The Homey" is on the lowest rung of the social ladder. Homey being distinctly a derogatory term, a term which is the last word in opprobrium and condemnation. The genuine "hepcat" has nothing but scorn and contempt for the "Homey." How can he be so stupid? He's a stay-at-home, he reads heavy books about the goings-on in the 14th and 15th Century, while drawing his breath in the 20th. He's distinctly a mama's boy, under the influence of feminine domination; he doesn't even know as much about life as does the unenlightened Lane, the Cat, and the Skull.*

According to the Hepcat's viewpoint, both the Square, and the Homey miss a great deal in life.

"The Perfect Lamb" also ranks along with The Homey, for while he's no mama's boy, he is always on the outside looking in. "The Perfect Rum" is a male who falls in this same category.

There is also, by the same attribute, The Perfect Lane. Lanes are usually referred to as having made figurative trips to "Spain," or "Fort Wayne," or "Spokane." The Square, on the other hand, is most generally to be found, "hunting for Miss St. Claire," or "trying to be in there like the Bear."

The Homey, by popular consent in the world of Jive talk, usually evolves into the "Home from Rome."

"Jackson" in its original derivation referred to a colored fellow. (Phil Harris, please note.) While a stud is a male of any stature, width, color, or weight.

13. ADVANCED READING IN JIVE—SAM D. HOME'S SOLILOQUY

A Square ain't nothing but a Lane, and a Lane ain't nothing but a Rum, and a Rum ain't nothing but a Perfect Lamb; and a Perfect Lamb comes on like the Goodwill Hour—and tips away, Jackson, like the Widder Brown. If I was booted, truly booted, I'd lay a solid beg on my righteous scribe, and knock a scoff on the zoom on Turkey Day. In fact, I'd cop a trot to her frantic dommy, lay a mellow ring on the heavy buzz, give her Poppa Stoppa the groovy bend; and then lay my trill into the scoff-pad, hitch one of those most anxious lilywhites around my stretcher; cop a mellow squat and start forking. But my thinkpad is a drag, when it comes to a triple-quick-click; and that's why I'm out here eating fish-heads and scrambling for the gills, instead of being a round-tripper, good for a double-deuce of bags every play.

Every time I shoot for the side-pocket, I scratch. I hunch the pinball layout, Jack, and it's an unhipped tilt. I'm a true Rum: A Perfect Lamb that ain't been clipped. Instead of my groundpads being spread under my bantam's heavy oak, scarfing down some solid scarf, I'm out here with Mister Hawkins, wringling and twisting, ducking and dodging, and skulking close to the buildings: jumping to knock a stool in the greasy spoon and slice my chops on a bowl of beef and shinny beans with the deuce of demons I knocked on that last beg on the stem. Lawd! Who shall it be? Peace, Father, it's truly wonderful, or Uncle Sam Here I Come?

Picking up from the sentence following the one about the Goodwill Hour, Sam D. Home, in his soliloquy, really said:

"If I understood things and was really smart, I'd have asked my girl friend to invite me to dinner on Thanksgiving Day. In fact, right now, I'd run to her comfortable home, ring the bell, bow to her father, and walk into the dining room, where I'd put a napkin around my neck, take a seat and start eating. But my thinking is faulty when it comes to quick thinking, that is why I'm out on the street trying to promote

---

* A related definition of a "Homey" is a new arrival from one's hometown or a new arrival to a large Northern city from the South. See Harold Wentworth and Stuart Berg Flexner, *Dictionary of American Slang* (New York, 1967), p. 265. See also Chapter Three, "Homeboy," of *The Autobiography of Malcolm X* (New York, 1964). —ED.

a free dinner, instead of hitting home runs like good ballplayers do. Every time I put forth an effort, I fail to achieve my purpose. Everything I do turns out wrong. I'm really a simple fellow playing in hard luck. Instead of having my feet under my girl friend's dinner table eating a good dinner, I'm out here in the wintry gale, trying to make my way without freezing to death to the lunch wagon for a bowl of chili for 20 cents I just borrowed from somebody on the Avenue. What shall it be, Father Divine's Restaurant and Heavenly Kingdom, or do I join the United States Army?"

So contagious is the inclination to talk in this jive lingo that already certain aspects of it have and are emerging in the commercial world, in the movies, the daily comic sheets, over the radio and on popular recordings. Orson Welles, the playwright-actor, told the author one of his plays will have a jive theme. The movie hit, "Second Chorus" with Fred Astaire and Artie Shaw, featured an overdose of jive talk and jive dancing, freshly imported from Harlem. Popular comic strip characters in "Terry and the Pirates" were found talking in a really "hipped" manner to escape from a dire predicament.

Some high-brow psychiatrist might say that jive is the language of the "infantile-extrovert," but be that as it may, one can wander up Harlem way, night or day; pause for a bus or a cab, and one's ears are suddenly assailed by a bombardment of "Whatcha know, ole man?" "I'm like the bear, just ain't nowhere, but here to dig for Miss St. Clair". . . . "An' she laid the twister to her slammer on me, ole man, understand, and I dug the jive straight up an' down, three ways, sides and flats" . . . . Or: "Gimme some skin, ole man. That's

righteous. Jackson, truly reecheous. In fact, it's roacheous. I'm gonna put that right in my pocket so it won't get wet". . . . "I'm playing the dozens with my uncle's cousins; eatin' onions an' wiping my eyes" . . . . "The heavy sugar I'm laying down, ole man, understand, is harder than Norwegian lard. Lay a little of that fine skin on me, stud-hoss."

Such jargon is reminiscent of Tibet, Afghanistan, as unintelligible to the uninitiate as listening to a foreign dictator's harangue over a shortwave broadcast. One is confused and bewildered over this seemingly incomprehensible idiom. You forget about taking a cab or bus, and, lured by a sense of the occult and exotic, edge in closer to hear more, completely enchanted by the scene which greets your eyes—fellows in wide-brimmed fuzzy hats, pistol-cuffed trousers with balloon-like knees and frock-like coats the length of a clergyman's; you listen in breathless fascination as they exchange verbal bombshells, rhymed and lyrical, and although you do not know it, you are listening to the new poetry of the proletariat.

You glance about you in dismay. What has happened to the Harlem you thought you knew so well, or about which you read so much? Where are the poets, the high-brow intellectuals, the doctor-writers, and musicians, who spoke Harlem's language in the days of the Black Renaissance—that period ushered in by Carl Van Vechten and his "Nigger Heaven?" Harlem, apparently, has side-tracked her intellectuals. So, although you are unaware of it as yet, they have invented this picturesque new language, *the language of action*, which comes from the bars, the dance-halls, the prisons, honkey-tonks, gin mills, etc., wherever people are busy living, loving, fighting, working or conniving to get the better of one another.

You tap your nearest companion, a serious-looking man in the crowd, on the shoulder and ask him, "What kind of colored folk are these? What are they talking about?"

His answer is this, "They're talking the new jive language, my friend." As you listen to further parlance on the part of the zoot-suiters, gradually it dawns upon you that you are listening to the essence of slang gleaned from all nations, the cities, hamlets, and villages. You're listening to a purifying process in which expressions are tried and discarded, accepted or rejected, as the case may be. They are discussing politics, religion, science, war, dancing, business, love, economics, and the occult. They're talking of these things in a manner that those, orthodox in education and culture, cannot understand, This jive language may be a defense mechanism, or it may only be a method of deriving pleasure from something the uninitiated cannot understand. Little of it appears in print.

In a thousand and one places— poolrooms, night-clubs, dressing-rooms, back stage, kitchens, ballrooms, theatre lobbies, gymnasiums, jail cells, buffet flats, cafes, bars and grills—on a thousand and one street corners, when the sun shines warmly and they have a half-hour to kill, creators of the new Harlemese are busily adding words and expressions to their rapidly growing vocabulary of Jive. No aerial gunner ever had more ammunition for emergency use than a jiver's repertoire when encountering his gang. Each new phrase, each rhyme is received with delight. Like copyreaders and editorial writers on newspapers, jive addicts take infinite care of their latest brain-child. They trim and polish, rearrange, revise, reshuffle and recast certain phrases until they have the best and most concise expression that can be devised. Reputations as "jivers" are eagerly sought, and advanced apostles, real masters of the jargon, are looked up to with awe and admiration by their less accomplished disciples.

Story in Harlem Slang

ZORA NEALE HURSTON

One way for the reader to test his ability to understand jive, or at least the jive of the 1940's, is by looking at the following vignette couched in the vernacular idiom of that era. Actually, a good many of the slang items are still current, a fact which belies the commonly held notion that all slang is ephemeral and extremely short-lived. One reason for this is that it has taken fifteen to twenty years for the American Negro folk speech of Harlem in the 1930's to reach middle-class white Americans. One must remember that Harlem culture, including music and folk speech, was glorified by both Negro and white writers —a glorification that did not please some Negro critics—and this extension or transformation of the "Nigger Heaven" stereotype has no doubt contributed to the continued currency of Harlem folk speech.

Zora Neale Hurston, always an imaginative reporter of American Negro folklore, elected to demonstrate the vital nature of folk speech, not by presenting merely a long glossary as most conventional folklorists are wont to do, but by delineating a typical street encounter with its conversations. Thus the reader not only sees slang lexical items in context, but he also has an opportunity to observe hustlers in action.

WAIT TILL I light up my coal-pot and I'll tell you about this Zigaboo called Jelly. Well, all right now. He was a sealskin brown and papa-tree-top-tall. Skinny in the hips and solid built for speed. He was born with this rough-dried hair, but when he laid on the grease and pressed it down overnight with his stocking-cap, it looked just like that righteous moss, and had so many waves you got seasick from looking. Solid, man, solid!

Reprinted from *The American Mercury*, vol. 45 (July, 1942), pp. 84–96, by permission of *The American Mercury*.

His mama named him Marvel, but after a month on Lenox Avenue, he changed all that to Jelly. How come? Well, he put it in the street that when it came to filling that long-felt need, sugar-curing the ladies' feelings, he was in a class by himself and nobody knew his name, so he had to tell 'em. "It must be jelly, 'cause jam don't shake." Therefore, his name was Jelly. That was what was on his sign. The stuff was there and it was mellow. Whenever he was challenged by a hard-head or a frail eel on the right of his title he would eye-ball the idol-breaker with a slice of ice and put on his ugly-laugh, made up of scorn and pity, and say: "Youse just dumb to the fact, baby. If you don't know what you talking 'bout, you better ask Granny Grunt. I wouldn't mislead you, baby. I don't need to—not with the help I got." Then he would give the pimp's[1] sign, and percolate on down the Avenue. You can't go behind a fact like that.

So this day he was airing out on the Avenue. It had to be late afternoon, or he would not have been out of bed. All you did by rolling out early was to stir your stomach up. That made you hunt for more dishes to dirty. The longer you slept, the less you had to eat. But you can't collar nods all day. No matter how long you stay in bed, and how quiet you keep, sooner or later that big gut is going to reach over and grab that little one and start to gnaw. That's confidential right from the Bible. You got to get out on the beat and collar yourself a hot.

So Jelly got into his zoot suit with the reet pleats and got out to skivver around

and do himself some good. At 132nd Street, he spied one of his colleagues on the opposite sidewalk, standing in front of a café. Jelly figured that if he bull-skated just right, he might confidence Sweet Back out of a thousand on a plate. Maybe a shot of scrap-iron or a reefer. Therefore, Jelly took a quick backward look at his shoe soles to see how his leather was holding out. The way he figured it after the peep was that he had plenty to get across and maybe do a little more cruising besides. So he stanched out into the street and made the crossing.

"Hi there, Sweet Back!" he exploded cheerfully. "Gimme some skin!"

"Lay de skin on me, pal!" Sweet Back grabbed Jelly's outstretched hand and shook hard. "Ain't seen you since the last time, Jelly. What's cookin'?"

"Oh, just like de bear—I ain't nowhere. Like de bear's brother, I ain't no further. Like de bear's daughter—ain't got a quarter."

Right away, he wished he had not been so honest. Sweet Back gave him a top-superior, cut-eye look. Looked at Jelly just like a showman looks at an ape. Just as far above Jelly as fried chicken is over branch water.

"Cold in hand, hunh?" He talked down to Jelly. "A red hot pimp like you *say* you is, ain't got no business in the barrel. Last night when I left you, you was beating up your gums and broadcasting about how hot you was. Just as hot as July-jam, you told me. What you doing cold in hand?"

"Aw, man, can't you take a joke? I was just beating up my gums when

---

[1] In Harlemese, *pimp* has a different meaning than its ordinary definition as a procurer for immoral purposes. The Harlem pimp is a man whose amatory talents are for sale to any woman who will support him, either with a free meal or on a common law basis; in this sense, he is actually a male prostitute.

I said I was broke. How can I be broke when I got de best woman in Harlem? If I ask her for a dime, she'll give me a ten dollar bill; ask her for drink of likker, and she'll buy me a whiskey still. If I'm lying, I'm flying!"

"Gar, don't hang out dat dirty washing in my back yard! Didn't I see you last night with dat beat chick, scoffing a hot dog? Dat chick you had was beat to de heels. Boy, you ain't no good for what you live."

"If you ain't lying now, you flying. You ain't got de first thin. You ain't got nickel one."

Jelly threw back the long skirt of his coat and rammed his hand down into his pants pocket. "Put your money where your mouth is!" he challenged, as he mock-struggled to haul out a huge roll. "Back your crap with your money. I bet you five dollars!"

Sweet Back made the same gesture of hauling out non-existent money.

"I been raised in the church. I don't bet, but I'll doubt you. Five rocks!"

"I thought so!" Jelly crowed, and hurriedly pulled his empty hand out of his pocket. "I knowed you'd back up when I drawed my roll on you."

"You ain't drawed no roll on me, Jelly. You ain't drawed nothing but your pocket. You better stop dat booger-booing. Next time I'm liable to make you do it." There was a splinter of regret in his voice. If Jelly really had had some money, he might have staked him, Sweet Back, to a hot. Good Southern cornbread with a piano on a platter. Oh, well! The right broad would, or might, come along.

"Who boogerbooing?" Jelly snorted. "Jig, I don't have to. Talking about *me* with a beat chick scoffing a hot dog! You must of not seen me, 'cause

last night I was riding round in a Yellow Cab, with a yellow gal, drinking yellow likker and spending yellow money. Tell 'em 'bout me, tell 'em!"

"Git out of my face, Jelly! Dat broad I seen you with wasn't no pe-ola. She was one of them coal-scuttle blondes with hair just as close to her head as ninety-nine is to a hundred. She look-ted like she had seventy-five pounds of clear bosom, guts in her feet, and she look-ted like six months in front and nine months behind. Buy you a whiskey still! Dat broad couldn't make the down payment on a pair of sox."

"Sweet Back, you fixing to talk out of place." Jelly stiffened.

"If you trying to jump salty, Jelly, that's your mammy."

"Don't play in de family, Sweet Back. I don't play de dozens. I done told you."

"Who playing de dozens? You trying to get your hips up on your shoulders 'cause I said you was with a beat broad. One of them lam blacks."

"Who? Me? Long as you been knowing me, Sweet Back, you ain't never seen me with nothing but pe-olas. I can get any frail eel I wants to. How come I'm up here in New York? You don't know, do you? Since youse dumb to the fact, I reckon I'll have to make you hep. I had to leave from down south 'cause Miss Anne used to worry me so bad to go with me. Who, me? Man, I don't deal in no coal. Know what I tell 'em? If they's white, they's right! If they's yellow, they's mellow! If they's brown, they can stick around. But if they come black, they better git way back! Tell 'em bout me!"

"Aw, man, you trying to show your grandma how to milk ducks. Best you can do is to confidence some kitchen-mechanic out of a dime or two. Me,

I knocks de pad with them cack-broads up on Sugar Hill, and fills 'em full of melody. Man, I'm quick death and easy judgment. Youse just a home-boy, Jelly. Don't try to follow me."

"Me follow *you!* Man, I come on like the Gang Busters, and go off like The March of Time! If dat ain't so, God is gone to Jersey City and you know He wouldn't be messing 'round a place like that. Know what my woman done? We hauled off and went to church last Sunday, and when they passed 'round the plate for the *penny* collection, I throwed in a dollar. De man looked at me real hard for dat. Dat made my woman mad, so she called him back and throwed in a twenty dollar bill! Told him to take dat and go! Dat's what he got for looking at me 'cause I throwed in a dollar,"

"Jelly, de wind may blow and de door may slam; dat what you shooting ain't worth a damn!"

Jelly slammed his hand in his bosom as if to draw a gun. Sweet Back did the same.

"If you wants to fight, Sweet Back, the favor is in me,"

"I was deep-thinking then, Jelly. It's a good thing I ain't short-tempered. 'T'aint nothing to you, nohow. You ain't hit me yet."

Both burst into a laugh and changed from fighting to lounging poses.

"Don't get too yaller on me, Jelly. You liable to get hurt some day."

"You over-sports your hand your ownself. Too blamed astorperious. I just don't pay you no mind. Lay de skin on me!"

They broke their handshake hurriedly, because both of them looked up the Avenue and saw the same thing. It was a girl and they both remembered that it was Wednesday afternoon. All of the domestics off for the afternoon with their pay in their pockets. Some of them bound to be hungry for love. That meant a dinner, a shot of scrap-iron, maybe room rent and a reefer or two. Both went into the pose and put on the look.

"Big stars falling!" Jelly said out loud when she was in hearing distance. "It must be just before day!"

"Yeah, man!" Sweet Back agreed. "Must be a recess in Heaven—pretty angel like that out on the ground."

The girl drew abreast of them, reeling and rocking her hips.

"I'd walk clear to Diddy-Wah-Diddy to get a chance to speak to a pretty lil' ground-angel like that," Jelly went on.

"Aw, man, you ain't willing to go very far. Me, I'd go slap to Ginny-Gall, where they eat cow-rump, skin and all."

The girl smiled, so Jelly set his hat and took the plunge.

"Baby," he crooned, "what's on de rail for de lizard?"

The girl halted and braced her hips with her hands. "A Zigaboo down in Georgy, where I come from, asked a woman that one time and the judge told him 'ninety days.' "

"Georgy!" Sweet Back pretended to be elated ."Where 'bouts in Georgy is you from? Delaware?"

"Delaware?" Jelly snorted. "My people! My people! Free schools and dumb jigs! Man, how you going to put Delaware in Georgy? You ought to know dat's in Maryland."

"Oh, don't try to make out youse no northerner, you! Youse from right down in 'Bam your ownself!" The girl turned on Jelly.

"Yeah, I'm *from* there and I aims to stay from there."

"One of them Russians, eh?" the girl

retorted. "Rushed up here to get away from a job of work."

That kind of talk was not leading towards the dinner table.

"But baby!" Jelly gasped. "Dat shape you got on you! I bet the Coca Cola Company is paying you good money for the patent!"

The girl smiled with pleasure at this, so Sweet Back jumped in.

"I know youse somebody swell to know. Youse real people. You grins like a regular fellow." He gave her his most killing look and let it simmer in. "These dickty jigs round here tries to smile. S'pose you and me go inside the café here and grab a hot?"

"You got any money?" the girl asked, and stiffened like a ramrod. "Nobody ain't pimping on me. You dig me?"

"Aw, now, baby!"

"I seen you two mullet-heads before. I was uptown when Joe Brown had you all in the go-long last night. Dat cop sure hates a pimp! All he needs to see is the pimps' salute, and he'll out with his night-stick and whip your head to the red. Beat your head just as flat as a dime!" She went off into a great blow of laughter.

"Oh, let's us don't talk about the law. Let's talk about us," Sweet Back persisted. "You going inside with me to holler 'let one come flopping! One come grunting! Snatch one from de rear!' "

"Naw indeed!" the girl laughed harshly. "You skillets is trying to promote a meal on me. But it'll never happen, brother. You barking up the wrong tree. I wouldn't give you air if you was stopped up in a jug. I'm not putting out a thing. I'm just like the cemetery—I'm not putting out, I'm taking in! Dig?"

"I'll tell you like the farmer told the potato—plant you now and dig you later."

The girl made a movement to switch on off. Sweet Back had not dirtied a plate since the day before. He made a weak but desperate gesture.

"Trying to snatch my pocketbook,* eh?" she blazed. Instead of running, she grabbed hold of Sweet Back's draping coat-tail and made a slashing gesture. "How much split you want back here? If your feets don't hurry up and take you 'way from here, you'll *ride* away. I'll spread my lungs all over New York and call the law. Go ahead. Bed-bug! Touch me! And I'll holler like a pretty white woman!"

The boys were ready to flee, but she turned suddenly and rocked on off with her ear-rings snapping and her heels popping.

"My people! My people!" Sweet Back sighed.

"I know you feel chewed," Jelly said, in an effort to make it appear that he had had no part in the fiasco.

"Oh, let her go," Sweet Back said magnanimously. "When I see people without the periodical principles they's supposed to have, I just don't fool with 'em. What I want to steal her old pocket-book with all the money I got? I could buy a beat chick like her and give her away. I got money's mammy and Grand-ma change. One of my women, and not the best one I got neither, is buying me ten shag suits at one time."

He glanced sidewise at Jelly to see

---

* "Pocketbook" is, anti-Freudians notwithstanding, sometimes used as a slang euphemism for vagina. See Maya Angelou, *I Know Why the Caged Bird Sings* (New York, 1969), p. 268. —ED.

if he was convincing. But Jelly's thoughts were far away. He was remembering those full, hot meals he had left back in Alabama to seek wealth and splendor in Harlem without working. He had even forgotten to look cocky and rich.

GLOSSARY OF HARLEM SLANG

Air out—*leave, flee, stroll*

Astorperious—*haughty,* biggity

Aunt Hagar—Negro race (also Aunt Hagar's chillun)

Bad hair—*Negro type hair*

Balling—*having fun*

Bam, and down in Bam—*down South*

Battle-hammed—*badly formed about the hips*

Beating up your gums—*talking to no purpose*

Beluthahatchie—*next station beyond Hell*

Big boy—*stout fellow. But in the South, it means fool and is a prime insult.*

Blowing your top—*getting very angry; occasionally used to mean, "He's doing fine!"*

Boogie-woogie—*type of dancing and rhythm. For years, in the South, it meant secondary syphilis.*

Brother-in-black—*Negro*

Bull-skating—*Bragging*

Butt sprung—*a suit or a skirt out of shape in the rear*

Coal scuttle blonde—*black woman*

Cold—*exceeding, well, etc., as in "He was cold on that trumpet!"*

Collar a nod—*sleep*

Collar a hot—*eat a meal*

Color scale—*high yaller, yaller, high brown, vaseline brown, seal brown, low brown, dark black*

Conk buster—*cheap liquor; also an intellectual Negro*

Cruising—*parading down the Avenue. Variations:* oozing, percolating, and free-wheeling. *The latter implies more briskness.*

Cut—*doing something well*

Dark black—*a casually black person. Superlatives:* low black, *a blacker person;* lam black, *still blacker; and* damn black, *blackest man, of whom it is said: "Why, lightning bugs follows him at 12 o'clock in the day, thinking it's midnight.*

Dat thing—*sex of either sex*

Dat's your mammy—*same as, "So is your old man."*

Diddy-wah-diddy—*a far place, a measure of distance. (2) another suburb of Hell, built since way before Hell wasn't no bigger than Baltimore. The folks in Hell go there for a big time.*

Dig—*understand. "Dig me?" means, "Do you get me? Do you collar the jiver?"*

Draped down—*dressed in the height of Harlem fashion; also* togged down.

Dumb to the fact—*"You don't know what you're talking about."*

Dusty butt—*cheap prostitute*

Eight-rock—*very black person*

Every postman on his beat—*kinky hair*

First thing smoking—*a train. "I'm through with this town. I mean to grab the first thing smoking."*

Frail eel—*pretty girl*

Free schools—*a shortened expression of deprecation derived from "free schools and dumb Negroes," sometimes embellished with "free schools, pretty yellow teachers and dumb Negroes."*

Function—*a small, unventilated dance, full of people too casually bathed*

Gator-faced—*long, black face with big mouth*

Getting on some stiff time—*really doing well with your racket*

Get you to go—*power, physical or otherwise, to force the opponent to run*

Ginny Gall—*a suburb of Hell, a long way off*

Git up off of me—*quit talking about me, leave me alone*

Go when the wagon comes—*another way of saying, "You may be acting biggity now, but you'll cool down when enough power gets behind you."*

Good hair—*Caucasian-type hair*

Granny Grunt—*a mythical character to whom most questions may be referred*

Ground rations—*sex, also under rations*

Gum beater—*a blowhard, a braggart, idle talker in general*

Gut-bucket—*low dive, type of music, or expression from same*

Gut-foot—*bad case of fallen arches*

Handkerchief-head—*sycophant type of Negro; also an* Uncle Tom

Hauling—*fleeing on foot.* "Man! He cold hauled it!"

I don't deal in coal—"*I don't keep company with black women.*"

I'm cracking but I'm facking—"*I'm wise-cracking, but I'm telling the truth.*"

Inky dink—*very black person*

I shot him lightly and he died politely—"*I completely outdid him.*"

Jar head—*Negro man*

Jelly—*sex*

Jig—*Negro, a corrupted shortening of* zigaboo

Jook—*a pleasure house, in the class of gut-bucket; now common all over the South*

Jooking—*playing the piano, guitar, or any musical instrument in the manner of the Jooks (pronounced like "took") (2) Dancing and "scronching" ditto.*

Juice—*liquor*

July jam—*something very hot*

Jump salty—*get angry*

Kitchen mechanic—*a domestic*

Knock yourself out—*have a good time*

Lightly, slightly and politely—*doing things perfectly*

Little sister—*measure of hotness:* "Hot as little sister!"

Liver-lip—*pendulous, thick, purple lips*

Made hair—*hair that has been straightened*

Mammy—*a term of insult. Never used in any other way by Negroes.*

Miss Anne—*a white woman*

Mister Charlie—*a white man*

Monkey chaser—*a West Indian*

Mug man—*small-time thug or gangster*

My people! My people!—*Sad and satiric expression in the Negro language: sad when a Negro comments on the backwardness of some members of his race; at other times, used for satiric or comic effect*

Naps—*kinky hair*

Nearer my God to Thee—*good hair*

Nothing to the bear but his curly hair—"*I call your bluff,*" or "*Don't be afraid of him; he won't fight.*"

Now you cookin' with gas—*now you're talking, in the groove, etc.*

Ofay—*white person*

Old cuffee—*Negro (genuine African word for the same thing)*

Palmer House—*walking flat-footed, as from fallen arches*

Pancake—*a humble type of Negro*

Park ape—*an ugly, underprivileged Negro*

Peckerwood—*poor and unloved class of Southern whites*

Peeping through my likkers—*carrying on even though drunk*

Pe-ola—*a very white Negro girl*

Piano—*spare ribs (white rib-bones suggest piano keys)*

Pig meat—*young girl*

Pilch—*house or apartment; residence*

Pink toes—*yellow girl*

Playing the dozens—*low-rating the ancestors of your opponent*

Red neck—*poor Southern white man*

Reefer—*marijuana cigaret, also a* drag

Righteous mass or grass—*good hair*

Righteous rags—*the components of a Harlem-style suit*

Rug-cutter—*originally a person frequenting house-rent parties, cutting up the rugs of the host with his feet; a person too cheap or poor to patronize regular dance halls; now means a good dancer.*

Russian—*a Southern Negro up north.* "Rushed up here," *hence a Russian.*

Scrap iron—*cheap liquor*

Sell out—*run in fear*

Sender—*he or she who can get you to go, i.e., has what it takes. Used often as a compliment:* "He's a solid sender!"

Smoking, or smoking over—*looking someone over*

Solid—*perfect*

Sooner—*anything cheap and mongrel,*

now applied to cheap clothes, or a shabby person.

Stanch, or stanch out—*to begin, commence, step out*

Stomp—*low dance, but hot man!*

Stormbuzzard—*shiftless, homeless character*

Stroll—*doing something well*

Sugar Hill—*northwest corner of Harlem, near Washington Heights, site of newest apartment houses, mostly occupied by professional people. (The expression has been distorted in the South to mean a Negro red light district.)*

The bear—*confession of poverty*

The big apple, also the big red apple— *New York City.*

The man—*the law, or powerful boss*

Thousand on a plate—*beans*

Tight head—*one with kinky hair*

Trucking—*strolling. (2) dance step from the strolling motif*

V and X—*five-and-ten-cent store*

West Hell—*another suburb of Hell, worse than the original*

What's on the rail for the lizard?—*suggestion for moral turpitude*

Whip it to the red—*beat your head until it is bloody*

Woofing—*aimless talk, as a dog barks on a moonlight night* [The term might also be related to "wolf." For a reference to "wolfin', " see Will Thomas, *The Seeking* (New York: A. A. Wyn, Inc., 1953), p. 129. —ED.]

Young suit—*ill-fitting, too small. Observers pretend to believe you're breaking in your little brother's suit for him.*

Your likker told you—*misguided behavior*

Zigaboo—*a Negro*

Zoot suit with the reet pleat—*Harlem style suit, padded shoulders, 43-inch trousers at the knee with cuff so small it needs a zipper to get into, high waistline, fancy lapels, bushels of buttons, etc.*

The Language of Soul

CLAUDE BROWN

    By now, it should have become perfectly clear that folk speech is closely tied to the Negro's notion of group identity. That sense or notion of identity is summed up in the concept of "soul." "Soul" is not easy to define. It refers to the essence or quintessence of Negro-ness—and for this reason it has been compared with the concept of "Negritude" found in Africa. Soul is manifested in a variety of objects, e.g., music (soul music) and food (soul food), but its general characteristics tend to be more subjective than objective. It seems to have more to do with style or feeling than with substance.

    The identification of "soul" with "Negro" is not new and may well derive from an African concept. In any case, there appears to be good evidence from slavery times that the equation existed then. Individuals who speculated in the purchase and sale of slaves were called "Negro-drivers" or "soul-drivers." If "Negro-driver" was the same as "soul-driver," then in some sense "Negro" and "soul" were equivalent and interchangeable.

    In addition to the lexical evidence, there is also the great emphasis placed upon "soul" by the earliest Negro writers. Frederick Douglass in his celebrated Narrative, *first published in 1845, spoke of his holding Sunday school classes as "great days to my soul" and that he taught his fellow unfortunates "because it was the delight of my soul to be doing something that looked like bettering the condition of my race." In 1901, Booker T. Washington published his famous* Up From Slavery, *and one paragraph in that book anticipated much of the argument presented by Claude Brown in his essay "The Language of Soul." In the course of offering advice about public speaking, Booker T. Washington made the following remark:*

    Although there are certain things such as pauses, breathing, and pitch of voice

Reprinted from *Esquire*, vol. 69 (April, 1968), pp. 88, 160, 162, by permission of the Sterling Lord Agency.

that are very important, none of these can take the place of soul *in an address. When I have an address to deliver, I like to forget all about the rules for the proper use of the English language, and all about rhetoric and that sort of thing, and I like to make the audience forget all about these things, too.*

A strikingly analogous reflection was made by jazz musician Dizzy Gillespie when he spoke about expressing his "soul" with his trumpet. During an interview, he made the following comment:

You got to get your moods. You got to get your chords. You're thinking all the time. . . . Guys are always askin', me, "How do you get from a B-minor chord to an A flat?" They always talk about my attack. "What is that?" they say, "I'm playin' the same notes, but it comes out different." But you can't teach the soul.

In both cases, the formal, mechanical rules for speaking or playing cannot account for soul. Moreover, whereas rules of rhetoric or principles of musical modulation can be taught, soul cannot be taught. Claude Brown makes much the same point when he remarks that white Americans try in vain to borrow a soulful expression from American Negroes. "They get hung up in diction and grammar, and when they vocalize the expression it's no longer a soulful thing."

The fact that white Americans are trying to copy "soul" is itself an important point. Soul as found in present day folk speech has a positive value, and this represents a significant change from previous attitudes toward Negro dialect. During the nineteenth century and early twentieth century, dialect was frequently used to poke fun at Negroes. One observer astutely noted, for example, that southern white writers often had Negroes in their novels speaking in dialect whereas whites spoke "perfect" standard English. Since white southerners obviously spoke in dialect in real life, this practice was little more than another insidious form of Jim Crow. Southern white writers defended their use of Negro dialect, arguing that it was a true and authentic form of folk speech. But the fact that they were defensive about using Negro dialect indicates that the "deviations" from "standard" English had negative connotations.

In "The Language of Soul," we find an important reversal in attitude, a reversal which is very much in harmony with the general "Black is Beautiful" philosophy. If black is not ugly but beautiful, then Negro dialect is likewise nothing to be ashamed of, but rather it is something to be proud of (as in "I'm black and I'm proud"). In this new context, the Negro is far from being apologetic for his dialect of English. Instead he makes fun of the poor "ofay" (white person) who is apparently incapable of articulating Negro dialect correctly, that is, with "soul." This development signals a new importance for folk speech in developing race pride and in fostering a positive self-image.

For typical references to Negro- or soul-drivers in slavery times, see Gilbert Osofsky, ed., Puttin' On Ole Massa (*New York, 1969), pp. 128, 177, 191, 211. For the remarks by Frederick Douglass, see the* Narrative of the Life of Frederick Douglass (*New York, 1968), p. 90. It was probably no accident, incidentally, that Du Bois entitled his famous book published in 1903,* The Souls of Black Folk. *For the quote from Booker T. Washington, see* Three Negro Classics (*New York, 1965), p. 161. For the interview with Dizzy Gillespie, see Richard O. Boyer, "Bop,"* The New Yorker, 24 (*July 3, 1948), pp. 28–37. For the idea that neo-Confederate writers Jim Crow the Negro by using dialect in contrast to the King's English spoken by southern white characters in novels,*

see Earl Conrad, *"The Philology of Negro Dialect,"* Journal of Negro Educa-
tion, *13 (1944), pp. 150–54. For an ardent defense of the use of dialect in
novels written by white authors, see Margaret Long, "Strictly Subjective,"
New South 16, no. 10 (November, 1961), pp. 2–3, 11. For additional samples of
the rapidly growing literature on soul, see Ulf Hannerz, "The Significance of
Soul," in* Soul, *ed. Lee Rainwater (Chicago, 1970), pp. 15–30; Roger D.
Abrahams,* Positively Black *(Englewood Cliffs, 1970), pp. 136–50; and Chapter
VII, "Soul and Solidarity," in Charles Keil,* Urban Blues *(Chicago, 1966), pp.
164–90. For more about Claude Brown, see his best seller,* Manchild in the
Promised Land *(New York, 1965).*

PERHAPS THE most soulful word in the world is "nigger." Despite its very definite fundamental meaning (the Negro man), and disregarding the deprecatory connotation of the term, "nigger" has a multiplicity of nuances when used by soul people. Dictionaries define the term as being synonymous with "Negro," and they generally point out that it is regarded as a vulgar expression. Nevertheless, to those of chitlins-and-neck-bones background the word "nigger" is neither a synonym for Negro nor an obscene expression.*

"Nigger" has virtually as many shades of meaning in Colored English as the demonstrative pronoun "that," prior to application to a noun. To some Americans of African ancestry (I avoid using the term Negro whenever feasible, for fear of offending the Brothers X, a pressure group to be reckoned with), nigger seems preferable to "Negro" and has a unique kind of sentiment attached to it. This is exemplified in the frequent —and perhaps even excessive—usage

of the term to denote either fondness or hostility.

It is probable that numerous transitional niggers and even established ex-soul brothers can—with pangs of nostalgia—reflect upon a day in the lollipop epoch of lives when an adorable lady named Mama bemoaned her spouse's fastidiousness with the strictly secular utterance: "Lord, how can one nigger be so hard to please?" Others are likely to recall a time when that drastically lovable colored woman, who was forever wiping our noses and darning our clothing, bellowed in a moment of exasperation: "Nigger, you gonna be the death o' me." And some of the brethren who have had the precarious fortune to be raised up, wised up, thrown up or simply left alone to get up as best they could, on one of the nation's South Streets or Lenox Avenues, might remember having affectionately referred to a best friend as "My nigger."

The vast majority of "back-door Americans" are apt to agree with Webster

* The usage appears to depend upon the context and upon the relationship existing between the speaker and his audience. If a white person used it in speaking to a Negro, the word would normally be offensive. If a Negro used the term in speaking to another Negro, the term might not be offensive. If a Negro used the term to another Negro *with a white person present*, it would probably be offensive. For examples of the latter, see Claude Brown, *Manchild in the Promised Land* (New York, 1965), p. 132; Nathan C. Heard, *Howard Street* (New York, 1968), p. 104. For an account of how a northern Negro had to learn *not* to take offense when called "nigger" by black friends, see Will Thomas, *The Seeking* (New York, 1953), pp. 48–49. —ED.

—a nigger is simply a Negro or Black man. But the really profound contemporary thinkers of this distinguished ethnic group—Dick Gregory, Redd Foxx, Moms Mabley, Slappy White, etc.— are likely to differ with Mr. Webster and define "nigger" as "something else"—a soulful "something else." The major difference between the nigger and the Negro, who have many traits in common, is that the nigger is the more soulful.

Certain foods, customs and artistic expressions are associated almost solely with the nigger: collard greens, neck bones, hog maws, black-eyed peas, pigs' feet, etc.* A nigger has no desire to conceal or disavow any of these favorite dishes or restrain other behavioral practices such as bobbing his head, patting his feet to funky jazz, and shouting and jumping in church. This is not to be construed that all niggers eat chitlins and shout in church, nor that only niggers eat the aforementioned dishes and exhibit this type of behavior. It is to say, however, that the soulful usage of the term nigger implies all of the foregoing and considerably more.

The Language of Soul—or, as it might also be called, Spoken Soul or Colored English—is simply an honest vocal portrayal of black America. The roots of it are more than three hundred years old.

Before the Civil War there were numerous restrictions placed on the speech of slaves. The newly arrived Africans had the problem of learning to speak a new language, but also there were inhibitions placed on the topics of the slaves' conversation by slave masters and overseers. The slaves made up songs to inform one another of, say, the underground railroads' activity. When they sang *Steal Away* they were planning to steal away to the North, not to heaven. Slaves who dared to speak of rebellion or even freedom usually were severely punished. Consequently, Negro slaves were compelled to create a semi-clandestine vernacular in the way that the criminal underworld has historically created words to confound law-enforcement agents. It is said that numerous Negro spirituals were inspired by the hardships of slavery, and that what later became songs were initially moanings and coded cotton-field lyrics. To hear these songs sung today by a talented soul brother or sister or by a group is to be reminded of an historical spiritual bond that cannot be satisfactorily described by the mere spoken word.

The American Negro, for virtually all of his history, has constituted a vastly disproportionate number of the country's illiterates. Illiteracy has a way of showing itself in all attempts at vocal expression by the uneducated. With the aid of colloquialisms, malapropisms, battered and fractured grammar, and a considerable amount of creativity, Colored English, the sound of soul, evolved.

* For further discussion of soul food, see Viola Glenn, "The Eating Habits of Harlem," *Opportunity*, 13 (March, 1935), pp. 82–85; Clementine Paddleford, "What's Cooking in Harlem?" *Negro Digest*, 1 (October, 1943), pp. 11–12; Julian H. Lewis, "In Defense of Chittlins," *Negro Digest* 8 (April, 1950), pp. 74–78. See also Eleanore Ott, *Plantation Cookery of Old Louisiana* (New Orleans, 1938); Sue Bailey Thurman, ed., *The Historical Cookbook of the American Negro* (Washington, D. C., 1958), and Freda De Night, *The Ebony Cookbook: A Date with a Dish* (Chicago, 1962). —ED.

The progress has been cyclical. Often terms that have been discarded from the soul people's vocabulary for one reason or another are reaccepted years later, but usually with completely different meaning. In the Thirties and Forties "stuff" was used to mean vagina. In the middle Fifties it was revived and used to refer to heroin. Why certain expressions are thus reactivated is practically an indeterminable question. But it is not difficult to see why certain terms are dropped from the soul language. Whenever a soul term becomes popular with whites it is common practice for the soul folks to relinquish it. The reasoning is that "if white people can use it, it isn't hip enough for me." To many soul brothers there is just no such creature as a genuinely hip white person. And there is nothing more detrimental to anything hip than to have it fall into the square hands of the hopelessly unhip.

White Americans wrecked the expression "something else." It was bad enough that they couldn't say "sump'n else," but they weren't even able to get out somethin' else." They had to go around saying *something else* with perfect or nearly perfect enunciation. The white folks invariably fail to perceive the soul sound in soulful terms. They get hung up in diction and grammar, and when they vocalize the expression it's no longer a soulful thing. In fact, it can be asserted that spoken soul is more of a sound than a language. It generally possesses a pronounced lyrical quality which is frequently incompatible to any music other than that ceaseless and relentlessly driving rhythm that flows from poignantly spent lives. Spoken soul has a way of coming out metered without the intention of the speaker to invoke it. There are specific phonetic traits. To the soulless ear the vast majority of these sounds are dismissed as incorrect usage of the English language and, not infrequently, as speech impediments. To those so blessed as to have had bestowed upon them at birth the lifetime gift of soul, these are the most communicative and meaningful sounds ever to fall upon human ears: the familiar "mah" instead of "my," "gonna" for "going to," "yo" for "your." "Ain't" is pronounced "ain'"; "bread" and "bed," "bray-ud" and "bay-ud"; "baby" is never "bay-bee" but "bay-buh"; Sammy Davis Jr, is not "Sammee" but a kind of "Sam-eh"; the same goes for "Eddeh" Jefferson. No matter how many "man's" you put into your talk, it isn't soulful unless the word has the proper plaintive, nasal "maee-yun."

Spoken soul is distinguished from slang primarily by the fact that the former lends itself easily to conventional English, and the latter is diametrically opposed to adaptations within the realm of conventional English. Police (pronounced pō' lice) is a soul term, whereas "The Man" is merely slang for the same thing. Negroes seldom adopt slang terms from the white world and when they do the terms are usually given a different meaning. Such was the case with the term "bag." White racketeers used it in the Thirties to refer to the graft that was paid to the police. For the past five years soul people have used it when referring to a person's vocation, hobby, fancy, etc. And once the appropriate term is given the treatment (soul vocalization) it becomes soulful.

However, borrowings from spoken soul by white men's slang—particularly teen-age slang—are plentiful. Perhaps because soul is probably the most graphic language of modern times, everybody who is excluded from Soulville wants to usurp it, ignoring the formidable fettering to the soul folks that has brought the language about. Consider "uptight," "strung-out," "cop," "boss," "kill 'em," all now widely used outside Soulville. Soul people never question the origin of a slang term; they either dig it and make it a part of their vocabulary or don't and forget it. The expression "uptight," which meant being in financial straits, appeared on the soul scene in the general vicinity of 1953. Junkies were very fond of the word and used it literally to describe what was a perpetual condition with them. The word was pictorial and pointed; therefore it caught on quickly in Soulville across the country. In the early Sixties when "uptight" was on the move, a younger generation of soul people in the Black urban communities along the Eastern Seaboard regenerated it with a new meaning: "everything is cool, under control, going my way." At present the term has the former meaning for the older generation and the later construction for those under thirty years of age.

It is difficult to ascertain if the term "strung-out" was coined by junkies or just applied to them and accepted without protest. Like the term "uptight" in its initial interpretation, "strung-out" aptly described the constant plight of the junkie. "Strung-out" had a connotation of hopeless finality about it. "Uptight" implied a temporary situation and lacked the overwhelming despair of "strung-out."

The term "cop," (meaning "to get"), is an abbreviation of the word "copulation." "Cop," as originally used by soulful teenagers in the early Fifties, was deciphered to mean sexual coition, nothing more. By 1955 "cop" was being uttered throughout national Soulville as a synonym for the verb "to get," especially in reference to illegal purchases, drugs, pot, hot goods, pistols, etc. ("Man, where can I cop now?") But by 1955 the meaning was all-encompassing. Anything that could be obtained could be "copped."

The word "boss," denoting something extraordinarily good or great, was a redefined term that had been popular in Soulville during the Forties and Fifties as a complimentary remark from one soul brother to another. Later it was replaced by several terms such as "groovy," "tough," "beautiful" and most recently, "out of sight."* This last

* One must use caution in accepting all of Claude Brown's hypothetical etymological and chronological explanations. For example, it is extremely doubtful whether "out of sight" is really a recent outgrowth of "way out." For one thing, "out of sight" is not a new item in Negro speech. An instance is recorded in James David Corrothers, *The Black Cat Club; Negro Humor and Folk-Lore* (New York, 1902), p. 26, and it was used even earlier by the first major Negro novelist Charles W. Chesnutt in a letter written to his eldest daughter dated September 24, 1897. See Helen M. Chesnutt, *Charles Waddell Chesnutt: Pioneer of the Color Line* (Chapel Hill, 1952), p. 81.

Similarly, another "new" phrase, "right on," indicating enthusiastic assent or encouragement to a speaker may well have been in American Negro tradition in one form or another for over a hundred years. There were a number of popular ante-bellum Negro spirituals which contained phrases such as "Ride on, King Jesus." Jesus was frequently depicted as being mounted on a milk-white steed engaged in a race with Satan and it made sense for an exuberant congregation to urge on the Savior to victory. More direct linguistic evidence comes from a chance report of an elderly slave woman on a plantation in eastern Virginia during the Civil War who could hardly restrain her enthusiasm at the prospect of freedom near at hand. In listening to the sound of nearby Union

expression is an outgrowth of the former term "way out," the meaning of which was equivocal. "Way out" had an ad hoc hickish ring to it which made it intolerably unsoulful and consequently it was soon replaced by "out of sight," which is also likely to experience a relatively brief period of popular usage. "Out of sight" is better than "way out," but it has some of the same negative, childish taint of its predecessor.

The expression, "kill 'em," has neither a violent nor a malicious interpretation. It means "good luck," "give 'em hell," or "I'm pulling for you," and originated in Harlem from six to nine years ago.

There are certain classic soul terms which, no matter how often borrowed, remain in the canon and are reactivated every so often, just as standard jazz tunes are continuously experiencing renaissances. Among the classical expressions are: "solid," "cool," "jive" (generally as a noun), "stuff," "thing," "swing" (or "swinging"), "pimp," "dirt," "freak," "heat," "larceny," "busted," "okee doke," "piece," "sheet" (a jail record), "squat," "square," "stash," "lay," "sting," "mire," "gone," "smooth," "joint," "blow," "play," "shot," and there are many more.

Soul language can be heard in practically all communities throughout the country, but for pure, undiluted spoken soul one must go to Soul Street. There are several. Soul is located at Seventh and "T" in Washington, D.C., on One Two Five Street in New York City; on Springfield Avenue in Newark; on South Street in Philadelphia; on Tremont Street in Boston; on Forty-seventh Street in Chicago, on Fillmore in San Francisco, and dozens of similar locations in dozens of other cities.

As increasingly more Negroes desert Soulville for honorary membership in the Establishment clique, they experience a metamorphosis, the repercussions of which have a marked influence on the young and impressionable citizens of Soulville. The expatriates of Soulville are often greatly admired by the youth of Soulville, who emulate the behavior of such expatriates, as Nancy Wilson, Ella Fitzgerald, Eartha Kitt, Lena Horne, Diahann Carroll, Billy Daniels, or Leslie Uggams. The result—more often than not—is a trend away from spoken soul among the young soul folks. This abandonment of the soul language is facilitated by the fact that more Negro youngsters than ever are acquiring college educations (which, incidentally,

---

cannons, she greeted each blast with a subdued "ride on Massa Jesus." This use of the spiritual line is nearly identical with the modern hortatory usage of "right on." The shift from religious spiritual to secular speech which is implicit in the change from "ride on" to "right on" is also manifested in Negro folksong proper. In the 1920's, for example, there was a series of secular songs employing such lines as "Right on, Desperado Bill." It would appear that these songs may be the transitional link in the gradual evolution from "Ride on, King Jesus" to "Right on, Desperado Bill," to just plain "Right on." For representative texts of the spiritual, see J. B. T. Marsh, *The Story of the Jubilee Singers; With Their Songs* (Boston, 1880), p. 168, or Bruce Jackson, ed., *The Negro and His Folklore in Nineteenth Century Periodicals* (Austin, 1967), p. 333. See also Lawrence W. Levine, "Slave Songs and Slave Consciousness: An Exploration in Neglected Sources," in Tamara K. Hareven, ed., *Anonymous Americans: Explorations in Nineteenth-Century Social History* (Englewood Cliffs, N. J., 1971), p. 120. For the account of the greeting of Union cannon shots, see Bell Irvin Wiley, *Southern Negroes, 1861–1865* (New Haven, 1938), p. 19. For texts of "Right on, Desperado Bill," see Howard W. Odum and Guy B. Johnson, *The Negro and His Songs* (Chapel Hill, 1925), pp. 202–3. —ED.

is not the best treatment for the continued good health and growth of soul); integration and television, too, are contributing significantly to the gradual demise of spoken soul.

Perhaps colleges in America should commence to teach a course in spoken soul. It could be entitled the Vocal History of Black America, or simply Spoken Soul. Undoubtedly there would be no difficulty finding teachers. There are literally thousands of these experts throughout the country whose talents lie idle while they await the call to duty.

Meanwhile the picture looks dark for soul. The two extremities in the Negro spectrum—the conservative and the militant—are both trying diligently to relinquish and repudiate whatever vestige they may still possess of soul. The semi-Negro—the soul brother intent on gaining admission to the Establishment even on an honorary basis—is anxiously embracing and assuming conventional English. The other extremity, the Ultra-Blacks, are frantically adopting everything from a Western version of Islam that would shock the Caliph right out of his snugly fitting shintiyan to anything that vaguely hints of that big, beautiful, bountiful black bitch lying in the arms of the Indian and Atlantic Oceans and crowned by the majestic Mediterranean Sea. Whatever the Ultra-Black is after, it's anything but soulful.

Hidden Language:
Ghetto Children Know
What They're Talking About

JOHN M. BREWER

   The study of folk speech is much more than an amusing concern with quaint lexical items or turns of phrase. In fact, there are even more critical facets of folk speech studies than the relationship of folk speech to the central issue of group identity, important though that be. For the fact is that folk speech reflects the way people, ordinary people, talk. If one wishes to communicate with people, one needs to know the local lingo. Malcolm X makes this point very emphatically in criticizing black leaders who are unfamiliar with the language of the hustler. Here is his account:

   After a Harlem street rally, one of these downtown "leaders" and I were talking when we were approached by a Harlem hustler. To my knowledge I'd never seen this hustler before; he said to me, approximately: "Hey, baby! I dig you holding this all-originals scene at the track. . . . I'm going to lay a vine under the Jew's balls for a dime—got to give you a play. . . . Got the shorts out here trying to scuffle up on some bread. . . . Well, my man, I'll get on, got to go peck a little, and cop me some z's—" and the hustler went on up Seventh Avenue.

   I never would have given it another thought, except that this downtown "leader" was standing, staring after that hustler, looking as if he'd just heard Sanskrit. He asked me what had been said, and I told him. The hustler had said he was aware that the Muslims were holding an all-black bazaar at Rockland Palace, which is primarily a dancehall. The hustler intended to pawn a suit for ten dollars to attend and patronize the bazaar. He had very little money, but he was trying hard to make some. He was going to eat, then he would get some sleep.

   Malcolm X rightly observes that black leaders must be able to communicate with ghetto blacks as well as with "middle-class", well-educated Negroes. Exactly the same principle holds for ghetto children. And if this is so, then middle-class teachers, be they Negro or white, must make an effort to master the folk speech spoken in the ghetto. It is not enough to ask ghetto children to learn middle-class "standard English." The serious teacher must meet his student at least halfway by learning the student's language.

This makes sense even if one is narrowly committed to doctrinaire standard English to the exclusion of all slang; because, pedagogically speaking, one cannot teach any language, or any subject for that matter, without some knowledge of what the student already knows. Even if one considers what the student already knows to be completely wrong, one still needs to know the exact state of the student's knowledge.

From the folklorist's point of view, it does little good to label folk speech or slang as "wrong," "incorrect," or "non-standard." No spoken speech is "wrong" just because it doesn't fall neatly into a priori, Procrustean prescriptive categories. Unfortunately, generally speaking, teachers of language continue to be dominated by the rules of written *rather than* oral *language. Moreover, they tend to be prescriptive rather than descriptive. That is, they spend far more time trying to persuade unwilling students to accept long lists of "do's" and "don't's" than they do in examining "English as she is spoke" by the students.*

Folk speech exists, and regardless of the wishes or demands of formal education and educators, it effectively serves the needs of oral communication. The teacher can either ignore it—at his peril—or he can try to make some use of it. Preliminary studies have shown, for example, that reading materials based upon spoken, oral discourse have greatly facilitated the learning of reading by ghetto children. Since all children already know how to speak before they come to school, it seems sensible to tap the oral tradition in the classroom rather than waging what is almost invariably an unsuccessful battle to stamp it out.

In the following fascinating essay by John M. Brewer, an Assistant Superintendent of School-Community Affairs who has worked with slum children in the Pittsburgh school system, we get a firsthand account of just how useful a knowledge of ghetto folk speech can be and how a creative teacher can use the materials of folk speech and such verbal skills as playing the dozens to increase language learning in the classroom.

For the quotation by Malcolm X, see The Autobiography of Malcolm X (*New York, 1966*), *p. 310. For the possibilities of using oral speech to prepare workable materials for the teaching of reading, see William A. Stewart, "On the Use of Negro Dialect in the Teaching of Reading," in Joan C. Baratz and Roger W. Shuy, eds.,* Teaching Black Children to Read (*Washington, D.C., 1969*). *See also the Special Anthology Issue "Linguistic-Cultural Differences and American Education,"* The Florida Foreign Language Reporter, *vol. 7, no. 1 (Spring/Summer, 1969).*

BROKEN HOMES are "trees without roots."

Meat markets are "great flesh parlors."

Outsiders looking for thrills are "toys on a fairy lake."

This is the colorful, private speech of the children of America's ghettos, a "hidden language" of haunted phrases and striking subtlety. It is a language little known in the world outside, but for many it is more meaningful, more facile and more developed than the language of standard English.

During the period I was the principal of a large elementary school in the heart of a Negro slum, I became fascinated by this secret language developed by a rough-and-ready group of ghetto children. I found this idiom to be as dazzling as a diamond, invested with the bitter-sweet soulfulness bred by the struggle against poverty's dehumanizing forces.

I discovered that it was developed by the children even before they came to school, passed on from mother to child, and that a quarter of the students came from homes where it is the usual household speech. It is equipment for survival in the black ghetto. Normally it is used only in easy social settings like the home and after-school gatherings, and not in front of outsiders—which helps to explain why the children are often inarticulate when they try to use conventional English in talking to teachers, doctors, the school staff, etc.

As they advance in their schooling, these children also advance their hidden language vocabulary, become infatuated with this kind of verbal play and help it to flower with additions from the standard English they meet in class. They, and their parents, are fully aware of the aliveness of their words and make a serious effort to master the idiom. But, of course, this development conflicts with the formal school pattern and teachers who demand that only conventional English be used, and it often happens that verbally bright children suddenly clam up or become inarticulate in the classroom.

An illustration of the wonderful possibilities of the language of the ghetto helps one to judge how rich and interesting it is.

About 9:45 A.M. one day, Junebug—a small, wiry, shabbily dressed boy with large brown eyes—came into my office. As I looked up, it was obvious that he was hosed down and deep in the mud (embarrassed and had a problem). Very quickly I got up and asked, "Why are you stretched so thin by joy? Are you flying backwards?" ("Why are you so sad? Are you in trouble?")

Junebug took a cool view (looked up), cracked up (smiled) and answered, "My special pinetop (favorite teacher) is smoking (angry) and wants to eyeball (see) you fast." I said to him, "I'm stalled (puzzled.) What is this all about?"

He answered, "I wasted (punched) one of the studs (boys) for capping (insulting) me. Teach blasted (yelled) at me and told me to fade away (go) to the hub (office) and fetch you."

I stood up and told Junebug to cool it. "Don't put your head in the bowl and pull the chain" ("Don't do anything rash".) Hurriedly he grabbed my arm and said: "I hope I don't get a big slap on the rump."

As I headed up the stairs toward his classroom I was deeply concerned. What did he mean by that "slap-on-the-rump" remark? A paddling never fazed him before. Suddenly the message came through loud and clear: He had played the part of an unlikely wrongdoer to tell me something was wrong in his classroom. He was tough and cruel, cunning and ruthless, a master of all the skills needed to survive in his jungle; he was too shrewd to be trapped this way, with so many witnesses, without a motive. He was very fond of his teacher.

I knew his twisted code of honor, which did not allow him to be an informer. He had got in trouble himself so that I would see and uncover something about his class.

Very reluctantly I eased open the classroom door and entered the room. I could sense that the hum of industry was missing. The children—chronologically aged 11–13 but actually precocious young adults—were impenetrable, as though encased in glass, sitting stiffly at their desks. The teacher walked over to me and said, "Whatever has come over this class this morning defies interpretation by anyone—most of all myself."

In a booming voice I said to the class, "Operation Jappin' (teacher harassment) has shot its load (is all over)." Operation Jappin' goes like this:

The tomcat (the sly and ruthless student leading the operation) begins with a stinging hit (first attack) and the sandbaggin' starts—things are thrown, strange noises come out of nowhere, children are unresponsive. The tomcat tells all his tadpoles (classmates) that it is now time for the chicken to become an eagle (for more aggressive action) and they had better trilly along (join his group) because the sun has fallen on its belly (it's too late to back out).

The first step is to unzip the teacher (make her back down), so the tomcat takes the long dive (openly defies her), hoping she puts him in cold storage (punishes him) so he can then dress her in red tresses (insult her). He and his friends get bolder, and outflap (out wit) and scramble (gang up on) her daily. All morning they shoot her down with grease (play dirty tricks on her) until finally she is ready for the big sleep (gives in). They continue the heart-deep kicks (fun) until they are sure she is frozen on the needle (does not know what to do).

The tomcat then decides to wring (exploit) the scene. Now his glasses are on (he's in control), his ashes have been hauled away (his problems are gone). He sends hotcakes (notes) to some of the children demanding money; the rabbits (timid children) know they will be erased (beat up) unless they pay him. He tells them he is a liberty looter (good crook) who will protect them because he carries a twig (big club). Five-finger discount (stealing) pays off. The cockroaches crow (gang members are happy).

Poor Tiny Tim (the teacher), her nerve ends are humming (she is overwhelmed), her fleas (nice children) and bust-heads (smart children) have twisted the knob (lost respect for her). The tomcat doesn't have to waste any more hip bullets on her (continue the harassment)—after all, a cat can't tell a dog what to do (he is the new leader). He will keep his shoe laces tied (control everything). Hail the Stinking King.

Quickly I singled out the group I thought was capable of organizing Operation Jappin', and together we went to my office. I told Junebug to go to the outer office and sit down. In spite of the imperturbable look on his face, I knew he was aware that I had captured the scene (found out what was going on): these cub scouts (amateurs) were bleedin' (exposed).

The climate was a sticky one. I had to converse with them in their hidden language. But since I was a ghetto linguist, they could not victimize me by their idiomatic ambushes so neatly booby-trapped with sudden jolts and dead-end phrases.

I also had to ready them to pay their dues (accept disciplinary action). I could not offer them two tricks for one until they were ready to turn a somersault (promise them anything until they confessed). And I had to burn some time (give them time) to talk it over.

Finally, of course, I had to discipline the ringleaders. Operation Jappin' was sand-bagged. In the end, I couldn't help but feel sorry for Junebug, and yet how could I tell his teacher how he had sacrificed himself in her behalf? Conceivably all of this might terrify her.

Yet I had to try to provide a bridge between her world and his. It is imperative that teachers see the ways in which the hidden and formal languages cut across, support or collide with each other. In fact, the term "hidden language" is really a misleading one, because in the out-of-school setting it becomes the primary language while the formal language used in the schools is secondary.

I suspect that many teachers are unaware of this inversion. And they are baffled as well by the odd structure of the primary language of the street-corner society. The logic is nonlogic, for instance: "I am full of the joy of being up front" means I am disgusted with my circumstances. The appeal is illusion and fantasy: "It goes to the back of your head and pulls out beautiful things."

If one looks for substance instead of smut, meaning instead of obfuscation, it is possible to harness some of the positive features that lie behind the crust of degradation and depravation explicit in the hidden language. The schools in our urban ghettos are full of children who communicate this way.

It was to make clear the hidden dynamics of the hidden language—realistic, tough, practical, with a broad sweep of understanding—and to explore the inversion process that I began "Operation Capping."

Operation Capping can best be described as a "tug of war" between formal and restrictive language. The long-range goal was systematically to strip away the students' addition to a hidden language that thwarted their progress with the language of the school and textbook.

I developed a two-pronged approach. One was not to deny the validity of the child's world, his pragmatism, his unwillingness to be deluded, his suspicious nature and his perceptions, his quickness, toughness, and agile imagination. The other was to manipulate and redirect what was already a favorite pastime of the children, called "Capping," which in my youth was called "Playing the Dozens." In it, children try to outdo each other in trading insults and deprecating each other's family. For example: "Your Mama wasn't born, she was trapped"; "Your sisters are side-show bait"; "You ain't got no pappy, you're a S.O.B."; or "So's your Mama."

I decided to borrow this practice and give it a classy academic personality. The technique was simple, because the kids were already highly motivated to surpass each other in verbal intercourse. So I would meet a group for a "buzz session" (dictionary skills and English grammar) and introduce one of their well-known idioms, such as "pad," "crib" or "bread," and the children had to "cap" each other in formal English by providing a synonym.

As time passed we introduced antonyms and moved from simple sentences to complex ones. The kids were so highly competitive that they took up practices to which they previously were indifferent: They used the dictionary, read books, brought samples of word lists and resorted to all the conventional practices of the classroom. They had to win the capping game at any cost.

The spin-off from Operation Capping touched many sensitive and intriguing areas. The students discovered for themselves the built-in disadvantages of their idiomatic phrases: it didn't take them long to determine that these phrases didn't convey the meanings to others that their hidden language did: For example, they were stumped as they tried to find a standard English idiom for such hidden language phrases as: "rising on the wings of power" (a pocketful of money); "gold is my color" (pay me in advance); "trailing dark lines" (a hopeless search for something)"; "I'm on ice" (in trouble).

The students openly expressed a real concern about their verbal deficit in for-mal language. But at the end of Operation Capping, they had become less dependent on their hidden language to express themselves, and began to stockpile new standard words and phrases and to wrestle successfully with grammar for the first time.

They also had a purpose for reading, and their ability improved significantly. Learning became fun and exciting because they no longer labored under unfair handicaps. There was a change in their value system, and they had a new sense of identity.

I believe that the operation helped to provide richer opportunities for these children to experience the forces in the tug of war between their two languages and to come to know the language necessary for effective communication in the mainstream of contemporary American society.

VERBAL ART

The delight and facility with words so evident in the preceding sampling of American Negro folk speech is equally impressive in more extended verbal art forms. Throughout these forms one finds a number of recurrent stylistic features. The features include a preference for indirection, a pleasure in end and internal rhymes, and a penchant for playing with metaphors, such play often producing utterances with ambiguity and double meaning. Illustrations of these stylistic predilections may be observed in a gamut of folk materials running from the enigmatic discourse of courtship in ante-bellum times to the more recent symbolic statements of blues lyrics.

Many of the favorite American Negro forms of verbal art defy classification into the conventional European folklore genres. Playing the dozens could, one might suppose, be considered a type of verbal dueling, and there are unquestionably European analogues to proverbs and "boasts." On the other hand, the development of the American Negro near-epic "toast" and the finer points of the art of "signifying" do not seem to have many close parallels in European folklore. In any event, regardless of the degree of uniqueness of American Negro forms of verbal art, there can be no question of their continuing importance. No one can claim to know American Negro folklore well without some familiarity with the nature of "rapping" and "capping." Hopefully, even the most uninitiated reader will—by the time he gets to the final selection, "Street Smarts" by H. Rap Brown—be able to follow and appreciate all the allusions to the dozens, signifying, and the toasts as well as to other major categories of traditional American Negro verbal art.

Old-Time Negro Proverbs

J. MASON BREWER

  One of the most ancient forms of folklore is the proverb, and nowhere in the world is it more flourishing than in Africa. Yet proverbs are an example of what may be termed "fixed phrase" (as opposed to "free phrase") folklore, inasmuch as the specific wording of a proverb is as traditional as the content. Thus, if one cites the "Black is beautiful" proverb "The blacker the berry, the sweeter the juice," one is likely to use the identical wording every time. In contrast, the superstition that Friday the thirteenth is unlucky may be expressed in a variety of ways. This means that the proverb, unlike such free phrase forms of folklore as superstitions and folktales, is closely tied to language. This may be one reason why the great majority of African proverbs which surely came to the New World on the slave ships did not survive.

  One must also keep in mind that many proverbs are metaphorical, and it is extremely difficult to translate the metaphor of one language into another. A literal translation of a metaphor might be completely meaningless in the new language, and there may well not be any sort of even roughly equivalent metaphor available in the metaphorical repertoire of the new language. So while it was a relatively simple task to translate African trickster tales into English, it was nearly impossible to do the same for most African proverbs. Occasionally, one does find a successfully transplanted proverb. For example, a popular proverb to the effect that every time a fowl drinks it thanks God (which refers to the habit chickens have of throwing their heads back while they drink) is found among the Ashanti and in Jamaica. However, the identification of proverb parallels between African and New World Negro traditions has not yet been seriously undertaken.

  Notwithstanding the difficulties entailed in transplanting African proverbs in

Reprinted from *Publications of the Texas Folklore Society*, vol. 11 (1933), pp. 101–5, by permission of the author and the Texas Folklore Society.

the New World, the fundamental dependence upon proverbs for teaching deportment to children or for settling disputes must surely have continued. Yet there have been comparatively few American Negro proverbs reported. Whether this is a reflection of an actual paucity of proverbs or rather of the interests of folklore collectors in other forms (such as spirituals, worksongs, animal tales) remains to be seen. What is known is that the proverb is a major form of folklore throughout Africa and that it is an extremely popular form in the West Indies. (The fact that there are hundreds of "English language" proverbs in Jamaica and elsewhere in the West Indies makes it quite likely that there are more in the United States than have been reported by collectors thus far.) One suspects that the full story of the role of proverbs in American Negro life has yet to be told.

In the following brief essay, J. Mason Brewer, one of the few professionally trained Negro folklorists, provides some valuable insight into the nature of American Negro proverb tradition. Brewer, with the possible exception of Zora Neale Hurston, has been the most active Negro folklore collector at work in the United States. Influenced no doubt by his work at Indiana University with the eminent folktale specialist Stith Thompson, J. Mason Brewer has published many collections of folktales. His publications include: Humorous Tales of the South Carolina Negro (Orangeburg, South Carolina, 1945); The Word on the Brazos: Negro Preacher Tales from the Brazos Bottoms of Texas (Austin, 1953); "Dog Ghosts" and Other Texas Negro Folk Tales (Austin, 1958); and Worser Days and Better Times: The Folklore of the North Carolina Negro (Chicago, 1965). He has also published a very extensive anthology of American Negro folklore. See American Negro Folklore (Chicago, 1968). For more information about Brewer, see James W. Byrd, J. Mason Brewer: Negro Folklorist (Austin, Texas: Steck-Vaughn Co., 1967).

For other examples of American Negro proverbs, see J. A. Macan, Uncle Gabe Tucker: Reflections, Song, Sentiment (Philadelphia, 1883); J. Jenkins Hucks, Plantation Negro Sayings on the Coast of South Carolina in Their Own Vernacular (Georgetown, South Carolina, 1899) and the various collectanea in the Southern Workman, e.g., 23 (1894), p. 210; 27 (1898), pp. 145–46; 28 (1899), pp. 32–33; and 29 (1900), pp. 179–80. Other sources include Natalie Taylor Carlisle, "Old Time Darky Plantation Melodies," Publications of the Texas Folklore Society, 5 (1926), p. 137; Guy B. Johnson, Folk Culture on St. Helena Island, South Carolina (Chapel Hill, 1930), pp. 160–61; Kemp Malone, "Negro Proverbs from Maryland," American Speech, 4 (1929), p. 285; David Doar, "Negro Proverbs," Charleston Museum Quarterly, 2 (1932), pp. 23–24. Joel Chandler Harris also recorded some proverb texts, e.g., in Uncle Remus, His Songs and Sayings (New York, 1908). See also Langston Hughes and Arna Bontemps, eds., The Book of Negro Folklore (New York, 1958), pp. 118–21, and J. Mason Brewer, American Negro Folklore (Chicago, 1968), pp. 313–25.

For the Ashanti and Jamaican parallels, see R. Sutherland Rattray, Ashanti Proverbs (Oxford, 1916), p. 79, #200, and Kenneth B. M. Crooks, "Forty Jamaican Proverbs," Journal of Negro History, 18 (1933), p. 141, #28. See also Joseph J. Williams, Psychic Phenomena of Jamaica (New York, 1934), pp. 44–47. No doubt more parallels could be unearthed by anyone who took the trouble to examine collections from West Africa and the West Indies.

ONE MORNING when Uncle Israel, the old milk peddler, came to Aunt Patty's cabin, he was surprised to hear Hebe ask, "Uncle Israel, Mammy says huccom' de milk wattery in de mawnin'."

"Tell yo' mammy," replied Uncle Israel, "dat's de bes' sort o'milk. Dat's de dew on it. De cows been layin' in de dew."

"An' she tol' me to ax yuh," continued Hebe, "whut make de milk so blue."

"Yuh ax yo' mammy," replied Uncle Israel, "whut make she so black."

Uncle Israel proved himself equal to the emergency. It takes a great deal of audacity indeed to pronounce upon the origin and age of proverbs, but, encouraged by Uncle Israel's example, I shall in listing and explaining the meaning of a number that I have collected attempt to fix the period and circumstances of their origin. For the most part those here given have been taken from the speech of ex-slaves and elderly Negroes living in central Texas, if not on farms then with a rural background. However, such proverbs are to be heard in the homes of the best educated Negroes of the country as well as in those of the lowliest.

While the pithiest and most savory proverbs seem to have come directly out of the Negro's own wisdom as well as environment, some of them are but transmutations of older expressions into the language and experience of the Negro. Thus, as the Bible has it, "Whatsoever a man soweth, that shall he also reap." As the old-time Negro has it, *Yuh kin sow in mah fiel' ef yuh wants to, but when hit comes, hit'll be in your'n an' yuh won't know how it got dere.*

As a slave, so far as his life was reflected in song and proverb, the Negro's primary interest seems to have been in God and religion. The much exploited "Work Songs" and the proverbs dealing with work probably developed during and after Reconstruction, at a time when the master no longer provided food, when the Negro had to rustle for himself and family and could not logically continue to pray God to take him "home" and free him from slavery.

Ol' Massa take keer o' himself, but de niggah got to go ter God conveys about the same idea as that in a saying once current among vigorous frontiersmen: "Lord, take care of the poor and us rich devils will look out after ourselves."

God and Freedom were with many slaves synonymous. *Yuh mought as well die wid de chills ez wid de fever* not only goes gack to a common plantation malady but was interpreted for me as meaning that "you might as well get killed trying to escape as to remain a slave and die in slavery."

De quickah death, de quickah heaben, I heard an old woman say, and then she sang a song to enforce the idea of the proverb:

Oh Freedom, Oh Freedom,
Befoh Ah'd be uh slave
Ah'd be buried en mah grave
An' go home tuh mah Jesus an' be
    saved.

Much of the slave's time was spent in trying to find ways and means of escape. *Don' crow tel yuh git out o' de woods; dey mought be uh beah behin' de las' tree* meant "Don't be careless about talking to people you see, until you get to the Underground Railway. You might get caught and returned to your owner."

Don' say no mo' wid yo' mouf dan yo' back kin stan' is an admonition to slaves to speak briefly and seldom, not only to the master but to other slaves. Frequently the slaves would discuss the possibilities of escape among themselves, and be overheard by the overseer, some tattling slave, or the master himself; then his back paid for what his mouth had said.

You got eyes to see and wisdom not to see was an injunction to the slaves not to tell on each other about the neglect of duty, some clandestine visit to a neighboring plantation, the theft of a chicken or a pig, or any other misdemeanor.

Evah bell yuh heah ain't uh dinnah bell carries with it the idea that there was also a "rising bell" in the morning which called the slaves up for the day's work.

Of my entire collection I assign the most originality to a proverb given me by Aunt Milly Hicks, of Austin: *De one dat drap de crutch de bes' gits de mos' biscuits.* "What do you mean," I asked, "by drappin' de crutch?" "Dat means," explained Aunt Milly, "de one dat curt'sy de bes'." "Oh," I said, "you mean the one that could bow the most polite?" "Yas, suh, yas, suh, dat's hit," answered Aunt Milly, "an' Ah allus got de biscuits." This proverb carries with it more than Aunt Milly could express. It expresses the idea that the most polite slave got the easiest job on the plantation.

Don't let no chickens die in yo' han' implies the proverbial connection of the Negro with chickens. The idea is that when the dead chicken is on the ground instead of in his hand evidence against the darkey who has killed it is less incriminating.

As inevitable as chickens is cotton. The obvious meaning of *Dirt show up de quickes' on de cleanes' cotton* is that a bad deed shows up more distinctly on a person of good character than on a person of already bad repute.

Distant stovewood am good stovewood meant that the biggest trees don't grow on the edge of the woods and that if a man wanted big back logs for his fireplace, he would have to go to extra trouble to get them.

Muddy roads call de mile-post a liah belongs in the category of work proverbs.

Whut yuh don' hab in yo' haid yuh got ter hab in yo' feet. "Dat me'ns lak dis," said Uncle George McKay. "Lak ef yuh goes to de sto' fer some grub an' yuh fergits ter git it all, den yo' feet hab ter take yuh back anudder time fer whut yuh didn' git de fus' trip."

Dere's uh fambly coolness twixt de mule an' de singletree does not so much say that a mule sometimes kicks the singletree to which his traces are hooked as that two factors bound together, as man and wife, do not always work in harmony.

Although the ex-slave was grateful to God for his freedom and "God's chillun" were not supposed to dance, among the first of the freedman's free acts was a surrender to the rhythmic nature inherited from his African ancestors. He had, as a slave, developed into an excellent clog and tap dancer but had not been free to cultivate the social dance. The "platform dance" and the "cakewalk" came with Emancipation and the freedman revelled as much in dance and song as he had formerly revelled in church worship. Certain proverbs seem to date from this era of dancing and the freer courtship that came with it.

Don't take no mo' tuh yo' heaht dan yuh kick offen yo' heels meant, "Don't worry so much about jilts in love that you can't go to a dance and dance your troubles away."

Evahbody say "goodnight" ain't gone home may have evolved as a result of this social freedom enjoyed by the freed slave, especially by courting couples.

The philosophy of Negro gossip is summed up in the proverb, *Two niggahs'll draw fo' niggahs an' fo' niggahs draw eight.*

To the Negro religion is always Alpha and Omega. I began this paper with slave proverbs on God and religion. I shall end with a proverb connected with religion and possibly of Reconstruction days: *Stah won' shoot fer de sinnah.* I have been told that when during Reconstruction Negroes attended a revival or a camp-meeting and became converted, they would, if in doubt as to the authenticity of the conversion, ask, on the way home from the service, the Lord to "shoot" them a star. If then the convert saw a shooting star, it was a sign that he was really converted; but if he did not see a star shoot, there was still something lacking to his conversion, he had not yet been "born again," and he was still a sinner. Now some people claim that if a person keeps his gaze on one certain part of the sky for fifteen minutes, he will see a star fall and that, hence, there is nothing miraculous about the matter. Indeed, it is not likely that the gaze of man has anything to do with the falling or not falling of stars. The Negro, however, had unwavering faith in the belief and actually governed his decisions concern-ing conversion on the star sign. I recall hearing of only one instance in which a Negro who had asked for a shooting star failed to be convinced, when he saw it, that he had been born again and "washed in the blood of the Lamb."

A rousing revival was being conducted in Bell County, soon after the close of "the War," and finally Uncle Seth, who had not yet professed religion, was persuaded by his wife and children, members of the church, to attend the meetings. Before the services were over he had gone to the mourners' bench and professed religion. That night on the road home, however, his faith began to weaken. Knowing well the star test, Uncle Seth decided to try it out.

"Gawd," said Uncle Seth, "shoot me uh stah." In a few minutes he saw a star shoot across that part of the sky where he had his gaze directed. Not satisfied with this, however, when about halfway home, he repeated again, "Gawd, shoot me anudder stah." In a few minutes he saw another star shoot. This was not yet sufficient to get up Uncle Seth's faith; so when he was almost home, he said, "Gawd, looks lak hit's kinda hard fo' me to get up mah faith. Ah tells Yuh what Yuh do. Shoot me de moon." "The moon!" replied God. "I wouldn't shoot yuh de moon fer all de niggers in Texas."

Crude sayings of a crude people, humble, optimistic, good-humored. They have not all been collected.

> Dey's jes' ez good uh fish in de creek
>   ez evah been caught;
> Dey's jes' ez good uh timber in de
>   woods ez evah been bought.

Old-Time Courtship Conversation

FRANK D. BANKS AND PORTIA SMILEY

The following delightful descriptions of the traditional riddling conversations used on the occasion of courtship consists of three separate contributions which appeared in the pages of the Southern Workman in 1895. This important journal was published by Hampton Institute, where the first Negro folklore society was formed. It was in November, 1893 that this folklore society under the dedicated direction of Miss Alice M. Bacon began its work in the collection of American Negro folklore. Not only were students enrolled at Hampton asked to report folklore, but through the notices periodically placed in the Southern Workman, past graduates were asked to help the cause.

There were monthly meetings of the small but hardworking folklore society which was in fact an official branch of the larger American Folklore Society which was founded in 1888. The folklore movement at Hampton brought enthusiastic letters of support from Thomas W. Higginson, George W. Cable, Booker T. Washington, and W. W. Newell, then Secretary of the American Folklore Society. Leading folklorists of the day were invited to come to Hampton to address the local society. For example, William Wells Newell appeared on May 25, 1894 to speak on "The Importance and Utility of the Collection of Negro Folk-Lore." This address as well as most of the locally written papers presented at the society's meetings was published in the Southern Workman (which had succeeded the original Hampton School Record) in a column entitled "Folk-Lore and Ethnology." Although there was rarely much in the way of analysis, the folktales, legends, superstitions, and other folkloristic forms printed in the pages of the Southern Workman constitute a rich and authentic contribution to the known corpus of American Negro folklore.

For the letter sent out by Alice Bacon announcing the plans for collecting

Reprinted from *Southern Workman*, vol. 24 (1895), pp. 14–15, 78.

folklore, see Southern Workman, *22 (1893), pp. 180–81, or 24 (1895), pp. 154–56 (reprinted in Bruce Jackson, ed.,* The Negro and His Folklore in Nineteenth-Century Periodicals *(Austin, 1967), pp. 276–83). See also the "Proposal for Folklore Research at Hampton, Virginia,"* Journal of American Folklore, *6 (1893), pp. 305–9; and "Work and Methods of the Hampton Folklore Society,"* Journal of American Folklore, *11 (1898), pp. 17–21.*

For more of an idea of Alice Bacon's approach to folklore, see her paper "The Study of Folk-Lore," which was presented to a Congress on Africa held in Atlanta in 1895. (It was published in Africa and the American Negro *(Atlanta, 1896), pp. 187–94.) See also her article with Elsie Clews Parsons, "Folk-Lore from Elizabeth County, Virginia,"* Journal of American Folklore, *35 (1922), pp. 250–327, plus her many contributions to the "Folklore and Ethnology" columns in* Southern Workman. *For the address by Newell, see* Southern Workman, *23 (1894), pp. 131–32. For more about Hampton, see M. F. Armstrong and Helen W. Ludlow,* Hampton and Its Students *(New York, 1874) which includes "Cabin and Plantation Songs as Sung by the Hampton Students," pp. 171–255. See also Edwin A. Start, "General Armstrong and the Hampton Institute,"* New England Magazine, *vol. 6 (1892), 442–60. For a convenient list of most of the folklore articles contained in the* Southern Workman *during the years from 1893 to 1901, see Jackson, op. cit., pp. 361–66.*

I[1]

The American slave's life was a desert of suffering certainly, but in it there were oases whose shades and springs yielded comforts whose delights were all the keener for their infrequency.[*]

He had his holidays and his social seasons, and there were hours when, his day's task done, he poured his story of admiration and love into the ears of some dusky maiden whose presence brought to him a joy as sweet, perhaps sweeter, than that which his smart young master felt in the society of the free woman whom he loved and honored.

The slave girl had to be won as surely as did her fair young mistress, and her black fellow in slavery who aspired to her hand had to prove his worthiness to receive it.

Instances were not a few where the black knight laid down his life in defence of the honor of his lady-love, but of course milder proofs of worthiness were the rule.

Among the slaves there were regular forms of "courtship," and almost every

---

[1] Paper read before the Hampton (Va.) Folk-Lore Society, April 30, 1894.
[*] The first of the three contributions was written by Frank D. Banks. It was also published in the *Journal of American Folklore*, 7 (1894), pp. 147–49. In the introduction to its publication in *Southern Workman*, an introduction presumably written by Alice Bacon, an attempt is made to adduce an African origin of this courtship practice. Specifically, a folktale from Heli Chatelain, *Folk Tales of Angola*, Memoirs of the American Folklore Society, no. 1 (Boston and New York, 1894), pp. 119, 401, is cited in which one finds a reasonably convincing African parallel to the figurative speech employed in plantation courtship. Newell also commented upon the parallel although he thought the riddling formulas might be related to European ballad and folktale tradition in which individuals win royal spouses by successfully answering riddles. See W. W. Newell, "Plantation Courtship," *Journal of American Folklore*, 8 (1895), p. 106. However, it seems likely that the tradi-

large plantation had an experienced old slave who instructed young gallants in the way in which they should go in the delicate matter of winning the girls of their choice.

I have distinct recollection of "Uncle Gilbert," a bald, little, dark man, who carried his spectacles on his forehead the most of the time.

"Uncle Gilbert" was the shoemaker on a plantation where there were a hundred slaves, whose good young master, "Pete," allowed them to receive company Sundays and some evenings in the week from all the surrounding neighborhood.

What gay times there were on that plantation in the days befo' de wah!

"Uncle Gilbert" was very learned in the art of "courtship," and it was to his shop the slave lads went for instruction in "courtship's words and ways."

The old man had served a half dozen masters, had won and buried as many wives, and had travelled much. It was therefore conceded by the people of all the neighborhood that nobody thereabouts was a greater authority on wooing than he.

"Uncle Gilbert" held the very generally accepted opinion that "courtin' is a mighty ticklish bizness," and that he who would "git a gal wuth havin' mus' know how to talk fur her."

I never had the honor of being one of "the old man's" pupils, being too young when I knew him to make inquiry along the courtship line, but I tracked many young men to Uncle Gilbert's shop in the interest of general gossip.

The courtship idea, of course, belongs to people of every clime and race. People only differ in expressing it.

The American slave's courtship words and forms are the result of his attempt at imitating the gushingly elegant manners and speech of his master.

Uncle Gilbert's rule of courtship was that a "young man mus' tes' an' prove a gal befo' offerin' her his han'. Ef er gal gives a man as good anser as he gives her queston, den she is all right in min'. Ef she can look him squar in de face when she talks to him, den she kin be trusted; and ef her patches is on straight, an' her close clean, den she is gwine ter keep de house straight and yer britches mended. Sich er ooman is wuth havin'."

---

tion is African, not European. An unpublished study of the Coniagui made in 1941, for example, describes an element of courtship behavior as follows;

I have good reason to suppose that the love life of the Coniagui is rather a subtle affair. One has only to observe, in the bustle of the market or amid the silence of the bush, how a young man courts the girl of his choice, to become convinced of this.

Repartee is an important element in striking up an acquaintance. It might even be described as a verbal duel, full of proverbs and quips. The pair both want to touch each other, and indulge in a series of fencings and parryings in the hope of attaining their desire. Each measures the quickwittedness and intelligence of the other, as they try themselves in that "art of conference" in which Montaigne discovered all the elements of athletic sport.

The brief citation which unfortunately fails to include concrete examples of the fencings and parryings is included by Monique Gessain in her essay "Coniagui Women (Guinea)," in Denise Paulme, ed., *Women of Tropical Africa* (Berkeley and Los Angeles, 1963), pp. 17–46 (the passage from the unpublished study by B. Maupoil appears on p. 25). —ED.

SAMPLE OF A "COURTSHIP" CONVERSATION

HE: My dear kin' miss, has you any objections to me drawing my cher to yer side, and revolvin' de wheel of my conversation around de axle of your understandin'?

SHE: I has no objection to a gentleman addressin' me in a proper manner, kin' sir.

HE: My dear miss, de worl' is a howlin' wilderness full of devourin' animals, and you has got to walk through hit. Has you made up yer min' to walk through hit by yersef, or wid some bol' wahyer?

SHE: Yer 'terrigation, kin' sir, shall be answered in a ladylike manner, ef you will prove to me dat it is not for er form and er fashion dat you puts de question.

HE: Dear miss, I would not so impose on a lady like you as to as' her a question for a form an' a fashion. B'lieve me, kin' miss, dat I has a pertickler objick in ingagin' yer in conversation dis afternoon.

SHE: Dear kin' sir, I has knowed many a gentleman to talk wid wise words and flatterin' looks, and at de same time he may have a deceivin' heart. May I as' yer, kin' gentleman, ef you has de full right to address a lady in a pertickler manner?

HE: I has, kin' miss. I has seen many sweet ladies, but I has never up to dis day an' time lef' de highway of a single gentleman to foller dese beacon lights. But now, kin' miss, as I looks in yer dark eyes, and sees yer hones' face, and hears yer kind voice, I mus' confess, dear lady, dat I would be joyous to come to yer beck and call in any time of danger.

SHE: Den, kin' sir, I will reply in anser to your 'terrigation in de fus place, sence I think you is a hones' gentleman, dat I feels dat a lady needs de pertection of a bol' wahyer in dis worl' where dere's many wil' animals and plenty of danger.

HE: Den, kin' honored miss, will you condescen' to encourage me to hope dat I might, some glorious day in de future, walk by yer side as a perteckter?

SHE: Kin' sir, ef you thinks you is a bol' warrior I will condescend to let you pass under my observation from dis day on, an' ef you proves wuthy of a confidin' ladies' trus', some lady might be glad to axcept yer pertection—and dat lady might be me.

This brings us to the point where the two agree to become lovers, and as love's language is not reducible to writing and repetition we will leave them, hoping that when all has been arranged that we shall be among the many white and black guests who will assemble to give congratulations and to partake of the big supper which "ole mistis" and "ole marster" will surely give in celebration of the event here foreshadowed.

II

To Miss Portia Smiley, of Calhoun, Alabama, we are indebted for the following delicious bits of sentiment.*

1. Dear lady, I come down on justice an' qualification to advocate de law condemnin' de lady dat was never condemn befo'—not dat I'se gwine to condemn you, but I can condemn many odders.

2. Kin' lady, went up on high gum an' came down on little Pe de,† where many goes but few knows.

* These examples contributed by Portia Smiley first appeared in the *Southern Workman*, 24 (1895), p. 15, and were immediately reprinted in the *Journal of American Folklore*, 8 (1895), pp. 155–56. Portia Smiley did make other collections of folklore, e.g., "Folk-Lore from Virginia, South Carolina, Georgia, Alabama, and Florida," *Journal of American Folklore*, 32 (1919), pp. 357–83. —ED.
† Allusions to Peedee country were apparently commonly used as a frame of reference. See Ed Mott, *The Black Homer of Jimtown* (New York, 1900), pp. 13, 114, 231. As it happens, the area is rich in folklore. See Robert Duncan Bass, "Negro Songs from the Pedee Country," *Journal of American Folklore*, 44 (1931), pp. 418–36. —ED.

3. Kin' lady, are yo' a standin' dove or a flyin' lark?* Would you decide to trot in double harness, and will you give de mos excrutish pleasure of rollin' de wheels of de axil, accordin' to your understandin'? If not my tracks will be col' an' my voice will not be heard aroun' your do! I would bury my tomahawks an' dwell upon de subtell of mos' any T.

4. Kin' lady, ef I was to go up between de heavens an' de yearth an drop down a grain of wheat over ten acres of land an' plow it up wid a rooster fedder, would you marry me?

5. Good miss, ef dere was a beautiful bloom, how could you get it widout reachin', sendin', walkin', or goin' at it? (Answer: Get it by love.)

6. Kin' lady, s'pose you was to go 'long de road an' meet a pet rabbit, would you take it home an' call it a pet o' yourn?

7. Good lady, ef you was to come down de riber an' you saw a red stran' o' thread, black o' white, which one would you chose to walk on? (In the answer, the color of the thread given is the color of the man she would accept.)

8. Oh, good kin' lady, kin you go up 'twix' heaven an' de yearth an' bring me a blue morena wid a needle an' thread in it?

9. Kin' lady, since I have been trav'lin' up hill, valley, an' mountain, I nebber seed a lady dat suit my fancy mo' so den you does. Now is you a towel dat had been spun, or a towel dat had been woven? (Answer: If spun, single.)

10. Good lady, I was in a garden in my dream, an' I saw de lovelies' table, an' on de table was a fine cake an' a glass of wine, an' a beautiful lady was walkin' in de garden, and you were de lady. If you saw a peas hull in de garden which one would you choose, one wid one pea in it or a hull full of peas. (Answer: The hull with one pea is a single man, the hull full of peas is a widower with children.)

11. Good lady, ef I was to give you a handkerchief to wash an' iron, how would you do it widout water or iron? (Answer: Iron it with love.)

Of a kind similar to No. 9 in Miss Smiley's collection, the Hampton Folk-Lore Society has contributed the following:

Are you a rag on the bush or a rag off the bush? (Answer: If rag on the bush, free, if off, engaged.)

I saw three ships on the water, one full-rigged, one half-rigged, and one with no rigging at all. Which would you rather be? (Full-rigged, married; half-rigged, engaged; no rigging, single.)

Sometimes the girl wishes to find out her friend's intentions. *If so*, it may be done without loss of dignity through the following circumlocution:

Suppose you was walkin' by de side o' de river an' dere was three ladies in a boat, an' dat boat was overturned, which lady would you save, a tall lady or a short lady or a middle-sided lady?

If the young man declares his desire to save a lady corresponding in height to his questioner, she may rest assured

---

* There is a parallel for this verse included in the "Courtship Rhyme Section" of Thomas W. Talley, *Negro Folk Rhymes* (New York, 1922), p. 135. Talley's text is as follows;

HE: Is you a flyin' lark or a settin' dove?

SHE: I'se a flyin' lark, my honey Love.

HE: Is you a bird o' one fedder, or a bird o' two?

SHE: I'se a bird o' one fedder, w'en it comes to you.

HE: Den, Mam;

I has desire, an' quick temptation,
To jine my fence to yo' plantation.

that his intentions are serious. He may perhaps add the following tender avowal:

Dear miss, ef I was starvin' an' had jes one ginger-cake, I would give you half, an' dat would be de bigges' half.

Should a girl find herself unable to understand the figurative speech of her lover, she may say, "Sir, you are a huckleberry beyond my persimmon," and may thus retire in good form from a conversation in which her readiness in repartee has not been equal to her suitor's skill in putting sentimental questions.

III

Notes From Alabama

From one of our students who, upon promotion to the senior class took her year out in Miss Washington's school at Mt. Meigs, Ala., we have received the following collection.

Courtship

HE: Kin' lady, what's all de bes' news wid you?

SHE: Honorable mister, at dis time presen' my ears is a waitin' an' a listenin' to hear from your sweet little lips some words. Thirty years I's been lookin' to de eas' an' lookin' to de wes' to see some one to suit my fancies mo' so dan you has.

HE: Kin' lady, I has so much expression on my mind, ten thousan' tongues cannot explain it. Oh kin' gal, at this time presen' has you ever foun' a head of cabbage you desires to cut down?

SHE: Oh yes, sir, I has foun' at dis time presen' a head of cabbage I desires to cut down. I was comin' on a journey when I met some little runnin' vines in de road. Dose little runnin' vines has spread from one side of de road to de oder—dey's spread from heart to heart.

HE: Dem vines is love, will you gratify me de honor to come an' pay your visits through good manners, good behavior an' good character?

SHE: You am as de apple of my eyes an' also de darlin' of my heart. "De rose is red, de violet's blue, Sugar am sweet and so is you." Dere is no hin' rence in de wayside for your conversation to be passed. If it is to be, raise your right han' an say "I" if not, cas' it away.

HE: Kin' lady, I would not wish to wear out my boots an' shoes in vain all my days.

SHE: Oh, you won't wear dem out in vain, not by no means, so ever, my word am my bon' an' my bon' am my security.

HE: Kin' gal, will you turn ober to me twenty-one presents de balance of you life.

SHE: I will.

A few other forms of proposal came from the same source.

"Dear lady, if you was travellin' an seed three bottles sittin' in de road, one ob dem full, de udder half-full, an de udder wid 'bout a gill in it, which one ob dem would you choose?"

(If the reply is full, the lady is married, if half-full she is engaged, but if she chooses the bottle with about a gill in it, she is free from matrimonial promises of all kinds.)

QUESTION: "Dear lady, if you should 'ceive a letter, what would you do wid it?"

ANSWER: "I would place it in de norf corner ob my trunk an' ebry time I would tink ob it I would fill it full of love and return it."

"Dear lady, suppose you an' I was sittin' at de table wid but one dish ob soup an' but one spoon, would you be willin' to eat out ob de dish an' spoon wid me?"

"If you was passin' by
An seed me hangin' high
Would you cut me down and lie
Or would you let me hang there an
    die?"

"I hears dat you is a dove flyin' from lim' to lim' wid no where to res' your weary wing. I's in de same condition an hopes you kin fin' a place to res' your heart."

Double Meaning in the Popular Negro Blues

GUY B. JOHNSON

There appears to be little doubt that veiled symbolic messages are extremely common in American Negro folklore. One obvious reason for the frequency of concealed content was the very nature of slavery. Communication between one slave and another was always under the scrutiny of the plantation master or one of his representatives. Thus it is perfectly logical that in joke and song, the American Negro found a much needed outlet for the symbolic expression of protest and for the opportunity to speak of vital subjects. On the other hand, the practice of pasquinading leaders through folklore is widespread in Africa. By describing the wives of a character in a folktale in specific detail, the African storyteller makes it abundantly clear that the tale is meant to reflect upon the actions of a tribal leader who has wives with those same characteristics. Similarly, metaphorically rich proverbs may be cited to comment upon an event in daily life. The African rhetorical aesthetic seems to demand that indirection be used whenever possible. From this one could have predicted that American Negroes would continue to turn to one of the traditional vehicles for the effective communication of symbolic messages: folklore.

One problem in the decoding of symbolic messages is making the jump from the literal to the metaphorical meaning. In a spiritual, for example, it may be clear that the literal reference is to crossing the River Jordan. But if one believes there is a symbolic interpretation to this action, the question arises as to precisely what is being symbolized. Does crossing the River Jordan mean escaping up north? Does it refer to "crossing" the ocean back home to Africa? Does it refer to leaving life on earth to enter heaven? Of course, there is no reason to assume that there is only one "correct" symbolic interpretation. Any one of these plus presumably other interpretations might be "correct" for a given individual singer or his audience. In this case, an advocate of the symbolic approach

Reprinted from the *Journal of Abnormal and Social Psychology*, vol. 22 (1927–28), pp. 12–20, by permission of the author and the American Psychological Association.

would probably be safe only in suggesting that crossing the River Jordan implied some kind of escape. Whether the escape was from south to north or from this life to a better life after death simply cannot be definitively determined.

Of all the taboos of Negro life in the South, none created more anxiety than those having to do with sex. The double standard in which white males sought Negro partners but white females were off-limits to Negro males has been much discussed. In any case, it was obviously not safe for Negroes to discuss the subject of sex openly in front of southern whites. A white woman had merely to accuse a Negro male of looking at her in order to precipitate a charge of rape, which not infrequently ended with a mob lynching. If blues did present in part statements about the basic pleasures and sorrows of life, it should come as no surprise to learn that they spoke of sexuality and that they did so in symbolic form.

In this essay written by Guy B. Johnson, one of several University of North Carolina faculty members who specialized in American Negro folklore, we find some of the most common sexual references in blues discussed. Many of the phrases, e.g., "Easy Rider" and "Rock and Roll," continue to be current although it is doubtful whether many of the white people who know and use the phrases have any conscious idea of their possible sexual significance. For further discussion of sexual symbolism in the blues, see Samuel Charters, The Poetry of the Blues *(New York: Avon, 1970), pp. 122–51, and Paul Oliver,* The Meaning of the Blues *(New York: Collier, 1963), pp. 131–53. The reader should realize that the sexual symbolism found in the blues is just one of the many types of symbolism expressed in this genre. The fact that a white sociologist chose this particular aspect to investigate and that he elected to publish his results in a journal concerned with "abnormal" psychology perhaps tells us more about white culture than black! For a more complete treatment of blues symbolism, see the works by Charters and Oliver mentioned above.*

THOSE WHO are acquainted with the popular blues songs[1] of today, especially with what are known as the "race blues," have doubtless often had occasion to suspect that these songs are not always what they seem. A little research into Negro vulgar expressions and the origin of the blues will show such a suspicion to be well founded. After a long acquaintance with Negroes and Negro songs, the writer feels that there is no doubt of the presence of double meanings of a sex nature in the blues, and he wishes to present certain data in relation to that subject.

The blues, arising originally from the common Negro folk, have been widely exploited as a form of popular song. The word "blues" has such a market value today that song writers and composers of dance music attach it to many pieces which have no resemblance whatever to the original Negro article. In so far as one may speak of the original

---

[1] For information on the blues as a type of Negro song, see Odum and Johnson, *Negro Workaday Songs*, Chap. II; Scarborough, *On the Trail of Negro Folk-Songs*, Chap. X; and Handy, *Blues: An Anthology*. The use of the term "blues" has become very loose. In fact, many Southern Negroes distinguish just two classes of colored songs today: spirituals and blues. In the present article the writer would not restrict the meaning of "blues" to those songs bearing blues titles but would let it include the majority of popular Negro secular songs of today.

blues, they may be thought of as the wail of the despondent Negro lover. All peoples have their lonesome songs, but there was something naïve, something different in the Negro's melancholy songs which set them apart and marked them for preservation. Once they were introduced to the public,[2] they became nationally popular. At first they were interpreted by Negroes who had grown up with them, so to speak. But the exploitation of this kind of song has become so profitable that practically every writer of popular songs has tried his hand at it. Many of the best sellers today are written by white men.

Indeed, the production of blues today is like the production of Fords or of Ivory Soap. Since the phonograph holds the center of the stage at present as far as the distribution of songs is concerned, it is the phonograph record companies that produce most of the blues. Several of the major phonograph companies maintain "race record" departments, employ Negro artists, and make special efforts to cultivate the Negro trade. The 1925 general catalogues of the three largest producers of "race records" listed a total of 1,330 titles, of which 1,160 or 87 per cent were secular and therefore blues according to the regular Negro usage of the word today. The total sales of blues records by these three companies alone last year were around six million records. While the majority of these went to Negroes, there was a tremendous sale to white people. Thus it is evident that the blues as they are issued on phonograph records at present are no small item in the social life of the country. It is these popular blues that we shall now examine.

Needless to say, the double meanings in the blues are of a sexual nature. Not that other types of double meanings are not found in Negro songs,[3] but merely that such as are present in the blues would almost inevitably be of sexual significance because the blues deal with the man-woman relation.

We may divide the double meanings into two general groups: (1) those meanings pertaining specifically to the sex organs and (2) those relating to the sex act or to some other aspect of sex life. Of course, it is understood that this division is merely one of convenience in presentation and that the two classes of meanings frequently coincide.

Relatively few symbols for the sex organs are found in the blues, but these few are worked to the utmost. By far the most common of these terms is *jelly roll*. As used by the lower class Negro it stands for the vagina, or for the female genitalia in general, and sometimes for sexual intercourse. Doubtless it is the only word which many Negroes have to designate the female organs. Its use among Negroes of the lower class is so extensive that few will deny its meaning when they encounter it in the blues. Yet, because of its decent meaning, it passes fairly well in popular song society, being used occasionally even in white songs. The following lines from popular phonograph blues will illustrate the usage of jelly roll in these songs:

[2] The first piece to appear in print under the name of blues was *Memphis Blues*, 1910, by a Negro, W. C. Handy. Handy's works are nearly all based on folk themes.

[3] There are, for example, many hidden references to the white man in the Negro's songs. This is an interesting field of research in which little has been done.

I ain't gonna give nobody none o'
  this jelly roll.
Nobody in town can bake sweet jelly
  roll like mine.
Your jelly roll is good.

Of course, respectable persons are supposed to get the impression that something to eat is meant. But no Negro laborer contends that jelly roll means something to eat when he sings stanzas like the following:

I don't know but I've been tol',
Angels in heaven do the sweet jelly
  roll.

Dupree was a bandit,
He was brave an' bol',
He stole that diamon' ring
For some of Betty's jelly roll.

Another term for the female organs is *cabbage*. While not as common as jelly roll, it is used to such an extent that its lower meaning is readily recognized by the ordinary Negro when he hears it in a song. The line, "Anybody here want to try my cabbage," illustrates the use of this symbol in the blues. Other symbols are *keyhole* and *bread*. The former is found infrequently, but the latter, sometimes found as *cookie* and *cake*, is almost as common as *jelly roll* in everyday Negro slang. A Negro youth, wishing to express superlatively his estimate of his sweetheart's sexual equipment, often refers to it as *angel-food cake*. The old Negro

song, *Short'nin' Bread*, had a vulgar meaning, and even when recorded in its supposedly innocent versions retains an undercurrent of sexual meaning:

Two little niggers layin' in bed,
One turned over to the other an' said,
"My baby loves short'nin', short'nin'
  bread,
My baby loves short'nin' bread."

Symbols for the male organs are more difficult to find. There are numerous references to "thing" and "it," but these are usually descriptive of the sex act itself rather than the male organ. In fact, it is doubtful if there is a clearcut example of male symbolism in the blues. This is probably due to the fact that Negro vulgarisms for the male organs are not suited to double usage, that is, they are not easily clothed with conventional meanings which would give them safe passage into respectable circles.*

Expressions carrying double meanings relating to the act of cohabitation are much more numerous in the blues than are symbols for the sex organs. Many persons will be surprised, no doubt, to learn that the word *jazz* deserves to head this list. Used both as a verb and as a noun to denote the sex act, it has long been common vulgarity among Negroes in the South, and it is very likely from this usage that the term "jazz music" was derived.[4]

---

* The particular choice of words in this sentence, specifically the reference to concealing vulgarisms (in clothing!) sufficiently to give them "safe passage into respectable circles" suggests that sexual double meanings are not peculiar to the blues. —ED.

4 Jazz music originated in Negro pleasure houses—"jazz houses," as they are sometimes called by Negroes. The writer would like to add one more to the list of rather asinine theories on the origin of the term jazz. It is his opinion that the word was suggested by Negro preachers in their tirades on the wicked woman, Jezebel. [For useful surveys of the various etymologies proposed for "jazz," see Peter Tamony, "Jazz, the Word," *Jazz: A Quarterly of American Music*, 1 (October, 1958), pp. 33–42, and Alan P. Merriam and Fradley H. Garner, "Jazz, the Word," *Ethnomusicology*, 12 (1968), pp. 373–96. —ED.]

It is almost unbelievable that such vulgarity could become so respectable, but it is true nevertheless. Of course, much of the use of the word "jazz" in popular songs is without vulgar intent, but the fact remains that its original connotation was indecent and that several million people are aware of its original meaning. In such lines as

> I got the jazz-me blues,
> I want a jazzy kiss,
> Those jazzin' babies blues,

the word retains its vulgar meaning.

Strange to say, the majority of the expressions in the blues relating to the sex act are sung from the point of view of woman and are mostly concerned with the quality of the movements made by the male during coitus. The following expressions are frequent. They are presented with brief explanatory comments.

"My man rocks me with one steady roll." Here the woman boasts of the steady movement with which her man executes the act. Numerous vulgar versions of this song have been in vogue in the Negro underworld for several years, and their kinship with the phonograph version is indisputable. In the phonograph piece the song is stuffed with pointless rigamarole between the frequent repetitions of the refrain line, "My man rocks me with one steady roll." The following folk stanzas collected by the writer not long ago show the line of thought in the undeleted versions:

> Looked at the clock, clock struck one,
> Come on, daddy, let's have some fun.
>
> Looked at the clock, clock struck
>   two,

> Believe to my soul you ain't half
>   through.
>
> Looked at the clock, clock struck
>   three,
> Believe to my soul, you gonna kill
>   poor me.
>
> Looked at the clock, clock struck
>   four,
> If the bed breaks down we'll finish on
>   the floor.
>
> My daddy rocks me with one steady
>   roll,
> Dere ain't no slippin' when he once
>   takes hold.

"Do it- a long time, papa." Here the vulgar meaning is obscured by the usual means. One is led to believe that "do it" refers to something innocuous like kissing or dancing. But the sex meaning is too plain to be hidden so easily. The woman wants her partner to prolong coitus.

"Daddy, ease it to me." Here the woman requests the man to perform the act in an "easy" way. This way of speaking has considerable currency among both whites and Negroes of the lower classes. "Play me slow" has the same connotation.

"Easy rider." This apt expression is used to describe a man whose movements in coitus are easy and satisfying. It is frequently met both in Negro folk songs and in formal songs. "I wonder where my easy rider's gone," is a sort of by-word with Southern Negroes. There is an interesting circumstance connected with this expression which throws light upon the question of how vulgar meanings get over into art songs from folk songs. W. C. Handy, mentioned above as the author of the first popular blues, noticed the widespread use of "easy rider" as well as the existence of various folk songs based on that theme. He wrote a song, *Yellow Dog Blues*, in which he used the phrase. In this song there is a race horse and jockey (sic!) involved. The jockey deserts his horse, goes back South, and the horse wonders "where my easy rider's gone." If one judged the song on its own merits alone, Handy's efforts seemed to fall flat. But the song had symbolic meanings which were rooted deep in folk sources, and such popularity as it enjoyed among Negroes was doubtless derived from the fact that to them it was an old friend in disguise.

"Shake it," "shake that thing," etc.[5] Such expressions are very frequent in the blues. Ostensibly they refer to dancing, but they are really Negro vulgar expressions relating to coitus. Here is a stanza from a recent popular piece:

Why, there's old Uncle Jack,
The jelly-roll king,
Got a hump on his back
From shakin' that thing,
Yet he still shakes that thing.
For an ole man how he can shake
    that thing!
An' he never gets tired o' tellin'
    young folks how to shake that
    thing.

The type of double meaning most frequently found in the blues is not one which hinges upon a particular word or phrase, but one which depends upon the general content of an expression.

The following lines are good examples of this kind of double meaning:

"I got what it takes to bring you back." Most students of Negro folk song have come across one or more vulgar versions of this theme. The expression forms the refrain of a popular blues of the same name. It is sung from the point of view of woman, and in its darker meaning it refers to the woman's sexual attractions as something which will eventually bring back the straying lover.

"Mama's got something I know you want." This is similar to the above expression. Even in its whitewashed form its meaning is clear, but it probably passes because it contains no specifically indecent words. Following is the concluding stanza of the popular song:

Mama's got something sho' gonna
    surprise you,
Mama's got something gonna
    hypnotize you,
Mama's got something I know you
    want.

"I'm busy and you can't come in." The kinship of the popular song of this name with the folk song of similar name is indisputable. The writer has several variations of the latter. Usually the woman is represented as being sexually engaged with a man, so that she refuses to let her other "daddy" come in. The latter sings, in one of the semi-vulgar versions:[6]

[5] A note on "shake the shimmy" may be of interest here. Chemise is pronounced "shimmy" by most Negroes and a great many whites in the South. In its original meaning it described the effect produced when a woman made a movement or did a dance step which caused her breasts to shake. This caused her "shimmy" to shake. The expression could easily have been a Negro household usage before it got into the dance halls.

[6] See Odum and Johnson, *The Negro and His Songs*, pp. 189–90.

Lawd, I went to my woman's do'
Jes' lak I been doin' befo';
She says, "I got my all-night trick,
        baby,
An' you can't git in.
"Come back 'bout half pas' fo',
If I'm done I'll open de do',
Got my all-night trick, baby,
An' you can't git in."

"I got your bath water on." Here the original meaning was related to the sexually stimulating effect of a warm bath. Like so many other blues, it "gets by" because the song contains no words which are vulgar *per se*.

Additional lines from the popular blues in which this undercurrent of vulgarity runs are as follows:

It's right here for you; if you don't
        get it, 'tain't no fault of mine.
I'm gonna see you when your troubles
        are just like mine.
If I let you get away with it once,
        you'll do it all the time.
You've got what I've been looking for.
How can I get it when you keep on
        snatching it back?
Put it where I can get it.
If you don't give me what I want,
        I'm gonna get it somewhere else.

Lest the reader bring the charge that the writer is merely reading suggestive meanings into the blues, the writer will present certain lines of reasoning which substantiate his claims.

First, there is the circumstance already mentioned, namely, the fact of the presence of the above expressions in their vulgar meanings among the common Negro folk. Anyone who is at all acquainted with Negroes of the laboring class knows this to be true.

Furthermore, several prominent Negro leaders who grew up in the South have readily admitted to the writer the existence of these vulgarities and have vouched for the reality of double meanings in the blues. Some of these folk expressions were not indecent in their intention, for they were in ordinary and semi-respectable usage among Negroes. Especially was this true of the terms for various parts of the body, such as penis, vagina, anus, rectum, etc., for many Negroes—and whites, too, for that matter—knew no terms for these parts other than the vulgar ones.

Next we may consider the origins of Negro popular songs in general. Naturally the everyday songs of the Negro adventurer and roustabout abounded in suggestiveness and indecency. Houses of prostitution, gambling dens, and other resorts, especially in the cities along the Mississippi, were the clearing houses for such songs. Some of these songs of the Negro underworld have made the ascent to the realm of decency. In the lowest type of cabarets they can be heard in their original versions. Passing on up through the various grades of cabarets and vaudeville shows, they lose objectionable words and phrases here and there until they finally become either decent or indecent, as you will. Then song writers, white and black, adopt them and alter them just enough to "get by."

W. C. Handy, who, as stated above, published the first song under the title of blues, spoke as follows in a conference with Dorothy Scarborough: "Each one of my blues is based on some old Negro song of the South. . . . I can tell you the exact song I used as a basis for any one of my blues."[7]

James Weldon Johnson, one of the most prominent Negro leaders and authors of today, has written as follows of the origin of Negro ragtime songs:

The earliest ragtime songs, like Topsy, "jes' grew." Some of these earliest songs were taken down by white men, the words slightly altered or changed, and published under the names of the arrangers. . . .

Later there came along a number of colored men who were able to transcribe the old songs and write original ones. I was, about that time, writing words to music for the music show stage in New York. I was collaborating with my brother and the late Bob Cole. I remember that we appropriated about the last one of the old "jes' grew" songs. It was a song which had been sung for years all through the South. The words were unprintable, but the tune was irresistible, and belonged to nobody. We took it, re-wrote the verses, telling an entirely different story from the original, left the chorus as it was, and published the song. . . . The song was, "Oh, Didn't He Ramble!"[8]

There is every reason to suppose that this process of borrowing from unprintable folk songs has continued to operate. Indeed, the process is singularly accelerated today by the situation in the phonograph record business. Nearly all of the leading blues artists are persons who grew up in ordinary Negro society in the South. Their acquaintance with a great many Negro vulgar songs and expressions can be taken for granted. Furthermore, their employers encourage them to make their own blues. What more natural

than that they should draw upon their old songs? The writer has frequently met the remark, after repeating the words of some late blues to a Negro laborer, "Why I've known a song like that for ten years—except mine wouldn't do to put on a record."

The writers of the blues have been fortunate in their materials in several respects. Some of the Negro's terms for the sex organs were not known extensively outside of the lower strata of Negro society, therefore the writers found it easy to smuggle them into their songs and to invest them with passably respectable meanings. Furthermore, as regards the songs whose indecent meanings are not dependent upon words but upon general interpretation, they had little difficulty, for in such cases there is always the better or proper meaning. One takes his choice. In still other cases the authors could retain the folk phrases and change the contents of the songs. Handy's *Yellow Dog Blues*, mentioned above, is a case in point. The following might also be cited, a stanza from an old folk song:

> Thirty days in jail
> With my back turned to the wall;
> "Look here, Mr. Jailer,
> Put another gal in my stall."

This was originally sung by the *man*, and it had an actual basis in the custom which some jailers followed of locking Negro men and women in the same cell. Now comes a popular song based on the folk theme, but of course it is sung from the point of view of the woman!

[7] Scarborough, *On the Trail of Negro Folk-Songs*, p. 265. See also the introduction to W. C. Handy's *Blues: An Anthology*.
[8] Johnson, *The Book of American Negro Poetry*, pp. xi, xii.

There is one other phenomenon which might be mentioned as tending to substantiate the foregoing statement concerning the origin of some of the blues. Negro churchmen and educators almost without exception oppose vigorously the singing of blues. They are attempting to attach a stigma to the blues, and in so doing they often brand every song which is not a spiritual as something to be sung no longer by respectable Negroes. In their opposition to blues and other popular secular pieces there is an implicit recognition of the undercurrent of vulgarity which runs through many of these songs.

The writer is not passing upon the question of the good or bad of the state of affairs which he has described. Neither is he touching upon the subject of double meanings in white popular songs. Double meaning in secular song is after all nothing new. Folk song students know that many standard folk songs have come up out of the slime. But it is doubtful if any group ever has carried its ordinary vulgarities over into respectable song life so completely and successfully as the American Negro. And the ease with which the Negro has put this thing over leads one to suspect that the white man, too, enjoys seeing "the other meaning."

"I Can Peep Through Muddy Water and Spy Dry Land": Boasts in the Blues

MIMI CLAR MELNICK

Boasting is one of the traditional means for the expression of masculinity. It may occur in conversational form, in tall tales, in folksong, and in many other guises. No doubt some kind of boasting mechanism exists in nearly every society. What is of particular interest is the list of items considered to be "boastworthy" in a given culture. The values of a society or of a segment of a society could in theory be extrapolated by analyzing the content of the "boasts" of that society, bearing in mind of course that boasts inevitably involve a certain amount of unadulterated exaggeration. For this reason, the following analysis of the boasts found in Negro blues should prove enlightening.

For another valuable study of the blues undertaken by Mimi Clar Melnick, a folklorist trained at UCLA, see "Folk Belief and Custom in the Blues," Western Folklore, *19 (1960), pp. 173–89.*

EXAMINATION OF a representative number of blues texts* reveals a whole body of what Botkin has called "tall talk" or "the art of making a noise in language."[1] Embedded in the songs is a wealth of Negro lore akin to the ballyhoo of the "backwoods boaster, ringtailed roarer, half-horse half-alligator" tradition—lore which additionally reveals something of the status symbols, social attitudes, cultural phenomena and psychological opera-

---

* The present examples are largely the work of male blues singers; hence the discussion primarily concerns the male boaster. Female boasts will be indicated.

[1] See Benjamin Botkin, *A Treasury of American Folklore* (New York, 1944), p. 272, for discussion of the backwoods boaster.

Reprinted from *Folklore International: Essays in Traditional Literature, Belief, and Custom in Honor of Wayland Debs Hand.* Ed. D. K. Wilgus (Hatboro, Pennsylvania: Folklore Associates, Inc., 1967), pp. 139–49, by permission of the author and Folklore Associates.

tives present in Negro communities at particular times and places.

Like the backwoods boaster, and in the cleverest possible language, the blues singer dreams of personal greatness, follows certain formulas for success, brags of his accomplishments, and in no uncertain terms establishes himself as a hero. Unlike the windy narratives of his backwoods prototype, however, the blues man's bombast accomplishes more than the letting off of pent-up masculine steam. His boasts provide him with an outlet for his aggressions and frustrations, lend him a means for expressions of protest, and are generally designed to help him *be somebody* with the greatest possible style and color.

What, then, is the Negro blues boaster seeking? Largely, he is after status, and he gains it in a number of ways. First, he must exhibit tangible possessions which verify his personal importance and symbolize his own worth—possessions such as expensive ("sharp") clothes, fancy cars, women (pretty and in large quantity), and in some instances liquor and weapons. The most powerful of his possessions, however, is money, for without this most omnipotent charm, the above items are difficult to attain. To possess "plenty money" puts everything and everyone at the boaster's disposal; a loss of money, therefore, means a loss of power.

Status also comes from the individual's style of living: his appearance, which he enhances with clothes and other possessions; his personality, which he colors with individual quirks in speech, gesture, and mannerism. Values are also placed on certain types of behavior:[2] the big spender, the big drinker, the good lover.

Status similarly arrives in personal and material success, accomplishment in a job (legal or illegal), conquest in affairs with the opposite sex. Whatever the situation, the singer strives for superiority as a means of establishing the importance of his role in competitive society.[3]

Finally, status lies in the boaster's own identity, and wherever possible, in order to compensate for feelings of inferiority, he blows up his ego as a male, as the holder of an important social or economic position, and as an

---

[2] These values are so well defined as often to extend beyond the speaker himself. A singer will sometimes do another man's boasting for him, repeating an admired feat in the third person and thus both identifying with and envying another man's accomplishment. Deeds outlined by the singer illuminate the universal goals of his society. An excellent example of third-person boast is Ray Charles' "It Should've Been Me," parts of which appear later in this paper; another instance is Muddy Waters' "Long Distance Call" (Chess LP 1427):

> Hear my phone ringing; sound like a long distance call (2)
> When I pick up the receiver, a voice say 'Another mule kickin' in your stall.'

[3] Some personal boasts take the form of a future conjecture; the boaster could accomplish certain things provided conditions were right. Such texts are in the nature of wishes and daydreams and often begin with such standard lines as "If I could holler like a mountain jack." Note Muddy Waters' "Rollin' Stone":

> I wish I was a catfish, swimmin' in the deep blue sea,
> I would have all you good lookin' women fishin'—fishin' after me.

individual. On his own, the singer wins admiration for his masculinity, for his use of clever language, for acts of strength and cunning, and for his style of living which would include feats of drinking and gambling as well as particular modes of dress and speech.

From his possessions, the man earns respect and power (from money and weapons), envy (for number of women, expensive cars, amount of money), and acceptance by his group, which places high values on these things.

In his associates, the boaster offers further proof of his virility (in the number and type of women[4] he conquers). He inspires awe for his connections with impressive companions and thus backs up the fact of his own importance. There is also a strong identification with objects of power and speed—trains, weapons, cars, even large cities—which sometimes perform the boaster's feats for him or which lend him, through his intimacy with them, the attributes of a kind of superman.

In short, what the singer wishes to be is a hero, respected and idolized as Somebody. The hero to which he aspires is strong, tough, clever, shrewd, sharp, smooth, and above all, hip. Under close scrutiny, however, this hero will be seen to emerge a *winner* rather than a *leader*.

The great body of blues boasts deals with male prowess. Here stands the Negro equivalent of the ring-tailed roarer, yelling out his masculinity, beating his chest in song.

> I was raised on the desert, born in a
>   lion's den (2)
> Says my chief occupation—taking
>   "monkey men's" women.[5]
>
> I got a axe and a pistol on the
>   graveyard, friend
> That shoot tombstone boozers (?)
>   wearin' balls and chain
> I'm drinkin' TNT, I'm smokin'
>   dynamite,
> I hope some screwball start a fight.[6]
>
> I am Peetie Wheet Straw, the devil's
>   son-in-law (2)
> The woman I married, old Satan was
>   her paw.[7]
>
> Got my boots laced up, wise as a old
>   night owl (2)
> Like a wolf in the moonlight, baby,
>   it's my time to howl.[8]

As evidenced by Examples (1) and (4), this type of boast often identifies with animals, allowing the singer to assume the characteristics of whatever animal he chooses.[9] Sexual allusion is frequent, and the performer will often cloak his meaning in colorful images which reaffirm his virility and sexual capacities. The rambler takes pride in his ability to steal women:

> I'm known as the "rambler," I'm
>   known in every man's town (2)

---

[4] A well dressed, good-looking woman is highly valued since she reflects the boaster's good taste and is also a product of his spending (which he makes quite clear).

[5] Texas Alexander, "Water Bound Blues," as found in Paul Oliver, *Blues Fell This Morning* (New York, 1961), p. 117. [For further discussion of the monkey man, a henpecked male unable to dominate his woman, see Marshall and Jean Stearns, "Frontiers of Humor: American Vernacular Dance," *Southern Folklore Quarterly*, 30 (1966), pp. 227–35, reprinted in this volume. —Ed.]

[6] Muddy Waters, "I'm Ready," Chess LP 1427. All records are LP unless otherwise indicated.

[7] Peetie Wheetstraw, "Peetie Wheet Straw," *Journal of American Folklore*, LII (1939), p. 108.

[8] Mercy Dee, "I Been a Fool," Arhoolie FS 101.

[9] Animals most often mentioned: cat, wolf, mule, ram, lion, owl, duck.

Even the little birds begin weepin'
    when that evening sun goes
    down.[10]

The "rooster" comes on strong ("Look out, here I come") with an assurance he means what he says ("I ain't jivin'"):

But now I'm growin' old,
Yes, now I'm growin' old,
And I got what it takes to git all you
    hip chicks told.[11]
All you pretty little chicks with
    your curly hair
I know you feel like I ain't nowhere
But stop what you're doin', baby,
    come over here,
I'll prove to you baby that I ain't
    no square.
'Cause I'm ready, ready as anybody
    can be.
I am ready for you, I hope you ready
    for me.[12]

He has a stable of women, and as he prowls about he has little fear of the consequences of his actions:

My papa told me, my mother sat
    down and cried,
She say, "You're too young a man,
    son, to have tha' many women
    you guide (got)."
I looked at my mother dear and I
    didn't even crack a smile,
I said, "The women kill me, I don'
    min' dying."[13]

What kind of love is that you make?
The world start to tremblin' and the
    buildin' shake
Love me and hug me oncet (sic) again
Let the roof and walls come
    tumblin' in.[14]

I want you to love me, till the hair
    stand on my head (2)
I want you to love me, baby, till you
    know I wished I was dead.[15]

Further grounds for braggadocio come from attributes of appearance, prestige attached to certain jobs,[16] association with supernatural forces, bravery and readiness to do battle (often fortified by liquor and weapons), and the degree of hipness surrounding one's appearance and actions. One or more of these qualities may be observed in the following:

I'm gon' push on this old car, boys,
    and that ain't no jive.
Yes, I gotta push on this old car, man
    that ain't no jive.
When I went around Dead Man's
    Curve, speedometer said no
    95.[17]

This is the hammer that killed John
    Henry, but it won't kill me,
But it won't kill me, but it won't
    kill me. (2)[18]

If you want to have plenty women,
    why not work at the Chicago
    Mill? (2)

[10] Lonnie Johnson, "Rambler's Blues," Oliver, *op. cit.*, p. 227.
[11] Joe Turner, "Watch That Jive," Savoy MG 14016. See also Sunnyland Slim, "Shake It," Prestige/Bluesville 1016.
[12] Muddy Waters, "I'm Ready," Chess 1427.
[13] Willie Mabon, "I Don't Know," Chess 1531 (78 rpm)
[14] Joe Turner, "Lipstick, Powder, and Paint," Atlantic 8023.
[15] Muddy Waters, "I Want You to Love Me," Chess 1427.
[16] Examples of prestige jobs mentioned in blues: steel mill workers, oil driller, guitar player.
[17] Roosevelt Sykes, "Slidell Blues," Delmark DL 607.
[18] Mississippi John Hurt, "Spike Driver Blues," Oliver, *op. cit.*, p. 29.

You don't have to give them nothin',
    ooh well, jest tell them that
    you will.[19]

I been drinkin' gin like never before,
I feel so good, I want you to know,
One more drink, I wish you would
It takes a whole lot of lovin' to
    make me feel good.[20]

My baby don't have to work, she don't
    have to rob and steal (2)
I give her everything she needs, I am
    her drivin' wheel.[21]

You may bury my body down by the
    highway side
(Babe I don't care where you bury
    my body when I'm dead and
    gone (spoken).)

You may bury my body, ooh, down
    by the highway side.
So my old evil spirit can get a
    Greyhound bus and ride.[22]

The prowess of the female blues singer lies largely in her ability to attract men and to entice them away from other women. Some women boast of attributes of their appearance—skin color, age, build, clothes, hair; others claim attractiveness despite physical drawbacks; and some independent souls claim ability to get along without any men:

I'm a big fat mama, got the meat
    shakin' on my bones (2)
An' ev'y time I shake some silly girl's
    losing her own.[23]

I'll bet my money I can take any
    woman's man in town (2)
I can take your man and I won't have
    to run him down.[24]

Now my hair is nappy and I don't
    wear no clothes of silk (2)
But the cow that's black and ugly
    has often got the sweetest
    milk.[25]

Lordy, Lordy, I'm gettin' up in years
    (2)
But mama ain't too old to shift her
    gears.[26]

More detail regarding those attributes prized in females comes from verses sung by men proudly describing their special woman[27] or the females whose admiration they seek. Extremes in ugliness as well as beauty are spoken of boastfully:

My mother-in-law is the ugliest
    woman I ever seen.
That woman so skinny she can hide
    behind a broom.
She's some skinny.
Her teeth hang down all over her
    lips.
Her mouth is so doggone pointed she
    could eat an apple through
    a picket fence
Got a mouth like a chicken.
That's some ugly woman.
Her legs is so skinny she got to tie
    knots in her legs to make
    knees.
Boy that's some skinny woman—

---

[19] Peetie Wheatstraw, "Chicago Mill Blues," Oliver, *op. cit.*, p. 31.

[20] Muddy Waters, "I'm Ready," Chess 1427.

[21] Roosevelt Sykes, "Drivin' Wheel," Prestige/Bluesville 1006.

[22] Robert Johnson, "Me and the Devil Blues," Columbia CL 1654.

[23] Ida Cox, Vocalion 05298 (78 rpm).

[24] Rosetta Howard, "Rosetta's Blues," Ian Lang, *Jazz in Perspective* (New York, 1947), p. 124.

[25] Sara Martin, "Mean Tight Mama," Oliver, *op. cit.*, p. 79.

[26] Ida Cox, "Four Days Creep," Lang, *op. cit.*, p. 118.

[27] Many verses describe the magnetism of women of various skin shades. Variants of "Brownskin woman make a rabbit chase a hound" are abundant: "Black gal'll make a tadpole hug a whale"; "Yaller gal'll make a hound dog quit his trail," etc.

Every time she pass the junk yard the
    scale rattle,
Rattles for them bones.
She's some ugly woman, boy, you
    should see her.[28]

So doggone evil, you'd throw a rock
    in a hearse (2)
When you tell me those lies, that's
    when it really hurts.[29]

She's copper-colored mama, Lord,
    her shape is a solid dream (2)
She's the loveliest woman I swear I've
    ever seen.[30]

Extremes in good and evil character
traits and unique abilities also rate
admiration:

My baby is a Texas tornado, and she
    howls just like the wind. (2)
She'll blow the house down, Lord if
    I ask her where she been.[31]

I got the meanest woman you most
    ever saw.
She sleeps with an ice pick in her
    hand, man,
And she fights all in her dreams.[32]

The woman I love, she got dimples
    in her jaw,
The clothes she's wearin' is made
    out of the best of clawth.
She kin take and wash and she kin
    hang 'em upside the wall,
She kin throw 'em out the window
    and run out and catch 'em a
    little bit befo' they fall.[33]

She's there to love me, both day
    and night;

Never grumbles or fusses; always
    treats me right.
Never runnin' in the streets, and
    leavin' me alone;
Shd knows a woman's place is right
    there now in her home.[34]

Women are often compared to high-
speed slick objects and machinery, as
in Roosevelt Sykes "Satellite Baby":[35]

Well you talk about your Sputnik
    and your Hound Dog Crew
I got a rocket baby faster than the
    Asiatic flu.
I got a satellite baby, with a red hot
    style that's new.
She got more speed than Sputnik
    Number Two.

Women are among the blues man's
more important possessions. The ownership of a good-looking companion is
valued, as is an excess number of females
whom the singer can credit to his name.

Every time my woman smiles she
    shows the diamonds in her teeth
    (2)
She wears fine clothes, and patent
    leather shoes on her feet.[36]

I got a girl for Monday, Tuesday,
    Wednesday, Thursday, and
    Friday too (2),
I'm gon' (sweeten up?) on Saturday
    what the women through the
    week goin' to do.[37]

The singer proclaims his intentions

[28] Jack Dupree, "Mother-in-Law Blues," Atlantic 8045.
[29] Joe Turner, "That's When it Really Hurts," Savoy MG 14012.
[30] Doc Clayton, "Copper Colored Mama," Oliver, *op. cit.*, p. 85.
[31] Bill Broonzy, "Texas Tornado," *New Yorker* Oct. 25, 1958, p. 104.
[32] Sonny Boy Williamson, "I Been Dealin' With the Devil," in *Jazz Journal*, 8 (April 1955), p. 1.
[33] Willie Mabon, "I Don't Know," Chess 1531 (78 rpm).
[34] Ray Charles, "I Got a Woman," Atlantic 8006.
[35] Prestige/Bluesville 1014.
[36] Washboard Sam, "River Hip Woman," found in Oliver, *op. cit.*, p. 84.
[37] Blind Lemon Jefferson, "Chock House Blues," Riverside RLP 12-136.

to bestow lavish gifts in return for feminine favors, often threatening to revoke the presents if his woman cheats on him. The higher the demand on his partner, the higher the singer's own worth.

> I gave you all my money and everyting too
> A fine Cadillac, tell me watcha gonna do,
> You got to watch yourself (3)
> 'Cause I've got my eye on you.[38]
>
> Now if you shake it, I'll buy you a diamond ring (2)
> If you don't shake it, baby, you know you won't get a doggone thing.[39]
> Now everybody wants to know about the clothes.
> But them fine dresses I been buyin' you, you don't wear them no mo'.
>
> Won't be any more washin', an' hangin' upside the wall,
> An' throwin' 'em out the window an' runnin' out and catch 'em befo' they fall.[40]
>
> I'm mad (3)
> And you have the nerve to try to be glad.
>
> On big parties, I throw money on the floor (2)
> And leave it for the sweeper, and walk on out the door.[41]

Large amounts of money, flashily displayed and easily spent, are important in winning over the opposite sex, in elevating the ego and in gilding the individual's style of living.

> As I was walkin' down the street last night
> A pretty little girl came into sight.
> I bowed and smiled and asked her name,
> She said, "Hold it, bud, I don't play that game."
> I reached into my pocket and to her big surprise,
> There was Lincoln starin' her dead in the eye.[42]
>
> Jimmy Bell in town, Lordy, walkin' 'round
> He got greenback enough, sweet babe,
> To make a man a suit (3)
> He got greenback enough, sweet babe, make a man a suit.[43]
>
> If you follow me, babe, I turn your money green (2)
> I'll show you more money than Rockefeller ever seen.[44]

Other status boosters are fine cars (Cadillacs most often mentioned), clothes, diamonds, musical instruments, and, occasionally, food, household items and fashionable spas.

A fairly unique instance of envious status comparison occurs in Ray Charles' "It Should've Been Me,"[45] where he extols the prowess of rival males and laments his own inability to score in a similar manner with the women he desires:[46]

---

[38] Little Walter, "You Better Watch Yourself," Chess 1428.
[39] Joe Turner, "Watch That Jive," Savoy MG 14016.
[40] Willie Mabon, "I'm Mad," Chess 1538 (78 rpm).
[41] Peetie Wheetstraw, "Mister Livingood," Oliver, *op. cit.*, p. 302.
[42] Ray Charles, "Greenbacks," Atlantic 8006.
[43] Cat Iron, "Jimmy Bell," Folkways FA 2389.
[44] Furry Lewis, "I'll Turn Your Money Green," Folkways FA 3823.
[45] Atlantic 1021 (78 rpm).
[46] See note 2 regarding third person boasts.

As I passed by a real fine hotel,
A chick walked out; she sure was
    swell.
I gave her the eye and started to carry
    on,
When a Cadillac cruised up, and
    swish!
She was gone.

Chorus:
It should've been me, with that
    real fine chick (2)
Hey, hey, hey, hey, drivin' that
    Cadillac.

When I got to the corner, I saw a
    sharp cat
With a $300 suit on and a $100 hat.
He was standin' on the sidewalk by
    a Dynaflow,
When a voice within said, "Come on,
    daddy, let's go."

(*Chorus.*)

Travel is a valuable status symbol, often an ace in the hole in time of stress. Travel usually means a change in status, mostly for the better ("I'm gonna change my way of livin'"). A journey can be a threat to keep a woman in line ("If you don't believe I'm leaving, count the days I'm gone"); or it can be used to acquire specific items (money, whiskey, a new girlfriend). Far-off destinations give added glamour; the singer will mention specific places such as Texas or Chicago, or he will tell of an ideal world of some sort ("Goin' where orange blossoms bloom").

Running and walking are resorted to as modes of transportation, but the most valued conveyance is the train. An admired object of speed and power, the train acts to rescue or to return the blues man, who strongly identifies with it

and who personifies it as a friend, enemy, or ally. Even the length of trains is important ("The train I ride is 18 coaches long"), as the singer closely associates himself with an object that helps compensate for his own inferiority.

I'm goin' to Texas, Mama
Just to hear the wild ox moan,
Lord help my cryin' time I'm goin'
    to Texas
Mamma to hear the wild ox moan.
And if they moan to suit me,
I'm going to bring a wild ox home![47]

I'm going so far, can't hear your
    rooster crow. (2)[48]

Course I know my baby, she's goin'
    to jump and shout (2)
When the train rolls up and I come
    walkin' out.[49]

Gonna grab me a cab and motor on
    down
Be kinda sharp when I hit the town
Yeah, baby, don't like to boast
But I'm kinda sharp when I hit the
    coast.[50]

A trip is not the only threat at a man's disposal when his self-integrity is at stake. Warnings of every nature of physical violence assume boastful proportions as the singer exaggerates dire threats of murder, destruction, lawbreaking, fisticuffs and even suicide. The boastful threat is most often a retaliation for unfaithfulness, with the pistol acting as the commonest weapon for violence against a girlfriend or a rival.

Well, I feel like snappin', pistol in your
    face,

[47] Text from Harold Courlander, *Negro Folk Music U.S.A.* (New York and London, 1963), p. 141.
[48] Furry Lewis, Label "X" LVA 3032.
[49] Big Maceo, "County Jail Blues," Oliver, *op. cit.*, p. 219.
[50] Joe Turner, "I'm in Sharp When I Hit the Coast," Savoy MG 14012.

I'm goin' let some graveyard, Lawd,
  be your restin' place.
Woman I'm troubled, I be all worried
  in mind.
Well baby, I can't never be satisfied,
  and I jes' can't keep from
  cryin'.[51]

I love my baby but my baby won't
  behave (2)
I'm gonna buy me a hard-shootin'
  pistol and I'm gonna lay my
  baby in her grave.[52]

I'm gonna get me a picket off a
  graveyard fence (2)
Gonna beat you brownskins till you
  learn good sense.[53]

Give me gunpowder, give me dynamite
  (2)
Yes, I'm gonna wreck the city, gonna
  blow it up tonight.[54]

Gonna build me a scaffold, I'm gonna
  hang myself.
Cain't git the man I love, don't want
  nobody else.[55]

Me and the Devil was walkin' side by
  side (2)
I'm gon' to beat my woman until I get
  satisfied.[56]

Boastful threats contain frequent
mention of bargains and intimate association with the devil—

  Well, I'm sold to the devil
  Trouble is all I crave
  I'd rather see you dead

And laying in your grave.[57]

—as well as reference to powerful
hoodoo charms[58] at the singer's disposal:

  Get me some toad frogs' hips, I'm
    gonna,
  Gonna put it all together, I'm
    gonna,
  Gonna mix it up together, I'm gonna,
  Gonna whip it all up good, I'm
    gonna,
  Gonna kill that old dirty ground
    hog.
  I betcha my bottom dollar then, man,
    he
  He won't root there no more.
  (No he ain't gonna root no more
    then!)[59]

  I'm goin' down in New Orleans,
    mmmmm, get me a mojo hand
    (2)
  I'm gonna show all you good-lookin'
    women just how to treat
    your man.[60]

  I got a black cat bone, I got a mojo,
    too
  I got the John The Conqueror Root,
    I'm gonna mess with you
  I'm gonna make you girls lead me by
    my hand
  Then the world'll know the
    hoochie-coochie man.[61]

  I don't need no money, I got luck
    oil on my hand

[51] Muddy Waters, "I Can't Be Satisfied," Chess 1427.
[52] Tampa Red, "Goodbye Baby," Prestige/Bluesville 1030.
[53] Stovepipe No. 1, "Court St. Blues," Oliver, *op. cit.*, p. 94.
[54] Violet Mills, "Mad Mama's Blues," *Ibid.*, p. 199.
[55] Text from Langston Hughes and Arna Bontemps, *The Book of Negro Folklore* (New York, 1958), p. 382.
[56] Robert Johnson, "Me and the Devil Blues," Columbia CL 1654.
[57] "Evil Hearted Me," *The Josh White Song Book* (Chicago, 1963), p. 51.
[58] See my article "Folk Belief and Custom in the Blues" *Western Folklore*, XIX, (1960), pp. 173–89, for discussion of hoodoo charms mentioned in blues texts.
[59] John Lee Hooker, "Groundhog Blues," Chess 1438.
[60] Muddy Waters, "Louisiana Blues," Chess 1427.
[61] Muddy Waters, "Hoochie Coochie," Chess 1427.

I don't want no woman, boys, always
    raising sand.[62]

The hoodoo articles serve to add considerably to the singer's heroic stature, and may be employed for power, luck, status, or as weapons with which to control enemies or attract the opposite sex. Muddy Waters boasts that his greatness was prophesied even before his birth:

That gypsy woman told my mother
Just befo' I was born
I got a boy child's comin'
Gonna be a rollin' stone
He gonna make pretty womens
Jump and shout
Then the world wanna know
What this all about.[63]

A particular status is gained from dealings in sin and from defiance of law and order. Complete indifference to the consequences of liquor, reefers, drugs, gambling, women and assorted crimes lends the badman boaster a kind of wildman glamour as well as a high position in his competitive society. Status is also gained from serving time in jail, the greater number of years the better and more impressive.

I'm a man from the gutter, women in
    your dive at night (2)
I'm evil and mean and funny, so don't
    come back with that line of
    jive.[64]

I love to fuss and fight, (2)
Lawd, and get sloppy drunk
Off a bottle 'n ball,
And walk the streets all night.[65]

I'm going to the big house and I don't
    even care.
Don't you hear me talkin' to you,
    scoldin' 'em out dere
I'm goin' down and I don't even care
I might get fo', five years, Lawd, and
    I might get the chair.[66]

Gimme a pigfoot
An' a bottle of beer.
Send me gate I don't care.
Gimme a reefer
An' a gang of gin
Slay me 'cause
I'm in my sin.[67]

[62] Bill Broonzy, "When I've Been Drinking," Okeh 06303, Columbia 37474 (78 rpm).
[63] Muddy Waters, "Hoochie Coochie," Chess 1427.
[64] George Hannah, "Gutter Man Blues," Oliver, op. cit., p. 197.
[65] Charlie Patton, "Elder Green," Origin OJL-1.
[66] Jesse James, "Lonesome Day Blues," Decca 7213 (78 rpm).
[67] Bessie Smith, "Gimme a Pigfoot," Okeh 8945 (78 rpm).

The Dozens:
Dialectic of Insult

JOHN DOLLARD

Of all the elaborated forms of verbal art found in American Negro folklore, none is more central in the life of a Negro adolescent male than "the dozens." "The dozens" is a type of verbal dueling in which usually male antagonists address pointed barbs, often in rhymed couplet form, at one another. The battle of words normally takes place in front of an audience—in fact many of the scoring "put-downs" are really designed to elicit approbation from the interested observers in attendance.

One of the ways young boys achieve status in their peer group is by being especially adept at playing the dozens. For this reason, it is obviously to a boy's advantage to build up as large a repertoire of rhymes as possible so as to be able to outlast any opponent. Though some phrases employed in the dozens are fixed, there is room for improvisation. Certainly there is ample opportunity for strategy in making what appear to be virtually instant decisions as to precisely when to counter a particular rhyme insult with a given retort.

There is no question of the lasting influence this verbal ritual has among many American Negro male adults. One can see possible reflections of the dozens in predictions—made in rhymed couplets—by Negro prizefighters as to the very round in which a future opponent will fall or in the selection of a rhyming put-down title, "Change the Joke and Slip the Yoke" by Ralph Ellison in his literary "verbal duel" with Stanley Edgar Hyman in the Partisan Review *in 1958 (reprinted in this volume).*

Although there were occasional allusions to the dozens over the years during the first decades of the twentieth century, it was not really until 1939 that the ritual was described in any detail. In that year, Yale psychologist John Dollard, writing the lead article in the first volume of American Imago, *a psycho-*

Reprinted from *American Imago*, vol. 1 (1939), pp. 3–25, by permission of the author and Dr. George B. Wilbur.

analytic journal founded by Sigmund Freud, among others, and modeled after the celebrated earlier journal Imago, *devoted the entire essay to this remarkable example of verbal duelling. Although Dollard's discussion of the possible origins of the dozens now appears to be inadequate, and despite the fact that his hypothesis that the ritual functions primarily as an outlet for the Negro's frustration over his treatment by whites—i.e., the Negro takes out his aggression against a fellow Negro rather than the real white enemy—is questionable to say the least, the paper remains something of a classic.*

For some of the more recent "dozens" scholarship, see Roger D. Abrahams, "Playing the Dozens," Journal of American Folklore, 75 (1962), pp. 209–20, *reprinted next in this volume.*

IT IS a common observation of anthropologists that the field worker will recognize intuitively a series of character types among his informants, types which correspond closely to the people who surround the worker at home.* It is not so common, but perhaps equally important, to notice that there are forms of behavior among other peoples which have been worked up, traditionally patterned and consolidated for which the emotional background is also present in our own society. It is as though one recognized at home the raw material which has been elaborated into public and well recognized norms of behavior abroad. For example, in our society, a friendship may exist as a spontaneous optional relationship between two men. Among the Dahomey,[1] on the contrary, such a relationship will appear as a feature of the "best friend" pattern, and it will be defined that every man has routinely a best friend who performs certain well recognized services for him and receives a return in kind. What is a sporadic invention in the one case, appearing and dying with its instigators, is a patterned affair in the other. Psychotics in American hospitals display disorders of perception which are individual variants from our social practices; whereas in Tanino society as Murdock[2] has found, medicine men must (unconsciously) falsify their experience in a somewhat similar way in order to qualify for their craft. So, also, the "joking relationship," familiar to students of primitives, sometimes exists between Americans as a personal invention in human relations.

I have seen a joking relationship arise between two friends in exactly this spontaneous way; indeed these two men are noted for this behavior and provide much amusement to others in their particular circle. The jests fly—about infidelity, though each seems a faithful husband—about impotence, though both are apparently adequately married and have children—about homosexual tendencies, although neither exhibits such to public percep-

---

* The material used in this paper has been gathered in considerable part in the course of a study of Negro children carried on under the aegis of the American Youth Commission. Thanks for the opportunity to do this work but no blame for the nature of the material may be accorded to the Commission.

[1] Herskovits, M. J. "The Best Friend in Dahomey." *Negro*, an anthology edited by Nancy Cunard, London, Wishart & Company, 1934, pp. 627–32.

[2] Murdock, G. P. Unpublished Field Notes on the Tanino of Central Oregon.

tion. It is, in fact, just matters presumed to be farthest from fact which have the greatest currency in these jests. It is only by innuendoes and indirect references that the forbidden subjects may be touched on. A sally on the part of the one calls for a retort usually of a kind which would be most offensive if it were meant seriously. Both friends seem to have an unconscious perception and agreement on how far the joking may go. It does not touch upon actual weaknesses. It is done only when other persons are present. A playful attitude surrounds the whole affair, and it apparently gives great satisfaction to the participants. It is from such a behavioral ground that "the Dozens" springs.

The Dozens is a pattern of interactive insult which is used among some American Negroes. Apparently it exists in all three class groups within the Negro caste. It is guided by well recognized rules which at once permit and govern the emotional expression. It is evidently played by boys and girls and by adolescents and adults. Adolescents frequently make use of rhymes to express the forbidden notions. It is for some a game the only purpose of which seems to be the amusement of participants and onlookers, and as a game it may best be described as a form of aggressive play; in other circumstances the play aspect disappears and the Dozens leads directly to fighting. It is important to note that the Dozens is a collective game. It takes place before a group and usually involves two protagonists. Group response to the rhymes or sallies of the leaders is crucial; individuals do not play the Dozens alone. With group response comes the possibility of reward for effective slanders and feelings of shame and humiliation if one is bested.

Several ways of referring to the game are known. Adolescent informants talked about "playing" the Dozens. Others talked about "giving" a person in the Dozens and still others talked about "putting" a person in the Dozens. All of these expressions will be found used in the illustrative material.

The themes about which joking is allowed seem to be those most condemned by our social order in other contexts. Allegations are made that the person addressed by the speaker has committed incest, or that the speaker has taken liberties with the mother or sister of the one addressed; accusations of passive homosexuality are made, it is suggested that the cleanliness taboos have been broken, cowardice is alleged, and defects of the person of the one addressed, such as stupidity, crossed eyes, or inferiority, are played upon. There seems to be a taboo on mentioning dead relatives of either speaker. No references to menstruation or castration have been discovered.

Nothing is known to me about the history of the Dozens pattern. It does not appear to be noticed in a series of fourteen contemporary texts and studies which were assayed at random. The origin of the title, "the Dozens," is not known to me. What is known is that there is an obscene rhyme which is used in playing the Dozens which has twelve units in it. It goes in part as follows:

> "I—your mammy one;
> She said, 'You've just begun.'
> ....
> I—her seven;
> She said, 'I believe I'm in Heaven.'
> ....
> I—her twelve;
> She swore she was in Hell."

It may be that this pattern of twelve rhymes has given its name to the whole behavior form.

The Dozens pattern is known to exist in Mississippi and Louisiana. It was by chance that two Negro observers who had gone to school in a large northern city also reported it from there. It is known also among New Haven Negroes. No attempt at widespread sampling has been made and no thorough study of the pattern except in one area of the deep South. Although there are no thorough geographical data, it seems exceedingly likely that the Dozens is played very widely among American Negroes.

It is not at all certain that the Dozens pattern is limited to Negroes but it is only from them that I have data on it. Certainly many of the same insults are exchanged by whites in situations of provocation. Further study may well show that it is a lower-class pattern which exists among whites also.*

The evidence is confusing at many points; for example, on how frequently physical combat follows the game. Some informants believe it to be quite common and some quite rare. There is also much data presented for one city or area that is missing for others. This is due to systematic defects in the study, which was not organized in the first place to assemble information on the Dozens pattern.

The data will be classified under the rubrics Northern-Southern, large-city–small-city, adults-adolescents, boys-girls, and social class. In regard to the latter, two distinctions will be made: lower-class, on the one hand, and middle- and upper-class, lumped together, on the other.[3]

At this point it is necessary to agree on one fact about the material; some condemned words and concepts must be used if the necessary scientific interpretation is to be made. Only the briefest references to these data will be made, just enough in fact to give the impact of the actual material.

SOUTHERN: BIG CITY: ADOLESCENT: LOWER-CLASS

One of the first impressions about the Dozens was the reluctance of two small boys with their lower-class gang to begin playing it. One asked the other, "Do you want to play the Dozens?"

The other boy said, "Yes."

The first boy said, "You start."

The second boy said, "No, you start." Finally one of them started. The boys behaved, in fact, like nations; each one of them reconciled to a war but neither willing to accept the responsibility of being the aggressor. It was apparent that some fear or anxiety was operative in both boys.

My best informants were ten lower-class Negro children in a big Southern city. In the course of prolonged interviewing with each of these children none of them spontaneously mentioned the Dozens to me. I had to find out about it finally by actually seeing them

---

* On this point, see Millicent R. Ayoub and Stephen A. Barnett, "Ritualized Verbal Insult in White High School Culture," *Journal of American Folklore*, 78 (1965), pp. 337–44, and Bruce Jackson, "White Dozens and Bad Sociology," *Journal of American Folklore*, 79 (1966), pp. 374–77. —ED.

[3] For the sake of this paper the term "class" will be used as an arbitrary way of dividing the data and no further defense of its utility will be made.

play the game. Even then, I did not recognize at first that the behavior was patterned but thought of it only as an interpersonal quarrel. Once discovered and questioning begun, the boys reacted with furtive amusement in some cases, occasionally with embarrassment and sometimes with outright and deceitful denials. With Raymond, for example, his embarrassment was obvious when I first questioned him. Tom giggled at my question and refused to reply. Some children denied knowing the rhymes altogether at first but later, however, proved to be familiar with many of them. These showed marked shame and secrecy about the game, claimed they never played it and evinced indignation in the face of questioning. These reactions of concealment and shame convinced me that playing the Dozens is not an orgy of licentious expression for lower-class Negroes; all know that the themes treated are in general forbidden, some refuse to play the game and still others are very resentful and defensive at the mere thought of it.

The rhymed Dozens are played apparently predominantly by children; all of my informants on rhyming happened to be from twelve to sixteen years old. Perhaps rhyming in children tends to be done because they are still in the age when rhymes are read and quoted to them. Perhaps again the forbidden content can express itself behind the facade of the rhyme, a facade which grown-ups do not need. Younger children, moreover, are less emancipated from family controls and must find some covering while expressing anti-social accusations.

Sex themes are by far the most common and they frequently relate to the female relatives of the challenged person. Raymond came forward with the following rhymes, among many others:

"I saw your ma
At Tulane and Broad;
She was coming out
Of the red light yawd."

....
"Your ma behind
Is like a rumble seat.
It hang from her back
Down to her feet."

The reference in the first rhyme is obvious. The second is also an intimate and derogatory reference to the mother.

The Dozens is also played among these adolescents without the use of rhymes and without direct erotic references. For instance, one day Willy was joking Jimmy to the following effect: that Jimmy should go and get a machine gun. He kept on iterating this while Jimmy attempted feebly to retort in kind. Willy was stressing the point that he could lick Jimmy fist to fist and that Jimmy would need a machine gun to defend himself. Willy kept "jiving" him until Jimmy finally left, saying that he was coming back but not meaning to and not doing it; he thus escaped from the fight which might have followed. Delbert reported that Herbert had been put in the Dozens by another boy in the following manner: the boy said, "Your mama needs a bath." This was a fighting matter to Herbert, and he had answered, "Go on home, nigger," and had chased the boy home. Apparently the other fellow was unwilling to back up his words with deeds.

Sometimes homosexuality was the subject of jest among these boys; for example, Joe was kidding Steve in my hearing along the following lines: he kept saying that Steve had always got the "next dish" from Mr. Ting out at the camp. Steve had kept answering, "That's good," meaning that that was his business. Steve attempted to retort but could not seem to find anything as good; finally he wanted to fight about it. Later, I queried what the "next dish" meant. They explained to me that when Steve was at the camp he would get a nice dish of corn flakes while the other boys got oatmeal with worms in it, and that this often happened at the camp, or at least the boys from there said so. I asked what Steve had to do to get the next dish. They explained to me that Steve would have to "give some of his behind" in order to get it. The boys said they did not know whether this was true; maybe it was just malicious gossip. Anyway, it made good subject matter for attacking Steve.

This introduced a very common aspect of the Dozens game. Although there are stereotyped rhymes and general challenges which can be made to anybody, it is good technique to attack the other fellow at his weak point, if that be found. In checking up on this, I asked Bill, "Suppose a fellow's daddy were in jail, what would you say then?"

He said, "The boys would kid you that your daddy was a thief or a jailbird."

I said, "Suppose a boy's sister had an illegitimate child?"

He said, "The boys would kid you something like this: 'Aw, your sister is an ole two-cent street-walker.' " He said they would find out and kid you if there was something wrong with your family, and if there were nothing wrong with it they would make something up. Bill also said that when the boys played the Dozens with Willy

they accused him of being a "snoteater." Apparently this behavior had been observed in Willy. Willy was also a constant target for affronts on the score of irregularities in his family set-up. It seemed that his father had deserted the mother when Willy was a child, had never been married to her, and that therefore Willy had never had a consolidated family situation. The boys constantly and savagely joked Willy about this matter, and it was said that he invariably fought; although a lower-class boy, Willy was both secretive and protective as to his mother's behavior. Probably he did not want to sink out of the lower class into the limbo of class-lessness with the illegitimate. Members of the primary group have a keen eye for the weaknesses and defects of fellow participants and are invariably able to bring them forward in the case of any sadistic game.

Some boys refuse to play the Dozens and immediately issue a warning to this effect once it is proposed. Bill was one of these. He said that he had heard a lot of the rhymes and used to use them himself, but stated that he could not remember any of them now. He said he did not like to play this game and always told the boys to stop "giving him in." In explanation, he said the game almost always ended in a fight. It was through this game that he had got into so many fights with Willy. It was bound to lead to a fight, he felt, because it almost always ended up by the other fellow saying something about your mother, daddy or sister, and in this case there was nothing else one could do.

Sam also said that if there was something you objected to in the course of the rhymes you would have to fight, and that the game frequently ended in a fight. Raymond said that if one of the children ran out of rhymes first he would feel humiliated and begin to fight. Apparently, if one has no effective comeback he must resort to his fists. Fighting seems to be known in the in-group in this neighborhood since Bill and Willy who fight so much were both old friends and belong to the same gang.

SOUTHERN: BIG CITY: ADOLESCENTS: MIDDLE-CLASS

In middle class much the same features are observed in playing the Dozens that have been noticed for lower-class, big city boys. It may be that through defects in information some differences appear which would be found not to exist in a more complete survey, or the contrary may be true for the same reason. There seems some slight tendency, on the existing evidence, for a greater suppression of vulgar expressions. An experienced observer writes:

"I saw a group of four boys between thirteen and eighteen, apparently lower-middle-class, keep the game going for fifty minutes. They jeered at everything from one's inferiority at checkers to another's withered leg and T.B. There was careful avoidance of any jeering at mothers, sisters or girl friends." Another observer notes that rhymes need not be used, and that reference to caste status, such as "your mammy is a nigger," has a particular sting among middle-class boys. This observer cites the following rhymes as an example of the non-obscene type:

"You weren't born fair,
I sure can swear.

You were born by an alligator
And suckled by a mare."

Though not obscene, the above could certainly be classified as an offensive personal reference, imputing animal characteristics to the one addressed. Another rhyme on the margin of the obscene follows:

"If you wanta play the Dozens,
Play them fast.
I'll tell you how many bull-dogs
Your mammy had.

She didn't have one;
She didn't have two;
She had nine damned dozens
And then she had you."

One can imagine how such a rhyme is pulled out with triumph in a heated altercation. The same reference to animal origins is noted. This rhyme, however, definitely does cast a slur on the person's mother, contrary to the opinion that middle-class boys do not use such jests.

Another experienced observer distinguishes between the "dirty" Dozens and the ordinary Dozens. Apparently the latter would be jesting without particular reference to the person's family.

The informant about the dirty Dozens stressed that in them references are made to mother, sisters, father and brothers, and that the mother is most continuously involved. He says: "Slangs are passed about one's mother and rhymes are made up about her. Slangs such as these are passed: 'I am your paw'; 'I did it to your maw'; 'I slept with your maw last night,' etc. Of course, there are a lot of other slangs and rhymes used, but these are just a few so as to give you an idea. There is really no truth to the slangs used and no sense to the rhymes but it just sets one to burning up because of the heckling and the laughter of the onlookers fanning the flame."

This observer has noted the very considerable role of the crowd of onlookers in the Dozens game. It is the laughter, applause and the derision of the crowd which stirs the participants to ever renewed attempts to out-do the other in invective. The crowd is essential both to the rewards and punishments which attend the Dozens behavior. The way the Dozens occur in actual nature is also suggested by this informant through the following interchange:

JOE: Nigger, if I was as ugly as you I would kill myself.

JAMES: You ain't so hot yourself. Your hair looks like a wire fence.

JOE: Your paw's hair look like a wire fence, nigger.

JAMES: You are my paw.

JOE: If I am your paw I must have done it to your maw.

ONLOOKERS: Oh, oh! He told you about your maw. I would not take that if I was you. Go ahead and tell him something back. (The dialogue becomes increasingly offensive and insults are tossed back and forth on the themes of illegitimacy and incest. More laughter from the onlookers, and then:) Why don't you two fight and get it over with? Hit him, Joe. If you don't hit him, James, you are a sissy. (They push the two boys and as a result a fight ensues.)

The above gives the impression of a collective transaction whose object it is to create a sort of impromptu prize fight. It would seem that the crowd, anxious for a battle, eggs the participants on and finally ridicules them into

having a fight. The boys themselves would seem to be willing to drop the matter on some occasions, if it were not for fear of public ridicule.

It may be that fighting is a less customary activity and is therefore more feared among middle-class boys, or it may be that the participants in the above case were exceptionally intimidated. The Dozens is not always played solely by two protagonists with a circle of onlookers. An example has been given of four boys who played it as a group, each against the other three. Another informant confirms this impression that it may be a group game as well as one used between two individuals.

Another informant remarks that the dirty Dozens usually follows after two boys begin to joke one another before a crowd. At first no obscene words or references are used. Later, however, the "weaker kidder" who "can't take it" will fight back by telling the other about his "mammy," and thus the dirty Dozens begins. It is at this point also that the onlookers play an important part, as where they jump in by saying, "Aw, he told you about your mother. I wouldn't stand for that. Don't be a sissy. Tell him something back. I just know this is a fight," etc. Again, the boys surrounding the two may burst into laughter and "make small" of the boy for whom the remark was intended, thus arousing his anger, and he begins to tell his opponent about his mother also. We are told that "the kidding continues like this, with the group around pushing fire, first siding with one and then the other so as to keep the kidding up."

I am sure that this behavior must be analogous to that which occurs in small-boy gangs all over America, which is not heavily patterned but which springs up spontaneously through the needs and hostilities of the individual children themselves. It is assumed that most people, young and old alike, are willing to see a prize fight or a grudge fight, if they can only get someone else to do the fighting.

There is considerable disagreement about how often the Dozens game ends up in a fight. In some cases the audience is definitely disappointed if there is no fight and the "weaker kidder" will be booed and laughed at as he leaves the crowd. Most informants seem to agree that when the Dozens is played with an out-group member it generally ends up in physical fighting. Even in the in-group if the joking becomes sufficiently exasperating and extreme it will often end in fisticuffs. The in-group, of course, has a difficult problem here. It must maintain its solidarity, which includes friendly relationships between the two Dozens participants. It must, therefore, exercise a certain control over in-group hostilities if it is to be capable of mass action against some other gang. The informants seem to be agreed that playing the dirty Dozens is most likely to lead to fights between in-group members. Even there, however, references to "your mother" may sometimes be made without leading to actual fighting. One observer stresses the importance of the etiquette of some Dozens playing groups which compels an individual to control his temper and not actually fight. The one who fights first tends to be viewed as the "weaker kidder" and the one who "can't take it." Fighting itself proves that you have run out of effective verbal retort and that you have been bested by your opponent. It may be that the taboo on fighting is a matter of preservation of the in-group, or it may, on the other hand, be a special feature of the character structure of middle-class boys to avoid open violence and limit their aggressions to the verbal mode.

Another informant stresses the entertainment value of the Dozens. He says, "In my group, the 'dozens' pattern was very well known—especially on trips to other towns or cities. It generally began when the 'life of the party' wanted to break the monotony of a long trip without entertainment and would start kidding (according to the 'dozens') some of his very intimate pals. He would be sure to joke with the 'right person' of the group, because there was always some person who cried, 'I don't play that!' Because the leader chose the other person with whom to play the 'dozens,' there were generally no fights." It would be interesting to know how the "right person" is chosen in this case. Presumably, it would be a fellow who "could take it" and who would not damage the mood of the group by open hostility. It is especially important to see in the case of this pattern not only how it permits some hostilities to be expressed but also how it carries with it a sanction which tends to limit those aggressions which would damage the unity of the boys' group.

Two informants agree that girls put one another in the Dozens as well as boys, and that the game may be played between girls and girls, and girls and boys. In this case, the girls use the same "slangs and rhymes" that the boys use, and their games often end up in physical fighting too. The game begins with girls, as with boys, with the "clean" Dozens and then proceeds to the dirty

Dozens, where one tells the other "about your mother or father."

In a study of forty-three adolescent children in the middle- and upper-class groups, conducted in a large city, no reference to the Dozens pattern was made by the interviewers reporting on the children; this was true in spite of the fact that in some cases ten to twenty interviews had been obtained. There was no precise questioning on the score of the existence of the Dozens pattern, however, and the children may not have thought it important enough to report, especially since the interviewers did not ask about it. Delicacy of feeling on the part of either informant or interviewer may also have resulted in withholding information, especially about the dirty Dozens. In view of my own experience in interviewing on this pattern, it is believed that the lack of appearance of material on the Dozens testifies not to its absence but either to neglect or withholding of the relevant information.

SOUTHERN: BIG CITY: ADULT

The Dozens pattern is also played by adults. "Adult" is here given to mean anyone in age from seventeen or eighteen on up. One thing is clear, and that is that adults do not use the rhymes which are characteristic of adolescents. They depend rather on directly improvised insults and curses, and seem to be altogether more crude and direct in their expressions. I refer here only to lower-class adults. The jibes tend to include incidents of promiscuity of a man's mother or sister and literal references are made to homosexual practices.

I have no evidence on the occurrence of Dozens behavior among middle-class or upper-class Negro men in this city, although I have often observed the same friendly and unpatterned joking among them that I have in similar white groups.

SOUTHERN: SMALL CITY: ADOLESCENT: ALL CLASSES

The Dozens in this town is characterized, as elsewhere, mainly by obscene rhymes and references. There seems to be no distinction between the clean and dirty Dozens.

The Dozens game very commonly ends in fighting, especially in the lower-class group. In the middle- and upper-class, on the other hand, it is said to be done largely for amusement and fighting is interdicted. A case of two boys in a typical patter is described as follows:

FIRST BOY: Who is yo' gittin' slop fo'?
SECOND: Fo' yo' mammy, you nigger!
FIRST: I ain't said nothin' 'bout yo' black mammy and I'm goin' to beat yo' up 'cause I don't play that wid yo'. (The fight starts when the first boy leads.)

In this city there is another name for the Dozens, "joaning." Frequent references to caste are made. The word "nigger" is used, as is the word "black." Among middle-class boys such references would lead to fights, but this is not necessarily the case with the lower class. Such an interchange as the following may not provoke a fight if it takes place between boys both of whom belong to a friendly group:

FIRST BOY: Nigger, you can't see nothin'.
SECOND: You know who kin.

FIRST: Who?
SECOND: Yo' big black mammy.

If, however, the boys belong to hostile groups, for instance, ones from different parts of the town, a fight is almost certain to occur.

"Joaning" is reported by children from middle- and upper-class families. Here are rhymes which come from three of the most prominent members of the high school class:

> "Keep on joanin'
> You'll make me mad.
> I'll tell you the trouble
> Your grandmaw had.
>
> She had ninety-nine puppies
> And a dog named Belle.
> If you don't like that
> You may go to Hell."

The rhyming, it may be admitted, is slightly better than that of lower-class children, but it contains the same obscene references to family members and the same forcing of incestuous or adulterous phantasies on the person addressed.

Girls in this town are said to play the Dozens as well as boys. The informant says that "fourteen and fifteen year old middle-class girls take an active part in the Dozens as they take part with the boys at the meetings of their various class clubs."

No information is available on the playing of this game by adults in this town, although undoubtedly it is done by lower-class men. The role of the group of onlookers is also not stressed but there seems no reason to believe that it is not a feature of the play.

SOUTHERN: SMALL TOWN AND RURAL DATA

In my own work in "Southerntown" I did not get direct information on the Dozens probably because of my lack of direct participation with lower-class people. I did, however, hear about it but did not recognize it at that time as a patterned activity. I thought of it as just ordinary "joking." In the nine histories of middle-class adults which I gathered no reference was made to the Dozens, although I have little doubt that my informants knew about it. It seems very unlikely that they played it, however, if one may judge from their character structures in other respects.

Cohn[4] writing of Negro behavior in the Mississippi Delta speaks of the game as a "prolific source of shootings and stabbings." He describes it further as "a form of Rabelaisian banter engaged in by two or more Negroes . . . Aspersion after aspersion is cast by each on the mammy of the other. Finally a pistol explodes or a knife flashes." Cohn is undoubtedly reporting on lower-class behavior although he does not specify to this effect.

Bradford[5] also puts a reference to the Dozens in the mouth of his "John Henry," who is a rural Louisiana Negro. He writes: " . . . Maybe de happy dust cross me up, and de preacher put me in de dozens . . ." This reference is somewhat obscure, but it seems to have to do with the occasion when the preacher was pleading with John Henry to repent of his sins. It is, nevertheless, one of the rare references to the pattern and seems to imply that it

---

[4] Cohn, D. L., *God Shakes Creation*. New York: Harper & Brothers, 1935, p. 161.
[5] Bradford, Roark, *John Henry*. New York: The Literary Guild, 1931, p. 213.

is common knowledge in rural Louisiana.

NORTHERN: BIG CITY: ALL CLASSES

There happens to be some casual and isolated information on the playing of the Dozens in a large city on the borderline between North and South. A particular middle-class observer, thinking back to his adolescence, states that obscene rhymes and references were not the chief foci of the Dozens in his group. The reason seems simple; references to female relatives brought about either an immediate fight or a rather permanent break in friendly relationships. This was not true of lower-class boys in the same school. In the middle and upper classes, the constant themes utilized were those which played around various types of inferiority, cowardice or stupidity. This observer feels that jibes about sex matters were more freely allowed in lower class. But, at the same time, there were stricter taboos in the lower-class group about allowing the Dozens to lead to fights. He feels that the middle- and upper-class children, with a higher sense of "personal honor" were much quicker to become insulted and resort to fisticuffs over the Dozens. This "higher sense of personal honor" may mean that there is a severer repression of the forbidden tendencies among middle-class children and that when one is accused of wanting to do something which he has severely repressed he becomes anxious and will fight to give an emphatic denial to the accusation. Lower-class children with possibly less severe repressions would not become so anxious and therefore not be so likely to fight. This tentative analysis does not take account of individual differences which there certainly must be.

There is another scrap of evidence with regard to a northern city. An upper-class Negro woman said the pattern existed in her high school group in the following form: a simple reference to "your ma" or "your mother" was a fighting challenge. The woman herself did not know why one had to fight when she heard this but did know that fight one must. Perhaps the repressive influence of class and school had elided from expression the rest of the Dozens pattern, and we have in the condensed expression a sort of stump of the full behavior structure.

NORTHERN: SMALL CITY: ALL CLASSES

The Dozens is known in another and smaller northern city. It is played both by boys and girls and by adolescents and adults. In this city the Dozens is always "dirty." Both fixed rhymes and impromptu retorts are used; content and form are about the same as the examples already reported. Among adolescents at least a rhymed retort is considered to have a superior demoralizing effect on one's opponent. The informant stated that at hearing a telling rhyme she will sometimes say with admiration, "Let me put my foot down (pat my foot) and listen to that one." It seems to be a game played primarily by lower-class people although younger people of middle-class status also participate; it seems unlikely that middle- or upper-class adults use it. In this city the Dozens is viewed as a dangerous game. One does not initiate it unless he is expecting it to end in a fight and fighting is said to be the usual outcome—in this case not only fist-fighting but often also knife- and gun-play. The clean or non-dirty Dozens is not recognized as the same game but is played under another name; it is called "working plays" on another person. One refers to it in this way: "I worked a play" on so-and-so, or "I ranked" so-and-so, meaning "set him back on his heels." The one who is about to initiate the Dozens is said often to clap his hands and tap his foot as a sign that he is about to begin the joking. At this sign others may warn him off continuing or gather around to see the fun or fight. The watching crowd plays a crucial role here as in the South.

ANALOGOUS PRACTICES IN OTHER SOCIETIES

No attempt at a complete ethnographical survey of joking behavior will be made at this point. I desire only to show by one or two references that similar behavior forms have been known and transmitted in remote parts of the earth. No relationship is presumed between the American Negro Dozens and any other similar form.

Mead[6] has described the "joking relationship" among her Manus informants. The "joking relationship" is a special relationship between specified kinsmen in which matters may be jested about which would be unthinkable outside of the terms of the relationship itself. She refers to the main features of the pattern in the following form: it is public; through it the participants simulate hostility and anger; and their behavior consists mainly of obscene taunts and jests. Mead notes[7] that on no account may the twitted person actually become hostile, except, of course, by way of jesting retort in kind. Among the Tikopia, Firth[8] found a joking relationship to exist between terminological brothers. Such brothers may be technical kinsmen despite such great differences in rank as that between chief and commoner. The jeers fly back and forth very much as already described here, and the laughter of the watching crowd is an essential feature. Obscene references are the characteristic material of these jokes. A pattern somewhat similar to the Dozens is found in the song contests of the Aleutians as described by Weyer[9] who, in turn, refers to Weniaminow; here two opponents sing derisive songs before a group, each one capping the insults offered by the other. Occasionally such competitions end in blows and even death. Thomas[10] (paraphrasing Thalbitzer) notes the use of similar song competitions, called "drum fights," among the Greenland Eskimo. He observes that the utility of the pattern seems to lie in the

---

[6] Mead, Margaret, "Kinship in the Admiralty Islands," *Anthropological Papers of the American Museum of Natural History*, vol. XXXIV, part II (1934), p. 252.

[7] *Ibid.*, p. 249.

[8] Firth, Raymond, *We, The Tikopia* (London: George Allen & Unwin, Ltd., 1936).

[9] Weyer, E. M., *The Eskimos* (New Haven: Yale University Press, 1932), pp. 226–227.

[10] Thomas, W. I., *Primitive Behavior* (New York & London: McGraw-Hill Book Company, Inc., 1937).

public ridicule of an opponent with whom an actual private quarrel exists.

SUMMARY

The Dozens is a pattern of inter-active insult widely distributed among American Negroes. Adolescents tend to carry on the game by means of rhymes whereas adults speak without rhymes and often improvise. The clean Dozens are distinguished from the dirty Dozens everywhere, though not always by name. In the latter, accusations of incestuous or adulterous behavior are made on the part of the accused or his near rela-tives; in the former, jeers concerning the inferiority, stupidity or cowardice of the one addressed, or his relatives, are the stock in trade. The collective aspect of Dozens play is very important since the watching crowd serves as a sounding board for all insults, magnify-ing them and compelling adequate rejoinder. Fights are most likely to terminate the play when the chief protagonists are members of exclusive out-groups. They often occur when the players in a middle-class group resort to the obscene slanders of the dirty Dozens. When the two players are members of an in-group in any class there is a tendency to put a premium on not fighting; not "letting the other fellow get your goat" is the form which this sanction takes. Both boys and girls play the Dozens.

INTERPRETATION

Every culture item should be exam-ined from the standpoint of its function in the contemporary social order. "Function" is here taken to mean the expressive value of the pattern from the impulse standpoint. The basic assump-tion is that such a culture item as the Dozens exists because it is in a general way adaptive. Such adaptive utility should be revealed by close study even in the case of relatively trivial patterns.

From the historical point of view, the Dozens pattern is seen as a collec-tive creation, fashioned in the adjustive struggle of the Negro caste. It is impos-sible to say at the present moment whether the pattern itself has been borrowed from Western European cul-ture and refashioned by Negroes in the last one hundred and fifty years or whether it has been borrowed or adapted from the native African heritage of our colored people. It is always possible, too, that the game has been indepen-dently invented by American Negroes.

Whatever be the truth here, the fact would remain that this borrowing, adaptation or invention could only occur in case the pattern formed a balancing element within the current structure of Negro life. In the latter case, we have a behavior element which is integrated with other fundamental aspects of Negro society of the present day. It is the contention here that the Dozens behavior is expressive of impulses gener-ated and fashioned in living individuals by other portions of their life experience.

It may then be asked, since the Dozens deals in a general way with aggressive behavior, what are the circumstances of life for Negroes which would facilitate the existence of aggres-sive patterns? In answering this question we will note at the outset that the Dozens is an in-caste pattern. It does not countenance jeering openly at white people, but it confines aggressive expres-sion within Negro society. The reason for this limitation seems obvious, i.e., the punishing circumstances which come into play when Negroes display direct hostility for whites.

In general, we would expect aggression to be overtly expressed when two circumstances are present, i.e., when frustration levels are high, and when social pressure against aggressive behavior is weak.[11] That frustration levels are high among Negroes, especially lower-class Negroes, would seem to emerge from the following considerations. Negroes are included in the most depressed economic group in the country, that is, lower-class people, white and colored, in the southern United States.[12] The strivings toward social self-aggrandizement of middle-class Negroes are markedly limited by caste barriers; the under-representation in positions of business leadership and some of the professions is a case in point. Negroes are not permitted, in the southern states, to make their protests effective through political means. They are excluded from full participation in our society in a polite social sense. They are ringed around with a threatening series of rebuffs, scorn and humiliation when they attempt to change their status. "Not Wanted Here" is a sign that the Negro sees when he claims full membership in our system. Since Negroes know what rights they should have from the standpoint of our democratic customs, these limitations constitute frustrations of a severe order. These frustrations regularly raise their aggressive responses in turn. We will arbitrarily leave out of consideration for the moment the substitute satisfactions available to Negroes which diminish frustration levels somewhat. One would expect, therefore, in Negroes a readiness to aggression which would constitute from the societal standpoint a constant market for patterns permissive of aggressive expression. It is suggested that the Dozens is one of these.

To take up the second consideration, we may expect overt aggression from people when social pressures against such expression are weak. It is regularly presumed that aggressive responses will be expressed if it is not too dangerous to do so. I have suggested in another place[13] that Negroes are to a considerable degree "outside the law." Aggressive behavior on the part of Negroes is condoned, punished less severely than similar behavior in whites and is, on the whole, rather expected of them; this is true, of course, only when such expressions are confined to members of the Negro caste. Negro society constitutes a frontier area of relative lawlessness within white society, where the social punishment for aggressive expressions is diminished much below our standard practice. Such a circumstance makes it immediately plausible why a pattern such as the Dozens can appear.

This makes clear the general point of view advanced here on the Dozens game; it is a valve for aggression in a depressed group. Some psychological comments in explanation of the game

---

[11] Dollard, J., Doob, L. W., Miller, N., Mowrer, O. H., and Sears, R. R., *Frustration and Aggression* (New Haven: Yale University Press, 1939), Chap. VI, pp. 110–41.

[12] National Emergency Council, *Report on Economic Conditions of the South* (Washington, 1938), pp. 21–23.

[13] Dollard, John, *Caste and Class in a Southern Town* (New Haven: Yale University Press, 1937), pp. 279–80.

itself are in order. It is undoubtedly set in motion by aggressive tendencies which have been mobilized in other situations and are ready for expression. It has been noted that the point of the game seems to be to bring up matters painful to the other person. The physical self of the addressed person is derogated; he is sometimes accused of incestuous behavior; adulterous acts are alleged on the part of persons "sacred" to him, i.e., those toward whom the accused does not himself have conscious sexual wishes. It seems to be generally agreed that it is just such accusations as the latter which provoke an intense anger in the accused person and differentiate the ordinary Dozens from the dirty Dozens. It is evidently this element of exposure of the other person's unconscious wishes which is crucial. When the taunting speaker hits his unconscious mark he describes a repressed wish struggling for expression in his hearer.[14] This ripping of the repressive veil in the person addressed immediately raises his level of anxiety. Anxiety is itself a punishing state of affairs, and the inevitable response is aggression toward the first speaker by the accused and taunts in kind. If the game goes on, anxiety in each participant or perhaps especially in one becomes so great that verbal attacks will no longer hold the aggression mobilized and only blows will suffice. It is in this way that the all-important interactive element of the game can be explained. If fighting is wanted by the group but does not occur, it is probable that the one addressed is more afraid of the speaker than he is of his own anxiety.

The foregoing makes clear only how direct aggression is elicited in the Dozens game. No doubt in addition to the direct frustrations administered while the game is being played, much aggressive response is irrationally overtoned by the general readiness to aggression of the participants. It is at this point that the high frustration level among Negroes resulting from their general circumstances of life comes to bear.

We are now in a position to discuss why it seems to be the case that middle-class boys will fight quicker than lower-class boys when the dirty Dozens is played. The middle-class boys are in general *mobile* boys and because of this feature of their social position they are required to make exceptional impulse sacrifices in order to develop the skills incident to social advancement. Impulse renunciation in this case is regularly brought about in the course of the life history of each one of them by repression of counter-mores tendencies. With these stronger repressive forces operating the middle-class people will develop more anxiety when presented with the verbal equivalent of their repressed wishes and hence react more strongly with aggression. The expectation would be, what some informants allege is the fact, that they will fight more readily. This consideration might explain also why Negroes in the North react to the game with fighting more regularly than do southern Negroes; northern Negroes are in general more mobile and stronger repressive forces are in operation.

---

[14] The fundamental conceptions of Freud have made this analysis possible. Many of them are used here, such as "wish," "repression," "anxiety."

Following along these same lines it becomes clear why boys will fight with out-gang members more readily than with fellow members of their own small group. Barriers against aggression are low where outsiders are concerned and high where in-group members are concerned. In-group members are threatened with loss of status if they are "not able to take it." "Ability to take it" would be defined from this standpoint as an ability to stand the anxiety raised by the presentation of the forbidden fantasy. In-groupers must learn to tolerate this anxiety since aggression is penalized within the primary group by fear of loss of group esteem and cooperation. This fear is often great enough to get the accused person to bear his anxiety and not fight.

It is indeed one of the fears of the writer of this paper that by the presentation of so much forbidden material he will do to the reader what the Dozens players do to one another, and with the same results. It can only be hoped that the psychological analysis is sufficiently discerning to minimize punitive action.

Another obvious psychological element of the Dozens is the enjoyment of forbidden themes by the speaker and the crowd; this enjoyment is the negative of the discomfiture of the one addressed. It must be remembered that fantasy and verbal expression of forbidden acts are in themselves gratifying since they stand next door to overt muscular execution of these acts. Nor is it to be presumed that "cultural patterning" is the sole explanation of the form the insults take. One must follow Freud exactly at this point and suppose that the accusations made by the speaker represent in most cases repressed wishes of his own; the accusations follow too closely the familiar catalogue of the repressed tendencies— i.e., incest, homosexuality, peeping, phallic display, and the like—for any other presumption to be justified.

Equally clear is the fact that the aggression involved in exposing the other person is enjoyed by each respondent. Long stifled tendencies to damage others can be ventilated by this means. There is an aggrandizement of self involved in besting or humiliating the other person and a concurrent denial of weakness in the own self. In addition, one may guess that in verbalizing the forbidden notions the speaker experiences a triumph over repressive forces in himself, a triumph sweet to the child-animal in all of us.

It is never amiss to rebut again the fallacy that Negroes are fundamentally different from whites. This rebuttal is easy in considering the foregoing evidence. Since Negroes repress the same tendencies as do whites it is obvious that they are governed by the same moral imperatives as whites are. Since they manifest anxiety at the prospect of emergence of the same forbidden tendencies they are "human" in sharing the same culture controls. They have obviously the same taboos on incestuous behavior, homosexuality, adulterous activities and possession of extreme Negroid characteristics which whites have. Their family loyalties show the marks of being fashioned by the same repressive forces. The conclusion could not be otherwise since they are fellow participants in our Western European culture heritage.

In conclusion we may indicate the interactive mounting of aggression as an important theme for social research. The problem of summation of aggressive response has already been discussed by Bateson[15] in reference to the splitting of small groups in a primitive society. It has long been known by diplomats that it is dangerous to humiliate an important nation twice on the same score. The building up of aggressive responses, started sometimes from trivial causes, must be carefully studied since to know the mechanisms involved may offer means of control. What we want to know is how aggressive expression may get out of social control and become disruptive of social life. Patterns of aggressive expression, like the Dozens, are undoubtedly valuable, but if unchecked interaction teases out of individuals or nations the ultimate in repressed aggression that pattern is a dangerous one to human society.

[15] Bateson, Gregory, *Naven* (Cambridge, England: The University Press, 1936), pp. 183–86.

Playing the Dozens

ROGER D. ABRAHAMS

Academic discussion of the dozens did not progress appreciably after Dollard's pioneering essay until folklorist Roger Abrahams, Professor of English and Anthropology at the University of Texas, undertook his fieldwork in a section of the Philadelphia ghetto. Professor Abrahams found that texts similar to those reported by Dollard were in common use and in the course of writing his important book-length treatment of urban Negro folklore, he devoted some attention to the dozens.

Abrahams' approach to the dozens differs somewhat from Dollard's. Whereas Dollard sought to interpret the ritual in the light of race relations, Abrahams believed the dozens were a male ritual reflecting the tensions caused by the particulars of American Negro family structure. As Abrahams puts it, "Not only is the [the Negro man] a black man in a white man's world, but he is a male in a matriarchy." Abrahams argues that the adolescent boy would like to "put down" his own mother (both in the Oedipal sexual sense and in the sense of rejecting the female centered home life to enter the world of men), but he accomplishes this by putting down the mother of his opponent who he knows will in turn "attack" the first speaker's mother. This is admittedly a highly speculative interpretation—and it would not really explain the psychological functioning of the dozens as practiced by females. Nevertheless, the reader may decide for himself as to the plausibility of Abrahams' hypothesis.

One problem with both Dollard's and Abrahams' interpretations of the dozens is that they ignore any possible African source for the dozens. Dollard left the question of origins open by stating that "It is impossible to say at the present moment whether the pattern itself has been borrowed from Western European culture and refashioned by Negroes in the last one hundred and fifty

Reprinted from the *Journal of American Folklore*, 75 (1962), pp. 209–20, by permission of the author and the American Folklore Society.

years or whether it has been borrowed or adapted from the native African heritage." Dollard also allowed the possibility of indigenous development when he observed, "It is always possible, too, that the game has been independently invented by American Negroes." Still, Dollard does tend to argue that the ritual evolved as an outlet for the display of aggressive behavior which would ideally or more properly have been directed at white society. Abrahams, on the other hand, related the ritual to the allegedly matriarchal "absent-father" household in American Negro culture.

Without denying the validity of either Dollard's or Abrahams' interpretations—for there is no reason why one ritual cannot serve a variety of psychological functions—one might still seek an analogous ritual in African societies in the hope that such a ritual might shed light upon the American Negro dozens.

In 1963, anthropologist Donald C. Simmons contributed a brief note to the Journal of American Folklore *entitled "Possible West African Sources for the American Negro 'Dozens'." Unfortunately, Simmons did not find an exact West African analogue for the dozens, so he listed a number of possible sources, e.g., tone riddles, curses, and stereotyped sarcasm plus retorts to curses. Despite some slight similarity of content in the few tone riddles and curses cited with that found in the dozens, the would-be parallels are not really very convincing. The stereotyped sarcasm and curse retorts are a little more promising, but even Professor Simmons himself does not appear to be overly impressed with his own data. He reminds the reader that the mere similarity of folkloristic form can only "suggest" rather than "prove" provenience; and, in his final sentence, he hints that the American Negro dozens may in fact be a form fashioned to satisfy new needs.*

Yet there are reports in the African ethnographic literature which may be relevant. In 1906, an account of the Kafirs, natives of South Africa, included the following remarks: "Boys of the same age tease one another by well known methods. One boy will say to another, ' Your mother is an ugly old thing . . . . Your mother is a crow,' and so on. Strange to say, they do not tease one another about their father . . . . The great insults centre round speaking evil of the mother and grandmother." This is certainly suggestive but hardly conclusive. More persuasive is a report by Philip Mayer made in 1951 based upon his fieldwork among the Gusii (sometimes referred to as the Kisii), a Bantu people whose home lies in the highlands of the southern district of Nyanza Province in East Africa. In Mayer's essay, "The Joking of 'Pals' in Gusii Age-Sets," we find a description of a game or play which involves insult exchange. The game is especially common in adolescence but may be continued in old age. The addressee is not supposed to get angry but he is rather expected to return in kind. Mayer notes that a frequent kind of verbal insult consists of the "use of expressions normally considered indecent, obscene or unutterable." He reported, "Even in my presence, pals used exchanges like these: You excrement, stop treading on me! Excrement yourself, get away!" But, Mayer continues, the true measure of the unique lack of restraint of the pals and the climax of their intimacy is their exchanging of pornographic references to the other's mother and particularly the imputation that the opponent is prepared for incestuous relations with his mother. "Eat your mother's anus!" is a specimen of this kind, or even the direct "copulate with your mother!"

Here then we have a Bantu people practicing a form of verbal dueling among boys in the same age set who are not regarded as quasi-kin but who share a common initiation ceremony, and the high point of the dueling involves a "pornographic" reference to the opponent's mother. This would appear to be quite similar to the dozens as it is reported by Dollard, Abrahams, and others.

If the dozens is a derivative of an African ritual, then it is clear that it did not arise autochthonously in the New World in response to the need for an outlet for displaced aggression. (In fairness to Dollard, one must note that the dozens could have taken on this function regardless of a probable African origin.) Mayer's reporting that the Gusii justify the "copulate with your mother" insult on the grounds that the participants sang the "esimbore" together on the triumphal journey homeward from the place of circumcision does lend credence to Abrahams' theory of dozens dynamics. The song text sung by the initiates refers to the mother's sexual parts and to "intercourse with mother." In this respect, the dozens would appear to be related to all of those rites of passage in which boys become men. As Bruno Bettelheim and others have pointed out, initiation rites frequently involve males denying or repudiating female procreativity. Often the young males are born anew, this time from males rather than from females. The irony is that in the very act of asserting one's masculinity, one is forced to do so in imitation of, or in reaction to, the female role. Thus one way to deny the female procreative role is to deny one's mother. The male's principal weapon is his phallus, and thus, by having intercourse with one's mother, one asserts his total priapic superiority over female procreativity. The Oedipal advantages of such symbolic ritual are, of course, obvious enough. In the dozens, not only are "mothers" sexually attacked, but males attack one another. Abrahams, in his explanation of "to down" as placing someone at a verbal disadvantage, has noted that it may also imply putting someone down sexually, that is, in the female, passive, receiving position. Thus the dozens is a battle to express masculinity. Each male tries to assert his virility by at-tacking his opponent or his opponent's female relatives. He can do so positively *by asserting that he has had sexual liaisons with his antagonist's mother or sister; or he can proceed in* negative *fashion by denying his opponent's virility or that of his opponent's male relatives (father or brother) rather than positively asserting his own virility. Seen in this broad perspective, the dozens would appear to be part of a larger set of rituals by means of which a young man attempts to prove his masculinity to his male peers' satisfaction while repudiating his dependence upon the female members of his family.*

For Simmons' note, see Donald C. Simmons, "Possible West African Sources for the American Negro 'Dozens'," Journal of American Folklore, *76 (1963), pp. 339–40. For possible African analogues, see Dudley Kidd,* Savage Childhood *(London, 1906), p. 198, and especially Philip Mayer, "The Joking of 'Pals' in Gusii Age-Sets,"* African Studies, *10 (1951), pp. 27–41. For a fascinating though controversial discussion of the symbolism of male initiation rites, see Bruno Bettelheim,* Symbolic Wounds: Puberty Rites and the Envious Male *(New York, 1962). For more of Roger Abrahams' stimulating analyses of urban American Negro folklore, see his* Deep Down in the Jungle: Negro Narrative Folklore from the Streets of Philadelphia, *revised edition (Chicago, 1970). For criticisms of Abrahams' analysis of the dozens, see Charles Keil,* Urban Blues *(Chicago, 1966), pp. 20–29.*

"PLAYING THE DOZENS" is one of the most interesting folkloristic phenomena found among contemporary Negroes, because in its operation it reflects so many of the cultural imperatives of the group from whom it is most often encountered, the lower-class Negro adolescent. Since both the forms and the culture are of importance, I will attempt to interrelate the two, pointing out how both function.

One of the most important aspects of folklore, and one which is too seldom investigated, is the way in which lore, both in form and substance, reflects the values and the special problems of a group and the individuals within it. Though adult lore is often a more complex and mature expression of values and problems, the lore of the child and the adolescent provides us with important indexes to a part of the group's life which we otherwise might not see. For the child and the adolescent are going through the process of identity formation, experiencing periods of pronounced anxiety different in nature and intensity from later problems. In the lore of the younger groups we are able to see the performers developing their technical resources within the confines permitted by both their peers and adults, and at the same time attempting to find adequate release for their anxieties. Our knowledge of

personality formation tells us that often the permanent techniques, values, and attitudes operative on the adult level (both conscious and unconscious) are formed during childhood and adolescence, especially if there is any kind of neurosis involved. Any folklore derives directly from the psychosocial needs of the age group which spawns it. But there is an interrelationship of lore between different age groups: a development from age to age (which is especially strong in cases of arrested development) and an effect of adult forms and attitudes upon the lore of the younger members of the group. Thus investigating the lore of the young can cast light both on the life of the young and on that of the whole group at the same time.

The process of "playing the dozens" is illustrative of these psychosocial remarks. It is an early example of the infantile fixation illustrated by the use of agonistic rhymed verbal forms, a neurotic symptom which is observable in many Negro males through much of their lives. More germane to the purposes of this study, the dozens stands as a mechanism which helps the Negro youth adapt to his changing world and trains him for similar and more complex verbal endeavors in the years of his manhood. The dozens are commonly called "playing"[1] or "sounding,"[2] and

[1] There has been some speculation as to the origin and history of the game under this name. John Dollard in "The Dozens: The Dialectic of Insult," *American Imago*, I (1939), pp. 3–24 (referred to as Dollard henceforth) feels that the name may have come from one of the rhymes which went from one to twelve describing the obscenities "mother" engaged in. Paul Oliver in *Blues Fell This Morning* (London, 1960, p. 128) says of its history, "Putting in the Dozens' developed as a folk game in the late nineteenth century," but he gives no documentation for this. Peter Tamony, in a letter, suggests the derivation of the name may come from "DOZEN," v., to stun, stupefy, daze, which can be used both transitively and intransitively (*OED*). If this were true, its etymology would concur with many other Negro words which come eminently from English parlance of the eighteenth century. This would attach an English name to a phenomenon possibly brought from Africa. Newbell Niles Puckett (*Folk Beliefs of the Southern Negro*, Chapel Hill, 1926, p. 23) quoting

the nature of the terms indicates the kind of procedure involved; "playing" illustrates that a game or contest is being waged, and "sounding" shows that the game is vocal. It is, in fact, a verbal contest which is an important part of the linguistic and psychosocial development of the Negroes who indulge in this verbal strategy. This discussion is based on two years of research among lower-class Negroes in one neighborhood in South Philadelphia, and has been enlarged through observations of other similar groups in Texas.

"Sounding" occurs only in crowds of boys.[3] One insults a member of another's family; others in the group make disapproving sounds to spur on the coming exchange. The one who has been insulted feels at this point that he must reply with a slur on the protagonist's family which is clever enough to defend his honor (and therefore that of his family). This, of course,

---

Kingsley says, "The dominant affection in the home is the intense devotion of the African for his mother, more fights being occasioned among boys by hearing something said in disparagement of their mothers than by all other causes put together." This would place the game, or something like it, quite far back historically. The first mention I have found of the game with this name is from a popular "race" record by "Speckled Red" (Rufus Perryman) as quoted in Oliver, p. 128. [There are still other possible but generally unconvincing theories as to the origin of the term "dozens." Charles S. Johnson, in his book *Growing Up in the Black Belt: Negro Youth in the Rural South* (Washington, D.C., 1941, reprinted New York, 1967), pp. 184–85, suggests it may have come from the game of dice. Twelve is one of the worst throws in shooting craps, hence to be "put in the dozens" is to be put in a bad or losing position. See Roger D. Abrahams, *Deep Down in the Jungle*, revised edition (Chicago, 1970), pp. 260–61 for a more recent survey of explanations. One interesting point about the term is that it is sometimes singular rather than plural. For instance, in a text dating from 1915–1916 in Auburn, Alabama, reported by Newman Ivey White, we find: "I don't play the dozen/And don't you ease me in." [*American Negro Folk Songs* (Hatboro, Pennsylvania, 1965,) p. 365.] The singular form is also employed in a recent brief report of the practice from Mississippi. See James E. Spears, "Playing the Dozen," *Mississippi Folklore Register*, vol. III, no. 4 (Winter, 1969), pp. 127–29. The repeated occurrence of a single "dozen" suggests that twelve may be some kind of unit. But the question remains unit of what? One possibility, albeit extremely speculative, is that the reference is to *teeth*. In an essay on Negro language based upon an interview with Dan Burley, there is a curious passing reference to playing the dozens as meaning "clacking the teeth rapidly." See Stanley Frank, "Now I Stash Me Down to Nod," *Esquire*, 21 (June, 1944), p. 53. The association of dozens to teeth is strengthened by the fact that a popular riddle reported among American Negro groups for teeth often refers to "twenty-four" horses (although other numbers also occur). See Archer Taylor, *English Riddles from Oral Tradition* (Berkeley and Los Angeles, 1951), especially riddles 503 ff., 507, 510. There are also references in Negro writing to "flashing two perfect dozen of the thirty two" meaning teeth. See Iceberg Slim, *Pimp: The Story of My Life* (Los Angeles: Holloway House, 1969), p. 160. If the dozens referred to teeth, then putting someone in the dozens would be placing someone in a position to be chewed up. Such a metaphor for an act of oral aggressive behavior would not be inappropriate. On the other hand, this suggested origin is just as hypothetical as all the others proposed. —Ed.]

2 This is the more common way of referring to the game today. "Dozens" is not even understood by some Negroes now.

3 One will occasionally find girls making dozens-type remarks, but for the most part not in the organized fashion of the boys. The boys do not generally play in front of girls, except where one boy is trying to put another down. In this case the game can lead to a physical fight. Dollard seems to have encountered more girl "players" than I have. It certainly could not perform any similar psychosocial function among females, but the mechanism does exist as an expression of potential hostility by either sex.

leads the other (once again, due more to pressure from the crowd than actual insult) to make further jabs. This can proceed until everyone is bored with the whole affair, until one hits the other (fairly rare), or until some other subject comes up that interrupts the proceedings (the usual state of affairs).

When the combatants are quite young (just entering puberty), they are obviously trying out some of the words and concepts they have overheard and are just beginning to understand. Thus, their contest is liable to be short, sweet, and uncomplicated, but the pattern is established:

> I hear your mother plays third base
> for the Phillies.
> Your mother is a bricklayer, and
> stronger than your father.
> Your mother eats shit.
> Your mother eats shit and mustard.

Here the emphasis is on a reversal of roles, with the mother playing the male role, a realization of a basic fact of lower-class Negro family life.

As sexual awareness grows, the vilification of the mother is changed to sexual matters, the contests become more heated and the insults more noteworthy. Many of them take the form of rhymes or puns, signaling the beginning of the bloom of verbal dexterity which comes to fruition later in the long narrative poem called the "toast," and indicating the necessity of applying strict formal structure to highly volatile matters. A sample of a fracas involving two fourteen- or fifteen-year-olds might run as follows: Someone mentions the name of someone else's mother in the course of a joking conversation—"Constance," for instance. At this point someone in the crowd says,

"Yeah, Constance was real good to me last Thursday." Then Constance's son has to reply in kind, "I heard Virginia (the other's mother) lost her titty in a poker game." "Least my mother ain't no cake; everybody get a piece." The other might reply:

> I hate to talk about your mother,
> She's a good old soul.
> She's got a ten-ton pussy
> And a rubber asshole.
> She got hair on her pussy
> That sweep the floor.
> She got knobs on her titties
> That open the door.

And this in turn elicits any of the numerous retorts which are listed in the following pages. Eventually the boys' verbal dexterity increases to the point at which they can achieve more through subtlety and innuendo than through rhymes and obvious puns.

Somewhere between the ages of sixteen and twenty-six, "playing" begins to lose its effect and passes out of frequent use as an institution. When someone indicates that he wants to start, the one who is supposed to be insulted may reply, "Oh man, don't play with me." If he needs a more clever retort, he may rely on the proverb, "I laugh, joke, and smoke, but I don't play." Yet the game is never really forgotten. Any time within the period in which the boys are still running in groups of their own sex, an argument which arises can be complicated and enlivened by some fleeting derogatory reference to a member of the other's family. It has been reported to me many times that the dozens is often invoked by Negroes in the army, under those very tense and restrictive conditions of regimentation for which the young Negro is not completely suited. When it is used under such circumstances, it almost invariably leads to a fight. Similarly, when used by older males in a verbal battle, in such places as a bar or a poolroom, it also ends in a battle. As such, the institution functions quite differently among men than among adolescents.

Among the older males the references to the family of the other are fleeting, and not necessarily directed against any specific aspect of life. Among adolescents, especially the younger ones, the insults are much more rigidly constructed and are directed toward or against certain things. Most prominently, they are concerned with sexual matters. Usually both the rhymes and the taunts are directed against the other's mother, alleging sexual wantonness:

> I fucked your mother on an electric
> wire.
> I made her pussy rise higher and
> higher.
> I fucked your mother between two
> cans.
> Up jumped a baby and hollered,
> "Superman."

> At least my mother ain't no doorknob,
> everybody gets a turn.

Sometimes the rhymes just place the the other's mother in an embarrassing position:

> I saw your mother flying through
> the air.
> I hit her on the ass with a rotten
> pear.

Another common subject is the effeminacy or homosexuality of father or brother:

> Least my father ain't pregnant in
> the stomach.

> Least my brother ain't no store; he
> takes meat in the back.

Whether the game involves rhymes or not, the language which is used is different from the everyday language of contestants. Such linguistic (or paralinguistic) elements as changes in pitch, stress, and sometimes syntax, provide the signals of contest. Just as counting-out introduces us to the world of the children's game, with its resultant suspension of reality, or the phrase "Have you heard the one about ... ?" leads us into the permissive world of the joke, so when someone of this group makes a dozens-type preliminary remark, it can be predicted that he is about to construct a hypothetical playfield on which a verbal contest is to be played.

These contrastive linguistic features outline the rules of the game, a verbal battle. Within specific forms, the rules seem to say, "You can insult my family, but don't exceed the rules because we are dealing with something perilously close to real life." The most prominent linguistic features are (1) the reliance upon formulaic patterns, (2) the use of rhyme within these patterns, and (3) the change of speech rhythms from natural ones to ones that conform to the demands of the formula. These are the strictest boundaries imposed by this game. As the youths learn to use words more securely, any contrived witticism will supply the needed formulaic requirement. Until such an age, it is easier to be clever within the confines of the appointed rhyme form. The use of rhyme is a type of wit.

The verses used in this contest show that "sounding" is a device from a transitional period of life. The technique, length, rhyme, meter, and restriction of form are very like the verses used by children; in subject they look more toward adult attitude and expression.

> Roses are red,
> Violets are blue.
> I fucked your mama,
> And now it's for you.

The rhyme

> I fucked your mother between two
>   tracks.
> It stung so hard, the train fell back.

is very similar to these lines from a children's rhyme:

> Just before your mother died
> She called you to her side.
> She gave you a pair of drawers.
> Before your father died.
> She put 'em in the sink.
> The sink begin to stink.
> *She put 'em on on the track.*
> *The train backed back.*
> She put 'em on the fence.
> Ain't seen 'em since.

Negro children use tricks, catches, and taunts which utilize much the same strategy as the dozens' rhymes:

> Red, red, peed in bed,
> Wiped it up with jelly-bread.
>
> Brown, brown, go to town,
> With your britches hanging down.

But the importance of the verbal contest is something closer to the agonistic structure of adult discourse.

A device which links the dozens to childhood behavior is that of "signifying." This is a technique of indirect argument or persuasion that underlies many of the strategies of children and is utilized more subtly in the dozens. The unity of approach of both "signifying" and the dozens is illustrated in a toast from an older age group, called "The Signifying Monkey and the Lion." In this verse narrative we have a dialogue between a malicious, childlike monkey and a headstrong lion,[4] in which the monkey is trying to get the lion involved in a fight with the elephant. The monkey is a "signifier," and one of the methods he uses for inflaming the lion is to indicate that the elephant has been "sounding" on the lion.

> Now the lion came through the jungle
>   one peaceful day,
> When the signifying monkey stopped
>   him, and this is what he started
>   to say:
> He said, "Mr. Lion," he said, "A
>   bad-assed motherfucker down
>   your way,"
> He said, "Yeah! The way he talks
>   about your folks is a certain
>   shame.
> "I even heard him curse when he
>   mentioned your grandmother's
>   name."
> The lion's tail shot back like a
>   forty-four
> When he went down that jungle in
>   all uproar.

It is significant in this regard that the monkey is childlike, and for his "signify-

[4] For further discussion of "signifying" in relation to Negro life and folklore, see my article "The Changing Concept of the Negro Hero," in *The Golden Log*, no. XXXI, Publications of the Texas Folklore Society, ed. Mody C. Boatright, Wilson M. Hudson, Allen Maxwell (Dallas, 1962), p. 125 ff. [But see especially the essay "Signifying" by Claudia Mitchell-Kernan which appears next in this volume. —ED.]

ing" he gets killed in most endings to this toast. "Signifying" is a children's device, and is severely "put down" by adults. They say, "Signifying is worse than dying," at the same time recognizing that they themselves easily fall into the same pattern, by saying "Signification is the nigger's occupation." Thus the dozens uses many of the techniques of childhood discourse, but places them in a context that leads directly to adult modes of expression. Both the reliance on rhyme and wit and the use of "signifying" remain as major parts of adult male expression, but in considerably mutated form. The dozens signals this mutation.

Many have commented upon the institution of playing the dozens, but few have discussed the function which it performs in the life of the young Negro.[5] John Dollard's article, "The Dozens: The Dialectic of Insult," perceptively points out that the game acts

as a release mechanism for the anxieties of Negro youths; his article stands as a unique document in the field. But his uncertainty as to the manner of release, and a misunderstanding of its psychosocial importance, leads me to make further remarks on the way in which the dozens function. Specifically, Dollard does not seem to differentiate between the dozens as played by youths and by adults. Further, he sees the game as a displaced aggression against the Negro's own group instead of against the real enemy, the whites, a reading which I find untenable not because it is wholly wrong, but because it is too easy.[6]

Certainly these rhymes serve as a clever expression of the growing awareness of the adolescent performers, especially of matters of sex. But "growing awareness" signals the fact that dozens are an expression of boys in transition to manhood. In fact, "sound-

---

[5] R. F. Berdie (*Journal of Abnormal and Social Psychology*, XLII, 1947, pp. 120–21) describes the game accurately in a note. William Elton, in two notes (*American Speech*, XXV, 1950, pp. 148–49, 230–33) indicates a number of places in which the term is to be encountered in contexts literary and scholarly. He ties the practice up with the "joking relationship," especially among the Dahomeans and the Ashanti, an attribution which is both strange and unsound, the two phenomena being similar only in the socially permissive and initiatory functions. But "joking relationships" develop their permissiveness out of a familistic structure, and the dozens do not. See also *American Notes and Queries*, I (Dec. 1941), p. 133; Robert C. Elliott, *The Power of Satire* (Princeton, 1960), pp. 73–74; Dollard, *op. cit.*

[6] Dollard's arguments are tenable from an outside view, because almost any aggression committed by the underprivileged group within a society can be seen as a "substitute aggression," a principle similar to sublimation. But looking at the problem generically, the psychosocial problem of a healthy ego development exists before any sociological situation incurs itself upon the individuals, and the dislocation of the ego through the mother-dominated system will create an anxiety situation that is only aggravated by the fact that the values which grow out of such a system often produce illegal or immoral acts in the white man's eyes. The result, as many have pointed out, is a double standard of law, with acts of violence being tolerated within the Negro group to a great extent, especially in the South. For a discussion of such problems in a vein similar to Dollard's arguments, see Hortense Powdermaker, "The Channeling of Negro Aggression by the Cultural Process," *American Journal of Sociology*, XLVIII (1943), pp. 750–58. (I am indebted to Alan Dundes for this citation.) For a corroboration of my thesis, see *The Eighth Generation*, ed. John H. Rohrer and Munro S. Edmondson (New York, 1960) pp. 158 ff., which is an excellent recent study of gang-values.

ing" is one of the major ways in which boys are enabled to become men in the limited sense in which Negro males from the lower class ever attain a sense of masculinity.

The Negro man from the lower class is confronted with a number of social and psychological impediments. Not only is he a black man in a white man's world, but he is a male in a matriarchy. The latter is his greatest burden. Family life is dominated by the mother. Often a boy grows up in a home which only sporadically has an older male in it; marriage is seldom longstanding, if it occurs at all. Casual alliances are much more the standard. Women, then, are not only the dispensers of love and care, but also of discipline and authority. Women find it easier to support themselves, either through jobs or relief, than to "worry" about any man. This tends to reinforce a matriarchal system which goes back at least to slavery days, and perhaps farther.[7] The concomitant of this system is a series of attitudes which are far-reaching in their importance in the lives of those living under it; most important of these is the absolute and divisive distrust which members of one sex have for the other. Young girls brought up by their mothers are taught early and often about how men are not to be trusted. Men learn to say the same thing about the women.

Growing up in this matriarchal system, the boys receive little guidance from older males. There are few figures about during their childhood through whom the boys can achieve any sort of positive ego identity.* Thus their ideas of masculinity are slow to appear under the tutelage of their mothers. Yet when they reach puberty, they must eminently be rejected as men by the women in the matriarchy; and thus a period of intense anxiety and rootlessness is created at the beginning of adolescence. The results often are an open resorting to the apparent security of gang existence in which masculinity can be overtly expressed.

Typically, of course, the little boys who are recruited into gangs come out of matriarchal families. Often they have little or no contact with their fathers. It does not appear that they get markedly different maternal treatment from that accorded to little girls, but it seems clear that vesting all parental authority in a woman would have rather different consequences for boys and girls, and the spirit of rebellion against authority so prominent in the gang is mainly derived from this source. The matriarchs make no bones about their preference for little girls, and while they often manifest real affection for their boy children, they are clearly convinced that all little boys must inexorably and deplorably become men, with all the pathologies of that sex.[8]

Life for the boy is a mass of oppositions. He is both a part of his mother-oriented family and yet not a part of it. His emotional attachments are wholly to his mother; but as a male he must seek his masculine identity, and consequently must be rejected from

[7] For an excellent, if biased, review of the scholarship, see Melville J. Herskovits, *The Myth of the Negro Past*. (Boston, 1941; rev. ed., 1958), pp. 179 ff.
[8] Rohrer and Edmondson, p. 161. The preference for girls is by no means the absolute rule.
* This may be an overstatement. It is, after all, not just the father who can serve as a source or model for male ego identity. Any older male residing in a household not to mention the young boy's peer group could and probably does provide male models. The fact that there may be conflicting norms of maleness, e.g., as taught by a boy's mother, and as taught by the boy's peers, may, however, be relevant to the dozens. —ED.

his family to some extent because of this. The rejection will occur anyhow, for with puberty comes a distrust from the female members. The result is generally a violent reaction against the world of women which has rejected him, to a life filled with expressions of virility and manliness. Femininity and weakness become the core of the despicable; the expression for these reactions is the gang.

Thus an organizational form that springs from the little boy's search for a masculinity he cannot find at home becomes first a protest against femininity and then an assertion of hypervirility. On the way it acquires a structuring in which the aspirations and goals of the matriarchy or the middle class are seen as soft, effeminate, and despicable. The gang ideology of masculine independence is formed from these perceptions, and the gang then sees its common enemy not as a class, nor even perhaps as a sex, but as the "feminine principle" in society.[9]

However, before any such metamorphosis can occur, the transition must be made by the boy from his mother-oriented to the gang-oriented values. This means a complete reversal of values, after all, and in order to achieve this changeover, a violent and wildly permissive atmosphere must be established through which the boys can express the subsequent emotions involved. The dozens evolved exactly to fit this need.

At the beginning of this stage, the boy cannot openly attack his own mother (and her values) either to himself or to his peers. His emotional stability will not allow him to do this, for his oedipal attractions fasten his affections on his mother. But his

impulses are not unified in this, for his mother (or some other woman) has been the source of authority from which he must react in order to achieve manhood. And the fact that it has been a woman who has thus threatened his potential virility with her values and her authority makes the reversal of his attitudes that much more potentially explosive. Yet reverse them he must, for not to do so would be to place oneself in a vulnerable position with his peers and with the older males. So he must in some way exorcize her influence. He therefore creates a playground which enables him to attack some other person's mother, in full knowledge that that person must come back and insult his own. Thus someone else is doing the job for him, and between them they are castigating all that is feminine, frail, unmanly. (This is why the implications of homosexuality are also invoked.) By such a ritualizing of the exorcism procedure, the combatants are also beginning to build their own image of sexual superiority, for these rhymes and taunts not only free otherwise repressed aggressions against feminine values, but they also affirm their own masculine abilities. To say "I fucked your mother" is not only to say that womanly weakness is ridiculous, but that the teller's virility has been exercised. In this way the youths prepare themselves for the hyper-masculine world of the gang.

But the dozens functions as more than simply a mutual exorcism society. It also serves to develop one of the devices by which the nascent man will have to defend himself—the verbal contest. Such battle in reality is much more important to the psychical growth

[9] *Ibid.*, p. 163.

of the Negro than actual physical battle. In fact, almost all communication among this group is basically agonistic, from the fictive experience of the narratives to the ploying of the proverbs. Though the children have maneuvers which involve a kind of verbal strategy, it is the contest of the dozens which provides the Negro youth with his first opportunity to wage verbal battle.

It is not gratuitous that this *agon* should first arise at the period of emerging sexual awareness. Through the dozens the youth has his first real chance of declaring the differences between male and female and of taking sides in the struggle. The feminine world that has gripped and yet rejected him has been rejected in kind and by a complete negation. (It is not unusual for such complete rejection to occur toward something that has so nearly seduced us to its values.) Significantly, this first "manly" step is done with a traditional manly tool, the power of words. Thus this declaration of sexual awakening and independence also provides the youth with a weapon of sexual power, one which he will have to cultivate and use often.[10]

The importance of these contests is heightened when one realizes that they are indulged in by the very ones who are most conscious of their appearance of virility to the outside. Being bested in a verbal battle in a group of this sort has immense potential repercussions because of the terror of disapproval, of being proved ineffectual and therefore effeminate, in the eyes of peers. This leads to the apparent paradox that those who are most afraid of public humiliation have institutionalized a procedure of humiliation for the purpose of releasing aggressions and repressed instincts, while at the same time learning verbal skills.

It is astonishing to find that the same people for whom ridicule's destructive power holds such terror institutionalize it for therapeutic purposes; they turn its primary function inside out as it were, and ridicule properly conducted becomes a thing to be enjoyed for the health of society.[11]

This is only a seeming paradox,

---

[10] This type of insult contest is not limited to this group. It is found in many groups throughout Africa and Europe, at least. Johann Huizinga in *Homo Ludens, A Study of the Play Element in Culture* (Boston, 1950), p. 65, describes it as follows:

> The nobleman demonstrates his virtue by feats of strength, skill, courage, wit, wisdom, wealth, or liberality. For want of these he may yet excel in a contest of words, that is to say, he may either himself praise the virtues in which he wishes to excel his rivals, or have them praised for him by a poet or a herald.
>
> This boosting of one's own virtue as a form of contest slips over quite naturally into contumely of one's adversary, and this in its turn becomes a contest in its own right. It is remarkable how large a place these bragging and scoffing matches occupy in the most diverse civilizations.

Earlier he has equated virtue and virility, so that the sexual nature of these contests is within his plan. Elliott (cf. *op. cit.*) devotes a major part of his book showing how satire derives from just such contests. He adds the factor of the magic quality of words and how they can have power over an adversary. Oliver, p. 128, sees the dozens as also coming from the idea of casting spells with words. He indicates that the game developed out of a contest of real enmities, with an offended man "putting his foot up" (jamming the door of his cabin with his foot) and singing a blues that "put the Dozens" at the expense of his enemy, "calling out his name." This would agree in many respects with Tamony's derivation of the word (cf. *op. cit.*).

[11] Elliott, p. 78.

however, for the dozens situation calls for extreme permissiveness, which must apply as much to the audience as to the contestants. Beyond this, one would not play the dozens with just anyone, but someone who was safe to play it with.[12] The boys then are developing the tools of battle on their own home field.

As with so many other child and adolescent phenomena, the Negro men from this background never seem to reject "playing" completely. When men do "sound," however, it provides a very different kind of release than when adolescents do. Such maneuvers indicate flatly that the players are in some way victims of a fixation, needing a kind of release mechanism that allows them to get rid of some of their tensions. But with men, the dozens is often used as an obvious prelude to a physical fight.

As an institutionalized mechanism, the dozens is most important to the lower-class Negro youth in search of his masculine identity. It represents a transition point in his life, that place at which he casts off a woman's world for a man's, and begins to develop the tools by which he is to implement his new found position, in a member of a gang existence.

The following is a group of dozens rhymes and replies collected from Negro youths in one neighborhood of South Philadelphia between September 1958 and June 1960.

1

I fucked your mother in a horse and
    wagon.

She said, " 'Scuse me, mister, my pussy's
    draggin'."

2

I fucked your mother between two
    cans.
Up jumped a baby and hollered,
    "Superman."

3

I fucked your mother between two
    tracks.
It stung so hard, the train fell back.

4

I fucked your mother in a bowl of rice.
Two children jumped out shootin'
    dice.
One shot seven and one shot eleven.
God damn, them children ain't goin'
    to Heaven.

5

I fucked your mother in a car.
She hit me in the eye with a
    fucking bar.

6

I fucked your mother between two cars.
Out popped a baby shouting,
    "Vanguard."

7

I fucked your mother on an electric
    wire.
I made her pussy rise higher and
    higher.

8

I fucked your mother on City Hall.
William Penn said, "Don't take it
    all."

9

I fucked your mother on a ten-ton truck.
She said, "God damn, baby, you sure
    can fuck."

10

I fucked your mother in a bowl of piss.

---

[12] As stated above, the dozens is used by older Negroes to start a fight, especially in the army and prison situations. But here we are primarily concerned with youths.

She said, "Hold it, baby, I got to
    shit."
I said, "Shit on, baby, while I fuck
    you down."
She said, "But baby, it's supposed to
    be black, not brown."

11

I fucked your mother from day to day.
Out came a baby and what did it say?
He say, "Looka here, Pop, you
    grind so fine.
Please give me some of that fucking
    wine."

12

I fucked your mother from hill to
    hill.
Up popped a baby named Mr. Sill.

13

I fucked your mother from booty to
    booty.[13]
Out came a baby called Mr. Sanooty.

14

I fucked your mother from house to
    house.
Out came a baby named Minnie
    Mouse.

15

I saw your mother last night,
She was an awful old soul.
I stuck my dick in her hole.
She said, "Gimme some more."

16

Your mother chased me, I chased
    your mother on a sycamore tree.
The tree split, she shit, all I got was
    a little bit.

17

Roses are red,
Violets are blue.
I fucked your mama,
And now it's for you.

18

Yes, your mother's of the
    neighborhood.
She's got a rutabaga [Studebaker?]
    pussy, turned up ass,
She can wiggle, she can woggle,
She can do it so good.
She got the best old hole in the
    neighborhood.
Some people call it the G. I. jam.
A stingin' motherfucker, but good god
    damn.

19

I saw your mother flying through
    the air.
I hit her in the ass with a rotten pear.

20

I saw your mother down by the river.
I hit her in the ass with two pounds
    of liver.

21

Fee, fie, fo, fum,
Your mother's a bum.

22

Ring-a-ling-a, ting, ting, tong.
Your mother's related to old King
    Kong.

23

Don't talk about my mother 'cause
    you'll make me mad.
Don't forget how many your mother
    had.
She didn't have one, she didn't have
    two,
She had eighty motherfuckers look
    just like you.

24

I hate to talk about your mother,
She's a good old soul.
She got a ten-ton pussy

---

[13] "Booty" is an argot term for the female organs, or for the sexual act with a female. See Oliver, p. 189. In this sense the word may go back, as Peter Tamony has suggested in a personal letter, once again to eighteenth-century English; see "Buckinger's Boot" in Francis Grose, *Classical Dictionary of the Vulgar Tongue* (London, 1931), reprint edition, ed. Eric Partridge), p. 56.

And a rubber asshole.
She got hairs on her pussy
That sweep the floor.
She got knobs on her titties
That open the door.

25

I can tell by your toes
Your mother wear brogues.

26

I can tell by your toes
Your mother drink Tiger Rose.

27

I can tell by your knees
Your mother eats surplus cheese.

28

I can tell by your knees
Your mother climbs trees.

29

I heard
Your mother drink Thunderbird.

30

I saw your mother last night,
She was a hell of a sight.
I threw her in the grass.
I stuck my dick in her ass.
I said, "Ooh, bop-a-doo."
Then she said, "How do you do?"

DOZENS' REPLIES

At least my mother ain't no rope
    fighter.
At least my mother don't work in a
    coalyard.
At least my mother ain't no cake—
    everybody get a piece.[14]
At least my mother ain't no
    doorknob—everybody gets a
    turn.
Least my father ain't tall as a pine
    tree, black as coal, talk more
    shit than the radio.
Least my mother ain't no railroad
    track, lay all around the
    country.
At least when my mom fuck around,
    She don't use no Royal Crown
    (hair dressing oil).
Least my father ain't pregnant in the
    stomach.
Least my father ain't pregnant in the
    nose, expecting boogies.
Least my brother ain't no store; he
    takes meat in the back.
Least my brother ain't no store, stand
    on the counter tempting
    everybody.
Your mother lost her titty in a poker
    game.

14 The word "cake," meaning any potential female sexual partner, has probably come from this saying, and has found wide acceptance in jazz circles; see *Dictionary of American Slang*, ed. Harold Wentworth and Stuart Berg Flexner (New York, 1960), p. 84.

Signifying

CLAUDIA MITCHELL-KERNAN

The importance of "signifying" has already been briefly touched upon, but the specific techniques employed and the range of nuances involved have yet to be made clear. Fortunately, a young black anthropological linguist at Harvard, Claudia Mitchell-Kernan, has described in some detail this crucial form of verbal art. Although much of her data comes from her doctoral fieldwork in an urban, West Coast black community, it is almost certain that her brilliant analysis is applicable to oral style in other parts of the country.

After a number of fascinating discussions of conversational data, Professor Mitchell-Kernan makes some insightful comments on the celebrated toast "The Signifying Monkey." Her praiseworthy attention to socio-linguistic context—including her childhood recollection of the first time she heard this classic narrative—makes this one of the finest studies of this genre of folklore to have been made thus far. (For full texts of "The Signifying Monkey," the first line of which often begins "Deep down in the jungle," see Roger Abrahams, Deep Down in the Jungle, *revised edition (Chicago, 1970), pp. 113–19, 142–56; Langston Hughes and Arna Bontemps,* The Book of Negro Folklore *(New York, 1958), pp. 363–66; Richard M. Dorson,* American Negro Folktales *(New York, 1967), pp. 98–99.)*

It is quite likely though hardly easily demonstrable that the origins of "signifying" lie in African rhetoric. For an excellent study of the importance of indirection and allusion in an African socety, see Ethel M. Albert, "'Rhetoric,' 'Logic,' and 'Poetics' in Burundi: Culture Patterning of Speech Behavior," in John J. Gumperz and Dell Hymes, The Ethnography of Communication, *American Anthropologist, 66, no. 6, Part 2 (1964), pp. 35–54. For further consideration of urban Negro speech strategies, see Thomas Kochman,*

Reprinted from Claudia Mitchell-Kernan, *Language Behavior in a Black Urban Community*, Monographs of the Language-Behavior Laboratory, University of California, Berkeley, Number Two (February, 1971), pp. 87–129, by permission of the author.

" 'Rapping' in the Black Ghetto," Trans-Action, vol. 6, no. 4 (February, 1969), pp. 26–34, or the expanded version of the same paper "Toward an Ethnography of Black American Speech Behavior," in Norman E. Whitten, Jr. and John F. Szwed, eds., Afro-American Anthropology: Contemporary Perspectives (New York, 1970), pp. 145–62. For an interesting application of signifying to poetry, see Carolyn M. Rodgers, "Black Poetry—Where It's At," Negro Digest, vol. 18 (September, 1969), pp. 7–16.

1. INTRODUCTION*

A number of individuals interested in Black verbal behavior have devoted attention to the "way of talking" which is known in many Black communities as *signifying*. (See Abrahams 1964; Kochman 1969.) *Signifying* can be a tactic employed in game activity— verbal dueling—which is engaged in as an end in itself and it is *signifying* in this context which has been the subject of most previous analyses. *Signifying*, however, also refers to a way of encoding messages or meanings which involves, in most cases, an element of indirection. This kind of *signifying* might be best viewed as an alternative message form, selected for its artistic merit, and may occur embedded in a variety of discourse. Such *signifying* is not focal to the linguistic interaction in the sense that it does not define the entire speech event. While the primacy of either of these uses of the term *signifying* is difficult to establish, the latter deserves attention due to its neglect in the literature.

According to Abrahams, *signifying*

. . . can mean any number of things; in the case of the toast,† it certainly refers to the monkey's ability to talk with great innuendo, to carp, cajole, needle and lie. It can mean in other instances the propensity to talk around a subject, never quite coming to the point. It can mean "making fun" of a person or situation. Also it can denote speaking with the hands and eyes, and in this respect encompasses a whole complex of expressions and gestures. Thus it is "signifying" to stir up a fight between neighbors by telling stories; it is signifying to make fun of the police by parodying his motions behind his back, it is signifying to ask for a piece of cake by saying, "My brother needs a piece of that cake." It is, in other words, many facets of the smart-alecky attitude. (Abrahams 1964: 54).

While the present researcher never obtained consensus from informants in their definition of *signifying*, most informants felt that some element of indirec-

* The research upon which this essay is based was conducted in a large West Coast city. The data reported here was collected over a span of years, from 1965–1969 in several short periods and an intensive period of one year's duration. The author gratefully acknowledges the financial support of a number of institutions. The Anthropology Department of the University of California, Berkeley, provided support for the pilot work carried out during the summer of 1965; The Social Science Research Council made possible the extended period of research; the Ford Foundation provided support for follow-up research. The author is also indebted to Brent Berlin, Ben Blount, Lilyan Brudner, Jan Brukman, Susan Ervin-Tripp, John Gumperz, Edward Hernandez, Paul Kay, Dan Slobin, Brian Stross, and her husband Keith Kernan, all of whom provided helpful comments on earlier versions of this essay.
† See Abrahams for texts.

tion was criterial to *signifying* and many would label the parodying of the policeman's motions *marking** and the request for cake *shucking*, in the examples above.

Kochman differentiates two forms of *signifying* and classifies them in terms of their function:

When the function of signifying is *directive* the *tactic* employed is indirection, i.e., the signifier reports or repeats what someone else has said about the listener; the "report" is couched in plausible language designed to compel belief and arouse feelings of anger and hostility. There is also the implication that if the listener fails to do anything about it—what has to be done is usually quite clear—his status will be seriously compromised. ... when the function of signifying is to arouse feelings of embarrassment, shame, frustration, or futility, to diminish someone's status, the tactic employed is direct in the form of a taunt.... (Kochman 1969: 32)

Kochman reports that the verbal insult game known in other regions as "Playing the Dozens," "Joning," "Screaming," and "Sounding" is called "Signifying" in Chicago. He notes that the term *sounding*, elsewhere used to label the game as a speech event, is in Chicago used descriptively to refer to initial remarks designed ". . . to sound out the other person to see whether he will play the game." (1969:32) Thus *sounding* is related to sequencing rules

in the strategy employed in playing the "game" in Chicago. As a child in the Chicago area I can remember that *sounding* and *signifying* referred to contrasting tactics used in *Sounding*† (as a verbal insult game), the former referring to direct insults and the latter to indirect insults in the game context. The terms were distinguished by their message form rather than by their position of occurrence in a sequence. Closely related was the activity of "Playing the Dozens" which then involved broadening the target of the insults to include derogatory remarks about the family of the addressee, particularly his mother. In "Playing the Dozens" one could either *sound on* the addressee's ancestors or *signify* about them. *Sounding* and *Playing the Dozens* categorically involved verbal insult (typically joking behavior); *signifying* did not. Labels which refer to sequencing would appear to indicate further elaboration perhaps reflecting greater stylization of the insult game.

It should be noted that the composition of the present sample differs from the samples of both Kochman and Abrahams. The latter two are weighed heavily in favor of male informants and the present favors female informants. The factor of composition, particularly the sex of informants, is important, due to the much greater likelihood of males engaging in *Sig-*

---

* Elsewhere in her monograph (pp. 137–43), Claudia Mitchell-Kernan discusses "Marking" (related to "mocking"). It includes the individuating of characters in folktales as well as making fun of real people through the use of special speech mannerisms. It is not so much what is said as the way it is said, e.g., the mannerism is intended to comment upon the designated character's background, personality, or motivation. —ED.

† Since many of the terms are used on more than one level of contrast (i.e., as labels for the game or speech event and as labels for tactics employed in the game) when they are used superordinately (as labels for the speech event) they will be capitalized.

nifying, Sounding, and *Playing the Dozens* as speech events. There is in addition a marked tendency for such activity to be far more typical of certain age-groups than others. These factors may slant interpretation, particularly because the insult dimension looms large in contexts where verbal dueling is focal. While the terminological use of *signifying* to refer to a particular kind of language specialization defines the Black community as a speech community in contrast to non-Black communities, it should be emphasized that further intra-community terminological specialization reflects social structural divisions within the community and related activity specializations. An admirable instance of *signifying* might well involve a remark laced with taboo terms for a twelve year old boy. A thirty year old woman or man would not likely utilize the same criterion for judging effectiveness.

In lieu of beginning our discussion of *signifying* with a precise definition of the term, we will proceed by way of analogy to inform the reader of its various meanings as applied in interpretation.

The Standard English concept of signifying seems etymologically related to the use of this term within the Black community. An audience, for example, may be advised to signify "yes" by standing or to signify its disapproval of permissive education by saying "aye." It is possible to say that an individual signified his poverty by wearing rags. In the first instance we explicitly state the relationship between the meaning and the act, informing the audience that in this context the action or word will be an adequate and acceptable means of expressing approval. In the second instance the relationship between rags and poverty is implicit and stems from conventional associations. These same meanings of signifying are in currency in the Black community. What is unique in Black English usage is the way in which signifying is extended to cover a range of meanings and events which are not covered in its Standard English usage. In the Black community it is possible to say, "He is signifying" and "Stop signifying"— sentences which would be anomalous elsewhere.

In the context of new analyses we hear the rhetorical question "What does all of this signify?" Individuals posing this question proceed to tell us what some words or events mean by placing major emphasis on the implications of the thing which is the subject of interpretation and, more often than not, posing inferences which are felt to logically follow. Such interpretations rely on the establishment of context which may include antecedent conditions and background knowledge as well as the context in which the event occurred.

Within the political arena we accept such interpretations as natural and tend to feel that they serve to foster understanding of phenomena which might otherwise pose difficulties. We tend to enjoy a common competence at one level of decoding meaning, that is, we can supply dictionary entries for words in sentences and, dependent upon their arrangement, we arrive at a kind of interpretation of meaning. When we use the term "meaning" in reference to analyses offered by Sevareid or Reston we refer to the *signification* or *significance* of the words of our leaders as suggested by these commentators.* Signified meaning in the Black sense has much in common with these kinds of interpretations.

The Black concept of *signifying* incorporates essentially a folk notion that dictionary entries for words are not always sufficient for interpreting meanings or messages, or that meaning goes beyond such interpretations. Complimentary remarks may be delivered in a left-handed fashion. A particular utterance may be an insult in one context and not another. What pretends to be informative may intend to be persuasive. The hearer is thus constrained to attend to all potential meaning carrying symbolic systems in speech events—the total universe of discourse. The context embeddedness of meaning is attested to by both our reliance on the given context and, most importantly, by our inclination to construct additional context from our background knowledge of the world. Facial expression and tone of voice serve to orient us to one kind of interpretation rather than another. Situational context helps us to narrow meaning. Personal background knowledge about the speaker points us in different directions. Expectations based on role or status criteria enter into the sorting process. In fact, we seem to process all manner of information against a background of assumptions and expectations. . . .

2. MORE FORMAL FEATURES OF SIGNIFYING

Labeling a particular utterance "*signifying*" involves the recognition and attri-

bution of some implicit content or function, which is potentially obscured by the surface content or function. The obscurity may lie in the relative difficulty it poses for interpreting (1) the meaning or message the speaker is adjudged as intending to convey; (2) the addressee—the person or persons to whom the message is directed; (3) the goal orientation or intent of the speaker. A precondition for the application of the term *signifying* to some speech act is the assumption that the meaning decoded was consciously and purposely formulated at the encoding stage. In reference to function the same condition must hold.

3. SOME EXAMPLES OF SIGNIFYING WITH ACCOMPANYING EXPLANATIONS

The present section will be devoted to the presentation of a series of examples of speech acts which are labeled signifying in the community in question. The examples will be followed by interpretations which are intended to clarify messages and meanings which are being conveyed in each case.

(1) The interlocutors here are Barbara, an informant, Mary, one of her friends, and the researcher. The conversation takes place in Barbara's home and the episode begins as I am about to leave.

BARBARA: What are you going to do Saturday? Will you be over here?

R: I don't know.

BARBARA: Well, if you're not going to be doing anything, come by. I'm going to cook some chit'lins. (rather jokingly) Or are you one of those Negroes who don't eat chit'lins?

* The references are to television commentator Eric Sevareid and journalist-columnist James Reston. —ED.

MARY: (interjecting indignantly) That's all I hear lately—soul food, soul food. If you say you don't eat it you get accused of being saditty (affected, considering oneself superior). (Matter of factly) Well, I ate enough black-eyed peas and neckbones during the depression that I can't get too excited over it. I eat prime rib and T-bone because I like to, not because I'm trying to be white. (Sincerely) Negroes are constantly trying to find some way to discriminate against each other. If they could once get it in their heads that we are all in this together maybe we could get somewhere in this battle against the man.

(Mary leaves)

BARBARA: Well, I wasn't signifying at her, but like I always say, if the shoe fits, wear it.

While the manifest topic of Barbara's question was food, Mary's response indicates that this is not a conversation about the relative merits of having one thing or another for dinner. Briefly, Barbara was, in the metaphors of the culture, implying that Mary (and/or I) were assimilationists.

First of all, let us deal with the message itself, which is somewhat analogous to an allegory in that the significance or meaning of the words must be derived from known symbolic values. An outsider or non-member (perhaps not at this date) might find it difficult to grasp the significance of eating chit'lins or not eating chit'lins. Barbara's "one of those Negroes that" places the hearer in a category of persons which, in turn, suggests that the members of that category may share other features, in this case, negatively evaluated ones, and indicates that there is something here of greater significance than mere dietary preference.

Chit'lins are considered a delicacy by many Black people and eating chit'lins is often viewed as a traditional dietary habit of Black people. Changes in such habits may be viewed as gratuitous aping of whites thus implying derogation of these customs. The same sort of sentiment often attaches to other behaviors such as changes in church affiliation of upwardly mobile Blacks. Thus, not eating or liking chit'lins may be indicative of assimilationist attitudes, which in turn imply a rejection of one's Black brothers and sisters. It is perhaps no longer necessary to mention that assimilation is far from a neutral term intra-culturally. Blacks have traditionally shown ambivalence toward the abandonment of ethnic heritage. Many strong attitudes attached to certain kinds of cultural behavior seem to reflect a fear of cultural extermination.

It is not clear at the outset to whom the accusation of being an assimilationist was aimed. Ostensibly, Barbara addressed her remarks to me. Yet Mary's seems to indicate that she felt herself to be the real addressee in this instance. The signifier may employ the tactic of obscuring his addressee as part of his strategy. In the following case the remark is, on the surface, directed toward no one in particular.

(2) I saw a woman the other day in a pair of stretch pants, she must have weighed 300 pounds. If she knew how she looked she would burn those things.

Such a remark may have particular significance to the 235 pound member of the audience who is frequently seen about town in stretch pants. She is likely to interpret this remark as directed at her, with the intent of providing her with the information that she looks singularly unattractive so attired.

The technique is fairly straightforward, the speaker simply selects a topic which is selectively relevant to his audience. A speaker who has a captive audience, such as a minister, may be accused of *signifying* by virtue of his text being too timely and selectively *à propos* of segments of his audience.

It might be proposed that Mary intervened in the hope of rescuing me from a dilemma, by asserting the absence of any necessary relationships between dietary habits and assimilationist attitudes. However, Barbara's further remarks lend credence to the original hypothesis, and suggest that Mary was correct in her interpretation, that she was the target of the insinuation.

BARBARA: I guess she was saying all that for your benefit. At least, I hope she wasn't trying to fool me. If she weren't so worried about keeping up with her saditty friends, she would eat less T-bone steak and buy some shoes for her kids once in a while.

Although Mary never explicitly accuses Barbara of signifying, her response seems tantamount to such an accusation as is evidenced by Barbara's denial. Mary's indignation registers quite accurately the spirit in which some signifying is taken. This brings us to another feature of *signifying*: the message often carries some negative import for the addressee. Mary's response deserves note. Her retaliation also involves *signifying*. While talking about obstacles to brotherhood she intimates that behavior such as that engaged in by Barbara is typical of artificially induced sources of schism which are in essence superficial in their focus, and which, in turn, might be viewed as a comment on the character of the individual who introduces divisiveness on such trivial grounds.

Barbara insulted Mary, her motive perhaps being to injure her feelings or lower her self-esteem. An informant asked to interpret this interchange went further in imputing motives by suggesting possible reasons for Barbara's behavior. He said that the answer was buried in the past. Perhaps Barbara was repaying Mary for some insult of the past, settling a score, as it were. He suggested that Barbara's goal was to raise her own self-esteem by asserting superiority of a sort over Mary. Moreover, he said that this kind of interchange was probably symptomatic of the relationship between the two women and that one could expect to find them jockeying for position on any number of issues. "Barbara was trying to *rank* Mary," to put her down by typing her. This individual seemed to be defining the function of *signifying* as the establishment of dominance in this case.

Terry Southern narrates an excellent example of this allegorical kind of *signifying* message form in the anthology *Red Dirt Marijuana*. Here we find two brothers *signifying* at each other in an altercation leading to a razor duel in which both men are killed. One of the brothers, C. K., tells the following story:

(3)

C. K.: There was these two boys from Fort Worth, they was over in Paris, France, and with the Army, and they was standin' on the corner without much in partic'lar to do when a couple of *o-fay* chicks come strollin' by, you know what I mean, a couple of nice French gals—and they was very nice indeed with the exception that one of them appeared to be considerable *older* than the other one, like she might be the great grandmother of the other one or somethin' like that, you see. So these boys was diggin' these chicks and one of them say: "Man, let's make a move, I believe we do awright there!" And the other one say: "Well, now, similar thought occurred to me as well, but . . . er . . . uh . . . how is we goin decide who takes the *grandmother*? I don't want no old bitch like that!" So the other one say: "How we *decide*? Why man, I goin take the grandmother! I the one see these chicks first, and I gets to take my choice!" So the other one say: "Well, now you talking! You gets the grandmother, and I gets the young one—that's fine! But tell me this, boy,—how comes you wants the old lady, instead of the fine young gal?" So the other one say: "Why, don't you know? Ain't you with it? She been *white* . . . LONGER!"

BIG NAIL: You ain't change much, is you boy?

This story was not told for its pure entertainment value. C. K.'s message to Big Nail was that the fellow who preferred the grandmother was his allegorical counterpart. This alleged social type is the target of some ethnic humor and has been explored particularly by Cleaver in his book, *Soul on Ice*. Such an allegation would be considered a deep insult by many.

The preceding messages are indirect not because they are cryptic (i.e., difficult to decode), but because they somehow force the hearer to take additional steps. To understand the significance of not eating chit'lins or a yen for a grandmotherly white woman, one must voyage to the social world and discover the characteristics of these social types and cultural values and attitudes toward them.

The indirect message may take any number of forms, however, as in the following example.

(4) The relevant background information lacking in this interchange is that the husband is a member of the class of individuals who do not wear suits to work.

WIFE: Where are you going?

HUSBAND: I'm going to work.

WIFE: (You're wearing) a suit, tie and white shirt? You didn't tell me you got a promotion.

The wife, in this case, is examining the truth value of her husband's assertion (A) I'm going to work, by stating the obvious truth that (B) he is wearing a suit. Implicit is the inappropriateness of this dress as measured against shared background knowledge. In order to account for this discrepancy, she advances the hypothesis (C) he has received a promotion and is now a member of the class of people who wear suits to work. (B) is obviously true and if (C) is not true then (A) must also be false. Having no reason to suspect that (C) is true, she is *signifying* that he is not going to work, moreover, he is lying about his destination.

Now the wife could have chosen a more straightforward way of finding an acceptable reason for her husband's unusual attire. She might have asked, for example, "Why are you wearing a suit?" And he could have pleaded some unusual circumstances. Her choice to entrap him suggests that she was not really seeking information but more than likely already had some answers in mind. While it seems reasonable to conclude that an accusation of lying is implicit in the interchange, and one would guess that the wife's intent is equally apparent to the husband, this accusation is never made explicit. This brings us to some latent advantages of indirect messages, especially those with negative import for the receiver. Such messages, because of their form—they contain both explicit and implicit content—structure interpretation in such a way that the parties have the option of avoiding a real confrontation (cf. Brown 1958:314 for a similar discussion). Alternately, they provoke confrontations without at the same time exposing unequivocally the speaker's intent. The advantage in either case is for the speaker because it gives him control of the situation at the receiver's expense. The speaker, because of the purposeful ambiguity of his original remark, reserves the right to subsequently insist on the harmless interpretation rather than the provocative one. When the situation is such that there is no ambiguity in determining the addressee, the addressee faces the possibility that if he attempts to confront the speaker, the latter will deny the message or intent imputed, leaving him in the embarrassing predicament of appearing contentious.

Picture, if you will, the secretary who has become uneasy about the tendency of her knee to come into contact with the hand of her middle-aged boss. She finally decides to confront him and indignantly informs him that she is not that kind of a girl. He responds by feigning hurt innocence, "How could you accuse me of such a thing?" If his innocence is genuine, her misconstrual of the significance of these occasions of body contact possibly comments on her character more than his. She has no way of being certain and she feels foolish. Now a secretary skilled in the art of *signifying* could have avoided the possibility of "having the tables turned" by saying, "Oh, excuse me Mr. Smith, I didn't mean to get my knee in your way." He would have surely understood her message if he were guilty and a confrontation would have been avoided. If he were innocent, the remark would have probably been of no consequence.

When there is some ambiguity with reference to the addressee, as in the first example, the hearer must expose himself as the target before the confrontation can take place. The speaker still has the option of retreating and the opportunity, while feigning innocence, to jibe, "Well, if the shoe fits, wear it."

The individual who has a well-known reputation for this kind of *signifying* is felt to be sly and, sometimes, not man or woman enough to come out and say what he means.

Signifying does not, however, always have negative valuations attached to it; it is clearly thought of as a kind of art—a clever way of conveying messages. In fact, it does not lose its artistic merit even when it is malicious. It takes some skill to construct messages with multi-level meanings, and it sometimes takes equal expertise in unravelling the puzzle presented in all of its many implications. Just as in certain circles the clever punster derives satisfaction and is rewarded by his hearers for constructing a multi-sided pun, the signifier is also rewarded for his cleverness.

The next example was reported by an informant to illustrate the absence of negative import as a criterial feature of signifying.

(5) After I had my little boy, I swore I was not having any more babies. I thought four kids was a nice-sized family. But it didn't turn out that way. I was a little bit disgusted and didn't tell anybody when I discovered I was pregnant. My sister came over one day and I had started to show by that time. ROCHELLE: Girl, you sure do need to join the Metrecal for lunch bunch.

GRACE: (non-committally) Yea, I guess I am putting on a little weight.

ROCHELLE: Now look here, girl, we both standing here soaking wet and you still trying to tell me it ain't raining.

Grace found the incident highly amusing. She reports the incident to illustrate Rochelle's clever use of words, the latter's intent being simply to let her know in a humorous way that she was aware of her pregnancy. "She was teasing—being funny." Such messages may include content which might be construed as mildly insulting except that they are treated by the interlocutors as joking behavior.

(6) What a lovely coat, they sure don't make coats like that any more. (Glossed: Your coat is out of style).

(7) You must be going to the Ritz this afternoon. (Glossed: You're looking tacky).

(8) The following interchange took place in a public park. Three young men in their early twenties sat down with the researcher, one of whom initiated a conversation in this way:

I: Mama, you sho is fine.

R: That ain no way to talk to your mother.

(laughter)

I: You married?

R: Um hm.

I: Is your husband married?

(laughter)

R: Very.

(The conversation continues with the same young man doing most of the talking. He questions me about what I am doing and I tell him about my research project. After a couple of minutes of discussing "rapping" *I* returns to his original style.)

I: Baby, you a real scholar. I can tell you want to learn. Now if you'll just cooperate a li'l bit, I'll show you what a good teacher I am. But first we got to get into my area of expertise.

R: I may be wrong but seems to me we already in your area of expertise.

(laughter)

I: You ain' so bad yourself, girl. I ain't heard you stutter yet. You a li'l fixated on your subject though. I want to help a sweet thang like you all I can. I figure all that book learning you got must mean you been neglecting other areas of your education.

II: Talk that talk! (Gloss: Olé)

R: Why don't you let me point out where I can best use your help.

I: Are you sure you in the best position to know?

(laughter)

I: I'mo leave you alone, girl. Ask me what you want to know. Tempus fugit, baby.

(laughter)

The folk label for the kind of talking engaged in by *I* is *rapping*, defined by Kochman as ". . . a fluent and lively way of talking characterized by a high degree of personal style," which may be used when its function is referential or directive—to get something from someone or get someone to do something. The interchange is laced with innuendo —*signifying* because it alludes to and implies things which are never made explicit.

The utterance which initiated the conversation was intended from all indications as a compliment and was accepted as such. The manner in which it was framed is rather stylized and jocularly effusive, and as such makes the speaker's remarks less bold and presumptuous and is permissive of a response which can acknowledge the compliment in a similar and jokingly impersonal fashion. The most salient purpose of the compliment was to initiate a conversation with a strange woman. The response served to indicate to the speaker that he was free to continue, probably any response (or none at all) would not have terminated his attempt to engage the hearer, but the present one signaled to the speaker that it was appropriate to continue in his original style. The factor of the audience is crucial, because it obliges the speaker to continue attempting to engage the addressee once he has begun. The speaker at all points has a surface addressee, but the linguistic and non-linguistic responses of the other two young men indicate that they are very aware of being integral participants in this interchange. The question "Is your husband married?" is meant to suggest to the hearer, who seeks to turn down the speaker's advances by pleading marital ties, that such bonds should not be treated as inhibitory except when one's husband has by his behavior shown similar inhibition.

The speaker adjusts his *rap* to appeal to the scholarly leanings of his addressee, who responds by suggesting that he is presently engaging in his area of virtuosity. *I* responds to this left-handed compliment by pointing out that the researcher is engaging in the same kind of speech behavior and is apparently an experienced player of the game— "I ain't heard you stutter yet"—which is evidenced by her unfaltering responses. At the same time he notes the narrowness of the speaker's interests, and states the evidence leading him to the conclusion that there must be gaps in her knowledge. He benevolently offers his aid. His maneuvers are offensive and calculated to produce defensive responses. His repeated offers of aid are

intended ironically. A member of the audience interjects "Talk that talk!" This phrase is frequently used to signal approval of some speaker's virtuosity in using language skillfully and colorfully and, moreover, language which is appropriate and effective to the social context. The content of the message is highly directive but the speaker indicates by many paralinguistic cues, particularly a highly stylized leer, that he does not expect to be taken seriously; he is parodying a tête à tête and not attempting to engage the hearer in anything other than conversation. He is merely demonstrating his ability to use persuasive language. He is "playing a game," and he expects his addressee and audience to recognize it as such. He signals that the game is over by saying, "I'mo leave you alone" and redirects the conversation. The juxtaposition of the lexical items, which typically are not paired, evokes more humor by the dissonant note it strikes.

Another tactic of the signifier is to allude to something which somehow has humor value or negative import for the hearer in a casual fashion—information dropping.

(9) Thelma, these kids look more and more like their fathers every day. (Signifying about the fact that the children do not all have the same father.)

(10) What time is it? (May in certain contexts be taken to mean, it's time for you to go. It will be said that the person was signifying that it's time to go home.)

(11) Who was that fox (pretty girl) I saw you with last night. Sure wish you'd introduce me to her. (Signifying: I saw you with a woman who was not your wife.) If said in the presence of the addressee's wife this kind of *signifying* is felt to have a highly

malicious intent, because it drops information which is likely to involve negative consequences for the addressee.

(12)

I: Man, when you gon pay me my five dollars?

II: Soon as I get it.

I: (to audience) Anybody want to buy a five dollar nigger? I got one to sell.

II: Man, if I gave you your five dollars, you wouldn't have nothing to signify about.

I: Nigger, long as you don't change, I'll always have me a subject.

4. THE DIRECTIVE ASPECT OF SIGNIFYING

The kind of *signifying* discussed above, involving metaphoric reference and metaphorical significance, may be directive as measured against either the speaker's intent or the effect it causes. The most obvious cases are those in which metaphoric reference is used to insult or provoke a confrontation with the hearer, and such intent is realized by the hearer's taking umbrage. This sort of *signifying* might also be considered directive when the hearer recognizes such intent, but the goal is not realized because the hearer chooses for some reason not to be engaged. However, even when the speaker's end is not realized, the directive element remains from the perspective of intent. (cf. Hymes 1967:22)

At the age of seven or eight I encountered what I believe is a version of the tale of the "Signifying Monkey." In this story a monkey reports to a lion that an elephant has been maligning the lion and his family. This stirs the lion into attempting to impose sanctions against the elephant. A battle ensues in which the elephant is victor and the lion returns extremely chafed at the monkey. In this instance, the recounting of this story is a case of signifying for directive purposes. I was sitting on the stoop of a neighbor who was telling me about his adventures as a big game hunter in Africa, a favorite tall-tale topic, unrecognized by me as tall-tale at the time. A neighboring woman called to me from her porch and asked me to go to the store for her. I refused, saying that my mother had told me not to, a lie which Mr. Waters recognized and asked me about. Rather than simply saying I wanted to listen to his stories, I replied that I had refused to go because I hated the woman. Being pressured for a reason for my dislike, and sensing Mr. Water's disapproval, I countered with another lie, "I hate her because she say you were lazy," attempting I suppose, to regain his favor by arousing ire toward someone else. Although I had heard someone say that he was lazy, it had not been this woman. He explained to me that he was not lazy and that he didn't work because he had been laid-off from his job and couldn't find work elsewhere, and that if the lady had said what I reported, she had not done so out of meanness but because she didn't understand. Guilt-ridden, I went to fetch the can of Milnot milk. Upon returning, the tale of the "Signifying Monkey" was told to me, a censored prose version in which the monkey is rather brutally beaten by the lion after having suffered a similar fate in the hands of the elephant. I liked the story very much and righteously approved of its ending, not realizing at the time that he was *signifying* at me. Mr. Waters reacted to my response with a great deal of amusement. It was several days later in the context of retelling the tale to another child that I understood its timely telling. My apology and admission of lying were met by affectionate humor, and I was told that I was finally getting to the age where I could "hold a conversation," i.e., understand and appreciate implications.

There are, of course, other messages which may intend to bring about some action on the part of the hearer and often succeed in doing so. The directive dimension of *signifying* seems most relevant to native speakers when intent (goals) is aggressive and outcome is bellicose and involves a third party. In this connection, there is a kind of speech act which is labeled *signifying* which does not necessarily involve metaphoric reference. Such speech acts are labeled signifying because ends are salient (although implicit), and the message involves a party other than speaker and addressee. *Ends* are measured against the message's inherent potential to bring about certain effects or from the actual outcome, if known. These effects theoretically involve the ensuance of some kind of ill-will, aggression, or disturbance in the relationship between, not speaker and addressee, but addressee and some third party. This is a special category of *signifying* which does not have a separate label but which is a type distinguished from others by native speakers. It is thus not *ends* alone which differentiate this form from others, but ends which are actually or potentially bellicose, paired with the speaker's intention to direct aggression toward a third party. This is the proverbial

signifying of the narrative poem "The Signifying Monkey."*

One of the most interesting points brought up by informants in reference to this kind of signifying was that this tactic was highly ineffectual in realizing its goal. It fails chiefly because the hearer recognizes the message as *signifying*. It is said that the individual who allows himself to be led by such a tactic would have to be naive, gullible and foolish to an uncommon degree.

In the metaphorical type of *signifying*, the speaker attempts to transmit his message indirectly and it is only by virtue of the hearers defining the utterance as signifying that the speaker's intent (to convey a particular message) is realized. In third-party *signifying*, the speaker may realize his aim only when the converse is true, that is, if the addressee fails to recognize the speech act as *signifying*. In the toast summarized above, the monkey succeeds in goading the lion into a rash act because the lion does not define the monkey's message as *signifying*.

According to Abrahams, "It is significant that the monkey is child-like, and for his signifying he gets killed in many endings to this toast." (1964:55) The monkey's behavior and the child's behavior may have something in common, but seeing too much of the child in the monkey would seem to pose a rather bizarre moral order—if there is a moral to the story. From the point of view of informants, the monkey is wily, contriving and villainous, traits not ordinarily associated with children. The monkey is frequently allowed to triumph in this tale, even to the extent of duping the lion a second time. If

* See Abrahams for texts.

childishness is to figure in the tale, the lion's behavior would seem to parody that of a child more accurately. The lion is victimized, as it were, because he is too credulous. He fails to consider guile and duplicity. His naive view of the world is responsible for his failure or inability to sensibly process intent. He is an innocent and does not operate with basic adult assumptions.

While most Black people would agree that the monkey's behavior is villainy of the worst sort, if any vicarious identification were to occur, it would tend to be with the monkey and certainly not the lion; a tendency which Abrahams notes in quoting informants as saying, "Signifying is the nigger's occupation." The lion is a fool, and it is not so much that he gets his just desserts, but that he is a puppet who moves when his strings are pulled. He wins an occasional battle, but does so mindlessly.

This poem is sometimes recited as an allegory; the animals representing racial types. The monkey may be portrayed as Black or white and similarly the lion. When both monkey and lion are Black, they are not of a kind in other respects.

There seems something of symbolic relevance from the perspective of language in this poem. The monkey and lion do not speak the same language; the lion is not able to interpret the monkey's use of language, he is an outsider, un-hip, in a word. To anyone in the know, the monkey's intent should be transparent. If the lion were hip, he could not have been duped.

We are not always told whether the elephant was actually guilty of the slander reported, but this seems of little importance. Truth or falsity does not lift the asocial taint from the monkey's behavior. For the most part,

the monkey is not seen as motivated by a grudge against either the elephant or the lion—he is stirring up trouble for its own sake. For this reason, he is an adversary to be feared because, not possessing human motives, his intent is relatively more difficult to process. No matter how much his deeds are condemned, however, there is a touch of admiration for his skill and cunning and a touch of disdain for his victim.

Informants tend not to see themselves as potential victims of this kind of verbal behavior and categorize those who permit themselves to be goaded by hearsay as fools. The mere reporting of calumny should be sufficient grounds for suspecting the motives of the speaker. Having grounds to suspect motive should also lead one to question truth value. Crucially, however, because of the potential such reporting has for causing feuds, one should assume that the signifier's goal is to do just that. The outcome of a feud being unpredictable, the signifier is setting the stage for a confrontation which could lead to serious consequences for either party or both. Jeopardizing both parties, at best he is indifferent to the welfare of both. It is the signifier who should be the target of righteous indignation, if any.

When asked if all victims of signifying were fools, an informant felt this to be the case, although she objected to the connotation of victim. She felt that what makes signifying work is underlying animosity on the part of the hearer toward the third party. The hearer must be disposed to believe that the remarks attributed to the third party were actually said. Thus a necessary condition for *signifying* to achieve its goal is a state of ill-will, in which, according to informants, the reported message is used as an excuse for a confrontation, and is no more than a precipitating cause.

When *signifying* takes the form of the speaker's reporting slander alleged to a third party, it is frequently assumed that his ends (goals) are directive. If ends are read from the perspective of outcomes, the hearer most commonly will read the directive intent and the speaker may be the target of ire. If, however, the alleged slanderer becomes the focus of indignation, a state of ill-will is implied. While some individuals who engage in this kind of signifying are said to have much in common with the monkey—their motivations seemingly inexplicable—actual accounts render the signifier far less enigmatic. The signifier is commonly characterized as motivated by animosity or envy, negatively valued but nevertheless very human traits. Not all "tale bearing" is called signifying. In fact, labeling such a speech act signifying appears to be a function of the hearer's knowing or suspecting ill-will on the part of the speaker toward either himself or the third party.

In this kind of signifying, indirection derives from a hearer's attributing implicit directive intent to a speaker's message. The message must have inherent potential for either causing a disturbance in the relationship between the hearer and a third party, or creating ill-will on the hearer's part for the third party. The overwhelming sentiment toward such remarks and the speaker is resentment.

5. SIGNIFYING AS A FORM OF VERBAL ART

We have discussed some of the art characteristics of *signifying* in an attempt to adequately describe and define this speech act. All other conditions permitting, a style which has artistic merit is more likely to be selected than one which does not, because of positive cultural values assigned to the skillful use of speech. We would like to examine briefly the artistic characteristics of *signifying*.

No attempt will be made here to formulate an all-encompassing definition of art. That we may differ in our conceptions of art is made patently clear, for example, by Abrahams summarizing statement that signifying is ". . . many facets of the smart-alecky attitude." (1964: 54) That our appreciation differs has, more than likely, been communicated in these pages. For our purposes, what is art is simply what native speakers judge witty, skillful and worthy of praise. This is a working definition at best. It nevertheless serves to limit our field of discourse and, more importantly, to base our judgments on the native speaker's own point of view.

It is true that poor attempts at signifying exist. That these attempts are poor art rather than non-art is clear from comments with which some of them are met. Needless and extreme circumlocution is considered poor art. In this connection, Labov has similar comments about *sounding* (1968: vol. II). He cites peer group members as reacting to some *sounds* with such metalinguistic responses as "That's phony" and "That's lame." *Signifying* may be met with similar critical remarks. Such failures, incidentally, are as interesting as the successes, for they provide clues to the rules by violating one or more of them while, at the same time, meeting other criteria.

One of the defining characteristics of *signifying* is its indirect intent or metaphorical reference. This indirection appears to be almost purely stylistic. It may sometimes have the function of being euphemistic or diplomatic, but its art characteristics remain in the forefront even in such cases. Without the element of indirection, a speech act could not be considered *signifying*.

Indirection means here that the correct semantic (referential interpretation) or signification of the utterance cannot be arrived at by a consideration of the dictionary meaning of the lexical items involved and the syntactic rules for their combination alone. The apparent significance of the message differs from its real significance. The apparent meaning of the sentence signifies its actual meaning.

Meaning conveyed is not apparent meaning. Apparent meaning serves as a key which directs hearers to some shared knowledge, attitudes, and values or signals that reference must be processed metaphorically. The words spoken may actually refer to this shared knowledge by contradicting it or by giving what is known to be an impossible explanation of some obvious fact. The indirection, then, depends for its decoding upon shared knowledge of the participants, and this shared knowledge operates on two levels.

It must be employed, first of all, by the participants in a speech act in the recognition that *signifying* is occurring and that the dictionary-syntactical meaning of the utterance is to be ignored. Secondly, this shared knowledge must be employed in the reinterpretation of the utterance. It is the cleverness used in directing the attention of the hearer and audience to this shared knowledge upon which a speaker's artistic talent is judged.

Topic may have something to do with the artistic merit of an act of *signifying*. Although practically any topic may be signified about, some topics are more likely to make the overall act of signifying more appreciated. Sex is one such topic. For example, an individual offering an explanation for a friend's recent grade slump quipped, "He can't forget what happened to him underneath the apple tree," implying that the young man was preoccupied with sex at this point in his life and that the preoccupation stemmed from the relative novelty of the experience. A topic which is suggested by on-going conversation is appreciated more than one which is peripheral. Finally, an act of *signifying* which tops a preceding one, in a verbal dueling sense, is especially appreciated.

Kochman cites such an example in the context of a discussion of *rapping*:

A man coming from the bathroom forgot to zip his pants. An unescorted party of women kept watching him and laughing among themselves. The man's friends hip (inform) him to what's going on. He approaches one woman—"Hey, baby, did you see that big Cadillac with the full tires, ready to roll in action just for you?" She answers, "No, motherfucker, but I saw a little gray Volkswagen with two flat tires."

As mentioned earlier, *signifying* may be a tactic used in rapping, defined by Kochman as ". . . a fluent and lively way of talking, always characterized by a high degree of personal style." (1969:27)

Verbal dueling is clearly occurring; the first act of *signifying* is an indirect and humorous way of referring to shared knowledge—the women have been laughing at the man's predicament. It is indirect in that it doesn't mention what is obviously being referred to. The speaker has cleverly capitalized on a potentially embarrassing situation by taking the offensive and, at the same time, displaying his verbal skill. He emphasizes the sexual aspect of the situation with a metaphor that implies power and class. He is however, as Kochman says, "capped." The woman wins the verbal duel by replying with an act of *signifying* which builds on the previous one. The reply is indirect, sexual and appropriate to the situation. In addition, it employs the same kind of metaphor and is, therefore, very effective.

Motherfucker is a rather common term of address in such acts of verbal dueling. The term *nigger* also is common in such contexts. For example: "Nigger, it was a monkey one time wasn't satisfied till his ass was grass." and "Nigger, I'm gon be like white on rice on your ass."

These two examples are illustrative of a number of points of good *signifying*. Both depend on a good deal of shared cultural knowledge for their correct semantic interpretation. It is the intricacy of the allusion to shared knowledge that makes for the success of these speech acts. The first refers to the toast, "The Signifying Monkey." The monkey signified at the lion until he got himself in trouble. A knowledge of this toast is necessary for an interpretation of the message. "Until his ass was grass" can only be understood in the light of its common use in the speech of members of the culture—meaning, until he was beaten up—and occurs in

such forms as "His ass was grass and I was the lawnmower." What this example means is something like: "You have been signifying at me and like the monkey, you are treading on dangerously thin ice. If you don't stop, I am likely to become angry and beat you!"

"Nigger, I'm gon be like white on rice on your ass" is doubly clever. A common way of threatening to beat someone is to say, "I'm gonna be all over your ass." And how is white on rice?— all over it. Metaphors such as these may lose their effectiveness over time due to overuse. They lose value as clever wit.

The use of the term *nigger* in these examples is of interest. It is often coupled with the use of code features which are furthest removed from SE.* That is, the code utilizes many linguistic markers which differentiate Black speech from SE or white speech. Frequently, more such markers than might ordinarily appear in the language of the speaker are used. Interestingly, the use of the term *nigger* with other BE markers has the effect of "smiling when you say that." The use of SE with *nigger*, in the words of an informant is "The wrong tone of voice" and may be taken as abusive.

It would seem that the use of these terms and this style of language serve the same function. They both serve to emphasize that BE is being used and that what is being engaged in is a Black speech act. This serves a function other than simply emphasizing group solidarity. It signals to the hearer that this is an instance of Black verbal art and should be interpreted in terms of the subcultural rules for interpreting such speech acts.

---

* SE is Standard English; BE is Black English. BE is surely a far better term than the value-laden term used by some white linguists: NNE, Non-Standard Negro English! —ED.

Such features serve to define the style being used, indicate its tone, and to describe the setting and participants as being appropriate to the use of such an artistic style. Further, such features indicate that it should be recognized that a verbal duel is occurring and that what is said is meant in a joking, perhaps also threatening, manner. A slight switch in code may carry implications for other components in the speech act. Because verbal dueling treads a fine line between play and real aggression, it is a kind of linguistic activity which requires strict adherence to socio-linguistic rules. To correctly decode the message, a hearer must be finely tuned to values which he observes in relation to all other components of the speech act. To do so he must rely on his conscious or unconscious knowledge of the socio-linguistic rules attached to this usage. Meaning, often assumed by linguists to be signaled entirely through code features, is actually dependent upon a consideration of other components of a speech act (cf. Gumperz 1964:196). A remark taken in the spirit of verbal dueling may, for example, be interpreted as insult by virtue of what on the surface seems to be merely a minor change in personnel or a minor change in topic. Crucially, paralinguistic features must be made to conform appropriately to the rules. Change in posture, speech rate, tone of voice, facial expression, etc., may signal a change in meaning. The audience must also be sensitive to these cues. A change in meaning may signal that members of the audience must shift their responses and that metalinguistic comments may no longer be appropriate.

It is this focus in Black culture—the necessity of applying sociolinguistic rules, in addition to the frequent appeal to shared background knowledge for correct semantic interpretation—that accounts for some of the unique character and flavor of Black speech. There is an elaboration of the ability to carefully and skillfully manipulate other components of the speech act in relation to code to signal meaning, rather than pure syntactic and lexical elaboration.

6. SUMMARY

Signifying is defined by message form and function. All messages involve a topic and a function. If we examine the social rules which govern the use of the message form, we find that they relate to the topic and ends of the message and not to the form itself. That is to say, if the topic is permissive of joking, and the goal is appropriate to the setting and the participants, this message form is appropriate. In instances where such harmony obtains, this message form adds an intensity or potency factor to the component defined by Hymes as *ends*. The same is true when topic and ends are judged inappropriate to setting and participants. Thus, if the goal is to make an observation which has humor value and this outcome obtains, the joke is more effective, funnier. If the outcome finds the hearer insulted, *signifying* causes the insult to be more grave. *Key* is used here, following Hymes, as the tone or spirit in which *signifying* is taken and relates to the goals hearers and audience attribute to the speaker. Such goals are governed by rules of usage which dictate how particular ends may be appropriately realized and under what circumstances a given purpose is socially acceptable. Thus, if it is inappropriate for a fifteen-year-old boy to accuse his mother of lying, it is also inappropriate for him to imply she is lying. With regard to topics to which some form of taboo is attached, *signifying*, due to its metaphorical reference, may represent an attempt to be deliberately euphemistic. In such cases, where taboo is not absolute, the use of *signifying* may remove the taboo stigma.

The form of *signifying*, in which the speaker's disguised directive intent is considered an effort to disturb relations between addressee and a third party, is considered a highly antisocial act and, in the context of everyday social interaction, is taboo. It may be met by calculated coldness on the part of the addressee or a more active form of censure, depending on temperament.

It may, however, be employed as a technique in verbal dueling, where the emphasis is recognizably game behavior. Verbal dueling is essentially a kind of speech event, in which a variety of speech acts may be performed competitively, including *signifying*, *sounding* and *playing the dozens*, where competition is apparent and the goal is essentially to get the better of another individual verbally (cf. Labov 1968; Abrahams 1964). Verbal dueling, as a speech event, occurs, if not exclusively

between males, almost so. This is not to say that no woman ever engages in such speech acts as *sounding* or *playing the dozens*, but when she does, they are typically not in the context of the speech event "verbal dueling." Because verbal dueling permits a great deal of license (not absolute in any sense), women cannot be suitably competitive because other social norms require more circumspection in their verbal behavior.

Verbal joking behavior has a high frequency of occurrence among solidary Blacks. By joking behavior we mean simply teasing and ridicule, which override in many respects norms of politeness which operate in other nonjoking contexts. In the context of joking behavior, remarks, which might ordinarily find a hearer taking umbrage, are taken in good sport in accordance with expectation. *Signifying* frequently occurs in such contexts, as mentioned earlier, and tends to make joking more effective, chiefly due to the artistry involved in metaphorical reference. Metaphorical reference would never be any individual's primary, or even predominant, means of conveying meaning. It has the status of an artistic variant more than anything else.

REFERENCES

ABRAHAMS, ROGER D. *Deep Down in the Jungle: Negro Narrative Folklore from the Streets of Philadelphia*. Hatboro, Pennsylvania, Folklore Associates, 1964.
BROWN, ROGER. *Words and Things*. Glencoe, Il.: Free Press, 1958.
GUMPERZ, JOHN J. "Linguistic and Social Interaction in Two Communities," in "The Ethnography of Communication," ed. J. J. Gumperz and D. Hymes. *American Anthropologist*, 66 (1964) no. 6, Part 2, pp. 137–53.
HYMES, DELL. "Models of the Interaction of Language and Social Setting," in "Problems of Bilingualism," ed. J. MacNamara. *Journal of Social Issues*, 23 (1967) no. 2, pp. 8–28.
KOCHMAN, THOMAS. " 'Rapping' in the Black Ghetto." *Trans-Action*, 6 (1969) no. 4, pp. 26–34.
LABOV, WILLIAM, *et al*. *A Study of the Non-Standard English of Negro and Puerto Rican Speakers in New York City*. Cooperative Research Project No. 3288, vols. I and II (1968).

Toasts

WILLIAM LABOV, PAUL COHEN, CLARENCE ROBINS, AND JOHN LEWIS

"The Signifying Monkey" is only one example of a genre of American Negro folklore called the toast. There are other equally popular toasts, e.g., "The Titanic" or "Shine," and "Stagolee" (which also exists in folksong form). Toasts are narrative poems, which are frequently epical in nature, involving an extended battle between protagonists. They represent one of the most elaborate poetic forms of American Negro oral art.

Genteel middle-class readers, black as well as white, will no doubt find the following detailed discussion of the content and stylistic features of toasts highly distasteful. It is true that much of the toast's lexicon consists of words which are adjudged obscene by the norms of middle-class morality. It is very likely in fact that the inclusion of this treatment of the toast (along with the previous discussions of the dozens) will unfortunately result in censors' attempts to keep this volume out of many libraries, private and public. Nevertheless, no amount of goody-goody sermonizing can in any way alter the fact that the toast is a dynamic form of contemporary American Negro folklore. Any survey of American Negro folklore which claims to offer comprehensive coverage simply cannot ignore the toast.

Although the approach to the data in the following essay is essentially linguistic rather than folkloristic, we shall see in the toasts discussed here some of the values of urban ghetto youth. The materials were elicited in the course of an intensive study of the speech behavior of two Harlem gangs, the Jets and the Cobras. Since the same toasts are known in Philadelphia (as reported by Roger Abrahams) and in Oakland, one can assume that they are indeed traditional. Particularly noteworthy are the delineations of male and female roles. Certainly there is an incredible contrast between the nineteenth-century southern rural

Reprinted from William Labov, Paul Cohen, Clarence Robins, and John Lewis, *A Study of the Non-Standard English of Negro and Puerto Rican Speakers in New York*, vol. II, "The Use of Language in the Speech Community," Cooperative Research Project No. 3288 (New York: Columbia University, 1968), pp. 55–75, by permission of William Labov.

Negro picture of male-female interaction as depicted in the riddling language of plantation courtship formulas and the images presented in twentieth-century northern urban Negro toasts. Of course, the courtship formulas were addressed by men directly to women whereas the toasts tend to be "men only" folklore.

In the toasts, as in the ghetto, the hustler and the pimp are culture heroes of a sort. The black pimp, for example, not only makes his living from the money taken from white tricks (tricks being clients of the pimp's ho's [whores]), but he reverses the traditional dependence pattern in that he is one male who is not *dominated by a female. Rather he dominates his "stable" of ho's. No doubt the widespread admiration of ghetto youth for successful pimps and for their ability to manipulate the system to their personal advantage will not be easily understood by most white readers who tend to regard "pimping" as a very low-ranking activity. However, the evidence from some of the toasts is absolutely clear cut.*

For further consideration of toasts, see Roger D. Abrahams, Deep Down in the Jungle, *revised edition (Chicago, 1970), pp. 97–172. For a better idea of the significance of pimping, see Iceberg Slim,* Pimp: The Story of My Life *(Los Angeles: Holloway House, 1969) and Nathan C. Heard,* Howard Street *(New York, 1968, paperback edition 1970). See also Horace Cayton,* Long Old Road *(New York, 1965), pp. 144–48; and Claude Brown,* Manchild in the Promised Land *(New York, 1965), pp. 37, 104, 109–11, 242–43, 261–63.*

ONE OF the most elaborate and highly developed features of the NNE sub-culture* is the body of oral epic poetry known as *toasts* or sometimes as *jokes*. The lack of communication between NNE and other sub-cultures is most vividly illustrated by the fact that this body of poetry is almost completely unknown to white society, but every Negro man or woman who has contact with the vernacular culture is aware of some of these toasts and is familiar with the tradition. Until recently, white collectors of folklore knew nothing of this material, which must be ranked at the very highest level of achievement in terms of poetic and narrative values. The recent volume of Roger D. Abrahams, *Deep Down in the Jungle* (1964), has done a great deal to repair this lack of knowledge. Abrahams collected a number of toasts from adult Philadelphia informants, including many that we also encountered. He gives several versions of each, with some valuable background and general analysis. Abrahams justly describes his materials as "the greatest flowering of Negro verbal talent." The toasts collected by John Lewis from some of his adult informants seem in some ways to be of even higher quality: we will quote some below to exemplify toasts at their highest level. We will also be concerned with toasts as they are known to adolescent members of the NNE peer groups we have studied, to show the level of verbal skills achieved by some members of the Jets and Cobras.

In the following account, we will draw upon the toasts given by "Saladin," a Negro leader prominent in the nationalist movement in Harlem, to John Lewis. A number of these toasts were

---

* NNE is an abbreviation for Non-Standard Negro English. —ED.

not known before, and among them are such highly developed works as "The Fall."

Toasts are long oral epic poems. Most often there are many complex metrical arrangements, and even within most toasts the meter varies much more freely than in other oral literature. "The Fall," for example, has a quatrain of the form AA B CC B where the first and third are four-foot lines with internal rhyme, and the second and fourth lines have three feet apiece. Toasts are compositions of some size, both in conception and length. "The Fall," for example, has 249 lines. The opening lines show the complexity of the form, the wealth of rhetorical devices used, and the wide scope of the unknown author's view. Toasts are recited in a rhythmic, slightly musical "rifting" style.

> Who's the lame who says he knows the
>   game
> And where did he learn to play?
> For I'd like to tell of how I fell
> And the tricks fate played on me.
> Now if you gather roun' I'll run it
>   down
> And unravel my history.
> It was a Saturday night, the jungle
>   was bright
> As the game stalked their prey;
> And the cold was crime on the neon
>   line,
> And the weak was doomed to pay,
> Where crime begun, where daughter
>   fought son,
> And your father stayed in jail,
> As your mom lied awoke with her
>   heart almost broke
> As they loaded that train to hell;

> Where blood was shed for the sake
>   of bread
> And winos were rolled for their
>   port,
> By the right of a hand of some
>   murphy man*
> Of the words some conman spoke,
> Where the addicts prowl where the
>   tiger growl
> And search for that lethal blow,
> Where the winos crump for that can
>   heat rump
> You'll find their graves in the snow;
> Where girls of vice sell love for a
>   price
> And even the law's corrupt,
> But you keep on tryin' as you go down
>   cryin',
> "Say man, it's a bitters cup."

"The Fall" is about a man of the street who gets a very able whore to work for him. As in many toasts, there are lines where the man reciting the poem inserts his own name as if he had indeed composed it:

> She was a brownskin moll like a
>   Chinese doll
> Walkin' in the ways of sin
> Up and down she trod with a wink
>   'n a nod
> To the nearest whorehouse den.
> But it wasn't by chance that I caught
>   her glance
> For I intended to steal this dame.
> And I smiled with glee as I thought
>   "Oh golly, gee,
> It's time for old Saladin to game. . . ."
> I said "Bitch, dry your tears,
> The old kind lover's here.
> And I'm stakin' my claim at a
>   piece of this game
> And vowin' to have no peers."

---

* According to Iceberg Slim, a "Murphy" refers to a con game played on suckers looking for whores. There are apparently many different types of "Murphys," see Iceberg Slim, *Pimp: The Story of My Life* (Los Angeles, 1970), pp. 38–40, 316. See also Claude Brown, *Manchild in the Promised Land* (New York, 1965), pp. 154–56. —ED.

Now, Jack, the whore looked at me like
    a slave set free
Said "Daddy, I'll be your girl."
And her man didn't stir as I split
    with her.
We made it all over the world.

There follow many observations on the professional problems of the pimp's trade, and the kind of trouble that most whores give. But this particular girl was exceptional:

But a whore got to go to be a real
    class whore
To beat this triple bitch of mine,
Like a sex machine she stood
    between
Raindrops, snow, and hail.
She stood on hot bricks to have her
    tricks*
Come cyclone, blizzard or gale.
She tricked with the Frenchmen
    torpedo 'n the henchmen
To her they were all the same.
She tricked with the Greeks,
    Arabs and freaks
And breeds I cannot name.
She tricked with the Jews, Apaches and
    Siouxs
She even tricked in the house of God.
For there wasn't a son of a gun who
    this whore couldn't shun
That played to claim a rod.

The hero confesses without shame that

he spent all of the money coming in on dope. But as his "habit got taller," his "money got smaller." When finally his whore takes sick, the narrator decides to get him another woman. He is roundly denounced by her for this idea; she warns him,

"May the black coats of sorrow pick
    your ass up tomorrow
If you walk beyond that door."

The protagonist then explains the ethics of the trade to her in the following language:

"Whore, you ain't no lame, you
    know the game,
Then call it cop and blow.
You had your run, now you done,
I'm goin' to get me another whore.
I can't make no swag off no swayback
    nag
Whose thoroughbred days are past,
Why I'd look damn silly puttin' a
    cripple filly
On a track that's way too fast.
I might have put you in charge of a
    whore house lodge,
Or give you some girl of your own
    to rule,
But you spoke of hell and sending me
    to jail,
Bitch, you must be a goddam fool.
Cause a whore ain't shit without a good
    man's wit,
And one monkey don't stop no show.

---

* The use of the term "trick" for a prostitute's customer goes back at least to the first decades of the twentieth century. In a song text reported but not explained by Odum and Johnson, there is a reference to someone's being unable to enter his woman's room because she has an "all-night trick," that is, a customer who has paid to stay through the night. For the text, see Howard W. Odum and Guy B. Johnson, *The Negro and His Songs* (Chapel Hill, 1925), pp. 189–90 (or this volume, pp. 263–4), or Louis Armstrong, *Satchmo, My Life in New Orleans* (Englewood Cliffs, 1954), p. 8. It is tempting to speculate about the use of the term in Negro tradition in connection with the term "trick" as used in conjuration. Love charms which could magically force a man to seek a woman were, after all, one extremely popular type of conjuration. One informant from South Carolina reported that "trickin' a man" referred to making a man do what one wanted him to do without hurting him. See Harry Middleton Hyatt, *Hoodoo-Conjuration-Witchcraft-Rootwork* (Washington, D.C., 1970), vol. I, p. 668. For examples of conjure tricks, see Hyatt, pp. 260–69, or the essay "Conjuring and Conjure-Doctors" by Leonora Herron and Alice M. Bacon in this volume. —ED.

In a hour or two I'll have me a goddam
    slew
Of bitches out there to whore.
So step aside cause I'm fixin' to
    slide,
I mean, get the fuck up off my back
Cause my poke is low and I need me
    a whore
To run me a steady track."

The complex rhetoric of this statement is
worth noting. The race-track metaphor
is extended over the whole second
quatrain, and then reintroduced in the
final line. The author shows great skill
in incorporating apothegms—short,
proverbial sentences—which make his
general point with force. First he
observes, "a whore ain't shit without a
good man's wit," and then adds "One
monkey don't stop no show": a rhetoric
is used to express the basic values of the
sub-culture which the hero represents.

The whore's claim to special consideration in the light of her past achievement is here abruptly denied. *Gratitude*
or *pity* are not terms which appear in
the rules of the game being played here.
In the speaker's eyes, the world is
abruptly divided into those who know
the game and play according to the rules,
and those who are ignorant of the rules
—the lames. There is no claim that the
game pays off—in fact it is played without profit. The underlying attitude is
one of despair—since there is no hope
of any good outcome, the only satisfaction is from playing with dignity,
and according to the rules. The end
result in this case is "the fall." The whore
denounces the hero to the police: "You
should have seen the shit that bitch had
writ all over the police report," and he
winds up in prison. Adhering to the code
which he endorsed in rebuking her,
the hero concludes with the following

statement:

Now as I sit in my six by six cell in the
    county jail
Watchin' the sun rise in the east,
The morning chills give slumber to the
    slumbering beast,
Farewell to the nights, and the neon
    lights,
Farewell to one and all;
Farewell to the game, may it still be
    the same
When I finish doin' this fall.

There is a more explicit statement of
this fundamental attitude in another
toast called "Honky-Tonk Bud." Bud
is "a hipcat stud" who is arrested by a
federal *agent provocateur* on a narcotics
charge. The judge gives Bud the conventional opportunity to speak: "Before
I pass sentence on you, have you anything to say?" The hero confronts the
judge in the following passage:

Now Bud looked down with a halfway
    frown,
In his hand was a brown felt hat.
He looked at Judge Stern. He said
    "you'll never learn,"
Then he told him where it was at.
He said "I'm not cryin' cause the
    agent was lyin'
And left you all with a notion,
That I was a big wheel in the
    narcotics field
I hope the fag cops a promotion.
It's all the same, it's all in the game
I dug when I sat down to play.
That you take all odds, deal all low
    cards,
It's the dues the dope fiend must pay."

It is important to observe that in both
"The Fall" and "Honkey-Tonk Bud,"
the most important events are speech
events. Though the actual course of
events goes against the hero, he triumphs

over his opponents by his words. Bud goes to jail, but it is clear that his moral statement has shaken the forces of the law. The fact that he foresaw the outcome, and did not avoid it by refusing to play the game, gives him a moral superiority within this value system. The implication is that others would not have the courage to face such penalties:

Now the judge looked at Bud cause
    he was a down stud,
He had done this with many men.
He said, "It would shock the nation
    if I gave you probation
So I must give you from five to ten."
Now here's a note I want the repo'ter
    to repo't,
Bud lost with a grin,
But those who know will tell you for
    sho'
That that same grin went out with
    him.

Two recurrent themes of the toasts are found in these extracts—the moral despair of the hero, and the use of scorn and overpowering verbal force to win an encounter. These themes are also found in one of the most widely known toasts,

"The Sinking of the Titanic."* The commercial ballad of this name contains some blunt references to the fact that most of the poor people drowned because they were down below, while the rich survived. In the toast, the spokesman of the oppressed is Shine, a Negro stoker. He comes to the captain of the ship with repeated reports that the ship is leaking:

Shine ran on deck and said "Cap'n,
    cap'n, I was downstairs
      beatin' my meat
And the water rose above my feet."

The captain sends Shine back down again with the false assurance that all is well:

The captain said, "Shine, Shine, have
    no doubt
I told you we got ninety-nine pumps
    to pump the water out."

Finally, Shine sees that the ship is going to sink, and he jumps overboard and begins to swim to shore. The captain, a beautiful woman, and other representatives of society appeal to Shine for

* For numerous texts of this toast plus analysis, see Roger Abrahams, *Deep Down in the Jungle*, revised edition (Chicago, 1970), pp. 79–81, 101–3, 120–29. See also Neil A. Eddington, "Genital Superiority in Oakland Negro Folklore: A Theme," *Papers of the Kroeber Anthropological Society*, 33 (Fall, 1965), pp. 99–105, which is reprinted in this volume. A version collected by Langston Hughes is contained in Hughes and Bontemps, *Book of Negro Folklore* (New York, 1958), pp. 366–67, but the text has evidently been heavily expurgated. Abrahams, p. 121, rightly remarks that it is impossible to date accurately the origin of this piece inasmuch as the story could have existed prior to the sinking of the Titanic and simply have been attached to this event in view of the magnitude of the tragedy. However, if we assume that April 14–15, 1912 is a "terminus a quo" or "point after which" the particular narrative must have arisen, then we may be able to narrow the possible time period in which the story at least in its present form probably first began. Obviously, a story about the sinking of the Titanic could not have circulated before that date. Then comes the difficult task of locating the first printed text or allusion to the narrative. A passing reference in July, 1920, provides one "terminus ad quem" or "point before which" the story must have existed. Newman Ivey White in his essay "Racial Traits in the Negro Song," *Sewanee Review*, 28 (1920), pp. 396–404, speaks of the grotesque and exaggerated humor of such songs as the one about the *Titanic* in which the hero, on deck when the ship strikes the iceberg, "bestirs himself so briskly that he is shooting craps in Liverpool when she sinks." This would mean that the toast as we know it today must have started sometime between April, 1912, and July, 1920. —ED.

help. They offer all they have, but Shine rebukes them sharply by reminding them how unimportant their values are compared to life itself. (Note that in this toast the regular lines are interspersed with prose transitions.)

After a bit the captain saw the boat
    was gon' sink.
He said, "Shine, Shine, save poor me,
I'll make you the Captain of the
    seven long seas."
Shine said, "Captain on land, captain
    on sea
If you wanna live, motherfucker, you
    better swim like me!"

A pregnant woman asks Shine for help, but she receives no more special consideration than the whore in "The Fall":

She said, "Shine, Shine, save poor me,
My little baby has a papa to see!"
Shine said, "You round here lookin'
    like a pregnant pup.
Go find that motherfucker that
    knocked your ass up."

The last appeal to Shine is from a baby:

After a bit, Shine met up with a baby.
    The baby was cryin'.
Shine said, "Baby, baby, please don't
    cry,
All y'all little motherfuckers got a
    time to die."
He said "You got eight little
    fingers and two little thumbs,
And your black ass goes when the
    wagon comes."

Shine's rebuke to the baby is cast in the same despairing terms that are used by other tragic heroes. When Achilles is asked for mercy, he too argues that we all must die, and that no one can get special consideration.

Ay, friend, thou too must die: why
    thus lamentest thou?
Patroklos too is dead, who was
    better far than thou.
Seest thou not also what manner of
    man am I for might and
    goodliness?
Yet over me too hang death and
    forceful fate.

(Iliad XXI)

Shine is unique among the heroes of toasts in that he survives and triumphs over his enemies in actual deeds. In later stanzas, we find him strolling through Central Park while two lovers pass him:

Shine was strollin' through the park
    one day,
Met two lovebirds comin' his way.
One lovebird said to the other,
"Under your dress your heart lies,
That's what makes my love rise:
Shakespeare, Shakespeare,
    Shakespeare."

He ridicules the sentimentality of the lovers and rejects at the same time the most revered literary figure of the dominant society:

Shine kept on walkin'.
On Shine's way back Shine met
    these two lovebirds again.
Shine tried to remember what they said.
Shine said "Under your dress your
    pussy lies,
That's what makes my dick rise:
Bullshit, bullshit, bullshit."

Shine gives us the most explicit statement of the point of view which underlies all of the toasts: total rejection of the values of white middle-class society. The heroes are all "bad":* they claim the virtues of courage, physical strength,

---

* For further discussion of this point, see H. C. Brearley, "Ba-ad Nigger," *South Atlantic Quarterly*, 38 (1939), pp. 75–81, reprinted in this volume. —ED.

clarity and coolness of mind, and knowledge of the rules of the game and ways of the world. They explicitly reject respect for the law; romantic love; pity and gratitude; chivalry or special consideration for women. Note that these are the virtues which characterize a "gentleman": Shine, Honkey-Tonk Bud and the narrator of "The Fall" are heroes, but they are not gentlemen. Furthermore, the heroes of the toasts defy the values of middle-class society in respect to language: in their use of taboo words and their scorn for sentimental and abstract verbiage. They do not, however, reject the esthetic values of poetry: the intricate system of rhyme, meter and metaphor shows a great emphasis on the poetic aspect of verbal skill. Shakespeare is not rejected as a poet, but as a symbol of hypocritical romantic poetry. Shine's rejection of Shakespeare is roughly equivalent to Romeo's rejection of the empty romantic style which he used before he fell in love with Juliet. Note that when Elizabethan heroes are desperate, they also fail to behave as gentlemen: witness Hamlet with his mother, the violence of Romeo, or Hamlet wrestling with Laertes in Ophelia's grave.

The heroes of the toasts are *bad* by virtue of the same series of "delinquent" or "bad" actions which were noted above in connection with delinquent subculture. They violate the norms of white society in fighting, stealing, cursing, fornication, the illegal use of drugs and the excessive use of alcohol. Furthermore, their attitude toward women is the reverse of that endorsed by middle-class society: they reject chivalry, exploit women and show even more violence toward them than toward men. Some of the violence toward women seems unmotivated. For example, in the toast based on the history of Stagolee,* there are several occasions on which the hero shoots a woman dead on the slightest provocation:

Now some dirty bitch turned out the
    light,
But I had Billy Lyon in my
    god-damned sight.
One little bitch hollered,
    "Stackolee, please!"
I shot that bitch clean to her
    knees.
The other one hollered, "Call the
    law!"
I shot that bitch in the god-damned
    jaw.

But there are toasts which express the hero's anger toward women as a justifiable reaction to bad treatment. The toast called "The Letter" is about a pimp who goes to jail and is deserted by his whore. He begins with the general statement:

I played the game an' I'm here to
    say
There's some no good bitches and crime
    don't pay.
They'll get you into trouble and
    that ain't no doubt,
Know motherfuckin' well they can't
    get your black ass out.

He gets a "penny post-card from the no-good whore" which is quite blunt:

* For texts and discussion of Stackolee or Stagolee, see Abrahams, *Deep Down in the Jungle*, revised edition (Chicago, 1970), pp. 129–42. For additional studies, see Richard E. Buehler, "Stacker Lee: A Partial Investigation into the Historicity of a Negro Murder Ballad," *Keystone Folklore Quarterly*, 12 (1967), pp. 187–91, and Bruce Jackson, "Stagolee Stories: A Badman Goes Gentle," *Southern Folklore Quarterly*, 29 (1965), pp. 228–33. —ED.

I went to see your lawyer, but he
     wasn't in,
Be up to see you soon, but God
     knows when.
But don't worry while they got your
     ass up there
Breakin' up rocks like a grizzly bear
I'm a try my damnedest to keep you
     black ass there.
Love, Rose."

When the hero gets out of jail, he meets his whore standing on the corner, "Bare-headed, damn near blind," and she asks him for a dime. He uses a familiar routine to put her down—one used by Shine and others, but developed with an especially vindictive force here:

I said, "Bitch before you get the price
     of nothin'
A grape got to grow as large as a
     pumpkin.
Rockefeller can't have a motherfuckin'
     cent,
You got to wash and wring you
     drawers for the police precinct
Grab the United States and throw
     it over in Rome
Take a baseball bat and run your
     mammy away from home,
Do like the Hebrew children and
     walk through fire,
Bring me the rock that killed Goliath,
Dig up Moses an' kiss him in the
     crack of his ass,
Look up a camel's back and blow the
     hump out his ass
And if you do all this in
     record-breaking time
I might give you a nickel but not a
     whole motherfuckin' dime."*

This rhetoric of contraries shows the familiar juxtaposition of styles and cultures characteristic of the NNE: Biblical references side by side with the language of the street, geography alongside physiology. But the antagonism toward women is the predominant message. It is not merely a question of lack of respect for women, but rather a serious hostility deeply embedded in the street culture. In considering various educational tactics, one must bear in mind that this hostility makes it particularly difficult for women teachers to deal successfully with the male members of the NNE culture.

The rhymes of the toasts. The quotations given above show that the rhymes used in the toasts are based on the sound patterns of the NNE vernacular. We can immediately see the rules of consonant cluster simplification in such end rhymes as *corrupt* and *cup*; *girl* and *world*; *toll* and *cold*; *cross* and *lost*. Final voiceless stops are often merged in glottal stop, as shown by such rhymes as *port* and *spoke*; *sleet* and *deep*. The half-line, *and winos are rolled for their port* was originally heard by us as . . . *rolled for their poke*. Phonetically the form was simply [poʔ]. But John Lewis pointed out that winos do not have *pokes* (wallets); what they do have is *port*. Obviously the line makes more sense with *port*, after one takes into account the operation of several linguistic rules: (1) final *t* going to glottal stop; (2) vocalization of pre-

---

* This toast is a variant of "A Hard-Luck Story." See Abrahams, pp. 158–60. We see once again a statement of the crucial question as to who takes money from whom. A "ho'" takes money from her "tricks." Thus she is superior to men who pay her. The pimp takes money from his "ho," and he is thus superior to her. Her asking him for money is understood as an attempt on her part to convert him from "superior" pimp to "inferior" trick. This is why, according to the rules of the "game," the pimp adamantly refuses to pay her what she asks. —Ed.

consonantal *r*; and (3) deletion of post-vocalic schwa. The regular operation of these rules is shown in numerous rhymes such as *note* and *report* in Honkey-Tonk Bud: *Now here's a note I want the repo'ter to repo't.* Similarly, we find *blow* rhyming with *floor*: *A crack an' a blow sent me to the flo'.*

There are other rhymes in the toasts which reflect various Southern vowel systems. There is a merger of short and long /e/ befor *l*, so that *jail* rhymes with *hell*; *male* with *Jezobel*; *fell* with *tale*; and *tail* with *hell*. The word *get* is of course [gɪt], so that it rhymes with *hit* (or even with *quits*). The merger of *i* and *e* before nasals is of course quite regular. When this is combined with the deletion of final *t, d,* we have such rhymes as *in* and *friend, sin* and *end.* Finally, it is worth noting that the monophthongization of the diphthongs /ay/ and /aw/ before *l* is complete enough to allow the rhyme of *piles* and *bowels.*

Archaic language in the toasts. The toasts preserve mythical figures of folklore such as Stagolee, the Titanic, and John Henry, and along with them archaic or literary expressions which were known to the original composers. In "The Fall" we hear of "the bitter cup" and "the slumbering beast." In "The Night before Xmas" as delivered by Larry, (see below) we hear "Stranger, stranger, who may thou be?" Mixed with this and other formal language, there is a great deal of slang—some old, and some current. In general, there is some separation of style by quatrain; the beginning and the ending of "The Fall" are more formal than the middle. But even in the beginning, we find such a mixed quatrain as:

Where the addicts prowl, where the
        tiger growl

And search for that lethal blow;
Where the winos crump for that can
        heat rump
You'll find their graves in the snow.

Here we find two fairly obscure slang terms—*crump* and *rump*—following *prowl* and *lethal.* Not only are older slang terms embedded (and eventually transformed) in the toasts, but there are also preserved beliefs and past history of the culture which may be obscure to outsiders. For example, at one point the narrator complains about whores who are drug addicts:

Turnin' dollar tricks to make
        up a fix
And the Chinaman is doin' all the
        pimpin'.

One cannot understand the last line without knowing that drugs were originally introduced into Harlem by the Chinese, and that the Chinaman is still the abstract symbol for the drug supplier. Since the money is going to the Chinaman, he is metaphorically doing the pimping. There is another Chinaman mentioned when the whore falls sick:

But the deadliest blow came when
        this whore
Took sick and could not sin.
The Chinaman spoke, no motherfuckin'
        joke,
I knew this was the end.

We have not been able to identify the Chinaman who appears here as a symbol of death and fate. He is mentioned again a few lines later:

But when lockjaw set in, believe me,
        friend,
The Chinaman took his toll;
For her ass was dead, the lips was
        red,

The lips on her cunt was cold.

To many readers, the toasts may appear altogether obscure. Certainly an extended gloss could be given on almost every line. The process of creative oral transmission insures that the style of the toasts will be mixed, and that many contributions from many generations will co-exist.

The rhythm of the toasts. It was noted above that "The Fall" is written in a complex quatrain form with internal rhyme; the first and third lines are iambic tetrameter with internal rhyme, the second and fourth are trimeter. "The Sinking of the Titanic" makes skillful use of prose transitions, such as:

Shine start strokin' on.
After a bit Shine met up with a
    shark. The shark said:

The line *Shine start strokin' on* occurs between each episode and seems to arouse special enthusiasm among listeners. The prose transitions set off the regular meter of following verses by contrast:

"Shine, Shine, you swim so fine
You miss one stroke and your black
    ass is mine."

Note that the epithets which are inserted in such passages are often additions to the meter that break up the regular feet, avoiding an over-regular pattern such as *You miss one stroke and your ass is mine.*

The word *motherfucker* is used over and over again in just this way; by itself it would occupy a full half-line *A mótherfúcker*, but it is never used this way. Instead we have such intricate rhythms as:

Shine said, "You round here lookin'
    like a pregnant pup,
Go find that motherfucker that
    knocked your ass up."

The rapid alternation of a polysyllabic half-line with a slow regular line is characteristic:

Baby, baby, please don't cry
All y'all little motherfuckers got a
    time to die.

The well known "Signifying Monkey" shows even more complex rhythms though the rhyme scheme is simply AA BB CC, etc. The version given by Saladin uses a rapid, pattering meter which requires considerable practice and skill in delivery:

Lean your ear over here for a minute
I'm a tell you 'bout the jungles and
    a certain monkey in it.
Now this monkey, he ain't had no
    name
But his signifyin' shit was a
    motherfuckin' shame.

Signifying here means the use of verbal deceit to get others into trouble. The monkey starts a fight between the lion and the elephant:

Everything was going good in the
    jungle for a spell
Till this monkey decided he would
    raise him some hell
He said, "Mr. Lion, Mr. Lion,
    there's a big burly motherfucker
    comin' your way
Talks shit about you from day to
    day."

Again, *motherfucker* is a decoration on the basic rhythm which prevents any reversion to a doggerel meter. For example, when the monkey decides to get the zebra involved, he uses these lines:

> The zebra said, "Yeah! yeah!
>   Describe 'im!"
> He said, "He's a big burly
>   motherfucker, weigh about ten
>   thousand pounds,
> When he walk, he shake the
>   motherfuckin' grounds."
> Say, "He a big peanut-eatin'
>   motherfucker, big long flappy
>   ears,
> Been turnin' out these parts for the
>   last ten years."

Note that the toasts use the basic grammatical pattern of the NNE vernacular, but they are not confined to the simple syntax of typical personal narrative. Instead, we have such complex nominalizations as *a big peanut-eatin' motherfucker*, which show the elaboration of experienced adult story tellers.

The best way to illustrate the complexity of the meter of the toasts is to compare them with an example of another type of folk poetry from the white community. "The Story of Adam and Eve" is a poem circulated in writing, which describes sexual intercourse in close detail. The meter is the over-regular anapestic tetrameter pattern, which is usually referred to as "doggerel," and most familiar to us in "The Night Before Christmas."

> Adam and Eve, as everyone knows,
> Lived in the garden without any
>   clothes.
> In this garden there were two little
>   leaves,
> One covered Adam and the other Eve.
> As the story goes, needless to say
> Along came the wind, and blew them
>   away.
> The wonderful sight that caused Adam
>   to stare

> Was Eve's brown little body all
>   covered with hair.
> And the wonderful thing that smarted
>   Eve's eyes
> Was Adam's big thing that started
>   to rise. . . .

This poem is circulated in the Negro community, but it is very distant from the toasts in vocabulary, meter and rhyme. Doggerel inserts meaningless words to preserve the dactylic line, usually conventional "poetic" elements such as *all* in *all covered with hair*. The toasts insert meaningful though optional epithets to add variety to the meter.

"Adam and Eve" shows an SE grammar in the very first line: *as everyone knows*. We find such lines as "And ás nature hád them in éach other's chárms". Not only is the possessive *'s* foreign to the vernacular, but the 18th-century rhetoric of abstract *nature* is foreign to the street rhetoric and Biblical rhetoric used by the toasts.

"Adam and Eve" also forms a striking contrast to the toasts in its attitude towards women. It is a woman's poem (Mr. Lewis obtained this version from a woman) in which men and women play an equal part on the surface. But the sexual details show a concentration on the woman's point of view:

> She clung to Adam as if in a bad
>   dream,
> Her pussy was throbbing and spilling
>   with cream.

The toasts do not share this personal, subjective attitude toward sex, and of course do not take the woman's view at all. Woman is seen as an object, in a much more mechanical light:

> Like a sex machine she stood between
> Raindrops, snow and hail

She stood on hot bricks to lure her
tricks
Come cyclone, blizzard or gale.

Here again, we note the metrical style of the toast uses the attributive *hot* to form a half-line with double primary stress, avoiding the doggerel effect of something like *She stayed on the bricks to lure her tricks.* In both style and content, the toasts depart sharply from the doggerel of the "Adam and Eve" type, plainly derived from a literary tradition.

Telling and transmission of the toasts. The toasts show the combined effects of conservatism and flux that are typical of oral literature. Each teller is entitled to make his own modifications or additions. Sometimes a whole section of another toast is incorporated into the basic framework: that is the case with our version of "The Sinking of the Titanic," which adds to Shine's other exploits a familiar account of how Shine outwitted the Devil. Some toasts, like "The Fall," bear the mark of a single originator of genius from one end to the other; others show no such internal consistency, and are plainly the result of many re-combinations.

A great many toasts are told in jail, and some of the most expert tellers of toasts have spent a good deal of time in jail. It may seem that one reason is the time required to commit several hundred lines to memory. But we find that many adolescent boys know long toasts, and that the structure of the toasts, combined with their great intrinsic interest, makes it possible for one to memorize them with surprising ease. John Lewis played tape recordings of Saladin's toasts a number of times to friends; one day, the tape recorder was

out of commission, and he found to his own surprise that he had learned without realizing it the greater part of many toasts.

The toasts are delivered in a rhetorical style which is quite different from ordinary speech. The meter is emphasized, and the whole style is far from casual. Some speeches are recited in a special voice qualifier. In "The Fall," for example, Saladin uses an excited falsetto in quoting the whore at the moment the police break in:

"That's he! That's he!" she shouted
with glee
"That's the son of a bitch with the con
man's pitch
That made a whore out of me!"

It is important to note that the toasts are heard as very funny. They get belly-laughs from tellers and listeners alike, especially where somebody is shown as beat-up and down-and-out. At such points, the middle-class listener is apt to feel a certain sympathy for the victim which keeps him from laughing. Everybody laughs when they hear (in "The Fall"):

She tricked with the Greeks, Arabs
and freaks
And breeds I cannot name;
She tricked with the Jews, Apaches
and Siouxs. . . .

But it is members of the NNE culture who laugh aloud at passages such as these:

The bitch had the piles, the inflamed
bowels,
For a month she could not pee;
I was shot to hell when her arches fell
Things really looked bad for me.

My woman cried, she damn near died
When I made off with her mink,
But stayed in my role and I stole an'
    I stole
Everything but the kitchen sink.

It is clear that the toasts, and the audience who respond to toasts, are not sentimental. There is no immediate rush of sympathy for the unfortunate and the down-trodden. Though individuals may feel a great deal of sympathy and act accordingly, it is not a part of the social ethic and it is not expressed by the group. Since it is this audience itself which is the receiver in real life of the same hard luck, it might be simpler to say that the members of the street culture do not show self-pity.

Adolescent versions of the toasts. The toasts which we have been quoting so far are the adult versions, representing the fully developed form. This rich body of poetry is well known to the Jets and Cobras. Everyone is familiar with the toasts, though not everyone is able to recite them. It is a matter of common knowledge among the peer groups that some members "know a lot of jokes." The toasts are included with ordinary anecdotes; the same term—"jokes"—is used for both.

The verbal leaders of the Jets and Cobras often excel at a wide variety of verbal skills. Little Stevie W. is one: he is small, only thirteen years old at the time of the study, and from the lower status 200's block. But he was the best singer of the Jets; in the videotaped group sessions, Stevie gives solo performances. He is given a personal handshake from Stanley, President; "Very good, my man, very good!" Stevie is the only member of the 200's block to achieve recognition from the

central core of the Jets, but as we will see, he finds it very difficult at other times to break into the closed circle of the core members. Stevie leads the Jets in their performance of the Jets' song. In a word, Stevie is adept at almost every form of verbal skill in the vernacular culture—though not in the classroom situation. He speaks very fast, with very precise articulation, in a high-pitched voice.

Stevie gave us the following version of "The Night Before Xmas," in a level, high-pitched chant, using roughly the same rhythm as in his version of the Jets' own song. It begins with a parody of "The Night Before Christmas." It is worth noting that this is in the same anapestic rhythm as "Adam and Eve" cited above, but it quickly departs from that meter except in the few lines that are direct imitations:

It was the night before Xmas and all
    through the pad
Reefers and cocaine was all we had.
The [nod] in the corner, coppin' a nod,
One more scratch he swore he was God.
As I went to the phone to dial with
    care
Wishing the reefer man would soon be
    there.
All of a something I heard the clatter
I ran to the door to see what was the
    matter.
As I opened the door, in my surprise
Five shiny badges was shinin' in my
    eyes.

This far, the poem follows the same line as parodies of traditional children's rhymes. The "good" activities of Christmas are replaced with the "bad" activities of the drug addicts. However, the narrative then takes a different line, following the melodramatic implications of the situation, and showing full familiarity with the details of the real-life confrontation:

> Before the cops began to get rough
> I ran to the bathroom, get rid of the stuff.
> As they bang, I stuffed into my vein,
> All I couldn't stuff I flushed down the drain.
> They caught me. But I didn't give a damn.
> They put me in that dark dingy cell
> While I was in there, I met my friend named Snake.
> Me and Snake planned a prison break.
> Over the wall through the muddy grass,
> Snake got caught but I was too fuckin' fast.

This hardly measures up to the standard of "The Fall." Snake does not reappear; he is inserted simply for the sake of the rhyme. The next two lines are an isolated incident following a traditional rhyme (*coal* with *old* after the final consonant is deleted parallel to *grass* and *fast* in the last two lines above):

> I went to my girl's house, she threw on the coal,
> I say "What's wrong, baby, my love gettin' old?"

At this point, the toast merges with "Stagolee," a well-known epic about a bad man who kills quite a few bystanders in the bar called "The Bucket of Blood" in the course of his feud with Billy Lyons. Here only the most famous lines are excerpted from Stagolee, and the toast ends abruptly without arrest or trial.

> As I slipped and slide through the mud,
> I came to this place called "The Bucket of Blood."

I asked this man for a bite to eat,
He gave me some dirty water and a fucked-up piece of meat.

The toast now takes on the character of an ideological confrontation. The hero has sufficient justification for any anti-social action: he has been arrested and imprisoned for the use of drugs, betrayed by his girl, and treated as if he did not exist in a public bar. He asserts his identity in the following lines:

> I say . . . "*Man*, do you realize who I am?"
> He say, "I don't give a damn."
> I pulled out my forty-four,
> I shot him *all* in his head.
> This bitch ran out there, said, "Is he dead? Is he dead?
> I say, "If you don't think he's dead count the bullets in his head."

Defiance of authority here includes the rejection of the whole range of middle-class values as noted in our earlier discussion. The same toast was given us by Larry of the Jets, a member of the core hang-out group of the "six best fighters." Larry does not take the same prominent stance as a verbal leader, since he has other claims to status. In fact he is reluctant to take a central role in the group, but his verbal skill is a matter of social knowledge. In a single interview with Larry, fairly early in the history of his contacts with the Jets, John Lewis used his insider's knowledge of Larry's skill to overcome his reluctance to recite toasts before the microphone.

JOHN L.: In the cats you hang out with, is there a cat who cracks a lot of jokes?
LARRY: No.

JOHN L.: Well . . . How about you, man?
. . . Well, like some guys tell me you would

tell some jokes. Whyntcha tell me a couple of jokes.

LARRY: [laughs] I 'on' know no *jokes*... I've gotta be—I've gotta be *high* to talk *that* shit. I mean, you know. ...

JOHN L.: You can tell a couple of jokes man.

LARRY: I don't know nuttin' now, man.

JOHN L.: Well, you know some jokes. ... Run it down, man! You gotta lotta tape there, baby!

At this point, Larry starts to weaken under the persistence of the interviewer and his inside knowledge. This exchange should make it clear that middle-class investigators will not find it easy to extract the verbal skills of peer group members in a formal situation, and only fairly sophisticated techniques and intimate knowledge will reveal the competence we are after.

LARRY: Lawww... Lemme see a joke. ... Who told you that I knew jokes, man?

JOHN L.: Oh I know you know 'em.

LARRY: I don' know no jokes.

JOHN L.: You know some jokes man. C'mon.

LARRY: Lemmee see. ...

JOHN L.: Some of 'em real natural.

LARRY: Awright, lemme tell you where I spent my X's Day—you heard that?

JOHN L.: Un-uh.

LARRY: You lyin'! You did!

JOHN L.: No, I didn' hear it.

LARRY: Well, you see it was. ...

The toast is then delivered as if it was Larry's own personal experience—not only a poem composed by him, but an account of something that had happened to him. His version follows the same outlines as that of Stevie, but it has some details which were lost in the version cited by the thirteen-year-old. For example, the junky sitting on the bed is described as

> One nod, he knew he was hard.
> Two nods, he swore he was far.
> One more nod, he swore to hell he
>   was God.

Stevie's "Over the wall, through the muddy grass" is here given as

> High water slippery grass,
> They caught Snake and bust his ass.

The bar becomes the "Tip Top Beat" (rhyming with "fucked-up piece of meat"). The final violent episodes preserve several phrases missing in Stevie's version which are important to the rhythm and style of the toast:

> And I said, "Bartender, bartender,
> Do you know who I am?"
> And the bartender replied to me,
> "No, and don't give a goddamn."
> And that's when I took out my
>   forty-four*
> And shot him dead in his head.
> This old raggedy bitch come runnin'
>   out,
> "Is he dead? Is he dead?"

---

* Shooting someone with a "forty-four" seems to be a formula in the toasts. There are many such formulas and this may tell us something about the composition of toasts. Even a cursory examination of toast texts reveals the same dependence upon on-the-spot improvisation so characteristic of American Negro folklore generally. Sermons and blues can be generated using combinations and re-combinations of traditional formulas. The same may also be true for the toast. For example, the formula having to do with proving death by counting the bullets in the victim's head appears in a toast entitled "Jesse James" reported by Abrahams (pp. 163–64). It seems likely, therefore, that the oral-formulaic approach could be applied with profit not only to toasts but to

"Count the bullet holes in his
    motherfuckin' head."

"The Bucket of Blood" appeared in
Larry's toasts as the site of a confrontation between two western gunmen:
Bad Man Dan and Two Gun Green.
This is a version of the tall-tale braggadocio found in traditional frontier
folklore—here adopted into NNE
style. Though the locale is New Orleans,
where many of the Negro badmen such
as Stackolee lived, the rest of the toast
plainly reflects the western frontier.
Larry's version of this toast is given on
this page, as far as he remembered it;
some of his own stylistic interpolations
are indicated in brackets—typical of his
narrative style as well.

It was a cold winter night down
    in New Or-lean,
When Bad Man Dan met Two
    Gun Green.
It was at the Bucket of Blood
    when those two met,
I was the bartender, that day I'll
    never forget.
Lucy Brown, the biggest   5
    money-makin' hole in town,
Had every faggot bleedin' from
    they ass,
Backed into a dick a little too fast.
What? Who's that stranger standin'
    in the light,
No wonder I can't pull no whores
    tonight.
Who's that stranger standin' in the   10
    dark,
No one here, no one but a fart.

"Stranger, stranger, who may thou
    be?"
When the stranger replied to me,
"My name is Nailhead, I come
    from Montana,
Where motherfuckers never go to   15
    bed.
I got a big enough chuckle-buck
    hair backed bone,
Fuck anything hair grows upon.
I died,—yeah, but not as a natural
    death,
I died because a frog climbed up my
    ass and tickled me to death.
I walked through the streets with   20
    war, lightning and thunder,
I walked through the graveyard and
    put the dirt to wonder.
[Tha's right.] I threw a baby up on
    the roof,
Run until he drown in a glass of
    water; therefore it's proof."
And that's when Bad Man Dan
    walked in the bar.
[Yeah—] Couldn't see too far.   25
Then here comes Green. So Green
    says,
"I make a black pencil light brown,
Snuff your mammy's ass without a
    frown,
I was born between two butcher
    knives,
Baptised in the dust of a Colt   30
    forty-five.
[Yeah!] Then Dan fired at Green.
    [Yeah! Um hm!]
"I walked through the graveyard with
    raw lightning and thunder,
I walked through your mother's heart,
    put that baby under to wonder.
I put a baby on to slaughter.

---

most of the major improvisational genres of American Negro folklore. (I am indebted to Gerald
Davis for first calling my attention to the possible application of the oral-formulaic approach to
blues and sermons.) For the oral-formulaic approach, see Albert B. Lord, *The Singer of Tales* (Cambridge, Mass., 1960). For an application of this approach to Negro sermons, see Bruce Rosenberg, "The Formulaic Quality of Spontaneous Sermons," *Journal of American Folklore*, 83 (1970),
pp. 3–20, or his book-length treatment, *The Art of the American Folk Preacher* (New York,
1970). —ED.

I run to the ocean and drown a drop 35
of water [Y'know?]
[Y'know?] Then that's when one hell
of a bet
Started makin' the set." [Y'know.]
Then Bad Man Dan took off for
Green.
What'd poor Green did? Sat up
there and creamed. [Y'know?]
Then Bad Man Dan shot him four 40
in the head.
Green ran out there.
One to the slide—
One to the face—
Another one way out of reach.
[Y'know.]
Then. . . . Then . . . I forgot the rest, 45
man.

It is apparent that Larry does not have complete control of his material. Whereas Saladin's toasts are well integrated from start to finish, this version of "Bad Man Dan" has several incoherent aspects. Lines 5–7 seem to have little connection with the rest. Then the mysterious stranger appears in lines 8–12, and makes his boast in 14–23. This statement plainly overlaps Bad Man Dan's boast of 32–36—it uses the same rhymes and roughly the same images— though Dan's speech is better put together. The actual gun battle between Dan and Green is not too clear, and at this point Larry's narrative breaks off. We can see a gradual development of skill in Larry's versions, but it remains true that the only accomplished tellers of toasts we have encountered so far are adults.

We find the knowledge of toasts, and delight in the sound of them, among Negro adolescents throughout the country. As an example, we may quote from a group session recorded in the "Irish Channel" district of New Orleans with three fourteen-year-old Negro boys: Andrew, Gill and Armand.

WL: Do you know any toasts? . . . Do any fellows around here know toasts? . . .
ANDREW: Who?
WL: Like . . . "The Sinking of the Titanic" . . .
    "Shine, Shine, have no . . ."
GILL: Yeah! "Shine, Shine, save poor me,
    Give you more pussy than you ever did see!" [laugh]

The first request for "toasts" met blank stares; as noted above, the superordinate terms vary widely from place to place. (In New Orleans, as among the Jets, toasts are known as "jokes.") Even the title, "The Sinking of the Titanic," was of little help. But the beginning of the favorite line immediately aroused a response in Gill, the verbal leader of the group.

WL: You know any more about Shine?
GILL: Lessee . . . Lemme see. Shine—lemme see—You know tha's on a ship and the ship was sinkin', an' then a lady say—
ANDREW: The shark say—
GILL: Yeah, a lady say,
    "Shine, Shine, save poor me,
    I'll give you more pussy than you ever did see."

Gill is not the only one who knows this toast; Andrew wants to start at a later episode, but Gill pushes him aside. He uses prose transitions just as in the version quoted above; but in Gill's version, Shine's first reply has been lost.

GILL: Then Shine didn' say nuthin'.
    Shine kept swimmin'.

(In the version given by Abrahams, Shine has an elaborate reply: "Pussy ain't nothin' but meat on the bone / You

may fuck it or suck it or leave it alone
/ I like cheese but I ain't no rat / I like
pussy, but not like that.")

GILL: Then—uh—this man say,
   "Shine, Shine, save poor me,
   I'll give you more booty than you ever
      did see."
   Then Shine say,
   "Booty on land, booty on sea."

The rest of this reply is lost too. *Booty* is
a term used by Negro children equivalent
to "ass"; it has the same full range of
meanings, including the homosexual
one intended here.

GILL: An' den he met the shark. An' the
      shark say,
   "I'm a eat you, Shine."
   Shine say, he say—uh—
   "Shark on land, shark on sea,
   No black motherfucker gonna eat me."

Gill's prose transitions carry more of
the narrative, and the amount of
poetry retained has shrunk. Note that
the epithet *black* (pejorative at the time
that this toast originated) is transferred
to the shark from other contexts. The
balance of Gill's version of this toast is
a "signifying" episode, where Shine
plays the same role to the shark and the
whale that the monkey plays to the elephant and the lion. But in this case,
Shine isn't out just to "raise a little
hell"; he uses his verbal skill to confuse
and confound the enemy, and so come
safe to shore.

GILL: Then he kep' goin'. Then he met a
      whale. He say,

"Mr. Whale, that shark back there say he
   the king of the ocean, king of the sea."
And then the whale say,
"I'm the king of the ocean, I'm the king of
   the sea,
No black motherfucker gonna mess with
   me."
An' then the whale met the shark and
   say,
"What did you tell Shine, Mr. Shark, that
   you're the king of the ocean, the king of
   the sea?" An' the shark say, "No, Mr.
Whale, you got it wrong."
And then Shine got asho'.

After Gill finishes, Andrew says, "They
have another one that goes like this. . ."
and then proceeds to tell one of the
well-known jokes of Negro folklore. No
distinction in principle is thus made
between the poetic form of the epic
and the prose anecdote. At the same
time, the audience and the teller plainly
respond to the poetic form. Prose uses
a plain, conversational prose style.
Poetry is delivered in a raised, "projecting" style, where the rhyme, the
meter and the metaphors are all given
their full weight.

In this fragment from New Orleans
we can see how knowledge of the toasts
is reflected among NNE adolescents.
There is considerable deterioration in
production; but the influence of the full
form is plainly present, and the standards of verbal performance are also
present to guide the further development of verbal skills. The free re-sec-
tioning and re-combination of toasts is
characteristic of an oral tradition which
is very much alive.

Meet "Mr. Franklin": An Example of Usage

NATHAN AND JOANNE KANTROWITZ

> *Verbal art clearly depends upon individual words as building blocks, and so it may not be out of order to consider one individual word in some depth. The study of a single word would normally fall under the rubric of folk speech rather than verbal art. However, because of the importance of this particular word as manifested in the dozens and in toasts, it was decided to include the discussion of it at this point.*

Each lexical item has its own special life history and usage rules. It is one thing to know about playing the dozens and the telling of toasts, but it is quite another to understand the nuances of a single critical slang term. The following discussion is part of a larger study of a prison vocabulary made by Nathan Kantrowitz while he was employed as Sociologist-Actuary for the Illinois Department of Public Safety from 1957 to 1963 at the Joliet-Stateville Penitentiary. His wife Joanne, who holds a Ph.D. in English from the University of Chicago, assisted in the analysis of the data gathered.

The word discussed by the Kantrowitzes is one which many middle-class whites and Negroes find extremely offensive. Overtly, at any rate, the word would seem to concern mother-son incest, which is clearly a source of anxiety whatever credence one places in Freud's delineation of the Oedipus Complex. The anxiety about the word is signalled in part by the existence of a number of jokes about it. For example, two Negro mothers meet on a street. One asks the other, "How's your new baby doing?" "Fine, he learned half of a word today." "Really? What was it?" "Mother!" Still another joke has to do with the alleged widespread use of the word. Two Negro men pass one another on the street. One says, "Howdy motherfucker." The other replies, "Howdy reverend." Whether or not one believes preachers would use the word in public, it is safe to say that one would have

This selection was taken from Nathan and Joanne Kantrowitz, "Stateville Names: A Prison Vocabulary," unpublished manuscript, 1963, pp. xxxi-xxxviii, by permission of the authors.

to know the word in order to appreciate the joke that the NAACP elected Alabama Governor George Wallace "Mother of the Year!"

The euphemism noted here, "Mister Franklin," is only one of a number of traditional ones. Almost any available local name with the requisite "m" and "f" initials would serve equally well. Thus in Chicago, the name "Marshall Field" is used, while in the Washington, D.C. area one can hear "Maryland Farmer" used for the same purpose.

The following discussion concerns prison usage only. However, there is no doubt that the word enjoys great popularity in not only ghetto culture but among the general public, both black and white. The word is common, for example, in integrated urban elementary schools. The age of the term is not known. Folk speech authority Peter Tamony has found a reference in print to the term in John O'Hara's 1934 novel Appointment in Samara, but suggests (personal communication) that it goes back at least to the 1920's. Of course, if there is anything to the suggested African origin of the dozens as discussed earlier in this volume, then it is possible that the English language item is merely a translation of a much older idiom. In any event, regardless of the antiquity of the term, and with or without the blessing of middle-class morality, the locution is becoming more and more popular. Comedian Lenny Bruce and writer Norman Mailer, among others, have helped to bring the word to the attention of the general public. For further discussion of the word, see Edward Sagarin, The Anatomy of Dirty Words (New York, 1962), pp. 139–40, and especially Roger Abrahams, Deep Down in the Jungle (Hatboro, Pennsylvania, 1964), pp. 261–62, whose data confirm the present analysis.

ALTHOUGH SOME people may not consider obscenities and lesser pejoratives an important element in communication and group cohesion, such terms constitute a large proportion of the words used in the male society of prisons, and serve to differentiate the "in's" from the "out's." Some men make a ritual use of oaths by making every noun in all conversations carry a string of obscenities, and others are unconsciously more inventive by also substituting an obscenity for the noun itself. A man may begin by saying "He's the dirtiest son of a bitch" when referring to any custodial officer, and then follow it by his real comment which may even be a statement of regard or respect. In face-to-face conversation, usage tends to be the same whether an inmate is talking to another inmate or to a guard: the reference will be restricted to the third person. In the first or second person, an oath is only used among friends and in joking manner, since swearing at another convict will probably lead to a fight and caution is the commonest device of accommodating strangers or enemies. As humor, however, the use of oaths can become elaborate in games and entertainments such as "playing the dozens," a contest in the invention of curses, or "telling toasts" where participants recite, sometimes for hours, ballads or current popular song lyrics in which the amusement is the clever substitution of obscenity for sentiment and other "respectable" emotions.

The commonest words used are *motherfucker* (easily the favorite among oaths), *bitch*, *whore*, *slut*, *cocksucker* (more common among Negroes), *faggot* or *fag*, and *punk*. Since these constitute the largest part of the pejorative vocabulary of most prisoners, the mere listing of terms does not adequately convey the meanings as they are used in prison. As in the argot generally, their real significance frequently depends on the rhythm, tone, and emphasis of the spoken word to convey subtle shadings of difference. To suggest the range of nuance ultimately possible in this area, we take the most popular term as an example.

Mister Franklin in polite society, *MF* for short, or *motherfucker* is one of the commonest oaths used in Stateville. Omitting what is probably a large minority of the inmates who never or very rarely use the word, and a second large minority who use it as a fill-in word, *motherfucker* functions for the rest of the prison population as a relatively common term with a variety of meanings. The background of its usage varies considerably. One man recalled hearing it for the first time as a grade school child in Dayton, Ohio among poor whites and Negroes. Another recalls hearing it in the middle 1940's in Chicago among white grade school children; still another was raised in Chicago orphanages but had never heard it until 1948 at the United States Disciplinary Barracks in Fort Leavenworth, Kansas, where it was used among whites and Negroes as a "fighting word." However, at Stateville, it became common prior to the late 1940's where it was primarily a term used among Negroes, and considered only an extremely derogatory term, again a "fighting word." Since about 1956, it has become common among both races, and has developed a wide range of positive and negative meaning.

Used alone, as in "He's a motherfucker," the word never has a specific meaning, but depends on inflection, facial expression, gesture, and context to express extreme distaste or extreme admiration. Syllable stress controls the amount of emotional "charge" or "voltage." When used alone, the degree of stress on the first or third syllable is an index of the emotion—the heavier the stress, the more emotion. Emphasis on the first syllable is generally complimentary; on the third, it expresses contempt, anger or hostility. Thus, in context, the term expresses the highest praise—"Is he smart?" "He's a MOtherfucker"—or conversely, the deepest disdain—"Is he a deadbeat?" "He's a motherFUcker."

An added adjective, however, creates a wider range of meaning. My informants unanimously agree that such combinations are common throughout Stateville, and, in present-day Chicago, common among Negro groups and in Jazz circles. Used with adjectives such as *rotten, stupid* or *phony*, the word intensifies the adjective and has no meaning beyond that of emphasis. But, with ten specific adjectives, it forms distinctively new words with their own nuances which vary according to context and reference. *Good motherfucker* implies admiration, approval, or respect regardless of application to persons or situations, and *dirty motherfucker* and *stinking motherfucker* are always considered derogatory terms; the latter is, perhaps, the stronger.

In contrast to such clear usage, *sweet motherfucker* and *fine motherfucker* are synonyms which undergo considerable change. Used with the first person, I'm a *fine motherfucker* or I'm a *sweet motherfucker* indicates an expansive individual who may or may not be a braggart: "...a soap-box stud . . . he brags about his Cadillacs." When used for the second person (among very good friends) as a term of address, *say, sweet motherfucker,* or as a greeting, *hello, sweet motherfucker,* it carries a joking sexual connotation. Used to greet a stranger, however, it becomes an extremely aggressive homosexual term: It's the same as saying "if you let me fuck you, I would." When describing a third person, *he's a sweet motherfucker* usually carries a strong sexual connotation—not that the person discussed is a homosexual, but that he may be desired for homosexual activity. It does not imply that the person described has homosexual traits. Sometimes, *he's a sweet motherfucker* means only a good fellow, someone to be trusted, someone who "takes care of the business"—and the "business" can be homosexuality, gambling, fighting, or breaking prison rules. With the third-person, then, the term always conveys approval, usually has heavy sexual overtones, but sometimes indicates approval for other talents. When used to describe objects or events, *fine motherfucker* and *sweet motherfucker* maintain the general aura of approval. Generally, they indicate something that is physically or mentally easy, usually with the connotation of favorable circumstances. Thus, a "soft" or "good" prison job, a good movie, a good meal, or a well-executed deception of the authorities may be described as a *sweet* or *fine motherfucker.*

Less complex, *jive motherfucker* is a very common phrase which is never used in the first person. *You're a jive motherfucker* always refers to a liar or a fake who is undependable or talks too much. Among friends, though, its meanings range from a pseudo-reprimand to teasing or even approval. With the third-person, its emotional charge is stronger and extremely superlative. In discussing a stranger the term may imply extreme approval or disapproval, depending on context. If the discussion concerns a mutual friend, however, the speaker is always expressing extreme affection and respect. Conversely, referring to an enemy, it states extreme hatred or contempt. When applied to events or objects, *jive motherfucker* indicates an element different from reality, i.e., a phony or a fake, as in the second person reference. *Jazzy motherfucker,* a term seemingly related to a basis in popular music, has quite a different meaning. Infrequently used with the first person, but common with the second and third person, it describes someone fluent, glib, animated. In impersonal contexts, it generally suggests something good or desirable.

Other combinations include *mean motherfucker* which, in the first person— "I'm a mean motherfucker"—is equivalent to "I'm tough" or "Don't mess with me," indicating someone who is not to be trifled with or, referring to the second or third person, someone who is evil or vicious. *Rough motherfucker,* on the other hand, indicates an individual who is physically tough, and always implies respect. *Bad motherfucker,* used with the first person is synonymous with *mean* or *rough,* but referring to the second person, context is again the indicative element. To acquaintances or friends, it is a compliment, but it would not be addressed to strangers because they could consider it an insult. In conversation, the phrase is either a compliment or an insult: when referring to a man's intelligence, it is the former; when discussing someone who didn't pay debts, the latter.

Added to the above widespread variety of meanings are the phenomena of other shadings which catch on within specific groups. For example, in the TV College, at the time of this study, examinations had the following characteristics: A *mean motherfucker, rough motherfucker, bad motherfucker, tough motherfucker* applies to "fair" exams and indicates respect for both the exam and examiner. But *stinking motherfucker* and *dirty motherfucker* indicates a "trick" exam, where "you don't think much of the test or the man who gave it."

The range of meaning for *motherfucker* may appear to extend into non-meaning, but, while there is an element of truth in such a simplification, the word has several interesting characteristics. Certainly, once one is accustomed to the word, it seems to lose all literal meaning and, with it, one's sense of moral disapproval. It could just as well be *father lover* or *country tractor* if the group agreed to use either word in a similar fashion. Certainly, it seems much more flexible than other comparable oaths: words like *bitch* and *bastard* retain

a gender and the connotation of a mother one must apologize for or defend. As used in the Stateville prison, *motherfucker* seems to have a more general meaning of *person* or *thing*. Its connotations are supplied by context, emphasis, and/or the character of the adjective joined to it. As such, it is a word of great flexibility and of many uses. It retains, however, one distinctive characteristic: appropriateness. An inmate may call himself or his friends a *motherfucker*, but it is not a word used lightly beyond that boundary. Spoken to strangers or of enemies, it is still a "fighting word"; among friends, it symbolizes intimacy and trust.

Perhaps the reader has found this an over-detailed explanation of a single, undoubtedly disreputable word. And it may be. But it should also function as a cautionary tale for those concerned with the collection and study of words. Our example is an extreme case, but it illustrates the dangers of accepting entries in glossaries as "complete." As every linguist knows, you don't learn an argot from a dictionary, or, as a wise old philosopher once said, "You got the words, but the tune ain't right!"

Street Smarts

H. RAP BROWN

*Having considered such forms of American Negro verbal art as the
dozens, signifying, boasts, and toasts, we may perhaps begin to understand
the rhetoric used by black militants. Whether one is sympathetic to militant
causes or not, one does need to know what the causes are. Militants, of course,
are busy telling people what the causes are. However, white Americans are not
always able to understand the militants because they do not know enough about
black styles of speech. This ignorance on the part of most whites not only
impedes their understanding of the black community, but it perpetuates an
obsolescent education system which black students are forced to enter.*

*In traditional American education, black students are penalized for not
conforming to white linguistic norms—one recalls such terms as "Non-Standard
English" or "culturally deprived." Moreover, the considerable verbal skills that
black students do possess are not rewarded—partly because most white school
teachers are almost totally unaware that Negro folk speech and verbal art have
their own highly developed forms. As a result, black children are bored in school
and white teachers become more firmly convinced that black children lack
"verbal skills."*

In the following brief selection from Die Nigger Die, *Rap Brown says
all this, only he says it using the conventions of black verbal art. He is "telling
it like it is," but the question remains as to whether American educators will
continue to "fight" street talk (without even knowing precisely what it is) or
whether they will attempt to make courses and curricula relevant to "real life."
(The term "street smarts" was chosen to title this selection from Rap Brown's
book because it is a slang locution referring to the clever use of language and
intelligence to manipulate others, an expertise normally acquired in the process*

of learning street culture.) The reader is invited to see if he can read Rap Brown's thoughts without being stymied by "obscenities" and with some genuine appreciation of the power and beauty of the verbal art styles which he so masterfully employs.

THE STREET is where young bloods get their education. I learned how to talk in the street, not from reading about Dick and Jane going to the zoo and all that simple shit. The teacher would test our vocabulary each week, but we knew the vocabulary we needed. They'd give us arithmetic to exercise our minds. Hell, we exercised our minds by playing the Dozens.

> I fucked your mama
> Till she went blind.
> Her breath smells bad,
> But she sure can grind.

> I fucked your mama
> For a solid hour.
> Baby came out
> Screaming, Black Power.

> Elephant and the Baboon
> Learning to screw.
> Baby came out looking
> Like Spiro Agnew.

And the teacher expected me to sit up in class and study poetry after I could run down shit like that. If anybody needed to study poetry, she needed to study mine. We played the Dozens for recreation, like white folks play Scrabble.

In many ways, though, the Dozens is a mean game because what you try to do is totally destroy somebody else with words. It's that whole competition thing again, fighting each other. There'd be sometimes 40 or 50 dudes standing around and the winner was determined by the way they responded to what was said. If you fell all over each other laughing, then you knew you'd scored. It was a bad scene for the dude that was getting humiliated. I seldom was. That's why they call me Rap, 'cause I could rap. (The name stuck because Ed would always say, "That my nigger Rap," "Rap my nigger.") But for dudes who couldn't, it was like they were humiliated because they were born Black and then they turned around and got humiliated by their own people, which was really all they had left. But that's the way it is. Those that feel most humiliated humiliate others. The real aim of the Dozens was to get a dude so mad that he'd cry or get mad enough to fight. You'd say shit like, "Man, tell your mama to stop coming around my house all the time. I'm tired of fucking her and I think you should know that it ain't no accident you look like me." And it could go on for hours sometimes. Some of the best Dozens players were girls.

Signifying is more humane. Instead of coming down on somebody's mother, you come down on them. But, before you can signify you got to be able to rap. A session would start maybe by a brother saying, "Man, before you mess with me you'd rather run rabbits, eat shit and bark at the moon." Then, if he was talking to me, I'd tell him:

> Man, you must don't know who I am.
> I'm sweet peeter jeeter the womb
>   beater
> The baby maker the cradle shaker
> The deerslayer the buckbinder the
>   women finder

Known from the Gold Coast to the
 rocky shores of Maine
Rap is my name and love is my game.
I'm the bed tucker the cock plucker
 the motherfucker
The milkshaker the record breaker the
 population maker
The gun-slinger the baby bringer
The hum-dinger the pussy ringer
The man with the terrible middle
 finger.
The hard hitter the bullshitter the
 poly-nussy getter
The beast from the East the Judge the
 sludge
The women's pet the men's fret and the
 punks' pin-up boy.
They call me Rap the dicker the ass
 kicker
The cherry picker the city slicker the
 titty licker
And I ain't giving up nothing but
 bubble gum and hard times and
 I'm fresh out of bubble gum.
I'm giving up wooden nickels 'cause I
 know they won't spend
And I got a pocketful of splinter
 change.
I'm a member of the bathtub club: I'm
 seeing a whole lot of ass but I ain't
 taking no shit.
I'm the man who walked the water and
 tied the whale's tail in a knot
Taught the little fishes how to swim
Crossed the burning sands and shook
 the devil's hand
Rode round the world on the back of a
 snail carrying a sack saying AIR
 MAIL.
Walked 49 miles of barbwire and
 used a Cobra snake for a necktie
And got a brand new house on the
 roadside made from a cracker's hide,
Got a brand new chimney setting on
 top made from the cracker's skull
Took a hammer and nail and built the
 world and calls it "THE BUCKET
 OF BLOOD."

Yes, I'm hemp the demp the women's
 pimp
Women fight for my delight.
I'm a bad motherfucker. Rap the
 rip-saw the devil's brother 'n law.
I roam the world I'm known to wander
 and this .45 is where I get my
 thunder.
I'm the only man in the world who
 knows why white milk makes yellow
 butter.
I know where the lights go when you
 cut the switch off.
I might not be the best in the world,
 but I'm in the top two and my
 brother's getting old.
And ain't nothing bad 'bout you but
 your breath.

Now, if the brother couldn't come
back behind that, I usually cut him
some slack (depending on time, place
and his attitude). We learned what the
white folks call verbal skills. We learned
how to throw them words together.
America, however, has Black folk in a
serious game of the Dozens. (The dirty
muthafucka.) Signifying allowed you a
choice—you could either make a cat
feel good or bad. If you had just destroyed someone or if they were just
down already, signifying could help
them over. Signifying was also a way of
expressing your own feelings:

Man, I can't win for losing.
If it wasn't for bad luck, I wouldn't
 have no luck at all.
I been having buzzard luck
Can't kill nothing and won't nothing
 die
I'm living on the welfare and things is
 stormy
They borrowing their shit from the
 Salvation Army
But things bound to get better 'cause
 they can't get no worse

I'm just like the blind man, standing
  by a broken window
I don't feel no pain.
But it's your world
You the man I pay rent to
If I had your hands I'd give 'way both
  my arms.
Cause I could do without them
I'm the man but you the main man
I read the books you write
You set the pace in the race I run
Why, you always in good form
You got more foam than Alka
  Seltzer. . . .

Signifying at its best can be heard when brothers are exchanging tales. I used to hang out in the bars just to hear the old men "talking shit." By the time I was nine, I could talk Shine and the Titanic, Signifying Monkey, three different ways, and Piss-Pot-Peet, for two hours without stopping.

Sometimes I wonder why I even bothered to go to school. Practically everything I know I learned on the corner. Today they're talking about teaching sex in school. But that's white folks for you. They got to intellectualize everything. Now how you gon' intellectualize screwing? At the age when little white kids were finding out that there was something down there to play with, we knew where it went and what to do with it after it got there. You weren't a man if you hadn't gotten yourself a little piece by the time you were seven. When the white kids were out playing Hide and Go Seek, we were playing Hide and Go Get It. One dude would count to a hundred while the girls hid. Once the girls were hidden, you went and found one and you got it. That was the game. Hide and Go Get It. None of that ol' simple tagging a tree and yelling, "I got in free." Yeah, we got in free.

Some of the dudes started pimping early for their sisters and, sometimes, even their mama. Survival'll make you do anything, jim. Anything! You'd be walking down the street one night and some white dude in a car would pull up next to you and say, "Hey, boy, you got a sister?" or, "You know any nice colored girls?" So whitey would get him a little taste of black gold for $10 or $15 and Black people helped him. It shows you just how low you can get when you sell your own women to a white man—or any man for that matter. But it's particularly bad when they're sold to white men. To this day, you can find the snakes in the Black community on the weekends trying to buy some Black pussy. And Black men see 'em, know what they're there for and don't run 'em out. Not even the so-called big, bad militants.

FOLK BELIEF

Of all the subject subdivisions of folklore, there is none about which people are more self-conscious than the area of superstition or folk belief. Even though all peoples hold some form of folk belief (including folk medical practices), there seems generally to be considerable reluctance to admit that one is superstitious. (One must realize that even the decision to go ahead and walk under a ladder because one does *not* believe that this will result in bad luck remains related to folk belief. The very fact that one even thinks about the superstition indicates that such beliefs continue to influence our lives and thought. So it is that if a person feels that taking an umbrella to work will "cause" it not to rain that day, or that washing one's automobile will "cause" it to rain, he is indulging in the "omnipotence of thought" common to many superstitions. The egocentricity of such omnipotence of thought is truly amazing—to think that the actions of a single individual could definitely affect the future weather conditions of an entire region!)

In any sector of human life where there is uncertainty and accompanying anxiety, one may expect to find a battery of customs and beliefs whose function it is to relieve or at least minimize that anxiety. This is why in the area of health there is an especially large number of prophylactic or curative practices. Even if the concern is only with hiccoughs or warts, the principles of sympathetic magic are often the same as those involved in combating more deadly diseases.

In the study of American Negro folklore, there has been less emphasis upon folk belief than upon other types of folklore, e.g., animal tales or spirituals. Certainly this holds true for black folklorists. One reason for this was the notion found in the white stereotype of the Negro to the effect that superstitious behavior and fear were an intrinsic part of Negro character. Since whites believed that all Negroes were superstitious, one could hardly expect Negro scholars to go out and collect large quantities of superstitions inasmuch as such materials would surely have been used to support the stereotype. Negroes are superstitious; so are whites; and so are *all* the peoples of the world. So long as there are un-resolved sources of anxiety, there will be superstitions. (In academic student folk-lore, there are superstitions having to do with examination anxiety, e.g., some students insist upon buying their examination blue books from the same store each time or upon using the same pen or wearing the same clothes or sitting in the same seat in the classroom, etc. in order to be assured of doing well on a test.)

Probably some readers will be as upset or outraged about discussions of American Negro folk belief as others will be about seeing the language of the ghetto street in print. Hopefully, they will realize that, value judgments notwith-standing, one must begin with what exists. Even if one were to argue that all superstition should be stamped out, one could not proceed to do this without knowing precisely what the superstition was. However, before one jumps on the bandwagon to eliminate all forms of superstition, one should keep in mind that there are such things as psychoso-matic illnesses. If this is so, then their will probably always need to be some type of faith healing to undo the dam-age caused by the human mind. The modern medical use of placebos con-tinues the ancient art of faith healing. If the mind causes illness, it can also "cause" health.

Conjuring & Conjure-Doctors

LEONORA HERRON AND ALICE M. BACON

Unfortunately, probably largely because of the stereotype, most of the research on Negro superstition has been carried out by white scholars. Perhaps the one most notable exception is Zora Neale Hurston, whose detailed study of "hoodoo" remains a major contribution. (It was first published as "Hoodoo in America," Journal of American Folklore, 44 [1931], pp. 317–417, and later reprinted as a section of her Mules and Men [Philadelphia, 1935].) Among the larger collections of superstitions are the Yale doctoral dissertation of Newbell Niles Puckett, Folk Beliefs of the Southern Negro (Chapel Hill, 1926, Dover paperback edition, 1969) and the recent enormous 1843 page, two-volume Hoodoo-Conjuration-Witchcraft-Rootwork (Washington, D.C.: American University Bookstore, 1970) by Harry M. Hyatt. Yet there were early attempts by black students to report superstitions and one of these essays had to do with conjuration.

The art of conjuration is one which has captured the imagination of not only the folk but also a good many creative writers. The beginnings of American Negro literature are full of short stories with conjure as the principal topic. Unfortunately, in such literary accounts, one can not always be sure of the accuracy of the conjuring practice as fictional writers are often wont to add embellishment. For this reason, modern students must be grateful that conjuration was one of the subjects investigated by members of the Hampton Folklore Society. From a series of student papers written in the mid 1870's, Leonora Herron and Alice M. Bacon, librarian and teacher respectively at Hampton Institute, were able to determine some of the most characteristic features of both the conjure doctor and his techniques of conjuration. The above-mentioned voluminous report of the years of fieldwork carried out by Harry

Reprinted from Southern Workman, 24 (1895), pp. 117–18, 193–94, 209–11.

Hyatt provides ample confirmations of the authenticity of the sketches made by these early, dedicated students of American Negro folklore.

For further details of the specific practices discussed in the following essays, the reader should consult the works of Puckett and Hyatt. For an idea of the distribution of a particular practice in different parts of the United States, see Wayland Hand, ed., Popular Beliefs and Superstitions from North Carolina, *volumes 6 and 7 of* The Frank C. Brown Collection of North Carolina Folklore *(Durham, 1961, 1964), which has valuable comparative notes.*

I*

The Negro's belief in conjuration and magic is very probably a relic of African days, though strange and incongruous growths rising from association with the white race, added to and distorted it from time to time, till it became a curious conglomerate of fetichism, divination, quackery, incantation and demonology.

Overt and natural means of obtaining justice being forbidden the Negro, was it surprising that, brought up in ignorance, and trained in superstition, he should invoke secret and supernatural powers to redress his wrongs and afford him vengeance on those of his fellows whom envy, jealousy or anger prompted him to injure?

The agent of this vengeance was usually the Conjure Doctor. This individual might be a man or a woman, white or colored, but was found in every large Negro community, where though held in fear and, horror, his supernatural powers were still implicitly believed in. The source of these powers is but ill defined. One authority says: "I have always heard that those doctors sold themselves to the Devil before they were given this power." Another, in speaking

of a certain old woman who was a conjure doctor, says: "She said she had a special revelation from God, as do all the conjure doctors I have ever heard of." One rather noted conjure doctor described by several of our writers, claimed his power in virtue of being the "seventh son of a seventh son," and having been "born with seven cauls over his face." It is said by some, however, that women who conjure sometimes give instruction in the art, and that if a conjure doctor is asked where he got his teaching, he will tell you of some old person who has been dead for years as having been his teacher.

The conjure doctor's business was of two kinds: to conjure, or "trick," a person, and to cure persons already "conjured." They were appealed to upon the least pretext to exert their powers in the former way. Jealousy or envy of a more fortunate neighbor or associate was a frequent cause for appealing to the conjure doctor, who would be requested to "trick" the object of the ill feeling. A quarrel between the two neighbors, even over the merest trifle, would result in a visit to the conjure doctor and the subsequent illness, or death perhaps, of one of the parties. Love affairs gave plenty of employment to the

* Part I of this study was written by Leonora Herron. An introductory note indicated it was compiled from a series of essays on conjure-doctors written in 1878 by Hampton students. Some of the essays were published in *Southern Workman.* —ED.

conjure doctors, as they were believed to be able to "work their roots" so to make one person return another's affection, and, if the affair resulted unhappily, the slighted party sought revenge in having the other "tricked" so that no rival should be more successful.

In slavery times, there are frequent records of the conjure doctor's being appealed to to save the slave from punishment, to enable him to escape the "patrolers" or, in the case of a runaway, to enable him to return home without suffering from his master's anger.

In all these cases there was the most implicit faith in the conjure doctor's power. Disliked and feared as these men and women were, gruesome as were the beliefs about them, the confidence in their abilities was unbounded; and deliberate open impostors as most of them evidently were, they were nevertheless able to wring from their victims the money they could so little spare from the needs of every day life.

Some curious things are told of the personal appearance of these doctors. Almost all agree that they are usually tall and very dark; and a distinguishing mark seems to be extreme redness of the eyes. One describes them as "always on the lookout, full of superstition, and long, exciting tales." Another calls them "singular and queer, seeming always in a deep study, looking at some distant object," and adds: "I have never seen one that could look a man straight in the eyes. They never sleep like any one else. It's more like the sleep of a cat. At the slightest noise or pain they are up telling their fortunes to see if any one is trying to injure them."

One conjure doctor is pictured as having the remarkable gift of "turning as green as grass moss, and when he was just as black as a man could very well be; and his hair covered his neck, and around his neck he had a string, and he had lizards tied on it. He carried a crooked cane. He'd throw it down and he would pick it up and say something, and throw it down, and it would wriggle like a snake, and he would pick it up and it would be as stiff as any other cane."

In one account, the conjure doctors are represented as going along looking very sanctified, with leathern bags on their arms. They are not called conjure doctors in their presence but are addressed as doctor. They seem to have exacted respectful treatment, for we have testimony that a conjure doctor meeting a person who refused to bow to him, would threaten to conjure the person.

Powers of all kinds are attributed to these doctors. The healing art in various degrees is their gift, and the so-called "diseases" which they possess exclusive power to cure are, as one of our informers puts it, these: tricks, spells and poison.

The power of snake-charming seems to be quite generally attributed to them. One is told of who claimed that he could turn a horse to a cow, and kill a man or woman and bring them to life again by shaking up his little boxes. He could also whistle in the key-hole after the doors were locked, and make them fly open. Others are told of who "can trick, put snakes, lizards, terrapins, scorpions and different other things in you, fix you so you can't walk, can't sleep, or sleep all the time, and so you can't have any use of your limbs. They could put you in such a state that you would linger and pine away or so that you would go blind or crazy."

II*

It is difficult here to make any classification of the things used in conjuring which will have any value except as a mere arbitrary distinction for the sake of ease in enumerating and remembering in some intelligible order the great variety of media for the charms cited by the authors of the compositions from which our data are drawn. We will however, for the sake of convenience, classify into

1. Poisons.
2. Charms.

Of poisons derived from substances known or believed to be poisonous and administered in food or drink a number of cases are cited. A drink of whiskey is poisoned and offered to the victim; an apple is poisoned and given in church on Sunday. One instance is given of "toad heads, scorpion heads, hair, nine pins and needles baked in a cake and given to a child who became deathly sick." By another of our writers it is said that "some go in the woods and get lizards and little ground dogs and snakes and dry them and then powder them all up together in liquor and give them to drink, or pick a chance and put in their food so they can eat it." Another case is mentioned of a conjurer who caught a snake, cut his head off, hung him up by his tail and let the blood drop into a can. Then he went out and caught a lizard, killed him, took his blood and mixed it with the snake's blood. This mixture was done up in a bundle and sent to the victim. He drank it up, and in two minutes was lying on the floor speech-

less. In this case the victim was saved by an old doctor who was brought in and rubbed him about twelve hours. One woman swallowed a lizard in a cup of coffee and was poisoned thereby. In another case cabbage, presumably poisoned, was given to the victim with evil results. Again, horse hair is put into the food or a preparation of poisonous snakes and lizards is mixed with the whiskey. The theory in regard to the poisonous effects of hair is thus stated by a boy whose own hair had been baked in bread and given him to eat. The conjure-doctor told him that if he had eaten it the hair would cling round his heart strings and would have afflicted him so that he would not be able to work and after a while it would kill him. It required no belief in the supernatural whatever to make one afraid of persons whose business it is to devise poisons to place in the food of their victims, and, if the evidence of our collection of compositions is to be trusted, there was on the plantations in the old days a vast amount of just that sort of thing. That the poison did not always produce the desired effect was due rather to a lack of knowledge than to a lack of zeal on the part of the conjurer, and if roots and herbs, snakes and lizards, hairs and other disgusting objects could be worked into the food and drink of the victim it was undoubtedly the most certain way of despatching the business to the satisfaction of his enemy. But this method of revenge, because it was the most direct and certain, was the most easily discovered, and we find that other methods seem to have been more popular. Just as poisoning

---

* Part II of this study was written by Miss Alice Bacon. It deals with the techniques of conjuration rather than with the conjure-doctor. An introductory headnote indicates the basis of the essay was a collection of student compositions written in 1875. —ED.

is less direct and therefore safer than clubbing or shooting, so "fixing" by means of a charm is safer than either, and charms seem to have been relied on for working evil, to a very great extent.

The form of the charm which comes most near to the simple poisoning, of which we have already given examples, is the passing of the spell to the victim by handing to him some conjured article or placing it where he can pick it up. In these examples it is contact alone that transmits the evil; the charmed or poisoned thing need not be eaten. A sweet potato on a stump in the victim's potato patch has been known to cause pain just as soon as it was touched by the one for whom it was intended. A woman, picking up chips, picked up a small bundle folded in rags; the next chip stuck to her hand and she was conjured. A pair of new shoes just come from the shoe-maker causes such pain that the victim cannot walk. He continues to grow weaker and thinner and to suffer even after the shoes are removed and at last dies of the effect of conjured shoes. A bottle of cologne presented to a girl by her unsuccessful rival puts her eyes out when she smells of it. Something put on the gate-post causes swelling of the hands. One instance is, of a girl who detects her father-in-law putting something into her shoes after she is supposed to have gone to sleep. She burns the shoes and so avoids the trick; the shoes in burning make a noise like a bunch of fire works. In another case a small red bag, (presumably filled with occult miniatures) is fixed to the sole of the victim's foot. In one case a carving knife is conjured, supposing that the cook will be the first person to use it, but the charm goes astray because the seamstress has occasion to use the knife,

and the charm goes from it to her. Some conjurers accomplish their ends by throwing hair balls at their victims.

But charms seem to be most frequently conveyed by even more indirect methods than those thus far enumerated. A baby is conjured by the presence in its crib of something all wrapped up in hair and all kinds of other queer looking things. The bundle when burned showed strange variety of colors. A colored man got angry at a woman and tricked her by the following complicated charm. He took some blue cloth and cut out several chickens and sewed them up after filling them with some kind of dust and a lot of needles and pins. He covered these with feathers so that they looked precisely like real chickens, and then sewed them up in his victim's bed. Conjure balls, snakes and all kinds of reptiles are often found in the beds of those who have been "conjured." In other cases the fatal bundle or bottle is secreted in some corner of the room in which the victim lives or is placed in the road over which he most often walks. A charm in the shape of a small rubber ball may be placed in the chimney corner, or poison may be put in a bottle and buried in the path, (in some cases upside down). A sick woman, who had almost pined away to skin and bones, sent for a conjure-doctor. He went at once to the hearth, took up a brick and found sticking in a cloth six pins and needles. He took them up, put salt on them, and threw them in the river. The needles and pins were said to be the cause of so many pains. In other cases poisonous balls of various sizes, filled with roots, herbs and other mixtures, were put in the road. They would have no effect on any but the intended victim. These charms or tricks seem to have been made personal by securing something from the body of the victim, as a strand of his hair, or some earth from his foot prints.

If you fail to get near enough to your victim to place the spell in his room or his hand or his bed or his path, you may yet, if you are skillful, succeed in carrying out your fell design by simply burying your charm under his doorstep or in his yard where he may never see it or come in contact with it, but where it can work untold evil to him and his— under the doorstep if you can, near the house if you can't do that, but failing of that, almost anywhere in the yard will do if the spell is potent. A black bottle containing a liquid mixture and nine pins and nine needles is a favorite charm. Sometimes a bundle containing salt, pepper and a silver five cents; sometimes needles, pins, hairs, snake-heads. Again, it is salt, red pepper, anvil dust and a kind of root that conjure doctors always carry in their pockets. In the latter case, our informant tells us that "when putting this down they have a ceremony and request the devil to cause this to have the desired effect," specifying in the request the part of the body of the victim which it is desired to injure. A small red flannel bag filled with new pins, small tacks and other things, and buried under the gate-sill made a horse refuse to enter the gate. After working over the horse for an hour, the driver looked under the sill, found the charm and removed it, and the horse walked quietly in at the gate. Jelly-fish taken out of the water, dried, powdered and put into small bags are used for conjuring. In one case, when search was made for the charm there was found in the ground a tin cup seven inches deep and three in diameter, called a "conjure cup." It contained little balls, some like lumps of tar and some like

sulphur and other different colors. When burned these balls gave "beautiful blazes." In one case a bottle full of snakes was buried by the doorstep. The first one to come out in the morning stepped over it and fell. A preserve jar found buried in one garden contained "a snake and several other insects and something else wrapped in cloth," which the finder did not open but threw away. In one case, where there was reason to suspect conjuring, a bottle filled with roots, stones, and a reddish powder was found under the doorstep, and in the yard more bottles with beans, nails and the same powder. The man burned them up and got well. Again a package in the shape of a brick was found and inside of it a "tin trunk and a great many articulate creatures." Another of our writers tells us that "some of their simplest things are salt, pepper, needles, pins, black bottles and all kinds of roots. I have seen one of their roots which they called "devil's shoe string." It is a long, wiry-looking root resembling the smallest roots of a sweet potato-vine."

With this variety of gruesome and disgusting things, did the plantation conjurers essay to work evil among the credulous people with whom they were surrounded. The next phase of our study is to inquire what were the evils that were laid to their door as the result of their dealing in roots, herbs, snakes, and mysteries.

The disease which is caused by conjuring may be recognized in its early stages, in the first place by the suddenness of the attack. The victim is seized with a sharp pain in some part of her body; later, swelling and other symptoms follow, but the beginning of the attack can usually be traced to a sharp pain which followed directly upon handling, stepping over, or swallowing the charm. Another, and perhaps the surest sign that the disease is the result of a spell or trick, is that the patient grows worse rather than better under treatment of regular physicians. When this is the case it is well to call in a conjure doctor at once or it may be too late, for there are cases where even after the spell is removed the victim fails to recover from the injuries it has already wrought.

As the disease develops itself the symptoms become more severe and terrible in their nature. In many cases snakes and lizards are seen running up and down under the flesh, or are even known to show their heads from the sufferer's mouth. One example is given of a woman possessed by a lizard that "would run up and down her throat and hollow when she would be a-talking." Another case is of a man whose food did him no good. The conjure doctor told him that he had been conjured and that inside of him were a number of small snakes which ate up the food as fast as he ate it. Another woman who had lizards crawling in her body was obliged to eat very often to keep the lizards from eating her. This possession by reptiles of various kinds seems to be a part in almost every evil wrought by the conjurer, and instances are too numerous and too horrible for a more detailed review of them in this paper. Sometimes when direct evidence of these reptiles fails to appear during the life of the patient, a post mortem brings them to light and establishes the truth of the doctor's diagnosis.

Another evidence that the disease is of a magical origin is in the strange noises made by the patient. Numerous instances are given of sufferers who howled or barked like dogs. One example is given of a woman who "howled like a dog, crowed like a cock, barked like a fox and mewed like a cat and made all sorts of noises before she died." One boy used to walk on all fours and howl like a dog. Another man who was conjured "would have ways like a dog, growling and gritting his teeth."

From these symptoms it is but a brief step to insanity of all kinds, and many cases are cited where the insane patient is regarded as "conjured" by his relative. One woman, could not go further than a mile. "When she had walked a mile she would get out of her head so she would have to stop, so she could gather her mind to go back." A girl when conjured "ran wild and drowned herself." One woman "who was very sick and almost crazy was conjured to her bed for several months. And now she has some kind of spells that come upon her, when she lies like one dead for about an hour. She cannot bear any kind of medicine to be used about her. She says that she can hear all that is said to her but cannot speak." It is unnecessary to cite all the instances given in the compositions. They are numerous enough to go far towards proving that insanity on the plantation was often laid to "conjuration" and consequently took in the patient the form that the belief in conjuration would naturally give it, just as in New Testament times it was believed to be demoniacal possession and took that form in its manifestations.

When it is once decided that the sufferer from mysterious symptoms of any kind has been conjured, there remains no hope except through the conjure doctor. He must be sent for at once, as delay is always dangerous and often fatal. There are few settlements of colored people in which the belief in conjuration is prevalent, in which there is not to be found some person distinguished for his skill as a conjure doctor. Of their personal peculiarities it is not my part to speak. Of that you already have learned through Miss Herron's paper, but their special methods of procedure when summoned to cure disease, we must try to get some general idea from the mass of testimony presented by the compositions.

The conjure doctor has five distinct services to render to his patient. (1) He must tell him whether he is conjured or not. (2) He must find out who conjured him. (3) He must search for and find the "trick" and destroy it. (4) He must cure the patient. (5) He will if the patient wishes turn back the trick upon the one who made it. But as a rule before he does anything for the patient he demands and receives a large fee. Should he find business slack he will sometimes take it upon himself to secure patients by visiting certain persons and telling them that they have been or are about to be conjured, and often presenting irrefragable proofs in the shape of a pin stuck in the north side of a distant tree, or a bottle dug up at a certain designated spot in the yard; he extracts a payment of money for his services in preventing the evil sure to follow if he is not engaged by a good-sized retainer to prevent it. A conjure doctor summoned to attend a case of mysterious illness in a family will frequently begin his examination by putting a small piece of silver into the mouth or hand of the sufferer. Should the silver turn black, there is no doubt about the diagnosis. The silver piece is not always tried; in some cases the very nature of the seizure proclaims at once

to the doctor that it is the work of conjurers. The next step is to study the nature of the disease and search out and destroy the trick by which it was caused. In one case the conjure doctor recognized the disease by the trembling of the patient's fingers as he came in at the door. The poison had not then taken much effect upon the patient but the conjure doctor assured the sufferer that, without attention it would kill her. In another case the doctor informed his patient that the charm was fixed to work with the moon and tides. When the tide was coming in he would be worse, when going out he would be better. A case is mentioned of a girl who had been suffering for a long time from a sore and swollen foot, until at last a conjure doctor was called to her relief:

As soon as he saw the foot he said that she was conjured and that it was done by an old man who wanted to marry her, and that it was done at church one night. Then he said, "I will try to cure you in the name of the Lord." Then he asked her for a pin and scratched her foot on the side and got some blood and he rubbed some cream on it and said, "God bless her," and he called her name, and the next morning this girl, who had been ill for nine months, walked out of doors without crutch or cane.

In another case in which a bright silver piece held in the patient's hand had turned perfectly black in five minutes, the patient was cupped three times. In each case the cupping horn came away filled with live lizards, frogs and snakes that had had their abode in her. Later she was bathed in an infuson of mullein and moss made with boiling water in a tub. After the bath the water was thrown towards the sunset and this line repeated: "As the sun sets in the West so should the works of the Devil end in judgement." This treatment did her good and she recovered rapidly. Another doctor sawed a tree in the middle and put the patient through it four times. He then cupped him and buried the things that came out of him under a tree at sunset. Still another doctor would begin his treatment by making the patient swallow a small piece of silver. He said the conjuration would stick to the silver and his medicine would cure the person conjured. Another practitioner arrived when sent for with a bottle filled with herbs, roots, and leaves; with these he made a tea which acted as an emetic and the patient threw up a variety of reptiles. Again a conjure doctor came and chewed some roots and did a great many other things. In one light case of tricking, the patient was merely given some roots to carry in his pocket and something to rub with.

Either after or before the cure of the patient is well under way, the doctor will make an effort to find the "trick" or "conjure" and to identify the miscreant who has caused the trouble. He may be able to tell immediately and without visiting the spot, just where the cause of the trouble is buried. An instance is given of an old man who was visited by a woman who lived twelve miles away. He was able to tell the patient after one look at her sore foot exactly the spot in her own yard where, if she would dig, she would find a large black bottle, containing a mixture, placed there by one of her neighbors to trick her. She went home, dug and found it was as he said. In other cases the detection of the trick seems to be more difficult and the doctor is obliged to have recourse to cards or other means of obtaining the truth. One of our writers tells us of ǀa conjure doctor who, on visiting a patient,

cut his cards and told her that she was poisoned by a woman who wanted her place and that the conjure bottle was under the sill of her door. Every time she stepped over the sill one drop of the poison dried up, and when the last drop dried she would die. The conjure doctors seemed to have an objection to name the enemy who had cast the spell. In some cases they would simply undertake to describe him, in other cases a more complicated device was resorted to: "They would find a bundle of roots under the doorstep or floor. After they had found the roots they would ask for a flat iron. They would take the iron and a piece of brown paper and draw the image of the person who put the roots there."

After the enemy has been identified the conjure doctor may be of further use in securing revenge for the injured person. There are many instances cited where the charm has been turned against the one who sent it. This the conjure doctor may do by a variety of devices, some of which easily commend themselves to the ignorant minds with which he deals. It is said that if any one tricks you and you discover the trick and put that into the fire, you burn your enemy, or if you throw it into the running water you drown him. One instance is given of a conjure laid down in the path of a young man. He saw it in time, picked it up with two sticks, carried it into the house, and put it in the fire. This took great effect upon the old man "who danced and ran and hollowed and jumped and did a little of everything, but still the bundle burned," until at last the old man acknowledged everything he had done. Another of our writers tells us that, "If the composition used in conjuring can be found and given to the conjure-doctor, he will throw the charm from the person conjured to the one who did it. This affects him so strongly that he will come to the house and ask for something. If he gets it his charm will return, if not it will end on himself." One writer cites the case of a man who had been made lame by a lizard in his leg who was told by a conjure-doctor what to do, and as a result his enemy went about as long as he lived with that lizard in his leg.

And now for the ounce of prevention that is worth the pound of cure in conjuration as in other things. Silver in the shoe or hung around the neck seems to be the most universal counter-charm. A horse shoe nailed over the door or even hidden under the sill will keep out conjurer's spells as well as hags and witches. A smooth stone in the shoe was recommended in one case, in another case, a goose quill filled with quicksilver worn below the knee. In one case where a man had been under the care of a conjure doctor and recovered, the doctor would not allow him to visit unless he wore a silver coin in his shoe and a silver ring on his right hand.

Superstitions & Folklore of the South

CHARLES W. CHESNUTT

Having had the pattern of conjuration delineated, the reader might like to consider several accounts of conjuration from different parts of the country. For details from North Carolina, we are greatly indebted to Charles W. Chesnutt who, a contemporary of poet Paul Laurence Dunbar, is generally regarded as being the first distinguished American Negro author of short stories and novels. In many of his stories, Chesnutt drew heavily upon his personal knowledge of the folklore found in Fayetteville, North Carloina and the surrounding area. Even though he spent some of his most creative years in Cleveland, Ohio, he never stopped finding inspiration from the folklore of his North Carolina days.

Chesnutt's interest in folklore was clearly more than casual. The very fact that he wrote an essay specifically devoted to folklore is evidence enough. (This essay is surely one of the earliest studies of Negro folklore made by a Negro writer, apart from those made by members of the Hampton Folklore Society and such articles as "Negro Folk-Lore and Dialect," The Arena, 17 [1897], pp. 186–92, by Professor W. S. Scarborough.) Chesnutt was really very sophisticated about folklore, and he carefully distinguished between folklore on the one hand and literature based on folklore on the other, a distinction not always made by later critics of Chesnutt's writings. Chesnutt himself spoke to this point in an autobiographical essay entitled "Post-Bellum—Pre-Harlem," where he remarked that although many of his stories were sometimes referred to as folktales, they were not. With the exception of his first story "The Goophered Grapevine" which appeared in the August, 1887 issue of the Atlantic Monthly, his stories, he claimed, were the fruit of his own imagination "in which respect they differ from the Uncle Remus stories which are avowedly folk tales." On the other hand, as Chesnutt candidly confesses in the following valuable essay, he

Reprinted from *Modern Culture*, vol. 13 (1901), pp. 231–35.

was frequently astonished to discover that some of his "original" creative ideas turned out to be folkloristic materials in disguise that he had learned in his childhood.

For more about Chesnutt, see John Livingston Wright, "Charles W. Chesnutt: One of the Leading Novelists of the Race," The Colored American Magazine, *4 (1902), pp. 153–56, or the biography written by his daughter but based largely on his diary journal entries and his personal correspondence, Helen M. Chesnutt,* Charles Waddell Chesnutt: Pioneer of the Color Line *(Chapel Hill, 1952). Indications of the high regard contemporary men of letters had for Chesnutt include the fact that George W. Cable once sought young Chesnutt's services as secretary and Chesnutt's invitation to attend a special 70th birthday celebration for Mark Twain. There was also the special notice of his work by William Dean Howells. See Philip Butcher,* George W. Cable: The Northampton Years *(New York, 1959), pp. 92–97; "Mark Twain,"* The Colored American Magazine, *10 (1906), pp. 5–7; William Dean Howells, "Mr. Charles W. Chesnutt's Stories,"* Atlantic Monthly, *85 (1900), pp. 699–701. (Howell's comments were not always entirely favorable, see "A Psychological Counter-Current in Recent Fiction,"* North American Review, *173 [1901], pp. 872–88 [esp. pp. 881–83].) See also Helen M. Chesnutt,* Charles Waddell Chesnutt, *pp. 43–47, 213–15. For a consideration of Chesnutt as a marginal man, see S. P. Fullinwider,* The Mind and Mood of Black America *(Homewood, Illinois, 1969) pp. 77–84.*

For Chesnutt's treatment of folktales, see Robert A. Smith, "A Note on the Folktales of Charles W. Chesnutt," College Language Association Journal, *5 (1962), pp. 229–32. See also Chesnutt's essay, "Post-Bellum—Pre-Harlem,"* The Crisis, *38 (1931), pp. 193–94. For a study of Chesnutt's use of the Fayetteville locale, see Sylvia Lyons Render, "Tar Heelia in Chesnutt,"* College Language Association Journal, *9 (1965), pp. 39–50. For indications of the continuing esteem in which Chesnutt is held, see John W. Parker, "Chesnutt as a Southern Town Remembers Him,"* The Crisis, *56 (1946), pp. 205–6, 221, and "Chesnutt Marker,"* The Crisis, *68 (1961) pp. 494–95. Among Chesnutt's works are* The Conjure Woman *(Boston, 1899),* The Wife of His Youth and Other Stories of the Color Line *(Boston, 1899),* The House Behind the Cedars *(Boston, 1900),* The Marrow of Tradition *(Boston, 1901), and* The Colonel's Dream *(New York, 1905). Serious students of Chesnutt should probably consult the special collection including manuscript and correspondence materials housed at Fisk University (The Charles Waddell Chesnutt Collection, Erastus Milo Cravath Memorial Library, Fisk University, Nashville, Tennessee).*

DURING A recent visit to North Carolina, after a long absence, I took occasion to inquire into the latter-day prevalence of the old-time belief in what was known as "conjuration" or "goopher," my childish recollection of which I have elsewhere embodied into a number of stories. The derivation of the word "goopher" I do not know, nor whether any other writer than myself has recognized its existence, though it is in frequent use in certain parts of the South.

The origin of this curious superstition itself is perhaps more easily traceable.* It probably grew, in the first place, out of African fetichism, which was brought over from the dark continent along with the dark people. Certain features, too, suggest a distant affinity with Voodooism, or snake worship, a cult which seems to have been indigenous to tropical America. These beliefs, which in the place of their origin had all the sanctions of religion and social custom, become, in the shadow of the white man's civilization, a pale reflection of their former selves. In time, too, they were mingled and confused with the witchcraft and ghost lore of the white man, and the tricks and delusions of the Indian conjurer. In the old plantation days they flourished vigorously, though discouraged by the "great house," and their potency was well established among the blacks and the poorer whites. Education, however, has thrown the ban of disrepute upon witchcraft and conjuration. The stern frown of the preacher, who looks upon superstition as the ally of the Evil One; the scornful sneer of the teacher, who sees in it a part of the livery of bondage, have driven this quaint combination of ancestral traditions to the remote chimney corners of old black aunties, from which it is difficult for the stranger to unearth them. Mr. Harris, in his Uncle Remus stories, has, with fine literary discrimination, collected and put into pleasing and enduring form, the plantation stories which dealt with animal lore, but so little attention has been paid to those dealing with so-called conjuration, that they seem in a fair way to disappear, without leaving a trace behind. The loss may not be very great, but these vanishing traditions might furnish valuable data for the sociologist, in the future study of racial development. In writing, a few years ago, the volume entitled *The Conjure Woman*,

---

* It is still believed by some that Chesnutt may have been the first to record in print the use of "goopher" as a synonym for conjuration. See Sylvia Lyons Render, "Tar Heelia in Chesnutt," *College Language Association Journal*, 9 (1965), p. 44. But it is clear, as Chesnutt himself notes, that the term was in common use throughout the South. Actually, the term "goopher" was used repeatedly by an earlier Negro writer. See William Wells Brown, *My Southern Home* (Upper Saddle River, N. J.: The Gregg Press, 1968), pp. 11, 70, 74, 79–81, 124. This work first published in 1880 refers to the 1830's and 1840's. For more about Brown, see William Edward Farrison, *William Wells Brown: Author and Reformer* (Chicago, 1969).

Hyatt's recent detailed accounts of "goofer dust" come from informants from Alabama, Arkansas, Georgia, Louisiana, Maryland, as well as several from Fayetteville, North Carolina, Chesnutt's original source. Goofer dust is often associated with "graveyard dirt" and may be dust taken from a cemetery grave. Goofer dust can be used for a variety of purposes. For example, its placement in a victim's shoe will cause the unfortunate person's foot to swell or become sore. Forms of goofer dust made from the heads of snakes, scorpions, or lizards could be used to re-create the same sort of creatures, live, inside the body of the victim. For further information, see Harry Middleton Hyatt, *Hoodoo-Conjuration-Witchcraft-Rootwork* (Washington, D. C.: American University Bookstore, 1970), vol. I, pp. 221–27. Regardless of whether or not the original term "goopher" or "goofer" is an Africanism, it is tempting to speculate about the relationship of "putting the goofer" on someone—bringing them under one's control, or making them "goofy"—to the modern slang words built upon "goof." To be "goofed" is to be under the influence of marijuana and "to goof," meaning to make a mistake, was originally a jazz term. Both of these meanings are not that different from being "under the influence" of a magical agent. Of course, the modern agent is more likely to be a "goof ball" (a drug) rather than Chesnutt's "goopher dust." —ED.

I suspect that I was more influenced by the literary value of the material than by its sociological bearing, and therefore took, or thought I did, considerable liberty with my subject. Imagination, however, can only act upon data—one must have somewhere in his consciousness the ideas which he puts together to form a connected whole. Creative talent, of whatever grade, is, in the last analysis, only the power of rearrangement—there is nothing new under the sun. I was the more firmly impressed with this thought after I had interviewed half a dozen old women, and a genuine "conjure doctor"; for I discovered that the brilliant touches, due, I had thought, to my own imagination, were after all but dormant ideas, lodged in my childish mind by old Aunt This and old Uncle That, and awaiting only the spur of imagination to bring them again to the surface. For instance, in the story, "Hot-foot Hannibal," there figures a conjure doll with pepper feet. Those pepper feet I regarded as peculiarly my own, a purely original creation. I heard, only the other day, in North Carolina, of the consternation struck to the heart of a certain dark individual, upon finding upon his doorstep a rabbit's foot—a good omen in itself perhaps—to which a malign influence had been imparted by tying to one end of it, in the form of a cross, two small pods of red pepper!

Most of the delusions connected with this belief in conjuration grow out of mere lack of enlightenment. As primeval men saw a personality behind every natural phenomenon, and found a god or a devil in wind, rain, and hail, in lightning, and in storm, so the untaught man or woman who is assailed by an unusual ache or pain, some strenuous symptom of serious physical disorder, is prompt to accept the suggestion, which tradition approves, that some evil influence is behind his discomfort; and what more natural than to conclude that some rival in business or in love has set this force in motion?

Relics of ancestral barbarism are found among all peoples, but advanced civilization has at least shaken off the more obvious absurdities of superstition. We no longer attribute insanity to demoniac possession, nor suppose that a king's touch can cure scrofula. To many old people in the South, however, any unusual ache or pain is quite as likely to have been caused by some external evil influence as by natural causes. Tumors, sudden swellings due to inflammatory rheumatism or the bites of insects, are especially open to suspicion. Paralysis is proof positive of conjuration. If there is any doubt, the "conjure doctor" invariably removes it. The credulity of ignorance is his chief stock in trade—there is no question, when he is summoned, but that the patient has been tricked.

The means of conjuration are as simple as the indications. It is a condition of all witch stories that there must in some way be contact, either with the person, or with some object or image intended to represent the person to be affected; or, if not actual contact, at least close proximity. The charm is placed under the door-sill, or buried under the hearth, or hidden in the mattress of the person to be conjured. It may be a crude attempt to imitate the body of the victim, or it may consist merely of a bottle, or a gourd, or a little bag, containing a few rusty nails, crooked pins, or horsehairs. It may be a mysterious mixture thrown surreptitiously upon the person to be injured, or merely a line drawn across a road or path, which line it is fatal for a certain man or woman to cross. I heard of a case of a laboring man who went two miles out of his way, every morning and evening, while going to and from his work, to avoid such a line drawn for him by a certain powerful enemy.

Some of the more gruesome phases of the belief in conjuration suggest possible poisoning, a knowledge of which baleful art was once supposed to be widespread among the imported Negroes of the olden time. The blood or venom of snakes, spiders, and lizards is supposed to be employed for this purpose. The results of its administration are so peculiar, however, and so entirely improbable, that one is supposed to doubt even the initial use of poison, and figure it in as part of the same general delusion. For instance, a certain man "swelled up all over" and became "pieded," that is, pied or spotted. A white physician who was summoned thought that the man thus singularly afflicted was poisoned, but did not recognize the poison nor know the antidote. A conjure doctor, subsequently called in, was more prompt in his diagnosis. The man, he said, was poisoned with a lizard, which at that very moment was lodged somewhere in the patient's anatomy. The lizards and snakes in these stories, by the way, are not confined to the usual ducts and cavities of the human body, but seem to have freedom of movement throughout the whole structure. This lizard, according to the "doctor," would start from the man's shoulder, descend to his hand, return to the shoulder, and pass down the side of the body to the leg. When it reached the calf of the leg the lizard's head would appear right under the skin. After it had been perceptible for three days the lizard was to be cut out with a razor, or the man would die. Sure enough, the lizard manifested its presence in the appointed place at the appointed time; but the patient would not permit the surgery, and at the end of three days paid with death the penalty of his obstinacy. Old Aunt Harriet told me, with solemn earnestness, that she herself had taken a snake from her own arm, in sections, after a similar experience. Old Harriet may have been lying, but was, I imagine, merely self-deluded. Witches, prior to being burned, have often confessed their commerce with the Evil One. Why should Harriet hesitate to relate a simple personal experience which involved her in no blame whatever?

Old Uncle Jim, a shrewd, hard old sinner, and a palpable fraud, who did not, I imagine, believe in himself to any great extent, gave me some private points as to the manner in which these reptiles were thus transferred to the human system. If a snake or a lizard be killed, and a few drops of its blood be dried upon a plate or in a gourd, the person next eating or drinking from the contaminated vessel will soon become the unwilling landlord of a reptilian tenant. There are other avenues, too, by which the reptile may gain admittance; but when expelled by the conjure doctor's arts or medicines, it always leaves at the point where it entered. This belief may have originally derived its existence from the fact that certain tropical insects sometimes lay their eggs beneath the skins of animals, or even of men, from which it is difficult to expel them until the larvae are hatched. The *chico* or "jigger" of the West Indies and the Spanish Main is the most obvious example.*

* There is good reason to believe that "jigger" or "chigger" is an Africanism. See Lorenzo Dow Turner, *Africanisms in the Gullah Dialect* (Chicago, 1949), p. 195. —ED.

Old Aunt Harriet—last name uncertain, since she had borne those of her master, her mother, her putative father, and half a dozen husbands in succession, no one of which seemed to take undisputed precedence—related some very remarkable experiences. She at first manifested some reluctance to speak of conjuration, in the lore of which she was said to be well-versed; but by listening patiently to her religious experiences—she was a dreamer of dreams and a seer of visions—I was able now and then to draw a little upon her reserves of superstition, if indeed her religion itself was much more than superstition.

"W'en I wuz a gal 'bout eighteen er nineteen," she confided,

de w'ite folks use' ter sen' me ter town ter fetch vegetables. One day I met a' ole conjuh man name' Jerry Macdonal', an' he said some rough, ugly things ter me. I says, says I, "You mus' be a fool." He did n' say nothin', but jes' looked at me wid 'is evil eye. W'en I come 'long back, date ole man wuz stan'in' in de road in front er his house, an' w'en he seed me he stoop' down an' tech' de groun', jes' lack he wuz pickin' up somethin', an' den went 'long back in 'is ya'd. De ve'y minute I step' on de spot he tech', I felt a sha'p pain shoot thoo my right foot, it tu'n't under me, an' I fell down in de road. I pick' myself up' an' by de time I got home, my foot wuz swoll' up twice its nachul size. I cried an' cried an' went on, fer I knowed I'd be'n trick' by dat ole man. Dat night in my sleep a voice spoke ter me an' says: "Go an' git a plug er terbacker. Steep it in a skillet er wa'm water. Strip it lengthways, an' bin' it ter de bottom er yo' foot." I never didn' use terbacker, an' I laid dere, an' says I ter myse'f, "My Lawd, w'at is dat, w'at is dat!" Soon ez my foot got kind er easy, dat voice up an' speaks ag'in: "Go an' git a plug er terbacker. Steep it in a skillet er wa'm water, an' bin'

it ter de bottom er yo' foot." I scramble' ter my feet, got de money out er my pocket, woke up de two little boys sleepin' on de flo', an' tol' 'em ter go ter de sto' an' git me a plug er terbacker. Dey didn' want ter go, said de sto' wuz shet, an' de sto' keeper gone ter bed. But I chased 'em fo'th, an' day found' de sto' keeper an' fetch' de terbacker—dey sho' did. I soaked it in de skillet, an' stripped it 'long by degrees, till I got ter de een', w'en I boun' it under my foot an' roun' my ankle. Den I kneel' down an' prayed, an' next mawnin' de swelin' wuz all gone! Dat voice wus de Spirit er de Lawd talkin' ter me, it sho' wuz! De Lawd have mussy upon us, praise his Holy Name!

Very obviously Harriet had sprained her ankle while looking at the old man instead of watching the path, and the hot fomentation had reduced the swelling. She is not the first person to hear spirit voices in his or her own vagrant imaginings.

On another occasion, Aunt Harriet's finger swelled up "as big as a corn-cob." She at first supposed the swelling to be due to a felon. She went to old Uncle Julius Lutterloh, who told her that some one had tricked her. "My Lawd!" she exclaimed, "how did they fix my finger?" He explained that it was done while in the act of shaking hands. "Doctor" Julius opened the finger with a sharp knife and showed Harriet two seeds at the bottom of the incision. He instructed her to put a poultice of red onions on the wound over night, and in the morning the seeds would come out. She was then to put the two seeds in a skillet, on the right hand side of the fire-place, in a pint of water, and let them simmer nine mornings, and on the ninth morning she was to let all the water simmer out, and when the last drop should have gone, the one that put the seeds in her hand was to go out of this world! Harriet, however, did not pursue the treatment to the bitter end. The seeds, once extracted, she put into a small phial, which she corked up tightly and put carefully away in her bureau drawer. One morning she went to look at them, and one of them was gone. Shortly afterwards the other disappeared. Aunt Harriet has a theory that she had been tricked by a woman of whom her husband of that time was unduly fond, and that the faithless husband had returned the seeds to their original owner. A part of the scheme of conjuration is that the conjure doctor can remove the spell and put it back upon the one who laid it. I was unable to learn, however, of any instance where this extreme penalty had been insisted upon.

It is seldom that any of these old Negroes will admit that he or she possesses the power to conjure, though those who can remove spells are very willing to make their accomplishment known, and to exercise it for a consideration. The only professional conjure doctor whom I met was old Uncle Jim Davis, with whom I arranged a personal interview. He came to see me one evening, but almost immediately upon his arrival a minister called. The powers of light prevailed over those of darkness, and Jim was dismissed until a later time, with a commission to prepare for me a conjure "hand" or good luck charm, of which, he informed some of the children about the house, who were much interested in the proceedings, I was very much in need. I subsequently secured the charm, for which, considering its potency, the small sum of silver it cost me was no extravagant outlay. It is a very small bag of roots and herbs, and, if used according to directions, is guaranteed to insure me good luck and "keep me from losing my job." The directions require it to be wet with spirits nine mornings in succession, to be carried on the person, in a pocket on the right hand side, care being taken that it does not come in contact with any tobacco. When I add that I procured, from an equally trustworthy source, a genuine graveyard rabbit's foot, I would seem to be reasonably well protected against casual misfortune. I shall not, however, presume upon this immunity, and shall omit no reasonable precaution which the condition of my health or my affairs may render prudent.

An interesting conjure story which I heard, involves the fate of a lost voice. A certain woman's lover was enticed away by another woman, who sang very sweetly, and who, the jilted one suspected, had told lies about her. Having decided upon the method of punishment for this wickedness, the injured woman watched the other closely, in order to find a suitable opportunity for carrying out her purpose; but in vain, for the fortunate one, knowing of her enmity, would never speak to her or remain near her. One day the jilted woman plucked a red rose from her garden, and hid herself in the bushes near her rival's cabin. Very soon an old woman came by, who was accosted by the woman in hiding, and requested to hand the red rose to the woman of the house. The old woman, suspecting no evil, took the rose and approached the house, the other woman following her closely, but keeping herself always out of sight. When the old woman, having reached the door and called out the mistress of the house, delivered the rose as requested, the recipient thanked the giver in a loud voice, knowing the old woman to be somewhat deaf. At the moment she spoke, the woman in hiding reached up and caught her rival's voice, and clasping it tightly in her right hand, escaped, unseen, to her own cabin. At the same instant the afflicted woman missed her voice, and felt a sharp pain shoot through her left arm, just below the elbow. She at first suspected the old woman of having tricked her through the medium of the red rose, but was subsequently informed by a conjure doctor that her voice had been stolen, and that the old woman was innocent. For the pain he gave her a bottle of medicine, of which nine drops were to be applied three times a day, and rubbed in with the first two fingers of the right hand, care being taken not to let any other part of the hand touch the arm, as this would render the medicine useless. By the aid of a mirror, in which he called up her image, the conjure doctor ascertained who was the guilty person. He sought her out and charged her with the crime which she promptly denied. Being pressed, however, she admitted her guilt. The doctor insisted upon immediate restitution. She expressed her willingness, and at the same time her inability

to comply—she had taken the voice, but did not possess the power to restore it. The conjure doctor was obdurate and at once placed a spell upon her which is to remain until the lost voice is restored. The case is still pending, I understand; I shall sometime take steps to find out how it terminates.

How far a story like this is original, and how far a mere reflection of familiar wonder stories, is purely a matter of speculation. When the old mammies would tell the tales of Brer Rabbit and Brer Fox to the master's children, these in turn would no doubt repeat the fairy tales which they had read in books or heard from their parents' lips. The magic mirror is as old as literature. The inability to restore the stolen voice is foreshadowed in the Arabian Nights, when the "Open Sesame" is forgotten. The act of catching the voice has a simplicity which stamps it as original, the only analogy of which I can at present think being the story of later date, of the words which were frozen silent during the extreme cold of an Arctic winter, and became audible again the following summer when they had thawed out.*

---

* This final example cited by Chesnutt is a standard traditional tall tale or lie. See tale type 1889F, "Frozen Words Thaw," in Antti Aarne and Stith Thompson, *The Types of the Folktale* (Helsinki, 1961), p. 511. —ED.

Braziel Robinson
Possessed of Two Spirits

ROLAND STEINER

From North Carolina, we move south to Georgia for an account of an actual conjurer dating from the turn of the century. The following information was reported by a Georgia doctor from Grovetown, Columbia County, Georgia. Many of the familiar details such as the caul and the potent "graveyard dirt" are present. The uniformity of supernatural phenomena is striking.

Of particular interest is the distinction allegedly made between good and bad spirits on the basis of color. The fact that "good" spirits are always white and "bad" spirits are always black definitely supports Eldridge Cleaver's argument that folklore does contain and perpetuate inherent racism and that folklore can be destructive of race pride.

For other contributions to folklore by Roland Steiner, see his "Observations on the Practice of Conjuring in Georgia," Journal of American Folklore, 14 (1901), pp. 173–80; "Seeking Jesus," Journal of American Folklore, 14 (1901), p. 172; "Sol Lockhart's Call," Journal of American Folklore, 13 (1900), pp. 67–70; and "Superstitions and Beliefs of Central Georgia," Journal of American Folklore, 12 (1899), pp. 261–71.

BRAZIEL ROBINSON, recently deceased, is a Negro of about seventy-five years of age, and came to our plantation immediately after the war to test the question whether he was really free or not, and had the right to move from his former master's place. He soon established a reputation as a foreseer of events, as a root-doctor, would advise Negroes when to plant their garden, when to expect rain, administered in a medical way to the many wants of the community in which he lived. Braziel had a peculiar habit, when any one asked him a ques-

Reprinted from the *Journal of American Folklore*, 13 (1900), pp. 226–28, by permission of the American Folklore Society.

tion, of asking you please to give him a chew of tobacco, so that he could collect his thoughts before answering you.

The following statement is given in his own words:

I am not a preacher, but a member of the church, but I can make a few remarks in church, I have a seat in conference, I can see spirits, I have two spirits, one that prowls around, and one that stays in my body. The reason I have two spirits is because I was born with a double caul. People can see spirits if they are born with one caul, but nobody can have two spirits unless they are born with a double caul, very few people have two spirits. I was walking along and met a strange spirit, and then I heard a stick crack behind me and turned round and heard my prowling spirit tell the strange spirit it was me, not to bother me, and then the strange spirit went away and left me alone. My two spirits are good spirits, and have power over evil spirits, and unless my mind is evil, can keep me from harm. If my mind is evil my two spirits try to win me, if I won't listen to them, then they leave me and make room for evil spirits and then I'm lost forever, mine have never left me, and they won't if I can help it, as I shall try to keep in the path.

Here he took the quid of tobacco out of his mouth, and rolling it in his hand for a few minutes, resumed:

Spirits are around about all the time, dogs and horses can see them as well as people, they don't walk on the ground, I see them all the time, but I never speak to one unless he speaks to me first, I just walk along as if I saw nothing, you must never speak first to a spirit. When he speaks to me and I speak back I always cross myself, and if it is a good spirit, it tells me something to help me, if it is a bad spirit, it disappears, it can't stand the cross. Sometimes two or more spirits are together, but they are either all good, or all bad spirits, they don't mix like people on earth, good and bad together.

Good spirits have more power than bad spirits, but they can't help the evil spirits from doing us harm. We were all born to have trouble, and only God can protect us. Sometimes the good spirits let the evil spirits try to make you fall, but I won't listen to the evil spirits.

When a person sees a spirit, he can tell whether it is a good spirit or a bad spirit by the color, good spirits are always white, and bad spirits are always black. When a person sees a bad spirit, it sometimes looks like a black man with no head, and then changes into a black cat, dog, or hog, or cow, sometimes the cow has only one horn and it stands out between the eyes. I never saw them change into a black bird; a man told me he saw one in the shape of a black owl; but I have seen good spirits change into white doves, but never saw one in shape of a cat, have seen them in the shape of men and children, some with wings and some without, then I have seen them look like a mist or a small white cloud. When a person is sick and meets good spirits near enough to feel the air from their bodies, or wings, he generally gets well. Any one can feel a spirit passing by, though only a few can see it. I've seen a great many together at one time, but that was generally about dusk. I never saw them flying two or three along together. Good and bad spirits fly, but a bad spirit can't fly away up high in the air, he is obleeged to stay close to the ground. If a person follows a bad spirit, it will lead him into all kinds of bad places, in ditches, briers. A bad spirit is obleeged to stay in the body where it was born, all the time. If one has two spirits, the one outside wanders about, it is not always with you. If it is near and sees any danger, it comes and tells the spirit inside of you, so it can keep you from harm. Sometimes it can't, for the danger is greater than any spirit can ward off, then one's got to look higher.

I've heard spirits talk to themselves, they talk in a whisper like, sometimes you can tell what they're saying, and sometimes you can't. I don't think the spirit in the body has to suffer for the sins of the body it is in, as it is always telling you to do right. I can't tell, some things are hidden from us.

People born with a caul generally live to be old. The caul is always buried in a graveyard.

Children born with a caul talk sooner than other children, and have lot more sense.

I was conjured in May 1898, while hoeing cotton, I took off my shoes and hoed two rows, then I felt strange, my feet begun to swell, and then my legs, and then, I couldn't walk. I had to stop and go home. Just as I stepped in the house, I felt the terriblest pain in my jints, I sat down and thought, and then looked in my shoes, I found some yaller dirt, and knew it was graveyard dirt, then I knew I was conjured, I then hunted about to find if there was any conjure in the house and found a bag under my door-step. I opened the bag and found, some small roots about an inch long, some black hair, a piece of snake skin, and some graveyard dirt, dark-yaller, right off some coffin. I took the bag and dug a hole in the ɔublic road in front of my house, and buried it with the dirt out of my shoes, and throwed some red pepper all around the house. I didn't get any better, and went and saw a root-doctor, who told me he could take off the conjure, he gave me a cup of tea to drink and biled up something and put it in a jug to wash my feet and legs with, but it ain't done me much good, he ain't got enough power, I am gwine to see one in Augusta, who has great power, and can tell me who conjured me. They say root-doctors have power over spirits, who will tell them who does the conjuring; they ginerally uses yerbs

gathered on the changes of the moon, and must be got at night. People git conjur from the root-doctors and one root-doctor often works against another, the one that has the most power does the work.

People gits most conjured by giving them snake's heads, lizards, and scorpions, dried and beat up into powder and putting it in the food or water they drink, and then they gits full of the varmints, I saw a root-doctor cut out of a man's leg a lizard and a grasshopper, and then he got well. Some conjur ain't to kill, but to make a person sick or make him have pain, and then conjur is put on the ground in the path where the person to be conjured goes, it is put down on a young moon, a growing moon, so the conjur will rise up and grow, so the person stepping over it will git conjured. Sometimes they roll it up in a ball and tie it to a string and hang it from a limb, so the person to be conjured, coming by, touches the ball, and the work's done, and he gits conjured in the part that strikes the ball, the ball is small and tied by a thread so a person can't see it. There are many ways to conjur, I knew a man that was conjured by putting graveyard dirt under his house in small piles and it almost killed him, and his wife. The dirt made holes in the ground, for it will always go back as deep as you got it, it goes down to where it naturally belongs.

Only root-doctors can git the graveyard dirt, they know what kind to git and when, the hants won't let everybody git it, they must git it thro' some kind of spell, for the graveyard dirt works trouble 'til it gits back inter the ground, and then wears off. It must git down to the same depth it was took from, that is as deep as the coffin lid was from the surface of the ground.

Mojo

RUTH BASS

From Georgia, we move to Mississippi to confirm the consistency of conjuration techniques. Despite occasional overly literary embellishments, Ruth Bass, a native white Mississippian appears to have succeeded in capturing both the sense and the spirit of folk belief. Most of the annoying patronizing condescension which invariably permeates southern white accounts of Negro superstition seems to be absent. Praiseworthy details are presented with sufficient sensitivity and sympathy as to partly (though not completely!) excuse the romantic references to possible origins in an African jungle. The personages of Menthy and Old Divinity are unforgettable, and most readers will be grateful to Ruth Bass for her poignant vignettes.

CONJUR IS a strange thing. Some conjurers are born that way. Some learn their magic through long, slow years of patient meditating and watching of signs, and others, like young Donis, have conjur thrust upon them by accident. Donis picked up a hat that had been blown from another Negro's head in a whirlwind. He handed the hat back to the man. A few hours later the owner of the hat stooped to untangle the traces from his black mule's leg. He was laugh-ing. The mule became frightened and kicked the man to death. He had died laughing aloud, and his death was attributed to Donis who had taken the hat from the devil in the whirlwind. Men would no longer work around him. He could not get a place to stay or to eat. Eventually he was forced to live away from his fellows in a tumble-down cabin on the edge of the swamp and follow conjuring as a trade. Sometimes a gal will come down from one of the

Reprinted from *Scribner's Magazine*, 87 (1930), pp. 83–90, by permission of Meredith A. Bass.

plantations begging him for a love-charm; or a half-scared buck will come, willing to pay for a trick that will bring his wandering woman back home. But mostly Donis will be alone with the swamp and the silence—and the powers of conjuration. For magic is a lonely thing and when it falls upon a native of the Bayou Pierre swamp-lands there is no escape from it.

In these swamp-lands there are different ways by which a conjurer can be identified. If you are a double-sighted person and can see ghosts, if you happen to have been born on Christmas Day, or are a seventh son, you are born for magic. Others say, if you are an albino, or have three birthmarks on your left arm, or a luck-mole on your right arm, or if you have one blue eye and one black, you are born to conjure and it will be no trouble for you to learn the art of gri-gri. Of the several conjurers I have known in Mississippi, each one had some distinguishing physical characteristic. One was tall and dark with grave eyes. One was an undersized, dwarfed mulatto, almost an albino, with green eyes and a cunning little face. I remember one who had a twisted back and walked with a sickening, one-sided limp. But the most powerful conjurer I know today is a tall, dark woman. Her straight-backed, small-breasted figure seems in some strange way to suggest unusual strength. Her eyes are grave and wise, terribly wise in the ways of ghosts and devils and mojo, as well as in the practice of medicine. "Dat sickness ain't nat'ul an' doctor's medicine am bound tuh be agin hit," they say and send for Menthy. Menthy will come, grave and dark, to work her cures. A strange conglomeration of superstition and folk-lore these cures are.

She might prescribe the sucking of alum, or rubbing the limbs with grave-yard dirt. Her specific for all diseases brought on by tricks or conjur is to mix some mutton suet with powdered blue-stone and quinine and rub this salve on the bottoms of the patient's feet every morning. No one can harm the person who uses this salve, because it contains the fat of a lamb, and the lamb "am so innercint." For diagnosis Menthy will put a piece of silver in the hand or mouth of the sufferer. If the silver turns black, he has been conjured and must be treated accordingly. To locate the conjurer she uses the blood of a fat chicken. This is put into the hand of the patient and the hand slapped; whichever way the blood flies—well, the origin of the trick lies in that direction. One conjurer, a blue-gum Negro called a "Ponton," or cross between a horse and a man, uses tea made from the burned lining of the gizzard of a frizzly chicken pounded up with prince-feathers, to relieve a trick. Still another—an old, wrinkled, black woman—claims that water in which silver has been boiled is very effective.

As a preventive against being tricked Menthy prescribes nutmeg worn on a string around the neck, or the red foot of a jay-bird carried in the pocket. Others advise carrying the paw of a mole or a little ball of "he-garlic." One old man from up the swamp carries the right eye of a wolf in his right sleeve as a guard against the evil eye. The little old, black, wrinkled woman claims that she can prevent a woman from ever having children by giving her tea brewed from black haw and dogwood roots. Menthy accomplishes this by giving the woman dog-fennel to chew. She makes salves by boiling collard leaves and vinegar or vinegar and clay. But Tully, the hunchback conjurer who has a crippled body but unusual "strength uv haid," makes salve out of earthworms fried in lard. He cures rheumatism with the gall from animals, and headache with a poultice of jimson-weeds. To cure chills and fever he rubs red pepper up and down the patient's back to warm up the system. Others put red pepper into the sufferer's shoes. Menthy prescribes bathing in sun-warmed water and wrapping up in leaves of "Palma Christian." All over Mississippi one will find hog's-hoof tea prescribed for pneumonia or pine-top tea sweetened with honey, or sweetgum ball tea. Menthy cures consumption by giving the patient hot blood from the heart of a young bull and by rubbing goose grease on the chest. To cure toothache, she picks the teeth with a sliver from a pine-tree that was struck by lightning and then throws the pick into running water. The best-known general household remedy, given for all manner of diseases, is May-water. May-water is water caught in the first rain that falls in the month of May.

The strangest cure I think I ever heard of in Mississippi was when Overlea, a seventh son and a born double-sighter, loosed five white pigeons that had never known freedom, for a sick child. When the pigeons crossed water the child was cured. Overlea, they say, can "split a storm" by sticking an axe into the corner of the room or into the ground. He can produce rain by crossing two matches and sprinkling salt on them, or by hanging up a "snake-shed." He can call fair weather by sleeping with certain flowers under his head. Yes, magic is still a practised and powerful thing among the Negroes of some parts of the South today.

It was Menthy, feared and respected as she is all over the Bottoms, who told me how to become a conjurer. It seems that the secret of the whole thing is to know the signs. First, last, and always, know the signs, and nothing will be hidden from you. If a person knows the signs, he can always tell what is going to happen. One thing the conjurer always does is to learn some secret name by which he calls himself when working spells. This name is never revealed to any one. Then he learns to meditate. If he knows the signs and knows how to meditate, all he has to do is lie down on his back, fold his arms, and watch the visions swing by. There are a few signs that are more or less common to all mojo-workers.

They always carry a beauty rock (a small, clear pebble) in their pockets and they are careful never to drink from a gourd after another conjurer. They always watch out for cats, pigs, and woodpeckers. From various sources I learned why these three creatures are watched out for. Woodpeckers are conjur-birds, always tapping at things and digging out secrets. Pigs can see the wind. When you hear pigs squealing uncommon loud—well, that's a sure sign of a change in the weather. The pigs are squealing at what they see on the wind. If a person wishes to see the wind, he must put a little of the water that runs out of the corner of the pig's eye in his own eyes. Cats were first made of Jesus' glove, and that's why it's so unlucky to kill a cat. Always watch out for cats.

Then the student of mojo must learn how to lay the tricks. Red flannel is almost always used in making tricks. To hoodoo a person, Menthy takes a bunch of hair or wool, a rabbit's paw, and a chicken gizzard. She ties these up in a red flannel rag and fastens the bundle to some implement which the man to be conjured is in the habit of using. She assures me that as soon as the person catches sight of the trick his eyes will bulge out, and he will break into a cold sweat. He gradually grows weak and will eventually fall away to a mere shadow. Some conjurers put their tricks into the person's shoes; others into his sweet-potato patch or his wood-pile, or rub it on his razor or butcher-knife. Menthy's grandpappy, who from all accounts was a most powerful witch-doctor, could make the wind a bearer of devilment. He would dust his hands with powdered devil's-shoestring and devil's-snuff, then hold them up so the wind would blow the dust toward the person he wished to conjure. Jimson-weed pounded with the dried head of a snake will fly on the wind and work the trick also. However, except in extreme cases, Menthy herself is averse to using the wind to carry tricks. She would only shake her head when I asked her why. Probably because too many people can see the wind nowadays.

As a personal favor to a friend of long standing, Menthy disclosed to me, on special request, the most powerful trick known to any conjurer in the Bottoms. It is a dangerous business and can't be played with. You take the wing of a jay-bird, the jaw of a squirrel, and the fang of a rattlesnake and burn them to ashes on red-hot metal. Mix the ashes with a bit of grave dust, taken at sundown from the grave of the old and wicked, moisten with the blood of a pig-eating sow, and make into a cake. Put this cake into a little bag tied with ravellings from a shroud, name it for a person you wish to conjure, and bury it under his house. It will bring certain death to the victim. In making this trick, the forefinger of the left hand must be used. In fact, among conjurers of this section of the South it is a common practice to use this certain finger. This is the dog finger. The dog finger is the conjur finger and the left hand is the devil's hand.

So far as I have been able to discover, there seems to be a trick for every kind of occupation and desire in life. To the swamp Negroes nothing is inanimate, incapable of being tricked. I have heard a swamp Negress talking aloud to her pot because it was slow about boiling. She begged it to boil, pointed out the advantages of boiling over not boiling, and when it remained obstinate she resorted to a trick which consisted of rubbing her belly. The pot promptly cooked faster. To prevent things from boiling over, the cook rubs her head. I have often heard plantation folks use angry words to a fire because it refused to burn. And they say that if a fire burns with a blue flame it is making anger and you'd better "chunk" some salt in there to drive the devil away.

The swamp seems to be full of old and familiar friends, and those who live in its shadows are never lonely. The fisherman on the wet, shaded banks of the bayou talks to his fish-hook before he sets it to catch the sleepy catfish in the sluggish stream. He tells the hook how hungry his children and his old grandmammy are, and how easy it is to catch fish. Then he spits on the hook and sets it out. A hook that continually refuses to catch a fish is judged naturally bad-natured and perverse and is soon consigned to the bottom of the bayou.

One class of tricks always popular and useful is the great and powerful love-charm. Chewing of heart-root in the presence of a person will soften that person's heart toward you. To get control over a person, chew some shame-weed and rub it on your hands before shaking hands with the person you desire. To call a woman to you is a little more complicated and usually has to be done by a professional, though the common population tries its hand at most of the love-tricks. You pick up some dirt from the woman's foot-track, mingle it with some dust from your own track, mix with red onion juice, and tie in red flannel. This charm is carried in the left breast-pocket and acts as a magnet to draw the desired one to you. To bring a man and woman together, Menthy gets some hair from the head of each. She takes this to the woods and finds a young sapling that has grown up in a fork. She splits the tree a little at this fork and puts the hair in the split place. When this tree grows up the two will be eternally united. Menthy informs me that men are always coming to her for tricks to keep a wandering woman at home, and this is how she does it. Devil's-shoestring (a plant that grows abundantly in the Bottoms) mixed with snail-water, tracks from the woman's right foot, gunpowder, and bluestone. This mixture planted around the house is guaranteed to keep any woman at home. To break up a couple, Menthy takes some of the tracks of each while the ground is wet, rolls this up in brown paper, putting some whiskers of a cat and those of a dog in with it. She ties this up in a sack and leaves until the earth is dry. When it has dried she throws it all into the fire, and the two will henceforth fight like cats and dogs.

These are a few proofs that magic is a living thing in some parts of the South today. Where did it come from? How long has it existed? What part of it was brought from the African jungle?

How much of it has been acquired from the whites, who in turn had brought it from their own foreign forefathers? Most of us have lost our ancient mysteries in the creation and worship of machinery. We have left magic behind. As they have taken the out-of-date clothes and old-fashioned, battered furniture, they took our outworn wisdom. Planted in the swamp this patched and cut-down wisdom has lived and grown. Their mojo is not fakery. It is not trickery. It is magic. Swamps themselves are mysterious, and magic belongs there. Swamps are refuges for wild things that are in danger of extermination. Mojo is taking its last stand. It has retreated to the swamp-lands. Whatever its origin, whatever its future, it is no less interesting and no less an outward sign of the emotional and spiritual life of the rural Negroes in parts of the South today. I am convinced that volumes of unsurpassably interesting folk-knowledge exist among the plantation black folk of Mississippi and other Southern States. It seems certain that at least a part of this magic is of African origin. It is doubly certain that it is all in danger of passing away with the passing of plantation Negro life.

In these swamp-lands I have often found traces of the old magic called tree-talking. Here magic becomes a still more imponderable thing and carries with it a philosophy that is more or less pantheistic. It had its roots in the friendship of the jungle man for the mysterious, animated, and beautiful world in which he lived. The swamp people, like the jungle men, recognize life in everything about them. They impart a consciousness and a wisdom to the variable moods of material things, wind, water, trees. Details are vague and hard to find, but, so far as I have been able to ascertain, the basis of tree-talking is the cultivation of a friendship with a certain tree—any tree of any species will do. The young tree-talker goes to this tree, first with a teacher and later alone. He loves it and studies it under all conditions and seasons. He listens while the summer breezes whisper through it. He pays attention to the lashing of winter winds. He meditates under it by day and sleeps under it at night. Then, when he has learned its language, tree and man talk together. No one can explain it. It is simply magic, a magic that is still found in the Bayou Pierre swamp-land today. Among my acquaintances I number one tree-talker. The other conjurers point to Divinity when I mention tree-talking. More than once I have visited his cabin in the edge of the swamp, burning with curiosity, and I learned nothing tangible. I resolved to try again and on a warm afternoon in autumn I followed the swamp path along the bayou until I found him—and what he lived by.

Old Divinity sat on the little front porch of his cabin at the very edge of the swamp. It was late October, dry and still with a low-hanging sky. Leaves were beginning to drift from the big water-oak that dominated his clean-swept yard. A frizzly cock and three varicolored hens scratched and clucked in the shrivelled leaves under a fig-tree near the porch. Six white pigeons sat in a row on the roof, sunning their ruffled feathers. A brown leaf, whirled from the oak by a sudden gust of wind, fell on Divinity's knee. He laid a gnarled old hand on the leaf and held it there. A swarm of sulphur-yellow butterflies floated by. Silently, aimlessly, purposefully, they drifted eastward. Divinity sighed.

"Bes' tuh stay in one place an' take

whut de good Lawd sends, lak a tree." Here was my chance, it seemed.

"Yes, there's something of magic about a tree. I've heard that, for whoever can understand, there's a thing called tree-talking, Ever hear of it, Divinity?"

"Did Ah! Ma gran'mammy brung tree-tawkin' from de jungle. Ah's from a tree-tawkin' fambly, an' Ah ain't bin livin' undah this watah-oak evah since de surrendah foh nuthin'." I felt that I was near to looking into that almost inscrutable Negro soul. Here were pages of precious folk-knowledge and all of it in danger of passing with ninety-six-year-old Divinity. What could I say to draw out a bit of his jungle lore? I said nothing.

The old man fumbled through his numerous pockets for his sack of home-mixed tobacco and clay pipe. A flame flared up from his match, then the fragrance of burning deer-tongue slipped away on the soft air. Divinity rubbed his dry old hands together. I was afraid to seem too eager. Silence lay between us. Suddenly there came from the swamp pines and cypresses that crowded upon the little clearing, a soft murmur, a sound like the whimper of a company of comfortless creatures passing through the trees. We felt no wind and there was no perceptible movement in the tree-tops; but the gray swamp-moss swayed gently as though it were endowed with the power of voluntary motion.

"Heah dat? If yo heah murmurin' in de trees when de win' ain't blowin', dem's sperrits. Den effen yo know how tuh lissen yo kin git dey wisdom."

"Spirits of what, Divinity?"

"Why, de sperrits ob trees! Dey rustle de leaves tuh tract tenshun, den dey speaks tuh yo."

"So trees have spirits, have they?"

"Cose dey does." The old man with-

ered me with a glance, puffed out a cloud
of fragrant smoke and proceeded, in his
slow old voice, to tell me a few things
about spirits. Everything has spirit, he
told me. What is it in the jimson-weed
that cures asthma if it isn't the spirit
of the weed? What is that in the buckeye
that can drive off rheumatism unless it's
spirit? Yes, he assured me, everything
has spirit. To prove it he could take
me to a certain spring that was haunted
by the ghost of a bucket. Now if that
bucket didn't have a spirit where did its
ghost come from? To Divinity man is
only a rather insignificant partaker in the
adventure called life. The soul of man
is a living thing, but neither greater nor
less than the soul of anything else in
nature. To him it is stupid to think of
all other things as being soulless, insensi-
tive, dead. "Is eberything cept'n man
daid den? Dat red-burd yondah—" A
cardinal, like a living flame, flashed into
a dark pine, "Dat black bitch ob yourn
—what she got?" Old Divinity had hit
home. I stroked the soft head the old
spaniel rested on my knee. "Yessum,
mens an' dey rememberings keep on
livin' but dat ain't all; so do de wind an'
de trees an' de burds dat sing in 'em. Men
am a part uv hit, dat's all. Jes' a part uv
de livin' souls, no mo' an' no less. Men
ain't all."

"It's a pity more men don't know
this," I agreed, half to myself.

"Yessum. Hit's a sho pity," Divinity
agreed, half to himself. Then I asked
Divinity how men could learn this truth
of his. He assured me that some men
were born with it, though most people
had to find it out for themselves.

"What about you, Divinity, were you
born with wisdom, or did you learn it?"

"Me? Ah's de gran'son ob a witch,"
he answered proudly. "An' Ah's bawn

wid a veil ovah ma face. A pusson what
bawn wid a veil is er dubble-sighter." A
double-sighter, he told me gravely, was
a person who had two spirits, one that
wanders and one that stays in the body.
He was "strong in de haid." I gathered
that a double-sighter was one who looked not merely at things but into them—
and through them—one who could see
beauty and significance in things near
at hand. One spirit might be sitting on
the little porch meditating, but the other
would be swinging in the tree-tops.
Double-sighters, Divinity told me seriously, mixing great truths with sheerest
fancy, could see the wind. However, he
assured me that there was no cause for
worry if I hadn't been lucky enough to
have been born with a veil.

"No'm, yo' gotta watch de signs,
dat's all. Anybody what watch de signs
kin tell what comin'. Heah dat woodpecker? Woodpeckers is conjur-burds,
allus tappin' an' seekin'. Effen he come a
tappin' on yo' housetop hit's a sho'
sign ob death in dat fambly. He's a
nailin' down a coffin-lid, an' somebody
bettah git ready tuh go. Yessum, effen
yo' know de signs yo' knows enuff."
For instance, he said, when one feels a
warm breath of air on his neck at night,
that's a sign there's a spirit near and
wanting to talk to him. Sometimes
spirits were known to break a stick near
by or throw down a handful of leaves
to attract the attention. If the spirit is
your friend he will call you by name.
He asked me if I had ever been awakened
in the middle of the night with a feeling
that a voice had called my name. I
confessed that I had.

"Well, dat's a sperrit callin' yo'.
Don't nevah answer no strange voices at
night," he warned me. "Pepul's sperrits
wander at night an' effen dey's woke too

sudden-like de sperrit is likely tuh be left out walkin'." Then the old man was silent, while a mocking-bird sang from the fig-tree. Suddenly he pointed toward the swamp with his rattan cane.

"See dem buzzards ovah dah on dat daid cypress stump? Dey's a waitin' fuh tuh smell deaf. Atter while dey'll go sailin' off in a certain d'rection an' yo' kin be sho' somebody daid ovah dat way.

> " 'Deaf, he is a little man,
> An' he go from do' tuh do'.'

Dat what de ole song say. But de little man allus sen' a sign, effen you jes' knows how tuh watch fuh 'em."

"What are some of the signs of death?" I wanted to know, and these are some of the things he told me. There is the sign of the empty rocking-chair rocking. That's a sure sign. If a wild bird flies into your house that's a sure sign. To drop one's bread in taking it out of the stove means sure and sudden death. If a white measuring-worm gets on a person, that worm is just measuring the person's shroud. Sweeping out of the door after sundown is a sure sign that you are sweeping somebody's soul out. If a lamp goes out of its own accord, that's a sign. If you wash clothes on New Year's Day, you're washing one of your family away. To lie on two chairs is to measure your own grave. Then there are the bad signs, such as: don't stand a hoe alongside the house you live in; and don't ever take a fire from one room to another unless you first spit on the fire. A flock of crows around a house is a bad sign, and, if you see one lone crow fly over, then turn and come back—that's a certain sign of death. Then there is the infallible ticking of deathwatches (wood-beetles). "De deafwatches is heard mos' when a pusson is low sick; when de tickin' stop, de pusson die. Yessum, 'Deaf, he is a little man, an' he go from do' tuh do'.' "

The sun was reddening in the west. A breeze had sprung up, bringing a continual soft murmur from the swamp trees. Old Divinity sat silent. His pipe had gone out. No wonder he sat and thought of death, so lonely and so old, with no one to look to.

"Do you get very lonely, Divinity, now that all your children are gone?"

"No'm. When Jessmin, ma baby, lef', Ah felt sad at fust, but now Ah sets an' tawks tuh mase'f, er de trees an' de win'. Sometimes Ah tawks tuh God an' Jesus an' Saint Peter an' dem. Sometimes, when de win' be's right Ah heah de trains comin' an' goin'. Hit allus makes me sad, folks comin' an' goin'. Bettah tuh stay in one place an' take what de good Lawd sen', lak a tree." Dusk was creeping through the swamp. I rose to go. A killdeer went crying across the little patch back of the cabin.

"Tu'n col', Honey. Heah Killdee cryin' dat away, he callin' up de win'. Wintah comin'." Winter! "Ah, winter, touch that little cabin lightly," I wished, as I turned through the darkening swamp and left the old, old grandson of a witch sitting on his porch, while a lone killdeer called up the wind. Mojo? Call it what you will. The magic of the swamp had come upon me. I found myself talking with the wind!

The Little Man

RUTH BASS

Death is a source of anxiety for all men. In fact, one of the definitions of man is that he is the only animal who is consciously aware of the fact that his life will one day come to an end. Signs of impending death and the elaborate precautions which must be taken by the living during burials are probably found in some form among all peoples. Most folklorists in reporting death signs and customs simply enumerate discrete superstitions giving little or no context. There are countless books and articles which consist of no more than long lists of customs and beliefs among the so-and-so's. In this essay by Ruth Bass, we meet once again the delightful elder of Hazlehurst, Mississippi, Old Divinity. However, the meeting is sad because it is his passing which has occasioned the essay.

In this moving account of an actual service, Ruth Bass has managed to include a large number of traditional folk beliefs having to do with death. These beliefs are skillfully woven into a smooth narrative, a most pleasant and refreshing change from the dull catalog style of presentation common to professional folklorists.

For other treatments of American Negro signs and superstitions, see New-bell Niles Puckett, Folk Beliefs of the Southern Negro *(New York, 1970) and the various articles in periodicals, e.g., Thaddeus Norris, "Negro Superstitions,"* Lippincott's Magazine, *6 (1870), pp. 90–95 (reprinted in Bruce Jackson, ed.,* The Negro and His Folklore in Nineteenth-Century Periodicals, *Bibliographical and Special Series of the American Folklore Society, vol. 18 [Austin, Texas, 1967], pp. 134–43); Eli Shepard, "Superstitions of the Negro,"* Cosmopolitan, *5 (1888), pp. 47–50 (reprinted in Jackson, pp. 247–53); Susan Showers, "A Weddin' and a Buryin' in the Black Belt,"* New England Magazine, *18*

Reprinted from *Scribner's Magazine*, 97 (1935), pp. 120–23, by permission of Meredith A. Bass.

(1898), pp. 478–83 (reprinted in Jackson, pp. 293–301); "Beliefs and Customs Connected with Death and Burial," Southern Workman, *26 (1897), pp. 18–19; Clement Richardson, "Some Slave Superstitions,"* Southern Workman, *41 (1912), pp. 246–48; Martha Emmons, "Dyin' Easy,"* Publications of the Texas Folklore Society, *10 (1932), pp. 55–61; E. Horace Fitchett, "Superstition in South Carolina,"* The Crisis, *43 (1936), pp. 360–61, 370; Margaret Y. Jackson, "Folklore in Slave Narratives before the Civil War,"* New York Folklore Quarterly, *11 (1955), pp. 5–19; and Glenn Sisk, "Funeral Customs in the Alabama Black Belt, 1870–1910,"* Southern Folklore Quarterly, *23 (1959), pp. 169–71.*

CONJURE IS strange and powerful. It devises a remedy for every ailment that visits the Bayou Pierre swamps. But there is a little man in the swamp before whom the most powerful conjurer is helpless and whom no gri-gri, no trick, no mojo can keep away from one's doorstep.

Who dat knockin' at de do',
In a long, black robe an' silver shoe?
Don' look at me, deat'—
Look on down de road!

I got word yesterday that the little man in a long, black robe had called on Old Divinity. Old, old Divinity, one hundred and eight he measured his years, grandson of a witch, wisest and strongest in the head among conjurers, and, most likely, the last tree-talker that the Bayou Pierre swamp will ever know, has "ceasted"!*

I remembered how I had left him one day in spring, meditating under his old water-oak, gnarled and storm-tossed yet brightening with new leaves. It was evening and a breeze had come in from the west. The last white pigeon had circled over the cabin and settled with contented cooing into one of the boxes under the eaves. Suddenly a bull-bat swooped above the cabin, fell and rose with his long, thin cry. Swoop! Swoop! Spade!

"Hab mussy, Jedus! Ah ain' gwi' be wid yall long now, Honey. When a bull-bat go lak dat he diggin' a grabe. He diggin' Ol' 'Vinity's grabe now,"

"But, Divinity, you're not sick. You feel as well as——"

"Nemmine dat. De Li'l Man he go from do' to do', dat what de ol' song say;† and de Li'l Man he allus sen' he sign fust 'fo he come in—effen a body

---

* An introductory headnote places the locale as near Hazlehurst, Mississippi and provides several details of the life of Howard Divinity. During the Civil War, he was a servant with the Confederate Army, and for many years, he faithfully attended annual Confederate reunions. Once he attended an American Legion meeting held in California as guest of a group of soliders. He died on March 28, 1934 at approximately 100 years of age. —ED.

† The anthropomorphic conception of death as a little man who knocks on one's door seems to be traditional. In versions of the spiritual "Oh Lord, Remember Me," we find stanzas along the following lines:

O, Death he is a little man,
He goes from do' to do',
He kill some soul, and he wounded some,
Ah' he lef' some soul for to pray.

See H. G. Spaulding, "Under the Palmetto," *Continental Monthly*, 4 (1863), pp. 188–203. (An

know how ter read hit. Me, Ah done see um slip in de house many time, in he long, black robe an' shinin' shoe but he allus lookin' de odder way. He lookin' twoge me now' De bull-bat's diggin' over ma haid, Ah's ol' an' frail. Ah done hindered deat'—but Ah ain' gwi hinder um no mo'." He rubbed his gnarled, old hands lovingly along the gnarled, old tree trunk. There was no touch of sadness in his speech, just the simple, quiet voice in which he had so often "done wo' down de sun wid tawkin'." Yet in his whole manner there was a profound foreknowledge, a calm acquiescence to the inevitable, without a trace of fear or hate or bravado. It was the calm expression of a simple yet powerful philosophy that had made perfect peace with its environment and out of which had grown an attitude which gave to life that constant flow that enabled him to meet death as he would meet any other little man, with the admiration of the weak for the strong but without cringing.

So I had left him, musing on the melancholy mystery of death; but not alone, for I had heard his philosophy voiced time and again by all of the swamp and its folk, voiced with sweetness and patience and the saving grace of humor. "Deat' ain' nothin' but a robber an' he come to de big house same as de cabin," Old Con had said years ago as she pointed out to the spindle-legged white baby tagging her about the place, a certain blue plush sofa upon which my grandmother had been laid out. "But don' never pint yo finger twoge 'im,

Honey, ner twoge a grabe. Dat bad manners an' de Li'l Man don' lak hit. A body mock an' shame at deat', deat' gwi mock an' shame um back."

They know the meaning of omnipotence, these who have not yet denied the earth as their mother but submit daily to the mysterious power of nature, superhuman forces whose actions they can only partially control. They do not whine over evils but "tie de hankerchief ter fit de haid" and make a song of them, finding some jump-up words to set to a blue, or a reel, or a mourn tune as a defense against brooding and proof that what happens to them has happened to others and is a part of the way of the world. So long as they can't trick death they have accepted it and out of their sense of the fitness of things have formed a sort of friendship with the Little Man. They have met death in the big houses, in the cabins, in the cotton fields, and along the lonely swamp paths under those white mists that rise up from the bayou, and so dramatic is their impulse to weave together into a connected, coherent whole the fragments of knowledge and experience that life brings to them, that death has come to take form and personality. He is a visitor, a conjurer, a Little Man who comes to big house and cabin and whom it is wise to meet with proper manners and receive with proper style. And though the Little Man is so powerful and inexorable that no charm or gri-gri can touch him, and though he may be a robber and a highwayman, he's never a sneak thief for he always sends word of his whereabouts

excerpt from this article is reprinted in Jackson, *The Negro and His Folklore*. For the spiritual text, see pp. 69–70.) See also Thomas Wentworth Higginson, *Army Life in a Black Regiment* (New York, 1962), p. 201; Miles Mark Fisher, *Negro Slave Songs in the United States* (New York, 1969), pp. 72–73; and Newbell Niles Puckett, *Folk Beliefs of the Southern Negro* (New York, 1969), p. 79. —ED.

and intentions. He never slips up on a body who keeps his ears and eyes open to the signs.

To Old Divinity he sent a sign by a bull-bat, to Con by an empty rocking-chair a-rocking. Old Easter bought and made her shroud just a week before she was killed by a team of runaway mules, because her picture had suddenly fallen off the wall of her daughter's cabin. Francellette knew that her apparently healthy baby boy would die before he could walk because she found a white measuring worm measuring him for his little shroud. Manuel, a strapping buck who stumbled into a stable on Christmas Eve night while the animals were kneeling, was buried on New Year's Day. Viola's little Abby told of hearing soft singing as she played under a pine tree. Two days later she took a chill and died. She had heard the angels sing. Matt swept out her house after sundown because she was expecting company. Her old mammy was found dead in her bed the very next morning. The Little Man has signs a plenty. There is the sign of the death watch and of the "deat' drap," the sound of dropping water, slow and regular and mournful along the creek bank or levee, the sign of a wild bird flying into the house, the sign of a woodpecker tapping on one's roof, the sign of the last name a dying person calls, the sign of death bells ringing in the ears.

But, if it so happens that you are one of the unfortunates, weak in the head and unversed in the signs, all you have to do is watch the animals. The dog, especially, is the sacred animal of death. All dogs can smell the Little Man and a black bitch can see him.

"A body kin allus tell when a pusson low-sick," Cæsar assured me one night at a wake, "dey dawg'll leave um. Dawg lay rat on de bed while a pusson sick ontil he git low-sick, den hit leave. When a dawg see de Li'l Man alongside a body hit howls so's ter skeer off all de evil an' onfriendly sperrits. No'am, hit ain' nothin' kin 'duce a dawg ter stay 'round a pusson dat's fey."

"Fey?"

"Yessum, fey, marked wid deat'."

Long and loose-jointed Sam Daniels, who is an adept at "seein' thangs," told me: "Oncet Ah see de Li'l Man hisse'f in he long, black robe wid silver slippers wawkin' twoge de bayou an' a houn' dawg a followin' 'im, nothin' scusin' a houn' dawg." I have been assured more than once that that black bitch of mine is a "natchul deaf' smeller." Obediah, a professional hunter and hunting dog trainer, maintains that whoever, in his life, kicks a house dog or either a cattle dog or trained hunting dog, "He sperrit gwi' pass through mo' louder howlin' an' faster persuin' dan de sheeps do when de wood-runner take atter um. De ain' no friend gwi meet um on dey lonesome road ner neither call in de dawgs dat hang round de golden gates."

The spirits of animals can only be seen by their kind but they can be heard as the well-known song to that effect testifies:

> Old Joe's daid an' gone
> But his hant blows de hawn,
> An' his houn' howls still
> From de top er dat hill!

The dog aims to defend his master against the Little Man but cats, who can also sense death, act just the other way. The black robe and silver slippers seem to attract all manner of cats. When a person is dying this cat will slink in and try to be near. After death a body must never be left alone a minute for cats will gather from the whole community and try to get to a corpse. What they will do to the body is either unknown—or beyond description. Cows, horses, mules, goats, and chickens as well as owls and wolves can also sense death. If a horse neighs during a wake it's a sign that some other member of the family will go soon. A rooster crowing directly after sundown is a sign that some acquaintance of yours has just died or will die soon.

These are a few of the ways that the Little Man has of knocking at one's door. When he actually enters a cabin there are certain ways to receive him, certain manners that are more apt to please and propitiate the visitor. Immediately after the last breath passes from the dying, the clock is stopped and the hands left pointing to the hour and minute the soul left the body until after the funeral. All mirrors and glass-covered pictures are turned to the wall, for it is very bad to see one's reflection while a dead body lies in the room; almost as bad as seeing the reflection of the corpse itself. The shadow of the dead is apt to be seen lurking behind the shoulders of the living, or, worse still, the shadow may become enamored to its looks and continue to be held in the glass permanently. If the master of the house dies, someone, preferably a child of the house, must go out and tell the bees lest they leave the hive. "De bees is too busy ter watch fuh deat', de has ter be tol'." None of the kinfolks may assist in preparing the dead for burial. The women kin have to carry on the mourning which is a ritual and a form that is usually kept going all during the wake and the burial. It usually begins with:

"Thank Gawd, 'e didn' hafter die in

a stawm! Ah don' wanter die in a stawn, Oh Lawd—" This low and solemn wail drifts into a jump-up mourn that recites the good qualities of the deceased who because of them did not have to die in a storm, for to die amid thunder and lightning signifies that the devil has come for the soul. On the other hand rain soon after burial is a good sign that the soul rests peacefully. The emotions are freely released in mourns, consequently the Negro's unrepressed flow of song is sometimes heard best at this time. A strong woman voice sings a couplet in praise of the dead; a chorus of women voices follows with "All dat Ah got done gone!" or "We'll all rise togedder, to face de risin' sun! Oh Lawdy! Lawd hab mussy, if you please!" Then from a corner another takes up the story and so on until a wreath of song is thus woven for their dead kin. Probably no one present has ever known, or can ever repeat a single line of the body of the song, but the endless rhythm restores their spirits until they rise in triumphant shouts often ending in tears, convulsions, a sort of snake dance, or a swound. The men sit dry-eyed and silent.

Meanwhile the friends and neighbors are preparing the body. If a person dies with his mouth and eyes open it is a bad sign, so immediately after death the mouth is tied up and the eyes are closed and weighted down with coins. These coins, usually nickels, brightly polished, should be buried with the body as it is very bad to spend money that has been used for this purpose. The water used to wash the corpse must never be carried out of the room before the body is removed, nor the bed clothes on which the person died, neither should the ashes be taken from the fireplace nor the floor swept. As soon as the body is arrayed in its grave clothes a dish of salt is placed on the chest and a plate full of salt mixed with ashes is set under the cooling board, "ter take up de disease." These ashes are taken to the grave and sprinkled on the coffin. The body must never be left alone for an instant until it is left in the grave. It must be "set up" with. Those attending the "settin-up" or wake need have no fear for the spirit won't bother you until the body is buried. It seems that after death the spirit stays around home three days, around the grave three days, and then goes wandering.

That the spirits of the dead are free and able to come back to their former haunts is never doubted, hence the many signs and precautions to keep spirits from bothering the living. Homeless spirits gather in graveyards, deserted houses, beside streams of water, in the lofts of churches, and such lonely places, especially on dark and rainy nights. To mortals they may take the shapes of persons, cows, clouds, white mists, or wandering lights. They are most active on Friday nights, near the last quarter of the moon, and around midnight. At such times the air is full of spirits and if you cannot see them you must watch for signs of their presence. A warm current of air on your back is a sure sign. A rabbit or cat crossing one's path in the moonlight may be a spirit taking that form. A fresh smell like coffee sometimes indicates a lurking spirit. If you hear a sneeze at night always answer, "God bless you!" All animals and especially dogs and cats can see ghosts. Never turn away a stray dog or cat. Never force your horse on a path he does not want to take, at night. Many precautions are taken to prevent being bothered with spirits. Get some one to read a verse from the Bible, backwards, fold the page, place a

knife and fork in it and put it under your pillow before going to bed and no spirit will disturb your rest that night. Pour sweet milk on the ground before your step and the spirits will stop to lick it up. If the milk is satisfying the spirit will leave without entering. Sprinkle collard seeds on the floor if you have been hearing soft footsteps at night. Newspapers pasted on the walls will cause any spirit to stop and read every word on the papers before bothering you. A horseshoe placed in the fire, or salt sprinkled on the fire, or matches worn in the hair are also good. To lay the spirit of any particular person take a lock of his hair, a piece of his garment, or some very personal possession of his, place this in a hole bored in a tree and plug up the hole tightly with the same wood and bark taken out. The spirit will then take up its abode in this tree and can sometimes be heard rustling the leaves on windless nights. Dogs will avoid such trees.

If you are forced to work the field of a man who has died before the crop he began is harvested, go to the graveyard and take some dirt from the grave and two splinters of wood from the head and foot boards. Turn your back and walk directly to the field. In the middle of the field plant the two pieces of wood in the form of a cross. Throw pinches of the grave dust toward all parts of the land, at the same time asking the dead owner's pardon for taking over his crop. If you don't do this the mules won't plow for you. The dead will pull on the lines and make them walk down the cotton or corn.

If your enemy dies, secretly slip a few white chicken feathers into his coffin, or, if you are unable to do this, bury some feathers in a bottle on his grave. So long as the feathers are safe you won't be bothered.

On the other hand, if you are very strong in the head and wish to see or talk to a spirit for any particular purpose, this can be accomplished by looking over the left shoulder or under the up-raised left arm of a person who is possessed of double sight, or by looking back over your own left shoulder, or looking in the mirror over the shoulder of another person, or sometimes even by holding a rusty nail in your mouth. If these fail, there is an extreme measure that may be taken. Go into a graveyard at twelve o'clock noon or midnight, hold up a mirror before your eyes and drop a pair of scissors to the ground, call the name of the person you desire to see and ask him what you please. This is a risky business, so be sure to have your feet comfortable when you go into the graveyard.

On All Saints' Eve all the dead roam. It is then that suppers are cooked for the spirits. Two persons must cook the supper, without speaking and without using salt in any form. If one speaks the dogs will howl, chickens cackle, winds blow, and the fire burn blue! This food is served on the table with necessary plates and spoons and left all night. Some time during the night the essence or spirit of the food is eaten by the homesick and hungry spirits.

It is coming on to evening when I take the path through the swamp to Old Divinity's cabin for my last sight of the old tree-talker. Before the cabin the men have started a light wood fire on the clean-swept yard in preparation for the wake. They are sitting and squatting about the yard and door steps and gallery, Cæsar and Sam and Overlea and Joe Williams, Donis and Obediah,

several strange young bucks, and the inevitable fringe of children. They take off their hats and give me hidy. I go into the lamplit, firelit room and the familiar smell of ancient Negro cabins comes to me through the newer, stronger odor of living, black bodies; the smells of tobacco and deer tongue and hickory smoke and sage and vinegar and coffee and cologne and hair vigor all mingled into one. The old, old man lies on the cooling board dressed in his grave clothes, black pants and the moth-eaten and faded gray coat of an officer in the Confederate army. This coat Divinity had worn on all other dress occasions ever since the surrender for he had been inordinately proud of the fact that he had been a servant in the army for which the State of Mississippi paid him a pension. The dish of salt is placed on his chest amid the numerous medals that he has collected during his lifetime and pinned there himself. I notice a celluloid campaign button bearing the picture of James K. Vardeman, a World War service star, a dime with a hole in it, the picture of some baseball hero, such as is given as a prize in candy, and a thin silver medal of Saint Anthony with the Infant Jesus. Saint Anthony, pray for the old grandson of a witch, so withered, so tiny, hardly bigger than the Little Man himself! His face is like a bit of withered fire ash. His gnarled old hands lie empty at his sides. His mouth that had uttered wisdom akin to fantasy and fantasy akin to wisdom is tied up with a white rag. He who had lived long like a tree, and, gathered up peace and wisdom and strength like a tree—I turned back to the door through which the Little Man had led him.

The Negroes have gathered now from all the neighboring plantations for the wake. It is an occasion. All night long they will boil coffee and smoke and tell tales around the fires both inside and out of the cabin. Everyday life in the swamp is lonely, often somber and grave. There are few occasions for public gatherings and social intercourse. So among the lonesome and secluded plantations the people must make a pleasure of their necessities, court days, molasses makings, cotton loadings, ginnings, and funerals. They have an intense passion for funerals for here they are among their kind and their aching emotions may run free. They always get at least two days off for every death, first the burying and then some weeks or months later the funeral proper, "ter stir up de daid." They gather for miles and it makes no difference whether the deceased has been a friend or a stranger. As it is a very bad sign to meet a burial procession face to face, the individual who chances to do so always turns and accompanies any procession to the grave. To pass up a procession is simply crossing one's grave! A body must never wear new clothes to a burying lest he excite the envy of the dead and cause the spirit to pull at his shirt or coat tail. At the burying all expressions in word and song are spontaneous, uttered by the friends of the dead about the virtues of his past life. It is here that the most truly poetic jump-ups are improvised to fit old tunes and mourns. At the funeral preachers are given a chance with their carefully composed sermons. It is then that the evergreen is planted on the grave. These trees are identified with the departed and if the tree flourishes all is well with the soul.

Tomorrow afternoon they will pallbear Old Divinity to his resting place under the cedars and cape jessamines and arbor vitæ and boxwood. They will take with him his cup and saucer and medicine bottles, his walking stick, and perhaps his pipe or some other very personal possessions. Some familiar and used articles belonging to the dead are always placed on graves so that the spirit may not find itself in an entirely strange world. The cups and saucers and bottles are always cracked or broken in some way to free the spirit of the thing, that it may serve the dead beyond. On the graves of little children are placed some play-pretties, little doll heads, small cups, or toy animals. Frequently one finds a broken lamp brought to light the soul to glory. I have heard that in former times a pone of bread and a bottle of molasses were placed on the grave, "So's he kin sop his way ter de promised lan'." A cripple's crutch is always placed on his grave. Because Old Divinity was near kin to a witch, a double-sighter, born with a caul and a tree-talker, his carefully preserved caul and probably a bunch of powerful herbs will be thrown into his grave along with his drinking cup, to lay the spirit. Unless you bring the things a person liked with him, he'll come back after them. However, a clod of dirt brought from the grave directly after the burying and placed under the door step will discourage a returning spirit.

> Ah kin see ma dear ol' Pappy, face to face!
> Ah kin see ma dear ol' Pappy, face to face!
> We'll all rise togedder, to face de risin' sun,
> Oh, Lawdy! Lawd, hab mussy, if you please——

The wake proper has begun now. The women's voices rise and fall in a long swinging rhythm, following me down the path where the moon hangs white above the swamp. The pale mists float like wraiths along the low ground, rise, and stoop like low-lying clouds, like ghost women picking cotton. A heron croaks. An owl mocks. Why does the fog swallow all other sounds and make the world so still? But there is a sort of movement in the trees, a low whisper and a sigh. Trees! They are the oldest things in the swamp. The Little Man has passed them by! It is natural to think that they have gathered wisdom, since in their unchanging lives the past and the future are much the same. They have seen the time when Old Divinity was an unborn babe. They will see the time when his great-great-grandson will have counted his hundred years—but who will hear and understand their whispers? What are they trying to say to me to-night? No one will ever know—the Little Man has called the last tree-talker on the Bayou Pierre.

"Oh, Lawdy! Lawd, hab mussy, if you please!"

The Human Hand Threat

A. PHILIP RANDOLPH

There appears to be little doubt that the intimate connection between *superstition and the white racist stereotype of the Negro has discouraged research in this area. A propos of this, it is of interest that famed sociologist E. Franklin Frazier wrote a brief article in which he first listed a number of traditional cures for various ailments, but then he abruptly departed from the conventional listing of folk medicine items to suggest that it was the racism in the social environment which caused some illnesses. Thus he argued, riding on Jim Crow cars could literally make a Negro sick.*

A typical example showing how racism creeps into folklore scholarship itself is a study made by Floyd J. Anderson and Norman C. Meier entitled "The Rationality and Control-Strength of Superstitious Beliefs Among Negroes." The article begins with the statement that "It is commonly believed that superstitious beliefs have a higher control strength among Negroes than among whites." This assumption was presumably tested through the use of question-naires distributed at several schools. Students were asked to indicate to what extent they believed in the efficacy of a given number of specific superstitions. The investigators were "very surprised" when they discovered that the Negro college group turned out to be much less superstitious than the white college control group. They then offered the following explanation which, consciously or unconsciously, expresses the racist bias they were supposedly trying to investigate: *"The writers advance the possible explanation that instruction at the Negro college, particularly in sociology classes, has tended to relieve the Negro mind of* his normal inclination toward superstitious beliefs. . ." (*my emphasis*). *So much for purportedly objective social science!*

But the association of superstition with racist stereotypic thinking occurs in real life as well as in the ivory tower. In September of 1922, Negro labor leader

Reprinted from *The Messenger*, vol. 4 (1922), pp. 499–500, by permission of the author.

A. Philip Randolph received an unusual package. The story of that package and Randolph's interesting analysis of why it was sent to him shows very clearly the importance of superstition with respect to racism.

For the brief study by Frazier, see "Psychological Factors in Negro Health," The Journal of Social Forces, 3 (1925), pp. 488–90. For the study by Anderson and Meier, see Social Forces, 15 (1936), pp. 91–96. For references to the work of A. Philip Randolph, see the introduction to his "Dialogues of the Old and the New Porter," which appears in the "Folk Speech" section of this volume.

ON TUESDAY afternoon, about 2:30 o'clock, September 5, while sitting in my office, I received a package marked "from a friend." This anonymous sender forthwith aroused my suspicions. Immediately I began opening it. I noticed a whitish powder falling out of it. This confirmed my suspicions of there being some foul play intended. Hence, before I had taken all of the brown paper off the box, I telephoned the 38th Precinct Police Station on 135th Street, informed the detectives of the nature of the package, and, post-haste, they came over to my office, regarded the parcel cautiously, and then placed it in water to prevent an explosion in the event that its contents were explosive material.

To the utter amazement and horror of everyone, upon opening the package a human hand was found. In the box also was this letter:

Listen Randolph—

We have been watching your writings in all your papers for quite a while but we want you to understand before we act. If you are not in favor with your own race movement you can't be with ours. There is no space in our race for you and your creed. What do you mean by giving us a nigger? Do you know that our organization is made up of all whites?

We have sent you a sample of our good work, so watch your step or else you. . . . Now let me see your name in your nigger improvement association as a member, paid up too, in about one week from now.

Don't worry about lynching in South. If you were here you wouldn't talk about it. Now be careful how you publish this letter in your magazine or we may have to send your hand to some one else.

Don't think we can't get you and your crowd. Although you are in New York City it is just as easy as if you were in Georgia. If you can't unite with your own race we will find out what's the matter with you all. Don't be selfish. Give your friends a tip.

K.K.K.

All of us immediately set ourselves the task of suggesting some probable theory which would explain such an extraordinary incident. The theories, naturally, were numerous and varied, no one evidencing fright, but a dignified caution.

Of the many theories advanced, the one that seemed to be the most generally accepted, the most logical and real was that one which assigned the dastardly deviltry to the K. K. K.—the signer of the letter.

Their reasons given were: (1) the bitter hatred of the Klan for the position of THE MESSENGER and its editors on "social equality," economic and political. This position had been, time and again, buttressed up by the most exhaustive writing and platform propaganda from coast to coast. For quite some years the MESSENGER editors have been directing a systematic and vigorous campaign through the large white unions against the Klan.

Doubtless, Knights of the Invisible Empire have reported of this work to the Imperial Wizard. In the Socialist and Labor Movement, I have striven, at all times, to establish beyond the question of a doubt, the value and necessity of working class political, economic and social solidarity. Naturally, this would evoke the fire of this group of criminal, cut-throat, midnight riders, who vegetate in the shadows of murder and incendiarism. And to the utter amazement and surprise of this stone-age fraternity, the MESSENGER's work has found a marvelous reception, being recognized, as it is, by an increasingly growing body of unionists and white intellectuals. This, of course, riles these inglorious keepers of the virtues of white womanhood and the sacred principles (?) of Americanism. For it is proclaimed from the imperial throne of the imperial city, Atlanta, that it is "a violation of American ideals and of the fetish of white supremacy, for contact between the Negro and white people to be permitted or, for that matter, even advocated."

That the Klan outfit would be interested in terrifying me from continuing to carry on my work, is obvious from the foregoing.

But why would the Klan send a "human hand"? comes the query. This is why: it is well-nigh a part of the traditions and the folk-lore of Negro life in the South, that Negroes are easily frightened by anything which suggests the "dead." The proverbial "haunted house" plays its part in the fire-side tale

among Negroes. Everybody in the neighborhood can point out the "haunted house." Stories are current, too, of ghosts lurking around the graveyards, chasing passers-by. This is a vestige of primitive superstition. All races pass through this stage as is shown by the anthropologists. It arises from an effort to explain the behavior of natural phenomena. In the absence of the scientific knowledge which will enable people to understand causes of swoons, dreams, storms, earthquakes, floods, famines, droughts, etc., they have assigned as the cause some supernatural agency. The white South knew of this frailty of the old slave Negro. To the old white slave masters, all that was necessary to frighten the Negro field-hands almost out of their senses, was to throw a white sheet over their heads and prowl around the slave shacks in the night. The Negro slaves thought that the white sheeted forms were really ghosts.* Hence, they fled wildly through the fields, a picture of consternation and despair, or else they knelt down on their knees and prayed fervently to God to protect them from the devil, making effusive promises not to commit any more sins, to obey and follow him ever after, circumspectly.

This method of torturing the Negroes was employed quite generally along with cow-hide, to break the spirit of the most intractable, independent and militant Negro slaves; and, in accordance with the law of habit, it remains long after the conditions have passed that

---

* It is by no means certain that Negro slaves really thought the white-sheeted forms were ghosts. Quite the contrary, there is good evidence that they did *not!* The only thing that is certain is that *Klan members thought* that Negroes thought the hooded figures were ghosts. For an excellent discussion of this question, see H. Grady McWhiney and Francis B. Simkins, "The Ghostly Legend of the Ku-Klux Klan," *The Negro History Bulletin*, 14 (February, 1951), pp. 109–12, reprinted in this volume. —ED.

called it forth, and acts with a punctilious accuracy without the conscious attention of the agent.

This then explains why the "human hand" was sent from New Orleans, to the writer, a Negro, living in New York City. It does not occur to the Old South that there is a "New Negro"; that the "Uncle Toms" are passing, if, indeed, they have not already passed away.* The South can't understand how Negroes can grow up, feeling themselves the equal of any white man, advocating political, economic and social equality. Their treasured type of Negro is the so-called "good nigger," *the banjo darky, the me-too-boss, hat-in-hand, good-mornin'-massa species*. But this kind is dead or dying. In fact, it does not vegetate in the North, while only a few old, straggling, decrepit, moribund remnants survive in the South. Education, radical propaganda such as THE MESSENGER spreads, is the most deadly antidote to this vicious and virulent relic of the past. To the South to kill off this last symbol of Southern slave bourbonism is

the "most unkindest cut of all." Hence, to save this passing show of human iniquity, the Klan has sought to select and defend as the model of Negro leadership, Marcus Garvey, the leader of the Universal Negro Improvement Association, who during the month of June, held an interview with Acting Ku Klux Wizard Edward Young Clarke, and immediately thereafter through his paper, the Negro World, proclaimed to all of the fifteen million Negroes of the United States of America that they should cease fighting the Ku Klux Klan —the attitude which brought a thunderbolt of fury down upon his head. The attack was led by the writer, his associate, Chandler Owen, and Messrs. William Pickens and Robert W. Bagnall of the National Association for the Advancement of Colored People. Hard upon the heels of this attack, which was sponsored by the writer, the human hand was sent. Obviously the conclusion is that the Klan had come to the rescue of its Negro leader, Marcus Garvey, as is indicated in the letter of warning.†

---

* It also showed that the white Klan members really did not have a genuine knowledge of Negro folklore. Granted that a severed human hand was a grisly sight, but there is evidence that a dead man's hand was considered to be a powerful beneficial agent, e.g., to aid in gambling or to prevent a person from being arrested. See Hyatt, *Hoodoo-Conjuration-Witchcraft-Rootwork*, p. 545. Moreover, the term "hand," metaphorically speaking, refers to a whole host of useful magical agents. See Hyatt, pp. 519–669. However, if Klan members don't know much about Negro folklore, they do know a lot about committing brutal atrocities. Unfortunately, these barbaric bigots are still at work. A picture in *The Crisis*, 67 (1960), p. 318, shows their handiwork in the form of two sets of KKK initials carved in the abdomen of a Negro male. Note that this is in 1960, not 1920! — ED.

† Marcus Garvey was a West Indian by birth who advocated segregation. One of his schemes was a "back-to-Africa" movement where black men could be free from the evils of white civilization. Since he was committed to segregation, he was not at all hostile to some of the stated goals of the Ku Klux Klan who were obviously also segregationist in outlook. Garvey's position elicited heated attacks by the majority of American Negro leaders who had spent years of effort fighting to achieve integration. The schism between those American Negroes in favor of what might be termed "reverse racism," that is, a state, a school, or a dormitory for blacks only, and those more moderate American Negro groups in favor of integration continues. Unfortunately, this plaguing factionalism and division tends to weaken the overall black effort to achieve a better life in a less racist society. For a sample of Garvey's views, see Amy Jacques-Garvey, ed., *Philosophy and Opin-*

Still the work against treacherous, unscrupulous, disloyal Negro leaders as well as against the Klan will go on unabated. With redoubled efforts, I shall mobilize all of my energies in order to destroy black and white Ku Kluxism in America.

As an evidence of this resolve, the Sunday following the receiving of the hand, I assailed Marcus Garvey and the K. K. K. more violently than ever before, and it was hailed by the largest audience yet assembled which applauded more vociferously than ever before.

Thus the slogan under which this crusade began—Marcus Garvey Must Go!—will be reenforced with "and the Ku Klux Klan, too."

ion of Marcus Garvey (New York, 1923, paperback edition, 1970). For details of his organization, see Edmund David Cronon, *Black Moses: The Story of Marcus Garvey and the Universal Negro Improvement Association* (Madison, 1955). —Ed.

Contemporary Patterns of Malign Occultism Among Negroes in North Carolina

NORMAN E. WHITTEN, JR.

Lest the reader think that folk belief is strictly a thing of the past, the following study made by an anthropologist in central North Carolina should set the record straight. However, this interesting study does much more than demonstrate the continuity of a folk belief system. Professor Whitten of the University of Illinois tries to relate the various superstitions and conjuration techniques to the overall worldview of his informants. Ultimately, folklorists must get beyond the data collection stage and try to use their fascinating data for studies of worldview and ethos. For it is how a people thinks and how individuals perceive themselves in relation to the world they see around them that folklorists ought to be investigating. Far too often, articles and monographs concerned with folklore do no more than present raw, undigested data. If there is no analysis, then there may be no insight. Even inadequate or incorrect analysis may be better than no analysis at all if such analysis at least serves to stimulate thought and productive counterarguments. In any event, whether Professor Whitten's analysis of North Carolina Negro worldview is right or wrong, it is provocative, and it does show the great potential of superstitious behavior as a source for the study of values and worldview.

Professor Whitten has also studied black subcultures in Ecuador. See his Class, Kinship, and Power in an Ecuadorian Town: The Negroes of San Lorenzo *(Stanford, 1965). He is also co-editor with John Szwed of* Afro-American Anthropology: Contemporary Perspectives *(New York, 1970).*

WHITE FOLKS don' put much stock in roots and the like no mo'. They thinks that science has solved jes' about ever'thin—but there's lots of times they'd be better off if they'd pay mo' attention to us what knows. Why jes' las' month a white boy was sick—he

Reprinted from the *Journal of American Folklore*, 75 (1962), pp. 311–25, by permission of the author and the American Folklore Society.

jes' got sicker and sicker and no white doctor could he'p him a'tall. An ol' colored man that lives 'round here knowed what was wrong and he went to the fam'ly and tole them their li'l boy done had a snake in his lef' pulse. Somebody who done had it in fo' that family took a snake and powdered it and put it in that po' li'l boy's food. The old man said he could git it out but that boy's momma said she'd ruther see him daid than have any Negro mess with him. The next night that boy died and right in front of fo' people a snake came out'er his wrist.

Such cases are reported by rural and urban Negroes in central North Carolina.[1] These Negroes are usually, but by

no means always, from the lower social strata. They believe that they, and others, are the unfortunate victims of evil magic. Such persisting beliefs in a body of occult practices that plague a surprising number of Piedmont Negroes seem to be part of a pattern of magical thought brought to the Piedmont by the seventeenth- and eighteenth-century colonists from Europe.[2] From the white colonists these beliefs and practices diffused to the Negroes among whom they persist.[3] The purpose of this paper is to present the contemporary patterns of malign occultism found to be existing among Negroes living in central North Carolina.[4]

[1] A field investigation to collect and analyze aspects of Negro occult behavior was conducted by the author while he was a National Institute of Mental Health Trainee working under the auspices of the Social Research Section of the Institute for Research in Social Science, University of North Carolina. The data obtained in this study served as the body for the writer's M.A. thesis, in anthropology. Special thanks are due to Dr. John Gulick of the Department of Anthropology for his guidance and encouragement both during fieldwork and in collation of data. The writing of this paper was made possible by a National Institute of Mental Health training fellowship.

[2] The writer acknowledges the controversy on this point between those who hold that the Negroes' occult heritage is primarily African in origin and those who propound a European provenience. For a discussion of seventeenth- and eighteenth-century European occultism in the Piedmont area of North Carolina the reader might wish to consult Tom Peete Cross, "Witchcraft in North Carolina," *Studies in Philology*, XVI (1919), 217–87. A comparison of the beliefs and practices delineated by Cross for the European settlers may than be compared to the present-day beliefs of the Negro as presented in this paper. The evidence for Negro assimilation of European beliefs and the processes involved are given in Norman E. Whitten, Jr., "Aspects and Origins of Negro Occultism in Piedmont Village," unpublished M.A. thesis, (University of North Carolina, January, 1961). See also Richard M. Dorson, *American Folklore*, Chapter V (Chicago, 1959), pp. 166–99; and Guy B. Johnson, "The Speech of the Negro," *Folk-Ways*, ed. B. A. Botkin (Norman, Okla., 1930), p. 346. Melville J. Herskovits in *The Myth of the Negro Past* (New York, 1941), gives more weight to the African impress on American Negro occultism than do the above authors.

[3] The eleven male informants used for this study were assured strict anonymity. Suffice it to say here that they represented a cross-section of Negro life in central North Carolina. Three informants live in rural areas and eight live in urban areas. Of the latter, four are on the very bottom of the Negro class hierarchy, two held a somewhat higher position, and two could be considered as being solidly established in the Negro middle class. Of the rural informants, one old man was a "natural healer" by profession and also owned land which he rented to other Negroes; the other two were very poor "down-and-out" Negroes. No women were used as informants.

[4] In the literature on Negro occultism there exists a rich body of materials paralleling the content presented in this paper. Of the larger works one might wish to consult the following: Richard M. Dorson, *Negro Folktales in Michigan* (Cambridge, Mass., 1956), and *Negro Tales from Pine Bluff, Arkansas, and Calvin, Michigan* (Bloomington, 1958); *Drums and Shadows: Survival Studies among the Georgia Coastal Negroes*, by the Savannah Unit of the Georgia Writers' Project of the Work Projects Administration (Athens, 1940); Zora Neale Hurston, "Hoodoo in America," *Journal of*

MALEFICIA

Central to both the older white European and present day Negro occult beliefs and practices is the concept of maleficia.[5] Maleficia refer to misfortunes, attributed to evil, that cannot be explained or counteracted by science. Since maleficia are occult in nature, and since science is unable to deal with them, individuals are forced to cope with them by magical means. The central position of the malefice or malign event in both white European and Piedmont Negro occultism is significant in that evil magic is reported from the standpoint of victims, or potential victims, of maleficia rather than from the standpoint of a magical practitioner.

The malefice becomes articulate only after it has been decided that the afflicted has fallen victim to a "spell."[6] The spell is an unknown "something" that is the direct cause of maleficia. It is cast by a human being using occult means. The nature of spells will be discussed presently, but first let us examine three typical cases of maleficia drawn from field notes which give some indication of how the decision is made that the individual victim has fallen under a spell.

Stableboy had been paralyzed for about eight months. He had been to several physicians, all of whom asserted that he had a form of rheumatism for which there was no ready cure. His mother went to a "root doctor," and, after a brief conference, took Stableboy to see him. The root doctor had never seen Stableboy before but told him that he knew what was wrong and why he had come. The root doctor said that someone "had gone and done him in" and that only he could help. He gave Stableboy an "eight dose" and asked if he could "stand it" if he visited him in his sleep. With some trepidation Stableboy agreed. The next night the root doctor visited him in his sleep in the form of a "centipede with a thousand hands" and massaged his entire body. When he could stand this no longer he screamed, and the giant centipede vanished. When Stableboy awoke in the morning, he was well.

When Edward was young, he and two friends stopped to see three girls, one of whom Edward had been "going with." After two of the girls gave Edward's com-

American Folklore, XLIV (1931), 317-417, and *Mules and Men* (Philadelphia, 1935); Elsie Clews Parsons, "Tales from Guilford County, North Carolina," *Journal of American Folklore*, XXX (1917), 168–200, "Folk-Lore from Aiken, South Carolina," *Journal of American Folklore*, XXXIV (1921), 2–39, and "Folk-Lore from Elizabeth City County, Virginia," *Journal of American Folklore*, XXXV (1922), 250–327; Newbell Niles Puckett, *Folk Beliefs of the Southern Negro* (Chapel Hill, N. C., 1926).

[5] Maleficia (singular malefice): Jules Michelet gives the derivation of this term: "What is the derivation of maleficia . . .? 'It comes from maleficiendo (ill-doing) which signifies male de fide sentiendo (ill-thinking on matters of faith),'" *Satanism and Witchcraft*, tr., A. R. Allison (New York, 1939), p. 330. Russell H. Robbins, *Encyclopedia of Witchcraft and Demonology* (New York, 1959), p. 330, defines maleficia as "misfortunes, injuries and calamities suffered by persons, animals, or property, for which no immediate explanation could be found." It should also be noted that Robbins states that "Martin de Arles (1460) defined as maleficia all occurrences where the effect was more than could reasonably be expected in nature" (*Encyclopedia*, p. 331). An act of malefice was more than a crime against man; it was a crime against God by the enlistment of God's antithesis, the Devil.

[6] The writer has delineated the pattern whereby the recipient learns that he has fallen under a spell in "Events and Statuses Involved in a Pattern of Occult Behavior," *Research Previews*, VIII (Institute for Research in Social Science, University of North Carolina) (April, 1961), 9–16.

panions beer, Edward's girl brought him a very pretty glass of beer and told him to "drink it all up right away." The beer had a pretty, reddish color. Edward did as he was told and it "run him crazy"; he just could not keep away from the girl after this. His mother and other older women in the family knew what had happened. They became very angry and took Edward immediately to see a "longhead." The longhead said that the woman had put her "monthly" (menstrual blood) into the beer, making Edward desire her so much that he could not stay away from her. Much to Edward's and his family's relief the longhead removed the spell.

John is under the influence of a spell that prevents him from stopping his wife from running around with other men. He cannot even open his mouth to protest to her any more, and as the spell grows worse he finds it increasingly difficult to even approach her. He has finally given up and moved. He is sure that his wife has been "working a spell" because two years ago he found a "little bag of roots" in each of his boots. His wife had urged him to put them on, saying they would not hurt him— that they would be "good for him." John still takes his meals at home though his wife will not feed him until all others in the household have eaten. Whenever he succumbs to this schedule, he feels even worse and finds it impossible to even look at his wife.

These cases typify maleficia and, in a very general way, indicate the diagnostic pattern whereby an individual accepts the status of victim of malign occultism.[7] As soon as an individual decides that he is under the influence of a spell, the malefice has become patterned and can be critically examined. Let us now turn to the spells themselves.

THE NATURE OF SPELLS

In general, an individual may be thought to be under the influence of a spell when he consistently acts in an asocial manner, or in a manner that differs significantly from his usual behavior. The varied forms of behavior that characterize the victim of a spell include asocial behavior, insanity and general compulsive behavior to the detriment of the person's physical, psychological, and/or social well-being. For example, individuals are considered to be under the influence of a spell when unable to carry out their expressed wishes such as testifying in court when it benefits them to do so; associating with someone with whom they are emotionally involved; or avoiding someone whom they do not wish to be with. A spell is said to incapacitate one in the performance of his duties: a policeman who is unable to arrest an individual in the course of his duty, a jailer who cannot keep a given prisoner locked up, or a judge who cannot convict an obviously guilty person are all said to have "been rooted."

Afflictions which licensed physicians cannot immediately cure are often considered to be the results of spells. In such cases a professional conjurer helps the victim decide just what type of spell is causing his illness. Negroes who become insane, die under mysterious conditions, have strange afflictions called "running spells" and "fainting spells," or sudden onsets of diarrhea are also thought to be under the influence of some form of evil magic.

Local synonyms for the spell are "curse," "trick," "fix," "conjure," "root,"

---

[7] Many more examples of maleficia among Negroes may be found in *Drums and Shadows;* Dorson, *Michigan,* Chapter VII, pp. 100–19, and *Arkansas,* Chapter V, pp. 206–9; Hurston, "Hoodoo," pp. 400–11; Puckett; and Roland Steiner, "Observations on the Practice of Conjuring in Georgia," *Journal of American Folklore,* XIV (1901), 173–80.

and "hoodoo." Other less common terms are "wuwu," "hack," and "underworlded." An individual who is working a spell might also be referred to as "carrying a dirty undermining point."

The forms that local spells may take have many interesting characteristics. Words occasionally play a part. A Negro reported that one could steal a lock of another person's hair, place it in an eggshell or bottle, throw it in a stream, and say "damn you." As the egg floats down the stream, the individual's health fails and he eventually dies. Another source maintains that if one sprinkles salt around the area where unwanted guests have been and says, "Never come back" while he sweeps the salt out the door, the guests will never be able to return. Some people suspect that the conjurer may say certain words, but they are not sure, and have no idea what the words might be.

One desirous of delving into the occult arts in order to harm another may use one of the following methods (though by doing this he places himself in danger, for the spell may recoil—as we shall presently see). He may attempt to have his victim ingest some evil substance. For instance, when his intended victim is not looking, he may slip some powdered frog, toad, or snake into his food; or a woman may mix some of her menstrual blood into a man's food or drink to "run him crazy." One may also place conjure in a strategic position so that the recipient is forced to walk over it, or in some other way come close to it. For example, a common European and American occult act is that of placing a bag of roots, bones, or some magical powder under an intended victim's doorstep. Or, to employ a less common method, grave dust may be ironed into an unfortunate person's linen. Finally, one of evil intent may manipulate occult materials in some manner. That is, he may float his victim's hair down a stream in an eggshell; or he may burn sulphur in old shoes together with some nail parings from the fingers of a person whom he wishes to harm.

A rather general belief in "evil eye" exists, but no one seems willing to talk much about this. It is generally felt that Gypsies and some conjurers have the power to cast a spell by staring at the intended victim. More generally, "evil eye" is equated with mind reading more than it is with the ability to cast spells.

Certain nonhuman (and from the Negroes' position, unnatural) phenomena may precipitate, or establish the pattern of, a malefice. A black cat crossing in front of an individual and going left can cause him to become ill, go insane, or have bad luck. (To remove the effect, immediately turn around three times counterclockwise and spit in your hat.) Two young girls in a local town are supposed to have "running spells" that some unknown malefactor has placed on them. The spells are believed to be connected with the phases of the moon. The spells become so bad when the moon is full that the girls must be tied down to prevent them from injuring themselves.

Amulets are used to ward off spells. They are purchased from a "root doctor" (conjurer). Interestingly enough, there is also a fear of amulets. For example, a Negro policeman known to the writer will not even consider arresting an individual wearing an amulet, nor would he touch the amulet itself. No one seems sure whether or not a spell can be cast with the amulet. In general it protects the owner from spells, but it may also protect him from nonoccult occurrences (such as being arrested). Amulets also may be a characteristic symbol of a conjurer, or of one proficient in the occult arts.

Local names for amulets are "mojo," "monjo," "lucky hand," "hand," "goo-fuhdus," (possibly a derivation of "goof-er-dust"), "toby," and "jomo." These are all made by the conjurer and may consist of one or more of the following materials or some unknown substance wrapped in a little black, brown, or green cloth bag: roots, rats, lizards, snakes, spiders, frogs, snails, toads, bats (all usually dried and powdered), dimes, red dirt, steel wool, gray clay, and pumpkin seeds. Asafoedida, though worn around the neck in a little bag, seems to be a simple preventative measure against sore throat and cold rather than an amulet.

Many materials may be used as amulets by themselves. The "lucky bone" is a special bone obtained from an all-black cat. One gets the bone by boiling the cat completely and then throwing all the bones into a stream. The bone that floats upstream is the "lucky bone." The left hind foot of a rabbit, a "buckeye" (horse chestnut), a dime, or a horseshoe are all used for amulets. The dime is especially popular in that silver is said to have a powerful deterring force upon evil as well as being an excellent divining agent. Unlike other objects used for amulets, the horseshoe is hung over the door of a house and not worn. Rocks and pumpkins are also said to make very good amulets if one knows how to select and use them. Many say that only flint rocks have an occult character.

The amulet is usually kept hidden, but the pumpkin and rock are carried in plain sight. One old man in the local area puts a pumpkin on his head and does a dance in order to read minds. Individuals who carry a pumpkin, rock, or a "black bag of bones" are suspected of having occult knowledge and mysterious powers.[8]

THE HOMING-PRINCIPLE

There exists in the Piedmont area of North Carolina an interesting belief governing the "behavior" of the spell. This may be stated as follows: a spell, once created, can never be destroyed and, when removed, always returns to that individual of *malign motivation* from whom it originated. In no case would a spell return to a conjurer, for it is said that the conjurer is not really an evil man—only those who use his powers and knowledge to do harm to others are evil. This homing-principle or recoil effect is feared, but thought to be a "just thing." Interestingly enough, informants, when telling the author of this principle, all claimed that they alone knew of it. They would laugh and explain how any individual foolish enough

[8] None of the materials mentioned are new to those familiar with the literature on Negro occultism. All of the authors mentioned in footnotes 4 and 7 give some of these materials along with others that may be used in conjuring. *Drums and Shadows;* Dorson, *Michigan,* and *Arkansas;* and Puckett, *Folk Beliefs,* are handily indexed for quick reference and hence of special value. H. M. Wiltse gives a particularly elaborate recipe for making a harmful amulet under the heading "A Hoodoo Charm," in his "In the Field of Southern Folklore," *Journal of American Folklore,* XIII (1900), 212. In any discussion of occult materials it is well to take note of the following statement by Hurston: "It would be impossible for anyone to find out all the things that are being used as conjure in America. Anything may be conjure and nothing may be conjure according to the doctor, the time and the use of the articles" ("Hoodoo," p. 411).

to *desire* to harm another through occult means would inevitably fall victim to his own malign wishes. The joke is that the potential evildoer does not realize the danger in which he places himself. A spell also returns to its originator if he pays a conjurer to cast a spell for him and then stops payment.

This principle becomes most serious when an evil person, after casting a spell, or having one cast, dies, for then the spell has no home to return to and may well lead its victim to the grave. Cases such as the following have been given by all Negro respondents as well as by a white psychiatric social worker.

When Melville was born something was wrong with his mother, and by the time he was six, his mother had been to fifteen or twenty doctors. They had all been unable to help her. She finally went to a root doctor and was informed that her husband and three women had placed a spell upon her. But the women had since died, and this made removing the spell difficult because it could not be removed without sending it "back home." The root doctor went to the cemetery with the mother, and they dug up the dead women. The root doctor put some "funny salve" on the dead women, said some words inducing a frog from the deceased's mouths. He then turned the spell onto the frog.

The conjurer has a choice of either utilizing the homing-principle when he removes the spell or simply killing the originator of the spell. Reports indicate that conjurers made only the former choice (utilizing the homing-principle). However, in some cases the agent of the spell died because of the homing-principle.

A man came to Henry's house and hung his coat on a garden fence. A cow "got

the coat and sort of licked it all over and chewed it up pretty bad." The man got so mad that he cast a spell on the cow and its udders swelled up, the milk in them turning to blood. Henry's mother took the bloody milk to an "underworld doctor," and the doctor sent the spell back to the person who threw it. The spell could not die so it lodged in the man's genital organs. They swelled horribly and he died.

One deviation from the homing-principle is that it does not seem to apply to a woman who puts a spell on a man by mixing her menstrual blood into his food and/or drink. No explanation was given for this deviation though all informants were questioned about it.

COURT SPELLS

This is the major deviation from the homing-principle. Court spells are understood to mean the circumventing of legal sanctions by occult means (conjuration). Informants repeatedly have reported that conjurers cannot be arrested or held in jail, and that an individual can go to a conjurer for a spell to work on a court if he needs one. Bootleggers and other people on the "shady" side of the law frequently make use of court spells. Daniel, a local Negro policeman, told of a man who shot and killed another person while four people watched. He was a conjurer who could not be arrested, convicted, or kept in jail. He simply laughed at the police and went away free.

Another Negro policeman told the author that he was once living with a woman who "knew a lot about roots." She killed someone. Soon after this happened her aunt called her and told her how to avoid conviction. She followed instructions, broke two eggs, and threw them over her left shoulder; she went free.

It should be noted here that both of these examples were given by Negro policemen, and that they thought the events were quite humorous. Court spells may not always be occult in principle. There is one case of a woman who was to be tried for not paying bills over an extended period of time. She went to a conjurer, and he told her to come into court on a stretcher. She had two men carry her in on a stretcher and was acquitted.

THE CONJURER

Central to the whole occult complex in central North Carolina is the conjurer. This is the professional diviner, curer, agent finder, and general controller of the occult arts. Local synonyms for the conjurer are "root doctor," "herb doctor," "herb man," "underworld man," "conjure man," and "goofuhdus man." The principal function and role of the conjurer is to deal with and control the occult. This he does for a fee. To cast or remove a spell the conjurer charges from fifty to one hundred dollars. He charges smaller fees for other services. He is not affected by the homing-principle. Cases showing that the conjurer divines, casts, and removes spells are numerous. The following illustrates his divinatory and spell-removing powers:

Melville was ill and went to a root doctor who told him that a girl had taken a frog and hung it over a fire alive so that it would not burn but die slowly. She then let the heat dry it completely. When the frog was completely dry, the girl took a piece of brown paper and crumpled the frog up in it (according to the conjurer) and put this in

Melville's food. The food turned the same color that the frog had been and looked terrible. But Melville ate enough to fall under the woman's spell.

After divining this technique the conjurer told the victim the following:

Melville was told that he could not stay away from the woman who had "rooted him" (though he was married to another woman and this affair was seriously disrupting his life). The root doctor gave Melville a half pint of whiskey and told him to take it home and put it on the left hand corner of the mantel, asserting that it would turn green by morning. Melville was to drink the green whiskey as soon as he arose the next day and was not to look at the girl for the next three days. If he did this the spell would go away.

Melville drank the whiskey and said that he felt fine and "sort of braced up." He did not look at her for three days. Then he started seeing her again but every time he saw her he liked her less and less, until finally he hated her so much he never went back again. The woman fell in love with Melville, her love serving as punishment, as he never looked at her again.

The conjurer also performs smaller services for smaller fees:

Henry was gambling and became drunk. Later, when sober, he found that he missed his watch. He went to a root doctor and was told that for fifteen dollars she would get his watch back for him. She gave him three roots and told him to put one under his pillow, one on the left side of the mantel, and one by the door. Then he was to go to bed. He got up around 3:30 A. M. for someone was at the door. He asked who it was but received no answer. He went to the door and snatched it open. The woman who lived upstairs was there; she walked in without a word, placed the watch on the table, and walked back out.

John said that just the other day a friend

of his had a ham stolen and wanted to find out who stole it. He went to a root doctor who told him where the ham was hidden, but would not tell him who took it. The man went to the spot the root doctor told him to go to and found the ham.

One informant reported that, on one visit to a conjurer, the conjurer asked one hundred dollars to remove the spell, but was willing for only ten dollars to tell him in an indirect way who had cast the spell.

The major defining agents[9] of the conjurer (besides the conjurer himself) are individuals under a spell, or who have been under spells that a conjurer has successfully removed. It is very difficult to determine precisely who knows just where a conjurer may be located. There are no "full-time" conjurers in the immediate area under study. All report that most conjurers are to be found in and around Aiken, South Carolina. There are alleged to be "part-time" conjurers in Smithfield, Durham, and Pittsboro, North Carolina.

Other defining agents are the Negro police. When they are unable to apprehend or arrest a person, they "know" that they are confronted with a root doctor; and there is no use trying further.

It is often said that the best way to locate a root doctor is to go to a bus station in a strange town and from there get a taxi and ask the driver to take you to a conjurer. It seems then that cab-drivers, to some extent, serve to define the conjurer. That is, if, as the informants all say, a taxi driver is a major middleman between the recipient and the conjurer, then that individual whom a taxi driver claims is a conjurer may be well on his way toward the achievement of professional status.

The conjurer may be Negro or white, male or female. The variety of defining characteristics by which a conjurer is recognized and known is considerable. Any person acting in an unusual manner or carrying an unusual object or objects may be suspected. The following characteristics have been given independently by more than one informant. What makes the conjurer's use of the following significant in the eyes of the informants is his conspicuous use of one or more of the components that become his defining characteristics.

He will always have a characteristic symbol such as a "familiar" (a black cat or animated roots) or an amulet (usually composed of roots, a pumpkin, bones, or an unknown substance). He will usually have general extrasensory perceptive abilities. In particular, the conjurer is thought to have the powers of mind-reading and prediction of the future. However, he may have to use the familiar, the amulet, a deck of cards, or a little black book to aid him in his predictions.[10]

Another characteristic of the conjurer is that many people always seem to be in his house. Interestingly enough, all informants have used the phrase "like a prayer meeting" to describe the

---

[9] By "defining agents" we refer to those individuals within a configuration who determine, and state the nature of, a given status (in this case the status of the conjurer). The definition of a status from this standpoint may be implicit or explicit. By "status" we mean simply "a position in a particular pattern" (Ralph Linton, *The Study of Man*, New York, 1936, p. 113).

[10] Powdermaker also found that conjurers use little books. See Hortense Powdermaker, *After Freedom* (New York, 1939), Appendix E.

number of people in the conjurer's house.

The following are some examples of the characteristics of conjurers.

Familiar (taken from a tape-recording of an interview):

He took me in a dark room—so dark you couldn't see an' set the cat acrost the table so's I could see these big eyes lookin' at me—like diamonds sparklin', and he had a big bowl, and he figgered out what was wrong and who done it. Well, this was after I'd been cut [stabbed] by Flo, and he tole me that I wouldn't be able to testify against her, and wanted a hundred dollars to put the spell back on her so's I could testify.

Animated Roots:

Joe went to a root doctor to get a spell removed, but he was not sure the root doctor was any good. The root doctor gave him two roots and told him to hide them. Joe took them to his car, and locked them in the glove compartment of the car. Then he locked the car doors and returned to the root doctor's place. The root doctor asked where his "little buddies" were. As soon as he asked this, the roots came in the door and jumped up on the table.

Extrasensory perception:

Peter said that about a year ago he knew a boy that went to South Carolina to have a spell removed, but he didn't have any money with him. The root doctor told him to leave the money "some place" in the boy's home town where no one could find it. The boy did this, and the money disappeared; and he never heard from the root doctor again. Also, to the best of his knowledge the root doctor never visited this community.

Some mention is made of the use of cards for divination. There are some root doctors who use ordinary playing cards. They put the cards together and pray over them, and then shuffle them and repeat this several times. Then they start flipping them off one by one. They tell what each card means. Then they let the client ask questions and flip the cards, and they give an answer for each question according to what card appears. Melville said that the funny thing about these root doctors is that one never seems to be able to ask any questions when he gets there.[11]

Informants reported two classes of conjurers: the "real" professionals of South Carolina and the "small-time" conjurers near the local area. The small-time conjurers get their materials and instructions from one of the South Carolina conjurers, but they do not, in one old Negro's terms "know all the ins and outs" of conjuration. The difference between the two classes lies mainly in the degree of knowledge of occultism. It might be expressed in this way: the local conjurers know what to do but they do not know why; and the real, professional South Carolina conjurers know not only what to do, but also why they do it. There are indications that the local conjurers do not charge the high fee that the South Carolina conjurers do.

When asked if conjurers were good or bad people, all informants immediately asserted that they were good people with considerable community prestige. Only those who use them to work evil are bad. When asked why they considered the conjurer to be good, informants stated that he had knowledge and, as a result

---

[11] For further, rich case material on the conjurer, see Dorson, *Michigan*, Chapter VII, "Hoodoos and Two Heads," pp. 100–19.

of this knowledge, possessed ability to help people in trouble.

However when further questions such as, "How can the conjurer be a good person to be respected when he helps someone harm another person?" were asked, two types of response were obtained. In the first, the informant retracted his former statement and said that perhaps the conjurer was not such a good person after all. In the second type the response was that "everyone has to make a living," and that the conjurer is not at fault if a person chooses to use his knowledge for evil purposes. When questioned further on this point, informants answered that the conjurer who used his knowledge for personal gains could not be a good and respected person. All said that a conjurer would not do such a thing. A malign motivation, then, would seem to be more significant in determining whether an individual is good or evil than the deed itself. Presently, we shall see the relation of the broad concepts of good and evil to the entire occult complex.

THE GYPSY

There seems to be a general Gypsy-fear among the Negroes in the central North Carolina area. Gypsies are thought to have certain occult powers somewhat different from those of the usual conjurer. Whereas the conjurer uses roots, a familiar, or other symbols, the Gypsy is thought to be highly skilled in extrasensory perception, notably mind reading, palm reading, and prediction of the future. Extrasensory perception refers to the possession of a "sixth sense," or the ability of an individual to do something considered to be beyond

the range of ordinary human abilities. Palm reading is entered under the E. S. P. rubric because informants consider it to be on the same level of psychic ability as mind reading and clairvoyance. Negro respondents do not consider palm reading to be something that one can learn, but rather, an ability innate in some individuals (notably Gypsies).

Edward had two cousins who were going to see a circus. They wanted Edward to go with them and he did. They caught the train and got off at West Durham and, as they walked down the tracks, saw some Gypsy tents. One boy wanted to "git his fortune tole," and the other laughed, and said "This old fool cain't tell nothin'." When they arrived at the Gypsy tent, the first boy "had his fortune tole." When he was finished the Gypsy turned to the second boy (who had made fun of her) and asked him if he wanted his palm read too. He said he did. Then she laughed and said "This old fool cain't tell nothin'." The Gypsy then turned to Edward and looked at him and then called another girl to look too—they told him that his brother and sister were going to cheat him out of his land. Eventually his brother and sister did cheat him out of his land.

At times recipients of spells go to Gypsies to have spells removed, but no information has been obtained about a person going to a Gypsy to cast a spell. Gypsies are feared and regarded as evil because it is thought that if one is angered, he can point a finger and jabber at an individual and in this way place a spell on him. The Gypsy, then, differs from the conjurer in that he may be characterized by malign motivation, whereas the conjurer never is. Also, there is quite a financial difference between the Gypsy and the conjurer. The Gypsy asks small fees—a maximum of five to ten dollars, whereas the conjurer's usual fee ranges from fifty to one hundred dollars.[12]

WORLD VIEW

The occult beliefs and practices of central North Carolina Negroes exist within a broader belief system or world view quite similar to that of the seventeenth- and eighteenth-century Europeans.[13]

The Negroes' concept of the universe and man's place in it can be stated as follows. Every man has a profession and must find it; there are good and evil professions, and one can make his way in the world by following either the good or evil path. The good and the evil in life are absolute and were determined in the following way: there once was a war in Heaven and the Lord threw the Devil out. When the Devil left he took one-third of everything with him and went down to Hell. The Devil put his third to work in the world. As a result, in one Negro's terms, "Soothsayers and witches have always been on earth. These are the Bible names of underworld people, but today we [the Negroes] call them conjure men."

Besides the good and evil professions, there are good and evil material things all over the earth. The good professions use the good materials and work through the Lord, and the evil professions employ the evil materials to do the work of the Devil.[14]

Good and evil are not in a definite balance, as witnessed by such statements as: "The Devil took a third of everything," (not half) and "The Devil is mighty but the Lord is almighty." It must be noted however, that most persons stated that they are not so sure that the Devil is not just as powerful as the Lord.

Anyone may learn to make use of the good and the evil in life, and the use of evil alone does not necessarily make a person evil, though it usually does. Conjurers know about evil things, but they use this knowledge to combat evil and so are, on the whole, good.

It is said that men may choose evil or good means to get along in this life, but that they have a responsibility to their fellow man. Further, an individual is not considered to be responsible for his own sickness, but he is responsible if he causes the sickness of another individual. He will always be in danger of the homing-principle when he causes sickness in someone else.

Everything has its antithesis. For instance, for every disease there is an antidote if man can only find it. This is frequently expressed in the statement:

[12] Dorson, *Michigan*, found that Negroes distinguish between "hoodoo doctors," "fortune-tellers," and "healers" (p. 110). We find the same distinction to exist, with the additional feature that only Gypsies serve as fortunetellers.

[13] For a sample of references giving one the feel of the European worldview, see "The Witch of Wapping," *Reprints of English Books, 1475–1700*, No. 13, ed. Joseph A. Foster (London, 1939), pp. 2–5; Brother Francisco Maria Guazzo, *Compendium Maleficarum*, ed. Montague Summers (London, 1929), pp. 90, 100, 101, 121; Michelet, *Satanism*, pp. 4, 13, 84, 88, 89, 95–97; Robbins, *Encylopedia*, pp. 87, 398, 490–92; and Jakob Sprenger and Heinrich Kramer, *Malleus Maleficarum*, ed. Montague Summers (London, 1928), pp. 1–2, 14, 48, 52, 54, 60, 84, 95.

[14] For a fuller discussion of good and evil, natural and unnatural materials in the context of the broader Negro belief-system see Norman E. Whitten, Jr., "Notes on Negro Folk Medicine," *Folk Healthways Newsletter*, I (Oct. 1960), 5–8.

"We are walking over things every day that could cure us if we only knew about them."

There is a natural-unnatural dichotomy cutting across the good-evil one. For instance, there are poisons and cures that are good and evil respectively, but both are natural. A physician or folk practitioner (herbalist), sophisticated in the use of natural herb cures, deals with this aspect of good and evil. On the unnatural side there are, on the one hand, the occult spells and materials that are evil, and their good antidotes that only the conjurer can deal with (the only example of a good side to evil— also a part of the seventeenth- and eighteenth-century European belief framework). On the other hand, there is the "pursuit of the Lord" and coping with life through Him that the ministers and preachers deal with.[15]

This worldview can be stated more clearly by considering the Negro to have two frames of reference. The first frame of reference is that normative one of good and evil held by the white community as a whole, and most clearly articulated in the Negro subculture through the Negro church. It is stated, in this frame of reference that, regarding the natural, such phenomena as sickness and crime are bad, while law and health are good. In regard to the occult or unnatural, the Lord and His servants (ministers) are good and the Devil and his servants (conjurers) are evil.

The second frame of reference is the existential one pertaining to the immediate Negro milieu where often life can only be coped with by means normatively defined as evil. Here a breakdown of good and evil according to intent is found. Malign intent, either in crime (natural) or conjuration (unnatural), is evil, while either of these may be good if malign intent is not present and the results of the crime or occult behavior are satisfying to the individual involved.

THE ASSIMILATION OF SEVENTEENTH- AND EIGHTEENTH-CENTURY EUROPEAN OCCULTISM BY PIEDMONT NEGROES

Just what factors can be found to explain the existence of what seems to be an essentially seventeenth- and eighteenth-century European-type occult complex among Negroes in the Piedmont area of North Carolina?

Let us begin with the Negro-white ratio in the Piedmont area. Discussion here is based on the assumption that the smaller the proportion of Negroes to whites, the greater the opportunity Negroes would have to learn and incorporate white occult beliefs and practices. North Carolina had some large slave-holding plantations, but they did not determine the character of the state as they did in Virginia and the deep South.

[15] Vivian K. Cameron has found the natural-unnatural dichotomy to be manifested in much the same way: "two groups of practitioners are known and recognized not only by themselves but also by their particular clienteles as distinct from each other. One deals in what may be termed 'medicine,' that is, roots, herbs, barks, and teas, while the other is composed of those who work by means of magic. So clear cut is this feeling of difference between the members of the two groups that there is reason for deep insult if a practitioner of the medical type is mistaken for one of those who practices magic." *Folk-Beliefs Pertaining to Health of the Southern Negro*, unpublished M. A. thesis (Northwestern University, 1930), p. 239.

Johnson states that "the small slave holders actually shaped the character of slavery in the state because they were in the majority. Equally important . . . were the families, 72 percent of the total in 1860, who owned no slaves."[16] Exact figures for the eighteenth century are given by Basset,[17] who concluded: "while the colony was growing slowly and was thinly settled, the ratio of blacks to whites remained comparatively constant, but that after the French and Indian War the negroes began rapidly to gain."[18]

The next important question is, when the ratio of Negroes to whites rapidly began to increase, what was the source of the increase? Were these new Negroes descendants of New World Negroes or new imports from Africa? Pollitzer effectively answers this question: "Slaves imported to the United States after the ban of 1808 were destined primarily for the newly opened lands of the Gulf States rather than coastal Carolina."[19]

Turning from Negro-white ratios to the contact situation between whites and Negroes in the Piedmont area of North Carolina, we submit two factors greatly influencing the assimilation of European occult beliefs by eighteenth-century Negroes. These factors were the language spoken by the Negroes and the church attended by them.

Herskovits, in his book *The Myth of the Negro Past*, gives all of the words used by the Negro which he can find and trace to African origin. However, a few words do not make a language. Also, most of these words come from the Gullah dialect and, in the words of Johnson, "one might like to know how many Negroes speak gullah today and how many are likely to be speaking it fifty years hence."[20] Puckett submits the following: "Apart from such isolated cases . . . the African impress upon the English language was negligible. Everywhere English became the accepted method of communication and English folk beliefs and superstitions were given an enormous advantage over the African forms."[21]

A major institutional vehicle linking the Negro and white worldviews quite probably was, and certainly still is, the church. Looking at the history of acculturation in the Piedmont area we find that: "Although the negroes were allowed to join any church they might fancy, they were not allowed to

[16] Guion Johnson, *Ante Bellum North Carolina* (Chapel Hill, N. C., 1937), p. 469.

[17] John Spencer Bassett, *Slavery and Servitude in the State of North Carolina* (Baltimore, 1899), p. 22.

[18] *Ibid.*

[19] William S. Pollitzer, "The Negroes of Charleston (S.C.): A Study of Hemoglobin Types, Serology, and Morphology," *American Journal of Physical Anthropology*, XVI (1958), 241.

[20] Guy B. Johnson, review of M. Herskovits, *The Myth of the Negro Past*, in *American Sociological Review*, VII (April 1942), p. 289.

[21] Puckett, p. 20. The hypothesis that the Gullah dialect has been affected by the African background of its Sea Island Negroes is well supported by Lorenzo Dow Turner in his book *Africanisms in the Gullah Dialect* (Chicago, 1949). Unlike the situation in the Piedmont, the Negroes currently found on the Sea Islands were direct imports from the West African coast. They had no prior exposure to the English language and had little opportunity to learn it after their arrival (*Ibid*, pp. 1, 4–5). For a discussion of Negro dialect areas and their European proveniences see Johnson, "Speech."

have a church organization of their own."[22]

Communicating with English symbols and attending an institution devoted to explaining and justifying the real and supernatural, Negroes, in the context of a close contact situation dominated by whites, assimilated a body of occult beliefs and practices more European than African in character. The next question is, just how widespread were white occult beliefs and practices in the Piedmont? This question is readily answered by Tom Peete Cross, in his monograph "Witchcraft in North Carolina"; this monograph documents the occult beliefs and practices of the white settlers and asserts that they were, indeed, extensive.

Our concern with contemporary patterns of Negro occultism brings us finally to the question, after assimilating white beliefs in the Piedmont, why did the Negro retain them?

CONTEMPORARY SUPPORT FOR THE EXISTENCE OF NEGRO OCCULTISM IN THE PIEDMONT

The first factor may well be a lack of contact with the more scientific orientation of the white middle and upper classes. Pushed down economically, politically, and socially, and denied adequate educational opportunities, the Negro has not been able to keep up with the development of thought that has characterized most social strata of white Americans. This phenomenon is known to most anthropologists as "cultural lag." The dichotomy between natural and unnatural may also influence the persistence of occult beliefs and practices by allowing them to exist concomitantly with a developing scientific orientation. With this dichotomy, one can develop the natural side without necessarily rejecting what one has learned of the unnatural. The principal of a Negro high school gave the writer some indication of this when, while discussing Negro occultism, he made frequent reference to the "mysteries of the mind which science still knows nothing about and may never solve."

The proclivity of the American Negro to cope by magical means due to his social, political, and economic position in the greater American social structure may well be another crucial factor. Malinowski, among others, has presented evidence for the hypothesis that the greater the uncertainty regarding the

[22] Bassett, p. 50. Guy B. Johnson in his book *Folk Culture on St. Helena Island* (Chapel Hill, N. C., 1940), p. 127, points out that, regarding religious music, African elements that survived did so in a European framework. That the Negro turned to Christianity with a fervor born of the need to justify his depressed position in the emerging American social structure is supported by V. F. Calverton, "The Negro and American Culture," *Saturday Review of Literature*, XXII (21 Sept. 1940), 17f. See also Miles Mark Fisher, *Negro Slave Songs in the United States* (Ithaca, 1953), p. 31; and Johnson, "Speech," p. 358.

Fisher makes a strong case for the existence of Africanisms in American Negro religious music during the colonial period. His position is that Negro music of the colonial period was found in similar situations in Africa and the New World, functioned in similar manners, and that the African background of the Negro was conducive to the incorporation of Christianity. In no way do the ideas expressed in this paper contradict the thesis of Fisher. We are concerned with pattern, and he is concerned with situation and function. Similarities in the situation and function of Negro African and colonial music should be conducive to its assimilation into a European pattern. Note must also be taken of Amercan Negroes' secret religious meetings, which are carefully

means to an end, the greater the tendency to cope by magical means.[23] Due to his suppressed social position the Negro can find little satisfaction by coping directly with his frustrations and dissatisfactions. Misfortunes that befall him may have no real solution, though magical practices or the relegation of problems to magical causes may offer at least partial satisfaction by relieving some anxiety and tension.

Along somewhat the same lines, Dollard in his discussion of Negro magic states, "Magic accepts the status quo; it takes the place of political activity, agitation, organization, solidarity or any real moves to change status."[24] This is one way, Dollard feels, that Negroes express and justify accommodation to their status. He also feels that occult practices may serve as an outlet for aggressive behavior.

The pattern of Negro occultism may also be supported through publications such as the little book described by informants and the three books described by Powdermaker in her study of a Mississippi community.[25] Codifications of such folk beliefs were once used by white colonists. Now similar codifications seem to help these European superstitions remain with the great-grandchildren of their slaves and servants to whom these colonists, consciously and unconsciously, imparted their occult knowledge and rather specific fears of the unknown.

The Bible, with its references to witchcraft and sorcery, may also support the belief in malign forces antithetical to the "ways of the Lord." Also, Negro preachers may take Biblical references such as, "Thou shalt not suffer a witch to live,"[26] and "neither seek after wizards to be defiled by them,"[27] much more literally than do the middle- and upper-class white ministers.

A final support may be the failure of licensed physicians to give immediate diagnosis and cure for a Negro's symptoms. A comment from a physician such as, "There is nothing I can do to help you," or "come back next week and we'll have the results of the tests," may suggest to that Negro whose belief system already includes the above notions that his trouble is of an occult nature. All sources reported that a physician using scientific practices could not help an individual who was under a spell. It may also be that the older general practitioners utilized the concept of suggestion (and removed the spell) more often than the modern physician is prone to do. One physician in the area under investigation reported that he has taken off spells by performing a simple ritual in which he uses a drug to produce hot and cold flashes. Such practices could easily reinforce the existing occult pattern by validating, for the Negro, occult efficacy by including it in a scientific (medical) context. The physicians, of course, know that the only reason that the effects of a

---

examined by Fisher, *Slave Songs*, Chapter IV and V. These meetings may indeed have allowed some African patterns to be perpetuated. Regarding the interest of this paper, suffice it to say that the Piedmont is not mentioned as a trouble area for such meetings.

[23] Bronislaw Malinowski, *Magic, Science and Religion* (Glencoe, Ill., 1948), pp. 30–31.
[24] John Dollard, *Caste and Class in a Southern Town* (New York, 1937, 1949), p. 263.
[25] Powdermaker.
[26] Ex. 22: 18.
[27] Levit. 19: 26.

spell can be removed is that they are psychosomatically caused in the first place, but to some Negroes such practices only support the idea that "they's some things that jes' ain't natchel."

The above factors suggest what some of the supports for the existence of Negro occultism may be. They also suggest hypotheses for further study; while they are not to be taken as being conclusive at the present time, they are derived from full consideration of the field data.

* In an interesting discussion of seven case histories from Rochester, New York, a doctor has suggested that physicians should be aware of the influence of spells and hexes in connection with diagnosing illnesses of some of their patients. He even recommends that on those occasions when the patient indicates that something strange has happened to him, the doctor might do well to inquire specifically about the possibility of roots, conjure, hoodoo, etc. Without such an initiative on the doctor's part—an initiative which, of course, runs the great risk of being construed as an enormous insult—the patient might be reluctant to tell his scientific doctor the "truth" about his ailment as he perceives it. See David C. Tinling, "Voodoo, Root Work, and Medicine," *Psychosomatic Medicine*, 29 (1967), pp. 483–90. —ED.

Symbiosis: The Case of Hoodoo & the Numbers Racket

GEORGE J. MCCALL

If there is a misconception that folk belief is by and large a creature of the past, there is an equally great misconception that folk belief is peculiar to the rural South. If this were the case, then one would not expect to find superstition and conjuration rife in northern urban ghettoes. The fact is, though, that folk belief is infinitely flexible and can easily be adapted and transferred from old problems to new. The following investigation of the interrelationships existing between institutionalized gambling and traditional techniques of conjuration should serve to dispel the notion that city life is superstition-free.

THE PURPOSE of this study[1] is to investigate the relationship which exists between two pervasive institutions of the underworld—hoodoo[2] and the numbers racket.[3] Carlson, in his otherwise incisive analysis of the numbers racket,[4] interprets the relation as one of what he calls "parasitism," but in the usage

[1] This paper is heavily indebted to Albert J. Reiss, Jr. and to J. L. Simmons, who contributed helpful advice throughout the study. I am also grateful to Everett C. Hughes and Talcott Parsons for their comments on an earlier draft and to Martin U. Martel for many insights regarding Park's theoretical framework. [The original printed version of this paper began with a lengthy exposition of the theoretical formulations of Robert E. Park with regard to different types of symbiotic or survival relationships. The interested reader should consult this version for the discussion and references. —ED.]

[2] "Hoodoo," a term explained in some detail in subsequent sections, is one of several sometimes used to refer to the syncretistic blend of Christianity and African fetishism which still exerts considerable influence on the Negro in America. See, for example, Zora Neale Hurston, "Hoodoo in America," *Journal of American Folklore*, 44 (1931), pp. 317–417; and Norman E. Whitten, Jr.,

Reprinted in slightly abridged form from *Social Problems*, vol. 10 (Spring 1963), pp. 361–71, by permission of the author and The Society for the Study of Social Problems.

adopted here it might better be termed "exploitation," in that he sees hoodoo as *manifestly* profiting from association with the numbers racket without important consequences for the latter.

It is the thesis of the present paper that the relationship is rather one of mutualism, in that it is latently eufunctional for both institutions. In support of this interpretation, we shall present an examination of data culled from the writer's field observations in Harlem, from police reports, and from other documentary sources of various kinds.

HOODOO AND ITS CHARMS

"Hoodoo" represents the syncretistic blend of Christian and Nigritic[5] religious traditions in the United States, corresponding to *vodun* ("voodoo") and *obeah* in Haiti, *shango* in Trinidad, *candomble* and *macumba* in Brazil,

santeria in Cuba, and *cumina* in Jamaica. In twentieth century hoodoo, however, Catholic elements are less prominent than in the other variants, and Nigritic collective rituals have largely disappeared.[6] Instead, hoodoo has been assimilated to the bewildering variety of store-front spiritualist churches in its truly religious aspect,[7] leaving a heavy residue of sorcery and fetishism as the remaining native elements.

As with sorcery among other peoples, the major foci of hoodoo sorcery lie in the realms of health, love, economic success, and interpersonal power. In all these cases, hoodoo doctors—after careful spiritual "reading" of the client—prescribe courses of action (which always include some hoodoo ritual) and gladly sell him the charms, potions, and amulets the ritual requires.[8]

And lest such piney-woods practices be thought beneath the sophistication

---

"Contemporary Patterns of Malign Occultism Among Negroes in North Carolina," *Journal of American Folklore*, 75 (1962), pp. 311–25.

[3] By the "numbers racket" is meant here the illicit institution organized around those forms of gambling in which players bet on numbers within a specified range, one of which is later selected in a "random" fashion as the winner. The most popular variant currently is "mutuel racehorse policy," in which a three-digit number is derived from the published odds figures of the race-result chart of some given track. [As of 1971, the three digits used are the last three of the "handle," or the take at the track. For example, with a day's take of $1,321,403, the number would be 403. —Ed.] A most intensive analysis of the institution is found in Gustav G. Carlson, *Numbers Gambling: A Study of a Culture Complex*, unpublished Ph.D. dissertation, University of Michigan, 1940. Also useful are Capt. Frederick W. Egen, *Plainclothesman: A Handbook of Vice and Gambling Investigation* (New York: Arco Publishing Co., 1959), pp. 60–82; and *An Investigation of Law Enforcement in Buffalo* (New York: New York State Commission of Investigation, January, 1961), pp. 31–39.

[4] Carlson, *op. cit*, pp. 4–5, 89, 114–26.

[5] Following the usage of George Peter Murdock, in his *Africa: Its Peoples and Their Culture History* (New York: McGraw-Hill, 1959), pp. 14–16.

[6] Zora Neale Hurston, *Mules and Men*, (Philadelphia: Lippincott, 1935), pp. 221–35; and Newbell N. Puckett, *Folk Beliefs of the Southern Negro* (Chapel Hill, N.C.: University of North Carolina Press, 1926), pp. 520–82.

[7] St. Clair Drake and Horace R. Cayton, *Black Metropolis: A Study of Negro Life in a Northern City* (New York: Harcourt Brace, 1945), pp. 641–53; and Arthur Huff Fauset, *Black Gods of the Metropolis: Negro Religious Cults of the Urban North* (Philadelphia: University of Pennsylvania Press, 1944).

[8] Hurston, "Hoodoo in America," *op. cit.*; Robert Tallant, *Voodoo in New Orleans* (New York: Macmillan, 1946); and Whitten, *op. cit.*

of the urban Negro, consider that the writer has visited some 25 of these full-service establishments in Harlem alone.[9] In addition, the colorful window-signs of innumerable "readers" (who carry no line of religious goods) cry out from their store-front or walk-up locations. Marvel Cooke, writing in the *New York Amsterdam-News* of May 25, 1940, declares that "it is a conservative estimate that these people reap nearly $1,000,000 from approximately 50,000 or more Harlemites passing through their door annually." Similar takes are recorded in Chicago, Detroit, Philadelphia, and the other Negro centers of the North. Moreover, many other "doctors" and "readers" carry on thriving businesses by mail, advertising their goods and services in Negro newspapers and popular magazines.

Of the many hoodoo charms prescribed by these agents for securing good luck in gambling, perhaps the most popular is the fabled John the Conqueror Root, with its associated oils and incenses. One possible reason for the pre-eminence of this charm is its greater scope, as indicated in the enthusiastic pitch of a Lenox Avenue "doctor:"

Y'know, the women and the numbers, they's both jus' alike. Ain't neither of 'em can hold out long when yuh got Big Johnny workin' fo' yuh.

Other widely-sold items include pairs of lodestones (male and female, which must be carefully nourished with iron filings) and miniature bone hands (the increasing substitution of plastic in the manufacture of these hands is uniformly deplored by the older "doctors," and a few have refused to handle any but the

genuine article). Goldstones, snake vertebrae, and the well-known rabbit's foot are further examples of such gambling charms and are not infrequently encountered.

Among the magical perfumes recommended for gamblers' use, Lucky Dog is widely reputed to be the most powerful, although some experts hold out for Essence of Van Van, Three Jacks and a King, or Has-no-harra. Then too, sachets of Fast Luck or Money Drawing Powders are available for those who prefer a more subtle fragrance.

Turning to a few of the remaining Christian elements of hoodoo, we may note that certain of the Psalms have been credited with magical efficacy as symbols of prayer (e.g., for gambling, Psalms 4, 57, and 114), and these are sold in the form of medals or on parchment, in blood-red ink. The power of these Psalms is thought to be more fully realized if incorporated in a meticulous prayer ritual involving the burning of specially prescribed candles dressed with Prosperity Oil and supplemented by Lady Luck Incense. Experts hold that the ritual must be conducted on a special altar cloth, decked out with Bible and a lithograph or statue of the appropriate saint (Saint Anthony, in the case of gambling rituals).

All of these artifacts (among others) are associated with attempts to secure simple good luck in gambling. Another set is employed in the more interesting and important process of *divination*—specifically, in the attempt to supernaturally divine the specific three-digit number that will prove to be the winning combination on a given day.

Among the more ingenious devices

[9] Ronald Sullivan, writing in *The New York Times Magazine* of November 11, 1962, pp. 136–37, estimates that there are approximately 100 such shops in the whole of New York City.

for this purpose are the so-called Psalm Prayer Candles. When lit, these candles reveal a three-digit "Psalm number" as the wax melts away. Needless to say, these numbers are taken to be a revelation of the winning number, despite the fact that most candles are advertised in advance as containing 12 different numbers, one for each day.

Chief among the divining artifacts, however, are the ubiquitous "dream books," in which thousands of objects, events, or themes which might occur in a dream or unusual experience are assigned three-digit numbers.[10] Of those books now used in Harlem, the most popular include Rajah Rabo's Dream Book, the Three Witches Dream Book, Aunt Sally's Dream Book, The Harlem Pete Dream Book, and The Black Cat Dream Book. In some, the numbers are assigned in keeping with well-known hoodoo symbolisms, such as 769 for death or 369 for fecal matter, while in others the assignment seems essentially random. When questioned about the inconsistency between books, not all informants were able to explain as cleverly as one young "reader," who turned the potentially embarrassing situation to her own advantage:

Well, honey, some books works good fo' some people, 'n others works good fo' other ones. You jus' needs advice about which one'll work fo' you.

Some widely-known readers have specialized exclusively in numbers divination and operate largely by telephone and telegraph, advertising in the Negro press. By telegraphing "donations" of $10 to $20 to these big-time readers, one can obtain by return telegram the "blessing" of a certain Psalm—of three digits, of course. In the February 24, 1962, issue of The New York Courier, no fewer than 14 such specialists advertised their "hot money blessings," many of them openly mentioning the numbers game.

In fine, then, it is clear that a considerable proportion of the multimillion-dollar "take" of the hoodoo complex stems from its accommodation to the urban Negro's dedicated interest in "playing the numbers."[11] Up to this point, of course, the argument—though considerably more detailed—is in substantial agreement with Carlson's to the effect that the hoodoo complex profits enormously from its association with the numbers racket.

BELIEFS, BETS, AND BANKERS

What Carlson fails to bring out is the fact that the benefit is *reciprocated*, in that the hoodoo belief system bolsters the profits of the numbers racket in at least two important respects.

First of all, hoodoo *increases the volume of business in* numbers gambling, through evoking greater confidence in the bets by attaching supernatural significance to the numbers played. And then, should a bet still miss, there is almost always available a supernatural explanation of the failure.[12] The player may have used the wrong dream book or

[10] Harry B. Weiss, "Oneirocritica Americana: The Story of American Dream Books," *Bulletin of the New York Public Library*, (1944), pp. 519–41, 642–53.

[11] Drake and Cayton, *op. cit.*, pp. 470–94; Dan Wakefield, "Harlem's Magic Numbers," *The Reporter* (February 4, 1960), pp. 25–26; Julian Mayfield, *The Hit* (New York: Vanguard Press, 1956).

[12] In the metaphysical tradition of numerology, it is held that "The 'number field' is merely the

placed his bet with the wrong numbers "bank," or, most significantly, he may have failed to play separately all the permutations of his three lucky digits.

In such cases, the player will often stick by a particular hunch for long periods of time, even years, hopping from book to book, bank to bank, and betting the full "Combination" (set of permutations). As a less extreme example of this perseverance, one inveterate player had, at the time of interview, played regularly for some months a number listed for his birthday in a particular dream book, explaining that

God give me that number when I was born, so it must be lucky for me. My birthday ain't gonna change, so I reckon it'll always be lucky. . . . 'Course it don't hit every time, but I reckon it'll hit more often than any other one for me. So why mess around guessin' all the time?

Then too, should a player have a number revealed to him and fail to play it, yet see it win—the most tragic of all fates in the lore of the numbers game—he will curse his stupidity loudly and attempt to make up for it by playing that number long and hard thereafter.[13]

All these mechanisms, deriving from the hoodoo belief system, can be seen to yield the same result: a greater number of bets being placed, even in the face of failure to win.

Secondly, the hoodoo beliefs actually *increase the already overwhelming odds in favor of the "bank,"* by causing bets to cluster on certain numbers corresponding to commonly occurring hoodoo symbols, such as dreams of phalluses or of treading in feces. The utility of this clustering can be manifested in a number of ways. For example, in one variant of the numbers game in which a drawing is made from balls numbered 1 to 78, the "puller" may actually surreptitiously remove any ball on which bets have clustered heavily, then slip it back into the bag after the winner has been drawn, thus dramatically reducing the probability of having to pay off big.[14] In the "night number" variant in which the winning number is determined by rolling three ten-sided dice, the bankers often reserve the right to roll them again if they do not "like" the first number to come up (i.e., if the bets on it are too heavy).[15] Even in those variants in which the bank has no control over the winning number, such clustering naturally decreases the probability of anyone hitting the winner by sheer chance.

However, such clustering can also backfire, if a popular number actually turns up as the winner, for the bank must then pay off all the holders of that number at something like 500 to 1. Maisel relates an ironic instance of such a backfiring when a leading Cleveland numbers banker was sentenced to 6–60 years in prison. Betters in great numbers

---

normal location of the nine digits, and the naught or cipher. This formation, as applied to dreams, is not entirely stationary. In fact numbers are constantly on the move. That is the real safeguard to the [numbers] game, otherwise it would be a simple thing to 'hit,' day after day. Remember, the figures change positions each time a play is checked into the day's 'totals,' " *The Lucky Red Devil Combination Dream Book*, 1961 edition. (McKees Rocks, Pa.: Caro Book Co., 1961), p. 14.

13 Mayfield, *op. cit.*, pp. 190–91; Egen, *op. cit.*, p. 77; and Paul Oliver, *Blues Fell This Morning: The Meaning of the Blues* (New York: Horizon Press, 1960), p. 148.

14 Albert Q. Maisel, "Return of the Numbers Racket," *Collier's* (January 19, 1949) p. 22.

15 *An Investigation of Law Enforcement in Buffalo, op. cit.*, pp. 36–37.

immediately bought 660—the eventual winner—and the bank was forced to pay off heavily.[16] Such occasional catastrophes have led the smaller banks to establish "lay-off" systems similar to those in bookmaking, whereby bankers can insure themselves against heavy loss on a popular number through placing part of the bets with other banks (called "spreading the action").[17]

In addition, some banks have instituted "cut number" systems, in which the payoff rate on certain of the most popular numbers is reduced to 300 or 250 to 1. Thus a player who wishes to bet a dollar on one of these importantly symbolic (and hence well-played) numbers must give away as much as 70 cents for the privilege of making his bet at the unreduced odds of 1000 to 1 against him.[18]

THE MUTUALISM OF GAMES

In summary, then, we have seen that the association of hoodoo and the numbers racket is a mutually beneficial one.[19] The numbers bankers profit from the hoodoo beliefs that one can supernaturally manipulate one's fate in gambling, which beliefs serve to increase both the volume of betting and the odds against paying off heavily. In turn, the manufacturers and distributors of hoodoo goods and services receive the benefits of increased sales due to widespread interest in numbers gambling.

Is it, however, a case of true mutualism, as we have defined that concept above? Clearly, the criterion of mutual benefit is met, but are the requirements that the consequences be unintended and unrecognized by the actors similarly met?

Generally speaking, the hoodoo practitioners and the numbers bankers do not actively *intend* that their clients should divert any of their limited cash resources to the other; that is, it is a genuinely competitive relationship. (On the other hand, there seem to be some exceptions to this rule, in that a few individuals are said to occupy positions of power in both complexes, cashing in at both ends, as it were.)[20] Nonetheless, many of the personnel of each institution recognize that they do indirectly give business to, and receive it from, the other complex. Thus, on this level of conceptualization, the criteria for mutualism are not met, as Long seems to have realized in his own work:

A great deal of the communities' activities consist of undirected co-operation of particular social structures, each seeking particular goals and in doing so, meshing with others. While much of this might be explained in Adam Smith's terms, much of it could not be explained with a rational,

---

[16] Maisel, *op. cit.*, p. 73.

[17] *An Investigation of Law Enforcement in Buffalo, op. cit.*, pp. 37–38.

[18] *Ibid.*, p. 35.

[19] One of the persistent difficulties in functional analysis is specification of the desideratum in terms of which eu- or dysfunctionalities are to be judged. In the present paper, the cash income of the institutions has served as the primary index of their relative well-being. Other indicators—such as the number of participants, the ratio of staff to clients, the areal coverage of their services, the rate of cultural innovations within each complex, etc.—might also have been chosen, with essentially similar results, but none of these reveal the actual *mechanisms* of benefit so cleanly and directly as do the cash transactions themselves.

[20] Oliver, *op. cit.*, pp. 147–50; Maisel, *op. cit.*, p. 71; and Carlson, *op. cit.* pp. 112–13.

atomistic model of calculating individuals. . . . The behavior of X is not some disembodied rationality but, rather, behavior within an organized group activity that has goals, norms, strategies, and roles that give the very field and ground for rationality. . . .

It is the contention of this paper that the structured group activities that co-exist in a particular territorial system can be looked at as games. . . . Within each game there is a well-established set of goals whose achievement indicates success or failure for the participants, a set of socialized roles making participant behavior highly predictable, a set of strategies and tactics handed down through experience and occasionally subject to improvement and change, an elite public whose approbation is appreciated, and, finally, a general public which has some appreciation for the standing of the players.[21]

Long suggests, then, that the relevant symbionts are *games*, not categories, groups, or associations. To what extent do hoodoo and the numbers racket qualify as "games" in this sense?

Clearly, such an interpretation of the numbers racket is strictly correct, for its central activity is literally a game—a game of chance, which dictates goals, roles, and strategies and often commands the entire community as an interested and informed public. As has happened with so many play-forms of games (e.g., baseball, boxing, football, racing, etc.), it has become a "multi-situated game,"[22] requiring a vast proliferation of goals, roles, and strategies beyond those of the "gaming encounter" itself. Many of these extrinsic game-elements are oriented toward the ecologi-

cal struggle with other games of the community—the law enforcement game, the ecclesiastical game, the hoodoo game, etc.

Although the game-character of hoodoo is perhaps less obvious than that of the numbers racket, it is no less essential. Hoodoo is basically a game of men against the supernatural powers (rather than against chance), in which certain moves—in the form of rituals—are calculated to pay off in very specific valued outcomes. In some instances, the game can become an interpersonal one, as when two enemies bring to bear upon one another their most horrible "tricks" and counter-tricks. And because this is a game which depends so heavily on esoteric knowledge and ritual expertise (rather than chance), a whole body of supporting specialists has arisen to function as coaches and elite public.

This characterization of the game-structure of hoodoo and the numbers racket is, of course, much too brief and is intended only to suggest the applicability of Long's concepts to the present case. If this much be granted, we must note that the two games are truly distinct entities, so that the assertion of a relationship between them does not become tautological. As we have seen, one of the games involves man against chance for cash payoffs, with other men involved in holding the pot, recording bets, and allocating the money. The other game pits man—aided by expert human counsel—against the supernatural, for a wide variety of payoffs. Thus, the games differ in roles, goals, strategies,

---

[21] Norton E. Long, "The Local Community as an Ecology of Games," *American Journal of Sociology*, 64 (1958), pp. 251–61, especially 252–53.

[22] The concepts of "multi-situated game" and "gaming encounter" have been borrowed from Erving Goffman's analysis of game-structure in his "Fun in Games," in Goffman, *Encounters* (Indianapolis: Bobbs-Merrill, 1961) pp. 15–81, especially pp. 34–44.

and publics, and neither involves any essential consideration of the continued playing of the other. Furthermore, they are historically independent, hoodoo originating among the Negro slaves of the South, and the numbers game being introduced to this country by the early Italian immigrants to New York City.

How, then, do these games come to have latent, eufunctional consequences for one another? And whose actions are generating these consequences?

Sharing a common territorial field and collaborating for different and particular ends in the achievement of over-all social functions, the players in one game make use of the players in another and are, in turn, made use of by them. . . . Each is a piece in the chess game of the other, sometimes a willing piece, but, *to the extent that the games are different, with a different end in view.*[23]

It is in this framework that Park's conception of symbiosis can most clearly be seen to operate in human society, in that game-actions of the players in one game latently affect the out-come-structure of another game—and in the present case, these effects are mutual and beneficial, constituting an instance of true mutualism.

THE FUTURE OF THE RELATION

In looking back at the mechanisms of the mutualism between the two illicit games, it should be clear that without

substantial overlap in players, none of these mechanisms can operate effectively.[24] If hoodoo clients do not play the numbers on the basis of divination, hoodoo is of no more consequence to the numbers racket than is a political party or a social lodge. If numbers players do not buy gambling charms and divination artifacts, the numbers racket is likewise of no special importance to hoodoo.

Consequently, if a separation of clientele could be effected, both operations might be substantially weakened, possibly resulting in considerable saving of ill-spent cash for many Negro families. However, such a facile "solution" to this social problem seems unlikely to occur, for at least three important reasons.

First, the lore of each of the games contains references to how the other can be played for personal ends. Therefore, participation in one game has implications for the individual's "learning structure" *vis-à-vis* the other.[25] The more he learns about hoodoo, the more likely he is to learn about the numbers racket, and vice-versa. Given the fact that in the Negro sections of the larger cities the "opportunity structure" for participation in each is approximately the same, the learning structure probably accounts for most of the variance in predicting participation. On the other hand, because there is and has been such an extensive overlap in clientele, the learning structures available to the individual *before* participation in either

[23] Long, *op. cit.*, p. 253. Italics added.

[24] As Long notes, "the simultaneous playing of roles in two or more games is an important manner of linking separate games." *Ibid.*, p. 253.

[25] The use of "learning structure" and "opportunity structure" in this paragraph stems from Cloward's analysis of illegitimate means for securing legitimate ends, e.g., in this case, personal gain. See Richard A. Cloward, "Illegitimate Means, Anomie, and Deviant Behavior," *American Sociological Review*, 24 (1959), pp. 164–76.

are also roughly comparable; hence, it is "overdetermined" that a great many individuals will learn about (and probably play) both games.

Second, the two games, in their intersection, seem to have a certain integrative function for the Negro community, furnishing much of the content of casual conversation, imparting temporal structure to the day, and offering a sense of participation in a community-wide institution.[26]

Third, the proceeds from the numbers racket constitute a vital source of capital for other criminal activities.[27] Conse-quently, given the beneficial relationship of hoodoo to the numbers game, organized crime as a whole has a not inconsiderable stake in hoodoo, as do large numbers of politicians and law enforcement agents receiving bribes in return for their protection of numbers gambling.[28]

In light of this interdependence of powerful interests and the continuing influx of Negroes from the rural South—the heartland of hoodoo—it seems safe to conclude that the mutualism of hoodoo and the numbers racket will persist in the ghettos of the metropolitan North for some time to come.

[26] Mayfield, *op. cit.*, pp. 144–46; Julian Mayfield, "Numbers Writer: A Portrait," *The Nation* (May 14, 1960), pp. 424–25; and Wakefield, *op. cit.*

[27] Estes Kefauver, *et al*, *The Kefauver Committee Report on Organized Crime*, New York: Didier, 1951, p. 175. The racket is estimated to gross something between two and six billion dollars annually, largely in the Negro sections of Northern cities. See Maisel, *op. cit,*. and Harry C. Barnes and Negley Teeters, *New Horizons in Criminology* (3rd edition) (Englewood Cliffs, N.J.: Prentice-Hall, 1959), p. 30.

[28] Fred J. Cook, *A Two-Dollar Bet Means Murder* (New York: Dial Press, 1961), pp. 130–39.

FOLK MUSIC

It is generally agreed that one of the greatest, if not *the* greatest, contribution of American Negro culture to the world consists of a variety of different forms of folk music. From ragtime to jazz to swing to bebop to rock and roll; from spirituals to blues, the record of achievement is incredibly impressive. Not one but many books have been written on various portions of this rich heritage. In fact, the discussions of any one form, for example, the spirituals or blues or jazz, are so numerous and voluminous as to make it nearly impossible to survey the totality of American Negro folk music with any hope of completeness.

All that can reasonably be attempted within the limitations of the present volume is merely to sample some of the scholarship and to indicate where interested readers may turn for further information. If these representative essays can succeed in suggesting the beauty, power, and importance of some of the major forms of American Negro folk music, they will have served their purpose.

The Romance
of the Negro Folk Cry
in America

WILLIS LAURENCE JAMES

Cries, yells, and hollers may not appear to be folk music to the uninitiated, but upon reflection, one can see that such traditional forms do have musical characteristics. The following essay by Willis Laurence James is one of the few studies of these curious forms which stand somewhere in the area between the spoken and the sung word. Despite occasional overly romantic asides and a somewhat dubious hypothesis which would make the folk cry the principal source for gospel singing, blues, and jazz, Professor James, formerly the Chairman of the Department of Music at Spelman College, has written a provocative introduction to a fascinating subject.

For further consideration of this topic, see one of the few attempts to survey all American Negro folk music, Harold Courlander, Negro Folk Music, U.S.A. *(New York, 1963, paperback edition 1970), especially Chapter IV, "Cries, Calls, Whooping, and Hollering," pp. 80–88. See also the section entitled "Street Cries," in Langston Hughes and Arna Bontemps,* The Book of Negro Folklore *(New York, 1958), pp. 411–20, and Harriette Kershaw Leiding,* Street Cries of an Old Southern City *(Charleston, 1910).*

ANIMALS ARE capable of giving out sounds from their mouths which represent meanings and varying degrees of the powerful urge for expression. These sounds separate into two categories: those which man makes and those made by his lesser fellow inhabitants of this planet. Further, these sounds made by man fall into two categories—those which he learns how to make through instruction and by experimentation, and those which arise, seemingly, from no plan, or understood purpose, but which persist in his nature in all races and in all conditions of society.

The cry is an instant reminder of the

Reprinted from *Phylon*, vol. 16 (1950), pp. 15–30, by permission of *Phylon*.

primitive. It is the oldest form of vocal expression. From it arises all of the things associated with speech and musical tone concepts. When the newly born babe utters its cry, it gives therewith the true indication of life itself. There is something mysterious about the cry as it affects all animals, whether it be articulate or not. There is a certain something in it which says more than mere words may express. In fact, it may be said that the cry is more reliable in its general inarticulateness than when it is used as a purveyor of a definite idea, as in connection with speech. Speech may be false, but a spontaneous cry is never false. Therefore, it is evident that the cry is an expression of nature or impulse through natural spontaneous sound.

When one hears the newsboy on the streets crying his sales line, the experience brings him to the brink of musical beginnings. If the age of man has saved any one thing in the realm of communication and kept it active unto this day, as an unchanged factor in life, it is the cry in its several and different manifestations. There is no need to wonder how the music of ancient man sounded in principle. Merely go into the streets where you live, the villages where vendors abide, the waterfronts of remote places, the fields, the churches, and wherever people dwell and act out the patterns of life.

There are cries which are articulate in regard to speech and inarticulate in regard to music requirements. These are the types which can only be given the barest approximation in notation. They are the very primitive agents of expression which are yet heard in myriad ways—notably at contests, parades, disasters and various cases involving individuals.

Cries which are articulate from the standpoint of music, but not from the standpoint of words, represent the type which is heard less in urban areas. Perhaps they are older than song, if we are to consider song as the wedding of words to notes. It was those cries which Negroes made famous in the Old South. Being direct and, therefore, realistic importations from Africa, the cries baffled the white man. Because of their wordless nature, they sounded savage, wild, depraved and unworthy of civilized attention. The names for these plaintive and, I say, beautiful fragments and phrases were used in derision. Famous among those yet surviving names are "corn field holler," "nigger squall," "piney-woods whoop," "roustabout drunk-yell" and "loud mouthing." Many Negroes took to using these names for their cries and, no doubt, made some of the names used here. The last one seems to belong to this class:

Wordless cry:

The meter here is merely for convenience. A cry like this is the source for a series of startling variations, done in the freest manner imaginable—depending, of course, upon the gifts of the crier.

Sometimes, Negroes would give out a cry which was articulate in speech and music. When this was done, the groundwork for a song cry had been laid. Very often this led to the creation of a song akin to the "Water Boy" type, in which the cry and the song are joined together. One of the most lovely examples of this grouping is the one found in *Slave Songs of the United States*, Allen-Ware-Garrison, by the name of "I'm Gwine to Alabamy." Here is an illustration that points to the fact often not seen by most people,

that the Negro used his cry as a definite expression of feeling, although the cry of itself may have no words. There are variations of this old cry which carry beautiful verse as a part of the song:

When I see my ma in de mawnin',
Oh won't dat time be sweet!
Gwine to put my money in her
        welcome hand,
An' pretty little shoes on her feet.

It is obvious that this cry which precedes and links the verse to the main musical idea has sprung from no wild, base emotion. There are musical cries which use no verse, but simply cry out a short and oftime irregular musical statement, giving it variety by the addition or omission of a word here and there. For instance,

For the convenience of the reader (and in order to create better understanding on my part in the past) I have divided the cry into seven basic divisions. Commonest among these is the "call," an example of which was just seen above. Frequently the man who gives the orders to a group of men at work, such as a section gang, is referred to as the "caller." The train "caller" is familiar to all, and the car "caller" in parking

lots is also a familiar figure. The cry which asks for something for or from someone else, or pronounces judgment, is referred to, then, as a call. When a man is thirsty and calls the water-boy, or if he is tired and "calls on de boss," or if he is working and calls the procedure for getting the job done, these things will affect his mood and are reflected in his voice. The color, range, and dynamics of his cry will be different for each. The Negro has a warmth which causes him to be one of the world's greatest "callers."

These sounds have been observed to be connected in varying degrees of intensity and frequency with the following: Joy, sorrow, love, hate, pain, pleasure, comfort, and distress. These emotions are related to life in a pattern of great mixture and uncontrolled occurrence so that the factor of sound in its varying manifestations and types is synonymous with living itself.

The places, customs, mores, and occupations of man do have deep-seated effects upon his nature and do fashion the kind of person he will, in general, become. So we may say that people who live differently use sounds differently, but that the basic sound reservoir which previously has been referred to is unchangeably present in all men and is in all ways similar. This applies likewise to the lower species.

During World War II a large quota of Negro soldiers was stationed in the Atlanta University dormitory, which is directly in front of my house. White officers and Negro non-commissioned officers drilled and inspected these soldiers alternately. It was always possible to tell when the Negroes were in charge, though one were in the closed house. The white officers gave the commands, while the Negro officers called them. For comparison:

> White—Atten-n-tion!
> Negro—Atten-n-sho-wan-n!!

This difference ran throughout the entire procedure of maneuvers.

If one could go to a Negro baseball game of the old type—existing prior to the last war—the point would be brought to focus in a very different situation. At that time it was the custom for the umpire to give his decisions in a more dramatic manner than is now the case. The Negro umpire in the small Negro town felt himself called upon to be more than adjudicator. He was a performer. He used his hands, his feet and face as indicators. He "called" or sang, if you please, his decisions: Baw-oo-well! (Ball).

Though not a Negro cry, it is good for illustration to speak of one call as practiced on the radio at present. The call (chant) of the tobacco auctioneer is one of the most unique examples in the world. It is musical and, as far as language goes, may be said to be partly articulate and partly inarticulate. This call is among the most authoritative of the cries and the most generally useful. It is not as beautiful generally as many of the others. It is not a selling cry; for it is used mainly to assemble the buyers and terminate the sale. The tobacco really sells itself.

In the latter part of the last century and during the first decade of the present one, Negroes adopted the square dance of the white man, more in principle than in policy. As is well known, it is necessary to have someone call the figures. Right here is where the Negroes' social heritage—musical, oratorical and histrionic powers—got a chance for development through a new medium. There were scores of Negroes throughout the South who achieved lasting reputations as "set-callers." In fact, their popularity rose to such heights that they were in many cases professionals, being paid a fee to bring color and entertainment to the dance. They invented an entirely new system of "callin' sets." As they would call the figures, frequently they would dance very original solo steps and give out their calls in a musical phrase pattern. Their original sayings may be represented here by two specimens which were sure to "draw fire."

> If you like the way she look
> Hand de lady your pocketbook.
> Swing her fancy
> Come to de middle,
> But be careful
> Don't bust de fiddle.[1]

This next one seems to imply some connivance with the refreshment vendor.

> Sody water fine
> Wid de cakes just brown,
> Better buy yo' gal some
> Fo' she put you down.
> Lemonade cool
> And de glasses tall,
> Yo' better buy yo' gal some
> Fo' de others git it all.

It may appear at first sight that this call is a "dance cry." It is not considered as such for the reason that it belongs to an individual calling the dance sets, rather than to the dancers themselves. It is an appendage to the spirit of the dance and does not necessarily fit into the dance rhythm or music. It is more of an aside.

From the standpoint of sheer human interest, the most significant of all cries are what compose our second group. These are referred to as street cries. I have chosen selling cries for the reason that all cries heard in the streets are not selling cries and *vice-versa*. This cry is the most familiar, most often heard, and the most self-respecting of all cries.

No matter how humble the crier is, even if he possesses only a basket of frowsy collard greens, he represents what all business men aspire to be—a man who fashions and operates his own business. It should be noted that the selling cry denotes an independence which should be the envy of many a more prosperous merchant, if he but knew it. If business is not good in one spot, he can move at a moment's notice to another more desirable place.

Selling cries are personal expressions which belong to the maker, singer, or crier, who, in most cases, is the maker. No one need ask where the particular cry came from, as is so often done in regard to other folk material. For audacity and resourcefulness these selling cries stand alone as the finest single expression coming out of this segment of Negro folklore. There is often more imagination in one cry than would be expected in a dozen stanzas or phrases. As is obvious, this cry is a pendant and a species of the work song, being among its predecessors.

Religious cries are used principally by the Negro preacher in dispensing the "gravy" type of sermon. This is a phase of oratory which is peculiar to Negro life and culture. It is not merely fiery, frenzied declaiming, but a subtle, musical use of the voice which defies description. However, all of us have heard Negroes praying or preaching in this manner, in person or on the radio. The voice moves in short phrases preceded by a sort of buzzing, roaring sound which blends with the words and seems a part of them. However, the words themselves take on a clarion tone

[1] A worthy example of the excitement found in this dance is also shown in the delightfully humorous poem by Paul Laurence Dunbar, "The Party."

quality which moves through a chromate of sound, so as to emerge in unsuspecting blends and shapes. When a Negro preacher reaches the point where he feels the audience is ready to change the service into an informal feast of spontaneous rejoicing, he will oft lay aside any pretense of text and enter into a picturesque, oratorical cadenza, embellished with a very deftly controlled pantomime. This action will produce a type of religious excitement which in turn produces vocal "shouts" among the congregation. A favorite device of some Negro preachers is to select a strange word or phrase, and cry it over and over with variations of tone and inflection. Prayers which use cries are hauntingly beautiful. They seem to come more from the heart than from mere formal supplications. The prayer maker is too full for any utterance which is not colored tonally by his emotions. This is called "Zooning."

Field cries, or "corn field whoops" signify either a loneliness of spirit, due to the isolation of the worker, or serve as a signal to someone nearby, or merely as a bit of self-indulgence—about the same thing as singing to one's self. These cries are usually of an inarticulate nature as to the language and music factors. Briefer than most of the others, they yet often achieve a fascinating effect because they are frequently heard in silent, open country by persons who do not look for them. A field cry almost always proves an ideal motive which could bear rich fruit in the hands of a real composer.

The night cry, curiously enough, is exactly what it is called. Negroes working on farms in the day have, as do all men of similar occupation, a feeling of relaxation and self expression; and they have the urge to go visiting at night on a nearby plantation. This visit is usually undertaken to see someone of interest. Since it takes time to visit and return, the man will give out his night cry as he journeys along. He will also do the same thing when returning to his home. This avoids the visitor's being entirely separated from other human beings during any part of the visiting operation. Also, the cry may serve as a signal in dark night to a friend, or, as has been stated above, it may be a personal, disjointed serenade. At times, beautiful hunting cries are used to find the dogs and fellow "possum" huntsmen. The Negro's individuality, however, is not so well expressed in these stereotyped hunting versions as in the others. For sheer charm and mystic potency, no musical utterance can be more arresting than the cry of a gifted Negro moving in the night unseen, unknown. The degraded "whiskey squall" does not deserve consideration here, since it is an abnormal manifestation without rational dependability. Yet, it is a cry and has its roots in the others given here.

Dance cries, as has been pointed out, are among the oldest and most vital of all cries known to man. When the dance, on the folk level, reached a pitch of excitement where the dancers lost themselves in the joy of it all, the voice naturally gave out a response, which was also a form of rhythmic accompaniment of the movement of the feet. Since the main consideration was always the movement of the body, the cry imitated, in sound, some effect developed by primitive dance movements. Also, the words, more often than not, turned out to be mere sounds. Some of these were as follows:

1. Da, da, da.
2. Da, da, da-de-o.
3. Dum, a-lum, lum.
4. Ha-dee, lo, la.
5. Hi-dee, hi-dee-hoo (after Cab Calloway).
6. Doo-dah, doo-dah.

These same cries are used today in various places with about the same energy as was true formerly. The children use some of these in playing games and dancing to hand-claps, just as their elders.

However, for our interest, these dances show themselves to best advantage when looked at through the vista of the present dance development. The persons responsible for this are Louis Armstrong and Cab Calloway. Somehow, Armstrong and Calloway found the trick of using old folk cry principles to supplement the normal means of singing. This is a principle already shown as being a folk one. Being gifted in voice projection, Calloway invented or adopted a series of nonsense syllables and fitted them into his songs of jazz rhythms. When this was done, people realized the thing as a part of themselves, but they did not know why. They did not realize that they were listening to the cries of their vegetable man, their train caller, their charcoal vendor, their primitive ancestors, heated in the hot crucible of jazz, by the folk genius of Calloway and Armstrong until they ran into a new American alloy. It is possible that neither Calloway nor Armstrong realized what took place. If so, the more remarkable.

The response of the orchestra in imitating the cries of Armstrong and Calloway carried the cry into the orchestra itself. The rhythms and inflections have been picked up by orchestras in general during the last two decades. This has caused a vital development in dance music.

Water cries belong to all nations and people. There is a peculiar charm about the water and being borne upon its ever-changing bosom. This experience takes man into a sphere where he is not equipped naturally to dwell, and makes him feel himself the adventurer. To journey upon the water gives one a feeling akin to loneliness, even when in the company of others. It brings into sharp relief the things which go to make land and home important.

However, the need for variety and the love of travel and discovery have made man also love the water and build up a lore associated with it, and with it alone. Life upon the water is a different one, created by man for himself. Then, it is very natural that this situation would beget a type of folk art expression all its own.

Negroes in America have served on the rivers and their shores as workers— boatmen, roustabouts, longshoremen, raft-haulers and fishermen. Growing out of the lives of these men have come cries which are perhaps more plaintive than any of the others—especially those from the old Mississippi River boatmen.

These cries seem to possess the echo of the water in them. They are filled with a peculiar nostalgia. For some reason, too, they are very technical vocal pieces. Their brevity finds exception in a few calls of several broken measures in length. Most Negro water cries are sheer music, having no words. For this reason, it is difficult to identify them alone. Fortunately, many of these cries have been joined to songs which deal with the life on the river. This, with the help of old Negro river men of the past, enables us to get together those appearing hereafter.

Now, consider briefly, twenty of the elemental sounds produced in animals and see how many overlap in use by man and beasts. Note the great variety. The mere naming of the sounds demonstrates the point: laugh, snort, roar, hiss, whistle, song (hum), scream, moan, groan, grunt, coo, yell, yodle, growl, bark, bleat, mew, neigh, bay, whinny. It is very important and very interesting to note that the lower species and man are identified by sounds common to them. However, man has a rather unlimited range of sound formations based upon his ability to take any of the elemental sounds and combine them into new sound types such as words; for it is true that the languages of man do rely heavily upon the twenty sounds listed above. It is proof that man feels a basic dependence upon different animal sound types, since he has named them and is guided by them in many significant ways—love, fear, welcome, etc.

All of the aforesaid has been in support of the thesis that sounds are basic in animal nature and that man has more need for sounds and greater ability with sounds and a wider variety of sounds than any other living thing. Inarticulate sounds have greater meaning than ordinarily believed.

II

Mainly, the word "cry" is to be defined here as the most elemental song sound regardless of how or where one experiences it. Therefore we are to consider that certain sounds pro-duced through the mouth and the nose are not sung since these sounds do not emanate directly and essentially as a functional product of the larynx or voice box. Such sounds as vowels and their modifications are the main concern here, but there are other important types which must be considered. For instance, the laugh is the best known and most used of all inarticulate cries. The giggle is a close second. The vocal yawn and the scream are less frequent but equally familiar forms of the "cry." It is also notable how closely these sounds are wrapped up with deep human feelings.

When man or a lesser animal is thrown off normal physical and/or emotional balance by sudden crises he utters the primeval basic cries which spring from his innermost depths. It would seem that these sounds have lain dormant, awaiting their truest and best need for manifestation. They thus spring forth with fresh, startling, never failing vitality at the given moment, causing those who hear them to realize more vividly than could coherent language the distress or joy or surprise of the individual.

Types of crises seem to rob man of cultural veneer and the rational use of vocal sounds, and the main fact here is that they exist at given moments. There are other cries which are slightly less spontaneous and which are not caused by immediate crises which are more songlike or musical in that they cling to definite pitch movements. These cries are both brought together in Negro folk music expression—work song, blues, spirituals, jubilee, dance songs and songs of related character. These song cries are the main ingredient in all Negro folk music. It is basic in determining the distinguishable characteristic so highly prized and imitated in our present-day music in America.

The song cries of Negroes are divided into three categories: plain cries, which are the simplest in form and structure —some street cries and many of the so-called whoops and hollers; florid cries, which are the type which is the most prevalent and the most favored —the folk preaching, blues, spirituals, jazz, and the work songs are greatly indebted to this species which is not at all possible to set down in our present system of music; coloratura cries, which are among the most amazing and remarkable vocal feats in folk music. (Certain highly specialized and unusual feats as those accomplished by, for instance, Yma Sumac, are not typical of her race and are therefore considered as exceptional and inapplicable in this particular instance. However, they are very applicable in the general principle.) These cries are not as easily heard as the others and they are restricted in application because of their great complexity. Some of the best illustrations today can be found in some of the recordings of the Ward Sisters, Mahalia Jackson, Cab Calloway, Louis Armstrong, and some of the preaching records of the "Twenties Era." The plain and florid cries are really heard at all times when Negro music is sung or played in the authentic styles.

The greatest activity in the employment of the Negro folk cry in present-day music is to be found in the amazing rise of "gospel singing" in every state west of the Mississippi River and across the sea. As Negro churches became more European in decorum and program, the great mass of less European-ized Negroes began to look elsewhere for full-vented religious expressions in music and preaching. So, a great urge arose to use the Negro folk cry in connection with the religious antidote for segregation and all of the ills which bred it and were bred by it —poverty, sickness, social abuse and spiritual pain.

Although more advanced Negroes at first resented these "gospel songs," their creators and purveyors, they have gradually, very gradually, become more tolerant. Some churches where they were at first outlawed have carefully and quietly let down the bars to both the gospel song and gospel singers. Leading Negro newspapers speak in praise of Mahalia Jackson, the Ward Sisters, Rosetta Thorpe, Thomas Dorsey and several others as "outstanding artists." They perform at Carnegie Hall; they have a tremendous hold upon the record industry and, therefore, upon radio and television. More important, these gospel songs and singers are more numerous than any other active Negro music and musicians.

When one hears these songs he is conscious of a type of voice production which is strange and primitive but which seems to exhaust the innermost recesses of the singer's heart, mind, voice and soul. The folk listeners are similarly affected. Many faint, break forth in shouts, leap out of their seats, or scream incoherently.

Anyone who takes the time can easily see that the Negro has taken his cries— "whoops," "hollers," "calls"—and grafted them on to present-day song patterns whose practice goes back hundreds of years. This, and this alone, accounts for the great pull these songs exert on Negroes and white men of all classes here and in Europe. Rhythm is secondary but vital.

White men, in the South particularly, are imitating the Negro gospel singer —even in his physical activities while singing. This is vocal jazz in practice and in principle. I have seen numerous jazz audiences of Negroes and white men —even in New England—driven into hand clapping participation with Mahalia Jackson as singer and also as director at Music Inn, Lenox, Massachusetts.

Commercialization has drained all of the real spiritual value off and left gospel singing an anemic in terms of real, true, basic Negro religious fervor. Very often it creates this religious fervor but it differs from the spiritual in that it takes anything musical from any source and is governed by financial considerations and the white business man in its uses. However, the fact remains that the gospel song seems irresistibly here to stay and as long as it is based upon Negro cries it will remain. Further, like jazz, it will be learned by white men generally.

This principle of grafting the cry onto present-day music is noticed in another field—the present-day popular song and the crooner and stylist. The styles of singing in America have felt the indelible imprint of the Negro song cry to the extent that every very popular white singer in the field owes much to the Negro singer. The crooner would be impossible without the Negro vocal influence and, of course, every Negro song stylist today, especially the woman, is a living expression of the plain, florid and coloratura song cry of Negro origin. Without these sounds, we would not have American music in its present vigorous form.

American music is making our performers and composers too unique. Whether one likes it or not, a new type of vocal art is in process of development in this country. Its roots have long been accepted here and abroad by the great average mass of listeners and the constant flood of sound is bound to create a new type of listener in the course of fifty or, say, one hundred years. What the vocal amalgam will be like is a fascinating consideration. We must realize that our present European standard is the result of the confluence of singing of the folk, the church and the theatre. We have these same forces vigorously at work in Negro song and are transferring their essences into the main stream of American song. How these cries affect the instrumental music of our day is to be shown in a later section of this piece. Suffice it to say that man has not always sung as he does now and he certainly will not do so in the future in America. The constant change is pouring out of every radio and phonograph. Listen to any popular recording of thirty years ago and listen to those by today's stars—of either race and either sex. The contrast is startling.

When one hears a screaming bevy of bobby-soxers in the throes of ecstasy at concert or program featuring some famous crooner or stylist, he is listening to the cry answering the cry. How much more natural could it be? However, we are amazed at these outbursts because we do not realize that the bobby-soxer is far less inhibited than we of older origin and their ears have been adjusted to these cry sounds from birth. Moreover, these cry sounds are less veneered and have a much more direct contact with the spirits of these listeners than does the song itself.

In the not too distant past it was the songwriter—Herbert, Berlin, Friml, Ball, and Kern—who was famous. Today it is the popular singer who is famous. He uses the composer for a foil and places his vocal inventions in the foreground, using elements of, and/or, whole Negro cries.

For these reasons, I have never thought that Negro folk music was a logical sequence of developments—cry, work song, spiritual, blues, jazz, for the Negro has always possessed the fundamental ingredient for all these in his cries. It was a mere grafting on of these cries to the different needs and impulses and borrowed tunes and songs—just as is being done today. So much has been said about the twelve-bar blues, whereas, in fact, the structure is based upon a series of Negro cries. So is all Negro folk music in this country. The bars of the blues are a result of the Negro cry and dance in conjunction. The "silent bars" are used and were used by professional blues singers for the insertion of dance effects and "jive."

Because Negro cries have hitherto been so neglected from an analytical viewpoint, a concentrated list is given for clarity and re-emphasis: (a) Calls, (b) Selling (Street Cries), (c) Religious, (d) Field, (e) Night, (f) Dance, (g) Water. These divisions are all subject to further divisions in terms of music and speech and their various modifications.

It should be borne in mind that our consideration here, being a musical one, does not take into account all of the cries, such as those growing out of fear, distress, and grief in the purest sense.

In presenting the following examples, it becomes necessary to set some of the cries as "spoken" ones, since no system of notation is able to convey the sound impressions created through them. These types are definitely musical but they are also less than music in the accepted sense of the term. Then, too, the uses of them are so likely to change the inflections several times during the course of a day, that it becomes an unfair matter to the reader to give them too definite a tonal setting. Therefore, in reading these "spoken" cries one should imagine hearing them in terms of more familiar examples gleaned from the lips of Negroes in their own localities, or from past experiences. This "hit-or-miss" procedure is the best which can be offered.

Where the music could be set— and fortunately it frequently could be —great pains were taken to arrive at correct representations.

Call

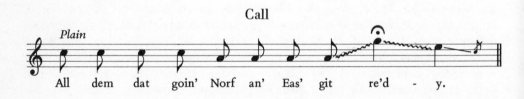

Plain

All   dem   dat   goin' Norf   an'   Eas'   git   re'd - y.

Speech Cries (Indefinite tonality)

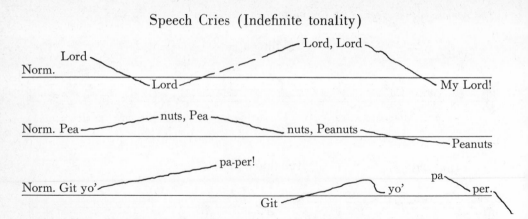

"Old Man River keeps rolling along" in art as well as in water. The connection between water and the Negro folk music is inseparable in this country. New Orleans was the Southern terminal point for the palatial river-boats and Negroes were the musicians for them. The famous Strekfus Line was the main source of living for many Negro musicians and workmen.

Long before, during and after slavery the Negro river singer was creating lonesome, strange, florid and coloratura cries about the river, women, towns, money, saloons, boats, white men, and black men. However, it must be repeated that many of these cries had no words at all. The voice was used as an instrument—as a horn, if you please, pure and simple.

It is certainly true that man's music comes from within and his instrument plays what is within him. He will always be moved by his relationship to his environment. So, as the boats were worked by musicians, the Negroes felt some of the same things which caused the singing Negroes to create the "water cries." Moreover, these musicians heard these sounds from Negro boatmen and shoremen as early as 1811 and worked them into jazz patterns and carried them inland after they left the boats.

It is no accident that the names St. Louis and New Orleans are connected with the greatest in Negro folk instrumental music. It is not mere chance that the most famous blues is called "St. Louis" and that the most famous jazz is called "New Orleans." Both are water towns.

These Negro cries were played in true form at times and were, as in vocal music, fitted on to the more definite, formal white music selections. Later these cries came into their own as seed for compositions.

The brazen instruments—not clarinets—were unable to convey the strange sounds as played normally. So Negroes began to use derby hats, sink-stoppers, plungers, handkerchiefs, whisk brooms, and anything else to modify the tone and give a more throaty quality to the instruments.

Negro cries have continued to be the chief ingredient of all true jazz to this day. The more Negro and white musicians become aware of this, the greater will be their understanding and ability as players and singers of Negro music.

Even when a jazz cornetist, trumpeter, clarinetist, saxophonist plays chords of the white man's origin based upon the European third and second —augmented, diminished, Major or

Minor,—he colors these with a certain oily sliding melancholy character which is obviously the result of the Negro cry impulse, or often as not the cry itself. Jazz is largely Negro cries sung or played or both.

The water ports of Charleston, Mobile, Jacksonville, Pensacola, Savannah and others all had remarkable influence on Negro folk music and should be given credit for it. For example, the influence of James Reese Europe, of Mobile, and of Eugene Mars Mikel of Charleston was of great importance in the assembling of Negro musicians—literate and illiterate——and singers, too. These men brought the cry into use on the eastern seaboard as a powerful force in popular and ragtime music.

The Negro cries were and are so natural to Negro musicians that they do not see the cry as an integral part of their nature. In fact, during my studies it has been noted that certain Negroes have been wont to ridicule Negro cries on the one hand and to find great pleasure in playing them on the other. Others have been greatly moved by these cries when or wherever they were heard.

In August, 1953, Eubie Blake, the famous composer of *Shuffle Along* and many other famous hits was at Music Inn. Mr. Blake has gone through ragtime, jazz, and classic music. He is now more than seventy and plays the piano wonderfully well. He was graduated from New York University at the age of sixty-odd, in the Schillinger System of Composition. He has known all levels of Negro musicians personally, intimately, having played with them.

One morning at a lecture of mine on Negro cries during the conference on Negro folk music, presided over by Marshall Stearns, I sang a florid Negro cry. Mr. Blake leaped halfway from his seat and yelled, "Oh, professor, professor, you hit me, you hit me." He placed both hands over his heart and continued with great emotion: "You make me think of my dear mother. She always sang like that. I can hear her now. That's the stuff I was raised on." He sat down quietly except for a deep sigh which had no audible competition from anyone. It was reverently quiet. I was forced to continue—unnecessarily. Eubie Blake was living testimony of the influences which had made him so musically unique without even formal training until he was old and famous and did not really need it much. He only knew then it was the cry which had guided him.

It is herewith suggested that the reader hear the following recordings in the order named: Ethnic Folkways Library 1484A and 1481B; Savoy 4023A, 4023B; Ethnic Folkways Library 1488B. These few records will reveal a lot. The Folkways records are sung by many old Negroes; the Savoy by young. Note the transference back and forth as cry patterns—plain, florid, coloratura.

The young "gospel singer," Roy Hamilton, who brings his natural and acquired song styles into the popular field, was born in Georgia. He has lived in the East, singing a combination of cries, blues, and European song styles. He is suddenly a sensation. Why? The question is answered already. Listen to his singing of *You'll Never Walk Alone*, *Ebb Tide* or *Beware* and the student will discover the unique application of African colors to the European song fabric.

Having done this, spirituals, work songs, jazz, gospel songs and popular songs should be listened to and noted for the influence of the cry, vocally and instrumentally. If this thesis is sound it should apply in general. It will. Only look for substances instead of identities —sounds instead of melodies—manner of tone projection rather than from what it is projected.

A cry on an instrument is as real and as meaningful as the cry from the human throat. It, too, is life suspended briefly in vibrant sound cast up from the innermost human depths—the source of all musical art.

Olin Downes, writing of eighty-seven-year-old Toscannini in the New York *Times*, February 7, 1954, and expressing his wonder at Toscannini's artistry said " . . . man is more than an animal; . . . the art which he has created is greater than man himself, and the guide to grander horizons than the race has yet known." Presently, it would seem that the Negro is supplying an important ingredient in this gradual process. The white man has been busy trying to find the cause of Negro musical uniqueness somewhere in Africa when the cause was always present with the Negro by his side, suffering and struggling for existence and pouring out his tension, despair, love, and, yes, hate in his strange native cries which in turn fascinated his white tormentor and made him his willing student and disciple and musical *confrère*.

Perhaps, as it seems, the Negro spoke a various language of races through his flexible spiritual nature, whereas the white man only discovered his own true nature in it as it grasped and shook him in his power. As unique and as powerful as the Negro's native musical urge is, it would not be of value as a thing apart from his fellowman—an unrelated entity in the cultural needs and graces of the world and less than a language of life.

To return once more to the greatest musician of our time, Toscannini, let us say that when the incomparable master stands before his orchestra and pleads: "Canta! Canta! Canta! preciso! Canta!" (Sing! Sing! Sing! truly! Sing!) he is asking for the most profound, poignant musical expression found on earth and he knows his men comprehend instinctively. At this point, in his lofty artistic height, he links himself with all classes of musicians—players, singers, conductors, composers—who work from within and seek truth in mere sound. One may also state this conversely and say that the simplest, humblest singer or player who reveals his soul is akin to the greatest. It only remains for his fellowman to comprehend and to place his contribution in the right cultural position by constant use, refinement and selection.

Negro "Shouts" from Georgia

ROBERT WINSLOW GORDON

It is not always meaningful to try to distinguish folksong as a separate entity. The folk cry, for example, is clearly related to a variety of specific functions, one of which is dancing. Another important form of Negro folksong intimately connected with dance is the "shout."

One of the earliest and most vivid accounts of the "shout" appeared in an unsigned article in The Nation *for May 30, 1867. It was mentioned in the process of reacting to Thomas Wentworth Higginson's pioneering article "Negro Spirituals," which had recently appeared in the* Atlantic Monthly. *However, one of the best descriptions is the following report by Robert Winslow Gordon, who was truly an eclectic collector of American folksong. Gordon, the first archivist of the Archive of American Folksong at the Library of Congress, wrote a series of articles on different types of folksong for the* New York Times Sunday Magazine *during 1927–1928. (These articles were later published as* Folk-Songs of America *[New York, 1938].) Gordon's articles were based upon materials which he had collected personally, though some were obtained from readers of his column "Old Songs That Men Have Sung" which appeared regularly in* Adventure Magazine *(1923–27). (Gordon's papers are deposited at the University of Oregon.)*

Higginson's essay on spirituals appeared in the Atlantic Monthly, *19 (1867), pp. 685–94 (reprinted in Bruce Jackson, ed.,* The Negro and His Folklore in Nineteenth-Century Periodicals *[Austin, 1967], pp. 82–102), and as Chapter 9 of his* Army Life in a Black Regiment *which was published in 1869. For Higginson's description of shouts, see* Army Life in a Black Regiment *(New York, 1962), p. 41. Another early description of the shout is found in H. G. Spaulding, "Under the Palmetto,"* Continental Monthly, *4 (1863), pp. 188–203 (the description is included in the excerpt reprinted by Jackson, op. cit., pp. 64–73).*

For other treatments of the shout, see Carl Carmer, Stars Fell on Alabama *(New York, 1934), pp. 24–27; Zora Neale Hurston, "Shouting," in Nancy Cunard, ed.*, Negro *(London, 1934), pp. 49–50; and Lydia Parrish*, Slave Songs of the Georgia Sea Islands *(New York, 1942), pp. 54–92. See also the account of the "ring shout" in Harold Courlander*, Negro Folk Music, U.S.A. *(New York, 1970), pp. 194–200.*

HARDLY LESS numerous than the spirituals were the "shouts" that once played an important part in both the social and the religious life of the Negro of plantation days. And though they are less known they are decidedly more typical, more nearly the Negro's own peculiar creation. To find them today is not easy. They have to a great extent passed from the church, where they originated, and are used but rarely, only on occasions of great celebration. And only the older Negroes have perpetuated the custom of shouting, the younger generation, so far as my own experience goes, never joining in.

The word has no reference to shouting in the ordinary sense. Technically the Negro "shout" is a peculiar combination of singing combined with a rhythmic shuffling dance, a "holy dance" as it is sometimes called. No song, no matter how boisterous is sufficient; the shuffling about in a circle is the prime essential.

The type of song used in shouting is peculiar and has had much to do with molding and changing spirituals. Yet, so far as I am aware no serious attempt has yet been made to explain its origin or to describe its various forms. Collectors have not attempted to separate and print as one group the songs used for this purpose, and this purpose only. This has resulted in unnecessary confusion.

As a matter of fact the same song may be used for two or three different purposes and have, consequently, several more or less fixed forms. With a large number of stanzas and a chorus or refrain it may be a regular church spiritual. Much shortened, with one or two special stanzas added, and with a refrain instead of a chorus, it may be a rowing song. Still more shortened, and with a chorus having an entirely different rhythm, it may be a favorite shout. And to add to the complications there may be two different ways of singing the spiritual itself, the "ole way" and "de new."

Many collectors are overanxious to "get all there is" and not sufficiently acquainted with Negro psychology. One of them approached an aged Negro singer with the request:

"Auntie, you know 'bout Phario?
　　Sing it to me."
"Wat you want 'em, boss—ol' way
　　or new?"
"All of it, auntie, every scrap—every
　　bit you know!"

Anxious to please, but a bit confused, she has very likely begun with the shouting version and then gone on with the longer and older spiritual. Praised, and urged hard to remember another verse or two, she has gone on to "de new way," and if still further urged had added verses from the rowing song, or even passed on to quite a different song that has similar lines.

A Negro of the older type will seldom

volunteer information and will never under ordinary circumstances contradict "de w'ite gem'man." " 'Taint manners!" If you make a misstatement and ask her for verification you will probably receive the courteous answer, "Yas, sir. Dat right, sir." Only in the kitchen, when she is instructing the youngsters of the white family in whose service she has been for years does she feel privileged to make direct and downright statements. Then no martinet could be more precise and exacting in laying down the law. In the case of the men the question of "manners" plays a smaller part, but the result is much the same. If the white gentleman is so ignorant, why bother to enlighten him? Do just what he asks and no more. Let him go on his way rejoicing; he will never know how much he missed, never be able to check up on any misinformation.

Hence in all scientific work with Negroes, direct statements and leading questions are to be avoided. Instead, the collector must constantly be on the watch for the slightest hints that might under skillful cross-examination produce hidden and unsuspected facts. It is well to approach all singers with an attitude of humble ignorance. At times this apparent ignorance may lead to your getting some extraordinary exaggerations and misstatements, but these can be checked with the stories of others approached in the same way. And at least you are armed with certain definite things for which to watch.

Often it may be a good plan to make a statement, giving as your authority some definite Negro in a nearby district, and intimating that you are a bit in doubt as to the accuracy of your information. That spur almost never fails. "Huh! W'at dat nigger know? I axe you. Don't know nottin'." And for the next five minutes your notebook fills rapidly with more material for later checking. Whatever stands continued tests is likely to be substantially accurate and reasonably complete.

The "shout" is old. In the district centering about Darien, Ga., where I am at present working, and from which all of the following texts were obtained, the custom can be traced back with certainty for more than seventy-five years, perhaps much more. Several apparently trustworthy traditions say that it was common in the period of 1812 during "de British War." The songs used for this "holy dance" as some call it, were extremely simple, consisting basically of a single stanza or "walk" and a single chorus usually with a quicker and more marked rhythm known as the "shout."

It was regularly permitted in all churches in the older days, but not as a part of the service. After that had closed, the wooden benches were pushed back and the centre of the floor was cleared to give room for the circle of shouters. This was done regularly on two fixed occasions—Christmas Eve and the last day of the old year, and at such other times as the desires of the congregation might demand it.

Any one might lead off by beginning the stanza or "walk." This was usually sung twice, all joining in as they formed a circle and marched about in time to the singing. Then began the chorus or shout proper. The peculiar swaying shuffle commenced and this chorus was sung over and over again without intermission for a considerable period. Occasionally, to give a moment's rest, or to break the monotony of the constant repetition, some leader would start the stanza again, and the walking would be resumed.

"'Ligion So Sweet" is an excellent example of the basic simplicity of structure found in most shouting songs and of the decided difference in rhythm between the stanza and the chorus. The slow and dignified measure of the "walk" changes to a double-quick, tripping measure in the "shout":

(WALK)

Keep a rollin' down de fountain,
Keep a rollin' down de fountain,
Keep a rollin' down de fountain,
Oh, de 'ligion so sweet!

(SHOUT)

Oh de 'ligion—oh de 'ligion
Oh de 'ligion—so sweet!
Oh de 'ligion—oh de 'ligion
Oh de 'ligion—so sweet!

And here is another favorite "all night" shout that shows the same simplicity and repetition:

(WALK)

Walk around de heavens,
We'll walk around de heavens,
Walk around de heavens, O Lord,
De room already dressed!

(SHOUT)

Oh, de room a'ready dressed—O
    Lord!
De room a'ready dressed, O Lord,
De room a'ready dressed, my God,
De room a'ready dressed!

The steps used while the chorus is sung and resung are varied. Though every singer will move exactly in time with the rhythm, and the tap and shuffle of the feet will accentuate it till the floor shakes, no two will perhaps adopt the same posture or use the same step. An aged auntie shuffles along with hands clasped and head slightly bowed, her feet never actually leaving the floor. A younger woman next to her alternately trips and stamps with her feet, her head thrown back and hands clapping time. Still another, hands on hips, glides and sways with a sidewise motion, facing now in and now out of the circle. The men are almost without exception patting and clapping time with hands held before them, and many are particular to keep their feet always at right angles, stepping and shuffling in a sort of herring-bone pattern. This is an added precaution on their part. For one of the deacons is "watchman," and woe to the member who forgets and "crosses feet." That would be dancing,* and would result in a summons before the conference on next communion Sunday and a severe warning if not a temporary expulsion from the church.

As the singing goes on the shouts will vary a good deal in type as well as in tone. Not all are as simple as the two already given. Occasionally instead of a constant repetition of a single chorus there will be a fixed sequence of verses. In the following example, one of the most elaborate I have found, "How long you goin' to hold um?" means how long are you going to hold fast to your religion without making a slip and falling from grace:

True believer, tell me now how long
    you goin' to hold um?

---

* The definition of "dancing" as "crossing one's feet" seems to be widespread. See, for example, Fanny D. Bergen, "On the Eastern Shore," *Journal of American Folklore*, 2 (1889), p. 298; Newbell Niles Puckett, *Folk Beliefs of the Southern Negro* (New York, 1969), p. 60; and Harold Courlander, *Negro Folk Music U.S.A.* (New York, 1970), p. 195. —ED.

Oh, tell me now how long you goin'
    to hold um?
Oh, tell me now how long you goin'
    to hold um?
Roll, Jerdan, roll!

Oh, my sin so heavy I can't get
    across,
Oh, oh, can't get across.
My sin so heavy I can't get across,
Roll, Jerdan, roll!

Oh, I throw my sin right middle ob
    de sea,
Oh, oh, right middle ob de sea.
Oh, I throw my sin right middle ob
    de sea,
Roll, Jerdan, roll!

True believer done wid de trouble o'
    de worl'
Oh, oh, de trouble o' de worl'
True believer done wid de trouble ob
    de worl'
Roll, Jerdan, roll!

I jus' begin wid de trouble o' de worl'
Oh, oh, de trouble o' de worl'
I jus' begin wid de trouble o' de worl'
Roll, Jerdan, roll!

Here the first stanza is the walk and
the next four the shout proper. The
whole song is repeated, and in the
successive singings "true believer" is
replaced as "Brudder Tember"—
"Mudder Charlotte"—"Sister Lucy"—
etc. In the choosing of the various names
much humor is shown. Brudder Tember,
whose name is of course, September,
is "watchman" and a pillar of the
church, while Sister Lucy, who joined
less than three months ago, is already
perilously close to dancing at the
present moment, and is being closely
watched by Mudder Charlotte, the
"godmother" of the church "what teach
de soul how to pray."

To have experienced shouting at its
best it would have been necessary to
attend one of the older churches at
Christmas or at New Year's. The service
held on Christmas Eve lasted all night
long, and interspersed with the shouts
were some of the very oldest spirituals,
including "The Twelve Blessings of
Mary." Moreover there were certain
special shouts that must traditionally
be used on this occasion. The "watchman" too had an added importance,
for it was his duty to scan the heavens
and announce the first appearance of
"de star."

Shortly after midnight, perhaps when
the "watchman" first went out to seek
the star, they were sure to start "Looka
Day."

Oh, true believer
Oh, oh, looka day
Day de comin'.

Looka day
Day de comin'
Looka day
Day de comin'.

When you jump,
Jump like a member.
When you hop,
Hop like a member.

No matter how many other shouts
were used, they would return to this
one again and again throughout the
night until finally the watchman reported
that the morning star had risen. Then
came:

Thought heard Father Johnny say
Call de nation great an' small
Look up de road at thy right hand
De star give its light!

Oh what a meeting, brothers
Oh what a meeting
Oh what a meeting
W'en de star give its light!

Oh what a shouting sisters,
Oh what a shouting
Oh what a shouting
W'en de star give its light!

This was immediately followed by "Baby Born Today," an extremely old traditional shout and differing from those commonly used in that it required a leader or foresinger to read out the lines while the rest repeated the refrain. There was no definite structure, lines being repeated at the will of the leader in varying combinations "jus' as de spirit moves."

Mother Mary, what is de matter?
Oh Jerusalem in de mornin'
Father Joseph, what is de matter?
Oh Jerusalem in de mornin'
A baby born today
Oh Jerusalem in de mornin'
Baby born today
Oh Jerusalem in de mornin'
Born in de manger
Oh Jerusalem in de mornin'
Born in de manger
Oh Jerusalem in de mornin'
They wrapped in swaddlin' clothes
Oh Jerusalem in de mornin'
The stall was His cradle
Oh Jerusalem in de mornin'
Born in de manger
Oh Jerusalem in de mornin'
Baby born today
Oh Jerusalem in de mornin'
Born in Bethlehem
Oh Jerusalem in de mornin'
Born in de manger
Oh Jerusalem in de mornin'
The stall was His cradle
Oh Jerusalem in de mornin'
And they wrapped in swaddlin'
        clothes
Oh Jerusalem in de mornin'
Jerusalem, Oh, Jerusalem
Oh Jerusalem in de mornin'
Baby born today
Oh Jerusalem in de mornin'! etc.

Finally the watchman announced that day was "broad clear" and began to sing the closing song:

De angels round de throne
De angels round de throne
De angels round de throne
Cryin' A-a-men.

Amen, Christians,
Amen, Christians,
I want to go to heaven
To see my father Abraham.

Once this song is sung all must depart and go home. No more singing, no more shouting. Hence if the group was not quite ready to break up, they attempted to stop him before he could start the song. The women would cluster about him and try to stop his mouth with their handkerchiefs. There was much laughter and good-natured tussling. If they succeeded, and that depended a good deal on whether or not he was willing to grant their plea for a short respite, he was led outside and two of the men were sometimes set to guard him.

The custom of shouting was never confined to the church. It was looked upon as a harmless recreation for all occasions in the old plantation days. Nearly every evening there was a shout down at the quarters, and after the war it continued long to be popular where any considerable number of Negroes lived near one another in a small community. Many a dear little Southern lady whose hair is now white has confessed to me that she used as a girl to beg the Negro women to shout for her and, if no men were present, had joined in with them—thus herself learning the art.

Outside the church the shout was one of the main social amusements. It was close enough to dancing to attract the young, and yet avoided all taint of worldliness. As a result some of the shouts were a curious mixture of the secular and the spiritual, of poetry, pathos and humor. "Side 'um, Darn'l" (go sideways, Daniel) is an excellent example. The step used for this was a modified chasse and very sprightly, though without any "crossin' of de feet."

Oh, Brudder Johnny
Oh, oh, side 'um Darn'l!

Little bit o' headache, little bit o'
        fever
Oh, oh, side 'um Darn'l!

When I git to Heaven, Heaven own me
Oh, oh, side 'um Darn'l!

Heaven know me; Heaven own me
Oh, oh, side 'um, Darn'l!

De true believer de Heaven people,
Oh, oh, side 'um Darn'l!

Several of the older Negroes have told me that there were two different groups of shouts, "de worldly and de spirichul." But others have denied this. Some songs were undoubtedly more fitted for church use and some for occasions of celebration. I doubt whether any exact line could be drawn. There were plenty of games that included modified dancing, such as "Peep Squirrel"—"Finger Ring"—and "Green Grow de Willow Tree" and it is possible that these were what my informants referred to as "worldly shouts."

Today both shouts and games are practically gone. Only on special occasions are the shouts now used. Just before a wedding, if the bride belongs to one of the old slave-owning families, it is possible that she will discover a group of old family servants at the door, come to "shout for de weddin'." If so, she may consider herself highly honored, for it is one of the greatest compliments they can pay her.

The whole subject is still practically untouched. My own investigations are as yet confined to a single district, and are inadequate to show many differences in type and custom that must have existed. But every example I have given is just as I took it from the mouth of some aged Negro, and with the exception of those given in the description of Christmas service I have seen every one of them shouted by a group.

The account of the old time Christmas service is practically word for word, as it was told to me by Mary C. Mann of Darien, whose memory and accuracy are both to be trusted.

The Social Implications
of the Negro Spiritual

JOHN LOVELL, JR.

The folk cry and the shout are at least related to folksong if they are not folksong proper, but to speak of folksong in the strictest sense, one must turn to such forms as the spiritual. Here is a species of American Negro folksong which has captured not only the imagination of all Americans but the hearts and minds of peoples all over the world. But if the popularity of the spirituals is widespread, so also is the range of scholarship dealing with them. Treatises by theologians stand alongside essays by students of folksong.

One reason, perhaps, for the large number of books and articles devoted to the spiritual—at least for those written by white scholars—is the association of the spiritual with the stereotype of the "good" docile Negro. The spirituals appeared on the surface to be "establishment" philosophy, that is, they seemed to argue that accepting one's lot, albeit a poor one, here on earth in the hope of a better life to come in heaven after death was the wisest course to follow. Violence was not encouraged (the "good" Negro is surely, from the white point of view, nonviolent), *and the nominal adherence to the principles of Christianity as expressed in the spirituals tended to reassure nervous slaveowners worrying about possible slave uprisings. The spirituals then were—and are—the music of "good" Negroes in contrast to the blues and jazz which were—and are—the music of "bad" Negroes. This dichotomy between the "good" sacred and the "bad" secular streams in American Negro music has continued even though, musicologically speaking, there are obvious similarities in form and style between, say, the spirituals and the blues just as there may be similarity in the verbal skills used by the preacher (sacred) and the hustler (secular).*

But there is a strong possibility that white interpretations of spirituals have been wrong. Several Negro scholars have convincingly demonstrated that the

Reprinted from *The Journal of Negro Education*, vol. 8 (1939), pp. 634–43, by permission of the author and Howard University.

spirituals represented statements about this world, not the next one, and that the philosophy expressed is not pro-establishment but anti-establishment. One of the best clarifications of this view is by John Lovell, Jr., a professor of English at Howard University. Despite the fact that Professor Lovell's essay was written in 1939, it remains one of the most articulate and succinct summaries of approaches to the spiritual.

The reader should realize that there are a number of high points of the spiritual literature. One of them is certainly W. E. B. Du Bois' classic essay on the "sorrow songs" which constitutes the fourteenth chapter of his Souls of Black Folk. *Also of interest is Mrs. Booker T. Washington's eloquent review of the emotional impact of the spirituals and their important role in the history of Fisk University. See "The Songs of Our Fathers,"* The Colored American Magazine, *8 (1905), pp. 245–53. Perhaps the most startling recent study has been the 1945 University of Chicago doctoral dissertation by Miles Mark Fisher, published as* Negro Slave Songs in the United States *(New York, 1953, paperback, New York, 1969), which argued that the early spirituals were symbolic messages summoning slaves to secret meetings and providing a vehicle for the expression of a hope to return to Africa. For a sample of some of the more conventional theological approaches to spirituals, see Howard Thurman,* The Negro Spiritual Speaks of Life and Death *(New York, 1947), or the same author's* Deep River: Reflections on the Religious Insight of Certain of the Negro Spirituals *(New York, 1955). For an entry into the extensive European scholarship devoted to the spiritual, see Theo Lehmann,* Negro Spirituals: Geschichte und Theologie *(Berlin, 1965). For an indication of the continuing discussion of the significance of spirituals and other folkloristic data in the context of slavery, see Sterling Stuckey, "Through the Prism of Folklore: The Black Ethos in Slavery,"* The Massachusetts Review, *9 (1968), pp. 417–37, and Lawrence W. Levine, "Slave Songs and Slave Consciousness: An Exploration in Neglected Sources," in Tamara K. Hareven, ed.,* Anonymous Americans: Explorations in Nineteenth-Century Social History *(Englewood Cliffs, N.J., 1971), pp. 99–130. See also John Lovell's magnum opus,* Black Song: The Forge and the Flame.

EARLY CRITICISM OF SPIRITUALS*

May 30, 1867 is an important date in the history of Negro culture. On that date, in the New York *Nation*, there appeared a notice of the first attempt to collect and understand Negro spirituals. One of the prospective compilers announced the forthcoming volume, and added almost shamefacedly: "No one up to this time has explored for preservation the wild, beautiful, and pathetic melodies of the Southern slaves."[1] Since then, a thousand pens have dipped themselves in the sunlight, and they have scribbled at least a million lines, in praise, in defense, in explanation, in interpretation, in eulogy of the Negro spiritual. They have mined out its religion, its psychology, its philosophy. But the vast wealth of the spiritual in terms of the social mind of a very powerful cul-

* Literature on the Spiritual and on the related topics I discuss here is voluminous and ubiquitous. The bibliography I suggest is far from complete, but is fully representative. [See end of article. —ED.]

[1] *Nation* (May 30, 1867), p. 428.

tural unit has just been scratched. In that respect, we have pierced only slightly deeper than we had on May 30, 1867.

James Weldon Johnson,[2] R. C. Harrison,[3] and Alain Locke[4] have sketched the periods of the creation and appreciation of the spiritual. They tell us that the spirituals were probably started on their way about 100 years before slavery died; that the heyday of the spiritual was about 1830 to 1865; that from 1865 to 1880 aroused Americans were collecting them, like fine orchids or trampled old masters; that from 1880 to 1910, men like Harris, Page, and Smith were using them for local color; that since 1910, Negroes, notably DuBois and Johnson, have rolled them through their subjective consciousnesses, with admirable results. White critics, like Krehbiel, Dorothy Scarborough, and Guy Johnson, have gone through them with a fine-tooth comb. The farthest advance any of these writers have made into the social meaning of the spiritual is found in Krehbiel, and DuBois. Krehbiel wrote:[5]

Is it not the merest quibble to say that these songs are not American? They were created in America under American influences and by people who are Americans in the same sense that any other element of our population is American—every element except the aboriginal.

Concerning the spiritual DuBois wrote some of America's finest prose.[6] He hinted at the African genius for transmuting trouble into song. His only social comment on the American spiritual, however, concerns "Nobody Knows the Trouble I've Seen," and that comment is incidental to a gorgeous picture:[7]

When struck with a sudden poverty, the United States refused to fulfill its promises of land to the freedmen, a brigadier-general went down to the Sea Islands to carry the news. An old woman on the outskirts of the throng began singing this song; all the mass joined her, swaying. And the soldier wept.

No literature can fail to look stunted when deprived of its social strength. Take away the fire of Elizabethan England and the grand tragedies of Shakespeare are just twice-told tales. Milton's "Lycidas" was just another elegy before Tillyard came along in the 1920's and showed that it was the cry of a young man against a system that threw stumbling-blocks before him on his road to fame. The high priests of the spiritual have worn themselves out with appeals to the gods of art and religion, and the people have not heard them, for they live in a social world. The result is that today white people look askance at explanations for the spiritual, and Negroes are ashamed to discuss it.

Sterling Brown,[8] two short years ago, prepared the first direct case for the social implications of the Negro spiritual. He brought Frederick Douglass and Harriet Tubman to the stand to testify that these "religious" songs

[2] *The Book of American Negro Spirituals*, (1937 ed.) pp. 10–23.
[3] *Texas and Southwestern Lore* No. 6, (1927), pp. 144–53.
[4] *The Negro and His Music*, pp. 10–21.
[5] *Afro-American Folksongs*, p. 26.
[6] "The Sorrow Songs" in *The Souls of Black Folk* (1903 ed.)
[7] *Ibid.*, p. 255.
[8] *Negro Poetry and Drama*, Ch. II.

had social meanings: for example, deliverance for the Israelites meant freedom for the slaves; Canaan meant Canada. With good evidence and keen insight, he says:[9]

Against the tradition of the plantation as a state of blessed happiness the spirituals speak out with power and tragic beauty. Too many rash critics have stated that the spirituals showed the slave turning his back on this world for the joys of the next. The truth is that he took a good look at this world and told what he saw.

But the pursuit of this point lay outside the scope of Brown's book. And so we still have 800 to 1,000 original songs, comprising an epic tradition in the class of the *Iliad*, the Songs of Roland, or the Lays of the Nibelungs, with no clear analysis of the soil from which they sprung or of the process of their growth. In other epic traditions, patient scholars have found the seeds of racial and national culture. They look there first. And yet for how many years have the dabblers in American "Negroitis" ignored or treated with disgraceful cavalierness the heart of the Negro spirituals!

SOIL OUT OF WHICH
SPIRITUAL GREW

What is this soil, capable of such rich products? Descriptions of it are fully available. There is, first of all, the African environment—not the romantic Africa of the movies but the Africa which puts blood and sand into the bodies of its natives. Woodson[10]

tells us of the social and political genius of the African tribes, from whom American slaves were recruited. He describes their metal workers, architects, their experts in industrial arts. None of the vicious tactics of slave-mongers, white or black; none of the patronizers or traducers of things African can obscure the cultural accomplishments of these people who, under new conditions, expressed themselves in the Negro spiritual. They left their imprint on America before the white man came, as seen in such terms as canoe, buckra, and tobacco.[11] In music, says Locke,[12] there is an African gulf-stream flowing completely around Southern America, the coast islands, Haiti, the Bahamas, the Eastern provinces of Cuba, Vera Cruz, Yucatan, Guiana; and influencing such well-known dances as the tango of the Argentine, the carioca of Trinidad, and the beguine of Guadeloupe. Weatherford[13] speaks highly of the Africans' trading and military ability, their agricultural science, and of the revelations of their social life through religious activities.

The horrors of the slave trade—in Africa, on the middle passage, and in America—could not take away the social consciousness of these people. Nor was their moral fibre loosened thereby. They realized that if they reached America, each of them had 15 to 20 partners who had been blotted out in the process of transferrence. They saw the American plantation system steadily and whole. Their memories stored up the pictures of masters, overseers,

---

[9] *Ibid.*, p. 18.

[10] *The Negro in Our History*, 1931 ed., pp. 37–52.

[11] *Ibid.*, p. 58. [The words canoe and tobacco seem to be American Indian, not African, in origin. —ED.]

[12] *Op. cit.*, p. 138.

[13] *The Negro from Africa to America*, pp. 33–36, 43.

auctioneers and buyers, patrollers, and other brutalizers of men. Read the slave narratives for their social implications, as Mrs. Robinson has done,[14] and you will see this remarkable mind at work.

Naturally, men as sensitive as these slaves were going to react definitely, and sometimes turbulently, to all these things. Sometimes they howled with alarm at brutalities;[15] but often they fought back, and learned the advantages of resistance.[16] Their physical reaction, seen in hundreds of recorded slave revolts and thousands of unrecorded ones,[17] is important enough. It destroys the almost universal belief that the African Negro is docile because he "accepted" slavery. Almost universally he did not accept slavery, and laws compelling every able-bodied white man to patrol duty around the plantations—or a sum for a substitute —and the consternation and fear in every nook and cranny of the slavocracy are devastating proof.

But the physical revolts are not so important as the mental revolts. Uprising slaves were shot or hanged and that was the end of them physically; but the mind of the slave seethed ceaselessly, and was a powerful factor in the abolition movement. *Gone With the Wind* resounds with "Go Down, Moses"

and "Jes a few more days ter tote de wee-ry load"[18] as well as with evidence of the pitiless progress of the group intelligence in: "that black grapevine telegraph system[19] which defies white understanding." Linda Brent, Douglass, Lewis and Milton Clarke, Josiah Henson, Elizabeth Keekley, Solomon Northrup, and a dozen others[20] tell what slaves were thinking, and how their thinking stimulated a great secret movement. Siebert[21] and Still[22] clinch the belief that the majority of slaves were collecting information, plotting and planning, seeking outlets, ammunition, supplies. A host of American writers, like Mark Twain, are further evidence. If the Negro spiritual came from the heart of the slave, it should be covered with such sentiments. It is. The demonstration of that fact in every particular is necessary.

THE SPIRITUAL AS CRITICISM OF EVERYDAY LIFE

The spiritual, then, is the key to the slave's description and criticism of his environment. It is the key to his revolutionary sentiments and to his desire to fly to free territory. With it, we can smash the old romantic molds, which are still turning out readymade Negroes.[23] But let us not put the empha-

---

[14] "Social Conditions of Slavery as Taken from Slave Narratives"—unpublished Master's thesis (Howard University, 1938.)

[15] Frederick Douglass, *My Bondage and My Freedom*, p. 123.

[16] *Ibid.*, p. 95.

[17] Herbert Aptheker, *Negro Slave Revolts in the United States, 1526–1860.*

[18] Pp. 306, 308, 349, etc.

[19] *Ibid.*, p. 813.

[20] Robinson, *op. cit., passim.*

[21] *The Underground Railroad from Slavery to Freedom*, 1898.

[22] *The Underground Railroad*, 1872.

[23] See the present writer's review of Richard Wright's *Uncle Tom's Children* in *Journal of Negro Education*, VIII (Jan. 1939): 71–73.

sis on the negative side. Most important of all, the Negro spiritual is a positive thing, a folk group's answer to life.

Many students of the spiritual are misled by the religious and folk elements into believing that the social contribution is nil. We have already quoted Weatherford to the effect that the African Negro mixed his social life and his religion so thoroughly that neither can be said to dominate perpetually. That is true of the American Negro, and of nearly all peoples. The English and Scottish popular ballads are solid folk stuff: hardly a one is without mystical tone, or reference to some religious practice in everyday life, and several are exclusively Christian stories, e.g., "St. Stephen and Herod," "Judas," "Dives and Lazarus." Their social implications are multitudinous.[24] American folk stuff is no different.[25] Casey Jones serenely mentions his "trip to the holy land,"[26] and many American ballads, non-Negro, begin like "Charles Guiteau": "Come all you tender Christians."[27] In her introduction, Miss Pound refers generously to the social revelations in these all-American songs, and dedicates her collection to, among others, "those who care for traditional pieces as social documents which reflect the life and tradition of those who preserve them."[28] Religion enhances the power and desire of the folk to reveal their deepest social selves. This is true no more of Negroes than of anybody else.

WHAT IS WRONG WITH EXTANT INTERPRETATIONS

This brings us to what is wrong with the extant interpretations of the spiritual, excluding Sterling Brown's. The answer is: two forms of sentimentalism, one from the gone-with-the-wind South, the other from the we-fought-for-freedom North. The first is rather obvious in Natalie Taylor Carlisle:[29]

As many Southerners have observed, the old time darky's trusting religious faith, his loyalty to his daily tasks, his love for "ole marse" and "ole mist'ess," and his richly flavored sayings make a very attractive memory.

It is less obvious, but no less present, in Howard Odum and Guy Johnson.[30] The second is plain in Higginson,[31] Allen and his associates,[32] and Krehbiel,[33] who wrote: "Slavery was the sorrow of the Southern blacks; religion was their comfort and refuge." It is less plain in James Weldon Johnson, DuBois, Locke, and Maud Cuney Hare,[34] who wrote: "These were hymns

---

[24] Francis J. Child, *English and Scottish Popular Ballads* (1898 ed.)
[25] Louise Pound, *American Ballads and Songs* (1922 ed.)
[26] *Ibid.*, p. 133.
[27] *Ibid.*, p. 146.
[28] *Ibid.*, p, vii.
[29] *Texas and Southwestern Folklore* No. 5 (1926) p. 137.
[30] *The Negro and His Songs:* chapters on "Presenting the Singer and His Song," "The Religious Songs of the Negro," and "Examples of Religious Songs."
[31] "Negro Spirituals" in *Atlantic Monthly*, XIX (June 1867): 685–94.
[32] *Slave Songs of the United States.*
[33] *Op cit.*, p. 29.
[34] *Negro Musicians and Their Music*, p. 54.

that glowed with religious fervor and constant belief in ultimate victory through the gateway of death." In these last, it is impassioned and beautiful, but sentimentalism still, and therefore thin as literary interpretation.

ESCAPE AND RELIGION

These interpretations harp on two connected theories: that the spiritual was exclusively a method of escape from a troublesome world to a land of dreams, before or after death; and that its chief motivation is pure religion. In opposition to the escape theory, let me submit the realistic interpretations of the whole system that are found in the slave narratives. These slaves knew that their masters suffered as much as they, economically and mentally, and said so. They did not perennially commiserate their lot, and they rarely wished themselves anyone else. They were not the kind of people to think unconcretely; and the idea that they put all their eggs into the basket of a heaven after death, as the result of abstract thinking, is absurd to any reader of firsthand materials in the social history of the slave. This is not to say that they were not intrigued by the possibilities of various escapes. They were interested in religion, underground railroads, swamps, abolition, colonization—anything that might provide a way out of the dark. But there was no exclusive surrender in songs and dreams.

George P. Jackson[35] has shown that some spirituals are perhaps derived from white camp-meetings. Let us accept that. The white camp-meeting was a frontier institution. The frontiersman's religion was one of his weapons. He enjoyed it ecstatically. But he did not separate it from the rest of his world. Mr. Jackson demonstrates that in the camp-meeting hymn the companionships of the rough journey to camp became the common pilgrimage to Canaan; the meetings and partings on the ground became the reunion of believers in Heaven; and the military suggestions of encampment suggested the militant host of the Lord. The sweetnesses of life were the delights of Heaven; the pains of life, the pains of hell.[36] The camp-meeting hymn parallels the spiritual in every respect, except that it is inferior poetry. The whites left the camp-meeting and went out to conquer the wilderness. The Negroes left spiritual singing and plotted to upset the system of slavery. In each case, the song was just a stimulation for the march.

Concerning the theory of pure religion, there is practically no evidence that the slave swallowed the American philosophies of religion, and much to the contrary. Professor Brown finds satirical parodies growing up side by side with the spirituals, like this:[37]

I don't want to ride in no golden
    chariot,
I don't want to wear no golden crown,
I want to stay down here and be
Just as I am without one plea.

Nat Turner was a preacher and knew his Bible well; but his religion was not pure in the best sense, for it led him to bloody massacres, coldly planned.

---

[35] *White Spirituals in the Southern Uplands.*
[36] *Ibid.*, p. 216.
[37] Brown, *op. cit.*, p. 21.

Douglass thinks Master Thomas's religion cheap and worthless when it did not improve his attitude toward his slaves,[38] and his thinking was representative on this subject. How could the slave accept seriously a religion which he saw making brutes of those who were handing it to him?

Most slaves, as most people, were mildly religious; a few, as always a few, were fanatical; but in the spiritual, religion is chiefly an arsenal of pointed darts, a storehouse of images, a means of making shrewd observations. Everybody talks about the keenness of imagery in the African, whether at home or in America.[39] Higginson shows[40] that an African word, Myo—from *mawa*, to die—is often substituted for Jordan. Natalie Carlisle, Harrison, Bales[41] present sharply-chiseled songs about woodchoppers, "long-tongue liars," and death scenes with doctor, mother, father, sister, actively participating. The slave had a genius for phrase-making and dramatic situations; the Biblical lore was a gold mine for him; he needed it to make a social point; that just about tells the story.

This is not to distort or belittle the slave's religion. That religion struck far more deeply than the gorgeous display of externals with little effect upon everyday living, which the American white man had set up. The present-day African is cynical of American religion and its missionaries in the same sense. The slave's religion is in his spiritual, yes, but not in the externals. It is in the principles he lives by, hid deep beneath the soil, and meaning something. It is a hard, thickly-rooted plant, not a flower of the empyrean. The things called religious in his spiritual are his artistic fancy at work. Witness his "Singin' wid a Sword in Ma Han'," for its marvellous flights and subtle double-meanings, or his introduction of modern arrangements, like a train, instead of boats and chariots. Remember that America got her first railroad only in 1828. Witness also his revision of camp meeting hymns:[42]

CAMP MEETING
(same as old Methodist Hymn)
And then away to Jesus
On wings of love I'll fly

NEGRO SPIRITUAL
Dey'll take wings and fly away,
For to hear de trumpet soun'
In dat mornin'

THE TRUE SOCIAL INTERPRETATION

Approaching the heart of the spiritual, we must recognize three fixed stars. First, there is the Negro's obsession for freedom, abundantly proved by every firsthand document connected with the slave himself. Douglass says of the spirituals:[43]

... they were tones, loud, long and deep, breathing the prayer and complaint of souls boiling over with the bitterest anguish. Every tone was a testimony against slavery,

[38] *Op. cit.*, pp. 193–200.
[39] Notable examples can be found in Krehbiel, *op. cit.*, p. 45; Hare, *op. cit.*, p. 64; *Book of American Negro Spirituals*, pp. 15–16; 23–24; etc.
[40] *Life in a Black Regiment*, pp. 274–75.
[41] *Texas and Southwestern Lore*, No. 5 (1926), pp. 88, 140, 143, 150–51.
[42] Jackson, *op. cit.*, p. 302.
[43] *Op. cit.*, p. 99.

and a prayer to God for deliverance from chains.

Second was the slave's desire for justice in the judgment upon his betrayers which some might call revenge. And third was his tactic of battle, the strategy by which he expected to gain an eminent future. These three are the *leit motif* of nearly every spiritual.

Higginson says the slaves were jailed in Georgetown, S.C. in 1862 for singing "We'll Soon Be Free." This song opens "We'll soon be free/When de Lord will call us home" and continues with such phrases as: "My brudder, how long fore we done suffering here" ... "It won't be long/Fore de Lord will call us home" ... "We'll walk de miry road/Where pleasure never dies" ... "We'll walk de golden street/Where pleasure never dies" ... "We'll soon be free/When Jesus sets me free" ... "We'll fight for liberty/When de Lord will call us home." Higginson was told by a little drummer-boy: "Dey tink *de Lord* mean for say *de Yankees*."[44] Aptheker,[45] on this same point, reports that the slaves were certain as far back as 1856 that the Republican party would free them. They smiled when whipped and said that Fremont and his men heard the blows they received.

Beginning with a song and a background like this, and others in the same category—such as "Many Thousands Go," a farewell to "peck o' corn," "pint o' salt," "hundred lash," "mistress' call"; and the spirituals on "the ole nigger-driver" or "the pater-roler get you"—it is easy, by the code found here, to work out into the open field of spirituals. Of course, the chariot in "Swing Low" is some arm of freedom reaching out to draw him in; and the number of times it succeeded shows that it was no hopeless hope. Of course "My Lord delibered Daniel ... why can't he deliber me" means just what it says. And the falling rocks and mountains hit the slave's enemies. You would never get the communities all over the South which tasted slave revolts, especially in 1831, 1856, and 1860,[46] to believe that these rocks and mountains were ethereal or that they couldn't fall at any time. You would never get post-Sherman Georgia to believe that there was no fire in hell for sinners. The slave song was an awesome prophecy, rooted in the knowledge of what was going on and of human nature, and not in mystical lore. Its deadly edge threatened; and struck.

THE SPIRITUAL'S FINEST TOUCH

These, however, are not the finest touches of the spiritual. The really significant poetry is found in the plans for the future. Take a simple spiritual like "I Got Shoes." "When I get to heav'm" means when I get free. It is a Walt Whitman "I," meaning any slave, present or future. If I personally don't, my children or grandchildren, or my friend on the other end of the plantation will. What a glorious sigh these people breathed when one of their group slipped through to freedom! What a tragic intensity they felt when

[44] *Atlantic Monthly*, XIX (June 1867): p. 602.
[45] *Op. cit.*, p. 58.
[46] Aptheker, *op. cit.*, p. 72.

one was shot down trying to escape!

So, the group-mind speaks in the group way, all for one, one for all. "When I get to heav'm, gonna put on my shoes" . . . that means he has talents, abilities, programs manufactured, ready to wear. On Douglass's plantation, the slaves bossed, directed, charted everything—horse-shoeing, cart-mending, plow-repairing, coopering, grinding, weaving, "all completely done by slaves."[47] But he has much finer shoes than that which he has no chance to wear. He does not mean he will outgrow work, but simply that he will make his work count for something, which slavery prevents. When he gets a chance, he says, he is going to "shout all ober God's heav'm"—make every section of his community feel his power. He knows he can do it.

Here this slave was, tearing down a wreck and building a new, solid world, and all along we thought he was romanticizing. We gave him credit for dainty little fantasies of song. He was writing some of the stoutest poetry ever created. His subjects are social living, democracy, revolution, morals, Nature, Death, Love, the subjects of all great poets.[48] Which do you prefer, gentle reader: the sentimental spiritual, or the thumping, two-fisted, uproarious, not-to-be-denied: "O no man can hinder me! O no man, no man, no man can hinder me!"

And so, we cannot accept the pretty little platitudes to be found in such excellently written books as Odum and Johnson's *The Negro and His Songs.* Satan is not a traditional Negro goblin; he is the people who beat and cheat the slave. King Jesus is not just the abstract Christ; he is whoever helps the oppressed and disfranchised, or gives him a right to his life. Babylon and Winter are slavery as it stands—note "Oh de winter, de winter, de winter'll soon be ober, children"; Hell is often being sold South, for which the sensitive Negro had the greatest horror. Jordan is the push to freedom. The "great 'sociation," the "welcome table," the "big baptizin'," the "union," "viewin' the land" were concrete things which fit into the scheme at one time or another.

A few spirituals were swinging, narrative verse. "Dust and Ashes" is a very imaginative story of the crucifixion, and "In dat Great Gittin'-up Mornin'" reveals a fine fancy at work on a few facts taken from Revelations. Either of these, in some versions, may run beyond a hundred stanzas. Good narrative verse is a composite of wit and awareness of striking experiences. That composite is much in evidence here.

SUMMARY: THE SPIRITUAL IS ESSENTIALLY SOCIAL

Let us try to sum up. The Negro slave was the largest homogeneous group in a melting-pot America. He analyzed and synthesized his life in his songs and sayings.[49] In hundreds of songs called spirituals, he produced an epic cycle;

---

[47] *Op. cit.*, p. 69.

[48] The present writer has projected four articles to follow this one, as follows: "Democracy in the Spiritual," "The Fighting Spiritual," "The Slave Looks at Progress," and "The Heav'm of the Negro Spiritual." [See John Lovell, *Black Song: The Forge and the Flame* (New York, 1972). —ED.]

[49] See Thomas W. Talley, *Negro Folk Rhymes: Wise and Otherwise,* 1922.

and, as in every such instance, he concealed there his deepest thoughts and ideas, his hard-finished plans and hopes and dreams. The exploration of these songs for their social truths presents a tremendous problem. It must be done, for, as in the kernel of the *Iliad* lies the genius of the Greeks, so in the kernel of the spiritual lies the genius of the American Negro. When it is done— when the Negro and his white helper have learned about the large soul of the Negro here imprisoned, respect for the Negro will rise, and his gifts will not be held in contempt. Men will know that he was fully civilized, though a slave. Men will appreciate the glowing words of Douglass:[50]

For much of the happiness—or absence of misery—with which I passed this year with Mr. Freeland, I am indebted to the genial temper and ardent friendship of my brother slaves. They were, every one of them, manly, generous and brave, yes; I say they were brave, and I will add, fine looking. It is seldom the lot of mortals to have truer and better friends than were the slaves on this farm. It is not uncommon to charge slaves with great treachery toward each other, and to believe them incapable of confiding in each other; but I must say, that I never loved, esteemed, or confided in men, more than I did in these. They were as true as steel, and no band of brothers could have been more loving.

Douglass tells how they resisted oppression and tyranny, how they worked together and never moved without mutual consultation. He provides another basis for our contention that the spiritual was a language well understood in all its burning import by the slave initiate, but harmless and graceful to an unthinking outsider.

Douglass captured the all-round greatness of the slave, reflected in the spiritual. Antonin Dvořák, Roland Hayes, Marian Anderson, Paul Robeson have captured it in their handling of spirituals. When some more of us do, American Negroes and Americans generally will want to seek democracy by moving out on the track laid by these slaves, who sang:

> You got a right,
> I got a right,
> We all got a right to the tree of life.

REFERENCES

I. BASIC COLLECTIONS AND STUDIES OF NEGRO SPIRITUALS

ALLEN, WILLIAM FRANCIS, WARE, CHARLES PICKARD, and GARRISON, LUCY MCKIM, *Slave Songs of the United States*. New York: Peter Smith, 1929 (c. 1867).

BARTON, WILLIAM E., *Old Plantation Hymns*, n.d.

BROWN, STERLING, *The Negro Poetry and Drama*. Washington: Associates in Negro Folk Education, 1937. Bronze Booklet No. 7.

DANN, HOLLIS ELLSWORTH, *Fifty-Eight Spirituals for Choral Use*. Boston: C. C. Birchard and Co., n.d.

DUBOIS, W. E. BURGHARDT, "The Sorrow Songs" in *Souls of Black Folk*, pp. 250–64. Chicago: A. C. McClurg and Co., 1903.

FENNER, THOMAS P., *Fifty Cabin and Plantation Songs* in *Hampton and Its Students*, ed. by Armstrong, M. F. and Ludlow, Helen W. New York: G. P. Putnam's Sons, 1874.

[50] *Op. cit.*, pp. 268–69.

HARRIS, JOEL CHANDLER, *Uncle Remus, His Songs and His Sayings*. New York: D. Appleton Co., 1892.

HIGGINSON, THOMAS WENTWORTH, "Negro Spirituals" in *Atlantic Monthly*, XIX (June 1867), 685–94.

KREHBIEL, HENRY EDWARD, *Afro-American Folksongs*. New York: G. Schirmer, n.d. (c. 1914).

JOHNSON, JAMES WELDON and JOHNSON, J. ROSAMUND, *The Book of American Negro Spirituals*. New York: Viking Press, 1937 (c. 1925).

————, *The Second Book of Negro Spirituals*. New York: Viking Press, 1926.

LOCKE, ALAIN LEROY, *The Negro and His Music*. Washington: Associates in Negro Folk Education, 1936.

ODUM, HOWARD W. and JOHNSON, GUY B., *The Negro and His Songs*. Chapel Hill: University of North Carolina Press, 1925.

SCARBOROUGH, DOROTHY, *On the Trail of Negro Folk-Songs*. Cambridge: Harvard University Press, 1925.

WHITE, CLARENCE CAMERON, *Forty Negro Spirituals*. Philadelphia: Theodore Presser, 1927

II.   PICTURES AND EXPLANATIONS OF SPIRITUAL BACKGROUNDS

APTHEKER, HERBERT, *Negro Slave Revolts in the United States, 1526–1860*. New York: International Publishers, n.d. (c. 1939). Reprinted from *Science and Society*, I (1937): 512–538; II (1938): 386–92.

DOUGLASS, FREDERICK, *My Bondage and My Freedom*. New York and Auburn: Miller, Orton and Mulligan, 1855.

HARE, MAUD CUNEY, *Negro Musicians and Their Music*. Washington: Associated Publishers, n.d. (c. 1936).

HIGGINSON, THOMAS WENTWORTH, *Army Life in a Black Regiment*. Boston: Houghton Mifflin and Co., 1900 (c. 1870).

JACKSON, GEORGE PULLEN, *White Spirituals in the Southern Uplands*. Chapel Hill: University of North Carolina Press, 1933.

MACON, J. A., *Uncle Gabe Tucker; or, Reflection, Song, and Sentiment in the Quarters*. Philadelphia: J. B. Lippincott, 1883.

METFESSEL, MILTON, *Phonophotography in Folk Music*. Chapel Hill: University of North Carolina Press, 1928.

MITCHELL, MARGARET, *Gone With the Wind*. New York: Macmillan Co., 1936.

Nation, IV: No. 100, Thursday, May 30, 1867: "Literary Notes."

ROBINSON, AVIS P., *Social Conditions of Slavery as Taken from Slave Narratives*. (Unpublished Master's Thesis, Howard University, 1938.)

SIEBERT, WILLIAM H., *The Underground Railroad from Slavery to Freedom*. New York: Macmillan Co., 1898.

STILL, WILLIAM, *The Underground Railroad*. Philadelphia: Porter and Coates, 1872.

TALLEY, THOMAS W., *Negro Folk Rhymes: Wise and Otherwise*. New York: Macmillan, 1922.

Texas Folk-Lore Society Publications, Nos. 1 to 7 (7 v.), 1916–1928.

WEATHERFORD, W. D., *The Negro from Africa to America*. New York: George H. Doran, n.d. (c. 1924).

WEEDEN, HOWARD, *Songs of the Old South*. (Verses and Drawings.) New York: Doubleday, Page and Co., 1900.

WOODSON, CARTER G., *The Negro in Our History*. Washington: Associated Publishers, n.d. (c. 1931).

III.   GENERAL BACKGROUND BOOKS AND ARTICLES

AUSTIN, MARY, *The American Rhythm*. Boston: Houghton, Mifflin and Co., 1930.

BARNES, NELLIE, *American Indian Verse*. Lawrence: University of Kansas Humanistic Studies, vol. II, No. 4, 1921.

CHILD, FRANCIS JAMES, *English and Scottish Popular Ballads*. 5 v. Boston: Houghton Mifflin and Co., n.d. (c. 1898).

HOFFMEISTER, KAREL, *Antonin Dvorak*, translated by Rosa Newmarch. London: John Lane, n.d. (c. 1928).

KENNEDY, R. EMMETT, *Black Cameos*. New York: Albert and Charles Boni, 1924.

LINTON, W. J., *Poetry of America*. London: George Bell and Sons, 1878.

LOVELL, JOHN, JR., "Negro-True" (review of Richard Wright, *Uncle Tom's Children*) in *Journal of Negro Education*, VIII (Jan. 1939): 71–73.

POUND, LOUISE, *American Ballads and Songs*. New York: Charles Scribner's Sons, n.d. (c. 1922).

Follow the Drinking Gourd

H. B. PARKS

In trying to unravel the mystery of the meaning of folksong or for that matter of any type of folklore, the final authority must be the folk. Analytic academics from their vantage point high up in the ivory tower may bring any number of theories to bear upon a given folksong, but most exegeses lack conviction if they are unaccompanied by significant informant interpretation and opinion. The collection of the "folk's" criticism of their own folklore is a sadly neglected art inasmuch as most professional folklorists-collectors are text-oriented to a nearly fanatical degree. Success in fieldwork is foolishly measured in terms of quantity instead of quality. So it is that folklorists brag of eliciting a hundred songs from this informant or a hundred tales from that one. In many respects, it would be far better for the study of folklore to have just one text explained in depth by one or more informants than to have one hundred texts presented without any explanation.

The following brief essay is an attempt to understand the meaning of one folksong. Although the author presents his findings in the form of anecdotal reminiscences, he does seem to have discovered the possible meaning of one song. The reader may test the necessity of having explanations of folksongs by asking himself or friends for the meaning of the phrase "follow the drinking gourd" prior to reading this study.

For a plea for the collection of folk criticism, that is, that there be field collections of "oral literary criticism" in addition to "oral literature," see Alan Dundes, "Metafolklore and Oral Literary Criticism," The Monist, 50 (1966), pp. 505–16.

Reprinted from *Publications of the Texas Folklore Society*, vol. 7 (1928), pp. 81–84, by permission of the Texas Folklore Society.

THE FOLLOWING story is a compilation of three incidents and an attempt to explain them. A number of years ago while a resident of Alaska I became much interested in folklore and consequently anything of this nature came to attract my attention quickly. I was a resident of Hot Springs, North Carolina, during the year of 1912 and had charge of the agricultural work of a large industrial school. This school owned a considerable herd of cattle, which were kept in the meadows on the tops on the Big Rich Mountains on the boundary between North Carolina and Tennessee. One day while riding through the mountains looking after this stock, I heard the following stanza sung by a little Negro boy, who was picking up dry sticks of wood near a Negro cabin:

> Foller the drinkin' gou'd,
> Foller the drinkin' gou'd;
> No one know, the wise man say,
> "Foller the drinkin' gou'd."

It is very doubtful if this part of the song would have attracted anyone's attention had not the old grandfather, who had been sitting on a block of wood in front of the cabin, slowly got up and, taking his cane, given the boy a sound lick across the back with the admonition not to sing that song again. This excited my curiosity and I asked the old man why he did not want the boy to sing the song. The only answer I could get was that it was bad luck.

About a year later I was in the city of Louisville and, having considerable time to wait for a train, I went walking about the city. My journey brought me to the riverfront, and while standing there watching the wharf activities I was very much surprised to hear a Negro fisherman, who was seated on the edge of the wharf, singing the same stanza on the same tune. The fisherman sang the same stanza over and over again without any variation. While I am unable to write the music that goes with this stanza, I can say that it is a jerky chant with the accented syllables very much prolonged.[1] When I asked the fisherman what he knew about the song, he replied that he knew nothing about it; he would not even converse with me. This seemed to be very peculiar, but because of the story of bad luck told by the grandfather in North Carolina I did not question the Negro further.

In 1918, I was standing on the platform of the depot at Waller, Texas, waiting for a train, when, much to my surprise, I heard the familiar tune being picked on a violin and banjo and two voices singing the following words:

> Foller the Risen Lawd,
> Foller the Risen Lawd;
> The bes' thing the Wise Man say,
> "Foller the Risen Lawd."

The singers proved to be two Negro boys about sixteen years of age. When they were asked as to where they learned the song, they gave the following explanation. They said that they were musicians traveling with a colored revivalist and that he had composed this song and that they played it and used it in their revival meetings. They also said the revivalist wrote new stanzas to fit the meetings.

These three incidents led me to

---

[1] In a fortunate hour I have met Mr. Carl A. Fehr, of Austin, and he has kindly transcribed the music from the best singing I could produce.

inquire into the subject, and I was very fortunate in meeting an old Negro at College Station, Texas, who had known a great many slaves in his boyhood days. After I had gained his confidence, this man told the following story and gave the following verses of the song.

He said that just before the Civil War, somewhere in the South, he was not just sure where, there came a sailor who had lost one leg and had the missing member replaced by a peg-leg. He would appear very suddenly at some plantation and ask for work as a painter or carpenter. This he was able to get at almost every place. He made friends with the slaves and soon all of the young colored men were singing the song that is herein mentioned. The peg-leg sailor would stay for a week or two at a place and then disappear. The following spring nearly all the young men among the slaves disappeared and made their way to the north and finally to Canada by following a trail that had been made by the peg-leg sailor and was held in memory by the Negroes in this peculiar song.

1 When the sun come back,
    When the firs' quail call,
    Then the time is come
    Foller the drinkin' gou'd.

Chorus: Foller the drinkin' gou'd,
    Foller the drinkin' gou'd;
    For the ole man say,
    "Foller the drinkin' gou'd."

2 The riva's bank am a very good road,
    The dead trees show the way,
    Lef' foot, peg foot goin' on,
    Foller the drinkin' gou'd.

Chorus:

3 The riva ends a-tween two hills,
    Foller the drinkin' gou'd;
    'Nuther riva on the other side
    Follers the drinkin' gou'd.

Chorus:

4 Wha the little riva
    Meet the grea' big un,

The ole man waits—
Foller the drinkin' gou'd.

Now my birthplace is in the North and I also belong to a family that took considerable part in the underground railroad movement; so I wrote about this story to the older members of the family in the North. One of my great-uncles, who was connected with the railroad movement, remembered that in the records of the Anti-Slavery Society there was a story of a peg-legged sailor, known as Peg-Leg Joe, who made a number of trips through the South and induced young Negroes to run away and escape through the North to Canada. The main scene of his activities was in the country immediately north of Mobile, and the trail described in the song followed northward to the head waters of the Tombigbee River, thence over the divide and down the Tennessee River to the Ohio. It seems that the peg-legged sailor would go through the country north of Mobile and teach this song to the young slaves and show them a mark of his natural left foot and the round spot made by the peg-leg. He would then go ahead of them northward and on every dead tree or other conspicuous object he would leave a print made with charcoal or mud of the outline of a human left foot and a round spot in place of the right foot. As nearly as could be found out the last trip was made in 1859. Nothing more could be found relative to this man.

The Negro at College Station said that the song had many verses which he could not remember. He quoted a number which, either by fault of memory or secret meaning, are unintelligible and are omitted. The ones given are in the phonetic form used by the College Station Negro and become rather simple when one is told that the "drinkin' gou'd" is the Great Dipper, that the "wise man" was the peg-leg sailor, and that the admonition is to go ever north, following the trail of the left foot and the peg-leg until "the grea' big un" (the Ohio) is reached, where the runaways would be met by the old sailor.*

The revivalist realized the power of this sing-song and made it serve his purpose by changing a few words, and in so doing pointed his followers to a far different liberty than the one the peg-leg sailor advocated.

---

* Regardless of the historicity of the "peg-leg" conductor of the underground railroad, there can be no doubt that the North Star was a most important guide for runaway slaves. There are frequent allusions to the North Star in slave narratives and often in endearing terms, e.g., "truly the slave's friend." See Gilbert Osofsky, ed., *Puttin' On Ole Massa: The Slave Narratives of Henry Bibb, William Wells Brown, and Solomon Northup* (New York, 1969), pp. 16, 131, 146, 205, 217. It was no doubt for such sentimental reasons that Frederick Douglass elected to call his abolitionist newspaper *The North Star*. Although the constellation Ursa Major bears the folk name of Big Dipper, in slavery times gourds were used rather than dippers. For example, one ex-slave account relates the following detail: "Sis and me went to the spring to get some water, and she had done dipped her water up and started to go, and I said, 'Hand me a drink,' and she handed me the dipper—I mean gourd, we didn't have no dippers then. . . ." See *Unwritten History of Slavery: Autobiographical Account of Negro Ex-Slaves*, Fisk University Social Science Source Documents No. 1 (Nashville, 1945), p. 113. See also Osofsky, *op. cit.*, p. 316. Of course, the North Star is not located in the Great or Big Dipper. Rather it lies in Ursa Minor, not Ursa Major, that is, it is the outermost star in the handle of the Little Dipper. Nevertheless, in the United States, the folk technique of finding Polaris, the North Star, involves the use of the Big Dipper. Drawing an imaginary line through the two end stars (called the Pointers) of the Big Dipper bowl, one extends that line approximately five times the distance between the "Pointers" to locate the North Star. So, follow the drinking gourd = follow the big dipper = follow the North Star = go north to freedom! —ED.

I Got the Blues

ALAN LOMAX

*It is difficult enough to seek an informant's "oral literary criticism" for
just one song, but the task of eliciting informant attitudes toward a whole genre
seems well nigh impossible. Yet famed folksong collector Alan Lomax made a
noteworthy stab at obtaining a picture of the blues as seen—or rather as felt—
by blues singers. Despite, or perhaps because of, an initial problem which resulted
simply from a white man trying to interview Negroes in Memphis in the 1940's,
Lomax was able to encourage an extraordinary rap session which he must
have recorded on tape. The report by Lomax seems to be an honest one inasmuch
as it includes his own mistakes. There is repeated evidence, for example, of the
blues singers putting Lomax on whether it is the* colored-people-are-always-
happy *"front" or the informants' refusal to tell Lomax that "Mister Charley"
was a generic name for the white man and not a particular white man. What
resulted was one of the best descriptions of what the blues are all about—and
there have been a great many descriptions.*

*The literature devoted to the blues is immense. A representative sampling
of some of the more valuable sources include Sterling Brown, "The Blues,"
Phylon, 13 (1952), pp. 286–92; E. Simms Campbell, "Blues are the Negroes'
Lament," Esquire, 12 (December, 1939), pp. 100, 276–80; Gene Bluestein, "The
Blues as a Literary Theme,"* The Massachusetts Review, *8 (1967), pp. 593–617;
Stephen E. Henderson, "Blues for the Young Blackman,"* Negro Digest, *16, no.
10 (August, 1967), pp. 10–17; Harry Oster, "The Blues as a Genre,"* Genre, *2
(1969), pp. 259–74. See also Leroi Jones,* Blues People *(New York, 1963);
Charles Keil,* Urban Blues *(Chicago, 1966); Paul Oliver,* The Meaning of
the Blues *(New York, 1963)—originally published with the title* Blues Fell
This Morning; *Harry Oster,* Living Country Blues *(Detroit, 1969); and*

Reprinted from *Common Ground*, vol. 8 (Summer, 1948), pp. 38–52, by permission of the
author and the American Council for Nationalities Service.

Samuel Charters, The Poetry of the Blues (*New York, 1970*). *Several of the latter works demonstrate that although the blues may have originally been primarily a rural phenomenon, they have become increasingly urbanized.*

It is not clear just when the blues began. Lafcadio Hearn, in writing about an old Negro local character named Henry in the Cincinnati Enquirer *for February 21, 1875, mentioned the latter's attitude toward his illness of old age. "With the expected 'blues' of sickness he thinks his friends are deserting him." This seems to be "blues" in the sense of sorrow or depression. See Lafcadio Hearn*, Children of the Levee (*Lexington, Kentucky, 1957*), *p. 60. See also the accounts of W. C. Handy, e.g., Dorothy Scarborough, "The 'Blues' as Folk-Songs,"* Publications of the Texas Folklore Society, *2 (1917), pp. 52–66, and William C. Handy,* Father of the Blues: An Autobiography of W. C. Handy, *ed. Arna Bontemps (*New York, 1955*).*

In considering the blues, regardless of their age, one must keep in mind that they are a secular form, poles apart in content from spirituals. Accordingly, they are likely to be disowned by some middle-class Negroes well before spirituals are disowned. For some indication of this sentiment, see two essays which appeared originally in Ebony *in 1957: Berta Wood, "Are Negroes Ashamed of the Blues?" and Leonard Feather, "Not Ashamed of the Blues," in Era Bell Thompson and Herbert Nipson, eds.,* White on Black (*Chicago, 1963*), *pp. 99–112. (Cf. "The Boston Songs,"* The Crisis, *9 (1915), p. 128, for a similar debate.) See also Leroi Jones,* Blues People, *pp. 128–29; Leroi Jones,* Black Music (*New York, 1968*), *pp. 11–12.*

Whether or not an individual chooses to take pride in the blues, there is no question of the blues' close association with Negro culture. Sterling Brown quotes Negro musicians as saying "You can't play the blues until you have paid your dues" with the latter phrase meaning "lived as a Negro in America." The same view is echoed by Leroi Jones: "Blues *means a Negro experience, it is the one music the Negro made that could not be transferred into a more general significance than the one the Negro gave it initially."*

If being a Negro is a prerequisite to playing the blues, it may also be one for understanding all the nuances of the blues. Samuel Charters, after observing that some blues express universal truths (and are hence comprehensible to the general public), contends that "the blues which are most closely involved with the reality of being a Negro in the United States will always have emotional overtones which will be almost impossible to sense" [by the non-Negro]. This is analogous to saying that only Negroes can have soul (which is not the same as saying that all Negroes have soul, which would be just as incorrect as claiming that all Negroes can play/understand blues). This folk conception is curious in the light of the longstanding white stereotype of the "sense of natural rhythm" which Negroes were alleged to possess. What we may have is the stereotype turned around such that a "liability" has become an "asset"! Just as the "Black is Beautiful" philosophy is an attempt to overturn the traditional black (evil)-white (good) symbolic dichotomy, so the concept of soul and the idea that only Negroes can sing or appreciate blues fully attempts to overturn the white racist musical aptitude stereotype. Black is evil in white society, but good in Negro society; musical aptitude (e.g., natural rhythm) thought by whites to be a stereotypic trait worthy of ridicule is converted into a desirable sensibility in the black community, a sensibility that whites cannot share. By similar reasoning, the

*"bad nigger" in white society is good in much of the Negro community where-
as the "good nigger" in the white society is regarded as a "bad" Uncle Tom
character in Negro society. This paradigm of reversals is essential to an understanding of the position blues occupy in contemporary Negro culture. If white
folks regarded blues as evil music (in contrast to the spirituals), then to the
extent that Negroes wished to form their own aesthetic judgments independent
of white values, it is reasonable for them to find a positive sense of identity in the
blues.*

*For the Negro-blues equational statements quoted above, see Sterling
Brown, "The Blues,"* Phylon, *13 (1952), p. 291; Leroi Jones,* Blues People, *p.
94; Samuel Charters,* The Poetry of the Blues, *pp. 13–14. For other works by
Lomax, see John A. Lomax and Alan Lomax,* Negro Folk Songs as Sung by
Leadbelly *(New York, 1936); Alan Lomax,* Mister Jelly Roll *(New York, 1952).
Lomax is much more than a collector of folksong. For a sampling of his sophis-
tication in folksong theory and method, see Alan Lomax,* Folk Song Style and
Culture, *American Association for the Advancement of Science Publication
No. 88 (Washington, D. C., 1968).*

I got the blues,
But I'm too damn mean to cry . . .

THE LAST chord sounded on Leroy's
guitar, the last blues of the evening.

"Well," Natchez told me, "I reckon
now you got an idea about the blues
around Memphis."

"I reckon I have," I said.

"Yeah, that *police* in Memphis had
you singin' the blues," he chuckled.
About that time the hard-faced man
who ran the honkey-tonk blew out the
lamp. Old Natchez picked up the nearly
empty gin bottle, Leroy and Sib grabbed
the guitars, and the four of us walked
out into the two o'clock dark. It was
black out there. You could feel the Delta
night rubbing itself against your cheek.

We sat down on the front step and
smoked. The stars hung just above our
heads, like fireflies caught in the dark
tangle of the night. I felt good. Sib,
Leroy, and Natchez had been singing
for several hours, and every blues had
been like another drink of raw gin.
The brights and shadows of their blues
reflected the wonderful and hateful

land of the South that had produced
all of us. We were warmed with the
undeniable vitality and humanity that
the blues carry beneath their melancholy.

I wasn't sure exactly where I was and
I didn't much care. The man who owned
the little country tonk was named Hamp,
they told me. This was Hamp's place,
somewhere out in the Arkansas black-
land across the river from Memphis. It
was a one-room shanty store that
doubled as a country bar-room at night,
a place where the people who made the
cotton in this fat land came to dance
and gamble and commit a bit of friendly
mayhem. Tonight it had been a refuge
for the three blues musicians and myself
—"where nobody gonna bother us,"
they said. "No laws or nothin'."

We had needed a hole to hide in.
When we had come racing across the
river bridge from Memphis into this
dark plain, we had had the feeling that
we were pursued, that we would like
to keep on going right out of this
world. We were running away from the
Memphis police and their attitudes

about human relations. Not that we had committed a crime; we had just forgotten, temporarily, that we were in the South.

I had hit Beale Street* in Memphis about the first cool of the evening, and, as usual, had begun to poke around for folk-singers. A Negro bartender told me I wasn't allowed in any of the Beale Street joints because of a new segregation ordinance. So I paraded Beale Street until I heard the music I wanted coming from a barber shop. Natchez and Leroy were playing their boxes to Sib's harmonica-blowing. When they had collected their tips, we sat down together in a vacant lot to talk blues, but a dribble-chinned Memphis cop interrupted our libations and harshly ordered us to move on. "We don't want no Washington Yankee foolin' around niggertown," he said. "If you like this nigger music, take it back North with you. We don't like it down here in the South."

With the cop pacing behind us, our feet dragged in a chain-gang walk up Beale Street. We piled into my car and headed out of town, and, by what was said, I knew that the Memphis cop had made these blues singers my friends. They tried to make a joke of the whole incident, but in the pauses between laughs Leroy kept saying, "Man, just as soon as I can rake and scrape money together, I'm gonna leave this country and they ain't *never* gonna see me down here again."

At Hamp's place we solaced ourselves with gin and with hours of the blues. Child of this fertile Delta land,

voice of the voiceless black masses, the blues crept into the back windows of America maybe forty years ago and since then has colored the whole of American popular music. Hill-billy singers, hot jazz blowers, crooners like Crosby, cowboy yodelers—all these have learned from the native folk blues. Now the blues is a big, lonesome wind blowing around the world. Now the whole world can feel, uncoiling in its ear, this somber music of the Mississippi. And yet no one had ever thought to ask the makers of these songs—these ragged meistersingers— —why they sang.

Now we sat together in the Delta night, smoking and saying little. Here was Natchez, who had helped to birth the blues forty years ago in this same Delta country. Here was young Leroy, making the blues for his own time. Finally here was Sib, the buffoon of the blues, who, like all fools, expressed in apish gestures the sorrows of life.

I turned to Natchez. You couldn't tell how old he was by looking at him. You just knew that he was old and strong, like the big live-oaks in these bottoms. "Natchez," I said, "tell me why you sing the blues."

There was a pause in which the insects and little animals of the night joined together in the sound that is the earth breathing in its sleep. Then Natchez began in his grave and hesitant way.

"Some people say that the blues is—a cow wantin' to see her calf, but I don't say it like that. I say it's a man that's got a good woman that turns

---

* For considerations of the importance of Beale Street with respect to the development of the blues, see George Lee, *Beale Street, Where the Blues Began* (New York, 1934), and Maude Greene, "The Background of the Beale Street Blues," *Tennessee Folklore Society Bulletin*, 7 (1941), pp. 1–10. —ED.

him down. Like when you sing—

If you see my milk cow, tell her to
hurry home,
'Cause I ain't had no lovin' since she
been gone . . .

Things like that happen, you know.
You want to see your lovin' babe, you
want to see her bad, and she be gone.
That gives you the blues:

I woke up this mornin' just about an
hour before day,
Reached and grabbed the pillow where
my baby used to lay. . . ."

Natchez paused and looked at Sib,
the stutterer—Sib, the slightly addled
one. On Sib's dark brow a frown was
eternally in conflict with the clownish
grin that twitched the corners of his
mouth. No one could sing Sib's blues
because they were a complete expression of Sib—his stammering speech,
his wild and idiot humors, his untram-
melled fancy. Natchez, who treated
him like a child, would yet sit back and
play for an hour while Sib indulged in
rhymes and stanzas which no other
singer could ever invent. "So what do
you think about it, Sib?" said Natchez
softly. "You must have some reason why
you have the blues."

Sib began to speak in his plaintive
way, the words tumbling out of him in
a rush as if he were afraid someone
might interrupt him at any moment.
"I'll tell you, Natchez, it really worries
me to think I had a sweet little girl
named Annie Belle. You know, we used
to go to school together and grew along
up together. So I wanted to love her
and I axed her mother for her and she
turnt me down. That cause me to sing
the blues:

Good mornin', little school girl,
Good mornin', little school girl,
May I go home wid you?
May I go home wid you?
You can tell your mama and your
papa
That Sib's a little school boy, too. . . .

"Her parents thought I wasn't the
right boy for Annie Belle. They turnt me
down, and then I just got to thinkin'
and that started me to drinkin' and from
that I got the blues."

Truly, they have sung ten thousand
blues verses about lack of love. Open the
big book of the blues and you will find all
the bitterness, all the frustration, all the
anger, and all the heartbreak that accompany love when people live precariously
in the slums.

Sib went on spurting words, but
Natchez interrupted him by directing
the question to Leroy. "Now what do
you think about the blues situation,
old Leroy?"

"Tell you, Natchez, the blues have
hope me a lot. Yes, sir, the blues will
help a man. When I has trouble, when
I'm feelin' low down and disgusted and
can't be satisfied, you know how it is
sometimes—

I woke up this mornin' with the blues
all round my bed,
Went to eat my breakfast, had blues
all in my bread. . . .

Then singin' a blues like that is the
onliest thing to ease my situation."

But Natchez wasn't satisfied. "Yeah,
you feel better. The blues helps a man to
explain his feelin's, but why do he feel
blue in the first place?"

"Here's my thought on it," Sib
came busting in. "We er-uh colored
people have had so *much* trouble, but

we's a people that tries to be happy anyway, you ever notice that? Because we never had so much, we tries to make the best of life. We don't have nothin', but we try to be jolly anyway; we don't let nothin' worry us too much. You take them old-fashioned country suppers." (As Sib talked, you could see him smacking his lips over the barbecued ribs and the field-ripe watermelons he had eaten.) "I thought I was a rich man when I'd go there with a dollar in my pocket. I never was used to much anyway, you understand? Always had to work."

He paused, and the puzzled and angry frown triumphed over the happy-go-lucky grin that twitched at his lips. "One year we cleaned up a whole big bottom where the willows was thick. The mud was so heavy I many times stalled four mules to a wagon down there. We'd work and clean up a bottom in the winter so we could plant it next summer. And I think this. You work hard all the year and you expectin' your money once a year, and, when that year wind up, you don't get nothin'; then you get the idea that 'I ain't doin' no good no way an' what's the use of livin'?' You know? You'll have all them funny thoughts like that."

Natchez, softly, "Sho, sho."

"And that gives you the blues, the po' man's heart disease. I remember I used to sing the blues down in that old black bottom—

I could hear my name,
My black name, a-ringin'
All up an' down the line.
I could hear my name,
My black name, a-ringin'
All up an' down the line.
Now I don't believe I'm doin' nothin'
But gradually throwin' away my
  time. . . ."

Sib put his harmonica to his lips and began to play. It was hardly music. It was a compound of shrieks and squeals and moans, like a farm in a tornado, where the cries of terror from the animals and the human beings are mixed with the noise of splitting planks and cracking timbers, and all are swallowed up in the howl of the storm. The words and phrases burst out in spasms through the harmonica as if Sib had learned to sing through the metal reeds because he was unable to express his feelings adequately in his own throat. Presently Natchez and Leroy joined Sib, underscoring his harmonica with their two guitars, until the song had run out in him. In the silence that followed, they chuckled quietly together. "That's the blues, man. That's purely it."

"You see what I mean about the blues expressin' a man's feelin', Natchez?" said Leroy.

"Yeah," Natchez replied. "It looks like the blues gits started thataway—when a man is goin' down some country road, whistlin, and singin' to himself somethin' or another like—

Hey, I feel like hollerin' and I feel like
  cryin',
Hey, I feel like hollerin' and I feel like
  cryin'.
I'm here today, Lawd, but tomorrow
  I'll be gone,
I'm here today, Lawd, but tomorrow
  I'll be gone.

He don't play no instrument or nothin'. He just hollers about what's worryin' him."

"They the *jump-up* blues," added Leroy. "They just *jump* up in your mind when you be down in trouble. Like those little numbers like they have over in *Tenn*essee." And Leroy began to sing in his rich baritone—

"Well, have you ever been to
     Nashville,
Well, have you ever been to Nashville,
Have you ever been to Nashville,
O Lawdy, to the Nashville pen?
Boys, if you don't stop stealin',
Boys, if you don't stop stealin',
Boys, if you don't stop stealin',
O buddy, you'll go back again . . . .

That's what I mean about the heart part. You singin' the way you feel from the heart."

"That's *right*, man," from Sib.

"Nobody could play behind them jumped-up blues," said Natchez, "because they ain't got no music to 'em. They ain't never been wrote down and won't never be, and I reckon all blues originated from just such stuff as that."

Out of the lonesome field hollers, out of the chain-gang chants, out of the full-throated choruses of the road builders, the clearers of swamps, the lifters and the toters—out of the biting irony, the power and savage strength and anger of worksongs—sprang the blues. Here was music with its tap root in African singing—Africa, the continent of communal work, the pre-eminent continent of the worksong. The worksong flowered under slavery and put forth its thorns after reconstruction. Forty-odd years ago singers like Natchez began to set these old cadences "to music," making their banjos, their guitars, and their pianos sound the work-gang chorus. Thus the old worksongs, given a regular harmonic form, became dance music in the unstable and uncertain world of the southern Negro worker. Here, from the experience of Leroy and Natchez, had come confirmation for my own notions about the origin of the blues.

"You sing about things you want to do or things you want to know or—"

Leroy continued—"things that really have happened to you."

"And," Natchez added, "some people that haven't had no hardship, they don't know how it is with the poor man that has had hardships and still has them."

"Yeah, classics and stuff like that," said Leroy, lumping musicians who played written music with all the secure and wealthy and privileged people in the world. "People like that don't know what the blues *is*."

"Naw, they couldn't play the blues if they wanted to," Sib said with great scorn.

"What I mean," explained Leroy, "it takes a man who *had* the blues to really *play* the blues. Yeah, you got to be *blue* to sing the blues, and that's the truth:

I was down in the bottom with the
     mud up to my knees,
I was workin' for my baby, she was so
     hard to please.

I worked all the summer, Lord, and all
     the fall,
Went home to take my Christmas,
     good pardner, in my overalls. . . ."

Natchez scrooched up on the step and spat far into the night. He could spit like a muleskinner. His voice rang now with authority.

"Let's come to a showdown now. Just where did the blues originate from? I'm thinkin' they didn't start in the North—in Chicago or New York or Pennsylvania."

"Naw, man, they started in the South," from Sib.

"From slavery, I'm thinkin'," Leroy muttered, half to himself.

"All right, then what we really want to know is why and how come a man in the South *have* the blues. Now I've worked on levee camps, in road camps, and in extra gangs on the railroad and everywhere. I've heard guys singin'—'Mm-mp' this and 'Mm-mp' that—and they was really expressin' their feelings from their heart the only way they knowed how.

"I've knowed guys that wanted to cuss out the boss and was afraid to go up to his face and tell him what they wanted to tell him. And I've heered a guy *sing* those things to the boss when he were out behind a wagon, hookin' up the horses. He'd make out like a horse stepped on his foot and he'd say, 'Get off my foot, goddamit!'—saying just what he wanted to say to his boss, only talkin' to the horse—'You got no business doin' me like that! Get offa my foot!' "

"That's just my idea, Natchez," Leroy broke in. "The blues is mostly revenge. You want to say something (and you know how we was situated so we couldn't say or do a lot of things we wanted to), and so you sing it. Like a friend of mine. He was workin' down on a railroad section gang a long time ago. I don't remember when it was. Anyhow, this friend of mine looked at the boss lyin' up in the shade sleepin' while him an' his buddies was out there shakin' those ties. He wanted to say something about it, but he couldn't you know. So that give him the blues and he sung a little number about—

> Ratty, ratty section,
> Ratty, ratty crew,
> The captain's gettin' ratty, boys,
> I b'lieve I'm gonna rat some, too.

Meanin' that he was signifying and getting his revenge through songs."

"And he didn't quit because he didn't know where he gonna find his next job," Natchez added.

"Yeah, and maybe he had one of those jobs you *couldn't* quit." Leroy chuckled.

"What you mean? Sumpin' like a chain-gang?" Sib asked.

"Naw, I mean one of the jobs only way you could quit was to run off," said Leroy.

"Man, how they gonna hold you?" from Sib, querulously.

"They hold you just like this, Sib, boy. You didn't have no payday on them jobs. They give you an allowance in the commissary store for you an' yo' woman. You draw on that allowance, so much a week, and after it was up, that's all you git. Most boys didn't know how to read and write and figger and so they charge them what they wants, like twenty-five dollars for a side of side-meat. And you gonna stay there till you paid for that meat, Sib, maybe gettin' twenty-five cents a day wages. When you take a notion to leave, they tell you, 'Well, you owe us four hundred dollars.' "

"Four hundred dollars! Aw, be quiet, man." Sib started to laugh his mad and infectious laugh.

"I said four hundred dollars," Leroy cut in. "Just for eatin' and sleepin'."

Natchez took up the story. "Suppose you be workin' a team of mules and one git his leg broke and have to be killed? That's your mule, then! Yessir, that dead mule is one you bought and you gonna work right on that job till you pay for him or slip off some way."

"Whyn't you say somethin' about it?" Sib inquired plaintively.

"Say something about it and you might go just like that mule," Natchez said seriously. "All odds are against you, even your own people."

"That's right," agreed Leroy. "The white man don't all the time do those things. It's some of your own people at times will do those dirty deeds because they're told to do them, and they do what they're told."

Treat a group of people as if they had no right to dignity, allow these people no security, make them bend their knees and bow their heads, and some of them will conform to slavery in their souls. Perhaps these so-called "Uncle Toms" are the most grievous result of the slavery system.

Natchez interrupted my reflections. "Looky here, Leroy. Did you ever work for the Loran brothers?"

"You mean those guys that built all these levees up and down the river from Memphis? Sho, man, I've worked for the bigges' part of the Loran family —Mister Isum Loran, Mister Bill Loran, Mister Charley Loran—all them. I think them Lorans are something like the Rockefeller family. When a kid is born, *he* Loran junior. They got Loran the second, Loran the third, Loran the fourth. They always been and they is now—Loran brothers—some of them big business mens in towns, some of them running extry gangs and levee camps and road camps. And *they* were peoples wouldn't allow a man to quit unless they got tired of him and drove him away."

"That's right," Leroy chuckled. "And you remember how the boys used to sing—

I axed Mister Charley—
What time of day:
He looked at me,
Threw his watch away.

I axed Mister Charley
Just to give me one dime.
'Go on, old nigger,
You a dime behind!'

I axed Mister Charley
Just to give me my time.
'Go on, old nigger,
You're time behind!'. . ."

I had heard this levee camp blues from one end of the South to the other. It was the epic of the muleskinner, the man who did the dirt-moving jobs before the bulldozer was developed, the Negro who, working his big mule-drawn scoop, piled up the levees, graded the roads, and dug the canals of the South. This muleskinning blues has thousands of verses, attached to the mournfulest wailing tune in the world, a tune I never was able to sing myself until they put me on KP in the Army, and the mess sergeant began to look like a levee camp boss looks to a muleskinner.

All the way from the Brazos bottoms of Texas to the tidewater country of Virginia I had heard Negro muleskinners chant their complaint against Mister Charley but, although I had asked a score of singers, I had never found one who could identify him. I grinned with excitement. Maybe here, under the knee of one of the Loran brothers' levees, I had at last discovered the identity of my elusive Mister Charley.

I asked my second question of the evening. "Who is this 'Mister Charley'?"

"Mister Charley Loran," Natchez immediately responded.

"What sort of a man is he?" I asked.

"Well," Leroy drawled, "now I couldn't hardly describe him to you. You know, it's hard for a colored man to talk like a white man anyhow."

(Leroy was talking for my benefit now. He had been reminded there was a white man listening there in the dark. He began to rib me gently.) "Mister Charley was one of them *real* Southerners; had a voice that would scare you to death whenever he'd come out with all that crap of his. Always in his shirt sleeves, I don't care how early in the mornin' and how cold it was."

"Night or day." Natchez began to chuckle with him. "Didn't make no difference to Mister Charley what time it was."

"Don't care how early he'd get up, *you* gonna get up, too. He'd holler—

Big bell call you, little bell warn you,
If you don't come now, I'm gonna
    break in on you. . . .

And he *meant* it."

"Sho he did," laughed Natchez. "He the man originated the old-time eight-hour shift down here. Know what I mean? Eight hours in the morning and eight more in the afternoon."

Sib kept adding eight to eight and getting sixteen and going off into peal after peal of high whinnying laughter. In this shared laughter I felt the three had again accepted me. I asked another question.

"I'd always heard of this Mister Charley in the song as 'the mercy man.' Is he the same as Charley Loran?"

"Naw, man, that's Mister Charley *Hulen*, the best friend we had down in this part of the country, really a friend to our people. He was the man we all run to when somebody mistreated us," Natchez told me.

"Otherwise known as 'the mercy man,'" Leroy added. "Now I remember an incident about Charley Hulen happen in Hughes, Arkansas. It's hard to believe it, but I know it for a fact. They had a Negro there name Bolden, run a honkeytonk and had a lot of property. In fact the sheriff of the county lived in one of Bolden's houses. But he wouldn't pay Bolden no rent, just stayed there and gave Bolden a whuppin' every time Bolden asked him for his money."

"That's what he did," said Natchez, listening, seeing it, feeling it in his guts.

"So this Bolden happen to be, as they say, one of Charley Hulen's niggers. He finally got up nerve to go tell Mister Charley what was goin' on. So Charley Hulen tells the *po*lice, say, 'Saturday evenin' at one o'clock, meet me. I'm killin' you or you kill me.' And that's what happen. He met that sheriff that Saturday and told him, 'I come to kill you. You been messin' with one of my niggers.'

"The *po*lice started after his gun and Charley Hulen shot him through the heart. So they pulled that *po*lice over out the street, and let the honky-tonk roll on." Softly, seeing it, wondering about it, he repeated, "Yeah, man, let the old honky-tonk roll *right* on."

"Toughest places I *ever* seen," said Natchez, "were some of them honkytonks, call them barrel-houses, in Charley Loran's camps. Negroes all be in there gamblin', you know, and some of them short guys couldn't quite reach up to the crap table—and I've seed them pull a *dead* man up there and stand on him."

"Yeah, stand on 'em. I've seed that," Leroy said

But Natchez had more to tell. "Down in them barrel-houses in Loran's levee camps I've seen them stand on a dead man and shoot craps all night long; and I've heard Loran come around and say, 'If you boys keep out the grave, I'll keep you out the jail.' Yeah, and I've heard him say, 'Kill a nigger, hire another. But kill a mule and I'll have to *buy* another.' "

"That's just what he believed, Natchez," Leroy said, in anger and at the same time with curious pride. "Peoples like him had another word, too. On those camps, when the fellows were wore down from carrying logs or doing some kind of heavy work, the bosses used to say, '*Burn out, burn up. Fall out, fall dead*!' That was the best you could do. You had to work yourself to death or you proved that you were a good man, that's all."

"Main thing about it is that some of those people down there didn't think a Negro ever get *tired*!" Natchez' ordinarily quiet voice broke with a sound that was half sob, half growl. "They'd work him—work him till he couldn't work, see! You couldn't *tell* 'em you was tired."

"Why couldn't you?" I asked.

"They'd crack you 'cross the head with a stick or maybe kill you. One of those things. You just had to keep on workin' whether you was tired or not. From what they call 'can to can't.' That mean you start to work when you just can see—early in the mornin'—and work right on till you can't see no more at night."

"Only man ever helped us about our work was Charley Hulen, the mercy man," said Leroy. "He used to come out and say, 'Those fellows are tired; give 'em some rest.' Ain't he the man, Natchez, cut them sixteen hours a day down to eight?"

"Right in this section he was," Natchez replied.

"How did he do it?" I asked.

"Why, he and his son, Little Charley, just didn't like the way things was going on, so they just come in and taken over, that's all. Otherwise they was the baddest men down through this part of the country. Both of them was ex-cowboys from Texas and sharpshooters. Could shoot like nobody's business. So after they taken over, that made it a lot better. And it's still better today."

"You mean the people were just scared of old man Hulen and his boy?" I asked.

"That's right," Leroy said. "I'll tell you how bad they was scared. You know they put up a law in Arkansas —no *hitchhikin'*. It made it kinda tough on a fellow to move around and change jobs if he wanted to. So, one afternoon I were hitchhikin' a ride to Little Rock and a fellow by the name of Mister Gotch stopped in his car. He were one of the baddest mens down in this country."

"He was so bad he was scared of hissef," Natchez chuckled.

"So Mister Gotch say to me, 'What you doin' hitchhikin', boy?' Called me 'boy.'

"I say, 'I'm tryin' to get home to work.'

"He say, 'Well, who do you work *for*?'

"I tell him"—Leroy imitated the mild and insinuating way he made his reply—" 'I work for Mister Charley Hulen.' You know what that man told me? He say, " 'Come on, I'll take you there!' "

Sib, Natchez, and Leroy threw back their heads and laughed, laughed quietly and long, as if they shared some old joke, burdened with irony, but bearable out of long acquaintance. "Any other time. . . . Or if you'd worked for another man. . . . Or if you hadn't been workin' . . . . You'd got a whuppin'. . . . Or went to jail or the farm and worked for no pay. . . . That's it, worked for no pay!" came bursting out between chuckles. "But, since I worked for Mister Charley Hulen, Mister Gotch taken me to his place. Scared to bother me, because I was one of Mister Charley's mens," Leroy went on.

"One of his *niggers*!"

"Yeah. So Mister Gotch took me in his car. Even gave me a drink!"

Natchez, shaking his head in wonder, chuckled. "They'll do that, too."

"You know, Leroy," Natchez said, "you and I worked in all kind of camps —levee camps, road camps, rock quarries and all—but what I want to get at is—how we lived in those places? I mean in tents and eatin' scrap food other people had refused, such as old bags of beans and stuff they couldn't sell."

Leroy, beginning to howl with laughter over the old and painful joke he recalled, interrupted, "And they had a name for it in the camp I was in—

La-la-loo!
If you don't like it,
He do!"

Natchez, chuckling with him, "Yeah, but you'll *like* it!"

"Unh-hunh, you might not like it when you first get there, but you'll like it before you leave." Leroy was still laughing.

Natchez went on, forcing us to savor the dirt, see the hoggish way the men had to live. "They'd just go out in those big truck gardens and pull up greens by the sackful, take 'em down to some lake or creek, sort of shake 'em off in the water, and cook 'em, roots, stalk, and all, in one of them big fifty-two gallon pots."

Leroy, beginning to laugh his big laugh again, broke in. "And if you found a worm in your greens and say, 'Captain, I found a worm here,' he'd say, 'What the hell you expect for nothing?' "

Natchez and Sib burst out in great yells of laughter, as Leroy hurried on to top his own story: "And then some fellow over 'long the table would holler, 'Gimme that piece of meat!' "

"Yeah, I've heard that—'Gimme that piece of meat! Don't throw it away!' " Natchez gasped out between the gusts of laughter that were shaking his whole body. Sib couldn't sit still any longer; his laughter was riding him too hard. He went staggering off down the dark path, beating his arms in the air, squealing and guffawing like a wild animal.

When we had recovered from this healing laughter, Leroy added thoughtfully, "Those guys seemed to get a kick out of the whole thing."

"Well, in them times what did you know? What did you know?" Natchez asked the night and the stars.

"Ham and eggs, pork and beans,
I would-a ate more, but the cook wasn't clean."

"Did you ever see those guys they called 'table-walkers'?" Natchez went on.

"Yeah, many times," said Leroy.

"I mean one of these guys had made up his mind he didn't care whether he died or no; was just tired of the way he'd been living and the kind of food he'd been eating. He'd snatch out his .45 revolver, get up on one end of the mess table and walk it, what I mean, walk right down the whole length, tromping his big dirty feets in everybody's plates, grabbin' up your food."

"Those guys were what you might call 'tough peoples,'" Leroy said respectfully.

"Yeah, 'cause they know they gonna get a whuppin' from the boss," Natchez agreed.

"He may have that .45, that so-called tough guy," Leroy went on, "but, when the white man come, *he'll* whup him with that .45 right on his hip. White man won't have no gun or nothin'. Just come in and say, 'Lay down there, fellow; I'm gonna whup you.'" Leroy spoke quietly, with bitter, weary irony. "So this tough guy gonna lay right down and the white man would kick the gun out of his scabbard and give him a whuppin'." There was a pause. We could all see the big, black figure cowering on the earth and the white man standing over him with a stick, beating him as he might a chicken-killing hound. After a moment, almost in a whisper, Leroy continued, "After this table-walker get his whuppin', he'd pick up that big pistol he toted and go on back to work.

Well, you kicked and stomped and beat me,
And you called that fun, and you called that fun.

If I catch you in my home town,
Gonna make you run, gonna make you run. . . ."

"Yeah," Natchez said. "Then maybe this guy that took the beating would come out there on the job and kill one of his buddies. I've seen that many times."

"If you were a good worker, you could kill anybody down there," Leroy added.

"What you mean is—" Natchez rapped this out—"you could kill anybody down there as long as you kill a *Negro!*"

"Any *Negro.*" Leroy's voice was flat and painstakingly logical, as if he were reading the rules out of a book. "If you could *work* better than him and you were *sorry!* But don't go killin' a good worker!"

"That's right," said Natchez. "You could kill anybody you want in those days, if you could work better than him.

Stagolee, he went a-walkin' in that red-hot broilin' sun;
He said, 'Bring me my big pistol, I wants my forty-one.'

Stagolee, he went a-walkin' with his .40 gun in his hand;
He said, 'I feel mistreated this mornin', I could kill most any man.'"

The small hot breeze of midnight had died away and the dawn wind had not yet begun to stir. The night wrapped around us a choking black blanket of stillness and quiet. The quiet voices of Natchez and Leroy moved on with the sureness and strength of the great river that had given them birth.

They were both entertainers. They had made their way safely and even pleasantly through their violent world, their guitars slung around their necks—like talismans. Wearing these talismans, they had entered into all the secret places of this land, had moved safely through its most dangerous jungles, past all its killers, who, seeing their talismans, had smiled upon them. They lived the magic life of fools. (Remember the hard drawling voice—"I got a nigger on my place that can keep you laughin' all day. I don't know where he gets all the stories he tells and them songs of his. Reckon he makes them up, nigger-like. And sing! Sing like a mockin'-bird. You ought to hear him. You'd split your sides.") Now these buffoons with their clear artist's vision were making a picture of their world, a terrifying picture of which they were not at all afraid. They were at home with it.

"You know, Natchez," said Leroy, "we had a *few* Negroes around here that wasn't *afraid* of white people. They actually talked back to them. People like that they called 'crazy'—'crazy niggers.' I wonder why do they call them crazy and bad because they speak up for their rights?"

"They afraid they might *ruin* the other Negroes, make *them* crazy enough to talk back," said Natchez. "I had a crazy uncle and they hung him. My uncle was a man that, if he worked, he wanted his pay. And he could figger as good as a white man. Fact of the matter, he had a better education than some of them and they would go to him for advice."

Leroy chuckled. "Um-hum, a lot of the white peoples down here are about as dumb as we are."

"Anyhow," Natchez went on, "this is how they found out my uncle was really a crazy nigger. One day his white boss come to his house and told him, say, 'Sam, I want you to git that woman of yours out of the house and put her to work.' Say, 'It's no woman on this plantation sits up in the shade and don't work but Mizz Anne.'

"An' my uncle say, 'Well, who is Mizz Anne?'

"The white man tell him, 'Mizz Anne is my wife.'*

"My uncle say, 'Well, I'm sorry, Mister Crowther, but my wife is named Anne, too, and *she* sets up in the shade and *she* don't come out in the field and work!'

"The man say, 'She *got* to come out there.'

"My uncle look at him. 'There's one Mizz Anne that's a *Negro* and *she* ain't gonna work in the field.'

"The white man jumps off his horse and my uncle whipped him and run him *and* his horse off his place." Natchez went on in a flat and weary voice to finish his story. "So the white man rode to town and he got him a gang and come back after my uncle. My uncle shot four or five of them, but they finally caught him and hung him. So that's the story of *him*! Yeah, that's the story of my *crazy* uncle."

"Lynched him," Sib muttered.

"Fifty or sixty of them come out

* Mizz Anne is, of course, the female counterpart to Mister Charley, i.e., it is the generic term for "Mrs. white man." The terms "Mister Charley" and "Miss Anne" would appear to date from ante-bellum times. See *Unwritten History of Slavery: Autobiographical Account of Negro Ex-Slaves*, Fisk University Social Science Source Documents No. 1 (Nashville, 1945), p. 247. It is difficult to determine with any degree of certitude why these two personal names came to be chosen for such purposes. According to the *Oxford English Dictionary* (Oxford, 1933), "charley" was a nineteenth-century slang term for a watchman. If this is at all relevant it may well *not* be, then "Mr. Charley" might have originally been "Mr. Watchman" or the obvious white guardian of property rights and material goods. However, this questionable speculation does not provide any clues as to the possible significance of the name "Mizz Anne" for the mistress of the plantation. —Ed.

there and killed him." Natchez began to speak with mounting rage. "That was on account of him trying to protect his own *wife*. Because he didn't want his own *wife* to work out on the farm when she had a new baby there at the house an' was expecting another one pretty soon!

"I've seed this happen, too. One boy I know was likin' the same girl a white man was likin'. The white man told the colored boy not to marry the colored girl, because *he* wanted her for hisself. The boy told him he loved the girl and was going to marry her, so the white guy say, 'You can't git no license here!'

"Well, the boy and girl ran off to another town and they got married and then come back home. The white fellow asked if they was really married and they told him they were. Now this girl figger if she showed him the license he would leave her go. She showed him the license, so they went and got her husband and killed him. Then they come back and got her—she was in a fam'ly way—and they killed her. Then they went and killed the boy's daddy and they killed his mother, and then, one of the brothers, *he* tried to fight and they killed *him*. So they killed twelve in that one family. That family was named Belcher, and all this happened at a place they call Longdale, Arkansas, way out in the woods from Goulds, Arkansas."

Without any more feeling than one would recall a storm or a flood or any other past disaster, Leroy commented, "Yeah, I heard of that, heard all about it."

"It was no protection at all that the poor peoples got in places like that back in those days," Natchez went on

with calm anger. "You try to fight back, then it's not just *you* they gonna get. It's anybody in your family. Like if I have three brothers and do something and they can't catch me, they'll catch the brothers."

"It don't matter to them—just anybody in the family," Leroy said.

"*You* might do things and get away. But why do something or another and get your whole family kilt? You know what I mean?"

"I know it!"

"That's what they got on you, see?"

"Yeah, that's what they got on you," observed Natchez. "And if your family have a girl *they* like, you might's well's to let them *have* her, because if you don't, they liable to do something outrageous. When they see a Negro woman they like, they *gonna* have her, if they want her, especially down here.

If I feel tomorrow, like I feel today,
If I feel tomorrow, like I feel today,
Stand right here and look a thousand
    miles away.

I'm goin' to the river, set down on the
    ground;
I'm goin' to the river, set down on the
    ground;
When the blues overtake me, I'll jump
    overboard and drown.

I feel my hell a-risin', a-risin' every
    day;
I feel my hell a-risin', a-risin' every
    day;
Someday it'll bust this levee and wash
    the whole wide world away. . . ."

"You know, they's another kind of Negro the white man call *bad*," Natchez went on. "A bad *seed*, a seed that ruins the rest of the Negroes, by opening their eyes and telling them things they don't know,"

"Otherwise he is a *smart* Negro," Leroy chuckled.

"Yeah," said Natchez. "He would git the *Chicago Defender*, for an instance, and bring it down here and read it to the Negroes."

"Speakin' of the *Chicago Defender*," Leroy interrupted, "I were in a place once they called Marigold, Mississippi. They had a restaurant there and in the back they had a room with a peephole in the door. I thought it was a crap game goin' on back there and I went back to see. Fact of the business, I were kind of stranded and I wanted to shoot some craps and make me a stake, if I could.

"And you know what they were doin' back there? They were readin' the *Chicago Defender* and had a lookout man on the door. If a white man had come in the restaurant, they'd stick the *Defender* in the stove. Burn it up. And start playin' checkers." Leroy laughed. "That's the way they had to smuggle the *Defender* down there. Now if they'd caught this fellow that *brought* the *Defender*, they'd have called him a bad nigger."

"Might-a killed him."

"Yeah. He was the kind they call a *really* bad Negro—a man that has the nerve to smuggle the *Defender* into Mississippi where they don't even allow the paper to be put off the train."

The *Chicago Defender* has more than a hundred thousand circulation among Negro readers. It is far from radical. It prints news about Negro life, much that does not appear in the non-Negro press.

"That's what makes the Negro so *tetchious* till today," Natchez said. "He have been denied in so many places

until if a gang of guys is, for an instance, standing in some certain place and they say to them *all*, 'You fellas, git back and don't stand there,' the Negroes in the crowd figger they're pointin' straight to *them*. A lot of times they don't mean that. They really mean they don't want *nobody* standin' there, but the Negro thinks, straight off, they referrin' to him because he's black."

Sib had been listening to his two older friends for a long time. He had had no experience of the deeps of the South—the work camps, the prison farms, the wild life of the river that they had known. He was a boy right off the farm, whose half-mad genius on his Woolworth harmonica was gradually leading him out into the world.

But Sib knew how it was to feel "black and tetchious."

"Well, boys, I'll tell you what happen to me. My mother, she bought a mule from er-uh Captain Jack, who was the boss of the county farm at my home. It was a nice mule. But, by me bein' young—you know how young boys are?—I rode this mule down, run him, you understand. After all, Captain Jack didn't have nothin' to say. He'd done sold the mule to my mother. And this mule finally got mired up in the bottom."

"You say married? Is that the mule you married?"

"Naw, naw, mired, mired up in the mud."

"That *must* be the mule you bought the hat for," Leroy cracked, and all three men burst into guffaws of country laughter, while Sib kept stuttering his story.

"Naw, it ain't! Now listen! Just this old mule got mired up and *died* down there in the bottom."

"I understand."

"Yeah. So er-uh Captain Jack, he told my mother that he was just crazy to git his hands on that stuttering fool of hers. Which was me. Said he was gonna do me just like I did the mule. Get me out there on the gang and—"

"I understand," said Natchez, now grave.

"And my mother had to just scuffle to keep me offa that gang. Ever' little move I'd make, he was watchin' me. And, after all, he done *sold* the mule and she done *paid* him. But he say I killed the mule and—"

Natchez interrupted sharply. "You see the main point is that word they have down here—'Kill a nigger, hire another one. Kill a mule, buy another one.' All these things, everything we've talked about, all these blues and everything, come under that one word. Fact of the business, back not long ago, a Negro didn't mean no more to a white man *than* a mule."

"Didn't mean as much," said Leroy.

"A black man," Natchez went on, "to what they looked at, was just a black face. I knew a man (they call him Mister White) had a plantation about fifty or sixty miles square and he didn't even want a Negro to come *through* his place. The government highway ran through his land, you know? What they call a pike, a main highway where everybody had to go, but he built a special road, ran all around his place, and when you got there it was a sign said 'NEGRO TURN.' You had to turn off the highway and go all around his plantation."

"I knew him, knew him well," Leroy muttered.

"And this Mister White had all white fences around his place. The trees, he painted them white as high as he could reach. All his cattle, his sheeps, goats, hogs, cows, mules, hosses, and everything on his place was white. Anytime one of his animals have a black calf or a black goat—whatsoever it was—Mister White give it to the niggers. Even down to the chickens. He had all white chickens, too. And when a chicken would hatch off some black chickens, he'd say, 'Take those chickens out and find a nigger and give 'em to him. Get rid of 'em. I won't have no nigger chickens on this plantation!' "

"I've seed all that, too," said Leroy. "And you know the time a Negro and a white man was standin' by a railroad crossin'? They was talkin', you know. The white man was tellin' the Negro what he wanted him to do. So along come another Negro drivin' a wagon with a white mule hitched to it. Well, the railin' was kinda high at this crossin' and the wheels got caught and the wagon stopped. This Negro who was drivin' begin to holler at that mule. 'Get up!' he says. 'Get along there.'

"So the white man holler up there and asked him, say, 'Hey you, don't you know that's a *white* mule you talkin' to?'

" 'Yassuh, boss,' the Negro tell him. 'Get up, *Mister* mule!' "

Natchez and Leroy began to guffaw, and, after a moment, when he got the point of the joke, Sib's laughter burst over him in torrents. Again he went staggering down the path, howling with glee and beating his arms helplessly in the air. So we all laughed together in the early morning breeze, blowing the blues out of our lungs and hearts in gusts of wild laughter.

"And how about that Prince Albert tobacco?" gasped Natchez, when he could speak again.

"I've heard of that," said Leroy.

"You know you couldn't go into one of these here little country stores and say, 'Gimme a can of Prince Albert'? Not with that white man on the can."

"What would you say?"

"Gimme a can of *Mister* Prince Albert!"

We were caught up in the gales of squalling laughter that racked Sib, until we must have looked like a party of madmen capering there in the dawn under the lee of the levee. We were howling down the absurdity, the perversity, and the madness that grips the land on which we stood, a beautiful and fecund land, rich in food and genius and good living and song, yet turned into a sort of purgatory by fear.

Now for an instant we understood each other. Now in this moment of laughter, the thongs and the chains, the harsh customs of dominance, the stupefying and brutalizing lies of race had lost their fallacious dignity, but only for an instant. The magic night had gone. Back in Memphis our night's friendship and understanding would vanish like this morning's mist under the pitiless southern sun. The blues would begin again their eternal rhythm, their eternal ironic comment:

The blues jumped a rabbit, run him a
    solid mile,
When the blues overtaken him, he
    hollered like a baby child. . . .

"Yeah," said Natchez, his face showing somberly now in the hard light of the July morning, "that's the way things go down around these little southern places—enough to give anybody the blues."

Protest & Irony in Negro Folksong

RUSSELL AMES

    Having sampled albeit ever so briefly some of the scholarship devoted to spirituals and blues, it may be worthwhile to consider some of the stylistic and functional similarities in these folksong forms. In particular, the use of folksong as a vehicle for the expression of social protest seems to be common in spirituals and blues as well as in other forms of Negro folksong. The widespread utilization of such songs as "We Shall Overcome" in connection with the Civil Rights movement is almost certainly a continuation of the technique of articulating wishful thinking in the form of folksong. In folksong, wrongs that need righting can be spelled out effectively. Frequently, understatement and irony are used to drive a point home. The subtlety of symbolic complaints and double meanings often give these folk statements much more poignancy and persuasive power than would normally be present in direct statements of social injustice.

    From Russell Ames' discussion, we learn that the rhetorical techniques and strategies found in Negro folksong are not limited to a single genre. In this sense (as in the musical discussions) it is probably a mistake to consider the various genres of American Negro folksong separately. Just as antiphonal singing style is a common feature in spirituals and worksongs, so the skillful use of irony is found throughout the range of Negro folksong.

    It should be pointed out that not all experts agree that protest is expressed in Negro folksong. With regard to spirituals, for example, R. Wilson Howe wrote in the Southern Workman, *"Nowhere in these songs can we trace any suggestion of hatred or revenge, two qualities usually developed under slavery." With regard to blues, Samuel Charters has made the unequivocal statement: "There is little social protest in the blues. . . . There is complaint, but protest has been stifled." See R. Wilson Howe, "The Negro and His Songs,"* Southern Work-

Reprinted from *Science and Society*, vol. 14 (1950), pp. 193–213, by permission of the author and *Science and Society*.

man, *51 (1922), pp. 381–83, and Samuel Charters*, The Poetry of the Blues, *(New York, 1970), p. 152.*

For further consideration of Negro protest songs, see Chapter 2, "Negro Songs of Protest" in John Greenway, American Folksongs of Protest *(New York, 1960), pp. 67–120. See also Lawrence Gellert*, Negro Songs of Protest *(New York, 1936) and* Me and My Captain *(New York, 1939). Also of interest is Philip Schatz, "Songs of the Negro Worker,"* New Masses, *5 (May, 1930), pp. 6–8.*

IN ANGLO-SAXON literary culture folksong has generally been put low on the artistic scale, and Negro song has suffered most. The Negro folksong is not as it has generally been thought an almost exclusively simple and emotional expression, or nonsensical, and artless and crude in form. At its best it is, like all folksong, sophisticated and ironic in its meanings, classical and subtle in its use of forms.[1]

In an excellent article on the spirituals, John Lovell, Jr. has shown how profoundly interpretations of Negro folksong need to be changed.[2] Most of us reject the sentimental picture of the spirituals as a reflection of "the old time darky's trusting religious faith, his loyalty to his daily tasks, his love for "ole marse" and "ole mist'ess"; but many may accept the traditional Northern view that religion was chiefly a comfort and a refuge from oppressive slavery, a view held even by W. E. B. DuBois, Alain Locke, and James Weldon Johnson. The reality was, according to Lovell, that while "the whites left the camp-meeting and went out to conquer the wilderness," the "Negroes left spiritual singing and plotted to upset the system of slavery."[3]

He contends that the spirituals, "Babylon" and "Winter" equalled slavery: the "Devil" was people who cheated and beat slaves; "King Jesus" was whoever helped the oppressed; "Hell" meant being sold South; "Jordan" was the push to freedom; the chariot in "Swing Low" was some arm of freedom reaching down to draw the slave in, as it many times did successfully through the underground railway; and "the great 'sociation," "the welcome table," "the big baptizin'," and the "union," were concrete plans and hopes.

Lovell's suggestions concerning the spirituals are not in themselves complete scholarly proof of his thesis, but they jibe with what we are learning of the secret cultural and political life of oppressed peoples through the ages, the revolutionary character of early Christianity, the underground organization of the medieval peasantry with their "witchcraft" and Devil-worship, which the English historian A. L. Morton and others have been investigating, and with the American Negro slave revolts, which Herbert Aptheker has recorded. As the editors of *The Negro Caravan* point out:

[1] See Russell Ames, "Art in Negro Folksong," *Journal of American Folklore*, LVI (October–December, 1943), pp. 251–52, 254.
[2] "The Social Implications of the Negro Spiritual," *Journal of Negro Education*, VIII (October, 1939).
[3] *Ibid.*, p. 639.

There are not many spirituals that speak openly of a love for freedom and a determination to be free. The slaves were not so naive as that; they knew, better than several of their historians, how close to hysteria the slave-holders really were, how rigid the control could be.[4]

The specifically political songs of slaves, even when more or less open and bold, were disguised in fantasy and humor, and sometimes employed ingenious concealing puns:

You mought be Carroll from Carrollton
Arrive here night afo' Lawd make
    creation
But you can't keep the World from
    moverin' around
And not turn her back from the
    gaining ground.[5]

The attack on the Carrolls was presumably robbed of its menace by laughter, but revolution had to be described as that of the earth, and the name of Nat Turner, leader of a slave rebellion could appear only, though it appeared repeatedly in the chorus, as "not turn her."

The censorship involved in Negro song—especially slave and chaingang song—should be extremely obvious:

Got one mind for white folks to see,

'Nother for what I know is me;
He don't know, he don't know my
    mind
When he see me laughing
Laughing just to keep from crying.[6]

But the obvious need of the oppressed for disguising his feelings and for self-censorship of his social ideas is by no means widely recognized. A careful collector of Negro folksongs, Newman I. White, remarks that "Every Southern white man . . . knows that the Negro does not say all he means or mean all he says; he is aware of a secretive strain [*sic*] in the Negro which attempts to keep certain things strictly within the race."[7] Elsewhere White recognizes the need of the Negro slave for discretion, for disguise of his meanings in song. But in general he adheres to a stereotype of the happy, humorous, thoughtless, fatalistic Negro.

White shows no evidence of having heard the kind of chaingang songs which Lawrence Gellert has recorded:

All the wrong, Captain, you do to me
Bound to come back to you—wait
    and see.
When it comes, white folks, shows you
    I'm a man,
Not a no-tail monkey, what get rattling
    his chain.[8]

[4] Sterling A. Brown, Arthur P. Davis, Ulysses Lee, *The Negro Caravan* (New York, 1941), p. 418.
[5] Lawrence Gellert, "Two Songs about Nat Turner," *The Worker Magazine* (June 12, 1949), p. 8.
[6] Lawrence Gellert, *Me and My Captain* (New York, 1936), p. 5. This collection is the second volume of Gellert's *Negro Songs of Protest*.
[7] Newman I. White, *American Negro Folk-Songs* (Cambridge, Mass., 1928), p. 29.
[8] Gellert, *op. cit.*, p. 19. [But it is precisely the lack of published parallels to many of Gellert's protest songs which has made some folksong scholars suspicious of Gellert's materials. However, Gellert's song texts, many of which appeared first in *New Masses* (November, 1930; January, 1931; and May, 1932), and later as "Negro Songs of Protest" in Nancy Cunard, ed., *Negro* (London, 1934), pp. 366–77, before appearing in book form, do seem to be authentic. The fact remains that it is not easy for a white man to collect Negro songs of protest in the South and also that the majority of southern gentleman and lady folksong collectors would not have been likely to have elicited them. For a statement of the suspicion about Gellert's texts and a partial rebuttal, see John Greenway, *American Folksongs of Protest* (New York, 1960), p. 86. —ED.]

Or the poetic keenness of this:

> Please, Bossman, tell me, what have I
>   done,
> How come you lock me 'way from the
>   light of the sun;
> I hear danger singing
> I hear danger moan,
> Crying who, crying who, crying you.[9]

The important fact, then, is not that there are few songs of open protest available to whites, but that the American Negro, more than most people, has had subtlety and irony forced upon his art. Yet White can conclude, concerning the Negro: "In his songs I find him, as I have found him elsewhere, a most naive and unanalytical-minded person, with a sensuous joy in his religion; thoughtless, careless, unidealistic, rather fond of boasting, predominantly cheerful, but able to derive considerable pleasure from a grouch; occasionally suspicious, charitably inclined toward the white man, and capable of a gorgeously humorous view of anything, particularly himself."[10]

Some Negroes, as well as some members of any people, conform to White's stereotype. The significant point is that resentment, frustration and protest, among all oppressed people, and especially among Negroes, is widespread and deeper than is generally suspected. A recent Philadelphia Early Childhood Project finds that in describing whites "the Negro child's feelings [are] often 'masked' in such responses as, 'they are nice. They smiles at you'."[11]

The number of printed and recorded Negro songs openly expressing rebellion is necessarily small; the number existing is certainly much larger. The frequency with which these are sung, that is, the extent to which they enter into life, is of course unknown. Not often do white ears hear this from the chaingang:

> My Bossman name was Sammy,
> The meanest dog I ever know.
> Speak soft, 'cause he got more
>   ear-sights
> Than old Devil down below. . . .
>
> If I had my sweet way
> Graveyard's place my Bossman'd lay.
> I even hates to hear his name,
> Could kill him like express train.[12]

Half-concealed and concealed protests have taken an infinite variety of forms. The following song, for example, is not so pointed as the powerful rhyme of the fourteenth-century English peasant revolt—"When Adam delved and Eve span, who was then the gentleman?"*—but it has the same basic meaning:

> Ef effer 'ligion wuz a thing dat
>   money could buy
>   Oh, reign, Marse Jesus, oh reign
> De rich would live an' de po' would
>   die,
>   Oh, reign, Marse Jesus, oh reign. . . .
>
> But de Lord, he 'owed, dat he wouldn't
>   have it so,
>   Reign, Marse Jesus, oh reign,
> So de rich mus' die, jes same as de po',
>   Oh reign, Marse Jesus, oh reign.[13]

---

[9] *Ibid.*, p. 29.

[10] White, *op. cit.*, p. 30.

[11] Catherine Mackenzie, "Prejudiced Can Be Unlearned," The New York *Times Magazine* (July 25, 1948), p. 16.

[12] Gellert, *op. cit.*, p. 6.

* For an extended discussion of this proverb, see Sylvia Resnikow, "The Cultural History of a Democratic Proverb," *Journal of English and Germanic Philology*, 36 (1937), pp. 391–405. —ED.

[13] White, *op. cit.*, p. 101.

Regardless of the attitudes of any individual singer, the objective social necessity of American Negro songs over a period of time was to create forms, patterns, habits, and styles which would conceal and protect the singer. Perhaps the commonest technique of concealment has been to disguise meaning in some kind of fantastic, symbolical, or nonsensical clothing. B. A. Botkin has pointed out that a "grotesque mixture of humor with criticism, realism with fantasy, runs through the hard-hitting songs of . . . the lumberjack, the cowboy, the coal miner, the wobbly, the sharecropper, the Okie. It is in the satirical tradition with a new twist—the trick of what Zora Neale Hurston has called 'hitting a straight lick with a crooked stick.' "[14]

Whenever bosses or other persons considered hostile were likely to hear, working people have had to sing differently or remain quiet, and that is why so many folksongs shift, line by line, or stanza by stanza, from sense to nonsense, from bitterness to humor, and that is also the reason why much of it seems unorganized. Gellert comments aptly: "What if the white man laughs and gauges the mentality of his charges by the nonsensical doggerel and ribald parodies he's permitted to hear? Educating him contrariwise with protest songs would proportionately diminish the convict's life expectancy on the road."[15]

In the following lines, a neat mixture of fantasy and social resentment can be seen:

Old massa had a great big house,
It was sixteen stories high,
And every story in that house
Was filled with chicken pie.[16]

This was probably first a minstrel song but it was taken up by Negroes and varied infinitely. A similar meaning and technique appears in:

Ole master had a fine buggy,
He filled it up wid peaches,
He run it against a sign board,
And busted it all ter pieces.
De hoss begun ter kick up,
De mule begun to prance,
De ole sow whistled
And de pigs all danced.[17]

The apparent glee of the above animals at the master's misfortune suggests one of the broadest fields of symbolism and disguise in Negro song, identification of the singer with animals.

In the great body of Negro songs, we find animal life symbolizing human life:

I tell you how this man think
Black man just like Betsey mule,
You got to beat 'em every day
To know that he's their rule.[18]

A threatening example:

I ain't gonna be your old work ox no
more. . .
You can never tell what your old work
ox gwine do.[19]

The mule again:

Massah had an old black mule,
His name was Simon Slick,

---

[14] B. A. Botkin, "The Folk-Say of Freedom Songs," *New Masses* (October 21, 1947), p. 16.

[15] Gellert, *op. cit.*, "Preface," p. 3.

[16] White, *op. cit.*, p. 155.

[17] *Ibid.*, p. 156.

[18] Gellert, *op. cit.*, p. 6.

[19] *Ibid.*, p. 7.

The only mule with screamin' eyes
An' how that mule could kick.

Chorus:

Hi yi for your greenback
Hi yi for your change,
Hi yi for your money, good Lord,
An' don't you differ with me.

He kicked the feathers from the goose,
He broke the elephant's back,
He stopped the Texas railroad train
An' he kicked it off the track.[20]

At other times the animal is not strong but clever:

Rabbit is a cunning thing
Rambles in the dark,
Never knows what trouble is
Till he hears old Rover bark.[21]

This is the brilliant Brer Rabbit of Harris' Uncle Remus stories, who outsmarts those who have more physical power—just as the bourgeois fox, in the medieval and renaissance Fox and Wolf stories, made fools of the knights in the form of the greedy, stupid wolf.

Sometimes the animal and the Negro are equally tough:

Well as I was going across the field
Great big black snake took and bit me
    on the heel.
Turned around and give him a grin.
Son-of-a-gun took and bit me again.
Great God! you shall be free,
Just when the good Lord sets you free.[22]

The qualities which the Negro admires in the snake, and their connection with freedom, are not hard to dig out of these lines. To a thoughtless singer, the song is little more than humorous parody of a spiritual; to a reasonably perceptive one, it has several layers and relations of meaning.

The theme of freedom is a persistent one, among the animal songs and elsewhere:

If I had my rather, I rather be a
    squirrel,
I would curl my tail on top of my back
    and run all around this world.[23]

This is another of the common illustrations of ingenuity and compression in folksong—an example of the expression of "the Big" in little which Emily Dickinson might have admired.

Occasionally the tone of the animal songs is defeatist.

'Way down yonder in de fork ob de
    branch
De jaybird say he ain't got much
    chance.[24]
Way up yonder on the ole green lake
The bull frog died with the belly ache,
Just cause he had nothin' else to do,
Just cause he had nothin' else to do.[25]

Defiance, endurance, action, and heroism, however, prevail in theme and mood despite the seeming passivity of the much sung blues songs. Heroes are, of course, vital and creative in the lives of any struggling or oppressed people: heroes give youth models for action. The Negro people have been especially attracted to the little David

[20] "Sung by Negro guitar picker" in Choctaw County, Alabama. White, *op. cit.*, p. 157.
[21] White, *op. cit.*, p. 233.
[22] *Ibid.*, p. 139.
[23] *Ibid.*, p. 239.
[24] *Ibid.*. p. 243.
[25] *Ibid.*, p. 244.

who killed Goliath, to the Joshua who fought the battle of Jericho till the walls (of slavery or discrimination) came tumbling down, to the Moses who led his people to freedom, to the John Henry who drove railroad spikes faster than a steam pile-driver though the effort killed him, and latterly to the Joe Louis who beat Nazi Max Schmeling, and to that extraordinary many-sided "Renaissance" man Paul Robeson, who will not be silenced.

Sometimes the hero is real, sometimes magical-fantastic, sometimes a good fighter for justice, sometimes a "bad" anarchistic rebel, sometimes a mixture of these. A minor hero is the humorous boaster; and yet he is more than that—he is a symbol of power and defiance and endurance:

I was born about four thousand years
  ago,
Ain't nothing ever happened that I
  don't know,
I seen King Pharoe's daughter seeking
  Moses on the water,
I can lick the man that says that that
  ain't so.[26]

The ballad hero Stackalee[27] has great strength and magical powers and is sometimes comparable to the Devil as, for example:

The Devil hollered out "Breakfast"!
And the big chef he rung the bell . . .
But when they put corn-bread on my
  plate
That's when war broke out in Hell.
The Devil hollered out
What in the hell can be going wrong . . .

I had kicked away table
One mile and one-half long.
Now, big Devil, keep still;
Little devil, don't you even mumble
  a word . . .
I will be . . . a bigger devil
Than the Devil ever was.

I out with my pistol
And covered the whole darn lousy
  crew . . .
I'll kill you big Devil
And all your young ones too.
Now the keys to this palace
Is the only thing I want to see . . .
I'm going to make the Devil
Hand over this Hell to me.[28]

Of the types of Negro song the blues is perhaps the most "Negro," the most traditional and consistent and formal—certainly the least respected. Its well-defined form—its pentatonic scale, its clichés in melody and phrase, subtly modified by context or by slight change in wording, which are common characteristics of folksong—has not been recognized even by such serious students of Negro song as Dorothy Scarborough, who wrote: "One could scarcely imagine a convention of any kind in connection with this Negroid free music."[29] Her error has something in common with Sterling Brown's comment that "crudities, incongruities, of course, there are in abundance—annoying changes of mood from tragedy to cheap farce." However, he went on to say: "But at their most genuine, they are accurate, imaginative transcripts of folk experience, with flashes of excellent poetry." And he concludes that "these blues belong . . . to the best of folk litera-

[26] *Ibid.*, p. 146.
[27] See B. A. Botkin, *Treasury of American Folklore* (New York, 1944), p. 124.
[28] Curtis Jones, "War Broke Out in Hell," Vocalion 04520.
[29] Dorothy Scarborough, *On the Trail of Negro Folk-Songs*, (Cambridge, Mass., 1925), p. 78.

ture."[30] It is surely a mistake to think that good poetry can ever be a matter of occasional flashes of originality and brilliance: it is the concept of the poet-novice that new and lovely phrases are the soul of poetry. A poem is a system of relationships, an organism, and everything in poetry depends on context.[31] The effectiveness of blues imagery usually comes from variation of traditional phrases rather than from any sudden originality.

The meaning of the blues is perhaps no better understood than its formal qualities. One of the better statements of its content comes from Alain Locke: "The dominant blues mood is a lament, beginning in a sentimental expression of grief or hard luck, sometimes ending in an intensification of the same mood and sometimes turned to ironical self-ridicule or fatalistic resignation. Self-pity tends to dominate. But irony and bitter disillusionment also occur."[32] This is a perceptive comment, but it does neglect the context, the conditions of informal and self-censorship, the necessity for disguise, or the habit of disguise. The seeming surface of the blues is one of lament and self-pity, now and then laced with irony. But much of this sentimental surface is protective, while the irony is an outcropping of the hard metal beneath. The deeper content of the blues has been stated by a blues singer, in the presence of Alan Lomax: "The blues is mostly revenge." And a friend answered: "That's right. Signifyin' and gettin' his revenge through song."[33]

Here we have suggested something of the essential nature of poetry. The fantasies of poetry are seldom purely passive or escapist, but are psychological preparation for action. A human problem, no longer a puzzle or a mystery when it is defined in poetry, is solved in poetry symbolically or fantastically, and this gives the singer the hope and assurance to go forward in real life to an actual completion of the task. The blues outline and sharpen consciousness of suffering and injustice.

That devoted collector of Negro song, John A. Lomax, more than thirty years ago in an article of which he must surely have been critical later on, made self-pity a major quality of all Negro folksong. He thought it deeply tragic that "Over and over, from many angles, the Negro expresses his feeling of a race inferiority, and sings of what seems to be to his mind his badge of shame—his color."[34] In short, color seemed to Lomax another source of self-pity. The quotations he gives, however, suggest a different emphasis:

I wouldn't marry a black gal, she so
        black, you know,
When I see her comin' she look like a
        crow.[35]

Such lines do express, in part, and for some singers, a feeling of inferiority, but they are probably more often simple examples of that old phenomenon—transfer of hate from the oppressor to the most vulnerable object at hand, since striking back at the oppressor is dangerous. Lighter-colored people, at

[30] Sterling A. Brown, "The Blues as Folk Poetry," *Folk-say* (1930), p. 339.
[31] See Cleanth Brooks, "Irony and 'Ironic' Poetry," *College English*, IX (February, 1948), p. 232.
[32] Alain Locke, *The Negro and His Music* (Washington, 1936), pp. 32–33.
[33] From an address delivered before the New York State Folklore Society, April 3, 1948.
[34] John Lomax, "Self-pity in Negro Folk-Songs," *The Nation* (August 9, 1917), pp. 141–44.
[35] *Ibid.*

times, transfer and hide resentments against the usually even lighter group called "whites" by attacks on darker individuals; but this does not mean that there is not a deep sympathy among the colored peoples. At least one blues singer understands this whole pattern of color thoroughly, and expresses it with a magnificent force and compression:

> Now, if you're white, you're right;
> And if you're brown, stick around;
> But if you're black—
> Oh, brother, git back, git back, git back![36]

Diverse attitudes are expressed. On the one hand the blues declare:

> If I got to hate somebody, rather it would be
> Judge and Jury and mean bossman, not Poor Black Man like me.[37]

and on the other:

> "All the odds are against you—even your own people."[38]

A more characteristic theme of Negro song, especially of the blues, is the utopian one, and it overshadows the theme of color in these lines, also quoted by John Lomax:

> Well, I'm goin' to buy me a little railroad of my own,
> Ain't goin' to let nobody ride but de chocolate to de bone.[39]

In another blues we hear a similar kind of longing:

> I'm going to buy me a Lincoln
> Just about two blocks long.[40]

And here, too:

> I'm goin' get in my airplane . . .
> I'm goin' ride all over
> Your town.[41]

These lines obviously reveal frustration and desire for certain possessions; less obviously but just as definitely they reveal desire for freedom, and more subtly they reflect an ambivalent, contradictory view of the Negro's future, ironical recognition that such dreams are hopeless, mixed with a very real belief that the Negro is capable of and will wring from the world a fuller life.

Irony is the major intellectual trait of Negro song and of all folksong. Botkin says: "Irony is perhaps best illustrated in Negro songs of protest, in the double meaning of the blues and spirituals."[42] Typical, on a rather obvious level, are these lines, sung by Bessie Smith:

> I don't mind being in jail
> But I got to stay there so long.[43]

Understanding of the relation between illusion and reality, the ridicule of idle speculation, is excellently expressed thus:

> Ef a toadfrog had wings, he'd be flyin' all aroun',

[36] William Broonzy.
[37] Gellert, *op. cit.*, p. 15.
[38] From an address delivered before the New York State Folklore Society, April 3, 1948.
[39] *Op. cit.*, p. 144
[40] Frankie Jones, "My Lincoln," Vocalion 04204.
[41] Sleepy John Estes, "Airplane Blues," Decca 7354.
[42] B. A. Botkin, "The Folk-say of Freedom Songs," *New Masses* (October 21, 1947), p. 16.
[43] "Jail-House Blues," Columbia 81226.

Would not have his bottom boppin'
 boppin' on de groun'.[44]

Occasionally the realism of the Negro worker comes into more direct conflict with the illusion fostered by official optimism.

I went down to the depot; I looked
 upon the board;
It say: there's good times here, they's
 better up the road.[45]

Here we can see that despair in the blues is by no means limited to simple emotional cries like "Hard times!" and "Poor me!" This comment is mature. Personal hardship is extended into an ironic attack on the whole legend of American prosperity.

The irony of much Negro song has done its work of disguise too effectively. Rebellious songs seem sad, humble and defeatist. The irony is not apparent at first hearing in lines like these:

I have walked the lonesome road
Till my feet is too sore to walk . . .
I begs grub from the people
Whoo-well-well, till my tongue is too
 stiff to talk . . .

Anybody can tell you people
That I ain't no lazy man . . .
But I guess I'll have to go to the
 poorhouse
Whoo-well-well, and do the best I can.

I am what I am
And all I was born to be . . .
Ahh, hard luck is in the family
Whoo-well-well, and it's rolling down
 on me.[46]

If a man who is not lazy has to beg food till his tongue is stiff, the prosperous rulers of his world are neither benevolent nor competent; what society is rather than what the singer was "born to be," explains his troubles. That he should go to the poorhouse—the hopeless end of the road down-hill—and there do the best he can, is all irony.

Ironic parodies of spirituals also increase our understanding of Negro folksong, helping to correct the stereotype of the simple, childish Negro, though they are usually more obvious in meaning than the "straight" spirituals, ballads, blues, and simple lyric poems:

I want to go to Heaven and I want to
 go right,
 Oh, how I long to be there.
I want to go to Heaven all dressed in
 white,
 Oh, how I long to go there.
I want to go to Heaven at my own
 expense,
 Oh, how I long to be there.
If I can't get through the gate I'll
 jump the fence,
 Oh, how I long to be there.[47]

If you get there before I do, all right,
Just scratch a hole and pull me
 through, all right, all right[48]

White thinks that such mockery is just fooling, and insists that when the Negro

sings his "you shall be free" refrain to all sorts of nonsense stanzas and proclaims freedom to elephants, chickens, and spareribs in the same measure as to mourners, the refrain has long lost its original camp-meeting meaning of freedom from sin, and it

[44] Brown, Davis, and Lee, *op. cit.*, p. 327.
[45] *Ibid.*, p. 430.
[46] Peetie Wheatstraw, "Road-Tramp Blues," Decca 7589.
[47] White, *op. cit.*, pp. 109–10.
[48] *Ibid.*, p. 111.

is surely very far indeed from any connection with the Negro's hope for freedom such as most writers about the spiritual have been fond of ascribing to this and similar spiritual lines.[49]

Though this interpretation seems reasonable—and doubtless holds true for some singers, or for all at some times, since there is delight in nonsense and incongruity for their own sakes—the fact remains that there is a Negro song tradition of using nonsense and animal symbolism for disguise.

Over and over again we get this kind of comment:

Old massa he done promised me
When he died he gwine to set me
    free . . .

Chorus: Oh, mourner, you shall be
       free
      When the good Lord set you
      free.[50]

More open, yet still ironical:

I don't want to ride in no golden
    chariot,
I don't want to wear no golden crown,
I want to stay down here and be
Just like I am.[51]

Similarly, in lines more secular, the irony is even more obvious:

Ole massa sol' me,
Speculator bought me,
Took me to Raleigh
To learn how to rock candy.[52]

Thus we see that there is an ancestry in both the spirituals and in other slave songs for the irony of the more popular modern blues.

The maturity of thought in the blues is expressed in a variety of social ideas aside from those dealing directly with race, rebellion and freedom. Sterling Brown writes with some truth, and perhaps with some illogicality, that the blues "show a warm-hearted folk, filled with a naïve wonder at life yet sophisticated about human relationships."[53] Certainly Negroes have been wise in evaluating white promises:

Say, all right, you black man,
Won't forget you nohow:
Come around to see me
'Bout for——ty year from now.[54]

The same profound distinction between talk and action is expressed more generally: "May mean good, but he *do* so doggone po'."[55]

That particular piece of profound psychology which is the core of thousands of novels, plays, and stories is stated succinctly and without melodrama in the blues:

When you love a man, he treats you
  lak a dog,
But when you don't love him, he'll
  hop aroun' you lak a frog.[56]

Volumes of sociology often express less of American life than a few blues songs do:

[49] *Ibid.*, p. 131.
[50] *Ibid.*, p. 134.
[51] *Ibid.*, p. 144.
[52] *Ibid.*, p. 162. "Rock candy" was a dance-step like "Jump Jimcrow" or "Ball the Jack."
[53] Brown, *op. cit.*, p. 339.
[54] Gellert, *op. cit.*, p. 10.
[55] Brown, Davis, and Lee, *op. cit.*, p. 338.
[56] *Ibid.*, p. 329.

Workin' on the project,
What a scared man you know . . .
Because every time I look around
Whoo-well-well, somebody's gettin'
    a 304 . . .[57]

First time I got my 304
Whoo-well-well, the furniture man
    come and taken my furniture
    away . . .
My partner got his 304, too . . .
So you better look out,
Whoo-well-well, because tomorrow
    it may be you.

Workin' on the project,
That 304 may make you cry;
Workin' on the project,
That 304 will *make* you cry.
There's one thing sure
Whoo-well-well, you can tell that
    project goodbye.[58]

Though the meaning here is everything
and there are no pretensions to colorful
or literary language, the slight change
from "that 304 may make you cry" to
"that 304 will *make* you cry," with its
force and its subtle implications of a
whole social and psychological situation,
is an excellent example of the way that
folksong, by slight change of traditional
phrase, achieves its classical effects.
The same theme[59] is dealt with ironically ("She'll give me a piece of paper";
"But she didn't say when.") by Washboard Sam in "CCC Blues":

I'm goin' down, I'm goin' down
To the CCC . . .
I know that the WPA
Won't do a thing for me.

I told her my name
And the place I stay;

She say she'll give me a piece of paper,
Come back some other day. . . .

I told her I had no people
And the shape I was in;
She said that she would help me
But she didn't say when.[60]

Since striking imagery is a commonly
praised characteristic of the blues style,
a few examples will suffice:

Trouble never layin' dead on the
    bottom dis here Worl'.

* * *

I think a match box won't hold my
    clothes.

* * *

High sherrif man, huh, six feet chalk.

* * *

White folks and nigger in great Co't
    house
Like Cat down Cellar wit' no-hole
    mouse.

* * *

Money thinks I'm dead.

* * *

Standin' here lookin' one thousand
    miles away.

* * *

I'm goin' down South where de
    weather suits my clothes.

* * *

You can't look it down: steel's got to
    be drove.

Folksong, however, offers more than
flashes of wisdom and color. It would
be hard to miss the bitter beauty of
"Look Over Yonder," which Gellert
says is sung "With Resentment," though
the meaning is partly concealed. This is
poetry of a high order—intense, subtle,
filled with shadow and fire, reaching

[57] A "304" obviously was the number of a W.P.A. discharge form.
[58] Peetie Wheatstraw (The Devil's Son-in-Law), "New Workin' on the Project," Decca 7379.
[59] See also Big Bills "Unemployment Stomp," Vocalion 04378.
[60] Bluebird, B-7993.

out and forward in space and time:

> Look over yonder, huh,
> Hot burning sun turning over;
> Look over yonder, huh,
> Hot burning sun turning over;
> And it won't go down,
> Oh, my Lord, it won't go down.
>
> I was a-hamm'ring, huh,
> Hamm'ring away last December;
> I was a-hamm'ring, huh,
> Hamm'ring away last December;
> Wind was so cold,
> Oh, my Lordy, wind so cold.
>
> Can't you all hear them, huh,
> Cuckoo birds a-holl'ring;
> Can't you all hear them, huh,
> Cuckoo birds a-holl'ring;
> Sure sign of rain,
> Oh, my Lord, sure sign of rain.
>
> My little woman, huh,
> She keep sending me letter;
> My little woman, huh,
> She keep sending me letter;
> Don't know I'm dead,
> Oh, my Lord, I'm worse than dead.
>
> Sometimes I wonder, huh,
> Wonder if other people wonder;
> Sometimes I wonder, huh,
> Wonder if other people wonder;
> Just like I do.
> Oh, my Lord, just like I do.[61]

It need not be claimed that songs like this are superior to other kinds of lyric poetry, but they have their peculiar virtues. It is most important to note that they are larger and more complex than they seem at first glance. In "Promise of Victory: a Note on the Negro Spiritual," A. L. Morton has expressed the complexity and scope to be found in "simple" songs as no other critic has.

Of a "typical emancipation song" he says that:

> It is hardly possible to say whether it is death or freedom or freedom in death which is the subject.

In a very real sense it is all three, and this is what gives these songs their extraordinary richness and depth. We feel that they exist on several planes at the same time, that the singer is aware of an opposition, which cannot perhaps be logically resolved but which is resolved emotionally.

> ...In them misery and defeat and weariness and cruelty, and man's last and greatest enemy, the fear of death, have been fairly encountered and overthrown. They are a new *Pilgrim's Progress* composed in the more universal language of song.[62]

All Negro singers and listeners cannot have been the same in skill and perception. Singers are more or less sensitive, thoughtful, socially conscious, and professional—and so are audiences —though it is understood that there is an especially strong link between the folksinger and the folk audience.[63] Even the most isolated contemporary literary poet does not really work alone or create with any great originality—he uses language, forms, ideas, and emotions given him by others (past and present), adding his small but perhaps significant contribution through a new arrangement of forms, enveloping some new materials. The materials used by the Negro singer are not "pure"; the influence of white folksong has been considerable, although much stronger upon the words than upon the music. The artistic qualities of Negro folksong, though distinct, are not basically different from those of folk art in general.

---

[61] Gellert, *op. cit.*, p. 17.

[62] A. L. Morton, *Language of Men* (London, 1945), p. 99.

[63] See George Thomson, *Marxism and Poetry* (New York, 1946). pp. 7–8.

Folk art is a way in which working people of agricultural communities and of certain trades clarify their experience. The precise forms in which Negro song has been known and loved are disappearing. But they will make their contribution to a new democratic culture, which is developing now and will grow better:

At night when the world, it seem most
    dark,
I toss and moan the whole night long,
'Bout all the wrong,
I can't do nothing but get mad.

But when it come, the morning light,
Then I just know the sun will pour
On my back door,
It come some soon sweet day.[64]

[64] "No Breakfast," Gellert, *op. cit.*, p. 31.

Social Influences
on Jazz Style:
Chicago, 1920-30

CHADWICK HANSEN

If there were any hostility on the part of middle-class whites and Negroes toward blues as "devil songs," this was a mere drop in the bucket compared to the intense feelings of antipathy aroused by and toward jazz. The early association of jazz with crime and sin made it extremely difficult for jazz to make its way into the mainstream of American musical culture. The initial incredible bias against jazz on the part of "classical" musicians, music teachers, and Negro leaders—whose various accounts of the achievements of the Negro rarely, if ever, referred to jazz—has been well documented in great detail by Morroe Berger in his excellent essay "Jazz: Resistance to the Diffusion of a Culture-Pattern",
which appeared in the Journal of Negro History *in 1947. (For psychoanalytic insights into the white resistance to jazz, see Aaron H. Esman, "Jazz—A Study in Cultural Conflict,"* American Imago, *8 [1951], pp. 219–26, and Norman H. Margolis, "A Theory on the Psychology of Jazz,"* American Imago, *11 [1954], pp. 263–91.) It may be difficult for future generations to imagine the numerous editorials written in the 1920's alone protesting the evil influence of jazz and urging that it be stamped out.*

The prejudice against jazz did have an impact upon jazz musicians, especially those who were in the process of migrating from the South, e.g., New Orleans, to the North, e.g., Chicago. In the following fascinating essay by Professor Chadwick Hansen of the Department of English at the University of Minnesota, we see the familiar story told once more of how Negroes were brainwashed into rejecting their own culture, in this instance, true jazz. Fortunately, the charismatic magnetism and popularity of jazz proved too much for prejudice. Not only did jazz become the best known music in America, but it soon

Reprinted from *American Quarterly*, vol. 12 (1960), pp. 493–507, by permission of the author, *American Quarterly*, and the University of Pennsylvania. Copyright, 1960, Trustees of the University of Pennsylvania.

conquered Europe and other parts of the world. Part of the history of the acceptance of jazz as "real music" is delineated by Hansen. (For critical reaction to Hansen's essay, see Neil Leonard, Jazz and the White Americans: The Acceptance of a New Art Form *[Chicago, 1962,] pp. 108–9.) But for the full story, one must venture into the voluminous literature devoted to jazz.*

For discussions of the possible origins of the word "jazz," see Peter Tamony, "Jazz, the Word," Jazz: A Quarterly of American Music, *1 (October, 1958), pp. 33–42, and Fradley H. Garner and Alan P. Merriam, "The Word, Jazz,"* The Jazz Review, *3 (1960), reprinted as "Jazz—The Word," in* Ethnomusicology, *12 (1968), pp. 373–96. Tamony's view is that the origin may be French or French creole. "Chassé" is a traditional dance step term and a "chassé-beau" would be a "dancing dandy." From chassé-beau, it is not far to "jazzbo," a word in Negro slang meaning a fancily dressed, hip male. However, for alternative hypotheses including Arabic and African origins, see the survey by Garner and Merriam.*

For a sample of the enormous jazz literature swelled by the ranks of enthusiasts and buffs, see Rudi Blesh, Shining Trumpets, A History of Jazz *(New York, 1946); Marshall Stearns,* The Story of Jazz *(New York, 1956); Andre Hodeir,* Jazz, Its Evolution and Essence *(London, 1956); Alfons M. Dauer,* Der Jazz, seine Ursprünge und seine Entwicklung *(Kassel, 1958); Francis Newton,* The Jazz Scene *(New York, 1960); Nat Hentoff and Albert McCarthy, eds.,* Jazz *(New York, 1961); Martin Williams, ed.,* Jazz Panorama *(New York, 1964); Leonard G. Feather,* The Book of Jazz *(New York, 1965); and Gunther Schuller,* The History of Jazz, *vol. 1 (New York, 1968). For an entrée into the truly formidable jazz literature, see Alan Merriam,* A Bibliogaphy of Jazz *(Philadelphia, 1954); Robert George Reisner,* The Literature of Jazz: A Selective Bibliography *(New York, 1959); and Carl Gregor,* International Jazz Bibliography: Jazz Books from 1919 to 1968 *(Strasbourg, 1969).*

The discography of jazz is just as much of a maze as the bibliography of jazz. There are literally thousands of recordings, and it is not easy to keep track of them. Some of the many discographical aids include Charles Edward Smith with Frederic Ramsey, Jr., Charles Payne Rogers, and William Russell, The Jazz Record Book *(New York, 1942); Charles Delaunay,* New Hot Discography: The Standard Directory of Recorded Jazz, *edited by Walter E. Schaap and George Avakian (New York, 1948); Hugues Panassié,* Discographie Critique des meilleurs disques de Jazz, 1920–1951 *(Paris, 1951); Rex Harris and Brian Rust,* Recorded Jazz: A Critical Guide *(Harmondsworth, Middlesex, England, 1958); Brian A. Rust, comp.,* Jazz Records, A-Z, 1897–1931, *2nd ed. (Hatch End, Middlesex, England, 1962); Brain A. Rust,* Jazz Records, A-Z, 1932–1942 *(Hatch End, Middlesex, England, 1965).*

BEFORE THE First World War jazz was primarily a music of the southern Negro, and especially of the Negro in and around New Orleans. It was, in the southerner's disdainful and distasteful phrase, "nigger music": one component of a subculture that was thoroughly segregated, detested and exploited by the dominant culture. But during and after the First World War, during the "Great Migration" of Negroes to the North, jazz moved north as well, and Chicago, which attracted more Negroes than any other northern city in the

Mississippi Valley, soon replaced New Orleans as the center of the jazz world.

Migration to the North placed the Negro jazz musician in a social environment radically different from that in which his music had been formed. He was, to be sure, still a member of a minority group, a subculture, but the dominant culture in the North was open to him to an extent that would have been unthinkable in the South. Furthermore, it opened up to him the possibility of further change, the possibility of suppressing the traits of his own subculture and acquiring the traits of the dominant white middle class.

The result was a series of social pressures on the jazz musician, which, operating throughout the decade of the twenties, effected a marked change in jazz style. By 1930 jazz was a new music; many of its own traditions had been abandoned and were replaced by elements adapted from the popular music of the white middle class.

The most important of these social pressures was the Negro's own recognition that in moving north he had made one step toward escaping from a vicious and degrading social situation, and his desire to continue this escape, rejecting the hated past and replacing it with something better.

The old southern spirituals were full of escape images, after emancipation as well as during slavery: the gospel train, which would take you away from your present misery; the promised land, for which you were bound; the delivery of the Lord's anointed out of Egypt or out of the lions' den; the journey to "the city of refuge." Secular folksong and folklore as well were permeated by the theme of escape, as in the legend of Lost John: "hounds couldn't catch him . . . he's long gone, Lost John." This pervasive Negro folk motif found concrete realization in the Great Migration.

It must be admitted that many of the Negroes who came north during the First World War and the twenties found the city a lonesome and impersonal place, and many of them were occasionally homesick for old friends and old places, familiar cooking and familiar smells. The common term for the South among these people was "down home." Almost none of them went back down home, however, for with their nostalgia went too many bitter memories. Their South had not been the South of magnolia blossoms and the cool grace and proportion of Greek-revival plantation houses. Their South was a land of fear and hatred, dirt and disease, malnutrition, degradation and violence. In 1921 Chicago's Negro newspaper, the *Defender*, carried an article which began, "A letter came from Jelly Roll Morton, and in it he claims that the report of his death, which is raging throughout the civilized world and the South, is exaggerated."[1] Morton put lightly what he and others felt deeply. They had escaped from the South to civilization; they had found a city of refuge.

The Black Belt of Chicago's South Side, where jazz musicians of the

[1] The sources for my quotations from *The Chicago Defender*, in the order in which they appear in the text, are as follows: November 12, 1921, p. 7; January 21, 1928, part 1, p. 8; September 13, 1924, part 1, p. 6; April 30, 1921, p. 8; April 28, 1928, part 1, p. 8; April 7, 1928, part 1, p. 10; May 19, 1928, part 1, p. 11; February 25, 1928, part 1, p. 8; January 28, 1928, part 1, p. 8; February 28, 1928, part 1, p. 8; March 10, 1928, part 1, p. 8; May 12, 1928, part 1, p. 10; May 19, 1928, part 1, p. 10; April 24, 1920, p. 6; December 6, 1924, part 1, p. 1; June 4, 1921, p. 6. I wish to thank Mrs. Roi Ottley, librarian of the *Defender*, for her consistent courtesy and helpfulness.

twenties and their audience were located, would hardly seem like paradise to most Americans. But the words of an old blues say "I've been down so long that it seems like up to me." Even the Chicago Black Belt seemed like up, since compared to down home it *was* up. Futhermore, it brought the Negro to a place where he could see a world that was even further up: the world of the middle-class Chicago white man.

E. Franklin Frazier speaks of what the motion pictures represented to the southern Negro who saw them for the first time: "an undreamed world of romance and adventure."[2] The world of the motion pictures and the advertisements, the slick magazines and the sentimental song—the world of American popular culture—looks rather tawdry to some Americans. But to many of the inhabitants of Chicago's South Side in the twenties it had the glitter of the dimly apprehended golden streets of heaven. It lay beyond them, but since they had been able to make the step from a very real hell to the purgatory of the Black Belt they knew they might make this step, too, and many of them began to try.

The militant *Chicago Defender* had played an important part in the Great Migration in the entire Mississippi Valley area, by urging southern Negroes to move north.[3] And the *Defender*, which had given many southern Negroes their first picture of the advantages of the North, also gave its readers a picture of the world of white, standard, middle-class culture, the next step in race progress. Dave Peyton, who led one of Chicago's Negro bands and wrote a regular column called "The Musical Bunch" for the *Defender*, gave classic form to this picture when he wrote, in 1928, under the subheading "Opportunity,"

In Chicago an opportunity is offered musicians [i.e., Negro musicians] in another field [i.e., another field than jazz] and we must make good if humanly possible. Friendship must be cast aside. It is the reckoning hour for our musicians. We have ballyhooed along for the past 10 or 12 years fooling ourselves. We have played music as we think it should be played without trying to find out if we are playing it correctly. So few of us have the time to visit the grand symphony orchestras, the deluxe picture houses and other places where things musically are done correctly. . . . With the coming of the new Regal theater in Chicago, operated by a corporation of theatrical magnates who know just what it's all about, a new era is dawning upon Race musicians. In the pits of the deluxe houses things are done machine like. . . . The orchestra leader must register with the picture operator and every department in the deluxe house, directly under the orders of the stage director, must function their part in the cogwheel [*sic*]. . . . The opportunity is here, the door has opened for us, we have entered . . . let's make good.

This is a fabulous picture in the true sense of the word: a picture of a world of fable in which music is played "correctly," rather than the way in which Negroes think it should be played. It is a "grand" and "deluxe" world. Since a symphony orchestra was to Peyton

---

[2] E. Franklin Frazier, *The Negro Family in the United States*, revised and abridged edition (New York: Dryden Press, 1948), p. 92.

[3] For the *Defender's* role in the Great Migration see Emmett J. Scott, *Negro Migration During the War*, Preliminary Economic Studies of the War No. 16 (New York, 1920), pp. 29–33, or Chap. x "The Uneasy Exodus," of Roi Ottley's *The Lonely Warrior* (Chicago, 1955).

nothing more than a large orchestra that played from a written score, the "grand symphony orchestra" and the pit orchestra of the "deluxe picture house" are musically one and the same. Peyton has chosen technology as the most logical source for the imagery that enables him to construct a world of mindless efficiency directed by a "corporation of theatrical magnates who know what it's all about." Having entered this world, it is the business of the Negro musician to make good.

The compulsion to conform to socially approved standards is, of course, a characteristic of the Negro who is on his way up in American society. Frazier quotes an instance from an earlier time, of an ex-slave who had been almost completely unmanageable during slavery but took up the middle-class white man's virtues of sobriety and respect for property after emancipation:

Since he has been freed, he has grown honest, quiet, and industrious; he educated his children and pays his debts. Mr. Barrow asked him, one day, what had changed him so. "Ah, master!" he replied, "I'm free now; I have to do right."[4]

There is an instructive parallel between the two cases. In the process of advancing in social status neither Peyton nor the ex-slave has gained any real freedom of choice: they have gained instead barely enough equality so that they are permitted the opportunity to fit themselves into a cultural pattern established by the white man. Both have accepted cultural masters: the ex-slave, the man who was formerly his literal master; Peyton, the "corporation of theatrical magnates."[5]

Since the traditional New Orleans jazz style was clearly identified in the Negro's mind with the southern past he had rejected, since it was clearly unlike the white man's popular music that was played in theaters run by "theatrical magnates," the *Defender's* staff had few kind words for jazz.[6] They were, however, always pleased by the success of individual jazz musicians. They were proud that A. J. Piron's orchestra was employed in the more expensive white restaurants in New Orleans: "the successful achievement of Piron and his orchestra in the South is another milestone covered by the

[4] Frazier, p. 130.
[5] "Advancing the race" is so common a concept among American Negroes that Drake and Clayton use it as the title of Chap. xxii of *Black Metropolis.* The primary meaning of the phrase is, of course, simply advancing toward equal status, but it has been characteristic for Negroes to assume that any cultural differences between Negro and white are a hindrance to equal status.
[6] The *Defender* staff was not unique in this. Morroe Berger, in "Jazz: Resistance to the Diffusion of a Culture Pattern," *Journal of Negro History*, XXXII (1947), pp. 465–66, writes: "Leaders of Negro communities have spoken out against the influence of jazz. This is to be expected of those 'race leaders' who believe that Negroes can improve their status mainly by acceptance of the standards of the white community, which clearly disapproved of jazz as barbaric and sensual—characterizations which Negroes have tried to dissociate from themselves. . . . The treatment of jazz by Negro writers reveals that it is not considered the kind of cultural achievement of the race that ought to be mentioned or recommended. . . . The most prominent chroniclers of Negro achievement in America . . . scarcely mention jazz in their books." Mr. Berger is dealing with Negro leaders and writers in general. I have chosen to depend primarily on the *Defender* because it represented militant Negro leadership in Chicago in the twenties, and may therefore be expected to have exercised more immediate influence on jazz men than the similar national attitudes which are Mr. Berger's subject.

Negro musician." They were proud that Tony Jackson, the New Orleans pianist, had written popular tunes which were known outside the Negro community (one of them is the perennial *Pretty Baby*), and added that "it is said that there are many of the better grade [vaudeville] acts using numbers which were sold to them outright by him." They were proud of the individual musician who could stand out as a star: "Louis [Armstrong] is the only musician I know of who stops the ball, just as an actor stops a show."

The Negro community was proud of an outstanding individual like Armstrong, since to most white men Negroes were nameless nonentities. Negroes' names were a matter of supreme indifference even to some of the recording companies which sold their music. Ferdinand "Jelly Roll" Morton's name was spelled "Fred Morton" on one of his early records, and "Jelly Roll Marton" on another.[7] Sometimes the names might be absent altogether from the record label, or a pseudonym invented by a record company executive might be used.

If a Negro musician could make himself a star the record companies would use his name, and learn to spell it correctly: Morton's name was never misspelled on his later recordings. The name of a star meant money to the record companies, and it meant status to the Negro community. A man who made a name for himself in music was a race hero to the Negro community for the same reason that Jackie Robinson and Ralph Bunche are race heroes today: because names are generally reserved for white men.

Negro musicians on the way up wanted more than names, however. On April 7, 1928 Dave Peyton announced in his column that:

Fess Williams and his Jazz Joy Boys of the Regal theater made some fine recordings for the Vocalion records which will soon be released. Manager Jack Kapps[8] says this is the first "Sweet Record" our musicians have recorded and it was perfect. Heretofore, our orchestras have been making jazz and hokum numbers, but Fess insisted that if they wanted him to record he would have to be given the same breaks as the white bands were getting and that is making real sweet musical song and dance records. Good for Fess.[9]

---

[7] Rialto 535 and Paramount 12050. Since Paramount's executives were Negroes, this misspelling may be attributed to the middle-class Negro's contempt for jazz musicians. Paramount's tastes are clearly indicated in the following paean to musical propriety, taken from their 1924 catalogue: "Paramount is proud to offer you records by the celebrated soprano—Florence Cole-Talbert. She is the premier concert star of the Race, and is known to millions from Coast to Coast because of her concert tours of the United States. These records are undoubtedly the highest type of Race music sold today." Mrs. Cole-Talbert's records are Paramount 12096: *Homing* and *Swiss Echo Song*, accompanied by Sammy Stewart's Symphonic Orchestra, and Paramount 12187: *The Kiss* (*Il Bacio*) and *The Last Rose of Summer*, accompanied by the Black Swan Symphony Orchestra. This portion of the catalogue is reprinted in *The Record Changer*, September 1950, p. 11.

[8] This is, of course, the late Jack Kapp, later co-founder and president of Decca Records.

[9] This was not actually the first sweet record made by Negroes, but it was probably the first Peyton knew of. *My Oriental Rose*, recorded by Fletcher Henderson and his Orchestra in 1922, and issued on Black Swan 2022, is sweet enough for the most saccharine taste, and there may have been sweet records made by Negroes before this one. Peyton's ignorance of Henderson's early recordings may be explained by the fact that Henderson and Black Swan were in New York and Peyton in Chicago, and by the absence of national Negro communication media at this time.

Peyton praised Fess Williams' preference for sweet music over jazz again, a month later:

Fess and his boys are doing sweet numbers and are the first of our orchestras to get into the legitimate line. Heretofore our orchestras have confined themselves to hot jazzy tunes.

He spoke of his own theater orchestra as playing "first class standard music" and as "highly trained symphony players [who] will characterize the screen classics with symphonic music and offer from time to time standard overtures, animated by interesting stage characterizations." It must have pained him to admit that among his "highly trained symphony players" was jazz drummer Jasper Taylor, whose chief contribution was a "washboard specialty." He advised Negro musicians: "if you are now in a jazz band, do not give up the proper study on your instrument. You may be called upon to render real service and to play good music."

Peyton's conception of good music is most clearly stated in the two following quotations:

Jazz is on the wane, and the better class of music is coming back into favor with the critical public. . . . The country raves about Leroy Smith's orchestra and Fletcher Henderson's orchestra, both of New York. [Henderson, at this time, was half way between sweet music and jazz. He had started his career with a band that sounded like a white popular band. In 1923 he began adding jazz musicians, and began the process of combining sweet and jazz that was to make him one of the famous men of the swing style in the thirties.] They have the goods, they have the same quality of Lopez, Whitman [sic], Paul Ash, Dornberger and other prominent [white, successful, sweet] orchestras. They play together, they play even, they sound like an orchestra and no individual stands out above the ensemble, unless in solo rendition. Practice and direction has made this efficiency and that is what the majority of our orchestras need. To know Paul Whiteman is to understand at last the phenomenon of American jazz. Whiteman did not invent jazz—he specifically disclaims this—but he was the first to write an orchestral score for jazz, and from its inception ten years ago right to the present he has been its acknowledged chief exponent all over the world.

Peyton was not the only *Defender* writer to prefer the correct social status of sweet music to jazz. Indeed, he is typical of the writers on music, whether their articles appear on the entertainment page, in the general news, or on that traditional home of genteel journalism, the Woman's Page. The *Defender's* writers were generally not interested in music as such. They were interested in status, and, as a result, the *Defender's* coverage of jazz in Chicago is inadequate throughout the twenties. A historian who wanted to trace the careers of jazz men would find more information in the advertisements of night clubs, theaters and phonograph record companies than in the news columns. The news columns would tell him that a particular blues singer had a large and expensive wardrobe. They would tell him that a theater built for Negroes was lavishly decorated. They would tell him that a vaudeville performer had entertained the "elite" of New York City. In the early twenties they would tell him when Negroes made recordings, since in the early twenties this was still an unusual event. But "race records" included popular music as well as jazz, and since the *Defender* writers preferred the former, the historian would not find much material even here.

The music criticism he would find would not differ significantly from Peyton's. For example, under the heading "Soft and Slow" he would find the following, by an anonymous "admirer of C. W. [sic] Handy":

There is a vast difference between "Blues" and Jazz. The public is just beginning to learn the distinction. Many orchestra leaders who have assumed that the two forms of music were the same, and who have been prejudiced against Jazz, have recently taken up "Blues" and are glad to get the genuine article. . . . The most effective way to play "Blues" is the soft, slow, croony way, and . . . it is not necessary to be an acrobat to play this wonderful music.[10]

He would find a description of a pop concert under a New York dateline and the heading "Handiwork of Handy Lauded":

At the Metropolitan Opera House here Sunday afternoon Vincent Lopez [the leader of a popular sweet band] and his augmented orchestra of 40 selected soloists rendered a symphonic "jazz" concert, in which everything and every note known to music was featured.

The chief offering at this concert was a "tone poem" entitled The Evolution of the Blues, by W. C. Handy and Joseph Nussbaum, "with orchestral development by the latter and Vincent Lopez."

It is an ironic inconsistency that the Defender's staff preferred sweet music to jazz, for in its political and social policy the Defender was no friend of white middle-class gentility. The Defender followed the radical social position of W. E. B. DuBois, rather than the polite conservatism of the Booker T. Washington tradition. Yet one should not expect the music criticism of a Negro newspaper in the twenties to be consistent with its political and social criticism. The Negro who disliked the social assumptions of the white middle class still had good reason to dislike traditional jazz, since traditional jazz was part of the white stereotype of the Negro.

In Peyton's account of Fess Williams' sweet records, what pleased him most was that "Fess insisted that if they wanted him to record he would have to be given the same breaks as the white bands were getting and that is making real sweet musical song and dance records." It is quite true that the white world expected Negroes to stick to jazz and leave "respectable" music to the white man. Jazz, the blues, and the spirituals were products of the Negro community, and the white world has put a racial tag on all of them. And this identification of the Negro with music of Negro origin has been a serious barrier to the Negro musician who wants to perform popular or classical music. The Defender gives the history of one such man, Carroll Clark, who had recorded for a company run by whites. The company's policy had been that this man's picture

must not be identified with the finer ballads, but with the type of song which has come to be identified in the popular mind with the smart, sophisticated "coon" who furnishes us with ragtime and jazz. Mr. Clark, a cultured Negro, with a fine and well trained voice, naturally rebelled against the imposition of this demand that he cheapen his art and belittle his race, and left the employ of the white concern.

[10] Handy's own recordings show that he played the blues in a sweet, popularized, "soft, slow, croony way." See, for example, Aunt Hagar's Blues, by Handy's Orchestra, Okeh 4789, recorded in the early twenties.

This racial identification still persists today. For example, a Negro concert singer is expected to include a number of spirituals in his repertory. This is foolish, since the Negro uses the same concert arrangements of spiritual melodies as the white concert singer, and these arrangements are a far cry from the spirituals as they are sung by a shouting congregation. But the concert audience likes to get its spirituals from a Negro. The music carries a racial tag, and the Negro singer is expected to accept it.

Negro newspaper men were not, of course, the only Negroes who compared the rough, disturbing vitality of jazz unfavorably with the sugary "correctness" of popular music. The impact of popular standards may be seen very clearly in the tastes of jazz musicians as well. Louis Armstrong announced his fondness for Guy Lombardo on a number of occasions, and insisted that the men in his Savoy Ballroom band, in 1928, would never miss a Sunday night Lombardo broadcast.[11] These attitudes are not limited to the twenties nor to New Orleans jazz men. As late as 1943 Duke Ellington, one of the best of the swing musicians, wrote the following tribute to the producers of the insipid confections we call "semi-classical" music:

Then, there is the school of Kostelanetz, Morton Gould and Dave Rose, who work with a different type of instrumentation [different from the instrumentation of the swing band]. I think they're wonderful, and the things they turn out are gorgeous. The music is beautiful to listen to and wonderful to write. It's the kind of thing everyone wishes he could write, and what we'd all like to be working on. It's such majestic music! Dave Rose is very modern, almost futuristic. Strayhorn [Ellington's staff arranger], too, has some ultra-modern ideas. His ideas are way ahead of those being used by most of the others, but he is reluctant to write them, as am I. Dave Rose has gone ahead and thus, in a sense, pioneered the modern field.[12]

To call the music of Kostelanetz, Gould and Rose "majestic," and to speak of their derivative popularizations of the late nineteenth-century European tradition as "very modern" seems fantastic. Only the worst of Duke Ellington's music has approached the slick emptiness of these popular semi-classicists. It is fortunate that Armstrong and Ellington, no matter how hard they may have tried, have never been able to sound quite like Lombardo, Kostelanetz, Gould and Rose.

The impact of the standards of popular music on jazz musicians may also be seen in their curious contempt for the man among them who does not read music. Many of the best early jazz musicians could not read, or learned to read late and badly. This did not in any way diminish their excellence as performers of a music which has always been at its best when improvised or played in "head" (memorized) arrangements. Yet when *Down Beat* asked for comments on Kid Ory, the best that pianist Eddie Beal could produce as a compliment to one of the greatest of the New Orleans jazz musicians was this:

The thing that comes to my mind first when thinking of Kid Ory is that he is one of the very few musicians of his era that could

---

[11] See "The Sweetest Music . . . ," *The Record Changer* (July–August, 1950), p. 26.
[12] Duke Ellington, "Duke Ellington on Arrangers," *Metronome* (October 1943), p. 35.

actually read music. In other words, he was one of the very few real musicians.[13]

Benny Goodman has said that some of the better jazz men he knew in Chicago "were terrifically talented guys, but most of them didn't read."[14] And a trombonist I talked with in Washington, D. C. told me he thought Sidney Bechet was wonderful—he could listen to Bechet all night long—but Bechet was "no musician," because he couldn't read.

It is said that some of the best of the older New Orleans cornetists used to hold one hand over the fingers that were manipulating the valves, if they thought a rival was watching them, so that the rival could not steal their fingering, and thus steal their phrases. But since the twenties the test for "real" musicianship has become reading, a technique that every hack in the Guy Lombardo band is sure to possess.

Big Bill Broonzy is rebelling against this definition of reality in music when he says:

Some Negroes tell me that the old style of blues is carrying Negroes back to the horse-and-buggy days and back to slavery ... and they say to me: "You should learn, go and take lessons and learn to play real music." Then I will ask them: "Ain't the blues real music?"

Yet Broonzy himself partially accepts the common phrase when he says, of a musician who had some experience with popular music, "He knew more about real music than I did, but I knew more about the real blues."[15]

It *is* a definition of reality rather than a peculiar use of the word "real" that we are dealing with here, since the Negro jazz musician did feel that he was playing "music as we think it should be played" rather than "correctly," in Peyton's words. The Negro jazz man felt that he was living in a world of musical make-believe, playing "hokum," a term which was synonymous with jazz not only for Peyton but for Negro jazz men in general.[16]

Even when the question of "reality" is not involved, the jazz musician's sense of playing a stigmatized music may be summed up in his use of the word "legitimate." From the beginnings of jazz to the present, all jazz musicians have referred to the man who played the notes as he saw them in the score—either the popular or the classical musician—as a legitimate musician, and to the music he played as legitimate, and have referred to all jazz techniques as illegitimate. The white jazz man, as well as the Negro, has used this curious classification, since both have been aware that their music lacks the social approval and status granted to classical and popular music. Now that jazz is becoming respectable, this classification may die out, but the fact that it is still widely used is evidence of the extraordinary pressures the jazz musician has had to acknowledge,

[13] *Down Beat* (August 10, 1951), p. 19.
[14] Benny Goodman and Irving Kolodin, *The Kingdom of Swing* (New York: Stackpole Sons, 1939), p. 74.
[15] William Broonzy and Yannick Bruynoghe, *Big Bill Blues* (London: Cassell & Company, Ltd., 1955), pp. 4, 87–88.
[16] Johnny Dodds, the New Orleans clarinetist, used this word for his own music all his life (see Charles Edward Smith, with Frederic Ramsey, Jr., Charles Payne Rogers and William Russell, *The Jazz Record Book* [New York, 1942] p. 116).

pressures to stop playing jazz and start playing "correctly."

I have outlined, in the attitudes of the *Defender's* staff and in the attitudes of jazz musicians themselves, one of the socially determined pressures toward change in jazz style during the decade of the twenties: the Negro's own compulsion to reject a music identified in his mind with a degraded past, and to replace it with the socially respectable popular music of the white middle-class majority. But the new social environment of Chicago exerted external as well as internal pressures on the jazz musician.

For one thing, the audience for jazz was changing. Much of it consisted of Negroes who were on their way up in American society and beginning to identify with the dominant popular culture. Many of the whites who were becoming an important part of the jazz audience could not understand a music too radically different from the popular music they were used to, and preferred sweetened jazz to the unadulterated variety. And when more members of the audience wanted popularization, the musician, like any other professional entertainer, felt obliged to satisfy them. Richard M. Jones, a pianist and band-leader, announced at the beginning of one of his recordings, in a mock preacher's tone: "We are gathered here to give the public what it wants—and the public wants good first-class music— and we gonna give 'em *Dusty Bottom*

Blues."[17] Jones was recording in 1926, when his public was already beginning to want something quite different from *Dusty Bottom Blues*. Jones made almost thirty records during the twenties, but he made only five in the thirties, since by 1930 his taste differed too greatly from that of his public.

It was during the twenties that jazz really spread beyond the Negro community and became popular with America at large. Jazz men had, of course, been playing for some white audiences long before, but it was in the twenties that they acquired a truly national audience and found themselves a part of the national entertainment industry, subject to all its requirements. And it was in the twenties that entertainment first began to acquire the centralization and standardization that have made it an industry.[18]

There were always a few night club owners who liked their jazz unsweetened and managed to find enough local customers to stay in business. But many club owners, and most of the people who dealt with a national, undifferentiated mass audience—record company, radio and motion picture executives, and the agents of the national booking agencies—preferred the safety of a kind of jazz that was not too different from the standard product of the entertainment industry. The record companies will serve as an example. In the early twenties, when jazz records sold only to the Negro community and were listed

[17] Richard M. Jones Jazz Wizards, *Dusty Bottom Blues*, Okeh 8431.
[18] Some idea of the centralization within this industry may be gained from Irving Kolodin's statement in "The Dance Band Business: a Study in Black and White," *Harper's Magazine*, CLXXXIII (June, 1941), p. 72: "These three booking offices [the Music Corporation of America, the Willam Morris Agency, and the General Amusements Corporation] *are* the band business, and every leader knows it." Mr. Kolodin remarks on the same page that booking "is a business that has flourished for only two decades."

only in special "Race" catalogues, the record company executives were content not to meddle musically with this profitable sideline. But when jazz began to be listed in the main catalogue they could not afford to let it alone. The company has a far larger economic stake in a nationally distributed record than in a record sold to a limited audience. And the nationally distributed record must strike an average of mass taste rather than the clearly defined taste of a special group, since the company must sell a large number of records simply to get its money back. In order to make money it must produce a certain proportion of "hits," and while a really original record may occasionally become a hit it is much more apt to lose money. Therefore the standard product is the safe product.

The musician who succeeds in the entertainment industry, then, is the musician who will produce the required standard product. Louis Armstrong, defending himself against the charge of wasting his talent on trivial popular tunes, said, "They put a piece of music up in front of you—you ain't supposed to tell the leader 'I don't want to do this.' And I was brought up that way."[19] Notice that "the leader" here is not the bandleader, since Armstrong leads his own band, but a metaphor for the entertainment industry.

Finally, it should not be forgotten that all of these pressures toward popularization were supplemented by the constant presence, in northern Negro communities, of popular music itself. The twenties, when Negroes had moved to the cities en masse, was also the period when the American entertainment industry first began to achieve mass distribution. Every radio, every phonograph, every sheet music counter was a channel for the standard variety of popular music.

It is hardly surprising, given the radical changes in the Negro jazz musician's social attitudes and environment, and the resulting social pressures upon him, that the first major change in jazz style was toward the socially sanctioned popular music of the white man, more than a change proceeding from innovations within jazz itself.

A convenient date for the ending of the first jazz style and the beginning of the second is 1930. Certainly it was about this time that this socially-determined impact of popular music on jazz had its most dramatic musical effects.

These effects may be seen very clearly by comparing two of Louis Armstrong's records. The first, *Yes! I'm in the Barrel*, by Louis Armstrong and his Hot Five, was recorded in 1925.[20] The composer credit is given to Armstrong: this is a jazz tune rather than a popular song made over into jazz. The instrumentation is cornet, clarinet, trombone, banjo and piano, a traditional New Orleans instrumentation except for the omission of bass and drums, which may have been left out because neither could be recorded well in 1925. All of the musicians but pianist Lil Armstrong are from New Orleans. The record opens with a three-note, stop-time riff against which Armstrong constructs the lead. (A riff is a short melodic or

---

[19] From a broadcast of "The Dave Garroway Show," September 5, 1954.
[20] Okeh 8261, reissued on Columbia ML-4383. The "barrel" in the title is an abbreviation of "barrelhouse," a low-class bar.

rhythmic pattern, repeated with minor variations. The equivalent term in European music is "ostinato." Stop-time leaves one or more accents of the meter unstated. The lead is the main melodic line.) At the end of this passage there is a marked sense of released tension as the band abandons the riff for the traditional New Orleans improvised ensemble style. The third section, a solo by clarinetist Johnny Dodds with rhythm accompaniment, is followed by a final ensemble passage, broken only by two short breaks by trombonist Kid Ory and Armstrong.

The second record, *Star Dust*, by Louis Armstrong and his Orchestra, was recorded in 1931.[21] The tune is, of course, a popular sentimental song, which must be made over into jazz. The instrumentation is two trumpets, trombone, three alto saxophones, tenor saxophone, piano, banjo, bass and drums, a band smaller than most of the white sweet bands of the period, but a step in that direction, especially in the saxophone section. Less than half the men are New Orleans musicians. The record consists of three parts: a trumpet solo by Armstrong, a vocal solo by Armstrong and a trumpet solo by Armstrong, with short bridge passages by the band. Armstrong is in magnificent form, better as a soloist than on *Yes! I'm in the Barrel*, since he has time to develop his ideas. His inventive trumpet and his gravelly voice break the sentimental melody into little pieces, and from those pieces build something new and exciting. But listen to the rest of the band! It plays in close harmony, with the mushy timbre of the saxophones dominating the orchestral sound. Behind the trumpet solos it plays a dispirited two-note riff, failing utterly to achieve the tension of the stop-time riff produced by the Hot Five. Behind the vocal solo and in the bridge passages it plays an arrangement of the melody so sickeningly sweet and sentimental that this band could not be distinguished from Guy Lombardo's except for Armstrong himself and for the fact that his rhythm section can keep interesting as well as accurate time.

Jazz has always borrowed from popular music, but this is something more than borrowing, something more than the adaptation of a melodic phrase or a harmonic device to a jazz framework. Here the very basis for Armstrong's jazz solos is a great, sticky, unassimilated glob of musical sweetness.

Armstrong's *Star Dust* is music with a split personality, jazz and sweet combined in a tissue of contradictions, the half-marvelous and half-monstrous issue of the socially-forced marriage of popular music to jazz. It is still clearly jazz because of Armstrong's dominating role as soloist: a role that satisfied both the Negro community's desire for a race hero and the entertainment industry's desire for an easily identifiable star. But the jazz solo is placed in a startlingly inappropriate setting, in the slushiest musical vulgarity of which popular music is capable.

Surely the southern Negro made a real social advance to the extent that he became acculturated to white middle-class society, for in spite of the faults of the latter it is clearly preferable to the social disorganization and degrada-

---

21 Okeh 41530 (second master), reissued on Columbia ML-4386.

tion of the southern Negro's subculture. But since the Negro's jazz tradition was preferable to the popular music of the white middle class, the results of acculturation on the musical level were equally clearly unfortunate. Jazz at the end of the twenties was an unsuccessful mixture of two disparate musical traditions. Reconciling these traditions, synthesizing jazz and sweet, was the difficult business of the jazz musicians of the thirties, and the result of their synthesis was the music we call swing.

The Acculturation of the Delta Negro

SAMUEL C. ADAMS, JR.

Although many American Negroes did migrate from the rural South to the urban North and West, taking their music with them, there were obviously many who did not leave the South. The question may be raised, what happened to the folklore of those who stayed in the South? We know that the process of urbanization has affected the content and style of much folklore as well as attitudes toward folklore. What is less obvious are the changes which have occurred in the folklore of the southern Negro. The influence of the city is felt in part through the mass media. Records, radio, and more recently television have had an impact upon traditional folklore, and it can no longer be assumed that any group in the United States is really isolated, no matter where they happen to live.

In this brief study by Samuel C. Adams, Jr., former U.S. Ambassador to the Republic of Niger and presently the Assistant Administrator for Africa of the Agency for International Development, we learn about some of the specific shifts in attitude which are found in a community in the Mississippi Delta, the Delta being one of the very richest sources of traditional American Negro folklore. From actual field-recorded comments of informants, we gain valuable insights into Delta Negro views of folksong and folk religion.

THE IMPACT of city ways is affecting the folk heritage of Negroes on the King and Anderson, a Delta plantation, and in this process the influence is felt unevenly by the folk culture. A basic explanation lies in the differential factors associated with acculturation; this is found in the extent of acculturation already achieved as well as by the prestige and reward values accompanying the addition of new cultural traits.

In an effort to test this assumption,

Reprinted from *Social Forces*, vol. 26 (1947), pp. 202–5, by permission of the author and the University of North Carolina Press.

one hundred Negro sharecropper families on the King and Anderson plantation were studied. The locale of the community as well as the region of the Mississippi Delta, though not completely isolated, is not urban but is, at present, reacting to modern civilization or the culture of the city.[1] Clarksdale, Mississippi, the trade and culture center of this plantation area is the seat of urban influence, and from this city the influence of the outside world comes to the people.

Church activity represents the institutional behavior of the Negro; while folktales and folksongs, the spontaneous expressions. The data on the religious behavior were obtained from ministers, deacons, the churched and non-churched, and by participant observation. Data on folktales and folksongs were obtained through informal listening and recording of songs and tales; by interviewing the older and younger generations of the community. Information on their past and present preferences in the kinds of music, tales, and stories constitute the basis for what is to follow.

I

Negro folktales and folksongs were the literature of folk society. In the past the isolated world of the plantation gave an added significance to this type of expression. "Yes I can remember them old times," says one informant. "We just farmed, went to church, went visiting, stayed around home sitting by the fireside telling them old tales, and then that was just about all."

In this way of life custom was supreme, and hopes, fears, and frustrations expressed themselves in songs.

> Oh the time is so hard
> Oh the time is so hard
> Oh mother the time is so hard
> Oh Lordy the time is so hard
> Oh I'm going away
> Where the time ain't so hard

Sources of expressive behavior of the Negro were found in the immediate world of their religious and work life experience. The field hands moved back and forth, up and down rows of tall cotton stalks, and picked with nine-foot cotton sacks on their shoulders. They sang loudly and jubilantly all along the way: "Children, I got heaven on my mind. And it keeps me singing all the time."

Moreover, in the early days of the Delta plantations the rampages of the Mississippi River occupied a great deal of the time and attention of the plantation Negro. "Them floods came, and they'd sing when the work was going on. About anything. Sometime one person be singing one thing and pass by somebody else, and if it fitted how the other fellow was feeling or thinking he would pick it up; just like he be walking along—quit talking and start singing."

This former world of experience no longer exists, and this means that the condition which once fostered the development and maintenance of the folk literature is less effective. This has come about as a result of the breakdown of isolation, increase in literacy, in the growing importance of the press and other printed matter; the awakening interest of the people toward the movies,

[1] Louis Wirth, "Urban Society and Civilization," *American Journal of Sociology*, *XLV* (March 1940), p. 744.

the radio, the juke-box, and general city ways. The present-day Negroes on the King and Anderson plantation are ceasing to be a folk people.[2]

The "gang singing" is rapidly disappearing. Cotton pickers say now "Ain't got no time for no singin'." Moreover, the influence of mechanization is to make a man "not want to sing." A young informant emphatically states:

There ain't nothing about a tractor that makes a man want to sing. The thing keeps so much noise, and you so far away from the other folks. There ain't a thing to do but sit up there and drive.

Also, mechanization changes the content of songs:

Friend, I'm married unto Jesus
And we's never been apart
I've a telephone in my bosom
I can ring him up from my heart
I can get him on the air [radio]
Down on my knees in prayer

One of the consequences of the city life is the decline of the customary control on the one hand and the increase in the authority of the sheriff on the other hand. This secular authority is incorporated in a song:

When I was lying in Clarksdale jail
I seen a louse as long as a rail
Cut off his head nine feet from his tail
And still he was long as a ten foot rail
Hard times, po' boy
Hard times, po' boy

Old Capt. Quinn I most all forgot
He's the meanest old white man we
    had in the lot

For $5.00 he'd run you right well
For $25.00 he'd run you to hell
Hard times, po' boy
Hard times, po' boy

The tales which flourish today on the plantation are mainly the worldly stories. These stories have their place in the new scheme of living, peculiar to the younger generation. The fact that on the plantation the stories about Hitler and other international characters exist, shows clearly that the plantation is no longer an isolated world.

The spirituals can no longer be said to be the natural expression of the mind and the mood of these plantation Negroes of today, for the natural idiom of the Negro proletarian, the blues, is used to express the mood of the present. In the past the plantation Negro sang of "Pearly Gates and Golden Slippers," now the plantation Negro sings:

I'm just a po' cold nigger
Me and the white man and the boll
    weevil
All living off of cotton
The white man and the boll weevil

All getting fat
And here's po' me
I ain't got a dime
I'm just a po' cold nigger

The plantation Negro knows that "he has a place" in the city and with this awareness he delights in telling stories or reciting poems that show the Negro "besting the white man." There is an evidence of growing race consciousness on the part of the Delta Negro:

[2] Specifically, the facts: 50 families have radios; 30 are subscribers to urban newspapers; 28 out of the 100 families reported that some members of the families go to Clarksdale at least once in every two weeks, while the remaining 72 families go three times a week; 30 families have automobiles; most all the plantation families frequented the movies, the juke joints, special city events, and expressed attitudes of the felt prestige of the civilization of the city. These are regarded as measures of the degree of participation in urban life.

Think something of yourself you
    crazy dunce
No matter if you was a slave once
Every nation done been a slave once
They didn't draw up and act a dunce
Think because you a nigger
You just can't get no bigger

With the rise of race consciousness
among Negroes, songs not only became
less expressive and spontaneous, but the
songs seem to have some purpose other
than mere expression. Some of the purposes are to ridicule whites, or to make
subtle protest against the bulwark of
racial segregation; others to stimulate
racial pride. Judging from the reasons
given for preferring Negro music one
can see clearly the growing race consciousness.[3] A youngster who frequents
the movies of Clarksdale says:

I just like it best cause I can't get nothing
out of what no white man do; but boy I get
a thrill out of what the colored do. Because
that's one thing they can do better'n white
folks. Sometimes I have the radio on and
hear whites and turn it off.

Likewise, Sue Flowers, one of the active
members of the plantation church,
comments:

I like Negro music the best. Heard that
before I ever heard any other, and I'm
used to it and can enjoy it the best. It seems
to me like praising God through my own
color, and I loves my color and I'll go further to praise them than whites. Ain't nothing no white man do sincere.

Today when a plantation Negro
sings he is more likely to sing a popular
song than a spiritual or folksong. Of
the kinds of songs known by Negro
sharecroppers on this Delta plantation,
approximately 47 percent are popular

songs, and 19 percent, spirituals; 30
percent, church hymns; 4 percent,
work songs.

Although both the younger and older
generations are familiar with popular
songs, the former is far more acquainted
with them than the latter. Of the favorite
songs of the older generation nearly
29 percent were popular songs (songs
definitely other than church or religious
songs); 32 percent hymns, 22 percent
spirituals; 14 percent blues; and 2
percent lullabies and work songs. In
contrast, the younger generation listed
more than twice the number of blues as
given by the older generation: 30 percent
blues as favorites, and 38 percent other
popular songs; 8 percent hymns; 22
percent spirituals; and 2 percent work
songs.

These findings would indicate that
the folktales and folksongs are now
showing the effect of juke-boxes, radios,
and movies on spontaneous expression.
It shows, further, that as acculturation
advances, the less prestige value folk
expressions seem to have. This is evidenced by noting that the plantation
people chose as favorites more songs
which definitely had no local origin.
Thus, the extent of acculturation can
be explained not only by the prestige
and reward values accompanying new
cultural traits, but by the fact that the
urban cultural traits had opportunity
to spread, came to be needs, and are
now appreciated.

II

The investigation of church activity,
likewise, reveals the effect of the impact

---

[3] It should be noted that these subjects have little idea as to Negro music, but the fact that they
conceive of certain music as being "Negro music" is an important expression of race consciousness,
racial identity, and loyalty.

of civilization on rural Negro life. This process reflects itself not so much in the further incorporation of the white man's religious rituals and practices as in the disorganization of the Negro plantation religious life. The church was irrefutably the center of Negro plantation life, for it was the socially accepted channel through which the people gave formal expression to their religious and social emotions. So compelling was the desire to express their religious emotions, that the people came together wherever they could; they assembled in the seed house, in the barns, and in any other available building on the plantation.

But as the Negro feels the impact of city ways, there emerges in the community a duality of attitudes toward the church and minister. Everywhere there is the growing pervasive skepticism of the pretentiousness of the church, the declining authority of the church and minister, and the growing disinterested attitudes of plantation youth toward things religious and sacred. The younger generation are largely indifferent either as to the necessity of joining the church, or, if they are already members, as to the "putting out" of the church. Their comments and stories ridicule ministers.

Some of the ministers in the Delta are aware of the secularizing influence of the city. Others, though few in number, try to reverse the inevitable change by stressing the values of the traditional way of life. One of them is reported to preach sermons against formal education: he points out to the congregation how much better things were in the past, "when men and women wasn't out searching for idolatry and education." Another minister likened an educated person to a mad dog, against

which the community had to arm itself. Once when a country agricultural agent tried to improve the quality of the hogs within the area by new breeding, a minister replied by choosing as his sermon topic "Blood Don't Make Meat."

In a feeble effort to stem this inevitable tide, or to swim with it, some ministers are adopting secular means. But this causes conflict within the church. Some innovations are felt to mean a decline in the spiritual values of the church; especially is this true of the older generation. Matilda Mae Jones, fifty years old, reveals her attitude of disgust toward the changes. She says:

Songs they sing in church now feel like fire burning. What do I mean? Well that's how I feel. You know how fire burns; all fast and jumpy, and leapy like. Well that's just the way these swing church songs are now. Yes sir, most churches now call themselves getting on time or something the other. Getting so some churches got people that don't pray like they used to. Praying, I'm telling you, seem to be getting out of style. Just now, they got the Lord's prayer set to notes. Long time ago people used to sing, rock, and moan. Call that "rocking Daniel"; but now they only want you to rock when you rock up to put that money down. They done put a new touch on "Give Me That Old Time Religion," and now they got it in another tune. They don't have no time to bring up "Hallies" like, "I'm Going Home on the Morning Train, The Evening Train May Be Too Late." The other day, the church lasted all the day, but that wasn't with preaching and singing. They was trying to get money.

On the other hand, the younger generation favors these changes.

Even the church entertainment shows a considerable degree of urban influence. Churches sponsor "Heaven and Hell" parties, to go to which—according to one informant,

You buys a ticket, which tells you which a way you'll be going: to Heaven or to Hell. No you can't go to both of them. I guess you got to do what the ticket says. Well, if you gets a ticket to Heaven, they serves you ice cream and cake, and you just sits around and talks and play games. However if you gets a ticket to Hell, they serves you hot cocoa, and red hot spaghetti, and they dance, play cards, checks, and do most anything.

The fact that more plantation families belong to the burial association than to the church may be regarded as significant. A sociological import lies in the fact that the burial association is a secular institution. Sue Sampson's account may be considered as an indication of the present trend. She says:

I really think it's better to belong to it than the church. Members have to be particular about one another's wives and husbands. You see, you can give a person laws when he's going to the church but the lodge is the thing when it comes to compelling you to stick to your laws.

Now I can tell you in just about a summary way what the lodge means to me. The other night an old sad-looking woman pinched me, and I was so mad, I wanted to kill her. If she just hadn't been a lodge member and just a church member to me, I probably would have. But I couldn't do a thing cause she was a member of the lodge. So I just smiled and acted kind of nice.

With the increasing participation in urban life, the mental horizon of the people is slowly expanding. George Johnson, a 63-year-old Delta plantation Negro, who has been on the plantation all of his life as a sharecropper, now has radio. He has learned to read and expresses rather articulately the effect of literacy on traditional religious notions. He says:

There ain't nothing I can do about this unfair life here, but I got my God and my kind of God allows for all things to be right. I don't believe that God is a person. I just don't. Most folks see God all up in the sky with the stars. I used to see him as a gray-haired old man. People long time ago took things they thought rather than what they knew. Now I learned all this like I told you. I just been to the sixth grade, but I ain't stopped learning yet. Yes sir, I learned all this in a book called *The Miracle Power*. There ain't no such thing as seeing a ghost. God is the spirit. I been having some books here that explains all about the stars and I know that God isn't a gray-haired old man sitting up there.

The impact of civilization and the resulting changes in church, minister, and religious behavior in general can be summarized as follows: new forms of ridiculing ministers; declining rates of attendance; greater emphasis upon pecuniary and secular values than upon the spiritual life of the community; and, the substitution of other activities for the past all inclusive functions of the church. These factors indicate that the church is no longer the vital institution. Owing to the fact that there exist vested interests, the rigidity of sentiments and habits, social and cultural sanctions of its institutional role, the old plantation church tends to resist present forces of cultural change. There is, therefore, the wide gulf between the attitudes and the traditional religious values.

III

The foregoing discussion indicates that acculturation is in evidence in the Delta. The acquiring of new culture traits means change in the attitudes, sentiments, and values of the people who make these new traits as vital parts of their daily activities. It is a widely recognized fact that a well established institution resists innovations. Conflict is thus inevitable.

It seems apparent that under the conditions of racial discrimination the religious practices of the plantation Negro are not subject to great change. Moreover, in the cultural conflict situation there is very little prestige to be had by incorporating more of the white man's religious cultural traits, while, on the other hand, in other areas of Negro plantation life, there are yet prestige and reward values accompanying the acceptance of new cultural traits from the city. A hypothesis here proposed is that the acculturation of an excluded group will take the form of a S-curve. In other words, there is a period of rapid incorporation of alien traits in the beginning but this process slows down when group conflict becomes evident. As the group becomes articulate in its protest against caste or other limitations, the members begin to create its own history and group loyalty.

FOLK NARRATIVE

Just as important as the songs of a people are the stories of that people. In traditional narrative forms, the various adventures of popular folk heroes are set forth. The details of these adventures and the particular lifestyles of these folk characters can very often be extremely important sources for an understanding of the values of a people. What kind of a character is Brer Rabbit? What kind of a character is John Henry? Is there anything in common between a small rabbit and a large steel-driving man? They are two of the folk characters whose exploits are celebrated in American Negro folk narrative.

"Folk narrative" is being construed here in a broad sense. Accordingly, there are narrative forms considered other than the more conventional genres of *folktale* and *legend*. For example, family legends or "memorates" represent an important form of American Negro folk narrative. "Memorate" is a technical folkloristic term intended to designate narratives related by individuals about a purely personal experience of their own. Every family has its share of memorates which may be told whenever and wherever families get together for reunions. Occasionally, specific memorates may become known outside the original family circle, and they may in time become local legends. However, the majority of memorates never leave the intimate limits of the family about whom or one of whose members the events allegedly refer. In any case, memorates are part of American Negro folk narrative even if they are not considered as often as are the well-known animal tales and the tales of "John and Old Marster."

Uncle Remus
& the Malevolent Rabbit

BERNARD WOLFE

    There is no doubt that the most common form of folk narrative is the folktale. American Negro folklore is especially rich in folktales, and of these folktales, none are more celebrated than the adventures of Brer Rabbit. Much of the fame of Brer Rabbit is credited to Joel Chandler Harris, an Atlanta newspaperman, whose collections of Uncle Remus stories are known in many parts of the world.

    Unfortunately, the enjoyment of Brer Rabbit stories has been somewhat threatened by the particular literary context employed by Harris. The context consists of a faithful "Uncle Tom" Negro telling amusing stories for the little white boy, son of the plantation owners. Clearly, this painful reminder of slavery times in which a grown Negro man is depicted as the playmate or nursemaid of a "boy" is offensive to contemporary American Negroes and some whites. Because of this, the Joel Chandler Harris collections of Negro tales are not used in some racially mixed elementary schools. The sad thing about this is that as a result of the official or voluntary ban against Uncle Remus, black children may grow up deprived of a knowledge of the marvelous rabbit trickster figure, a figure who ranks with the finest inventions of the folk imagination ever created. One must keep in mind that Joel Chandler Harris did not invent Brer Rabbit or the stories about him. The tales existed long before Harris was born. He simply told the tales, and, as a matter of fact, he re-told them—still another reason why his versions of the tales should not be the ones used in schools.

    Anyone seriously interested in learning about Brer Rabbit should consult the numerous tales collected from Negro informants by folklorists. In other words, one should go back to the source, that is, to the folk, and not rely upon literary reworkings of folktales. Merely banning Joel Chandler Harris and not

Commentary, vol. 8 (1949), pp. 31–41. Copyright © 1949 by American Jewish Committee, reprinted from *Commentary* per permission of *Commentary* and the Harold Matson Company, Inc.

replacing his works with authentic versions of folktales would seem to be a case of throwing out the baby with the bathwater. Brer Rabbit is a vital, dynamic part of the American Negro folk heritage and his delightful exploits deserve a wide audience.

In this unusual essay, Bernard Wolfe brilliantly describes the marked contrast between the white racist context of the Uncle Remus storytelling context and the essentially protest, anti-establishment orientation of the tales themselves. If one accepts the details of Wolfe's analysis, one is tempted to doubt that Joel Chandler Harris fully understood the meaning of the tales he genuinely loved and tried to preserve. Wolfe points out that in the white European trickster cycle, the central character is the fox, and that in American Negro tradition, the fox has been replaced by the rabbit. In fact, the fox is quite often the dupe in American Negro tradition. In the light of his analysis, Wolfe might have pointed out that this makes good sense. If a Reynard type fox is the white trickster figure, then what better form of symbolic protest than to have the Negro rabbit trickster dupe the white fox. Cunning though the fox may be, he is no match for the ingenious rabbit!

One final point is that the essay illustrates once again the familiar result which occurs when a white man reports Negro folklore, namely, bias. It is probably true that whenever the culture of people X is described by a member of culture Y, there will almost inevitably be bias in that description—though surely there would also be bias if people X were described by a member of their own society. Wolfe's essay suggests that if a white man collects Negro folklore, the final result is likely to reveal as much about white values as about Negro values! In this instance, the utilization of American Negro folklore by Joel Chandler Harris is but one of a long line of white exploitations of Negro folklore (cf. composer Stephen Foster's "borrowing" of American Negro folk melodies). On the other hand, had Joel Chandler Harris not been interested in Negro folklore, one of the great stimuli to collectors of Negro folktales would have been absent, and many of the collections of tales inspired by Harris' efforts might never have been made.

For studies of Joel Chandler Harris, see Julia Collier Harris, The Life and Letters of Joel Chandler Harris *(Boston, 1918); Julia Collier Harris,* Joel Chandler Harris: Editor and Essayist *(Chapel Hill, 1931); Stella Brewer Brookes,* Joel Chandler Harris: Folklorist *(Athens, Georgia, 1950); and Paul M. Cousins,* Joel Chandler Harris *(Baton Rouge, 1968). For samples of the scholarship devoted to the Uncle Remus tales, see John Stafford, "Patterns of Meaning in* Nights with Uncle Remus," American Literature, *18 (1946), pp. 89–108; and Louise Dauner, "Myth and Humor in the Uncle Remus Fables,"* American Literature, *20 (1948), pp. 129–43. For analyses and rejections of the Uncle Remus stereotype, see F. C. Campbell, "An Ontological Study of the Dynamics of Black Anger in the United States,"* New South, *21, no. 2 (Spring, 1966), pp. 29–35, and Darwin T. Turner, "Daddy Joel Harris and His Old-Time Darkies,"* The Southern Literary Journal, *1 (1968), pp. 20–41.*

AUNT JEMIMA, Beulah, the Gold Dust Twins, "George" the Pullman-ad porter, Uncle Remus. . . . We like to picture the Negro as grinning at us. In Jack de Capi- tator, the bottle opener that looks like a gaping minstrel face, the grin is a kitchen utensil. At Mammy's Shack, the Seattle roadside inn built in the shape of a minstrel's head, you walk into the neon grin to get your hamburger.... And always the image of the Negro—as we create it—signifies some bounty—for us. Eternally the Negro gives—but (as they say in the theater) *really gives*—grinning from ear to ear.

Gifts without end, according to the billboards, movie screens, food labels, soap operas, magazine ads, singing commercials. Our daily bread: Cream O' Wheat, Uncle Ben's Rice, Wilson Ham ("The Ham What Am!"), those "happi-fyin'" Aunt Jemima pancakes for our "temptilatin'" breakfasts. Our daily drink, too: Carioca Puerto Rican Rum, Hiram Walker whiskey, Ballantine's Ale. Through McCallum and Propper, the Negro gives milady the new "dark Creole shades" in her sheer nylons;

through the House of Vigny, her "grotesque," "fuzzy-wuzzy" bottles of Golliwogg colognes and perfumes. Shoeshines, snow-white laundry, comfortable lower berths, efficient handling of luggage; jazz, jive, jitterbugging, zoot, comedy, and the wonderful tales of Brer Rabbit to entrance the kiddies. Service with a smile.... *

"The Negroes," writes Geoffrey Gorer, "are kept in their subservient position by the ultimate sanctions of fear and force, and this is well known to whites and Negroes alike. Nevertheless, the whites demand that the Negroes shall appear smiling, eager, and friendly in all their dealings with them."

But if the grin is extracted by force, may not the smiling face be a false face—and just underneath is there not

---

* There is a vast literature devoted to the white stereotype of the Negro. Of course, most of such stereotypes belong to white folklore, not Negro. On the other hand, it would be wrong to assume that Negro folklore has not been influenced by white stereotypes of Negroes. This is one of the issues debated by Hyman and Ellison earlier in this volume. In any event, the fact that Negro folklore such as the trickster tales of Brer Rabbit was initially collected by whites makes consideration of white stereotypes of Negroes very relevant. For representative samples of analyses of white stereotypes, see Sterling A. Brown, "Negro Character as Seen by White Authors," *Journal of Negro Education*, 2 (1933), pp. 180–201; R. Blake and W. Dennis, "The Development of Stereotypes Concerning the Negro," *Journal of Abnormal and Social Psychology*, 38 (1943), pp. 525–31; Guy B. Johnson, "The Stereotype of the American Negro," in Otto Klineberg, ed., *The Characteristics of the American Negro* (New York, 1944), pp. 3–22; Edgar Rogie Clark, "Negro Stereotypes," *Journal of Negro Education*, 17 (1948), pp. 545–49; Edgar A. Toppin, "The New York *Times*'s Idea of Humor about the Negro in the Early Part of the Twentieth Century," *The Negro History Bulletin*, 14, no. 9 (June, 1951), pp. 205–6; Lawrence M. Bott, "A Summary of 'The Negro' as Portrayed in *Harper's Magazine*, 1901–1924," *The Negro History Bulletin*, 14, no. 9 (June, 1951), pp. 208–9, 211–12, 216; Cecil L. Patterson, "A Different Drum: The Image of the Negro in the Nineteenth-Century Songster," *College Language Association Journal*, 8 (1964), pp. 44–50; Seymour L. Gross and John Edward Hardy, eds., *Images of the Negro in American Literature* (Chicago, 1966); Roger D. Abrahams, "The Negro Stereotype: Negro Folklore and the Riots," *Journal of American Folklore*, 83 (1970), pp. 229–49; and Roger D. Abrahams, *Positively Black* (Englewood Cliffs, 1970). There are also Negro stereotypes of whites, for example, see Tilman C. Cothran, "White Stereotypes in Fiction by Negroes," *Phylon*, 11 (1950), pp. 252–56, and the same author's "Negro Conceptions of White People," *American Journal of Sociology*, 56 (1951), pp. 458–67. Finally, the reader should realize that there are not only stereotypes, but also stereotypes of stereotypes. In other words, there are Negro conceptions of what the white stereotype of the Negro is and these conceptions may or may not coincide with the actual white stereotype of the Negro. Similarly, there are white notions of what the Negro stereotype of white people is. The point is that stereotypes and "stereotypes of stereotypes" seriously impede better race relations, and it is for this reason that stereotypes need to be clearly delineated and labeled as such. —Ed.

something else, often only half-hidden?

Uncle Remus—a kind of blackface Will Rogers, complete with standard minstrel dialect and plantation shuffle—has had remarkable staying power in our popular culture, much more than Daddy Long Legs, say, or even Uncle Tom. Within the past two years alone he has inspired a full-length Disney feature, three Hit Parade songs, a widely circulated album of recorded dialect stories, a best-selling juvenile picture book, a syndicated comic strip. And the wily hero of his animal fables, Brer Rabbit—to whom Bugs Bunny and perhaps even Harvey owe more than a little—is today a much bigger headliner than Bambi or Black Beauty, out-classing even Donald Duck.

For almost seventy years, Uncle Remus has been the prototype of the Negro grinner-giver. Nothing ever clouds the "beaming countenance" of the "venerable old darky"; nothing ever interrupts the flow of his "hearty," "mellow," "cheerful and good-humored" voice as, decade after decade, he presents his Brer Rabbit stories to the nation.

But Remus too is a white man's brainchild: he was created in the columns of the Atlanta *Constitution*, back in the early 1880's by a neurotic young Southern journalist named Joel Chandler Harris (1848–1908).

When Remus grins, Harris is pulling the strings; when he "gives" his folk stories, he is the ventriloquist's dummy on Harris's knee.

The setting for these stories never varies: the little white boy, son of "Miss Sally" and "Mars John," the plantation owners, comes "hopping and skipping" into the old Negro's cabin down in back of the "big house" and the story-telling session gets under way. Remus's face "breaks up into little eddies of smiles"; he takes his admirer on his knee, "strokes the child's hair thoughtfully and caressingly," calls him "honey." The little boy "nestles closer" to his "sable patron" and listens with "open-eyed wonder."

No "sanctions of fear and force" here, Harris insists—the relationship between narrator and auditor is one of unmitigated tenderness. Remus "gives," with a "kindly beam" and a "most infectious chuckle"; the little boy receives with mingled "awe," "admiration," and "delight." But, if one looks more closely, within the magnanimous caress is an incredibly malevolent blow.

Of the several Remus collections published by Harris, the first and most famous is *Uncle Remus: His Songs and His Sayings*. Brer Rabbit appears twenty-six times in this book, encounters the Fox twenty times, soundly trounces him nineteen times. The Fox, on the other hand, achieves only two very minor triumphs—one over the Rabbit, another over the Sparrow. On only two other occasions is the Rabbit victimized even slightly, both times by animals as puny as himself (the Tarrypin, the Buzzard); but when he is pitted against adversaries as strong as the Fox (the Wolf, the Bear, once the whole Animal Kingdom) he emerges the unruffled winner. The Rabbit finally kills off all three of his powerful enemies. The Fox is made a thorough fool of by all the weakest animals—the Buzzard, the Tarrypin, the Bull-Frog.

All told, there are twenty-eight victories of the Weak over the Strong; ultimately all the Strong die violent deaths at the hands of the Weak; and there are, at most, two very insignificant

victories of the Strong over the Weak.
. . . Admittedly, folk symbols are seldom
systematic, clean-cut, or specific; they are
cultural shadows thrown by the unconscious, and the unconscious is not governed by the sharp-edged neatness of the
filing cabinet. But still, on the basis of
the tally-sheet alone, is it too far-fetched
to take Brer Rabbit as a symbol—about
as sharp as Southern sanctions would
allow—of the Negro slave's festering
hatred of the white man?

It depends, of course, on whether
these are animals who maul and murder
each other, or human beings disguised
as animals. Here Harris and Remus seem
to differ. "In dem days," Remus often
starts, "de creeturs wuz santer'n 'roun'
same like fokes." But for Harris—so
he insists—this anthropomorphism is
only incidental. What the stories depict,
he tells us, is only the "roaring comedy
of animal life."

Is it! These are very un-Aesopian
creatures who speak a vaudeville dialect,
hold candy-pulls, run for the legislature,
fight and scheme over gold mines, compete for women in elaborate rituals of
courtship and self-aggrandizement, sing
plantation ditties about "Jim Crow,"
read the newspapers after supper, and
kill and maim each other—not in gusts
of endocrine Pavlov passion but cold-
bloodedly, for prestige, plotting their
crafty moves in advance and often using
accomplices. . . . Harris sees no malice
in all this, even when heads roll. Brer
Rabbit, he explains, is moved not by
"malice, but mischievousness." But
Brer Rabbit "mischievously" scalds the
Wolf to death, makes the innocent Possum die in a fire to cover his own crimes,
tortures and probably murders the Bear
by setting a swarm of bees on him—and,
after causing the fatal beating of the

Fox, carries his victim's head to Mrs.
Fox and her children, hoping to trick
them into eating it in their soup. . . .

One dramatic tension in these stories
seems to be a gastronomic one: *Will
the communal meal ever take place in the
"Animal" Kingdom?*

The food-sharing issue is posed in
the very first story. "I seed Brer B'ar
yistiddy," the Fox tells the Rabbit as
the story opens, "en he sorter rake me
over de coals kaze you en me ain't
make frens en live naborly." He then
invites the Rabbit to supper—intending
that his guest will be the main course in
this "joint" feast. Brer Rabbit solemnly
accepts the invitation, shows up, makes
the Fox look ridiculous, and blithely
scampers off: "En Brer Fox ain't kotch
'im yit en w'at's mo', honey, he ain't
gwine ter." The Rabbit can get along
very well without the communal meal;
but, it soon develops, Brer Fox and
his associates can't live without it.

Without food-sharing, no community. Open warfare breaks out immediately after the Fox's hypocritical invitation; and the Rabbit is invariably the
victor in the gory skirmishes. And after
he kills and skins the Wolf, his other
enemies are so cowed that now the communal meal finally seems about to take
place: "de animals en de creeturs, dey
kep' on gittin' mo' en mo' familious wid
wunner nudder—bunchin' der perwish-
uns tergidder in de same shanty" and
"takin' a snack" together too.

But Brer Rabbit isn't taken in.
Knowing that the others are sharing their
food with him out of fear, not genuine
communality, he remains the complete
cynic and continues to raid the Fox's
goober patch and the Bear's persimmon
orchard. Not until the closing episode

does the Fox make a genuine food-sharing gesture—he crawls inside Book-ay the Cow with Brer Rabbit and gratuitously shows him how to hack out all the beef he can carry. But the communal overture comes too late. In an act of the most supreme malevolence, the Rabbit betrays his benefactor to the farmer and stands by, "makin' like he mighty sorry," while the Fox is beaten to death. . . . And now the meal which aborted in the beginning, because the Fox's friendliness was only a ruse, almost does take place—with the Fox as the main course. Having brutally destroyed his arch enemy, Brer Rabbit tries to make Mrs. Fox cook a soup with her husband's head, and almost succeeds.

Remus is not an anthropomorphist by accident. His theme is a *human* one—neighborliness—and the communal meal is a symbol for it. His moral? There are no good neighbors in the world, neither equality nor fraternity. But the moral has an underside: the Rabbit can never be trapped.

Another tension runs through the stories: *Who gets the women?* In sex, Brer Rabbit is at his most aggressive—and his most invincible. Throughout he is engaged in murderous competition with the Fox and the other animals for the favors of "Miss Meadows en de gals."

In their sexual competition the Rabbit never fails to humiliate the Fox viciously. "I'll show Miss Meadows en de gals dat I'm de boss er Brer Fox," he decides. And he does: through the most elaborate trickery he persuades the Fox to put on a saddle, then rides him past Miss Meadows' house, digging his spurs in vigorously. . . . And in sex, it would seem, there are no false distinctions between creatures—all differences

in status are irrelevant. At Miss Meadows' the feuds of the work-a-day world must be suspended, "kaze Miss Meadows, she done put her foot down, she did, en say dat w'en dey come ter her place dey hatter hang up a flag er truce at de front gate en 'bide by it."

The truce is all to the Rabbit's advantage, because if the competitors start from scratch in the sexual battle the best man must win—and the best man is invariably Brer Rabbit. The women themselves want the best man to win. Miss Meadows decides to get some peace by holding a contest and letting the winner have his pick of the girls. The Rabbit mulls the problem over. He sings ironically,

> Make a bow ter de Buzzard en den ter
>   de Crow
> Takes a limber-toe gemmun fer ter
>   jump Jim Crow.

Then, through a tricky scheme, he proceeds to outshine all the stronger contestants.

Food-sharing, sex-sharing—the Remus stories read like a catalogue of Southern racial taboos, all standing on their heads. The South, wearing the blinders of stereotype, has always tried to see the Negro as a "roaringly comic" domestic animal. Understandably; for animals of the tame or domestic variety are not menacing—they are capable only of mischief, never of malice. But the Negro slave, through his anthropomorphic Rabbit stories, seems to be hinting that even the frailest and most humble of "animals" can let fly with the most blood-thirsty aggressions. And these aggressions take place in the two most sacrosanct areas of Southern racial etiquette: the gastronomic and the erotic.

The South, with its "sanctions of fear and force," forbids Negroes to eat at the same table with whites. But Brer Rabbit, through an act of murder, *forces* Brer Fox and all his associates to share their food with him. The South enjoins the Negro, under penalty of death, from coming near the white man's women—although the white man has free access to the Negro's women. But Brer Rabbit flauntingly demonstrates his sexual superiority over all the other animals and, as the undisputed victor in the sexual competition, gets his choice of *all* the women.

And yet, despite these food and sex taboos, for two solid centuries—for the Rabbit stories existed long before Harris put them on paper—Southerners chuckled at the way the Rabbit terrorized all the other animals into the communal meal, roared at the Rabbit's guile in winning the girls away from the Fox *by jumping Jim Crow*. And they were endlessly intrigued by the O. Henry spasm of the miraculous in the very last story, right after the Fox's death: "Some say dat . . . Brer Rabbit married ole Miss Fox. . . ."

An interesting denouement, considering the sexual fears which saturate the South's racial attitudes. Still more interesting that Southern whites should even have countenanced it, let alone revelled in it. . . .

Significantly, the goal of eating and sex, as depicted in Uncle Remus, is not instinct gratification. The overriding drive is for *prestige*—the South is a prestige-haunted land. And it is in that potent intangible that the Rabbit is always paid off most handsomely for his exploits. Throughout, as he terrorizes the Strong, the "sassy" Rabbit remains bland, unperturbed, sure of his invincibility. When he humiliates the Fox by turning him into a saddle-horse, he mounts him "same's ef he wuz king er de patter-rollers." ("Patter-rollers," Harris cheerfully points out, were the white patrols that terrorized Negro slaves so they wouldn't wander off the plantations.)

Brer Rabbit, in short, has all the jaunty topdog airs and attitudes which a slave can only dream of having. And, like the slave, he has a supremely cynical view of the social world, since he sees it from below. The South is the most etiquette-ridden region of the country; and the Rabbit sees all forms of etiquette as hypocritical and absurd. Creatures meet, address each other with unctuous politeness, inquire after each other's families, pass the time of day with oily clichés—and all the while they are plotting to humiliate, rob, and assassinate each other. The Rabbit sees through it all; if he is serene it is only because he can plot more rapidly and with more deadly efficiency than any of the others.

The world, in Brer Rabbit's wary eyes, is a jungle. Life is a battle-unto-the-death for food, sex, power, prestige, a battle without rules. There is only one reality in this life: who is on top? But Brer Rabbit wastes no time lamenting the mad unneighborly scramble for the top position. Because it is by no means ordained that the Weak can never take over. In his topsy-turvy world, to all practical purposes, the Weak *have* taken over. In one episode, the Rabbit falls down a well in a bucket. He can get back up only by enticing the Fox to climb into the other bucket. The Fox is duped: he drops down and the Rabbit rises, singing as he passes his enemy:

Good-by, Brer Fox, take keer yo' cloze
Fer dis is de way de worril goes
Some goes up en some goes down
You'll git ter de bottom all safe en
    soun'.

This is the theme song of the stories. The question remains, who sings it? The Rabbit is a creation of Uncle Remus's people; is it, then, Uncle Remus singing? But Uncle Remus is a creation of Joel Chandler Harris. . . .

There is a significant difference in ages—some hundreds of years—between Uncle Remus and Brer Rabbit. The Rabbit had been the hero of animal stories popular among Negroes from the early days of slavery; these were genuine folktales told by Negroes to Negroes and handed down in oral form. Uncle Remus was added only when Harris, in packaging the stories—using the Negro grin for gift-wrapping—invented the Negro narrator to sustain the dialect.

Harris, then, fitted the hate-imbued folk materials into a framework, a white man's framework, of "love." He took over the animal characters and situations of the original stories and gave them a human setting: the loving and lovable Negro narrator, the adoring white auditor. Within this framework of love, the blow was heavily padded with caresses and the genuine folk was almost emasculated into the cute folksy.

Almost, but not quite. Harris all his life was torn between his furtive penchant for fiction and his profession of journalism. It was the would-be novelist in him who created Remus, the "giver" of interracial caresses; but the trained journalist in him, having too good an eye and ear, reported the energetic folk blow in the caress. Thus the curious tension in his versions between "human" form and "animal" content.

Before Harris, few Southerners had ever faced squarely the aggressive symbolism of Brer Rabbit, or the paradox of their delight in it. Of course: it was part of the Southerner's undissected myth—often shared by the Negroes—that his cherished childhood sessions in the slave quarters were bathed in two-way benevolence. But Harris, by writing the white South and its Negro tale-spinners into the stories, also wrote in its unfaced paradoxes. Thus his versions helped to rip open the racial myth—and, with it, the interracial grin.

What was the slippery rabbit-hero doing in these stories to begin with? Where did he come from? As soon as Harris wrote down the oral stories for mass consumption, these questions began to agitate many whites. The result was a whole literature devoted to proving the "un-American" genealogy of Brer Rabbit.

Why, one Southern writer asks, did the Negro pick the Rabbit for a hero? Could it be because the Rabbit was "symbolic of his own humble and helpless condition in comparison with his master the owner of the plantation"? Perhaps the Rabbit represents the Negro "in revolt at . . . his own subordinate and insignificant place in society"?

But no: if the Negro is capable of rebelling against society—American society—even symbolically, he is a menace. The Negro must be in revolt against *Nature*, against the "subordinate and insignificant place" assigned to him by biological fate, not America. The writer reassures himself: the Negro makes animals act "like a low order of human intelligence, such as the Negro himself [can] comprehend." The Negro naturally feels "more closely in touch with [the lower animals] than with the white man who [is] so superior to him in every respect." No threat in Brer Rabbit; his genealogy, having no *American* roots, is a technical matter for "the psychologist or the student of folklore."

However, uneasy questions were raised; and as they were raised they were directed at Harris. Readers sensed the symbolic taunts and threats in the Rabbit and insisted on knowing whether they were directed against white America —or against "Nature." Harris took refuge from this barrage of questions in two mutually contradictory formulas: (1) he was merely the "compiler" of these stories, a non-intellectual, a lowly humorist, ignorant of "folkloristic" matters; and (2) Brer Rabbit was most certainly, as Southerners intuited, an undiluted African.

"All that I know—all that we Southerners know—about it," Harris protested, "is that every old plantation mammy in the South is full of these stories." But, a sentence later, Harris decided there *was* one other thing he knew: "One thing is certain—the Negro did not get them from the whites; *probably they are of remote African origin.*" And if they come from the Congo, they offer no symbolic blows to Americans; they are simply funny. So Harris warns the folklorists: "First let us have the folktales told as they were intended to be told, for the sake of amusement. . . ."

But if the folklorists *should* find in them something "of value to their pretension"? Then "let it be picked out and preserved with as little cackling as possible."

The South wavered; it could not shake off the feeling that Brer Rabbit's over-

tones were more than just funny. And Harris, too, wavered. To a British folklorist editor he wrote, suddenly reversing himself, that the stories were "more important than humorous." And in the introduction to his book he explains that "however humorous it may be in effect, its intention is perfectly serious. . . . It seems to me that a volume written wholly in dialect must have its solemn, not to say melancholy features."

What was it that Harris sporadically found "important," "solemn," even "melancholy" here? It turns out to be the *Americanism* of Brer Rabbit: "it needs no scientific investigation," Harris continues in his introduction,

to show why he [the Negro] selects as his hero the weakest and most harmless of all animals. . . . It is not virtue that triumphs, but helplessness. . . . Indeed, the parallel between the case of the 'weakest' of all animals, who must, perforce, triumph through his shrewdness, and the humble condition of the slave raconteur, is not without its pathos.

A suggestive idea. But such a "parallel" could not have been worked out in the African jungle, before slavery; it implies that Brer Rabbit, after all, was born much closer to the Mississippi than to the Congo. . . . This crucial sentence does not occur in later editions. Instead we read: "It would be presumptious [*sic*] in me to offer an opinion as to the origins of these curious myth-stories; but, *if ethnologists should discover that they did not originate with the African, the proof to that effect should be accompanied with a good deal of persuasive eloquence.*"

In this pressing sentence we can see Harris's whole fragmented psyche mirrored. Like all the South, he was caught in a subjective tug-of-war: his intelligence groped for the venomous American slave crouching behind the Rabbit, but his beleaguered racial emotions, in self-defense, had to insist on the "Africanism" of Brer Rabbit—and of the Negro. Then Miss Sally and Mars John could relish his "quaint antics" without recognizing themselves as his targets.

Against the African origin of Brer Rabbit one may argue that he is an eloquent white folk-symbol too, closely related to the lamb as the epitome of Christian meekness (the Easter bunny). May not the Negro, in his conversion to Christianity, have learned the standard Christian animal symbols from the whites? Could not his constant tale-spinning about the Rabbit's malevolent triumphs somehow, in some devious way, suggest the ascent of Christ, the meekness that shall inherit the earth; suggest, even, that the meek may stop being meek and set about inheriting the earth without waiting on the Biblical timetable?

But, there *is* more definite evidence as to Brer Rabbit's non-African origins —skimpy, not conclusive, but highly suggestive. Folklore study indicates that if the Negro did have stories about a rabbit back in Africa, they were not these stories, and the rabbit was most decidedly not this rabbit. Brer Rabbit's truer ancestor, research suggests, hails from elsewhere.*

"Most of these Negro stories," reported a Johns Hopkins ethnologist—one of the "cackling" folklorists— "... bear a striking resemblance to the large body of animal stories made on European soil, of which the most extensive is that known as the *Roman de Renard*. The episodes which form the substance of this French version circulated in the Middle Ages on the Flemish border. ... The principal actors ... are the fox, who plays the jokes, and the wolf, most frequently the victim of the fox."

In incident after incident, the Brer Rabbit situations parallel the Reynard the Fox situations: the same props appear, the same set-to's, the same ruses, the same supporting characters, often the same dialogue. But there is one big

---

* Wolfe's argument is at its weakest here in view of his lack of familiarity with the standard tools of folklore scholarship, for example, Stith Thompson, *Motif-Index of Folk Literature*, 6 vols, 2nd ed. (Bloomington, Indiana, 1955–58), and Antti Aarne and Stith Thompson, *The Types of the Folktale*, second revision, Folklore Fellows Communications 184 (Helsinki, 1961). Such tools could assist in positively identifying those tales which are widely distributed in Europe. As a matter of fact, it is quite likely that the American Negro rabbit *is* a direct "translation" of the African hare, especially since some of the same stories *are* told in Africa. (For further discussion and references, see Alan Dundes, "African Tales Among the North American Indians," reprinted earlier in this volume.) Moreover, for those tales which are African in origin, Wolfe's interpretations must be read with caution. He tends to perceive the tales' meaning almost entirely in the context of race relations. However, if a given folktale is indigenous to Africa, it presumably had meaning there, and the meaning might be totally unrelated to a race relations context. In other words, Wolfe's interpretations—and it is by no means clear that they represent the American Negro's own interpretations—reflect *his* concern with race. Of course, whatever an African tale may have meant to an original African audience, there is no doubt that the meaning of the same or a similar tale in the New World surely changed in accordance with the pressures and anxieties of the slavery context. Such processes of localization are perhaps easier to observe in the numerous cases of what appear to be European tales that have become attached to the Brer Rabbit cycle. Certainly, Wolfe's discussion of the Negro recasting of European trickster tales is by no means invalidated by his extremist denial of an African origin, and, indeed, for the most part his suggestive readings of the tales seem quite plausible. —Ed.

difference: "In *Uncle Remus* the parts are somewhat changed. Here the rabbit, who scarcely appears (under the name Couard) in the *Renard*, is the chief trickster. His usual butt is the fox...."

In Christian symbolism, then, the rabbit is the essence of meekness and innocence. And in an important part of white folk culture he stands for the impotent, the cowardly, as against the cunning fox. Suddenly, with the beginning of slavery, the Negro begins to tell stories in which the rabbit, now the epitome of belligerence and guile, crops up as the *hero*, mercilessly badgering the fox.

Could the Negroes have got the Reynard fables from the whites? Not impossible. The stories originated among the Flemish peasants. During the twelfth century they were written down in French, Latin, and German, in a variety of rhymed forms. The many written versions were then widely circulated throughout Western Europe. And more than a few of the first Negro slaves were brought to France, Spain, and Portugal; and some of their descendants were transplanted to America. Also, many early slaves were brought to plantations owned by Frenchmen—whether in the Louisiana Territory, the Acadian-French sections of North Carolina, or the West Indies.

And many white masters, of French and other backgrounds, told these delightful fox tales to their children. And, from the beginning of the slave trade, many Negroes—who may or may not have had pre-Christian rabbit fables of their own back in Africa—could have listened, smiling amiably, slowly absorbing the raw materials for the grinning folk "gift" that would one day be immortalized by Joel Chandler Harris,

Walt Disney, Tin Pan Alley, and the comics. . . .

The Harris research technique, we learn, was first-hand and direct. Seeing a group of Negroes, he approaches and asks if they know any Brer Rabbit stories. The Negroes seem not to understand. Offhandedly, and in rich dialect, Harris tells one himself—as often as not, the famous "Tar-Baby" story. The Negroes are transfixed; then suddenly, they break out in peals of laughter, kick their heels together, slap their thighs. Before long they are swapping Rabbit yarns with the white man as though he were their lifelong "hail-feller." "Curiously enough," Harris notes, "I have found few Negroes who will acknowledge to a stranger that they know anything of these legends; and yet to relate one of the stories is the surest road to their confidence and esteem."

Why the sudden hilarity? What magic folk-key causes these wary, taciturn Negroes to open up? Harris claims to have won their "esteem"; but perhaps he only guaranteed them immunity. He thinks he disarmed the Negroes—he may only have demonstrated that he, the white bossman, was disarmed.

And how much did the Negroes tell him when they "opened up"? Just how far did they really open up? Harris observes that "there are different versions of all the stories—the shrewd narrators of the mythology of the old plantation adapting themselves with ready tact to the years, tastes, and expectations of their juvenile audiences." But there seem to be gaps in Harris's own versions. At tantalizingly crucial points Uncle Remus will break off abruptly—"Some tells one tale en some tells nudder"—leaving the story dangling like a radio cliff-hanger. Did these gaps appear when the stories were told to Harris? When the slave is obliged to play the clown-entertainer and "give" his folk tales to his masters, young or old, his keen sense of the fitting might well delete the impermissible and blur the dubious—and more out of self-preservation than tact.

Of course, the original oral stories would not express the slave's aggressions straightforwardly either. A Negro slave who yielded his mind fully to his race hatreds in an absolutely white-dominated situation must go mad; and the function of such folk symbols as Brer Rabbit is precisely to prevent inner explosions by siphoning off these hatreds before they can completely possess consciousness. Folk tales, like so much of folk culture, are part of an elaborate psychic drainage system—they make it possible for Uncle Tom to retain his facade of grinning Tomism and even, to some degree, to believe in it himself. But the slave's venom, while subterranean, must nonetheless have been *thrillingly* close to the surface and its symbolic disguises flimsier, its attacks less roundabout. Accordingly his protective instincts, sensing the danger in too shallow symbolism, would have necessarily wielded a meticulous, if unconscious, blue pencil in the stories told to white audiences.

Harris tried hard to convince himself that Uncle Remus was a full-fledged, dyed-in-the-denim Uncle Tom—he describes the "venerable sable patron" as an ex-slave "who has nothing but pleasant memories of the discipline of slavery." But Harris could not completely exorcise the menace in the Meek. How often Remus steps out of his clown

role to deliver unmistakeable judgments on class, caste, and race! In those judgments the aggressions of this "white man's nigger" are astonishingly naked.

"Why the Negro Is Black" tells how the little boy makes the "curious" discovery that Remus's palms are white. The old man explains: "Dey wuz a time w'en all de w'ite folks 'us black—blacker dan me. . . . Niggers is niggers now, but de time wuz w'en 'uz all niggers tergedder. . . ." How did some "niggers" get white? Simply by bathing in a pond which washed their pigmentation off and using up most of the waters, so that the latecomers could only dabble their hands and feet in it.

But the stragglers who were left with their dark skin tone are not trapped —they may be able to wriggle out of it. In "A Plantation Witch," Remus, explaining that there are witches everywhere in the world that "comes en conjus fokes," hints that these witches may be Negroes who have slipped out of their skins. And these witches conjure white folks from all sides, taking on the forms of owls, bats, dogs, cats—and rabbits.

And in "The Wonderful Tar-Baby Story"—advertised on the dust-jacket as the most famous of all the Remus stories—Remus reverts to the question of pigmentation. ("There are few negroes that will fail to respond" to this one, Harris advises one of his folklore "legmen.") The Fox fashions a "baby" out of tar and places it on the side of the road; the Rabbit comes along and addresses the figure. Not getting any answer, he threatens: "Ef you don't take off dat hat en tell me howdy, I'm gwineter bus' you wide open." (Here the Rabbit's bluster reads like a parody of the white man's demand for the proper bowing-

and-scraping etiquette from the Negro; it is a reflection of the satiric mimicry of the whites which the slaves often indulged in among themselves.) He hits the Tar-Baby—his fist sticks in the gooey tar. He hits it with the other hand, then kicks it—all four extremities are stuck.

This is "giving" in a new sense; tar, blackness, by its very yielding, traps. Interesting symbol, in a land where the mere possession of a black skin requires you, under penalty of death, to yield, to *give*, everywhere. The mark of supreme impotence suddenly acquires the power to render impotent, merely by its flaccidity, its inertness; it is almost a Gandhi-like symbol. There is a puzzle here: it is the Rabbit who is trapped. But in a later story, "How Mr. Rabbit Was Too Sharp for Mr. Fox," it turns out that the Rabbit, through another cagey maneuver, gets the Fox to set him free from the tar-trap and thus avoids being eaten by his enemy. The Negro, in other words, is wily enough to escape from the engulfing pit of blackness, although his opponents, who set the trap, do their level best to keep him imprisoned in it. But it is not at all sure that anyone else who fell victim to this treacherous black yieldingness—the Fox, say—would be able to wriggle out so easily.

The story about "A Plantation Witch" frightens his young admirer so much that Remus has to take him by the hand and lead him home to the "big house." And for a long time the boy lies awake "expecting an unseemly visitation from some mysterious source." Many of the other stories, too, must have given him uneasy nights. For within the "gift" that Uncle Remus gives to Miss Sally's little boy is a nightmare, a nightmare in which whites are Negroes, the Weak torture and drown the Strong, mere blackness becomes black magic— and Negroes cavort with cosmic forces and the supernatural, zipping their skins off at will to prowl around the countryside terrorizing the whites, often in the guise of rabbits. . . .

Harris's career is one of the fabulous success stories of American literary history. Thanks to Uncle Remus, the obscure newspaperman was catapulted into the company of Mark Twain, Bret Harte, James Whitcomb Riley, and Petroleum V. Nasby; Andrew Carnegie and Theodore Roosevelt traveled to Atlanta to seek him out; he was quoted in Congress. And all the while he maintained—as in a letter to Twain—that

my book has no basis in literary merit to stand upon; I know it is the matter and not the manner that has attracted public attention . . . my relations towards Uncle Remus are similar to those that exist between an almanac-maker and the calendar . . .*

But how was it that Harris could apply his saccharine manner to such

---

* Mark Twain disagreed. In a letter to Joel Chandler Harris in 1881, Twain wrote, "You can argue *yourself* into the delusion that the principle of life is in the stories themselves and not in their setting, but you will save labor by stopping with that solitary convert, for he is the only intelligent one you will bag. In reality the stories are only alligator pears—one eats them for the sake of the dressing." Folklorist Elsie Clews Parsons who pointed out some years ago the absolute falsity of the "dressing," at least in terms of social context, of a Negro male telling stories to white children observed, "To be sure, now and then one hears of somebody who fancies alligator pears without dressing." Of course, almost any folklorist familiar with oral tales finds them infinitely superior to the literary, doctored derivatives no matter how delicious the dressing might be! See Elsie Clews Parsons, "Joel Chandler Harris and Negro Folklore," *The Dial*, 46 (1919), pp. 491–93. —ED.

matter, dress this malevolent material, these nightmares, in such sweetness and light? For one thing, of course, he was only recording the tottering racial myth of the post-bellum South, doing a paste-job on its fissioning false face. As it happened, he was peculiarly suited for the job; for he was crammed full of pathological racial obsessions, over and above those that wrack the South and, to a lesser degree, all of white America.

Even Harris's worshipful biographer, his daughter-in-law, can't prevent his story from reading like a psychiatric recital of symptoms. The blush and the stammer were his whole way of life. From early childhood on, we are told, he was "painfully conscious of his social deficiencies" and his "lack of size"; he felt "handicapped by his tendency to stutter" and to "blush furiously," believed himself "much uglier than he really was"; in his own words, he had "an absolute horror of strangers."

During his induction into the typographical union, Harris stutters so badly that he has to be excused from the initiation ceremony; trapped in a room full of congenial strangers, he escapes by jumping out of the window. "What a coarse ungainly boor I am," he laments, "how poor, small and insignificant. . . ." He wonders if he is mad: "I am morbidly sensitive . . . it is an affliction —a disease . . . the slightest rebuff tortures me beyond expression. . . . It is worse than death itself. It is *horrible*." Again, he speculates about his "abnormal quality of mind . . . that lacks only vehemence to become downright insanity. . . ." Harris's life, it appears, was one long ballet of embarrassment.

"I am nursing a novel in my brain," Harris announced archly more than once. All along he was consumed with the desire to turn out some "long work" of fiction, but, except for two inept and badly received efforts (published after his forty-eighth year), he never succeeded. Over and over he complained bitterly of his grinding life in the journalistic salt mines—but when the Century Company offered him a handsome income if he would devote all his time to creative work, he refused. This refusal, according to his daughter-in-law, "can be explained only by his abnormal lack of confidence in himself as a 'literary man.' "

The urge to create was strong in Harris, so strong that it gave him no peace; and he could not create. That is the central fact in his biography: his creative impulses were trapped behind a block of congealed guilts, granite-strong; the works he produced were not real gushings of the subjective but only those driblets that were able to seep around the edges of the block.

Harris's stammer—his literal choking on words—was like a charade of the novelist *manqué* in him, his blush was the fitful glow of his smothered self, a tic of the guilty blood. And that smothered self had a name: Uncle Remus.

Accused of plagiarizing folk materials, Harris replies indignantly: "I shall not hesitate to draw on the oral stories I know for incidents. . . . The greatest literary men, if you will remember, were very poor inventors." Harris all his life was a very poor inventor; his career was built on a merciless, systematic plagiarizing of the folk-Negro. Small wonder, then, that the "plantation darky" was such a provocative symbol for him. For, ironically, this lowly Negro was, when viewed through the blinders of stereotype, almost the walking image of Harris's ego-ideal—the un-selfconscious, "natural," free-flowing, richly giving creator that Harris could never become. Indeed, for Harris, as for many another white American, the Negro *seemed* in every respect to be a negative print of his own uneasy self: "happy-go-lucky," socializing, orally expressive, muscularly relaxed, never bored or passive, unashamedly exhibitionistic, free from self-pity even in his situation of concentrated pain, emotionally fluid. And every time a Remus opened his mouth, every time he flashed a grin, he wrote effortlessly another novel that was strangled a-borning in Harris.

"I despise and detest those false forms of society that compel people to suppress their thoughts," Harris wrote. But he was himself the most inhibited and abashed of men. What fascinates him in the Rabbit stories, he confesses, is "the humor that lies between *what is perfectly decorous in appearance* and *what is wildly extravagant in suggestion.*" But, a thorough slave to decorum, he was incapable of the "wildly extravagant," whether in his love-making ("My love for you," he informs his future wife, "is . . . far removed from that wild passion that develops itself in young men in their teens . . . it is not wild or unreasoning.") or in his writing.

Harris, then, was *awed* by Uncle Remus. It was the awe of the sophisticate before the spontaneous, the straitjacketed before the nimble. But was the Negro what Harris thought him to be? It is certainly open to question, for another irony of the South is that the white man, under his pretense of racial omniscience, actually knows the Negro not at all—he knows only the false face which he has forced on the Negro. It is the white man who manufactures the Negro grin. The stereotype reflects the looker, his thwart-ings and yearnings, not the person looked at; it is born out of intense subjective need.

Harris's racial awe was only an offshoot of the problem that tormented him all his life: the problem of identifying himself. He was caught in the American who-am-I dilemma, one horn of which is white, the other often black. And there is abundant proof that, at least in one compartment of his being, Harris defined himself by identifying with the Negro.

As a child, Harris started the game of "Gully Minstrels" with his white playmates; and later in life, whenever he felt "blue" and wanted to relax, he would jump up and exclaim, "Let's have some fun—let's play minstrels!" Often, in letters and newspaper articles, and even in personal relations, he would *jokingly* refer to himself as "Uncle Remus," and when he started a one-man magazine, he decided to name it *Uncle Remus's Magazine* instead of *The Optimist*! Frequently he would lapse into a rich Negro dialect, to the delight of his admirers, from Andrew Carnegie down to the local trolley conductor. And, like Uncle Remus, he even toys with the idea that whites are only blanched Negroes: "Study a nigger right close," he has one of his characters say, "and you'll ketch a glimpse of how white folks would look and do without their trimmin's."

Harris seems to have been a man in permanent rebellion against his own skin. No wonder: for he was driven to "give," and it was impossible for him to give without first zipping out of his own decorous skin and slipping into Uncle Remus's. To him the artist and the Negro were synonymous.

And Harris virulently *hated* the

Negro, too. "The colored people of Macon," he writes in his paper, "celebrated the birthday of Lincoln again on Wednesday. This is the third time since last October. . . ." And: "A negro pursued by an agile Macon policeman fell in a well the other day. He says he knocked the bottom out of the concern." Again:

There will have to be another amendment to the civil rights bill. A negro boy in Covington was attacked by a sow lately and narrowly escaped with his life. We will hear next that the sheep have banded together to mangle the downtrodden race.

The malice here is understandable. Can the frustrate—the "almanac-maker" —ever love unequivocally the incarnation of his own taboo self—the "calendar"? What stillborn novelist can be undilutedly tender towards the objectivization of his squelched alter-ego, whose oral stories he feels impelled to "draw on" all his life?

Most likely, at least in Harris, the love went deeper than the hate—the hate was, in some measure, a *defense* against the love. "*Some goes up en some goes down.*" Who sings this theme song? A trio: the Rabbit, Remus, *and* Harris. Literally, it is only a rabbit and a fox who change places. Racially, the song symbolizes the ascent of the Negro "Weak" and the descent of the white "Strong."

But to Harris, on the deepest personal level, it must have meant: the collapse of the "perfectly decorous" (inhibition, etiquette, embarrassment, the love that is never wild, the uncreative journalist-compiler, the blush and the stammer) and the triumph of the "wildly extravagant" (spontaneity, "naturalness," the unleashed subjective, creativity, "Miss Meadows en de gals,"

exhibitionism, the folk-novelist). The song must have been *deliciously* funny to him. . . .

The Remus stories are a monument to the South's ambivalence. Harris, the archetypical Southerner, sought the Negro's love, and pretended he had received it (Remus's grin). But he sought the Negro's hate too (Brer Rabbit), and revelled in it in an unconscious orgy of masochism—punishing himself, possibly, for not being the Negro, the stereotypical Negro, the unstinting giver.

Harris's inner split—and the South's, and white America's—is mirrored in the fantastic disparity between Remus's beaming face and Brer Rabbit's acts. And such aggressive acts increasingly emanate from the grin, along with the hamburgers, the shoeshines, the "happifyin' " pancakes.

Today Negro attack and counterattack becomes more straightforward. The NAACP submits a brief to the United Nations, demanding a redress of grievances suffered by the Negro people at the hands of white America. The election newsreels showed Henry Wallace addressing audiences that were heavily sprinkled with Negroes, protected by husky, alert, *deadpan* bodyguards—Negroes. New York Negroes voted for Truman—but only after Truman went to Harlem. The Gandhi-like "Tar-Baby" begins to stir: Grant Reynolds and A. Phillips Randolph, announcing to a Senate committee that they will refuse to be drafted in the next war, revealed, at the time, that many Negroes were joining their civil-disobedience organization—the first movement of passive resistance this country had seen.

Increasingly Negroes themselves

reject the mediating smile of Remus, the indirection of the Rabbit. The present-day animated cartoon hero, Bugs Bunny, is, like Brer Rabbit, the meek suddenly grown cunning—but without Brer Rabbit's facade of politeness. "To pull a Bugs Bunny," meaning to spectacularly outwit someone, is an expression not infrequently heard in Harlem.

There is today on every level a mass repudiation of "Uncle Tomism." Significantly the Negro comedian is disap-pearing. For bad or good, the *Dark Laughter* that Sherwood Anderson heard all around white New Orleans is going or gone.

The grin is faltering, especially since the war. That may be one of the reasons why, once more, the beaming Negro butler and Pullman porter are making their amiable way across our billboards, food labels, and magazine ads—and Uncle Remus, "fetchin' a grin from year to year," is in the bigtime again.

High John de Conquer

ZORA NEALE HURSTON

In the light of Joel Chandler Harris's rapport with his informants and his possible ambivalence toward Negro folktales, it is probably not surprising that he failed to collect, or at any rate to publish, examples of the extensive cycle of tales involving John and Old Master. In these tales, the animal symbolic guise of rabbit versus fox is dropped, and the antagonists are the clever slave and Old Massa or Marster.

In the following account of John by folklorist Zora Neale Hurston, we see the importance of a hero or trickster to a people. John symbolizes the inner man or the soul behind the laughing, singing facade. It is of interest that Miss Hurston claims that John de Conquer "had come from Africa." In one sense, he surely did. On the other hand, many of the tales in the John and Old Marster cycle are undeniably European, not African. (Note the allusion to John stopping off in Hell where, under the name of Jack, he married the Devil's youngest daughter. The name, John, after all is the standard name for folktale heroes throughout Europe: Jack in England, Jean or Petit-Jean in France, Hans or Hansel in Germany, Ivan in Russia, etc.)

Some black militants or separatists may be unhappy with several of Miss Hurston's sentiments, e.g., "But nationally and culturally, we are as white as the next one," or even the now somewhat dated World War II context which apparently led her to reveal the nature of John to help white folks. This revelation could conceivably be construed as an act of betrayal in allowing a white audience to share esoteric "in-group" knowledge that previously was known almost exclusively by Negroes. On the other hand, who could quarrel with her eloquent commentary on the fundamental meaning of such a fascinating folk figure? "Making a way out of no-way" and "Hitting a straight lick with a

Reprinted from *The American Mercury*, vol. 57 (1943), pp. 450–58, by permission of *The American Mercury*.

crooked stick" are beautiful metaphors for the gutsy philosophy of life required in a land where prejudice and racism abound.

For additional examples of this important cycle of folktales, see Harry Oster, "Negro Humor: John and Old Marster," which follows Miss Hurston's account in this volume. For further information on the root John de Conquer, see Harry Middleton Hyatt, Hoodoo-Conjuration-Witchcraft-Rootwork, *vol. I (Washington, D.C.: American University Bookstore, 1970), pp. 593–95. Inasmuch as Hyatt indicates the spelling is more often "Conker" than "Conquer," one is tempted to speculate about the relationship between John de Conquer and "conk" meaning "head" or "conk" meaning "hair-straightening." Of course, to conk someone on the head is to "conquer" him; and if one wished to conquer curly hair by straightening it, that might be a "conk" too. (And "conker" is not all that far removed from "conjure.") In any case, Hyatt reports that possession of High John de Conker root will give an individual power over a boss, e.g., it will guarantee that the possessor will be hired, a theory very much in accord with Miss Hurston's delineation of the root and the trickster figure.*

Finally it should be noted that the alleged connection between the "John" found in the name of the root called John de Conquer and the "John" who appears as a trickster figure in tales involving John and Old Marster may not be traditional. Most accounts of the root make no mention whatsover of a related trickster figure, and, by the same token, none of the various collections of "John and Marster" folktales refer to the root. It is just possible that Zora Neale Hurston, who one must remember was both creative writer and folklorist, simply decided to combine the root and the trickster figure for literary and esthetic reasons. Additional fieldwork is needed to determine whether the association of John the Conquer root with John the trickster figure is truly traditional or whether it is a striking example of poetic license.

MAYBE, NOW, we used-to-be black African folks can be of some help to our brothers and sisters who have always been white. You will take another look at us and say that we are still black and, ethnologically speaking, you will be right. But nationally and culturally, we are as white as the next one. We have put our labor and our blood into the common causes for a long time. We have given the rest of the nation song and laughter. Maybe now, in this terrible struggle, we can give something else— the source and soul of our laughter and song. We offer you our hope-bringer, High John de Conquer.

High John de Conquer came to be a man, and a mighty man at that. But he was not a natural man in the beginning.

First off, he was a whisper, a will to hope, a wish to find something worthy of laughter and song. Then the whisper put on flesh. His footsteps sounded across the world in a low but musical rhythm as if the world he walked on was a singing-drum. The black folks had an irresistible impulse to laugh. High John de Conquer was a man in full, and had come to live and work on the plantations, and all the slave folks knew him in the flesh.

The sign of this man was a laugh, and his singing-symbol was a drumbeat. No parading drum-shout like soldiers out for show. It did not call to the feet of those who were fixed to hear it. It was an inside thing to live by. It was sure to be heard when and where the work was the hardest, and the lot the most cruel. It helped the slaves endure. They knew that something better was coming. So they laughed in the face of things and sang, "I'm so glad! Trouble don't last always." And the white people who heard them were struck dumb that they could laugh. In an outside way, this was Old Massa's fun, so what was Old Cuffy laughing for?

Old Massa couldn't know, of course, but High John de Conquer was there walking his plantation like a natural man. He was treading the sweat-flavored clods of the plantation, crushing out his drum tunes, and giving out secret laughter. He walked on the winds and moved fast. Maybe he was in Texas when the lash fell on a slave in Alabama, but before the blood was dry on the back he was there. A faint pulsing of a drum like a goatskin stretched over a heart, that came nearer and closer, then somebody in the saddened quarters would feel like laughing, and say, "Now, High John de Conquer, Old Massa couldn't get the best of *him*. That old John was a case!" Then everybody sat up and began to smile. Yes, yes, that was right. Old John, High John could beat the unbeatable. He was top-superior to the whole mess of sorrow. He could beat it all, and what made it so cool, finish it off with a laugh. So they pulled the covers up over their souls and kept them from all hurt, harm and danger and made them a laugh and a song. Night time was a joke, because daybreak was on the way. Distance and the impossible had no power over High John de Conquer.

He had come from Africa. He came walking on the waves of sound. Then he took on flesh after he got here. The sea captains of ships knew that they brought slaves in their ships. They knew about those black bodies huddled down there in the middle passage, being hauled across the waters to helplessness. John de Conquer was walking the very winds that filled the sails of the ships. He followed over them like the albatross.

It is no accident that High John de Conquer has evaded the ears of white people. They were not supposed to know. You can't know what folks won't tell you. If they, the white people, heard some scraps, they could not understand because they had nothing to hear things like that with. They were not looking for any hope in those days, and it was not much of a strain for them to find something to laugh over. Old John would have been out of place for them.

Old Massa met our hope-bringer all right, but when Old Massa met him, he was not going by his right name. He was traveling, and touristing around the plantations as the laugh-provoking Brer Rabbit. So Old Massa and Old Miss and their young ones laughed with and at Brer Rabbit and wished him well. And all the time, there was High John de Conquer playing his tricks of making a way out of no-way. Hitting a straight lick with a crooked stick. Winning the jackpot with no other stake but a laugh. Fighting a mighty battle without outside-showing force, and winning his war from within. Really winning in a permanent way, for he was winning with the soul of the black man whole and free. So he could use it afterwards. For what shall it profit a man if he gain the whole world, and lose his own soul? You would have nothing but a cruel, vengeful grasping monster come to power. John de Conquer was a bottom-fish. He was deep. He had the wisdom tooth of the East in his head. Way over there, where the sun rises a day ahead of time, they say that Heaven arms with love and laughter those it does not wish to see destroyed. He who carries his heart in his sword must perish. So says the ultimate law. High John de Conquer knew a lot of things like that. He who wins from within is in the "Be" class. *Be* here when the ruthless man comes, and *be* here when he is gone.

Moreover, John knew that it is written where it cannot be erased, that nothing shall live on human flesh and prosper. Old Maker said that before He made any more sayings. Even a man-eating tiger and lion can teach a person that much. His flabby muscles and mangy hide can teach an emperor right from wrong. If the emperor would only listen.

II

There is no established picture of what sort of looking-man this John de Conquer was. To some, he was a big, physical-looking man like John Henry. To others, he was a little hammered-down, low-built man like the Devil's doll-baby. Some said that they never heard what he looked like. Nobody told them, but he lived on the plantation where their old folks were slaves. He is not so well known to the present generation of colored people in the same way that he was in slavery time. Like King Arthur of England, he has served his people, and gone back into mystery again. And, like King Arthur, he is not dead. He waits to return when his people shall call again. Symbolic of English power, Arthur came out of the water, and with Excalibur, went back into the water again. High John de Conquer went back to Africa, but he left his power here, and placed his American dwelling in the root of a certain plant. Only possess that root, and he can be summoned at any time.

"Of course, High John de Conquer got plenty power!" Aunt Shady Anne Sutton bristled at me when I asked her about him. She took her pipe out of her mouth and stared at me out of her deeply wrinkled face. "I hope you ain't one of these here smart colored folks that done got so they don't believe nothing, and come here questionizing me so you can have something to poke fun at. Done got shamed of the things that brought us through. Make out 'tain't no such thing no more."

When I assured her that that was not the case, she went on.

"Sho John de Conquer means power. That's bound to be so. He come to teach and tell us. God don't leave nobody ignorant, you child. Don't care where He drops you down, He puts you a notice. He don't want folks taken advantage of because they don't know. Now, back there in slavery time, us didn't have no power of protection, and God knowed it, and put us under watch-care. Rattlesnakes never bit no colored folks until four years after freedom was declared. That was to give us time to learn and to know. 'Course, I don't know nothing about slavery personal like. I wasn't born till two years after the Big Surrender. Then I wasn't nothing but a infant baby when I was born, so I couldn't know nothing but what they told me. My mama told me, and I know that she wouldn't mislead me, how High John de Conquer helped us out. He had done teached the black folks so they knowed a hundred years ahead of time that freedom was coming. Long before the white folks knowed anything about it at all.

"These young Negroes reads they books and talk about the war freeing the Negroes, but Aye, Lord! A heap sees, but a few knows. 'Course, the war was a lot of help, but how come the war took place? They think they knows, but they don't. John de Conquer had done put it into the white folks to give us our freedom, that's what. Old Massa fought against it, but us could have told him that it wasn't no use. Freedom just *had* to come. The time set aside for it was there. That war was just a sign and a symbol of the thing. That's the truth! If I tell the truth about everything as good as I do about that, I can go straight to Heaven without a prayer."

Aunt Shady Anne was giving the inside feeling and meaning to the outside laughs around John de Conquer. He romps, he clowns, and looks ridiculous, but if you will, you can read something deeper behind it all. He is loping on off from the Tar Baby with a laugh.

Take, for instance, those words he had with Old Massa about stealing pigs.

Old John was working in Old Massa's house that time, serving around the eating table. Old Massa loved roasted young pigs, and had them often for dinner. Old John loved them too, but Massa never allowed the slaves to eat any at all. Even put aside the left-over and ate it next time. John de Conquer got tired of that. He took to stopping by the pig pen when he had a strong taste for pig-meat, and getting himself one, and taking it on down to his cabin and cooking it.

Massa began to miss his pigs, and made up his mind to squat for who was taking them and give whoever it

was a good hiding. So John kept on taking pigs, and one night Massa walked him down. He stood out there in the dark and saw John kill the pig and went on back to the "big house" and waited till he figured John had it dressed and cooking. Then he went on down to the quarters and knocked on John's door.

"Who dat?" John called out big and bold, because he never dreamed that it was Massa rapping.

"It's me, John," Massa told him. "I want to come in."

"What you want, Massa? I'm coming right out."

"You needn't to do that, John. I want to come in."

"Naw, naw, Massa. You don't want to come into no old slave cabin. Youse too fine a man for that. It would hurt my feelings to see you in a place like this here one."

"I tell you I want to come in, John!"

So John had to open the door and let Massa in. John had seasoned that pig *down*, and it was stinking pretty! John knowed Old Massa couldn't help but smell it. Massa talked on about the crops and hound dogs and one thing and another, and the pot with the pig in it was hanging over the fire in the chimney and kicking up. The smell got better and better.

Way after while, when that pig had done simbled down to a low gravy, Massa said, "John, what's that you cooking in that pot?"

"Nothing but a little old weasly possum, Massa. Sickliest little old possum I ever did see. But I thought I'd cook him anyhow."

"Get a plate and give me some of it, John. I'm hungry."

"Aw, naw, Massa, you ain't hongry."

"Now, John, I don't mean to argue with you another minute. You give me some of that in the pot, or I mean to have the hide off of your back tomorrow morning. Give it to me!"

So John got up and went and got a plate and a fork and went to the pot. He lifted the lid and looked at Massa and told him, "Well, Massa, I put this thing in here a possum, but if it comes out a pig, it ain't no fault of mine."

Old Massa didn't want to laugh, but he did before he caught himself. He took the plate of brownded-down pig and ate it up. He never said nothing, but he gave John and all the other house servants roast pig at the big house after that.*

III

John had numerous scrapes and tight squeezes, but he usually came out like Brer Rabbit. Pretty occasionally, though, Old Massa won the hand. The curious thing about this is, that there are no bitter tragic tales at all. When Old Massa won, the thing ended up in a laugh just the same. Laughter at the expense of the slave, but laughter right on. A sort of recognition that life is not one-sided. A sense of humor that said, "We are just as ridiculous as anybody else. We can be wrong, too."

There are many tales, and variants of each, of how the Negro got his freedom through High John de Conquer. The best one deals with a plantation where the work was hard, and Old Massa mean. Even Old Miss used to pull her maids' ears with hot firetongs when they got her riled. So, naturally, Old John de Conquer was around that plantation a lot.

"What we need is a song," he told the people after he had figured the whole thing out. "It ain't here, and it ain't no place I knows of as yet. Us better go hunt around. This has got to be a particular piece of singing."

But the slaves were scared to leave. They knew what Old Massa did for any slave caught running off.

"Oh, Old Massa don't need to know you gone from here. How? Just leave your old work-tired bodies around for him to look at, and he'll never realize youse way off somewhere, going about your business."

At first they wouldn't hear to John, that is, some of them. But, finally, the weak gave in to the strong, and John told them to get ready to go while he went off to get something for them to ride on. They were all gathered up under a big hickory nut tree. It was noon time and they were knocked off from chopping cotton to eat their dinner. And then that tree was right where Old Massa and Old Miss could see from the cool veranda of the big house. And both of them were sitting out there to watch.

"Wait a minute, John. Where we going to get something to wear off like that. We can't go nowhere like you talking about dressed like we is."

"Oh, you got plenty things to wear. Just reach inside yourselves and get out all those fine raiments you been toting around with you for the last longest. They is in there, all right. I know. Get 'em out, and put 'em on."

* This was one of the first folktales published by Miss Hurston. See "'Possum or Pig?" *The Forum*, 76 (1926), p. 465. For other references to this very popular, often reported, folktale, see Richard M. Dorson, *American Negro Folktales* (New York, 1967), pp. 137–38. —ED.

So the people began to dress. And then John hollered back for them to get out their musical instruments so they could play music on the way. They were right inside where they got their fine raiments from. So they began to get them out. Nobody remembered that Massa and Miss were setting up there on the veranda looking things over. So John went off for a minute. After that they all heard a big sing of wings. It was John come back, riding on a great black crow. The crow was so big that one wing rested on the morning, while the other dusted off the evening star.

John lighted down and helped them, so they all mounted on, and the bird took out straight across the deep blue sea. But it was a pearly blue, like ten squillion big pearl jewels dissolved in running gold. The shore around it was all grainy gold itself.

Like Jason in search of the golden fleece, John and his party went to many places, and had numerous adventures. They stopped off in Hell where John, under the name of Jack, married the Devil's youngest daughter and became a popular character. So much so, that when he and the Devil had some words because John turned the dampers down in old Original Hell and put some of the Devil's hogs to barbecue over the coals, John ran for High Chief Devil and won the election. The rest of his party was overjoyed at the possession of power and wanted to stay there. But John said no. He reminded them that they had come in search of a song. A song that would whip Old Massa's earlaps down. The song was not in Hell. They must go on.

The party escaped out of Hell behind the Devil's two fast horses. One of them was named Hallowed-Be-Thy-Name, and the other, Thy-Kingdom-Come. They made it to the mountain. Somebody told them that the Golden Stairs went up from there. John decided that since they were in the vicinity, they might as well visit Heaven.

They got there a little weary and timid. But the gates swung wide for them, and they went in. They were bathed, robed, and given new and shining instruments to play on. Guitars of gold, and drums, and cymbals and wind-singing instruments. They walked up Amen Avenue, and down Hallelujah Street, and found with delight that Amen Avenue was tuned to sing bass and alto. The west end was deep bass, and the east end alto. Hallelujah Street was tuned for tenor and soprano, and the two promenades met right in front of the throne and made harmony by themselves. You could make any tune you wanted to by the way you walked. John and his party had a very good time at that and other things. Finally, by the way they acted and did, Old Maker called them up before His great workbench, and made them a tune and put it in their mouths. It had no words. It was a tune that you could bend and shape in most any way you wanted to fit the words and feelings that you had. They learned it and began to sing.

Just about that time a loud rough voice hollered, "You Tunk! You July! You Aunt Diskie!" Then Heaven went black before their eyes and they couldn't see a thing until they saw the hickory nut tree over their heads again. There was everything just like they had left it, with Old Massa and Old Miss sitting on the veranda, and Massa was doing the hollering.

"You all are taking a mighty long time for dinner," Massa said. "Get up from there and get on back to the field. I mean for you to finish chopping that cotton today it if takes all night long. I got something else, harder than that, for you to do tomorrow. Get a move on you!"

They heard what Massa said, and they felt bad right off. But John de Conquer took and told them, saying, "Don't pay what he say no mind. You know where you got something finer than this plantation and anything it's got on it, put away. Ain't that funny? Us got all that, and he don't know nothing at all about it. Don't tell him nothing. Nobody don't have to know where us gets our pleasure from. Come on. Pick up your hoes and let's go."

They all began to laugh and grabbed up their hoes and started out.

"Ain't that funny?" Aunt Diskie laughed and hugged herself with secret laughter. "Us got all the advantage, and Old Massa think he got us tied!"

The crowd broke out singing as they went off to work. The day didn't seem hot like it had before. Their gift song came back into their memories in pieces, and they sang about glittering new robes and harps, and the work flew.

IV

So after a while, freedom came. Therefore High John de Conquer has not walked the winds of America for seventy-five years now. His people had their freedom, their laugh and their song. They have traded it to the other Americans for things they could use like education and property, and acceptance. High John knew that that was the way it would be, so he could retire with his secret smile into the soil of the South and wait.

The thousands upon thousands of humble people who still believe in him, that is, in the power of love and laughter to win by their subtle power, do John reverence by getting the root of the plant in which he has taken up his secret dwelling, and "dressing" it with perfume, and keeping it on their person, or in their houses in a secret place. It is there to help them overcome things they feel that they could not beat otherwise, and to bring them the laugh of the day. John will never forsake the weak and the helpless, nor fail to bring hope to the hopeless. That is what they believe, and so they do not worry. They go on and laugh and sing. Things are bound to come out right tomorrow. That is the secret of Negro song and laughter.

So the brother in black offers to these United States the source of courage that endures, and laughter. High John de Conquer. If the news from overseas reads bad, and the nation inside seems like it is stuck in the Tar Baby, listen hard, and you will hear John de Conquer treading on his singing-drum. You will know then, that no matter how bad things look now, it will be worse for those who seek to oppress us. Even if your hair comes yellow, and your eyes are blue, John de Conquer will be working for you just the same. From his secret place, he is working for all America now. We are all his kinfolks. Just be sure our cause is right, and then you can lean back and say, "John de Conquer would know what to do in a case like this, and then he would finish it off with a laugh."

White America, take a laugh out of our black mouths, and win! We give you High John de Conquer.

Negro Humor:
John & Old Marster

HARRY OSTER

      Having been introduced to the folk character of John de Conquer by Zora Neale Hurston, the reader may now wish to consider some more specific examples of this important folktale cycle together with some analysis. Professor Harry Oster of the University of Iowa has been a dedicated collector of American Negro folklore, especially blues, for some years. In this sampling of the John and Marster cycle, Professor Oster not only presents authentic verbatim oral texts (as opposed to the literary, re-worked, blue-pencilled texts of folktales so often published by amateurs and dilettantes), but he also shows his attempts to elicit "oral literary criticism," that is, his informants' own interpretations of the tales they tell. In addition, Professor Oster offers his own analysis of several of the tales. Whether one agrees with every detail of his interpretation or not, one can at least see the difference between mere presentation of raw folktale texts and a collection of texts with some attempt at interpretation and analysis. For every one hundred folktales in print, one would be fortunate to find just one subjected to any kind of analytic treatment!

      One point to keep in mind while reading these texts is the fact that a black informant is telling the tales to a white folklorist. This may be a factor in the collection of any genre of Negro folklore by white folklorists, but it is obviously particularly crucial when the tales have to do with a clever black man tricking a white plantation owner. The collecting context may well have influenced which tales were told to the extent that some of John's best put-downs of Old Marster were omitted and occasional tales in which John receives punishment from Old Marster were included. Of course, even the latter type of tale in a civil rights context may be a form of put-down insofar as even the most apathetic white

Reprinted from the *Journal of the Folklore Institute*, vol. 5 (1968), pp. 42–57, by permission of the author, the Folklore Institute of Indiana University, and Mouton & Co.

liberal is likely to be embarrassed by an account of a white plantation owner administering a hundred-lash whipping to the slave trickster.

For other representative texts in the John and Marster cycle, see J. Mason Brewer, "John Tales," Publications of the Texas Folklore Society, 21 (1946), pp. 81–104; Fred O. Weldon, "Negro Folktale Heroes," Publications of the Texas Folklore Society, 24 (1959), pp. 170–89; John Q. Anderson, "Old John and the Master," Southern Folklore Quarterly, 25 (1961), pp. 195–97; and especially Richard M. Dorson, American Negro Folktales (New York, 1967), pp. 124–70. For Professor Oster's studies of the blues, see "The Blues as a Genre," Genre, 2 (1969), pp. 259–74, and his extensive collection, Living Country Blues (Detroit: Folklore Associates, 1969).

ONE OF the least discusssed and at the same time most significant areas in American Negro folklore is a cycle of humorous stories involving the relationship between a slave, usually called John, and Old Marster, who after the Civil War has often been referred to as Old Boss. Richard M. Dorson has written, "Seldom printed, the spate of the stories involving John and his old Marster provides the most engaging theme in American Negro lore."[1] While most of the discussions of the stories have been primarily concerned with the comparative study of the motifs and with examinations of their sources in the folklore of the British Isles and Africa, there are tantalizing areas for sociological and psychological analyses in the curious relationships between slave and master, in the subtle and sometimes ambiguous satirical overtones, and in the often wildly fanciful images suggestive of the strangeness of dreams.

As is true of much folk humor (and a great number of the world's folktales), the stories frequently appeal to the ordinary person's need to deaden the pangs of a sense of inferiority. If the principal character in the stories is a numskull, the listener will enjoy his superiority to the ridiculous stupidity of an anti-hero. With most of the following stories the narrator and his audience are apt to think of themselves as sophisticated individuals poking fun at a naive country Negro. Moreover, where the protagonist is physically puny or poverty-stricken, the narrator and his audience enjoy identifying with the little man who either through luck or through shrewd trickery defeats frighteningly powerful opponents.

An example of the trickster hero appears in the John and Old Marster cycle in "The Champion Swimmer."[2]

Now back in slavery times, Grandaddy told me this. Marster had a fellow, they call him Tom, had him under bondage. And Tom was a great swimmer, he could swim. And he told the Marster if he find "a man that'll outswim me I could outswim, would you let me go free?"

He said, "Yes, Old Tom, I can get a man can beat you swimmin'. And I'll let him go free."

[1] Richard M. Dorson, *Negro Folktales in Michigan* (Cambridge, Mass., 1956), p. 49.
[2] Told by Jim Daniels of Memphis, Tennessee; recorded by Vincent Kohler, December 31, 1966. Type 1612, "The Contest in Swimming." Motif K1761, "Bluff: provisions for the swimming match." For other variants see Elsie Clews Parsons, *Folk-Lore of the Antilles* (New York, 1943), III, pp. 284–85; J. Mason Brewer, *Humorous Folk Tales of the South Carolina Negro* (Orangeburg, 1945), pp. 3–4; and Dorson, *op. cit.*, p. 55.

He said, "Oh no. I can outswim anybody you bring me here."

Grandaddy said Marster went and got a fellow from overseas somewhere it was. They gonna swim across the Atlantic.

And he said, "Now, Tom, what would you need to swim a hike like that?"

He said, "I'll get the fellow here in the mornin'." He said, "We'll have him here in the mornin'."

He [Tom] said, "Well, what time, Boss?"

"Well, you have him here about seven o'clock in the mornin' 'cause it's gonna take that long a time."

So Marster brought the fellow there for Tom to swim by across the ocean. He said, "Now look after you get here, what is you gonna need?"

He said, "I'll tell you in the mornin' what I'll need to swim across there."

So, when he brought the fellow there he asked him what he was goin' to need to swim across there. He said, "I don't need nothin' but just need me a swimmin' trunk."

So he asked Tom what did he want. Tom said, "I want a barrel of flour, then I want me a cooking stove, and then I'm gonna need about a ton of coal. And I want a deck of cards."

Marster said, "What is you gonna do with the stove?"

Tom said, "I'm gonna cook and eat while I'm swimmin'."

"What you gonna do with the cards?"

"I be playin' cards till my food get done."

He said, "What else you gonna need, Tom?"

He said, "Well, I'll need a bed, and I'll need a dresser."

Say, "Tom, what you gonna do with the bed?"

Say, "I can lay down and sleep too while I'm swimmin'."

Say, "What you gonna do with the dresser?"

Say, "I can look in the glass, see how my feet are workin'."

The other swimmer he had there, he was gettin' nervous. He hadn't swim with no man that wanted all that.

He said, "Tom, think that's all you need?"

He said, "Well, I would want me a gun and about five boxes of shells."

Other one listened at him, who was gonna swim with him. He said, "Look, Tom, swimmin' you don't need no gun and shells."

"Yes, Sir, one of them ducks may fly across and I'd have to shoot him."

He said, "That many shells?"

He said, "Well, swimmin' that far, no tellin' what I'll run in, would come by me, flyin' over me or in the water. I got time to shoot him while I'm swimmin'. I can just naturally swim that good."

So Marster said to the other fellow, "Well, you ready to try him?" The other fellow he had there with him, this fellow told him, said, "No, any damned person want all that, Sir, that's just makin'a crop. I couldn't swim with him. Lay off that swimmin'."

In addition to the obvious vicarious pleasure and amusement which the audience finds in identifying with the weak but clever trickster, there is also a response of joyous laughter at the elaborate, fanciful buildup of the story to its climax. For most people life is drab and chaotic; hence when the folk artist or literary artist transforms the disorderly or commonplace into something which has structure and style, which sparkles with imaginatively pictured scenes, he stirs his audience to amused delight. Such a use of wit occurs in many blues lines, as in the familiar, "If you don't think I'm sinkin', just see what a hole I'm in." The conventional and depressing feeling of "I sure am in a mess of trouble" which everyone experiences is stated in witty and paradoxical metaphor, in cleverly balanced phrases. The audience reacts with bitter-sweet pleasure to the aptness of the artist's deft control over chaotic experience.

The tone of the stories is comic, but as is frequently true of minority groups, the humor often displays self-mockery. With notable frequency, the plot culminates with the defeat of the Negro: he is the ridiculous butt of a joke or more painfully the victim of a hundred lashes. A typical example of the former method of defeat is found in "John and the Stones," which is spoken semi-rhythmically or sung over a guitar accompaniment.[3]

Spoken:

Look-a here, a guy, call him John.
In Marster's time, told John, say, "John,
All you colored people believe in God?"
He told him, he say, "Yassuh, Boss, I believe in God."
He says, uh, "Where do you pray at, John?"
John said, "Boss, I prays over yonder by that big oak tree."
He says, "What time you start to prayin', John?"
He says, "Boss, around about 6:30, Boss."

Well Old Marster he had two little boys, you know,
An' they got a sack an' got some stones in it.

He put 'em up in that tree.
Old John down on his knees.

Sung:

"Oh Lord, have mercy, oh Lord, have mercy.
Give me religion, Lord, give me religion, Lord,
If you give me truly foundation religion,
Drop somethin' on my head, let me feel it."

Spoken:

Little boy dropped one of them stones [on his] head.

Sung:

Hit him on the head, say "Baff!"
He said, "Now thank you, Jesus, thank you, Jesus.
If you give me truly foundation,
Lord, drop a little harder."

Spoken:

Boy dropped a little bigger stone, you know.

Sung:

He said, "I thank you, Jesus, thank you, Jesus,
Thank you, Jesus, thank you, Jesus.
Lord, you give my truly foundation religion,
Drop a little bit harder."

Spoken:

Well, you know, the little boy, you know,
He said, "Drop a little harder,"

[3] Performed by Emmanuel Dunn, originally a native of Mississippi; recorded in Iowa City, Iowa, by Harry Oster, November 7, 1963. Motif K1971, "Man behind statue (tree) speaks and pretends to be God (spirit)." There are a number of stories in the John and Old Marster cycle centering on deception at the praying tree. Sometimes John's faith is ridiculed; less frequently, Old Marster's. For an example of the latter, see Dorson, "Old Boss and John at the Praying Tree," *Negro Folktales in Michigan*, pp. 65–67: various heavy objects are dropped on Marster's head; he is horse-whipped and fooled into setting John free. In J. Mason Brewer, "How McGruder's Prayer Was Answered," *Mexican Border Ballads and Other Lore* (Austin, 1946), pp. 96–97, there is a significant variation on the typical pattern in that a semi-sophisticated trickster, in this case John, is outwitted by another Negro, the ignorant McGruder, a case of mother wit besting half-baked wisdom.

He had a great big old stone, you know.

Sung:

He turned that stone loose.
Hit Old John in the head.
Old John, knocked him out.
When Old John come back to, he said,
    "Look."
He looked up in the air, he said,
"Jesus, that the way you got to give
    me religion?
Knock me out? Take your religion
    on back to heaven.
I'm gonna stay down here and do the
    the best I can do.
Please, now."

Why do Negroes laugh at this story which makes one of them appear such a fool, the butt of Old Marster's sadistic joke at the expense of John's literal faith in God's intervention in his affairs? There is, of course, the obvious appeal of the numskull story. Most human beings enjoy laughing at the idiocies of an inferior member of their group because such a picture produces a sudden happy fulfillment of their own need for a sense of superiority. At the same time the story directs elements of sophisticated satire against the old-fashioned stereotype of the naive Negro who is gullible enough to have an intense reli-gious faith and to believe that there is any escape to a happier and more just place in either this world or a next one. The skillful use of the religious satire suggests the creative intelligence of a sophisticated, cynical observer, the narrator, who relishes his own superiority and savors the melancholy wisdom of the disenchanted—there is no pie in the sky, only stones.

In many of the tales in the cycle the contest of wit and trickery ends with Old Marster as the victim of the joke, often in the popular folk pattern of the strong formidable figure defeated by the weak ordinary person through cunning, trickery, or luck, as in the European and American Jack tales or the Negro Brer Rabbit tales. But even in such John and Old Marster stories the action is often seen through the mocking eyes of a sophisticated narrator who pierces both slave and master with the comic barb. This is true of "Two at the Gate."[4]

One I can remember my father used to tell me about it a lotta time when I was quite young in those days. An' so he'd sit down an' tell me what his father used to tell him an' his father told him. So the old story kep' a-goin'.

An' so he told me this one about one

---

[4] Told by Eddie "Son" House, originally a native of Mississippi; recorded in Iowa City, Iowa, by Harry Oster, April 24, 1965. Type 1791, "The Sexton Carries the Parson." Motif X424, "The Devil in the Cemetery." The background and elements of the tale are described in Stith Thompson, *The Folktale* (New York; 1946), pp. 213–14: "A sexton hears thieves in the cemetery cracking nuts and thinks it is the devil cracking bones. With the gouty parson on his back he comes upon the thieves who, thinking it is their companion with the sheep, call out. 'Is he fat?'—The sexton, dropping the parson, 'Fat or lean, here he is!' . . . This anecdote is certainly as old as the *Thousand and One Nights*, and appears in nearly every medieval and Renaissance tale collection. But it is widely told by oral story-tellers all over Europe and, for some reason, is about the best known of all anecdotes in America. It is found among the Canadian French; it has been told in Anglo-Saxon tradition in Indiana, the Ozarks, Canada, North Carolina, . . . Texas . . . and the West Indies. . . . And it is not absolutely necessary that the tale be told about a parson at all."—The master in the wheel chair in variants like that of Eddie "Son" House is apparently derived from the gouty priest. Cf. typical American Negro variants: Dorson, "Old Boss Wants into Heaven," *Negro Folktales in Michigan*, pp. 68–69 and "Dividing Souls," *Negro Tales from Pine Bluff, Arkansas, and Calvin, Michigan* (Bloomington, 1958), pp. 48–50.

of the slaves, how he tricked his—in a way—tricked his master into somethin' that he wasn't expectin'.

So his master couldn't walk so he had this guy, his slave, to roll him aroun' in a wheelchair. An' so that night he let him off. An' so this guy, this colored guy, he goes to see his girl friend that night. So the moon was shinin' an' the weather was good. An' so he goes to see his girl friend.

An' at the same time it was two more Negroes went out stealin' one night, stealin' chickens. An' so they had these gunny sacks with them to put the chickens in after they steal 'em. They steal the chickens, then they would tie thei' legs together so in case-a one would get a-loose he couldn't get very far. They could ketch him easy. So, anyway they stole the chickens an' they put 'em in the sacks. An' so in walkin' along goin' back home, one says to the other, says, "Say, listen, we got to divide these chickens an' whereabouts?" Says, "We don't wanta sit alongside the road to do it. Somebody may come along an' see us with the chickens. Say, wonder where could we go?"

So the other guy says, "I tell you a good place we won't be bothered with nobody. Nobody passin' or nothin'. They sho' ain't comin' there."

He says, "Where's that?"

He says, "Let's stop in the cemetery. Say, nobody visits there, not at night, especially."

He say, "That's right, that is a good place."

So they stopped at the cemetery. An' goin' in at the gate two of the old hens got out the bag an' the other one stopped to try an' get'm. He says, "No, that's all right. Let's hurry on in here an' we can get these two when we be comin' out. Say, they can't get nowhere, thei' legs tied."

"Okay, yeah, that's right!"

So they went up there in the cemetery. An' either one of them didn't have any kind o' education or nothin'. They didn't know how to count good. So he says, "I'll tell

you how we'll do it. Since you an' I ne'er one don't know how to count, say, as I get one chicken out I'll say, 'That one yours,' an' I get the next one, I'll say, 'This one mine.' We can divide'm like that."

He says, "Yeah, that's a good idea."

So they was doin' that. An' this guy was comin' back from his girl friend's. It was gettin' kinda late an' the road went right by the cemetery. So he got along there an' he heard 'em countin'. One said, "This one mine, that one yours." Well, he knowed that was the cemetery. "Oh my God!" he said, "Must be Judgment Day! God an' the Devil dividin' souls!"

So he took out an' run home. He got home, poundin' on the door, "Wake up Old Marster, wake up, wake up!"

He said, "What's the matter with you?"

Say, "Wake up, it's Judgment Day!"

He says, "You crazy?"

Says, "No, I'm not crazy. God an' the Devil is down there in the cemetery dividin' souls, right now. If you don't believe it, get up an' get in your chair, an' I'll roll you down there an' let you hear 'em yourself."

He says, "All right, I'm goin', an' I'm gonna take my shotgun with me. An' if you fool me down there, an' they ain't that, I'm gonna shot ya."

He say, "Well okay, you welcome, Old Boss, you welcome. Get in your chair."

So they rolled him on down there an' rolled him up to the gate, near the gate. An' he say, "Now you listen." An' they was near about through countin', "This one mine, that one yours."

Say, "You hear'm, don't ya?" Old Boss then he commenced to get interested in it too. He believed it too hisself then.

An' so way after a while they got the last chickens in. An' the other one remembered, says "Wait a minute."

He says, "What?"

"Say, you remember we got two at the gate."

An' Old Marster thought he was talkin' about him an' the guy he had hired wheel-in' him. He says, "It's two at the gate."

Then the Negro said, "Yeah, say, Old Boss, two at the gate, talkin' about us!"

An' Old Marster jumped out the wheel chair—he hadn't walked in years, jumped out the wheel chair. He say, "You can bring the chair on with you."

That's the first time he's walked in years. He thought it was Judgment Day too. He fooled him.

When I asked my informant, Eddie "Son" House, to explain why he liked the story, what in it made him laugh, he answered:

They would just be referrin' to in a way of how some of our people comin' up on the other man. This boss was always the smartest an' had the education an' learnin', an' he didn't. But through that an' bein' ignorant . . . sometime he work himself out o' somethin' he'd got into without an education, but it'd be just a smartness to try to get out of it, to fool the bossman.[5]

"Son" House found the story amusing and memorable as a result of the comic reversal of roles: the ignorant chicken thieves outwit the educated and supposedly wise master. But whatever slave first told this story (adapting a central motif from English tradition), he was engaging in double-edged satire, poking fun at the gullibility of both master and slave. The original teller and those who repeated the story relished the discomfiture of the Olympian Old Marster, but the sophisticated narrator and the amused listeners also relished their sense of superiority to those above them in power and those below them in intelligence.

Humor of greater complexity occurs in some of the tales in the cycle, as for example in "Tom an' Old Marster"[6] and "John an' the Owl." (Like "John and the Stones," both narratives are spoken semi-rhythmically or sung over a guitar accompaniment.)

Tom an' Old Marster

This here's about George an' Tom here,
Ain't nothin' to make ya feel good.
Ya know, ah, Old Marster told Tom,
ya know,
He said, "Tom." "Yassuh."
"I want you to take over my
plantation."
"Yassuh, I sure will."
Had a lot o' folks on the plantation, ya
know;
An' so, uh, Geor' an' Tom got
together, ya know;
They gonna do their stealin' together,
ya know.
So Tom told Geor', say, "Geor',"
Say, "Looka here,
Old Marster got me over his
plantation.
He jest put the swing [control] in our
hand, didn't he?"
"Sho' did, boy," said, "Say, looka here,
boy,
Say, tonight, let's go 'cross the river,

5 Interview with Eddie "Son" House; recorded in Iowa City, by Harry Oster, April 24, 1965.
6 Performed by Robert Pete Williams, a native of Louisiana; recorded in Iowa City, Iowa, by Harry Oster, February 10, 1965. A narrative related to a widely told Negro tale. Cf., for example, Portia Smiley, "Master Disguised" in "Folk-Lore from Virginia, South Carolina, Georgia, Alabama, and Florida," *Journal of American Folk-Lore*, XXXII (1919), p. 362; Arthur H. Fauset, "Master Gone to Philanewyork" in "Negro Folk Tales from the South (Alabama, Mississippi, Louisiana)," *Journal of American Folk-Lore*, XL (1927), pp. 266–67; Zora N. Hurston (no title is given for the story, but the malapropism for the big city is "Phily-Me-York"), *Mules and Men* (Philadelphia, 1935), pp. 112–14; Dorson, "Old Marster Takes a Trip," *Negro Folktales in Michigan*, p. 59 and "Master's Gone to Philly-Me-York," *Negro Tales from Pine Bluff, Arkansas, and Calvin, Michigan*, pp. 44–46.

An' get us a hog, ya know."
That's where he kept all his hog, ya
  know.
But they had to go 'cross there in a
  skiff.
Some people can swim, some can't ya
  know.
Just like me, I can't swim.
So, ur, ah, okay,
Old Marster kinda got hip to that, ya
  know;
He went an' painted his face, ya know;
I done told you what he did.
He met Tom, he say, "Oh, Tom."
He say, "Yeah," he say, "That you,
  Geor'?"
"Yeah, let's go." There we go.
They goin' to the river, ya see.
They got'm a skiff, ya know.
He say, "Say, roll me a cigarette
  there, Geor'."
He say, "All right, old pardner."
He's doin' so good, goin' 'cross there,
  ya know.
Old Tom, he's talkin' as they're jest
  paddlin' an' goin', ya know.
"How ya gettin' along, old pardner?"
"I'm doin' all right."

So they got on the other side, ya
  know.
"Ah, looka here, say, you shell the
  corn";
Told Geor' shell the corn, ya know.
They say, "Call him." "You call him."
"Geor', no, you call him." "No, you
  call him."
See, Old Marster didn't want to call
  him, see,
'Cause he knowed that Tom could
  ketch on to his voice, ya see;
There is a difference between Tom's
  voice an' Old Marster's voice,
'Cause Old Marster is white, ya know.
He say, "You call him."
He say, "Oo—ooh pig, oo—ooh pig!"
So after a while here come the hog,
Comin' up there, ugh, ugh, ooh, ooh.
He say, "Shell him the corn."

He say, "All right, shell the corn."
Come eat, slip, slurp, slip, slurp,
Uh, uh, uh, uh, it's all right.
Tom say, he say, "Give me the axe,
  Geor'."
Old Tom he took that ya know,
Throw him the corn, ya know, throw
  him the corn.
Hmuh, hmuh, hmuh [smacking
  grunting sounds],
[Axe] Bee! [Hog] Eeh! "There he go,
  he got him, let's go."
They got that hog, ya see.
They drug it over to the skiff, ya see,
An' they put it in the skiff, ya see;
"Oh Geor', we got a big one there."
"Yeah, man, it'll last us a while, won't
  it?"
"That's true, boy."
Still goin' in the skiff, ya know.
"How are ya doin', Geor'?"
"I'm doin' all right, boy. You doin' all
  right?"
"Yeah, I'm doin' fine."
"Say, Geor', hah, roll me a cigarette."
"All right,"—rollin' him a cigarette,
  ya know.
Jes' smokin' it, ya know, Tom, he
  lookin' back there.
"Hey, what's the matter wit' you, boy?"
"What you talkin' about?"
"You gettin' mighty bright back there."
"Oh, go on ahead, paddle, man."
Said, "Don't pay no attention to me."
Old Marster, you see, was gettin' that
  black off his face, ya know.
He say, "Go ahead on, boy, keep on
  paddlin', don't pay me no mind."
They went on a little further, got in the
  middle ways of the river ya know,
He look back, ya know;
He say, "Geor', Geor', huh? What
  the matter wit' you?"
Old Marster say, "Well, Tom, I got ya,
  ah!"

All right, Old Tom he got back, ya
  see, swimmin' on out an' gone home,
  ya see,

An' Old Marster out there, ya know,
   tryin' to paddle best he could wit'
   his hand, ya see;
Got onto the bank, an' so ya see,
So, all right, blow it [whistles], ya see.
He was headed towards Tom's house,
   ya know;
Got there, ya know, he say,
"Oh Tom!" Tom didn't wanta answer;
"Oh Tom!" Tom wouldn't answer;
Call him three time', las' time he call
   him,
"Tom, you hear me?"
"Yassuh, Old Marster."
Say, "Boy, ya know I caught ya
   stealin' my hog,
Ya know that, don't ya?"
"Nossuh, Old Marster, you got the
   wrong man, not me."
"Sure enough, I got you tonight."
He say, "You thought that was George
   wit' ya,
But that was me wit' ya.
I had ya fooled, I had my face
   painted."
"Yassuh, Marster, well, you got me to
   the fact,
You done caught me."
Say, "Come on out there, I'm gonna
   give you a hundred lashes."
Old Marster put a hundred lashes on
   him, ya see;
Ha, ha, he said, "Now look, I'm gonna
   whip ya,
An' I want ya to stay right on the place,
An' ya better not move,
An' I want ya to be to work the next
   mornin'."
"Yassuh, Old Marster."
So he put him a hundred lashes on
   him.

An' so the next mornin', well uh, Old
   Tom right back there to work.
But he was walkin' to work but he
   stopped,
But he thought he'd run that time.
So he went, "Old Marster?" "What?"
"Here I am, huh, I'm here."
"All right, you better be here,
Go on out there an' go to work."
That's Old Marster an' Old Tom.

Although the story ends on a grim note with the violent punishment of the trapped slave, the tone of Robert Pete Williams' narration was one of amusement, and he frequently punctuated his account with chuckles. I asked him if he found the story funny.

WILLIAMS: "It's not too funny, but it's funny in a way."

OSTER: "What makes it funny?"

WILLIAMS: "I can't find anything in it funny, but just the talk about the time, an' what happened at the time, ya see. Well, if I was workin' for you, an' you ketch me stealin', you got me here, an' you ketch me stealin', well, you just pay me, an' run me away, you pay me an' run me away. But in them days, they didn't pay 'em an' run 'em away. They whipped, still stayed on the place. They didn't give 'em no settlement at all. Ya see they put it like this,

Figger's a figger, an' ought a ought,
All for the white man an' none for the
   nigger.

See what I'm talkin' about? [Laughs.][7]

Apparently Williams was amused by

---

[7] Interview with Robert Pete Williams; recorded in Iowa City, Iowa, by Harry Oster, February 10, 1965. [This is a classic bit of folklore reflecting racism. However, it is normally arranged so that "figger" rhymes with "nigger." As reported by William Pickens, for example, it is:

"A nought's a nought, and a figger's a figger—
All fer de white man—none fer de nigger!"

See William Pickens, *Bursting Bonds* (Boston, 1923), p. 26. —ED.]

the narrative as reflected by his responses to his own performance, but when pressed for an explanation he could not explain his reaction beyond noting that the story struck him as worthy of attention as a true account of the old days. When a Negro got into trouble, he was not run off the plantation but instead he was whipped and then returned to work as before. His attitude toward the proverbial lines which he quotes suggests that he finds it amusing to describe even a temporary reversal of the roles of white and black.

Clearly, there are unconscious factors behind the circulation of this and similar tales. The discussions of wit in the writings of Freud and Reik suggest probable explanations. For example, the insights Reik expresses in his book *Jewish Wit* are essentially applicable to the mechanisms of much of the humor of most despised and/or persecuted minority groups. He writes:

[The] emotional process in the listener to an aggressive or obscene joke [operates] in the region "between fright and laughter." The first reaction to hearing such a joke is unconscious alarm. This emotion is aroused by an unexpected attack on highly esteemed persons or institutions, for instance religion, marriage, etc., which we conceived of as sacred or at least very precious and inviolable. In a sense one could speak of the initial shock effect of jokes of this kind. There must be in all of us an unconscious wish to attack those respected persons or highly regarded social institutions. The latent anxiety connected with this temptation is for a moment increased when we hear a cynical or obscene witticism assailing them. For a split second all inhibitions seem to be removed, but then the intensified fear reaction is recognized as overdue or superfluous and the alarm is suddenly stopped. The effect is laughter; in cases where the anxiety was not intensive, it is smiling.[8]

To apply the theory specifically to this tale of Tom and Old Marster, the slave (or later the country Negro) resents the power and wealth of the boss. The scene of Tom and the master with his face painted black is a dangerous fantasy in which the teller and the listener imagine an intriguing and also terrifying situation, a man-to-man confrontation in which the usual walls are down. The listener vicariously enjoys Tom's killing his master's hog, chatting and smoking with him on apparently equal terms. One must, however, return to the bitter reality from which there appears to be no real escape. The slave must work or die; the sharecropper (it would have appeared to many country Negroes) can only go on to another plantation within the same repressive system. Thus the old-time Negro who feels he has to work within the system uses tales of this sort as a defensive psychological mechanism. He identifies with and is amused by the transgressions against the system, but finally returns to work. The effect is that of a sentiment expressed in many Negro blues, "I'm laughin' just to keep from cryin'."

Another tale built on a similar psychological mechanism is "John an' the Owl."[9]

[8] Theodor Reik, *Jewish Wit* (New York, 1962), pp. 233–34.
[9] Performed by Emmanuel Dunn; recorded in Iowa City, Iowa, by Harry Oster, November 7, 1963. A rare tale, probably because of the taboo-ridden damning of God. When Dunn first told me this story in 1962 in Baton Rouge, Louisiana, he omitted this final motif; as I later learned, he was uncomfortable at saying something so blasphemous. Motif J1811, "Criminal confesses because of misunderstood animal cries," roughly covers the first part of the tale; motif J1390, "Retorts concerning thefts," the conclusion in which God is damned.

Spoken:

Old John he stole his Marster's sheep;
He went out in the woods an' he
            killed that sheep,
So Old John butchered that sheep an'
            he carried it on home.

Sung:

His family was hongry,

Spoken:

Didn't have nothin' to eat,
So when he was comin' back alone,
He was ridin' a little donkey,
Old owl way down on ole snag,
Old owl holler, "Yesterday evenin',
You stole that sheep, sheep, sheep."
Old John begin to get worried, you
            know;
He was worried an' he said,

Sung [a moaning spiritual tune]:
"Mm, hmm, ———————————."

Spoken:

So his mind struck him,
"You better pray, that may be Jesus."
Old John didn't know that was a owl;
He thought it was Jesus because his
            mind
Hinted to him that was Jesus.
An' Jesus gonna tell his Old Marster
'Bout he stole one o' his sheep.
Old John he got down off his donkey,
He started to pray, he say,

Sung:

"Oh Lawd, oh Lawd, if You just
            forgive me,
You know, Jesus, You know, Jesus,
My family was hongry,
An' I had nothin' to eat,
I went an' stole the sheep,
An' I butchered the sheep.

Sung:

I carried it on home for my family to
            eat;
Oh Lawd, forgive me, Jesus,
I won't be this guilty no mo'."

Spoken:

Well, the owl he look down, you know,

Seen him comin', crawlin' on his
            knees;
He didn't know what to make o' that,
            if it was a man.
The poor owl was hongry himself.
The owl said, "Yesterday evenin'
You stole that sheep, sheep, sheep."
Well, Old John he crawl near 'bout to
            that snag.

Sung:

"Oh Lawd, oh Lawd, You must forgive
            me, Jesus this time,
I'll never be that guilty no mo'."

Spoken:

Old owl he got long feathers on the
            side o' his head,
Make them look like ears.
Well, that time Old John had crawl to
            the bottom o' the snag;
He look up at him, he say,
"Long-eared Jesus an' feather-legged
            God,
I told You just forgive me,
I never be that guilty no mo'."
Old owl, he said it again,
"Yesterday evenin' you stole that sheep,
            sheep, sheep."
He looked up again, he say,
"Oh Lawd, long-eared Jesus,
            feather-legged God,
Told You Goddamn,
If You just forgive me,
I never be that guilty no mo'.
Told You, Goddamn,
My family was hongry,
I didn't have nothin' to eat,
Goddamn, You know, Jesus,
That is a po' way to be,
When yo' family hongry,
You got to get somethin' to eat.
Now You can go on down,
Tell Old Marster that I stole the sheep,
I tole You, Goddamn,
If You just forgive me,
Goddamn, I never be this guilty no
            mo';
Now You can go down an' tell Ole
            Marster,

Goddamn, I done stole one of his
    sheeps,
I done kill that sheep,
Now me an' my family gonna eat that
    sheep up,
An' Goddamn You!"

The account is built around a central ironic contrast. On the one hand, there is the credulous John who has faith in God's mercy, on the other, the sophisticated Negro who is telling the story. John commits a crime to feed his starving family; when confronted with the awesome figure of a horned owl on a tree at night, he takes it for a menacing Jesus, on the side of law rather than mercy, in league with Old Marster. The figure to whom John prays and humbles himself takes on Godlike status through John's predisposition to believe in Jesus. Ironically, the owl is a suffering fellow creature, like John, desperate for something to eat. In the context the picture is wildly comic: John moves closer and closer to the snag, praying more and more fervently to "long-eared, featherlegged Jesus," while the owl keeps relentlessly and unforgivingly intoning his accusation. At the same time, the situation has seriously ironic implications. Implicit in it is the suggestion that the scene represents the essence of religion— a suffering, guilt-ridden simpleton, praying for forgiveness to a creation of his own imagination, born of his own will to believe. The tale concludes with the simple John losing his faith and approaching the attitude of the cynical and skeptical narrator. Finally, the powerful conclusion in which John damns God retains ironic comicality since John invokes God in damning God —unable to abandon completely a pattern of speech and thought which have so long been part of him.

Although the discussion of the foregoing tales in the John and Old Marster cycle makes no claim to explaining the psychological aspects of all the plot patterns, the principles throw light on the functional dynamics of many of them. The numskull motifs are satisfying to the egos of narrator and listener. At a more complex level, many of the tales are told within an ironic framework in which the values and beliefs of an old-fashioned country Negro, an Uncle Tom, are seen through the eyes of a cynical, disillusioned Negro. In these stories there is a striking and ironically comic incongruity between two opposed views of reality. The story sometimes ends with the archetypal country Negro stumblingly reaching a conclusion like that of the narrator. The latter overcomes his latent anxiety in attacking powerful institutions like slavery, plantation ownership, and God by sharing his social anxiety and guilt feelings with the listener. "When he succeeds in making his audience laugh, he has attained not only approval, but acknowledgement and momentary admiration."[10] While such tales have been important as entertainment, they have also functioned significantly as a mechanism for emotional survival. If one can treat bitter but inescapable reality as a joke, even grim laughter produces a release which blunts tensions and brings about a catharsis of the emotions.

[10] Reik, *Jewish Wit*, p. 234.

The Steel-Drivin' Man

LEON R. HARRIS

There are many tales of Brer Rabbit and many tales of John and Old Marster, but there is only one basic story of John Henry. Nevertheless, John Henry in some ways is as important a folk hero as Brer Rabbit and John. If we consider these heroes in terms of a kind of evolutionary sequence through time, we have first the clever, small animal opposing the larger animal power structure, and then the clever slave opposing the plantation power structure. With John Henry, we have a post-slavery hero, a free Negro who works for wages— even though in the particular version of the story to be presented here John Henry is attempting to earn enough money to purchase his wife-to-be, which indicates that the setting is still slavery times.

The identification of American Negroes with John Henry may be accounted for by a variety of factors. Puckett's study of the names of American Negro slaves revealed that the two most popular male names were John and Henry. If this is so, then the name John Henry would presumably possess maximum appeal. But there are other reasons for the popularity of the story. The plight of the sharecropper or worker who, though technically free, was still economically dependent upon the plantation system was and is a poignant one. It is sad to say that the outlets for Negro creativity and energy have remained relatively few in number. To driving steel has been added professional sports and some portions of the entertainment industry, but unfortunately many areas of both labor (e.g., unions with official or unofficial racist quotas) and management have remained effectively closed to qualified Negro applicants. In this particular version of John Henry, the economic dependency is signaled by the poor percentage offered by the Captain. The white man stands to win five hundred dollars, of which John Henry is promised fifty—if John Henry wins. Presumably, if John Henry loses, he gets nothing—and in fact since he dies in making the effort, he doesn't receive even the fifty dollars. In other words, financially, John Henry does

Reprinted from *The Messenger*, vol. 7 (1925), pp. 386–87, 402, by permission of A. Philip Randolph.

not benefit much from all his labor—the white man does. To the extent that the song or legend encapsulates the evils of exploitation, it may have special appeal for people who have themselves had personal experience with such exploitation.

Also in this particular version, one finds yet another form of exploitation. The "enemy" is the Yankee from the North. Now while it is perfectly obvious that any agent of technology who provides machinery that is designed to put manual laborers out of work is an "enemy," the fact that he is cast as a Yankee may have other implications. Although there were, to be sure, "Yankee drummers" and carpetbaggers, the identity of the enemy in this version provides a North-South conflict. Specifically, the Negro serves as a "tool"—literally and figuratively of the white southerner in defeating the northern intruder. This example of the southern white's manipulation of Negro energy to aid in opposing a northern intruder is perhaps analogous to the Confederate Army's pressing Negroes into service in construction crews or as servants to assist in the struggle against the Union Army, an army which was ostensibly fighting in part to end slavery. In both cases, the Negro is forced into a position of working to help maintain the status quo, a pro-southern status quo which includes slavery or economic exploitation. The northerner in this story is depicted as nothing but a business-oriented opportunist who offers the Negro little other than the eventual unemployment caused by new technology. Though there were and are such Yankees, this is clearly a stereotype figure.

It should be noted that the version of John Henry presented by Leon Harris is not particularly typical, but then again John Henry exists in so many diverse forms—ballad, worksong, legend—that it is difficult to select just one typical version. In his book on John Henry, Professor Guy B. Johnson reports a song version of John Henry which had been sent to him by Leon R. Harris of Moline, Illinois. Harris wrote in a letter to Johnson that he had been a "Rambler" all his life ever since he had run away from the "white folks" when he was twelve years old. Harris, who had worked in railroad grading camps "from the Great Lakes to Florida" and "from the Atlantic to the Missouri River" claimed that his song version was the Virginia and West Virginia version and that he had first heard the song in 1904. The legend text presented here is similar though not identical to the song text from Harris published by Johnson.

One reason why this text rather than any of the hundreds of other texts was selected is that the collector was himself a black railroad grader—as opposed to the white academic folklorists who collected the majority of the other texts. Another reason is that the text appeared originally in a Negro periodical, The Messenger, *intended for a Negro audience (and also appeared in* Phylon *in slightly altered form in 1957).*

For the song text collected by Leon R. Harris, see Guy B. Johnson, John Henry: Tracking Down a Negro Legend *(Chapel Hill, 1929), pp. 90–95. For a comprehensive survey of the considerable John Henry scholarship, see Richard M. Dorson, "The Career of 'John Henry'," which immediately follows the Leon R. Harris version in this volume.*

MANY A rare character has lived and died and no historian has heard of him. But should you visit the particular neighborhood from whence he sprung, or the community that acknowledges his heroism, you will often hear his name lauded in song and story. Old men tell tales about him to their children and to their children's children, and, as mothers rock their babies to sleep, they recite his story while they sing their lullabies.

But the memory of such a one is cherished more by those who travel in his footsteps; who occupy the same station in life, or, who follow the same work or trade, than by any others. Napoleon was a great hero of France, but Napoleon was a soldier, therefore the French soldiers love him best. Lord Nelson was a great British hero, but he was a sailor, hence the English sailors claim him as their own. Every American Negro—and many white Americans— have heard of John Henry, the man who ran and won the greatest race in the world, but his name is worshipped by the "graders." He is the Hero of the "graders."

I would like to tell you this story just as the old man told it to us. We were running a railroad grade through the Allegheny foothills and had reached a spot only a short distance from John Henry's birth-place. For two days and two nights it had been raining. It was one of those cold, constant winter rains, not hard, but seemingly endless, and our camp looked like a soggy swamp.

All of our "rainy day work" was completed. We had sheared and dressed up the mules, greased the wheelers and the harness. The blacksmiths had sharpened the picks, the scrapers and the drills.

It was on the morning of the third day and still it was raining. The white folks were down in their shanty playing poker, and we had gathered in the mess shanty. Some of the fellows—the young bloods—were shooting dice, and playing "skin" for matches, but we old hands had crowded up close to our hard-coal salamander, and were listening intently to the endless stories, told in turn, of each other's experiences of grade and camp life.

The old man was with us. We had learned to like him very well even though he was a "pick-up," for such we call all the hands procured from the various neighborhoods through which we happen to be passing. Such fellows, you know, are usually "green-horns." They don't know a "lead mule" from a "toter."

But the old man was different. He said he was "an ole grader" and we soon found out he told the truth. He could make a sledge hammer talk. He could make a pick whistle. And then we discovered that he was fond of grade life, so fond indeed that he could not resist its call. For when he had heard the echoes of our blastings; the "skinners" yelling to their mule-teams; the curses of the bosses; the ring of the sledges and picks, and the camp-fire's laughter and song—for all this, in concert, is the "call of the grade"—he had come to us.

It was the old man's turn to recite, but right then we were interrupted. Shine, a "skinner," our darkest one and the clown of the camp, entered bearing a sledge hammer and a hand drill. He had come direct from the white folk's shanty. The engineer had covered him with flour and someone had given him a taste or two of moonshine corn liquor.

"Howdy niggahs*," he commenced, "how's you all dis mawnin'. 'Lo ole man!

---

* It is interesting to compare the 1925 *Messenger* version of Harris's essay with the one in *Phylon* in 1957. Although it is substantially the same essay, there are a number of minor detail changes. For example, "Howdy niggahs" in 1925 has been replaced by "Hi, Folkses" in 1957. It is not completely clear whether this change reflects the change in time or the change in audience or both— *Phylon* in contrast to the *Messenger* is read by *both* blacks and whites, which might make the

Wot you doin' sittin' up heah lookin' lak Rain-In-De-Face?"

He dropped the hammer and hand drill, threw his head back, opened wide his mouth and began singing:

"Keeps on a-rainin', podnor,
Niggah can't make no time."

"Ye, ye, yaw-aw," laughed Shine, "ye, ye, yaw-aw! Yere, cullud folkses, dis de way Ole Man does in meetin'."

Shine put his hands to his sides and began a ludicrous dance, keeping time to his hops and jumps by singing the old plantation song:

"O, it rained fo'ty days an' fo'ty nights widout stoppin',
People all prayed dat de watah'd stop droppin'—
O, didn't hit rain, Lawd,
Didn't hit rain!"

"Wish you'd git outta heah," growled the old man.

"Say, Ole Man," said Shine, "Ise jist gotta hab some eggsecize, yere me? I haint wuked none fo'a week. Bleeb Ise'll play John Henry."

He picked up the hand drill he had brought, stuck it the ground, and dextrously swinging the heavy sledge began to drive, keeping time to his strokes by singing the "John Henry" song—

"O John Henry-huh, he drib steel-huh,
lak a man-huh he did-huh,

John Henry-huh, he drib steel-huh,
lak a man-huh, lak a man-huh,
"O John Henry-huh, he war a steel-huh,
dribbin' man-huh, he war-huh,
John Henry-huh, he war a steel-huh,
dribbin' man-huh, dribbin' man-huh!

The fire of youth danced in the old man's eyes while Shine was singing, and when the song ended he exclaimed:

"Dat's wot e war, sawn, dat's wot he war! John 'Enry suttinly war a steel dribbin' man. Yassah! I knowed John 'Enry, and he suttinly war a steel dribbin' man. Yassah! But you, Monkey,"—he said, turning fiercely on Shine.

"O dry hup, Ole Man," said Shine, "an' go milk dem see-dere-ribs cows yuh got back dere in de pines. Wot you know 'bout John Henry?"

Well, we could hardly blame Shine. It did indeed seem like a bald sacrilege for any *living* human being to say that he had really known John Henry. Known John Henry? Seen John Henry? He the noblest "grader" of them all? He the strongest man who ever drove a piece of steel? Why we did not know when *we* had heard the great name mentioned first. We well remembered, that years before, when we were young, when we first began the "life of the grade"—and the work was much harder then than now—that ofttimes the picks and sledges would become intolerably heavy; the curses of the driving bosses unendurable; and we would falter and grow faint at heart, but then, right

---

in-group use of "nigger" inappropriate. Other changes include "steel dribbin' " being replaced by "steel drivin' " and "grader" replaced by "railroader." Of course, there is some evidence that both versions "suffer" from literary embellishment. The account does not really have the ring of oral tradition to it. On the other hand, there is a sense of the genuine involvement of the author with the subject matter and that may compensate in part for the lack of a verbatim transcription of an oral telling of John Henry. Readers who wish to compare the two versions of Leon R. Harris for themselves should see "That Steel Drivin' Man," *Phylon*, 18 (1957), pp. 402–6. —Ed.

then, some old "grader" would see, would understand, and would come to us and slap us on the back.

"Sawn, be a man," he would say. "A man lak John Henry war." I say that we were young. We did not know who this John Henry was, but we certainly learned to respect the memory of the one they cherished so deeply. Then we would take fresh heart. Yet, we would overcome our puerile trials, our imaginary impossibilities, for, woe be unto the "grader" who refused to follow in John Henry's steps! But now, now we were the "old graders" and so likewise we admonished our young men. Yes, all of us, like Shine, doubted the old man's veracity, and the interruption continued while he told the story.

John Henry was a "free man" the old man told us. While a mere lad he had saved his master from a watery grave. For his heroic act he was given his liberty, and more, the former master became his best friend. He always called the old plantation his home.

Physically, John Henry was a mighty man. He was over six feet tall. He weighed more than two-hundred-and-fifty pounds. He could muscle and toss a hundred-pound anvil with one hand. He was a pure Negro and the old man said, "He war pow'ful ugly and war allus grinnin', jist lak Shine dar —but his 'art war as tendah as an 'oman's."

What noble deed would John Henry not do? He would give his last crust of bread to a hungry child. He would sit up all night at the bedside of a sick slave and then work hard the following day, and the work was arduous indeed, but John Henry did not care. He was the best worker in the country.

John Henry was employed by Captain

Walters, a railroad contractor. The Captain was a southerner of the old school. He loved his "niggahs" as he called them, and they loved him.

The Captain also employed many slaves, hiring them from their masters until he completed his contracts. He divided his army of workers into gangs, as best suited each individual's ability. There was the "plow gang" and the "wheeler gang," the "pick-and-shovel gang" and the "skinners," and last, but most important of all, the "blasting gang," which included the steel drivers.

John Henry was a steel driver. The Captain had never seen a man drive steel as well as he did. No one on the job professed to be able to drive as well. Probably it was because he was a "free man," and was receiving into his own hand three silver dollars per week, but the old man told us that back on the old plantation a lassie, Lucy by name, was boss of the plantation kitchen, and John Henry was driving steel for her. John Henry loved her. He wanted her to be his wife but first, he wanted her to be free, as he was. For years he had been saving his money to buy the girl, to pay for the home, and as he drove his steel into the solid rock to make the opening for the powder charge—often the echo of his hammer would speak to him his sweetheart's name—and his "buddies" had christened his hammer "Lucy" because John Henry repeated that name so often.

John Henry loved that servant of his, his hammer. It weighed ten pounds more than any other there. It occupied a special place in the tool shanty. No one touched it but him, for had they done so they would have touched John Henry's heart.

Well, one day, the Captain landed

a contract for a few miles of road through the heart of the Virginia mountains. The work began in June and John Henry was happy. It was a rough country. There was much rock. This would make overtime work compulsory and that meant for him, more money. They knew he was happy for he began to sing a new song to the echo of his hammer—

> "Ef ah makes-huh, June, July an'
>   Augus-huh,
> Ise gwine home-huh, Ise gwine
>   home-huh,
> O ef ah makes-huh, June, July an'
>   Augus'-huh,
> Ise a-comin' home, Lucy-huh, Ise
>   a-comin' home-huh!"

This would he sing as his drill went down, and he grinned much, despite the heat and the perspiration.

But one day there arrived at the camp an enemy to John Henry and to all good steel-driving men. He came in the garb of a Yankee drummer, an agent for a so-called, "steam-drill." This new machine was guaranteed to drill a hole faster than any ten men could drill one in the old way with sledge hammer and steel.

That Yankee was determined to sell one to the Captain. He followed him around for days. But the old southerner was obdurate. He did not believe in the much advertised scientific improvements. It takes money to make improvements, despite their economical value in the end. Besides, he was working Negroes, and Negro labor cost him little. In those days a "nigger" was but a machine anyway— a tool to do the white man's work. Why pay for the use of brains when the use of muscle was so cheap? To rid himself of the Yankee the Captain told him:

"Suh, I have a niggah here who can

take his hammah and steel and beat that three-legged steam contraption of yours to a frazzle, suh. And ah'll bet yuh five hundred dollars on the spot that he can, suh."

"And I'll take your bet provided, that if I win you'll give me an order," said the wily Yankee. And thus it was settled.

The Captain was not at all afraid he would lose his money, the old man told us. He made it his business the next day to visit the "blasting gang" just as John Henry was setting his drill. He noticed how fervently the swarthy driver gripped his sledge, and, with what apparent ease he forced the steel down into the solid rock. He saw the hot perspiration pouring from the seasoned muscles, and then, the grin illuminating the ugly features, and the old Captain chuckled. He called the driver aside.

"John, John, come here John."

"John, I've bet that fool Yankee that you and your hammer can beat that steam contraption he's got. Think you can John?"

"Yassah Cap'n, yassah, yassah."

"Well John, we'll have the race tomorrow and you do it. You beat him and I'll give you—ah—I'll give you fifty dollars."

John Henry had never been so happy before in all his life. Fifty dollars! Fifty dollars! Why to him it meant everything. It meant that Lucy would be free. It meant that Lucy would be his wife. It meant that Lucy and he would have a home of their own. Is it any wonder then, that when night had fallen, he rubbed from his hammer every speck of dirt, placed it reverently away, and as he lay there among the jutting rocks, gazing at the stars, the melody of his songs reverberated throughout those rugged mountains louder and sweeter than his buddies'—that night in the grading camp?

The Yankee did not do right, the old man told us, for he never arrived the next day until the sun was hot, and it was a day in July. But John Henry did not care. He had been singing and grinning all the morning. They chose a spot favored by the Yankee, and, as all the hands crowded around, set their drills.

The race began! It was steam against muscle: brain against brawn; progress against retrogression; Yankee against Southerner; head against heart. John Henry kissed his hammer. The Yankee opened a valve.

John Henry did not sing as he usually did when driving steel. He could not spare the breath. But he drove, ah, how he did drive! With every stroke you could almost see the drill go down and, though the Yankee used much steam, the mark on the Negro's steel was approaching the surface of the stone faster than the mark on his own. And, as the mark on John Henry's steel entered the aperture, finally becoming invisible, he poised his sledge for one more mighty stroke—to clinch the argument, as it were—to make good. The sledge descended—it struck—but dropped from his hands. He staggered and fell full length upon the rocks. His face was ashen. His lips were pale. His buddies stooped over him, fanned him and some ran for water, but he only weakly beckoned for his hammer. Some one laid it in his arms. He touched it to his lips

and his kiss and his blood mingled upon the iron head.

"Lucy—Lucy—O Lucy," he whispered.

The old Captain pushed through the crowd, bent over the stricken driver, and tenderly raised his head.

"John, John," he said. "You've beat that steam contraption. You've beat the Yankee."

"We've beat him, Cap'n?"

The steel driver opened his eyes and saw the glow of victory on the contractor's wrinkled face.

"Why Cap'n, we did beat him! We beat him shor," he said and died.

It was Shine who broke the solemn stillness in our shanty after the old man had concluded his story.

"Ump," he grunted, "Ole Man you is a grader, sho anuff. Guess ah'll haf tuh go down tuh de white fo'ks an' bum some mo' cawn on dat."

He picked up the hammer and drill and departed, and as he trudged through the oozy mud we heard him singing:

"Dis ole hammah, Lawdy, Lawdy hit
   kilt John 'Enry;
Kilt 'im dead, Lawd, Lawd, kilt 'im
   dead—
O dis ole hammah, Lawdy, Lawdy,
   kilt John 'Enry;
But hit won't kill me, podnor—no,
   Lawdy hit won't kill me."

No it won't Shine. There was only one John Henry. There will never be another. He is the Hero of the Graders!

The Career of "John Henry"

RICHARD M. DORSON

Anyone seriously interested in studying a particular legend or folksong has eventually to discover what the state of knowledge is concerning that legend or song. Unfortunately, it is not always a simple matter to locate previous discussions of a particular item. As a matter of fact, it is sometimes a major task simply to locate other texts of the legend in question. In the following essay, one of the leading American folklorists, Professor Richard M. Dorson, Director of the Folklore Institute at Indiana University, surveys the John Henry scholarship. The story of how this ballad and legend have become one of the best known examples of American folklore is a most fascinating one.

Yet after learning about all the books and articles written about John Henry and his various appearances in children's books, all of which is so admirably summarized by Professor Dorson, the nagging question remains: why did this particular bit of American Negro folklore achieve the widespread popularity that it has? "Why" questions are always difficult to answer, but it is tempting to speculate that there may be many different reasons for the story's appeal, perhaps even different reasons for different audiences. For example, in the black community, one could understand the enjoyment of a plot in which a strong black hero wins a contest, a basically unfair contest in which, at first glance, the white man appears to possess all the power (steam drill = power). There is also the fear common to many manual workers, black and white, that automation and technology will put them out of work. Thus while machines obviously benefit management, they don't obviously benefit labor, or at least unskilled labor. But are these interpretations sufficient to explain the ballad and legend's extraordinary popularity in white *America?*

It is possible, though by no means easily demonstrable, that the story of John Henry allays the stereotypic white fears of the "bad nigger," that is, the rough, tough, aggressive militant who refuses to "stay in his place." Rather, John Henry is the strong, loyal, gentle Uncle Tom worker, the ideal "good nigger," whose total strength is devoted to doing the white man's assigned job. John Henry, strong as he is, constitutes no threat or danger to the white captain. In fact, his very death in the performance of his "duty" provides a final proof that he is harmless. He dies in the traces, toiling till the very end so that a white man will win a bet with another white man. Even the phallic interpretation of the tunnel digging discussed by Professor Dorson would be supported insofar as poor John Henry doesn't get to enjoy his wife since he dies immediately after the contest. In terms of the white stereotype, the super-phallic black male dies with his "hammer in his hand," that is, the phallic hammer is no longer a threat to any woman, white or black. If this is at all valid, then it is easy to see that the white appreciation of the story might be quite different from the black appreciation of the story. Black awareness of the unfortunate aspects of John Henry's fate—the victory is, after all, a Pyrrhic one—is indicated by versions including the verse to the effect that the old hammer which killed John Henry can't or won't kill the singer, implying that black people are no longer going to be killed by working for the white man! (See also Eldridge Cleaver, Soul on Ice [New York, 1968], p. 164.)

Of course, there is no one correct interpretation of John Henry any more than there is one correct version of John Henry. Nor is there one correct interpretation of any item of folklore. Each reader must decide for himself what he thinks the meaning or meanings of John Henry are. Hopefully, he will be better able to decide after reading Professor Dorson's thorough survey.

For other treatments of American Negro folklore by Professor Dorson, see Chapter V, "The Negro," of his book American Folklore *(Chicago, 1959) or his excellent anthology* American Negro Folktales *(New York, 1967).*

FOR THIRTY-SEVEN years after the completion of the Big Bend Tunnel in West Virginia, where John Henry presumably defeated the steam drill, his ballad escaped attention.* Then in 1909 it received a short and cryptic note in the pages of the *Journal of American Folklore.* A collector of folksongs from the North Carolina mountains, Louise Rand Bascom, coveted a ballad on "Johnie Henry," of which she possessed only the first two lines.

Johnie Henry was a hard-workin' man,
He died with his hammer in his hand.

Her informant declared the ballad to be sad, tearful and sweet, and hoped to secure the rest "when Tobe sees Tom, an' gits him to larn what he ain't forgot of hit from Muck's pickin'."[1] Apparently, Tobe never did see Tom, but the key stanza was enough to guide other collectors. In the next decade, five contributors to the *Journal* expanded knowledge of the work song and the ballad carrying the name of John Henry. In 1913 the pioneer collector of Southern folk rhymes and folksongs, E. C. Perrow, printed four snatches of the hammer song and the first full ballad text, though

---

* A shorter, unannotated version of this article appeared in *An American Primer*, edited by Daniel J. Boorstin (Chicago and London: University of Chicago Press, 1966; reprinted by the New American Library, Mentor Books, 1968). —ED.
[1] "Ballads and Songs of Western North Carolina," *Journal of American Folklore*, XXII (1909), p. 249.

from a manuscript. Perrow noted that workmen on southern railroads knew a considerable body of verse about the famous steel-driving man, John Henry.[2] An as yet little-known collector, John Lomax, printed a splendid text of eleven stanzas in 1915, saying this was the ballad sung along the Chesapeake and Ohio Railroad in Kentucky and West Virginia, but he provided no source at all, nor the tune.[3] The next year W. A. McCorkle, governor of West Virginia from 1893 to 1897, published an article in the *Journal* mixing John Henry with John Hardy, a Negro desperado hung in West Virginia in 1894. His view was followed by the folksong collector John H. Cox in the *Journal* in 1919 and again in his standard collection of 1925, *Folk-Songs of the South*, in which he mingled ballad texts of the two Negroes.[4] However the confusion between the two folksong characters became apparent to Newman I. White, who separated their texts in his *American Negro Folk-Songs* of 1928.[5]

Meanwhile two scholars had dedicated themselves to the task of recovering and weighing every last scrap of evidence surrounding John Henry. A professor of sociology at the University of North Carolina, Guy B. Johnson, included a chapter of texts on "John Henry, Epic of the Negro Workingman," in *Negro Workaday Songs*, a collection he made in 1926 with Howard W. Odum.[6] At this time Johnson believed

the song hero to be a "myth," but he changed his mind during the next three years and ended up accepting Big Bend Tunnel as the factual basis for the ballad. Johnson interviewed many Negroes and advertised his quest in Negro newspapers in five states, even staging John Henry contests to secure song texts and information. The resulting harvest of letters and statements revealed a pervasive and widespread tradition, deeply enough rooted to manifest all the vagaries and inconsistencies of popular legend. Nearly every state in the South, and several in the North, claimed John Henry as their offspring. One particularly circumstantial account placed the steam-drill contest in Alabama in 1882—but no documentary support could be found. However, struck by the relative stability of the ballad as compared with the fluctuations in narrative accounts, Johnson searched for and uncovered a printed broadside by one W. T. Blankenship, undated, which presumably both drew upon and contributed to the singing of the ballad. Johnson presented his book-length study in 1929—*John Henry, Tracking Down a Negro Legend.*[7]

Coincidentally, a second sleuth had been pursuing John Henry, and trailed him to Big Bend Tunnel before Johnson. Louis W. Chappell, an associate professor of English in West Virginia University, published *John Henry, A Folklore Study* in 1933.[8] It took the form of a minutely detailed critique of Johnson's

[2] "Songs and Rhymes from the South," *Journal of American Folklore*, XXVI, pp. 163–65.

[3] "Some Types of American Folk-Song," *Journal of American Folklore*, XXVIII, p. 14.

[4] "John Hardy," *Journal of American Folklore*, XXXII, pp. 505–20; and *Folk-Songs of the South* (Cambridge, Mass., 1925), pp. 175–88. The same identification of John Henry with John Hardy was made by Dorothy Scarborough, *On the Trail of Negro Folk-Songs* (Cambridge, Mass. 1925), pp. 218–22.

[5] (Cambridge, Mass.: Harvard University Press, 1928), pp. 189–91, "John Henry."

[6] (Chapel Hill: University of North Carolina Press).

[7] *Ibid.*

[8] (Jena: Frommannsche Verlag, Walter Biedermann).

methods and interpretation, mainly because they preceded, and derived from, his own. Chappell accused Johnson of using without acknowledgement a preliminary report he had made in 1925 on his findings at Big Bend Tunnel. The evidence painstakingly gathered and skillfully evaluated by Chappell builds a powerful case for the historicity of John Henry at Big Bend.[9]

With Chappell's exhaustive monograph, the scholarly probe into John Henry virtually ceased, and the two main questions—the relationship of John Henry to John Hardy and the factual basis for the steam-drilling contest—were laid to rest. Popular interest in the Negro hero, however, continued to grow.

Already, in his inquiry into the John Henry tradition, Guy B. Johnson had anticipated its potentialities for the creative arts. "I marvel" (he wrote) "that some of the 'new' Negroes with an artistic bent do not exploit the wealth of John Henry lore. Here is material for an epic poem, for a play, for an opera, for a Negro symphony. What more tragic theme than the theme of John Henry's martyrdom?"[10] A response was not long in coming. Within two years, a book-length story of *John Henry* had been published and distributed by the Literary Guild. Its author, Roark Bradford, while not a "new

Negro," had grown up on a Southern plantation near the Mississippi River and seen Negroes closely. Exploring Southern Negro culture for literary themes, he struck a profitable formula with fictional works depicting the childlike Negro conception of the world based on Scripture. Bradford achieved his greatest success with *Ol' Man Adam an' His Chillun* (1928), rendered by Marc Connolly into the Broadway hit, *The Green Pastures*. The revelation of a tragic Negro folk legend seemed timed to assist his literary career. In Bradford's *John Henry*, the contest with the machine occupies only 5 out of 223 pages, but it serves as the dramatic climax for such structure as the book possesses. A cotton-rolling steam winch on the levee replaces the rock-boring steam drill, and New Orleans and the Mississippi River form the locale. John Henry is a cotton-loading roustabout, when he is working; much of the time he is loving and leaving his girl Julie Anne, who follows him into death after his fatal contest with the new machine. At other times, he performs great feats of lifting, eating, and brawling. The whole narrative is written in a repetitive, rhythmic stage dialect, interspersed with plaintive little songs and centering around Negro literary stereotypes. The sporting man, the hell-busting preacher, the woman of easy acquaintance, the old conjure

---

[9] Between the two monographic studies, various related items were published. Chappell demanded an explanation from Johnson in *American Speech*, VI (Dec. 1930), pp. 144 ff. Lowry C. Wimberly wrote a note in admiration of Johnson's *John Henry* and praised the ballad as great literature, for its theme "of the individual pitting his lone strength and courage against an environment" and "its ringing hammer music" and portrayal of "the struggle of sentient humanity against the unfeeling machine" (*Folk-Say, A Regional Miscellany*, ed. B. A. Botkin [Norman, Okla., 1930], "Steel-Drivin' Man," pp. 413–15.) Gordon H. Gerould in his well-known study, *The Ballad of Tradition* (Oxford, 1932), pp. 264–68, discussed the confusion of "John Henry" with "John Hardy," speculated that "John Henry" was of Negro origin, and reprinted a 22-stanza text from Johnson, pp. 289–92. Louise Pound lauded Johnson's *John Henry* in her review in the *Journal of American Folklore*, XLIII (1930), pp. 126–27.

[10] Johnson, *op. cit.*, p. 150.

mammy are all present. John Henry is a new stereotype for the Negro gallery, but a well-established one in American lore —the frontier boaster—and he reiterates his tall-tale outcries on nearly every page.

In 1939 an adaptation of *John Henry*, billed as a play with music, appeared on the Broadway stage. Co-author with Roark Bradford was Jacques Wolfe, who supplied the musical scores for the song numbers. The play followed closely the original story, which contained obvious elements for a musical drama. Paul Robeson starred as John Henry. The Broadway production closed after a short run.[11]

The book and the play of Roark Bradford, with attendant newspaper reviews and magazine articles,[12] popularized the name of John Henry, and fixed him in the public mind as a Negro Paul Bunyan. In many ways, the growth of the John Henry legend and pseudo-legend parallels that of the giant logger, who was well-established as a national property by the 1930's. Bradford's *John Henry* resembles James Stevens' *Paul Bunyan* of 1925 as a fictional portrayal of an American "folk" hero based on a slender thread of oral tradition—in one case a few northwoods anecdotes, in the other a single ballad. Bradford,

like Stevens, created the picture of a giant strong man, although with a somber rather than a rollicking mien, as befit a Negro hero. In 1926 Odum and Johnson called John Henry the "black Paul Bunyan of the Negro workingman." Carl Sandburg made the comparison the following year in *The American Songbag*, saying both heroes were myths. Newspapers referred to John Henry as the "Paul Bunyan of Negroes," "the Paul Bunyan of his race, a gigantic river roustabout whose Herculean feats of work and living are part of America's folklore."[13]

In the later history of the two traditions, the parallelism persists. Writers, poets, and artists attempted to wrest some deeper meaning from the Paul Bunyan and John Henry legends and failed. But both figures lived on triumphantly in children's books of American folk heroes and in popular treasuries of American folklore.

The first presentation of John Henry as a folk hero came in 1930 in a chapter of *Here's Audacity! American Legendary Heroes*, by Frank Shay, who had published books of drinking songs. His account of "John Henry, the Steel-Driving Man," followed Guy B. Johnson's preliminary essay of 1927 on "John Henry: A Negro Legend."[14]

[11] Published by Harper and Brothers (New York & London: 1939). Josh White played the part of Blind Lemon, a folk singer, and in his 25th anniversary album (*ca. 1955*) recorded "The Story of John Henry," based on songs in the stage production (Elektra Records 123-A).

[12] *Time* and *Newsweek* carried notices on Jan. 22, 1940, and *Theatre Arts* in its March issue (XXIV, pp. 166–67). Roark Bradford wrote a piece for *Collier's* on "Paul Robeson in John Henry" (Jan. 13, 1940), pp. 105 f.

[13] Howard W. Odum and Guy B. Johnson, *Negro Workaday Songs* (Chapel Hill, 1926), p. 221; Carl Sandburg, *The American Songbag* (New York, 1927), p. 24 ("In southern work camp gangs, John Henry is the strong man, or the ridiculous man, or anyhow the man worth talking about, having a myth character somewhat like that of Paul Bunyan in work gangs of the Big Woods of the North"); R. M. Dorson, "Paul Bunyan in the News, 1939–1941" *Western Folklore*, XV (1956), p. 193, citing newspaper notices of the Bradford-Wolfe music-drama in which John Henry was likened to Paul Bunyan.

[14] The chapter "John Henry, the Steel Driving Man" in Frank Shay, *Here's Audacity!* (New York, 1930), pp. 245–53, was based on Guy B. Johnson's chapter in *Ebony and Topaz, A Collectanea*, ed. Charles S. Johnson (New York, 1927), pp. 47–51, "John Henry—A Negro Legend."

Shay's formula was repeated by a number of other writers for the juvenile market, all of whom inevitably included the story of John Henry and his contest with the steam drill in their pantheon of American comic demigods. Such folk-hero books were written by Carl Carmer (1937), Olive Beaupré Miller (1939), Anne Malcolmson (1941), Carmer again (1942), Walter Blair (1944), and Maria Leach (1958).[15]

Other authors of children's books found it rewarding to deal individually and serially with Paul Bunyan and his kin. Consequences were *John Henry, the Rambling Black Ulysses*, by James Cloyd Bowman (1942), *John Henry and the Double-Jointed Steam Drill* by Irwin Shapiro (1945), and *John Henry and His Hammer*, by Harold W. Felton (1950). Of these, Bowman's nearly three hundred pages went far beyond the ballad story to give a full-length improvisation of John Henry's career, from a slave boy on the old plantation through the Civil War to freedom times. John Henry encourages unruly freedmen to mine coal, cut corn, pick cotton, and drive railroad ties. He outsmarts confidence men and gamblers, stokes the *Robert E. Lee* to victory over the *Natchez*, and at long last dies with his hammer in his hand at the Big Bend Tunnel. But a final chapter presents an alternate report, that John Henry recovered from overwork and resumed his ramblin' around. In Shapiro's much briefer story, John Henry never dies at all, but after beating the steam drill pines away to a ghost, until his old pal John Hardy convinces him that he should learn to use the machine he conquered, and the tale ends with John Henry drilling through the mountain, and the steam drill shivering to pieces in his hands! So for American children John Henry unites the Negroes in faithful service to their white employers and accepts the machine. In these children's books, the full-page illustrations of a sad-faced Negro giant swinging a hammer contributed as much as the printed words to fixing the image of John Henry.[16] In the 1930's, Palmer Hayden completed twelve oil paintings, now hanging in the Harmon Foundation in New York, on the life story of John Henry.[17]

Folklore treasuries and folksong collections also continued to keep the story and song steadily before the public. In his best-selling *A Treasury of American Folklore* (1944), currently in its twenty-third printing, B. A. Botkin reprinted accounts of John Henry in oral hearsay, balladry, and fiction; he gave him further notice in *A Treasury of Southern Folklore* (1949) and *A Trea-*

---

[15] The titles are Carmer, *The Hurricane's Children* (New York and Toronto, 1937), "How John Henry Beat the Steam Drill Down," pp. 122–28; Miller, *Heroes, Outlaws and Funny Fellows* (New York, 1939), "John Henry's Contest with the Big Steam Drill," pp. 147–57; Malcolmson, *Yankee Doodle's Cousins* (Boston, 1941), "John Henry," pp. 101–7; Carmer, *America Sings* (New York, 1942), "John Henry," pp. 174–79; Blair, *Tall Tale America* (New York, 1944), "John Henry and the Machine in West Virginia," pp. 203–19; Leach, *The Rainbow Book of American Folk Tales and Legends* (Cleveland and New York, 1958), "John Henry," pp. 33–35.

[16] One such volume, *Their Weight in Wildcats* (Boston, 1946), carried only the name of the illustrator, James Daugherty, on the title page. The selection of hero tales reprinted from earlier volumes was made by an editor, Paul Brooks, at Houghton-Mifflin, the publisher. For John Henry he reprinted the statements of one of Guy B. Johnson's informants, Leon R. Harris of Moline, Illinois. Brooks saw in John Henry only "brute strength and dumb courage" (p. 170).

[17] Ray M. Lawless, *Folksingers and Folksongs in America* (New York, 1960), pp. 12–13.

sury of Railroad Folklore, done with Alvin C. Harlow (1953).[18] The lavishly illustrated *Life Treasury of American Folklore* (1961) offered a picture of John Henry spiking ties on a railroad track rather than driving steel in a tunnel, and in a skimpy headnote to the retelling of the ballad story revived the discredited hypothesis that the contest might have occurred in Alabama in 1882.[19] John A. and Alan Lomax, naturally sympathetic to the ballad hero first presented in a full text by the elder Lomax in 1915, always included John Henry ballads, some adapted and arranged, some recorded in the field, in their popular folksong compilations: *American Ballads and Folksongs* (1934), *Our Singing Country* (1941), *Folksong U.S.A.* (1947), and *The Folksongs of North America* (1960). "John Henry" was the opening song in their first book, and in *Our Singing Country* they called it "probably America's greatest single piece of folklore." In the latest and most ornate garland, Alan Lomax (the sole author), having meanwhile shifted from a Marxian to a Freudian analysis, found John Henry equally receptive to his altered insights. The steel-driver shaking the mountain is a phallic image; singers know that John Henry died from love-

making, not overwork:

> This old hammer—WHAM!
> Killed John Henry—WHAM!
> Can't kill me—WHAM!
> Can't kill me—WHAM!

Thus the hammer song vaunted the sexual virility of the pounder.[20] Lomax had returned full cycle to the psychoanalytic views of Chappell. The steel-driver also appealed to social reformers. In *American Folk Songs of Protest* (1953; reprinted as a paperback in 1960), John Greenway called "John Henry" the "best-known (and best) Negro ballad, the best-known Negro work song, the best song of protest against imminent technological unemployment."[21]

While collected folksongs and literary retellings of the John Henry theme poured into print, only one or two folktales landed in the net of collectors. A curious folk narrative, mixing tall-tale elements of the Wonderful Hunt, the Great Eater, and Schlaraffenland with heroic and erotic legends, was told to Howard Odum in 1926 by a Negro construction camp worker in Chapel Hill.[22] Yet subsequent Negro tale collections added only one substantial text to the John Henry tradition, while a whole cycle of trickster John tales dating from

[18] *A Treasury of American Folklore* (New York, 1944), pp. 230–40; *A Treasury of Southern Folklore* (New York, 1949), pp. 748–49; *A Treasury of Railroad Folklore* (New York, 1953), pp. 402–5.
[19] The Editors of Life, *Life Treasury of American Folklore* (New York, 1961), pp. 168–69. Other popular publications to retell the story of John Henry and reprint a ballad text are Freeman H. Hubbard, *Railroad Avenue* (New York, 1945), pp. 58–64, "The Mighty Jawn Henry"; *The Book of Negro Folklore*, ed. Langston Hughes and Arna Bontemps (New York, 1958), "John Henry," pp. 345–47; *American Heritage*, XIV (Oct., 1963), pp. 34–37, 95, Bernard Asbell, "A Man Ain't Nothin' but a Man."
[20] Alan Lomax, *The Folk Songs of North America* (New York, 1960), pp. 551–53. For the work song, cf. Chappell, p. 99. Support for Lomax's position is given by Roger D. Abrahams in his note and ballad text on John Henry as a sexual hero of South Philadelphia Negroes (*Deep Down in the Jungle*, Hatboro, Pa., 1964), p. 80.
[21] (Philadelphia: University of Pennsylvania Press), p. 107. Reprinted as paperback by A. S. Barnes & Co. (Perpetua edition, 1960).
[22] *Negro Workaday Songs*, pp. 238–40.

slavery times were being uncovered.[23] A folktale volume of 1943, prepared by the Federal Writers' Project in North Carolina, contained a graphic and fantastic prose tradition of John Henry's birth, deeds, and death in the contest with the steam drill on the Santa Fe Railroad. Data are given on the informant, an aged Negro of Lillington, North Carolina, who asserted John Henry was born north of him on the Cape Fear River, and worked with him on the Santa Fe road, but the text is obviously edited.[24] The talented Negro novelist and folklorist, Zora Neale Hurston, explicitly asserted in *Mules and Men* (1935) that the ballad was the only folklore item connected with John Henry.[25]

The greatest impact of John Henry on American culture has come outside the printed page through commercial recordings. In 1962 the most widely recorded folksong sold to the public was "John Henry." That year the Phonolog Record Index listed some fifty current renditions of the ballad "John Henry"

and fifteen of the work song "Nine Pound Hammer." As many popular singers have made recordings for the general public as have folksingers for collectors in the field. The Library of Congress Copyright Catalogue reveals over one hundred song titles devoted to John Henry from 1916 on, embracing all kinds of musical arrangements from simple melodic line and text to full orchestral composition. Arrangers staking out claims include: the well-known American composer, Aaron Copland; the Negro song-compiler, John W. Work; the musicologist, Charles Seeger; the celebrated Negro ex-convict, Huddie Ledbetter (Lead Belly); W. C. Handy, the "father of the blues"; concert arranger, Elie Siegmeister; and popular singer Bob Gibson. Chronologically, only ten copyrights are registered before 1937, ten in the period 1938–1945, twenty from 1946–1954, and eighty from 1955–1963.[26] While the general popularity of "John Henry" has dramatically climbed in the past decade, fresh field texts are rarely reported.[27] Still the

[23] There is no connection between the trickster John cycle and John Henry, as Alan Lomax suggests (*The Folk Songs of North America*, p. 553). For folktales of John the slave and his Old Marster, see R. M. Dorson, *Negro Folktales in Michigan* (Cambridge, Mass. 1956), Chap. 4, and *Negro Tales from Pine Bluff, Arkansas, and Calvin, Michigan* (Bloomington, Ind., 1958), pp. 43–62.

[24] *Bundle of Troubles and Other Tarheel Tales*, ed. W. C. Hendricks (Durham, N. C., 1943), pp. 37–51, "John Henry of the Cape Fear." (Told by Glasgow McLeod to T. Pat Matthews.)

[25] Hurston, *Mules and Men* (Philadelphia and London, 1935), p. 306. She prints nine "verses of John Henry, the king of railroad track-laying songs," pp. 80–81, 309–12.

[26] This information was kindly supplied to me by Joseph C. Hickerson, Reference Librarian in the Archive of Folk Song, Library of Congress.

[27] Field-collected texts are reported by G. Malcolm Laws, *Native American Balladry* (Philadelphia: 1950), p. 231. "John Henry" is I 1 in his index. He refers to thirty-nine recordings from eleven states and the District of Columbia in the Library of Congress folk song archives, including five releases. He cites, in addition to works already mentioned, Mellinger E. Henry, *Folk-Songs from the Southern Highlands* (New York, 1938), pp. 441–42, 446–48, for a text and many references. In *Folk-Songs of Virginia, A Descriptive Index and Classification* (Durham, N. C., 1949), p. 294, Arthur K. Davis lists six John Henry texts collected between 1932 and 1934. Only one full text of eight stanzas is presented in *The Frank C. Brown Collection of North Carolina Folklore*, Vol. II, *Folk Ballads* (Durham, N.C., 1952), pp. 623–27. The editors, H. M. Belden and A. P. Hudson, say, "Few if any folk songs of American origin have been so extensively and intensively studied as John Henry."

commerical recordings are frequently traditional or semitraditional in source.[28]

Popular singers and recording artists have altered the formless sequence of independent stanzas which comprised the folk ballad into a swift-moving, tightly knit song story. John Henry has shifted from the sphere of Negro laborers and white mountaineers into the center of the urban folksong revival and the entertainment world of jukebox and hootenanny, radio and television. The earlier texts from tradition show the usual variation characteristic of folklore. John Henry drives steel chiefly on the C&O, but once it is located in Brinton, New Jersey, and he also drives on the AC and L, and Air Line Road, the L and N, and the Georgia Southern Road. He comes from Tennessee most often, but also from East Virginia, Louisiana, and Mobile, Alabama. His hammer weighs nine, ten, twelve, sixteen, twenty and thirty pounds; sometimes he carries a hammer in each hand. His girl is named Julie Ann, Polly Ann, Mary Ann, Martha Ann, Nellie Ann, Lizzie Ann, and Mary Magdalene. In one unique text, John Henry's partner kills him with the hammer. Among the visitors to his grave are, in one instance, Queen Elizabeth.

Yet the shifts and twists of tradition are perhaps less surprising than the tenacity and recurrence of key phrases, lines, and stanzas. Analyzing his thirty-odd texts, Guy Johnson determined that the three most frequent stanzas, and therefore probably the earliest, were the opening stanza of John Henry sitting on his papa's (or mama's) knee, the declaration to his captain, "A man ain't nothin' but a man," and the verse about his gal dressed in red, Polly Ann. Otherwise, the story line varied considerably, and Johnson observed, "The stanza, not the song, is the unit" (p. 87), a conclusion later supported by Alan Lomax. Phonograph, radio, and record-player have however given the episodic stanzas of the ballad a structure and symmetry; already in 1929 Johnson could list eleven examples of "John Henry" on commercial records, and in 1933 Chappell added eleven more. One of the most astute folksong scholars in America, Phillips Barry, believed that mountain white song tradition, perhaps in the person of John Henry's white woman, helped stabilize the ballad. He pointed to its parallelism with the opening stanza of the well-known old English ballad of "Mary Hamilton":

When I was a babe and a very little
    babe,
And stood at my mither's knee,
Nae witch nor warlock did unfauld
    The death I was to dree.

"Mary Hamilton" and other English

[28] Some representative examples of commercially released "John Henry" recordings currently available, which appear indebted at least indirectly to traditional southern Appalachian sources, are Laurel River Valley Boys, *Music for Moonshiners* (Judson L3031); Mainer's Mountaineers, *Good Ole Mountain Music* (King 666); Bill Monroe and His Blue Grass Boys, *New John Henry Blues* (Decca 45–31540); George Pegram and Walter Parham, *Banjo Songs from the Southern Mountains* (Riverside RLP 12–610); Harry Smith, *Anthology of American Folk Song* (Folkways; re-recordings of early hillbilly and race records), No. 18, Williamson Brothers and Curry, "Gonna Die with my Hammer in my Hand" and No. 80, Mississippi John Hurt, "Spike Driver Blues"; Merle Travis, *Back Home* (Capital T891). Neil Rosenberg and Mayne Smith kindly furnished me information for this list from their personal record collections.

and Scottish ballads lingered in the Southern mountains and so could easily have influenced the new ballad.[29]

Today the ballad of John Henry lives on in remarkably stable form for an anonymous oral composition. It has been refashioned by the urban folksong revival into a national property, shared by singers and composers, writers and artists, listeners and readers. The ballad commemorates an obscure event in which several lines of American history converged—the growth of the railroads, the rise of the Negro, the struggle of labor. Various interpreters have read in the shadowy figure of John Henry symbols of racial, national and sexual strivings. Negro and white man, teenager and tot, professor and performer, have levied upon the John tradition. The explanation for these multiple appeals lies in the dramatic intensity, tragic tension, and simple poetry combined in one unforgettable American folk ballad.[30]

[29] Phillips Barry, review of L. W. Chappell, *John Henry*, in *Bulletin of the Folk-Song Society of the Northeast*, VIII (1934), pp. 24–26. As further evidence of "non-tunnel" influences, Barry cites a "John Hardy" tune transferred to "John Henry" but known only to white mountaineers.

[30] That new surprises are still possible in the career of John Henry was shown in the remarkable paper by MacEdward Leach presented at the regional meeting of the American Folklore Society at Duke University on April 23, 1964, "John Henry in Jamaica," suggesting the possibility of the John Henry tradition's originating among Jamaican Negroes. [For this Jamaican origin hypothesis, see MacEdward Leach, "John Henry," in Bruce Jackson, ed., *Folklore and Society* (Hatboro, Pennsylvania, 1966), pp. 93–106. —ED.]

"Ba-ad Nigger"

H. C. BREARLEY

In the light of the brutal history of slavery, it is not surprising that American Negroes needed to reassure themselves that they were not afraid. Much of the lifestyle surrounding the "peculiar institution" was very frightening—as the various ex-slave narratives attest. Small wonder that at least within the group, different forms of boasting and hyperbole were enjoyed.

No one could take pride in being "too light to fight and too thin to win," but one could find much needed ego support in maintaining one's roughness, toughness, meanness, or badness. Sometimes the folk expression was simply uttered to show the world that one was not afraid. A beautiful example of such is "to walk on the edge of a rainbow and dare the sun to shine." This implies that one is not afraid to fly high even though the path be most precarious and perhaps also that one is not afraid to defy the natural universe—presumably strong sunshine would soon destroy the all too fragile rainbow. But most often the boast speaks directly of badness. A typical intensifying simile is: "I'm so bad I'd jump into a lion's cage wearing a hamburger (or porkchop, in some versions) jacket."

In this brief essay by H. C. Brearley, who taught sociology at Clemson College and at George Peabody College, some of the "desirable" features of badness are set forth. Crucial is the premise that "bad" is good, which, as previously noted in this volume, is analogous to "black" being beautiful in the context of white society with its longstanding symbolic associations of good with white and evil with black. This premise is absolutely essential for any kind of an understanding of such "bad" folk heroes as Stagolee or Railroad Bill. Though one might argue that Brer Rabbit and trickster John occasionally operated "outside the law" in order to gain their ends, they are rarely, if ever, mean or bad. Guile and deceit are the hallmarks of these tricksters, not indul-

Reprinted from *The South Atlantic Quarterly*, vol. 38 (1939), pp. 75–81, by permission of the Duke University Press.

gence in braggadocio. John Henry is a strong man, but he is generally modest and humble. He is definitely not a trickster. Stagolee is no trickster either, but then again he is not a modest strong man like John Henry. The badman is an important character in American Negro folk narrative, especially in the urban ghettoes (though in ghetto culture there is also a trickster figure in the person of the pimp).

In addition to delineating "badness," Brearley also consciously or unconsciously describes a number of significant Southern white attitudes. One of the most "striking" is the curious notion that Negroes have respect or regard only for whites who beat them physically! For example, Brearley actually goes so far as to claim that the Southern white who in the case of an insult, real or imagined, from a Negro does not take the law into his own hands in vigilante style risks losing the respect of both Negroes and whites. This is, if true, an incredible rationalization for the necessity of lynchings! On the other hand, Brearley's insights into Negro attitudes toward the police may be a little more helpful. His "defense" of the "bad" Negro includes the statement that the bad man wishes only to arouse the fury of the whites and then "get away with it." If this is correct, it might be analogous to the inflammatory rhetoric employed by many "bad" black militants. This rhetoric, which has metaphorical *and connotative significance for black audiences is* literally *understood or rather misunderstood by frightened white audiences. All in all, Brearley's essay, whatever its deficiencies or excesses, deals with an important topic whose importance extends far beyond the realm of folk narrative.*

For an early ante-bellum reference to the specific phrase "bad nigger," see Benjamin Drew, A North-Side View of Slavery *(New York, 1968), pp. 219–20; see also E. C. Perrow, "Songs and Rhymes from the South,"* Journal of American Folklore, *25 (1912), p. 155, n. 1. For more recent discussions of the "bad nigger," see William H. Grier and Price M. Cobbs,* Black Rage *(New York, 1969), pp. 54–55, and William H. Wiggins, Jr., "Jack Johnson as Bad Nigger: the Folklore of His Life,"* The Black Scholar, *II, 5 (January, 1971), pp. 35–46. For other examples of boasts involving intensifying similes, see Roger D. Abrahams,* Deep Down in the Jungle *(Hatboro, Pa., 1964), pp. 240–42 or in the revised edition (Chicago, 1970), pp. 252–54. For essays dealing with the different types of Negro heroes and tricksters, see Fred O. Weldon, "Negro Folktale Heroes,"* Publications of the Texas Folklore Society, *24 (1959), pp. 170–89; Marshall Fishwick, "Uncle Remus vs. John Henry: Folk Tension,"* Western Folklore, *20 (1961), pp. 77–85; Roger D. Abrahams, "The Changing Concept of the Negro Hero,"* Publications of the Texas Folklore Society, *31 (1962), pp. 119–32; Bill R. Hampton, "On Identification and Negro Tricksters,"* Southern Folklore Quarterly, *31 (1967), pp. 55–65.*

A NEGRO youth yet in his teens seats himself upon a much whittled bench in front of a tottering general store near the railway tracks. Ceremoniously he adjusts his hat at a rakish angle, picks up his banjo, and sings to an approving circle of listeners:

I'se Wild Nigger Bill
  Frum Redpepper Hill,
I never did wo'k, an' I never will.
I'se done kill de boss;
  I'se knocked down de hoss:
I eats up raw goose widout apple sauce!

Such folksongs, expressing the Negro's admiration for recklessness and bravado, may be heard almost any day on the back streets of the villages and towns of the lower South. In Negro folk literature the "bad" man plays a role hardly secondary to that of the trickster, so well exemplified by the Brer Rabbit of Joel Chandler Harris's *Uncle Remus.*

In all folktales the daredevil is a constantly recurring character. From primitive champions like Beowulf to train-robbers like Jesse James and killers like John Dillinger the imagination of men has often cast an aura over the lives of those who dare to rebel against fate or authority or law.

In many Negro communities, however, this emphasis upon heroic deviltry is so marked that the very word *bad* often loses its original significance and may be used as an epithet of honor. This use of *bad* as a term of admiration is quite likely an importation from Africa, for Herskovits has found a similar terminology among the blacks of the Surinam district of Dutch Guiana, among the Negroes of the West Indies, and among the natives of the province of Dahomey in West Africa. In some parts of the South, however, there is a change in pronunciation to indicate whether or not the word carries approval. If the speaker wishes to use the term with the ordinary connotation, he pronounces it after the manner of Webster. But if he is describing a local hero, he calls him "ba-ad." The more he prolongs the *a*, the greater is his homage.

If this esteem for "bad" men is really African in origin, contact with the whites has not destroyed it. On the contrary, it has doubtless been strengthened by the traditional European approbation of rebels and outlaws. Besides, the Negro's love of derringdo may be partly an overcompensation for the generally observed docility of the natives of central West Africa and for the enforced servility of slavery and later Jim Crow-ism.*

But regardless of its origin, the tradi-

---

* These and the preceding remarks speculating about a possible African origin for the "bad nigger" aroused the ire of anthropologist Melville J. Herskovits. In a short critique of Brearley's essay, Herskovits dismisses out of hand the notion that the Negro heroic outlaw is a survival of an African tradition. He points out that to the best of his knowledge the African outlaw is a phenomenon which he has never come upon. Similarly, Herskovits attacks what he calls the stereotype of the docile Negro. He noted that the area of West Africa to which Brearley refers is known for the warring empires of its earlier history.

Herskovits' position was essentially as follows: although he was a firm believer in the existence of African retentions in the New World and in the importance of such retentions, he deplored excesses in the would-be identification and interpretations of alleged retentions. In Brearley's case, Herskovits felt that the African origin argument was inappropriate and indefensible. Moreover, Herskovits suggested that Brearley had, by his interpretation, somewhat distorted the available evidence. Herskovits might also have pointed out that the search for an African origin in this particular instance could conceivably have had a racist motivation, albeit an unconscious one. If the "bad nigger" is bad (by white standards), then obviously it would be an excellent culture trait to derive from "primitive," "savage," "bad" Africa! The fact is that the badman is a white folk hero too (as Brearley initially observes), and it is much more likely that the Negro community borrowed the badman from white tradition—though like the English language spiritual, it became transformed into something quite different from the original white model. For Herskovits' comments, see "A Letter to the Editors: Some Comments by Professor Herskovits," *The South Atlantic Quarterly*, 39 (1940), pp. 350–51.

Actually, the ante-bellum usage of the phrase "bad nigger" provides a clue to the most plausible theory for its origin and subsequent popularity. According to one John Little, a fugitive slave

tion of the glory of the "bad" man still flourishes and definitely motivates the conduct of many Negroes, especially in the rural South. Even Jesus Christ has been portrayed by a Negro circuit rider as a man "who wouldn't stand no foolin' wid. Why, he could pop off a lion's head jus like he was a fryin' size chicken!" No one in the congregation would fail to understand this tribute or to admire such courage and power.

The songs of Lead Belly, the tough troubadour brought to notice by Lomax, are exceptional chiefly for their high quality. On every holiday hundreds of other boastful songsters arouse the envy of Negro audiences by similar ballads and tales of amorous and murderous exploits.

The geographical extent of this tradition of the "bad" Negro is, however, difficult to state with exactness. Evidences of it have been found from Texas to Virginia. Dabney's reminiscences show it to have been prevalent among Cincinnati Negroes during the eighties and nineties, but several competent observers deny its importance among present-day Northern city dwellers. In West Virginia, according to Laing, Negroes native to the state look with disfavor upon those moving in from farther South because "they brag about how mean they is" and because "they'll kill you in a minute." This pattern of behavior is, then, more characteristic of the Negro of the lower South, since it is well known throughout the Cotton Belt.

Open expression of admiration for a "ba-ad nigger" is doubtless a comparatively recent development. Even if his type existed during slavery, the singing of ballads in his honor was not a very politic method of securing the favor of masters and overseers. Besides, his lawless activities were greatly circumscribed by the authority of the owners and the watchfulness of the "patterollers." Occasionally, however, a "bad" slave resisted punishment and fled to the swamps or the hills. This was a desperate recourse and usually led to his death or recapture and sale to a distant plantation.

The "bad" Negro of today has,

---

who found freedom and self-respect in Canada in the middle of the nineteenth century, a "bad nigger" (and he used the phrase in quotation marks which indicates its traditionality) is the Negro who is put in the stocks or put in irons. Little reports that local people seeing someone in irons would say: "Boy, what have you got that on you for? That shows a damned bad nigger . . . if you weren't a bad nigger you wouldn't have them on." The point is that being labeled "bad" by Southern white plantation owners in the sense of being dangerous, obstreperous, and the like indicated to black people that the individual in question was unwilling to submit passively to the oppression of slavery. Thus "bad niggers" were Negroes with spirit, Negroes who were willing to fight the system. "Bad" didn't mean evil at all. As Little puts it, "The man who was 'a bad nigger' in the South is here [Canada] a respected, independent farmer."

Thus the white's meant-to-be-insulting epithet of "bad nigger" became virtually a badge of honor in the black community. If the white slaveowners deemed one a "bad nigger," that was high praise indeed. Here then we may have a remarkable folk transformation of an outgroup's intended term of opprobrium into a positive compliment as understood by members of the in-group. For John Little's autobiographical report, see Benjamin Drew, *A North-Side View of Slavery. The Refugee: or the Narratives of Fugitive Slaves in Canada. Related by Themselves, with An Account of the History and Condition of the Colored Population of Upper Canada* (New York: Negro Universities Press, 1968, originally published in 1856), pp. 198–224 (see esp. pp. 203, 219–20). —ED.

however, an almost unlimited field of operations. One of his most effective methods of demonstrating his prowess is to "break up" a picnic, ball game, or "frolic." In Odum's *Rainbow Round My Shoulder* a Negro rowdy vividly describes the exploits of one "Graveyard Kid" and comments enviously, "Thought I was bad enough, but he sho got me beat." One rainy day this Graveyard Kid, disgusted with his duties as stable boy in a construction camp, went to his shack and "git in one hand a thirty-eight special an' in other a ortermatic an' jump up on that table while about fohty of us boys was eatin' supper an' go trompin, down the middle of it, steppin' in beans and bread, an' every other kind o' food his big feet hit." Meanwhile he announced loudly, "Now, boys, any of you don't like this don't have to take it, 'cause it ain't no doctor's 'scription. Nobody got to take it. If anybody meaner than I is don' like it, jes let me know." Intimidated by the two revolvers, "nobody never open his mouth."

Such dramatic exhibitions of recklessness and egotism have been enacted hundreds of times. If successful, they are sure to raise the status of the desperado. Bad-Lan' Stone understood his audience when he threatened,

Don't you never dare slight my repertation,
Or I'll break up this jamberee.

If the bravo is often able to terrorize the onlookers, he may become more than a local celebrity and may even have ballads sung in his honor, such as those telling of the deeds of Stagolee, Roscoe Bill, Eddy Jones, and other heroes. Many bloody affrays are, of course, occasioned by these attempts to secure prestige. Songs portraying this motive are very common.

I went down town de yudder night,
A 'raisin' san' an' a-wantin' a fight;
Had a forty-dollar razzer an' a gatlin' gun
Fer to shoot dem niggers down one by one.

Usually, however, the days of boasting are few. A rival "bad" Negro comes upon the scene. Shortly afterwards, money is being collected to provide funeral expenses for one of the combatants, as is described in one of the ballads about Stagolee:

Some give a nickel, some give a dime;
I didn't give a red copper cent, 'cause
He's no friend o' mine:
Stagolee done kill dat bully now.

Fohty dollar coffin, eighty dollar hack,
Carried po' man to cemetery but failed to bring him back;
Lawdy, Lawdy, one mo' rounder gone.

As the stanzas above suggest, there are other character types that resemble in one way or another the true "bad" Negro. The "bully" is generally one who secures his reputation at the expense of unarmed men or of those of inferior strength. The "rounder" is usually a ne'er-do-well, depending more upon chicanery than courage. He is often, however, a favorite with the women, as is the "nachel bohn Eastman," who boasts that he does not have to work— " 'cause I got it writ on the tail o' my shirt." Such near heroes are, none the less, distinctly inferior in status to the genuine "ba-ad nigger."

Negro women, like their sisters the world over, give the "bad" man his full share of praise. Indeed, the desire for feminine approval is one of the strongest motives for attempting this role. As one ballad puts it:

I'm de rough stuff o' dark-town alley,
I'm de man dey hates to see.
I'm de rough stuff o' dis alley,
But de womens all falls for me.

Many "bad" Negroes confine their bravado strictly to members of their own race. Often a man who is the very personification of arrogance in his dealings with other Negroes will be quite deferential in his treatment of whites. But others consider their triumph incomplete if they are unable to flaunt themselves in the face of a white man, especially of one who is known to go armed or to be "rough on niggers." On the other hand, the white, especially if he is of inferior social status, feels that any slight from a Negro is a humiliation that must be instantly revenged. These antagonistic attitudes make frequent interracial slayings difficult to avoid.

Two Negro women had a fight. A white man living nearby interfered. One of the women, according to her report, "cussed him out. And he took it." The next day she spent several hours going through the Negro village proudly describing her intimidation of the white man. If he had picked up a stick and knocked her unconscious, as the folkways demanded, she would have had far more regard for him.

The would-be "bad" Negro has, needless to say, little difficulty in arousing the anger of the whites. The interracial situation is so loaded with explosive prejudices that a triviality may easily lead to hostilities. A Negro may enrage a white man merely by calling him by his given name or asking him a simple question in a sneering voice. Again, he may resort to bantering wit, at which he is an adept, as when a colored fisherman replies to a passerby's question, "What are you catching?" with the saucy rejoinder, "Catching cold." Besides such verbal affronts, there is always the possibility of more overt conflicts, as collisions on the sidewalk, insulting gestures, and minor obscenities.

The white overseer is a favorite target for these more or less subtle shafts. In a Louisiana cane field a laborer replied to the young foreman's rebuke by asking, "Who taught you to cut cane?" Had the foreman attempted to ignore this indignity, he might as well have resigned his position. This method of securing prestige by "sassing the boss" is not, of course, confined to the Negro. It has been observed among the Shanty Irish, Italian miners, and other groups of day laborers. Essentially, it is an unsophisticated form of egotism, but among Negroes it serves also as an expression of racial antagonism and as a means of developing the reputation of being "ba-ad."

The policeman rather than the foreman provides, however, the supreme test of daring. Here is a white man, armed, the embodiment of authority. Whoever gets the better of him has reached the highest goal of the "bad" Negro. In a small town a Negro man choked the local constable into insensibility. Immediately the hero was dubbed "Jack Johnson," after the famous Negro boxer. This admiration made him overbold. Shortly afterwards, possibly to maintain his reputation, he killed a policeman with a baseball bat and ended his life in the electric chair.

Perhaps the most famous of all "bad" Negroes is Railroad Bill, about whose career dozens of ballads have been composed. This hero, whose real name was Morris Slater, shot a policeman with a rifle and escaped on a freight train. Sheriff McMillan went to capture the desperado, but:

Railroad Bill was de worst ole coon,
    Killed McMillan by de light o' de
        moon;
It's lookin' fer Railroad Bill.

As Carl Carmer says, "Railroad Bill is a god of Negro mythology. A rifle was the symbol of his godhead. A freight train was his chariot. The white gods pursued him—but he escaped." Not for long, however. The bullets of "the law" finally found their mark and "laid him down" on the "coolin' board" of the undertaker.*

Such a hostile attitude toward officers of the law is one of the important causes of killings involving both whites and Negroes. In the more than thirteen-hundred cases of interracial homicide studied by the writer approximately fifty percent concern police officials, either as the slain or as the slayer.† The "bad" Negro pattern of behavior is certainly one reason for this bloodshed, although there are such contributing causes as the arrogance of officers and the Negro's fear of the third degree and "the white folks' law."

In defense of the "bad" Negro it should be added, however, that he rarely premeditates interracial murder. He prefers to arouse the fury of the whites and then "get away with it." This is no easy task, for the Southern white who in such a matter does not take the law into his own hands loses the respect of both Negroes and whites. If the disturber becomes too bold, the community may seize upon some relatively unimportant incident as a pretext for "quieting" the offender. This is the explanation of not a few seemingly unprovoked lynchings.

In spite of these "miscalculations" the "bad" Negro enjoys so much prestige that he has imitators even among the whites, especially in sections where the Negroes predominate in number. The white who essays this role often feels it incumbent upon him to "shoot up the town" once or twice a year, preferably during the Christmas celebrations. In one Southern village the lone policeman is said to run ahead of the desperado, shouting to bystanders, "Get out of the way; a bad man's coming!"

* One of the fullest accounts of Railroad Bill may be found in Carl Carmer, *Stars Fell on Alabama* (New York, 1934), pp. 122–25. According to Carmer, Morris Slater from the pine woods of Escambia County, Alabama, shot and killed Sheriff E. S. McMillan on July 3, 1895. Slater, known as "Railroad Bill," was himself killed nearly a year later in March, 1896. One of the earliest texts dates from 1906 in Mississippi. See Newman I. White, *American Negro Folk-Songs* (Hatboro, Pennsylvania, 1965), pp. 358–59. Other relatively early (1909) texts are those reported from Alabama and Mississippi by E. C. Perrow, "Songs and Rhymes from the South," *Journal of American Folklore*, 25 (1912), p. 155. Perrow specifically describes Railroad Bill as a "bad nigguh" who terrified Alabama some years ago. For additional tests of Railroad Bill, see Thomas W. Talley, *Negro Folk Rhymes* (New York, 1922), p. 94 (this appears to be the source for the first stanza cited in Brearley's essay); Howard W. Odum and Guy B. Johnson, *The Negro and His Songs* (Chapel Hill, 1925), pp. 198–203; Alan Lomax, *The Rainbow Sign* (New York, 1959), p. 64; and Richard M. Dorson, *American Negro Folktales* (New York, 1967), p. 356. —ED.
† For Brearley's findings, see H. C. Brearley, *Homicide in the United States* (Chapel Hill, 1932). —ED.

Usually the "bad man," white or black, is less formidable than he seems. Vanity is his compelling motive, not revenge. Loudly he boasts of the killing power of his weapons, but rarely does he use his "thirty-eight special" or his "fohty fo." If his name is commonplace, he feels moved to adopt a more colorful one—"Cotton-eyed Joe," "Big Bad Wolf." Hardly ever is he of the killer type. With him the risk of slaying or of being slain is but a part of the price to be paid for prestige and glory.

The person of mixed blood, it is generally believed, is more likely than the black to attempt the part of the "bad" Negro. This is probably true, for the average mulatto feels superior to the blacks and often welcomes a chance to demonstrate his importance. Besides, he resents even more than does the black the racial discriminations practiced by the whites. His "almost but not quite" status is a precarious one and needs to be bolstered by public approval. If he has luck and courage, he may, by playing successfully the role of the "bad" Negro, be assured of the prestige he yearns for.

This pattern of conduct is, consequently, a very significant one in the life of the South. As a local hero and a racial demigod the "bad" Negro not only enjoys an esteem far out of proportion to his social worth, but he also induces the young and suggestible to imitate his recklessness and criminality. To understand the rural Negro of the lower South, it is necessary to keep in mind the potency of his desire to be known as a "ba-ad nigger."

The Ghostly Legend
of the Ku-Klux Klan

H. GRADY MCWHINEY AND FRANCIS B. SIMKINS

    Most of the folk narratives discussed thus far are fictional. Certainly the Brer Rabbit cycle and the John–Old Marster cycle are. The historicity of John Henry or of Stagolee or of Railroad Bill remains a moot point, but in a very real sense it makes little difference ultimately whether the ballads and tales are based upon fiction or fact. (The story of John Henry is powerful whether there was an actual steel-driver named John Henry or whether there was not. In this context, it is not history but what the folk make of history that is most important.) On the other hand, generically speaking, legend as opposed to folktale is usually believed to be true, that is, a legend is believed to be literally true whereas a folktale can only be metaphorically "true" (insofar as a human foible is portrayed, for example, or a piece of foolishness or wisdom is displayed). Since legend is frequently (though not always) accompanied by belief, it is a singularly important type of folk narrative.

    Inasmuch as legend is almost invariably set in the real world (in contrast to fairy tales which are set in another world, a fantasy world), it is often mixed with history, much to the despair of most historians. Since legend, like all folklore, is commonly—but wrongly—assumed to be fictional, or at least spurious as history, historians often pride themselves on their success in weeding out legendary elements so as to arrive at "pure" history—what actually happened at a given point in time—unadulterated by legend. What some historians fail to realize is that traditional legends may be as valuable as "pure" history as primary source material for an understanding of how ordinary people perceived historical events and personages.

    In this valuable study of the traditional stereotypes and legends which partly explain the nature of that particularly virulent form of racism—the Ku-Klux

Reprinted from *The Negro History Bulletin*, vol. 14 (February, 1951), pp. 109–12, by permission of Grady McWhiney and *The Negro History Bulletin*.

Klan—the reader can see how the folklore of a group is used to support the ideology of that group. In this instance, one might justifiably argue that the subject of this essay is white folklore, not Negro folklore, and therefore that the study does not belong in a volume concerned with American Negro folklore. However, the subject is really white folklore about Negroes, and it is folklore which, historically speaking, has had considerable impact upon Negro life in the United States.

In a way, the essay may be said to deal with white misconceptions about Negro folklore. For example, some Southern whites believe that Negroes are "congenitally superstitious," as the authors of this study put it. The thesis of the authors is that many of the rituals and practices of the Ku-Klux Klan are based upon white beliefs about Negro folklore, e.g., the Negro's alleged penchant for superstition. If these white beliefs are nothing more than unfounded stereotypes, then many of the derivative rituals and practices, such as wearing white sheet hoods, would appear to be sheer self-delusion on the part of the racist Klan members. In any event, the issue of whose folklore is involved is really the crucial one. If what whites have claimed was Negro folklore turns out to be white folklore about Negroes, then this is an important point. (This is directly analogous to Hyman's assumption that the "darky" entertainer is part of Negro folklore and Ellison's contention in rebuttal that the "darky" entertainer is white, not black!) Furthermore, to the extent that Negroes in a white school system run the risk of being brainwashed, it is imperative that the record be set straight lest young Negro students come to accept as Negro folklore what uninformed white teachers claim is Negro folklore. In this context, it will hopefully be deemed appropriate to include a discussion of white folklore about Negroes in a book devoted to Negro folklore. For further discussion of the Ku-Klux Klan and folklore, see Gladys-Marie Fry, The Night Riders: A Study in the Social Control of the Negro *(Knoxville, Tennessee, 1973).*

THE CONCEPT of the South as a distinct region of the United States is largely based on a series of legends little changed by the researches of the realists. Among these persistent stereotypes are the myths about the Sewanee River, Kentucky colonels, beaux and belles under the moonlight, the inability of the white man to work under the August sun, and the success of the planters' sons and daughters in avoiding toil. The Negro as the central character of Southern history has inevitably evolved into the most distinctive participant in the Southern legend.

In the imaginings of the South's numerous storytellers the Negro takes two forms—the Good "Darky"* and

* The white stereotype of the good "darky" shows once again the failure of white people to understand Negro culture. A Negro mask has been falsely perceived by whites as reality. As in the case of black militant rhetoric, something metaphorical has been wrongly understood literally. To the extent that playing the fool may be a wise ploy, the mask or "front" was part of the Negro survival kit. But the white failure to see a "front" as a "front," suggests the wise white may be the fool after all. For an interesting account of the "good nigger" as mask, see L. M. Hussey, "Homo Africanus," *American Mercury*, 4 (1925), pp. 83–89. For a fictional account of "frontin'" involving a middle-class Negro woman and her Negro maidservant, see Marita Bonner, "Black Fronts," *Opportunity*, 16 (1938), pp. 210–14. —ED.

the Bad Negro. The former is represented as bowing at the proper time and always agreeing with his reputed betters. He is characterized as slow, easy-going, unadapted to severe climates, irresponsible, good-natured, mercurial, and naturally fond of sweet 'taters, 'possum, and the banjo. The Good "Darky" is supposed to be so congenitally superstitious that the stratagems of all the Yankee schoolma'ams from Cape Cod to Philadelphia do not dispel his delusions. In the legend he is so persistently under the influence of nightly apparitions that the mere mention of a ghost makes him shake as actively as Step'in Fetch'it under the influence of an Arctic breeze.

This concept of the Good "Darky" is no small factor in explaining one of the significant facts of American history: the survival of the Southern view of life and thought despite the setbacks of the Civil War and Reconstruction. Thereby does the South live as a cultural entity. Fantastic as this attitude may appear to the objective observer, it is a means through which the white man asserts his superior caste status. It gives even the lowly poor white a chance to laugh at a creature adjudged meaner than the poor white himself. It allows the Southern mind to float back to the "good old days" before the war with illusions of "mint juleps," "grand balls," "gracious ladies," and loyal slaves suited to the interests of leisure-class idealism.

Of equal importance in the white man's mind is the legend of the Bad Negro. He is characterized as a huge brute with a large, flat nose and lust-crazed eyes. Of necessity, he is arrogant, untrustworthy, sneaky, and vicious. His primary interest is the deflowerment of white ladies or the murder of former masters. This creation was expressed in *The Clansman* and other writings of the Reverend Thomas Dixon, Jr., of North Carolina.[1] Dixon's imaginings as projected in the moving picture *The Birth of a Nation* were imposed upon the popular mind with such compelling effectiveness that race riots were narrowly averted. Indirectly the concept of the black hands around the white throats of the Southern maidens gave all true sons of Dixie a creature to hate and fear.

The Good "Darky" and the Bad Negro have become a main convention of Southern literature. It has its kindliest expression in the winsome creations of Irwin Russell. It has most sinister expression in the fulminations of Dixon. The attempt in the 1920's of the white South Carolinians, DuBose Heyward and Julia Peterkin, to endow the Negro with the varied emotions of normal men was only temporarily successful. Their writings have been followed by a return to type: the humorous mercurial fellow of Roy Octavus Cohen; the credulous preacher of *Green Pastures;* the kowtowing servitors of *Gone with the Wind.* Such Negroes figure in books of non-Southerners; they appear in the works of serious historians,[2] and have become too precious a part of the Southern legend to be rejected wherever the South is esteemed.

Such beliefs concerning the Negro culminate in the Southern conception

---

[1] Thomas Dixon, Jr., *The Clansman* (New York, 1905); *The Traitor* (New York, 1907); *The Leopard's Spots* (New York, 1902); *The Fall of a Nation* (New York, 1916); *The Black Hood* (New York, London, 1924).
[2] Claude G. Bowers, *The Tragic Era* (Cambridge, 1929), pp. 306–7; and Walter L. Fleming, *Documentary History of Reconstruction* (Cleveland, 1906), II, pp. 447–48.

of the Ku-Klux Klan of the Reconstruction period. The mythology surrounding the magic letters *KKK* is still vivid in the minds of the Southern people eighty years after the organization's supposed death. The ride of the hooded knights under a mythical Forrest and a mythical Gordon is considered as real as the ride of Confederate cavalrymen behind the real Nathan B. Forrest and the real John B. Gordon. Southerners hold to the aberration that the sole purpose of the Ku-Klux Klan was to prevent the deflowerment of Southern womanhood, to re-establish White Supremacy, and to drive infamous carpetbaggers back to their Northern homes. The degree to which the present authors believe this to be untrue is set forth elsewhere.[3]

An explanation of the full scope and purpose of the Ku-Klux Klan awaits the critical appraisal of the historian; such an ambitious task is beyond the limits of this paper. Its sole objective is to question the legend that ghostly affectations were an important means of effecting the klan's ambitions.

The great body of literature about the hooded order is loaded with assertions about knights in ghostly disguise using weird demonstrations as a certain method of effecting the return of the blacks to their traditional position of subordination. Such behavior is presented as a vivid example of the black man's inherent tendency to be superstitious as opposed to artificially imposed urges of the Negro to seek political and social equality. The first klansmen, says Susan

L. Davis, a historian sympathetic to the klan, "rode slowly through the streets of Pulaski [Tennessee] waving to the people and making grotesque gestures, which created merriment to the unsuperstitious, and to the superstitious, great fear." Elaborating, this interpreter of the motives of the actors in the Ku-Klux drama emphasizes how idle Negroes thought they had seen ghosts and hastily returned to their masters asking for work.[4]

John C. Lester and Daniel L. Wilson, two of the original members of the dreaded organization, loosely assert that the klan "swept noiselessly by in the darkness with gleaming death's-heads, skeletons, and chains" striking "terror into the hearts of the evil-doer."[5]

"Pretty soon," says Stanley F. Horn, the organization's most comprehensive historian, "the Ku-Klux were being referred to generally as the 'ghosts of the Confederate dead,' and a Negro preacher in Tennessee electrified his congregation by telling them that he had seen one of the spirits rise from the grave of a murdered Confederate soldier who was buried near his church." Not satisfied with this test of the reader's credulity, Mr. Horn relates the story of a klansman drinking a bucket of water to the utter horror of his Negro host. " 'That's good,' he would say, smacking his lips. 'That's the first drink I've had since I was killed at the Battle of Shiloh; and you get mighty thirsty down in Hell!' "[6] Already had this story been related, with implied endorsement of its authenticity, by Walter L. Fleming,

[3] Francis B. Simkins, "The Ku-Klux Klan in South Carolina, 1868–1871," *Journal of Negro History*, XII (October, 1927), pp. 606–47.

[4] Susan L. Davis, *Authentic History Ku-Klux Klan, 1865–1877* (New York, 1924), p. 8.

[5] John C. Lester and Daniel L. Wilson, *Ku-Klux Klan* (Nashville, Tenn., 1884), p. 98.

[6] Stanley F. Horn, *Invisible Empire* (Boston, 1939), pp. 18–19.

the most careful of the Southern historians of Reconstruction.[7]

These and other interesting cases of black men quailing before ghosts are based on the recollections of the white klansmen themselves or on hearsay recorded by willing retailers of a myth too precious not to be accepted. They form a part of the specious data which fit too well in the pattern of the Negro legend to be questioned by any but the most outlandish historian. Miss Davis gives no proof that it was the "grotesque gestures" of the first klansmen which created "great fear" among "the superstitious" and caused them to return to their traditional tasks. Messrs. Lester and Wilson do not bother to give proof that their death heads, skeletons and chains were the cause of the terror they say their cavalcade of disguised horsemen inspired. Mr. Horn fails to give the direct testimony of the Negro preacher or even so much as this preacher's name for the assertion that this black believed he had seen spirits rising from the grave of a Confederate soldier. Horn's and Fleming's story about the heavy-drinking visitor from hell is obviously based on the testimony of Joseph H. Speed of Marion, Alabama, in 1871 before the committee of Congress which was then investigating the activities of the klan. Speed's recollections have the value of being nearly contemporary, but they were based on hearsay and are not substantiated by the testimony of the heavy-drinking klansman or of the horrified Negro.[8]

That the Ku-Klux Klan fulfilled its historic mission of frightening Negroes is not to be denied; indeed Fleming cannot be successfully challenged when he asserts that the hooded order was a crucial factor in restoring White Supremacy in a number of states.[9] But, there are other explanations aside from rationalizations about ghostly blandishments which can be used to explain this denouement. Let it be remembered that there were other organizations of Southern white men as effective as the klan in forcing the Negro into social and political subordination. They were the Pale Faces and Knights of the White Camelia in Louisiana, the White Brotherhoods in Mississippi and the Red Shirts in South Carolina. The members of these organizations wore no disguises and about their memory clings no ghostly legends. They accomplished their purpose by violence or threats of violence. They, the historians tell us, rode about the country brandishing weapons and frequently using them. Obviously the Negroes were frightened into submission.

Is this not also true of the Ku-Klux raiders? Is it not reasonable to assume that the "superstitious" blacks were realists enough to be terrorized by the weapons hidden beneath the ghostly robes of the klansmen rather than by ghostly decorations of which the robes were a part? That the klansmen used the methods of violence as extensively as any of the other white terroristic organizations is attested by the number of crimes they committed. Their woundings, murders, whippings and even rapes

[7] Walter L. Fleming, *The Sequel of Appomattox* (New Haven, 1919), p. 254.
[8] Unites States Congress: *Report of Joint Select Committee to Inquire into the Condition of Affairs in the Late Insurrectionary States*, 42nd Cong., 2nd sess., 13 vols. (Washington, 1872), VIII, p. 432. This document is hereafter referred to as *Ku-Klux Reports*.
[9] Fleming, *The Sequel of Appomattox*, pp. 291–92.

became so widespread that responsible leaders of white opinion became alarmed and ordered the hooded order disbanded.

The most reliable way to approach the problem of whether or not Negro victims of the klan were frightened by its ghostly affectations is to let these victims speak for themselves. They do this to the number of 167 in confessions embodied in the thirteen volumes of testimony taken in 1871–1872 by a committee of Congress investigating the activities of the klan. The validity of this evidence has been attacked on the ground that it came from an illiterate group who inherited mendacious habits from slavery and who were black stooges mouthing the sentiments of the white politicians who put them on the witness stand. The answer to this challenge is suggested by Homer C. Hockett, a critic of historical evidence, when he says that a contemporary account, given by a naive person, is more likely to be accurate than a partisan memoir.[10] In other words, there is reason to believe that these Negroes, because they were uneducated and unsophisticated, would not have been ashamed to confess their belief in the efficacy of ghosts as would have been people better educated and more sophisticated. They had no motive while being questioned by congressional investigators for exercising their supposed proclivity for lying. They were perhaps under obligation to their Republican mentors to assert that Democratic violence was visited upon them; but they were under obligation to no one to assert that they did not believe in ghosts. What they said or did not say on this point was seemingly spontaneous, the outpourings of their simple hearts. This was something of no immediate concern to the practical politicians of both parties on the investigating committee.

The Congressional committee questioned the 167 subjects of Ku-Klux visitations concerning their names, places of residence, political affiliations, political activities, and the ways in which witnesses said that they were approached by the klansmen. In all cases those questioned said that they were ordered to stay out of politics and to conform in other respects to the Southern white's conception of proper social behavior for Negroes. As a means of enforcing their wishes the white visitors in all cases used or threatened violence. This behavior was likely to take forms as far removed from the gentle actions of ghosts as earthly conduct can be. This meant beatings, woundings, and killings with clubs and guns wielded by men too real to have been regarded as gravedwellers. "They said they wanted him [my horse] for a charger to ride to hell. I tell it to you just like they repeated it to me," stated Joseph Gill, a Negro of Huntsville, Alabama, in explaining how so-called ghosts addressed him in the unmistakable tones of living exmasters of slaves. This Negro knew that his white neighbors were doing the talking.[11]

It is interesting to note that in not one of the confessions of the Negro victims of the klan, did the investigating committee ask the Negroes if they believed their klan visitors were ghosts. This is true despite the fact that the victims admitted that the visitors often called themselves ghosts and often dressed accordingly.

[10] Homer C. Hockett, *Introduction to Research in American History* (New York, 1948), p. 91.
[11] *Ku-Klux Reports*, IX, p. 813 (Huntsville, Ala., October 12, 1871).

Why was this question not asked? It was because such an inquiry would have appeared obviously stupid when addressed to persons who were able to prove that the fear of actual physical violence was the only reason why they were frightened by their klan visitors. Had this not been true, the Democratic members of the congressional committee would not have lost the opportunity to defend the thesis that the klan accomplished its glorious purpose by nothing less harmful than ghostly affectations. Thereby the klan could have been freed of the stigma of violence, and the desire of the American people to laugh at the supposed credulous Negro could have been gratified. But, this golden opportunity to explain the effectiveness of the klan in the nonviolent terms of ghostly apparitions did not come until public opinion had time to envelop the klan in the haze of the Negro legend.

As has been previously mentioned, many Ku-Klux raiders claimed they came from hell or wore disguises designed to create that illusion. The fact that this contention was not believed is proved by the ability of a goodly number —thirty-six of the 167—of the witnesses testifying before the congressional committee to identify by name one or more members of each of the attacking parties.

William Coleman, a Negro farmer of Macon, Mississippi, gave a typical demonstration of ability to identify the alleged ghosts. He was asked by the chairman of the congressional committee if those who had whipped him were disguised. After an affirmative answer, the next question was: "Did you know any of them?"

ANSWER: Of course I did. I ought to know them, my neighbors; and I knocked off the faces and horns fighting, and then they knocked down the one that I ran between his legs; when they struck him, his horns and everything flew about; of course I knowed him. I don't know as I would know his ashes, unless I saw him burned.
QUESTION: Did you see that they had horns?
ANSWER: They had horns on them.*
QUESTION: They said they rode from Shiloh?
ANSWER: They said they rode from Shiloh in two hours and come to kill me.
QUESTION: Did they say they were the spirits of the Confederate dead?
ANSWER: They didn't tell me nothing about spirits. They said they come from Shiloh but said nothing about spirits.[12]

Hampton Hicklin of York County, South Carolina clearly proved that he did not believe that the disguises of his attackers were effective in creating the desired illusion:

QUESTION: All had on disguises?
ANSWER: Yes, sir.
QUESTION: What sort?
ANSWER: They had on these false-faces and white covers.
QUESTION: Were their heads covered?
ANSWER: No, sir, their heads were not covered, but their faces were. I could see their hair.[13]

One of the clearest proofs of a victim being able to identify elaborately

---

* Plantation owners often told their slaves that Yankees were devils with horns and tails. For a fictional account, see Corinne Dean, "Horns and Tails," *The Crisis*, 47 (1940), pp. 202–204, 210. —ED.
[12] *Ibid.*, XI, pp. 483–84 (Macon, Miss., November 6, 1871).
[13] *Ibid.*, V, p. 1567 (Yorkville, S. C., July 27, 1871).

disguised attackers was the testimony of Lucy McMillan, a forty-five year old widow of Spartanburg District, South Carolina. Concretely did she describe the ghostly disguises:

They had just such cloth as this white cotton frock made into old gowns; and some had black faces, and some red, and some had horns on their heads.

With equal emphasis did she prove that the harm they did was that of real men:

I was afraid of them; there was so much talk of Ku-Klux drowning people, and whipping people, and killing them. My house was only a little piece from the river, so I laid out at night in the woods. The Sunday evening after Isham McCrary was whipped I went up, and a white man, John Mc-Millan, came along and said to me, "Lucy, you had better stay at home, for they will whip you any how." I said if they have to, they might whip me in the wood, for I am afraid to stay there. Monday night they came in and burned my house down; I dodged out alongside of the road not far off.

Clearly did she prove that she was able to identify her visitors:

I saw them. I was sitting right not far off, and as they came along the river I knew some of them. I knew John McMillan, and Kennedy McMillan, and Billy Bush, and John Hunter. They were all together. I was not far off, and I saw them.

In explaining how she knew them she said, "They came a-talking and I knew their voices."[14]

Although many of the klan's victims were not able to identify their disguised assailants they could dispel the make-believe. Joseph Gill who had been whipped by klansmen at Briar Forks

in Madison County, Alabama, in 1868 gave detailed proof of this fact. The klansmen, he told the Congressional committee,

had gowns on just like your overcoat, that came down to the toes, and some would be red and some black, like a lady's dress, only open before. The hats were made of paper, and at the top about as thick as your ankle; and down around the eyes it was bound around like horse-covers, and on the mouth there was hair of some description, I don't know what. It looked like a mustache, coming down to the breast, and you couldn't see none of the face, nor nothing; you couldn't see a thing of them. Some of them had horns about as long as my finger, and made black.

But when Joseph Gill was asked to give names, he gave the following perplexed reply:

O, you are too hard for me, sir. I can't tell that. I couldn't see their faces to tell who they were.[15]

The secrecy on which the ghostly make-believe was based was at times carelessly betrayed. Joseph Davis, a Negro of Columbus, Mississippi, was in 1871 forced to accompany local klansmen on several raids.[16] Christina Page of Columbia, South Carolina, was hired to make disguises for Jim Rodger and John Gist, members of the local klan den.[17] The list of such testimonies can be extended indefinitely as a means of cutting deeply into the hypothesis of the supernatural effectiveness of the Ku-Klux Klan. Occasionally Negroes caused amusement by the manner in which they saw through the ghostly. "Had they disguises on?" asked the

[14] *Ibid.*, IV, pp. 604–05 (Spartanburg, S. C., July 10, 1871).
[15] *Ibid.*, IX, pp. 813–14 (Huntsville, Ala., October 12, 1871).
[16] *Ibid.*, XII, p. 810 (Columbus, Miss., November 13, 1871).
[17] *Ibid.*, IV, p. 1142 (Columbia, S. C., July 20, 1871).

members of the Congressional committee. Lydia Anderson of Macon, Mississippi, replied, "Yes, sir; they all wore dresses."[18]

It is interesting to speculate concerning why the klansmen wore disguises if, as we claim, these habiliments were not effective in frightening the Negroes. An adequate explanation is that disguises were used to conceal identity in the desperate business of lawlessness and crime in which the klansmen were engaged. These costumes afforded convenient concealment for weapons; the more elaborate the disguise the more effective was the concealment of the personal characteristics of the night-riders. Cherishing the well-known inability of the white man to understand the Negro as well as the Negro understands the white man, the whites perhaps in many cases were foolishly convinced that they were deceiving their black victims. Moreover, Southerners, like other Americans, black and white, were fond of ritual and costume as a means of creating collective enthusiasm. This mummery manifests itself in numerous other secret organizations such as the Odd Fellows, the Masons, and the Knights of Columbus. All of these organizations wear costumes as elaborate as those of the klansmen without any desire to create the superstitious illusions. The original klansmen of Pulaski said that their purpose in founding their organization was the delight of masquerading before their girlfriends, their mothers, and each other.

Can it not be concluded that the supposed ghostly effectiveness of the klansmen was an afterthought invented to fit into the white man's inherited stereotype of the American Negro? Such a concept survives because it fits so well into the conventional assumption that the Negro is a superstitious creature believing in ghosts in general and especially believing in them at the time the Ku-Klux Klan was creating a momentous crisis in the black man's career. But, the hollowness of this supposition is indicated by the fact that it was not claimed by contemporaries and not admitted by the black victims.

[18] *Ibid.*, XI, p. 510 (Macon, Miss., November 6, 1871).

Caddy Buffers:
Legends of a Middle-Class Negro Family in Philadelphia

KATHRYN L. MORGAN

   If one accepts the notion that a folk is any group whatsoever sharing at least one common linking factor, then an individual family would have to be considered a folk. If an individual family is a folk, then one would expect it to have its own folklore. And families do have their own traditions, rituals, sayings, and stories. Sometimes what families believe to be their own peculiar, unique traditions turn out to be related to the folklore of other families or even of families belonging to a different culture. On the other hand, some family folklore is unique—at least in content, though the form may be comparable to the form of folklore in other families.
   One important type of family folklore is intimately related to family history. Examples of this type of family folklore would include the legend and the memorate. Family legends are usually quite local and may or may not be known outside the family circle. The "memorate," a term proposed by the Swedish folklorist von Sydow, refers to narratives told by individuals about a purely personal experience of their own. One can in theory distinguish between first-person memorates in which individuals relate anecdotes or reminiscences about events in which they themselves participated, and derivative memorates in which relatives (or friends) of the original participant recount the narrative. "I wasn't actually there myself, but this happened to my father, aunt, grandmother, neighbor, etc." Presumably, a first-person memorate destined to become a full-fledged legend known by an entire community might first become a derivative memorate told by persons connected in some way with one or more of the original participants in, or observers of, the events described in the narrative.
   In the following extraordinary collection and analysis of a group of family legends or memorates, the reader should be able to see just how important

Reprinted from *Keystone Folklore Quarterly*, vol. 11 (1966), pp. 67–88, by permission of the author and the Pennsylvania Folklore Society.

folklore is at the most local level. Professor Kathryn L. Morgan who teaches folklore at Swarthmore College has tapped her own personal traditions to illustrate the nature of family folklore. Her notion that memorates serve as critical ego supports or "buffers" against the world outside the family is an apt and useful one. While some might object to a professional folklorist recording his own traditions (and those of his parents and children) on the grounds that he may be too personally involved with the informants and the data to be objective, it could be argued that it is precisely the subjective sense of involvement which makes Professor Morgan's study so valuable. This is not just a folklorist writing about somebody else's folklore; this is a folklorist writing with fervor and conviction about her own folklore.

The fact that the folklore presented in this essay is "middle-class" folklore makes it all the more unique. All people, whatever their socio-economic condition, have folklore. The idea that American Negro folklore is to be found only among rural Southerners or urban ghetto dwellers is false. All American Negroes have some American Negro folklore. The amount will vary from individual to individual, just as interest in folklore will vary from individual to individual. And this raises another point.

One of the topics treated in the Caddy "buffers" is the light complexioned Negro who "passes" for white. The author's experience, in view of her opinion that she was "the most Negroid looking member in the family in several generations" has clearly influenced the folklore she has chosen to remember and to report. (Any storyteller's repertoire is influenced by his particular background and personality.) The problem of being a black man in a white man's "world" can be especially difficult for those Negroes who try to pass or who could pass if they wished. Should they be black people with white skins or should they turn their backs on black culture? Certainly, there is resentment felt by some American Negroes against those who are adjudged to be seeking to become white men with black skins. (One term of derision is "oreo" for such an individual. The term comes from a standard commercially prepared cookie which has two disc-shaped chocolate wafers separated by sugar cream filling. An "oreo" is thus brown outside but white inside, hence, a Negro who has internalized white values. Possibly a similar explanation accounts for the use of the term "Bosco" as in the dozens line "Your mother eat Bosco." Bosco is a commercial chocolate preparation, but metaphorically speaking it is badly diluted when mixed with white milk.) The whole question of the relationship between folklore and self- or group identity lies at the very heart of both the Caddy buffers and Kathryn Morgan's sensitive analysis of them.

For further discussion of the memorate as a folklore genre, see C. W. von Sydow, Selected Papers on Folklore *(Copenhagen, 1948), pp. 73–74; Laurits Bøker,* Folk Literature (Germanic) International Dictionary of Regional European Ethnology and Folklore, *vol. II (Copenhagen, 1965), pp. 195–96; and Lauri Honko, "Memorates and the Study of Folk Beliefs,"* Journal of the Folklore Institute, *1 (1964), pp. 5–19. One valuable source for American Negro memorates is the large number of autobiographies written by ex-slaves. For a sample of this important literary genre, see James B. Cade, "Out of the Mouths of Ex-Slaves,"* Journal of Negro History, *22 (1935), pp 294–337; B. A. Botkin,* Lay My Burden Down: A Folk History of Slavery *(Chicago, 1945); Charles H. Nichols, Jr., ed.,* Many Thousands Gone: The Ex-

Slaves' Account of Their Bondage and Freedom (*Leiden, 1963*); *Arna Bontemps*, Great Slave Narratives (*Boston, 1969*); *Gilbert Osofsky, ed.*, Puttin' On Ole Massa (*New York, 1969*); *and especially* Unwritten History of Slavery, *Autobiographical Account of Ex-Slaves, Social Science Source Documents, no. 1* (*Nashville, Tennessee: Fisk University, 1945*). *For further references, see the "Bibliographic Note" in Osofsky, pp. 407–9.*

THE AMOUNT of blood which establishes whether or not one is a Negro American is determined not by nature but by law. The lesson for folklore then is clearly written, for whenever a people are isolated by choice or by force, to a limited or total extent, they develop a folkway.[1] Dorson[2] applies this theory to the Negro American by pointing out that:

While they take their raw material from a variety of sources, the colored folk have squeezed and shaped the dough into their very own folk property.

This folk property ranges all the way from the old Southern tradition found in Joel Chandler Harris' Uncle Remus[3] to Roger Abrahams' Philadelphia Jungle[4] and Hughes and Bontemps'[5] sophisticated lore of Harlem. But despite these varieties there are three things which are common to most Negro Americans. First, regardless of where we live today we are apt to have had Southern roots and since the majority of Negro American folklore belongs to the plantation culture of the old South[6] we have been exposed in some way to the lie that the Negro American is content with his lot, a fantasy which is strong in Southern

tradition. Lacy,[7] a Southern folklorist, directly relates Southern lore to the transmission of prejudiced concepts. He illustrates how the fountainheads of Southern lore pour out streams of distrust and prejudice by saying:

We find it lurking tenaciously in the background of our minds ready to reveal itself at an unguarded moment. The child is introduced to racial prejudice early in his life. The names which he hears applied to the Negro such as "coon," "darky," "nigger," and "burr head" gives an early impression that the Negro is an object of humor and scorn. He buys fireworks called "nigger chasers," nuts called "nigger toes," makes a toy called a "nigger shooter," and recites a jingle about catching "a nigger by his toe."

Second, there is a tie that binds us all no matter what our education, socioeconomic status, hair texture or skin color. If we are known to be a Negro, we have experienced in some degree the humiliations common to Negroes throughout the United States. And third, the majority of us are aware, consciously or unconsciously, of the tendency of scholars to lump us all under the single term "Negro," present us en masse or

[1] Louis E. Lomax, *The Negro Revolt*, (New York, 1965), p. 58.
[2] Richard M. Dorson, *American Folklore* (Chicago, 1959), p. 186.
[3] Joel Chandler Harris, *Nights with Uncle Remus: Myths and Legends of the Old Plantation* (New York, 1883).
[5] Roger D. Abrahams, *Deep Down in the Jungle, Negro Narrative Folklore from the Streets of Philadelphia* (Hatboro, Pa., 1964).
[5] Langston Hughes, and Arna Bontemps, *The Book of Negro Folklore* (New York, 1958).
[6] Richard M. Dorson, *op. cit.*, 2, pp. 180–81.
[7] James M. Lacy, "Folklore of the South and Racial Discrimination," *Publications of the Texas Folklore Society*, XXXII (1958), pp. 101–2.

as a "problem," diffusing our various heritages, experiences and points of view practically to the threshold of non-existence.

These facts are important in that they may shed some light on the almost total absence of middle-class Negro folklore. Such a lack is explained only in small part by a conspiracy of silence; the major force at work is that the more conscious one is of adding to a negative stereotype, the more indifferent one becomes to outward expression and self-advertisement. Thus the collection of lore from the middle-class Negro folk may be more difficult than the collection from those less fortunate or less inhibited.

Since the handicaps suffered by Negroes, even those with only a trace of Negro blood, are typically the socially imposed handicaps peculiar to a lower caste rather than engendered by racial inheritance,[8] the question arises as to what devices are available to use for enhancing our self esteem. The answer is of course that we, like all peoples, create "buffers." P. D. Ouspensky,[9] the mystic philosopher, describes buffers as the internal contrivances created by man which enable him to live with his contradictions and conflicts.

From time immemorial, slaves and members of seriously oppressed groups have used buffers to overcome fear, anxiety, and anger. It is traditional among Negro American parents throughout the United States, in their struggle to reduce the anatomy of prejudice to fit the understanding of their children, to supply the children with buffers.

Martin Luther King[10] describes such moments in "A Letter from A Birmingham Jail" when he says:

You suddenly find your tongue twisted as you seek to explain to your six-year-old daughter why she can't go to the public amusement park that has just been advertised on television and you see the tears welling up when she is told that Funtown is closed to colored children, and see the ominous clouds of inferiority beginning to form in her little mental sky, and see her beginning to distort her personality by unconsciously developing a bitterness toward white people.

And, Saunders Redding[11] as he describes how he felt when he tried to explain to his six-year-old son why the little white boy would not play with him anymore:

In his eyes was the look of a wound and I knew how it could grow and become infected and pump its poison into every tissue, to every brain cell. I did not know how to deal with it. Words were poultices to seal the infection in. I could recall them from my own childhood in answer to "why." For children are not born with answers.

And, Ernest J. Gaines[12] in his short story dialogue between a Negro woman and a Negro teenager:

I hope they all aren't like me, the boy said. Unfortunately I was born too late to believe in your God. Let's hope that the ones who come after will have your faith if not in your God, then in something else, something that they can lean on. I haven't anything. For me, the wind is pink; the grass is black.

[8] Gordon W. Allport, *The Nature of Prejudice* (New York, 1954), p. 304.

[9] P. D. Ouspensky, *In Search of the Miraculous* (New York, 1949), pp. 154–55, 156–60, 163, 165, 258.

[10] Martin Luther King, "Letter From A Birmingham Jail," *The Christian Century* (June, 1963), pp. 767–73.

[11] Saunders Redding, *On Being Negro In America* (New York) p. 81.

[12] Ernest J. Gaines, "The Sky Is Grey," *Negro Digest* (August 1963.)

The "something else" for us as Negro American children were family legends centering around my great-grandmother affectionately known to us as "Caddy." Caddy legends have served as "buffers" for the children in our family for four generations. Although there are many similar narratives in folk histories[13] dealing with the ordeals of slavery, with its whippings, rapes, murder, escapes and pursuits, they did not belong to us, as did the legends of Caddy. The other narratives along with the Negro spirituals, finally belonged to the world but Caddy was ours. She was among the first generation of freed mulatto slaves who, when emancipated, were decidedly underprivileged people. The struggle for survival in the remnants of a slave economy was difficult for her as she was illegitimate, the offspring of a master-slave relationship, illiterate and unskilled. She also had two very young illegitimate children conceived by former masters which she had to care for. Her children, Albert and Adeline, were born slaves and were freed along with her when they were about three and four years old. Adeline died at a very early age but Albert, who later became my grandfather, worked along with Caddy in Lynchburg, Virginia, until he met and married Kate who was later to become my grandmother. She was also the product of a master-slave relationship. Both Kate and Albert were unskilled and illiterate but they worked along with Caddy to help buy property and save money to enable the children of the third generation to go to school. The children were my mother Marjorie, her sisters Rosebud and Adeline and her brothers Prince, Jimmie, Benny and William. There were other members of our family in Lynchburg including numerous cousins, uncles and aunts.

In 1915–16 selected members of the family who could pass for white were sent to Philadelphia, Pennsylvania, to explore the possibilities for employment for themselves and other members of the family able to pass. Those who could not pass remained in Lynchburg and worked at whatever odd jobs they could find. My mother, Marjorie, one of the members able to pass, was sent to Philadelphia each summer during her vacation to visit her sisters both of whom were passing.

She met and married my father during one of her summer excursions and as a result, we had the dubious distinction of being the first generation born in the North with acceptable social status but no money. My father, who was in school when he married, left school and worked as a postal clerk. My mother struggled patiently to raise the children, browbeat the landlords and made the money stretch by preparing nourishing but inexpensive Southern meals.

She always attempted to instill in us some private sense of honor and dignity, which in her estimation would help us survive in this unnatural Northern vacuum suspended between the black and white worlds. Both parents attempted to destroy by example and discipline the stereotyped image of the Negro American which was constantly before us as children. The creature of stupid hangdog expression, lazy lipped mumbling speech, buckeyes, white teeth,

---

[13] B. A. Botkin, ed., *Lay My Burden Down, A Folk History of Slavery* (Chicago, 1965); Richard M. Dorson, *Negro Tales From Pine Bluff, Arkansas and Calvin, Michigan* (Bloomington, 1958), pp. 110–27.

loud and gaudy clothes and hunched over prowlike walk, was hated with a passion in our house.

There was no denying that Hattie McDaniel and Louise Beavers, the perennial maids and mammies of the movies, were the female stars of the day and Stepin Fetchit (Lincoln Perry) with his eye-rolling bewildered expression, head scratching and drooping dialect, the most popular colored motion picture personality in the country. In school we were reading about "Little Black Sambo," and our textbooks were chock-full of disparaging things about Negroes and their African background. The lies that Negroes were inferior and that slaves were sleek, well fed and happy under the patronizing and loving "ole Massa" had not yet been destroyed by the social scientists. As our teachers were all white we learned no Negro History in school. There was no evidence in our school books that Negroes had any part at all in building this great democracy. Many parents in our neighborhood were distressed by this image and proceeded to set the children's teeth on edge by constantly trying to make them into carbon copies of the typical middle-class white Protestant American Boy and Girl. James Baldwin[14] vividly describes the results of such parental distress by saying:

One's hair was always being attacked with hard brushes and combs and Vaseline; it was shameful to have "nappy" hair. One's legs and arms and face were always being greased, so that one would not look "ashy" in the wintertime. One was always being scrubbed and polished as though in the hope that a stain could be washed away. I hazard to say that the Negro children of my generation, anyway, had an earlier and more painful acquaintance with soap than any

other children anywhere. The women were forever straightening and curling their hair and using bleaching creams. And yet it was clear that none of this effort would release one from the stigma and danger of being a Negro; this effort merely increased the shame and rage. There was not, no matter where one turned, any acceptable image of oneself, no proof of one's existence.

This was in a world of Goldilocks and Shirley Temple curls. Considering that one's ideas, convictions, views, and conception of the world is mostly repertoire or taken from books, or has been created by imitating ready-made models, is it any wonder that accounts of Negro family valor and Negro history were fervently and desperately passed down by word of mouth from generation to generation?

This was our folklore and it was functional. It was the antidote used by our parents and our grandparents and our great-grandparents to help counteract the poison of self-hate stirred up by the cesspool of contradictions found in the home of the brave and the land of the free.

There is something very personal about writing about the members of one's family when one is a middle-class Negro American. It is like having a second ego which urges one to "polish up" the English, overdramatize the positive values expressed in the lore and suppress pertinent facts which may reflect negatively on the family image or contribute to the stereotype of the Negro American. Fortunately in the process of maturing, one can recognize these emotional and intellectual collisions and meet them head on. One recognizes the beginning of the tradition of handing down family legends of former slaves

14 James Baldwin, *Nobody Knows My Name* (New York, 1961), p. 73.

when one reads the narratives of the slaves themselves. In "The Bell and the Light"[15] related by a former slave, he is reported to have said:

The bigger ones don't care so much about hearing it now but the little ones never tire of hearing how their grandpa brought emancipation to loads of slaves he could touch and feel but never could see.

My mother Marjorie, aged sixty-one, is the major tradition bearer in our family. She told me the legends before I was old enough to go to school. I have kept them alive by telling them to my daughter Susan, age ten, who in turn has told several of them to her younger cousins.

I cannot truthfully say that I remember the exact circumstances surrounding the first telling of the legends, as I have forgotten over the years. I know they were often repeated. They were usually told in the kitchen while my mother was preparing a meal or performing some other chore. She never sat to tell them and sometimes we would have to follow her from room to room to hear the end of a legend. They were never told as a series. I was the most avid listener, as I was the only girl and my mother, when she was exasperated with me, would say I was "Just like Caddy." I never let her know that as far as I was concerned this was a most desired compliment. It was my life's ambition to be like Caddy when I was a little girl, as Caddy did all the daring things I secretly wanted to do. Frankly, Caddy comes to my rescue even now when some obstacle seems insurmountable to me. I cannot remember the first time I was

told about Caddy being sold on the block when she was eight years old, but all during my childhood I remember having a sense of well-being in the knowledge that nobody could sell me.

CADDY

Caddy was only eight years old when she was sold on the block. After that she was always being sold. She was sent from plantation to plantation but she would always run away. She grew to be a beautiful young girl and that made the white women hate her. The white men loved her and sometimes she was taken to live in the big houses. Big houses or not, Caddy didn't want to be a slave. She would run away. When she was caught, she was usually hung in the barn and whipped across her naked back with a cat-o-nine-tails. This didn't stop Caddy from running. She would run and she would be caught and she would be whipped. Do you think she'd cry when they whipped her with a cat-o-nine-tails? Not Caddy. It would take more than a cat-o-nine-tails to make Caddy cry in front of white trash.[16]

(*Marjorie Lawson told to Kathryn Morgan*)

15 B. A. Botkin, *op. cit.*, p. 185.
16 Similar slave narratives can be found in B. A. Botkin, ed. *Lay My Burden Down* (Chicago, 1961). References made to children being sold on the block by "Cato—Alabama," p. 86; "Joanna Draper —Mississippi," p. 98; "Katie Rowe—Arkansas," p. 105; An account epitomizing the extreme cruelty of whippings in the "Story of Ben Simpson," p. 75.

Susan reacted to this legend in a somewhat different manner than I did at her age, if I am to judge by her outward manifestations and questions. She expressed concern that "Caddy wouldn't like her very much" because she has lots of white friends. She also asked what made people "trash." It never occurred to me to ask such a question, as I was already prejudiced against "white trash" before I knew what "white" was. When I was a child, we merely lumped all white people into two compartments —good and trash. It was very simple. Those who treated you decently were good. Those who did not were trash. Although I had white classmates, they were not my friends as we were not closely involved with one another. We lived in separate worlds. Susan finally decided that she did not know any trash personally but had heard about "trash" from one of her white schoolmates while she was visiting her. It seemed that Ann, her friend, was going to allow Susan to play with a doll which was left at Ann's house until Ann realized that she had better not because her friend "didn't like coloreds." Susan assumed that Ann's friend was an example of "trash." She also encountered what she termed "trash" the first time she was chased and called a "dirty little nigger" by a woman who accused her of playing on her lawn. Susan came home full of glee to tell me how she took time to explain to the woman what a "nigger" really was and how she was "niggardly" not to let children play on her lawn. She wanted to know if it was all right to "sass" the woman the way she did since she was "trash." I told her she handled the situation very well.

CADDY
VERSION II

Sometimes you think it would be nice to be a slave girl where you wouldn't have to be worried about financial problems and things. But when you hear this story I believe that it will change your mind. It's about a girl named Caddy. Caddy was my great-great grandmother. She was only eight when she was sold on the slave block. After that she was always being sold. She had to be sent from plantation to plantation because she would always run away and sass the mistress. She would even sass people who weren't her mistresses. Well, she grew to be a beautiful young girl and that made all the white women hate her out of pure jealousy. The white masters loved her and sometimes she was taken into the big houses to live. That didn't make any difference to Caddy. Big house, little house, great house, small house, it was all the same because they were just taking her in so that she would be more convenient for them. Sometimes she would run away so that she wouldn't be a convenient little handy hand, but was usually caught and then she was taken into the barn and hung up by her thumbs and whipped across her back with a cat-o-nine-tails. It would hurt real bad but do you think Caddy would cry? Ah, you bet not! It would take more than a cat-o-nine-tails to make Caddy cry in front of poor white trash. Maybe they were rich in money, but they were poor in brains. Caddy hated trash black or white. Usually they had to sell Caddy because she was too hard to handle and would always be running away.

(Recorded by Susan Morgan)

We found the legend of "What Caddy Did When She Heard That Lee Had Surrendered" the most delightful of all. We would ask our mother who never said "bad" words, unless they could be attributed to Caddy who it was said "used vile language all the time," to repeat the part where Caddy flipped up her dress over and over again. I would go to my room and practice flipping up my dress and saying "kiss my ass" in front of a mirror. As a teenager I remember how wonderful I thought it would be to be able to tell the whole white world to "kiss my ass." When Susan recorded this legend she giggled and repeated the last line over and over.

WHAT CADDY DID WHEN SHE HEARD THAT LEE HAD SURRENDERED

Caddy had been sold to a man in Goodman, Mississippi. It was terrible to be sold in Mississippi. In fact, it was terrible to be sold anywhere. She had been put to work in the fields for running away again. She was hoeing a crop when she heard the General Lee had surrendered. Do you know who General Lee was? He was the man who was working for the South in the Civil War. When General Lee surrendered that meant that all the colored people were free! Caddy threw down that hoe, she marched herself up to the big house, then, she looked around and found the mistress. She went over to the mistress, she flipped up her dress and told the white woman to do something. She said it mean and ugly. This is what she said: *Kiss my ass.*[17]

(*Told by Marjorie Lawson recorded by Susan Morgan*)

I was taught to believe that my "aristocratic" blood would help me overcome any insult or hardship I might encounter at the hands of trash. This legend, while lessening somewhat the feelings of racial inferiority, did not erase them. In fact, there was a period in my life when I underwent intense internal conflict between feelings of inferiority on one hand and feelings of superiority on the other. I never questioned the implication that my African ancestors were kings and queens and my white ancestors were "quality" whites. I was often told "they may be your color, but they're not your kind!" This reference,

of course, was made to other Negroes who, assigned to the lowest stratum of the second-class citizenry, accounted for the appalling incidence of crime, coarse conduct and family disorganization. It took me a very long time to realize that any profit gained from the mass of colored folk would be a temporary and shameful profit. I now know that no person in America is safe as long as the bulk of America's Negroes live in such darkness. When I related this legend to Susan I stressed responsibility rather than aristocracy.

HOW CADDY FOUND HER MOTHER

Caddy went out to find her mother in Virginia. She had two small children. They weren't by the same fathers but both the men were aristocrats, that means masters of fine plantations.

Caddy was very proud of her children's blood. She used to always tell them, "There ain't no poor white blood running through your veins." Caddy told them that all the time. She told it to Albert and Adeline when they were little, and she told it to Kate when she became Albert's wife. That's one thing we can say with pride. There is no trash in our blood. It's good *aristocratic blood.* Caddy worked her way with those two children from Mississippi to Virginia. She was looking for her mother. She worked very hard because she aimed to make that aim. She met up with many troubles and hardships but she kept on. Then she found her mother. Aunt Liza was still living on a plantation but she was old and she was sick. Caddy took her to live with her and took care of her until she died. Caddy believed that you should take care of your family because your family are all that you have. Aunt Liza didn't die until she was ninety-two years old. That's a pretty old age as ages

---

[17] In *Lay My Burden Down*, pp. 223–53, there are many accounts of the various reactions of slaves and their owners when they were made aware of the emancipation proclamation. See "They Danced All Night," p. 226; "He Cussed Till He Died," p. 233; and "Death of A Plantation," pp. 235–36.

go. Caddy took care of her until the day she died. Caddy was a strong woman. Not in muscles but a strong woman in heart.[18]

(*Recorded by Susan Morgan*)

The next legend stresses the need for respectability and character. These two qualities were indicative of the "better class." I venture to say that I was the most Negroid looking member in the family in several generations. Two of my brothers were blond with blue eyes and white skin, the other looked just like an Indian with silky black hair. All could "pass" for something other than Negro American. As a result my mother drilled Character, Respectability and Brains into me, to make up for my not being "good-looking." Good-looking according to the standards of the times meant being as white as possible, with hair as straight as possible and features as fine as possible.

I can remember hearing almost daily the saying "it isn't what's on the outside that counts, it's what's on the inside," but I also remember being cautioned not to mention the fact that I had to have my hair straightened.

WHY CADDY GOT MR. GORDON OUT OF JAIL

Caddy got married to a Mr. Gordon. Getting married in those days wasn't like getting married today. You know you didn't have all the frills, the long white dress, the blue dress, and the long cape, the big aisle with the music going don don don don—and the man with the vest and all that. Caddy never even bothered to go to a preacher. It was just enough for two people to want to be married. Anyway, Caddy wanted a last name for her children. Mr. Gordon was willing to give them his. That's how papa became Albert *Gordon* and Adeline, well, that's how she became Adeline Gordon. It's very important for children to have an honest last name. Now Mr. Gordon wasn't a very good man but he did have a last name and he did let Caddy have it for the children, so Caddy was willing to put up with his laziness and didn't say too much. You know, equal-equal. Finally, though, he left Caddy and got himself another "wife." Caddy "got married" to a Mr. Rucker. Mr. Rucker was a very good man. Hard working and all that. But he died early. Caddy worked hard and saved her money. One day she heard that Mr. Gordon had gotten himself into some kind of trouble and was going to have to go to jail. You know what Caddy did? She went to the bank. And then she went to the courthouse. And then she went right up the middle aisle. She stood before the judge and then she reached down under her skirt and put the money on the table. She said, "Judge, I don't want no nigger with my children's name going to Jail so here I am to bail him out." Now everybody respected Caddy, even the judge, so he let Mr. Gordon go. Caddy was that kind of woman. Respectable. Caddy told Mr. Gordon that as long as her children had *his* last name she didn't want him laying around in any jail. Then she gave him some money and sent him home to his wife. Caddy was like that. Respected.[19]

(*Recorded by Susan Morgan*)

[18] In *Lay My Burden Down*, "Cato—Alabama," pp. 84–85 recalls that "They was the best quality white folks and they was always good to me, 'cause I's one of their blood . . . Tha's what makes me so mixed up with Indians, African and white blood. Sometimes it mattered to me, sometimes it didn't. It don't no more 'cause I'm not too far from the end of my days."

[19] For references to the various standards used for Negro class structure see E. Franklin Frazier, *Black Bourgeoisie* (Glencoe, Ill., 1949); Richard Bardolph, *The Negro Vanguard* (New York, 1961).

For a description of marriage customs among slaves see: *Lay My Burden Down*, "Tines Kendricks: Georgia," p. 70.

WHY CADDY GOT MR. GORDON OUT OF JAIL

VERSION II

Caddy got married to a Mr. Gordon. Getting married in those days wasn't like getting married today. Caddy never bothered to go to a preacher or anything. It was enough for two people to want to be married. Anyway, Caddy wanted a last name for her children and Mr. Gordon was willing to give them his. That's how papa became Albert *Gordon* and Adeline, Adeline *Gordon*. It's important for children to have an honest last name. Now Mr. Gordon was not a very good man, but he did have an honest last name and he let Caddy have it for the children. So Caddy put up with his laziness and didn't say too much. Finally though, he left Caddy and got himself another "wife." Caddy "got married" to a Mr. Rucker. Now Mr. Rucker was a good man, hard-working and all but he died early. Caddy worked hard and saved her money. One day she heard that Mr. Gordon had gotten himself in some kind of trouble and was going to be sent to jail. Caddy went to the bank. She marched herself right up to the courthouse. Marched right up the middle aisle. Stood before that judge. She reached down under her skirt and put the money on the table. She said, "Judge, I don't want no nigger with my children's name going to jail so I'm here to bail him out." Now everybody respected Caddy, even the judge, so he let Mr. Gordon go. Caddy was that kind of woman. Respectable. Caddy told Mr. Gordon that as long as he had *her* children's name she didn't want him laying around in jail. Then she gave him money and sent him home to his "wife." Caddy was like that. Respected.

(Recorded by Kathryn Morgan)

About the age of four my brother Raphael became very ill and had to be hospitalized on and off for a period of fourteen years. This made money very scarce in our house and even with help from the other members of the family there were times when we ate by candlelight because the electricity had been cut off. As children it was difficult for us to understand why my mother took down the eviction notices as soon as the constable left. My mother always managed to put "good shoes on our feet and good food in our stomachs," and tell us how Caddy made her money and bought property in spite of adverse conditions. We sacrificed for years and I can never remember a time when we had enough money and weren't dodging the bill collectors, but we always felt it was worth it if "Ray C" could get better. He did. He was inducted into the army and died at nineteen in World War II. My mother was the first mother in the neighborhood to receive a gold star for her window and an American flag.

HOW CADDY MADE HER MONEY AND BOUGHT HER PROPERTY

Caddy couldn't read or write but she sure could count money. She was never one penny short. Albert and Kate couldn't read or write either but Caddy taught them how to work hard and count money too. She said that there was only one way children could learn how to read and write. The grown-ups had to work hard and save the money. Caddy had all kinds of ways to make money. She was a midwife for the poor whites and Negroes. She would go around to all the restaurants and good houses on the other side of the tracks, pick out the spotted fruit that had been thrown in the garbage. Then she would come home, cut the spots off and make preserves and pies and go back and sell them to the same folks who had thrown the fruit away!

She would come to Philadelphia about once a month and buy up rag barrels which she had sent back "home." Then she would sort the rag barrels and the clothes she could patch up she would sell to the poor whites and to the Negroes. Then she would make quilts out of rags and sell them too. That's how Caddy made her money and bought her property.

(*Recorded by Kathryn Morgan*)

Every summer we went "home" to the South to visit Albert and Kate. My uncle William would drive up from Lynchburg and get us. My father never went with us and once I remember asking him "why?" He replied that he "didn't want to get lynched." I did not know what "lynched" meant, and since I loved going South I could not understand my father's attitude. My mother told me some years later that my father hated the South and prided himself on "never having set foot below the Mason-Dixon Line." My mother explained that he never went with us because he was "hot tempered" and was concerned that he might do something to bring harm to us all if someone should mistake my mother for a white woman married to a half-breed "nigger." She then told me the following legend concerning how Caddy brought the girls to Philadelphia. It was not until years later that I could understand my father's insistence on remaining in the North.

WHY CADDY BROUGHT THE GIRLS TO PHILADELPHIA

Caddy couldn't read or write but she was truly a great woman. She brought the whole family to Philadelphia on the excursions when she came up to buy the rags sometimes. Kate couldn't come because it made her sick to ride on the train. In fact, Kate had to walk everywhere she went. Albert couldn't come very often because he had to work. But Caddy would bring the children if they made good marks in school. They usually got good marks. Kate would whip them every day for a week if they didn't. They couldn't linger after school to look in the store windows or anything. Kate and

Albert were very strict like that. The children used to love to come to Philadelphia with Caddy because there they could pass and have fun. Caddy loved the trolley cars and the children used to ride all over the city with her. They had cousins who were passing and they stayed with their cousins. Caddy said that she and Cousin Dave had talked it over and they decided it was better to pass in the day and come home at night to a neighborhood that was colored. She said that way they wouldn't have to live with poor white trash. Living with poor white trash would be hell. Caddy said it was bad enough having to work with them all day but you could stand it as long as you knew it was temporary and you could come home to your own people at night. She used to tell them terrible stories about people who passed over all the way and married white. She used to say they would come up with black nappy-haired babies and tell terrible things about what happened to them. She said you never can tell what's going to come out or pop up, so it's best not to take chances that way. Later when Rosebud and Adeline were grown, they came to Philadelphia to live with Cousin Dave and passed and got good jobs. Marjorie was still in school and Caddy would only bring her during vacation.

Since Marjorie was the youngest girl and William was the youngest boy they were the ones who had to stay home and get ready to go to the seminary for colored students. They didn't really want to go to seminary. They wanted to come to Philadelphia and pass. It sounded like so much fun. You see, they were never allowed to have fun in Kate and Albert's house, Kate and Albert were so strict that the only time the children had fun was when Caddy came over and did something terrible like use a lot of cuss words in front of Albert and Kate. Caddy had a vile tongue and Albert and Kate were trying to raise the children right. They didn't like Caddy to cuss. But they didn't say anything. Kate tried to say something about it once but it didn't work so she gave up. During vacation Marjorie was glad to come to Philadelphia with Caddy. They would sit in the kitchen and wait for Cousin Dave and Rosebud and Adeline to come home and tell them what the whites would say about "niggers." Whites didn't know that they were colored. Caddy would be smoking her pipe. Sometimes she would laugh so hard she would almost swallow the smoke. She would spend hours telling them how to get even with the white trash that talked about "niggers." She knew some very terrible ways to get even too. She would tell them to Adeline and to Cousin Dave. Rosebud and Dave tried some of them but Adeline never would. Caddy used to tell her that the reason she was so simple was because she thought she was white for sure. She used to warn Adeline that she was in for a rude awakening. She really did like Adeline a lot though. She just didn't want her to get hurt because she was so soft. Caddy used to say that there was nothing more cowardly than trash. Especially white trash. That is why they have to talk so big and act so ugly. Caddy couldn't stand colored people who simpered around white folks either. She said the best thing to do is mind your business, don't linger, don't talk, don't believe and never act afraid no matter how scared you really are. Caddy said you could only die once. Better to die for something than nothing. You have to fight every inch of the way to be free, every inch of the way to be free.

(Recorded by Kathryn Morgan)

My uncle William finally came to Philadelphia to live with us and I could not understand why he insisted I learn how to fight when my mother was trying so hard to make me into a "little lady." I remember going into the cellar with Uncle Bill, my brothers and my father for boxing lessons but I can not remember ever having to defend myself physically. After my mother told us the fol-

lowing two legends, "How Caddy Taught William Not To Be A Coward" and "How Caddy Made Marjorie Walk Over the Bridge," I could understand my Uncle William a little better. Recently I asked my brother Donald, who is a marvelous story teller with a keen sense of humor and a vivid imagination, what these legends meant to him. He recalled that the only time he found it a little unhandy to "stand up and fight" was when the Germans caught him squatting on a makeshift john in France in World War II.

HOW CADDY TAUGHT WILLIAM NOT TO BE A COWARD

William had to walk by the poor white section one day by himself because he was late coming home from school. Some trash boys saw him and he saw them and he got scared and they chased him all the way home. Caddy and Kate were in Kate's kitchen when he ran in puffing for breath. Kate asked him what was wrong and he told her what happened. Kate beat him for running. Then Caddy beat him again. Caddy told him if he ever ran away from trash again she was going to beat his ass every day and that's what happened. William would run and Caddy would beat him— every day for about a week. Poor William. The other children used to cry because he got so many beatings. Then Kate would beat them so they couldn't be wasting good tears for nothing. Finally William caught one of the white trash and beat him almost to death. When he came home that day he wasn't out of breath and he didn't look scared anymore. Caddy and Kate told him he had done the right thing and Kate gave him an extra piece of hoe cake which he loved. Then Caddy went to get the shotguns. She and Kate took turns sitting at the kitchen window with the shotguns all that day and all night. Kate was meaner than Caddy and she would have blown somebody's head off for sure. Albert went to bed with his shotgun because he had to get up and go to work in the morning. Caddy sent for all the boy cousins. Cousin Dave's younger children and all the children had to walk back and forth from school together for a long time. Nothing happened but Kate and Caddy sat up a whole week all night and all day taking turns—just in case. Kate said nothing happened because we were respected and Caddy said it didn't hurt to be respected by high and low alike.[20]

HOW CADDY MADE MARJORIE FIND A WAY TO WALK ON THE BRIDGE

Marjorie had to walk over the bridge every day to get to school and every day she would meet this trash boy who would make her get off the bridge and walk in the street where the horses walked. She did this every day. He would wait for her on the bridge and when she got ready to walk across he would push her off into the street. Caddy found out what was happening. I don't know who told her but she called Marjorie in the kitchen and she said "Maggie, you will have to find a way to walk on the bridge. You are just as white as the trash that pushed you off of the bridge and if the bridge is for white they can't push you off because you are just as white as they are. It's up to you to find your own way to walk across the bridge." Now when Caddy told you you had to find your own way, you had better find it. Marjorie went to her room to think up a way. The only way she could think of was her mama's old rusty hat pin. She put it in her bookbag the next day so nobody would see it and she went off to school as usual. Sure enough after school there he was waiting on the bridge, and when he went to push her she took the hat pin and stuck it clean through his arm. Then she ran home and told Caddy what she had

done. Well, Caddy said she had found a way but it was the wrong way, but she wouldn't let any body bother Marjorie because she had told her to find a way and Marjorie had found the only way she could. Years later Marjorie's brother Benny was working in a factory and a foreman came up to him and asked him if he had a sister. He said, "Yes." Caddy always taught the children not to say. "Yas suh, No suh and Yas 'um and No Mum" to white folks. The foreman said, "Is her name Maggie?" Marjorie's brother said "yes." The foreman pulled up his sleeve and showed him a deep scar on his arm. Then he said to him, "I almost lost an arm because of Maggie, but you know one thing? She was right."

The most recent Caddy legend I heard was told to me by my mother several months ago while we were waiting in line at the supermarket. It seemed to strengthen my belief that Caddy has really left us rich in the ability to laugh, to perceive, to struggle, and to strive for wisdom.

As told to me by Marjorie Lawson this legend had no title; Marjorie started to talk about Caddy as we sometimes do when we have a bit of time:

You know Caddy was a mid-wife for the poor whites and Negroes and she had to go from house to house to deliver babies. Many times she tended the other sick people while she was in the house. One day she came home cussing and fussing because somebody had put a diaper on an old man who was not able to control his bladder. Caddy said, "you work hard all your life so you can get a bed of your own, then, when you get old, somebody straps you up so you can't even piss on it."

[20] For accounts of self-defense see Richard M. Dorson, *Negro Tales From Pine Bluff, Arkansas, and Calvin, Michigan* (Bloomington, 1958), "Will Kimbro Defends Himself," pp. 230–32. For traditional themes dealing with the Negro's fight for his rights, see Botkin, *Burden*, "The Slave's Chance," pp. 174–78.

Marjorie and I laughed so loud we attracted attention and had to remember where we were. I imagine people wondered what the white woman with her colored friend found so hilarious!

Every so often during my lifetime I somehow manage to delude myself into believing that I am superior to the mass of Negro humanity because of some superficial individual achievement. Whenever this happens I try to remember the following legends and stumble back to reality.

DON'T FORGET HOW IT WAS TO BE A SLAVE

Caddy suffered a lot. She suffered most all of her life, but she was a fighter. That's what she taught the children to be—fighters. You know, one day she was peeling apples in a big house and the mistress said something to her and she sassed that woman back. The mistress took the knife and cut Caddy's arm straight through to the bone and Caddy didn't have anybody to help take care of it or anything, so she just keep rubbing salt into it until it got well. She used to show the children the marks on her back from the cat-o-nine tails. They were thumb deep, but she didn't want them to forget what slavery was like.

(Recorded by Kathryn Morgan)

The last time Marjorie saw Caddy she was running for the trolley. She was trying to make a train home. She was nintey-six and she said she "was a little bit tired," just a "little bit tired." She died about a week later. She wasn't sick a day in her life and she had a very easy death. Before she died she took time to tell Kate to get her in the ground quick. She said to Kate, "Kate, don't let a lot of niggers pray and speak in the 'unknown tongue' over me." You know, next to trash Caddy hated preachers and church-going hypocrites more than anything in this world, and she let everybody know it including the church-going hypocrites and the preachers. Nobody questioned Kate either, they knew better than to do that. Kate never talked much and she never cried, not even when Caddy died. But nobody questioned Kate. She just buried Caddy with no praying and that was that.

If we ask what is most distinctive in this small contribution to the science of folklore, we must first make it clear that there cannot be anything absolutely unique in the experience of any race, any country or any individual. To say that internal conflict, race hatred and contempt were destroyed by these accounts would be untrue. They served the purpose of diminishing feelings of racial inferiority imposed upon us as children. I am sure that Caddy had many counterparts throughout the land, and, although I have attempted to relate the essence of the incidents as I remember them, I know there is much implied wisdom learned and transmitted by those children of the soil to their descendants which is missing. And, so, relatively honest analysis of the family lore reveals that it is on the whole essentially impersonal, it reflects emotion and experience which is deeper, wider and older than the emotion and wisdom of one individual. It is passionate without any loss of serenity and it is in the deepest sense— human.

APPENDIX: CHART OF THE TRANSMISSION OF THE CADDY BUFFERS

Caroline—"Caddy"—Born slave, offspring of unknown slave and master—freed at time of
         emancipation.

Albert—Born slave, son of Caddy—freed at the time of emancipation at about age 3.

Kate—Born slave, wife of Albert, picked by Caddy for wife of Albert due to family "blood"
         requirements as stipulated by Caddy. Kate was daughter of slave and
         master. Kate was freed at the time of the emancipation.

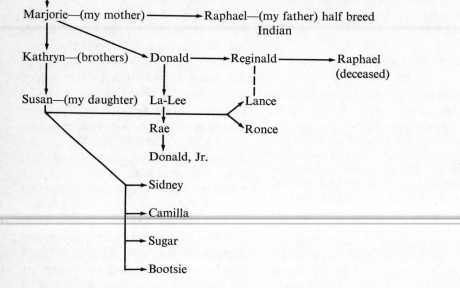

Marjorie—(my mother)————→Raphael—(my father) half breed
                            Indian

Kathryn—(brothers) ↖Donald————→Reginald————————→Raphael
                                     (deceased)

Susan—(my daughter) La-Lee   Lance

                      Rae   Ronce

                      Donald, Jr.

                → Sidney

                → Camilla

                → Sugar

                → Bootsie

FOLK HUMOR

No attempt to tap the laughing barrel would be complete without a look at traditional humor. For it is what makes a people laugh that reveals the soul of that people. Unfortunately, humor is one of the most difficult of all topics to study. One reason for this is that the humor of a people depends upon the entire culture, and an outsider, e.g., the typical anthropologist or folklorist, rarely possesses sufficient grasp of the whole culture of the people he visits to be able to understand all the nuances of the humor. In other words, humor is too delicate and too subtle for the casual fieldworker to handle with anything like sophistication. After all, even some "natives" are sometimes unable to understand a complex pun or an elaborate double-entendre. In every culture, there are surely always people who fail to grasp the point of a witty remark or who do not know precisely at what point to laugh as a particular humorous tale is related. This may be why there are so few rigorous anthropological, sociological or folkloristic investigations of humor.

The study of American Negro humor languishes along with the study of humor in general. Although there are a fair number of collections of jokes and humorous songs, there is virtually no analysis. Yet jokes, like other folkloristic materials, require interpretation. Whatever else humor may mean, it would seem at the very least to provide a way of facing or perhaps temporarily escaping the hard realities of life. Crying is one outlet, but laughing is to be preferred. The blues line "laughing to keep from crying" is an admirably succinct folk theory of humor!

Anyone genuinely interested in humor must eventually grapple with in-group humor. It is really in the in-group jokes and understandings that a group tests the solidarity of its members. Those who understand are "with it"; those who do not understand are *not* "with it." The very nature of esoteric humor is such as to make it extremely difficult for anyone outside the culture even to collect texts, much less understand the texts. Thus, for example, there are no doubt many

American Negroes who have never heard a white person tell a "Rastus and Liza" joke—the Rastus and Liza cycle being perhaps the most vicious and widespread white anti-Negro joke cycle. The rules of joke telling would normally preclude a white person relating jokes of this type to a Negro. By the same token most whites have not heard some of the favorite chestnuts in American Negro tradition—nor would they necessarily understand them if they heard them. For example, one of the standard joking responses to the greeting "What's new?" is "White folks still in the lead" which may imply, first of all, that there's nothing new: things are the the same as they've always been. It may be making fun of the Negro's inferior social position vis-à-vis the white world,

but it may also hint that the ballgame isn't over and that one day the white folks may no longer be in the lead.

As is the case for so much of American Negro folklore, much of the content of traditional humor deals with race relations. Sources of anxiety make the best subjects for humor and consequently race prejudice is a common theme in Negro jokes. On the other hand, much humor is entirely intra-group rather than inter-group, and one often finds one Negro group making fun of another, much as Dominicans and Franciscans tell jokes about Jesuits though all fall technically under the rubric of Catholicism. Nothing is too sacred for humor, and that is why the analysis of folk humor may provide an unequaled picture of a people.

Frontiers of Humor:
American Vernacular Dance

MARSHALL AND JEAN STEARNS

Humor is found not only in jokes but in all forms of folklore. There may be humor in proverbs, in folksongs, and in many other folkloristic genres. One rich source for the study of humor consists of the large body of skits which are performed both on stage and off. Not all skits are traditional, but many of them do represent long-standing "routines" which include singing, dancing, and general verbal sparring.

In the following brief look at some of the "man-and-wife" acts popular in Negro vaudeville, we obtain an idea of the nature of this vein of traditional humor. Especially valuable is the delineation through comedy of male and female role norms. The "man-and-wife" team who conducted the research, Marshall and Jean Stearns of Hunter College, were particularly interested in jazz. In fact, The Story of Jazz *by Marshall Stearns remains one of the best introductory books on the subject. Those readers who wish to learn more about traditional Negro dances and skits should consult Marshall and Jean Stearns, "Vernacular Dance in Musical Comedy,"* New York Folklore Quarterly, *22 (1966), pp. 251–61, and* Jazz Dance: The Story of American Vernacular Dance *(New York, 1968).*

"...I hope that Negro 'low' comedy persists even long after all the gangsters on television are named Smith and Brown."—*LeRoi Jones*

IN NEGRO vaudeville and nightclubs during the late twenties, teams of comedy dancers multiplied. They had evolved a knockabout style that combined acrobatics with eccentric dancing —anything that would attract attention —and employed it to project a type of humor that reflected Negro life in the South.

From *Southern Folklore Quarterly*, vol. 30 (1966), 227–35 by permission of Jean Stearns, and Southern Folklore Quarterly.

These teams were part of a tradition. Before the Civil War, white minstrelsy had adopted the two-man team: the comedian and the straight man, or The Plantation Hand and The Dandy. Both danced. After the Civil War, Negro tentshows developed comedians with a rhythmic style and the dancing became formalized: The Dandy strutted and The Plantation Hand shuffled. Among other things, they excelled at an "inside" humor in which, along with everything else, they laughed at themselves.

Perhaps the first popular blend of these elements on Broadway took place at the turn of the century in the performances of Williams and Walker. With the aid of the vernacular dance —George Walker did the Strut or Cakewalk and Bert Williams the Shuffle and a bit of the Grind—they introduced a kind of bittersweet humor. They were a great hit but the blend still had a long way to go.*

By the beginning of the first World War, the South had produced one of its own specialties in comedy, the man-and-wife team, and these teams had become the best-paid acts on the embryonic T.O.B.A. (Theater Owners Booking Association), the Negro vaudeville circuit. The impulse for these teams came from Negro folkways, pointing up the conflict between a vainglorious and henpecked husband, and a practical and domineering wife—with searing satire that white people did not understand and often considered vulgar if not dangerous.

By 1915 one of the most popular teams in the South was Stringbeans and Sweetie May. They played only Negro theaters and their act was created of, by, and for Negroes. They attracted so much business, according to legend, that manager after manager hired them for as long as they would play his theater. Offstage, Stringbeans was a person of importance—his real name was Budd LeMay—and his wife a highly respected woman. Audiences knew they were married, which gave their pantomime a particular relevance.

A performance by Stringbeans and Sweetie May in the mid-teens at the Globe Theater in Jacksonville, Florida, went like this:

Sweetie May trucks provocatively onstage, cuts a neat buck-and-wing and sings a blues. She is an outrageous flirt and the men in the audience are shouting encouragement as Stringbeans strolls out of the wings. Tall and lanky with a flashing diamond in one of his front teeth, he wears a dilapidated jacket with padlocks instead of buttons. He stops, listens to the shouts, and gives a loud and contemptuous sniff. The force of his presence is so powerful that the audience falls silent.

As Stringbeans concentrates on polishing his padlocks, Sweetie May eyes him critically: "Stop cuttin' the fool, Beans," she commands, "don't you see them intelligent peoples out front watchin' you?" Stringbeans explains: on the way to the theater a white cop stopped him, noticed the padlocks, and told him that he had been in jail often enough to know about locks and keep away from them. "So I tol'

---

* For sample appreciations of Williams and Walker in their own day, see R. C. Murray, "Williams and Walker, Comedians, Being an Appreciation of their Talent," *The Colored American Magazine*, 9 (1905), pp. 496–502; and Lester A. Walton, "Williams and Walker on Broadway," *The Colored American Magazine*, 14 (1908), pp. 226–30. —ED.

him the truth *an' he believed me*," says Stringbeans with a grin that changes abruptly into an accusing glare at the audience as he announced, "I don't want no colored folks 'round this town stealin' my clothes."

The insult to Jacksonville and the inadequacy of padlocks in any such a situation is merely the surface of the joke; that the white policeman believed Stringbeans, although the poorest member of the audience would not have worn that jacket to a dog fight, is more to the point; basically, the joke concerns the gullibility of white people, while Stringbeans plays the role of the trickster.

Stringbeans then lopes to the piano and announces "The Sinking of the Titanic." Standing at full height, he reaches down to the keyboard as he sings like an early Ray Charles:

> Listen no-good womens
> Stop kickin' us men aroun'
> Cause us men gonna be your iceberg
> And send you sinkin' down
>
> Sinkin' like Titanic
> Sinkin' sinkin' down
> Oh you no good womens listen
> You sure is bottom bound
>
> White folks got all the money
> Colored folks got all the signs
> Signs won't buy you nothin'
> Folks, you better change you mind
>
> Sinkin' like Titanic
> Sinkin' sinkin' down
> If you don't change your way of livin'
> You sure is bottom bound

This is the battle of the sexes and, apart from the enlightened comment that "white folks got all the money, colored folks got all the signs" (that is, voodoo signs or superstitions), Stringbeans is threatening "no-good womens" of his own color who, just like the people on the Titanic who refused passage to prizefighter Jack Johnson (as the audience is well aware), are "bottom bound."

This threat is foolish bravado, based upon an immutable fact of Negro life in the South. Stringbeans has broached a problem which he returns to at the end of the act.

As he attacks the piano, Stringbeans' head starts to nod, his shoulders shake, and his body begins to quiver. Slowly, he sinks to the floor of the stage. Before he submerges, he is executing the Snake Hips like a one-man Laocoön, shouting the blues and, as he hits the deck still playing the piano, performing a horizontal grind which would make today's rock-and-roll dancers seem like staid citizens.

At the end of the act, Stringbeans stands on his head, turns his pockets inside out so that a few pennies fall on the stage, and pleads, "Don't, Baby ... Don't Baby ... Don't Baby!" Sweetie May wants to know "Don't what?" and adds aggressively "I ain't done nothin' to you—*yet*" Stringbeans continues to beg like a masochistic Milquetoast until he cuts short the refrain suddenly and emphatically: "Don't—leave me a damn cent!"

Stringbeans is commenting upon the problem of a male Negro in a matriarchy by pantomiming the plight of the well-known "Monkey Man" in a moment of petulant rebellion. The Monkey Man is the servile mate who without protest turns over his hard-earned money to a woman.

After the Civil War, the Negro was suddenly "free" to earn his own living, a situation which as in slave days continued to give the woman an advantage over the man. Considered harmless and manageable, she was in demand as a domestic with bed and board supplied; he was considered a potential trouble-maker and lucky to get an ill-paid job as a manual laborer. Thus the wife was relatively independent, the boss who kept the family together—or tore it apart. The husband who stayed and put up with it all became a Monkey Man and a standing joke.

With the mother-wit of a healthy human being, Stringbeans is demonstrating a recipe for survival. He is not "laughing to keep from crying"—although this cannot be too far from his true feelings—but simply ventilating the absurdities of a chronic situation.

Among the many followers of Stringbeans and Sweetie May were Butterbeans and Susie (Mr. and Mrs. Jodie Edwards) who, at one time, formed a trio with Stringbeans. They are better known because they came North later and made a series of successful recordings. (Their first recording "When My Man Shimmies," Okeh 8147, was issued in 1922; their latest, Festival M-7000, in 1962.)

Between duets, Susie sang the blues and cakewalked while Butterbeans performed his eccentric dance. He was famous for his Heebie Jeebies, a dance routine known in the trade as the "Itch," where he scratched in syncopated rhythms. "That Butterbeans, he wore the tightest pants and kept his hands in his pockets and looked like he was itching to death," says dancer James Cross who is Stump in the team of Stump and Stumpy, "and when he took his hands out of his pockets and started to scratch all around the beat, the audience flipped."

Butterbeans and Susie spent little time pantomiming a male in a matriarchy (they *looked* the part) but made it verbally explicit—alternately singing, interrupting, and heckling each other. In one of their own numbers, "Get Yourself a Monkey Man," the forthright Susie describes exactly what she wants: "the man I got he's a hard-workin' man, he works hard all the time; and on Saturday night when he brings me his pay, he better not be short one dime."

Butterbeans' opinion of such a man is very low: "He's a bran' new fool and a Monkey Man." He believes in treating women rough: "I'd whip your head every time you breathe; rough treatment, Susie, is 'zactly what you need." This bloodthirsty declaration is contradicted by the baby-face and timorous bearing of Butterbeans, who is clearly indulging in delusions of grandeur. In fact, Butterbeans himself is the Monkey Man.

In their version of a standard tune, "Until the Real Thing Comes Along," Susie sings the original lyrics with feeling, swearing eternal devotion and establishing a more romantic mood than many popular singers. Then Butterbeans, apparently swept off his feet and madly in love, carries on with lyrics of his own: "I'd fight all the animals in the jungle or even in the zoo, I'd grab a lion and smack his face and tear a tiger in two!" Susie interjects an encouraging "Yeah" at this point. "If that ain't love, it'll have to do," he continues while Susie asks breathlessly "Till when, till when?" and Butterbeans answers: "Until another *fool* come along."

Butterbeans and Susie not only make the ignominy of the Monkey Man of Southern Negro life hilariously explicit but they also expose the saccharine fantasies of Tin Pan Alley. In direct contradiction to Western notions of chivalry, their objective is vilification in high style, insults that scandalize the middle-class ear. The source of this tradition, incidentally, is the West African song of allusion, reinterpreted in the West Indies as the political calypso, in New Orleans as the "signifying" song, and in the South more generally as "The Dozens."

A one-sided version which well-mannered people sometimes found hard to take survived during the twenties and thirties in the stage shows featuring Negro bands. As Ivy Anderson sang a sad blues in front of the Duke Ellington orchestra, drummer Sonny Greer, safely ensconced behind a mountain of percussion, talked back between pauses in the lyrics—rudely and with a straight face. "I got the blues," sings Ivy and Sonny interjects, "That ain't the worst you gonna get, Baby!" In Harlem, this was one of the traditional ways to encourage a vocalist.

In 1965 concerts, pianist Billy Kyle in Louis Armstrong's sextet fell back into the tradition of making rude remarks as the well-proportioned Jewel Brown sang. "I Left My Heart in San Francisco," she intoned, while Mr. Kyle observed loudly, "I see you brought the rest of it along." To some in the audience his remarks seemed to be in shockingly bad taste, but Miss Brown rather enjoyed them, feeling no doubt that they called attention to certain indisputable facts.

Not all the early man-and-wife teams were married. "Two-Story Tom," so-called because of his height and the floor of a house on which he liked to work, picked up a partner in each town as he traveled the circuits. Her part was

not large. He was a fine buck dancer with a genius for satirizing the stereotype of the "bad" Negro who is supposed to flash a razor, shoot crap, and get into fights. "When I start after you," he roars, "you'll run so fast you'll cut out a new street."

The possibilities of embroidering upon the mask of the "bad" Negro who "don't take nothin' from nobody" —a mean and militant John Henry— are almost endless. A stereotype, an example of wishful thinking by Black or white, or even a reality, such a rich subject for satire was taboo in many situations and therefore a prime source of inside humor.

Meanwhile the emphasis was shifting toward violence. In the late twenties, with migration from South to North and country to city, as well as exposure to more integrated audiences, man-and-wife teams succumbed to knockabout two-man teams. To a city audience, the problems of a male in a matriarchy (although increasingly applicable to white families) had less appeal than outright conflict, and the acts changed accordingly.

The best teams who mined this vein, for both Negro and—less frequently— white audiences, were devoted to dancing in jazz rhythms. Among them were Bilo and Asher, Cook and Brown, Moke and Poke, Stump and Stumpy, Chuck and Chuckles, and Red and Struggy. They played nightclubs (mostly Negro) and vaudeville circuits and, once in a long while, a Broadway musical. The best of them sometimes appeared in films.

Cook and Brown were working with Ben Bernie at the College Inn in Chicago around 1930. Their knockabout style was new and when they came East to open at the Cotton Club in 1934, they met with no competition. "Later on," says Brown, "Moke and Poke, Stump and Stumpy, Son and Sonny, and other teams of dancing comedians showed up."

The act combines flash dancing, that is, the most difficult acrobatic stunts, with an undeclared war between Cook and Brown. The irrepressible five-foot Brown interrupts the routine in order to show off, while the short-tempered six-foot Cook knocks him back into line. It looks like bone-crunching mayhem but is actually care-fully-rehearsed acrobatics. "Brownie can fall like a champion," says Cook, "he drops, slides the length of the stage, and bounces up in a reverse split thumb-ing his nose."

The more or less hidden theme is the little guy who proves indestructible, and the similarity to Negro folk symbols such as the Gray Goose and the Boll Weevil is clear; the headlong conflict is pantomimed strenuously and the humor is based upon cheerful survival amidst chaos.

Another team, Stump and Stumpy, transplants the tradition of Stringbeans and Sweetie May, making a distinction between Northern and Southern Negroes. It occurs in a skit at the Apollo Theater in Harlem. Both dark-skinned, they are seated happily in a nightclub "up North." Behind Stump and out of his sight stands a light-skinned and threatening bouncer-waiter, a napkin over his arm. His glowering presence sobers Stumpy who is facing him. Stump, unaware of the threat, tries to cheer up his buddy: "Whatsa matter, man? You up No'th now, let's have a ball!" He is convinced that his troubles are over since he has left the South.

Stumpy, watching the bouncer, tries to hush Stump who is becoming noisier and noisier. "You up No'th, man!" Stump cries.

At last Stumpy catches Stump's eye and nods fearfully at the bouncer. Stump turns around, puzzled at first by the figure towering above him. For a moment his newly-won confidence does not falter. He pulls his buddy's coat, points wildly at the bouncer, and commands: "Straighten that fool *out*, man, straighten that fool *out*!" Where-upon the bouncer picks him up and, as the audience screams with laughter, thrashes him unmercifully. The act finishes with flash dancing.

The assumption of the Southern Negro that once you come North your troubles are over is widespread and many in the audience recognize their own shattered illusions in the skit: the thrashing that Stump receives seems fitting (the *real* fool gets straightened out by one of a lighter shade of his own color); another difficult situation has been faced, placed in more bearable perspective, and even reduced to laugh-able proportions.

In the fifties, when jazz-based dance was being driven out of musicals by prestige-laden ballet and modern dance (it never really got on television), this style of comedy went off on a tangent of its own. The trend was toward stand-up, one-line comedians in the style of Bob Hope. Yet the inside humor of Stringbeans and Sweetie May still per-sisted, brought up to date by single comedians working in the new style. Some of them had been around a long time.

In a white world which thought of "racial" humor in terms of Stepin Fetchit and Amos 'n' Andy (they were "putting on" white people in their own way) the tradition surfaced in the "new" humor of Slappy White, Red Foxx, Nipsey Russell, Moms Mabley, Dick Gregory, Godfrey Cambridge, Flip Wilson, and others. (Bill Cosby garnered fame by *not* talking about the Negro.) It swiftly became big business because of its great appeal in nightclubs, theaters, on television and, especially, recordings where visibility is nil.

This inside humor is welcomed because these comedians are laughing at everybody including Negroes, and often because it is daring, since it deals with controversial subjects in which many people have deep emotional investments pro and con. Listening to a comedian pick his way through the constantly-changing nuances of sanctioned attitudes on such an explosive topic can be exhausting as well as exhilarating. And always, of necessity, the humor is genial and broadly appealing.

This humor can have a healthy impact. Dick Gregory's fantasy on what would happen if Governor Wallace discovered a drop of Negro blood in his veins makes debate temporarily irrelevant. It is no solution but it can clear the air of cant. To be able to appreciate such humor necessitates an understanding of the situation upon which it is based, and leads to a healthy questioning of prejudice.

Some years ago when the play *Purlie Victorious*, a marvel of inside humor, opened on Broadway and later appeared as a film, it was not much of a success. The white audience wanted to enjoy it

—isolated individuals laughed loudly— but the majority did not know what to make of it. This humor was new to them, they were puzzled, and there was no telling when to laugh.

In March, 1966, a bit of fooling in the ancient tradition of Stringbeans and Sweetie May popped up on prime-time TV. Sammy Davis portrayed a nervous Negro applying for a white-collar job and discovering that his interviewer is another Negro. Davis' obsequious formality dissolves into a hilarious parody of super-hip gestures and jargon, while interviewer Nipsey Russell remains stiffly dignified. Switching roles and obtaining the upper hand, Davis becomes instantly and pompously reserved.

In contrast to the rest of a rather bland show, the skit seemed hysterically out of place. Whether the critics were not watching (the show was soon to be cancelled) or the skit was simply unintelligible to them, no mention of it appeared in the New York papers. Limited inquiry indicated that the general public did not know what to make of it.

As the public is educated by exposure to this humor, the intricacies of black-white relationships will be better understood. Better still, the mainstream of American humor will be notably enriched. Best of all, it will no longer be *inside* humor. "Once you get past this racial business," says comedian Godfrey Cambridge who is proud of having learned from Butterbeans and Susie, "you begin to go somewhere."

Humor as a Technique in Race Conflict

JOHN H. BURMA

There are numerous anthologies of Negro humor, some of them compiled by leading Negro men of letters. However, the materials are almost invariably presented with little or no interpretation. One could argue, of course, that jokes are self-explanatory and that their meanings are perfectly obvious to members of the in-group. But then again, this may not be the case at all. For one thing, there may be more than one way of interpreting a given joke. To illustrate the possibility of multiple meanings for a single joke, let us consider the following text collected from an Alabama Negro informant in 1964: Governor Wallace of Alabama died and went to heaven. After entering the pearly gates, he walked up to the door of a splendid mansion and knocked. A voice inside exclaimed, "Who dat?" Wallace shook his head sadly and said, "Never mind, I'll go the other way."

First of all, we can see an expression of "wishful thinking," a common feature of jokes. In the very first line, Governor Wallace died—and this could easily represent wishful thinking on the part of an Alabama Negro in view of Wallace's adamant intransigence in opposing integration and violating Negro civil rights. But the multiple meanings may occur with regard to what is understood by the stereotyped dialect "Who dat?" Clearly, the implication is that a Negro is inside the mansion. But individuals differ as to the identity of the Negro voice. Some think it is God; others think it might be St. Peter. A few whites assume it is a doorman or other menial. Clearly, an individual's interpretation of this element of the joke may depend upon his own particular attitude toward race relations. There is a world of difference between assuming God or St. Peter is a Negro and thinking heaven has Negro servants. Similarly, some individuals take it that heaven has been completely taken over by Negroes: other individuals assume only that heaven is now integrated. Again, the views

Reprinted from *American Sociological Review*, 2 (1946), pp. 710–15, by permission of the the author and The American Sociological Association.

or fears of an individual with regard to race will affect his interpretation of a joke. In any event, whoever the person answering the knock on the door may be, Governor Wallace decides not to enter but rather to go to hell instead. Note that Governor Wallace is not forced to go to hell by Black Power militants. What is it precisely which makes him go to hell? It is his own prejudice which sends him to hell, an understandable sentiment from an Alabama Negro joke teller. In terms of the joke's premise, Governor Wallace would sooner go to hell before setting foot in a house in which there was so much as one Negro. This in no way exhausts the interpretative possibilities of this joke, but the point is that jokes leave a great deal unsaid—this is one of their most charmingly effective characteristics. Nevertheless, for those interested in the analysis of folklore, an effort must be made to make the implicit explicit, because to hear is not necessarily to understand.

In the following essay by sociologist John H. Burma, we have one of the relatively few attempts to analyze the content of Negro jokes, especially those dealing with Negro-white relations. In these jokes, we find stereotypes presented, but these stereotypes, offensive though they may be, do exist and they must be held up to the light of reason if they are ever to be eliminated. Naturally, there is always the risk that readers will remember only the jokes and not the analysis, in which case publication of the jokes may unfortunately be little more than an unwitting means of further perpetuating the stereotypes. One can only hope that, in the final analysis, humor and its study will prove to be a positive force in reducing racism and in creating better understanding between black and white Americans.

For what is still a classic work in the study of humor, see Sigmund Freud, Wit and Its Relation to the Unconscious *(New York, 1961). Also useful is G. Legman,* Rationale of the Dirty Joke *(New York, 1968). For a summary of theories of humor, see Ralph Piddington,* The Psychology of Laughter: A Study in Social Adaptation *(New York, 1963). For representative anthologies of Negro jokes, see James David Corrothers,* The Black Cat Club: Negro Humor and Folk-Lore *(New York, 1902); T. P. Sullivan,* Plantation and Up-to-Date Humorous Negro Stories *(Chicago, 1905); William Pickens,* American Aesop: Negro and Other Humor *(Boston, 1926, reprinted New York, 1969); J. H. Johnson and Ben Burns, eds.,* The Best of Negro Humor *(Chicago, 1945); J. Mason Brewer, ed.,* Humorous Folktales of the South Carolina Negro *(Orangeburg, South Carolina, 1945); Roger D. Abrahams,* Deep Down in the Jungle *(Hatboro, Pennsylvania, 1964, reprinted Chicago, 1970); Philip Sterling,* Laughing on the Outside: The Intelligent White Reader's Guide to Negro Tales and Humor *(New York, 1965); Langston Hughes, ed.,* The Book of Negro Humor *(New York, 1966).*

For other representative studies of humor and race relations, see Milton L. Barron, "A Content Analysis of Intergroup Humor," American Sociological Review, *15 (1950), pp. 88–94; Russell Middleton and John Moland, "Humor in Negro and White Subcultures,"* American Sociological Review, *24 (1959), pp. 61–69; Russell Middleton, "Negro and White Reactions to Racial Humor,"* Sociometry, *20 (1959), pp. 175–83; Louis E. Lomax, "The American Negro's New Comedy Act,"* Harper's Magazine, *222 (June, 1961), pp. 41–46; D. J. Bennett, "The Psychological Meaning of Anti-Negro Jokes,"* Fact, *1, no. 2 (March–April, 1964), pp. 53–59; Hamner Cobbs, "Give Me the Black Belt,"*

The Alabama Review, *16 (1964), pp. 163–80; Irwin D. Rinder, "A Note on Humor as an Index of Minority Group Morale,"* Phylon, *26 (1965), pp. 117–21; Alan Morrison, "Negro Humor: An Answer to Anguish,"* Ebony, *22, no. 7 (May 1967), pp. 99–100, 102, 104–6, 108, 110, and Norine Dresser, "The Metamorphosis of the Humor of the Black Man,"* New York Folklore Quarterly, *26 (1970), pp. 216–28. See also William Schechter,* The History of Negro Humor in America *(New York: Fleet Press Corporation, 1970).*

THE TYPE of group behavior we call race relations contains many aspects which must be classified as conflict patterns of behavior. In conflict, the involved parties make use of a variety of techniques to gain ascendancy or temporary advantage. Since subtle barbs often strike more telling blows than gratuitous insult or rational argument, not infrequently these techniques include humor, satire, irony and wit.[1]

Humor lends itself particularly well to use as a conflict device because of its almost boundless limits in subject matter, and because its nature is such that it often contains more or less well concealed malice. Jowett has said that every amusing story must of necessity be unkind, untrue, or immoral. Thomas Hobbes believed that humor arises from a conception of superiority in ourselves by comparison with the inferiority of others. Crothers has called it the "frank enjoyment of the imperfect," and more recently James L. Ford has said that humor "is founded on the deathless principle of seeing someone get the worst of it."[2] It is not surprising that humor frequently is used as a conflict technique.

Throughout the history of minority-majority group relations in this country the set of techniques which we may denominate by the general term "humor" has played a definite role in inter-personal and inter-group relationships. Apparently all minority groups suffer derogation in this manner, and apparently all use the same weapon in return. In the United States, this has been particularly true with reference to Negroes and Jews, but quite noticeable also in connection with Catholics, Mormons, Quakers, Italians, Greeks, Germans, Irish, Chinese, Japanese, Indians, Mexicans and others. Such use of humor may be considered as a universal phenomenon. Valid studies can be made of humor as a conflict technique in connection with any American minority group, but for purposes of cohesion and integration a single minority group, the Negro, will be discussed here.

An obvious division of "race-conscious" humor into four categories immediately presents itself. That is, the joke may be (1) by Negroes and pro-Negroes; (2) by Negroes and anti-white; (3) by whites and pro-white; or (4) by whites and anti-Negro. Types two and four are by all odds the most common and particularly fit the present discussion.

In any conflict it is most gratifying to cause one's adversary to appear ludicrous in his own eyes. Where this is not

[1] ——, "Wit is a Weapon," *Nation,* 939 November 28, 1934, p. 609.
[2] All quoted in Milton Wright, *What's Funny—and Why* (McGraw-Hill, 1939), pp. 6–8.

possible, very considerable satisfaction can be secured by making your opponent appear ludicrous in your eyes. It is exactly this which humor does. It is difficult to the point of impossibility to assign malice a specific role in "race" humor. One person may relate a humorous situation somewhat derogatory to a minority group and do it in all good will; possibly in his own mind taking into account only the situation itself and attaching it to a minority group only because he himself heard it told that way. He may think of himself as a liberal and as having nothing but good will for the minority involved. In other cases the same situation may be related by a different person. To him the real humor is in the discomfiture of the butt of the joke. He would see nothing of humor in the situation if the butt were of his own group. It should be pointed out further that a given joke may not appear derogatory to the majority who circulate it, but may be deemed scurrilous by the more sensitive minority who are more or less unintentionally involved.

In many instances the bit of humor is in itself merely a tool, and thus may be manipulated as any user sees fit. Thus there are many maliciously humorous situations which are related by whites with the Negro as the butt of the humor and related by Negroes with the white as the recipient of the barb. Many jokes become "race conscious" or "racially humorous" merely by the addition of color to the persons involved. For example, when a *colored* boy could not do his geometry, his *white* teacher says he

should be ashamed, for when George Washington was his age he was a surveyor. To which the Negro youth replies, "Yes, and when he was your age he was President." With the simple addition of color, the barb of the humor no longer particularly strikes at teachers (pupil-teacher conflict and "teacher" stereotypes), but now becomes symbolic of the Negro-white conflict and draws its humor from the discomfiture of the stereotyped superior white.

In any event, most Negro-white wit makes one race or the other appear as the butt of the humor. In the case of jokes by whites about Negroes, it is typical that some stereotyped characteristic or supposed characteristic is the point of the humor. Stories about Negroes and chickens, chicken houses, and chicken stealing depend for part or most of their humor on the stereotyped insatiable appetite of the Negro for chicken. To a person who does not have a comparable stereotype, they hold little or no humor.[3] Very much like the above and also very common are stories centering in the thickness and hardness of the Negro's skull and the blackness of his skin.

A high percentage of humor of any type centers in the various aspects of sex, and this is true of jokes by whites about Negroes.[4] Given the not uncommon stereotyped conception of the Negro as a sexually uninhibited person, it is not surprising that a myriad of jokes exist which relate to the sexual exploits or delinquencies of the Negro, particularly Negro girls. Some depend upon sex, and some depend almost

[3] Cf. David L. Cohen, "White Folks are Easy to Please," *Saturday Review of Literature, 27,* (November 25, 1944), p. 12.
[4] Cf. Gunnar Myrdal, *An American Dilemma* (New York: Harpers, 1944), p. 38.

entirely upon the above-mentioned stereotype.[5] A typical example of the latter is the rather lengthy story concerning the Negro man being charged with rape by a Negro girl. He explains his side of the story and concludes by telling the white jurors, "and you know as well as I do that there ain't never been *no* nigger gal raped." This convulses the jury, who immediately free him. Needless to say, without the proper stereotype, such stories are completely humorless.

Another favorite type of humor by whites about Negroes lampoons the pomposity, avarice, ignorance, and emotionalism of the stereotyped "nigger preacher" and his congregation. A large proportion of these situations might be humorous regardless of the racial angle, as is true of many other types of "Negro" jokes. Such, for example, is the case in which the visiting Negro minister catches the chief Deacon abstracting 50¢ from the collection; he remonstrates, and the Deacon replies, "Bless you, Brother, I been leadin' off with that same 50¢ piece for nearly eight years." So, too, the case of the Negro minister raising funds who tells his congregation, "The church has been walking (loud amens); but it ought to run (loud amens); it ought to do more, it ought to fly (loud amens); but to fly it needs money;" (dead silence, then one voice, "Let her walk, Brother, let her walk"). Such humor does not depend wholly on its racial connotations, but the possession of the proper stereotype adds considerably to the enjoyment of the listener.

To most Caucasians the notion of jokes by Negroes lampooning whites comes somewhat as a surprise. Yet as an actuality such humor may out-date its white counterpart. For many decades Negroes were usually in a position in which their conflict and defense techniques against the whites had to be covert rather than overt. This favored the growth of the more subtle type of humor as a weapon of both offense and defense.[6] Some modern stories still retain this subtlety of derogation; as for example the two Negro maids who were comparing notes:

"At my place I have a terrible time; all day it's 'Yes, Ma'am,' 'Yes, Ma'am,' 'Yes, Ma'am.' "

"Me, too," says the other, "but with me it's 'No, Sir,' 'No, Sir,' 'No, Sir.' "

It must be noted especially in this connection that humor lies primarily in the individual's reaction to a situation, not in the situation itself. Nothing in the whole field of humor is more common than the observation that a situation which is uproariously funny to one person will serve only to amuse someone else mildly, and will leave a third party blank and uncomprehending. An incident concerning a deaf man may be quite humorous to those who hear well, but completely devoid of humor for those who are hard of hearing Thus it is typical that whites see little if anything of humor in many jokes by Negroes concerning whites, and vice-versa. This holds true regardless of whether malice is intended or not. It is to be expected, for example, that the jokes here used as illustrations

[5] For a more detailed discussion of Negro-white sexual stereotypes see John Dollard, *Caste and Class in a Southern Town* (New Haven: Yale Univ. Press, 1937), Chap. VII and pp. 394–98.
[6] For a discussion of covert types of Negro aggression see Dollard, *op. cit.*, Chap. 14, passim, and W. E. B. DuBois, *The Souls of Black Folk* (Chicago: McClurg & Co., 1903), pp. 204–5.

of anti-white humor will seldom appear humorous to white readers, and vice-versa. So marked is the influence of one's viewpoint that an occasional story is told by both Negroes and whites, each thinking it is a joke on the other party. One such example concerns the new Negro foreign language professor who attempts to vote in the Southern town in which his college is located. He must pass a literacy test. He is given a newspaper and asked what it says. He reads from it. He is given in succession Spanish, French, and German papers, from which he reads. Then he is given a Chinese paper and triumphantly asked what it says. Unable to read Chinese, he throws it down saying, "It says Negroes can't vote in———!"

It is unfortunate that many of the most illustrative jokes against whites, like those against Negroes are too crude and obscene for the printed word. In them the real power of the pent-up animosity of the Negro appear most clearly and starkly. These bits of humor very commonly involve "the retort discourteous" by a Negro girl[7] to a white woman or to a white man. Less frequently is a Negro man involved; seldom is the alleged conversation between a Negro man and white woman, except in the case of stories transmitted solely by oral methods. One of the rare exceptions to this is the story of the white woman who enters a street car; a white soldier surrenders his seat which is next to a Negro civilian. She says "I won't sit next to that 4F nigger."

The Negro calmly asks, "Have you a son in the service?"

"I have two, both overseas."

"Good," says the Negro, "tell them to look for the right arm I left over there."

The lady got off at the next stop.*

To the Negro any joke is particularly humorous if it shows Jim Crow "back-firing" on a Southerner. Rather common is the situation in which a Negro is treated as a "darky" and then is discovered to be the superior of the white in distinction, education or rank. Typical is the situation during the late war in which a Southern officer stationed in England was seated next to a Negro at an official dinner. He completely ignores the Negro until the end of the meal, when he condescends to remark, "Rastus, Ah reckon you all miss yo' watermelon." It soon develops that the Negro is the guest-of-honor, a renowned Oxford scholar, and a high colonial official who makes a brilliant speech. Naturally the officer fidgets very uncomfortably and when the Negro sits down he says sarcastically to the officer, "Yes, Rastus sho' do miss his watermelon."

A back-firing Jim Crow story now going the rounds reputedly concerns a high officer in the National Urban League. This Negro wishes to purchase a car in Atlanta. The white salesman greets him warmly, but constantly refers to him as "boy." All is arranged, but the "boy" says he wishes to wait a day to make the final decision. When he returns he is greeted with "Glad to see you, boy. You'll be proud of this car; not another boy in Atlanta will have a better one."

"Sorry," the Negro replies, "but the deal is off. I read the law last night

---

[7] For a discussion of different standards of caste behavior for Negro men and women, see Dollard, *op. cit.*, pp. 288–89.

* For a fuller version of the "lost arm" joke, see Maya Angelou, *I Know Why the Caged Bird Sings* (New York, 1969), pp. 207–208. —ED.

and it says minors in Georgia cannot purchase cars; and since I am a boy, as you have so frequently reminded me, it would be illegal to buy a car from you." With which he exits.

As often as not the stories of the back-fire of Jim Crow attitudes contain a sort of double bitterness toward the restrictions and toward the attitudes of the whites who impose such restrictions.[8] When such attitudes and such restrictions both react against the white, the story is doubly appreciated. For example, in an Eastern college city a torrid romance between a light-skinned colored boy and a white girl was interrupted by the draft. A year later he was back on furlough; to his surprise she had become a mother.

"Why didn't you write me you were married?"

"I'm not; and this is your child."

"Why didn't you tell me; I would have come home and married you."

"I know, but I talked it over with my family and they decided they'd rather have an illegitimate child in the family than a nigger."

As a matter of fact, colored people very commonly laugh at the absurdity of Jim Crow incidents or the variegated nuances of the color line. They could hardly accept the white world's daily boorishness in any other way and retain their mental equilibrium.[9] This may account for the following story told the author by Negroes in three different areas; in each case it was recounted as an actual incident.

"I went into the store at———to get some tobacco. I asked for 'Prince Albert' and the clerk said 'See the man on that can? He's white. Say "Mister Prince Albert." ' I thought for a minute and then said 'No thank you, sir; I believe I'll just take Bull Durham; I don't have to "mister" him.' "*

Negroes as a whole recognize that some whites are more their foes than are others. Thus Rankin, Bilbo, Dies, Talmadge, Eastland, G. L. K. Smith, the KKK, DAR, and "Southern crackers" receive more than their share of barbed sallies. So do the poll tax, sharecropping, segregated schools, southern politics, segregation in the army, and the like.

Not infrequently "race" humor has a grim and even macabre quality. Such is the famous cartoon which appeared first in the *People's Voice* of New York after the Detroit riots. It portrayed two small white boys looking at hunting trophies hanging on the wall of father's den. Among them is the mounted head of a Negro. One small boy says proudly, "Dad got that one in Detroit last week." To many whites the idea is devoid of humor; yet many Negroes thought it unusually funny and it was reprinted a number of times.

Langston Hughes attributes another such story to a late college president.[10] In its essentials the incident is that the president was descending the train steps at Atlanta when he heard a scream behind him. A white woman had caught her heel and was falling head first down

[8] B. F. Doyle, *The Etiquette of Race Relations in the South*, (Univ. of Chicago Press, 1937), p. 163.

[9] See Myrdal, *op. cit.*, pp. 38–39, 1931, and Dollard, *op. cit.*, Chap. 14, passim.

* This version differs from the text reported by Alan Lomax in his essay "I Got the Blues" (see p. 486) in that in this case the Negro protagonist refuses to buy Prince Albert tobacco rather than comply with the parodied "Mister" etiquette. —ED.

[10] *The Best of Negro Humor* (Chicago: Negro Digest Publications, 1945), p. 96.

the steps. The Negro raised his arms to catch her and then quickly dropped them to his sides and let her fall. At this point his Negro audiences usually were swept by gales of laughter, for that was the end of the joke. To them it was funny, for they well knew that in Atlanta something very serious was likely to happen to any Negro who for any reason put his arms around a white woman. She was hurt badly, but it was a good joke on Jim Crow. Much the same technique was used by Jay Jackson when the Negro hero of his comic strip "Bungleton Green" is unable to make whites believe saboteurs are about to blow up the local war plant. He deliberately trips a white girl and then catches her in his arms. Pursued by the angry lynch-bent mob, he leads them direct to the saboteurs and then explains the necessity for his dangerous action. It is this same hero and his girl friend whose well-chosen, sonorous phrases, clear enunciation, and philosophical speeches are constantly contrasted with the poorly enunciated, ungrammatical and illogical speech of the white Southerners.

A refinement of this technique is frequently used by one of the largest Negro magazines. Its page, "The African Way," contains numerous jokes in which the untutored African savage makes a fool of the white man or ridicules satirically the white man's beliefs, actions, or culture. Also, during the war many jokes circulated by Negroes had a double flavor, for the whites involved were designated as German Nazis or Italian Fascists. This enabled the humorist to "kill two birds with one stone," so that such jokes were frequently particularly malicious and especially successful.

It must not be inferred that most jokes told by Negroes are "race conscious" jokes. This is no more true than to infer that all jokes told by whites are for purposes of minority group defamation. What is true is that from the huge welter of humor, wit, and satire which is current today, both written and oral, it is possible to isolate and examine a not inconsequential amount of humor which has as its primary purpose the continuation of race conflict.[11] Even more common is the borderline type; its chief purpose is humor, but it has secondary aspects which definitely can be related to racial competition and conflict and the social and cultural patterns which have arisen from them.

It might be argued that "race conscious" humor is not actually a conflict technique, since much of it is humorous even if not racially applied, and that racial connotations are chiefly fortuitous. This may be true for a given bit of wit, but not for the totality. Any persons or groups who are the butt of jokes thereby suffer discriminatory treatment and are indirectly being relegated to an inferior status. This is, in turn, typical of conflict in general and gives additional support to the fact that humor is one of the mechanisms rather frequently pressed into use in the racial conflicts of America.

[11] Cf. Myrdal, *op. cit.*, p. 38.

Jokes Among Southern Negroes: The Revelation of Conflict

ARTHUR J. PRANGE, JR., AND M. M. VITOLS

It is difficult enough for a white man to collect Negro folklore, but in the case of Negro jokes concerning whites, the chances of success in collecting are even less. In this study by two white doctors in North Carolina, a subterfuge was employed in order to obtain Negro joke texts. The artifice of asking a Negro colleague on a hospital staff to collect jokes from Negro patients raises all sorts of serious questions about fieldwork ethics. Shouldn't a collector always tell his informants what he is collecting and what he intends to do with the material he obtains? The sneaky methodology employed by the doctors is almost analogous to using a hidden microphone or a concealed tape recorder. In other words, shouldn't one always have one's informants' consent before recording their conversations? Of course, there is inevitably the counter-argument that complete honesty about the recording of data almost certainly precludes the elicitation of some kinds of sensitive data. The question is: does the "ultimate scientific value" of data take precedence over moral and ethical considerations? Those who believe "science" comes first should realize that the very decision that it is more important to collect Negro jokes than to worry about how they are collected is itself a value judgment!

There is no one satisfactory easy answer to such questions, and presumably each folklore collector has to make up his own mind about his responsibilities to his informants and his and their understanding of the nature of the "privileged communication" which takes place between them. For further consideration of the ethical plight of the fieldworker, see Kenneth S. Goldstein, A Guide for Field Workers in Folklore (*Hatboro, Pennsylvania, 1964*), *pp. 56–59.*

The joke texts collected by the doctors do appear to be traditional for the

Reprinted from the *Journal of Nervous and Mental Disease*, vol. 136, (1963), pp. 162–67. Copyright 1963, The Williams & Wilkins Co. Reproduced by permission.

most part although the authors, not being folklorists, fail to analyze the texts as fully as they might have. Nevertheless, in view of the sparse state of scholarship devoted to Negro humor, this essay does constitute a contribution toward our understanding of Southern Negro humor.

"W'ite fo'lks lib in a fine brick house,
Lawd, de yalluh gal do's de same;
De old nigger lib in de Columbus jail
But hit's a brick house jes' de same."
(10).

COMMENTS ABOUT the psychological aspects of jokes and joking have usually fallen into three main categories: the structure and function of the joke itself; the meaning of telling a joke; and the manner in which the act of joking characterizes interpersonal relations. Freud (3) showed that a joke is so constructed as to allow conflictual material to slip past the censor and enter consciousness. The joke can reveal otherwise unacceptable material in an indirect and partly disguised manner. Repressive energy is liberated; tension is reduced, and we laugh. Zwerling (12) has shown that the favorite joke of a patient is often related to a central unconscious conflict. Bergler (1) has pointed out the aggressive and often denigrating intention in the telling of salacious jokes. In the motive of the joker, he finds the frequent wish to undress not only the subject of the joke but the listener as well. Brant (2) has described the taboo of joking in certain kinships and its permissibility in others. Generally speaking, joking implies intimacy.

Aside from these more formal aspects of humor, something is known of the subject from common knowledge. First, the joke teller has a certain ego investment in his story. For example, the employee is expected to laugh at his boss's joke; his problem is to recognize the punchline. Second, the listener

knows, more or less intuitively, that the intent of the joke is apt to be related to the personality and concerns of the joker. As mentioned above, Zwerling has commented on this relationship at the individual diagnostic level. In the study of culture, attention has also been paid to joking. Jewish culture has been extensively studied through an examination of its humor (*cf.* 4). La Barre (5) has similarly investigated the content of drinking songs of young unmarried men. He concluded that such songs reflected a shared concern about genital functioning and a rejection of homosexuality. La Barre's method, that is, insight into shared conflict via the study of humor, furnishes the point of departure for the present paper. The above comments about the nature of jokes and joking are accepted as valid by the present writers, who do not attempt to prove these points, but to use them as a means of further investigation.

To this end, it occurred to us that a study of Negro jokes might advance the understanding of Negro culture. It was assumed that jokes and joking play the same psychodynamic functions for Negroes as for others—allowing the release of tension through the partial disguise of threatening material and the like. The variables involved, then, would be the extent to which joking is used and the material with which it deals. On the first point no comment is offered except the opinion that joking is important in the lives of contemporary Southern Negroes. This has always been the consensus, and the observation has often been employed to support the notion that Negroes are happy people. However, it is just as plausible to invoke this observation to argue that Negroes are unhappy. Several authors have written that Negro humor was born of necessity under the stimulus of adversity and has had survival value (5, 10).

The subjects at hand were the patients and Negro employees of Cherry Hospital, the only public facility for the hospitalization of Negro mental patients in North Carolina.* It was recognized that what is characteristic about this material cannot be attributed solely to the fact that the subjects were Negroes. They were also males of Southern rural origin, and members of the lower economic class. In this connection, however, the opinion of the writers is perfectly expressed by Kardiner and Ovesey (6): "...we cannot avoid the conclusion that the dominant conflicts of the Negro are created by the caste situation, and that those of class are secondary."

A professional, non-medical, Negro member of the staff who had the confidence and respect of most Negro hospital personnel and many of the patients acted as chronicler. He was instructed to jot down at once, in the language in which they were told, all jokes that he heard one Negro tell another. The arrangement was kept secret. After about three weeks (Spring, 1961) the help of another Negro professional

was engaged, but soon thereafter the word leaked out to hospital society that "the doctors" were collecting Negro jokes. At once the joke supply withered to a few insipid, stereotyped stories, and then died altogether. In the meantime 18 jokes were collected, and there is ample reason to think that they are not only authentic but also those not commonly heard by whites.[1]

All 18 jokes were told by Negro men to other Negro men. Sometimes our informant was the intended hearer, but more often he merely overheard. A few of the stories were between patients who were in good remission and had full ground privileges, but the bulk were between Negro personnel (attendants, workers).

There are probably as many ways to classify these jokes as there are readers of this paper. Rather than attempt a classification, we shall merely offer a few comments as they seem appropriate.

A rather striking number of jokes refer to race relations: 13 of 18 (72 per cent). Seven of 18 (39 per cent) refer to genital sexuality, and this may not differ much from the distribution of "white" jokes. Perhaps the most meaningful "control" for the reader will be his own experience.

The farms of a Negro and a white man joined. They agreed to make true what each other dreamed. Mr. Ed went to John's house and told him that he dreamed that he had half of John's land and cattle. John gave it to him. John dreamed he got his

---

* The second author was the Superintendent, Cherry State Hospital, Goldsboro, North Carolina. The first author was a member of the Department of Psychiatry of the University of North Carolina School of Medicine in Chapel Hill. —ED.

[1] One year later, in an attempt to expand the data, the same technique was used. Defenses were still up, however; the plot was quickly discovered, and only two more jokes (not included in the present material) were obtained.

cattle and land back and Mr. Ed's car. Mr. Ed gave it to him. Mr. Ed returned and said, "John, I dreamed I got all your corn, my car back, and your wife Sallie was working as a servant in my house." John agreed but couldn't sleep that night. At three o'clock the next morning he knocked on Mr. Ed's door.

"Mr. Ed, I had another dream. Want to hear it?"

"Yes, John. What was it?"

"Well, I dreamed I got my corn back, and I got Sallie back, and I dreamed you won't goin' to dream no dam mo.' "*

A Negro went to court for kicking a white man's behind. The judge asked, "John, what is this about you kicking someone?"

"Well, Capum, what would you do if someone called you a black son of a bitch?"

"Well, John," said the judge smiling, "nobody will ever call me that."

"Well, Capum, spose they call you the kind of a son of bitch you is?"

"Give him 30 days!"

This joke expresses defiance, but the last line, without which the joke would be structurally improved, tells us that the Negro paid dearly for his jest.

A colored couple were sharecroppers on a white man's farm. The wife had a baby that was quite evidently half white. The man was talking to his employer about it and said, "Some white man has been fooling with my wife."

The boss said, "Oh, I don't know. White people have different complexions and so do animals. Look at those sheep. They are white usually but now and then there is a black one. See, there are three black ones in that one flock."

"Yassuh, I sees all dat and I understands puffectly. Now, boss, I wants to make a 'greement with you. I'll leave your ewe sheep alone if you will stay away from my ole woman."

A Negro was a helper in a construction gang. A white lady passed. The Negro said, "Lawd, will I ever?"

He was overheard by a white man who said, "No, nigger, never."

The Negro said, "Long as there's life there's hope."

The white man said, "Yes. Long as there's a nigger there's a rope, too."

A Negro mother mothered five illegitimate children. One was fair with straight hair. One day she heard him bragging to the rest of his brothers and sisters about his color and hair. "Shut your mouth, you half-white rascal. If I hadn't got behind in my insurance you would have been as black as the rest of um."

Obviously the main point of this joke is to express the idea that the Negro woman had been coerced into sexual relations with the white insurance collector. However, a sub-theme is the prestige value of having a light skin. The same idea is expressed when a Negro dislikes or disapproves of a lighter Negro. The former may say of the latter: "That's white wasted." Of course, this attitude is laden with conflict. When resentful over some slight or wrong, one Negro may say to another, "That's damn white of you." It appears that these two slogans arose in the North and only recently have penetrated Southern Negro vernacular.

A Negro got off the bus in the South

* This is a standard dream contest folktale which seems to have been widely told in colonial times with white and Indian protagonists. See Richard M. Dorson, *American Folklore* (Chicago, 1959), p. 22, or Dorson, *American Negro Folktales* (New York, 1967), pp. 344–45. For a discussion of the tale, see Roger Abrahams, *Deep Down in the Jungle* (Hatboro, 1964), pp. 255–58 (in the revised edition, Chicago, 1970, pp. 188–92). —ED.

broke, friendless, hungry, and lost. The first man he saw was a policeman. "What time is it, boss?"

The cop struck him two licks with his club and said, "Two o'clock, nigger. Why?"

"Nothing, capum. I'se just glad it ain't twelve."

The officers of the law were chasing a Negro. He overtook a train and climbed aboard. "How fast will this train run, Mister?"

"Forty-five miles an hour," said the brakeman.

"Pshaw, man, I'll see you." He overtook a man riding a motorcycle at 55 miles and hopped aboard. "Mister, is this all the fasta this thing can run?"

"That's right."

"I got to do better than this." He hopped off and tore out. In his flight he ran across a buck deer. The buck mounted the top of small trees, lakes, hills, and fields. The Negro reached over and whispered into his ear, "Say bud, is de white folks after you, too?"

Two Negroes broke a road gang once. After running a long way one stopped to pray. His buddy caught him by the arm and said, "Oh man, come on here. Don't you know God is white folks, too?"

The last is the most poignant joke of our collection. In four sentences it expresses the Negro's sense of intimidation, of not belonging, rootlessness, his religious devotion and concern for his fellows.

A Negro man was plowing his cotton when a missionary stopped him to talk about the salvation of his soul.

"Do you want to go to heaven, Jim?" asked the missionary.

"No sah," answered Jim.

"What! How terrible! Don't you want to go to heaven when you die?"

"Oh, yassuh, I wants to go to hebben when I dies, but I thought you meant right now. I can't go right now. De bossman'll skin me alive if I don't finish plowing dis cotton patch."

A Negro was questioned by a judge after six straight weeks of arrest on Saturday night. The judge asked, "What is it that brings you up here every Monday morning?"

The Negro said, "Judge, you jest ought to be a nigger one Sadday night. You wouldn't ever want to be a white man no mo'."*

By tradition, at least, Southern culture is more tolerant toward Negro than white libidinous expression. Probably by way of overcompensation this joke is an exaggerated statement of the advantage.

Teddy Roosevelt went to Alabama and passed an old Negro guarding a watermelon patch. The Negro had been given orders by his boss to give no one a melon. "Do you know who I am?" said Mr. Roosevelt, upon being refused.

"Mister, I don't care who you is."

"Uncle, I am Mr. Roosevelt, the President of the United States."

"Mister, I don't care if you is Booker T. Washington. You ain't getting none of dese watermelons."†

There is an element of defiance here, of course, but we are especially interested in the Negro's proud comparison of Teddy Roosevelt and Booker T. Washington. It seems likely that this

* For other texts of the Saturday night joke, see Richard M. Dorson, *American Negro Folktales* (New York, 1967), pp. 185–86. For an early reference to the importance of Saturday as a day of revelry, see William Wells Brown, *My Southern Home* (Upper Saddle River, N. J., 1968), p. 167. —ED.

† For a similar joke involving Teddy Roosevelt and Booker T. Washington, but without the watermelon stereotype, see Philip Sterling, *Laughing on the Outside* (New York, 1965), p. 194. —ED.

joke has been imbedded in Southern Negro folklore, unchanged for fifty years. It is somewhat surprising that the characters have not been replaced by modern contemporaries. Washington, of course, was a Southern Negro folk hero, of which there are few. More recently he has become, to militant Negroes, a folk villain as the very archetype of "Uncle Tomism."

A Negro, an Indian and a white man were trying to get a goat out of the barn. The white man went in and came out holding his nose. The Indian went in and came out holding his nose. The Negro said, "Wait. Damn if I can't get him." He went in and the goat came out holding his nose.

Many races, nationalities, fraternities and the like have used this joke to express their notion of their worth *vis-à-vis* others.* Here, the joke is turned against the teller, suggesting the mechanism of identification with the aggressor. The unfavorable comparison of the Negro to the Indian is unexpected since the members of remnant Indian tribes in eastern North Carolina generally are thought to be lower on the social scale than Negroes.

In the present sample of Southern Negro humor, frank self-derogation appeared only once. This may represent a somewhat lower frequency than found in the humor of other minority groups.

A white man was walking through colored town one day when he heard a Negro woman call her small son, who was playing in the street. "Elec, Elec, come here to me. Elec, Elec, don't you hear me? Electricity! You better come here before I skin you alive."

The white man said, "Did you call the boy Electricity? Isn't that an unusual name for a child?"

"No sah, I don't think it's so unusual. My name is Dinah and my old man's name is Mose. Now don't dynamo's generate electricity?"

"I guess you got something at that," said the white man.

This joke is somewhat puzzling: the Negro teller makes fun of the ignorance of the Negro mother in the story. Still she expresses a kind of logic, a point that the white man concedes. But why is the second character in the story white, and for that matter, why a man? Negroes have sometimes functioned as jesters in white households; they still often do in modern novels of the South. This joke may express, among

---

* This is indeed a well-traveled international joke. For example, in 1966, in Denmark, a nationwide collection via the mass media proved this joke to be one of the most popular in that country. The protagonists are from the three areas of Denmark: Jutland, Funen, and Zealand where Copenhagen is located. See Carsten Bregenhøj, *Jyde, Fynbo og Sjaellaender* (Copenhagen, 1969). As the authors observe, the joke is nearly always used to make fun of "others." This makes it almost a certainty that the text of the joke reported here is a garbled one. The initially stated sequential order of the protagonists "A Negro, an Indian and a white man" shows that the last named white man is meant to be the butt of the joke. The fact that he was not strongly suggests that the joke may have been altered for white consumption. Whether the original informant guessed that the joke might be turned over to the white doctors or whether the black collaborator made an "editorial" change in the joke is not clear. It is perfectly conceivable that the black collaborator only turned over those jokes he felt were non-threatening to the white power structure at the hospital. If so, that might explain why a number of the jokes reported contain such sickeningly saccharine expressions of the white racist stereotype of Negroes, e.g., the faithful retainer guarding watermelons. If this is the case—and the attitudes and predicament of the black collaborator are not discussed at all by the authors—then one of the best jokes of all might be said to be on the authors! —ED.

other things, a persisting cultural con-
straint for Negroes to entertain others.*

The following jokes are presented in
summary to complete the spectrum of
the material. Unlike the preceding jokes,
they make no reference to white-Negro
relations.

An old Negro man bids farewell to his
penis, which must be amputated.

A Negro preacher proposes to seduce
the women of his congregation.

A wife mistakes the purpose of her husband's treatment of his penis for insect
bite.

A freed slave finds a conjure doctor
more effective than the Lord in finding
him a place to go.

An old dog teaches a young dog that
what cannot be eaten, drunk or fornicated
with should be urinated upon.†

COMMENT

These jokes were difficult to obtain,
and the very fact that they are so closely
guarded makes it more likely that they
contain important material. There is
an obvious preoccupation with relations

to whites and an underlying sense of
being intimidated. On the basis of this
small sample, one can say that the fact
of being Negro is the most frequent
concern in Negro humor. Even in the
jokes that have no obvious inter-racial
meaning, the characters are always
identified by race. It is never the case
that "one man said to another" but that
"one Negro said to another." In a similar
way the characters in the jokes speak
in Negro dialect; one might almost
say "stage" Negro dialect. To be sure,
there is such a thing as Southern
Negro dialect, but it is not as turgid as
the vernacular of these jokes. In many
cases the stories were told in dialect
by Negroes who ordinarily speak with
only a trace of it.

These jokes make no specific reference to anything that is topical in American culture as a whole. There is no
mention of current politicians, of the
antics of movie stars, the escapades of
space travelers. Probably this phenomenon of omission is explicable mainly
by preoccupation with race relations but

---

* The authors may have missed the point of this joke. First of all, the Negro mother isn't ignorant
at all. The white man in the joke—as well as the white men analyzing the joke—merely think she
is. The white man doesn't understand the language, e.g., names, used by Negroes. Through the
rather elaborate word play construction, the Negro woman puts down the white man by showing
his ignorance, in this case, his ignorance of sexual technique. The child is the product of the sexual
potency of Mose and Dinah. (The exigencies of the pun may have required the woman's name to
come first, but it is interesting nonetheless as a possible reflection of a female-centered family
structure.) Given the context of the South with its double standard such that white men had sexual
access to black women but black men were forbidden access to white women, the characters of
the joke make good sense. The black woman through word play is telling the white man he doesn't
know the basic facts of sexuality. The choice of a power metaphor for sexuality is really quite
clever in view of the "generator" pun: "Now don't dynamos *generate* electricity?" It is difficult, if
not impossible, to "prove" the validity of this interpretation, but it certainly would explain why
the second character in the story is white and why he is a man. A less complete interpretation
of this joke, an interpretation perhaps somewhat influenced by a feminist context, was offered by
Natalie Shainess, "Images of Woman: Past and Present, Overt and Obscured," *American Journal
of Psychotherapy*, 23 (1969), p. 80, who took the occasion to chide the authors for their inadequate
analysis. (I am indebted to the authors for this reference.) —ED.
† For a version of "The Old Dog and the Young Dog," see Roger Abrahams, *Deep Down in the
Jungle* (Hatboro, 1964), pp. 235–36, revised edition (Chicago, 1970), pp. 246–47. —ED.

it may be owing in part to the fact that our subjects are Negro and Southern, rural and poor. As has been noted previously in another context, (9) the fact that Southern Negroes live close to elemental realities spares them some sources of unhappiness. It probably also limits their subjects of humor.

Some other observations may be permissible. These jokes seem both stereotyped and old. They give the reader the feeling that they have been handed down, like heirlooms. This would be in contradistinction to the jokes of middle-class whites, which probably have a mean life span of a year or so at most. In white middle-class circles one risks disapprobation by telling an old joke. These Southern Negro jokes apparently are told and retold because they make a crucial point and because there is no felt need to clothe the point in new disguises.

Another noteworthy omission is reference to homosexuality. The incidence of homosexuality in the population from which our subjects come is not known, but it has been observed to occur more frequently under conditions of heterosexual deprivation such as hospitalization. In the judgment of the writers, it is not usually a preferred form of sexual expression but neither is it the source of much conflict when it is employed.

There is no contemporary control group, nor a group representative of previous times. The closest approach

to the latter was offered by Puckett (10), who, writing in 1926, found themes of the devices of unfaithful wives, the mishaps of white masters, and the ignorance of Irishmen. In 1944 Myrdal (8) emphasized the cynicism and stark fear in Negro humor. His findings more nearly resemble the present material and support the writers' impression that there have been qualitative changes in Negro humor responsive to social climate.

SUMMARY

This small collection of jokes sustains the idea that the Southern Negro is enormously preoccupied with the fact of being Negro. It may be the overriding consideration in his everyday life. This is not an astonishing finding, but it may be difficult for a member of a majority group to grasp. According to his humor, the Southern Negro fears whites but can sometimes defy them in a disguised way. There is conflict about whether whites should be envied; there is acknowledgment of some advantage in being Negro.

We do not maintain that this sample of humor necessarily accurately portrays the lot of the Southern Negro. In fact, some references—e.g., to Teddy Roosevelt and lynching—are museum pieces of anachronism.* It is, however, submitted that these jokes may reflect the Southern Negro's perception of his lot and that this is a reality in itself.

* One could argue that lynching should always have been an anachronism, but it wasn't and unfortunately still isn't. The slaying of civil rights workers, the assassinations of religious and political leaders (e.g., Martin Luther King, Medgar Evers), as well as the less publicized attacks on ordinary black citizens suggest that lynching-type activities are hardly "museum pieces of anachronism." Indeed, one is tempted to suggest that this and some of the other commentaries by the authors demonstrate quite convincingly why there is still a great need for Negro jokes about problems in race relations. —ED.

REFERENCES

1. BERGLER, E. Mystery fans and the problems of potential murders. Amer. J. Ortho-psychiat., *15*: 309–317, 1945.
2. BRANT, C. S. On joking relationships. Amer. Anthropologist, *50*: 160–162, 1948.
3. FREUD, S. Wit and its relation to the unconscious. *The Basic Writings of Sigmund Freud*, pp. 633–762. Modern Library, New York, 1938.
4. GROTJAHN, M. *Beyond Laughter*, pp. 21–25. Blakiston, New York, 1957.
5. JOHNSTON, H. H. *The Negro in the New World*. Macmillan, New York, 1910.
6. KARDINER, A. and OVESEY, L. Psychodynamic inventory of the Negro personality. *In Mark of Oppression*, pp. 301–317. Norton, New York, 1951.
7. LA BARRE, W. Psychopathology of drinking songs: Study of content of the 'normal' unconscious. Psychiatry, *2*: 203–212, 1939.
8. MYRDAL, G. *An American Dilemma*. Harper, New York, 1944.
9. PRANGE, A. J., JR. and VITOLS, M. M. Cultural aspects of the relatively low incidence of depression in southern Negroes. Internat. J. Soc. Psychiat., *8*: 102–112, 1962.
10. PUCKETT, N. N. *Folk Beliefs of the Southern Negro*, p. 8. Univ. of North Carolina Press, Chapel Hill, 1926.
11. TALLEY, T. W. *Negro Folk Rhymes Wise and Otherwise*. Macmillan, New York, 1922.
12. ZWERLING, I. The favorite joke in diagnostic and therapeutic interviewing. Psycho-analyt. Quart., *24*: 104–114, 1955.

Jokes Negroes Tell on Themselves

LANGSTON HUGHES

Some of the ethical questions arising when a white folklorist tries to collect Negro jokes are removed when a Negro folklorist collects jokes from Negro informants. Of course, there is still the crucial matter of being honest with informants and the potentially agonizing decision to publish in-group data, thereby making it available to people outside the group.

In this case, Langston Hughes, poet, author and playwright, and one of the best known Negro men of letters, has written a brief survey of traditional in-group humor. Langston Hughes had a lifelong interest in folklore and it was he, along with Arna Bontemps, who put together the first comprehensive anthology of American Negro folklore, The Book of Negro Folklore, *in 1958. Hughes was also an expert on humor as the countless delightful episodes of his near-folk character "Simple" attest. (The character's name, Jesse B. Semple, is a play on just be simple.) All in all, it would be difficult to find a Negro folklorist with better credentials than Langston Hughes to discuss Negroes' jokes on themselves.*

For details of Hughes' life, see his autobiographical works, The Big Sea, An Autobiography *(New York, 1963) and* I wonder as I wander, An Autobiographical Journey *(New York, 1964). See also James A. Emanuel,* Langston Hughes *(New York, 1967) and Milton Meltzer,* Langston Hughes: A Biography *(New York, 1968). For an indication of the many literary works of Langston Hughes, see Therman B. O'Daniel, "Langston Hughes: A Selected Classified Bibliography,"* College Language Association Journal, *11 (1968), pp. 349–66 (part of a Special Langston Hughes number) and also Donald C. Dickinson,* A Bibliography of Langston Hughes 1902–1967 *(Hamden, Connecticut: Archon Books, 1967).*

Reprinted from *Negro Digest*, vol. 9, no. 8 (June, 1951), pp. 21–25, by permission of Harold Ober Associates Incorporated. Copyright © 1951 by Langston Hughes.

THEY SAY once there was a Negro in Atlanta who had made up his mind to commit suicide, so one day he went down to the main street and took the freight elevator up to the top of the highest building in town, in fact, the highest skyscraper in Georgia. Negroes could not ride the passenger elevators, but he was so anxious to commit suicide that he did not let Jim Crow stand in his way. He rode as freight. Once at the top of the building, he took off his coat, drew a deep breath, approached the ledge and jumped off. He went hurtling through the air and was just about to hit the sidewalk when he saw a white woman come around the corner. He knew he had better not fall on that white woman, so he curved and went right on back up.

There was another Negro who one day came to a strange town in Mississippi where he had never been before. When he got off the bus he did not see any of the race around, so he asked a white man, "Where do the colored folks hang out here?"

The white man pointed at a great big tree in the public square and said, "Do you see that limb?"

Negroes in Arkansas, when you ask them what life is like in Tennessee, will tell you the white folks are so bad in Memphis that black folks can't even drink white milk. But if you ask Negroes in Tennessee what it is like in Arkansas, they will say, "Man, in that state you better not even put your black feet in no white shoes!"

There are innumerable variations on the use of the word *white* in the South. They say, for example (presumably in fun), that the reason Negroes eat so many black-eyed peas in Dixie, and in Louisiana so many red beans, is because for years after the Emancipation, colored people did not dare ask a storekeeper for white beans. Red beans or black-eyed peas, okay. But it was not until folks began using the term *navy beans*, that Negroes had the nerve to purchase white beans, too. In a Wylie Avenue hash-house one day I heard a Negro say to another one at the counter, "Here you are up North ordering white bean soup. Man, I know you are really free now." Everybody laughed.*

Some of these types of jokes are even laid on animals. They say there was once a black cat in Mobile who decided to head for Chicago because he had always heard that up North there was no color line. Hardly had that cat gotten to Chicago than he met a white cat. Desirous of being shown

* One of the most interesting Negro jokes about "white" culture concerns a young Negro girl who addresses a question to a mirror on a wall: "Mirror, mirror on the wall, who's the fairest one of all?" And the mirror answers, "Snow White, you black bitch, and don't you forget it." This text suggests the futility of Negroes attempting to use white folklore. White folklore, symbolized by the fairy tale of Snow White (Aarne-Thompson tale type 709) reflects white society, not black. The very name of the heroine demonstrates again the built-in symbolic color bias of "white" society. The moral so-to-speak is that Negroes should not expect to get ego support from white stories with magical mirrors which continue to reflect the same old prejudice. Negroes need to have recourse to their own folklore where, with cultural mirrors like "The blacker the berry, the sweeter the juice," they can take pride in being black: "I'm black and I'm proud." "Black is Beautiful!"

For texts of the folktale parody, see Langston Hughes, ed., *The Book of Negro Humor* (New York, 1966), p. 2 (where the item is given as being part of one of comedienne Jackie "Moms" Mabley's routines). —ED.

about a bit,

> The black cat said to the white cat,
> "Let's go round the town."
> But the white cat said to the black cat,
> "You better set your black self
>   down."

In some places, so another pleasantry goes, white folks are so mean they will not give a Negro the time of day. A colored man said to a white man, "What time is it, sir?"

The white man asked the Negro, "Do you play chess?"

The Negro said, "Yes, sir."

The white man said, "Then it's your time to move."

These, and hundreds of other jokes of a similar nature which Negroes tell on themselves, belong in the category of:

> White is right,
> Yellow mellow,
> But black, get back!

Their humor is the humor of frustration and the laughter with which these sallies are greeted, for all its loudness, is a desperate laughter. White people often do not understand such humor at all. Negroes do, and such jokes told at appropriate moments amuse them no end.

Shortly after the big Detroit race riots, a cartoon appeared in a Negro newspaper that Harlemites thought highly, if wryly, hilarious. But no white person to whom I have ever shown it even cracks a smile, let alone laughs aloud. The cartoon pictures a wall in a sportsman's den on which the heads of the game he has bagged are hung— a deer's head, an elk's head, a tiger's head. Among them, mounted like the others, is a Negro head. Two little white boys are looking at the head. One little boy, pointing at the Negro's head, tells the other youngster, "My daddy got that one in Detroit last week."

Most such jokes, however, are at the expense of the South. In Harlem they say a young mother-to-be, about to bear her first child, decided to go back down South to be with her mother when the great event came. Her young husband tried to keep her from going, pointing out to her that aside from having better hospital facilities, New York had no Jim Crow wards, and colored physicians could attend patients in the hospitals. In the South one often has to have a white doctor since many hospitals there will not permit Negro doctors to practice inside their walls. Still the expectant mother insisted on going home to mama.

The father in Harlem waited and waited for news of the birth of his child. No news came. The ninth month passed. The tenth month passed. Finally he phoned his wife and told her something must be wrong, to go to the hospital anyhow and be examined. She went. The white physician marvelled that her child had not yet come. Putting his earphones to his ears and baring her abdomen, he pressed his instrument against her flesh to listen for the pre-natal heartbeats of the unborn child. Instead, what he heard, quite clearly and distinctly inside the body of the mother, was a Sugar Chile Robinson type of voice singing the blues:

> I won't be born down here!
> I won't be born down here!
> If you want to know
> What it's all about—
> As long as South is South,

I won't come out!
No, I won't be born down here!

He wasn't. She had to come on back to New York to have her baby. Harlemites swear that that colored child had plenty of sense.

A great many jokes with which Negroes regale each other, but seldom tell white folks, are hardly complimentary to racial intelligence. Jokes relating to tardiness are among them. Some such jokes even go so far as to blame the darkness of race upon a lack of punctuality on that morning long ago in the dawning of creation when the Lord called upon mankind to wash in the River of Life. They say that everybody promptly went down to the water to wash—except the Negroes. The Negroes lingered and loitered along the way, dallied and played, and took their own good time getting down to the river. When they got there, the other folks had used up all the water and had emerged whiter than snow. In the river bed after so much washing, the Negroes found only a little mud. Into the mud they waded with their bare feet. Late, in their desperation, they bent down and put the palms of their hands in the mud, too. By that time, even the mud was used up. Therefore, to this day, nothing is light about Negroes except the palms of their hands and the soles of their feet. Late, always late.

Other jokes relate to behavior and how a Negro (insofar as these jokes go) will always snarl things up, even in heaven. They say the first time a Negro went to heaven, all the other angels became excited when they heard he was coming and had prepared a great welcome for him. Even Saint Peter and the Lord were moved at the prospect

of greeting the first member of the darkest race into celestial glory. In honor of the occasion the Gates of Pearl were shining and the Streets of Gold had been polished until each cobblestone gleamed. But what did that Negro do?

That Negro was so excited when he first got his wings that he took off then and there at top speed and would not stop flying. He flew, and he flew, and he flew, and he flew. In his crown of gold and his snow white robes he lifted up his wings and flew like mad from the East to the West, from the North to the South, up and down and all throughout the universe. He whizzed by the Golden Throne at 100 miles per hour, wings spread like a Constellation. He flew around God's footstool so fast the Cherubims thought he was greased lightening. He went past Saint Peter at such speed that he started a tailwind on the Golden Streets. Finally Saint Peter said, "Whoa!" But that Negro did not stop.

Peter sent a band of angels out to catch him but they could not get anywhere near that Negro. Gabriel blew his horn but he paid him no mind. He was a flying soul! He made wings do what wings had never been known to do before. He looped a loop in the sky, then he looped another loop, and tied a knot. That Negro was gone, solid gone! He scattered feathers all over heaven and stirred up such a gale that the Lord God himself stood up and cried, "Stop!"

When he stopped, that Negro skidded bang! into the Pearly Gates, broke one wing smack off, knocked his crown into eternity, snagged his robes wide open, and fell panting at the foot of the Throne.

Saint Peter just looked at him and said, "Just like a Negro!"*

In the category of the bawdy joke there are hundreds illustrating the prevalent folk belief in the amorous prowess of the Negro male. Many such jokes cut across the color line in boastful fashion. They say a white man came home one cold winter night to find his golden blond wife on the living room divan deep in the loving arms of a great big dark Negro. Petrified, in his astonishment the white man forgot to close the front door. The icy winds rushed in. Thinking his wife was being raped, in a frenzy he cried, "Darling, what shall I do to this Negro?"

She sighed from the couch, "Just shut the door so he won't catch cold."

Even in hell, according to the joke makers, a Negro is hell. Since for so long Negroes had had such a hard time on earth, as compensation, up until the end of the Civil War all of them automatically went to heaven when they died. But after Lincoln signed the Emancipation Proclamation and things got a little easier for Negroes on this globe, the Lord decided to send a few colored folks to hell. The first Negro consigned to the Devil was a tall strapping man of color who in his day had been a great lover from St. Louis to the Gulf. Because his boudoir skills left him so little time for grace, the Lord said, "Send that Negro to hell." So Peter threw him out of heaven.

No sooner did the Negro set foot in hell than he grabbed the Devil's daughter and ruined her. Ten minutes later he enticed the Devil's wife behind a hot rock and ruined her. About this time the Devil's mother came along. The Negro grabbed her and ruined her. The Devil suddenly became aware of this mighty despoilation. Trembling, for the first time since he had been ruler of hell, he fell to his knees and called on God for help, "Lord *please*, take this Negro out of here before he ruins me!"

Whether or not hell then began to draw the color line, the story does not say. But Negro jokes often draw a color line through their humor in such a fashion that only a Negro can appreciate them. Certain aspects of the humor of minority groups are often so inbred that they are not palatable for outside consumption. There are thousands of Jewish jokes that rarely reach the ears of Gentiles, and if they did they might be embarrassing to the ears of both groups. So it is with Negro humor—a part of it is intended only for Negroes. To others such jokes are seldom funny anyhow. The point is lost for often the nuances are too subtle for alien comprehension. A joke is not a joke when nobody laughs.

* In a version of this joke reported in William H. Grier and Price M. Cobbs, *Black Rage*, there is a different ending. After flying around heaven in reckless fashion "scaring the hell out of cherubim and seraphim," the newly arrived Negro is grounded by "the management" and his wings removed. A black brother comes along and scolds him for having abused his privileges: "and now here you sit grounded with no wings!" The protagonist's response is, "But I was a flying son of a bitch while I had 'em, wasn't I!" In Langston Hughes' 1951 version, there is only implicit approval for the "flying" excesses, e.g., "That Negro was gone, solid gone!" In the later 1969 version, the pleasure in flying circles around the establishment is explicitly signaled by the punchline. See *Black Rage* (New York, 1969), p. 95. For still another version of this joke, see K. Leroy Irvis, "Negro Tales from Eastern New York," *New York Folklore Quarterly*, 11 (1955), p. 171. —ED.

Genital Superiority in Oakland Negro Folklore: A Theme

NEIL A. EDDINGTON

> *In his essay on Negro jokes, Langston Hughes mentions that there are "hundreds illustrating the prevelant folk belief in the amorous prowess of the Negro male" (emphasis added). William H. Grier and Price M. Cobbs in their book* Black Rage *state (p. 53) that "The mythology and folklore of black people is filled with tales of sexually prodigious men." The theme of genital superiority appears to be a widespread one, and it seems to be shared by both Negroes and whites. In fact, it is not clear whether the notion was originally part of the white stereotype of the Negro which was eventually borrowed by the Negro or whether the notion started in Negro culture. Evidence from other cultures suggests that it is quite common for a "dominant" group to attribute greater sexual capacity and drive to members of an oppressed minority, e.g., during World War II, some Germans claimed that Jews possessed super sexual appetites. In any case, regardless of what the origin of the belief of the sexual superiority of Negro males may be, there is no doubt that this theme is a vital one, and it has had considerable influence upon the behavior of both individual Negroes and whites. It is quite likely that the frequency of white men's castrating Negroes in the South and the incredible, obsessive fear in the South that white women stand in perpetual danger of being attacked by a rapacious Negro male are closely related to this sexual stereotype.*
>
> *As in the case of any stereotype, there is always the question of its relationship to ethnographic reality. In short, are American Negro males especially expert in matters sexual or not? If they are, then there are several possible relationships to the stereotype: (1) Negroes are sexually superior, and this is why the folklore has arisen; or (2) white men, because of their own peculiar Puritan attitudes toward sex (and toward their wives), attributed greater sexual ap-*

Reprinted from the *Papers of the Kroeber Anthropological Society*, no. 33 (Fall, 1965), pp. 99–105, by permission of the author and the Kroeber Anthropological Society.

petites to Negroes, and Negroes came to accept this stereotype as valid, and some individuals believing it to be true, tried to act in accordance with it. In other words, once people become familiar with a stereotype, they consciously or unconsciously try to act it out. For example, it is possible that some fat people upon discovering the folk axiom that "fat people are usually jolly" may well give the outward appearance of being jolly since they have come to believe that this is the expected if not inevitable behavior. In this way, what started out as fiction begins to verge on fact. Even if American Negro males are no more or no less sexually adept than any other group of males in the world—which is probably nearer the truth—the existence of the stereotype as a formative influence on behavior cannot be denied.

In sum then, what is most critical about the theme of supermasculinity among Negro males is that it is believed to be true by some Negroes and some whites. Because it is believed to be true, it continues to affect attitudes and behavior of both Negroes and whites. Yet despite the theme's undoubted significance, there has been little discussion of its manifestation in folklore other than casual allusions. For this reason, the following brief essay by anthropologist Neil Eddington, based upon folklore which he collected himself in Oakland, California, should prove of interest.

For a discussion of the tendency to attribute greater sexual appetite and competence to an "enemy," see Robert Seidenberg, "The Sexual Basis of Social Prejudice," The Psychoanalytic Review, *39 (1952), pp. 90–95. For a consideration of the effect of the notion of "genital superiority" on Negro males, see William N. Grier and Price M. Cobbs,* Black Rage *(New York, 1969), pp. 53, 74, 77. For a highly speculative essay suggesting that the white stereotype of the Negro's genital superiority may underlie the elephant joke cycle in which phallic elephants are often castrated, see Roger D. Abrahams and Alan Dundes, "On Elephantasy and Elephanticide,"* The Psychoanalytic Review, *56 (1969), pp. 225–41.*

An exploration of the variability which exists within the genre of Negro humor can only be accomplished with a consideration of the major themes in Negro folklore.[1] One dominant theme which has been delineated is that of genital superiority of the Negro over his so-called white oppressor. As Abrahams pointed out in his paper on the "dozens" in Negro folklore, "both the forms and the culture are of importance," and it is the purpose of this paper to show how the two are interrelated (1962). There are at least two aspects of this theme which require elaboration: (1) Can the content of the assertion be explained in terms of virility striving?[2] and (2) Why is the assertion of dominance by the Negro over his white oppressor couched in terms of genital superiority?

Genital superiority can be seen as an expression of virility striving, and virility striving can be explained in terms of

[1] This research was carried out by a special grant from the Department of Anthropology, University of California, Berkeley, in 1963. I would like to thank John Ingham for his stimulating ideas and his discussion of some of the data.

[2] That this theme also has implications for affecting one-to-one social relationships also should be noted.

the developmental consequences of being socialized in an absent father family. There exists a number of empirical studies which show that males raised in absent father families show tendencies toward cross-sex identification and virility striving can be understood as a compensation for this cross-sex identification. (Burton and Whiting 1961). The empirical evidence for absent father families among lower class Negro families is well documented (Frazier 1939; Rainwater 1964; Moyninan 1965).

The motivation to relate to the white in terms of superiority can be understood in part by the self-hate hypothesis of Kardiner and Ovesey in their explorations in the personality of the American Negro (1951). The notion, in an oversimplified form, is to the effect that the Negroes basic identification is with the white oppressor and reality factors prevent achievement of this identification; the resulting frustration causes self-hate that, in turn, feeds back to cause them to strive harder to achieve the goal of "being white" and the cycle is repeated. It is my contention that if the Negro is consistently blocked in attaining his goal of "being white," he will utilize certain escape mechanisms which, while still not allowing attainment of his goal, will allow the Negro to achieve a type of superiority over the white.

One such mechanism is that of folklore, which affords the Negro a device he can utilize to escape his white dominated world of reality for a fantasy world in which he is the dominant individual. This is why a study of Negro folklore themes is important, for it is here we see a reflection of values and special problems which face the Negro. Hence we see Negro folklore as being derived in part from the psychosocial needs of the Negro.

As shown by Kardiner and Ovesey, it is a consistent feature of human personality that it tends to become organized about the main problems of adaptation, and this main problem tends to polarize all other aspects of adaptation toward itself. This central problem of Negro adaptation is oriented toward the discrimination he suffers and the consequences of this discrimination in regard to his self-esteem. This self-esteem suffers because he is constantly receiving an unpleasant image of himself in relation to the white. But the Negro can escape this impasse merely by retreating to his world of fantasy, a world in which he is not only superior to the white in matters of sexual prowess but also a world in which he can possess the white man's most valuable treasure, his woman (one aspect of the rape complex of the white southerner [Cash 1941]).

The process by which the Negro utilizes this theme of genital superiority will now be analyzed in terms of the previous psychological statements, as follows:

(1)

This is the luck to the duck
That swimmer on the lake
He fucked his grandma
Through a mistake
He take the little duck
Took her to his heart
Here's grandma fucking fart
Now, ladies and gentlemen,
It has come to the test
To see what nation
Can fuck the best
Get back white folks
Get in your class

The genital superiority stated in this rhyme is evident in that it is a direct challenge to the whites as a nation to pit themselves against the Negro. We can see that the ultimate outcome is decided before the contest begins in that the Negro tells the white to get in his class, which is obviously not equal to the class of the Negro. Other themes are present here but the point of the rhyme is again, which nation can perform the sexual act best.

(2)

There were three travelling salesmen; one was Negro, one was white, and one was, uh, Italian. So, uh, they all, uh, they was going out together riding in 'is car and they came by this farmer's house and the farmer had three daughters. They asked him, "Could we spend the night here?" and the farmer said, "Yes. I have three daughters. I will let either one of you—each one of you sleep with one of my daughters; but the first thing you gotta do is tell me how many times you fuck my daughter, the next morning when you get up."

So, uh, they said, "All right, we'll tell you."

"And the way I want you to tell me—the way that you—I want you to tell me is by the way you say good morning to me—I'll know how many times you've got."

So the first morning—the next morning, they all met—that evening they all went to bed with the daughters—the girls; and, uh, early that next morning the white man (he was first) he got up. He spoke, "Good morning" so, uh, he didn't get it but one time. The next morning—the next guy was the Italian—he got up—"Good morning, this morning." He got it—couple of times. So here come the Negro. He come in there. "Good mornin' this mornin'! How's every-

thing this mornin'? If this mornin' was as good as tomorrow mornin', I'll be back the next mornin'!"

This tale is a variant of a tale which exists in the white oral tradition. Two of the three combatants in the tale are obvious, the third, an Italian, is not so in his relation to the Negro. The informant was asked at a later date as to the distinction between white and Italian and the following answer was given. "He's kind of a Spanish type stud, you know they is pretty good lovers too." The "too" is in reference to the Negro and we can see by this remark that the status of the Negro as a sexual partner is enhanced even more by this comparison. As to the fact that the Italians are "pretty good lovers," it is evident the Negro is far superior by his repetitious "good morning" greeting, with the white a distant third.*

(3)

Yeh, that reminds me—these three guys, uh, they was in court. Uh, this time, uh, one was—they—one white boy, one Negro, and one Italian. The other one—the judge wanted to—they had caught a man and a lady out having an intercourse, and the judge wanted to find out actually what happened—what did the boys see. He wanted to know, you know, for real.

So, that day in court he called the white boy up. The boy say, he—the judge say, "Now, son, you gotta tell me; what did you see?"

He say, uh, "Uh, I saw 'em fucking, judge."

The judge said, "If you don't tell me the truth, I say, I'm gonna fine you ten dollars."

So, well, he said, "Well, judge, I saw them fucking, that's all."

---

* For another version in which there are three whores (Puerto Rican, Irish, and Negro), see Roger D. Abrahams, *Deep Down in the Jungle* (Hatboro, 1964), pp. 216–17, revised edition (Chicago, 1970), pp. 231–32. —ED.

So he told 'em, "Fine him ten dollars!" So he call the Italian guy come up there, and he came up there and he said, "What did you see? Uh, what did you see—John?"

He said, "Uh, just I saw, I saw a man on top of a lady; that was all I saw."

"Fine him!" So they called the Negro up there. He—come up there and he said, "Now will tell—I want you to tell me: what did you see?"

The boy said, "Alright. I'm going to tell you just exactly what I saw. Alright judge boy, I saw ten toes up, ten toes down, two asses going round, a big gang going out and in. If they ain't fucking you can fine me ten."

This is an interesting variation to the extent that while witnessing the same sexual act, the Negro is far more articulate in his description of the act. Again reaffirming his genital superiority is the fact he is better able to describe the act, which implies he knows more about what's taking place. I would also like to note that he differentiates between the Italian and the other two actors in the tale. This is done by calling the white and the Negro "boy" which is a common term of the white southerner when he is addressing a Negro. This could be a way of the Negro getting back at the white or it might be a mechanism for giving the Negro equal status with the white. The judge is called "boy" too. Since the Negro does not identify with the Italian as an oppressor, no special term is used to set him off.

(4)

On the fifth of May was a hell-fire day, during the time, you remember the Titanic, you know. They had this Negro on this ship. His name was Shine.

Shine was sitting on the ship, when he told the Captain, say, "Captain, Captain, I go it. The ship got a leak in it."

So the Captain told Shine, said, "I've got sixteen pumps to pump all the water." So Shine went on back and didn't pay no such.

Shine came back and he come running fast, said, "Captain, Captain, the water is above my head!" Shine said he couldn't bail it on time.

Shine jumped off the ship and went round it six times like a motorboat, prrrrrrrr. So here come the captain. "Shine, Shine, (save po) me. I make you the richest man you ever wanna see."

Shine said, "I've been a po man all along. I still a po man."

So here come the captain's wife. Say, "Shine, Shine," save po me—I'll give you as much white pussy as pussy you'll ever want to see."

Shine said, "There's pussy on land, there's pussy on sea; dunk your ass and swim like me."

So Shine went on out to sea, while the people on the ship were singing, "Nearer My God to Thee"—them whales on the sea telling Shine, "Bring your big black ass to me."

So Shine went on up north, bought him a hundred women, fucked them all but two. Went up town, got him some oyster stew. He come back and fucked them too.

Shine was so bad; he died and went to hell. The ole Devil busted in the glass. Shine took that big dick and bust him in the ass. So the Devil say he couldn't put up with Shine, so he sent him to Heaven.

Shine got to Heaven, said he's gonna fuck Saint Peter. So he fucked Saint Paul, said he ain't gonna stop until his roll is called.

(5)

Well, there was, uh—during the time the Titanic sunk, there was a colored guy by the name of Shine. That's the way he made his name, because he was the only, uh, colored on the ship at the time. He was the only one that uh,—was the survivor of the ship 'cause he swum that ocean. And this is the ways the story goes:

The 30th of May was a hell-of-a-day
That's the day when the Titanic sunk.
The black-assed guy on the name—on
that ship by the name of Shine.
Could swim the ocean in two seconds
time.
Shine was sitting up on the deck one
day
He said, "Captain, Captain, don't you
know,
There's water down you deck forty-four
feet deep."
The Captain said, "Shine, go on back
and do your act."
"I got forty-four pumps to keep the
water back."

Shine went on. Shine looked at the water, came back up. He said, "I'm gonna tell you one thing. I'm not gonna tell you no more; this ship is sinking."

The Captain looked down; he found it out. The Captain sound the alarm. Ole Shine got on—got on the, uh, deck and said to jump off, to swim.

Shine de—uh—the captain's, uh, daughter was on the deck. She said, "Shine," with her titties all wrapped around her neck. She say, "Shine, Shine," she say, "poor me I give you all you ever need."

Shine looked at her. He say, "Yours is good; that I know; but it's better on the other side of the shelf."

Shine came on; he was about to make his last leap off. Some more women grab his, say, "Shine, Shine, if you save poor me, I'll give you all you EVER will see."

Shine say, "Yours is good I know, but you got to save your ass and swim like me."

Shine jumped in the water, started swimming. Shine met a shark. Shine looked at the shark. He say, "Your eyes make

glit, your teeth make grit; but this one black ass you'll never get."

Shine kept—kept on wailing. Shine looked at the whale. The whale looked at Shine. The whale said, "Nearer my God to Thee, bring you black ass to me."

Shine looked at him; say, "This is one ass you never get," and he swim on to the shore.

[I'd have to come to the end of this; it's too prolonging] and here the informant stopped the tale.

In this quasi-folk epic of Shine, with versions given by two informants during the same recording session, we see conscious references to the genital superiority of the Negro and also the rejection, on the part of Shine, of the white male and his women.

The first version of this tale,* as we can see by the reading, is a more blatant version. The probable reason for this is that the informant relating it is in a higher state of intoxication than the other informant, therefore is somewhat less inhibited by the presence of the recorder.

A close comparison of the two versions will show the basic themes of wish-fulfillment and genital superiority to exist. However, only an analysis of the first version will be attempted, and only as it relates to this paper.

The tale begins with the Negro Shine (the only Negro on board) on the ill-fated ship Titanic (which shows that even the white man's ship is no good). Even though Shine informs the captain of the leak, he will not accept Shine's word as to the extent of the leak (which

---

* For other versions of Shine, see Roger D. Abrahams, *Deep Down in the Jungle* (Hatboro, 1964), pp. 111–23, revised edition (Chicago, 1970), pp. 120–29. Eddington's first text of Shine has evidently been combined with the story of the phallic trickster's visit to hell and his sexual attacks on the devil and his family, a milder version of which was reported by Langston Hughes in his sampling of jokes Negroes tell on themselves (see p. 641 in this volume). —ED.

reaffirms the lack of trust between the white and the Negro).

Shine then leaps from the ship and propels himself (by means of twirling his penis like the propellors of a motor-boat, which was indicated by the fact that the informant moved his index finger in a circular motion in the area of his genitals), around the ship six times which again shows that the penis of the Negro is superior to any mechanical phallus the white can build, regardless of size.

Emphasis is placed on this by the fact that the white captain now affirms the superiority of Shine's genitals by the fact that he offers him riches in an attempt to get him to pull the ship. Quite naturally, Shine rejects the offer, again reaffirming his hostility for the fate of the white.

Next we find the white woman offering her supposedly supreme gift, for isn't it true that that's what all Negroes secretly yearn for (a common idea circulated in white culture). But Shine again asserting the Negroes superiority, rejects the offer of copulation with the white female. He states the fact that she is no better than he is, and anyway, Shine says he can get that sort of thing anywhere.

Shine then swims to the North (opposite from the traditional South of the Negro) and copulates with a hundred women while all the whites drown. The supreme act of contempt by the Negro for the white.

In the end Shine dies, and goes to hell, but again he is able to escape the common fate of all Negroes, and like Christ dying on the cross and thereby gaining redemption for all whites, Shine attacks the white devil with his penis, his ultimate weapon, and redeems all Negroes and gains them admission to the white's heaven.

At the conclusion of the tale Shine is asserting his genital superiority over all whites by sexually assaulting all the white's religious heroes.

In closing, it may be stated that in continuing the collecting of Negro folklore this theme has been consistently observed by the ethnographer. This is especially true of the "ghetto" situation, where individuals have no means, other than overt physical action, but the folkloric encounter to escape the oppression of their situation.

REFERENCES

ABRAHAMS, R. D. 1962 "Playing the dozens." *Journal of American Folklore*, 75: 209–21.

BURTON, R. V. and J. W. M. WHITING. 1961 "The Absent Father and Cross-sex Identity." in *Merrill-Palmer Quarterly of Behavior and Development* 7: 85–95.

CASH, W. J. 1941 *The Mind of the South*. Garden City, Doubleday.

FRAZIER, E. F. 1939 *The Negro Family in the United States*. Chicago.

KARDINER, ABRAHAM and LIONEL OVESEY. 1951 *The Mark of Oppression*. New York, The World Publishing Co.

MOYNIHAN, D. P. 1965 "Employment, Income, and the Ordeal of the Negro Family." *Daedalus*, Fall, pp. 760–61.

MYRDAL, GUNNAR. 1944 *American Dilemma*. New York, Harper and Brothers.

RAINWATER, LEE. 1964 "Marital Sexuality in Four Cultures of Poverty." *Journal of Marriage and the Family*, vol. 26, no. 4 (November), pp. 457–66.

Jokes and Black Consciousness: A Collection with Interviews

PAULETTE CROSS

> One of the longstanding needs in the study of American Negro folklore
> has been for more Negro folklorists. Although there have been a number of excel-
> lent black folklorists, e.g., Zora Neale Hurston, J. Mason Brewer, Arthur
> Huff Fauset, Sterling Brown, Langston Hughes, etc., there have not been nearly
> enough. There must be many more black folklorists to collect and analyze the
> endlessly rich folklore heritage of black Americans. W. E. B. Du Bois in review-
> ing The Book of American Negro Spirituals in 1925 bemoaned the fact that for
> such a long time the Negro had to depend upon white critics for the presentation
> and analysis of his folksongs. Here is how he put it. "It is one thing for a race
> to produce artistic material," he said, "it is quite another thing for it to produce
> the ability to interpret and criticize this material."
>
> Hopefully, more and more black students will want to seek professional
> training in folklore at the graduate level. Only when this happens is there likely
> to be an end to the mere accumulation of folklore texts and a beginning of the
> difficult but very rewarding task of analyzing the folklore. The analysis may be
> historical, psychological, sociological, literary, linguistic, philosophical, political,
> or whatever. The important thing is that American Negro folklore will be better
> understood in terms of communication, values, and worldview so that ultimately
> the American Negro may better understand himself and be better understood by
> others.
>
> As a sample of the ideal situation in which a black student of folklore col-
> lects folklore from black informants, elicits the informants' own interpretations
> of their folklore, and adds his own analysis of that folklore, we offer the fol-
> lowing exceptional essay by Paulette Cross, formerly an undergraduate student
> at Indiana University and later a graduate student at Columbia University.
> Miss Cross, who is interested in Black Studies, wrote the paper as part of an

Reprinted from *The Folklore Forum*, vol. 2, no. 6 (November, 1969), pp. 140–61, by permission of the author and *The Folklore Forum*.

Introduction to Folklore course taught by Barbara Kirshenblatt-Gimblett at Indiana University in the fall of 1969. Although there are only seven joke texts from just two informants, this undergraduate essay represents one of the finest and most insightful studies of Negro humor yet made. Although Miss Cross may not be an expert interviewer in every respect—she sometimes erred in "leading" her informants or failing to follow up different points and the context was not ideal insofar as a female collector was collecting "male" jokes from male informants—there is no doubt that her interviews are crammed full of superb raw data, and they may serve as a model for the kind of contextual considerations and "oral literary criticism" which all folklorists should be striving to elicit. If there is anyone who thinks that folklore and its collection and analysis are not relevant to contemporary society, he should be asked to read "Jokes and Black Consciousness" by Paulette Cross.

For the remarks by Du Bois, see "Review of The Book of American Negro Spirituals," The Crisis, *31, no. 1 (November, 1925), p. 31.*

THE INTENT of this paper is to present jokes told by black Americans which relate to the black view of white Americans and of some aspects of white culture. The main purpose of collecting jokes of this sort was to discern why the informants tell the jokes, how these jokes relate to black American attitudes about white America, and how the informants feel these jokes serve their purposes and the needs of their audience. Much attention has been given to the ensuing conversations with the informants in hopes of eliciting from them their attitudes toward the jokes and their opinions on the "black problem" in this country. Thus we may be able to see some ways in which this pressing problem might relate to the types of jokes being narrated. It is hoped that the reader will achieve a greater understanding of why these types of jokes are being told by black Americans. It is also to be hoped that a greater awareness and understanding may be achieved by whites about blacks in America through the ideas and attitudes expressed. Indeed many of the attitudes reflected in this paper are among the dominant lines of thought expounded by the Black Power movement in America.

THE JOKES AND THE INTERVIEWS

INFORMANT 1: RONALD TYLOR*

The first group of three jokes was collected from Ronald Tylor on November 4, 1968. Mr. Tylor is a 23-year-old graduate student at Indiana University. He is a native of Milwaukee, Wisconsin, and gives his religion as Orisha Voodoo. The jokes were collected at the apartment of the informant, although I had originally discussed collecting possibilities and his general attitudes earlier at a dance. The informant told the jokes over tea and coffee, and afterwards we discussed why he felt that white people were "funny."

THE JOKES

1. There's this uh—black cat from the north, ya know, he's a bad nigga, and he went down to the south, ya know, driving his uh—white Eldorado Cadillac, and he drove into this gas station in Southern

* The names of the informants have been changed.

Indiana. Right in front of him was another black man in an old beat-up pick-up truck. And the filling station attendant walked out and he said uh—whatcha want boy? And the black cat in the pick-up truck said uh—gimmie a dolla wortha regula. And the station attendant said, gimmie a dolla's worth of regula—what? The black man said, ah uh, please mista charlie. So mista charlie gave him a dolla's worth of regula and charged him a dolla fifty and said naw git on out a heah boy. So the black cat in the pick-up truck left. So then the nigga from the north, he pulls up in this uh—white Eldorado Cadillac, in his sharkskin suit, silk socks, Stetson hat, Stacy Adams shoes, just clean, you know. And uh— right away the white boy is really impressed, you know. So the nigga reaches over and pushes a button and the window slides down a little bit and the white cat say, whaddyah want boy? And the nigga say uh—fill it up. And the white boy say fill it up, what? He say fill it up man, I ain't got all day, come on, fill it up. The white boy say, fill it up, what? With gas, fool, come on I ain't got all day. So the white boy went inside the filling station and he got his rifle and he came back out with his rifle and he looked dead in the nigga's eye and he pointed over at a bush about 200 yards away and he said, nigga, see that fly on that bush 200 yards away? And the nigga say, yea, I see it; so the white boy took the rifle, aimed and fired and he killed this fly without touching the bush and he looked back at the nigga waitin for the nigga to respond with uh—if you please mista charlie but instead the nigga pushed this button and rolled the window all the way down and leaned over and pushed a button to the glove compartment, and pulled out a saucer. And he said hold that boy, to the white cat, and he reached over to his glove compartment and pulled out an apple and he reached in his inside coat pocket and he pulled out a razor and he

threw the apple in the air and he grabbed the razor and sliced around in the air with all kinda fast beautiful motions so quick and so fast, that he peeled the apple, cored the apple, and sliced it so thin in that split second with that razor, that when it hit the saucer it was applesauce. And the white boy said, what uh—what was that uh—regula or ethyl?*

2. There's this nigga who went to the "Sip," you know, uh—Mississippi, that is, and uh—he was wandering around to different restaurants and things like that, after the civil rights bill had passed, you know. So he sat down at one restaurant counter and the waitress said uh—I'm sorry but we don't serve niggas here. And he said, well, you're going to serve me and she said well I'll go get the manager, so she went and got the manager and the manager came over and he said uh—Ain't you heard what the waitress said, we don't serve niggas heah. An the black cat said well look, you're going to serve me cause I'm the president of the local chapter of the NAACP and if you don't serve me we're going to picket your store and we're going to sit in here. So the white dude said, ahh, ahh, all right, I'll serve ya, I'll serve ya, what you want? The nigga said, I want a fried chicken. So he said, ahh, all right. So while the cook was frying the chicken the manager went over and talked to some young toughs about town and then he went on back inside. About twenty-five minutes later, the chicken was done and the waitress brought it out and sat it on the nigga's plate. And the nigga put the little napkin around his neck and about that time about seven or eight toughs that was standin' in the corner, walked up and surrounded the nigga, you know, and he's sittin' there and he looked and he saw 'em. And they said, goan nigga, goan, its yo chicken, you ordered it, goan, but the manager told us, whatever you do

---

* For another version of this first joke, see Roger D. Abrahams, *Deep Down in the Jungle* (Hatboro, 1964), pp. 226–27, revised edition (Chicago, 1970), pp. 237–38. For the second joke, see Abrahams, *Positively Black* (Englewood Cliffs, 1970), pp. 68–69. —ED.

that chicken, we goan do to you. So the black man looked around at 'em a coupla times and he picked up the salt and he sprinkled salt on the chicken, put the salt down and he looked at 'em a coupla times and he picked up the chicken in his hands and he rolled it around, and around in his hands til the tail was up, and then he kissed it, smack. And he looked at 'em a coupla times.

3. They workin' down in this general store, ya see, down somewhere, in some southern state, they all alike. And uh—aw, this was a real hick town. The dudes around the general store would sit around, you know, and be talkin' nonsense. So they were all sittin' around one day, so uh—one day, one of 'em (all of 'em were white) proposed that they would have a penis weighing contest since uh—the manager had just got a new scale for weighing meat, so they decided to have a little contest, you know. Course there was po' Sam over in the corner, he was the nigga they had hired to do all the work, you know, sweeping the floor. So they said come on, everybody put in their dolla, you know, there was about twenty of 'em I suppose, so everybody put in a dolla and the one who had the heaviest one would get all the money. So po' Sam was over there workin' and they said, come on over here Sam, put you dolla in. But he said, naw, naw, thats alright I don't want to get in on it. They said, come on Sam, put yo dolla in, you wanta keep yo job heah? He said, aw yea, I wanna keep my job. So he put his dolla in cause they figured they was just goan git another dolla from another nigga. So anyway they started weighing and there's this one cat in town, his name was John the lover, you know, and John the lover was supposed to have the biggest thing around. So he threw it on the scale and his thing was fourteen pounds. And they said, damn, John, you sho got a biggun, John, look like you done won all the money. Yea, but, then there was ole Sam, Samuel, not Sam the sweeper; this was a white boy named Sam and he figured he was a lover

too cause he slept with everybody's wife in the county so he figured he musta had him somethin'. So he threw it up on the scale but it only weighed about thirteen and a half pounds, you know, so he said, well I guess uh—uh—I didn't win that so everybody figured that ole lovin' John had all the money, you know. So they went around weighin' and everybody had various weights around eight pounds, nine pounds, etcetera, etcetera. Then somebody said, aw wait, we done forgot ole po' Sam the sweeper. So they said, come on over here Sam. And Sam said, uh—uh—naw, naw, that's alright, that's okay, I don't want to get in on it. Come on over here Sam, you want to keep yo job? Sam said, aw yeah, I wanna keep my job. They said, okay Sam, weigh it. So Sam took it out and threw it on the scale and it broke the scale, boy. So they said, damn, look like ole po' Sam done won all the money. So they gave Sam the money and Sam went runnin' home to Nellie his wife. So he broke in and said, Nellie, Nellie, look at all the money I done won down at the general store and Nellie say, Sam you been gamblin'? He say, naw, naw, Nellie I waten gamblin'. She say, how you win this money? What you doin' wit all this money? How'd you win this money? He said, uh, well uh, uh, uh, uh, we had a contest. She say what kinda contest was it? He say, it was a duh, uh, uh, a, a, dick weighing contest. She say, you mean you done won all this money showin' yo dick? He say, HUH, I only showed half of it.

THE INTERVIEW

COLLECTOR: The jokes that you told me you knew at that dance, where did you first hear them?

INFORMANT: Oh, around; I can't really remember exactly where I first heard them. Oh I think usually at bullshit sessions, you know.

C: I see; why do you usually tell them and where?

I: I tell jokes about white people cause they're funny. I tell 'em when I'm with the fellas. Depending on the company though, I sometimes tell 'em around females, you know, when we're all high.

C: Because white people are funny or because the jokes are funny?

I: Well, because number 1, white people are funny and number 2, because the jokes are funny. Well, a lot of the jokes aren't necessarily funny. The jokes a lot of times are not on white people. Many times they about black people, uh—on Chinese or Jews or something like that. But, sometimes, you know, it's a way of relief. If you can laugh at someone then you don't have to hate 'em so much.

C: Oh I see; I take it that you don't particularly care for them?

I: For whom?

C: White people.

I: Oh I don't mind them. They're negligible you know.

C: I see; they're negligible?

I: Um hum.

C: Why have you gotten so wrapped up in this black nationalist movement? Oh I don't really mean wrapped up. . . .

I: Oh, I'm definitely wrapped up in it. That's a good statement. Well, because I don't believe we're going to get anything through white America. I don't believe that we're going to get anything unless we can address the power structure in America as a group of people, you know. As long as we have these little fractionated and divided organizations they don't really constitute enough numbers to really make any demands on the government. And it's obvious that the government is not going to do anything for us. It hasn't done anything, oh let's see, for about say for 200 years when it could have. It's not going to do anything for us now.

C: Oh yes, I remember, not too long ago, that I had told you that I had gone to hear the lecture on the "supposed myth of black sexual superiority" and you told me at that time that I should have stood up during the

lecture and told everyone that black men are sexually superior. Don't you remember telling me that?

I: Oh, yea, you started expounding about the sexual myth, and I said you should have told the lecturer that all of it's true, you know. Because it is true despite how it became true, you know, uh—no matter what you say about well uh—a person's body is a person's body. But if its wrapped up in somebody's mind that this particular body is superior uh—more superior than this particular body and everybody thinks that, then the body IS superior. It's like God, you know; everybody thinks there's a God.

C: Would you say that it's all psychological, then?

I: I wouldn't say that its ALL psychological, but I. . . .

C: Then, exactly what is it that you're trying to say?

I: Okay; well, it goes into a big long, long, thing about uh—how black people were allowed to use their bodies, you know, I mean slavery, etcetera, etcetera, you know, they became menial people you know, and uh—the white people they didn't do any work, didn't use their bodies and they tried to excel in the area of the mind. And they became very unused to using their bodies, you know, and uh—like they can't dance, you know, I don't care what you say, you know, there's a lot of 'em who will get out and try a little thing but they really can't dance, you know, and it wasn't until the twist came along that they really tried dancing and the Beatles, you know; before then they wouldn't even try. And uh—it's just that black people have been conditioned to, you know, responding physically and white people have been conditioned to intellectualize across the experience and over the experience, you know, and try to pretend that a man is defined by his ability to use fourteen-syllable words, instead of his ability to beat somebody's ass, you know. And if you're superior in this aspect of the body, the strength of the body, then I suppose quite naturally you'll be superior sexually, you know. And even if this weren't true, it's so hung-up in everybody's mind, black and white in America, that for all practical purposes all the mythology is true.

C: What about yourself? How do you rate yourself as far as sex is concerned?

I: Rate myself? I don't understand what you mean.

C: All right then, what category would you put yourself in if there was a grading scale from good to bad, using the numbers one through ten?

I: I couldn't do that, I mean I've never rated myself like that before. I don't like comparisons.

C: All right, fair enough, then do you psychologically feel you are superior sexually or physically, or just how do you feel about YOURSELF, SEXUALLY?

I: I've been told that I'm quite good.

C: Have females actually come out and told you that?

I: Yeah.

C: What about that joke in which Sam wins all the money because of his huge size?

I: What about it?

C: Well you use comparisons in that joke; if you don't like comparisons then why do you use them in your jokes?

I: Ah hell, jokes are meant to be funny.

C: In that same joke, what does Sam mean to you?

I: White Sam? The white or black Sam?

C: The black man that won all of the money. Do you think he is the typical stereotype?

I: Yes, I guess I might say that he is, you know. Most white people think that we are big, black, stupid, and ugly. And I guess that ole po' Sam kinda would fall in that category. But in a way, Sam is actually the smart one though, after all; he did win all the money. This all sorta fits in with what I said earlier about white people being so damned funny.

C: How is that?

I: Well they try to dance like niggas, you know, and they look funny trying to dance like niggas, you know. And uh—they're

really stupid in assuming a lot of things that they assume which makes them very funny, you know, like there were people on that "Black America" series on TV who went along saying that uh—oh when they had the niggras on their plantation that the niggras were happy, you know, and they danced and did all that, you know, and this ole fool couldn't see that the reason that the niggas was dancin' and singin' while they were using their sledge hammers was so that they could get rid of some of their ambition and some of their desire to use the sledge hammer on this white boy, you see. And of course they thought the niggas was happy you know, but it was really a cover-up for what they were really thinking, you know. Just like ole po' Sam; he was smart cause he only showed half of his, uh—rod, you know. He didn't want them dumb white boys to know how powerful he really was.

C: I see, I see. What does "John the lover" mean to you? Why do you think that was important enough to be included in the joke?

I: Hmmm, let me see; well, for one thing them white boys and girls are pretty promiscuous. I hate to generalize like that but they always talk about black people having such low morals and all that, you know, they seem to forget that we as a group of people are only products of our environment, you know, and since we only had them to copy from it was only natural that some of us might follow suit. They blamed us for what a lot of their "genteel society" folks was actually doing behind each others' backs. It was them who first brought about that "double standard," you know. "John the lover" simply personifies the hypocrisy of their society.

C: Okay, I understand. Do you feel that "John the lover" typifies the whole of their society?

I: Yeah, I would definitely say the majority. It brings attention to their degeneracy.

C: What would you say was the most important function of that joke or what aspects of that joke do you think really come across when you tell it to someone else?

I: Well, actually, the most important things about that joke is the fact that it shows how dumb them white suckers really are. Here they are with nothin' to do so they have a silly-ass DICK weighin' contest. The niggas are all out workin' too hard to be thinkin' about having such a stupid contest. Plus this, they end up losing all of their money to that big nigga who is supposed to be the epitome of "nigga-ness." And lastly, it shows that sexually they ain't worth a damn and that "stupid" nigga has won on all three counts.

C: Are you happy for "nigga Sam" then?

I: Yeah, in a way, but he still wasn't as domineering in that joke like he should have been. Like, in that first joke I told, that nigga from the north really made that white boy look like a fool.

C: Oh yeah, I see what you mean. By the way, why did you call him a "cat"?

I: Well it's cool to be called a "cat," you know, hip, or the new term is really "in."

C: I take it that you really approved of the actions of that black cat from the north?

I: Yeah, I really do. For one thing, he's the typical stereotype that whites have about city niggas, you know. They think that all any nigga wants to do is to make a little money and then spend it all on a big car, like that Cadillac. Only in the joke, it shows that that city nigga ain't so dumb after all. Also he's clean to boot.

C: What do you mean by "clean?"

I: You know, uh—really dressed sharp, uh—pressed, let me see, he really knows how to dress with good expensive clothes that match. In other words, he dresses with very good taste.

C: Oh, I see. When you mentioned that he was a "bad nigga," does that mean the same as cool or clean?

I: Yeah, about the same.

C: What does that black man in the pick-up truck mean to you or what makes him important?

I: He typifies the "black sambo" type, you know, the old accomodating "colored" man. He's important because he shows that there are two types of blacks in this country today, the passive "uncle Tom" type and on the other hand you have the type of black man who isn't going to take any shit from anybody. In a way, this last type sort of fits in with my views on violence.

C: What type of violence?

I: You know, organized to help the black man in this country. To help him get that white monkey off his back.

C: I don't understand what you mean. What do you mean by white monkey?

I: I mean that white leech that's bleeding my people dry. He's been promising a whole lot but he ain't done nothin' yet.

C: Why did you put an emphasis on the word "colored" in your statement about the passive accomodating colored man?

I: Because as I said before, there are two types of blacks in this country, the so-called colored who would prefer being called colored since it doesn't seem so close to black and more closer to being white. And then there's the black man that's proud of being black and being called black; he doesn't try to assimilate his cultural value within the mainstream of the white society by trying to be something he ain't and by demeaning his own values by attempting to replace them with something that is close to whiteness. What does "colored" mean? It means something that's mixed. Even though I know that as a race we are quite mixed physically, as a cultural entity we are quite unique and distinctive.

C: I see what you mean. How does that black cat in your joke fit in with your views on violence? Do you think that would really solve the problem?

I: The way it is, is that being in America and being defined as an American citizen and being granted by the Constitution uh—the rights of an American citizen in America, then there's no reason for me to be able to exercise these rights. But violence is not the issue; the only issue is my rights and I'll go to any resort necessary to obtain my rights. In that joke about the dude from the north, well that cat is simply showin' that he ain't afraid of nothing. And that's the essence of the whole black problem in this country today. Blacks, I'll say most blacks, especially our generation, are no longer afraid to stand up and take what belongs to us through our association with this country and that is simply the rights that were defined in the Constitution. Even though this joke depicted a northern nigga, it's true of all the blacks in this country today except for those few who haven't made up their mind on whether or not they want to play white or be proud of what they are. Even in that second joke I told you about that black man going to that restaurant in Mississippi he showed those whites that he was no fool. No type of threats are going to stop us blacks from showing the rest of the world how hypocritical and sick these white Americans really are.

C: I noticed that when you referred to particular white persons you spoke of them as being "boys" or that "White boy." Do you say this because many whites have called black men "boys" for so long? What is your reason for saying this?

I: No, not really. The reason why I say this is because I define a man as, number 1, somebody who will protect his women and uh—someone who treats other individuals as men. And these white boys don't protect their women. All they protect is their dollar, and they treat everybody else as though they were devils.

C: In your first joke you said that the gas station was in Southern Indiana, was there any particular reason for using Southern Indiana?

I: Yeah, for one thing, as far as I'm concerned Southern Indiana is grossly prejudiced. In fact, there aren't too many places in the north that aren't. Also the gas station attendant typified how ridiculous these whites really are. The fact that he placed so much value on the blacks saying "if you please mista charlie."

C: What about specific whites that you

know? How are the white students in your classes? Do they fall in the category of most of the whites you described in the jokes?

I: Well, no. Not all of them at least but then those few only get to know you on a very elementary level. They don't care to really associate with you outside of class because their true opinions of you have already been formed a long time ago, when they were kids.

C: Do you know any that you would call friends?

I: No, there aren't any that I would call a friend. They're entirely too two-faced. You could never depend on them if you were in a tight squeeze.

C: How do you think those jokes would be received by your black peers? Do you think your black brothers would like them?

I: Oh, I know they would. Mainly because even though they are jokes and meant to be laughed at, they paint quite an ugly picture of what has evolved here in America among the two races. I'm sure that you could find actual instances of similar if not the same circumstances that have actually taken place. Like I said before, a black man has to laugh in order to keep his sanity.

OBSERVATIONS ON RONALD TYLOR'S JOKES

There is one theme which dominates two of the jokes told by Ronald Tylor. This dominant theme is the sheer foolishness of the whites involved in the first two jokes. Although this same theme is present in the third joke, it does not assume a central role in this last joke. In the third joke it might be called a counter-theme running concurrently with the major or most important theme. In many cases these minor themes aid or influence the significance of the major or dominant theme.

In examining joke 1, I found that it was significant because of the many counter-themes running through it.

One counter-theme of this joke is the fact that the Negro from the north is so "clean," to use the informant's phrase. The fact of the Negro being so well-dressed serves to demonstrate a stereotype which most Negroes can readily identify. He is a figure quite familiar to the average American black and there is something about him which draws contempt as well as admiration. Even with all his finery, he is still not highly regarded in the black community, as he represents a pimp figure or even the image of gigolo or gambler. Even Tylor, despite his admiration for this character, realizes that this type of Negro is one of the "typical" negative stereotypes harbored by whites. This is clear when he states: "They [whites] think that all any nigga wants to do is to make a little money and then spend it all on a big car—only in the joke it shows that that city nigga ain't so dumb after all." This is, however, a stereotype that many middle-class blacks also have of their lower-class brothers. Mr. Tylor also felt that even though the black "cat" had these possibly negative attributes, this black "dude" was still "smart." He made the gas station attendant too, feel, and act foolish.

It is clear that Tylor feels alienated from the Negro in the old pick-up truck. Yet this character is made to look humorous in a rather contemptuous way. He is what Tylor and most blacks today would call a "typical Tom." Likewise, the gas station attendant is definitely a stereotype of what many blacks would call a "red-necked cracker." He is not only dull-witted but also sadistic and receives obvious pleasure and a sense of superiority from the subjugation of his black victims. He appears ridiculous to the point of absurdity because he places so much value on being called by a particular respectful title. Another important counter-theme in this joke is the black "cat's" use of the razor. The Negro has long been regarded as quite skilled and adept at using razors, knives, and other cutlery. The black "cat" fits well into this Negro stereotype since his agility with the razor helps him to perform an impossible feat, that of changing an apple to applesauce in front of the awed attendant. That the black's more primitive weapon defeats the white's rifle would appear to be a factor also.

The second joke, which also uses the dominant theme of revealing the absurdity and foolishness of whites, is somewhat similar to the first joke in that it also uses "typical" stereotypes. The stereotypes are the waitress, manager, and the young toughs in the restaurant, and all represent that part of southern white America which was so greatly publicized during the numerous civil rights marches and sit-ins which took place in the south a few years ago. This joke, which portrays the aggressiveness and bitterness of the whites involved, also demonstrates the reserved "coolness" of the Negro NAACP president. Since Tylor mentioned that this Negro ventured into the restaurant *after* the civil rights bill had been passed, it is evident that this particular Negro is using his position and his threats to assess the value and power of the recently passed bill. When the NAACP president appears "cornered" by his white antagonists, he remains calm and calculating in the face of potential disaster. He kisses the tail of the chicken, thus indicating that these white roughnecks could just as well kiss his ass. Thus the NAACP man saves face at the same time that he saves his own "ass." Once again the whites look ridiculous in their attempts to threaten a black man. These white stereotypes fit well into the "cracker" category and thus the joke helps the black man justify his fight for equality by featuring disreputable, violent and openly hostile whites.

This joke functions as a mild tension reliever for the black telling the joke as well as for the blacks listening to it. It is not as aggressive in nature as the first joke, but it does illustrate the same kind of "ultra-cool," "cunning" black "cat." However, this black "cat" is a respected man in his community.

The third joke is similar to the first two in that it also uses stereotypes, and has as one of its themes the foolishness and absurdity of whites. In this joke, however, the above theme is not the dominant characteristic of the joke. The dominant theme here is that of sexual superiority. This joke is significant because one of its main characters is an accommodating "Tom" type, "po' ole nigga Sam." The Negro, Sam, has a twofold function. He does represent the contemptible "Tom" but nevertheless redeems himself by triumphing over the whites and then by telling his wife Nelly that he only showed half of his private parts. Thus he exhibits his crafty and cunning character. By acting dumb and, as Tylor put it, as "the epitome of 'nigganess'" Sam becomes a symbol of sexual superiority woven more or less within the stereotype of the black "buck."

An important counter-theme is one in which "John the lover" and white Sam symbolize the supposed promiscuity of many whites. Not only is this supposedly inherent in lower-class whites, but is also supposedly prevalent among the "high society folks." As before, the "cracker" stereotype appears in this joke through those whites who are "sittin' around and talkin' nonsense" in the rural general store. They appear ridiculous in that they decide to have an absurd "dick weighin'" contest. By using black Sam to get his money they figure on once again outsmarting a "po' nigga." However, they themselves are taken over by their own game.

Nelly, Sam's wife, is another stereotype, of the chattering, questioning, domineering black woman. Not only is she not appreciative of the money Sam has received but she must know every detail as to how he acquired the money. She functions as an extra catalyst to make the joke funny.

In this type of joke, the listeners more or less expect that "po' ole Sam" will outdo all the whites by his huge size. However, the fact that he only showed half of himself indicates that Sam did not want to show his true sexual power. This aspect of Sam's personality is what Ronald Tylor feels is particularly "smart." He outsmarts the whites by winning all of the money, but he also is crafty enough to realize that by revealing his true sexual potential he might only make himself more vulnerable to the maliciousness of the whites. In a sense, this last part of the joke is related to what Tylor said about why many Negroes conspicuously danced and played in the old south. He states that "the reason that the niggas was dancin' and singin' while they were using their sledge hammers was so that they could get rid of some of their ambition and some of their desire to use the sledge hammer on this white boy." In relation to this last part of the joke, Mr. Tylor's statement helps us to realize that there has always been an attitude of crafty guile in the everyday relations that many blacks have had with whites, especially in the south, an attitude definitely reflected in much black folklore.

It is difficult to surmise the effects that these jokes would have if told in the presence of a group, black or white. I can only guess that if these jokes were told in the presence of a black group they would probably be interpreted in much the same way that Tylor interpreted them. It would no doubt be interesting to record the reactions of whites after they had heard the same jokes. But to speculate here on their hypothetical reactions would be pointless.

INFORMANT 2: KEITH NEWTON*

Keith Newton, who related four jokes, is a native of Raleigh, North Carolina, and was at the time of collection (December 17, 1968) an undergraduate student at Indiana University. Mr. Newton is 22, Black American, and a member of no particular church, although he regards himself as "fairly religious." The jokes were collected at his apartment after the informant and his girlfriend had finished dinner. Present also were two white friends of Mr. Newton. As we sat around I asked if anyone knew any jokes and both of the informant's white friends told several, after which Mr. Newton told his four. All of the jokes were recorded, but those told by the whites were not

* The informants' names have been changed.

in any way racially "tinged." The whites seemed to enjoy Mr. Newton's jokes, but had left before I conducted my interview with him.

THE JOKES

1. One time there was this girl and her mother, they stayed together, her father was dead. And the girl's mother always told her that when she got sixteen, she would let her go out on her first date. So it just so happened that the girl turned sixteen and the big girls were having a party, ya know, and she wanted to go out with the big girls. And it just so happened that she went out with a colored boy that night. So the girl's mother waited up that night waiting for her daughter to come home. So, finally that night about 12:30 the girl came home and she just walked slowly past her mama. Her mama say, chile, what the matta wit you, come here. She say, what you want mama. I want you to tell me everything that happened tonight. What's wrong? Why you acting so strange? The girl say mama, my new dress is tore, my titties are sore, and I don't think I'll be able to pee no more.

2. One time there were these two hillbillies that stayed up in the mountains, a granddaughter and her grandmother. And the granddaughter got a colored boyfriend from nearby. And uh—she wanted to have sex with her boyfriend but she couldn't think of a way that she could do it without her grandmother finding out about it. So she finally told her boyfriend that she was going to cut a hole in the floor and for him to come that night and stick hisself up through the floor and she was going to get on him. So that night about nine o'clock she cut a hole in the floor, and sho 'nough he came and stuck hisself up through the floor and she got on him. And they were having a good time. Finally, the grandmother came in and

said, granddaughter, what in the world are you doing? Get out of here. And the boy was under the floor and he didn't know what was going on so he just left hisself sticking up in there. So the old grandmama looked around and she didn't see nobody lookin' at her, so she took off all her clothes and she jumped on. And it started getting good to the dude under the floor and after a while he just started risin' and risin' so the grandmother said, granddaughter, granddaughter, come here quick and bring the axe. The granddaughter came in with the axe and said, what you want me to do, chop it down? The grandmother said, hell, naw, chop a hole in the ceiling, I'm goan ride this muthafucka to heaven.*

3. One time there were these three men left on this island alive and they didn't have but one sandwich. Since they knew they were going to die, they all agreed that all of them could not eat the sandwich and get full so they decided that they would go to sleep and whoever had the best dream would get the sandwich when they woke up the next morning. So the next day they got up, ya know, and the white man say, well, I dreamed I had eight million dollars and I was the richest man in the world. The other two men said, ahh, how can you dream that you had eight million dollars and be the richest man in the world? That ain't no good. So the Jew man say, I dreamed I had ten beautiful wives and all of 'em were treatin' me good. So the other two said, ahh, that ain't no good. So the white man and Jew man said, black man, what you dream? He say, I dreamed you all were trying to shit me so I got up and ate that sandwich.†

4. There was this honky family and this man had a daughter who had just turned

sixteen. And her father had always promised her that when she turned sixteen he was going to have her satisfied. So his daughter said, daddy, daddy, you know what you told me, that when I turned sixteen you were going to have me satisfied. So her father said alright. So her father went down to the corner to look for a suitable man. First, he sent a honky man to his daughter but she say, daddy, he too little. Next, he sent a Jew man to his daughter but she say, daddy he too fat. Finally, he sent a black man to his daughter and said that he was just right. So the girl's father waited on the corner. He was waiting for them to get through. So after a while it was about twelve o'clock midnight. And finally his little son came runnin' down to the corner and said, daddy, daddy, you know that black man you sent home, well, he done satisfied sister, sister Sue, Mary Lou, he done packed me and he waitin' on you, so get yo ass on down there.

THE INTERVIEW

COLLECTOR: Why were most of your jokes racial jokes? Did you tell them specifically because your white friends were here?

INFORMANT: No, I don't think so. I suppose I told them because I just know more racial jokes than any other types.

C: Why is that? What reason do you think has helped you to remember so many racial jokes?

I: I really don't know, I guess it could be because racial jokes during this day and age are just funnier, that's all.

C: Okay. Why do you tell these types of jokes?

I: To get a laugh.

C: Why do you think other black people

---

* For a different tale involving a lecherous grandmother who takes her granddaughter's place with a young man, see Roger D. Abrahams, *Deep Down in the Jungle* (Hatboro, 1964), pp. 203–5, revised edition (Chicago, 1970), pp. 217–20. —ED.

† This is a version of Aarne-Thompson tale type 1626, Dream Bread, which is widely distributed around the world and which was already popular by the middle ages, e.g., it appears in the *Gesta Romanorum*. For a discussion of this well known folktale, see Paul F. Baum, "The Three Dreams or 'Dream Bread' Story," *Journal of American Folklore*, 30 (1917), pp. 378–410. —ED.

might tell these same jokes or other types of racial jokes which would be similar to these?

I: Well there's a reason for it. I would say that jokes are basically the verbal transmission of a particular people's experience. So I would say that these black jokes which are derogatory towards whites simply tell you something about black experience in this country as far as white people are concerned. The jokes that I told, the racial ones that is, are part of a myth that has been perpetuated by whites against blacks and one that blacks have partaken of and have come to dislike. These jokes represent a true feeling, a human feeling. But it's the kind of thing that's self-defeating. These are negative jokes. It's a kind of thing where black people turn hate against themselves because they were not able to externalize the hate that they felt for their white oppressors. So they started to hate themselves and they adopted this sort of superior sex attitude about themselves. This was only a carry-over from the established principle of white supremacy which said that black men were very animalistic and sexually charged and this kind of thing.

C: If you feel that these jokes are self-defeating and negative, then why do you tell them?

I: Well, because they're funny and to get a laugh.

C: I see. Well, what do you think about the myth that black people are supposed to be superior sexually? You can be very truthful.

I: (Laughs) Oh, I'm going to be truthful all right. A black person is not superior sexually. A man is what he thinks he is. And this is what the consequence of slavery and exploitation has been. It has been one that breeds super humans. As of now, black people probably could be sexually superior although I doubt it, because everybody shares a common human experience which is devoid of color, and I think sex is one of these things. It's functional. It's of man to be sexually oriented. But I don't think that there's a necessity for black men to be supe-

rior but I think it's one of the possible effects of exploitation of a superior complex which trapped them in the socio-economic position which blacks are in.

C: I don't mean to be personal but what do you think about yourself? Do you think that sexually you're really good in comparison to the average white man?

I: I think it all relates to understanding oneself, of one's environment and where one came from. I don't compare myself with anyone, especially somebody white. I, you know, I, seek to know myself. I think I fulfill this pretty well, in all terms, in all aspects. So that I'm not concerned whether I'm equal or superior to a white cat. That's not the basis of how I judge my sexual life. It's really immaterial. And this is what black pride is about. This is what throwing off the chains of three hundred years of servitude is about. It's about coming to realize that your being is not contingent upon a white experience.

C: You mentioned that you would not want to compare yourself sexually with anyone. Then you said that you especially would not want to compare yourself to somebody white. Why is that? Why did you say, especially somebody white?

I: Okay, that's relatively an easy question. Uh, for all these years that I mentioned, three hundred-or-so-odd years, we were trapped in a white experience, a white lifestyle and through this we were never fully able to realize our being, our life-styles. So that, once you have conquered that, once you realize that you do have a distinctive cultural pattern, a distinctive cultural experience on a black basis then this is addressing oneself to the question of color and realizing that there remains a humanitarian point of view devoid of color. When black becomes positive, then at that point you have conquered the white experience. So that, THAT becomes negated, so that you dedicate yourself then to defining yourself within yourself. Which says that if I have to compare, then I compare among my own.

Because I am black and I relate to black. So that when I say ESPECIALLY A WHITE PERSON, this means that that is a phase past. That's the first phase of rediscovery. That's an identity that was lost through three-hundred years of subjugation. The primary task of every black person in this country today, and that is the thing of not divorcing oneself from white culture but to realize that the white culture has taken on an assumed role. This has been put on top of what we are. So to divorce oneself from that is to look back into the base and look back into the beginning. I guess you could say that in a sense it is "a going home."

C: Alright, you said that you don't think that black people should divorce themselves from white culture so I take it that you're not a separatist.

I: Oh, I'm definitely a separatist.

C: Well, if you are a separatist then how do you explain what you said about white culture?

I: (Laughs) Okay, let's examine separation. Separation doesn't necessarily mean geographic relocation or all these things. What it means in terms of relating to our present condition and in terms to this country, is that black people, Spanish people, Italians, everybody who happens to dwell in this country can call themselves an American, and in this we have a common bond, and in this we have a common experience, the American experience. So when I say separation I do not mean geographic separation, though I would not fail to advocate this either, you know. But it does mean that blacks have a right to define themselves and to determine their destinies. It means that black people must determine who they are and where they want to go and they must do this from a black base, from a black perspective. Then all groups in this country must realize that they have a common stake, a common point of experience, which is the American one. This means that everybody looks across the board and realizes

that as a black I can realize my blackness and cannot relate my blackness in totality with your whiteness and etcetera. But this means that we look at each other saying that we do not understand each other fully but that we can work to understand the common experience, the American experience. And that's, that's very definitely separation. Very definitely separation. I think that this is the sort of utopian atmosphere that we would seek to achieve. I think in the interim we will have to strive for uh—geographic separation, partitioning and all that.

C: Keeping in mind what you said about separation, what do you personally think about interracial dating and marriages?

I: I think uh—anybody who can't deal with his own before self-discovery is deluding himself or herself. Anybody who cannot deal with his own people through self-discovery is experiencing a hell of a psychological trauma. I'm not saying that interracial dating or marriages are wrong. I think it is wrong if the people involved have not come to the discovery of themselves. Anybody that's black and dating a white person, if he has to compromise any of his black being to experience a white thing, well then I think he's definitely lost. I know, I'm speaking from personal experience.

C: I see. If you had a daughter would you mind her marrying someone white?

I: (Laughs) Yeah, I'd mind. But in that position as a father all I would be able to do was offer counsel. I would just hope that I had raised her well enough so that she would understand herself well enough so that if she went into that type of situation she would definitely know that she was black and anybody that took her, if the cat was white he would understand that she was black first. He would not look at her as being a white woman in a black skin.

C: What about your friends that just left, do you think that they would be that understanding?

I: Yeah, I think so. I've known them for

quite a while and I really think that they do understand the racial situation in this country. Of course they are exceptions.

C: How do you think they really felt about those jokes you told? Do you think that you might have offended them?

I: No, I don't think so. Hell, we always kid around like that. That's certainly not the first time. They understand.

C: I see; what if they had started telling jokes about black people, do you think that would have bothered you?

I: Naw, naw, I don't think that it would. Like I said, we always kid around like that.

C: Why did most of the jokes that you told demean white sexuality?

I: Oh, I don't know, it just makes the jokes funnier, that's all.

C: Those jokes that you told about the young girl going out with the Negro boy and the one about the grandmother having sex with her granddaughter's boyfriend and also the one where the father finds a man to satisfy his daughter—well, do you really believe that whites are that promiscuous and have such low morals?

I: No, not really. Like I said before, the jokes are meant to be funny. But I do know that a lot of white girls are pretty wild that way. They are pretty forward.

C: How do you know that? That's a pretty rash statement.

I: Well, I basically know from my own experience. I've dated quite a few in the past. And the ones that I've dated were pretty blunt about a lot of things, especially sex.

C: But couldn't you say that you would find that among any race and not just one in particular?

I: Yeah, that's true, but I've found that white girls are just more willing to jump into bed. A lot of 'em do it because of that sexual myth, and then a lot of 'em do it because they feel it's the thing to do and then a lot of 'em do it because I think they

think that's what most black boys expect them to do. Black women are much harder to get in bed. I don't know how they react to white men though; they probably act just like them white girls do to us black boys. I guess it's because we're all opposites. They say opposites attract, ya know.

C: Hmmm. In that one joke you said that the sixteen-year-old girl came home from her date and told her mother that she wasn't able to go to the toilet any more and that her breasts were sore—why is that? What do you think her colored boyfriend had done to her?

I: Well, as far as that joke is concerned, that black boy had really put it on her mind.

C: I don't understand, he had put what on her mind?

I: (Laughs) His . . . you know, his . . . , they had intercourse. And he really did the job.

C: Oh, I see. Do you think a white boy could have really done the job?

I: Oh, yeah, I suppose he could. It's funnier to use a black boy since most people think black men are supposed to be sexually superior.

C: Do you really think that hillbillies don't care who they have sex with? That joke about the grandmother having sex with her granddaughter's boyfriend was pretty low.

I: I don't really know what they actually do, but you know how you hear that real low-class people and high society people will do anything. Well, in a way I don't doubt that.

C: Do you mean in relation to white people or would you include low-class Negroes?

I: No, not really. I've heard that a lot of low-class blacks will do most anything but I know that there are some things that they won't do.

C: And what's that?

I: Well, just to mention a couple, I'm pretty sure that they don't engage in oral sex and I'm also pretty sure that there aren't any black grandmothers who would have sex with their granddaughter's boyfriends.

C: What makes you think that that's true of whites?

I: Oh, I don't know, it just seems like something that a hillbilly might do But then, it's only a joke.

C: In one of the jokes you used the word "honky" to describe a family—what does that mean?

I: It's just a way of relating to whites, like they been relating to us and callin' us niggas.

C: I see; then it's a derogatory term then?

I: Yeah, in a way it is.

C: In that joke about the black man satisfying all of those people—what does "pack" mean?

I: It's a street term for anal intercourse.

C: I see. What does that joke mean to you?

I: It just shows how this black man was so superior sexually that he could satisfy all those different people and was still waitin' for more.

C: Do your jokes always receive such a good response?

I: Oh yeah, everytime I've told them I've had a lot of laughs from them.

C: Have you ever told those jokes in the company of other whites with whom you were less friendly?

I: No, as a matter of fact I haven't.

C: What do you think would be the reaction of the average white man who heard these jokes told by a black man?

I: Well, I really don't think they would like those jokes. (Laughs)

C: Why is that?

I: Well, nobody likes to hear derogatory statements about their own kind, whether the statements are true or not or whether they're just jokes. I know that they tell jokes about us that I would not particularly want to hear them say, but then I probably would laugh at the same joke if it was told by another black man.

C: What about your friends though? Those fellows that were here?

I: Oh them, oh well, they're different. They understand, like I said before, they are a little more intelligent.

C: I see. In that joke about the three men on the island with the one sandwich—well, why do you think that's funny?

I: Well, mainly 'cause most whites are so interested in makin' that dollar that they think about it so much that they end up starvin'. (Laughs)

C: I was under the impression that Jews are always concerned about making money. How is it that in your joke he was so interested in women that he dreamed about them?

I: Oh, I don't know. I guess it was just the way I said it. But you could change the joke and make it different, depending on what you wanted emphasized. In fact, you could change it so the black man was made to look like the fool. I'm sure that's how a white person would do it. They would probably tell it so that the black man was interested in only having sex or how many broads he could screw or somethin' like that.

C: I see. In general, how do you feel about white people?

I: I dislike the image of what white stands for. I dislike the atrocities that I've seen committed against the vast majority of the people of the world. I dislike violently what white people stand for. In terms of white people I recognize the possibility of them being humanized. I see them as human forms, people who have not yet been civilized. People who are striving to become human beings. So I pity white people in general.

C: So, you're saying that they are not civilized but you do see them in their human form?

I: Yes.

C: But basically you don't feel that they are civilized.

I: Yeah, yeah, I guess that's one way of putting it. A civilized man is one that practices what he preaches. A man who respects people. Civilization could, but only a small part, be measured by technological advances and these sort of things such as we've evolved in this country. It's only civilized in terms of the manner that it's used. It's a world of white machines that happen to be in human forms who possibly could become full-fledged human beings and join the world of civilization. But this has yet to come.

C: How do you feel about Don and Mike? [the whites present at the joke telling] Since they're white, how do you feel about them? Do you feel that they're uncivilized?

I: On a person to person basis I don't think you can say that they are uncivilized. Let me say this; I made a generalization about the image of white America and I said that it was an uncivilized and savage one. I think that there are people within that general context that have been able to solve certain problems, who have been able to look at themselves through various means and found that there is a common human experience and though we can't relate to the same music, though we can't relate to the same styles, we can relate to life itself and we can establish friendships on these bases. That's how I respond to these two fellas.

C: I've noticed that lately a lot of black men refer to white men as boys, you know, there seems to be an emphasis placed on saying "white boy." Why is that? Do you have any idea?

I: Well, part of it is revenge. Yeah, since they've been used to calling us boys I suppose it's our way of getting back at them. However, the best of us, Le Roi Jones, Donald Lee, uh—most black writers have come to realize that there has been no— and even white people are beginning to point this out—that there has been no assertive male image in the white world—in the white society. The pattern has been one of a **FAGGOT**, you know. From the time

of the European ascension, you know, they started out with them cats wearing a whole lot of powder and perfume and stuff. True, you've had some men—possibly men. But the image that has been given off by the white society has been one of a faggot male. It is a matriarchal society. You come to realize that the backbone of the white society is female oriented. So when a lot of black men speak of those whites as being "white boys," there's a reason for this. One of the reasons why black male images were not allowed to exist and why so many slaves were castrated for looking at white women was that these white faggots recognized the intrinsic male image of the black. You look around and you see uh— this is what your fashion trends tell you. This is what the esthetics of the white race tell you, their books, their music, the way they wear their hair, men's furnishing, you know, colognes. And then you look at the white women, and you see she's wearing pants, you know. Women in the white society own 70% of the wealth and determine which way it's used. And then you see the ads on television, you need a woman to sell a cigarette, you need a woman to sell cars, you need a woman to do this, you need a woman to do that, you know. It's a very female image dominated society. So it's a very real thing to say that there is a "white boy." Yeah, let's not call him a boy, let's call him a "white thing" that possesses the ingredients of being a man, you know, but has no sense of direction, that has no sense of manhood.

C: All right, then you're saying in a sense that as far as heterosexual love or heterosexual relationships are concerned, in your opinion or the opinion that you've gotten from the white culture, you feel that heterosexually, black people are superior. Right?

I: No, I, I didn't mention the word superior. I said that heterosexually, in terms of a man image and a female image—and you can draw correlations from any body of knowledge, you know, on both sides, from the black view and from the white view. From the black view drawing from the esthetics that have been established in folklore, music, and what little written body that has existed, you get the fact that there has always been very definitely a male image. The image of a man, of a woman lamenting for a man. Then you look at the other side of the spectrum and you see from the ascension of Europe and through the period of colonialism, you see the English High Court in wigs and pettipants and frivolous things like that. This fag image dominates, you know. And then you come to realize what the woman's role has been. The woman in the white society has been almost a dualism. She's been part man, part woman. And then you come to realize that in 1968, this year, the number of movies that come out dealing with the theme of homosexuality. Not black homosexuality; since blacks have participated in this white experience there has been that problem. But those people who have been able to divorce themselves from the white experience, coming back to black, establish an identity of male and female. Just look at the Catholic Church and the popes in terms of what the male image is, in terms of nature itself, they are against that trend, they are against nature. They are a bunch of PUNKS. Celibates, who go around saying "don't mess with women," who are very passive; they are feminine oriented. You can see what effect this had on slavery and the black man, the fact that he was castrated and lynched for looking at white women or in trying to assume the leadership in founding a black family, you know. It was due to the fact that there was no counterpart in the white race, there was no white male image strong enough to deal with the male image of the black man in this country. When you are not able to deal with a problem on the basis of understanding, because you have not defined yourself as a man, and you see a man and you realize that he could usurp you, you have to kill him to preserve yourself and this is what was done.

C: Okay I see. I don't understand why you mentioned the cologne though. I know a lot of black fellas wear cologne, you know, like Jade East, Canoe, Dante, Brut, and others.

I: Okay, I, I, I'll deal with that. Uh—it's not what you wear, you know. It's not what you partake of, it's the manner that you relate this to yourself. Black cats wear a lot of things, you know. Some black cats are really sharp dressers, but there aren't too many black cats that don't deal from a man's standpoint. There's not too many black cats that get bossed around by black women. There's not too many black cats that don't hesitate to walk out the door if they find it necessary. In short, there aren't that many black cats who don't portray a positive male image. They don't run behind their women, you know, they lead the pack. You might take issue with this and say that most sociologists have said that the Negro family was a matriarchy; well, that's true up to a point. But it wasn't really a family unit 'cause that male was not there. That male was out being a male, preserving a male image, and, if necessary, he did it on the block. But rather than be what the white man had become, he walked out. Okay, he smoked pot and drank and in many cases became a drunkard—well as far as I'm concerned, that's very definitely a positive male image.

C: Are you saying, then, that black men could not assert themselves as males in the home?

I: That's part of it, yeah, white society and their economic deprivation and all these other factors had the influence to kill any Negro or any black who challenged the system in terms of going out and being able to support a family, or of taking his family out without fearing for his life, and fearing for the lives of his family for the very fact of being black. He could not go out and get a job therefore he could not support a family. So he walked out to the block and spent a hundred years on the block. He waited on the block until that fag image of white society had weakened. You know, the whole white system crumbles, but it doesn't crumble because of pressure exerted by black people. It crumbles because it was defective in the building. Of course there is some black pressure on it, but this is only a response and reaction to the internal decay of the white world. However, if you're not thoroughly aware of all the channels, and incuts and outcuts, you could very easily disagree. But I assure you that this is a point that has been picked up and is being expanded every day.

C: Do you think white people are funny? You know, funny in a cynical sense.

I: I think that they're sort of pathetic. I don't think you can use the word funny in relation to them. I don't think they know how to relate to life. They're too busy tryin' to make that dollar.

C: Oh yes, there was another thing I wanted to ask you about one of your jokes. In one of the jokes you mentioned that the Negro boy under the floor started rising, what did you mean by that?

I: Well, you know, he started to get larger. I think it's significant because that's what white people expect.

C: I don't understand. What do you mean?

I: They think that black men are supposed to be extraordinarily large so the joke is funny because the dude gets larger and larger right in the act.

C: What was the point behind the black man who ate the sandwich while the other two fellows slept?

I: Oh, the fact that he outsmarted them, I suppose. While they were dreaming about money and women, he ate. (Laughs)

C: Even though you said that those jokes had a negative aspect to them, did you enjoy telling them?

I: Oh yeah, I always do. Even around my few white buddies like Don and Mike. They're not stupid, they know how their people are.

OBSERVATIONS ON KEITH NEWTON'S JOKES

Three of the jokes collected from Keith Newton, numbers 1, 2, and 4, can be grouped into a single category, mainly because the dominant theme running through all three is one of sex. They deal with promiscuous white families who have little regard for the sexual welfare and safety of their daughters and granddaughters. Also, these jokes are similar in that all the families involved appear to be southern or hillbilly in character.

Joke 1 is common and can be used to refer to black sexual superiority or really any other type of racial sexual superiority. This joke can best be understood by the words of Keith Newton, to the effect that "that black boy really put it on her mind," or, in other words, "he really did the job." It supposedly describes how well the black boy handled himself sexually. He handled himself so well in fact that the white girl was quite worn out when she returned home. From the informant's viewpoint it seems that this is the masculine thing to do. Joke 2, which also deals with sex, is oriented a little differently from joke 1. It deals with the low morals of a granddaughter as well as her grandmother. The promiscuity of the two is extreme. The fact that the black man under the floor starts "risin' and risin' " illustrates the size and power of his penis. It also brings into focus the alleged sexual superiority of black men in general. The jokes serve to help reinforce the black sexual superiority myth in the minds of many blacks.

Joke 4, which is sexually oriented, involves a father and his daughter. The father, after promising his daughter that he will have her "satisfied," proceeds to find a suitable male for her. Naturally, since a black is telling the joke, the white man is unfit, obviously because of his small size. This factor, as far as most blacks are concerned, would make him incapable of satisfying anybody. The second man, the Jew, is too fat. The third man, the black, is, of course, "just right," although what "just right" means is not completely spelled out. The fact that the black man takes so long with the white man's daughter simply testifies to his prowess as a lover and the supposed prowess of all blacks as lovers. The black man's ability to satisfy so many different people in so many different ways is another testimonial to his superior abilities.

Even though all three jokes deal specifically with black sexual superiority, I think it important to note that the most important factor in these jokes (according to the informant) is the promiscuity of the whites involved. It is ironic, I think, that he should feel that this factor is what really makes the jokes funny. If these same jokes were switched around and told by whites, I am sure that black promiscuity might well be similarly expressed.

Joke 3 can be changed so that the black man is made to look foolish. It serves the purpose of illustrating how much smarter the black man is in comparison to both the white man and the Jew. The fact that the white man dreams about money is indicative of how many blacks feel about whites who covet the precious dollar. The fact that the Jew is made to dream about women is not so important (and, indeed, seems inconsistent with the usual Jewish stereotype in jokes), since Mr. Newton states that the order could be arranged so that either

white or Jew could fit in the same category. This joke simply functions to show that the black man refuses to be fooled by the trickery of the two whites involved. It also illustrates, as I stated in the analysis of Mr. Tylor's jokes, that a state of crafty guile has existed between many blacks and whites. This is exemplified by the fact that the black man eats the sandwich while the two white men sleep.

These jokes were received quite well by the small group who heard them at Mr. Newton's apartment. The two white students, Mike and Don, seemed to truly enjoy the jokes as a form of humorous expression. In attempting to understand how these two young men actually felt about these jokes, I can only surmise that the jokes probably helped them feel more secure in terms of their relationship with Keith. Since they could laugh at some aspects of their culture and not be offended, or at least see the humor, they had achieved or were in the process of achieving what Newton called "relating through the common experience." I think that they laughed at the absurdity of the jokes and accepted them on the basis of their humorous content.

It is quite obvious that Newton felt that he could tell these jokes in their presence and still receive hearty laughs. His justification for doing so was because these two young men were "exceptions," that they were a little "more intelligent" than the average white American and could easily relate to Keith's blackness and the black humor inherent in the jokes. As far as the stereotypes in the jokes are concerned, I think that both whites only focused on the absurdity of the situations involved and probably never realized that Keith actually felt that there were many whites who were just as promiscuous. It would have been interesting to note their reactions when Keith stated: "I do know that a lot of white girls are pretty wild that way," or that "white girls are just more willing to jump into bed" than black women. But making assumptions or guessing at what might have been said or done if the interview had been carried out under different circumstances is useless from an objective standpoint.

SOME FINAL REMARKS

In attempting to assess the total value of the information compiled in this paper, I have run into difficulties because of the varied beliefs and ideas of the informants. I think the most significant factor is the fact that the reader participates in ideas that are of great importance to the American public. Through the statements of both informants the reader is given a quick glance at many of the tenets inherent in the Black Nationalist movement in this country.

At first I felt that this could not be done by simply interviewing two informants. I felt that I needed more information from more informants (say, about ten) to give the reader more of a cross-section of opinions in a particular area. However, after thoroughly examining both conversations I found that, even as short as they are, there is one significant factor in both. In Ronald Tylor the reader gets what I think is a fairly good example of a steadfast militant. Perhaps he is not a Stokely Carmichael or an H. Rap Brown, but the seeds of discontent are there just the same. In Keith Newton, the reader gets a fine example of a black person who is unable to compromise with himself. He hasn't made up his mind whether or not he wants to be militant (even mildly militant) or more moderate in his actions and viewpoints. His ideas may seem contradictory. Newton speaks about blacks and whites being sexual equals— "A man is what he thinks he is."— and later he speaks of "white America's faggot male." Ronald Tylor at least admits that he feels that "It's [black sexual superiority] so wrapped up in the minds of blacks and whites in America that for all practical purposes it's true." Keith Newton has some white friends because those he has are "exceptions" to the rule. Ronald Tylor speaks of having no white friends at all. In short, we see two individuals who are part of an important social and political trend, yet who represent different points of view within that trend. To a point they reflect some of the problems dividing black Americans and preventing them from achieving a greater cohesiveness.

Yet their jokes, though they are in many ways different in terms of both style and content, show a common interest in that they all direct laughter at aspects of America much hated in black society. These jokes and others like them displace wounded pride and anger and replace it with a certain joviality. Thus the jokes, insofar as they evoke laughter, underscore the value of humor as a "defensive mechanism." Yet insofar as they reflect unpleasant social realities they emphasize the facts of the black experience in America and the unanimity of the black response to an oppressive system.

Suggestions for Further Reading in American Negro Folklore

There are hundreds of books and articles which deal directly or indirectly with various aspects of American Negro folklore. Some are excellent while others are not. Unfortunately, one cannot always tell from the title of the book or article whether the item in question is worth reading or not. In any case, the first step in seeking further reading in the field of American Negro folklore is simply discovering what the available sources are.

Generally speaking, there are two principal places to begin a search for treatments of American Negro folklore. One is in the overall scholarship devoted to American Negro culture, and the other is the scholarship concerned with American folklore. It is regrettable but to be expected that coverage of Negro folklore in either type of scholarship is at best partial. Thus, for example, one finds sections on folklore in such standard references as Erwin K. Welsch, The Negro in the United States; A Research Guide (*Bloomington, Indiana, 1965*); *Monroe N. Work,* A Bibliography of the Negro in Africa and America (*New York, 1965*); *Elizabeth W. Miller,* The Negro in America: A Bibliography 2nd ed. (*Cambridge, Mass., 1970*); *and Dorothy B. Porter,* A Working Bibliography on the Negro in the United States (*Ann Arbor, 1969*), *and* The Negro in the United States: A Selected Bibliography (*Washington, D. C., 1970*); *but such sections are far from being comprehensive. Other valuable bibliographical aids include the nine-volume* Dictionary of the Schomburg Collection of Negro Literature and History (*Boston, 1962*); Index to Selected Periodicals Received in the Hallie Q. Brown Library, Decennial Cumulative 1950–1959 (*Boston, 1961*); *and Janheinz Jahn,* A Bibliography of Neo-African Literature from Africa, America, and the Caribbean (*New York, 1965*), *but again the coverage of folklore is casual. The same situation applies to folklore bibliographical aids. Thus the annual spring issue of the periodical* Southern Folklore Quarterly, *an issue devoted exclusively to bibliography, does contain entries on Negro folklore, but articles appearing in other than folklore journals*

670

may or may not be listed. The same situation holds true for Abstracts of Folklore Studies. (*For a list of bibliographical aids in folklore, see Alan Dundes, ed.,* The Study of Folklore [*Englewood Cliffs, 1965*], pp. 477–78.) *So the upshot of all this is that there is really no up-to-date comprehensive bibliography of American Negro folklore.*

The bibliographical sources which readers may find it most profitable to consult include Myrtle Funkhouser, "Folklore of the American Negro: A Bibliography," Bulletin of Bibliography and Dramatic Index, *16 (1937–1939), pp. 28–29, 49–51, 72–73, 108–10, 136–37, 159–60, which is limited in scope and suffers from repeated entries though there is at least an attempt at annotation. More useful is Charles Haywood, "The Negro" in his* A Bibliography of North American Folklore and Folksong, *2nd revised edition, vol. I (New York, 1961), pp. 430–560. Despite occasional inaccuracies in citation, this is probably the best bibliographical source for American Negro folklore presently available. Haywood's subject subdivisions include spirituals, work songs, blues, minstrelsy as well as sections on Creole and the West Indies.*

Fortunately, some of the bibliographical void is filled by anthologies, surveys, and specialized bibliographical essays. For example, access to nineteenth-century materials is afforded by Bruce Jackson's anthology, The Negro and His Folklore in Nineteenth-Century Periodicals (*Austin, Texas, 1967*). *For early sources of Negro music, see Damon S. Foster, "The Negro in Early American Songsters,"* Papers of the Bibliographical Society of America, *28, part 2 (1934), pp. 132–63; Dena J. Epstein, "Slave Music in the United States Before 1860, A Survey of Sources,"* Music Library Association Notes, *20 (1963), pp. 195–212, 377–90. Also useful is the anthology edited by Bernard Katz,* The Social Implications of Early Negro Music in the United States (*New York, 1969*). *For later materials, see Alan P. Merriam, "An Annotated Bibliography of African and African-Derived Music Since 1936,"* Africa, *21 (1951), pp. 319–29, and Darius L. Thieme, "Negro Folk Song Scholarship in the United States,"* African Music, *2 (1960), pp. 67–72.*

One reason why bibliographies are badly needed is that the writings on American Negro folklore are so widely scattered. Important articles may appear in American folklore journals, e.g., Journal of American Folklore, Journal of the Folklore Institute, Southern Folklore Quarterly, Western Folklore, Publications of the Texas Folklore Society, New York Folklore Quarterly, Keystone Folklore Quarterly, North Carolina Folklore, Tennessee Folklore Society Bulletin, Kentucky Folklore Record, Mississippi Folklore Register, *etc., or in leading black periodicals, e.g.,* College Language Association (*CLA*) Journal, The Crisis, Journal of Negro Education, Journal of Negro History, Negro Digest, Black World, Negro History Bulletin, Phylon, *etc. Sometimes there are indexes to these periodicals, e.g., Tristram P. Coffin,* An Analytical Index to the Journal of American Folklore (*Philadelphia, 1958*); *Joan Ruman Perkal,* Western Folklore Twenty-Five Year Index (*Berkeley and Los Angeles, 1969*); *Dorothy B. Porter,* Index to the Journal of Negro Education, *vols. 1–31 (1932–1962) (Washington, D. C., 1963), but for the most part, cumulative indices for journals are lacking. Moreover, as anyone who takes the trouble to look at the sources of the essays included in the present volume can easily see, key articles may be published in a great variety of periodicals. Students need to check such helpful abstract services as* Psychological Abstracts, Sociological

Abstracts, *African Abstracts, Abstracts of English Studies, etc., if they wish
to guard against missing important articles appearing in periodicals in other
disciplines.*

*Another way of learning more about the field of American Negro folklore
is by reading survey articles. There are a number of such articles, and they vary
in quality from very poor, superficial, intellectually shallow sketches to valuable,
insightful, summary discussions. Sometimes the surveys are part of more general
works. For example, there is a useful chapter on Negro folklore in Richard M.
Dorson,* American Folklore (*Chicago, 1959*), *pp. 166–98, and there is a chapter
entitled "Negro Folk Music in the New World" in Bruno Nettl,* Folk and Traditional Music of the Western Continents (*Englewood Cliffs, 1965*), *pp. 169–87,
but these merely whet the appetite of the interested reader. And the same may
be said for most of the various survey articles, e.g., A. O. Stafford, "Folk
Literature of the Negro,"* The Crisis, *10 (1915), pp. 296–99; Arthur Huff
Fauset, "American Negro Folk Literature," in Alain Locke, ed.,* The New
Negro (*New York, 1968, first published in 1925*), *pp. 238–44, and cf. Fauset's
bibliography "Negro Folk Lore," also in* The New Negro, *pp. 442–45; Thomas
W. Talley, "The Origin of Negro Traditions,"* Phylon, *3 (1942), pp. 371–76;
4 (1943), pp. 30–38; Melville J. Herskovits, "Some Next Steps in the Study of
Negro Folklore,"* Journal of American Folklore, *56 (1943), pp. 1–7; J.
Mason Brewer, "American Negro Folklore,"* Phylon, *6 (1945), pp. 354–61; J.
Mason Brewer, "Negro Folklore in North America: A Field of Research,"*
New Mexico Quarterly, *17 (1946), pp. 27–33, reprinted as "Afro-American
Folklore,"* Journal of American Folklore, *60 (1947), pp. 377–83; Sterling A.
Brown, "Negro Folk Expression,"* Phylon, *11 (1950), pp. 318–27; Daniel J.
Crowley, "Negro Folklore, an Africanist's View,"* Texas Quarterly, *5 (1962),
pp. 65–71; Norman E. Whitten, Jr. and John F. Szwed, "The Romance of Afro-
American Folklore" in the introduction to their* Afro-American Anthropology,
Contemporary Perspectives (*New York, 1970*), *pp. 30–34.*

*What then can the non-scholar or layman turn to if he wishes to learn
more about American Negro folklore? He might begin by perusing several basic
background books, e.g., John P. Davis, ed.,* The American Negro Reference
Book (*Englewood Cliffs, 1965*); *Melville J. Herskovits,* The Myth of the
Negro Past (*Boston, 1958*); *John Hope Franklin,* From Slavery to Freedom: A
History of American Negroes (*New York, 1956*); *E. Franklin Frazier,* Black
Bourgeoisie (*New York, 1957*); *August Meier,* Negro Thought in America,
1880–1915 (*Ann Arbor, 1963*); *E. Franklin Frazier,* The Negro Family in the
United States (*Chicago, 1966*); *Norman E. Whitten, Jr. and John F. Szwed,*
Afro-American Anthropology, Contemporary Perspectives (*New York, 1970*).
*He might then profit from reading several descriptions of Southern rural Negro
community life, e.g., T. F. Woofter, Jr.,* Black Yeomanry: Life on St. Helena
Island (*New York, 1930*) *or Hylan Lewis,* Blackways of Kent (*Chapel Hill,
1955*) *and several descriptions of northern urban ghetto life, e.g., Elliot Liebow,*
Tally's Corner: A Study of Negro Streetcorner Men (*Boston, 1967*) *or Ulf
Hannerz,* Soulside: Inquiries into Ghetto Culture and Community (*New
York, 1969*).

*After studying American Negro culture in general, the reader may be
better prepared to look at American Negro folklore. He may elect to turn to
anthologies of the folklore itself, e.g., Langston Hughes and Arna Bontemps,*

The Book of Negro Folklore (*New York, 1958*), *available in paperback, and/or J. Mason Brewer*, American Negro Folklore (*Chicago: Quadrangle Books, 1968*). *He may then decide to examine more specialized works which, thanks to paperback editions or reprintings, are readily available. For folktale, he could start with Richard M. Dorson*, American Negro Folktales (*New York, 1967*), *and Zora Neale Hurston's classic* Mules and Men (*New York, 1970*); *for folk music, Harold Courlander's* Negro Folk Music U.S.A. (*New York, 1970*); *for spirituals, Miles Mark Fisher*, Negro Slave Songs in the United States (*New York, 1969*); *for blues, Paul Oliver*, The Meaning of the Blues (*New York, 1963*) *or Samuel Charters*, The Poetry of the Blues (*New York, 1970*); *for superstitions, Newbell Niles Puckett*, Folk Beliefs of the Southern Negro (*New York, 1969*); *for urban Negro folklore, Roger D. Abrahams*, Deep Down in the Jungle (*Chicago, 1970*) *and Charles Keil*, Urban Blues (*Chicago, 1966*).

This is by no means an exhaustive list of suggested further readings in American Negro folklore, but, together with bibliographical information provided throughout this volume, it should give the interested reader some idea of what is available or at least clues as to where to go to look for himself to find out what might be available. The reader should remember only that it is difficult if not impossible to appreciate folklore through reading. Folklore is spoken, sung, danced, acted. The record of folklore found in print is a poor reflection of the dynamic "stuff" of living folklore. Nevertheless, reading further in American Negro folklore may be worthwhile and rewarding insofar as as it sensitizes the reader to recognize, enjoy, and better understand one of the great folk heritages of the world.